A. W. Whetstone,
June 24, 1903.
L. S. A.

Henry W. Longfellow.
1879

THE COMPLETE

POETICAL WORKS

OF

HENRY WADSWORTH LONGFELLOW

Household Edition

WITH ILLUSTRATIONS

BOSTON AND NEW YORK
HOUGHTON, MIFFLIN AND COMPANY
The Riverside Press, Cambridge

The Riverside Press, Cambridge, Mass., U. S. A.
Electrotyped and Printed by H. O. Houghton & Company.

PUBLISHERS' NOTE.

THE present Household Edition of Mr. Longfellow's Poetical Works contains his three long poems in dramatic form, The Divine Tragedy, The Golden Legend, and the New England Tragedies, which were formerly published in a separate volume under the general title of Christus: a Mystery. All of his other verse which he cared to preserve is included in this volume, with the exception of his translation of Dante's Divina Commedia, which is published separately.

BIOGRAPHICAL SKETCH.

HENRY WADSWORTH LONGFELLOW was born in Portland, Maine, February 27, 1807. He was a classmate of Hawthorne at Bowdoin College, graduating there in the class of 1825. He began the study of law in the office of his father, Hon. Stephen Longfellow; but receiving shortly the appointment of professor of modern languages at Bowdoin, he devoted himself after that to literature, and to teaching in connection with literature. Before beginning his work at Bowdoin he increased his qualifications by travel and study in Europe, where he stayed three years. Upon his return he gave his lectures on modern languages and literature at the college, and wrote occasionally for the *North American Review* and other periodicals. The first volume which he published was an *Essay on the Moral and Devotional Poetry of Spain*, accompanied by translations from Spanish verse. This was issued in 1833, but has not been kept in print as a separate work. It appears as a chapter in *Outre-Mer*, a reflection of his European life and travel, the first of his prose writings. In 1835 he was invited to succeed Mr. George Ticknor as professor of modern languages and literature at Harvard College, and again went to Europe for preparatory study, giving especial attention to Switzerland and the Scandinavian countries. He held his professorship until 1854, and continued to live in Cambridge until his death, March 24, 1882, occupying a house known from a former occupant as the Craigie house, and also as Washington's headquarters, that general having so used it while organizing the army that held Boston in siege at the beginning of the Revolution. Everett, Sparks, and Worcester, the lexicographer, at one time or another lived in this house, and here Longfellow wrote most of his works.

In 1839 appeared *Hyperion, a Romance*, which, with more narrative form than *Outre-Mer*, like that gave the results of a poet's entrance into the riches of the Old World life. In the same year was published *Voices of the Night*, a little volume containing chiefly poems and translations which had been printed separately in periodicals. *The*

Psalm of Life, perhaps the best known of Longfellow's short poems, was in this volume, and here too were *The Beleaguered City* and *Footsteps of Angels*. *Ballads and other Poems* and *Poems on Slavery* appeared in 1842 ; *The Spanish Student*, a play in three acts, in 1843 ; *The Belfry of Bruges and other Poems* in 1846; *Evangeline* in 1847 ; *Kavanagh, a Tale*, in prose, in 1849. Besides the various volumes comprising short poems, the list of Mr. Longfellow's works includes *The Golden Legend, The Song of Hiawatha, The Courtship of Miles Standish, Tales of a Wayside Inn, The New England Tragedies*, and a translation of Dante's *Divina Commedia*. Mr. Longfellow's literary life began in his college days, and he wrote poems almost to the day of his death. A classification of his poems and longer works would be an interesting task, and would help to disclose the wide range of his sympathy and taste ; a collection of the metres which he used would show the versatility of his art, and similar studies would lead one to discover the many countries and ages to which he went for subjects. It would not be difficult to gather from the volume of Longfellow's poems hints of personal experience, that biography of the heart which is of more worth to us than any record, however full, of external change and adventure. Such hints may be found, for example, in the early lines, *To the River Charles*, which may be compared with the much later *Three Friends of Mine*, IV., V. ; in *A Gleam of Sunshine, To a Child, The Day is Done, The Fire of Driftwood, Resignation, The Open Window, The Ladder of St. Augustine, My Lost Youth, The Children's Hour, Weariness*, and other poems ; not that we are to take all sentiments and statements made in the first person as the poet's, for often the form of the poem is so far dramatic that the poet is assuming a character not necessarily his own ; but the recurrence of certain strains, joined with personal allusions, helps one to penetrate the slight veil with which the poet, here as elsewhere, half conceals and half reveals himself. The friendly associations of the poet may also be discovered in several poems directly addressed to persons or distinctively alluding to them, and the reader will find it pleasant to construct the companionship of the poet out of such poems as *The Herons of Elmwood, To William E. Channing, The Fiftieth Birthday of Agassiz, To Charles Sumner*, the *Prelude* to *Tales of a Wayside Inn, Hawthorne*, and other poems. An interesting study of Mr. Longfellow's writings will be found in a paper by W. D. Howells, in the *North American Review*, vol. civ.

CONTENTS.

CONTENTS.

LIST OF ILLUSTRATIONS.

———◆———

VOICES OF THE NIGHT.

Πότνια, πότνια νὺξ,
ὑπνοδότειρα τῶν πολυπόνων βροτῶν,
Ἐρεβόθεν ἴθι· μόλε μόλε κατάπτερος
Ἀγαμεμνόνιον ἐπὶ δόμον·
ὑπὸ γὰρ ἀλγέων, ὑπό τε συμφορᾶς
διοιχόμεθ’, οἰχόμεθα.

EURIPIDES.

PRELUDE.

PLEASANT it was, when woods were green,
　And winds were soft and low,
To lie amid some sylvan scene,
Where, the long drooping boughs between,
Shadows dark and sunlight sheen
　Alternate come and go ;

Or where the denser grove receives
　No sunlight from above,
But the dark foliage interweaves
In one unbroken roof of leaves,
Underneath whose sloping eaves
　The shadows hardly move.

Beneath some patriarchal tree
　I lay upon the ground ;
His hoary arms uplifted he,
And all the broad leaves over me
Clapped their little hands in glee,
　With one continuous sound ;—

A slumberous sound, a sound that brings
　The feelings of a dream,
As of innumerable wings,
As, when a bell no longer swings,
Faint the hollow murmur rings
　O’er meadow, lake, and stream.

And dreams of that which cannot die,
　Bright visions, came to me,
As lapped in thought I used to lie,
And gaze into the summer sky,
Where the sailing clouds went by,
　Like ships upon the sea ;

Dreams that the soul of youth engage
　Ere Fancy has been quelled ;

Old legends of the monkish page,
Traditions of the saint and sage,
Tales that have the rime of age,
　And chronicles of Eld.

And, loving still these quaint old themes,
　Even in the city’s throng
I feel the freshness of the streams,
That, crossed by shades and sunny
　　gleams,
Water the green land of dreams,
　The holy land of song.

Therefore, at Pentecost, which brings
　The Spring, clothed like a bride,
When nestling buds unfold their wings,
And bishop’s-caps have golden rings,
Musing upon many things,
　I sought the woodlands wide.

The green trees whispered low and mild
　It was a sound of joy !
They were my playmates when a child,
And rocked me in their arms so wild !
Still they looked at me and smiled,
　As if I were a boy ;

And ever whispered, mild and low,
　“ Come, be a child once more ! ”
And waved their long arms to and fro,
And beckoned solemnly and slow ;
O, I could not choose but go
　Into the woodlands hoar, —

Into the blithe and breathing air,
　Into the solemn wood,
Solemn and silent everywhere !
Nature with folded hands seemed there
Kneeling at her evening prayer !
　Like one in prayer I stood.

Before me rose an avenue
  Of tall and sombrous pines ;
Abroad their fan-like branches grew,
And, where the sunshine darted through,
Spread a vapor soft and blue,
  In long and sloping lines.

And, falling on my weary brain,
  Like a fast-falling shower,
The dreams of youth came back again,
Low lispings of the summer rain,
Dropping on the ripened grain,
  As once upon the flower.

Visions of childhood ! Stay, O stay !
  Ye were so sweet and wild !
And distant voices seemed to say,
" It cannot be ! They pass away !
Other themes demand thy lay ;
  Thou art no more a child !

" The land of Song within thee lies,
  Watered by living springs ;
The lids of Fancy's sleepless eyes
Are gates unto that Paradise,
Holy thoughts, like stars, arise,
  Its clouds are angels' wings.

' Learn, that henceforth thy song shall
    be,
  Not mountains capped with snow,
Nor forests sounding like the sea,
Nor rivers flowing ceaselessly,
Where the woodlands bend to see
  The bending heavens below.

" There is a forest where the din
  Of iron branches sounds !
A mighty river roars between,
And whosoever looks therein
Sees the heavens all black with sin,
  Sees not its depths, nor bounds.

" Athwart the swinging branches cast,
  Soft rays of sunshine pour ;
Then comes the fearful wintry blast ;
Our hopes, like withered leaves, fall fast ;
Pallid lips say, ' It is past !
  We can return no more ! '

" Look, then, into thine heart, and
    write !
  Yes, into Life's deep stream !
All forms of sorrow and delight,
All solemn Voices of the Night,
That can soothe thee, or affright, —
  Be these henceforth thy theme."

HYMN TO THE NIGHT.

Ἀσπασίη, τρίλλιστος.

I HEARD the trailing garments of the
    Night
  Sweep through her marble halls !
I saw her sable skirts all fringed with
    light
  From the celestial walls !

I felt her presence, by its spell of might,
  Stoop o'er me from above ;
The calm, majestic presence of the Night,
  As of the one I love.

I heard the sounds of sorrow and delight,
  The manifold, soft chimes,
That fill the haunted chambers of the
    Night,
  Like some old poet's rhymes.

From the cool cisterns of the midnight
    air
  My spirit drank repose ;
The fountain of perpetual peace flows
    there, —
  From those deep cisterns flows.

O holy Night ! from thee I learn to bear
  What man has borne before !
Thou layest thy finger on the lips of Care,
  And they complain no more.

Peace ! Peace ! Orestes-like I breathe
    this prayer !
  Descend with broad-winged flight,
The welcome, the thrice-prayed for, the
    most fair,
  The best-beloved Night !

A PSALM OF LIFE.

WHAT THE HEART OF THE YOUNG MAN
SAID TO THE PSALMIST.

TELL me not, in mournful numbers,
  Life is but an empty dream !
For the soul is dead that slumbers,
  And things are not what they seem

Life is real ! Life is earnest !
  And the grave is not its goal ;
Dust thou art, to dust returnest,
  Was not spoken of the soul.

Not enjoyment, and not sorrow,
  Is our destined end or way ;

But to act, that each to-morrow
  Find us farther than to-day.

Art is long, and Time is fleeting,
  And our hearts, though stout and
      brave,
Still, like muffled drums, are beating
  Funeral marches to the grave.

In the world's broad field of battle,
  In the bivouac of Life,
Be not like dumb, driven cattle !
  Be a hero in the strife !

Trust no Future, howe'er pleasant !
  Let the dead Past bury its dead !
Act, — act in the living Present !
  Heart within, and God o'erhead !

Lives of great men all remind us
  We can make our lives sublime,
And, departing, leave behind us
  Footprints on the sands of time ; —

Footprints, that perhaps another,
  Sailing o'er life's solemn main,
A forlorn and shipwrecked brother,
  Seeing, shall take heart again.

Let us, then, be up and doing,
  With a heart for any fate ;
Still achieving, still pursuing,
  Learn to labor and to wait.

THE REAPER AND THE FLOWERS.

THERE is a Reaper, whose name is Death,
  And, with his sickle keen,
He reaps the bearded grain at a breath,
  And the flowers that grow between.

" Shall I have naught that is fair ? "
    saith he ;
  " Have naught but the bearded grain ?
Though the breath of these flowers is
    sweet to me,
  I will give them all back again."

He gazed at the flowers with tearful eyes,
  He kissed their drooping leaves ;
It was for the Lord of Paradise
  He bound them in his sheaves.

"My Lord has need of these flowerets
    gay,"
  The Reaper said, and smiled ;
" Dear tokens of the earth are they,
  Where he was once a child.

" They shall all bloom in fields of light,
  Transplanted by my care,
And saints, upon their garments white,
  These sacred blossoms wear."

And the mother gave, in tears and pain,
  The flowers she most did love ;
She knew she should find them all again
  In the fields of light above.

O, not in cruelty, not in wrath,
  The Reaper came that day ;
'T was an angel visited the green earth,
  And took the flowers away.

THE LIGHT OF STARS.

THE night is come, but not too soon ;
  And sinking silently,
All silently, the little moon
  Drops down behind the sky.

There is no light in earth or heaven
  But the cold light of stars ;
And the first watch of night is given
  To the red planet Mars.

Is it the tender star of love ?
  The star of love and dreams ?
O no ! from that blue tent above,
  A hero's armor gleams.

And earnest thoughts within me rise,
  When I behold afar,
Suspended in the evening skies,
  The shield of that red star.

O star of strength ! I see thee stand
  And smile upon my pain ;
Thou beckonest with thy mailed hand,
  And I am strong again.

Within my breast there is no light
  But the cold light of stars ;
I give the first watch of the night
  To the red planet Mars.

The star of the unconquered will,
  He rises in my breast,
Serene, and resolute, and still,
  And calm, and self-possessed.

And thou, too, whosoe'er thou art,
  That readest this brief psalm,
As one by one thy hopes depart,
  Be resolute and calm.

O fear not in a world like this,
  And thou shalt know erelong,
Know how sublime a thing it is
  To suffer and be strong.

FOOTSTEPS OF ANGELS.

WHEN the hours of Day are numbered,
  And the voices of the Night
Wake the better soul, that slumbered,
  To a holy, calm delight ;

Ere the evening lamps are lighted,
  And, like phantoms grim and tall,
Shadows from the fitful firelight
  Dance upon the parlor wall ;

Then the forms of the departed
  Enter at the open door ;
The beloved, the true-hearted,
  Come to visit me once more ;

He, the young and strong, who cherished
  Noble longings for the strife,
By the roadside fell and perished,
  Weary with the march of life !

They, the holy ones and weakly,
  Who the cross of suffering bore,
Folded their pale hands so meekly,
  Spake with us on earth no more !

And with them the Being Beauteous,
  Who unto my youth was given,
More than all things else to love me,
  And is now a saint in heaven.

With a slow and noiseless footstep
  Comes that messenger divine,
Takes the vacant chair beside me,
  Lays her gentle hand in mine.

And she sits and gazes at me
  With those deep and tender eyes,
Like the stars, so still and saint-like,
  Looking downward from the skies.

Uttered not, yet comprehended,
  Is the spirit's voiceless prayer,
Soft rebukes, in blessings ended,
  Breathing from her lips of air.

O, though oft depressed and lonely,
  All my fears are laid aside,
If I but remember only
  Such as these have lived and died !

FLOWERS.

SPAKE full well, in language quaint and
  olden,
  One who dwelleth by the castled Rhine,
When he called the flowers, so blue and
  golden,
  Stars, that in earth's firmament do
  shine.

Stars they are, wherein we read our history,
  As astrologers and seers of eld ;
Yet not wrapped about with awful mys
  tery,
  Like the burning stars, which they
  beheld.

Wondrous truths, and manifold as won
  drous,
  God hath written in those stars above ;
But not less in the bright flowerets un-
  der us
  Stands the revelation of his love.

Bright and glorious is that revelation,
  Written all over this great world of
  ours ;
Making evident our own creation,
  In these stars of earth, these golden
  flowers.

And the Poet, faithful and far-seeing,
  Sees, alike in stars and flowers, a part
Of the self-same, universal being,
  Which is throbbing in his brain and
  heart.

Gorgeous flowerets in the sunlight shin-
  ing,
  Blossoms flaunting in the eye of day,
Tremulous leaves, with soft and silver
  lining,
  Buds that open only to decay ;

Brilliant hopes, all woven in gorgeous
  tissues,
  Flaunting gayly in the golden light ;
Large desires, with most uncertain is-
  sues,
  Tender wishes, blossoming at night !

These in flowers and men are more than
  seeming ;
  Workings are they of the self-same
  powers,
Which the Poet, in no idle dreaming,
  Seeth in himself and in the flowers.

Everywhere about us are they glowing,
  Some like stars, to tell us Spring is
    born ;
Others, their blue eyes with tears o'er-
  flowing,
Stand like Ruth amid the golden corn ;

Not alone in Spring's armorial bearing,
  And in Summer's green-emblazoned
    field,
But in arms of brave old Autumn's wear-
  ing,
  In the centre of his brazen shield ;

Not alone in meadows and green alleys,
  On the mountain-top, and by the brink
Of sequestered pools in woodland valleys,
  Where the slaves of nature stoop to
    drink ;

Not alone in her vast dome of glory,
  Not on graves of bird and beast alone,
But in old cathedrals, high and hoary,
  On the tombs of heroes, carved in stone ;

In the cottage of the rudest peasant,
  In ancestral homes, whose crumbling
    towers,
Speaking of the Past unto the Present,
  Tell us of the ancient Games of Flow-
    ers ;

In all places, then, and in all seasons,
  Flowers expand their light and soul-
    like wings,
Teaching us, by most persuasive reasons,
  How akin they are to human things.

And with childlike, credulous affection
  We behold their tender buds expand ;
Emblems of our own great resurrection,
  Emblems of the bright and better land.

THE BELEAGUERED CITY.

I HAVE read, in some old, marvellous tale,
  Some legend strange and vague,
That a midnight host of spectres pale
  Beleaguered the walls of Prague.

Beside the Moldau's rushing stream,
  With the wan moon overhead,
There stood, as in an awful dream,
  The army of the dead.

White as a sea-fog, landward bound,
  The spectral camp was seen,

And, with a sorrowful, deep sound,
  The river flowed between.

No other voice nor sound was there,
  No drum, nor sentry's pace ;
The mist-like banners clasped the air,
  As clouds with clouds embrace.

But when the old cathedral bell
  Proclaimed the morning prayer,
The white pavilions rose and fell
  On the alarmed air.

Down the broad valley fast and far
  The troubled army fled ;
Up rose the glorious morning star,
  The ghastly host was dead.

I have read, in the marvellous heart of
  man,
  That strange and mystic scroll,
That an army of phantoms vast and wan
  Beleaguer the human soul.

Encamped beside Life's rushing stream,
  In Fancy's misty light,
Gigantic shapes and shadows gleam
  Portentous through the night.

Upon its midnight battle-ground
  The spectral camp is seen,
And, with a sorrowful, deep sound,
  Flows the River of Life between.

No other voice nor sound is there,
  In the army of the grave ;
No other challenge breaks the air,
  But the rushing of Life's wave.

And when the solemn and deep church-
  bell
  Entreats the soul to pray,
The midnight phantoms feel the spell,
  The shadows sweep away.

Down the broad Vale of Tears afar
  The spectral camp is fled ;
Faith shineth as a morning star,
  Our ghastly fears are dead.

MIDNIGHT MASS FOR THE DY-
ING YEAR.

YES, the Year is growing old,
  And his eye is pale and bleared !
Death, with frosty hand and cold,
  Plucks the old man by the beard,
    Sorely, sorely !

The leaves are falling, falling,
  Solemnly and slow;
Caw ! caw ! the rooks are calling,
  It is a sound of woe,
    A sound of woe !

Through woods and mountain passes
  The winds, like anthems, roll ;
They are chanting solemn masses,
  Singing, " Pray for this poor soul,
    Pray, pray ! "

And the hooded clouds, like friars,
  Tell their beads in drops of rain,
And patter their doleful prayers ;
  But their prayers are all in vain,
    All in vain !

There he stands in the foul weather,
  The foolish, fond Old Year,
Crowned with wild flowers and with
    heather,
  Like weak, despised Lear,
    A king, a king !

Then comes the summer-like day,
  Bids the old man rejoice !
His joy ! his last ! O, the old man gray
  Loveth that ever-soft voice,
    Gentle and low.

To the crimson woods he saith,
  To the voice gentle and low

Of the soft air, like a daughter's breath,
  " Pray do not mock me so !
    Do not laugh at me ! "

And now the sweet day is dead ;
  Cold in his arms it lies ;
No stain from its breath is spread
  Over the glassy skies,
    No mist or stain !

Then, too, the Old Year dieth,
  And the forests utter a moan,
Like the voice of one who crieth
  In the wilderness alone,
    " Vex not his ghost ! "

Then comes, with an awful roar,
  Gathering and sounding on,
The storm-wind from Labrador,
  The wind Euroclydon,
    The storm-wind !

Howl ! howl ! and from the forest
  Sweep the red leaves away !
Would, the sins that thou abhorrest,
  O Soul ! could thus decay,
    And be swept away !

For there shall come a mightier blast,
  There shall be a darker day ;
And the stars, from heaven down-cast
  Like red leaves be swept away !
    Kyrie, eleyson !
    Christe, eleyson !

EARLIER POEMS.

[These poems were written for the most part during my college life, and all of them before the age of nineteen. Some have found their way into schools, and seem to be successful. Others lead a vagabond and precarious existence in the corners of newspapers ; or have changed their names and run away to seek their fortunes beyond the sea. I say, with the Bishop of Avranches on a similar occasion : " I cannot be displeased to see these children of mine, which I have neglected, and almost exposed, brought from their wanderings in lanes and alleys, and safely lodged, in order to go forth into the world together in a more decorous garb."]

AN APRIL DAY.

  WHEN the warm sun, that brings
Seed-time and harvest, has returned
    again,
'T is sweet to visit the still wood, where
    springs
  The first flower of the plain.

  I love the season well,
When forest glades are teeming with
    bright forms,
Nor dark and many-folded clouds foretell
  The coming-on of storms.

  From the earth's loosened mould
The sapling draws its sustenance, and
    thrives ;

Though stricken to the heart with winter's
　　cold,
　　The drooping tree revives.

The softly-warbled song
Comes from the pleasant woods, and col-
　　ored wings
Glance quick in the bright sun, that
　　moves along
　　The forest openings.

When the bright sunset fills
The silver woods with light, the green
　　slope throws
Its shadows in the hollows of the hills,
　　And wide the upland glows.

And when the eve is born,
In the blue lake the sky, o'er-reaching
　　far,
Is hollowed out, and the moon dips her
　　horn,
　　And twinkles many a star.

Inverted in the tide
Stand the gray rocks, and trembling
　　shadows throw,
And the fair trees look over, side by side,
　　And see themselves below.

Sweet April ! many a thought
Is wedded unto thee, as hearts are wed ;
Nor shall they fail, till, to its autumn
　　brought,
　　Life's golden fruit is shed.

AUTUMN.

WITH what a glory comes and goes the
　　year !
The buds of spring, those beautiful har-
　　bingers
Of sunny skies and cloudless times, enjoy
Life's newness, and earth's garniture
　　spread out ;
And when the silver habit of the clouds
Comes down upon the autumn sun, and
　　with
A sober gladness the old year takes up
His bright inheritance of golden fruits,
A pomp and pageant fill the splendid
　　scene.

There is a beautiful spirit breathing
　　now
Its mellow richness on the clustered
　　trees,

And, from a beaker full of richest dyes,
Pouring new glory on the autumn woods,
And dipping in warm light the pillared
　　clouds.
Morn on the mountain, like a summer
　　bird,
Lifts up her purple wing, and in the
　　vales
The gentle wind, a sweet and passionate
　　wooer,
Kisses the blushing leaf, and stirs up
　　life
Within the solemn woods of ash deep-
　　crimsoned,
And silver beech, and maple yellow-
　　leaved,
Where Autumn, like a faint old man,
　　sits down
By the wayside a-weary. Through the
　　trees
The golden robin moves. The purple
　　finch,
That on wild cherry and red cedar feeds,
A winter bird, comes with its plaintive
　　whistle,
And pecks by the witch-hazel, whilst
　　aloud
From cottage roofs the warbling blue-
　　bird sings,
And merrily, with oft-repeated stroke,
Sounds from the threshing-floor the busy
　　flail.

O what a glory doth this world put on
For him who, with a fervent heart, goes
　　forth
Under the bright and glorious sky, and
　　looks
On duties well performed, and days well
　　spent !
For him the wind, ay, and the yellow
　　leaves,
Shall have a voice, and give him eloquent
　　teachings.
He shall so hear the solemn hymn that
　　Death
Has lifted up for all, that he shall go
To his long resting-place without a tear.

WOODS IN WINTER.

WHEN winter winds are piercing chill,
　　And through the hawthorn blows the
　　gale,
With solemn feet I tread the hill,
　　That overbrows the lonely vale.

O'er the bare upland, and away
    Through the long reach of desert
        woods,
The embracing sunbeams chastely play,
    And gladden these deep solitudes.

Where, twisted round the barren oak,
    The summer vine in beauty clung,
And summer winds the stillness broke,
    The crystal icicle is hung.

Where, from their frozen urns, mute
        springs
    Pour out the river's gradual tide,
Shrilly the skater's iron rings,
    And voices fill the woodland side.

Alas! how changed from the fair scene,
    When birds sang out their mellow lay,
And winds were soft, and woods were
        green,
    And the song ceased not with the day!

But still wild music is abroad,
    Pale, desert woods! within your
        crowd;
And gathering winds, in hoarse accord,
    Amid the vocal reeds pipe loud.

Chill airs and wintry winds! my ear
    Has grown familiar with your song;
I hear it in the opening year,
    I listen, and it cheers me long.

HYMN OF THE MORAVIAN NUNS OF BETHLEHEM.

AT THE CONSECRATION OF PULASKI'S BANNER.

WHEN the dying flame of day
Through the chancel shot its ray,
Far the glimmering tapers shed
Faint light on the cowled head;
And the censer burning swung,
Where, before the altar, hung
The crimson banner, that with prayer
Had been consecrated there.
And the nuns' sweet hymn was heard
        the while,
Sung low, in the dim, mysterious aisle.

    "Take thy banner! May it wave
    Proudly o'er the good and brave;
    When the battle's distant wail
    Breaks the sabbath of our vale.

When the clarion's music thrills
To the hearts of these lone hills,
When the spear in conflict shakes,
And the strong lance shivering
        breaks.

"Take thy banner! and, beneath
The battle-cloud's encircling wreath,
Guard it, till our homes are free!
Guard it! God will prosper thee!
In the dark and trying hour,
In the breaking forth of power,
In the rush of steeds and men,
His right hand will shield thee then.

"Take thy banner! But when night
Closes round the ghastly fight,
If the vanquished warrior bow,
Spare him! By our holy vow,
By our prayers and many tears,
By the mercy that endears,
Spare him! he our love hath shared!
Spare him! as thou wouldst be
        spared!

"Take thy banner! and if e'er
Thou shouldst press the soldier's
        bier,
And the muffled drum should beat
To the tread of mournful feet,
Then this crimson flag shall be
Martial cloak and shroud for thee."

The warrior took that banner proud,
And it was his martial cloak and shroud!

SUNRISE ON THE HILLS.

I STOOD upon the hills, when heaven's
        wide arch
Was glorious with the sun's returning
        march,
And woods were brightened, and soft
        gales
Went forth to kiss the sun-clad vales.
The clouds were far beneath me; bathed
        in light,
They gathered mid-way round the wood
        ed height,
And, in their fading glory, shone
Like hosts in battle overthrown,
As many a pinnacle, with shifting glance,
Through the gray mist thrust up its
        shattered lance,
And rocking on the cliff was left
The dark pine blasted, bare, and cleft.

The veil of cloud was lifted, and below
Glowed the rich valley, and the river's
    flow
Was darkened by the forest's shade,
Or glistened in the white cascade ;
Where upward, in the mellow blush of
    day,
The noisy bittern wheeled his spiral way.

I heard the distant waters dash,
I saw the current whirl and flash,
And richly, by the blue lake's silver
    beach,
The woods were bending with a silent
    reach.
Then o'er the vale, with gentle swell,
The music of the village bell
Came sweetly to the echo-giving hills ;
And the wild horn, whose voice the wood-
    land fills,
Was ringing to the merry shout,
That faint and far the glen sent out,
Where, answering to the sudden shot,
    thin smoke,
Through thick-leaved branches, from the
    dingle broke.

If thou art worn and hard beset
With sorrows, that thou wouldst forget,
If thou wouldst read a lesson, that will
    keep
Thy heart from fainting and thy soul
    from sleep,
Go to the woods and hills ! No tears
Dim the sweet look that Nature wears.

THE SPIRIT OF POETRY.

THERE is a quiet spirit in these woods,
That dwells where'er the gentle south-
    wind blows ;
Where, underneath the white-thorn, in
    the glade,
The wild flowers bloom, or, kissing the
    soft air,
The leaves above their sunny palms out-
    spread.
With what a tender and impassioned voice
It fills the nice and delicate ear of thought,
When the fast ushering star of morning
    comes
O'er-riding the gray hills with golden
    scarf ;
Or when the cowled and dusky-sandaled
    Eve,
In mourning weeds, from out the western
    gate,

Departs with silent pace ! That spirit
    moves
In the green valley, where the silver
    brook,
From its full laver, pours the white cas-
    cade ;
And, babbling low amid the tangled
    woods,
Slips down through moss-grown stones
    with endless laughter.
And frequent, on the everlasting hills,
Its feet go forth, when it doth wrap itself
In all the dark embroidery of the storm,
And shouts the stern, strong wind. And
    here, amid
The silent majesty of these deep woods,
Its presence shall uplift thy thought
    from earth,
As to the sunshine and the pure, bright
    air
Their tops the green trees lift. Hence
    gifted bards
Have ever loved the calm and quiet
    shades.
For them there was an eloquent voice in
    all
The sylvan pomp of woods, the golden
    sun,
The flowers, the leaves, the river on its
    way,
Blue skies, and silver clouds, and gentle
    winds,
The swelling upland, where the sidelong
    sun
Aslant the wooded slope, at evening,
    goes,
Groves, through whose broken roof the
    sky looks in,
Mountain, and shattered cliff, and sunny
    vale,
The distant lake, fountains, and mighty
    trees,
In many a lazy syllable, repeating
Their old poetic legends to the wind.

And this is the sweet spirit, that doth
    fill
The world ; and, in these wayward days
    of youth,
My busy fancy oft embodies it,
As a bright image of the light and beauty
That dwell in nature ; of the heavenly
    forms
We worship in our dreams, and the soft
    hues
That stain the wild bird's wing, and flush
    the clouds

When the sun sets.   Within her tender
eye
The heaven of April, with its changing
light,
And when it wears the blue of May, is
hung,
And on her lip the rich, red rose.   Her
hair
Is like the summer tresses of the trees,
When twilight makes them brown, and
on her cheek
Blushes the richness of an autumn sky,
With ever-shifting beauty.   Then her
breath,
It is so like the gentle air of Spring,
As, from the morning's dewy flowers, it
comes
Full of their fragrance, that it is a joy
To have it round us, and her silver voice
Is the rich music of a summer bird,
Heard in the till night, with its passion-
ate cadence.

BURIAL OF THE MINNISINK.

On sunny slope and beechen swell,
The shadowed light of evening fell ;
And, where the maple's leaf was brown,
With soft and silent lapse came down,
The glory, that the wood receives,
At sunset, in its golden leaves.

Far upward in the mellow light
Rose the blue hills.   One cloud of white,
Around a far uplifted cone,
In the warm blush of evening shone ;
An image of the silver lakes,
By which the Indian's soul awakes.

But soon a funeral hymn was heard
Where the soft breath of evening stirred

The tall, gray forest ; and a band
Of stern in heart, and strong in hand,
Came winding down beside the wave,
To lay the red chief in his grave.

They sang, that by his native bowers
He stood, in the last moon of flowers,
And thirty snows had not yet shed
Their glory on the warrior's head ;
But, as the summer fruit decays,
So died he in those naked days.

A dark cloak of the roebuck's skin
Covered the warrior, and within
Its heavy folds the weapons, made
For the hard toils of war, were laid ;
The cuirass, woven of plaited reeds,
And the broad belt of shells and
beads.

Before, a dark-haired virgin train
Chanted the death dirge of the slain ;
Behind, the long procession came
Of hoary men and chiefs of fame,
With heavy hearts, and eyes of grief,
Leading the war-horse of their chief.

Stripped of his proud and martial
dress,
Uncurbed, unreined, and riderless,
With darting eye, and nostril spread,
And heavy and impatient tread,
He came ; and oft that eye so proud
Asked for his rider in the crowd.

They buried the dark chief; they freed
Beside the grave his battle steed ;
And swift an arrow cleaved its way
To his stern heart !   One piercing neigh
Arose, and, on the dead man's plain,
The rider grasps his steed again.

TRANSLATIONS.

[Don Jorge Manrique, the author of the following poem, flourished in the last half of the fifteenth century. He followed the profession of arms, and died on the field of battle. Mariana, in his History of Spain, makes honorable mention of him, as being present at the siege of Uclés; and speaks of him as " a youth of estimable qualities, who in this war gave brilliant proofs of his valor. He died young; and was thus cut off from long exercising his great virtues, and exhibiting to the world the light of his genius, which was already known to fame." He was mortally wounded in a skirmish near Cañavete, in the year 1479.

The name of Rodrigo Manrique, the father of the poet, Conde de Paredes and Maestre de Santiago, is well known in Spanish history and song. He died in 1476; according to Mariana, in the town of Uclés; but, according to the poem of his son, in Ocaña. It was his death that called forth the poem upon which rests the literary reputation of the younger Manrique. In the language of his historian, " Don Jorge Manrique, in an elegant Ode, full of poetic beauties, rich embellishments of genius, and high moral reflections, mourned the death of his father as with a funeral hymn." This praise is not exaggerated. The poem is a model in its kind. Its conception is solemn and beautiful; and, in accordance with it, the style moves on, — calm, dignified, and majestic.]

COPLAS DE MANRIQUE.

FROM THE SPANISH.

O LET the soul her slumbers break,
Let thought be quickened, and awake ,
Awake to see
How soon this life is past and gone,
And death comes softly stealing on,
How silently !

Swiftly our pleasures glide away,
Our hearts recall the distant day
With many sighs ;
The moments that are speeding fast
We heed not, but the past, — the past,
More highly prize.

Onward its course the present keeps,
Onward the constant current sweeps,
Till life is done ;
And, did we judge of time aright,
The past and future in their flight
Would be as one.

Let no one fondly dream again,
That Hope and all her shadowy train
Will not decay ;
Fleeting as were the dreams of old,
Remembered like a tale that 's told,
They pass away.

Our lives are rivers, gliding free
To that unfathomed, boundless sea,
The silent grave !
Thither all earthly pomp and boast
Roll, to be swallowed up and lost
n one dark wave.

Thither the mighty torrents stray,
Thither the brook pursues its way,
And tinkling rill.
There all are equal ; side by side
The poor man and the son of pride
Lie calm and still.

I will not here invoke the throng
Of orators and sons of song,
The deathless few ;
Fiction entices and deceives,
And, sprinkled o'er her fragrant leaves,
Lies poisonous dew.

To One alone my thoughts arise,
The Eternal Truth, the Good and Wise,
To Him I cry,
Who shared on earth our common lot,
But the world comprehended not
His deity.

This world is but the rugged road
Which leads us to the bright abode
Of peace above ;
So let us choose that narrow way,
Which leads no traveller's foot astray
From realms of love.

Our cradle is the starting-place,
Life is the running of the race,
We reach the goal
When, in the mansions of the blest,
Death leaves to its eternal rest
The weary soul.

Did we but use it as we ought,
This world would school each wandering
thought

To its high state.
Faith wings the soul beyond the sky,
Up to that better world on high,
For which we wait.

Yes, the glad messenger of love,
To guide us to our home above,
The Saviour came ;
Born amid mortal cares and fears,
He suffered in this vale of tears
A death of shame.

Behold of what delusive worth
The bubbles we pursue on earth,
The shapes we chase,
Amid a world of treachery !
They vanish ere death shuts the eye,
And leave no trace.

Time steals them from us, chances
        strange,
Disastrous accident, and change,
That come to all ;
Even in the most exalted state,
Relentless sweeps the stroke of fate ;
The strongest fall.

Tell me, the charms that lovers seek
In the clear eye and blushing cheek,
The hues that play
O'er rosy lip and brow of snow,
When hoary age approaches slow,
Ah, where are they ?

The cunning skill, the curious arts,
The glorious strength that youth imparts
In life's first stage ;
These shall become a heavy weight,
When Time swings wide his outward gate
To weary age.

The noble blood of Gothic name,
Heroes emblazoned high to fame,
In long array ;
How, in the onward course of time,
The landmarks of that race sublime
Were swept away !

Some, the degraded slaves of lust,
Prostrate and trampled in the dust,
Shall rise no more ;
Others, by guilt and crime, maintain
The scutcheon, that, without a stain,
Their fathers bore.

Wealth and the high estate of pride,
With what untimely speed they glide,
How soon depart !

Bid not the shadowy phantoms stay,
The vassals of a mistress they,
Of fickle heart.

These gifts in Fortune's hands are found,
Her swift revolving wheel turns round,
And they are gone !
No rest the inconstant goddess knows,
But changing, and without repose,
Still hurries on.

Even could the hand of avarice save
Its gilded baubles, till the grave
Reclaimed its prey,
Let none on such poor hopes rely ;
Life, like an empty dream, flits by,
And where are they ?

Earthly desires and sensual lust
Are passions springing from the dust,
They fade and die ;
But, in the life beyond the tomb,
They seal the immortal spirit's doom
Eternally !

The pleasures and delights, which mask
In treacherous smiles life's serious task,
What are they, all,
But the fleet coursers of the chase,
And death an ambush in the race,
Wherein we fall ?

No foe, no dangerous pass, we heed,
Brook no delay, but onward speed
With loosened rein ;
And, when the fatal snare is near,
We strive to check our mad career,
But strive in vain.

Could we new charms to age impart,
And fashion with a cunning art
The human face,
As we can clothe the soul with light,
And make the glorious spirit bright
With heavenly grace,

How busily each passing hour
Should we exert that magic power,
What ardor show,
To deck the sensual slave of sin,
Yet leave the freeborn soul within,
In weeds of woe !

Monarchs, the powerful and the strong,
Famous in history and in song
Of olden time.

Saw, by the stern decrees of fate,
Their kingdoms lost, and desolate
Their race sublime.

Who is the champion? who the strong?
Pontiff and priest, and sceptred throng?
On these shall fall
As heavily the hand of Death,
As when it stays the shepherd's breath
Beside his stall.

I speak not of the Trojan name,
Neither its glory nor its shame
Has met our eyes;
Nor of Rome's great and glorious dead,
Though we have heard so oft, and read,
Their histories.

Little avails it now to know
Of ages passed so long ago,
Nor how they rolled;
Our theme shall be of yesterday,
Which to oblivion sweeps away,
Like days of old.

Where is the King, Don Juan? Where
Each royal prince and noble heir
Of Aragon?
Where are the courtly gallantries?
The deeds of love and high emprise,
In battle done?

Tourney and joust, that charmed the eye,
And scarf, and gorgeous panoply,
And nodding plume,
What were they but a pageant scene?
What but the garlands, gay and green,
That deck the tomb?

Where are the high-born dames, and where
Their gay attire, and jewelled hair,
And odors sweet?
Where are the gentle knights, that came
To kneel, and breathe love's ardent flame,
Low at their feet?

Where is the song of Troubadour?
Where are the lute and gay tambour
They loved of yore?
Where is the mazy dance of old,
The flowing robes, inwrought with gold,
The dancers wore?

And he who next the sceptre swayed,
Henry, whose royal court displayed
Such power and pride;

O, in what winning smiles arrayed,
The world its various pleasures laid
His throne beside!

But O how false and full of guile
That world, which wore so soft a smile
But to betray!
She, that had been his friend before,
Now from the fated monarch tore
Her charms away.

The countless gifts, the stately walls,
The royal palaces, and halls
All filled with gold;
Plate with armorial bearings wrought,
Chambers with ample treasures fraught
Of wealth untold;

The noble steeds, and harness bright,
And gallant lord, and stalwart knight,
In rich array,
Where shall we seek them now? Alas!
Like the bright dewdrops on the grass,
They passed away.

His brother, too, whose factious zeal
Usurped the sceptre of Castile,
Unskilled to reign;
What a gay, brilliant court had he,
When all the flower of chivalry
Was in his train!

But he was mortal; and the breath,
That flamed from the hot forge of Death,
Blasted his years;
Judgment of God! that flame by thee,
When raging fierce and fearfully,
Was quenched in tears!

Spain's haughty Constable, the true
And gallant Master, whom we knew
Most loved of all;
Breathe not a whisper of his pride,
He on the gloomy scaffold died,
Ignoble fall!

The countless treasures of his care,
His villages and villas fair,
His mighty power,
What were they all but grief and shame,
Tears and a broken heart, when came
The parting hour?

His other brothers, proud and high,
Masters, who, in prosperity,
Might rival kings;

Who made the bravest and the best
The bondsmen of their high behest,
Their underlings ;

What was their prosperous estate,
When high exalted and elate
With power and pride ?
What, but a transient gleam of light,
A flame, which, glaring at its height,
Grew dim and died ?

So many a duke of royal name,
Marquis and count of spotless fame,
And baron brave,
That might the sword of empire wield,
All these, O Death, hast thou concealed
In the dark grave !

Their deeds of mercy and of arms,
In peaceful days, or war's alarms,
When thou dost show,
O Death, thy stern and angry face,
One stroke of thy all-powerful mace
Can overthrow.

Unnumbered hosts, that threaten nigh,
Pennon and standard flaunting high,
And flag displayed ;
High battlements intrenched around,
Bastion, and moated wall, and mound,
And palisade,

And covered trench, secure and deep,
All these cannot one victim keep,
O Death, from thee,
When thou dost battle in thy wrath,
And thy strong shafts pursue their path
Unerringly.

O World ! so few the years we live,
Would that the life which thou dost give
Were life indeed !
Alas ! thy sorrows fall so fast,
Our happiest hour is when at last
The soul is freed.

Our days are covered o'er with grief,
And sorrows neither few nor brief
Veil all in gloom ;
Left desolate of real good,
Within this cheerless solitude
No pleasures bloom.

Thy pilgrimage begins in tears,
And ends in bitter doubts and fears,
Or dark despair ;
Midway so many toils appear,
That he who lingers longest here
Knows most of care.

Thy goods are bought with many a groan,
By the hot sweat of toil alone,
And weary hearts ;
Fleet-footed is the approach of woe,
But with a lingering step and slow
Its form departs.

And he, the good man's shield and shade,
To whom all hearts their homage paid,
As Virtue's son,
Roderic Manrique, he whose name
Is written on the scroll of Fame,
Spain's champion ;

His signal deeds and prowess high
Demand no pompous eulogy,
Ye saw his deeds !
Why should their praise in verse be
    sung ?
The name, that dwells on every tongue,
No minstrel needs.

To friends a friend ; how kind to all
The vassals of this ancient hall
And feudal fief !
To foes how stern a foe was he !
And to the valiant and the free
How brave a chief !

What prudence with the old and wise :
What grace in youthful gayeties ;
In all how sage !
Benignant to the serf and slave,
He showed the base and falsely brave
A lion's rage.

His was Octavian's prosperous star,
The rush of Cæsar's conquering car
At battle's call ;
His, Scipio's virtue ; his, the skill
And the indomitable will
Of Hannibal.

His was a Trajan's goodness, his
A Titus' noble charities
And righteous laws ;
The arm of Hector, and the might
Of Tully, to maintain the right
In truth's just cause ;

The clemency of Antonine,
Aurelius' countenance divine,
Firm, gentle, still ;
The eloquence of Adrian,
And Theodosius' love to man,
And generous will ;

In tented field and bloody fray,
An Alexander's vigorous sway
And stern command ;
The faith of Constantine ; ay, more,
The fervent love Camillus bore
His native land.

He left no well-filled treasury,
He heaped no pile of riches high,
Nor massive plate ;
He fought the Moors, and, in their fall,
City and tower and castled wall
Were his estate.

Upon the hard-fought battle-ground,
Brave steeds and gallant riders found
A common grave ;
And there the warrior's hand did gain
The rents, and the long vassal train,
That conquest gave.

And if, of old, his halls displayed
The honored and exalted grade
His worth had gained,
So, in the dark, disastrous hour,
Brothers and bondsmen of his power
His hand sustained.

After high deeds, not left untold,
In the stern warfare, which of old
'T was his to share,
Such noble leagues he made, that more
And fairer regions, than before,
His guerdon were.

These are the records, half effaced,
Which, with the hand of youth, he traced
On history's page ;
But with fresh victories he drew
Each fading character anew
In his old age.

By his unrivalled skill, by great
And veteran service to the state,
By worth adored,
He stood, in his high dignity,
The proudest knight of chivalry,
Knight of the Sword.

He found his cities and domains
Beneath a tyrant's galling chains
And cruel power ;
But, by fierce battle and blockade,
Soon his own banner was displayed
From every tower.

By the tried valor of his hand,
His monarch and his native land
Were nobly served ;

Let Portugal repeat the story,
And proud Castile, who shared the glory
His arms deserved.

And when so oft, for weal or woe,
His life upon the fatal throw
Had been cast down ;
When he had served, with patriot zeal,
Beneath the banner of Castile,
His sovereign's crown ;

And done such deeds of valor strong,
That neither history nor song
Can count them all ;
Then, on Ocaña's castled rock,
Death at his portal came to knock,
With sudden call,

Saying, "Good Cavalier, prepare
To leave this world of toil and care
With joyful mien ;
Let thy strong heart of steel this day
Put on its armor for the fray,
The closing scene.

" Since thou hast been, in battle-strife,
So prodigal of health and life,
For earthly fame,
Let virtue nerve thy heart again ;
Loud on the last stern battle-plain
They call thy name.

"Think not the struggle that draws
near
Too terrible for man, nor fear
To meet the foe ;
Nor let thy noble spirit grieve,
Its life of glorious fame to leave
On earth below.

" A life of honor and of worth
Has no eternity on earth,
'T is but a name ;
And yet its glory far exceeds
That base and sensual life, which leads
To want and shame.

" The eternal life, beyond the sky,
Wealth cannot purchase, nor the high
And proud estate ;
The soul in dalliance laid, the spirit
Corrupt with sin, shall not inherit
A joy so great.

" But the good monk, in cloistered cell,
Shall gain it by his book and bell,
His prayers and tears :

And the brave knight, whose arm en-
    dures
Fierce battle, and against the Moors
His standard rears.

"And thou, brave knight, whose hand
    has poured
The life-blood of the Pagan horde
O'er all the land,
In heaven shalt thou receive, at length,
The guerdon of thine earthly strength
And dauntless hand.

"Cheered onward by this promise sure,
Strong in the faith entire and pure
Thou dost profess,
Depart, thy hope is certainty,
The third, the better life on high
Shalt thou possess."

"O Death, no more, no more delay;
My spirit longs to flee away,
And be at rest;
The will of Heaven my will shall be,
I bow to the divine decree,
To God's behest.

"My soul is ready to depart,
No thought rebels, the obedient heart
Breathes forth no sigh;
The wish on earth to linger still
Were vain, when 't is God's sovereign
    will
That we shall die.

"O thou, that for our sins didst take
A human form, and humbly make
Thy home on earth;
Thou, that to thy divinity
A human nature didst ally
By mortal birth,

"And in that form didst suffer here
Torment, and agony, and fear,
So patiently;
By thy redeeming grace alone,
And not for merits of my own,
O, pardon me!"

As thus the dying warrior prayed,
Without one gathering mist or shade
Upon his mind;
Encircled by his family,
Watched by affection's gentle eye
So soft and kind;

His soul to Him, who gave it, rose;
God lead it to its long repose,
Its glorious rest!

And, though the warrior's sun has set,
Its light shall linger round us yet,
Bright, radiant, blest.

THE GOOD SHEPHERD.

FROM THE SPANISH OF LOPE DE VEGA.

SHEPHERD! who with thine amorous,
    sylvan song
  Hast broken the slumber that encom-
    passed me,
  Who mad'st thy crook from the ac-
    cursed tree,
  On which thy powerful arms were
    stretched so long!
Lead me to mercy's ever-flowing foun-
    tains;
  For thou my shepherd, guard, and
    guide shalt be;
  I will obey thy voice, and wait to see
  Thy feet all beautiful upon the moun-
    tains.
Hear, Shepherd! thou who for thy flock
    art dying,
  O, wash away these scarlet sins, for
    thou
Rejoicest at the contrite sinner's vow.
O, wait! to thee my weary soul is crying,
  Wait for me! Yet why ask it, when
    I see,
  With feet nailed to the cross, thou 'rt
    waiting still for me!

TO—MORROW.

FROM THE SPANISH OF LOPE DE VEGA.

LORD, what am I, that, with unceasing
    care,
  Thou didst seek after me, that thou
    didst wait,
  Wet with unhealthy dews, before my
    gate,
  And pass the gloomy nights of winter
    there?
O strange delusion! that I did not greet
  Thy blest approach, and O, to Heaven
    how lost,
  If my ingratitude's unkindly frost
  Has chilled the bleeding wounds upon
    thy feet.
How oft my guardian angel gently cried,
  "Soul, from thy casement look, and
    thou shalt see

How he persists to knock and wait
    for thee ! "
And, O ! how often to that voice of sor-
    row,
    " To-morrow we will open," I replied,
And when the morrow came I an-
    swered still, "To-morrow."

THE NATIVE LAND.

FROM THE SPANISH OF FRANCISCO DE
ALDANA.

CLEAR fount of light ! my native land
    on high,
·   Bright with a glory that shall never
    fade !
    Mansion of truth ! without a veil or
    shade,
Thy holy quiet meets the spirit's eye.
There dwells the soul in its ethereal
    essence,
    Gasping no longer for life's feeble
    breath ;
But, sentinelled in heaven, its glori-
    ous presence
With pitying eye beholds, yet fears
    not, death.
Beloved country ! banished from thy
    shore,
    A stranger in this prison-house of clay,
The exiled spirit weeps and sighs for
    thee !
Heavenward the bright perfections I
    adore
Direct, and the sure promise cheers
    the way,
That, whither love aspires, there shall
    my dwelling be.

THE IMAGE OF GOD.

FROM THE SPANISH OF FRANCISCO DE
ALDANA.

O LORD ! who seest, from yon starry
    height,
    Centred in one the future and the past,
    Fashioned in thine own image, see
    how fast
The world obscures in me what once
    was bright !
Eternal Sun ! the warmth which thou
    hast given,
    To cheer life's flowery April, fast de-
    cays ;

Yet, in the hoary winter of my days,
    Forever green shall be my trust in
    Heaven.
Celestial King ! O let thy presence pass
    Before my spirit, and an image fair
    Shall meet that look of mercy from on
    high,
As the reflected image in a glass
    Doth meet the look of him who seeks
    it there,
    And owes its being to the gazer's eye.

THE BROOK.

FROM THE SPANISH.

LAUGH of the mountain ! — lyre of bird
    and tree !
    Pomp of the meadow ! mirror of the
    morn !
    The soul of April, unto whom are
    born
    The rose and jessamine, leaps wild in
    thee !
Although, where'er thy devious current
    strays,
    The lap of earth with gold and silver
    teems,
    To me thy clear proceeding brighter
    seems
Than golden sands, that charm each
    shepherd's gaze.
How without guile thy bosom, all trans-
    parent
    As the pure crystal, lets the curious
    eye
    Thy secrets scan, thy smooth, round
    pebbles count !
How, without malice murmuring, glides
    thy current !
    O sweet simplicity of days gone by!
    Thou shun'st the haunts of man, to
    dwell in limpid fount !

THE CELESTIAL PILOT.

FROM DANTE.   PURGATORIO, II.

AND now, behold ! as at the approach of
    morning,
    Through the gross vapors, Mars grows
    fiery red
    Down in the west upon the ocean floor
Appeared to me, — may I again behold
    it !

A light along the sea, so swiftly com-
ing,
    Its motion by no flight of wing is
    equalled.
And when therefrom I had withdrawn a
little
    Mine eyes, that I might question my
    conductor,
    Again I saw it brighter grown and
    larger.
Thereafter, on all sides of it, appeared
    I knew not what of white, and under-
    neath,
    Little by little, there came forth an-
    other.
My master yet had uttered not a word,
    While the first whiteness into wings
    unfolded ;
    But, when he clearly recognized the
    pilot,
He cried aloud : " Quick, quick, and
    bow the knee !
    Behold the Angel of God ! fold up thy
    hands !
    Henceforward shalt thou see such
    officers !
See, how he scorns all human arguments,
    So that no oar he wants, nor other sail
    Than his own wings, between so dis-
    tant shores !
See, how he holds them, pointed straight
    to heaven,
    Fanning the air with the eternal pin-
    ions,
    That do not moult themselves like
    mortal hair ! "
And then, as nearer and more near us
    came
    The Bird of Heaven, more glorious he
    appeared,
    So that the eye could not sustain his
    presence,
But down I cast it ; and he came to
    shore
    With a small vessel, gliding swift and
    light,
    So that the water swallowed naught
    thereof.
Upon the stern stood the Celestial Pilot !
    Beatitude seemed written in his face !
    And more than a hundred spirits sat
    within.
" *In exitu Israel de Ægypto !* "
    Thus sang they all together in one
    voice,
    With whatso in that Psalm is after
    written.

Then made he sign of holy rood upon
    them,
    Whereat all cast themselves upon the
    shore,
    And he departed swiftly as he came.

THE TERRESTRIAL PARADISE.

FROM DANTE.   PURGATORIO, XXVIII.

LONGING already to search in and round
    The heavenly forest, dense and living-
    green,
    Which tempered to the eyes the new-
    born day,
Withouten more delay I left the bank,
    Crossing the level country slowly,
    slowly,
    Over the soil, that everywhere breathed
    fragrance.
A gently-breathing air, that no muta-
    tion
    Had in itself, smote me upon the fore-
    head,
    No heavier blow, than of a pleasant
    breeze,
Whereat the tremulous branches readily
    Did all of them bow downward to-
    wards that side
    Where its first shadow casts the Holy
    Mountain ;
Yet not from their upright direction bent
    So that the little birds upon their tops
    Should cease the practice of their tune-
    ful art ;
But, with full-throated joy, the hours of
    prime
    Singing received they in the midst of
    foliage
    That made monotonous burden to
    their rhymes,
Even as from branch to branch it gath-
    ering swells,
    Through the pine forests on the shore
    of Chiassi,
    When Æolus unlooses the Sirocco.
Already my slow steps had led me on
    Into the ancient wood so far, that I
    Could see no more the place where I
    had entered.
And lo ! my further course cut off a
    river,
    Which, tow'rds the left hand, with its
    little waves,
    Bent down the grass, that on its mar-
    gin sprang.

All waters that on earth most limpid are,
Would seem to have within themselves some mixture,
Compared with that, which nothing doth conceal,
Although it moves on with a brown, brown current,
Under the shade perpetual, that never
Ray of the sun lets in, nor of the moon.

BEATRICE.

FROM DANTE. PURGATORIO, XXX., XXXI.

EVEN as the Blessed, at the final summons,
Shall rise up quickened, each one from his grave,
Wearing again the garments of the flesh,
So, upon that celestial chariot,
A hundred rose *ad vocem tanti senis,*
Ministers and messengers of life eternal.
They all were saying, "*Benedictus qui venis,*"
And scattering flowers above and round about,
"*Manibus o date lilia plenis.*"
Oft have I seen, at the approach of day,
The orient sky all stained with roseate hues,
And the other heaven with light serene adorned,
And the sun's face uprising, overshadowed,
So that, by temperate influence of vapors,
The eye sustained his aspect for long while ;
Thus in the bosom of a cloud of flowers,
Which from those hands angelic were thrown up,
And down descended inside and without,
With crown of olive o'er a snow-white veil,
Appeared a lady, under a green mantle,
Vested in colors of the living flame.
. . . . . .
Even as the snow, among the living rafters
Upon the back of Italy, congeals,

Blown on and beaten by Sclavonian winds,
And then, dissolving, filters through itself,
Whene'er the land, that loses shadow, breathes,
Like as a taper melts before a fire,
Even such I was, without a sigh or tear,
Before the song of those who chime forever
After the chiming of the eternal spheres ;
But, when I heard in those sweet melodies
Compassion for me, more than had they said,
" O wherefore, lady, dost thou thus consume him ? "
The ice, that was about my heart congealed,
To air and water changed, and, in my anguish,
Through lips and eyes came gushing from my breast.
. . . . . .
Confusion and dismay, together mingled,
Forced such a feeble "Yes ! " out of my mouth,
To understand it one had need of sight.
Even as a cross-bow breaks, when 't is discharged,
Too tensely drawn the bow-string and the bow,
And with less force the arrow hits the mark ;
So I gave way beneath this heavy burden,
Gushing forth into bitter tears and sighs,
And the voice, fainting, flagged upon its passage.

SPRING.

FROM THE FRENCH OF CHARLES D'ORLEANS.

XV. CENTURY.

GENTLE Spring ! in sunshine clad,
Well dost thou thy power display !
For Winter maketh the light heart sad,
And thou, thou makest the sad heart gay.
He sees thee, and calls to his gloomy train,

The sleet, and the snow, and the wind,
    and the rain ;
And they shrink away, and they flee in
    fear,
    When thy merry step draws near.

Winter giveth the fields and the trees,
    so old,
    Their beards of icicles and snow ;
And the rain, it raineth so fast and cold,
    We must cower over the embers low ;
And, snugly housed from the wind and
    weather,
Mope like birds that are changing feather.
But the storm retires, and the sky grows
    clear,
    When thy merry step draws near.

Winter maketh the sun in the gloomy
    sky
    Wrap him round with a mantle of
    cloud ;
But, Heaven be praised, thy step is
    nigh ;
    Thou tearest away the mournful
    shroud,
And the earth looks bright, and Winter
    surly,
Who has toiled for naught both late and
    early,
Is banished afar by the new-born year,
    When thy merry step draws near.

THE CHILD ASLEEP.

FROM THE FRENCH.

SWEET babe ! true portrait of thy father's
    face,
    Sleep on the bosom that thy lips have
    pressed !
Sleep, little one ; and closely, gently
    place
    Thy drowsy eyelid on thy mother's
    breast.

Upon that tender eye, my little friend,
    Soft sleep shall come, that cometh not
    to me !
I watch to see thee, nourish thee, defend ;
    'T is sweet to watch for thee, alone for
    thee !

His arms fall down ; sleep sits upon his
    brow ;
    His eye is closed ; he sleeps, nor dreams
    of harm.

Wore not his cheek the apple's ruddy
    glow,
    Would you not say he slept on Death's
    cold arm ?

Awake, my boy ! I tremble with af-
    fright !
    Awake, and chase this fatal thought !
    Unclose
Thine eye but for one moment on the
    light !
    Even at the price of thine, give me
    repose !

Sweet error ! he but slept, I breathe
    again ;
    Come, gentle dreams, the hour of
    sleep beguile !
O, when shall he, for whom I sigh in
    vain,
    Beside me watch to see thy waking
    smile ?

THE GRAVE.

FROM THE ANGLO-SAXON.

FOR thee was a house built
Ere thou wast born,
For thee was a mould meant
Ere thou of mother camest.
But it is not made ready,
Nor its depth measured,
Nor is it seen
How long it shall be.
Now I bring thee
Where thou shalt be ;
Now I shall measure thee,
And the mould afterwards.

Thy house is not
Highly timbered,
It is unhigh and low ;
When thou art therein,
The heel-ways are low,
The side-ways unhigh.
The roof is built
Thy breast full nigh,
So thou shalt in mould
Dwell full cold,
Dimly and dark.

Doorless is that house,
And dark it is within ;
There thou art fast detained
And Death hath the key.

Loathsome is that earth-house,
And grim within to dwell.
There thou shalt dwell,
And worms shall divide thee.

Thus thou art laid,
And leavest thy friends
Thou hast no friend,
Who will come to thee,
Who will ever see
How that house pleaseth thee ;
Who will ever open
The door for thee,
And descend after thee ;
For soon thou art loathsome
And hateful to see.

KING CHRISTIAN.

A NATIONAL SONG OF DENMARK.

FROM THE DANISH OF JOHANNES EVALD.

KING CHRISTIAN stood by the lofty mast
  In mist and smoke ;
His sword was hammering so fast,
Through Gothic helm and brain it
    passed ;
Then sank each hostile hulk and mast,
  In mist and smoke.
"Fly !" shouted they, "fly, he who can!
Who braves of Denmark's Christian
  The stroke ?"

Nils Juel gave heed to the tempest's roar,
  Now is the hour !
He hoisted his blood-red flag once more,
And smote upon the foe full sore,
And shouted loud, through the tempest's
    roar,
  " Now is the hour !"
" Fly !" shouted they, " for shelter fly !
Of Denmark's Juel who can defy
  The power ?"

North Sea ! a glimpse of Wessel rent
  Thy murky sky !
Then champions to thine arms were sent ;
Terror and Death glared where he went ;
From the waves was heard a wail, that
    rent
  Thy murky sky !
From Denmark, thunders Tordenskiol',
Let each to Heaven commend his soul,
  And fly !

Path of the Dane to fame and might !
  Dark-rolling wave !
Receive thy friend, who, scorning flight,
Goes to meet danger with despite,
Proudly as thou the tempest's might,
  Dark-rolling wave !
And amid pleasures and alarms,
And war and victory, be thine arms
    My grave !

THE HAPPIEST LAND.

FROM THE GERMAN.

THERE sat one day in quiet,
  By an alehouse on the Rhine,
Four hale and hearty fellows,
  And drank the precious wine.

The landlord's daughter filled their cups,
  Around the rustic board ;
Then sat they all so calm and still,
  And spake not one rude word.

But, when the maid departed,
  A Swabian raised his hand,
And cried, all hot and flushed with wine,
  " Long live the Swabian land !

" The greatest kingdom upon earth
  Cannot with that compare ;
With all the stout and hardy men
  And the nut-brown maidens there."

"Ha !" cried a Saxon, laughing,
  And dashed his beard with wine ;
" I had rather live in Lapland,
  Than that Swabian land of thine !

" The goodliest land on all this earth,
  It is the Saxon land !
There have I as many maidens
  As fingers on this hand !"

" Hold your tongues ! both Swabian
    and Saxon !"
  A bold Bohemian cries ;
" If there 's a heaven upon this earth,
  In Bohemia it lies.

" There the tailor blows the flute,
  And the cobbler blows the horn,
And the miner blows the bugle,
  Over mountain gorge and bourn.'

And then the landlord's daughter
Up to heaven raised her hand,
And said, "Ye may no more contend, —
There lies the happiest land!"

THE WAVE.

FROM THE GERMAN OF TIEDGE.

"WHITHER, thou turbid wave?
Whither, with so much haste,
As if a thief wert thou?"

"I am the Wave of Life,
Stained with my margin's dust;
From the struggle and the strife
Of the narrow stream I fly
To the Sea's immensity,
To wash from me the slime
Of the muddy banks of Time."

THE DEAD.

FROM THE GERMAN OF STOCKMANN.

How they so softly rest,
All they the holy ones,
Unto whose dwelling-place
Now doth my soul draw near!
How they so softly rest,
All in their silent graves,
Deep to corruption
Slowly down-sinking!

And they no longer weep,
Here, where complaint is still!
And they no longer feel,
Here, where all gladness flies!
And, by the cypresses
Softly o'ershadowed,
Until the Angel
Calls them, they slumber!

THE BIRD AND THE SHIP.

FROM THE GERMAN OF MÜLLER.

THE rivers rush into the sea,
By castle and town they go;
The winds behind them merrily
Their noisy trumpets blow.

"The clouds are passing far and high,
We little birds in them play;
And everything, that can sing and fly,
Goes with us, and far away.

"I greet thee, bonny boat! Whither,
or whence,
With thy fluttering golden band?" —
"I greet thee, little bird! To the wide
sea
I haste from the narrow land.

"Full and swollen is every sail;
I see no longer a hill,
I have trusted all to the sounding gale,
And it will not let me stand still.

"And wilt thou, little bird, go with us?
Thou mayest stand on the mainmast
tall,
For full to sinking is my house
With merry companions all." —

"I need not and seek not company,
Bonny boat, I can sing all alone;
For the mainmast tall too heavy am I,
Bonny boat, I have wings of my own.

"High over the sails, high over the
mast,
Who shall gainsay these joys?
When thy merry companions are still, at
last,
Thou shalt hear the sound of my
voice.

"Who neither may rest, nor listen may,
God bless them every one!
I dart away, in the bright blue day,
And the golden fields of the sun.

"Thus do I sing my merry song,
Wherever the four winds blow;
And this same song, my whole life long,
Neither Poet nor Printer may know."

WHITHER?

FROM THE GERMAN OF MÜLLER.

I HEARD a brooklet gushing
From its rocky fountain near,
Down into the valley rushing,
So fresh and wondrous clear.

I know not what came o'er me,
Nor who the counsel gave;
But I must hasten downward,
All with my pilgrim-stave;

Downward, and ever farther,
And ever the brook beside;

And ever fresher murmured,
  And ever clearer, the tide.

Is this the way I was going?
  Whither, O brooklet, say!
Thou hast, with thy soft murmur,
  Murmured my senses away.

What do I say of a murmur?
  That can no murmur be;
'T is the water-nymphs, that are singing
  Their roundelays under me.

Let them sing, my friend, let them
      murmur,
  And wander merrily near;
The wheels of a mill are going
  In every brooklet clear.

BEWARE!

FROM THE GERMAN.

I KNOW a maiden fair to see,
  Take care!
She can both false and friendly be,
  Beware! Beware!
  Trust her not,
She is fooling thee!

She has two eyes, so soft and brown,
  Take care!
She gives a side-glance and looks down,
  Beware! Beware!
  Trust her not,
She is fooling thee!

And she has hair of a golden hue,
  Take care!
And what she says, it is not true,
  Beware! Beware!
  Trust her not,
She is fooling thee!

She has a bosom as white as snow,
  Take care!
She knows how much it is best to show,
  Beware! Beware!
  Trust her not,
She is fooling thee!

She gives thee a garland woven fair,
  Take care!
It is a fool's-cap for thee to wear,
  Beware! Beware!
  Trust her not,
She is fooling thee!

SONG OF THE BELL.

FROM THE GERMAN.

BELL! thou soundest merrily,
When the bridal party
  To the church doth hie!
Bell! thou soundest solemnly.
When, on Sabbath morning,
  Fields deserted lie!

Bell! thou soundest merrily;
Tellest thou at evening,
  Bed-time draweth nigh!
Bell! thou soundest mournfully,
Tellest thou the bitter
  Parting hath gone by!

Say! how canst thou mourn?
How canst thou rejoice?
  Thou art but metal dull!
And yet all our sorrowings,
And all our rejoicings,
  Thou dost feel them all!

God hath wonders many,
Which we cannot fathom,
  Placed within thy form!
When the heart is sinking,
Thou alone canst raise it,
  Trembling in the storm!

THE CASTLE BY THE SEA.

FROM THE GERMAN OF UHLAND.

" HAST thou seen that lordly castle,
  That Castle by the Sea?
Golden and red above it
  The clouds float gorgeously.

" And fain it would stoop downward
  To the mirrored wave below;
And fain it would soar upward
  In the evening's crimson glow."

" Well have I seen that castle,
  That Castle by the Sea,
And the moon above it standing,
  And the mist rise solemnly."

" The winds and the waves of ocean,
  Had they a merry chime?

Didst thou hear, from those lofty chambers,
    The harp and the minstrel's rhyme?"

"The winds and the waves of ocean,
    They rested quietly,
But I heard on the gale a sound of wail,
    And tears came to mine eye."

"And sawest thou on the turrets
    The King and his royal bride?
And the wave of their crimson mantles?
    And the golden crown of pride?

"Led they not forth, in rapture,
    A beauteous maiden there?
Resplendent as the morning sun,
    Beaming with golden hair?"

"Well saw I the ancient parents,
    Without the crown of pride;
They were moving slow, in weeds of woe,
    No maiden was by their side!"

THE BLACK KNIGHT.

FROM THE GERMAN OF UHLAND.

'T was Pentecost, the Feast of Gladness,
When woods and fields put off all sad-
    ness.
    Thus began the King and spake:
"So from the halls
Of ancient Hofburg's walls,
    A luxuriant Spring shall break."

Drums and trumpets echo loudly,
Wave the crimson banners proudly,
    From balcony the King looked on;
In the play of spears,
Fell all the cavaliers,
    Before the monarch's stalwart son.

To the barrier of the fight
Rode at last a sable Knight.
    "Sir Knight! your name and scutch-
      eon, say!"
"Should I speak it here,
Ye would stand aghast with fear;
    I am a Prince of mighty sway!"

When he rode into the lists,
The arch of heaven grew black with
    mists,
    And the castle 'gan to rock;

At the first blow,
Fell the youth from saddle-bow,
    Hardly rises from the shock.

Pipe and viol call the dances,
Torch - light through the high halls
    glances;
    Waves a mighty shadow in;
With manner bland
Doth ask the maiden's hand,
    Doth with her the dance begin.

Danced in sable iron sark,
Danced a measure weird and dark,
    Coldly clasped her limbs around;
From breast and hair
Down fall from her the fair
    Flowerets, faded, to the ground.

To the sumptuous banquet came
Every Knight and every Dame;
    'Twixt son and daughter all dis-
      traught,
With mournful mind
The ancient King reclined,
    Gazed at them in silent thought.

Pale the children both did look,
But the guest a beaker took:
    "Golden wine will make you whole!"
The children drank,
Gave many a courteous thank:
    "O, that draught was very cool!"

Each the father's breast embraces,
Son and daughter; and their faces
    Colorless grow utterly;
Whichever way
Looks the fear-struck father gray,
    He beholds his children die.

"Woe! the blessed children both
Takest thou in the joy of youth;
    Take me, too, the joyless father!"
Spake the grim Guest,
From his hollow, cavernous breast:
    "Roses in the spring I gather!"

SONG OF THE SILENT LAND.

FROM THE GERMAN OF SALIS.

Into the Silent Land!
Ah! who shall lead us thither?

Clouds in the evening sky more darkly
    gather,
And shattered wrecks lie thicker on the
    strand.
Who leads us with a gentle hand
Thither, O thither,
Into the Silent Land ?

Into the Silent Land !
To you, ye boundless regions
Of all perfection ! Tender morning-
    visions
Of beauteous souls ! The Future's pledge
    and band !
Who in Life's battle firm doth stand,
Shall bear Hope's tender blossoms
Into the Silent Land !

O Land ! O Land !
For all the broken-hearted
The mildest herald by our fate allotted,
Beckons, and with inverted torch doth
    stand
To lead us with a gentle hand
To the land of the great Departed,
Into the Silent Land !

L'ENVOI.

YE voices, that arose
After the Evening's close,
And whispered to my restless heart repose !

Go, breathe it in the ear
Of all who doubt and fear,
And say to them, " Be of good cheer ! "

Ye sounds, so low and calm,
That in the groves of balm
Seemed to me like an angel's psalm !

Go, mingle yet once more
With the perpetual roar
Of the pine forest, dark and hoar !

Tongues of the dead, not lost,
But speaking from death's frost,
Like fiery tongues at Pentecost !

Glimmer, as funeral lamps,
Amid the chills and damps
Of the vast plain where Death encamps !

BALLADS

AND OTHER POEMS.

THE SKELETON IN ARMOR.

"SPEAK ! speak ! thou fearful guest !
Who, with thy hollow breast
Still in rude armor drest,
    Comest to daunt me !
Wrapt not in Eastern balms,
But with thy fleshless palms
Stretched, as if asking alms,
    Why dost thou haunt me ? "

Then, from those cavernous eyes
Pale flashes seemed to rise,
As when the Northern skies
    Gleam in December ;
And, like the water's flow
Under December's snow,
Came a dull voice of woe
    From the heart's chamber.

"I was a Viking old !
My deeds, though manifold,

No Skald in song has told,
    No Saga taught thee !
Take heed, that in thy verse
Thou dost the tale rehearse,
Else dread a dead man's curse ;
    For this I sought thee.

" Far in the Northern Land,
By the wild Baltic's strand,
I, with my childish hand,
    Tamed the gerfalcon ;
And, with my skates fast-bound,
Skimmed the half-frozen Sound,
That the poor whimpering hound
    Trembled to walk on.

"Oft to his frozen lair
Tracked I the grisly bear,
While from my path the hare
    Fled like a shadow ;

Oft through the forest dark
Followed the were-wolf's bark,
Until the soaring lark
   Sang from the meadow.

" But when I older grew,
Joining a corsair's crew,
O'er the dark sea I flew
   With the marauders.
Wild was the life we led ;
Many the souls that sped,
Many the hearts that bled,
   By our stern orders.

" Many a wassail-bout
Wore the long Winter out ;
Often our midnight shout
   Set the cocks crowing,
As we the Berserk's tale
Measured in cups of ale,
Draining the oaken pail,
   Filled to o'erflowing.

" Once as I told in glee
Tales of the stormy sea,
Soft eyes did gaze on me,
   Burning yet tender ;
And as the white stars shine
On the dark Norway pine,
On that dark heart of mine
   Fell their soft splendor.

" I wooed the blue-eyed maid,
Yielding, yet half afraid,
And in the forest's shade
   Our vows were plighted.
Under its loosened vest
Fluttered her little breast,
Like birds within their nest
   By the hawk frighted.

" Bright in her father's hall
Shields gleamed upon the wall,
Loud sang the minstrels all,
   Chanting his glory ;
When of old Hildebrand
I asked his daughter's hand,
Mute did the minstrels stand
   To hear my story.

" While the brown ale he quaffed,
Loud then the champion laughed,
And as the wind-gusts waft
   The sea-foam brightly,
So the loud laugh of scorn,
Out of those lips unshorn,
From the deep drinking-horn
   Blew the foam lightly.

" She was a Prince's child,
I but a Viking wild,
And though she blushed and smiled
   I was discarded !
Should not the dove so white
Follow the sea-mew's flight,
Why did they leave that night
   Her nest unguarded ?

" Scarce had I put to sea,
Bearing the maid with me,
Fairest of all was she
   Among the Norsemen !
When on the white sea-strand,
Waving his armed hand,
Saw we old Hildebrand,
   With twenty horsemen.

" Then launched they to the blast,
Bent like a reed each mast,
Yet we were gaining fast,
   When the wind failed us ;
And with a sudden flaw
Came round the gusty Skaw,
So that our foe we saw
   Laugh as he hailed us.

" And as to catch the gale
Round veered the flapping sail,
Death ! was the helmsman's hail,
   Death without quarter !
Mid-ships with iron keel
Struck we her ribs of steel ;
Down her black hulk did reel
   Through the black water !

" As with his wings aslant,
Sails the fierce cormorant,
Seeking some rocky haunt,
   With his prey laden,
So toward the open main,
Beating to sea again,
Through the wild hurricane,
   Bore I the maiden.

" Three weeks we westward bore,
And when the storm was o'er,
Cloud-like we saw the shore
   Stretching to leeward ;
There for my lady's bower
Built I the lofty tower,
Which, to this very hour,
   Stands looking seaward.

" There lived we many years ;
Time dried the maiden's tears ;
She had forgot her fears,
   She was a mother ;

"Should not the dove so white,
Follow the seamew's flight."   Page 26.

Death closed her mild blue eyes,
Under that tower she lies ;
Ne'er shall the sun arise
    On such another !

" Still grew my bosom then.
Still as a stagnant fen !
Hateful to me were men,
    The sunlight hateful !
In the vast forest here,
Clad in my warlike gear,
Fell I upon my spear,
    O, death was grateful !

" Thus, seamed with many scars,
Bursting these prison bars,
Up to its native stars
    My soul ascended !
There from the flowing bowl
Deep drinks the warrior's soul,
Skoal ! to the Northland ! *skoal !* "
    Thus the tale ended.

THE WRECK OF THE HESPERUS.

It was the schooner Hesperus,
    That sailed the wintry sea ;
And the skipper had taken his little
    . daughter,
    To bear him company.

Blue were her eyes as the fairy-flax,
    Her cheeks like the dawn of day,
And her bosom white as the hawthorn
    buds,
    That ope in the month of May.

The skipper he stood beside the helm,
    His pipe was in his mouth,
And he watched how the veering flaw
    did blow
    The smoke now West, now South.

Then up and spake an old Sailòr,
    Had sailed to the Spanish Main,
" I pray thee, put into yonder port,
    For I fear a hurricane.

' Last night, the moon had a golden
    ring,
    And to-night no moon we see ! "
The skipper, he blew a whiff from his
    pipe,
    And a scornful laugh laughed he.

Colder and louder blew the wind,
    A gale from the Northeast,

The snow fell hissing in the brine,
    And the billows frothed like yeast.

Down came the storm, and smote amain
    The vessel in its strength ;
She shuddered and paused, like a fright-
    ed steed,
    Then leaped her cable's length.

"Come hither ! come hither ! my little
    daughter,
    And do not tremble so ;
For I can weather the roughest gale
    That ever wind did blow."

He wrapped her warm in his seaman's
    coat
    Against the stinging blast ;
He cut a rope from a broken spar,
    And bound her to the mast.

" O father ! I hear the church-bells ring,
    O say, what may it be ? "
" 'T is a fog-bell on a rock-bound
    coast ! " —
    And he steered for the open sea.

" O father ! I hear the sound of guns,
    O say, what may it be ? "
" Some ship in distress, that cannot live
    In such an angry sea ! "

" O father ! I see a gleaming light,
    O say, what may it be ? "
But the father answered never a word,
    A frozen corpse was he.

Lashed to the helm, all stiff and stark,
    With his face turned to the skies,
The lantern gleamed through the gleam
    ing snow
    On his fixed and glassy eyes.

Then the maiden clasped her hands and
    prayed
    That savèd she might be ;
And she thought of Christ, who stilled
    the wave,
    On the Lake of Galilee.

And fast through the midnight dark and
    drear,
    Through the whistling sleet and
    snow,
Like a sheeted ghost, the vessel swept
    Tow'rds the reef of Norman's Woe

And ever the fitful gusts between
   A sound came from the land ;
It was the sound of the trampling surf
   On the rocks and the hard sea-sand.

The breakers were right beneath her bows,
   She drifted a dreary wreck,
And a whooping billow swept the crew
   Like icicles from her deck.

She struck where the white and fleecy
     waves
   Looked soft as carded wool,
But the cruel rocks, they gored her side
   Like the horns of an angry bull.

Her rattling shrouds, all sheathed in ice,
   With the masts went by the board ;
Like a vessel of glass, she stove and sank,
   Ho ! ho ! the breakers roared !

At daybreak, on the bleak sea-beach,
   A fisherman stood aghast,
To see the form of a maiden fair,
   Lashed close to a drifting mast.

The salt sea was frozen on her breast,
   The salt tears in her eyes ;
And he saw her hair, like the brown sea-
     weed,
   On the billows fall and rise.

Such was the wreck of the Hesperus,
   In the midnight and the snow !
Christ save us all from a death like this,
   On the reef of Norman's Woe !

THE LUCK OF EDENHALL.

FROM THE GERMAN OF UHLAND.

Of Edenhall, the youthful Lord
Bids sound the festal trumpet's call ;
He rises at the banquet board,
And cries, 'mid the drunken revellers all,
" Now bring me the Luck of Edenhall ! "

The butler hears the words with pain,
The house's oldest seneschal,
Takes slow from its silken cloth again
The drinking-glass of crystal tall ;
They call it The Luck of Edenhall.

Then said the Lord : "This glass to
     praise,
Fill with red wine from Portugal ! "

The graybeard with trembling hand
     obeys ;
A purple light shines over all,
It beams from the Luck of Edenhall.

Then speaks the Lord, and waves it light :
" This glass of flashing crystal tall
Gave to my sires the Fountain-Sprite ;
She wrote in it, *If this glass doth fall,*
Farewell then, O Luck of Edenhall !

" 'T was right a goblet the Fate should be
Of the joyous race of Edenhall !
Deep draughts drink we right willingly ;
And willingly ring, with merry call,
Kling ! klang ! to the Luck of Eden-
     hall ! "

First rings it deep, and full, and mild,
Like to the song of a nightingale ;
Then like the roar of a torrent wild ;
Then mutters at last like the thunder's
     fall,
The glorious Luck of Edenhall.

" For its keeper takes a race of might,
The fragile goblet of crystal tall ;
It has lasted longer than is right ;
Kling ! klang ! — with a harder blow
     than all
Will I try the Luck of Edenhall ! "

As the goblet ringing flies apart,
Suddenly cracks the vaulted hall ;
And through the rift, the wild flames
     start ;
The guests in dust are scattered all,
With the breaking Luck of Edenhall !

In storms the foe, with fire and sword ;
He in the night had scaled the wall,
Slain by the sword lies the youthful
     Lord,
But holds in his hand the crystal tall,
The shattered Luck of Edenhall.

On the morrow the butler gropes alone,
The graybeard in the desert hall,
He seeks his Lord's burnt skeleton,
He seeks in the dismal ruin's fall
The shards of the Luck of Edenhall.

"The stone wall," saith he, " doth fall
     aside,
Down must the stately columns fall ;
Glass is this earth's Luck and Pride ;
In atoms shall fall this earthly ball
One day like the Luck of Edenhall ! "

THE ELECTED KNIGHT.

FROM THE DANISH.

Sir Oluf he rideth over the plain,
　Full seven miles broad and seven miles
　　wide,
But never, ah never can meet with the
　　man
　A tilt with him dare ride.

He saw under the hillside
　A Knight full well equipped ;
His steed was black, his helm was barred ;
　He was riding at full speed.

He wore upon his spurs
　Twelve little golden birds ;
Anon he spurred his steed with a clang,
　And there sat all the birds and sang.

He wore upon his mail
　Twelve little golden wheels ;
Anon in eddies the wild wind blew,
　And round and round the wheels they
　　flew.

He wore before his breast
　A lance that was poised in rest ;
And it was sharper than diamond-stone,
　It made Sir Oluf's heart to groan.

He wore upon his helm
　A wreath of ruddy gold ;
And that gave him the Maidens Three,
　The youngest was fair to behold.

Sir Oluf questioned the Knight eftsoon
　If he were come from heaven down ;
" Art thou Christ of Heaven," quoth he
　" So will I yield me unto thee."

" I am not Christ the Great,
　Thou shalt not yield thee yet ;
I am an Unknown Knight,
　Three modest Maidens have me be
　　dight."

" Art thou a Knight elected,
　And have three Maidens thee bedight
So shalt thou ride a tilt this day,
　For all the Maidens' honor ! "

The first tilt they together rode
　They put their steeds to the test ;
The second tilt they together rode,
　They proved their manhood best.

The third tilt they together rode,
　Neither of them would yield ;
The fourth tilt they together rode,
　They both fell on the field.

Now lie the lords upon the plain,
　And their blood runs unto death ;
Now sit the Maidens in the high tower
　The youngest sorrows till death.

THE CHILDREN OF THE LORD'S SUPPER.

FROM THE SWEDISH OF BISHOP TEGNÉR.

Pentecost, day of rejoicing, had come.　The church of the village
Gleaming stood in the morning's sheen.　On the spire of the belfry,
Decked with a brazen cock, the friendly flames of the Spring-sun
Glanced like the tongues of fire, beheld by Apostles aforetime.
Clear was the heaven and blue, and May, with her cap crowned with roses,
Stood in her holiday dress in the fields, and the wind and the brooklet
Murmured gladness and peace, God's-peace ! with lips rosy-tinted
Whispered the race of the flowers, and merry on balancing branches
Birds were singing their carol, a jubilant hymn to the Highest.
Swept and clean was the churchyard.　Adorned like a leaf-woven arbor
Stood its old-fashioned gate ; and within upon each cross of iron
Hung was a fragrant garland, new twined by the hands of affection.
Even the dial, that stood on a mound among the departed,
(There full a hundred years had it stood,) was embellished with blossoms.
Like to the patriarch hoary, the sage of his kith and the hamlet,
Who on his birthday is crowned by children and children's children,

So stood the ancient prophet, and mute with his pencil of iron
Marked on the tablet of stone, and measured the time and its changes,
While all around at his feet, an eternity slumbered in quiet.
Also the church within was adorned, for this was the season
When the young, their parents' hope, and the loved-ones of heaven,
Should at the foot of the altar renew the vows of their baptism.
Therefore each nook and corner was swept and cleaned, and the dust was
Blown from the walls and ceiling, and from the oil-painted benches.
There stood the church like a garden ; the Feast of the Leafy Pavilions
Saw we in living presentment.   From noble arms on the church wall
Grew forth a cluster of leaves, and the preacher's pulpit of oak-wood
Budded once more anew, as aforetime the rod before Aaron.
Wreathed thereon was the Bible with leaves, and the dove, washed with silver,
Under its canopy fastened, had on it a necklace of wind-flowers.
But in front of the choir, round the altar-piece painted by Hörberg,
Crept a garland gigantic ; and bright-curling tresses of angels
Peeped, like the sun from a cloud, from out of the shadowy leaf-work.
Likewise the lustre of brass, new-polished, blinked from the ceiling,
And for lights there were lilies of Pentecost set in the sockets.

Loud rang the bells already ; the thronging crowd was assembled
Far from valleys and hills, to list to the holy preaching.
Hark ! then roll forth at once the mighty tones of the organ,
Hover like voices from God, aloft like invisible spirits.
Like as Elias in heaven, when he cast from off him his mantle,
So cast off the soul its garments of earth ; and with one voice
Chimed in the congregation, and sang an anthem immortal
Of the sublime Wallin, of David's harp in the North-land
Tuned to the choral of Luther ; the song on its mighty pinions
Took every living soul, and lifted it gently to heaven,
And each face did shine like the Holy One's face upon Tabor.
Lo ! there entered then into the church the Reverend Teacher.
Father he hight and he was in the parish ; a Christianly plainness
Clothed from his head to his feet the old man of seventy winters.
Friendly was he to behold, and glad as the heralding angel
Walked he among the crowds, but still a contemplative grandeur
Lay on his forehead as clear as on moss-covered gravestone a sunbeam.
As in his inspiration (an evening twilight that faintly
Gleams in the human soul, even now, from the day of creation)
Th' Artist, the friend of heaven, imagines Saint John when in Patmos,
Gray, with his eyes uplifted to heaven, so seemed then the old man ;
Such was the glance of his eye, and such were his tresses of silver.
All the congregation arose in the pews that were numbered.
But with a cordial look, to the right and the left hand, the old man
Nodding all hail and peace, disappeared in the innermost chancel.

Simply and solemnly now proceeded the Christian service,
Singing and prayer, and at last an ardent discourse from the old man.
Many a moving word and warning, that out of the heart came,
Fell like the dew of the morning, like manna on those in the desert.
Then, when all was finished, the Teacher re-entered the chancel,
Followed therein by the young.   The boys on the right had their places,
Delicate figures, with close-curling hair and cheeks rosy-blooming.
But on the left of these there stood the tremulous lilies,
Tinged with the blushing light of the dawn, the diffident maidens, —
Folding their hands in prayer, and their eyes cast down on the pavement
Now came, with question and answer, the catechism.   In the beginning

Answered the children with troubled and faltering voice, but the old man's
Glances of kindness encouraged them soon, and the doctrines eternal
Flowed, like the waters of fountains, so clear from lips unpolluted.
Each time the answer was closed, and as oft as they named the Redeemer,
Lowly louted the boys, and lowly the maidens all courtesied.
Friendly the Teacher stood, like an angel of light there among them,
And to the children explained the holy, the highest, in few words,
Thorough, yet simple and clear, for sublimity always is simple,
Both in sermon and song, a child can seize on its meaning.
E'en as the green-growing bud unfolds when Springtide approaches,
Leaf by leaf puts forth, and warmed, by the radiant sunshine,
Blushes with purple and gold, till at last the perfected blossom
Opens its odorous chalice, and rocks with its crown in the breezes,
So was unfolded here the Christian lore of salvation,
Line by line from the soul of childhood.   The fathers and mothers
Stood behind them in tears, and were glad at the well-worded answer.

Now went the old man up to the altar; — and straightway transfigured
(So did it seem unto me) was then the affectionate Teacher.
Like the Lord's Prophet sublime, and awful as Death and as Judgment
Stood he, the God-commissioned, the soul-searcher, earthward descending
Glances, sharp as a sword, into hearts that to him were transparent
Shot he; his voice was deep, was low like the thunder afar off.
So on a sudden transfigured he stood there, he spake and he questioned.

"This is the faith of the Fathers, the faith the Apostles delivered,
This is moreover the faith whereunto I baptized you, while still ye
Lay on your mothers' breasts, and nearer the portals of heaven.
Slumbering received you then the Holy Church in its bosom;
Wakened from sleep are ye now, and the light in its radiant splendor
Downward rains from the heaven; — to-day on the threshold of childhood
Kindly she frees you again, to examine and make your election,
For she knows naught of compulsion, and only conviction desireth.
This is the hour of your trial, the turning-point of existence,
Seed for the coming days; without revocation departeth
Now from your lips the confession; Bethink ye, before ye make answer,
Think not, O think not with guile to deceive the questioning Teacher.
Sharp is his eye to-day, and a curse ever rests upon falsehood.
Enter not with a lie on Life's journey; the multitude hears you,
Brothers and sisters and parents, what dear upon earth is and holy
Standeth before your sight as a witness; the Judge everlasting
Looks from the sun down upon you, and angels in waiting beside him
Grave your confession in letters of fire upon tablets eternal.
Thus, then, — believe ye in God, in the Father who this world created?
Him who redeemed it, the Son, and the Spirit where both are united?
Will ye promise me here, (a holy promise!) to cherish
God more than all things earthly, and every man as a brother?
Will ye promise me here, to confirm your faith by your living,
Th' heavenly faith of affection! to hope, to forgive, and to suffer,
Be what it may your condition, and walk before God in uprightness?
Will ye promise me this before God and man?" — With a clear voice
Answered the young men Yes! and Yes! with lips softly-breathing
Answered the maidens eke.   Then dissolved from the brow of the Teacher
Clouds with the lightnings therein, and he spake in accents more gentle,
Soft as the evening's breath, as harps by Babylon's rivers.

"Hail, then, hail to you all!   To the heirdom of heaven be ye welcome
Children no more from this day, but by covenant brothers and sisters!

Yet, — for what reason not children? Of such is the kingdom of heaven.
Here upon earth an assemblage of children, in heaven one Father,
Ruling them all as his household, — forgiving in turn and chastising,
That is of human life a picture, as Scripture has taught us.
Blest are the pure before God ! Upon purity and upon virtue
Resteth the Christian Faith : she herself from on high is descended.
Strong as a man and pure as a child, is the sum of the doctrine,
Which the Divine One taught, and suffered and died on the cross for
O, as ye wander this day from childhood's sacred asylum
Downward and ever downward, and deeper in Age's chill valley,
O, how soon will ye come, — too soon ! — and long to turn backward
Up to its hill-tops again, to the sun-illumined, where Judgment
Stood like a father before you, and Pardon, clad like a mother,
Gave you her hand to kiss, and the loving heart was forgiven,
Life was a play and your hands grasped after the roses of heaven !
Seventy years have I lived already ; the Father eternal
Gave me gladness and care ; but the loveliest hours of existence,
When I have steadfastly gazed in their eyes, I have instantly known them,
Known them all again ; — they were my childhood's acquaintance.
Therefore take from henceforth, as guides in the paths of existence,
Prayer, with her eyes raised to heaven, and Innocence, bride of man's childhood
Innocence, child beloved, is a guest from the world of the blessed,
Beautiful, and in her hand a lily ; on life's roaring billows
Swings she in safety, she heedeth them not, in the ship she is sleeping.
Calmly she gazes around in the turmoil of men ; in the desert
Angels descend and minister unto her ; she herself knoweth
Naught of her glorious attendance ; but follows faithful and humble,
Follows so long as she may her friend ; O do not reject her,
For she cometh from God and she holdeth the keys of the heavens. —
Prayer is Innocence' friend ; and willingly flieth incessant
'Twixt the earth and the sky, the carrier-pigeon of heaven.
Son of Eternity, fettered in Time, and an exile, the Spirit
Tugs at his chains evermore, and struggles like flame ever upward.
Still he recalls with emotion his Father's manifold mansions,
Thinks of the land of his fathers, where blossomed more freshly the flowerets,
Shone a more beautiful sun, and he played with the wingèd angels.
Then grows the earth too narrow, too close ; and homesick for heaven
Longs the wanderer again ; and the Spirit's longings are worship ;
Worship is called his most beautiful hour, and its tongue is entreaty.
Ah ! when the infinite burden of life descendeth upon us,
Crushes to earth our hope, and, under the earth, in the graveyard,
Then it is good to pray unto God ; for his sorrowing children
Turns he ne'er from his door, but he heals and helps and consoles them.
Yet is it better to pray when all things are prosperous with us,
Pray in fortunate days, for life's most beautiful Fortune
Kneels before the Eternal's throne ; and with hands interfolded,
Praises thankful and moved the only giver of blessings.
Or do ye know, ye children, one blessing that comes not from Heaven ?
What has mankind forsooth, the poor ! that it has not received ?
Therefore, fall in the dust and pray ! The seraphs adoring
Cover with pinions six their face in the glory of him who
Hung his masonry pendent on naught, when the world he created.
Earth declareth his might, and the firmament utters his glory.
Races blossom and die, and stars fall downward from heaven,
Downward like withered leaves ; at the last stroke of midnight, millenniums
Lay themselves down at his feet, and he sees them, but counts them as nothing
Who shall stand in his presence ? The wrath of the judge is terrific,

Casting the insolent down at a glance.   When he speaks in his anger
Hillocks skip like the kid, and mountains leap like the roebuck.
Yet, — why are ye afraid, ye children ?   This awful avenger,
Ah ! is a merciful God !   God's voice was not in the earthquake,
Not in the fire, nor the storm, but it was in the whispering breezes.
Love is the root of creation ; God's essence ; worlds without number
Lie in his bosom like children ; he made them for this purpose only.
Only to love and to be loved again, he breathed forth his spirit
Into the slumbering dust, and upright standing, it laid its
Hand on its heart, and felt it was warm with a flame out of heaven.
Quench, O quench not that flame !   It is the breath of your being.
Love is life, but hatred is death.   Not father, nor mother
Loved you, as God has loved you ; for 't was that you may be happy
Gave he his only Son.   When he bowed down his head in the death-hour
Solemnized Love its triumph ; the sacrifice then was completed.
Lo ! then was rent on a sudden the veil of the temple, dividing
Earth and heaven apart, and the dead from their sepulchres rising
Whispered with pallid lips and low in the ears of each other
Th' answer, but dreamed of before, to creation's enigma, — Atonement !
Depths of Love are Atonement's depths, for Love is Atonement.
Therefore, child of mortality, love thou the merciful Father ;
Wish what the Holy One wishes, and not from fear, but affection ;
Fear is the virtue of slaves ; but the heart that loveth is willing ;
Perfect was before God, and perfect is Love, and Love only.
Lovest thou God as thou oughtest, then lovest thou likewise thy brethren ;
One is the sun in heaven, and one, only one, is Love also.
Bears not each human figure the godlike stamp on his forehead ?
Readest thou not in his face thine origin ?   Is he not sailing
Lost like thyself on an ocean unknown, and is he not guided
By the same stars that guide thee ?   Why shouldst thou hate then thy brother
Hateth he thee, forgive !   For 't is sweet to stammer one letter
Of the Eternal's language ; — on earth it is callèd Forgiveness !
Knowest thou Him, who forgave, with the crown of thorns on his temples?
Earnestly prayed for his foes, for his murderers ?   Say, dost thou know him ?
Ah ! thou confessest his name, so follow likewise his example,
Think of thy brother no ill, but throw a veil over his failings,
Guide the erring aright ; for the good, the heavenly shepherd
Took the lost lamb in his arms, and bore it back to its mother.
This is the fruit of Love, and it is by its fruits that we know it.
Love is the creature's welfare, with God ; but Love among mortals
Is but an endless sigh !   He longs, and endures, and stands waiting,
Suffers and yet rejoices, and smiles with tears on his eyelids.
Hope, — so is called upon earth, his recompense, — Hope, the befriending,
Does what she can, for she points evermore up to heaven, and faithful
Plunges her anchor's peak in the depths of the grave, and beneath it
Paints a more beautiful world, a dim, but a sweet play of shadows !
Races, better than we, have leaned on her wavering promise,
Having naught else but Hope.   Then praise we our Father in heaven,
Him, who has given us more ; for to us has Hope been transfigured,
Groping no longer in night ; she is Faith, she is living assurance.
Faith is enlightened Hope ; she is light, is the eye of affection,
Dreams of the longing interprets, and carves their visions in marble.
Faith is the sun of life ; and her countenance shines like the Hebrew's,
For she has looked upon God ; the heaven on its stable foundation
Draws she with chains down to earth, and the New Jerusalem sinketh
Splendid with portals twelve in golden vapors descending.
There enraptured she wanders. and looks at the figures majestic,

Fears not the wingèd crowd, in the midst of them all is her homestead.
Therefore love and believe ; for works will follow spontaneous
Even as day does the sun ; the Right from the Good is an offspring,
Love in a bodily shape ; and Christian works are no more than
Animate Love and faith, as flowers are the animate Springtide.
Works do follow us all unto God ; there stand and bear witness
Not what they seemed, — but what they were only.   Blessed is he who
Hears their confession secure ; they are mute upon earth until death's hand
Opens the mouth of the silent.   Ye children, does Death e'er alarm you ?
Death is the brother of Love, twin-brother is he, and is only
More austere to behold.   With a kiss upon lips that are fading
Takes he the soul and departs, and, rocked in the arms of affection,
Places the ransomed child, new born, 'fore the face of its father.
Sounds of his coming already I hear, — see dimly his pinions,
Swart as the night, but with stars strewn upon them !   I fear not before him
Death is only release, and in mercy is mute.   On his bosom
Freer breathes, in its coolness, my breast ; and face to face standing
Look I on God as he is, a sun unpolluted by vapors ;
Look on the light of the ages I loved, the spirits majestic,
Nobler, better than I ; they stand by the throne all transfigured,
Vested in white, and with harps of gold, and are singing an anthem,
Writ in the climate of heaven, in the language spoken by angels.
You, in like manner, ye children beloved, he one day shall gather,
Never forgets he the weary ; — then welcome, ye loved ones, hereafter !
Meanwhile forget not the keeping of vows, forget not the promise,
Wander from holiness onward to holiness; earth shall ye heed not ;
Earth is but dust and heaven is light ; I have pledged you to heaven.
God of the universe, hear me ! thou fountain of Love everlasting,
Hark to the voice of thy servant !   I send up my prayer to thy heaven !
Let me hereafter not miss at thy throne one spirit of all these,
Whom thou hast given me here !   I have loved them all like a father.
May they bear witness for me, that I taught them the way of salvation,
Faithful, so far as I knew, of thy word ; again may they know me,
Fall on their Teacher's breast, and before thy face may I place them,
Pure as they now are, but only more tried, and exclaiming with gladness,
Father, lo ! I am here, and the children, whom thou hast given me ! "

Weeping he spake in these words ; and now at the beck of the old man
Knee against knee they knitted a wreath round the altar's enclosure.
Kneeling he read then the prayers of the consecration, and softly
With him the children read ; at the close, with tremulous accents,
Asked he the peace of Heaven, a benediction upon them.
Now should have ended his task for the day ; the following Sunday
Was for the young appointed to eat of the Lord's holy Supper.
Sudden, as struck from the clouds, stood the Teacher silent and laid his
Hand on his forehead, and cast his looks upward ; while thoughts high and holy
Flew through the midst of his soul, and his eyes glanced with wonderful bright
        ness.
" On the next Sunday, who knows ! perhaps I shall rest in the graveyard !
Some one perhaps of yourselves, a lily broken untimely,
Bow down his head to the earth ; why delay I ? the hour is accomplished.
Warm is the heart ; — I will ! for to-day grows the harvest of heaven.
What I began accomplish I now ; what failing therein is
I, the old man, will answer to God and the reverend father.
Say to me only, ye children, ye denizens new-come in heaven,
Are ye ready this day to eat of the bread of Atonement ?
What it denoteth, that know ye full well, I have told it you often.

Of the new covenant symbol it is, of Atonement a token,
Stablished between earth and heaven. Man by his sins and transgressions
Far has wandered from God, from his essence. 'T was in the beginning
Fast by the Tree of Knowledge he fell, and it hangs its crown o'er the
Fall to this day ; in the Thought is the Fall; in the Heart the Atonement.
Infinite is the fall, — the Atonement infinite likewise.
See ! behind me, as far as the old man remembers, and forward,
Far as Hope in her flight can reach with her wearied pinions,
Sin and Atonement incessant go through the lifetime of mortals.
Sin is brought forth full-grown'; but Atonement sleeps in our bosoms
Still as the cradled babe ; and dreams of heaven and of angels,
Cannot awake to sensation ; is like the tones in the harp's strings,
Spirits imprisoned, that wait evermore the deliverer's finger.
Therefore, ye children beloved, descended the Prince of Atonement,
Woke the slumberer from sleep, and she stands now with eyes all resplendent
Bright as the vault of the sky, and battles with Sin and o'ercomes her.
Downward to earth he came and, transfigured, thence reascended,
Not from the heart in like wise, for there he still lives in the Spirit,
Loves and atones evermore. So long as Time is, is Atonement.
Therefore with reverence take this day her visible token.
Tokens are dead if the things live not. The light everlasting
Unto the blind is not, but is born of the eye that has vision.
Neither in bread nor in wine, but in the heart that is hallowed
Lieth forgiveness enshrined ; the intention alone of amendment
Fruits of the earth ennobles to heavenly things, and removes all
Sin and the guerdon of sin. Only Love with his arms wide extended,
Penitence weeping and praying; the Will that is tried, and whose gold flows
Purified forth from the flames ; in a word, mankind by Atonement
Breaketh Atonement's bread, and drinketh Atonement's wine-cup.
But he who cometh up hither, unworthy, with hate in his bosom,
Scoffing at men and at God, is guilty of Christ's blessed body,
And the Redeemer's blood ! To himself he eateth and drinketh
Death and doom ! And from this, preserve us, thou heavenly Father !
Are ye ready, ye children, to eat of the bread of Atonement ? "
Thus with emotion he asked, and together answered the children,
" Yes !" with deep sobs interrupted. Then read he the due supplications,
Read the Form of Communion, and in chimed the organ and anthem :
" O Holy Lamb of God, who takest away our transgressions,
Hear us ! give us thy peace ! have mercy, have mercy upon us ! "
Th' old man, with trembling hand, and heavenly pearls on his eyelids,
Filled now the chalice and paten, and dealt round the mystical symbols.
O, then seemed it to me as if God, with the broad eye of midday,
Clearer looked in at the windows, and all the trees in the churchyard
Bowed down their summits of green, and the grass on the graves 'gan to shiver.
But in the children (I noted it well ; I knew it) there ran a
Tremor of holy rapture along through their ice-cold members.
Decked like an altar before them, there stood the green earth, and above it
Heaven opened itself, as of old before Stephen ; they saw there
Radiant in glory the Father, and on his right hand the Redeemer.
Under them hear they the clang of harpstrings, and angels from gold clouds
Beckon to them like brothers, and fan with their pinions of purple.

Closed was the Teacher's task, and with heaven in their hearts and their faces,
Up rose the children all, and each bowed him, weeping full sorely,
Downward to kiss that reverend hand, but all of them pressed he
Moved to his bosom, and laid, with a prayer, his hands full of blessings,
Now on the holy breast, and now on the innocent tresses.

MISCELLANEOUS.

THE VILLAGE BLACKSMITH.

UNDER a spreading chestnut-tree
  The village smithy stands ;
The smith, a mighty man is he,
  With large and sinewy hands ;
And the muscles of his brawny arms
  Are strong as iron bands.

His hair is crisp, and black, and long,
  His face is like the tan ;
His brow is wet with honest sweat,
  He earns whate'er he can,
And looks the whole world in the face,
  For he owes not any man.

Week in, week out, from morn till night,
  You can hear his bellows blow ;
You can hear him swing his heavy sledge,
  With measured beat and slow,
Like a sexton ringing the village bell,
  When the evening sun is low.

And children coming home from school
  Look in at the open door ;
They love to see the flaming forge,
  And hear the bellows roar,
And catch the burning sparks that fly
  Like chaff from a threshing-floor.

He goes on Sunday to the church,
  And sits among his boys ;
He hears the parson pray and·preach,
  He hears his daughter's voice,
Singing in the village choir,
  And it makes his heart rejoice.

It sounds to him like her mother's voice,
  Singing in Paradise !
He needs must think of her once more,
  How in the grave she lies ;
And with his hard, rough hand he wipes
  A tear out of his eyes.

Toiling, — rejoicing, — sorrowing,
  Onward through life he goes ;
Each morning sees some task begin,
  Each evening sees it close ;
Something attempted, something done,
  Has earned a night's repose.

Thanks, thanks to thee, my worthy
    friend,
  For the lesson thou hast taught !

Thus at the flaming forge of life
  Our fortunes must be wrought ;
Thus on its sounding anvil shaped
  Each burning deed and thought.

ENDYMION.

THE rising moon has hid the stars ;
Her level rays, like golden bars,
  Lie on the landscape green,
  With shadows brown between.

And silver white the river gleams,
As if Diana, in her dreams,
  Had dropt her silver bow
  Upon the meadows low.

On such a tranquil night as this,
She woke Endymion with a kiss,
  When, sleeping in the grove,
  He dreamed not of her love.

Like Dian's kiss, unasked, unsought,
Love gives itself, but is not bought ;
  Nor voice, nor sound betrays
  Its deep, impassioned gaze.

It comes, — the beautiful, the free,
The crown of all humanity, —
  In silence and alone
  To seek the elected one.

It lifts the boughs, whose shadows deep
Are Life's oblivion, the soul's sleep,
  And kisses the closed eyes
  Of him, who slumbering lies.

O weary hearts ! O slumbering eyes !
O drooping souls, whose destinies
  Are fraught with fear and pain,
  Ye shall be loved again !

No one is so accursed by fate,
No one so utterly desolate,
  But some heart, though unknown,
  Responds unto his own.

Responds, — as if with unseen wings,
An angel touched its quivering strings ;
  And whispers, in its song,
  "Where hast thou stayed so long?"

THE TWO LOCKS OF HAIR.

FROM THE GERMAN OF PFIZER.

A YOUTH, light-hearted and content,
  I wander through the world ;
Here, Arab-like, is pitched my tent
  And straight again is furled.

Yet oft I dream, that once a wife
  Close in my heart was locked,
And in the sweet repose of life
  A blessed child I rocked.

I wake ! Away that dream, — away !
  Too long did it remain !
So long, that both by night and day
  It ever comes again.

The end lies ever in my thought ;
  To a grave so cold and deep
The mother beautiful was brought ;
  Then dropt the child asleep.

But now the dream is wholly o'er,
  I bathe mine eyes and see ;
And wander through the world once more,
  A youth so light and free.

Two locks — and they are wondrous
    fair —
  Left me that vision mild ;
The brown is from the mother's hair,
  The blond is from the child.

And when I see that lock of gold,
  Pale grows the evening-red ;
And when the dark lock I behold,
  I wish that I were dead.

IT IS NOT ALWAYS MAY.

No hay pájaros en los nidos de antaño.
                    Spanish Proverb.

THE sun is bright, — the air is clear,
  The darting swallows soar and sing,
And from the stately elms I hear
  The bluebird prophesying Spring.

So blue yon winding river flows,
  It seems an outlet from the sky,
Where waiting till the west-wind blows,
  The freighted clouds at anchor lie.

All things are new ; — the buds, the
    leaves,
  That gild the elm-tree's nodding crest,

And even the nest beneath the eaves ; —
  There are no birds in last year's nest !

All things rejoice in youth and love,
  The fulness of their first delight !
And learn from the soft heavens above
  The melting tenderness of night.

Maiden, that read'st this simple rhyme,
  Enjoy thy youth, it will not stay ;
Enjoy the fragrance of thy prime,
  For O, it is not always May !

Enjoy the Spring of Love and Youth,
  To some good angel leave the rest ;
For Time will teach thee soon the truth,
  There are no birds in last year's nest !

THE RAINY DAY.

THE day is cold, and dark, and dreary ;
  It rains, and the wind is never weary ;
The vine still clings to the mouldering
    wall,
But at every gust the dead leaves fall,
  And the day is dark and dreary.

My life is cold, and dark, and dreary ;
It rains, and the wind is never weary ;
My thoughts still cling to the mouldering
    Past,
But the hopes of youth fall thick in the
    blast,
  And the days are dark and dreary.

Be still, sad heart ! and cease repining ;
Behind the clouds is the sun still shining ;
Thy fate is the common fate of all,
Into each life some rain must fall,
  Some days must be dark and dreary.

GOD'S – ACRE.

I LIKE that ancient Saxon phrase, which
    calls
  The burial-ground God's-Acre ! It is
    just ;
It consecrates each grave within its walls,
  And breathes a benison o'er the sleep-
    ing dust.

God's-Acre ! Yes, that blessed name im-
    parts
  Comfort to those, who in the grave
    have sown

The seed that they had garnered in their
          hearts,
    Their bread of life, alas ! no more their
          own.   .

Into its furrows shall we all be cast,
    In the sure faith, that we shall rise
          again
At the great harvest, when the archan-
          gel's blast
    Shall winnow, like a fan, the chaff and
          grain.

Then shall the good stand in immortal
          bloom,
    In the fair gardens of that second birth ;
And each bright blossom mingle its per-
          fume
    With that of flowers, which never
          bloomed on earth.

With thy rude ploughshare, Death, turn
          up the sod,
    And spread the furrow for the seed we
          sow ;
This is the field and Acre of our God,
    This is the place where human harvests
          grow !

TO THE RIVER CHARLES.

RIVER ! that in silence windest
    Through the meadows, bright and free,
Till at length thy rest thou findest
    In the bosom of the sea !

Four long years of mingled feeling,
    Half in rest, and half in strife,
I have seen thy waters stealing
    Onward, like the stream of life.

Thou hast taught me, Silent River !
    Many a lesson, deep and long ;
Thou hast been a generous giver ;
    I can give thee but a song.

Oft in sadness and in illness,
    I have watched thy current glide,
Till the beauty of its stillness
    Overflowed me, like a tide.

And in better hours and brighter,
    When I saw thy waters gleam,
I have felt my heart beat lighter,
    And leap onward with thy stream.

Not for this alone I love thee,
    Nor because thy waves of blue
From celestial seas above thee
    Take their own celestial hue.

Where yon shadowy woodlands hide thee,
    And thy waters disappear,
Friends I love have dwelt beside thee,
    And have made thy margin dear.

More than this ; — thy name reminds me
    Of three friends, all true and tried ;
And that name, like magic, binds me
    Closer, closer to thy side.

Friends my soul with joy remembers !
    How like quivering flames they start,
When I fan the living embers
    On the hearth-stone of my heart !

'T is for this, thou Silent River !
    That my spirit leans to thee ;
Thou hast been a generous giver,
    Take this idle song from me.

BLIND BARTIMEUS.

BLIND Bartimeus at the gates
Of Jericho in darkness waits ;
He hears the crowd ; — he hears a breath
Say, " It is Christ of Nazareth ! "
And calls, in tones of agony,
Ἰησοῦ, ἐλέησόν με !

The thronging multitudes increase ;
Blind Bartimeus, hold thy peace !
But still, above the noisy crowd,
The beggar's cry is shrill and loud ;
Until they say, " He calleth thee ! "
Θάρσει, ἔγειραι, φωνεῖ σε !

Then saith the Christ, as silent stands
The crowd, " What wilt thou at my
          hands ? "
And he replies, " O give me light !
Rabbi, restore the blind man's sight.
And Jesus answers, Ὕπαγε ·
Ἡ πίστις σου σέσωκέ σε !

Ye that have eyes, yet cannot see,
In darkness and in misery,
Recall those mighty Voices Three,
Ἰησοῦ, ἐλέησόν με !
Θάρσει, ἔγειραι, ὕπαγε !
Ἡ πίστις σου σέσωκέ σε !

THE GOBLET OF LIFE.

FILLED is Life's goblet to the brim;
And though my eyes with tears are dim,
I see its sparkling bubbles swim,
And chant a melancholy hymn
    With solemn voice and slow.

No purple flowers, — no garlands green,
Conceal the goblet's shade or sheen,
Nor maddening draughts of Hippocrene,
Like gleams of sunshine, flash between
    Thick leaves of mistletoe.

This goblet, wrought with curious art,
Is filled with waters, that upstart,
When the deep fountains of the heart,
By strong convulsions rent apart,
    Are running all to waste.

And as it mantling passes round,
With fennel is it wreathed and crowned,
Whose seed and foliage sun-imbrowned
Are in its waters steeped and drowned,
    And give a bitter taste.

Above the lowly plants it towers,
The fennel, with its yellow flowers,
And in an earlier age than ours
Was gifted with the wondrous powers,
    Lost vision to restore.

It gave new strength, and fearless mood;
And gladiators, fierce and rude,
Mingled it in their daily food;
And he who battled and subdued,
    A wreath of fennel wore.

Then in Life's goblet freely press,
The leaves that give it bitterness,
Nor prize the colored waters less,
For in thy darkness and distress
    New light and strength they give!

And he who has not learned to know
How false its sparkling bubbles show,
How bitter are the drops of woe,
With which its brim may overflow,
    He has not learned to live.

The prayer of Ajax was for light;
Through all that dark and desperate fight,
The blackness of that noonday night,
He asked but the return of sight,
    To see his foeman's face.

Let our unceasing, earnest prayer
Be, too, for light, — for strength to bear
Our portion of the weight of care,
That crushes into dumb despair
    One half the human race.

O suffering, sad humanity!
O ye afflicted ones, who lie
Steeped to the lips in misery,
Longing, and yet afraid to die,
    Patient, though sorely tried!

I pledge you in this cup of grief,
Where floats the fennel's bitter leaf!
The Battle of our Life is brief,
The alarm, — the struggle, — the relief
    Then sleep we side by side.

MAIDENHOOD.

MAIDEN! with the meek, brown eyes,
In whose orbs a shadow lies
Like the dusk in evening skies!

Thou whose locks outshine the sun,
Golden tresses, wreathed in one,
As the braided streamlets run!

Standing, with reluctant feet,
Where the brook and river meet,
Womanhood and childhood fleet!

Gazing, with a timid glance,
On the brooklet's swift advance,
On the river's broad expanse!

Deep and still, that gliding stream
Beautiful to thee must seem,
As the river of a dream.

Then why pause with indecision,
When bright angels in thy vision
Beckon thee to fields Elysian?

Seest thou shadows sailing by,
As the dove, with startled eye,
Sees the falcon's shadow fly?

Hearest thou voices on the shore,
That our ears perceive no more,
Deafened by the cataract's roar?

O, thou child of many prayers!
Life hath quicksands, — Life hath snares!
Care and age come unawares!

Like the swell of some sweet tune,
Morning rises into noon,
May glides onward into June.

Childhood is the bough, where slumbered
Birds and blossoms many-numbered ; —
Age, that bough with snows encumbered.

Gather, then, each flower that grows,
When the young heart overflows,
To embalm that tent of snows.

Bear a lily in thy hand ;
Gates of brass cannot withstand
One touch of that magic wand.

Bear through sorrow, wrong, and ruth,
In thy heart the dew of youth,
On thy lips the smile of truth.

O, that dew, like balm, shall steal
Into wounds that cannot heal,
Even as sleep our eyes doth seal ;

And that smile, like sunshine, dart
Into many a sunless heart,
For a smile of God thou art.

EXCELSIOR.

THE shades of night were falling fast,
As through an Alpine village passed
A youth, who bore, 'mid snow and ice,
A banner with the strange device,
        Excelsior !

His brow was sad ; his eye beneath,
Flashed like a falchion from its sheath,
And like a silver clarion rung
The accents of that unknown tongue,
        Excelsior !

In happy homes he saw the light
Of household fires gleam warm and bright ;
Above, the spectral glaciers shone,
And from his lips escaped a groan,
        Excelsior !

" Try not the Pass ! " the old man said ;
" Dark lowers the tempest overhead,
The roaring torrent is deep and wide ! "
And loud that clarion voice replied,
        Excelsior !

" O stay," the maiden said, " and rest
Thy weary head upon this breast ! "
A tear stood in his bright blue eye,
But still he answered, with a sigh,
        Excelsior !

' Beware the pine-tree's withered branch !
Beware the awful avalanche ! "
This was the peasant's last Good-night,
A voice replied, far up the height,
        Excelsior !

At break of day, as heavenward
The pious monks of Saint Bernard
Uttered the oft-repeated prayer,
A voice cried through the startled air,
        Excelsior !

A traveller, by the faithful hound,
Half-buried in the snow was found,
Still grasping in his hand of ice
That banner with the strange device,
        Excelsior !

There in the twilight cold and gray,
Lifeless, but beautiful, he lay,
And from the sky, serene and far,
A voice fell, like a falling star,
        Excelsior !

MEZZO CAMMIN.

Written at Boppard on the Rhine, August 25,
1842, just before leaving for home.

Half of my life is gone, and I have let
    The years slip from me and have not
        fulfilled
    The aspiration of my youth, to build
    Some tower of song with lofty parapet.
Not indolence, nor pleasure, nor the fret
    Of restless passions that would not be
        stilled,
    But sorrow, and a care that almost
        killed,
    Kept me from what I may accomplish
        yet ;
Though, half-way up the hill, I see the
        Past
    Lying beneath me with its sounds and
        sights, —
    A city in the twilight dim and vast,
With smoking roofs, soft bells, and
        gleaming lights, —
    And hear above me on the autumnal
        blast
    The cataract of Death far thundering
        from the heights.

POEMS ON SLAVERY.

[The following poems, with one exception, were written at sea, in the latter part of October, 1842. I had not then heard of Dr. Channing's death. Since that event, the poem addressed to him is no longer appropriate. I have decided, however, to let it remain as it was written, in testimony of my admiration for a great and good man.]

TO WILLIAM E. CHANNING.

The pages of thy book I read,
  And as I closed each one,
My heart, responding, ever said,
  " Servant of God ! well done ! "

Well done ! Thy words are great and
    bold ;
  At times they seem to me,
Like Luther's, in the days of old,
  Half-battles for the free.

Go on, until this land revokes
  The old and chartered Lie,
The feudal curse, whose whips and yokes
  Insult humanity.

A voice is ever at thy side
  Speaking in tones of might,
Like the prophetic voice, that cried
  To John in Patmos, " Write ! "

Write ! and tell out this bloody tale ;
  Record this dire eclipse,
This Day of Wrath, this Endless Wail,
  This dread Apocalypse !

THE SLAVE'S DREAM.

Beside the ungathered rice he lay,
  His sickle in his hand ;
His breast was bare, his matted hair
  Was buried in the sand.
Again, in the mist and shadow of sleep,
  He saw his Native Land.

Wide through the landscape of his dreams
  The lordly Niger flowed ;
Beneath the palm-trees on the plain
  Once more a king he strode ;
And heard the tinkling caravans
  Descend the mountain-road.

He saw once more his dark-eyed queen
  Among her children stand ;

They clasped his neck, they kissed his
    cheeks,
  They held him by the hand ! —
A tear burst from the sleeper's lids
  And fell into the sand.

And then at furious speed he rode
  Along the Niger's bank ;
His bridle-reins were golden chains,
  And, with a martial clank,
At each leap he could feel his scabbard
    of steel
  Smiting his stallion's flank.

Before him, like a blood-red flag,
  The bright flamingoes flew ;
From morn till night he followed their
    flight,
O'er plains where the tamarind grew,
Till he saw the roofs of Caffre huts,
  And the ocean rose to view.

At night he heard the lion roar,
  And the hyena scream,
And the river-horse, as he crushed the
    reeds
  Beside some hidden stream ;
And it passed, like a glorious roll of
    drums,
  Through the triumph of his dream.

The forests, with their myriad tongues,
  Shouted of liberty ;
And the Blast of the Desert cried aloud,
  With a voice so wild and free,
That he started in his sleep and smiled
  At their tempestuous glee.

He did not feel the driver's whip,
  Nor the burning heat of day ;
For Death had illumined the Land of
    Sleep,
  And his lifeless body lay
A worn-out fetter, that the soul
  Had broken and thrown away !

THE GOOD PART,

THAT SHALL NOT BE TAKEN AWAY.

SHE dwells by Great Kenhawa's side,
  In valleys green and cool ;
And all her hope and all her pride
  Are in the village school.

Her soul, like the transparent air
  That robes the hills above,
Though not of earth, encircles there
  All things with arms of love.

And thus she walks among her girls
  With praise and mild rebukes ;
Subduing e'en rude village churls
  By her angelic looks.

She reads to them at eventide
  Of One who came to save ;
To cast the captive's chains aside
  And liberate the slave.

And oft the blessed time foretells
  When all men shall be free ;
And musical, as silver bells,
  Their falling chains shall be.

And following her beloved Lord,
  In decent poverty,
She makes her life one sweet record
  And deed of charity.

For she was rich, and gave up all
  To break the iron bands
Of those who waited in her hall,
  And labored in her lands.

Long since beyond the Southern Sea
  Their outbound sails have sped,
While she, in meek humility,
  Now earns her daily bread.

It is their prayers, which never cease,
  That clothe her with such grace ;
Their blessing is the light of peace
  That shines upon her face.

THE SLAVE IN THE DISMAL SWAMP.

IN dark fens of the Dismal Swamp
  The hunted Negro lay ;
He saw the fire of the midnight camp,
And heard at times a horse's tramp
  And a bloodhound's distant bay.

Where will-o'-the-wisps and glow-worms
    shine,
  In bulrush and in brake ;
Where waving mosses shroud the pine,
And the cedar grows, and the poisonous
    vine
  Is spotted like the snake ;

Where hardly a human foot could pass,
  Or a human heart would dare,
On the quaking turf of the green morass
He crouched in the rank and tangled
    grass,
  Like a wild beast in his lair.

A poor old slave, infirm and lame ;
  Great scars deformed his face ;
On his forehead he bore the brand of
    shame,
And the rags, that hid his mangled frame,
  Were the livery of disgrace.

All things above were bright and fair,
  All things were glad and free ;
Lithe squirrels darted here and there,
And wild birds filled the echoing air
  With songs of Liberty !

On him alone was the doom of pain,
  From the morning of his birth ;
On him alone the curse of Cain
Fell, like a flail on the garnered grain,
  And struck him to the earth !

THE SLAVE SINGING AT MID-NIGHT.

LOUD he sang the psalm of David !
He, a Negro and enslaved,
Sang of Israel's victory,
Sang of Zion, bright and free.

In that hour, when night is calmest,
Sang he from the Hebrew Psalmist,
In a voice so sweet and clear
That I could not choose but hear,

Songs of triumph, and ascriptions,
Such as reached the swart Egyptians,
When upon the Red Sea coast
Perished Pharaoh and his host.

And the voice of his devotion
Filled my soul with strange emotion ;
For its tones by turns were glad,
Sweetly solemn, wildly sad.

Paul and Silas, in their prison,
Sang of Christ, the Lord arisen,
And an earthquake's arm of might
Broke their dungeon-gates at night.

But, alas! what holy angel
Brings the Slave this glad evangel?
And what earthquake's arm of might
Breaks his dungeon-gates at night?

THE WITNESSES.

In Ocean's wide domains,
    Half buried in the sands,
Lie skeletons in chains,
    With shackled feet and hands.

Beyond the fall of dews,
    Deeper than plummet lies,
Float ships, with all their crews,
    No more to sink nor rise.

There the black Slave-ship swims,
    Freighted with human forms,
Whose fettered, fleshless limbs
    Are not the sport of storms.

These are the bones of Slaves;
    They gleam from the abyss;
They cry, from yawning waves,
    "We are the Witnesses!"

Within Earth's wide domains
    Are markets for men's lives;
Their necks are galled with chains,
    Their wrists are cramped with gyves.

Dead bodies, that the kite
    In deserts makes its prey;
Murders, that with affright
    Scare school-boys from their play!

All evil thoughts and deeds;
    Anger, and lust, and pride;
The foulest, rankest weeds,
    That choke Life's groaning tide!

These are the woes of Slaves;
    They glare from the abyss;
They cry, from unknown graves,
    "We are the Witnesses!"

THE QUADROON GIRL.

The Slaver in the broad lagoon
    Lay moored with idle sail;
He waited for the rising moon,
    And for the evening gale.

Under the shore his boat was tied,
    And all her listless crew
Watched the gray alligator slide
    Into the still bayou.

Odors of orange-flowers, and spice,
    Reached them from time to time,
Like airs that breathe from Paradise
    Upon a world of crime.

The Planter, under his roof of thatch,
    Smoked thoughtfully and slow;
The Slaver's thumb was on the latch,
    He seemed in haste to go.

He said, "My ship at anchor rides
    In yonder broad lagoon;
I only wait the evening tides,
    And the rising of the moon."

Before them, with her face upraised,
    In timid attitude,
Like one half curious, half amazed,
    A Quadroon maiden stood.

Her eyes were large, and full of light,
    Her arms and neck were bare;
No garment she wore save a kirtle bright,
    And her own long, raven hair.

And on her lips there played a smile
    As holy, meek, and faint,
As lights in some cathedral aisle
    The features of a saint.

"The soil is barren, — the farm is old";
    The thoughtful planter said;
Then looked upon the Slaver's gold,
    And then upon the maid.

His heart within him was at strife
    With such accursed gains:
For he knew whose passions gave her life,
    Whose blood ran in her veins.

But the voice of nature was too weak;
    He took the glittering gold!
Then pale as death grew the maiden's cheek,
    Her hands as icy cold.

The Slaver led her from the door,
    He led her by the hand,
To be his slave and paramour
    In a strange and distant land!

THE WARNING.

BEWARE ! The Israelite of old, who tore
   The lion in his path, — when, poor
   and blind,
He saw the blessed light of heaven no
   more,
   Shorn of his noble strength and forced
   to grind
In prison, and at last led forth to be
A pander to Philistine revelry, —

Upon the pillars of the temple laid
   His desperate hands, and in its over-
   throw
Destroyed himself, and with him those
   who made
   A cruel mockery of his sightless woe ;

The poor, blind Slave, the scoff and jest
   of all,
Expired, and thousands perished in the
   fall !

There is a poor, blind Samson in this
   land,
   Shorn of his strength and bound in
   bonds of steel,
Who may, in some grim revel, raise his
   hand,
   And shake the pillars of this Common-
   weal,
Till the vast Temple of our liberties
A shapeless mass of wreck and rubbish
   lies.

THE SPANISH STUDENT.

DRAMATIS PERSONÆ.

VICTORIAN } HYPOLITO }	*Students of Alcalá.*
THE COUNT OF LARA } DON CARLOS }	*Gentlemen of Madrid.*
THE ARCHBISHOP OF TOLEDO.	
A CARDINAL.	
BELTRAN CRUZADO	*Count of the Gypsies.*
BARTOLOMÉ ROMAN	*A young Gypsy.*
THE PADRE CURA OF GUADARRAMA.	
PEDRO CRESPO	*Alcalde.*
PANCHO	*Alguacil.*
FRANCISCO	*Lara's Servant.*
CHISPA	*Victorian's Servant.*
BALTASAR	*Innkeeper.*
PRECIOSA	*A Gypsy Girl.*
ANGELICA	*A poor Girl.*
MARTINA	*The Padre Cura's Niece.*
DOLORES	*Preciosa's Maid.*

Gypsies, Musicians, &c.

ACT I.

SCENE I. — *The* COUNT OF LARA'S *chambers. Night. The* COUNT *in his dressing-gown, smoking and conversing with*
DON CARLOS.

   Lara. You were not at the play to-
night, Don Carlos ;
How happened it ?
   Don C. I had engagements else-
where.
Pray who was there ?
   Lara. Why. all the town and court.

The house was crowded ; and the busy
   fans
Among the gayly dressed and perfumed
   ladies
Fluttered like butterflies among the
   flowers.
There was the Countess of Medina Celi ;
The Goblin Lady with her Phantom
   Lover,
Her Lindo Don Diego ; Doña Sol,
And Doña Serafina, and her cousins.
   Don C. What was the play ?
   Lara.   It was a dull affair ;

One of those comedies in which you see,
As Lope says, the history of the world
Brought down from Genesis to the Day
    of Judgment.
There were three duels fought in the first
    act,
Three gentlemen receiving deadly
    wounds,
Laying their hands upon their hearts,
    and saying,
"O, I am dead!" a lover in a closet,
An old hidalgo, and a gay Don Juan,
A Doña Inez with a black mantilla,
Followed at twilight by an unknown
    lover,
Who looks intently where he knows she
    is not!
    Don C. Of course, the Preciosa danced
    to-night?
    Lara. And never better. Every foot-
    step fell
As lightly as a sunbeam on the water.
I think the girl extremely beautiful.
    Don C. Almost beyond the privilege
    of woman!
I saw her in the Prado yesterday.
Her step was royal, — queen-like, — and
    her face
As beautiful as a saint's in Paradise.
    Lara. May not a saint fall from her
    Paradise,
And be no more a saint?
    Don C.   Why do you ask?
    Lara. Because I have heard it said
    this angel fell,
And though she is a virgin outwardly,
Within she is a sinner; like those panels
Of doors and altar-pieces the old monks
Painted in convents, with the Virgin
    Mary
On the outside, and on the inside Venus!
    Don C. You do her wrong; indeed,
    you do her wrong!
She is as virtuous as she is fair.
    Lara. How credulous you are! Why
    look you, friend,
There's not a virtuous woman in Madrid,
In this whole city! And would you per-
    suade me
That a mere dancing-girl, who shows
    herself,
Nightly, half naked, on the stage, for
    money,
And with voluptuous motions fires the
    blood
Of inconsiderate youth, is to be held
A model for her virtue?

    Don C.   You forget
She is a Gypsy girl.
    Lara.   And therefore won
The easier.
    Don C. Nay, not to be won at all!
The only virtue that a Gypsy prizes
Is chastity. That is her only virtue.
Dearer than life she holds it. I remem-
    ber
A Gypsy woman, a vile, shameless bawd,
Whose craft was to betray the young and
    fair;
And yet this woman was above all bribes.
And when a noble lord, touched by her
    beauty,
The wild and wizard beauty of her race,
Offered her gold to be what she made
    others,
She turned upon him, with a look of
    scorn,
And smote him in the face!
    Lara.   And does that prove
That Preciosa is above suspicion?
    Don C. It proves a nobleman may be
    repulsed
When he thinks conquest easy. I believe
That woman, in her deepest degrada-
    tion,
Holds something sacred, something un-
    defiled,
Some pledge and keepsake of her highest
    nature,
And, like the diamond in the dark, re-
    tains
Some quenchless gleam of the celestial
    light!
    Lara. Yet Preciosa would have taken
    the gold.
    Don C. (*rising*). I do not think so.
    Lara.   I am sure of it.
But why this haste? Stay yet a little
    longer.
And fight the battles of your Dulcinea.
    Don C. 'T is late. I must begone,
    for if I stay
You will not be persuaded.
    Lara.   Yes; persuade me.
    Don C. No one so deaf as he who will
    not hear!
    Lara. No one so blind as he who will
    not see!
    Don C. And so good night. I wish
    you pleasant dreams,
And greater faith in woman.   [*Exit.*
    Lara.   Greater faith!
I have the greatest faith; for I believe
Victorian is her lover. I believe

That I shall be to-morrow ; and there-
after
Another, and another, and another,
Chasing each other through her zodiac,
As Taurus chases Aries.

(*Enter* FRANCISCO *with a casket.*)

                  Well, Francisco,
What speed with Preciosa ?
  Fran.   None, my lord.
She sends your jewels back, and bids me
    tell you
She is not to be purchased by your gold.
  Lara. Then I will try some other way
    to win her.
Pray, dost thou know Victorian ?
  Fran.   Yes, my lord ;
I saw him at the jeweller's to-day.
  Lara. What was he doing there ?
  Fran.   I saw him buy
A golden ring, that had a ruby in it.
  Lara. Was there another like it ?
  Fran.   One so like it
I could not choose between them.
  Lara.   It is well.
To-morrow morning bring that ring to me.
Do not forget. Now light me to my bed.
                      [*Exeunt.*

SCENE II. — *A street in Madrid.* Enter
CHISPA, *followed by musicians, with a
bagpipe, guitars, and other instruments.*

  Chispa. Abernuncio Satanas ! and a
plague on all lovers who ramble about at
night, drinking the elements, instead of
sleeping quietly in their beds. Every
dead man to his cemetery, say I ; and
every friar to his monastery. Now, here's
my master, Victorian, yesterday a cow-
keeper, and to-day a gentleman ; yesterday a student, and to-day a lover ; and
I must be up later than the nightingale,
for as the abbot sings so must the
sacristan respond. God grant he may
soon be married, for then shall all this
serenading cease. Ay, marry ! marry !
marry ! Mother, what does marry mean ?
It means to spin, to bear children, and
to weep, my daughter ! And, of a truth,
there is something more in matrimony
than the wedding-ring. (*To the musicians.*) And now, gentlemen, Pax vobiscum ! as the ass said to the cabbages.
Pray, walk this way ; and don't hang
down your heads. It is no disgrace to
have an old father and a ragged shirt.

Now, look you, you are gentlemen who
lead the life of crickets ; you enjoy hunger by day and noise by night. Yet, I
beseech you, for this once be not loud,
but pathetic ; for it is a serenade to a
damsel in bed, and not to the Man in the
Moon. Your object is not to arouse and
terrify, but to soothe and bring lulling
dreams. Therefore, each shall not play
upon his instrument as if it were the only
one in the universe, but gently, and with
a certain modesty, according with the
others. Pray, how may I call thy name,
friend ?
  First Mus. Gerónimo Gil, at your
service.
  Chispa. Every tub smells of the wine
that is in it. Pray, Gerónimo, is not
Saturday an unpleasant day with thee ?
  First Mus. Why so ?
  Chispa. Because I have heard it
said that Saturday is an unpleasant
day with those who have but one shirt.
Moreover, I have seen thee at the tavern,
and if thou canst run as fast as thou
canst drink, I should like to hunt hares
with thee. What instrument is that ?
  First Mus. An Aragonese bagpipe.
  Chispa. Pray, art thou related to the
bagpiper of Bujalance, who asked a
maravedí for playing, and ten for leaving off ?
  First Mus. No, your honor.
  Chispa. I am glad of it. What other
instruments have we ?
  Second and Third Musicians. We
play the bandurria.
  Chispa. A pleasing instrument. And
thou ?
  Fourth Mus. The fife.
  Chispa. I like it ; it has a cheerful,
soul-stirring sound, that soars up to my
lady's window like the song of a swallow.
And you others ?
  Other Mus. We are the singers, please
your honor.
  Chispa. You are too many. Do you
think we are going to sing mass in the
cathedral of Córdova ? Four men can
make but little use of one shoe, and I see
not how you can all sing in one song.
But follow me along the garden wall.
That is the way my master climbs to the
lady's window. It is by the Vicar's
skirts that the Devil climbs into the
belfry. Come, follow me, and make no
noise.   [*Exeunt.*

SCENE III. — PRECIOSA'S *chamber. She
stands at the open window.*

  Prec. How slowly through the lilac-
      scented air
Descends the tranquil moon! Like
      thistle-down
The vapory clouds float in the peaceful
      sky;
And sweetly from yon hollow vaults of
      shade
The nightingales breathe out their souls
      in song.
And hark! what songs of love, what
      soul-like sounds,
Answer them from below!

SERENADE.

    Stars of the summer night!
        Far in yon azure deeps,
    Hide, hide your golden light!
        She sleeps!
    My lady sleeps!
        Sleeps!

    Moon of the summer night!
        Far down yon western steeps,
    Sink, sink in silver light!
        She sleeps!
    My lady sleeps!
        Sleeps!

    Wind of the summer night!
        Where yonder woodbine creeps,
    Fold, fold thy pinions light!
        She sleeps!
    My lady sleeps!
        Sleeps!

    Dreams of the summer night!
        Tell her, her lover keeps
    Watch! while in slumbers light
        She sleeps!
    My lady sleeps!
        Sleeps!

(*Enter* VICTORIAN *by the balcony.*)

  Vict. Poor little dove! Thou trem-
      blest like a leaf!
  Prec. I am so frightened! 'T is for
      thee I tremble!
I hate to have thee climb that wall by
      night!
Did no one see thee?
    Vict.   None, my love, but thou.
  Prec. 'T is very dangerous; and when
      thou art gone
I chide myself for letting thee come here

Thus stealthily by night. Where hast
      thou been?
Since yesterday I have no news from thee.
    Vict. Since yesterday I have been in
      Alcalá.
Erelong the time will come, sweet
      Preciosa,
When that dull distance shall no more
      divide us;
And I no more shall scale thy wall by
      night
To steal a kiss from thee, as I do now.
  Prec. An honest thief, to steal but
      what thou givest.
    Vict. And we shall sit together un-
      molested,
And words of true love pass from tongue
      to tongue,
As singing birds from one bough to an-
      other.
  Prec. That were a life to make time
      envious!
I knew that thou wouldst come to me
      to-night.
I saw thee at the play.
    Vict.   Sweet child of air!
Never did I behold thee so attired
And garmented in beauty as to-night!
What hast thou done to make thee look
      so fair?
  Prec. Am I not always fair?
    Vict.   Ay, and so fair
That I am jealous of all eyes that see
      thee,
And wish that they were blind.
  Prec.   I heed them not;
When thou art present, I see none but
      thee!
    Vict. There's nothing fair nor beau-
      tiful, but takes
Something from thee, that makes it
      beautiful.
  Prec. And yet thou leavest me for
      those dusty books.
    Vict. Thou comest between me and
      those books too often!
I see thy face in everything I see!
The paintings in the chapel wear thy
      looks,
The canticles are changed to sarabands,
And with the learned doctors of the
      schools
I see thee dance cachuchas.
  Prec.   In good sooth,
I dance with learned doctors of the
      schools
To-morrow morning.

Vict. And with whom, I pray?
Prec. A grave and reverend Cardinal,
and his Grace
The Archbishop of Toledo.
Vict. What mad jest
Is this?
Prec. It is no jest; indeed it is not.
Vict. Prithee, explain thyself.
Prec. Why, simply thus.
Thou knowest the Pope has sent here
into Spain
To put a stop to dances on the stage.
Vict. I have heard it whispered.
Prec. Now the Cardinal,
Who for this purpose comes, would fain
behold
With his own eyes these dances; and the
Archbishop
Has sent for me —
Vict. That thou mayst dance before
them!
Now viva la cachucha! It will breathe
The fire of youth into these gray old
men!
'T will be thy proudest conquest!
Prec. Saving one.
And yet I fear these dances will be
stopped,
And Preciosa be once more a beggar.
Vict. The sweetest beggar that e'er
asked for alms;
With such beseeching eyes, that when I
saw thee
I gave my heart away!
Prec. Dost thou remember
When first we met?
Vict. It was at Córdova,
In the cathedral garden. Thou wast
sitting
Under the orange-trees, beside a fountain.
Prec. 'Twas Easter-Sunday. The full-
blossomed trees
Filled all the air with fragrance and with
joy.
The priests were singing, and the organ
sounded,
And then anon the great cathedral bell.
It was the elevation of the Host.
We both of us fell down upon our knees,
Under the orange boughs, and prayed to-
gether.
I never had been happy till that moment.
Vict. Thou blessed angel!
Prec. And when thou wast gone
I felt an aching here. I did not speak
To any one that day. But from that day
Bartolomé grew hateful unto me.

Vict. Remember him no more. Let
not his shadow
Come between thee and me. Sweet
Preciosa!
I loved thee even then, though I was
silent!
Prec. I thought I ne'er should see thy
face again.
Thy farewell had a sound of sorrow in it.
Vict. That was the first sound in the
song of love!
Scarce more than silence is, and yet a
sound.
Hands of invisible spirits touch the strings
Of that mysterious instrument, the soul,
And play the prelude of our fate. We
hear
The voice prophetic, and are not alone.
Prec. That is my faith. Dost thou be-
lieve these warnings?
Vict. So far as this. Our feelings and
our thoughts
Tend ever on, and rest not in the Present.
As drops of rain fall into some dark well,
And from below comes a scarce audible
sound,
So fall our thoughts into the dark Here-
after,
And their mysterious echo reaches us.
Prec. I have felt it so, but found no
words to say it!
I cannot reason; I can only feel!
But thou hast language for all thoughts
and feelings.
Thou art a scholar; and sometimes I
think
We cannot walk together in this world!
The distance that divides us is too great!
Henceforth thy pathway lies among the
stars;
I must not hold thee back.
Vict. Thou little sceptic!
Dost thou still doubt? What I most
prize in woman
Is her affections, not her intellect!
The intellect is finite; but the affections
Are infinite, and cannot be exhausted.
Compare me with the great men of the
earth;
What am I? Why, a pygmy among
giants!
But if thou lovest, — mark me! I say
lovest,
The greatest of thy sex excels thee not!
The world of the affections is thy world,
Not that of man's ambition. In that
stillness

Which most becomes a woman, calm and
holy,
Thou sittest by the fireside of the heart,
Feeding its flame.   The element of fire
Is pure.   It cannot change nor hide its
nature,
But burns as brightly in a Gypsy camp
As in a palace hall.   Art thou con-
vinced?
  Prec. Yes, that I love thee, as the
good love heaven;
But not that I am worthy of that heaven.
How shall I more deserve it?
  Vict.   Loving more.
  Prec. I cannot love thee more; my
heart is full.
  Vict. Then let it overflow, and I will
drink it,
As in the summer-time the thirsty sands
Drink the swift waters of the Manzanares,
And still do thirst for more.
  A Watchman (in the street). Ave
Maria
Purissima!   'T is midnight and serene!
  Vict. Hear'st thou that cry?
  Prec.   It is a hateful sound,
To scare thee from me!
  Vict.   As the hunter's horn
Doth scare the timid stag, or bark of
hounds
The moor-fowl from his mate.
  Prec.   Pray, do not go!
  Vict. I must away to Alcalá to-
night.
Think of me when I am away.
  Prec.   Fear not!
I have no thoughts that do not think
of thee.
  Vict. (giving her a ring). And to re-
mind thee of my love, take this;
A serpent, emblem of Eternity;
A ruby, — say, a drop of my heart's
blood.
  Prec. It is an ancient saying, that
the ruby
Brings gladness to the wearer, and pre-
serves
The heart pure, and, if laid beneath the
pillow,
Drives away evil dreams.   But then,
alas!
It was a serpent tempted Eve to sin.
  Vict. What convent of barefooted
Carmelites
Taught thee so much theology?
  *Prec. (laying her hand upon his
mouth).*   Hush! hush!

Good night! and may all holy angels
guard thee!
  Vict. Good night!   good night!
Thou art my guardian angel!
I have no other saint than thou to pray
to!
  (He descends by the balcony.)
  Prec. Take care, and do not hurt thee.
Art thou safe?
  Vict. (from the garden). Safe as my
love for thee!   But art thou
safe?
Others can climb a balcony by moon-
light
As well as I.   Pray shut thy window
close;
I am jealous of the perfumed air of
night
That from this garden climbs to kiss thy
lips.
  *Prec. (throwing down her handker-
chief).* Thou silly child! Take
this to blind thine eyes.
It is my benison!
  Vict.   And brings to me
Sweet fragrance from thy lips, as the soft
wind
Wafts to the out-bound mariner the
breath
Of the beloved land he leaves behind.
  Prec. Make not thy voyage long.
  Vict.   To-morrow night
Shall see me safe returned.   Thou art the
star
To guide me to an anchorage.   Good
night!
My beauteous star!   My star of love,
good night!
  Prec. Good night!
  Watchman (at a distance). Ave Maria
Purissima!

SCENE IV. — *An inn on the road to Alcalá.*
BALTASAR *asleep on a bench. Enter*
CHISPA.

  Chispa. And here we are, half-way to
Alcalá, between cocks and midnight.
Body o' me! what an inn this is!   The
lights out, and the landlord asleep.
Holá! ancient Baltasar!
  Bal. (waking). Here I am.
  Chispa. Yes, there you are, like a one-
eyed Alcalde in a town without inhabi-
tants.   Bring a light, and let me have
supper.

Bal. Where is your master ?

Chispa. Do not trouble yourself about him. We have stopped a moment to breathe our horses ; and, if he chooses to walk up and down in the open air, looking into the sky as one who hears it rain, that does not satisfy my hunger, you know. But be quick, for I am in a hurry, and every man stretches his legs according to the length of his coverlet. What have we here ?

Bal. (*setting a light on the table*). Stewed rabbit.

Chispa (*eating*). Conscience of Portalegre ! Stewed kitten, you mean !

Bal. And a pitcher of Pedro Ximenes, with a roasted pear in it.

Chispa (*drinking*). Ancient Baltasar, amigo ! You know how to cry wine and sell vinegar. I tell you this is nothing but Vino Tinto of La Mancha, with a tang of the swine-skin.

Bal. I swear to you by Saint Simon and Judas, it is all as I say.

Chispa. And I swear to you by Saint Peter and Saint Paul, that it is no such thing. Moreover, your supper is like the hidalgo's dinner, very little meat and a great deal of tablecloth.

Bal. Ha ! ha ! ha !

Chispa. And more noise than nuts.

Bal. Ha ! ha ! ha ! You must have your joke, Master Chispa. But shall I not ask Don Victorian in, to take a draught of the Pedro Ximenes ?

Chispa. No ; you might as well say, " Don't - you - want - some ?" to a dead man.

Bal. Why does he go so often to Madrid ?

Chispa. For the same reason that he eats no supper. He is in love. Were you ever in love, Baltasar ?

Bal. I was never out of it, good Chispa. It has been the torment of my life.

Chispa. What ! are you on fire, too, old hay-stack ? Why, we shall never be able to put you out.

Vict. (*without*). Chispa !

Chispa. Go to bed, Pero Grullo, for the cocks are crowing.

Vict. Ea ! Chispa ! Chispa !

Chispa. Ea ! Señor. Come with me, ancient Baltasar, and bring water for the horses. I will pay for the supper to-morrow.   [*Exeunt.*

SCENE V. — VICTORIAN'S *chambers at Alcalá.* HYPOLITO *asleep in an armchair. He awakes slowly.*

Hyp. I must have been asleep ! ay,
     sound asleep !
And it was all a dream. O sleep, sweet
     sleep !
Whatever form thou takest, thou art fair,
Holding unto our lips thy goblet filled
Out of Oblivion's well, a healing draught !
The candles have burned low ; it must
     be late.
Where can Victorian be ? Like Fray
     Carrillo,
The only place in which one cannot find
     him
Is his own cell. Here's his guitar, that
     seldom
Feels the caresses of its master's hand.
Open thy silent lips, sweet instrument !
And make dull midnight merry with a
     song.

(*He plays and sings.*)

     Padre Francisco !
     Padre Francisco !
What do you want of Padre Francisco ?
     Here is a pretty young maiden
     Who wants to confess her sins !
Open the door and let her come in,
I will shrive her from every sin.

(*Enter* VICTORIAN.)

Vict. Padre Hypolito ! Padre Hypolito !

Hyp. What do you want of Padre Hypolito ?

Vict. Come, shrive me straight ; for,
     if love be a sin,
I am the greatest sinner that doth live.
I will confess the sweetest of all crimes,
A maiden wooed and won.

Hyp.   The same old tale
Of the old woman in the chimney-corner,
Who, while the pot boils, says, "Come
     here, my child ;
I 'll tell thee a story of my wedding-day."

Vict. Nay, listen, for my heart is full ;
     so full
That I must speak.

Hyp.   Alas ! that heart of thine
Is like a scene in the old play ; the curtain
Rises to solemn music, and lo ! enter
The eleven thousand virgins of Cologne !

Vict. Nay, like the Sibyl's volumes,
     thou shouldst say ;

Those that remained, after the six were
  burned,
Being held more precious than the nine
  together.
But listen to my tale. Dost thou re-
  member
The Gypsy girl we saw at Córdova
Dance the Romalis in the market-place ?
  Hyp. Thou meanest Preciosa.
  Vict.   Ay, the same.
Thou knowest how her image haunted me
Long after we returned to Alcalá.
She 's in Madrid.
  Hyp.   I know it.
  Vict.   And I 'm in love.
  Hyp. And therefore in Madrid when
  thou shouldst be
In Alcalá.
  Vict.   O pardon me, my friend,
If I so long have kept this secret from thee ;
But silence is the charm that guards such
  treasures,
And, if a word be spoken ere the time,
They sink again, they were not meant
  for us.
  Hyp. Alas ! alas ! I see thou art in
  love.
Love keeps the cold out better than a
  cloak.
It serves for food and raiment. Give a
  Spaniard
His mass, his olla, and his Doña Luisa —
Thou knowest the proverb. But pray
  tell me, lover,
How speeds thy wooing ? Is the maiden
  coy ?
Write her a song, beginning with an *Ave ;*
Sing as the monk sang to the Virgin
  Mary,

  Ave ! cujus calcem clare
  Nec centenni commendare
  Sciret Seraph studio !

  Vict. Pray, do not jest ! This is no
  time for it !
I am in earnest !
  Hyp.   Seriously enamored ?
What, ho ! The Primus of great Alcalá
Enamored of a Gypsy ? Tell me frankly,
How meanest thou ?
  Vict.   I mean it honestly.
  Hyp. Surely thou wilt not marry her !
  Vict.   Why not ?
  Hyp. She was betrothed to one Bar-
  tolomé,
If I remember rightly, a young Gypsy
Who danced with her at Córdova.

  Vict.   They quarrelled,
And so the matter ended.
  Hyp.   But in truth
Thou wilt not marry her.
  Vict.   In truth I will.
The angels sang in heaven when she was
  born !
She is a precious jewel I have found
Among the filth and rubbish of the world.
I 'll stoop for it ; but when I wear it here,
Set on my forehead like the morning
  star,
The world may wonder, but it will not
  laugh.
  Hyp. If thou wear'st nothing else upon
  thy forehead,
'T will be indeed a wonder.
  Vict.   Out upon thee
With thy unseasonable jests ! Pray tell
  me,
Is there no virtue in the world ?
  Hyp.   Not much.
What, think'st thou, is she doing at this
  moment ;
Now, while we speak of her ?
  Vict.   She lies asleep,
And from her parted lips her gentle breath
Comes like the fragrance from the lips of
  flowers.
Her tender limbs are still, and on her
  breast
The cross she prayed to, ere she fell asleep,
Rises and falls with the soft tide of
  dreams,
Like a light barge safe moored.
  Hyp.   Which means, in prose,
She 's sleeping with her mouth a little
  open !
  Vict. O, would I had the old magician's
  glass
To see her as she lies in childlike sleep !
  Hyp. And wouldst thou venture ?
  Vict.   Ay, indeed I would !
  Hyp. Thou art courageous. Hast thou
  e'er reflected
How much lies hidden in that one word,
  now ?
  Vict. Yes ; all the awful mystery of
  Life !
I oft have thought, my dear Hypolito,
That could we, by some spell of magic,
  change
The world and its inhabitants to stone,
In the same attitudes they now are in,
What fearful glances downward might
  we cast
Into the hollow chasms of human life !

What groups should we behold about the death-bed,
Putting to shame the group of Niobe !
What joyful welcomes, and what sad farewells !
What stony tears in those congealed eyes !
What visible joy or anguish in those cheeks !
What bridal pomps, and what funeral shows !
What foes, like gladiators, fierce and struggling !
What lovers with their marble lips together !

Hyp. Ay, there it is ! and, if I were in love,
That is the very point I most should dread.
This magic glass, these magic spells of thine,
Might tell a tale were better left untold.
For instance, they might show us thy fair cousin,
The Lady Violante, bathed in tears
Of love and anger, like the maid of Colchis,
Whom thou, another faithless Argonaut,
Having won that golden fleece, a woman's love,
Desertest for this Glaucè.

Vict.   Hold thy peace !
She cares not for me.   She may wed another,
Or go into a convent, and, thus dying,
Marry Achilles in the Elysian Fields.

Hyp. (*rising*). And so, good night !
Good morning, I should say.

(*Clock strikes three.*)

Hark ! how the loud and ponderous mace of Time
Knocks at the golden portals of the day !
And so, once more, good night !   We 'll speak more largely
Of Preciosa when we meet again.
Get thee to bed, and the magician, Sleep,
Shall show her to thee, in his magic glass,
In all her loveliness.   Good night !
                                        [*Exit.*
Vict.   Good night !
But not to bed ; for I must read awhile.

(*Throws himself into the arm-chair which* HYPOLITO *has left, and lays a large book open upon his knees.*)

Must read, or sit in revery and watch
The changing color of the waves that break

Upon the idle sea-shore of the mind !
Visions of Fame ! that once did visit me,
Making night glorious with your smile, where are ye ?
O, who shall give me, now that ye are gone,
Juices of those immortal plants that bloom
Upon Olympus, making us immortal ?
Or teach me where that wondrous mandrake grows
Whose magic root, torn from the earth with groans,
At midnight hour, can scare the fiends away,
And make the mind prolific in its fancies !
I have the wish, but want the will, to act !
Souls of great men departed !   Ye whose words
Have come to light from the swift river of Time,
Like Roman swords found in the Tagus' bed,
Where is the strength to wield the arms ye bore ?
From the barred visor of Antiquity
Reflected shines the eternal light of Truth,
As from a mirror !   All the means of action —
The shapeless masses, the materials —
Lie everywhere about us.   What we need
Is the celestial fire to change the flint
Into transparent crystal, bright and clear.
That fire is genius !   The rude peasant sits
At evening in his smoky cot, and draws
With charcoal uncouth figures on the wall.
The son of genius comes, foot-sore with travel,
And begs a shelter from the inclement night.
He takes the charcoal from the peasant's hand,
And, by the magic of his touch at once
Transfigured, all its hidden virtues shine,
And, in the eyes of the astonished clown,
It gleams a diamond !   Even thus transformed,
Rude popular traditions and old tales
Shine as immortal poems, at the touch
Of some poor, houseless, homeless, wandering bard,
Who had but a night's lodging for his pains.
But there are brighter dreams than those of Fame,

Which are the dreams of Love !　Out of
　　the heart
Rises the bright ideal of these dreams,
As from some woodland fount a spirit
　　rises
And sinks again into its silent deeps,
Ere the enamored knight can touch her
　　robe !
'T is this ideal that the soul of man,
Like the enamored knight beside the
　　fountain,
Waits for upon the margin of Life's
　　stream ;
Waits to behold her rise from the dark
　　waters,
Clad in a mortal shape !　Alas ! how
　　many
Must wait in vain !　The stream flows
　　evermore,
But from its silent deeps no spirit rises !
Yet I, born under a propitious star,
Have found the bright ideal of my
　　dreams.
Yes ! she is ever with me.　I can feel,
Here, as I sit at midnight and alone,
Her gentle breathing ! on my breast can
　　feel
The pressure of her head ! God's benison
Rest ever on it !　Close those beauteous
　　eyes,
Sweet Sleep ! and all the flowers that
　　bloom at night
With balmy lips breathe in her ears my
　　name !

　　　(*Gradually sinks asleep.*)

ACT II.

SCENE I. — PRECIOSA's *chamber. Morning.*
PRECIOSA *and* ANGELICA.

　Prec. Why will you go so soon ?　Stay
　　yet awhile.
The poor too often turn away unheard
From hearts that shut against them with
　　a sound
That will be heard in heaven.　Pray,
　　tell me more
Of your adversities.　Keep nothing from
　　me.
What is your landlord's name ?
　Ang.　　　　The Count of Lara.
　Prec. The Count of Lara ?　O, beware
　　that man !
Mistrust his pity, — hold no parley with
　　him !

And rather die an outcast in the streets
Than touch his gold.
　Ang.　　　You know him, then !
　Prec.　　　　　　As much
As any woman may, and yet be pure.
As you would keep your name without a
　　blemish,
Beware of him !
　Ang.　　　Alas ! what can I do !
I cannot choose my friends.　Each word
　　of kindness,
Come whence it may, is welcome to the
　　poor.
　Prec. Make me your friend.　A girl
　　so young and fair
Should have no friends but those of her
　　own sex.
What is your name ?
　Ang.　　　Angelica.
　Prec.　　　　　That name
Was given you, that you might be an
　　angel
To her who bore you !　When your in-
　　fant smile
Made her home Paradise, you were her
　　angel.
O, be an angel still !　She needs that
　　smile.
So long as you are innocent, fear nothing.
No one can harm you !　I am a poor
　　girl,
Whom chance has taken from the public
　　streets.
I have no other shield than mine own
　　virtue.
That is the charm which has protected
　　me !
Amid a thousand perils, I have worn it
Here on my heart !　It is my guardian
　　angel.
　Ang. (*rising*).　I thank you for this
　　counsel, dearest lady.
　Prec. Thank me by following it.
　Ang.　　　　　Indeed I will.
　Prec. Pray, do not go.　I have much
　　more to say.
　Ang. My mother is alone.　I dare not
　　leave her.
　Prec. Some other time, then, when
　　we meet again.
You must not go away with words alone.

　　　(*Gives her a purse.*)

Take this.　Would it were more.
　Ang.　　　I thank you, lady.
　Prec. No thanks.　To-morrow come
　　to me again.

I dance to-night, — perhaps for the last time.

But what I gain, I promise shall be yours,
If that can save you from the Count of Lara.

Ang. O, my dear lady ! how shall I be grateful
For so much kindness ?

Prec.   I deserve no thanks,
Thank Heaven, not me.

Ang.   Both Heaven and you.

Prec.   Farewell.
Remember that you come again to-morrow.

Ang. I will. And may the Blessed Virgin guard you,
And all good angels.   [*Exit.*

Prec.   May they guard thee too,
And all the poor ; for they have need of angels.

Now bring me, dear Dolores, my basquiña,
My richest maja dress, — my dancing dress,
And my most precious jewels ! Make me look
Fairer than night e'er saw me ! I 've a prize
To win this day, worthy of Preciosa !

(*Enter* BELTRAN CRUZADO.)

Cruz. Ave Maria !

Prec. O God ! my evil genius !
What seekest thou here to-day ?

Cruz.   Thyself, — my child.

Prec. What is thy will with me ?

Cruz.   Gold ! gold !

Prec. I gave thee yesterday ; I have no more.

Cruz. The gold of the Busné, — give me his gold !

Prec. I gave the last in charity to-day.

Cruz. That is a foolish lie.

Prec.   It is the truth.

Cruz. Curses upon thee ! Thou art not my child !
Hast thou given gold away, and not to me ?
Not to thy father ? To whom, then ?

Prec.   To one
Who needs it more.

Cruz. No one can need it more.

Prec. Thou art not poor.

Cruz.   What, I, who lurk about
In dismal suburbs and unwholesome lanes ;

I, who am housed worse than the galley slave ;
I, who am fed worse than the kennelled hound ;
I, who am clothed in rags, — Beltran Cruzado, —
Not poor !

Prec. Thou hast a stout heart and strong hands.
Thou canst supply thy wants ; what wouldst thou more ?

Cruz. The gold of the Busné ! give me his gold !

Prec. Beltran Cruzado ! hear me once for all.
I speak the truth. So long as I had gold,
I gave it to thee freely, at all times,
Never denied thee ; never had a wish
But to fulfil thine own. Now go in peace !
Be merciful, be patient, and erelong
Thou shalt have more.

Cruz.   And if I have it not,
Thou shalt no longer dwell here in rich chambers,
Wear silken dresses, feed on dainty food,
And live in idleness ; but go with me,
Dance the Romalis in the public streets,
And wander wild again o'er field and fell ;
For here we stay not long.

Prec.   What ! march again ?

Cruz. Ay, with all speed. I hate the crowded town !
I cannot breathe shut up within its gates !
Air, — I want air, and sunshine, and blue sky,
The feeling of the breeze upon my face,
The feeling of the turf beneath my feet,
And no walls but the far-off mountain-tops.
Then I am free and strong, — once more myself,
Beltran Cruzado, Count of the Calés !

Prec. God speed thee on thy march !
— I cannot go.

Cruz. Remember who I am, and who thou art !
Be silent and obey ! Yet one thing more.
Bartolomé Román —

Prec. (*with emotion*). O, I beseech thee !
If my obedience and blameless life,
If my humility and meek submission
In all things hitherto, can move in thee

One feeling of compassion ; if thou art
Indeed my father, and canst trace in me
One look of her who bore me, or one tone
That doth remind thee of her, let it plead
In my behalf, who am a feeble girl,
Too feeble to resist, and do not force me
To wed that man !   I am afraid of him !
I do not love him ! On my knees I beg
thee
To use no violence, nor do in haste
What cannot be undone !
    Cruz.   O child, child, child !
Thou hast betrayed thy secret, as a bird
Betrays her nest, by striving to conceal
it.
I will not leave thee here in the great city
To be a grandee's mistress. Make thee
ready
To go with us ; and until then remember
A watchful eye is on thee.   [*Exit.*
    Prec.   Woe is me !
I have a strange misgiving in my heart !
But that one deed of charity I 'll do,
Befall what may ; they cannot take that
from me.

Scene. II —*A room in the* Archbishop's
Palace. The Archbishop *and a* Cardinal *seated.*

    Arch. Knowing how near it touched
the public morals,
And that our age is grown corrupt and
rotten
By such excesses, we have sent to Rome,
Beseeching that his Holiness would aid
In curing the gross surfeit of the time,
By seasonable stop put here in Spain
To bull-fights and lewd dances on the
stage.
All this you know.
    Card.   Know and approve.
    Arch.   And further,
That, by a mandate from his Holiness,
The first have been suppressed.
    Card.   I trust forever.
It was a cruel sport.
    Arch.   A barbarous pastime,
Disgraceful to the land that calls itself
Most Catholic and Christian.
    Card.   Yet the people
Murmur at this ; and, if the public
dances
Should be condemned upon too slight
occasion,
Worse ills might follow than the ills we
cure.

As *Panem et Circenses* was the cry
Among the Roman populace of old,
So *Pan y Toros* is the cry in Spain.
Hence I would act advisedly herein ;
And therefore have induced your Grace
to see
These national dances, ere we interdict
them.

    (*Enter a Servant.*)

    Serv. The dancing-girl, and with her
the musicians
Your Grace was pleased to order, wait
without.
    Arch. Bid them come in.   Now shall
your eyes behold
In what angelic, yet voluptuous shape
The Devil came to tempt Saint Anthony.

(*Enter* Preciosa, *with a mantle thrown
over her head. She advances slowly, in
modest, half-timid attitude.*)

    Card. (*aside*). O, what a fair and
ministering angel
Was lost to heaven when this sweet
woman fell !
    Prec. (*kneeling before the* Archbish-
op). I have obeyed the order of
your Grace.
If I intrude upon your better hours,
I proffer this excuse, and here beseech
Your holy benediction.
    Arch.   May God bless thee,
And lead thee to a better life.   Arise.
    Card. (*aside*). Her acts are modest,
and her words discreet !
I did not look for this ! Come hither,
child.
Is thy name Preciosa ?
    Prec.   Thus I am called.
    Card. That is a Gypsy name.   Who
is thy father ?
    Prec. Beltran Cruzado, Count of the
Calés.
    Arch. I have a dim remembrance of
that man :
He was a bold and reckless character,
A sun-burnt Ishmael !
    Card.   Dost thou remember
Thy earlier days ?
    Prec.   Yes ; by the Darro's side
My childhood passed.   I can remember
still
The river, and the mountains capped
with snow ;
The villages, where, yet a little child,
I told the traveller's fortune in the
street :

The smuggler's horse, the brigand and
    the shepherd ;
The march across the moor ; the halt at
    noon ;
The red fire of the evening camp, that
    lighted
The forest where we slept ; and, further
    back,
As in a dream or in some former life,
Gardens and palace walls.
    Arch.   'T is the Alhambra,
Under whose towers the Gypsy camp was
    pitched.
But the time wears ; and we would see
    thee dance.
    Prec. Your Grace shall be obeyed.

(*She lays aside her mantilla. The music
of the cachucha is played, and the dance
begins. The* ARCHBISHOP *and the* CAR-
DINAL *look on with gravity and an occasional frown ; then make signs to each
other ; and, as the dance continues, become more and more pleased and excited ;
and at length rise from their seats, throw
their caps in the air, and applaud vehemently as the scene closes.*)

SCENE III. — *The Prado. A long avenue of trees leading to the gate of Ato-
cha. On the right the dome and spires of
a convent. A fountain. Evening,* DON
CARLOS *and* HYPOLITO *meeting.*

    Don C. Holá ! good evening, Don
        Hypolito.
    Hyp. And a good evening to my
        friend, Don Carlos.
Some lucky star has led my steps this
    way.
I was in search of you.
    Don C.   Command me always.
    Hyp. Do you remember, in Quevedo's
        Dreams,
The miser, who, upon the Day of Judg-
    ment,
Asks if his money-bags would rise ?
    Don C.   , I do ;
But what of that ?
    Hyp.   I am that wretched man.
    Don C. You mean to tell me yours
        have risen empty ?
    Hyp. And amen ! said my Cid the
        Campeador.
    Don C. Pray, how much need you ?
    Hyp.   Some half-dozen ounces,
Which, with due interest —
    Don C. (*giving his purse*).   What, am
        I a Jew

To put my moneys out at usury ?
Here is my purse.
    Hyp. Thank you. .A pretty purse,
Made by the hand of some fair Madri-
    leña ;
Perhaps a keepsake.
    Don C.   No, 't is at your service.
    Hyp. Thank you again. Lie there,
        good Chrysostom,
And with thy golden mouth remind me
    often,
I am the debtor of my friend.
    Don C.   But tell me,
Come you to-day from Alcalá ?
    Hyp.   This moment.
    Don C. And pray, how fares the brave
    · Victorian ?
    Hyp. Indifferent well ; that is to say,
        not well.
A damsel has ensnared him with the
    glances
Of her dark, roving eyes, as herdsmen
    catch
A steer of Andalusia with a lazo.
He is in love.
    Don C.   And is it faring ill
To be in love ?
    Hyp.   In his case very ill.
    Don C. Why so ?
    Hyp. For many reasons. First and
        foremost,
Because he is in love with an ideal ;
A creature of his own imagination ;
A child of air ; an echo of his heart ;
And, like a lily on a river floating,
She floats upon the river of his thoughts !
    Don C. A common thing with poets.
        But who is
This floating lily ? For, in fine, some
        woman,
Some living woman, — not a mere
        ideal, —
Must wear the outward semblance of his
        thought.
Who is it ? Tell me.
    Hyp.   Well, it is a woman !
But, look you, from the coffer of his heart
He brings forth precious jewels to adorn
    her,
As pious priests adorn some favorite
    saint
With gems and gold, until at length she
    gleams
One blaze of glory. Without these, you
    know,
And the priest's benediction, 't is a doll.
    Don C. Well, well ! who is this doll?

Hyp. Why, who do you think?
Don C. His cousin Violante.
Hyp. Guess again.
To ease his laboring heart, in the last
    storm
He threw her overboard, with all her
    ingots.
Don C. I cannot guess; so tell me
    who it is.
Hyp. Not I.
Don C. Why not?
Hyp. (mysteriously). Why? Because
    Mari Franca
Was married four leagues out of Sala-
    manca!
Don C. Jesting aside, who is it?
Hyp. Preciosa.
Don C. Impossible! The Count of
    Lara tells me
She is not virtuous.
Hyp. Did I say she was?
The Roman Emperor Claudius had a wife
Whose name was Messalina, as I think;
Valeria Messalina was her name.
But hist! I see him yonder through the
    trees,
Walking as in a dream.
Don C. He comes this way.
Hyp. It has been truly said by some
    wise man,
That money, grief, and love cannot be
    hidden.

(*Enter* VICTORIAN *in front.*)

Vict. Where'er thy step has passed is
    holy ground!
These groves are sacred! I behold thee
    walking
Under these shadowy trees, where we
    have walked
At evening, and I feel thy presence now;
Feel that the place has taken a charm
    from thee,
And is forever hallowed.
Hyp. Mark him well!
See how he strides away with lordly
    air,
Like that odd guest of stone, that grim
    Commander
Who comes to sup with Juan in the
    play.
Don C. What ho! Victorian!
Hyp. Wilt thou sup with us?
Vict. Holá! amigos! Faith, I did
    not see you.
How fares Don Carlos?
Don C. At your service ever.

Vict. How is that young and green-
    eyed Gaditana
That you both wot of?
Don C. Ay, soft, emerald eyes!
She has gone back to Cadiz.
Hyp. Ay de mí!
Vict. You are much to blame for let-
    ting her go back.
A pretty girl; and in her tender eyes
Just that soft shade of green we some-
    times see
In evening skies.
Hyp. But, speaking of green eyes,
Are thine green?
Vict. Not a whit. Why so?
Hyp. I think
The slightest shade of green would be
    becoming,
For thou art jealous.
Vict. No, I am not jealous.
Hyp. Thou shouldst be.
Vict. Why?
Hyp. Because thou art in love.
And they who are in love are always
    jealous.
Therefore thou shouldst be.
Vict. Marry, is that all?
Farewell; I am in haste. Farewell, Don
    Carlos.
Thou sayest I should be jealous?
Hyp. Ay, in truth
I fear there is reason. Be upon thy
    guard.
I hear it whispered that the Count of
    Lara
Lays siege to the same citadel.
Vict. Indeed!
Then he will have his labor for his
    pains.
Hyp. He does not think so, and Don
    Carlos tells me
He boasts of his success.
Vict. How's this, Don Carlos?
Don C. Some hints of it I heard from
    his own lips.
He spoke but lightly of the lady's vir-
    tue,
As a gay man might speak.
Vict. Death and damnation!
I'll cut his lying tongue out of his mouth,
And throw it to my dog! But no, no,
    no!
This cannot be. You jest, indeed you
    jest.
Trifle with me no more. For otherwise
We are no longer friends. And so, fare-
    well! [*Exit.*

Hyp. Now what a coil is here ! The
    Avenging Child
Hunting the traitor Quadros to his death,
And the great Moor Calaynos, when he
    rode
To Paris for the ears of Oliver,
Were nothing to him ! O hot-headed
    youth !
But come ; we will not follow. Let us
    join
The crowd that pours into the Prado.
    There
We shall find merrier company ; I see
The Marialonzos and the Almavivas,
And fifty fans, that beckon me already.
                        [*Exeunt.*

SCENE IV. — PRECIOSA'S *chamber. She
is sitting, with a book in her hand, near
a table, on which are flowers. A bird
singing in its cage. The* COUNT OF LARA
enters behind unperceived.

  Prec. (*reads*.)

    All are sleeping, weary heart !
    Thou, thou only sleepless art !

Heigho ! I wish Victorian were here.
I know not what it is makes me so rest-
    less !

      (*The bird sings.*)

Thou little prisoner with thy motley
    coat,
That from thy vaulted, wiry dungeon
    singest,
Like thee I am a captive, and, like thee,
I have a gentle jailer. Lack-a-day !

    All are sleeping, weary heart !
    Thou, thou only sleepless art !
    All this throbbing, all this aching,
    Evermore shall keep thee waking,
    For a heart in sorrow breaking
    Thinketh ever of its smart !

Thou speakest truly, poet ! and me-
    thinks
More hearts are breaking in this world of
    ours
Than one would say. In distant vil-
    lages
And solitudes remote, where winds have
    wafted
The barbed seeds of love, or birds of pas-
    sage
Scattered them in their flight, do they
    take root,
And grow in silence, and in silence per-
    ish.

Who hears the falling of the forest leaf ?
Or who takes note of every flower that
    dies ?
Heigho ! I wish Victorian would come.
Dolores !

(*Turns to lay down her book, and perceives
        the* COUNT.)

            Ha !
Lara.   Señora, pardon me
Prec. How 's this ? Dolores !
Lara.   Pardon me —
Prec.   Dolores !
Lara. Be not alarmed ; I found no
    one in waiting.
If I have been too bold —
    Prec. (*turning her back upon him*).
                You are too bold !
Retire ! retire, and leave me !
    Lara.   My dear lady,
First hear me ! I beseech you, let me
    speak !
'T is for your good I come.
    Prec. (*turning toward him with indig-
        nation*). Begone ! begone !
You are the Count of Lara, but your
    deeds
Would make the statues of your ancestors
Blush on their tombs ! Is it Castilian
    honor,
Is it Castilian pride, to steal in here
Upon a friendless girl, to do her wrong ?
O shame ! shame ! shame ! that you, a
    nobleman,
Should be so little noble in your thoughts
As to send jewels here to win my love,
And think to buy my honor with your
    gold !
I have no words to tell you how I scorn
    you !
Begone ! The sight of you is hateful to
    me !
Begone, I say !
    Lara. Be calm ; I will not harm you
    Prec. Because you dare not.
    Lara.   I dare anything !
Therefore beware ! You are deceived in
    me.
In this false world, we do not always
    know
Who are our friends and who our ene-
    mies.
We all have enemies, and all need friends.
Even you, fair Preciosa, here at court
Have foes, who seek to wrong you.
    Prec.   If to this
I owe the honor of the present visit,

You might have spared the coming.
Having spoken,
Once more I beg you, leave me to my-
self.

Lara. I thought it but a friendly part
to tell you
What strange reports are current here in
town.
For my own self, I do not credit them ;
But there are many who, not knowing
you,
Will lend a readier ear.

Prec. There was no need
That you should take upon yourself the
duty
Of telling me these tales.

Lara. Malicious tongues
Are ever busy with your name.

Prec. Alas !
I 've no protectors. I am a poor girl,
Exposed to insults and unfeeling jests.
They wound me, yet I cannot shield
myself.
I give no cause for these reports. I live
Retired ; am visited by none.

Lara. By none ?
O, then, indeed, you are much wronged !

Prec. How mean you ?

Lara. Nay, nay ; I will not wound
your gentle soul
By the report of idle tales.

Prec. Speak out !
What are these idle tales ? You need
not spare me.

Lara. I will deal frankly with you.
Pardon me ;
This window, as I think, looks toward
the street,
And this into the Prado, does it not ?
In yon high house, beyond the garden
wall,—
You see the roof there just above the
trees,—
There lives a friend, who told me yester-
day,
That on a certain night, — be not of-
fended
If I too plainly speak, — he saw a man
Climb to your chamber window. You
are silent !
I would not blame you, being young and
fair —

*[He tries to embrace her. She starts back,
and draws a dagger from her bosom.]*

Prec. Beware ! beware ! I am a Gypsy
girl !

Lay not your hand upon me. One step
nearer
And I will strike !

Lara. Pray you, put up that dagger.
Fear not.

Prec. I do not fear. I have a heart
In whose strength I can trust.

Lara. Listen to me
I come here as your friend, — I am your
friend, —
And by a single word can put a stop
To all those idle tales, and make your
name
Spotless as lilies are. Here on my knees,
Fair Preciosa ! on my knees I swear,
I love you even to madness, and that
love
Has driven me to break the rules of cus-
tom,
And force myself unasked into your
presence.

(VICTORIAN *enters behind.*)

Prec. Rise, Count of Lara ! That is
not the place
For such as you are. It becomes you
not
To kneel before me. I am strangely
moved
To see one of your rank thus low and
humbled ;
For your sake I will put aside all an-
ger,
All unkind feeling, all dislike, and
speak
In gentleness, as most becomes a woman,
And as my heart now prompts me. I
no more
Will hate you, for all hate is painful to
me.
But if, without offending modesty
And that reserve which is a woman's
glory,
I may speak freely, I will teach my heart
To love you.

Lara. O sweet angel !

Prec. Ay, in truth.
Far better than you love yourself or me.

Lara. Give me some sign of this, —
the slightest token.
Let me but kiss your hand !

Prec. Nay, come no nearer.
The words I utter are its sign and token.
Misunderstand me not ! Be not de-
ceived !
The love wherewith I love you is not
such

As you would offer me. For you come
    here
To take from me the only thing I have,
My honor. You are wealthy, you have
    friends
And kindred, and a thousand pleasant
    hopes
That fill your heart with happiness ;
    but I
Am poor, and friendless, having but one
    treasure,
And you would take that from me, and
    for what ?
To flatter your own vanity, and make
    me
What you would most despise.   O sir,
    such love,
That seeks to harm me, cannot be true
    love.
Indeed it cannot.   But my love for you
Is of a different kind.   It seeks your
    good.
It is a holier feeling.   It rebukes
Your earthly passion, your unchaste
    desires,
And bids you look into your heart, and
    see
How you do wrong that better nature in
    you,
And grieve your soul with sin.
    Lara.   I swear to you,
I would not harm you ; I would only
    love you.
I would not take your honor, but restore
    it,
And in return I ask but some slight
    mark
Of your affection.   If indeed you love
    me,
As you confess you do, O let me thus
With this embrace —
    Vict. (*rushing forward*). Hold ! hold !
    This is too much.
What means this outrage ?
    Lara.   First, what right have you
To question thus a nobleman of Spain ?
    Vict. I too am noble, and you are no
    more !
Out of my sight !
    Lara.   Are you the master here ?
    Vict. Ay, here and elsewhere, when
    the wrong of others
Gives me the right !
    Prec. (*to* LARA). Go ! I beseech you,
    go !
    Vict. I shall have business with you,
    Count, anon !

Lara. You cannot come too soon !
                                    [*Exit.*
    Prec.   Victorian !
O, we have been betrayed !
    Vict.   Ha ! ha ! betrayed !
'T is I have been betrayed, not we !—not
    we !
    Prec. Dost thou imagine —
    Vict.   I imagine nothing ;
I see how 't is thou whilest the time away
When I am gone !
    Prec.   O speak not in that tone !
It wounds me deeply.
    Vict.   'T was not meant to flatter.
    Prec. Too well thou knowest the pres-
        ence of that man
Is hateful to me !
    Vict.   Yet I saw thee stand
And listen to him, when he told his love.
    Prec. I did not heed his words.
    Vict.   Indeed thou didst,
And answeredst them with love.
    Prec.   Hadst thou heard all —
    Vict. I heard enough.
    Prec.   Be not so angry with me.
    Vict. I am not angry ; I am very
        calm.
    Prec. If thou wilt let me speak —
    Vict.   Nay, say no more.
I know too much already. Thou art
    false !
I do not like these Gypsy marriages !
Where is the ring I gave thee ?
    Prec.   In my casket.
    Vict. There let it rest ! I would not
    have thee wear it :
I thought thee spotless, and thou art
    polluted !
    Prec. I call the Heavens to witness —
    Vict.   Nay, nay, nay !
Take not the name of Heaven upon thy
    lips !
They are forsworn !
    Prec. Victorian ! dear Victorian !
    Vict. I gave up all for thee ; myself,
        my fame,
My hopes of fortune, ay, my very soul !
And thou hast been my ruin ! Now, go
    on !
Laugh at my folly with thy paramour,
And, sitting on the Count of Lara's knee,
Say what a poor, fond fool Victorian
    was !

(*He casts her from him and rushes out.*)

    Prec. And this from thee !

                    (*Scene closes.*)

SCENE V. — *The* COUNT OF LARA'S *rooms. Enter the* COUNT.

Lara. There's nothing in this world so sweet as love,
And next to love the sweetest thing is hate!
I've learned to hate, and therefore am revenged.
A silly girl to play the prude with me!
The fire that I have kindled —

(*Enter* FRANCISCO.)

Well, Francisco,
What tidings from Don Juan?
Fran. Good, my lord;
He will be present.
Lara. And the Duke of Lermos?
Fran. Was not at home.
Lara. How with the rest?
Fran. I've found
The men you wanted. They will all be there,
And at the given signal raise a whirlwind
Of such discordant noises, that the dance
Must cease for lack of music.
Lara. Bravely done.
Ah! little dost thou dream, sweet Preciosa,
What lies in wait for thee. Sleep shall not close
Thine eyes this night! Give me my cloak and sword.   [*Exeunt.*

SCENE VI. — *A retired spot beyond the city gates. Enter* VICTORIAN *and* HYPOLITO.

Vict. O shame! O shame! Why do I walk abroad
By daylight, when the very sunshine mocks me,
And voices, and familiar sights and sounds
Cry, "Hide thyself!" O what a thin partition
Doth shut out from the curious world the knowledge
Of evil deeds that have been done in darkness!
Disgrace has many tongues. My fears are windows,
Through which all eyes seem gazing. Every face
Expresses some suspicion of my shame,
And in derision seems to smile at me!
Hyp. Did I not caution thee? Did I not tell thee
I was but half persuaded of her virtue?

Vict. And yet, Hypolito, we may be wrong,
We may be over-hasty in condemning!
The Count of Lara is a cursed villain.
Hyp. And therefore is she cursed, loving him.
Vict. She does not love him! 'T is for gold! for gold!
Hyp. Ay, but remember, in the public streets
He shows a golden ring the Gypsy gave him,
A serpent with a ruby in its mouth.
Vict. She had that ring from me!
God! she is false!
But I will be revenged! The hour is passed.
Where stays the coward?
Hyp. Nay, he is no coward;
A villain, if thou wilt, but not a coward.
I've seen him play with swords; it is his pastime.
And therefore be not over-confident,
He'll task thy skill anon. Look, here he comes.

(*Enter* LARA *followed by* FRANCISCO.)

Lara. Good evening, gentlemen.
Hyp. Good evening, Count.
Lara. I trust I have not kept you long in waiting.
Vict. Not long, and yet too long. Are you prepared?
Lara. I am.
Hyp. It grieves me much to see this quarrel
Between you, gentlemen. Is there no way
Left open to accord this difference,
But you must make one with your swords?
Vict. No! none!
I do entreat thee, dear Hypolito,
Stand not between me and my foe. Too long
Our tongues have spoken. Let these tongues of steel
End our debate. Upon your guard, Sir Count.

They fight. VICTORIAN *disarms the* COUNT.)

Your life is mine; and what shall now withhold me
From sending your vile soul to its account?
Lara. Strike! strike!

Vict.   You are disarmed.
I will not kill you.
I will not murder you. Take up your
sword.

FRANCISCO *hands the* COUNT *his sword,
and* HYPOLITO *interposes.*)

Hyp. Enough! Let it end here!
The Count of Lara
Has shown himself a brave man, and
Victorian
A generous one, as ever.   Now be friends.
Put up your swords ; for, to speak frank-
ly to you,
Your cause of quarrel is too slight a thing
To move you to extremes.
Lara.   I am content.
I sought no quarrel. A few hasty words,
Spoken in the heat of blood, have led to
this.
Vict. Nay, something more than that.
Lara.   I understand you.
Therein I did not mean to cross your
path.
To me the door stood open, as to others.
But, had I known the girl belonged to
you,
Never would I have sought to win her
from you.
The truth stands now revealed ; she has
been false
To both of us.
Vict.   Ay, false as hell itself !
Lara. In truth, I did not seek her ;
she sought me ;
And told me how to win her, telling me
The hours when she was oftenest left
alone.
Vict. Say, can you prove this to me?
O, pluck out
These awful doubts, that goad me into
madness !
Let me know all ! all ! all !
Lara.   You shall know all.
Here is my page, who was the messenger
Between us. Question him. Was it not
so,
Francisco ?
Fran.   Ay, my lord.
Lara.   If further proof
Is needful, I have here a ring she gave
me.
Vict. Pray let me see that ring ! It
is the same !

*Throws it upon the ground, and tramples
upon it.*)

Thus may she perish who once wore that
ring !
Thus do I spurn her from me ; do thus
trample
Her memory in the dust ! O Count of
Lara,
We both have been abused, been much
abused !
I thank you for your courtesy and frank-
ness.
Though, like the surgeon's hand, yours
gave me pain,
Yet it has cured my blindness, and I
thank you.
I now can see the folly I have done,
Though 't is, alas ! too late. So fare you
well !
To-night I leave this hateful town forever.
Regard me as your friend.   Once more
farewell !
Hyp. Farewell, Sir Count.

[*Exeunt* VICTORIAN *and* HYPOLITO

Lara. Farewell ! farewell ! farewell !
Thus have I cleared the field of my worst
foe !
I have none else to fear ; the fight is
done,
The citadel is stormed, the victory won !
[*Exit with* FRANCISCO.

SCENE VII. — *A lane in the suburbs.
Night.   Enter* CRUZADO *and* BAR
TOLOMÉ.

Cruz. And so, Bartolomé, the expedi-
tion failed.   But where wast thou for
the most part ?
Bart. In the Guadarrama mountains,
near San Ildefonso.
Cruz. And thou bringest nothing
back with thee ? Didst thou rob no one
Bart. There was no one to rob, save
a party of students from Segovia, who
looked as if they would rob us ; and a
jolly little friar, who had nothing in his
pockets but a missal and a loaf of bread.
Cruz. Pray, then, what brings thee
back to Madrid ?
Bart. First tell me what keeps thee
here ?
Cruz. Preciosa.
Bart. And she brings me back. Hast
thou forgotten thy promise ?
Cruz. The two years are not passed
yet. Wait patiently. The girl shall be
thine.

Bart. I hear she has a Busné lover.

Cruz. That is nothing.

Bart. I do not like it. I hate him, —the son of a Busné harlot. He goes in and out, and speaks with her alone, and I must stand aside, and wait his pleasure.

Cruz. Be patient, I say. Thou shalt have thy revenge. When the time comes, thou shalt waylay him.

Bart. Meanwhile, show me her house.

Cruz. Come this way. But thou wilt not find her. She dances at the play to-night.

Bart. No matter. Show me the house.
                              [*Exeunt.*

SCENE VIII. — *The Theatre. The orchestra plays the cachucha. Sound of castanets behind the scenes. The curtain rises, and discovers* PRECIOSA *in the attitude of commencing the dance. The cachucha. Tumult ; hisses ; cries of "Brava !" and "Afuera !" She falters and pauses. The music stops. General confusion.* PRECIOSA *faints.*

SCENE IX. — *The* COUNT OF LARA'S *chambers.* LARA *and his friends at supper.*

Lara. So, Caballeros, once more many thanks !
You have stood by me bravely in this matter.
Pray fill your glasses.

Don J.   Did you mark, Don Luis,
How pale she looked, when first the noise began,
And then stood still, with her large eyes dilated !
Her nostrils spread ! her lips apart ! her bosom
Tumultuous as the sea !

Don L.   I pitied her.

Lara. Her pride is humbled ; and this very night
I mean to visit her.

Don J.   Will you serenade her ?

Lara. No music ! no more music !

Don L.   Why not music ?
It softens many hearts.

Lara.   Not in the humor
She now is in. Music would madden her.

Don J. Try golden cymbals.

Don L.   Yes, try Don Dinero ;
A mighty wooer is your Don Dinero.

Lara. To tell the truth, then, I have bribed her maid.
But, Caballeros, you dislike this wine.
A bumper and away ; for the night wears.
A health to Preciosa.
            (*They rise and drink.*)

All.   Preciosa.

Lara (*holding up his glass*). Thou
    bright and flaming minister of Love !
Thou wonderful magician ! who hast stolen
My secret from me, and mid sighs of passion
Caught from my lips, with red and fiery tongue,
Her precious name ! O nevermore henceforth
Shall mortal lips press thine ; and never-more
A mortal name be whispered in thine ear.
Go ! keep my secret !
    (*Drinks and dashes the goblet down.*)

Don J.   Ite ! missa est !
            (*Scene closes.*)

SCENE X. — *Street and garden wall. Night. Enter* CRUZADO *and* BARTOLOMÉ.

Cruz. This is the garden wall, and above it, yonder, is her house. The window in which thou seest the light is her window. But we will not go in now.

Bart. Why not ?

Cruz. Because she is not at home.

Bart. No matter ; we can wait. But how is this ? The gate is bolted. (*Sound of guitars and voices in a neighboring street.*) Hark ! There comes her lover with his infernal serenade ! Hark !

SONG.

Good night ! Good night, beloved !
    I come to watch o'er thee !
To be near thee, — to be near thee,
    Alone is peace for me.

Thine eyes are stars of morning,
    Thy lips are crimson flowers !
Good night ! Good night, beloved,
    While I count the weary hours.

Cruz. They are not coming this way.

Bart. Wait, they begin again.

SONG (*coming nearer*).

Ah! thou moon that shinest
  Argent-clear above!
All night long enlighten
  My sweet lady-love!
Moon that shinest,
All night long enlighten!

Bart. Woe be to him, if he comes this
  way!
Cruz. Be quiet, they are passing
  down the street.

SONG (*dying away*).

The nuns in the cloister
  Sang to each other;
For so many sisters
  Is there not one brother!
Ay, for the partridge, mother!
The cat has run away with the partridge!
Puss! puss! puss!

Bart. Follow that! follow that!
Come with me. Puss! puss!

(*Exeunt. On the opposite side enter the*
COUNT OF LARA *and gentlemen, with*
FRANCISCO.)

Lara. The gate is fast. Over the
  wall, Francisco,
And draw the bolt. There, so, and so,
  and over.
Now, gentlemen, come in, and help me
  scale
Yon balcony. How now? Her light
  still burns.
Move warily. Make fast the gate, Francisco.

(*Exeunt. Re-enter* CRUZADO *and* BAR-
TOLOMÉ.)

Bart. They went in at the gate.
Hark! I hear them in the garden.
(*Tries the gate.*) Bolted again! Vive
Cristo! Follow me over the wall.

(*They climb the wall.*)

SCENE XI. — PRECIOSA'S *bedchamber.
Midnight. She is sleeping in an arm-
chair, in an undress.* DOLORES *watching her.*

Dol. She sleeps at last!

(*Opens the window, and listens.*)

          All silent in the street,
And in the garden. Hark!
Prec. (*in her sleep*). I must go hence!
Give me my cloak!
Dol. He comes! I hear his footsteps.

Prec. Go tell them that I cannot
  dance to-night;
I am too ill! Look at me! See the
  fever
That burns upon my cheek! I must go
  hence.
I am too weak to dance.

(*Signal from the garden.*)

Dol. (*from the window*). Who's there?
Voice (*from below*).   A friend.
Dol. I will undo the door. Wait till
  I come.
Prec. I must go hence. I pray you
  do not harm me!
Shame! shame! to treat a feeble woman
  thus!
Be you but kind, I will do all things for
  you.
I'm ready now, — give me my casta-
  nets.
Where is Victorian? Oh, those hateful
  lamps!
They glare upon me like an evil eye.
I cannot stay. Hark! how they mock
  at me!
They hiss at me like serpents! Save
  me! save me!

(*She wakes.*)

How late is it, Dolores?
Dol.   It is midnight.
Prec. We must be patient. Smooth
  this pillow for me.

(*She sleeps again. Noise from the garden,
and voices.*)

Voice. Muera!
Another Voice. O villains! villains!
Lara.   So! have at you!
Voice. Take that!
Lara.   O, I am wounded!
Dol. (*shutting the window*). Jesu
  Maria!

ACT III.

SCENE I. — *A cross-road through a wood
In the background a distant village spire.*
VICTORIAN *and* HYPOLITO, *as travelling
students, with guitars, sitting under the
trees.* HYPOLITO *plays and sings.*

SONG.

Ah, Love!
Perjured, false, treacherous Love!
  Enemy
Of all that mankind may not rue!
  Most untrue

To him who keeps most faith with thee.
    Woe is me !
The falcon has the eyes of the dove.
    Ah, Love !
Perjured, false, treacherous Love !

Vict. Yes, Love is ever busy with his
    shuttle,
Is ever weaving into life's dull warp
Bright, gorgeous flowers and scenes
    Arcadian ;
Hanging our gloomy prison-house about
With tapestries, that make its walls dilate
In never-ending vistas of delight.
    Hyp. Thinking to walk in those Arca-
dian pastures,
Thou hast run thy noble head against
the wall.

SONG (*continued*).

Thy deceits
Give us clearly to comprehend,
    Whither tend
All thy pleasures, all thy sweets !
    They are cheats,
Thorns below and flowers above.
    Ah, Love !
Perjured, false, treacherous Love !

Vict. A very pretty song. I thank
thee for it.
Hyp. It suits thy case.
Vict.   Indeed, I think it does.
What wise man wrote it ?
Hyp.   Lopez Maldonado.
Vict. In truth, a pretty song.
Hyp.   With much truth in it.
I hope thou wilt profit by it ; and in
earnest
Try to forget this lady of thy love.
Vict. I will forget her ! All dear rec-
ollections
Pressed in my heart, like flowers within
a book,
Shall be torn out, and scattered to the
winds !
I will forget her ! But perhaps hereafter,
When she shall learn how heartless is the
world,
A voice within her will repeat my name,
And she will say, " He was indeed my
friend ! "
O, would I were a soldier, not a scholar,
That the loud march, the deafening beat
of drums,
The shattering blast of the brass-throated
trumpet,
The din of arms, the onslaught and the
storm,

And a swift death, might make me deaf
forever
To the upbraidings of this foolish heart !
    Hyp. Then let that foolish heart up-
braid no more !
To conquer love, one need but will to
conquer.
Vict. Yet, good Hypolito, it is in
vain
I throw into Oblivion's sea the sword
That pierces me ; for, like Excalibar,
With gemmed and flashing hilt, it will
not sink.
There rises from below a hand that
grasps it,
And waves it in the air ; and wailing
voices
Are heard along the shore.
    Hyp.   And yet at last
Down sank Excalibar to rise no more.
This is not well. In truth, it vexes me.
Instead of whistling to the steeds of Time,
To make them jog on merrily with life's
burden,
Like a dead weight thou hangest on the
wheels.
Thou art too young, too full of lusty
health
To talk of dying.
    Vict.   Yet I fain would die !
To go through life, unloving and un-
loved ;
To feel that thirst and hunger of the
soul
We cannot still ; that longing, that wild
impulse,
And struggle after something we have
not
And cannot have ; the effort to be
strong ;
And, like the Spartan boy, to smile, and
smile,
While secret wounds do bleed beneath
our cloaks ;
All this the dead feel not, — the dead
alone !
Would I were with them !
    Hyp.   We shall all be soon.
Vict. It cannot be too soon ; for I am
weary
Of the bewildering masquerade of Life,
Where strangers walk as friends, and
friends as strangers ;
Where whispers overheard betray false
hearts ;
And through the mazes of the crowd we
chase

Some form of loveliness, that smiles, and beckons,
And cheats us with fair words, only to leave us
A mockery and a jest; maddened, — confused, —
Not knowing friend from foe.
  Hyp.   Why seek to know ?
Enjoy the merry shrove-tide of thy youth !
Take each fair mask for what it gives itself,
Nor strive to look beneath it.
  Vict.   I confess,
That were the wiser part. But Hope no longer
Comforts my soul. I am a wretched man,
Much like a poor and shipwrecked mariner,
Who, struggling to climb up into the boat,
Has both his bruised and bleeding hands cut off,
And sinks again into the weltering sea,
Helpless and hopeless !
  Hyp.   Yet thou shalt not perish.
The strength of thine own arm is thy salvation.
Above thy head, through rifted clouds, there shines
A glorious star. Be patient. Trust thy star !

(*Sound of a village bell in the distance.*)

  Vict. Ave Maria ! I hear the sacristan
Ringing the chimes from yonder village belfry !
A solemn sound, that echoes far and wide
Over the red roofs of the cottages,
And bids the laboring hind a-field, the shepherd,
Guarding his flock, the lonely muleteer,
And all the crowd in village streets, stand still,
And breathe a prayer unto the blessed Virgin !
  Hyp. Amen ! amen ! Not half a league from hence
The village lies.
  Vict.   This path will lead us to it,
Over the wheat-fields, where the shadows sail
Across the running sea, now green, now blue,

And, like an idle mariner on the main,
Whistles the quail. Come, let us hasten on.   [*Exeunt.*

SCENE II. — *Public square in the village of Guadarrama. The Ave Maria still tolling. A crowd of villagers, with their hats in their hands, as if in prayer. In front, a group of Gypsies. The bell rings a merrier peal. A Gypsy dance. Enter* PANCHO, *followed by* PEDRO CRESPO.

  Pancho. Make room, ye vagabonds and Gypsy thieves !
Make room for the Alcalde and for me !
  Pedro C. Keep silence all ! I have an edict here
From our most gracious lord, the King of Spain,
Jerusalem, and the Canary Islands,
Which I shall publish in the market-place.
Open your ears and listen !

(*Enter the* PADRE CURA *at the door of his cottage.*)

                 Padre Cura,
Good day ! and, pray you, hear this edict read.
  Padre C. Good day, and God be with you ! Pray, what is it ?
  Pedro C. An act of banishment against the Gypsies !

(*Agitation and murmurs in the crowd.*)

  Pancho. Silence !
  Pedro C. (*reads*). "I hereby order and command,
That the Egyptian and Chaldean strangers,
Known by the name of Gypsies, shall henceforth
Be banished from the realm, as vagabonds
And beggars ; and if, after seventy days,
Any be found within our kingdom's bounds,
They shall receive a hundred lashes each ;
The second time, shall have their ears cut off ;
The third, be slaves for life to him who takes them,
Or burnt as heretics. Signed, I, the King."
Vile miscreants and creatures unbaptized !
You hear the law ! Obey and disappear

Pancho. And if in seventy days you
    are not gone,
Dead or alive I make you all my slaves.

(*The Gypsies go out in confusion, showing
signs of fear and discontent.* PANCHO
follows.)

    Padre C. A righteous law ! A very
    righteous law !
Pray you, sit down.
    Pedro C.   I thank you heartily.

(*They seat themselves on a bench at the*
PADRE CURA'S *door. Sound of guitars
heard at a distance, approaching during the dialogue which follows.*)

A very righteous judgment, as you say.
Now tell me, Padre Cura, — you know
    all things, —
How came these Gypsies into Spain ?
    Padre C.   Why, look you ;
They came with Hercules from Palestine,
And hence are thieves and vagrants, Sir
    Alcalde,
As the Simoniacs from Simon Magus.
And, look you, as Fray Jayme Bleda says,
There are a hundred marks to prove a
    Moor
Is not a Christian, so 't is with the Gyp-
    sies.
They never marry, never go to mass,
Never baptize their children, nor keep
    Lent,
Nor see the inside of a church, — nor —
    nor —
    Pedro C. Good reasons, good, substan-
    tial reasons all !
No matter for the other ninety-five.
They should be burnt, I see it plain
    enough,
They should be burnt.

(*Enter* VICTORIAN *and* HYPOLITO *playing.*)

    Padre C. And pray, whom have we
    here ?
    Pedro C. More vagrants ! By Saint
    Lazarus, more vagrants !
    Hyp. Good evening, gentlemen ! Is
    this Guadarrama ?
    Padre C. Yes, Guadarrama, and good
    evening to you.
    Hyp. We seek the Padre Cura of the
    village ;
And, judging from your dress and rever-
    end mien,
You must be he.
    Padre C.   I am. Pray, what 's
    your pleasure ?

    Hyp. We are poor students, travel-
    ling in vacation.
You know this mark ?
(*Touching the wooden spoon in his hat
    band.*
    Padre C. (*joyfully*). Ay, know it, and
    have worn it.
    Pedro C. (*aside*). Soup-eaters ! by the
    mass ! The worst of vagrants !
And there 's no law against them. Sir,
    your servant.   [*Exit.*
    Padre C. Your servant, Pedro Crespo.
    Hyp.   Padre Cura,
From the first moment I beheld your face,
I said within myself, " This is the man ! "
There is a certain something in your
    looks,
A certain scholar-like and studious some-
    thing, —
You understand, — which cannot be mis-
    taken ;
Which marks you as a very learned man,
In fine, as one of us.
    Vict. (*aside*).   What impudence !
    Hyp. As we approached, I said to my
    companion,
" That is the Padre Cura ; mark my
    words ! "
Meaning your Grace. " The other man,"
    said I,
" Who sits so awkwardly upon the bench,
Must be the sacristan."
    Padre C.   Ah ! said you so ?
Why, that was Pedro Crespo, the al-
    calde !
    Hyp. Indeed ! you much astonish me !
    His air
Was not so full of dignity and grace
As an alcalde's should be.
    Padre C.   That is true.
He 's out of humor with some vagrant
    Gypsies,
Who have their camp here in the neigh-
    borhood.
There 's nothing so undignified as anger.
    Hyp. The Padre Cura will excuse our
    boldness,
If, from his well-known hospitality,
We crave a lodging for the night.
    Padre C.   I pray you !
You do me honor ! I am but too happy
To have such guests beneath my humble
    roof.
It is not often that I have occasion
To speak with scholars ; and *Emollit
    mores,*
Nec sinit esse feros, Cicero says.

Hyp. 'T is Ovid, is it not?
Padre C.   No, Cicero.
Hyp. Your Grace is right. You are
the better scholar.
Now what a dunce was I to think it
Ovid!
But hang me if it is not! (*Aside.*)
Padre C.   Pass this way.
He was a very great man, was Cicero!
Pray you, go in, go in! no ceremony.
                               [*Exeunt.*

SCENE III. — *A room in the* PADRE CURA'S
house, Enter the PADRE *and* HYPOLITO.

Padre C. So then, Señor, you come
from Alcalá.
I am glad to hear it. It was there I
studied.
Hyp. And left behind an honored
name, no doubt.
How may I call your Grace?
Padre C.   Gerónimo
De Santillana, at your Honor's service.
Hyp. Descended from the Marquis
Santillana?
From the distinguished poet?
Padre C.   From the Marquis,
Not from the poet.
Hyp.   Why, they were the same.
Let me embrace you! O some lucky
star
Has brought me hither! Yet once more!
— once more!
Your name is ever green in Alcalá,
And our professor, when we are unruly,
Will shake his hoary head, and say,
    " Alas!
It was not so in Santillana's time! "
Padre C. I did not think my name
remembered there.
Hyp. More than remembered; it is
idolized.
Padre C. Of what professor speak
you?
Hyp.   Timoneda.
Padre C. I don't remember any Ti-
moneda.
Hyp. A grave and sombre man, whose
beetling brow
O'erhangs the rushing current of his
speech
As rocks o'er rivers hang. Have you for-
gotten?
Padre C. Indeed, I have. O, those
were pleasant days,

Those college days! I ne'er shall see the
like!
I had not buried then so many hopes!
I had not buried then so many friends!
I 've turned my back on what was then
before me;
And the bright faces of my young com-
panions
Are wrinkled like my own, or are no
more.
Do you remember Cueva?
Hyp.   Cueva? Cueva?
Padre C. Fool that I am! He was
before your time.
You 're a mere boy, and I am an old
man.
Hyp. I should not like to try my
strength with you.
Padre C. Well, well. But I forget;
you must be hungry.
Martina! ho! Martina! 'T is my niece.

(*Enter* MARTINA.)

Hyp. You may be proud of such a
niece as that.
I wish I had a niece. *Emollit mores.*
(*Aside.*)
He was a very great man, was Cicero!
Your servant, fair Martina.
Mart.   Servant, sir
Padre C. This gentleman is hungry.
See thou to it.
Let us have supper.
Mart.   'T will be ready soon.
Padre C. And bring a bottle of my
Val-de-Peñas
Out of the cellar. Stay; I 'll go myself.
Pray you, Señor, excuse me.   [*Exit.*
Hyp.   Hist! Martina!
One word with you. Bless me! what
handsome eyes!
To-day there have been Gypsies in the
village.
Is it not so?
Mart. There have been Gypsies here.
Hyp. Yes, and have told your for-
tune.
Mart. (*embarrassed*). Told my for-
tune?
Hyp. Yes, yes; I know they did.
Give me your hand.
I 'll tell you what they said. They said,
— they said,
The shepherd boy that loved you was a
clown,
And him you should not marry. Was it
not?

Mart. (*surprised*). How know you
that ?

Hyp.   O, I know more than that.
What a soft, little hand ! And then they
said,

A cavalier from court, handsome, and tall
And rich, should come one day to marry
you,

And you should be a lady. Was it not ?
He has arrived, the handsome cavalier.

(*Tries to kiss her. She runs off. Enter*
VICTORIAN, *with a letter.*)

Vict. The muleteer has come.

Hyp.   So soon ?

Vict.   I found him
Sitting at supper by the tavern door,
And, from a pitcher that he held aloft
His whole arm's length, drinking the
blood-red wine.

Hyp. What news from Court ?

Vict.   He brought this letter only.
(*Reads.*)

O cursed perfidy ! Why did I let
That lying tongue deceive me ! Preciosa,
Sweet Preciosa ! how art thou avenged !

Hyp. What news is this, that makes
thy cheek turn pale,
And thy hand tremble ?

Vict.   O, most infamous !
The Count of Lara is a worthless villain !

Hyp. That is no news, forsooth.

Vict.   He strove in vain
To steal from me the jewel of my soul,
The love of Preciosa. Not succeeding,
He swore to be revenged ; and set on foot
A plot to ruin her, which has succeeded.
She has been hissed and hooted from the
stage,
Her reputation stained by slanderous lies
Too foul to speak of ; and, once more a
beggar,
She roams a wanderer over God's green
earth,
Housing with Gypsies !

Hyp.   To renew again
The Age of Gold, and make the shepherd
swains
Desperate with love, like Gasper Gil's
Diana.

Redit et Virgo !

Vict.   Dear Hypolito,
How have I wronged that meek, confid-
ing heart !
I will go seek for her ; and with my tears
Wash out the wrong I 've done her !

Hyp.   O beware !
Act not that folly o'er again.

Vict.   Ay, folly,
Delusion, madness, call it what thou wilt,
I will confess my weakness, — I still love
her !
Still fondly love her !

(*Enter the* PADRE CURA.)

Hyp.   Tell us, Padre Cura,
Who are these Gypsies in the neighborhood ?

Padre C. Beltran Cruzado and his
crew.

Vict.   Kind Heaven,
I thank thee ! She is found ! is found
again !

Hyp. And have they with them a pale,
beautiful girl,
Called Preciosa ?

Padre C.   Ay, a pretty girl.
The gentleman seems moved.

Hyp.   Yes, moved with hunger,
He is half famished with this long day's
journey.

Padre C. Then, pray you, come this
way. The supper waits. [*Exeunt.*

SCENE IV. — *A post-house on the road to
Segovia, not far from the village of Guadarrama. Enter* CHISPA, *cracking a
whip, and singing the cachucha.*

Chispa. Halloo ! Don Fulano ! Let
us have horses, and quickly. Alas, poor
Chispa ! what a dog's life dost thou lead!
I thought, when I left my old master
Victorian, the student, to serve my new
master Don Carlos, the gentleman, that
I, too, should lead the life of a gentleman ;
should go to bed early, and get up late.
For when the abbot plays cards, what
can you expect of the friars ? But, in
running away from the thunder, I have
run into the lightning. Here I am in
hot chase after my master and his Gypsy girl. And a good beginning of the week
it is, as he said who was hanged on Mon-
day morning.

(*Enter* DON CARLOS.)

Don C. Are not the horses ready yet ?

Chispa. I should think not, for the
hostler seems to be asleep. Ho ! within
there !   Horses ! horses ! horses ! (*He
knocks at the gate with his whip, and enter* MOSQUITO, *putting on his jacket.*)

Mosq. Pray, have a little patience.
I 'm not a musket.

Chispa. Health and pistareens ! I 'm

glad to see you come on dancing, padre ! Pray, what's the news ?

Mosq. You cannot have fresh horses ; because there are none.

Chispa. Cachiporra ! Throw that bone to another dog. Do I look like your aunt ?

Mosq. No ; she has a beard.

Chispa. Go to ! go to !

Mosq. Are you from Madrid ?

Chispa. Yes ; and going to Estrama-dura. Get us horses.

Mosq. What's the news at Court ?

Chispa. Why, the latest news is, that I am going to set up a coach, and I have already bought the whip.

(*Strikes him round the legs.*)

Mosq. Oh ! oh ! you hurt me !

Don C. Enough of this folly. Let us have horses. (*Gives money to* Mos-quito.) It is almost dark ; and we are in haste. But tell me, has a band of Gyp-sies passed this way of late ?

Mosq. Yes ; and they are still in the neighborhood.

Don C. And where ?

Mosq. Across the fields yonder, in the woods near Guadarrama. [*Exit.*

Don C. Now this is lucky. We will visit the Gypsy camp.

Chispa. Are you not afraid of the evil eye ? Have you a stag's horn with you ?

Don C. Fear not. We will pass the night at the village.

Chispa. And sleep like the Squires of Hernan Daza, nine under one blanket.

Don C. I hope we may find the Pre-ciosa among them.

Chispa. Among the Squires ?

Don C. No ; among the Gypsies, blockhead !

Chispa. I hope we may ; for we are giving ourselves trouble enough on her account. Don't you think so ? How-ever, there is no catching trout without wetting one's trousers. Yonder come the horses. [*Exeunt.*

SCENE V. — *The Gypsy camp in the for-est. Night. Gypsies working at a forge. Others playing cards by the firelight.*

Gypsies (*at the forge sing*).

On the top of a mountain I stand,
With a crown of red gold in my hand,

Wild Moors come trooping over the lea,
O how from their fury shall I flee, flee, flee !
O how from their fury shall I flee ?

First Gypsy (*playing*). Down with your John-Dorados, my pigeon. Down with your John-Dorados, and let us make an end.

Gypsies (*at the forge sing*).

Loud sang the Spanish cavalier,
And thus his ditty ran ;
God send the Gypsy lassie here,
And not the Gypsy man.

First Gypsy (*playing*). There you are in your morocco !

Second Gypsy. One more game. The Alcalde's doves against the Padre Cura's new moon.

First Gypsy. Have at you, Chirelin.

Gypsies (*at the forge sing*).

At midnight, when the moon began
To show her silver flame,
There came to him no Gypsy man,
The Gypsy lassie came.

(*Enter* BELTRAN CRUZADO.)

Cruz. Come hither, Murcigalleros and Rastilleros ; leave work, leave play ; lis-ten to your orders for the night. (*Speak-ing to the right.*) You will get you to the village, mark you, by the stone cross.

Gypsies. Ay !

Cruz. (*to the left*). And you, by the pole with the hermit's head upon it.

Gypsies. Ay !

Cruz. As soon as you see the planets are out, in with you, and be busy with the ten commandments, under the sly, and Saint Martin asleep. D'ye hear ?

Gypsies. Ay !

Cruz. Keep your lanterns open, and, if you see a goblin or a papagayo, take to your trampers. Vineyards and Dan-cing John is the word. Am I compre-hended ?

Gypsies. Ay ! ay !

Cruz. Away, then !

(*Exeunt severally.* CRUZADO *walks up the stage, and disappears among the trees Enter* PRECIOSA.)

Prec. How strangely gleams through the gigantic trees
The red light of the forge ! Wild, beck oning shadows
Stalk through the forest, ever and anon
Rising and bending with the flickering flame,

Then flitting into darkness! So within
    me
Strange hopes and fears do beckon to
    each other,
My brightest hopes giving dark fears a
    being
As the light does the shadow. Woe is
    me!
How still it is about me, and how
    lonely!

(BARTOLOMÉ *rushes in.*)

Bart. Ho! Preciosa!
Prec.   O Bartolomé!
Thou here?
  Bart.   Lo! I am here.
  Prec.   Whence comest thou?
  Bart. From the rough ridges of the
    wild Sierra,
From caverns in the rocks, from hunger,
    thirst,
And fever! Like a wild wolf to the
    sheepfold
Come I for thee, my lamb.
  Prec.   O touch me not!
The Count of Lara's blood is on thy
    hands!
The Count of Lara's curse is on thy
    soul!
Do not come near me! Pray, begone
    from here!
Thou art in danger! They have set a
    price
Upon thy head!
  Bart.   Ay, and I 've wandered long
Among the mountains; and for many
    days
Have seen no human face, save the
    rough swineherd's.
The wind and rain have been my sole
    companions.
I shouted to them from the rocks thy
    name,
And the loud echo sent it back to me,
Till I grew mad. I could not stay from
    thee,
And I am here! Betray me, if thou wilt.
  Prec. Betray thee? I betray thee?
  Bart.   Preciosa!
come for thee! for thee I thus brave
    death!
Fly with me o'er the borders of this
    realm!
Fly with me!
  Prec.   Speak of that no more. I
    cannot.
I 'm thine no longer.

  Bart.   O, recall the time
When we were children! how we played
    together,
How we grew up together; how we
    plighted
Our hearts unto each other, even in
    childhood!
Fulfil thy promise, for the hour has
    come.
I 'm hunted from the kingdom, like a
    wolf!
Fulfil thy promise.
  Prec.   'T was my father's promise.
Not mine. I never gave my heart to
    thee,
Nor promised thee my hand!
  Bart.   False tongue of woman!
And heart more false!
  Prec.   Nay, listen unto me.
I will speak frankly. I have never
    loved thee;
I cannot love thee. This is not my
    fault,
It is my destiny. Thou art a man
Restless and violent. What wouldst
    thou with me,
A feeble girl, who have not long to
    live,
Whose heart is broken? Seek another
    wife,
Better than I, and fairer; and let not
Thy rash and headlong moods estrange
    her from thee.
Thou art unhappy in this hopeless pas-
    sion.
I never sought thy love; never did
    aught
To make thee love me. Yet I pity
    thee,
And most of all I pity thy wild heart,
That hurries thee to crimes and deeds
    of blood.
Beware, beware of that.
  Bart.   For thy dear sake
I will be gentle. Thou shalt teach me
    patience.
  Prec. Then take this farewell, and
    depart in peace.
Thou must not linger here.
  Bart.   Come, come with me.
  Prec. Hark! I hear footsteps.
  Bart.   I entreat thee, come!
  Prec. Away! It is in vain.
  Bart.   Wilt thou not come?
  Prec. Never!
  Bart.   Then woe, eternal woe,
    upon thee!

Thou shalt not be another's. Thou
　　shalt die.　　　　　　　[*Exit.*
　Prec. All holy angels keep me in this
　　hour !
Spirit of her who bore me, look upon
　　me !
Mother of God, the glorified, protect
　　me !
Christ and the saints, be merciful unto
　　me !
Yet why should I fear death ? What is
　　it to die ?
To leave all disappointment, care, and
　　sorrow,
To leave all falsehood, treachery, and
　　unkindness,
All ignominy, suffering, and despair,
And be at rest forever ! O dull heart,
Be of good cheer ! When thou shalt
　　cease to die,
Then shalt thou cease to suffer and com-
　　plain !

(*Enter* VICTORIAN *and* HYPOLITO *behind.*)

　Vict. 'T is she ! Behold, how beauti-
　　ful she stands
Under the tent-like trees !
　Hyp.　　　　　A woodland nymph !
　Vict. I pray thee, stand aside. Leave
　　me.
　Hyp.　　　　　　Be wary.
Do not betray thyself too soon.
　Vict. (*disguising his voice*). Hist !
　　Gypsy !
　Prec. (*aside, with emotion*). That
　　voice ! that voice from heaven !
　　O speak again !
Who is it calls ?
　Vict.　　　　　A friend.
　Prec. (*aside*).　　'T is he ! 'T is he !
I thank thee, Heaven, that thou hast
　　heard my prayer,
And sent me this protector ! Now be
　　strong,
Be strong, my heart ! I must dissem-
　　ble here.
False friend or true ?
　Vict.　　A true friend to the true ;
Fear not ; come hither. So ; can you
　　tell fortunes ?
　Prec. Not in the dark. Come nearer
　　to the fire.
Give me your hand. It is not crossed,
　　I see.
　Vict. (*putting a piece of gold into her
　　hand*). There is the cross.
　Prec.　　　　　　Is 't silver ?

　Vict.　　　　　　No, 't is gold.
　Prec. There 's a fair lady at the Court,
　　who loves you,
And for yourself alone.
　Vict.　　　　　Fie ! the old story !
Tell me a better fortune for my money ;
Not this old woman's tale !
　Prec.　　　　You are passionate ;
And this same passionate humor in your
　　blood
Has marred your fortune. Yes ; I see
　　it now ;
The line of life is crossed by many
　　marks.
Shame ! shame ! O you have wronged
　　the maid who loved you !
How could you do it ?
　Vict.　　　　I never loved a maid ;
For she I loved was then a maid no
　　more.
　Prec. How know you that ?
　Vict.　　　　A little bird in the air
Whispered the secret.
　Prec.　　There, take back your gold !
Your hand is cold, like a deceiver's
　　hand !
There is no blessing in its charity !
Make her your wife, for you have been
　　abused ;
And you shall mend your fortunes,
　　mending hers.
　Vict. (*aside*). How like an angel's
　　speaks the tongue of woman,
When pleading in another's cause her
　　own !
That is a pretty ring upon your finger-
Pray give it me.　(*Tries to take the ring.*)
　Prec.　　No ; never from my hand
Shall that be taken !
　Vict.　　Why, 't is but a ring.
I 'll give it back to you ; or, if I keep it,
Will give you gold to buy you twenty
　　such.
　Prec. Why would you have this ring ?
　Vict.　　　　A traveller's fancy,
A whim, and nothing more. I would
　　fain keep it
As a memento of the Gypsy camp
In Guadarrama, and the fortune-teller
Who sent me back to wed a widowed
　　maid.
Pray, let me have the ring.
　Prec.　　　　No, never ! never !
I will not part with it, even when I
　　die ;
But bid my nurse fold my pale fingers
　　thus

That it may not fall from them. 'T is a
    token
Of a beloved friend, who is no more.
    Vict.   How ? dead ?
    Prec. Yes ; dead to me ; and worse
        than dead.
He is estranged ! And yet I keep this
    ring.
I will rise with it from my grave here-
    after,
To prove to him that I was never false.
    Vict. (*aside*). Be still, my swelling
        heart ! one moment, still !
Why, 't is the folly of a love-sick girl.
Come, give it me, or I will say 't is
    mine,
And that you stole it.
    Prec.   O, you will not dare
To utter such a falsehood !
    Vict.   I not dare ?
Look in my face, and say if there is
    aught
I have not dared, I would not dare for
    thee !

    (*She rushes into his arms.*)

    Prec. 'T is thou ! 't is thou ! Yes ;
        yes ; my heart's elected !
My dearest-dear Victorian ! my soul's
    heaven !
Where hast thou been so long ? Why
    didst thou leave me ?
    Vict. Ask me not now, my dearest
        Preciosa.
Let me forget we ever have been parted !
    Prec. Hadst thou not come —
    Vict. I pray thee, do not chide
        me !
    Prec. I should have perished here
        among these Gypsies.
    Vict. Forgive me, sweet ! for what I
        made thee suffer.
Think'st thou this heart could feel a
    moment's joy,
Thou being absent ? O, believe it
    not !
Indeed, since that sad hour I have not
    slept,
For thinking of the wrong I did to
    thee !
Dost thou forgive me ? Say, wilt thou
    forgive me ?
    Prec. I have forgiven thee. Ere those
        words of anger
Were in the book of Heaven writ down
    against thee,
I had forgiven thee.

    Vict.   I 'm the veriest fool
That walks the earth, to have believed
    thee false.
It was the Count of Lara —
    Prec.   That bad man
Has worked me harm enough. Hast
    thou not heard —
    Vict. I have heard all. And yet speak
        on, speak on !
Let me but hear thy voice, and I am
    happy ;
For every tone, like some sweet incanta-
    tion,
Calls up the buried past to plead for me.
Speak, my beloved, speak into my heart,
Whatever fills and agitates thine own.

    (*They walk aside.*)

    Hyp. All gentle quarrels in the pas-
        toral poets,
All passionate love scenes in the best
    romances,
All chaste embraces on the public stage,
All soft adventures, which the liberal
    stars
Have winked at, as the natural course
    of things,
Have been surpassed here by my friend,
    the student,
And this sweet Gypsy lass, fair Preci-
    osa !
    Prec. Señor Hypolito ! I kiss your
        hand.
Pray, shall I tell your fortune ?
    Hyp.   Not to-night ;
For, should you treat me as you did
    Victorian,
And send me back to marry maids for-
    lorn,
My wedding day would last from now
    till Christmas.
    Chispa (*within*). What ho ! the Gyp-
        sies, ho ! Beltran Cruzado !
Halloo ! halloo ! halloo ! halloo !

(*Enters booted, with a whip and lantern*

    Vict.   What now
Why such a fearful din ? Hast thou
    been robbed ?
    Chispa. Ay, robbed and murdered ;
        and good evening to you,
My worthy masters.
    Vict. Speak ; what brings thee here ?
    Chispa (*to* PRECIOSA). Good news from
        Court ; good news ! Beltran Cru-
        zado,
The Count of the Calés, is not your fa-
    ther,

But your true father has returned to Spain
Laden with wealth.   You are no more a Gypsy.

Vict.   Strange as a Moorish tale !

Chispa.   And we have all
Been drinking at the tavern to your health,
As wells drink in November, when it rains.

Vict.   Where is the gentlemen ?

Chispa.   As the old song says,
    His body is in Segovia,
    His soul is in Madrid.

Prec.   Is this a dream ?   O, if it be a dream,
Let me sleep on, and do not wake me yet !
Repeat thy story !   Say I 'm not deceived !
Say that I do not dream !   I am awake ;
This is the Gypsy camp ; this is Victorian,
And this his friend, Hypolito !   Speak ! speak !
Let me not wake and find it all a dream !

Vict.   It is a dream, sweet child !   a waking dream,
A blissful certainty, a vision bright
Of that rare happiness, which even on earth
Heaven gives to those it loves.   Now art thou rich,
As thou wast ever beautiful and good ;
And I am now the beggar.

Prec. (*giving him her hand*).   I have still
A hand to give.

Chispa. (*aside*).   And I have two to take.
I 've heard my grandmother say, that Heaven gives almonds
To those who have no teeth.   That 's nuts to crack.
I 've teeth to spare, but where shall I find almonds ?

Vict.   What more of this strange story ?

Chispa.   Nothing more.
Your friend, Don Carlos, is now at the village
Showing to Pedro Crespo, the Alcalde,
The proofs of what I tell you.   The old hag,
Who stole you in your childhood, has confessed ;

And probably they 'll hang her for the crime,
To make the celebration more complete.

Vict.   No ; let it be a day of general joy ;
Fortune comes well to all, that comes not late.
Now let us join Don Carlos.

Hyp.   So farewell,
The student's wandering life !   Sweet serenades,
Sung under ladies' windows in the night,
And all that makes vacation beautiful !
To you, ye cloistered shades of Alcalá,
To you, ye radiant visions of romance,
Written in books, but here surpassed by truth,
The Bachelor Hypolito returns,
And leaves the Gypsy with the Spanish Student.

SCENE VI. — *A pass in the Guadarrama mountains.   Early morning.   A muleteer crosses the stage, sitting sideways on his mule, and lighting a paper cigar with flint and steel.*

SONG.

If thou art sleeping, maiden,
  Awake and open thy door,
'T is the break of day, and we must away,
  O'er meadow, and mount, and moor.

Wait not to find thy slippers,
  But come with thy naked feet ;
We shall have to pass through the dewy grass,
  And waters wide and fleet.

(*Disappears down the pass.   Enter a Monk.   A shepherd appears on the rocks above.*)

Monk.   Ave Maria, gratia plena.   Olá ! good man !

Shep.   Olá !

Monk.   Is this the road to Segovia ?

Shep.   It is, your reverence.

Monk.   How far is it ?

Shep.   I do not know.

Monk.   What is that yonder in the valley ?

Shep.   San Ildefonso.

Monk.   A long way to breakfast.

Shep.   Ay, marry.

Monk.   Are there robbers in these mountains ?

Shep.   Yes, and worse than that.

Monk. What ?
Shep. Wolves.
Monk. Santa Maria ! Come with me to San Ildefonso, and thou shalt be well rewarded.
Shep. What wilt thou give me ?
Monk. An Agnus Dei and my benediction.

(*They disappear. A mounted Contrabandista passes, wrapped in his cloak, and a gun at his saddle-bow. He goes down the pass singing.*)

SONG.

Worn with speed is my good steed,
And I march me hurried, worried ;
Onward, caballito mio,
With the white star in thy forehead !
Onward, for here comes the Ronda,
And I hear their rifles crack !
Ay, jaléo ! Ay, ay, jaléo !
Ay, jaléo ! They cross our track.

(*Song dies away. Enter* PRECIOSA, *on horseback, attended by* VICTORIAN, HYPOLITO, DON CARLOS, *and* CHISPA, *on foot, and armed.*)

Vict. This is the highest point. Here let us rest.
See, Preciosa, see how all about us
Kneeling, like hooded friars, the misty mountains
Receive the benediction of the sun !
O glorious sight !
Prec. Most beautiful indeed !
Hyp. Most wonderful !
Vict. And in the vale below,
Where yonder steeples flash like lifted halberds,
San Ildefonso, from its noisy belfries,
Sends up a salutation to the morn,
As if an army smote their brazen shields,
And shouted victory !
Prec. And which way lies
Segovia ?
Vict. At a great distance yonder.
Dost thou not see it ?
Prec. No. I do not see it.
Vict. The merest flaw that dents the horizon's edge.
There, yonder !
Hyp. 'T is a notable old town,
Boasting an ancient Roman aqueduct,
And an Alcázar, builded by the Moors,
Wherein, you may remember, poor Gil Blas
Was fed on *Pan del Rey*. O, many a time

Out of its grated windows have I looked
Hundreds of feet plumb down to the Eresma,
That, like a serpent through the valley creeping,
Glides at its foot.
Prec. O yes ! I see it now,
Yet rather with my heart than with mine eyes,
So faint it is. And all my thoughts sail thither,
Freighted with prayers and hopes, and forward urged
Against all stress of accident, as in
The Eastern Tale, against the wind and tide
Great ships were drawn to the Magnetic Mountains,
And there were wrecked, and perished in the sea ! (*She weeps.*)
Vict. O gentle spirit ! Thou didst bear unmoved
Blasts of adversity and frosts of fate !
But the first ray of sunshine that falls on thee
Melts thee to tears ! O, let thy weary heart
Lean upon mine ! and it shall faint no more,
Nor thirst, nor hunger ; but be comforted
And filled with my affection.
Prec. Stay no longer !
My father waits. Methinks I see him there,
Now looking from the window, and now watching
Each sound of wheels or footfall in the street,
And saying, " Hark ! she comes ! " O father ! father !

(*They descend the pass.* CHISPA *remains behind.*)

Chispa. I have a father, too, but he is a dead one. Alas and alack-a-day Poor was I born, and poor do I remain. I neither win nor lose. Thus I wag through the world, half the time on foot, and the other half walking ; and always as merry as a thunder-storm in the night. And so we plough along, as the fly said to the ox. Who knows what may happen ? Patience, and shuffle the cards ! I am not yet so bald that you can see my brains ; and perhaps, after all, I shall some day go to Rome, and come back Saint Peter. Benedicite ! [*Exit.*

(A pause. Then enter BARTOLOMÉ *wildly, as if in pursuit, with a carbine in his hand.)*

Bart. They passed this way ! I hear their horses' hoofs !
Yonder I see them ! Come, sweet cara-millo,
This serenade shall be the Gypsy's last !

(Fires down the pass.)

Ha ! ha ! Well whistled, my sweet cara-millo !
Well whistled ! — I have missed her ! — O my God !

(The shot is returned. BARTOLOMÉ *falls).*

THE BELFRY OF BRUGES

AND OTHER POEMS.

CARILLON.

IN the ancient town of Bruges,
In the quaint old Flemish city,
As the evening shades descended,
Low and loud and sweetly blended,
Low at times and loud at times,
And changing like a poet's rhymes,
Rang the beautiful wild chimes
From the Belfry in the market
Of the ancient town of Bruges.

Then, with deep sonorous clangor
Calmly answering their sweet anger,
When the wrangling bells had ended,
Slowly struck the clock eleven,
And, from out the silent heaven,
Silence on the town descended.
Silence, silence everywhere,
On the earth and in the air,
Save that footsteps here and there
Of some burgher home returning,
By the street lamps faintly burning,
For a moment woke the echoes
Of the ancient town of Bruges.

But amid my broken slumbers
Still I heard those magic numbers,
As they loud proclaimed the flight
And stolen marches of the night ;
Till their chimes in sweet collision
Mingled with each wandering vision,
Mingled with the fortune-telling
Gypsy-bands of dreams and fancies,
Which amid the waste expanses
Of the silent land of trances
Have their solitary dwelling ;
All else seemed asleep in Bruges,
In the quaint old Flemish city.

And I thought how like these chimes
Are the poet's airy rhymes,
All his rhymes and roundelays,
His conceits, and songs, and ditties,
From the belfry of his brain,
Scattered downward, though in vain,
On the roofs and stones of cities !
For by night the drowsy ear
Under its curtains cannot hear,
And by day men go their ways,
Hearing the music as they pass,
But deeming it no more, alas !
Than the hollow sound of brass.

Yet perchance a sleepless wight,
Lodging at some humble inn
In the narrow lanes of life,
When the dusk and hush of night
Shut out the incessant din
Of daylight and its toil and strife,
May listen with a calm delight
To the poet's melodies,
Till he hears, or dreams he hears,
Intermingled with the song,
Thoughts that he has cherished long ;
Hears amid the chime and singing
The bells of his own village ring-ing,
And wakes, and finds his slumberous eyes
Wet with most delicious tears.

Thus dreamed I, as by night I lay
In Bruges, at the Fleur-de-Blé,
Listening with a wild delight
To the chimes that, through the night,
Rang their changes from the Belfry
Of that quaint old Flemish city.

THE BELFRY OF BRUGES.

IN the market-place of Bruges stands
the belfry old and brown ;
Thrice consumed and thrice rebuilded,
still it watches o'er the town.

As the summer morn was breaking, on
that lofty tower I stood,
And the world threw off the darkness,
like the weeds of widowhood.

Thick with towns and hamlets studded,
and with streams and vapors gray,
Like a shield embossed with silver,
round and vast the landscape lay.

At my feet the city slumbered. From
its chimneys, here and there,
Wreaths of snow-white smoke, ascending, vanished, ghost-like, into air.

Not a sound rose from the city at that
early morning hour,
But I heard a heart of iron beating in
the ancient tower.

From their nests beneath the rafters sang
the swallows wild and high ;
And the world, beneath me sleeping,
seemed more distant than the sky.

Then most musical and solemn, bringing
back the olden times,
With their strange, unearthly changes
rang the melancholy chimes,

Like the psalms from some old cloister,
when the nuns sing in the choir ;
And the great bell tolled among them,
like the chanting of a friar.

Visions of the days departed, shadowy
phantoms filled my brain ;
They who live in history only seemed to
walk the earth again ;

All the Foresters of Flanders, — mighty
Baldwin Bras de Fer,
Lyderick du Bucq and Cressy Philip,
Guy de Dampierre.

I beheld the pageants splendid that
adorned those days of old ;
Stately dames, like queens attended,
knights who bore the Fleece of
Gold

Lombard and Venetian merchants with
deep-laden argosies ;
Ministers from twenty nations ; more
than royal pomp and ease.

I beheld proud Maximilian, kneeling
humbly on the ground ;
I beheld the gentle Mary, hunting with
her hawk and hound ;

And her lighted bridal-chamber, where
a duke slept with the queen,
And the armed guard around them, and
the sword unsheathed between.

I beheld the Flemish weavers, with Namur and Juliers bold,
Marching homeward from the bloody
battle of the Spurs of Gold ;

Saw the fight at Minnewater, saw the
White Hoods moving west,
Saw great Artevelde victorious scale the
Golden Dragon's nest.

And again the whiskered Spaniard all
the land with terror smote ;
And again the wild alarum sounded from
the tocsin's throat ;

Till the bell of Ghent responded o'er lagoon and dike of sand,
"I am Roland ! I am Roland ! there is
victory in the land !"

Then the sound of drums aroused me
The awakened city's roar
Chased the phantoms I had summoned
back into their graves once more.

Hours had passed away like minutes ;
and, before I was aware,
Lo ! the shadow of the belfry crossed
the sun-illumined square.

MISCELLANEOUS.

A GLEAM OF SUNSHINE.

THIS is the place. Stand still, my steed,
  Let me review the scene,
And summon from the shadowy Past
  The forms that once have been.

The Past and Present here unite
  Beneath Time's flowing tide,
Like footprints hidden by a brook,
  But seen on either side.

Here runs the highway to the town ;
  There the green lane descends,
Through which I walked to church with
    thee,
  O gentlest of my friends !

The shadow of the linden-trees
  Lay moving on the grass ;
Between them and the moving boughs,
  A shadow, thou didst pass.

Thy dress was like the lilies,
  And thy heart as pure as they :
One of God's holy messengers
  Did walk with me that day.

I saw the branches of the trees
  Bend down thy touch to meet,
The clover-blossoms in the grass
  Rise up to kiss thy feet.

" Sleep, sleep to-day, tormenting cares,
  Of earth and folly born! "
Solemnly sang the village choir
  On that sweet Sabbath morn.

Through the closed blinds the golden sun
  Poured in a dusty beam,
Like the celestial ladder seen
  By Jacob in his dream.

And ever and anon, the wind,
  Sweet-scented with the hay,
Turned o'er the hymn-book's fluttering
    leaves
  That on the window lay.

Long was the good man's sermon,
  Yet it seemed not so to me ;
For he spake of Ruth the beautiful,
  And still I thought of thee.

Long was the prayer he uttered,
  Yet it seemed not so to me ;
For in my heart I prayed with him,
  And still I thought of thee.

But now, alas ! the place seems changed;
  Thou art no longer here :
Part of the sunshine of the scene
  With thee did disappear.

Though thoughts, deep-rooted in my
    heart,
  Like pine-trees dark and high,'
Subdue the light of noon, and breathe
  A low and ceaseless sigh ;

This memory brightens o'er the past,
  As when the sun, concealed
Behind some cloud that near us hangs
  Shines on a distant field.

THE ARSENAL AT SPRINGFIELD.

THIS is the Arsenal. From floor to ceil-
    ing,
  Like a huge organ, rise the burnished
    arms ;
But from their silent pipes no anthem
    pealing
  Startles the villages with strange
    alarms.

Ah ! what a sound will rise, how wild
    and dreary,
  When the death-angel touches those
    swift keys !
What loud lament and dismal Miserere
  Will mingle with their awful sympho-
    nies !

I hear even now the infinite fierce cho-
    rus,
  The cries of agony, the endless groan,
Which, through the ages that have gone
    before us,
  In long reverberations reach our own.

On helm and harness rings the Saxon
    hammer,
  Through Cimbric forest roars the
    Norseman's song,

And loud, amid the universal clamor,
  O'er distant deserts sounds the Tartar
    gong.

I hear the Florentine, who from his pal-
    ace
  Wheels out his battle-bell with dread-
    ful din,
And Aztec priests upon their teocallis
  Beat the wild war-drums made of ser-
    pent's skin;

The tumult of each sacked and burning
    village;
  The shout that every prayer for mercy
    drowns;
The soldiers' revels in the midst of pil-
    lage;
  The wail of famine in beleaguered
    towns;

The bursting shell, the gateway wrenched
    asunder,
  The rattling musketry, the clashing
    blade;
And ever and anon, in tones of thunder,
  The diapason of the cannonade.

Is it, O man, with such discordant
    noises,
  With such accursed instruments as
    these,
Thou drownest Nature's sweet and kind-
    ly voices,
  And jarrest the celestial harmonies?

Were half the power, that fills the world
    with terror,
  Were half the wealth, bestowed on
    camps and courts,
Given to redeem the human mind from
    error,
  There were no need of arsenals or
    forts:

The warrior's name would be a name ab-
    horred!
  And every nation, that should lift
    again
Its hand against a brother, on its fore-
    head
  Would wear forevermore the curse of
    Cain!

Down the dark future, through long
    generations,
  The echoing sounds grow fainter and
    then cease;

And like a bell, with solemn, sweet vi-
    brations,
  I hear once more the voice of Christ
    say, "Peace!"

Peace! and no longer from its brazen
    portals
  The blast of War's great organ shakes
    the skies!
But beautiful as songs of the immortals
  The holy melodies of love arise.

NUREMBERG.

In the valley of the Pegnitz, where across
    broad meadow-lands
Rise the blue Franconian mountains,
    Nuremberg, the ancient, stands.

Quaint old town of toil and traffic, quaint
    old town of art and song,
Memories haunt thy pointed gables, like
    the rooks that round them throng:

Memories of the Middle Ages, when the
    emperors, rough and bold,
Had their dwelling in thy castle, time-
    defying, centuries old;

And thy brave and thrifty burghers boast-
    ed, in their uncouth rhyme,
That their great imperial city stretched
    its hand through every clime.

In the court-yard of the castle, bound
    with many an iron band,
Stands the mighty linden planted by
    Queen Cunigunde's hand;

On the square the oriel window, where
    in old heroic days
Sat the poet Melchior singing Kaiser
    Maximilian's praise.

Everywhere I see around me rise the
    wondrous world of Art:
Fountains wrought with richest sculpture
    standing in the common mart;

And above cathedral doorways saints and
    bishops carved in stone,
By a former age commissioned as apostles
    to our own.

In the church of sainted Sebald sleeps
    enshrined his holy dust,
And in bronze the Twelve Apostles guard
    from age to age their trust:

In the church of sainted Lawrence stands
  a pix of sculpture rare,
Like the foamy sheaf of fountains, rising
  through the painted air.

Here, when Art was still religion, with a
  simple, reverent heart,
Lived and labored Albrecht Dürer, the
  Evangelist of Art ;

Hence in silence and in sorrow, toiling
  still with busy hand,
Like an emigrant he wandered, seeking
  for the Better Land.

Emigravit is the inscription on the tombstone where he lies ;
Dead he is not, but departed, — for the
  artist never dies.

Fairer seems the ancient city, and the
  sunshine seems more fair,
That he once has trod its pavement, that
  he once has breathed its air !

Through these streets so broad and stately,
  these obscure and dismal lanes,
Walked of yore the Mastersingers, chanting rude poetic strains.

From remote and sunless suburbs came
  they to the friendly guild,
Building nests in Fame's great temple,
  as in spouts the swallows build.

As the weaver plied the shuttle, wove he
  too the mystic rhyme,
And the smith his iron measures hammered to the anvil's chime ;

Thanking God, whose boundless wisdom
  makes the flowers of poesy bloom
In the forge's dust and cinders, in the
  tissues of the loom.

Here Hans Sachs, the cobbler-poet, lau-
  reate of the gentle craft,
Wisest of the Twelve Wise Masters, in
  huge folios sang and laughed.

But his house is now an ale-house, with
  a nicely sanded floor,
And a garland in the window, and his
  face above the door ;

Painted by some humble artist, as in
  Adam Puschman's song,
As the old man gray and dove-like, with
  his great beard white and long.

And at night the swart mechanic comes
  to drown his cark and care,
Quaffing ale from pewter tankards, in
  the master's antique chair.

Vanished is the ancient splendor, and
  before my dreamy eye
Wave these mingled shapes and figures,
  like a faded tapestry.

Not thy Councils, not thy Kaisers, win
  for thee the world's regard ;
But thy painter, Albrecht Dürer, and
  Hans Sachs thy cobbler-bard.

Thus, O Nuremberg, a wanderer from a
  region far away,
As he paced thy streets and court-yards,
  sang in thought his careless lay :

Gathering from the pavement's crevice,
  as a floweret of the soil,
The nobility of labor, — the long pedigree
  of toil.

THE NORMAN BARON.

Dans les moments de la vie où la réflexion de-
vient plus calme et plus profonde, où l'intérêt et
l'avarice parlent moins haut que la raison, dans
les instants de chagrin domestique, de maladie,
et de péril de mort, les nobles se repentirent de
posséder des serfs, comme d'une chose peu agré-
able à Dieu, qui avait créé tous les hommes à son
image.
  THIERRY, *Conquête de l'Angleterre.*

In his chamber, weak and dying,
Was the Norman baron lying ;
Loud, without, the tempest thundered,
    And the castle-turret shook.

In this fight was Death the gainer,
Spite of vassal and retainer,
And the lands his sires had plundered,
    Written in the Doomsday Book.

By his bed a monk was seated,
Who in humble voice repeated
Many a prayer and pater-noster,
    From the missal on his knee ;

And, amid the tempest pealing,
Sounds of bells came faintly stealing,
Bells, that from the neighboring kloster
    Rang for the Nativity.

In the hall, the serf and vassal
Held, that night, their Christmas was-
    sail ;

Many a carol, old and saintly,
    Sang the minstrels and the waits ;

And so loud these Saxon gleemen
Sang to slaves the songs of freemen,
That the storm was heard but faintly,
    Knocking at the castle-gates.

Till at length the lays they chanted
Reached the chamber terror-haunted,
Where the monk, with accents holy,
    Whispered at the baron's ear.

Tears upon his eyelids glistened,
As he paused awhile and listened,
And the dying baron slowly
    Turned his weary head to hear.

" Wassail for the kingly stranger
Born and cradled in a manger !
King, like David, priest, like Aaron,
    Christ is born to set us free ! "

And the lightning showed the sainted
Figures on the casement painted,
And exclaimed the shuddering baron,
    " Miserere, Domine ! "

In that hour of deep contrition
He beheld, with clearer vision,
Through all outward show and fashion,
    Justice, the Avenger, rise.

All the pomp of earth had vanished,
Falsehood and deceit were banished,
Reason spake more loud than passion,
    And the truth wore no disguise.

Every vassal of his banner,
Every serf born to his manor,
All those wronged and wretched crea-
    tures,
    By his hand were freed again.

And, as on the sacred missal
He recorded their dismissal,
Death relaxed his iron features,
    And the monk replied, " Amen ! "

Many centuries have been numbered
Since in death the baron slumbered
By the convent's sculptured portal,
    Mingling with the common dust :

But the good deed, through the ages
Living in historic pages,
Brighter grows and gleams immortal,
    Unconsumed by moth or rust.

RAIN IN SUMMER.

How beautiful is the rain !
After the dust and heat,
In the broad and fiery street,
In the narrow lane,
How beautiful is the rain !

How it clatters along the roofs,
Like the tramp of hoofs !
How it gushes and struggles out
From the throat of the overflowing
    spout !

Across the window-pane
It pours and pours ;
And swift and wide,
With a muddy tide,
Like a river down the gutter roars
The rain, the welcome rain !

The sick man from his chamber looks
At the twisted brooks ;
He can feel the cool
Breath of each little pool ;
His fevered brain
Grows calm again,
And he breathes a blessing on the rain.

From the neighboring school
Come the boys,
With more than their wonted noise
And commotion ;
And down the wet streets
Sail their mimic fleets,
Till the treacherous pool
Ingulfs them in its whirling
And turbulent ocean.

In the country, on every side,
Where far and wide,
Like a leopard's tawny and spotted hide,
Stretches the plain,
To the dry grass and the drier grain
How welcome is the rain !

In the furrowed land
The toilsome and patient oxen stand ;
Lifting the yoke-encumbered head,
With their dilated nostrils spread,
They silently inhale
The clover-scented gale,
And the vapors that arise
From the well-watered and smoking soil.
For this rest in the furrow after toil
Their large and lustrous eyes

Seem to thank the Lord,
More than man's spoken word.

Near at hand,
From under the sheltering trees,
The farmer sees
His pastures, and his fields of grain,
As they bend their tops
To the numberless beating drops
Of the incessant rain.
He counts it as no sin
That he sees therein
Only his own thrift and gain.

These, and far more than these,
The Poet sees!
He can behold
Aquarius old
Walking the fenceless fields of air;
And from each ample fold
Of the clouds about him rolled
Scattering everywhere
The showery rain,
As the farmer scatters his grain.

He can behold
Things manifold
That have not yet been wholly told,—
Have not been wholly sung nor said.
For his thought, that never stops,
Follows the water-drops
Down to the graves of the dead,
Down through chasms and gulfs profound,
To the dreary fountain-head
Of lakes and rivers under ground;
And sees them, when the rain is done,
On the bridge of colors seven
Climbing up once more to heaven,
Opposite the setting sun.

Thus the Seer,
With vision clear,
Sees forms appear and disappear,
In the perpetual round of strange,
Mysterious change
From birth to death, from death to birth,
From earth to heaven, from heaven to
earth;
Till glimpses more sublime
Of things, unseen before,
Unto his wondering eyes reveal
The Universe, as an immeasurable wheel
Turning forevermore
In the rapid and rushing river of Time.

TO A CHILD.

DEAR child! how radiant on thy mother's knee,
With merry-making eyes and jocund
smiles,
Thou gazest at the painted tiles,
Whose figures grace,
With many a grotesque form and face,
The ancient chimney of thy nursery!
The lady with the gay macaw,
The dancing girl, the grave bashaw
With bearded lip and chin;
And, leaning idly o'er his gate,
Beneath the imperial fan of state,
The Chinese mandarin.

With what a look of proud command
Thou shakest in thy little hand
The coral rattle with its silver bells,
Making a merry tune!
Thousands of years in Indian seas
That coral grew, by slow degrees,
Until some deadly and wild monsoon
Dashed it on Coromandel's sand!
Those silver bells
Reposed of yore,
As shapeless ore,
Far down in the deep-sunken wells
Of darksome mines,
In some obscure and sunless place,
Beneath huge Chimborazo's base,
Or Potosi's o'erhanging pines!
And thus for thee, O little child,
Through many a danger and escape,
The tall ships passed the stormy cape;
For thee in foreign lands remote,
Beneath a burning, tropic clime,
The Indian peasant, chasing the wild
goat,
Himself as swift and wild,
In falling, clutched the frail arbute,
The fibres of whose shallow root,
Uplifted from the soil, betrayed
The silver veins beneath it laid,
The buried treasures of the miser, Time.

But, lo! thy door is left ajar!
Thou hearest footsteps from afar!
And, at the sound,
Thou turnest round
With quick and questioning eyes,
Like one, who, in a foreign land,
Beholds on every hand
Some source of wonder and surprise!
And, restlessly, impatiently,
Thou strivest, strugglest, to be free.

" From under the sheltering trees,
    The farmer sees
    His pastures."   Page 82.

The four walls of thy nursery
Are now like prison walls to thee.
No more thy mother's smiles,
No more the painted tiles,
Delight thee, nor the playthings on the
    floor,
That won thy little, beating heart before ;
Thou strugglest for the open door.

Through these once solitary halls
Thy pattering footstep falls.
The sound of thy merry voice
Makes the old walls
Jubilant, and they rejoice
With the joy of thy young heart,
O'er the light of whose gladness
No shadows of sadness
From the sombre background of memory
    start.

Once, ah, once, within these walls,
One whom memory oft recalls,
The Father of his Country, dwelt.
And yonder meadows broad and damp
The fires of the besieging camp
Encircled with a burning belt.
Up and down these echoing stairs,
Heavy with the weight of cares,
Sounded his majestic tread ;
Yes, within this very room
Sat he in those hours of gloom,
Weary both in heart and head.

But what are these grave thoughts to
    thee ?
Out, out ! into the open air !
Thy only dream is liberty,
Thou carest little how or where.
I see thee eager at thy play,
Now shouting to the apples on the tree,
With cheeks as round and red as they ;
And now among the yellow stalks,
Among the flowering shrubs and plants,
As restless as the bee.
Along the garden walks,
The tracks of thy small carriage-wheels
    I trace ;
And see at every turn how they efface
Whole villages of sand-roofed tents,
That rise like golden domes
Above the cavernous and secret homes
Of wandering and nomadic tribes of
    ants.
Ah, cruel little Tamerlane,
Who, with thy dreadful reign,
Dost persecute and overwhelm
These hapless Troglodytes of thy realm !

What ! tired already ! with those sup-
    pliant looks,
And voice more beautiful than a poet's
    books,
Or murmuring sound of water as it flows.
Thou comest back to parley with repose :
This rustic seat in the old apple-tree,
With its o'erhanging golden canopy
Of leaves illuminate with autumnal hues,
And shining with the argent light of
    dews,
Shall for a season be our place of rest.
Beneath us, like an oriole's pendent
    nest,
From which the laughing birds have
    taken wing,
By thee abandoned, hangs thy vacant
    swing.
Dream-like the waters of the river
    gleam ;
A sailless vessel drops adown the stream,
And like it, to a sea as wide and deep,
Thou driftest gently down the tides of
    sleep.

O child ! O new-born denizen
Of life's great city ! on thy head
The glory of the morn is shed,
Like a celestial benison !
Here at the portal thou dost stand,
And with thy little hand
Thou openest the mysterious gate
Into the future's undiscovered land.
I see its valves expand,
As at the touch of Fate !
Into those realms of love and hate,
Into that darkness blank and drear,
By some prophetic feeling taught,
I launch the bold, adventurous thought,
Freighted with hope and fear ;
As upon subterranean streams,
In caverns unexplored and dark,
Men sometimes launch a fragile bark,
Laden with flickering fire,
And watch its swift-receding beams,
Until at length they disappear,
And in the distant dark expire.

By what astrology of fear or hope
Dare I to cast thy horoscope !
Like the new moon thy life appears ;
A little strip of silver light,
And widening outward into night
The shadowy disk of future years ;
And yet upon its outer rim,
A luminous circle, faint and dim,
And scarcely visible to us here,

Rounds and completes the perfect
    sphere ;
A prophecy and intimation,
A pale and feeble adumbration,
Of the great world of light, that lies
Behind all human destinies.

Ah ! if thy fate, with anguish fraught,
Should be to wet the dusty soil
With the hot tears and sweat of toil, —
To struggle with imperious thought,
Until the overburdened brain,
Weary with labor, faint with pain,
Like a jarred pendulum, retain
Only its motion, not its power, —
Remember, in that perilous hour,
When most afflicted and oppressed,
From labor there shall come forth rest.

And if a more auspicious fate
On thy advancing steps await,
Still let it ever be thy pride
To linger by the laborer's side ;
With words of sympathy or song
To cheer the dreary march along
Of the great army of the poor,
O'er desert sand, o'er dangerous moor.
Nor to thyself the task shall be
Without reward ; for thou shalt learn
The wisdom early to discern
True beauty in utility ;
As great Pythagoras of yore,
Standing beside the blacksmith's door,
And hearing the hammers, as they smote
The anvils with a different note,
Stole from the varying tones, that hung
Vibrant on every iron tongue,
The secret of the sounding wire,
And formed the seven-chorded lyre.

Enough ! I will not play the Seer ;
I will no longer strive to ope
The mystic volume, where appear
The herald Hope, forerunning Fear,
And Fear, the pursuivant of Hope.
Thy destiny remains untold ;
For, like Acestes' shaft of old,
The swift thought kindles as it flies,
And burns to ashes in the skies.

THE OCCULTATION OF ORION.

I saw, as in a dream sublime,
The balance in the hand of Time.
O'er East and West its beam impended ;
And day, with all its hours of light,
Was slowly sinking out of sight,

While, opposite, the scale of night
Silently with the stars ascended.

Like the astrologers of eld,
In that bright vision I beheld
Greater and deeper mysteries.
I saw, with its celestial keys,
Its chords of air, its frets of fire,
The Samian's great Æolian lyre,
Rising through all its sevenfold bars,
From earth unto the fixed stars.
And through the dewy atmosphere,
Not only could I see, but hear,
Its wondrous and harmonious strings,
In sweet vibration, sphere by sphere,
From Dian's circle light and near,
Onward to vaster and wider rings,
Where, chanting through his beard of
    snows,
Majestic, mournful, Saturn goes,
And down the sunless realms of space
Reverberates the thunder of his bass.

Beneath the sky's triumphal arch
This music sounded like a march,
And with its chorus seemed to be
Preluding some great tragedy.
Sirius was rising in the east ;
And, slow ascending one by one,
The kindling constellations shone.
Begirt with many a blazing star,
Stood the great giant Algebar,
Orion, hunter of the beast !
His sword hung gleaming by his side,
And, on his arm, the lion's hide
Scattered across the midnight air
The golden radiance of its hair.

The moon was pallid, but not faint ;
And beautiful as some fair saint,
Serenely moving on her way
In hours of trial and dismay.
As, if she heard the voice of God,
Unharmed with naked feet she trod
Upon the hot and burning stars,
As on the glowing coals and bars,
That were to prove her strength, and try
Her holiness and her purity.

Thus moving on, with silent pace,
And triumph in her sweet, pale face,
She reached the station of Orion.
Aghast he stood in strange alarm !
And suddenly from his outstretched arm
Down fell the red skin of the lion
Into the river at his feet.
His mighty club no longer beat

The forehead of the bull ; but he
Reeled as of yore beside the sea,
When, blinded by Œnopion,
He sought the blacksmith at his forge,
And, climbing up the mountain gorge,
Fixed his blank eyes upon the sun.

Then, through the silence overhead,
An angel with a trumpet said,
" Forevermore, forevermore,
The reign of violence is o'er ! "
And, like an instrument that flings
Its music on another's strings,
The trumpet of the angel cast
Upon the heavenly lyre its blast,
And on from sphere to sphere the words
Re-echoed down the burning chords, —
" Forevermore, forevermore,
The reign of violence is o'er ! "

THE BRIDGE.

I stood on the bridge at midnight,
    As the clocks were striking the hour,
And the moon rose o'er the city,
    Behind the dark church-tower.

I saw her bright reflection
    In the waters under me,
Like a golden goblet falling
    And sinking into the sea.

And far in the hazy distance
    Of that lovely night in June,
The blaze of the flaming furnace
    Gleamed redder than the moon.

Among the long, black rafters
    The wavering shadows lay,
And the current that came from the
    ocean
    Seemed to lift and bear them away ;

As, sweeping and eddying through them,
    Rose the belated tide,
And, streaming into the moonlight,
    The seaweed floated wide.

And like those waters rushing
    Among the wooden piers,
A flood of thoughts came o'er me
    That filled my eyes with tears.

How often, O how often,
    In the days that had gone by,
I had stood on that bridge at midnight
    And gazed on that wave and sky !

How often, O how often,
    I had wished that the ebbing tide
Would bear me away on its bosom
    O'er the ocean wild and wide !

For my heart **was** hot and restless,
    And my life was full of care,
And the burden laid upon me
    Seemed greater than I could bear.

But now it has fallen from me,
    It is buried in the sea ;
And only the sorrow of others
    Throws its shadow over me.

Yet whenever I cross the river
    On its bridge with wooden piers,
Like the odor of brine from the ocean
    Comes the thought of other years.

And I think how many thousands
    Of care-encumbered men,
Each bearing his burden of sorrow,
    Have crossed the bridge since then.

I see the long procession
    Still passing to and fro,
The young heart hot and restless,
    And the old subdued and slow !

And forever and forever,
    As long as the river flows,
As long as the heart has passions,
    As long as life has woes ;

The moon and its broken reflection
    And its shadows shall appear,
As the symbol of love in heaven,
    And its wavering image here.

TO THE DRIVING CLOUD.

Gloomy and dark art thou, O chief of the mighty Omahas ;
Gloomy and dark as the driving cloud, whose name thou hast taken !
Wrapt in thy scarlet blanket, I see thee stalk through the city's
Narrow and populous streets, as once by the margin of rivers
Stalked those birds unknown, that have left us only their footprints.
What, in a few short years, will remain of thy race but the footprints ?

How canst thou walk these streets, who hast trod the green turf of the prairies !
How canst thou breathe this air, who hast breathed the sweet air of the mountains ?
Ah ! 't is in vain that with lordly looks of disdain thou dost challenge
Looks of disdain in return, and question these walls and these pavements,
Claiming the soil for thy hunting-grounds, while down-trodden millions
Starve in the garrets of Europe, and cry from its caverns that they, too,
Have been created heirs of the earth, and claim its division !

Back, then, back to thy woods in the regions west of the Wabash !
There as a monarch thou reignest.   In autumn the leaves of the maple
Pave the floors of thy palace-halls with gold, and in summer
Pine-trees waft through its chambers the odorous breath of their branches.
There thou art strong and great, a hero, a tamer of horses !
There thou chasest the stately stag on the banks of the Elkhorn,
Or by the roar of the Running-Water, or where the Omaha
Calls thee, and leaps through the wild ravine like a brave of the Blackfeet !

Hark ! what murmurs arise from the heart of those mountainous deserts ?
Is it the cry of the Foxes and Crows, or the mighty Behemoth,
Who, unharmed, on his tusks once caught the bolts of the thunder,
And now lurks in his lair to destroy the race of the red man ?
Far more fatal to thee and thy race than the Crows and the Foxes,
Far more fatal to thee and thy race than the tread of Behemoth,
Lo ! the big thunder-canoe, that steadily breasts the Missouri's
Merciless current ! and yonder, afar on the prairies, the camp-fires
Gleam through the night ; and the cloud of dust in the gray of the daybreak
Marks not the buffalo's track, nor the Mandan's dexterous horse-race ;
It is a caravan, whitening the desert where dwell the Camanches !
Ha ! how the breath of these Saxons and Celts, like the blast of the east-wind,
Drifts evermore to the west the scanty smokes of thy wigwams !

SONGS AND SONNETS.

SEAWEED.

When descends on the Atlantic
        The gigantic
Storm-wind of the equinox,
Landward in his wrath he scourges
        The toiling surges,
Laden with seaweed from the rocks :

From Bermuda's reefs ; from edges
        Of sunken ledges,
In some far-off, bright Azore ;
From Bahama, and the dashing,
        Silver-flashing
Surges of San Salvador ;

From the tumbling surf, that buries
        The Orkneyan skerries,
Answering the hoarse Hebrides ;

And from wrecks of ships, and drifting
        Spars, uplifting
On the desolate, rainy seas ; —

Ever drifting, drifting, drifting
        On the shifting
Currents of the restless main ;
Till in sheltered coves, and reaches
        Of sandy beaches,
All have found repose again.

So when storms of wild emotion
        Strike the ocean
Of the poet's soul, erelong
From each cave and rocky fastness,
        In its vastness,
Floats some fragment of a song :

From the far-off isles enchanted,
        Heaven has planted
With the golden fruit of Truth ;

From the flashing surf, whose vision
    Gleams Elysian
In the tropic clime of Youth ;

From the strong Will, and the Endeavor
    That forever
Wrestle with the tides of Fate ;
From the wreck of Hopes far-scattered,
    Tempest-shattered,
Floating waste and desolate ; —

Ever drifting, drifting, drifting
    On the shifting
Currents of the restless heart ;
Till at length in books recorded,
    They, like hoarded
Household words, no more depart.

THE DAY IS DONE.

The day is done, and the darkness
    Falls from the wings of Night,
As a feather is wafted downward
    From an eagle in his flight.

I see the lights of the village
    Gleam through the rain and the mist,
And a feeling of sadness comes o'er me
    That my soul cannot resist :

A feeling of sadness and longing,
    That is not akin to pain,
And resembles sorrow only
    As the mist resembles the rain.

Come, read to me some poem,
    Some simple and heartfelt lay,
That shall soothe this restless feeling,
    And banish the thoughts of day.

Not from the grand old masters,
    Not from the bards sublime,
Whose distant footsteps echo
    Through the corridors of Time.

For, like strains of martial music,
    Their mighty thoughts suggest
Life's endless toil and endeavor ;
    And to-night I long for rest.

Read from some humbler poet,
    Whose songs gushed from his heart,
As showers from the clouds of summer,
    Or tears from the eyelids start ;

Who, through long days of labor,
    And nights devoid of ease,
Still heard in his soul the music
    Of wonderful melodies.

Such songs have power to quiet
    The restless pulse of care,
And come like the benediction
    That follows after prayer.

Then read from the treasured volume
    The poem of thy choice,
And lend to the rhyme of the poet
    The beauty of thy voice.

And the night shall be filled with music
    And the cares, that infest the day,
Shall fold their tents, like the Arabs,
    And as silently steal away.

AFTERNOON IN FEBRUARY.

The day is ending,
The night is descending;
The marsh is frozen,
    The river dead.

Through clouds like ashes
The red sun flashes
On village windows
    That glimmer red.

The snow recommences ;
The buried fences
Mark no longer
    The road o'er the plain ;

While through the meadows,
Like fearful shadows,
Slowly passes
    A funeral train.

The bell is pealing,
And every feeling
Within me responds
    To the dismal knell ;

Shadows are trailing,
My heart is bewailing
And tolling within
    Like a funeral bell.

TO AN OLD DANISH SONG–BOOK.

WELCOME, my old friend,
Welcome to a foreign fireside,
While the sullen gales of autumn
Shake the windows.

The ungrateful world
Has, it seems, dealt harshly with thee,
Since, beneath the skies of Denmark,
First I met thee.

There are marks of age,
There are thumb-marks on thy margin,
Made by hands that clasped thee rudely,
At the alehouse.

Soiled and dull thou art ;
Yellow are thy time-worn pages,
As the russet, rain-molested
Leaves of autumn.

Thou art stained with wine
Scattered from hilarious goblets,
As the leaves with the libations
Of Olympus.

Yet dost thou recall
Days departed, half-forgotten,
When in dreamy youth I wandered
By the Baltic, —

When I paused to hear
The old ballad of King Christian
Shouted from suburban taverns
In the twilight.

Thou recallest bards,
Who, in solitary chambers,
And with hearts by passion wasted,
Wrote thy pages.

Thou recallest homes
Where thy songs of love and friend-
ship
Made the gloomy Northern winter
Bright as summer.

Once some ancient Scald,
In his bleak, ancestral Iceland,
Chanted staves of these old ballads
To the Vikings.

Once in Elsinore,
At the court of old King Hamlet,
Yorick and his boon companions
Sang these ditties.

Once Prince Frederick's Guard
Sang them in their smoky barracks ; —
Suddenly the English cannon
Joined the chorus !

Peasants in the field,
Sailors on the roaring ocean,
Students, tradesmen, pale mechanics,
All have sung them.

Thou hast been their friend ;
They, alas ! have left thee friendless !
Yet at least by one warm fireside
Art thou welcome.

And, as swallows build
In these wide, old-fashioned chimneys,
So thy twittering songs shall nestle
In my bosom, —

Quiet, close, and warm,
Sheltered from all molestation,
And recalling by their voices
Youth and travel.

WALTER VON DER VOGELWEID.

VOGELWEID the Minnesinger,
    When he left this world of ours,
Laid his body in the cloister,
    Under Würtzburg's minster towers.

And he gave the monks his treasures,
    Gave them all with this behest :
They should feed the birds at noontide
    Daily on his place of rest ;

Saying, " From these wandering min-
    strels
I have learned the art of song ;
Let me now repay the lessons
    They have taught so well and long."

Thus the bard of love departed ;
    And, fulfilling his desire,
On his tomb the birds were feasted
    By the children of the choir.

Day by day, o'er tower and turret,
    In foul weather and in fair,
Day by day, in vaster numbers,
    Flocked the poets of the air.

On the tree whose heavy branches
    Overshadowed all the place,
On the pavement, on the tombstone,
    On the poet's sculptured face,

On the cross-bars of each window,
    On the lintel of each door,
They renewed the War of Wartburg,
    Which the bard had fought before.

There they sang their merry carols,
    Sang their lauds on every side ;
And the name their voices uttered
    Was the name of Vogelweid.

Till at length the portly abbot
    Murmured, "Why this waste of food ?
Be it changed to loaves henceforward
    For our fasting brotherhood."

Then in vain o'er tower and turret,
    From the walls and woodland nests,
When the minster bells rang noontide,
    Gathered the unwelcome guests.

Then in vain, with cries discordant,
    Clamorous round the Gothic spire,
Screamed the feathered Minnesingers
    For the children of the choir.

Time has long effaced the inscriptions
    On the cloister's funeral stones,
And tradition only tells us
    Where repose the poet's bones.

But around the vast cathedral,
    By sweet echoes multiplied,
Still the birds repeat the legend,
    And the name of Vogelweid.

DRINKING SONG.

INSCRIPTION FOR AN ANTIQUE PITCHER.

COME, old friend ! sit down and listen !
    From the pitcher, placed between us,
How the waters laugh and glisten
    In the head of old Silenus !

Old Silenus, bloated, drunken,
    Led by his inebriate Satyrs ;
On his breast his head is sunken,
    Vacantly he leers and chatters.

Fauns with youthful Bacchus follow ;
    Ivy crowns that brow supernal
As the forehead of Apollo,
    And possessing youth eternal.

Round about him, fair Bacchantes,
    Bearing cymbals, flutes, and thyrses,

Wild from Naxian groves, or Zante's
    Vineyards, sing delirious verses.

Thus he won, through all the nations,
    Bloodless victories, and the farmer
Bore, as trophies and oblations,
    Vines for banners, ploughs for armor.

Judged by no o'erzealous rigor,
    Much this mystic throng expresses :
Bacchus was the type of vigor,
    And Silenus of excesses.

These are ancient ethnic revels,
    Of a faith long since forsaken ;
Now the Satyrs, changed to devils,
  · Frighten mortals wine-o'ertaken.

Now to rivulets from the mountains
    Point the rods of fortune-tellers ;
Youth perpetual dwells in fountains, —
    Not in flasks, and casks, and cellars.

Claudius, though he sang of flagons
    And huge tankards filled with Rhenish,
From that fiery blood of dragons
    Never would his own replenish.

Even Redi, though he chaunted
    Bacchus in the Tuscan valleys,
Never drank the wine he vaunted
    In his dithyrambic sallies.

Then with water fill the pitcher
    Wreathed about with classic fables ;
Ne'er Falernian threw a richer
    Light upon Lucullus' tables.

Come, old friend, sit down and listen !
    As it passes thus between us,
How its wavelets laugh and glisten
    In the head of old Silenus !

THE OLD CLOCK ON THE STAIRS.

L'éternité est une pendule, dont le balancier
dit et redit sans cesse ces deux mots seulement,
dans le silence des tombeaux : " Toujours !
jamais ! Jamais ! toujours ! "
                        JACQUES BRIDAINE.

SOMEWHAT back from the village street
Stands the old-fashioned country-seat.
Across its antique portico
Tall poplar-trees their shadows throw ;

And from its station in the hall
An ancient timepiece says to all, —
    " Forever — never !
    Never — forever ! "

Half-way up the stairs it stands,
And points and beckons with its hands
From its case of massive oak,
Like a monk, who, under his cloak,
Crosses himself, and sighs, alas !
With sorrowful voice to all who pass, —
    " Forever — never !
    Never — forever ! "

By day its voice is low and light ;
But in the silent dead of night,
Distinct as a passing footstep's fall,
It echoes along the vacant hall,
Along the ceiling, along the floor,
And seems to say, at each ·chamber-
    door, —
    " Forever — never !
    Never — forever ! "

Through days of sorrow and of mirth,
Through days of death and days of
    birth,
Through every swift vicissitude
Of changeful time, unchanged it has
    stood,
And as if, like God, it all things
    saw,
It calmly repeats those words of awe, —
    " Forever — never !
    Never — forever ! "

In that mansion used to be
Free-hearted Hospitality ;
His great fires up the chimney roared ;
The stranger feasted at his board ;
But, like the skeleton at the feast,
That warning timepiece never ceased, —
    " Forever — never !
    Never — forever ! "

There groups of merry children played,
There youths and maidens dreaming
    strayed ;
O precious hours ! O golden prime,
And affluence of love and time !
Even as a miser counts his gold,
Those hours the ancient timepiece told, —
    " Forever — never !
    Never — forever ! "

From that chamber, clothed in white,
The bride came forth on her wedding
    night ;

There, in that silent room below,
The dead lay in his shroud of snow ;
And in the hush that followed the prayer,
Was heard the old clock on the stair, —
    " Forever — never !
    Never — forever ! "

All are scattered now and fled,
Some are married, some are dead ;
And when I ask, with throbs of pain,
" Ah ! when shall they all meet again ?"
As in the days long since gone by,
The ancient timepiece makes reply, —
    " Forever — never !
    Never — forever ! "

Never here, forever there,
Where all parting, pain, and care,
And death, and time shall disappear, —
Forever there, but never here !
The horologe of Eternity
Sayeth this incessantly, —
    " Forever — never !
    Never — forever ! "

THE ARROW AND THE SONG.

I SHOT an arrow into the air,
It fell to earth, I knew not where ;
For, so swiftly it flew, the sight
Could not follow it in its flight.

I breathed a song into the air,
It fell to earth, I knew not where ;
For who has sight so keen and strong,
That it can follow the flight of song ?

Long, long afterward, in an oak
I found the arrow, still unbroke ;
And the song, from beginning to end,
I found again in the heart of a friend.

SONNETS.

THE EVENING STAR.

Lo ! in the painted oriel of the West,
  Whose panes the sunken sun incarna-
    dines,
  Like a fair lady at her casement, shines
The evening star, the star of love and
    rest !
And then anon she doth herself divest
  Of all her radiant garments, and re-
    clines
  Behind the sombre screen of yonder
    pines,

With slumber and soft dreams of love
  oppressed.
O my beloved, my sweet Hesperus !
  My morning and my evening star of
    love !
  My best and gentlest lady ! even thus,
As that fair planet in the sky above,
  Dost thou retire unto thy rest at night,
  And from thy darkened window fades
    the light.

AUTUMN.

THOU comest, Autumn, heralded by the
  rain,
  With banners, by great gales incessant
    fanned,
  Brighter than brightest silks of Samar-
    cand,
  And stately oxen harnessed to thy
    wain !
Thou standest, like imperial Charle-
  magne,
  Upon thy bridge of gold ; thy royal
    hand
  Outstretched with benedictions o'er
    the land,
  Blessing the farms through all thy
    vast domain !
Thy shield is the red harvest moon, sus-
  pended
  So long beneath the heaven's o'er-
    hanging eaves ;
  Thy steps are by the farmer's prayers
    attended ;
Like flames upon an altar shine the
  sheaves ;
  And, following thee, in thy ovation
    splendid,
  Thine almoner, the wind, scatters the
    golden leaves !

DANTE.

TUSCAN, that wanderest through the
  realms of gloom,
  With thoughtful pace, and sad, ma-
    jestic eyes,

Stern thoughts and awful from thy
  soul arise,
Like Farinata from his fiery tomb.
Thy sacred song is like the trump of
  doom ;
  Yet in thy heart what human sympa-
    thies,
  What soft compassion glows, as in
    the skies
  The tender stars their clouded lamps
    relume !
Methinks I see thee stand, with pallid
  cheeks,
  By Fra Hilario in his diocese,
  As up the convent-walls, in golden
    streaks,
The ascending sunbeams mark the day's
  decrease ;
  And, as he asks what there the stran-
    ger seeks,
  Thy voice along the cloister whispers,
    " Peace ! "

THE CROSS OF SNOW.

IN the long, sleepless watches of the
  night,
  A gentle face — the face of one long
    dead —
  Looks at me from the wall, where
    round its head
  The night-lamp casts a halo of pale
    light.
Here in this room she died; and soul
  more white
  Never through martyrdom of fire was
    led
  To its repose; nor can in books be
    read
  The legend of a life more benedight.
There is a mountain in the distant West
  That, sun-defying, in its deep ravines
  Displays a cross of snow upon its side.
Such is the cross I wear upon my breast
  These eighteen years, through all the
    changing scenes
  And seasons, changeless since the day
    she died.
    July 10, 1879.

TRANSLATIONS.

THE HEMLOCK TREE.

FROM THE GERMAN.

O HEMLOCK tree ! O hemlock tree ! how
    faithful are thy branches !
Green not alone in summer time,
    But in the winter's frost and rime !
O hemlock tree ! O hemlock tree ! how
    faithful are thy branches !

O maiden fair ! O maiden fair ! how
    faithless is thy bosom !
To love me in prosperity,
    And leave me in adversity !
O maiden fair ! O maiden fair ! how
    faithless is thy bosom !

The nightingale, the nightingale, thou
    tak'st for thine example !
So long as summer laughs she sings,
    But in the autumn spreads her
    wings.
The nightingale, the nightingale, thou
    tak'st for thine example !

The meadow brook, the meadow brook,
    is mirror of thy falsehood !
It flows so long as falls the rain,
    In drought its springs soon dry
    again.
The meadow brook, the meadow brook,
    is mirror of thy falsehood !

ANNIE OF THARAW.

FROM THE LOW GERMAN OF SIMON DACH.

ANNIE of Tharaw, my true love of old,
She is my life, and my goods, and my
    gold.

Annie of Tharaw, her heart once again
To me has surrendered in joy and in pain.

Annie of Tharaw, my riches, my good,
Thou, O my soul, my flesh, and my
    blood !

Then come the wild weather, come sleet
    or come snow,
We will stand by each other, however
    it blow.

Oppression, and sickness, and sorrow,
    and pain
Shall be to our true love as links to the
    chain.

As the palm-tree standeth so straight
    and so tall,
The more the hail beats, and the more
    the rains fall, —

So love in our hearts shall grow mighty
    and strong,
Through crosses, through sorrows,
    through manifold wrong.

Shouldst thou be torn from me to wander
    alone
In a desolate land where the sun is scarce
    known, —

Through forests I'll follow, and where
    the sea flows,
Through ice, and through iron, through
    armies of foes.

Annie of Tharaw, my light and my sun,
The threads of our two lives are woven
    in one.

Whate'er I have bidden thee thou hast
    obeyed,
Whatever forbidden thou hast not gain-
    said.

How in the turmoil of life can love stand,
Where there is not one heart, and one
    mouth, and one hand ?

Some seek for dissension, and trouble,
    and strife ;
Like a dog and a cat live such man and
    wife.

Annie of Tharaw, such is not our love ;
Thou art my lambkin, my chick, and my
    dove.

Whate'er my desire is, in thine may be
    seen ;
I am king of the household, and thou
    art its queen.

It is this, O my Annie, my heart's
    sweetest rest,
That makes of us twain but one soul in
    one breast.

This turns to a heaven the hut where we
    dwell ;
While wrangling soon changes a home
    to a hell.

THE STATUE OVER THE CATHE-DRAL DOOR.

FROM THE GERMAN OF JULIUS MOSEN.

FORMS of saints and kings are standing
    The cathedral door above ;
Yet I saw but one among them
    Who hath soothed my soul with love.

In his mantle, — wound about him,
    As their robes the sowers wind, —
Bore he swallows and their fledglings,
    Flowers and weeds of every kind.

And so stands he calm and childlike,
    High in wind and tempest wild ;
O, were I like him exalted,
    I would be like him, a child !

And my songs, — green leaves and
    blossoms, —
    To the doors of heaven would bear,
Calling even in storm and tempest,
    Round me still these birds of air.

THE LEGEND OF THE CROSS-BILL.

FROM THE GERMAN OF JULIUS MOSEN.

ON the cross the dying Saviour
    Heavenward lifts his eyelids calm,
Feels, but scarcely feels, a trembling
    In his pierced and bleeding palm.

And by all the world forsaken,
    Sees he how with zealous care
At the ruthless nail of iron
    A little bird is striving there.

Stained with blood and never tiring,
    With its beak it doth not cease,
From the cross 't would free the Saviour,
    Its Creator's Son release.

And the Saviour speaks in mildness :
    " Blest be thou of all the good !
Bear, as token of this moment,
    Marks of blood and holy rood !"

And that bird is called the crossbill ;
    Covered all with blood so clear,
In the groves of pine it singeth
    Songs, like legends, strange to hear.

THE SEA HATH ITS PEARLS.

FROM THE GERMAN OF HEINRICH HEINE.

THE sea hath its pearls,
    The heaven hath its stars ;
But my heart, my heart,
    My heart hath its love.

Great are the sea and the heaven,
    Yet greater is my heart,
And fairer than pearls and stars
    Flashes and beams my love.

Thou little, youthful maiden,
    Come unto my great heart ;
My heart, and the sea, and the heaven
    Are melting away with love !

POETIC APHORISMS.

FROM THE SINNGEDICHTE OF FRIEDRICH VON LOGAU.

SEVENTEENTH CENTURY.

MONEY.

WHEREUNTO is money good ?
Who has it not wants hardihood,
Who has it has much trouble and care,
Who once has had it has despair.

THE BEST MEDICINES.

JOY and Temperance and Repose
Slam the door on the doctor's nose.

SIN.

MAN-LIKE is it to fall into sin,
Fiend-like is it to dwell therein,
Christ-like is it for sin to grieve,
God-like is it all sin to leave.

POVERTY AND BLINDNESS.

A BLIND man is a poor man, and blind
  a poor man is ;
For the former seeth no man, and the
  latter no man sees.

LAW OF LIFE.

LIVE I, so live I,
  To my Lord heartily,
  To my Prince faithfully,
  To my Neighbor honestly.
Die I, so die I.

CREEDS.

LUTHERAN, Popish, Calvinistic, all these
  creeds and doctrines three
Extant are ; but still the doubt is, where
  Christianity may be.

THE RESTLESS HEART.

A MILLSTONE and the human heart are
  driven ever round ;
If they have nothing else to grind, they
  must themselves be ground.

CHRISTIAN LOVE.

WHILOM Love was like a fire, and
  warmth and comfort it bespoke ;
But, alas ! it now is quenched, and only
  bites us, like the smoke.

ART AND TACT.

INTELLIGENCE and courtesy not always
  are combined ;
Often in a wooden house a golden room
  we find.

RETRIBUTION.

THOUGH the mills of God grind slowly,
  yet they grind exceeding small ;
Though with patience he stands waiting,
  with exactness grinds he all.

TRUTH.

WHEN by night the frogs are croaking,
  kindle but a torch's fire,
Ha ! how soon they all are silent ! Thus
  Truth silences the liar.

RHYMES.

IF perhaps these rhymes of mine should
  sound not well in strangers' ears,
They have only to bethink them that it
  happens so with theirs ;
For so long as words, like mortals, call
  a fatherland their own,
They will be most highly valued where
  they are best and longest known.

CURFEW.

I.

SOLEMNLY, mournfully,
  Dealing its dole,
The Curfew Bell
  Is beginning to toll.

Cover the embers,
  And put out the light ;
Toil comes with the morning,
  And rest with the night.

Dark grow the windows,
  And quenched is the fire ;
Sound fades into silence, —
  All footsteps retire.

No voice in the chambers,
  No sound in the hall !
Sleep and oblivion
  Reign over all !

II.

THE book is completed,
  And closed, like the day ;
And the hand that has written it
  Lays it away.

Dim grow its fancies ;
  Forgotten they lie ;
Like coals in the ashes,
  They darken and die.

Song sinks into silence,
   The story is told,
The windows are darkened,
   The hearth-stone is cold.

Darker and darker
   The black shadows fall;
Sleep and oblivion
   Reign over all.

EVANGELINE.

A TALE OF ACADIE.

THIS is the forest primeval. The murmuring pines and the hemlocks,
Bearded with moss, and in garments green, indistinct in the twilight,
Stand like Druids of eld, with voices sad and prophetic,
Stand like harpers hoar, with beards that rest on their bosoms,
Loud from its rocky caverns, the deep-voiced neighboring ocean
Speaks, and in accents disconsolate answers the wail of the forest.

This is the forest primeval; but where are the hearts that beneath it
Leaped like the roe, when he hears in the woodland the voice of the huntsman
Where is the thatch-roofed village, the home of Acadian farmers, —
Men whose lives glided on like rivers that water the woodlands,
Darkened by shadows of earth, but reflecting an image of heaven?
Waste are those pleasant farms, and the farmers forever departed!
Scattered like dust and leaves, when the mighty blasts of October
Seize them, and whirl them aloft, and sprinkle them far o'er the ocean
Naught but tradition remains of the beautiful village of Grand-Pré.

Ye who believe in affection that hopes, and endures, and is patient,
Ye who believe in the beauty and strength of woman's devotion,
List to the mournful tradition still sung by the pines of the forest;
List to a Tale of Love in Acadie, home of the happy.

PART THE FIRST.

I.

IN the Acadian land, on the shores of the Basin of Minas,
Distant, secluded, still, the little village of Grand-Pré
Lay in the fruitful valley. Vast meadows stretched to the eastward,
Giving the village its name, and pasture to flocks without number.
Dikes, that the hands of the farmers had raised with labor incessant,
Shut out the turbulent tides; but at stated seasons the flood-gates
Opened, and welcomed the sea to wander at will o'er the meadows.
West and south there were fields of flax, and orchards and cornfields
Spreading afar and unfenced o'er the plain; and away to the northward
Blomidon rose, and the forests old, and aloft on the mountains
Sea-fogs pitched their tents, and mists from the mighty Atlantic
Looked on the happy valley, but ne'er from their station descended
There, in the midst of its farms, reposed the Acadian village.
Strongly built were the houses, with frames of oak and of hemlock,

Such as the peasants of Normandy built in the reign of the Henries.
Thatched were the roofs, with dormer-windows ; and gables projecting
Over the basement below protected and shaded the doorway.
There in the tranquil evenings of summer, when brightly the sunset
Lighted the village street and gilded the vanes on the chimneys,
Matrons and maidens sat in snow-white caps and in kirtles
Scarlet and blue and green, with distaffs spinning the golden
Flax for the gossiping looms, whose noisy shuttles within doors
Mingled their sound with the whir of the wheels and the songs of the maidens.
Solemnly down the street came the parish priest, and the children
Paused in their play to kiss the hand he extended to bless them.
Reverend walked he among them ; and up rose matrons and maidens,
Hailing his slow approach with words of affectionate welcome.
Then came the laborers home from the field, and serenely the sun sank
Down to his rest, and twilight prevailed.   Anon from the belfry
Softly the Angelus sounded, and over the roofs of the village
Columns of pale blue smoke, like clouds of incense ascending,
Rose from a hundred hearths, the homes of peace and contentment.
Thus dwelt together in love these simple Acadian farmers, —
Dwelt in the love of God and of man.   Alike were they free from
Fear, that reigns with the tyrant, and envy, the vice of republics.
Neither locks had they to their doors, nor bars to their windows;
But their dwellings were open as day and the hearts of the owners ;
There the richest was poor, and the poorest lived in abundance.

Somewhat apart from the village, and nearer the Basin of Minas,
Benedict Bellefontaine, the wealthiest farmer of Grand-Pré,
Dwelt on his goodly acres ; and with him, directing his household,
Gentle Evangeline lived, his child, and the pride of the village.
Stalworth and stately in form was the man of seventy winters ;
Hearty and hale was he, an oak that is covered with snow-flakes ;
White as the snow were his locks, and his cheeks as brown as the oak-leaves
Fair was she to behold, that maiden of seventeen summers.
Black were her eyes as the berry that grows on the thorn by the wayside,
Black, yet how softly they gleamed beneath the brown shade of her tresses !
Sweet was her breath as the breath of kine that feed in the meadows.
When in the harvest heat she bore to the reapers at noontide
Flagons of home-brewed ale, ah ! fair in sooth was the maiden,
Fairer was she when, on Sunday morn, while the bell from its turret
Sprinkled with holy sounds the air, as the priest with his hyssop
Sprinkles the congregation, and scatters blessings upon them,
Down the long street she passed, with her chaplet of beads and her missal,
Wearing her Norman cap and her kirtle of blue, and the ear-rings,
Brought in the olden time from France, and since, as an heirloom,
Handed down from mother to child, through long generations.
But a celestial brightness — a more ethereal beauty —
Shone on her face and encircled her form, when, after confession,
Homeward serenely she walked with God's benediction upon her.
When she had passed, it seemed like the ceasing of exquisite music.

Firmly builded with rafters of oak, the house of the farmer
Stood on the side of a hill commanding the sea ; and a shady
Sycamore grew by the door, with a woodbine wreathing around it.
Rudely carved was the porch, with seats beneath ; and a footpath
Led through an orchard wide, and disappeared in the meadow.
Under the sycamore-tree were hives overhung by a penthouse,
Such as the traveller sees in regions remote by the roadside,

Built o'er a box for the poor, or the blessed image of Mary.
Farther down, on the slope of the hill, was the well with its moss-grown
Bucket, fastened with iron, and near it a trough for the horses.
Shielding the house from storms, on the north, were the barns and the farm-yard,
There stood the broad-wheeled wains and the antique ploughs and the harrows ;
There were the folds for the sheep ; and there, in his feathered seraglio,
Strutted the lordly turkey, and crowed the cock, with the selfsame
Voice that in ages of old had startled the penitent Peter.
Bursting with hay were the barns, themselves a village.   In each one
Far o'er the gable projected a roof of thatch ; and a staircase,
Under the sheltering eaves, led up to the odorous corn-loft.
There too the dove-cot stood, with its meek and innocent inmates
Murmuring ever of love ; while above in the variant breezes
Numberless noisy weathercocks rattled and sang of mutation.

    Thus, at peace with God and the world, the farmer of Grand-Pré
Lived on his sunny farm, and Evangeline governed his household.
Many a youth, as he knelt in the church and opened his missal,
Fixed his eyes upon her as the saint of his deepest devotion ;
Happy was he who might touch her hand or the hem of her garment !
Many a suitor came to her door, by the darkness befriended,
And, as he knocked and waited to hear the sound of her footsteps,
Knew not which beat the louder, his heart or the knocker of iron ;
Or at the joyous feast of the Patron Saint of the village,
Bolder grew, and pressed her hand in the dance as he whispered
Hurried words of love, that seemed a part of the music.
But, among all who came, young Gabriel only was welcome ;
Gabriel Lajeunesse, the son of Basil the blacksmith,
Who was a mighty man in the village, and honored of all men ;
For, since the birth of time, throughout all ages and nations,
Has the craft of the smith been held in repute by the people.
Basil was Benedict's friend.   Their children from earliest childhood
Grew up together as brother and sister ; and Father Felician,
Priest and pedagogue both in the village, had taught them their letters
Out of the selfsame book, with the hymns of the church and the plain-song.
But when the hymn was sung, and the daily lesson completed,
Swiftly they hurried away to the forge of Basil the blacksmith.
There at the door they stood, with wondering eyes to behold him
Take in his leathern lap the hoof of the horse as a plaything,
Nailing the shoe in its place ; while near him the tire of the cart-wheel
Lay like a fiery snake, coiled round in a circle of cinders.
Oft on autumnal eves, when without in the gathering darkness
Bursting with light seemed the smithy, through every cranny and crevice,
Warm by the forge within they watched the laboring bellows,
And as its panting ceased, and the sparks expired in the ashes,
Merrily laughed, and said they were nuns going into the chapel.
Oft on sledges in winter, as swift as the swoop of the eagle,
Down the hillside bounding, they glided away o'er the meadow.
Oft in the barns they climbed to the populous nests on the rafters,
Seeking with eager eyes that wondrous stone, which the swallow
Brings from the shore of the sea to restore the sight of its fledglings ;
Lucky was he who found that stone in the nest of the swallow !
Thus passed a few swift years, and they no longer were children.
He was a valiant youth, and his face, like the face of the morning,
Gladdened the earth with its light, and ripened thought into action.
She was a woman now, with the heart and hopes of a woman.
" Sunshine of Saint Eulalie " was she called ; for that was the sunshine

Which, as the farmers believed, would load their orchards with apples ·
She, too, would bring to her husband's house delight and abundance,
Filling it full of love and the ruddy faces of children.

II.

Now had the season returned, when the nights grow colder and longer,
And the retreating sun the sign of the Scorpion enters.
Birds of passage sailed through the leaden air, from the ice-bound,
Desolate northern bays to the shores of tropical islands.
Harvests were gathered in ; and wild with the winds of September
Wrestled the trees of the forest, as Jacob of old with the angel.
All the signs foretold a winter long and inclement.
Bees, with prophetic instinct of want, had hoarded their honey
Till the hives overflowed ; and the Indian hunters asserted
Cold would the winter be, for thick was the fur of the foxes.
Such was the advent of autumn.   Then followed that beautiful season,
Called by the pious Acadian peasants the Summer of All-Saints !
Filled was the air with a dreamy and magical light ; and the landscape
Lay as if new-created in all the freshness of childhood.
Peace seemed to reign upon earth, and the restless heart of the ocean
Was for a moment consoled.   All sounds were in harmony blended.
Voices of children at play, the crowing of cocks in the farm-yards,
Whir of wings in the drowsy air, and the cooing of pigeons,
All were subdued and low as the murmurs of love, and the great sun
Looked with the eye of love through the golden vapors around him ;
While arrayed in its robes of russet and scarlet and yellow,
Bright with the sheen of the dew, each glittering tree of the forest
Flashed like the plane-tree the Persian adorned with mantles and jewels.

Now recommenced the reign of rest and affection and stillness.
Day with its burden and heat had departed, and twilight descending
Brought back the evening star to the sky, and the herds to the homestead.
Pawing the ground they came, and resting their necks on each other,
And with their nostrils distended inhaling the freshness of evening.
Foremost, bearing the bell, Evangeline's beautiful heifer,
Proud of her snow-white hide, and the ribbon that waved from her collar,
Quietly paced and slow, as if conscious of human affection.
Then came the shepherd back with his bleating flocks from the seaside,
Where was their favorite pasture.   Behind them followed the watch-dog,
Patient, full of importance, and grand in the pride of his instinct,
Walking from side to side with a lordly air, and superbly
Waving his bushy tail, and urging forward the stragglers ;
Regent of flocks was he when the shepherd slept ; their protector,
When from the forest at night, through the starry silence, the wolves howled.
Late, with the rising moon, returned the wains from the marshes,
Laden with briny hay, that filled the air with its odor.
Cheerily neighed the steeds, with dew on their manes and their fetlocks,
While aloft on their shoulders the wooden and ponderous saddles,
Painted with brilliant dyes, and adorned with tassels of crimson,
Nodded in bright array, like hollyhocks heavy with blossoms.
Patiently stood the cows meanwhile, and yielded their udders
Unto the milkmaid's hand ; whilst loud and in regular cadence
Into the sounding pails the foaming streamlets descended.
Lowing of cattle and peals of laughter were heard in the farm-yard,
Echoed back by the barns.   Anon they sank into stillness ;

Heavily closed, with a jarring sound, the valves of the barn-doors,
Rattled the wooden bars, and all for a season was silent.

In-doors, warm by the wide-mouthed fireplace, idly the farmer
Sat in his elbow-chair, and watched how the flames and the smoke-wreaths
Struggled together like foes in a burning city.   Behind him,
Nodding and mocking along the wall, with gestures fantastic,
Darted his own huge shadow, and vanished away into darkness.
Faces, clumsily carved in oak, on the back of his arm-chair
Laughed in the flickering light, and the pewter plates on the dresser
Caught and reflected the flame, as shields of armies the sunshine.
Fragments of song the old man sang, and carols of Christmas,
Such as at home, in the olden time, his fathers before him
Sang in their Norman orchards and bright Burgundian vineyards.
Close at her father's side was the gentle Evangeline seated,
Spinning flax for the loom, that stood in the corner behind her.
Silent awhile were its treadles, at rest was its diligent shuttle,
While the monotonous drone of the wheel, like the drone of a bagpipe,
Followed the old man's song, and united the fragments together.
As in a church, when the chant of the choir at intervals ceases,
Footfalls are heard in the aisles, or words of the priest at the altar,
So, in each pause of the song, with measured motion the clock clicked.

Thus as they sat, there were footsteps heard, and, suddenly lifted,
Sounded the wooden latch, and the door swung back on its hinges.
Benedict knew by the hob-nailed shoes it was Basil the blacksmith,
And by her beating heart Evangeline knew who was with him.
"Welcome!" the farmer exclaimed, as their footsteps paused on the threshold,
"Welcome, Basil, my friend!   Come, take thy place on the settle
Close by the chimney-side, which is always empty without thee ;
Take from the shelf overhead thy pipe and the box of tobacco ;
Never so much thyself art thou as when through the curling
Smoke of the pipe or the forge thy friendly and jovial face gleams
Round and red as the harvest moon through the mist of the marshes."
Then, with a smile of content, thus answered Basil the blacksmith,
Taking with easy air the accustomed seat by the fireside : —
"Benedict Bellefontaine, thou hast ever thy jest and thy ballad !
Ever in cheerfullest mood art thou, when others are filled with
Gloomy forebodings of ill, and see only ruin before them.
Happy art thou, as if every day thou hadst picked up a horseshoe."
Pausing a moment, to take the pipe that Evangeline brought him,
And with a coal from the embers had lighted, he slowly continued : —
"Four days now are passed since the English ships at their anchors
Ride in the Gaspereau's mouth, with their cannon pointed against us.
What their design may be is unknown ; but all are commanded
On the morrow to meet in the church, where his Majesty's mandate
Will be proclaimed as law in the land.   Alas ! in the mean time
Many surmises of evil alarm the hearts of the people."
Then made answer the farmer : — "Perhaps some friendlier purpose
Brings these ships to our shores.   Perhaps the harvests in England
By untimely rains or untimelier heat have been blighted,
And from our bursting barns they would feed their cattle and children."
"Not so thinketh the folk in the village," said, warmly, the blacksmith,
Shaking his head, as in doubt ; then, heaving a sigh, he continued : —
"Louisburg is not forgotten, nor Beau Séjour, nor Port Royal.
Many already have fled to the forest, and lurk on its outskirts,
Waiting with anxious hearts the dubious fate of to-morrow.

Arms have been taken from us, and warlike weapons of all kinds ;
Nothing is left but the blacksmith's sledge and the scythe of the mower."
Then with a pleasant smile made answer the jovial farmer : —
" Safer are we unarmed, in the midst of our flocks and our cornfields,
Safer within these peaceful dikes, besieged by the ocean,
Than our fathers in forts, besieged by the enemy's cannon.
Fear no evil, my friend, and to-night may no shadow of sorrow
Fall on this house and hearth ; for this is the night of the contract.
Built are the house and the barn.   The merry lads of the village
Strongly have built them and well ; and, breaking the glebe round about them,
Filled the barn with hay, and the house with food for a twelvemonth.
René Leblanc will be here anon, with his papers and inkhorn.
Shall we not then be glad, and rejoice in the joy of our children ? "
As apart by the window she stood, with her hand in her lover's,
Blushing Evangeline heard the words that her father had spoken,
And, as they died on his lips, the worthy notary entered.

III.

BENT like a laboring oar, that toils in the surf of the ocean,
Bent, but not broken, by age was the form of the notary public ;
Shocks of yellow hair, like the silken floss of the maize, hung
Over his shoulders ; his forehead was high ; and glasses with horn bows
Sat astride on his nose, with a look of wisdom supernal.
Father of twenty children was he, and more than a hundred
Children's children rode on his knee, and heard his great watch tick.
Four long years in the times of the war had he languished a captive,
Suffering much in an old French fort as the friend of the English.
Now, though warier grown, without all guile or suspicion,
Ripe in wisdom was he, but patient, and simple, and childlike.
He was beloved by all, and most of all by the children ;
For he told them tales of the Loup-garou in the forest,
And of the goblin that came in the night to water the horses,
And of the white Létiche, the ghost of a child who unchristened
Died, and was doomed to haunt unseen the chambers of children ;
And how on Christmas eve the oxen talked in the stable,
And how the fever was cured by a spider shut up in a nutshell,
And of the marvellous powers of four-leaved clover and horseshoes,
With whatsoever else was writ in the lore of the village.
Then up rose from his seat by the fireside Basil the blacksmith,
Knocked from his pipe the ashes, and slowly extending his right hand,
" Father Leblanc," he exclaimed, " thou hast heard the talk in the village,
And, perchance, canst tell us some news of these ships and their errand."
Then with modest demeanor made answer the notary public, —
" Gossip enough have I heard, in sooth, yet am never the wiser ;
And what their errand may be I know not better than others.
Yet am I not of those who imagine some evil intention
Brings them here, for we are at peace ; and why then molest us ? "
" God's name ! " shouted the hasty and somewhat irascible blacksmith ;
" Must we in all things look for the how, and the why, and the wherefore ?
Daily injustice is done, and might is the right of the strongest ! "
But, without heeding his warmth, continued the notary public, —
" Man is unjust, but God is just ; and finally justice
Triumphs ; and well I remember a story, that often consoled me,
When as a captive I lay in the old French fort at Port Royal."
This was the old man's favorite tale, and he loved to repeat it

When his neighbors complained that any injustice was done them.
" Once in an ancient city, whose name I no longer remember,
Raised aloft on a column, a brazen statue of Justice
Stood in the public square, upholding the scales in its left hand,
And in its right a sword, as an emblem that justice presided
Over the laws of the land, and the hearts and homes of the people.
Even the birds had built their nests in the scales of the balance,
Having no fear of the sword that flashed in the sunshine above them.
But in the course of time the laws of the land were corrupted ;
Might took the place of right, and the weak were oppressed, and the mighty
Ruled with an iron rod.   Then it chanced in a nobleman's palace
That a necklace of pearls was lost, and erelong a suspicion
Fell on an orphan girl who lived as maid in the household.
She, after form of trial condemned to die on the scaffold,
Patiently met her doom at the foot of the statue of Justice.
As to her Father in heaven her innocent spirit ascended,
Lo ! o'er the city a tempest rose ; and the bolts of the thunder
Smote the statue of bronze, and hurled in wrath from its left hand
Down on the pavement below the clattering scales of the balance,
And in the hollow thereof was found the nest of a magpie,
Into whose clay-built walls the necklace of pearls was inwoven."
Silenced, but not convinced, when the story was ended, the blacksmith
Stood like a man who fain would speak, but findeth no language ;
All his thoughts were congealed into lines on his face, as the vapors
Freeze in fantastic shapes on the window-panes in the winter.

Then Evangeline lighted the brazen lamp on the table,
Filled, till it overflowed, the pewter tankard with home-brewed
Nut-brown ale, that was famed for its strength in the village of Grand-Pré :
While from his pocket the notary drew his papers and inkhorn,
Wrote with a steady hand the date and the age of the parties,
Naming the dower of the bride in flocks of sheep and in cattle.
Orderly all things proceeded, and duly and well were completed,
And the great seal of the law was set like a sun on the margin.
Then from his leathern pouch the farmer threw on the table
Three times the old man's fee in solid pieces of silver ;
And the notary rising, and blessing the bride and the bridegroom,
Lifted aloft the tankard of ale and drank to their welfare.
Wiping the foam from his lip, he solemnly bowed and departed,
While in silence the others sat and mused by the fireside,
Till Evangeline brought the draught-board out of its corner.
Soon was the game begun.   In friendly contention the old men
Laughed at each lucky hit, or unsuccessful manœuvre,
Laughed when a man was crowned, or a breach was made in the king-row
Meanwhile apart, in the twilight gloom of a window's embrasure,
Sat the lovers, and whispered together, beholding the moon rise
Over the pallid sea and the silvery mist of the meadows.
Silently one by one, in the infinite meadows of heaven,
Blossomed the lovely stars, the forget-me-nots of the angels.

Thus was the evening passed.   Anon the bell from the belfry
Rang out the hour of nine, the village curfew, and straightway
Rose the guests and departed ; and silence reigned in the household.
Many a farewell word and sweet good-night on the door-step
Lingered long in Evangeline's heart, and filled it with gladness.
Carefully then were covered the embers that glowed on the hearth-stone,
And on the oaken stairs resounded the tread of the farmer.

Soon with a soundless step the foot of Evangeline followed.
Up the staircase moved a luminous space in the darkness,
Lighted less by the lamp than the shining face of the maiden.
Silent she passed the hall, and entered the door of her chamber.
Simple that chamber was, with its curtains of white, and its clothes-press
Ample and high, on whose spacious shelves were carefully folded
Linen and woollen stuffs, by the hand of Evangeline woven.
This was the precious dower she would bring to her husband in marriage,
Better than flocks and herds, being proofs of her skill as a housewife.
Soon she extinguished her lamp, for the mellow and radiant moonlight
Streamed through the windows, and lighted the room, till the heart of the maiden
Swelled and obeyed its power, like the tremulous tides of the ocean.
Ah! she was fair, exceeding fair to behold, as she stood with
Naked snow-white feet on the gleaming floor of her chamber!
Little she dreamed that below, among the trees of the orchard,
Waited her lover and watched for the gleam of her lamp and her shadow.
Yet were her thoughts of him, and at times a feeling of sadness
Passed o'er her soul, as the sailing shade of clouds in the moonlight
Flitted across the floor and darkened the room for a moment.
And, as she gazed from the window, she saw serenely the moon pass
Forth from the folds of a cloud, and one star follow her footsteps,
As out of Abraham's tent young Ishmael wandered with Hagar!

IV.

PLEASANTLY rose next morn the sun on the village of Grand-Pré.
Pleasantly gleamed in the soft, sweet air the Basin of Minas,
Where the ships, with their wavering shadows, were riding at anchor.
Life had long been astir in the village, and clamorous labor
Knocked with its hundred hands at the golden gates of the morning.
Now from the country around, from the farms and neighboring hamlets,
Came in their holiday dresses the blithe Acadian peasants.
Many a glad good-morrow and jocund laugh from the young folk
Made the bright air brighter, as up from the numerous meadows,
Where no path could be seen but the track of wheels in the greensward,
Group after group appeared, and joined, or passed on the highway.
Long ere noon, in the village all sounds of labor were silenced.
Thronged were the streets with people; and noisy groups at the house-doors
Sat in the cheerful sun, and rejoiced and gossiped together.
Every house was an inn, where all were welcomed and feasted;
For with this simple people, who lived like brothers together,
All things were held in common, and what one had was another's.
Yet under Benedict's roof hospitality seemed more abundant:
For Evangeline stood among the guests of her father;
Bright was her face with smiles, and words of welcome and gladness
Fell from her beautiful lips, and blessed the cup as she gave it.

    Under the open sky, in the odorous air of the orchard,
Stript of its golden fruit, was spread the feast of betrothal.
There in the shade of the porch were the priest and the notary seated;
There good Benedict sat, and sturdy Basil the blacksmith.
Not far withdrawn from these, by the cider-press and the beehives,
Michael the fiddler was placed, with the gayest of hearts and of waistcoats.
Shadow and light from the leaves alternately played on his snow-white
Hair, as it waved in the wind; and the jolly face of the fiddler

"Without, in the churchyard, waited the women." Page 103.

Glowed like a living coal when the ashes are blown from the embers.
Gayly the old man sang to the vibrant sound of his fiddle,
Tous les Bourgeois de Chartres, and *Le Carillon de Dunkerque*,
And anon with his wooden shoes beat time to the music.
Merrily, merrily whirled the wheels of the dizzying dances
Under the orchard-trees and down the path to the meadows ;
Old folk and young together, and children mingled among them.
Fairest of all the maids was Evangeline, Benedict's daughter !
Noblest of all the youths was Gabriel, son of the blacksmith !

So passed the morning away.   And lo ! with a summons sonorous
Sounded the bell from its tower, and over the meadows a drum beat.
Thronged erelong was the church with men.   Without, in the churchyard,
Waited the women.   They stood by the graves, and hung on the headstones
Garlands of autumn-leaves and evergreens fresh from the forest.
Then came the guard from the ships, and marching proudly among them
Entered the sacred portal.   With loud and dissonant clangor
Echoed the sound of their brazen drums from ceiling and casement, —
Echoed a moment only, and slowly the ponderous portal
Closed, and in silence the crowd awaited the will of the soldiers.
Then uprose their commander, and spake from the steps of the altar,
Holding aloft in his hands, with its seals, the royal commission.
" You are convened this day," he said, " by his Majesty's orders.
Clement and kind has he been ; but how you have answered his kindness,
Let your own hearts reply !   To my natural make and my temper
Painful the task is I do, which to you I know must be grievous.
Yet must I bow and obey, and deliver the will of our monarch ;
Namely, that all your lands, and dwellings, and cattle of all kinds
Forfeited be to the crown ; and that you yourselves from this province
Be transported to other lands.   God grant you may dwell there
Ever as faithful subjects, a happy and peaceable people !
Prisoners now I declare you ; for such is his Majesty's pleasure !"
As, when the air is serene in the sultry solstice of summer,
Suddenly gathers a storm, and the deadly sling of the hailstones
Beats down the farmer's corn in the field and shatters his windows,
Hiding the sun, and strewing the ground with thatch from the house-roofs,
Bellowing fly the herds, and seek to break their enclosures ;
So on the hearts of the people descended the words of the speaker.
Silent a moment they stood in speechless wonder, and then rose
Louder and ever louder a wail of sorrow and anger,
And, by one impulse moved, they madly rushed to the door-way.
Vain was the hope of escape ; and cries and fierce imprecations
Rang through the house of prayer ; and high o'er the heads of the others
Rose, with his arms uplifted, the figure of Basil the blacksmith,
As, on a stormy sea, a spar is tossed by the billows.
Flushed was his face and distorted with passion ; and wildly he shouted, —
" Down with the tyrants of England ! we never have sworn them allegiance !
Death to these foreign soldiers, who seize on our homes and our harvests !"
More he fain would have said, but the merciless hand of a soldier
Smote him upon the mouth, and dragged him down to the pavement.

In the midst of the strife and tumult of angry contention,
Lo ! the door of the chancel opened, and Father Felician
Entered, with serious mien, and ascended the steps of the altar.
Raising his reverend hand, with a gesture he awed into silence
All that clamorous throng ; and thus he spake to his people ;
Deep were his tones and solemn · in accents measured and mournful

Spake he, as, after the tocsin's alarum, distinctly the clock strikes.
"What is this that ye do, my children? what madness has seized you?
Forty years of my life have I labored among you, and taught you,
Not in word alone, but in deed, to love one another!
Is this the fruit of my toils, of my vigils and prayers and privations?
Have you so soon forgotten all lessons of love and forgiveness?
This is the house of the Prince of Peace, and would you profane it
Thus with violent deeds and hearts overflowing with hatred?
Lo! where the crucified Christ from his cross is gazing upon you!
See! in those sorrowful eyes what meekness and holy compassion!
Hark! how those lips still repeat the prayer, 'O Father, forgive them!'
Let us repeat that prayer in the hour when the wicked assail us,
Let us repeat it now, and say, 'O Father, forgive them!'"
Few were his words of rebuke, but deep in the hearts of his people
Sank they, and sobs of contrition succeeded the passionate outbreak,
While they repeated his prayer, and said, "O Father, forgive them!"

Then came the evening service. The tapers gleamed from the altar.
Fervent and deep was the voice of the priest, and the people responded,
Not with their lips alone, but their hearts; and the Ave Maria
Sang they, and fell on their knees, and their souls, with devotion translated,
Rose on the ardor of prayer, like Elijah ascending to heaven.

Meanwhile had spread in the village the tidings of ill, and on all sides
Wandered, wailing, from house to house the women and children.
Long at her father's door Evangeline stood, with her right hand
Shielding her eyes from the level rays of the sun, that, descending,
Lighted the village street with mysterious splendor, and roofed each
Peasant's cottage with golden thatch, and emblazoned its windows.
Long within had been spread the snow-white cloth on the table;
There stood the wheaten loaf, and the honey fragrant with wild-flowers;
There stood the tankard of ale, and the cheese fresh brought from the dairy;
And, at the head of the board, the great arm-chair of the farmer.
Thus did Evangeline wait at her father's door, as the sunset
Threw the long shadows of trees o'er the broad ambrosial meadows.
Ah! on her spirit within a deeper shadow had fallen,
And from the fields of her soul a fragrance celestial ascended, —
Charity, meekness, love, and hope, and forgiveness, and patience!
Then, all-forgetful of self, she wandered into the village,
Cheering with looks and words the mournful hearts of the women,
As o'er the darkening fields with lingering steps they departed,
Urged by their household cares, and the weary feet of their children.
Down sank the great red sun, and in golden, glimmering vapors
Veiled the light of his face, like the Prophet descending from Sinai.
Sweetly over the village the bell of the Angelus sounded.

Meanwhile, amid the gloom, by the church Evangeline lingered.
All was silent within; and in vain at the door and the windows
Stood she, and listened and looked, till, overcome by emotion,
"Gabriel!" cried she aloud with tremulous voice; but no answer
Came from the graves of the dead, nor the gloomier grave of the living.
Slowly at length she returned to the tenantless house of her father.
Smouldered the fire on the hearth, on the board was the supper untasted,
Empty and drear was each room, and haunted with phantoms of terror.
Sadly echoed her step on the stair and the floor of her chamber.
In the dead of the night she heard the disconsolate rain fall
Loud on the withered leaves of the sycamore-tree by the window.

Keenly the lightning flashed ; and the voice of the echoing thunder
Told her that God was in heaven, and governed the world he created!
Then she remembered the tale she had heard of the justice of Heaven ;
Soothed was her troubled soul, and she peacefully slumbered till morning.

V.

FOUR times the sun had risen and set ; and now on the fifth day
Cheerily called the cock to the sleeping maids of the farm-house.
Soon o'er the yellow fields, in silent and mournful procession,
Came from the neighboring hamlets and farms the Acadian women,
Driving in ponderous wains their household goods to the sea-shore,
Pausing and looking back to gaze once more on their dwellings,
Ere they were shut from sight by the winding road and the woodland.
Close at their sides their children ran, and urged on the oxen,
While in their little hands they clasped some fragments of playthings.

Thus to the Gaspereau's mouth they hurried ; and there on the sea-beach
Piled in confusion lay the household goods of the peasants.
All day long between the shore and the ships did the boats ply ;
All day long the wains came laboring down from the village.
Late in the afternoon, when the sun was near to his setting,
Echoed far o'er the fields came the roll of drums from the churchyard.
Thither the women and children thronged.   On a sudden the church-doors
Opened, and forth came the guard, and marching in gloomy procession
Followed the long-imprisoned, but patient, Acadian farmers.
Even as pilgrims, who journey afar from their homes and their country,
Sing as they go, and in singing forget they are weary and wayworn,
So with songs on their lips the Acadian peasants descended
Down from the church to the shore, amid their wives and their daughters.
Foremost the young men came ; and, raising together their voices,
Sang with tremulous lips a chant of the Catholic Missions : —
" Sacred heart of the Saviour ! O inexhaustible fountain !
Fill our hearts this day with strength and submission and patience ! "
Then the old men, as they marched, and the women that stood by the wayside
Joined in the sacred psalm, and the birds in the sunshine above them
Mingled their notes therewith, like voices of spirits departed.

Half-way down to the shore Evangeline waited in silence,
Not overcome with grief, but strong in the hour of affliction, —
Calmly and sadly she waited, until the procession approached her,
And she beheld the face of Gabriel pale with emotion.
Tears then filled her eyes, and, eagerly running to meet him,
Clasped she his hands, and laid her head on his shoulder, and whispered —
" Gabriel ! be of good cheer ! for if we love one another
Nothing, in truth, can harm us, whatever mischances may happen ! "
Smiling she spake these words ; then suddenly paused, for her father
Saw she slowly advancing. Alas ! how changed was his aspect !
Gone was the glow from his cheek, and the fire from his eye, and his footstep
Heavier seemed with the weight of the heavy heart in his bosom.
But with a smile and a sigh, she clasped his neck and embraced him,
Speaking words of endearment where words of comfort availed not.
Thus to the Gaspereau's mouth moved on that mournful procession.

There disorder prevailed, and the tumult and stir of embarking.
Busily plied the freighted boats ; and in the confusion

Wives were torn from their husbands, and mothers, too late, saw their children
Left on the land, extending their arms, with wildest entreaties.
So unto separate ships were Basil and Gabriel carried,
While in despair on the shore Evangeline stood with her father.
Half the task was not done when the sun went down, and the twilight
Deepened and darkened around ; and in haste the refluent ocean
Fled away from the shore, and left the line of the sand-beach
Covered with waifs of the tide, with kelp and the slippery sea-weed.
Farther back in the midst of the household goods and the wagons,
Like to a gypsy camp, or a leaguer after a battle,
All escape cut off by the sea, and the sentinels near them,
Lay encamped for the night the houseless Acadian farmers.
Back to its nethermost caves retreated the bellowing ocean,
Dragging adown the beach the rattling pebbles, and leaving
Inland and far up the shore the stranded boats of the sailors.
Then, as the night descended, the herds returned from their pastures ;
Sweet was the moist still air with the odor of milk from their udders ;
Lowing they waited, and long, at the well-known bars of the farm-yard, —
Waited and looked in vain for the voice and the hand of the milkmaid.
Silence reigned in the streets ; from the church no Angelus sounded,
Rose no smoke from the roofs, and gleamed no lights from the windows.

But on the shores meanwhile the evening fires had been kindled,
Built of the drift-wood thrown on the sands from wrecks in the tempest.
Round them shapes of gloom and sorrowful faces were gathered,
Voices of women were heard, and of men, and the crying of children.
Onward from fire to fire, as from hearth to hearth in his parish,
Wandered the faithful priest, consoling and blessing and cheering,
Like unto shipwrecked Paul on Melita's desolate sea-shore.
Thus he approached the place where Evangeline sat with her father,
And in the flickering light beheld the face of the old man,
Haggard and hollow and wan, and without either thought or emotion,
E'en as the face of a clock from which the hands have been taken.
Vainly Evangeline strove with words and caresses to cheer him,
Vainly offered him food ; yet he moved not, he looked not, he spake not
But, with a vacant stare, ever gazed at the flickering fire-light.
"*Benedicite!*" murmured the priest, in tones of compassion.
More he fain would have said, but his heart was full, and his accents
Faltered and paused on his lips, as the feet of a child on a threshold,
Hushed by the scene he beholds, and the awful presence of sorrow.
Silently, therefore, he laid his hand on the head of the maiden,
Raising his tearful eyes to the silent stars that above them
Moved on their way, unperturbed by the wrongs and sorrows of mortals.
Then sat he down at her side, and they wept together in silence.

Suddenly rose from the south a light, as in autumn the blood-red
Moon climbs the crystal walls of heaven, and o'er the horizon
Titan-like stretches its hundred hands upon mountain and meadow,
Seizing the rocks and the rivers, and piling huge shadows together.
Broader and ever broader it gleamed on the roofs of the village,
Gleamed on the sky and the sea, and the ships that lay in the roadstead.
Columns of shining smoke uprose, and flashes of flame were
Thrust through their folds and withdrawn, like the quivering hands of a martyr.
Then as the wind seized the gleeds and the burning thatch, and, uplifting,
Whirled them aloft through the air, at once from a hundred house-tops
Started the sheeted smoke with flashes of flame intermingled.

These things beheld in dismay the crowd on the shore and on shipboard.
Speechless at first they stood, then cried aloud in their anguish,
"We shall behold no more our homes in the village of Grand-Pré!"
Loud on a sudden the cocks began to crow in the farm-yards,
Thinking the day had dawned; and anon the lowing of cattle
Came on the evening breeze, by the barking of dogs interrupted.
Then rose a sound of dread, such as startles the sleeping encampments
Far in the western prairies or forests that skirt the Nebraska,
When the wild horses affrighted sweep by with the speed of the whirlwind,
Or the loud bellowing herds of buffaloes rush to the river.
Such was the sound that arose on the night, as the herds and the horses
Broke through their folds and fences, and madly rushed o'er the meadows.

Overwhelmed with the sight, yet speechless, the priest and the maiden
Gazed on the scene of terror that reddened and widened before them;
And as they turned at length to speak to their silent companion,
Lo! from his seat he had fallen, and stretched abroad on the sea-shore
Motionless lay his form, from which the soul had departed.
Slowly the priest uplifted the lifeless head, and the maiden
Knelt at her father's side, and wailed aloud in her terror.
Then in a swoon she sank, and lay with her head on his bosom.
Through the long night she lay in deep, oblivious slumber;
And when she woke from the trance, she beheld a multitude near her.
Faces of friends she beheld, that were mournfully gazing upon her,
Pallid, with tearful eyes, and looks of saddest compassion.
Still the blaze of the burning village illumined the landscape,
Reddened the sky overhead, and gleamed on the faces around her,
And like the day of doom it seemed to her wavering senses.
Then a familiar voice she heard, as it said to the people, —
"Let us bury him here by the sea. When a happier season
Brings us again to our homes from the unknown land of our exile,
Then shall his sacred dust be piously laid in the churchyard."
Such were the words of the priest. And there in haste by the sea-side,
Having the glare of the burning village for funeral torches,
But without bell or book, they buried the farmer of Grand-Pré.
And as the voice of the priest repeated the service of sorrow,
Lo! with a mournful sound, like the voice of a vast congregation,
Solemnly answered the sea, and mingled its roar with the dirges.
'T was the returning tide, that afar from the waste of the ocean,
With the first dawn of the day, came heaving and hurrying landward.
Then recommenced once more the stir and noise of embarking;
And with the ebb of the tide the ships sailed out of the harbor,
Leaving behind them the dead on the shore, and the village in ruins.

PART THE SECOND.

I.

MANY a weary year had passed since the burning of Grand-Pré,
When on the falling tide the freighted vessels departed,
Bearing a nation, with all its household gods, into exile,
Exile without an end, and without an example in story.
Far asunder, on separate coasts, the Acadians landed;
Scattered were they, like flakes of snow, when the wind from the northeast
Strikes aslant through the fogs that darken the Banks of Newfoundland.

Friendless, homeless, hopeless, they wandered from city to city,
From the cold lakes of the North to sultry Southern savannas,—
From the bleak shores of the sea to the lands where the Father of Waters
Seizes the hills in his hands, and drags them down to the ocean,
Deep in their sands to bury the scattered bones of the mammoth.
Friends they sought and homes ; and many, despairing, heart-broken,
Asked of the earth but a grave, and no longer a friend nor a fireside.
Written their history stands on tablets of stone in the churchyards.
Long among them was seen a maiden who waited and wandered,
Lowly and meek in spirit, and patiently suffering all things.
Fair was she and young ; but, alas ! before her extended,
Dreary and vast and silent, the desert of life, with its pathway
Marked by the graves of those who had sorrowed and suffered before her,
Passions long extinguished, and hopes long dead and abandoned,
As the emigrant's way o'er the Western desert is marked by
Camp-fires long consumed, and bones that bleach in the sunshine.
Something there was in her life incomplete, imperfect, unfinished ;
As if a morning of June, with all its music and sunshine,
Suddenly paused in the sky, and, fading, slowly descended
Into the east again, from whence it late had arisen.
Sometimes she lingered in towns, till, urged by the fever within her,
Urged by a restless longing, the hunger and thirst of the spirit,
She would commence again her endless search and endeavor ;
Sometimes in churchyards strayed, and gazed on the crosses and tombstones,
Sat by some nameless grave, and thought that perhaps in its bosom
He was already at rest, and she longed to slumber beside him.
Sometimes a rumor, a hearsay, an inarticulate whisper,
Came with its airy hand to point and beckon her forward.
Sometimes she spake with those who had seen her beloved and known him,
But it was long ago, in some far-off place or forgotten.
"Gabriel Lajeunesse !" they said ; "O yes ! we have seen him.
He was with Basil the blacksmith, and both have gone to the prairies ;
Coureurs-des-Bois are they, and famous hunters and trappers."
"Gabriel Lajeunesse !" said others ; "O yes ! we have seen him.
He is a Voyageur in the lowlands of Louisiana."
Then would they say, "Dear child ! why dream and wait for him longer ?
Are there not other youths as fair as Gabriel ? others
Who have hearts as tender and true, and spirits as loyal ?
Here is Baptiste Leblanc, the notary's son, who has loved thee
Many a tedious year ; come, give him thy hand and be happy !
Thou art too fair to be left to braid St. Catherine's tresses."
Then would Evangeline answer, serenely but sadly, "I cannot !
Whither my heart has gone, there follows my hand, and not elsewhere.
For when the heart goes before, like a lamp, and illumines the pathway,
Many things are made clear, that else lie hidden in darkness."
Thereupon the priest, her friend and father-confessor,
Said, with a smile, "O daughter ! thy God thus speaketh within thee !
Talk not of wasted affection, affection never was wasted ;
If it enrich not the heart of another, its waters, returning
Back to their springs, like the rain, shall fill them full of refreshment ;
That which the fountain sends forth returns again to the fountain.
Patience ; accomplish thy labor ; accomplish thy work of affection !
Sorrow and silence are strong, and patient endurance is godlike.
Therefore accomplish thy labor of love, till the heart is made godlike,
Purified, strengthened, perfected, and rendered more worthy of heaven !"
Cheered by the good man's words, Evangeline labored and waited.
Still in her heart she heard the funeral dirge of the ocean,

But with its sound there was mingled a voice that whispered, "Despair not!"
Thus did that poor soul wander in want and cheerless discomfort,
Bleeding, barefooted, over the shards and thorns of existence.
Let me essay, O Muse! to follow the wanderer's footsteps; —
Not through each devious path, each changeful year of existence;
But as a traveller follows a streamlet's course through the valley:
Far from its margin at times, and seeing the gleam of its water
Here and there, in some open space, and at intervals only;
Then drawing nearer its banks, through sylvan glooms that conceal it,
Though he behold it not, he can hear its continuous murmur;
Happy, at length, if he find the spot where it reaches an outlet.

II.

It was the month of May.   Far down the Beautiful River,
Past the Ohio shore and past the mouth of the Wabash,
Into the golden stream of the broad and swift Mississippi,
Floated a cumbrous boat, that was rowed by Acadian boatmen.
It was a band of exiles: a raft, as it were, from the shipwrecked
Nation, scattered along the coast, now floating together,
Bound by the bonds of a common belief and a common misfortune;
Men and women and children, who, guided by hope or by hearsay,
Sought for their kith and their kin among the few-acred farmers
On the Acadian coast, and the prairies of fair Opelousas.
With them Evangeline went, and her guide, the Father Felician.
Onward o'er sunken sands, through a wilderness sombre with forests,
Day after day they glided adown the turbulent river;
Night after night, by their blazing fires, encamped on its borders.
Now through rushing chutes, among green islands, where plumelike
Cotton-trees nodded their shadowy crests, they swept with the current,
Then emerged into broad lagoons, where silvery sand-bars
Lay in the stream, and along the wimpling waves of their margin,
Shining with snow-white plumes, large flocks of pelicans waded.
Level the landscape grew, and along the shores of the river,
Shaded by china-trees, in the midst of luxuriant gardens,
Stood the houses of planters, with negro-cabins and dove-cots.
They were approaching the region where reigns perpetual summer,
Where through the Golden Coast, and groves of orange and citron,
Sweeps with majestic curve the river away to the eastward.
They, too, swerved from their course; and, entering the Bayou of Plaquemine,
Soon were lost in a maze of sluggish and devious waters,
Which, like a network of steel, extended in every direction.
Over their heads the towering and tenebrous boughs of the cypress
Met in a dusky arch, and trailing mosses in mid-air
Waved like banners that hang on the walls of ancient cathedrals.
Deathlike the silence seemed, and unbroken, save by the herons
Home to their roosts in the cedar-trees returning at sunset,
Or by the owl, as he greeted the moon with demoniac laughter.
Lovely the moonlight was as it glanced and gleamed on the water,
Gleamed on the columns of cypress and cedar sustaining the arches,
Down through whose broken vaults it fell as through chinks in a ruin.
Dreamlike, and indistinct, and strange were all things around them;
And o'er their spirits there came a feeling of wonder and sadness, —
Strange forebodings of ill, unseen and that cannot be compassed.
As, at the tramp of a horse's hoof on the turf of the prairies,
Far in advance are closed the leaves of the shrinking mimosa,

So, at the hoof-beats of fate, with sad forebodings of evil,
Shrinks and closes the heart, ere the stroke of doom has attained it.
But Evangeline's heart was sustained by a vision, that faintly
Floated before her eyes, and beckoned her on through the moonlight.
It was the thought of her brain that assumed the shape of a phantom.
Through those shadowy aisles had Gabriel wandered before her,
And every stroke of the oar now brought him nearer and nearer.

Then in his place, at the prow of the boat, rose one of the oarsmen,
And, as a signal sound, if others like them peradventure
Sailed on those gloomy and midnight streams, blew a blast on his bugle.
Wild through the dark colonnades and corridors leafy the blast rang,
Breaking the seal of silence, and giving tongues to the forest.
Soundless above them the banners of moss just stirred to the music.
Multitudinous echoes awoke and died in the distance,
Over the watery floor, and beneath the reverberant branches ;
But not a voice replied ; no answer came from the darkness ;
And, when the echoes had ceased, like a sense of pain was the silence.
Then Evangeline slept ; but the boatmen rowed through the midnight,
Silent at times, then singing familiar Canadian boat-songs,
Such as they sang of old on their own Acadian rivers,
While through the night were heard the mysterious sounds of the desert,
Far off, — indistinct, — as of wave or wind in the forest,
Mixed with the whoop of the crane and the roar of the grim alligator.

Thus ere another noon they emerged from the shades ; and before them
Lay, in the golden sun, the lakes of the Atchafalaya.
Water-lilies in myriads rocked on the slight undulations
Made by the passing oars, and, resplendent in beauty, the lotus
Lifted her golden crown above the heads of the boatmen.
Faint was the air with the odorous breath of magnolia blossoms,
And with the heat of noon ; and numberless sylvan islands,
Fragrant and thickly embowered with blossoming hedges of roses,
Near to whose shores they glided along, invited to slumber.
Soon by the fairest of these their weary oars were suspended.
Under the boughs of Wachita willows, that grew by the margin,
Safely their boat was moored ; and scattered about on the greensward,
Tired with their midnight toil, the weary travellers slumbered.
Over them vast and high extended the cope of a cedar,
Swinging from its great arms, the trumpet-flower and the grapevine
Hung their ladder of ropes aloft like the ladder of Jacob,
On whose pendulous stairs the angels ascending, descending,
Were the swift humming-birds, that flitted from blossom to blossom.
Such was the vision Evangeline saw as she slumbered beneath it.
Filled was her heart with love, and the dawn of an opening heaven
Lighted her soul in sleep with the glory of regions celestial.

Nearer, ever nearer, among the numberless islands,
Darted a light, swift boat, that sped away o'er the water,
Urged on its course by the sinewy arms of hunters and trappers.
Northward its prow was turned, to the land of the bison and beaver.
At the helm sat a youth, with countenance thoughtful and careworn.
Dark and neglected locks overshadowed his brow, and a sadness
Somewhat beyond his years on his face was legibly written.
Gabriel was it, who, weary with waiting, unhappy and restless,
Sought in the Western wilds oblivion of self and of sorrow.
Swiftly they glided along, close under the lee of the island,

But by the opposite bank, and behind a screen of palmettos,
So that they saw not the boat, where it lay concealed in the willows,
All undisturbed by the dash of their oars, and unseen, were the sleepers,
Angel of God was there none to awaken the slumbering maiden.
Swiftly they glided away, like the shade of a cloud on the prairie.
After the sound of their oars on the tholes had died in the distance,
As from a magic trance the sleepers awoke, and the maiden
Said with a sigh to the friendly priest, "O Father Felician!
Something says in my heart that near me Gabriel wanders.
Is it a foolish dream, an idle and vague superstition?
Or has an angel passed, and revealed the truth to my spirit?"
Then, with a blush, she added, "Alas for my credulous fancy!
Unto ears like thine such words as these have no meaning."
But made answer the reverend man, and he smiled as he answered, —
"Daughter, thy words are not idle; nor are they to me without meaning.
Feeling is deep and still; and the word that floats on the surface
Is as the tossing buoy, that betrays where the anchor is hidden.
Therefore trust to thy heart, and to what the world calls illusions.
Gabriel truly is near thee; for not far away to the southward,
On the banks of the Têche, are the towns of St. Maur and St. Martin.
There the long-wandering bride shall be given again to her bridegroom,
There the long-absent pastor regain his flock and his sheepfold.
Beautiful is the land, with its prairies and forests of fruit-trees;
Under the feet a garden of flowers, and the bluest of heavens
Bending above, and resting its dome on the walls of the forest.
They who dwell there have named it the Eden of Louisiana."

With these words of cheer they arose and continued their journey.
Softly the evening came.   The sun from the western horizon
Like a magician extended his golden wand o'er the landscape;
Twinkling vapors arose; and sky and water and forest
Seemed all on fire at the touch, and melted and mingled together.
Hanging between two skies, a cloud with edges of silver,
Floated the boat, with its dripping oars, on the motionless water.
Filled was Evangeline's heart with inexpressible sweetness.
Touched by the magic spell, the sacred fountains of feeling
Glowed with the light of love, as the skies and waters around her.
Then from a neighboring thicket the mocking-bird, wildest of singers,
Swinging aloft on a willow spray that hung o'er the water,
Shook from his little throat such floods of delirious music,
That the whole air and the woods and the waves seemed silent to listen.
Plaintive at first were the tones and sad; then soaring to madness
Seemed they to follow or guide the revel of frenzied Bacchantes.
Single notes were then heard, in sorrowful, low lamentation;
Till, having gathered them all, he flung them abroad in derision,
As when, after a storm, a gust of wind through the tree-tops
Shakes down the rattling rain in a crystal shower on the branches.
With such a prelude as this, and hearts that throbbed with emotion,
Slowly they entered the Têche, where it flows through the green Opelousas,
And, through the amber air, above the crest of the woodland,
Saw the column of smoke that arose from a neighboring dwelling; —
Sounds of a horn they heard, and the distant lowing of cattle.

III.

NEAR to the bank of the river, o'ershadowed by oaks, from whose branches
Garlands of Spanish moss and of mystic mistletoe flaunted,
Such as the Druids cut down with golden hatchets at Yule-tide,
Stood, secluded and still, the house of the herdsman.   A garden
Girded it round about with a belt of luxuriant blossoms,
Filling the air with fragrance.   The house itself was of timbers
Hewn from the cypress-tree, and carefully fitted together.
Large and low was the roof; and on slender columns supported,
Rose-wreathed, vine-encircled, a broad and spacious veranda,
Haunt of the humming-bird and the bee, extended around it.
At each end of the house, amid the flowers of the garden,
Stationed the dove-cots were, as love's perpetual symbol,
Scenes of endless wooing, and endless contentions of rivals.
Silence reigned o'er the place.   The line of shadow and sunshine
Ran near the tops of the trees; but the house itself was in shadow,
And from its chimney-top, ascending and slowly expanding
Into the evening air, a thin blue column of smoke rose.
In the rear of the house, from the garden gate, ran a pathway
Through the great groves of oak to the skirts of the limitless prairie,
Into whose sea of flowers the sun was slowly descending.
Full in his track of light, like ships with shadowy canvas
Hanging loose from their spars in a motionless calm in the tropics,
Stood a cluster of trees, with tangled cordage of grapevines.

Just where the woodlands met the flowery surf of the prairie,
Mounted upon his horse, with Spanish saddle and stirrups,
Sat a herdsman, arrayed in gaiters and doublet of deerskin.
Broad and brown was the face that from under the Spanish sombrero
Gazed on the peaceful scene, with the lordly look of its master.
Round about him were numberless herds of kine, that were grazing
Quietly in the meadows, and breathing the vapory freshness
That uprose from the river, and spread itself over the landscape.
Slowly lifting the horn that hung at his side, and expanding
Fully his broad, deep chest, he blew a blast, that resounded
Wildly and sweet and far, through the still damp air of the evening
Suddenly out of the grass the long white horns of the cattle
Rose like flakes of foam on the adverse currents of ocean.
Silent a moment they gazed, then bellowing rushed o'er the prairie,
And the whole mass became a cloud, a shade in the distance.
Then, as the herdsman turned to the house, through the gate of the garden
Saw he the forms of the priest and the maiden advancing to meet him.
Suddenly down from his horse he sprang in amazement, and forward
Rushed with extended arms and exclamations of wonder;
When they beheld his face, they recognized Basil the blacksmith.
Hearty his welcome was, as he led his guests to the garden.
There in an arbor of roses with endless question and answer
Gave they vent to their hearts, and renewed their friendly embraces,
Laughing and weeping by turns, or sitting silent and thoughtful.
Thoughtful, for Gabriel came not; and now dark doubts and misgivings
Stole o'er the maiden's heart; and Basil, somewhat embarrassed,
Broke the silence and said, "If you came by the Atchafalaya,
How have you nowhere encountered my Gabriel's boat on the bayous?"
Over Evangeline's face at the words of Basil a shade passed.
Tears came into her eyes, and she said, with a tremulous accent,
"Gone? is Gabriel gone?" and, concealing her face on his shoulder,

All her o'erburdened heart gave way, and she wept and lamented.
Then the good Basil said, — and his voice grew blithe as he said it, —
"Be of good cheer, my child; it is only to-day he departed.
Foolish boy! he has left me alone with my herds and my horses.
Moody and restless grown, and tried and troubled, his spirit
Could no longer endure the calm of this quiet existence.
Thinking ever of thee, uncertain and sorrowful ever,
Ever silent, or speaking only of thee and his troubles,
He at length had become so tedious to men and to maidens,
Tedious even to me, that at length I bethought me, and sent him
Unto the town of Adayes to trade for mules with the Spaniards.
Thence he will follow the Indian trails to the Ozark Mountains,
Hunting for furs in the forests, on rivers trapping the beaver.
Therefore be of good cheer; we will follow the fugitive lover;
He is not far on his way, and the Fates and the streams are against him.
Up and away to-morrow, and through the red dew of the morning
We will follow him fast, and bring him back to his prison."

Then glad voices were heard, and up from the banks of the river,
Borne aloft on his comrades' arms, came Michael the fiddler.
Long under Basil's roof had he lived like a god on Olympus,
Having no other care than dispensing music to mortals.
Far renowned was he for his silver locks and his fiddle.
"Long live Michael," they cried, "our brave Acadian minstrel!"
As they bore him aloft in triumphal procession; and straightway
Father Felician advanced with Evangeline, greeting the old man
Kindly and oft, and recalling the past, while Basil, enraptured,
Hailed with hilarious joy his old companions and gossips,
Laughing loud and long, and embracing mothers and daughters.
Much they marvelled to see the wealth of the cidevant blacksmith,
All his domains and his herds, and his patriarchal demeanor;
Much they marvelled to hear his tales of the soil and the climate,
And of the prairies, whose numberless herds were his who would take them;
Each one thought in his heart, that he, too, would go and do likewise.
Thus they ascended the steps, and, crossing the breezy veranda,
Entered the hall of the house, where already the supper of Basil
Waited his late return; and they rested and feasted together.

Over the joyous feast the sudden darkness descended.
All was silent without, and, illuming the landscape with silver,
Fair rose the dewy moon and the myriad stars; but within doors,
Brighter than these, shone the faces of friends in the glimmering lamplight.
Then from his station aloft, at the head of the table, the herdsman
Poured forth his heart and his wine together in endless profusion.
Lighting his pipe, that was filled with sweet Natchitoches tobacco,
Thus he spake to his guests, who listened, and smiled as they listened : —
"Welcome once more, my friends, who long have been friendless and homeless,
Welcome once more to a home, that is better perchance than the old one!
Here no hungry winter congeals our blood like the rivers;
Here no stony ground provokes the wrath of the farmer.
Smoothly the ploughshare runs through the soil, as a keel through the water.
All the year round the orange-groves are in blossom; and grass grows
More in a single night than a whole Canadian summer.
Here, too, numberless herds run wild and unclaimed in the prairies;
Here, too, lands may be had for the asking, and forests of timber
With a few blows of the axe are hewn and framed into houses.
After your houses are built, and your fields are yellow with harvests,

No King George of England shall drive you away from your homesteads,
Burning your dwellings and barns, and stealing your farms and your cattle."
Speaking these words, he blew a wrathful cloud from his nostrils,
While his huge, brown hand came thundering down on the table,
So that the guests all started ; and Father Felician, astounded,
Suddenly paused, with a pinch of snuff half-way to his nostrils.
But the brave Basil resumed, and his words were milder and gayer: —
"Only beware of the fever, my friends, beware of the fever !
For it is not like that of our cold Acadian climate,
Cured by wearing a spider hung round one's neck in a nutshell ! "
Then there were voices heard at the door, and footsteps approaching
Sounded upon the stairs and the floor of the breezy veranda.
It was the neighboring Creoles and small Acadian planters,
Who had been summoned all to the house of Basil the Herdsman.
Merry the meeting was of ancient comrades and neighbors :
Friend clasped friend in his arms ; and they who before were as strangers,
Meeting in exile, became straightway as friends to each other,
Drawn by the gentle bond of a common country together.
But in the neighboring hall a strain of music, proceeding
From the accordant strings of Michael's melodious fiddle,
Broke up all further speech.   Away, like children delighted,
All things forgotten beside, they gave themselves to the maddening
Whirl of the dizzy dance, as it swept and swayed to the music,
Dreamlike, with beaming eyes and the rush of fluttering garments.

Meanwhile, apart, at the head of the hall, the priest and the herdsman
Sat, conversing together of past and present and future ;
While Evangeline stood like one entranced, for within her
Olden memories rose, and loud in the midst of the music
Heard she the sound of the sea, and an irrepressible sadness
Came o'er her heart, and unseen she stole forth into the garden.
Beautiful was the night.   Behind the black wall of the forest,
Tipping its summit with silver, arose the moon.   On the river
Fell here and there through the branches a tremulous gleam of the moonlight,
Like the sweet thoughts of love on a darkened and devious spirit.
Nearer and round about her, the manifold flowers of the garden
Poured out their souls in odors, that were their prayers and confessions
Unto the night, as it went its way, like a silent Carthusian.
Fuller of fragrance than they, and as heavy with shadows and night-dews,
Hung the heart of the maiden.   The calm and the magical moonlight
Seemed to inundate her soul with indefinable longings,
As, through the garden gate, and beneath the shade of the oak-trees,
Passed she along the path to the edge of the measureless prairie.
Silent it lay, with a silvery haze upon it, and fire-flies
Gleaming and floating away in mingled and infinite numbers.
Over her head the stars, the thoughts of God in the heavens,
Shone on the eyes of man, who had ceased to marvel and worship,
Save when a blazing comet was seen on the walls of that temple,
As if a hand had appeared and written upon them, " Upharsin."
And the soul of the maiden, between the stars and the fire-flies,
Wandered alone, and she cried, " O Gabriel ! O my beloved !
Art thou so near unto me, and yet I cannot behold thee ?
Art thou so near unto me, and yet thy voice does not reach me ?
Ah ! how often thy feet have trod this path to the prairie !
Ah ! how often thine eyes have looked on the woodlands around me !
Ah ! how often beneath this oak, returning from labor,
Thou hast lain down to rest, and to dream of me in thy slumbers !

When shall these eyes behold, these arms be folded about thee ?"
Loud and sudden and near the note of a whippoorwill sounded
Like a flute in the woods ; and anon, through the neighboring thickets,
Farther and farther away it floated and dropped into silence.
" Patience ! " whispered the oaks from oracular caverns of darkness :
And, from the moonlit meadow, a sigh responded, " To-morrow ! "

Bright rose the sun next day ; and all the flowers of the garden
Bathed his shining feet with their tears, and anointed his tresses
With the delicious balm that they bore in their vases of crystal.
" Farewell ! " said the priest, as he stood at the shadowy threshold ;
" See that you bring us the Prodigal Son from his fasting and famine,
And, too, the Foolish Virgin, who slept when the bridegroom was coming."
" Farewell ! " answered the maiden, and, smiling, with Basil descended
Down to the river's brink, where the boatmen already were waiting.
Thus beginning their journey with morning, and sunshine, and gladness,
Swiftly they followed the flight of him who was speeding before them,
Blown by the blast of fate like a dead leaf over the desert.
Not that day, nor the next, nor yet the day that succeeded,
Found they trace of his course, in lake or forest or river,
Nor, after many days, had they found him ; but vague and uncertain
Rumors alone were their guides through a wild and desolate country ;
Till, at the little inn of the Spanish town of Adayes,
Weary and worn, they alighted, and learned from the garrulous landlord,
That on the day before, with horses and guides and companions,
Gabriel left the village, and took the road of the prairies.

IV.

FAR in the West there lies a desert land, where the mountains
Lift, through perpetual snows, their lofty and luminous summits.
Down from their jagged, deep ravines, where the gorge, like a gateway,
Opens a passage rude to the wheels of the emigrant's wagon,
Westward the Oregon flows and the Walleway and Owyhee.
Eastward, with devious course, among the Wind-river Mountains,
Through the Sweet-water Valley precipitate leaps the Nebraska ;
And to the south, from Fontaine-qui-bout and the Spanish sierras
Fretted with sands and rocks, and swept by the wind of the desert,
Numberless torrents, with ceaseless sound, descend to the ocean,
Like the great chords of a harp, in loud and solemn vibrations.
Spreading between these streams are the wondrous, beautiful prairies,
Billowy bays of grass ever rolling in shadow and sunshine,
Bright with luxuriant clusters of roses and purple amorphas.
Over them wandered the buffalo herds, and the elk and the roebuck ;
Over them wandered the wolves, and herds of riderless horses ;
Fires that blast and blight, and winds that are weary with travel ;
Over them wander the scattered tribes of Ishmael's children,
Staining the desert with blood ; and above their terrible war-trails
Circles and sails aloft, on pinions majestic, the vulture,
Like the implacable soul of a chieftain slaughtered in battle,
By invisible stairs ascending and scaling the heavens.
Here and there rise smokes from the camps of these savage marauders ;
Here and there rise groves from the margins of swift-running rivers ;
And the grim, taciturn bear, the anchorite monk of the desert,
Climbs down their dark ravines to dig for roots by the brook-side,
And over all is the sky, the clear and crystalline heaven,
Like the protecting hand of God inverted above them.

Into this wonderful land, at the base of the Ozark Mountains,
Gabriel far had entered, with hunters and trappers behind him.
Day after day, with their Indian guides, the maiden and Basil
Followed his flying steps, and thought each day to o'ertake him.
Sometimes they saw, or thought they saw, the smoke of his camp-fire
Rise in the morning air from the distant plain ; but at nightfall,
When they had reached the place, they found only embers and ashes.
And, though their hearts were sad at times and their bodies were weary,
Hope still guided them on, as the magic Fata Morgana
Showed them her lakes of light, that retreated and vanished before them.

Once, as they sat by their evening fire, there silently entered
Into the little camp an Indian woman, whose features
Wore deep traces of sorrow, and patience as great as her sorrow.
She was a Shawnee woman returning home to her people,
From the far-off hunting-grounds of the cruel Camanches,
Where her Canadian husband, a Coureur-des-Bois, had been murdered.
Touched were their hearts at her story, and warmest and friendliest welcome
Gave they, with words of cheer, and she sat and feasted among them
On the buffalo-meat and the venison cooked on the embers.
But when their meal was done, and Basil and all his companions,
Worn with the long day's march and the chase of the deer and the bison,
Stretched themselves on the ground, and slept where the quivering fire-light
Flashed on their swarthy cheeks, and their forms wrapped up in their blankets
Then at the door of Evangeline's tent she sat and repeated
Slowly, with soft, low voice, and the charm of her Indian accent,
All the tale of her love, with its pleasures, and pains, and reverses.
Much Evangeline wept at the tale, and to know that another
Hapless heart like her own had loved and had been disappointed.
Moved to the depths of her soul by pity and woman's compassion,
Yet in her sorrow pleased that one who had suffered was near her,
She in turn related her love and all its disasters.
Mute with wonder the Shawnee sat, and when she had ended
Still was mute ; but at length, as if a mysterious horror
Passed through her brain, she spake, and repeated the tale of the Mowis ;
Mowis, the bridegroom of snow, who won and wedded a maiden,
But, when the morning came, arose and passed from the wigwam,
Fading and melting away and dissolving into the sunshine,
Till she beheld him no more, though she followed far into the forest.
Then, in those sweet, low tones, that seemed like a weird incantation,
Told she the tale of the fair Lilinau, who was wooed by a phantom,
That, through the pines o'er her father's lodge, in the hush of the twilight,
Breathed like the evening wind, and whispered love to the maiden,
Till she followed his green and waving plume through the forest,
And nevermore returned, nor was seen again by her people.
Silent with wonder and strange surprise, Evangeline listened
To the soft flow of her magical words, till the region around her
Seemed like enchanted ground, and her swarthy guest the enchantress.
Slowly over the tops of the Ozark Mountains the moon rose,
Lighting the little tent, and with a mysterious splendor
Touching the sombre leaves, and embracing and filling the woodland.
With a delicious sound the brook rushed by, and the branches
Swayed and sighed overhead in scarcely audible whispers.
Filled with the thoughts of love was Evangeline's heart, but a secret,
Subtile sense crept in of pain and indefinite terror,
As the cold, poisonous snake creeps into the nest of the swallow.

It was no earthly fear.   A breath from the region of spirits
Seemed to float in the air of night ; and she felt for a moment
That, like the Indian maid, she, too, was pursuing a phantom.
With this thought she slept, and the fear and the phantom had vanished.

Early upon the morrow the march was resumed ; and the Shawnee
Said, as they journeyed along, "On the western slope of these mountains
Dwells in his little village the Black Robe chief of the Mission.
Much he teaches the people, and tells them of Mary and Jesus ;
Loud laugh their hearts with joy, and weep with pain, as they hear him."
Then, with a sudden and secret emotion, Evangeline answered,
"Let us go to the Mission, for there good tidings await us !"
Thither they turned their steeds ; and behind a spur of the mountains,
Just as the sun went down, they heard a murmur of voices,
And in a meadow green and broad, by the bank of a river,
Saw the tents of the Christians, the tents of the Jesuit Mission.
Under a towering oak, that stood in the midst of the village,
Knelt the Black Robe chief with his children.   A crucifix fastened
High on the trunk of the tree, and overshadowed by grapevines,
Looked with its agonized face on the multitude kneeling beneath it.
This was their rural chapel.   Aloft, through the intricate arches
Of its aerial roof, arose the chant of their vespers,
Mingling its notes with the soft susurrus and sighs of the branches.
Silent, with heads uncovered, the travellers, nearer approaching,
Knelt on the swarded floor, and joined in the evening devotions.
But when the service was done, and the benediction had fallen
Forth from the hands of the priest, like seed from the hands of the sower,
Slowly the reverend man advanced to the strangers, and bade them
Welcome ; and when they replied, he smiled with benignant expression,
Hearing the homelike sounds of his mother-tongue in the forest,
And, with words of kindness, conducted them into his wigwam.
There upon mats and skins they reposed, and on cakes of the maize-ear
Feasted, and slaked their thirst from the water-gourd of the teacher.
Soon was their story told ; and the priest with solemnity answered : —
"Not six suns have risen and set since Gabriel, seated
On this mat by my side, where now the maiden reposes,
Told me this same sad tale ; then arose and continued his journey !"
Soft was the voice of the priest, and he spake with an accent of kindness ;
But on Evangeline's heart fell his words as in winter the snow-flakes
Fall into some lone nest from which the birds have departed.
"Far to the north he has gone," continued the priest ; "but in autumn,
When the chase is done, will return again to the Mission."
Then Evangeline said, and her voice was meek and submissive,
"Let me remain with thee, for my soul is sad and afflicted."
So seemed it wise and well unto all ; and betimes on the morrow,
Mounting his Mexican steed, with his Indian guides and companions,
Homeward Basil returned, and Evangeline stayed at the Mission.

Slowly, slowly, slowly the days succeeded each other, —
Days and weeks and months ; and the fields of maize that were springing
Green from the ground when a stranger she came, now waving above her,
Lifted their slender shafts, with leaves interlacing, and forming
Cloisters for mendicant crows and granaries pillaged by squirrels.
Then in the golden weather the maize was husked, and the maidens
Blushed at each blood-red ear, for that betokened a lover,
But at the crooked laughed, and called it a thief in the corn-field.
Even the blood-red ear to Evangeline brought not her lover.

"Patience !" the priest would say; "have faith, and thy prayer will be answered !
Look at this vigorous plant that lifts its head from the meadow,
See how its leaves are turned to the north, as true as the magnet ;
This is the compass-flower, that the finger of God has planted
Here in the houseless wild, to direct the traveller's journey
Over the sea-like, pathless, limitless waste of the desert.
Such in the soul of man is faith.   The blossoms of passion,
Gay and luxuriant flowers, are brighter and fuller of fragrance,
But they beguile us, and lead us astray, and their odor is deadly.
Only this humble plant can guide us here, and hereafter
Crown us with asphodel flowers, that are wet with the dews of nepenthe."

So came the autumn, and passed, and the winter, — yet Gabriel came not;
Blossomed the opening spring, and the notes of the robin and bluebird
Sounded sweet upon wold and in wood, yet Gabriel came not.
But on the breath of the summer winds a rumor was wafted
Sweeter than song of bird, or hue or odor of blossom.
Far to the north and east, it said, in the Michigan forests,
Gabriel had his lodge by the banks of the Saginaw River.
And, with returning guides, that sought the lakes of St. Lawrence,
Saying a sad farewell, Evangeline went from the Mission.
When over weary ways, by long and perilous marches,
She had attained at length the depths of the Michigan forests,
Found she the hunter's lodge deserted and fallen to ruin !

Thus did the long sad years glide on, and in seasons and places
Divers and distant far was seen the wandering maiden ; —
Now in the Tents of Grace of the meek Moravian Missions,
Now in the noisy camps and the battle-fields of the army,
Now in secluded hamlets, in towns and populous cities.
Like a phantom she came, and passed away unremembered.
Fair was she and young, when in hope began the long journey ;
Faded was she and old, when in disappointment it ended.
Each succeeding year stole something away from her beauty,
Leaving behind it, broader and deeper, the gloom and the shadow.
Then there appeared and spread faint streaks of gray o'er her forehead,
Dawn of another life, that broke o'er her earthly horizon,
As in the eastern sky the first faint streaks of the morning.

                                        V.

In that delightful land which is washed by the Delaware's waters,
Guarding in sylvan shades the name of Penn the apostle,
Stands on the banks of its beautiful stream the city he founded.
There all the air is balm, and the peach is the emblem of beauty,
And the streets still re-echo the names of the trees of the forest,
As if they fain would appease the Dryads whose haunts they molested.
There from the troubled sea had Evangeline landed, an exile,
Finding among the children of Penn a home and a country.
There old René Leblanc had died ; and when he departed,
Saw at his side only one of all his hundred descendants.
Something at least there was in the friendly streets of the city,
Something that spake to her heart, and made her no longer a stranger ;
And her ear was pleased with the Thee and Thou of the Quakers,
For it recalled the past, the old Acadian country,
Where all men were equal, and all were brothers and sisters.
So, when the fruitless search, the disappointed endeavor,

Ended, to recommence no more upon earth, uncomplaining,
Thither, as leaves to the light, were turned her thoughts and her footsteps
As from a mountain's top the rainy mists of the morning
Roll away, and afar we behold the landscape below us,
Sun-illumined, with shining rivers and cities and hamlets,
So fell the mists from her mind, and she saw the world far below her,
Dark no longer, but all illumined with love ; and the pathway
Which she had climbed so far, lying smooth and fair in the distance.
Gabriel was not forgotten.   Within her heart was his image,
Clothed in the beauty of love and youth, as last she beheld him,
Only more beautiful made by his deathlike silence and absence.
Into her thoughts of him time entered not, for it was not.
Over him years had no power ; he was not changed, but transfigured ;
He had become to her heart as one who is dead, and not absent ;
Patience and abnegation of self, and devotion to others,
This was the lesson a life of trial and sorrow had taught her.
So was her love diffused, but, like to some odorous spices,
Suffered no waste nor loss, though filling the air with aroma.
Other hope had she none, nor wish in life, but to follow
Meekly, with reverent steps, the sacred feet of her Saviour.
Thus many years she lived as a Sister of Mercy ; frequenting
Lonely and wretched roofs in the crowded lanes of the city,
Where distress and want concealed themselves from the sunlight,
Where disease and sorrow in garrets languished neglected.
Night after night, when the world was asleep, as the watchman repeated
Loud, through the gusty streets, that all was well in the city,
High at some lonely window he saw the light of her taper.
Day after day, in the gray of the dawn, as slow through the suburbs
Plodded the German farmer, with flowers and fruits for the market,
Met he that meek, pale face, returning home from its watchings.

Then it came to pass that a pestilence fell on the city,
Presaged by wondrous signs, and mostly by flocks of wild pigeons,
Darkening the sun in their flight, with naught in their craws but an acorn.
And, as the tides of the sea arise in the month of September,
Flooding some silver stream, till it spreads to a lake in the meadow,
So death flooded life, and, o'erflowing its natural margin,
Spread to a brackish lake, the silver stream of existence.
Wealth had no power to bribe, nor beauty to charm, the oppressor ;
But all perished alike beneath the scourge of his anger ; —
Only, alas ! the poor, who had neither friends nor attendants,
Crept away to die in the almshouse, home of the homeless.
Then in the suburbs it stood, in the midst of meadows and woodlands ;
Now the city surrounds it ; but still, with its gateway and wicket
Meek, in the midst of splendor, its humble walls seem to echo
Softly the words of the Lord : — " The poor ye always have with you."
Thither, by night and by day, came the Sister of Mercy.   The dying
Looked up into her face, and thought, indeed, to behold there
Gleams of celestial light encircle her forehead with splendor,
Such as the artist paints o'er the brows of saints and apostles,
Or such as hangs by night o'er a city seen at a distance.
Unto their eyes it seemed the lamps of the city celestial,
Into whose shining gates erelong their spirits would enter.

Thus, on a Sabbath morn, through the streets, deserted and silent,
Wending her quiet way, she entered the door of the almshouse.
Sweet on the summer air was the odor of flowers in the garden ;

And she paused on her way to gather the fairest among them,
That the dying once more might rejoice in their fragrance and beauty.
Then, as she mounted the stairs to the corridors, cooled by the east-wind,
Distant and soft on her ear fell the chimes from the belfry of Christ Church,
While, intermingled with these, across the meadows were wafted
Sounds of psalms, that were sung by the Swedes in their church at Wicaco.
Soft as descending wings fell the calm of the hour on her spirit ;
Something within her said, " At length thy trials are ended" ;
And, with light in her looks, she entered the chambers of sickness.
Noiselessly moved about the assiduous, careful attendants,
Moistening the feverish lip, and the aching brow, and in silence
Closing the sightless eyes of the dead, and concealing their faces,
Where on their pallets they lay, like drifts of snow by the roadside.
Many a languid head, upraised as Evangeline entered,
Turned on its pillow of pain to gaze while she passed, for her presence
Fell on their hearts like a ray of the sun on the walls of a prison.
And, as she looked around, she saw how Death, the consoler,
Laying his hand upon many a heart, had healed it forever.
Many familiar forms had disappeared in the night time ;
Vacant their places were, or filled already by strangers.

Suddenly, as if arrested by fear or a feeling of wonder,
Still she stood, with her colorless lips apart, while a shudder
Ran through her frame, and, forgotten, the flowerets dropped from her fingers,
And from her eyes and cheeks the light and bloom of the morning.
Then there escaped from her lips a cry of such terrible anguish,
That the dying heard it, and started up from their pillows.
On the pallet before her was stretched the form of an old man.
Long, and thin, and gray were the locks that shaded his temples ;
But, as he lay in the morning light, his face for a moment
Seemed to assume once more the forms of its earlier manhood ;
So are wont to be changed the faces of those who are dying.
Hot and red on his lips still burned the flush of the fever,
As if life, like the Hebrew, with blood had besprinkled its portals,
That the Angel of Death might see the sign, and pass over.
Motionless, senseless, dying, he lay, and his spirit exhausted
Seemed to be sinking down through infinite depths in the darkness,
Darkness of slumber and death, forever sinking and sinking.
Then through those realms of shade, in multiplied reverberations,
Heard he that cry of pain, and through the hush that succeeded
Whispered a gentle voice, in accents tender and saint-like,
" Gabriel ! O my beloved ! " and died away into silence.
Then he beheld, in a dream, once more the home of his childhood ;
Green Acadian meadows, with sylvan rivers among them,
Village, and mountain, and woodlands ; and, walking under their shadow,
As in the days of her youth, Evangeline rose in his vision.
Tears came into his eyes ; and as slowly he lifted his eyelids,
Vanished the vision away, but Evangeline knelt by his bedside.
Vainly he strove to whisper her name, for the accents unuttered
Died on his lips, and their motion revealed what his tongue would have spoken.
Vainly he strove to rise ; and Evangeline, kneeling beside him,
Kissed his dying lips, and laid his head on her bosom.
Sweet was the light of his eyes ; but it suddenly sank into darkness,
As when a lamp is blown out by a gust of wind at a casement.

All was ended now, the hope, and the fear, and the sorrow,
All the aching of heart, the restless, unsatisfied longing,

All the dull, deep pain, and constant anguish of patience !
And, as she pressed once more the lifeless head to her bosom,
Meekly she bowed her own, and murmured, " Father, I thank thee ! "

STILL stands the forest primeval ; but far away from its shadow,
Side by side, in their nameless graves, the lovers are sleeping.
Under the humble walls of the little Catholic churchyard,
In the heart of the city, they lie, unknown and unnoticed.
Daily the tides of life go ebbing and flowing beside them,
Thousands of throbbing hearts, where theirs are at rest and forever,
Thousands of aching brains, where theirs no longer are busy,
Thousands of toiling hands, where theirs have ceased from their labors,
Thousands of weary feet, where theirs have completed their journey !

Still stands the forest primeval ; but under the shade of its branches
Dwells another race, with other customs and language.
Only along the shore of the mournful and misty Atlantic
Linger a few Acadian peasants, whose fathers from exile
Wandered back to their native land to die in its bosom.
In the fisherman's cot the wheel and the loom are still busy ;
Maidens still wear their Norman caps and their kirtles of homespun,
And by the evening fire repeat Evangeline's story,
While from its rocky caverns the deep-voiced, neighboring ocean
Speaks, and in accents disconsolate answers the wail of the forest.

THE SEASIDE AND THE FIRESIDE.

DEDICATION.

As one who, walking in the twilight gloom,
  Hears round about him voices as it darkens,
And seeing not the forms from which they come,
  Pauses from time to time, and turns and hearkens ;

So walking here in twilight, O my friends !
  I hear your voices, softened by the distance,
And pause, and turn to listen, as each sends
  His words of friendship, comfort, and assistance.

If any thought of mine, or sung or told,
  Has ever given delight or consolation,
Ye have repaid me back a thousand-fold,
  By every friendly sign and salutation.

Thanks for the sympathies that ye have shown !
  Thanks for each kindly word, each silent token,
That teaches me, when seeming most alone,
  Friends are around us, though no word be spoken.

Kind messages, that pass from land to land ;
  Kind letters, that betray the heart's deep history,
In which we feel the pressure of a hand, —
  One touch of fire, — and all the rest is mystery !

The pleasant books, that silently among
  Our household treasures take familiar places,
And are to us as if a living tongue
  Spake from the printed leaves or pictured faces !

Perhaps on earth I never shall behold,
   With eye of sense, your outward form
      and semblance ;
Therefore to me ye never will grow old,
   But live forever young in my remem-
      brance.

Never grow old, nor change, nor pass
      away !
   · Your gentle voices will flow on forever,
When life grows bare and tarnished with
      decay,
   As through a leafless landscape flows a
      river.

Not chance of birth or place has made
      us friends,
   Being oftentimes of different tongues
      and nations,

But the endeavor for the selfsame ends,
   With the same hopes, and fears, and
      aspirations.

Therefore I hope to join your seaside
      walk,
   Saddened, and mostly silent, with
      emotion ;
Not interrupting with intrusive talk
   The grand, majestic symphonies of
      ocean.

Therefore I hope, as no unwelcome guest,
   At your warm fireside, when the lamps
      are lighted,
To have my place reserved among the
      rest,
   Nor stand as one unsought and unin-
      vited !

BY THE SEASIDE.

THE BUILDING OF THE SHIP.

"BUILD me straight, O worthy Master !
   Stanch and strong, a goodly vessel,
That shall laugh at all disaster,
   And with wave and whirlwind wres-
      tle ! "

The merchant's word
Delighted the Master heard ;
For his heart was in his work, and the
      heart
Giveth grace unto every Art.

A quiet smile played round his lips,
As the eddies and dimples of the tide
Play round the bows of ships,
That steadily at anchor ride.
And with a voice that was full of glee,
He answered, " Erelong we will launch
A vessel as goodly, and strong, and
      stanch,
As ever weathered a wintry sea ! "
And first with nicest skill and art,
Perfect and finished in every part,
A little model the Master wrought,
Which should be to the larger plan
What the child is to the man,
Its counterpart in miniature ;
That with a hand more swift and sure
The greater labor might be brought

To answer to his inward thought.
And as he labored, his mind ran o'er
The various ships that were built of yore,
And above them all, and strangest of all
Towered the Great Harry, crank and
      tall,
Whose picture was hanging on the wall,
With bows and stern raised high in air,
And balconies hanging here and there,
And signal lanterns and flags afloat,
And eight round towers, like those that
      frown
From some old castle, looking down
Upon the drawbridge and the moat.
And he said with a smile, " Our ship, I
      wis,
Shall be of another form than this ! "

It was of another form, indeed ;
Built for freight, and yet for speed,
A beautiful and gallant craft ;
Broad in the beam, that the stress of the
      blast,
Pressing down upon sail and mast,
Might not the sharp bows overwhelm ;
Broad in the beam, but sloping aft
With graceful curve and slow degrees,
That she might be docile to the helm,
And that the currents of parted seas,
Closing behind, with mighty force,
Might aid and not impede her course.

In the ship-yard stood the Master,
    With the model of the vessel,
That should laugh at all disaster,
    And with wave and whirlwind wrestle!

Covering many a rood of ground,
Lay the timber piled around;
Timber of chestnut, and elm, and oak,
And scattered here and there, with these,
The knarred and crooked cedar knees;
Brought from regions far away,
From Pascagoula's sunny bay,
And the banks of the roaring Roanoke!
Ah! what a wondrous thing it is
To note how many wheels of toil
One thought, one word, can set in mo-
    tion!
There's not a ship that sails the ocean,
But every climate, every soil,
Must bring its tribute, great or small,
And help to build the wooden wall!

The sun was rising o'er the sea,
And long the level shadows lay,
As if they, too, the beams would be
Of some great, airy argosy,
Framed and launched in a single day.
That silent architect, the sun,
Had hewn and laid them every one,
Ere the work of man was yet begun.
Beside the Master, when he spoke,
A youth, against an anchor leaning,
Listened, to catch his slightest mean-
    ing.
Only the long waves, as they broke
In ripples on the pebbly beach,
Interrupted the old man's speech.

Beautiful they were, in sooth,
The old man and the fiery youth!
The old man, in whose busy brain
Many a ship that sailed the main
Was modelled o'er and o'er again; —
The fiery youth, who was to be
The heir of his dexterity,
The heir of his house, and his daughter's
    hand,
When he had built and launched from
    land
What the elder head had planned.

"Thus," said he, "will we build this
    ship!
Lay square the blocks upon the slip,
And follow well this plan of mine.
Choose the timbers with greatest care;
Of all that is unsound beware;

For only what is sound and strong
To this vessel shall belong.
Cedar of Maine and Georgia pine
Here together shall combine.
A goodly frame, and a goodly fame,
And the UNION be her name!
For the day that gives her to the sea
Shall give my daughter unto thee!"

The Master's word
Enraptured the young man heard;
And as he turned his face aside,
With a look of joy and a thrill of pride,
Standing before
Her father's door,
He saw the form of his promised bride.
The sun shone on her golden hair,
And her cheek was glowing fresh and
    fair,
With the breath of morn and the soft
    sea air.
Like a beauteous barge was she,
Still at rest on the sandy beach,
Just beyond the billow's reach;
But he
Was the restless, seething, stormy sea!

Ah, how skilful grows the hand
That obeyeth Love's command!
It is the heart, and not the brain,
That to the highest doth attain,
And he who followeth Love's behest
Far excelleth all the rest!

Thus with the rising of the sun
Was the noble task begun,
And soon throughout the ship-yard's
    bounds
Were heard the intermingled sounds
Of axes and of mallets, plied
With vigorous arms on every side;
Plied so deftly and so well,
That, ere the shadows of evening fell,
The keel of oak for a noble ship,
Scarfed and bolted, straight and strong,
Was lying ready, and stretched along
The blocks, well placed upon the slip.
Happy, thrice happy, every one
Who sees his labor well begun,
And not perplexed and multiplied,
By idly waiting for time and tide!

And when the hot, long day was o'er,
The young man at the Master's door
Sat with the maiden calm and still,
And within the porch, a little more
Removed beyond the evening chill,

The father sat, and told them tales
Of wrecks in the great September gales,
Of pirates coasting the Spanish Main,
And ships that never came back again,
The chance and change of a sailor's life,
Want and plenty, rest and strife,
His roving fancy, like the wind,
That nothing can stay and nothing can
     bind,
And the magic charm of foreign lands,
With shadows of palms, and shining
     sands,
Where the tumbling surf,
O'er the coral reefs of Madagascar,
Washes the feet of the swarthy Lascar,
As he lies alone and asleep on the turf.
And the trembling maiden held her
     breath
At the tales of that awful, pitiless sea,
With all its terror and mystery,
The dim, dark sea, so like unto Death,
That divides and yet unites mankind!
And whenever the old man paused, a
     gleam
From the bowl of his pipe would awhile
     illume
The silent group in the twilight gloom,
And thoughtful faces, as in a dream;
And for a moment one might mark
What had been hidden by the dark,
That the head of the maiden lay at rest,
Tenderly, on the young man's breast!

Day by day the vessel grew,
With timbers fashioned strong and
     true,
Stemson and keelson and sternson-knee,
Till, framed with perfect symmetry,
A skeleton ship rose up to view!
And around the bows and along the
     side
The heavy hammers and mallets plied,
Till after many a week, at length,
Wonderful for form and strength,
Sublime in its enormous bulk,
Loomed aloft the shadowy hulk!
And around it columns of smoke, up-
     wreathing,
Rose from the boiling, bubbling, seething
Caldron, that glowed,
And overflowed
With the black tar, heated for the
     sheathing.
And amid the clamors
Of clattering hammers,
He who listened heard now and then
The song of the Master and his men : —

" Build me straight, O worthy Master,
     Stanch and strong, a goodly vessel,
That shall laugh at all disaster,
     And with wave and whirlwind wrestle!"

With oaken brace and copper band,
Lay the rudder on the sand,
That, like a thought, should have con-
     trol
Over the movement of the whole ;
And near it the anchor, whose giant
     hand
Would reach down and grapple with the
     land,
And immovable and fast
Hold the great ship against the bellow-
     ing blast!
And at the bows an image stood,
By a cunning artist carved in wood,
With robes of white, that far behind
Seemed to be fluttering in the wind.
It was not shaped in a classic mould,
Not like a Nymph or Goddess of old,
Or Naiad rising from the water,
But modelled from the Master's daugh-
     ter!
On many a dreary and misty night,
'T will be seen by the rays of the signal
     light,
Speeding along through the rain and the
     dark,
Like a ghost in its snow-white sark,
The pilot of some phantom bark,
Guiding the vessel, in its flight,
By a path none other knows aright!
Behold, at last,
Each tall and tapering mast
Is swung into its place ;
Shrouds and stays
Holding it firm and fast !

Long ago,
In the deer-haunted forests of Maine,
When upon mountain and plain
Lay the snow,
They fell, — those lordly pines !
Those grand, majestic pines !
'Mid shouts and cheers
The jaded steers,
Panting beneath the goad,
Dragged down the weary, winding road
Those captive kings so straight and tall,
To be shorn of their streaming hair,
And, naked and bare,
To feel the stress and the strain
Of the wind and the reeling main,
Whose roar

Would remind them forevermore
Of their native forests they should not
    see again.

And everywhere
The slender, graceful spars
Poise aloft in the air,
And at the mast-head day
White, blue, and red,
A flag unrolls the stripes and stars.
Ah! when the wanderer, lonely, friendless,
In foreign harbors shall behold
That flag unrolled,
'T will be as a friendly hand
Stretched out from his native land,
Filling his heart with memories sweet
    and endless !

All is finished ! and at length
Has come the bridal day
Of beauty and of strength.
To-day the vessel shall be launched !
With fleecy clouds the sky is blanched,
And o'er the bay,
Slowly, in all his splendors dight,
The great sun rises to behold the sight.

The ocean old,
Centuries old,
Strong as youth, and as uncontrolled,
Paces restless to and fro,
Up and down the sands of gold.
His beating heart is not at rest ;
And far and wide,
With ceaseless flow,
His beard of snow
Heaves with the heaving of his breast.
He waits impatient for his bride.
There she stands,
With her foot upon the sands,
Decked with flags and streamers gay,
In honor of her marriage day,
Her snow-white signals fluttering, blend-
    ing,
Round her like a veil descending,
Ready to be
The bride of the gray old sea.

On the deck another bride
Is standing by her lover's side.
Shadows from the flags and shrouds,
Like the shadows cast by clouds,
Broken by many a sunny fleck,
Fall around them on the deck.

The prayer is said,
The service read.

The joyous bridegroom bows his head ;
And in tears the good old Master
Shakes the brown hand of his son,
Kisses his daughter's glowing cheek
In silence, for he cannot speak,
And ever faster
Down his own the tears begin to run.
The worthy pastor —
The shepherd of that wandering flock,
That has the ocean for its wold,
That has the vessel for its fold,
Leaping ever from rock to rock —
Spake, with accents mild and clear,
Words of warning, words of cheer,
But tedious to the bridegroom's ear.
He knew the chart
Of the sailor's heart,
All its pleasures and its griefs,
All its shallows and rocky reefs,
All those secret currents, that flow
With such resistless undertow,
And lift and drift, with terrible force,
The will from its moorings and its
    course.
Therefore he spake, and thus said
    he : —
" Like unto ships far off at sea,
Outward or homeward bound, are we.
Before, behind, and all around,
Floats and swings the horizon's bound,
Seems at its distant rim to rise
And climb the crystal wall of the skies,
And then again to turn and sink,
As if we could slide from its outer
    brink.
Ah! it is not the sea,
It is not the sea that sinks and shelves,
But ourselves
That rock and rise
With endless and uneasy motion,
Now touching the very skies,
Now sinking into the depths of ocean.
Ah ! if our souls but poise and swing
Like the compass in its brazen ring,
Ever level and ever true
To the toil and the task we have to do,
We shall sail securely, and safely reach
The Fortunate Isles, on whose shining
    beach
The sights we see, and the sounds we
    hear,
Will be those of joy and not of fear !"

Then the Master,
With a gesture of command,
Waved his hand ;
And at the word,

Loud and sudden there was heard,
All around them and below,
The sound of hammers, blow on blow,
Knocking away the shores and spurs.
And see ! she stirs !
She starts, — she moves, — she seems to
    feel
The thrill of life along her keel,
And, spurning with her foot the ground,
With one exulting, joyous bound,
She leaps into the ocean's arms !

And lo ! from the assembled crowd
There rose a shout, prolonged and loud,
That to the ocean seemed to say,
"Take her, O bridegroom, old and gray,
Take her to thy protecting arms,
With all her youth and all her charms ! "

How beautiful she is !   How fair
She lies within those arms, that press
Her form with many a soft caress
Of tenderness and watchful care !
Sail forth into the sea, O ship !
Through wind and wave, right on-
    ward steer !
The moistened eye, the trembling lip,
Are not the signs of doubt or fear.

Sail forth into the sea of life,
O gentle, loving, trusting wife,
And safe from all adversity
Upon the bosom of that sea
Thy comings and thy goings be !
For gentleness and love and trust
Prevail o'er angry wave and gust ;
And in the wreck of noble lives
Something immortal still survives !

Thou, too, sail on, O Ship of State !
Sail on, O UNION, strong and great !
Humanity with all its fears,
With all the hopes of future years,
Is hanging breathless on thy fate !
We know what Master laid thy keel,
What Workmen wrought thy ribs of steel,
Who made each mast, and sail, and rope,
What anvils rang, what hammers beat,
In what a forge and what a heat
Were shaped the anchors of thy hope !
Fear not each sudden sound and shock,
'T is of the wave and not the rock ;
'T is but the flapping of the sail,
And not a rent made by the gale !
In spite of rock and tempest's roar,
In spite of false lights on the shore,
Sail on, nor fear to breast the sea !

Our hearts, our hopes, are all with thee,
Our hearts, our hopes, our prayers, our
    tears,
Our faith triumphant o'er our fears,
Are all with thee, — are all with thee !

CHRYSAOR.

JUST above yon sandy bar,
    As the day grows fainter and dimmer,
Lonely and lovely, a single star
    Lights the air with a dusky glimmer

Into the ocean faint and far
    Falls the trail of its golden splendor,
And the gleam of that single star
    Is ever refulgent, soft, and tender.

Chrysaor, rising out of the sea,
    Showed thus glorious and thus emu-
        lous,
Leaving the arms of Callirrhoe,
    Forever tender, soft, and tremulous.

Thus o'er the ocean faint and far
    Trailed the gleam of his falchion
        brightly ;
Is it a God, or is it a star
    That, entranced, I gaze on nightly !

THE SECRET OF THE SEA.

AH ! what pleasant visions haunt me
    As I gaze upon the sea !
All the old romantic legends,
    All my dreams, come back to me.

Sails of silk and ropes of sandal,
    Such as gleam in ancient lore ;
And the singing of the sailors,
    And the answer from the shore !

Most of all, the Spanish ballad
    Haunts me oft, and tarries long,
Of the noble Count Arnaldos
    And the sailor's mystic song.

Like the long waves on a sea-beach,
    Where the sand as silver shines,
With a soft, monotonous cadence,
    Flow its unrhymed lyric lines ; —

Telling how the Count Arnaldos,
    With his hawk upon his hand,
Saw a fair and stately galley,
    Steering onward to the land ; —

How he heard the ancient helmsman
  Chant a song so wild and clear,
That the sailing sea-bird slowly
  Poised upon the mast to hear,

Till his soul was full of longing,
  And he cried, with impulse strong, —
" Helmsman ! for the love of heaven,
  Teach me, too, that wondrous song !"

"Wouldst thou," — so the helmsman
    answered,
  " Learn the secret of the sea ?
Only those who brave its dangers
  Comprehend its mystery !"

In each sail that skims the horizon,
  In each landward-blowing breeze,
I behold that stately galley,
  Hear those mournful melodies ;

Till my soul is full of longing
  For the secret of the sea,
And the heart of the great ocean
  Sends a thrilling pulse through me.

TWILIGHT.

THE twilight is sad and cloudy,
  The wind blows wild and free,
And like the wings of sea-birds
  Flash the white caps of the sea.

But in the fisherman's cottage
  There shines a ruddier light,
And a little face at the window
  Peers out into the night.

Close, close it is pressed to the window,
  As if those childish eyes
Were looking into the darkness,
  To see some form arise.

And a woman's waving shadow
  Is passing to and fro,
Now rising to the ceiling,
  Now bowing and bending low.

What tale do the roaring ocean,
  And the night-wind, bleak and wild,
As they beat at the crazy casement,
  Tell to that little child ?

And why do the roaring ocean.
  And the night-wind, wild and bleak,
As they beat at the heart of the mother,
  Drive the color from her cheek ?

SIR HUMPHREY GILBERT.

SOUTHWARD with fleet of ice
  Sailed the corsair Death ;
Wild and fast blew the blast,
  And the east-wind was his breath.

His lordly ships of ice
  Glisten in the sun ;
On each side, like pennons wide,
  Flashing crystal streamlets run.

His sails of white sea-mist
  Dripped with silver rain ;
But where he passed there were cast
  Leaden shadows o'er the main.

Eastward from Campobello
  Sir Humphrey Gilbert sailed ;
Three days or more seaward he bore,
  Then, alas ! the land-wind failed.

Alas ! the land-wind failed,
  And ice-cold grew the night ;
And nevermore, on sea or shore,
  Should Sir Humphrey see the light

He sat upon the deck,
  The Book was in his hand ;
" Do not fear ! Heaven is as near,"
  He said, " by water as by land !"

In the first watch of the night,
  Without a signal's sound,
Out of the sea, mysteriously,
  The fleet of Death rose all around.

The moon and the evening star
  Were hanging in the shrouds ;
Every mast, as it passed,
  Seemed to rake the passing clouds.

They grappled with their prize,
  At midnight black and cold !
As of a rock was the shock ;
  Heavily the ground-swell rolled.

Southward through day and dark,
  They drift in close embrace,
With mist and rain, o'er the open main ;
  Yet there seems no change of place.

Southward, forever southward,
  They drift through dark and day ;
And like a dream, in the Gulf-Stream
  Sinking, vanish all away.

THE LIGHTHOUSE.

THE rocky ledge runs far into the sea,
　And on its outer point, some miles
　　away,
The Lighthouse lifts its massive ma-
　sonry,
　A pillar of fire by night, of cloud by
　　day.

Even at this distance I can see the
　tides,
　Upheaving, break unheard along its
　　base,
A speechless wrath, that rises and sub-
　sides
　In the white lip and tremor of the face.

And as the evening darkens, lo ! how
　bright,
　Through the deep purple of the twi-
　　light air,
Beams forth the sudden radiance of its
　light
　With strange, unearthly splendor in
　　the glare !

Not one alone ; from each projecting
　cape
　And perilous reef along the ocean's
　　verge,
Starts into life a dim, gigantic shape,
　Holding its lantern o'er the restless
　　surge.

Like the great giant Christopher it
　stands
　Upon the brink of the tempestuous
　　wave,
Wading far out among the rocks and
　sands,
　The night-o'ertaken mariner to save.

And the great ships sail outward and
　return,
　Bending and bowing o'er the billowy
　　swells,
And ever joyful, as they see it burn,
　They wave their silent welcomes and
　　farewells.

They come forth from the darkness, and
　their sails
　Gleam for a moment only in the blaze,
And eager faces, as the light unveils,
　Gaze at the tower, and vanish while
　　they gaze.

The mariner remembers when a
　child,
　On his first voyage, he saw it fade and
　　sink ;
And when, returning from adventures
　wild,
　He saw it rise again o'er ocean's brink.

Steadfast, serene, immovable, the same
　Year after year, through all the silent
　　night
Burns on forevermore that quenchless
　flame,
　Shines on that inextinguishable light !

It sees the ocean to its bosom clasp
　The rocks and sea-sand with the kiss
　　of peace ;
It sees the wild winds lift it in their
　grasp,
　And hold it up, and shake it like a
　　fleece.

The startled waves leap over it ; the
　storm
　Smites it with all the scourges of the
　　rain,
And steadily against its solid form
　Press the great shoulders of the hur-
　　ricane.

The sea-bird wheeling round it, with the
　din
　Of wings and winds and solitary
　　cries,
Blinded and maddened by the light
　within,
　Dashes himself against the glare, and
　　dies.

A new Prometheus, chained upon the
　rock,
　Still grasping in his hand the fire of
　　Jove,
It does not hear the cry, nor heed the
　shock,
　But hails the mariner with words of
　　love.

"Sail on !" it says, "sail on, ye stately
　ships !
　And with your floating bridge the
　　ocean span ;
Be mine to guard this light from all
　eclipse,
　Be yours to bring man nearer unto
　　man !"

THE FIRE OF DRIFT-WOOD.

DEVEREUX FARM, NEAR MARBLEHEAD.

WE sat within the farm-house old,
  Whose windows, looking o'er the bay,
Gave to the sea-breeze, damp and cold,
  An easy entrance, night and day.

Not far away we saw the port,
  The strange, old-fashioned, silent
    town,
The lighthouse, the dismantled fort,
  The wooden houses, quaint and brown.

We sat and talked until the night,
  Descending, filled the little room;
Our faces faded from the sight,
  Our voices only broke the gloom.

We spake of many a vanished scene,
  Of what we once had thought and
    said,
Of what had been, and might have been,
  And who was changed, and who was
    dead;

And all that fills the hearts of friends,
  When first they feel, with secret pain,
Their lives thenceforth have separate
    ends,
  And never can be one again;

The first slight swerving of the heart,
  That words are powerless to express,

And leave it still unsaid in part,
  Or say it in too great excess.

The very tones in which we spake
  Had something strange, I could but
    mark;
The leaves of memory seemed to make
  A mournful rustling in the dark.

Oft died the words upon our lips,
  As suddenly, from out the fire
Built of the wreck of stranded ships,
  The flames would leap and then expire.

And, as their splendor flashed and
    failed,
  We thought of wrecks upon the main,
Of ships dismasted, that were hailed
  And sent no answer back again.

The windows, rattling in their frames,
  The ocean, roaring up the beach,
The gusty blast, the bickering flames,
  All mingled vaguely in our speech;

Until they made themselves a part
  Of fancies floating through the brain,
The long-lost ventures of the heart,
  That send no answers back again.

O flames that glowed! O hearts that
    yearned!
  They were indeed too much akin,
The drift-wood fire without that burned,
  The thoughts that burned and glowed
    within.

BY THE FIRESIDE.

RESIGNATION.

THERE is no flock, however watched and
    tended,
  But one dead lamb is there!
There is no fireside, howsoe'er defended,
  But has one vacant chair!

The air is full of farewells to the dy-
    ing,
  And mournings for the dead;
The heart of Rachel, for her children
    crying,
  Will not be comforted!

Let us be patient! These severe afflic-
    tions
  Not from the ground arise,
But oftentimes celestial benedictions
  Assume this dark disguise.

We see but dimly through the mists and
    vapors;
  Amid these earthly damps
What seem to us but sad, funereal tapers
  May be heaven's distant lamps.

There is no Death! What seems so is
    transition;
  This life of mortal breath

Is but a suburb of the life elysian,
  Whose portal we call Death.

She is not dead, — the child of our affec-
    tion, —
  But gone unto that school
Where she no longer needs our poor pro-
    tection,
  And Christ himself doth rule.

In that great cloister's stillness and se-
    clusion,
  By guardian angels led,
Safe from temptation, safe from sin's
    pollution,
  She lives, whom we call dead.

Day after day we think what she is doing
  In those bright realms of air ;
Year after year, her tender steps pursu-
    ing,
  Behold her grown more fair.

Thus do we walk with her, and keep un-
    broken
  The bond which nature gives,
Thinking that our remembrance, though
    unspoken,
  May reach her where she lives.

Not as a child shall we again behold
    her ;
  For when with raptures wild
In our embraces we again enfold her,
  She will not be a child ;

But a fair maiden, in her Father's man-
    sion,
  Clothed with celestial grace ;
And beautiful with all the soul's expan-
    sion
  Shall we behold her face.

And though at times impetuous with
    emotion
  And anguish long suppressed,
The swelling heart heaves moaning like
    the ocean,
  That cannot be at rest, —

We will be patient, and assuage the feel-
    ing
  We may not wholly stay ;
By silence sanctifying, not concealing,
  The grief that must have way.

THE BUILDERS.

ALL are architects of Fate,
  Working in these walls of Time ;
Some with massive deeds and great,
  Some with ornaments of rhyme.

Nothing useless is, or low ;
  Each thing in its place is best ;
And what seems but idle show
  Strengthens and supports the rest.

For the structure that we raise,
  Time is with materials filled ;
Our to-days and yesterdays
  Are the blocks with which we build.

Truly shape and fashion these ;
  Leave no yawning gaps between ;
Think not, because no man sees,
  Such things will remain unseen.

In the elder days of Art,
  Builders wrought with greatest care
Each minute and unseen part ;
  For the Gods see everywhere.

Let us do our work as well,
  Both the unseen and the seen ;
Make the house, where Gods may dwell,
  Beautiful, entire, and clean.

Else our lives are incomplete,
  Standing in these walls of Time,
Broken stairways, where the feet
  Stumble as they seek to climb.

Build to-day, then, strong and sure,
  With a firm and ample base ;
And ascending and secure
  Shall to-morrow find its place.

Thus alone can we attain
  To those turrets, where the eye
Sees the world as one vast plain,
  And one boundless reach of sky.

SAND OF THE DESERT IN AN HOUR-GLASS.

A HANDFUL of red sand, from the hot
    clime
  Of Arab deserts brought,
Within this glass becomes the spy of
    Time,
  The minister of Thought.

How many weary centuries has it been
  About those deserts blown !
How many strange vicissitudes has seen,
  How many histories known !

Perhaps the camels of the Ishmaelite
    Trampled and passed it o'er,
When into Egypt from the patriarch's
    sight
    His favorite son they bore.

Perhaps the feet of Moses, burnt and
    bare,
  Crushed it beneath their tread ;
Or Pharaoh's flashing wheels into the air
  Scattered it as they sped ;

Or Mary, with the Christ of Nazareth
    Held close in her caress,
Whose pilgrimage of hope and love and
    faith
    Illumed the wilderness ;

Or anchorites beneath Engaddi's palms
    Pacing the Dead Sea beach,
And singing slow their old Armenian
    psalms
  In half-articulate speech ;

Or caravans, that from Bassora's gate
    With westward steps depart ;
Or Mecca's pilgrims, confident of Fate,
  And resolute in heart !

These have passed over it, or may have
    passed !
  Now in this crystal tower
Imprisoned by some curious hand at last,
  It counts the passing hour.

And as I gaze, these narrow walls ex-
    pand ;
  Before my dreamy eye
Stretches the desert with its shifting
    sand,
  Its unimpeded sky.

And borne aloft by the sustaining blast,
  This little golden thread
Dilates into a column high and vast,
  A form of fear and dread.

And onward, and across the setting sun,
  Across the boundless plain,
The column and its broader shadow
    run,
  Till thought pursues in vain.

The vision vanishes ! These walls again
    Shut out the lurid sun,
Shut out the hot, immeasurable plain ;
    The half-hour's sand is run !

BIRDS OF PASSAGE.

BLACK shadows fall
From the lindens tall,
That lift aloft their massive wall
  Against the southern sky ;

And from the realms
Of the shadowy elms
A tide-like darkness overwhelms
  The fields that round us lie.

But the night is fair,
And everywhere
A warm, soft vapor fills the air,
  And distant sounds seem near.

And above, in the light
Of the star-lit night,
Swift birds of passage wing their flight
  Through the dewy atmosphere.

I hear the beat
Of their pinions fleet,
As from the land of snow and sleet
  They seek a southern lea.

I hear the cry
Of their voices high
Falling dreamily through the sky,
  But their forms I cannot see.

O, say not so !
Those sounds that flow
In murmurs of delight and woe
  Come not from wings of birds.

They are the throngs
Of the poet's songs,
Murmurs of pleasures, and pains, and
    wrongs,
  The sound of winged words.

This is the cry
Of souls, that high
On toiling, beating pinions, fly,
  Seeking a warmer clime.

From their distant flight
Through realms of light
It falls into our world of night,
  With the murmuring sound of rhyme.

THE OPEN WINDOW.

THE old house by the lindens
    Stood silent in the shade,
And on the gravelled pathway
    The light and shadow played.

I saw the nursery windows
    Wide open to the air;
But the faces of the children,
    They were no longer there.

The large Newfoundland house-dog
    Was standing by the door;
He looked for his little playmates,
    Who would return no more.

They walked not under the lindens,
    They played not in the hall;
But shadow, and silence, and sadness
    Were hanging over all.

The birds sang in the branches,
    With sweet, familiar tone;
But the voices of the children
    Will be heard in dreams alone!

And the boy that walked beside me,
    He could not understand
Why closer in mine, ah! closer,
    I pressed his warm, soft hand!

KING WITLAF'S DRINKING-
HORN.

WITLAF, a king of the Saxons,
    Ere yet his last he breathed,
To the merry monks of Croyland
    His drinking-horn bequeathed, —

That, whenever they sat at their revels,
    And drank from the golden bowl,
They might remember the donor,
    And breathe a prayer for his soul.

So sat they once at Christmas,
    And bade the goblet pass;
In their beards the red wine glistened
    Like dew-drops in the grass.

They drank to the soul of Witlaf,
    They drank to Christ the Lord,
And to each of the Twelve Apostles,
    Who had preached his holy word.

They drank to the Saints and Martyrs
    Of the dismal days of yore,
And as soon as the horn was empty
    They remembered one Saint more.

And the reader droned from the pulpit,
    Like the murmur of many bees,
The legend of good Saint Guthlac,
    And Saint Basil's homilies;

Till the great bells of the convent,
    From their prison in the tower,
Guthlac and Bartholomæus,
    Proclaimed the midnight hour.

And the Yule-log cracked in the chim-
    ney,
    And the Abbot bowed his head,
And the flamelets flapped and flickered,
    But the Abbot was stark and dead.

Yet still in his pallid fingers
    He clutched the golden bowl,
In which, like a pearl dissolving,
    Had sunk and dissolved his soul.

But not for this their revels
    The jovial monks forbore,
For they cried, " Fill high the goblet!
    We must drink to one Saint more!"

GASPAR BECERRA.

By his evening fire the artist
    Pondered o'er his secret shame;
Baffled, weary, and disheartened,
    Still he mused, and dreamed of fame.

'T was an image of the Virgin
    That had tasked his utmost skill;
But, alas! his fair ideal
    Vanished and escaped him still.

From a distant Eastern island
    Had the precious wood been brought,
Day and night the anxious master
    At his toil untiring wrought;

Till, discouraged and desponding,
    Sat he now in shadows deep,
And the day's humiliation
    Found oblivion in sleep.

Then a voice cried, "Rise, O master!
    From the burning brand of oak

Shape the thought that stirs within
  thee!"
And the startled artist woke, —

Woke, and from the smoking embers
  Seized and quenched the glowing
    wood;
And therefrom he carved an image,
  And he saw that it was good.

O thou sculptor, painter, poet!
  Take this lesson to thy heart:
That is best which lieth nearest;
  Shape from that thy work of art.

PEGASUS IN POUND.

ONCE into a quiet village,
  Without haste and without heed,
In the golden prime of morning,
  Strayed the poet's winged steed.

It was Autumn, and incessant
  Piped the quails from shocks and
    sheaves,
And, like living coals, the apples
  Burned among the withering leaves.

Loud the clamorous bell was ringing
  From its belfry gaunt and grim;
'T was the daily call to labor,
  Not a triumph meant for him.

Not the less he saw the landscape,
  In its gleaming vapor veiled;
Not the less he breathed the odors
  That the dying leaves exhaled.

Thus, upon the village common,
  By the school-boys he was found;
And the wise men, in their wisdom,
  Put him straightway into pound.

Then the sombre village crier,
  Ringing loud his brazen bell,
Wandered down the street proclaiming
  There was an estray to sell.

And the curious country people,
  Rich and poor, and young and old,
Came in haste to see this wondrous
  Winged steed, with mane of gold.

Thus the day passed, and the evening
  Fell, with vapors cold and dim;
But it brought no food nor shelter,
  Brought no straw nor stall, for him.

Patiently, and still expectant,
  Looked he through the wooden bars,
Saw the moon rise o'er the landscape,
  Saw the tranquil, patient stars;

Till at length the bell at midnight
  Sounded from its dark abode,
And, from out a neighboring farm-yard
  Loud the cock Alectryon crowed.

Then, with nostrils wide distended,
  Breaking from his iron chain,
And unfolding far his pinions,
  To those stars he soared again.

On the morrow, when the village
  Woke to all its toil and care,
Lo! the strange steed had departed,
  And they knew not when nor where.

But they found, upon the greensward
  Where his struggling hoofs had trod,
Pure and bright, a fountain flowing
  From the hoof-marks in the sod.

From that hour, the fount unfailing
  Gladdens the whole region round,
Strengthening all who drink its waters,
  While it soothes them with its sound.

TEGNÉR'S DRAPA.

I HEARD a voice, that cried,
  "Balder the Beautiful
Is dead, is dead!"
And through the misty air
Passed like the mournful cry
Of sunward sailing cranes.

I saw the pallid corpse
Of the dead sun
Borne through the Northern sky.
Blasts from Niffelheim
Lifted the sheeted mists
Around him as he passed.

And the voice forever cried,
  "Balder the Beautiful
Is dead, is dead!"
And died away
Through the dreary night,
In accents of despair.

Balder the Beautiful,
God of the summer sun,
Fairest of all the Gods!
Light from his forehead beamed,

Runes were upon his tongue,
As on the warrior's sword.

All things in earth and air
Bound were by magic spell
Never to do him harm ;
Even the plants and stones ;
All save the mistletoe,
The sacred mistletoe !

Hœder, the blind old God,
Whose feet are shod with silence,
Pierced through that gentle breast
With his sharp spear, by fraud
Made of the mistletoe,
The accursed mistletoe !

They laid him in his ship,
With horse and harness,
As on a funeral pyre.
Odin placed
A ring upon his finger,
And whispered in his ear.

They launched the burning ship !
It floated far away
Over the misty sea,
Till like the sun it seemed,
Sinking beneath the waves.
Balder returned no more !

So perish the old Gods !
But out of the sea of Time
Rises a new land of song,
Fairer than the old.
Over its meadows green
Walk the young bards and sing.

Build it again,
O ye bards,
Fairer than before !
Ye fathers of the new race,
Feed upon morning dew,
Sing the new Song of Love !

The law of force is dead !
The law of love prevails !
Thor, the thunderer,
Shall rule the earth no more,
No more, with threats,
Challenge the meek Christ.

Sing no more,
O ye bards of the North,
Of Vikings and of Jarls !
Of the days of Eld
Preserve the freedom only,
Not the deeds of blood !

SONNET.

ON MRS. KEMBLE'S READINGS FROM SHAKESPEARE.

O PRECIOUS evenings ! all too swiftly
          sped !
  Leaving us heirs to amplest heritages
  Of all the best thoughts of the greatest
          sages,
  And giving tongues unto the silent
          dead !
How our hearts glowed and trembled as
          she read,
  Interpreting by tones the wondrous
          pages
  Of the great poet who foreruns the
          ages,
  Anticipating all that shall be said !
O happy Reader ! having for thy text
  The magic book, whose Sibylline
          leaves have caught
  The rarest essence of all human
          thought !
O happy Poet ! by no critic vext !
  How must thy listening spirit now
          rejoice
  To be interpreted by such a voice !

THE SINGERS.

GOD sent his Singers upon earth
With songs of sadness and of mirth,
That they might touch the hearts of men,
And bring them back to heaven again.

The first, a youth, with soul of fire,
Held in his hand a golden lyre ;
Through groves he wandered, and by
          streams,
Playing the music of our dreams.

The second, with a bearded face,
Stood singing in the market-place,
And stirred with accents deep and loud
The hearts of all the listening crowd.

A gray old man, the third and last,
Sang in cathedrals dim and vast,
While the majestic organ rolled
Contrition from its mouths of gold.

And those who heard the Singers three
Disputed which the best might be ;
For still their music seemed to start
Discordant echoes in each heart.

But the great Master said, "I see
No best in kind, but in degree ;
I gave a various gift to each,
To charm, to strengthen, and to teach.

"These are the three great chords of
   might,
And he whose ear is tuned aright
Will hear no discord in the three,
But the most perfect harmony."

SUSPIRIA.

TAKE them, O Death ! and bear away
   Whatever thou canst call thine own !
Thine image, stamped upon this clay,
   Doth give thee that, but that alone !

Take them, O Grave ! and let them lie
   Folded upon thy narrow shelves,
As garments by the soul laid by,
   And precious only to ourselves !

Take them, O great Eternity !
   Our little life is but a gust
That bends the branches of thy tree,
   And trails its blossoms in the dust !

HYMN

FOR MY BROTHER'S ORDINATION.

CHRIST to the young man said : "Yet
      one thing more ;
   If thou wouldst perfect be,
Sell all thou hast and give it to the poor,
   And come and follow me !"

Within this temple Christ again, unseen,
   Those sacred words hath said,
And his invisible hands to-day have been
   Laid on a young man's head.

And evermore beside him on his way
   The unseen Christ shall move,
That he may lean upon his arm and say,
   "Dost thou, dear Lord, approve ?"

Beside him at the marriage feast shall be,
   To make the scene more fair ;
Beside him in the dark Gethsemane
   Of pain and midnight prayer.

O holy trust ! O endless sense of rest !
   Like the beloved John
To lay his head upon the Saviour's breast,
   And thus to journey on !

THE BLIND GIRL OF CASTÈL-CUILLÈ.

FROM THE GASCON OF JASMIN.

> Only the Lowland tongue of Scotland might
> Rehearse this little tragedy aright ;
> Let me attempt it with an English quill ;
> And take, O Reader, for the deed the will.

I.

AT the foot of the mountain height
   Where is perched Castèl-Cuillè,
When the apple, the plum, and the al-
      mond tree
   In the plain below were growing
      white,
   This is the song one might perceive
On a Wednesday morn of Saint Joseph's
      Eve :

"The roads should blossom, the roads
      should bloom,
So fair a bride shall leave her home !
Should blossom and bloom with garlands
      gay,
So fair a bride shall pass to-day !"

This old Te Deum, rustic rites attending,
      Seemed from the clouds descending ;
   When lo ! a merry company
Of rosy village girls, clean as the eye,
   Each one with her attendant swain,
Came to the cliff, all singing the same
      strain ;
Resembling there, so near unto the sky,
Rejoicing angels, that kind Heaven has
      sent
For their delight and our encourage-
      ment.
      Together blending,
      And soon descending
      The narrow sweep
      Of the hillside steep,
      They wind aslant
      Towards Saint Amant,

Through leafy alleys
Of verdurous valleys
With merry sallies
Singing their chant :

"The roads should blossom, the roads
        should bloom,
So fair a bride shall leave her home !
Should blossom and bloom with garlands
        gay,
So fair a bride shall pass to-day ! "

It is Baptiste, and his affianced maiden,
With garlands for the bridal laden !

The sky was blue ; without one cloud of
        gloom,
The sun of March was shining brightly,
And to the air the freshening wind gave
        lightly
Its breathings of perfume.

When one beholds the dusky hedges
        blossom,
A rustic bridal, ah ! how sweet it is !
To sounds of joyous melodies,
That touch with tenderness the trem-
        bling bosom,
        A band of maidens
        Gayly frolicking,
        A band of youngsters
        Wildly rollicking !
            Kissing,
            Caressing,
With fingers pressing,
        Till in the veriest
Madness of mirth, as they dance,
They retreat and advance,
        Trying whose laugh shall be loud-
            est and merriest ;
While the bride, with roguish eyes,
Sporting with them, now escapes and
        cries :
        "Those who catch me
            Married verily
        This year shall be ! "

And all pursue with eager haste,
And all attain what they pursue,
And touch her pretty apron fresh and new,
And the linen kirtle round her waist.

Meanwhile, whence comes it that
        among
These youthful maidens fresh and
        fair,
So joyous, with such laughing air,

Baptiste stands sighing, with silent
        tongue ?
And yet the bride is fair and young !
Is it Saint Joseph would say to us all,
That love, o'er-hasty, precedeth a fall ?
        O no ! for a maiden frail, I trow,
        Never bore so lofty a brow !
What lovers ! they give not a single
        caress !
To see them so careless and cold to-day,
        These are grand people, one would
            say.
What ails Baptiste ? what grief doth him
        oppress ?

        It is, that, half-way up the hill,
        In yon cottage, by whose walls
        Stand the cart-house and the stalls,
        Dwelleth the blind orphan still,
        Daughter of a veteran old ;
        And you must know, one year ago,
        That Margaret, the young and ten-
            der,
        Was the village pride and splendor,
        And Baptiste her lover bold.
        Love, the deceiver, them ensnared ;
        For them the altar was prepared ;
        But alas ! the summer's blight,
        The dread disease that none can stay,
        The pestilence that walks by night,
        Took the young bride's sight away.

All at the father's stern command was
        changed ;
Their peace was gone, but not their love
        estranged.
Wearied at home, erelong the lover fled ;
        Returned but three short days ago,
        The golden chain they round him
            throw,
        He is enticed, and onward led
        To marry Angela, and yet
        Is thinking ever of Margaret.

        Then suddenly a maiden cried,
        " Anna, Theresa, Mary, Kate !
Here comes the cripple Jane ! "   And by
        a fountain's side
        A woman, bent and gray with years,
        Under the mulberry-trees appears,
        And all towards her run, as fleet
        As had they wings upon their feet.

        It is that Jane, the cripple Jane,
        Is a soothsayer, wary and kind.
        She telleth fortunes, and none complain.
        She promises one a village swain,

Another a happy wedding-day,
And the bride a lovely boy straight-
    way.
All comes to pass as she avers;
She never deceives, she never errs.

But for this once the village seer
Wears a countenance severe,
And from beneath her eyebrows thin and
    white
    Her two eyes flash like cannons
        bright
    Aimed at the bridegroom in waist-
        coat blue,
Who, like a statue, stands in view;
Changing color, as well he might,
When the beldame wrinkled and
    gray
Takes the young bride by the hand,
And, with the tip of her reedy wand
Making the sign of the cross, doth
    say : —
"Thoughtless Angela, beware!
Lest, when thou weddest this false
    bridegroom,
Thou diggest for thyself a tomb!"
And she was silent; and the maidens fair
Saw from each eye escape a swollen tear;
But on a little streamlet silver-clear,
    What are two drops of turbid rain?
Saddened a moment, the bridal train
Resumed the dance and song again;
The bridegroom only was pale with
    fear; —
        And down green alleys
        Of verdurous valleys,
        With merry sallies,
        They sang the refrain : —

"The roads should blossom, the roads
    should bloom,
So fair a bride shall leave her home!
Should blossom and bloom with garlands
    gay,
So fair a bride shall pass to-day!"

II.

And by suffering worn and weary,
But beautiful as some fair angel yet,
Thus lamented Margaret,
In her cottage lone and dreary : —

"He has arrived! arrived at last!
Yet Jane has named him not these three
    days past;

Arrived! yet keeps aloof so far!
And knows that of my night he is the
    star!
Knows that long months I wait alone,
    benighted,
And count the moments since he went
    away!
Come! keep the promise of that happier
    day,
That I may keep the faith to thee I
    plighted!
What joy have I without thee? what
    delight?
Grief wastes my life, and makes it mis-
    ery;
Day for the others ever, but for me
    Forever night! forever night!
When he is gone 't is dark! my soul is
    sad!
I suffer! O my God! come, make me
    glad.
When he is near, no thoughts of day in-
    trude;
Day has blue heavens, but Baptiste has
    blue eyes!
Within them shines for me a heaven of
    love,
A heaven all happiness, like that above,
    No more of grief! no more of lassi-
    tude!
Earth I forget, — and heaven, and all
    distresses,
When seated by my side my hand he
    presses;
    But when alone, remember all!
Where is Baptiste? he hears not when I
    call!
A branch of ivy, dying on the ground,
    I need some bough to twine around!
In pity come! be to my suffering kind!
True love, they say, in grief doth more
    abound!
    What then — when one is blind?

"Who knows? perhaps I am for-
    saken!
Ah! woe is me! then bear me to my
    grave!
    O God! what thoughts within me
        waken!
Away! he will return! I do but rave!
    He will return! I need not fear!
    He swore it by our Saviour dear;
    He could not come at his own will;
    Is weary, or perhaps is ill!
    Perhaps his heart, in this disguise,
    Prepares for me some sweet surprise!

But some one comes ! Though blind,
     my heart can see !
And that deceives me not ! 't is he ! 't is
     he !"

     And the door ajar is set,
     And poor, confiding Margaret
Rises, with outstretched arms, but sight-
     less eyes ;
'T is only Paul, her brother, who thus
     cries : —
     "Angela the bride has passed !
I saw the wedding guests go by ;
Tell me, my sister, why were we not
     asked ?
For all are there but you and I !"

     "Angela married ! and not send
To tell her secret unto me !
O, speak ! who may the bridegroom
     be ?"
     "My sister, 't is Baptiste, thy
     friend!"

A cry the blind girl gave, but nothing
     said ;
A milky whiteness spreads upon her
     cheeks ;
     An icy hand, as heavy as lead,
     Descending, as her brother speaks,
     Upon her heart, that has ceased to
     beat,
Suspends awhile its life and heat.
She stands beside the boy, now sore dis-
     tressed,
A wax Madonna as a peasant dressed.

     At length, the bridal song again
Brings her back to her sorrow and
     pain.

     "Hark ! the joyous airs are ring-
     ing !
Sister, dost thou hear them sing-
     ing ?
How merrily they laugh and jest !
Would we were bidden with the
     rest !
I would don my hose of homespun
     gray,
And my doublet of linen striped
     and gay ;
Perhaps they will come ; for they
     do not wed
Till to-morrow at seven o'clock, it is
     said !"

     "I know it !" answered Margaret ,
Whom the vision, with aspect black as
     jet,
Mastered again ; and its hand of ice
Held her heart crushed, as in a vice !
     "Paul, be not sad ! 'T is a holi-
     day ;
To-morrow put on thy doublet gay !
But leave me now for a while alone.''
Away, with a hop and a jump,
     went Paul,
And, as he whistled along the hall,
Entered Jane, the crippled crone.

     "Holy Virgin ! what dreadful heat !
I am faint, and weary, and out of
     breath !
But thou art cold, — art chill as
     death ;
My little friend ! what ails thee,
     sweet ?"
"Nothing ! I heard them singing home
     the bride ;
     And, as I listened to the song,
     I thought my turn would come
     erelong,
Thou knowest it is at Whitsuntide.
Thy cards forsooth can never lie,
To me such joy they prophesy,
Thy skill shall be vaunted far and
     wide
When they behold him at my
     side.
And poor Baptiste, what sayest
     thou ?
It must seem long to him ; — methinks
     I see him now !"
Jane, shuddering, her hand doth
     press :
     "Thy love I cannot all approve ;
We must not trust too much to happi-
     ness ; —
Go, pray to God, that thou mayst love
     him less !"
     "The more I pray, the more I
     love !
It is no sin, for God is on my side !"
It was enough ; and Jane no more re-
     plied.

Now to all hope her heart is barred and
     cold ;
     But to deceive the beldame old
     She takes a sweet, contented air ;
     Speak of foul weather or of fair,
     At every word the maiden smiles !
     Thus the beguiler she beguiles ;

So that, departing at the evening's close,
　　She says, "She may be saved ! she
　　　　nothing knows ! "

　　Poor Jane, the cunning sorceress !
Now that thou wouldst, thou art no
　　　　prophetess !
This morning, in the fulness of thy heart,
　　Thou wast so, far beyond thine art !

III.

Now rings the bell, nine times reverber-
　　ating,
And the white daybreak, stealing up the
　　sky,
Sees in two cottages two maidens wait-
　　ing,
　　　　How differently !

Queen of a day, by flatterers caressed,
　　The one puts on her cross and
　　　　crown,
　　Decks with a huge bouquet her
　　　　breast,
　　And flaunting, fluttering up and
　　　　down,
　　Looks at herself, and cannot rest.
　The other, blind, within her little
　　　　room,
　　Has neither crown nor flower's per-
　　　　fume ;
But in their stead for something gropes
　　apart,
　That in a drawer's recess doth lie,
And, 'neath her bodice of bright scarlet
　　dye,
　　Convulsive clasps it to her heart.

　The one, fantastic, light as air,
　　　　'Mid kisses ringing,
　　　　And joyous singing,
　Forgets to say her morning prayer !

The other, with cold drops upon her
　　brow,
　Joins her two hands, and kneels upon
　　　　the floor,
And whispers, as her brother opes the
　　　　door,
　　"O God ! forgive me now ! "

　And then the orphan, young and
　　　　blind,
　Conducted by her brother's hand,

Towards the church, through paths
　　unscanned,
　With tranquil air, her way doth
　　　　wind.
Odors of laurel, making her faint and
　　pale,
　Round her at times exhale,
And in the sky as yet no sunny ray,
　　But brumal vapors gray.

　Near that castle, fair to see,
Crowded with sculptures old, in every
　　part,
　Marvels of nature and of art,
　　And proud of its name of high
　　　　degree,
　A little chapel, almost bare
　At the base of the rock, is builded
　　　　there ;
　All glorious that it lifts aloof,
　Above each jealous cottage roof,
Its sacred summit, swept by autumn
　　gales,
　　And its blackened steeple high in air,
　　Round which the osprey screams
　　　　and sails.

　　"Paul, lay thy noisy rattle by ! "
Thus Margaret said.　"Where are we !
　　we ascend ! "
　　"Yes ; seest thou not our journey's
　　　　end ?
Hearest not the osprey from the belfry
　　cry ?
The hideous bird, that brings ill luck,
　　we know !
Dost thou remember when our father
　　said,
　　The night we watched beside his
　　　　bed,
　　'O daughter, I am weak and low ;
Take care of Paul ; I feel that I am
　　dying ! '
And thou, and he, and I, all fell to cry-
　　ing ?
Then on the roof the osprey screamed
　　aloud ;
And here they brought our father in his
　　shroud.
There is his grave ; there stands the
　　cross we set ;
Why dost thou clasp me so, dear Mar-
　　garet ?
　　Come in !　The bride will be here
　　　　soon :
Thou tremblest !　O my God ! thou art
　　going to swoon ! "

She could no more, — the blind girl,
	weak and weary !
A voice seemed crying from that grave
	so dreary,
"What wouldst thou do, my daugh-
	ter ?" — and she started,
	And quick recoiled, aghast, faint-
	hearted ;
But Paul, impatient, urges evermore
	Her steps towards the open door ;
And when, beneath her feet, the un-
	happy maid
Crushes the laurel near the house im-
	mortal,
And with her head, as Paul talks on
	again,
	Touches the crown of filigrane
	Suspended from the low-arched
	portal,
	No more restrained, no more afraid,
	She walks, as for a feast arrayed,
And in the ancient chapel's sombre
	night
	They both are lost to sight.

	At length the bell,
	With booming sound,
	Sends forth, resounding round,
Its hymeneal peal o'er rock and down
	the dell.
	It is broad day, with sunshine and
	with rain ;
	And yet the guests delay not
	long,
	For soon arrives the bridal train,
	And with it brings the village
	throng.

In sooth, deceit maketh no mortal gay,
For lo ! Baptiste on this triumphant
	day,
Mute as an idiot, sad as yester-morning,
Thinks only of the beldame's words of
	warning.

And Angela thinks of her cross, I wis ;
To be a bride is all ! The pretty lisper
Feels her heart swell to hear all round
	her whisper,
"How beautiful ! how beautiful she is !"

	But she must calm that giddy
	head,
	For already the Mass is said ;
	At the holy table stands the priest ;
The wedding ring is blessed ; Baptiste
	receives it ;

Ere on the finger of the bride he leaves
	it,
	He must pronounce one word at
	least !
'T is spoken ; and sudden at the grooms-
	man's side
"'T is he !" a well-known voice has
	cried.
And while the wedding guests all hold
	their breath,
Opes the confessional, and the blind
	girl, see !
"Baptiste," she said, "since thou hast
	wished my death,
As holy water be my blood for thee !"
And calmly in the air a knife suspended !
Doubtless her guardian angel near at-
	tended,
	For anguish did its work so well,
	That, ere the fatal stroke descended,
	Lifeless she fell !

	At eve, instead of bridal verse,
	The De Profundis filled the air ;
	Decked with flowers a simple hearse
	To the churchyard forth they bear ;
	Village girls in robes of snow
	Follow, weeping as they go ;
	Nowhere was a smile that day,
No, ah no ! for each one seemed to
	say : —

"The road should mourn and be veiled
	in gloom,
So fair a corpse shall leave its home !
Should mourn and should weep, ah,
	well-away !
So fair a corpse shall pass to-day !"

A CHRISTMAS CAROL.

FROM THE NOEL BOURGUIGNON DE GUI
BARÔZAI.

	I HEAR along our street
	Pass the minstrel throngs ;
	Hark ! they play so sweet,
On their hautboys, Christmas songs !
	Let us by the fire
	Ever higher
Sing them till the night expire !

	In December ring
	Every day the chimes ;
	Loud the gleemen sing
In the streets their merry rhymes.

Let us by the fire
Ever higher
Sing them till the night expire.

Shepherds at the grange,
Where the Babe was born,
Sang, with many a change,
Christmas carols until morn.
Let us by the fire
Ever higher
Sing them till the night expire !

These good people sang
Songs devout and sweet ;
While the rafters rang,
There they stood with freezing feet.
Let us by the fire
Ever higher
Sing them till the night expire.

Nuns in frigid cells
At this holy tide,

For want of something else,
Christmas songs at times have tried.
Let us by the fire
Ever higher
Sing them till the night expire !

Washerwomen old,
To the sound they beat,
Sing by rivers cold,
With uncovered heads and feet.
Let us by the fire
Ever higher
Sing them till the night expire.

Who by the fireside stands
Stamps his feet and sings ;
But he who blows his hands
Not so gay a carol brings.
Let us by the fire
Ever higher
Sing them till the night expire !

THE SONG OF HIAWATHA.

INTRODUCTION.

SHOULD you ask me, whence these sto-
ries ?
Whence these legends and traditions,
With the odors of the forest,
With the dew and damp of meadows,
With the curling smoke of wigwams,
With the rushing of great rivers,
With their frequent repetitions,
And their wild reverberations,
As of thunder in the mountains ?
I should answer, I should tell you,
" From the forests and the prairies,
From the great lakes of the Northland,
From the land of the Ojibways,
From the land of the Dacotahs,
From the mountains, moors, and fen-
lands,
Where the heron, the Shuh-shuh-gah,
Feeds among the reeds and rushes.
I repeat them as I heard them
From the lips of Nawadaha,
The musician, the sweet singer."
Should you ask where Nawadaha
Found these songs, so wild and wayward,
Found these legends and traditions,

I should answer, I should tell you,
" In the bird's-nests of the forest,
In the lodges of the beaver,
In the hoof-prints of the bison,
In the eyry of the eagle !
" All the wild-fowl sang them to him,
In the moorlands and the fen-lands,
In the melancholy marshes ;
Chetowaik, the plover, sang them,
Mahng, the loon, the wild-goose, Wawa,
The blue heron, the Shuh-shuh-gah,
And the grouse, the Musnkodasa ! "
If still further you should ask me,
Saying, " Who was Nawadaha ?
Tell us of this Nawadaha,"
I should answer your inquiries
Straightway in such words as follow.
" In the Vale of Tawasentha,
In the green and silent valley,
By the pleasant water-courses,
Dwelt the singer Nawadaha.
Round about the Indian village
Spread the meadows and the corn-fields,
And beyond them stood the forest,
Stood the groves of singing pine-trees,
Green in Summer, white in Winter,
Ever sighing, ever singing.

" And the pleasant water-courses,
You could trace them through the valley,
By the rushing in the Spring-time,
By the alders in the Summer,
By the white fog in the Autumn,
By the black line in the Winter ;
And beside them dwelt the singer,
In the vale of Tawasentha,
In the green and silent valley.
" There he sang of Hiawatha,
Sang the Song of Hiawatha,
Sang his wondrous birth and being,
How he prayed and how he fasted,
How he lived, and toiled, and suffered,
That the tribes of men might prosper,
That he might advance his people ! "
    Ye who love the haunts of Nature,
Love the sunshine of the meadow,
Love the shadow of the forest,
Love the wind among the branches,
And the rain-shower and the snow-storm,
And the rushing of great rivers
Through their palisades of pine-trees,
And the thunder in the mountains,
Whose innumerable echoes
Flap like eagles in their eyries ; —
Listen to these wild traditions,
To this Song of Hiawatha !
    Ye who love a nation's legends,
Love the ballads of a people,
That like voices from afar off
Call to us to pause and listen,
Speak in tones so plain and childlike,
Scarcely can the ear distinguish
Whether they are sung or spoken ; —
Listen to this Indian Legend,
To this Song of Hiawatha !
    Ye whose hearts are fresh and simple,
Who have faith in God and Nature,
Who believe, that in all ages
Every human heart is human,
That in even savage bosoms
There are longings, yearnings, strivings
For the good they comprehend not,
That the feeble hands and helpless,
Groping blindly in the darkness,
Touch God's right hand in that darkness
And are lifted up and strengthened ; —
Listen to this simple story,
To this Song of Hiawatha !
    Ye, who sometimes, in your rambles
Through the green lanes of the country,
Where the tangled barberry-bushes
Hang their tufts of crimson berries
Over stone walls gray with mosses,
Pause by some neglected graveyard,
For a while to muse, and ponder

On a half-effaced inscription,
Written with little skill of song-craft,
Homely phrases, but each letter
Full of hope and yet of heart-break,
Full of all the tender pathos
Of the Here and the Hereafter ; —
Stay and read this rude inscription,
Read this Song of Hiawatha !

THE SONG OF HIAWATHA.

I.

THE PEACE-PIPE.

ON the Mountains of the Prairie,
On the great Red Pipe-stone Quarry,
Gitche Manito, the mighty,
He the Master of Life, descending,
On the red crags of the quarry
Stood erect, and called the nations,
Called the tribes of men together.
    From his footprints flowed a river,
Leaped into the light of morning,
O'er the precipice plunging downward
Gleamed like Ishkoodah, the comet.
And the Spirit, stooping earthward,
With his finger on the meadow
Traced a winding pathway for it,
Saying to it, " Run in this way ! "
    From the red stone of the quarry
With his hand he broke a fragment,
Moulded it into a pipe-head,
Shaped and fashioned it with figures ;
From the margin of the river
Took a long reed for a pipe-stem,
With its dark green leaves upon it ;
Filled the pipe with bark of willow,
With the bark of the red willow ;
Breathed upon the neighboring forest,
Made its great boughs chafe together,
Till in flame they burst and kindled ;
And erect upon the mountains,
Gitche Manito, the mighty,
Smoked the calumet, the Peace-Pipe,
As a signal to the nations.
    And the smoke rose slowly, slowly
Through the tranquil air of morning,
First a single line of darkness,
Then a denser, bluer vapor,
Then a snow-white cloud unfolding,
Like the tree-tops of the forest,
Ever rising, rising, rising,
Till it touched the top of heaven,
Till it broke against the heaven,
And rolled outward all around it.
    From the Vale of Tawasentha,

From the Valley of Wyoming,
From the groves of Tuscaloosa,
From the far-off Rocky Mountains,
From the Northern lakes and rivers
All the tribes beheld the signal,
Saw the distant smoke ascending,
The Pukwana of the Peace-Pipe.

And the Prophets of the nations
Said : " Behold it, the Pukwana !
By this signal from afar off,
Bending like a wand of willow,
Waving like a hand that beckons,
Gitche Manito, the mighty,
Calls the tribes of men together,
Calls the warriors to his council ! "

Down the rivers, o'er the prairies,
Came the warriors of the nations,
Came the Delawares and Mohawks,
Came the Choctaws and Camanches,
Came the Shoshonies and Blackfeet,
Came the Pawnees and Omahas,
Came the Mandans and Dacotahs,
Came the Hurons and Ojibways,
All the warriors drawn together
By the signal of the Peace-Pipe,
To the Mountains of the Prairie,
To the great Red Pipe-stone Quarry.

And they stood there on the meadow,
With their weapons and their war-gear,
Painted like the leaves of Autumn,
Painted like the sky of morning,
Wildly glaring at each other ;
In their faces stern defiance,
In their hearts the feuds of ages,
The hereditary hatred,
The ancestral thirst of vengeance.

Gitche Manito, the mighty,
The creator of the nations,
Looked upon them with compassion,
With paternal love and pity ;
Looked upon their wrath and wrangling
But as quarrels among children,
But as feuds and fights of children !

Over them he stretched his right hand,
To subdue their stubborn natures,
To allay their thirst and fever,
By the shadow of his right hand ;
Spake to them with voice majestic
As the sound of far-off waters,
Falling into deep abysses,
Warning, chiding, spake in this wise : —
" O my children ! my poor children !
Listen to the words of wisdom,
Listen to the words of warning,
From the lips of the Great Spirit,
From the Master of Life, who made you
" I have given you lands to hunt in,

I have given you streams to fish in,
I have given you bear and bison,
I have given you roe and reindeer,
I have given you brant and beaver,
Filled the marshes full of wild-fowl,
Filled the rivers full of fishes ;
Why then are you not contented ?
Why then will you hunt each other ?

" I am weary of your quarrels,
Weary of your wars and bloodshed,
Weary of your prayers for vengeance,
Of your wranglings and dissensions ;
All your strength is in your union,
All your danger is in discord ;
Therefore be at peace henceforward,
And as brothers live together.

" I will send a Prophet to you,
A Deliverer of the nations,
Who shall guide you and shall teach you,
Who shall toil and suffer with you.
If you listen to his counsels,
You will multiply and prosper ;
If his warnings pass unheeded,
You will fade away and perish !

" Bathe now in the stream before you,
Wash the war-paint from your faces,
Wash the blood-stains from your fingers,
Bury your war-clubs and your weapons,
Break the red stone from this quarry,
Mould and make it into Peace-Pipes,
Take the reeds that grow beside you,
Deck them with your brightest feathers,
Smoke the calumet together,
And as brothers live henceforward ! "

Then upon the ground the warriors
Threw their cloaks and shirts of deer-
        skin,
Threw their weapons and their war-gear,
Leaped into the rushing river,
Washed the war-paint from their faces
Clear above them flowed the water,
Clear and limpid from the footprints
Of the Master of Life descending ;
Dark below them flowed the water,
Soiled and stained with streaks of crim-
        son,
As if blood were mingled with it !
From the river came the warriors,
Clean and washed from all their war-
        paint ;
On the banks their clubs they buried,
Buried all their warlike weapons.
Gitche Manito, the mighty,
The Great Spirit, the creator,
Smiled upon his helpless children !

And in silence all the warriors
Broke the red stone of the quarry,

Smoothed and formed it into Peace-
Pipes,
Broke the long reeds by the river,
Decked them with their brightest feath-
ers,
And departed each one homeward,
While the Master of Life, ascending,
Through the opening of cloud-curtains,
Through the doorways of the heaven,
Vanished from before their faces,
In the smoke that rolled around him,
The Pukwana of the Peace-Pipe !

II.

THE FOUR WINDS.

"Honor be to Mudjekeewis ! "
Cried the warriors, cried the old men,
When he came in triumph homeward
With the sacred Belt of Wampum,
From the regions of the North-Wind,
From the kingdom of Wabasso,
From the land of the White Rabbit.

He had stolen the Belt of Wampum
From the neck of Mishe-Mokwa,
From the Great Bear of the mountains,
From the terror of the nations,
As he lay asleep and cumbrous
On the summit of the mountains,
Like a rock with mosses on it,
Spotted brown and gray with mosses.

Silently he stole upon him,
Till the red nails of the monster
Almost touched him, almost scared him,
Till the hot breath of his nostrils
Warmed the hands of Mudjekeewis,
As he drew the Belt of Wampum
Over the round ears, that heard not,
Over the small eyes, that saw not,
Over the long nose and nostrils,
The black muffle of the nostrils,
Out of which the heavy breathing
Warmed the hands of Mudjekeewis.

Then he swung aloft his war-club,
Shouted loud and long his war-cry,
Smote the mighty Mishe-Mokwa
In the middle of the forehead,
Right between the eyes he smote him.

With the heavy blow bewildered,
Rose the Great Bear of the mountains ;
But his knees beneath him trembled,
And he whimpered like a woman,
As he reeled and staggered forward,
As he sat upon his haunches ;
And the mighty Mudjekeewis,

Standing fearlessly before him,
Taunted him in loud derision,
Spake disdainfully in this wise : —
"Hark you, Bear ! you are a coward
And no Brave, as you pretended ;
Else you would not cry and whimper
Like a miserable woman !
Bear ! you know our tribes are hostile,
Long have been at war together ;
Now you find that we are strongest,
You go sneaking in the forest,
You go hiding in the mountains !
Had you conquered me in battle
Not a groan would I have uttered ;
But you, Bear ! sit here and whimper,
And disgrace your tribe by crying,
Like a wretched Shaugodaya,
Like a cowardly old woman ! "

Then again he raised his war-club,
Smote again the Mishe-Mokwa
In the middle of his forehead,
Broke his skull, as ice is broken
When one goes to fish in Winter.
Thus was slain the Mishe-Mokwa,
He the Great Bear of the mountains,
He the terror of the nations.

"Honor be to Mudjekeewis ! "
With a shout exclaimed the people,
"Honor be to Mudjekeewis !
Henceforth he shall be the West-Wind,
And hereafter and forever
Shall he hold supreme dominion
Over all the winds of heaven.
Call him no more Mudjekeewis,
Call him Kabeyun, the West-Wind ! "

Thus was Mudjekeewis chosen
Father of the Winds of Heaven.
For himself he kept the West-Wind,
Gave the others to his children ;
Unto Wabun gave the East-Wind,
Gave the South to Shawondasee,
And the North-Wind, wild and cruel,
To the fierce Kabibonokka.

Young and beautiful was Wabun ;
He it was who brought the morning,
He it was whose silver arrows
Chased the dark o'er hill and valley ;
He it was whose cheeks were painted
With the brightest streaks of crimson,
And whose voice awoke the village,
Called the deer, and called the hunter.

Lonely in the sky was Wabun ;
Though the birds sang gayly to him,
Though the wild-flowers of the meadow
Filled the air with odors for him,
Though the forests and the rivers
Sang and shouted at his coming,

"Heaped the snow in drifts around it."   Page 145.

THE FOUR WINDS. 145

Still his heart was sad within him,
For he was alone in heaven.
 But one morning, gazing earthward,
While the village still was sleeping,
And the fog lay on the river,
Like a ghost, that goes at sunrise,
He beheld a maiden walking
All alone upon a meadow,
Gathering water-flags and rushes
By a river in the meadow.
 Every morning, gazing earthward,
Still the first thing he beheld there
Was her blue eyes looking at him,
Two blue lakes among the rushes.
And he loved the lonely maiden,
Who thus waited for his coming ;
For they both were solitary,
She on earth and he in heaven.
 And he wooed her with caresses,
Wooed her with his smile of sunshine,
With his flattering words he wooed her,
With his sighing and his singing,
Gentlest whispers in the branches,
Softest music, sweetest odors,
Till he drew her to his bosom,
Folded in his robes of crimson,
Till into a star he changed her,
Trembling still upon his bosom ;
And forever in the heavens
They are seen together walking,
Wabun and the Wabun-Annung,
Wabun and the Star of Morning.
 But the fierce Kabibonokka
Had his dwelling among icebergs,
In the everlasting snow-drifts,
In the kingdom of Wabasso,
In the land of the White Rabbit.
He it was whose hand in Autumn
Painted all the trees with scarlet,
Stained the leaves with red and yellow;
He it was who sent the snow-flakes,
Sifting, hissing through the forest,
Froze the ponds, the lakes, the rivers,
Drove the loon and sea-gull southward,
Drove the cormorant and curlew
To their nests of sedge and sea-tang
In the realms of Shawondasee.
 Once the fierce Kabibonokka
Issued from his lodge of snow-drifts,
From his home among the icebergs,
And his hair, with snow besprinkled,
Streamed behind him like a river,
Like a black and wintry river,
As he howled and hurried southward,
Over frozen lakes and moorlands.
 There among the reeds and rushes
Found he Shingebis, the diver,

Trailing strings of fish behind him,
O'er the frozen fens and moorlands,
Lingering still among the moorlands,
Though his tribe had long departed
To the land of Shawondasee.
 Cried the fierce Kabibonokka,
" Who is this that dares to brave me ?
Dares to stay in my dominions,
When the Wawa has departed,
When the wild-goose has gone south
      ward,
And the heron, the Shuh-shuh-gah,
Long ago departed southward ?
I will go into his wigwam,
I will put his smouldering fire out ! "
 And at night Kabibonokka
To the lodge came wild and wailing,
Heaped the snow in drifts about it,
Shouted down into the smoke-flue,
Shook the lodge-poles in his fury,
Flapped the curtain of the door-way.
Shingebis, the diver, feared not,
Shingebis, the diver, cared not ;
Four great logs had he for firewood,
One for each moon of the winter,
And for food the fishes served him.
By his blazing fire he sat there,
Warm and merry, eating, laughing,
Singing, " O Kabibonokka,
You are but my fellow-mortal ! "
 Then Kabibonokka entered,
And though Shingebis, the diver,
Felt his presence by the coldness,
Felt his icy breath upon him,
Still he did not cease his singing,
Still he did not leave his laughing,
Only turned the log a little,
Only made the fire burn brighter,
Made the sparks fly up the smoke-flue
 From Kabibonokka's forehead,
From his snow-besprinkled tresses,
Drops of sweat fell fast and heavy,
Making dints upon the ashes,
As along the eaves of lodges,
As from drooping boughs of hemlock,
Drips the melting snow in spring-time,
Making hollows in the snow-drifts.
 Till at last he rose defeated,
Could not bear the heat and laughter,
Could not bear the merry singing,
But rushed headlong through the door-
      way,
Stamped upon the crusted snow-drifts,
Stamped upon the lakes and rivers,
Made the snow upon them harder,
Made the ice upon them thicker,
Challenged Shingebis, the diver,

10

To come forth and wrestle with him,
To come forth and wrestle naked
On the frozen fens and moorlands.

Forth went Shingebis, the diver,
Wrestled all night with the North-Wind,
Wrestled naked on the moorlands
With the fierce Kabibonokka,
Till his panting breath grew fainter,
Till his frozen grasp grew feebler,
Till he reeled and staggered backward,
And retreated, baffled, beaten,
To the kingdom of Wabasso,
To the land of the White Rabbit,
Hearing still the gusty laughter,
Hearing Shingebis, the diver,
Singing, "O Kabibonokka,
You are but my fellow-mortal !"

Shawondasee, fat and lazy,
Had his dwelling far to southward,
In the drowsy, dreamy sunshine,
In the never-ending Summer.
He it was who sent the wood-birds,
Sent the robin, the Opechee,
Sent the bluebird, the Owaissa,
Sent the Shawshaw, sent the swallow,
Sent the wild-goose, Wawa, northward,
Sent the melons and tobacco,
And the grapes in purple clusters.

From his pipe the smoke ascending
Filled the sky with haze and vapor,
Filled the air with dreamy softness,
Gave a twinkle to the water,
Touched the rugged hills with smooth-
        ness,
Brought the tender Indian Summer
To the melancholy north-land,
In the dreary Moon of Snow-shoes.

Listless, careless Shawondasee !
In his life he had one shadow,
In his heart one sorrow had he.
Once, as he was gazing northward,
Far away upon a prairie
He beheld a maiden standing,
Saw a tall and slender maiden
All alone upon a prairie ;
Brightest green were all her garments,
And her hair was like the sunshine.

Day by day he gazed upon her,
Day by day he sighed with passion,
Day by day his heart within him
Grew more hot with love and longing
For the maid with yellow tresses.
But he was too fat and lazy
To bestir himself and woo her ;
Yes, too indolent and easy
To pursue her and persuade her.
So he only gazed upon her,

Only sat and sighed with passion
For the maiden of the prairie.

Till one morning, looking northward,
He beheld her yellow tresses
Changed and covered o'er with white-
        ness,
Covered as with whitest snow-flakes.
"Ah ! my brother from the North-
        land,
From the kingdom of Wabasso,
From the land of the White Rabbit !
You have stolen the maiden from me,
You have laid your hand upon her,
You have wooed and won my maiden,
With your stories of the North-land !"

Thus the wretched Shawondasee
Breathed into the air his sorrow ;
And the South-Wind o'er the prairie
Wandered warm with sighs of passion,
With the sighs of Shawondasee,
Till the air seemed full of snow-flakes,
Full of thistle-down the prairie,
And the maid with hair like sunshine
Vanished from his sight forever ;
Never more did Shawondasee
See the maid with yellow tresses !

Poor, deluded Shawondasee !
'T was no woman that you gazed at,
'T was no maiden that you sighed for,
'T was the prairie dandelion
That through all the dreamy Summer
You had gazed at with such longing,
You had sighed for with such passion,
And had puffed away forever,
Blown into the air with sighing.
Ah ! deluded Shawondasee !

Thus the Four Winds were divided ;
Thus the sons of Mudjekeewis
Had their stations in the heavens,
At the corners of the heavens ;
For himself the West-Wind only
Kept the mighty Mudjekeewis.

III.

HIAWATHA'S CHILDHOOD.

DOWNWARD through the evening twi-
        light,
In the days that are forgotten,
In the unremembered ages,
From the full moon fell Nokomis,
Fell the beautiful Nokomis,
She a wife, but not a mother.

She was sporting with her women
Swinging in a swing of grape-vines,

When her rival, the rejected,
Full of jealousy and hatred,
Cut the leafy swing asunder,
Cut in twain the twisted grape-vines,
And Nokomis fell affrighted
Downward through the evening twilight,
On the Muskoday, the meadow,
On the prairie full of blossoms.
"See ! a star falls !" said the people ;
" From the sky a star is falling ! "
There among the ferns and mosses,
There among the prairie lilies,
On the Muskoday, the meadow,
In the moonlight and the starlight,
Fair Nokomis bore a daughter.
And she called her name Wenonah,
As the first-born of her daughters.
And the daughter of Nokomis
Grew up like the prairie lilies,
Grew a tall and slender maiden,
With the beauty of the moonlight,
With the beauty of the starlight.

And Nokomis warned her often,
Saying oft, and oft repeating,
" O, beware of Mudjekeewis,
Of the West-Wind, Mudjekeewis;
Listen not to what he tells you ;
Lie not down upon the meadow,
Stoop not down among the lilies,
Lest the West-Wind come and harm
    you ! "
But she heeded not the warning,
Heeded not those words of wisdom,
And the West-Wind came at evening,
Walking lightly o'er the prairie,
Whispering to the leaves and blossoms,
Bending low the flowers and grasses,
Found the beautiful Wenonah,
Lying there among the lilies,
Wooed her with his words of sweetness,
Wooed her with his soft caresses,
Till she bore a son in sorrow,
Bore a son of love and sorrow.

Thus was born my Hiawatha,
Thus was born the child of wonder ;
But the daughter of Nokomis,
Hiawatha's gentle mother,
In her anguish died deserted
By the West-Wind, false and faithless,
By the heartless Mudjekeewis.

For her daughter, long and loudly
Wailed and wept the sad Nokomis ;
" O that I were dead ! " she murmured,
" O that I were dead, as thou art !
No more work, and no more weeping,
Wahonowin ! Wahonowin ! "
By the shores of Gitche Gumee,

By the shining Big-Sea-Water,
Stood the wigwam of Nokomis,
Daughter of the Moon, Nokomis.
Dark behind it rose the forest,
Rose the black and gloomy pine-trees,
Rose the firs with cones upon them ;
Bright before it beat the water,
Beat the clear and sunny water,
Beat the shining Big-Sea-Water.
There the wrinkled, old Nokomis
Nursed the little Hiawatha,
Rocked him in his linden cradle,
Bedded soft in moss and rushes,
Safely bound with reindeer sinews ;
Stilled his fretful wail by saying,
" Hush ! the Naked Bear will hear
    thee ! "
Lulled him into slumber, singing,
" Ewa-yea ! my little owlet !
Who is this, that lights the wigwam ?
With his great eyes lights the wigwam ?
Ewa-yea ! my little owlet ! "
Many things Nokomis taught him
Of the stars that shine in heaven ;
Showed him Ishkoodah, the comet,
Ishkoodah, with fiery tresses ;
Showed the Death-Dance of the spirits,
Warriors with their plumes and war-
    clubs,
Flaring far away to northward
In the frosty nights of Winter ;
Showed the broad, white road in heaven,
Pathway of the ghosts, the shadows,
Running straight across the heavens,
Crowded with the ghosts, the shadows.
At the door on summer evenings
Sat the little Hiawatha ;
Heard the whispering of the pine-trees,
Heard the lapping of the water,
Sounds of music, words of wonder ;
" Minne-wawa ! " said the pine-trees,
" Mudway-aushka ! " said the water.
Saw the fire-fly, Wah-wah-taysee,
Flitting through the dusk of evening,
With the twinkle of its candle
Lighting up the brakes and bushes,
And he sang the song of children,
Sang the song Nokomis taught him :
" Wah-wah-taysee, little fire-fly,
Little, flitting, white-fire insect,
Little, dancing, white-fire creature,
Light me with your little candle,
Ere upon my bed I lay me,
Ere in sleep I close my eyelids ! "
Saw the moon rise from the water
Rippling, rounding from the water,
Saw the flecks and shadows on it,

Whispered, "What is that, Nokomis?"
And the good Nokomis answered:
"Once a warrior, very angry,
Seized his grandmother, and threw her
Up into the sky at midnight;
Right against the moon he threw her;
'T is her body that you see there."

Saw the rainbow in the heaven,
In the eastern sky, the rainbow,
Whispered, "What is that, Nokomis?"
And the good Nokomis answered:
"'T is the heaven of flowers you see
    there;
All the wild-flowers of the forest,
All the lilies of the prairie,
When on earth they fade and perish,
Blossom in that heaven above us."

When he heard the owls at midnight,
Hooting, laughing in the forest,
"What is that?" he cried in terror;
"What is that?" he said, "Nokomis?"
And the good Nokomis answered:
"That is but the owl and owlet,
Talking in their native language,
Talking, scolding at each other."

Then the little Hiawatha
Learned of every bird its language,
Learned their names and all their secrets,
How they built their nests in Summer,
Where they hid themselves in Winter,
Talked with them whene'er he met them,
Called them "Hiawatha's Chickens."

Of all beasts he learned the language,
Learned their names and all their secrets,
How the beavers built their lodges,
Where the squirrels hid their acorns,
How the reindeer ran so swiftly,
Why the rabbit was so timid,
Talked with them whene'er he met them,
Called them "Hiawatha's Brothers."

Then Iagoo, the great boaster,
He the marvellous story-teller,
He the traveller and the talker,
He the friend of old Nokomis,
Made a bow for Hiawatha;
From a branch of ash he made it,
From an oak-bough made the arrows,
Tipped with flint, and winged with
    feathers,
And the cord he made of deer-skin.

Then he said to Hiawatha:
"Go, my son, into the forest,
Where the red deer herd together,
Kill for us a famous roebuck,
Kill for us a deer with antlers!"

Forth into the forest straightway
All alone walked Hiawatha

Proudly, with his bow and arrows;
And the birds sang round him, o'er him,
"Do not shoot us, Hiawatha!"
Sang the robin, the Opechee,
Sang the bluebird, the Owaissa,
"Do not shoot us, Hiawatha!"

Up the oak-tree, close beside him,
Sprang the squirrel, Adjidaumo,
In and out among the branches,
Coughed and chattered from the oak-tree,
Laughed, and said between his laughing,
"Do not shoot me, Hiawatha!"

And the rabbit from his pathway
Leaped aside, and at a distance
Sat erect upon his haunches,
Half in fear and half in frolic,
Saying to the little hunter,
"Do not shoot me, Hiawatha!"

But he heeded not, nor heard them,
For his thoughts were with the red deer;
On their tracks his eyes were fastened,
Leading downward to the river,
To the ford across the river,
And as one in slumber walked he.

Hidden in the alder-bushes,
There he waited till the deer came,
Till he saw two antlers lifted,
Saw two eyes look from the thicket,
Saw two nostrils point to windward,
And a deer came down the pathway,
Flecked with leafy light and shadow.
And his heart within him fluttered,
Trembled like the leaves above him,
Like the birch-leaf palpitated,
As the deer came down the pathway.

Then, upon one knee uprising,
Hiawatha aimed an arrow;
Scarce a twig moved with his motion,
Scarce a leaf was stirred or rustled,
But the wary roebuck started,
Stamped with all his hoofs together,
Listened with one foot uplifted,
Leaped as if to meet the arrow;
Ah! the singing, fatal arrow,
Like a wasp it buzzed and stung him!

Dead he lay there in the forest,
By the ford across the river;
Beat his timid heart no longer,
But the heart of Hiawatha
Throbbed and shouted and exulted,
As he bore the red deer homeward,
And Iagoo and Nokomis
Hailed his coming with applauses.

From the red deer's hide Nokomis
Made a cloak for Hiawatha,
From the red deer's flesh Nokomis
Made a banquet in his honor.

All the village came and feasted,
All the guests praised Hiawatha,
Called him Strong-Heart, Soan-ge-taha!
Called him Loon-Heart, Mahn-go-taysee!

IV.

HIAWATHA AND MUDJEKEEWIS.

OUT of childhood into manhood
Now had grown my Hiawatha,
Skilled in all the craft of hunters,
Learned in all the lore of old men,
In all youthful sports and pastimes,
In all manly arts and labors.

Swift of foot was Hiawatha;
He could shoot an arrow from him,
And run forward with such fleetness,
That the arrow fell behind him!
Strong of arm was Hiawatha;
He could shoot ten arrows upward,
Shoot them with such strength and swiftness,
That the tenth had left the bow-string
Ere the first to earth had fallen!

He had mittens, Minjekahwun,
Magic mittens made of deer-skin;
When upon his hands he wore them,
He could smite the rocks asunder,
He could grind them into powder.
He had moccasins enchanted,
Magic moccasins of deer-skin;
When he bound them round his ankles,
When upon his feet he tied them,
At each stride a mile he measured!

Much he questioned old Nokomis
Of his father Mudjekeewis;
Learned from her the fatal secret
Of the beauty of his mother,
Of the falsehood of his father;
And his heart was hot within him,
Like a living coal his heart was.

Then he said to old Nokomis,
"I will go to Mudjekeewis,
See how fares it with my father,
At the doorways of the West-Wind,
At the portals of the Sunset!"

From his lodge went Hiawatha,
Dressed for travel, armed for hunting;
Dressed in deer-skin shirt and leggings,
Richly wrought with quills and wampum;
On his head his eagle-feathers,
Round his waist his belt of wampum,
In his hand his bow of ash-wood,
Strung with sinews of the reindeer;
In his quiver oaken arrows,

Tipped with jasper, winged with feathers;
With his mittens, Minjekahwun,
With his moccasins enchanted.

Warning said the old Nokomis,
"Go not forth, O Hiawatha!
To the kingdom of the West-Wind,
To the realms of Mudjekeewis,
Lest he harm you with his magic,
Lest he kill you with his cunning!"

But the fearless Hiawatha
Heeded not her woman's warning;
Forth he strode into the forest,
At each stride a mile he measured;
Lurid seemed the sky above him,
Lurid seemed the earth beneath him,
Hot and close the air around him,
Filled with smoke and fiery vapors,
As of burning woods and prairies,
For his heart was hot within him,
Like a living coal his heart was.

So he journeyed westward, westward,
Left the fleetest deer behind him,
Left the antelope and bison;
Crossed the rushing Esconaba,
Crossed the mighty Mississippi,
Passed the Mountains of the Prairie,
Passed the land of Crows and Foxes,
Passed the dwellings of the Blackfeet,
Came unto the Rocky Mountains,
To the kingdom of the West-Wind,
Where upon the gusty summits
Sat the ancient Mudjekeewis,
Ruler of the winds of heaven.

Filled with awe was Hiawatha
At the aspect of his father.
On the air about him wildly
Tossed and streamed his cloudy tresses,
Gleamed like drifting snow his tresses,
Glared like Ishkoodah, the comet,
Like the star with fiery tresses.

Filled with joy was Mudjekeewis
When he looked on Hiawatha,
Saw his youth rise up before him
In the face of Hiawatha,
Saw the beauty of Wenonah
From the grave rise up before him.

"Welcome!" said he, "Hiawatha,
To the kingdom of the West-Wind!
Long have I been waiting for you!
Youth is lovely, age is lonely,
Youth is fiery, age is frosty;
You bring back the days departed,
You bring back my youth of passion,
And the beautiful Wenonah!"

Many days they talked together,
Questioned, listened, waited, answered;
Much the mighty Mudjekeewis

Boasted of his ancient prowess,
Of his perilous adventures,
His indomitable courage,
His invulnerable body.
  Patiently sat Hiawatha,
Listening to his father's boasting;
With a smile he sat and listened,
Uttered neither threat nor menace,
Neither word nor look betrayed him,
But his heart was hot within him,
Like a living coal his heart was.
  Then he said, "O Mudjekeewis,
Is there nothing that can harm you?
Nothing that you are afraid of?"
And the mighty Mudjekeewis,
Grand and gracious in his boasting,
Answered, saying, "There is nothing,
Nothing but the black rock yonder,
Nothing but the fatal Wawbeek?"
  And he looked at Hiawatha
With a wise look and benignant,
With a countenance paternal,
Looked with pride upon the beauty
Of his tall and graceful figure,
Saying, "O my Hiawatha!
Is there anything can harm you?
Anything you are afraid of?"
  But the wary Hiawatha
Paused awhile, as if uncertain,
Held his peace, as if resolving,
And then answered, "There is nothing,
Nothing but the bulrush yonder,
Nothing but the great Apukwa!"
  And as Mudjekeewis, rising,
Stretched his hand to pluck the bulrush,
Hiawatha cried in terror,
Cried in well-dissembled terror,
"Kago! kago! do not touch it!"
"Ah, kaween!" said Mudjekeewis,
"No indeed, I will not touch it!"
  Then they talked of other matters;
First of Hiawatha's brothers,
First of Wabun, of the East-Wind,
Of the South-Wind, Shawondasee,
Of the North, Kabibonokka;
Then of Hiawatha's mother,
Of the beautiful Wenonah,
Of her birth upon the meadow,
Of her death, as old Nokomis
Had remembered and related.
  And he cried, "O Mudjekeewis,
It was you who killed Wenonah,
Took her young life and her beauty,
Broke the Lily of the Prairie,
Trampled it beneath your footsteps;
You confess it! you confess it!"
And the mighty Mudjekeewis

Tossed upon the wind his tresses,
Bowed his hoary head in anguish,
With a silent nod assented.
  Then up started Hiawatha,
And with threatening look and gesture
Laid his hand upon the black rock,
On the fatal Wawbeek laid it,
With his mittens, Minjekahwun,
Rent the jutting crag asunder,
Smote and crushed it into fragments,
Hurled them madly at his father,
The remorseful Mudjekeewis,
For his heart was hot within him,
Like a living coal his heart was.
  But the ruler of the West-Wind
Blew the fragments backward from him,
With the breathing of his nostrils,
With the tempest of his anger,
Blew them back at his assailant;
Seized the bulrush, the Apukwa,
Dragged it with its roots and fibres
From the margin of the meadow,
From its ooze, the giant bulrush;
Long and loud laughed Hiawatha!
  Then began the deadly conflict,
Hand to hand among the mountains;
From his eyry screamed the eagle,
The Keneu, the great war-eagle,
Sat upon the crags around them,
Wheeling flapped his wings above them.
  Like a tall tree in the tempest
Bent and lashed the giant bulrush;
And in masses huge and heavy
Crashing fell the fatal Wawbeek;
Till the earth shook with the tumult
And confusion of the battle,
And the air was full of shoutings,
And the thunder of the mountains,
Starting, answered, "Baim-wawa!"
  Back retreated Mudjekeewis,
Rushing westward o'er the mountains,
Stumbling westward down the moun-
    tains,
Three whole days retreated fighting
Still pursued by Hiawatha
To the doorways of the West-Wind,
To the portals of the Sunset,
To the earth's remotest border,
Where into the empty spaces
Sinks the sun, as a flamingo
Drops into her nest at nightfall,
In the melancholy marshes.
  "Hold!" at length cried Mudjekee-
    wis,
"Hold, my son, my Hiawatha!
'T is impossible to kill me,
For you cannot kill the immortal.

I have put you to this trial,
But to know and prove your courage ;
Now receive the prize of valor !
   "Go back to your home and people,
Live among them, toil among them,
Cleanse the earth from all that harms it,
Clear the fishing-grounds and rivers,
Slay all monsters and magicians,
All the Wendigoes, the giants,
All the serpents, the Kenabeeks,
As I slew the Mishe-Mokwa,
Slew the Great Bear of the mountains.
   "And at last when Death draws near
        you,
When the awful eyes of Pauguk
Glare upon you in the darkness,
I will share my kingdom with you,
Ruler shall you be thenceforward
Of the Northwest-Wind, Keewaydin,
Of the home-wind, the Keewaydin."
   Thus was fought that famous battle
In the dreadful days of Shah-shah,
In the days long since departed,
In the kingdom of the West-Wind.
Still the hunter sees its traces
Scattered far o'er hill and valley ;
Sees the giant bulrush growing
By the ponds and water-courses,
Sees the masses of the Wawbeek
Lying still in every valley.
   Homeward now went Hiawatha ;
Pleasant was the landscape round him,
Pleasant was the air above him,
For the bitterness of anger
Had departed wholly from him,
From his brain the thought of vengeance,
From his heart the burning fever.
   Only once his pace he slackened,
Only once he paused or halted,
Paused to purchase heads of arrows
Of the ancient Arrow-maker,
In the land of the Dacotahs,
Where the Falls of Minnehaha
Flash and gleam among the oak-trees,
Laugh and leap into the valley.
   There the ancient Arrow-maker
Made his arrow-heads of sandstone,
Arrow-heads of chalcedony,
Arrow-heads of flint and jasper,
Smoothed and sharpened at the edges,
Hard and polished, keen and costly.
   With him dwelt his dark-eyed daugh-
        ter,
Wayward as the Minnehaha,
With her moods of shade and sunshine,
Eyes that smiled and frowned alternate,
Feet as rapid as the river,

Tresses flowing like the water,
And as musical a laughter ;
And he named her from the river,
From the water-fall he named her,
Minnehaha, Laughing Water.
   Was it then for heads of arrows,
Arrow-heads of chalcedony,
Arrow-heads of flint and jasper,
That my Hiawatha halted
In the land of the Dacotahs ?
   Was it not to see the maiden,
See the face of Laughing Water
Peeping from behind the curtain,
Hear the rustling of her garments
From behind the waving curtain,
As one sees the Minnehaha
Gleaming, glancing through the branch
        es,
As one hears the Laughing Water
From behind its screen of branches ?
   Who shall say what thoughts and
        visions
Fill the fiery brains of young men ?
Who shall say what dreams of beauty
Filled the heart of Hiawatha ?
All he told to old Nokomis,
When he reached the lodge at sunset,
Was the meeting with his father,
Was his fight with Mudjekeewis ;
Not a word he said of arrows,
Not a word of Laughing Water.

V.

HIAWATHA'S FASTING.

You shall hear how Hiawatha
Prayed and fasted in the forest,
Not for greater skill in hunting,
Not for greater craft in fishing,
Not for triumphs in the battle,
And renown among the warriors,
But for profit of the people,
For advantage of the nations.
   First he built a lodge for fasting,
Built a wigwam in the forest,
By the shining Big-Sea-Water,
In the blithe and pleasant Spring-time,
In the Moon of Leaves he built it,
And, with dreams and visions many,
Seven whole days and nights he fasted.
   On the first day of his fasting
Through the leafy woods he wandered ;
Saw the deer start from the thicket,
Saw the rabbit in his burrow,
Heard the pheasant, Bena, drumming,

Heard the squirrel, Adjidaumo,
Rattling in his hoard of acorns,
Saw the pigeon, the Omeme,
Building nests among the pine-trees,
And in flocks the wild goose, Wawa,
Flying to the fen-lands northward,
Whirring, wailing far above him,
"Master of Life !" he cried, despond-
    ing,
"Must our lives depend on these
    things ?"
    On the next day of his fasting
By the river's brink he wandered,
Through the Muskoday, the meadow,
Saw the wild rice, Mahnomonee,
Saw the blueberry, Meenahga,
And the strawberry, Odahmin,
And the gooseberry, Shahbomin,
And the grape-vine, the Bemahgut,
Trailing o'er the alder-branches,
Filling all the air with fragrance !
"Master of Life !" he cried, desponding,
"Must our lives depend on these
    things ?"
    On the third day of his fasting
By the lake he sat and pondered,
By the still, transparent water ;
Saw the sturgeon, Nahma, leaping,
Scattering drops like beads of wampum,
Saw the yellow perch, the Sahwa,
Like a sunbeam in the water,
Saw the pike, the Maskenozha,
And the herring, Okahahwis,
And the Shawgashee, the craw-fish !
"Master of Life !" he cried, despond-
    ing,
"Must our lives depend on these
    things ?"
    On the fourth day of his fasting
In his lodge he lay exhausted ;
From his couch of leaves and branches
Gazing with half-open eyelids,
Full of shadowy dreams and visions,
On the dizzy, swimming landscape,
On the gleaming of the water,
On the splendor of the sunset.
    And he saw a youth approaching,
Dressed in garments green and yellow
Coming through the purple twilight,
Through the splendor of the sunset ;
Plumes of green bent o'er his forehead,
And his hair was soft and golden.
    Standing at the open doorway,
Long he looked at Hiawatha,
Looked with pity and compassion
On his wasted form and features,
And, in accents like the sighing

Of the South-Wind in the tree-tops,
Said he, "O my Hiawatha !
All your prayers are heard in heaven,
For you pray not like the others ;
Not for greater skill in hunting,
Not for greater craft in fishing,
Not for triumph in the battle,
Nor renown among the warriors,
But for profit of the people,
For advantage of the nations.
    "From the Master of Life descending,
I, the friend of man, Mondamin,
Come to warn you and instruct you,
How by struggle and by labor
You shall gain what you have prayed for.
Rise up from your bed of branches,
Rise, O youth, and wrestle with me !"
    Faint with famine, Hiawatha
Started from his bed of branches,
From the twilight of his wigwam
Forth into the flush of sunset
Came, and wrestled with Mondamin ,
At his touch he felt new courage
Throbbing in his brain and bosom,
Felt new life and hope and vigor
Run through every nerve and fibre.
    So they wrestled there together
In the glory of the sunset,
And the more they strove and struggled,
Stronger still grew Hiawatha ;
Till the darkness fell around them,
And the heron, the Shuh-shuh-gah,
From her nest among the pine-trees,
Gave a cry of lamentation,
Gave a scream of pain and famine.
    "'T is enough !" then said Mondamin,
Smiling upon Hiawatha,
"But to-morrow, when the sun sets,
I will come again to try you."
And he vanished, and was seen not ;
Whether sinking as the rain sinks,
Whether rising as the mists rise,
Hiawatha saw not, knew not,
Only saw that he had vanished,
Leaving him alone and fainting,
With the misty lake below him,
And the reeling stars above him.
    On the morrow and the next day,
When the sun through heaven descend-
    ing,
Like a red and burning cinder
From the hearth of the Great Spirit,
Fell into the western waters,
Came Mondamin for the trial,
For the strife with Hiawatha ;
Came as silent as the dew comes,
From the empty air appearing,

Into empty air returning,
Taking shape when earth it touches,
But invisible to all men
In its coming and its going.
　Thrice they wrestled there together
In the glory of the sunset,
Till the darkness fell around them,
Till the heron, the Shuh-shuh-gah,
From her nest among the pine-trees,
Uttered her loud cry of famine,
And Mondamin paused to listen.
　Tall and beautiful he stood there,
In his garments green and yellow ;
To and fro his plumes above him
Waved and nodded with his breathing,
And the sweat of the encounter
Stood like drops of dew upon him.
　And he cried, "O Hiawatha !
Bravely have you wrestled with me,
Thrice have wrestled stoutly with me,
And the Master of Life, who sees us,
He will give to you the triumph !"
　Then he smiled, and said : "To-mor-
　　row
Is the last day of your conflict,
Is the last day of your fasting.
You will conquer and o'ercome me ;
Make a bed for me to lie in,
Where the rain may fall upon me,
Where the sun may come and warm me ;
Strip these garments, green and yellow,
Strip this nodding plumage from me,
Lay me in the earth, and make it
Soft and loose and light above me.
　"Let no hand disturb my slumber,
Let no weed nor worm molest me,
Let not Kahgahgee, the raven,
Come to haunt me and molest me,
Only come yourself to watch me,
Till I wake, and start, and quicken,
Till I leap into the sunshine."
　And thus saying, he departed ;
Peacefully slept Hiawatha,
But he heard the Wawonaissa,
Heard the whippoorwill complaining,
Perched upon his lonely wigwam ;
Heard the rushing Sebowisha,
Heard the rivulet rippling near him,
Talking to the darksome forest ;
Heard the sighing of the branches,
As they lifted and subsided
At the passing of the night-wind,
Heard them, as one hears in slumber
Far-off murmurs, dreamy whispers :
Peacefully slept Hiawatha.
　On the morrow came Nokomis,
On the seventh day of his fasting,

Came with food for Hiawatha,
Came imploring and bewailing,
Lest his hunger should o'ercome him,
Lest his fasting should be fatal.
　But he tasted not, and touched not,
Only said to her, "Nokomis,
Wait until the sun is setting,
Till the darkness falls around us,
Till the heron, the Shuh-shuh-gah,
Crying from the desolate marshes,
Tells us that the day is ended."
　Homeward weeping went Nokomis,
Sorrowing for her Hiawatha,
Fearing lest his strength should fail him,
Lest his fasting should be fatal.
He meanwhile sat weary waiting
For the coming of Mondamin,
Till the shadows, pointing eastward,
Lengthened over field and forest,
Till the sun dropped from the heaven,
Floating on the waters westward,
As a red leaf in the Autumn
Falls and floats upon the water,
Falls and sinks into its bosom.
　And behold ! the young Mondamin,
With his soft and shining tresses,
With his garments green and yellow,
With his long and glossy plumage,
Stood and beckoned at the doorway.
And as one in slumber walking,
Pale and haggard, but undaunted,
From the wigwam Hiawatha
Came and wrestled with Mondamin.
　Round about him spun the landscape,
Sky and forest reeled together,
And his strong heart leaped within him,
As the sturgeon leaps and struggles
In a net to break its meshes.
Like a ring of fire around him
Blazed and flared the red horizon,
And a hundred suns seemed looking
At the combat of the wrestlers.
　Suddenly upon the greensward
All alone stood Hiawatha,
Panting with his wild exertion,
Palpitating with the struggle ;
And before him, breathless, lifeless,
Lay the youth, with hair dishevelled,
Plumage torn, and garments tattered,
Dead he lay there in the sunset.
　And victorious Hiawatha
Made the grave as he commanded,
Stripped the garments from Mondamin,
Stripped his tattered plumage from him,
Laid him in the earth, and made it
Soft and loose and light above him ;
And the heron, the Shuh-shuh-gah,

From the melancholy moorlands,
Gave a cry of lamentation,
Gave a cry of pain and anguish !
   Homeward then went Hiawatha
To the lodge of old Nokomis,
And the seven days of his fasting
Were accomplished and completed.
But the place was not forgotten
Where he wrestled with Mondamin ;
Nor fŏrgotten nor neglected
Was the grave where lay Mondamin,
Sleeping in the rain and sunshine,
Where his scattered plumes and garments
Faded in the rain and sunshine.
   Day by day did Hiawatha
Go to wait and watch beside it ;
Kept the dark mould soft above it,
Kept it clean from weeds and insects,
Drove away, with scoffs and shoutings,
Kahgahgee, the king of ravens.
   Till at length a small green feather
From the earth shot slowly upward,
Then another and another,
And before the Summer ended
Stood the maize in all its beauty,
With its shining robes about it,
And its long, soft, yellow tresses ;
And in rapture Hiawatha
Cried aloud, " It is Mondamin !
Yes, the friend of man, Mondamin ! "
   Then he called to old Nokomis
And Iagoo, the great boaster,
Showed them where the maize was grow-
   ing,
Told them of his wondrous vision,
Of his wrestling and his triumph,
Of this new gift to the nations,
Which should be their food forever.
   And still later, when the Autumn
Changed the long, green leaves to yellow,
And the soft and juicy kernels
Grew like wampum hard and yellow,
Then the ripened **ears** he gathered,
Stripped the withered husks from off
   them,
As he once had stripped the wrestler,
Gave the first Feast of Mondamin,
And made known unto the people
This new gift of the Great Spirit.

VI.

HIAWATHA'S FRIENDS.

Two good friends had Hiawatha,
Singled out from all the others,
Bound to him in closest union,
And to whom he gave the right hand
Of his heart, in joy and sorrow ;
Chibiabos, the musician,
And the very strong man, Kwasind.
   Straight between them ran the path
      way,
Never grew the grass upon it ;
Singing birds, that utter falsehoods,
Story-tellers, mischief-makers,
Found no eager ear to listen,
Could not breed ill-will between them,
For they kept each other's counsel,
Spake with naked hearts together,
Pondering much and much contriving
How the tribes of men might prosper.
   Most beloved by Hiawatha
Was the gentle Chibiabos,
He the best of all musicians,
He the sweetest of all singers.
Beautiful and childlike was he,
Brave as man is, soft as woman,
Pliant as a wand of willow,
Stately as a deer with antlers.
   When he sang, the village listened ;
All the warriors gathered round him,
All the women came to hear him ;
Now he stirred their souls to passion,
Now he melted them to pity.
   From the hollow reeds he fashioned
Flutes so musical and mellow,
That the brook, the Sebowisha,
Ceased to murmur in the woodland,
That the wood-birds ceased from singing
And the squirrel, Adjidaumo,
Ceased his chatter in the oak-tree,
And the rabbit, the Wabasso,
Sat upright to look and listen.
   Yes, the brook, the Sebowisha,
Pausing, said, " O Chibiabos,
Teach my waves to flow in music,
Softly as your words in singing ! "
   Yes, the bluebird, the Owaissa,
Envious, said, " O Chibiabos,
Teach me tones as wild and wayward,
Teach me songs as full of frenzy ! "
   Yes, the robin, the Opechee,
Joyous, said, " O Chibiabos,
Teach me tones as sweet and tender,
Teach me songs as full of gladness ! "
   And the whippoorwill, Wawonaissa,
Sobbing, said, " O Chibiabos,
Teach me tones as melancholy,
Teach me songs as full of sadness ! "
   All the many sounds of nature
Borrowed sweetness from his singing ;
All the hearts of men were softened

By the pathos of his music ;
For he sang of peace and freedom,
Sang of beauty, love, and longing ;
Sang of death, and life undying
In the Islands of the Blessed,
In the kingdom of Ponemah,
In the land of the Hereafter.

Very dear to Hiawatha
Was the gentle Chibiabos,
He the best of all musicians,
He the sweetest of all singers ;
For his gentleness he loved him,
And the magic of his singing.

Dear, too, unto Hiawatha
Was the very strong man, Kwasind,
He the strongest of all mortals,
He the mightiest among many ;
For his very strength he loved him,
For his strength allied to goodness.

Idle in his youth was Kwasind,
Very listless, dull, and dreamy,
Never played with other children,
Never fished and never hunted,
Not like other children was he ;
But they saw that much he fasted,
Much his Manito entreated,
Much besought his Guardian Spirit.

"Lazy Kwasind !" said his mother,
"In my work you never help me !
In the Summer you are roaming
Idly in the fields and forests ;
In the Winter you are cowering
O'er the firebrands in the wigwam ;
In the coldest days of Winter
I must break the ice for fishing ;
With my nets you never help me !
At the door my nets are hanging,
Dripping, freezing with the water ;
Go and wring them, Yenadizze !
Go and dry them in the sunshine ! "

Slowly, from the ashes, Kwasind
Rose, but made no angry answer ;
From the lodge went forth in silence,
Took the nets, that hung together,
Dripping, freezing at the doorway,
Like a wisp of straw he wrung them,
Like a wisp of straw he broke them,
Could not wring them without breaking,
Such the strength was in his fingers.

"Lazy Kwasind !" said his father,
"In the hunt you never help me ;
Every bow you touch is broken,
Snapped asunder every arrow ;
Yet come with me to the forest,
You shall bring the hunting homeward."

Down a narrow pass they wandered,
Where a brooklet led them onward,

Where the trail of deer and bison
Marked the soft mud on the margin,
Till they found all further passage
Shut against them, barred securely
By the trunks of trees uprooted,
Lying lengthwise, lying crosswise,
And forbidding further passage.

" We must go back," said the old man,
" O'er these logs we cannot clamber ;
Not a woodchuck could get through them,
Not a squirrel clamber o'er them ! "
And straightway his pipe he lighted,
And sat down to smoke and ponder.
But before his pipe was finished,
Lo ! the path was cleared before him ;
All the trunks had Kwasind lifted,
To the right hand, to the left hand,
Shot the pine-trees swift as arrows,
Hurled the cedars light as lances.

"Lazy Kwasind !" said the young men,
As they sported in the meadow :
" Why stand idly looking at us,
Leaning on the rock behind you ?
Come and wrestle with the others,
Let us pitch the quoit together ! "

Lazy Kwasind made no answer,
To their challenge made no answer,
Only rose, and, slowly turning,
Seized the huge rock in his fingers,
Tore it from its deep foundation,
Poised it in the air a moment,
Pitched it sheer into the river,
Sheer into the swift Pauwating,
Where it still is seen in Summer.

Once as down that foaming river,
Down the rapids of Pauwating,
Kwasind sailed with his companions,
In the stream he saw a beaver,
Saw Ahmeek, the King of Beavers,
Struggling with the rushing currents,
Rising, sinking in the water.

Without speaking, without pausing,
Kwasind leaped into the river,
Plunged beneath the bubbling surface,
Through the whirlpools chased the beaver,
Followed him among the islands,
Stayed so long beneath the water,
That his terrified companions
Cried, " Alas ! good by to Kwasind !
We shall never more see Kwasind ! "
But he reappeared triumphant,
And upon his shining shoulders
Brought the beaver, dead and dripping
Brought the King of all the Beavers.

And these two, as I have told you,

Were the friends of Hiawatha,
Chibiabos, the musician,
And the very strong man, Kwasind.
Long they lived in peace together,
Spake with naked hearts together,
Pondering much and much contriving
How the tribes of men might prosper.

VII.

HIAWATHA'S SAILING.

" Give me of your bark, O Birch-Tree !
Of your yellow bark, O Birch-Tree !
Growing by the rushing river,
Tall and stately in the valley !
I a light canoe will build me,
Build a swift Cheemaun for sailing,
That shall float upon the river,
Like a yellow leaf in Autumn,
Like a yellow water-lily !
   " Lay aside your cloak, O Birch-Tree !
Lay aside your white-skin wrapper,
For the Summer-time is coming,
And the sun is warm in heaven,
And you need no white-skin wrapper ! "
   Thus aloud cried Hiawatha
In the solitary forest,
By the rushing Taquamenaw,
When the birds were singing gayly,
In the Moon of Leaves were singing,
And the sun, from sleep awaking,
Started up and said, " Behold me !
Gheezis, the great Sun, behold me ! "
   And the tree with all its branches
Rustled in the breeze of morning,
Saying, with a sigh of patience,
" Take my cloak, O Hiawatha ! "
   With his knife the tree he girdled ;
Just beneath its lowest branches,
Just above the roots, he cut it,
Till the sap came oozing outward ;
Down the trunk, from top to bottom,
Sheer he cleft the bark asunder,
With a wooden wedge he raised it,
Stripped it from the trunk unbroken.
   "Give me of your boughs, O Cedar !
Of your strong and pliant branches,
My canoe to make more steady,
Make more strong and firm beneath me ! "
   Through the summit of the Cedar
Went a sound, a cry of horror,
Went a murmur of resistance ;
But it whispered, bending downward,
" Take my boughs, O Hiawatha ! "
   Down he hewed the boughs of cedar,

Shaped them straightway to a frame-
   work,
Like two bows he formed and shaped
   them,
Like two bended bows together.
   " Give me of your roots, O Tamarack !
Of your fibrous roots, O Larch-Tree !
My canoe to bind together,
So to bind the ends together
That the water may not enter,
That the river may not wet me ! "
   And the Larch, with all its fibres,
Shivered in the air of morning,
Touched his forehead with its tassels,
Said, with one long sigh of sorrow,
" Take them all, O Hiawatha ! "
   From the earth he tore the fibres,
Tore the tough roots of the Larch-Tree,
Closely sewed the bark together,
Bound it closely to the framework.
   Give me of your balm, O Fir-Tree !
Of your balsam and your resin,
So to close the seams together
That the water may not enter,
That the river may not wet me ! "
   And the Fir-Tree, tall and sombre,
Sobbed through all its robes of darkness,
Rattled like a shore with pebbles,
Answered wailing, answered weeping,
"Take my balm, O Hiawatha ! "
   And he took the tears of balsam,
Took the resin of the Fir-Tree,
Smeared therewith each seam and fissure,
Made each crevice safe from water.
   " Give me of your quills, O Hedgehog !
All your quills, O Kagh, the Hedgehog !
I will make a necklace of them,
Make a girdle for my beauty,
And two stars to deck her bosom ! "
   From a hollow tree the Hedgehog
With his sleepy eyes looked at him,
Shot his shining quills, like arrows,
Saying, with a drowsy murmur,
Through the tangle of his whiskers,
"Take my quills, O Hiawatha ! "
   From the ground the quills he gathered,
All the little shining arrows,
Stained them red and blue and yellow,
With the juice of roots and berries ;
Into his canoe he wrought them,
Round its waist a shining girdle,
Round its bows a gleaming necklace,
On its breast two stars resplendent.
   Thus the Birch Canoe was builded
In the valley, by the river,
In the bosom of the forest ;
And the forest's life was in it,

All its mystery and its magic,
All the lightness of the birch-tree,
All the toughness of the cedar,
All the larch's supple sinews ;
And it floated on the river
Like a yellow leaf in Autumn,
Like a yellow water-lily.

Paddles none had Hiawatha,
Paddles none he had or needed,
For his thoughts as paddles served him,
And his wishes served to guide him ;
Swift or slow at will he glided,
Veered to right or left at pleasure.

Then he called aloud to Kwasind,
To his friend, the strong man, Kwasind,
Saying, "Help me clear this river
Of its sunken logs and sand-bars."

Straight into the river Kwasind
Plunged as if he were an otter,
Dived as if he were a beaver,
Stood up to his waist in water,
To his arm-pits in the river,
Swam and shouted in the river,
Tugged at sunken logs and branches,
With his hands he scooped the sand-bars,
With his feet the ooze and tangle.

And thus sailed my Hiawatha
Down the rushing Taquamenaw,
Sailed through all its bends and windings,
Sailed through all its deeps and shallows,
While his friend, the strong man, Kwa-
sind,
Swam the deeps, the shallows waded.

Up and down the river went they,
In and out among its islands,
Cleared its bed of root and sand-bar,
Dragged the dead trees from its channel,
Made its passage safe and certain,
Made a pathway for the people,
From its springs among the mountains,
To the waters of Pauwating,
To the bay of Taquamenaw.

VIII.

HIAWATHA'S FISHING.

FORTH upon the Gitche Gumee,
On the shining Big-Sea-Water,
With his fishing-line of cedar,
Of the twisted bark of cedar,
Forth to catch the sturgeon Nahma,
Mishe-Nahma, King of Fishes,
In his birch canoe exulting
All alone went Hiawatha.

Through the clear, transparent water
He could see the fishes swimming
Far down in the depths below him ;
See the yellow perch, the Sahwa,
Like a sunbeam in the water,
See the Shawgashee, the craw-fish,
Like a spider on the bottom,
On the white and sandy bottom.

At the stern sat Hiawatha,
With his fishing-line of cedar ;
In his plumes the breeze of morning
Played as in the hemlock branches ;
On the bows, with tail erected,
Sat the squirrel, Adjidaumo ;
In his fur the breeze of morning
Played as in the prairie grasses.

On the white sand of the bottom
Lay the monster Mishe-Nahma,
Lay the sturgeon, King of Fishes ;
Through his gills he breathed the water,
With his fins he fanned and winnowed,
With his tail he swept the sand-floor.

There he lay in all his armor ;
On each side a shield to guard him,
Plates of bone upon his forehead,
Down his sides and back and shoulders
Plates of bone with spines projecting !
Painted was he with his war-paints,
Stripes of yellow, red, and azure,
Spots of brown and spots of sable ;
And he lay there on the bottom,
Fanning with his fins of purple,
As above him Hiawatha
In his birch canoe came sailing,
With his fishing-line of cedar.

"Take my bait," cried Hiawatha,
Down into the depths beneath him,
"Take my bait, O Sturgeon, Nahma !
Come up from below the water,
Let us see which is the stronger !"
And he dropped his line of cedar
Through the clear, transparent water,
Waited vainly for an answer,
Long sat waiting for an answer,
And repeating loud and louder,
"Take my bait, O King of Fishes !"

Quiet lay the sturgeon, Nahma,
Fanning slowly in the water,
Looking up at Hiawatha,
Listening to his call and clamor,
His unnecessary tumult,
Till he wearied of the shouting ;
And he said to the Kenozha,
To the pike, the Maskenozha,
"Take the bait of this rude fellow,
Break the line of Hiawatha !"

In his fingers Hiawatha
Felt the loose line jerk and tighten ;

As he drew it in, it tugged so
That the birch canoe stood endwise,
Like a birch log in the water,
With the squirrel, Adjidaumo,
Perched and frisking on the summit.

Full of scorn was Hiawatha
When he saw the fish rise upward,
Saw the pike, the Maskenozha,
Coming nearer, nearer to him,
And he shouted through the water,
"Esa! esa! shame upon you!
You are but the pike, Kenozha,
You are not the fish I wanted,
You are not the King of Fishes!"

Reeling downward to the bottom
Sank the pike in great confusion,
And the mighty sturgeon, Nahma,
Said to Ugudwash, the sun-fish,
To the bream, with scales of crimson,
"Take the bait of this great boaster,
Break the line of Hiawatha!"

Slowly upward, wavering, gleaming,
Rose the Ugudwash, the sun-fish,
Seized the line of Hiawatha,
Swung with all his weight upon it,
Made a whirlpool in the water,
Whirled the birch canoe in circles,
Round and round in gurgling eddies,
Till the circles in the water
Reached the far-off sandy beaches,
Till the water-flags and rushes
Nodded on the distant margins.

But when Hiawatha saw him
Slowly rising through the water,
Lifting up his disk refulgent,
Loud he shouted in derision,
"Esa! esa! shame upon you!
You are Ugudwash, the sun-fish,
You are not the fish I wanted,
You are not the King of Fishes!"

Slowly downward, wavering, gleam-
ing,
Sank the Ugudwash, the sun-fish,
And again the sturgeon, Nahma,
Heard the shout of Hiawatha,
Heard his challenge of defiance,
The unnecessary tumult,
Ringing far across the water.

From the white sand of the bottom
Up he rose with angry gesture,
Quivering in each nerve and fibre,
Clashing all his plates of armor,
Gleaming bright with all his war-paint;
In his wrath he darted upward,
Flashing leaped into the sunshine,
Opened his great jaws, and swallowed
Both canoe and Hiawatha.

Down into that darksome cavern
Plunged the headlong Hiawatha,
As a log on some black river
Shoots and plunges down the rapids,
Found himself in utter darkness,
Groped about in helpless wonder,
Till he felt a great heart beating,
Throbbing in that utter darkness.

And he smote it in his anger,
With his fist, the heart of Nahma,
Felt the mighty King of Fishes
Shudder through each nerve and fibre,
Heard the water gurgle round him
As he leaped and staggered through it
Sick at heart, and faint and weary.

Crosswise then did Hiawatha
Drag his birch-canoe for safety,
Lest from out the jaws of Nahma,
In the turmoil and confusion,
Forth he might be hurled and perish.
And the squirrel, Adjidaumo,
Frisked and chattered very gayly,
Toiled and tugged with Hiawatha
Till the labor was completed.

Then said Hiawatha to him,
"O my little friend, the squirrel,
Bravely have you toiled to help me
Take the thanks of Hiawatha,
And the name which now he gives you
For hereafter and forever
Boys shall call you Adjidaumo,
Tail-in-air the boys shall call you!"

And again the sturgeon, Nahma,
Gasped and quivered in the water,
Then was still, and drifted landward
Till he grated on the pebbles,
Till the listening Hiawatha
Heard him grate upon the margin,
Felt him strand upon the pebbles,
Knew that Nahma, King of Fishes,
Lay there dead upon the margin.

Then he heard a clang and flapping,
As of many wings assembling,
Heard a screaming and confusion,
As of birds of prey contending,
Saw a gleam of light above him,
Shining through the ribs of Nahma,
Saw the glittering eyes of sea-gulls,
Of Kayoshk, the sea-gulls, peering,
Gazing at him through the opening,
Heard them saying to each other,
"'T is our brother, Hiawatha!"

And he shouted from below them,
Cried exulting from the caverns:
"O ye sea-gulls! O my brothers!
I have slain the sturgeon, Nahma;
Make the rifts a little larger,

With your claws the openings widen,
Set me free from this dark prison,
And henceforward and forever
Men shall speak of your achievements,
Calling you Kayoshk, the sea-gulls,
Yes, Kayoshk, the Noble Scratchers!"
  And the wild and clamorous sea-
        gulls
Toiled with beak and claws together,
Made the rifts and openings wider
In the mighty ribs of Nahma,
And from peril and from prison,
From the body of the sturgeon,
From the peril of the water,
They released my Hiawatha.

  He was standing near his wigwam,
On the margin of the water,
And he called to old Nokomis,
Called and beckoned to Nokomis,
Pointed to the sturgeon, Nahma,
Lying lifeless on the pebbles,
With the sea-gulls feeding on him.

  "I have slain the Mishe-Nahma,
Slain the King of Fishes!" said he;
"Look! the sea-gulls feed upon him,
Yes, my friends Kayoshk, the sea-gulls;
Drive them not away, Nokomis,
They have saved me from great peril
In the body of the sturgeon,
Wait until their meal is ended,
Till their craws are full with feast-
        ing,
Till they homeward fly, at sunset,
To their nests among the marshes;
Then bring all your pots and kettles,
And make oil for us in Winter."

  And she waited till the sun set,
Till the pallid moon, the Night-sun,
Rose above the tranquil water,
Till Kayoshk, the sated sea-gulls,
From their banquet rose with clamor,
And across the fiery sunset
Winged their way to far-off islands,
To their nests among the rushes.

  To his sleep went Hiawatha,
And Nokomis to her labor,
Toiling patient in the moonlight,
Till the sun and moon changed places,
Till the sky was red with sunrise,
And Kayoshk, the hungry sea-gulls,
Came back from the reedy islands,
Clamorous for their morning banquet.

  Three whole days and nights alternate
Old Nokomis and the sea-gulls
Stripped the oily flesh of Nahma,
Till the waves washed through the rib-
        bones,

Till the sea-gulls came no longer,
And upon the sands lay nothing
But the skeleton of Nahma.

IX.

HIAWATHA AND THE PEARL-FEATHER.

On the shores of Gitche Gumee,
Of the shining Big-Sea-Water,
Stood Nokomis, the old woman,
Pointing with her finger westward,
O'er the water pointing westward,
To the purple clouds of sunset.

  Fiercely the red sun descending
Burned his way along the heavens,
Set the sky on fire behind him,
As war-parties, when retreating,
Burn the prairies on their war-trail;
And the moon, the Night-sun, eastward,
Suddenly starting from his ambush,
Followed fast those bloody footprints,
Followed in that fiery war-trail,
With its glare upon his features.

  And Nokomis, the old woman,
Pointing with her finger westward,
Spake these words to Hiawatha:
"Yonder dwells the great Pearl-Feather,
Megissogwon, the Magician,
Manito of Wealth and Wampum,
Guarded by his fiery serpents,
Guarded by the black pitch-water.
You can see his fiery serpents,
The Kenabeek, the great serpents,
Coiling, playing in the water;
You can see the black pitch-water
Stretching far away beyond them,
To the purple clouds of sunset!
"He it was who slew my father,
By his wicked wiles and cunning,
When he from the moon descended,
When he came on earth to seek me.
He, the mightiest of Magicians,
Sends the fever from the marshes,
Sends the pestilential vapors,
Sends the poisonous exhalations,
Sends the white fog from the fen-lands,
Sends disease and death among us!

  "Take your bow, O Hiawatha,
Take your arrows, jasper-headed,
Take your war-club, Puggawaugun,
And your mittens, Minjekahwun,
And your birch-canoe for sailing,
And the oil of Mishe-Nahma,
So to smear its sides, that swiftly
You may pass the black pitch-water

Slay this merciless magician,
Save the people from the fever
That he breathes across the fen-lands,
And avenge my father's murder!"
   Straightway then my Hiawatha
Armed himself with all his war-gear,
Launched his birch-canoe for sailing;
With his palm its sides he patted,
Said with glee, "Cheemaun, my darling,
O my Birch-Canoe! leap forward,
Where you see the fiery serpents,
Where you see the black pitch-water!"
   Forward leaped Cheemaun exulting,
And the noble Hiawatha
Sang his war-song wild and woful,
And above him the war-eagle,
The Keneu, the great war-eagle,
Master of all fowls with feathers,
Screamed and hurtled through the heav-
     ens.
   Soon he reached the fiery serpents,
The Kenabeek, the great serpents,
Lying huge upon the water,
Sparkling, rippling in the water,
Lying coiled across the passage,
With their blazing crests uplifted,
Breathing fiery fogs and vapors,
So that none could pass beyond them.
   But the fearless Hiawatha
Cried aloud, and spake in this wise:
"Let me pass my way, Kenabeek,
Let me go upon my journey!"
And they answered, hissing fiercely,
With their fiery breath made answer:
"Back, go back! O Shaugodaya!
Back to old Nokomis, Faint-heart!"
   Then the angry Hiawatha
Raised his mighty bow of ash-tree,
Seized his arrows, jasper-headed,
Shot them fast among the serpents;
Every twanging of the bow-string
Was a war-cry and a death-cry,
Every whizzing of an arrow
Was a death-song of Kenabeek.
   Weltering in the bloody water,
Dead lay all the fiery serpents,
And among them Hiawatha
Harmless sailed, and cried exulting:
"Onward, O Cheemaun, my darling!
Onward to the black pitch-water!"
   Then he took the oil of Nahma,
And the bows and sides anointed,
Smeared them well with oil, that swiftly
He might pass the black pitch-water.
   All night long he sailed upon it,
Sailed upon that sluggish water,
Covered with its mould of ages,

Black with rotting water-rushes,
Rank with flags and leaves of lilies,
Stagnant, lifeless, dreary, dismal,
Lighted by the shimmering moonlight,
And by will-o'-the-wisps illumined,
Fires by ghosts of dead men kindled,
In their weary night-encampments.
   All the air was white with moonlight,
All the water black with shadow,
And around him the Suggema,
The mosquito, sang his war-song,
And the fire-flies, Wah-wah-taysee,
Waved their torches to mislead him;
And the bull-frog, the Dahinda,
Thrust his head into the moonlight,
Fixed his yellow eyes upon him,
Sobbed and sank beneath the surface;
And anon a thousand whistles,
Answered over all the fen-lands,
And the heron, the Shuh-shuh-gah,
Far off on the reedy margin,
Heralded the hero's coming.
   Westward thus fared Hiawatha,
Toward the realm of Megissogwon,
Toward the land of the Pearl-Feather,
Till the level moon stared at him,
In his face stared pale and haggard,
Till the sun was hot behind him,
Till it burned upon his shoulders,
And before him on the upland
He could see the Shining Wigwam
Of the Manito of Wampum,
Of the mightiest of Magicians.
   Then once more Cheemaun he patted,
To his birch-canoe said, "Onward!"
And it stirred in all its fibres,
And with one great bound of triumph
Leaped across the water-lilies,
Leaped through tangled flags and rushes,
And upon the beach beyond them
Dry-shod landed Hiawatha.
   Straight he took his bow of ash-tree,
On the sand one end he rested,
With his knee he pressed the middle,
Stretched the faithful bow-string tighter,
Took an arrow, jasper-headed,
Shot it at the Shining Wigwam,
Sent it singing as a herald,
As a bearer of his message,
Of his challenge loud and lofty:
"Come forth from your lodge, Pearl-
     Feather!
Hiawatha waits your coming!"
   Straightway from the Shining Wigwam
Came the mighty Megissogwon,
Tall of stature, broad of shoulder,
Dark and terrible in aspect,

Clad from head to foot in wampum,
Armed with all his warlike weapons,
Painted like the sky of morning,
Streaked with crimson, blue, and yellow,
Crested with great eagle-feathers,
Streaming upward, streaming outward.
    "Well I know you, Hiawatha!"
Cried he in a voice of thunder,
In a tone of loud derision,
"Hasten back, O Shaugodaya!
Hasten back among the women,
Back to old Nokomis, Faint-heart!
I will slay you as you stand there,
As of old I slew her father!"
    But my Hiawatha answered,
Nothing daunted, fearing nothing:
"Big words do not smite like war-clubs,
Boastful breath is not a bow-string,
Taunts are not so sharp as arrows,
Deeds are better things than words are,
Actions mightier than boastings!"
    Then began the greatest battle
That the sun had ever looked on,
That the war-birds ever witnessed.
All a Summer's day it lasted,
From the sunrise to the sunset;
For the shafts of Hiawatha
Harmless hit the shirt of wampum,
Harmless fell the blows he dealt it
With his mittens, Minjekahwun,
Harmless fell the heavy war-club;
It could dash the rocks asunder,
But it could not break the meshes
Of that magic shirt of wampum.
    Till at sunset Hiawatha,
Leaning on his bow of ash-tree,
Wounded, weary, and desponding,
With his mighty war-club broken,
With his mittens torn and tattered,
And three useless arrows only,
Paused to rest beneath a pine-tree,
From whose branches trailed the mosses,
And whose trunk was coated over
With the Dead-man's Moccasin-leather,
With the fungus white and yellow.
    Suddenly from the boughs above him
Sang the Mama, the woodpecker:
"Aim your arrows, Hiawatha,
At the head of Megissogwon,
Strike the tuft of hair upon it,
At their roots the long black tresses;
There alone can he be wounded!"
    Winged with feathers, tipped with jas-
        per,
Swift flew Hiawatha's arrow,
Just as Megissogwon, stooping,
Raised a heavy stone to throw it.

Full upon the crown it struck him,
At the roots of his long tresses,
And he reeled and staggered forward,
Plunging like a wounded bison,
Yes, like Pezhekee, the bison,
When the snow is on the prairie.
    Swifter flew the second arrow,
In the pathway of the other,
Piercing deeper than the other,
Wounding sorer than the other,
And the knees of Megissogwon
Shook like windy reeds beneath him,
Bent and trembled like the rushes.
    But the third and latest arrow
Swiftest flew, and wounded sorest,
And the mighty Megissogwon
Saw the fiery eyes of Pauguk,
Saw the eyes of Death glare at him,
Heard his voice call in the darkness;
At the feet of Hiawatha
Lifeless lay the great Pearl-Feather,
Lay the mightiest of Magicians.
    Then the grateful Hiawatha
Called the Mama, the woodpecker,
From his perch among the branches
Of the melancholy pine-tree,
And, in honor of his service,
Stained with blood the tuft of feathers
On the little head of Mama;
Even to this day he wears it,
Wears the tuft of crimson feathers,
As a symbol of his service.
    Then he stripped the shirt of wampum
From the back of Megissogwon,
As a trophy of the battle,
As a signal of his conquest.
On the shore he left the body,
Half on land and half in water,
In the sand his feet were buried,
And his face was in the water.
And above him, wheeled and clamored
The Keneu, the great war-eagle,
Sailing round in narrower circles,
Hovering nearer, nearer, nearer.
    From the wigwam Hiawatha
Bore the wealth of Megissogwon,
All his wealth of skins and wampum,
Furs of bison and of beaver,
Furs of sable and of ermine,
Wampum belts and strings and pouches,
Quivers wrought with beads of wampum,
Filled with arrows, silver-headed.
    Homeward then he sailed exulting,
Homeward through the black pitch-
        water,
Homeward through the weltering ser-
        pents,

With the trophies of the battle,
With a shout and song of triumph.
    On the shore stood old Nokomis,
On the shore stood Chibiabos,
And the very strong man, Kwasind,
Waiting for the hero's coming,
Listening to his song of triumph.
And the people of the village
Welcomed him with songs and dances,
Made a joyous feast, and shouted :
" Honor be to Hiawatha !
He has slain the great Pearl-Feather,
Slain the mightiest of Magicians,
Him, who sent the fiery fever,
Sent the white fog from the fen-lands,
Sent disease and death among us ! "
    Ever dear to Hiawatha
Was the memory of Mama !
And in token of his friendship,
As a mark of his remembrance,
He adorned and decked his pipe-stem
With the crimson tuft of feathers,
With the blood-red crest of Mama.
But the wealth of Megissogwon,
All the trophies of the battle,
He divided with his people,
Shared it equally among them.

X.

HIAWATHA'S WOOING.

" As unto the bow the cord is,
So unto the man is woman,
Though she bends him, she obeys him,
Though she draws him, yet she follows,
Useless each without the other ! "
    Thus the youthful Hiawatha
Said within himself and pondered,
Much perplexed by various feelings,
Listless, longing, hoping, fearing,
Dreaming still of Minnehaha,
Of the lovely Laughing Water,
In the land of the Dacotahs.
    " Wed a maiden of your people,"
Warning said the old Nokomis ;
" Go not eastward, go not westward,
For a stranger, whom we know not !
Like a fire upon the hearth-stone
Is a neighbor's homely daughter,
Like the starlight or the moonlight
Is the handsomest of strangers ! "
    Thus dissuading spake Nokomis,
And my Hiawatha answered
Only this : " Dear old Nokomis,
Very pleasant is the firelight,

But I like the starlight better,
Better do I like the moonlight ! "
    Gravely then said old Nokomis :
" Bring not here an idle maiden,
Bring not here a useless woman,
Hands unskilful, feet unwilling ;
Bring a wife with nimble fingers,
Heart and hand that move together,
Feet that run on willing errands ! "
    Smiling answered Hiawatha :
" In the land of the Dacotahs
Lives the Arrow-maker's daughter,
Minnehaha, Laughing Water,
Handsomest of all the women.
I will bring her to your wigwam,
She shall run upon your errands,
Be your starlight, moonlight, firelight,
Be the sunlight of my people ! "
    Still dissuading said Nokomis :
" Bring not to my lodge a stranger
From the land of the Dacotahs !
Very fierce are the Dacotahs,
Often is there war between us,
There are feuds yet unforgotten,
Wounds that ache and still may open ! "
    Laughing answered Hiawatha :
" For that reason, if no other,
Would I wed the fair Dacotah,
That our tribes might be united,
That old feuds might be forgotten,
And old wounds be healed forever ! "
    Thus departed Hiawatha
To the land of the Dacotahs,
To the land of handsome women ;
Striding over moor and meadow,
Through interminable forests,
Through uninterrupted silence.
    With his moccasins of magic,
At each stride a mile he measured ;
Yet the way seemed long before him,
And his heart outran his footsteps ;
And he journeyed without resting,
Till he heard the cataract's laughter,
Heard the Falls of Minnehaha
Calling to him through the silence.
" Pleasant is the sound ! " he murmured,
" Pleasant is the voice that calls me ! "
    On the outskirts of the forest,
'Twixt the shadow and the sunshine,
Herds of fallow deer were feeding,
But they saw not Hiawatha ;
To his bow he whispered, " Fail not ! "
To his arrow whispered, " Swerve not !"
Sent it singing on its errand,
To the red heart of the roebuck ;
Threw the deer across his shoulder,
And sped forward without pausing.

At the doorway of his wigwam
Sat the ancient Arrow-maker,
In the land of the Dacotahs,
Making arrow-heads of jasper,
Arrow-heads of chalcedony.
At his side, in all her beauty,
Sat the lovely Minnehaha,
Sat his daughter, Laughing Water,
Plaiting mats of flags and rushes ;
Of the past the old man's thoughts were,
And the maiden's of the future.

He was thinking, as he sat there,
Of the days when with such arrows
He had struck the deer and bison,
On the Muskoday, the meadow ;
Shot the wild goose, flying southward,
On the wing, the clamorous Wawa ;
Thinking of the great war-parties,
How they came to buy his arrows,
Could not fight without his arrows.
Ah, no more such noble warriors
Could be found on earth as they were !
Now the men were all like women,
Only used their tongues for weapons !

She was thinking of a hunter,
From another tribe and country,
Young and tall and very handsome,
Who one morning, in the Spring-time,
Came to buy her father's arrows,
Sat and rested in the wigwam,
Lingered long about the doorway,
Looking back as he departed.
She had heard her father praise him,
Praise his courage and his wisdom ;
Would he come again for arrows
To the Falls of Minnehaha ?
On the mat her hands lay idle,
And her eyes were very dreamy.

Through their thoughts they heard a
        footstep,
Heard a rustling in the branches,
And with glowing cheek and forehead,
With the deer upon his shoulders,
Suddenly from out the woodlands
Hiawatha stood before them.

Straight the ancient Arrow-maker
Looked up gravely from his labor,
Laid aside the unfinished arrow,
Bade him enter at the doorway,
Saying, as he rose to meet him,
" Hiawatha, you are welcome ! "

At the feet of Laughing Water
Hiawatha laid his burden,
Threw the red deer from his shoulders ;
And the maiden looked up at him,
Looked up from her mat of rushes,
Said with gentle look and accent,

" You are welcome, Hiawatha ! "

Very spacious was the wigwam,
Made of deer-skin dressed and whitened,
With the Gods of the Dacotahs
Drawn and painted on its curtains,
And so tall the doorway, hardly
Hiawatha stooped to enter,
Hardly touched his eagle-feathers
As he entered at the doorway.

Then uprose the Laughing Water,
From the ground fair Minnehaha,
Laid aside her mat unfinished,
Brought forth food and set before them,
Water brought them from the brooklet,
Gave them food in earthen vessels,
Gave them drink in bowls of bass-wood,
Listened while the guest was speaking,
Listened while her father answered,
But not once her lips she opened,
Not a single word she uttered.

Yes, as in a dream she listened
To the words of Hiawatha,
As he talked of old Nokomis,
Who had nursed him in his childhood,
As he told of his companions,
Chibiabos, the musician,
And the very strong man, Kwasind,
And of happiness and plenty
In the land of the Ojibways,
In the pleasant land and peaceful.

" After many years of warfare,
Many years of strife and bloodshed,
There is peace between the Ojibways
And the tribe of the Dacotahs."
Thus continued Hiawatha,
And then added, speaking slowly,
" That this peace may last forever,
And our hands be clasped more closely,
And our hearts be more united,
Give me as my wife this maiden,
Minnehaha, Laughing Water,
Loveliest of Dacotah women ! "

And the ancient Arrow-maker
Paused a moment ere he answered,
Smoked a little while in silence,
Looked at Hiawatha proudly,
Fondly looked at Laughing Water,
And made answer very gravely :
" Yes, if Minnehaha wishes ;
Let your heart speak, Minnehaha ! "

And the lovely Laughing Water
Seemed more lovely, as she stood there.
Neither willing nor reluctant,
As she went to Hiawatha,
Softly took the seat beside him,
While she said, and blushed to say it,
" I will follow you, my husband ! "

This was Hiawatha's wooing !
Thus it was he won the daughter
Of the ancient Arrow-maker,
In the land of the Dacotahs !

From the wigwam he departed,
Leading with him Laughing Water;
Hand in hand they went together,
Through the woodland and the meadow,
Left the old man standing lonely
At the doorway of his wigwam,
Heard the Falls of Minnehaha
Calling to them from the distance,
Crying to them from afar off,
"Fare thee well, O Minnehaha ! "

And the ancient Arrow-maker
Turned again unto his labor,
Sat down by his sunny doorway,
Murmuring to himself, and saying :
"Thus it is our daughters leave us,
Those we love, and those who love us !
Just when they have learned to help us,
When we are old and lean upon them,
Comes a youth with flaunting feathers,
With his flute of reeds, a stranger
Wanders piping through the village,
Beckons to the fairest maiden,
And she follows where he leads her,
Leaving all things for the stranger ! "

Pleasant was the journey homeward,
Through interminable forests,
Over meadow, over mountain,
Over river, hill, and hollow.
Short it seemed to Hiawatha,
Though they journeyed very slowly,
Though his pace he checked and slack-
ened
To the steps of Laughing Water.

Over wide and rushing rivers
In his arms he bore the maiden ;
Light he thought her as a feather,
As the plume upon his head-gear ;
Cleared the tangled pathway for her,
Bent aside the swaying branches,
Made at night a lodge of branches,
And a bed with boughs of hemlock,
And a fire before the doorway
With the dry cones of the pine-tree.

All the travelling winds went with
them,
O'er the meadow, through the forest ;
All the stars of night looked at them,
Watched with sleepless eyes their slum-
ber ;
From his ambush in the oak-tree
Peeped the squirrel, Adjidaumo,
Watched with eager eyes the lovers ;
And the rabbit, the Wabasso,

Scampered from the path before them,
Peering, peeping from his burrow,
Sat erect upon his haunches,
Watched with curious eyes the lovers.

Pleasant was the journey homeward !
All the birds sang loud and sweetly
Songs of happiness and heart's-ease ;
Sang the bluebird, the Owaissa,
"Happy are you, Hiawatha,
Having such a wife to love you ! "
Sang the robin, the Opechee,
"Happy are you, Laughing Water,
Having such a noble husband ! "

From the sky the sun benignant
Looked upon them through the branches,
Saying to them, "O my children,
Love is sunshine, hate is shadow,
Life is checkered shade and sunshine,
Rule by love, O Hiawatha ! "

From the sky the moon looked at
them,
Filled the lodge with mystic splendors,
Whispered to them, "O my children,
Day is restless, night is quiet,
Man imperious, woman feeble ;
Half is mine, although I follow ;
Rule by patience, Laughing Water ! "

Thus it was they journeyed home-
ward ;
Thus it was that Hiawatha
To the lodge of old Nokomis
Brought the moonlight, starlight, fire-
light,
Brought the sunshine of his people,
Minnehaha, Laughing Water,
Handsomest of all the women
In the land of the Dacotahs,
In the land of handsome women.

XI.

HIAWATHA'S WEDDING-FEAST.

You shall hear how Pau-Puk-Keewis
How the handsome Yenadizze
Danced at Hiawatha's wedding ;
How the gentle Chibiabos,
He the sweetest of musicians,
Sang his songs of love and longing ;
How Iagoo, the great boaster,
He the marvellous story-teller,
Told his tales of strange adventure,
That the feast might be more joyous.
That the time might pass more gayly,
And the guests be more contented.

Sumptuous was the feast Nokomis

Made at Hiawatha's wedding;
All the bowls were made of bass-wood,
White and polished very smoothly,
All the spoons of horn of bison,
Black and polished very smoothly.

She had sent through all the village
Messengers with wands of willow,
As a sign of invitation,
As a token of the feasting;
And the wedding guests assembled,
Clad in all their richest raiment,
Robes of fur and belts of wampum,
Splendid with their paint and plumage,
Beautiful with beads and tassels.

First they ate the sturgeon, Nahma,
And the pike, the Maskenozha,
Caught and cooked by old Nokomis;
Then on pemican they feasted,
Pemican and buffalo marrow,
Haunch of deer and hump of bison,
Yellow cakes of the Mondamin,
And the wild rice of the river.

But the gracious Hiawatha,
And the lovely Laughing Water,
And the careful old Nokomis,
Tasted not the food before them,
Only waited on the others,
Only served their guests in silence.

And when all the guests had finished,
Old Nokomis, brisk and busy,
From an ample pouch of otter,
Filled the red-stone pipes for smoking
With tobacco from the South-land,
Mixed with bark of the red willow,
And with herbs and leaves of fragrance.

Then she said, "O Pau-Puk-Keewis,
Dance for us your merry dances,
Dance the Beggar's Dance to please us,
That the feast may be more joyous,
That the time may pass more gayly,
And our guests be more contented!"

Then the handsome Pau-Puk-Keewis,
He the idle Yenadizze,
He the merry mischief-maker,
Whom the people called the Storm-Fool,
Rose among the guests assembled.

Skilled was he in sports and pastimes,
In the merry dance of snow-shoes,
In the play of quoits and ball-play;
Skilled was he in games of hazard,
In all games of skill and hazard,
Pugasaing, the Bowl and Counters,
Kuntassoo, the Game of Plum-stones.

Though the warriors called him Faint-Heart,
Called him coward, Shaugodaya,
Idler, gambler, Yenadizze,

Little heeded he their jesting,
Little cared he for their insults,
For the women and the maidens
Loved the handsome Pau-Puk-Keewis.

He was dressed in shirt of doeskin,
White and soft, and fringed with ermine,
All inwrought with beads of wampum;
He was dressed in deer-skin leggings,
Fringed with hedgehog quills and ermine
And in moccasins of buck-skin,
Thick with quills and beads embroidered.
On his head were plumes of swan's down,
On his heels were tails of foxes,
In one hand a fan of feathers,
And a pipe was in the other.

Barred with streaks of red and yellow,
Streaks of blue and bright vermilion,
Shone the face of Pau-Puk-Keewis.
From his forehead fell his tresses,
Smooth, and parted like a woman's,
Shining bright with oil, and plaited,
Hung with braids of scented grasses,
As among the guests assembled,
To the sound of flutes and singing,
To the sound of drums and voices,
Rose the handsome Pau-Puk-Keewis,
And began his mystic dances.

First he danced a solemn measure,
Very slow in step and gesture,
In and out among the pine-trees,
Through the shadows and the sunshine,
Treading softly like a panther.
Then more swiftly and still swifter,
Whirling, spinning round in circles,
Leaping o'er the guests assembled,
Eddying round and round the wigwam,
Till the leaves went whirling with him,
Till the dust and wind together
Swept in eddies round about him.

Then along the sandy margin
Of the lake, the Big-Sea-Water,
On he sped with frenzied gestures,
Stamped upon the sand, and tossed it
Wildly in the air around him;
Till the wind became a whirlwind,
Till the sand was blown and sifted
Like great snowdrifts o'er the landscape,
Heaping all the shores with Sand Dunes,
Sand Hills of the Nagow Wudjoo!

Thus the merry Pau-Puk-Keewis
Danced his Beggar's Dance to please them,
And, returning, sat down laughing
There among the guests assembled,
Sat and fanned himself serenely
With his fan of turkey-feathers.

Then they said to Chibiabos,
To the friend of Hiawatha,
To the sweetest of all singers,
To the best of all musicians,
"Sing to us, O Chibiabos!
Songs of love and songs of longing,
That the feast may be more joyous,
That the time may pass more gayly,
And our guests be more contented!"
    And the gentle Chibiabos
Sang in accents sweet and tender,
Sang in tones of deep emotion,
Songs of love and songs of longing;
Looking still at Hiawatha,
Looking at fair Laughing Water,
Sang he softly, sang in this wise:
    "Onaway! Awake, beloved!
Thou the wild-flower of the forest!
Thou the wild-bird of the prairie!
Thou with eyes so soft and fawn-like!
    "If thou only lookest at me,
I am happy, I am happy,
As the lilies of the prairie,
When they feel the dew upon them!
    "Sweet thy breath is as the fragrance
Of the wild-flowers in the morning,
As their fragrance is at evening,
In the Moon when leaves are falling.
    "Does not all the blood within me
Leap to meet thee, leap to meet thee,
As the springs to meet the sunshine,
In the Moon when nights are brightest?
    "Onaway! my heart sings to thee,
Sings with joy when thou art near me,
As the sighing, singing branches
In the pleasant Moon of Strawberries!
    "When thou art not pleased, beloved,
Then my heart is sad and darkened,
As the shining river darkens
When the clouds drop shadows on it!
    "When thou smilest, my beloved,
Then my troubled heart is brightened,
As in sunshine gleam the ripples
That the cold wind makes in rivers.
    "Smiles the earth, and smile the waters,
Smile the cloudless skies above us,
But I lose the way of smiling
When thou art no longer near me!
    "I myself, myself! behold me!
Blood of my beating heart, behold me!
O awake, awake, beloved!
Onaway! awake, beloved!"
    Thus the gentle Chibiabos
Sang his song of love and longing;
And Iagoo, the great boaster,
He the marvellous story-teller,

He the friend of old Nokomis,
Jealous of the sweet musician,
Jealous of the applause they gave him,
Saw in all the eyes around him,
Saw in all their looks and gestures,
That the wedding guests assembled
Longed to hear his pleasant stories,
His immeasurable falsehoods.
    Very boastful was Iagoo;
Never heard he an adventure
But himself had met a greater;
Never any deed of daring
But himself had done a bolder;
Never any marvellous story
But himself could tell a stranger.
    Would you listen to his boasting,
Would you only give him credence,
No one ever shot an arrow
Half so far and high as he had;
Ever caught so many fishes,
Ever killed so many reindeer,
Ever trapped so many beaver!
    None could run so fast as he could,
None could dive so deep as he could,
None could swim so far as he could;
None had made so many journeys,
None had seen so many wonders,
As this wonderful Iagoo,
As this marvellous story-teller!
    Thus his name became a by-word
And a jest among the people;
And whene'er a boastful hunter
Praised his own address too highly,
Or a warrior, home returning,
Talked too much of his achievements,
All his hearers cried, "Iagoo!
Here's Iagoo come among us!"
    He it was who carved the cradle
Of the little Hiawatha,
Carved its framework out of linden,
Bound it strong with reindeer sinews;
He it was who taught him later
How to make his bows and arrows,
How to make the bows of ash-tree,
And the arrows of the oak-tree.
So among the guests assembled
At my Hiawatha's wedding
Sat Iagoo, old and ugly,
Sat the marvellous story-teller.
    And they said, "O good Iagoo,
Tell us now a tale of wonder,
Tell us of some strange adventure,
That the feast may be more joyous,
That the time may pass more gayly,
And our guests be more contented!"
    And Iagoo answered straightway,
"You shall hear a tale of wonder,

"Can it be the sun descending." Page 167.

You shall hear the strange adventures
Of Osseo, the Magician,
From the Evening Star descended."

XII.

THE SON OF THE EVENING STAR.

CAN it be the sun descending
O'er the level plain of water ?
Or the Red Swan floating, flying,
Wounded by the magic arrow,
Staining all the waves with crimson,
With the crimson of its life-blood,
Filling all the air with splendor,
With the splendor of its plumage ?
    Yes ; it is the sun descending,
Sinking down into the water ;
All the sky is stained with purple,
All the water flushed with crimson !
No ; it is the Red Swan floating,
Diving down beneath the water ;
To the sky its wings are lifted,
With its blood the waves are reddened !
    Over it the Star of Evening
Melts and trembles through the purple,
Hangs suspended in the twilight.
No ; it is a bead of wampum
On the robes of the Great Spirit,
As he passes through the twilight,
Walks in silence through the heavens.
    This with joy beheld Iagoo
And he said in haste : " Behold it !
See the sacred Star of Evening !
You shall hear a tale of wonder,
Hear the story of Osseo,
Son of the Evening Star, Osseo !
    " Once, in days no more remembered,
Ages nearer the beginning,
When the heavens were closer to us,
And the Gods were more familiar,
In the North-land lived a hunter,
With ten young and comely daugh-
        ters,
Tall and lithe as wands of willow ;
Only Oweenee, the youngest,
She the wilful and the wayward,
She the silent, dreamy maiden,
Was the fairest of the sisters.
    " All these women married warriors,
Married brave and haughty husbands ;
Only Oweenee, the youngest,
Laughed and flouted all her lovers,
All her young and handsome suitors,
And then married old Osseo,
Old Osseo, poor and ugly,

Broken with age and weak with cough-
        ing,
Always coughing like a squirrel.
    " Ah, but beautiful within him
Was the spirit of Osseo,
From the Evening Star descended,
Star of Evening, Star of Woman,
Star of tenderness and passion !
All its fire was in his bosom,
All its beauty in his spirit,
All its mystery in his being,
All its splendor in his language !
    " And her lovers, the rejected,
Handsome men with belts of wampum,
Handsome men with paint and feathers,
Pointed at her in derision,
Followed her with jest and laughter.
But she said : ' I care not for you,
Care not for your belts of wampum,
Care not for your paint and feathers,
Care not for your jests and laughter ;
I am happy with Osseo !'
    " Once to some great feast invited,
Through the damp and dusk of evening
Walked together the ten sisters,
Walked together with their husbands ;
Slowly followed old Osseo,
With fair Oweenee beside him ;
All the others chatted gayly,
These two only walked in silence.
    " At the western sky Osseo
Gazed intent, as if imploring,
Often stopped and gazed imploring
At the trembling Star of Evening,
At the tender Star of Woman ;
And they heard him murmur softly,
' Ah, showain nemeshin, Nosa !
Pity, pity me, my father !'
    " ' Listen !' said the eldest sister,
' He is praying to his father !
What a pity that the old man
Does not stumble in the pathway,
Does not break his neck by falling !'
And they laughed till all the forest
Rang with their unseemly laughter.
    " On their pathway through the wood-
        lands
Lay an oak, by storms uprooted,
Lay the great trunk of an oak-tree,
Buried half in leaves and mosses,
Mouldering, crumbling, huge and hol-
        low.
And Osseo, when he saw it,
Gave a shout, a cry of anguish,
Leaped into its yawning cavern,
At one end went in an old man,
Wasted, wrinkled, old, and ugly ;

From the other came a young man,
Tall and straight and strong and hand-
   some.
"Thus Osseo was transfigured,
Thus restored to youth and beauty ;
But, alas for good Osseo,
And for Oweenee, the faithful !
Strangely, too, was she transfigured.
Changed into a weak old woman,
With a staff she tottered onward,
Wasted, wrinkled, old, and ugly !
And the sisters and their husbands
Laughed until the echoing forest
Rang with their unseemly laughter.

"But Osseo turned not from her,
Walked with slower step beside her,
Took her hand, as brown and withered
As an oak-leaf is in Winter,
Called her sweetheart, Nenemoosha,
Soothed her with soft words of kindness,
Till they reached the lodge of feasting,
Till they sat down in the wigwam,
Sacred to the Star of Evening,
To the tender Star of Woman.

"Wrapt in visions, lost in dreaming,
At the banquet sat Osseo ;
All were merry, all were happy,
All were joyous but Osseo.
Neither food nor drink he tasted,
Neither did he speak nor listen,
But as one bewildered sat he,
Looking dreamily and sadly,
First at Oweenee, then upward
At the gleaming sky above them.

"Then a voice was heard, a whisper,
Coming from the starry distance,
Coming from the empty vastness,
Low, and musical, and tender ;
And the voice said : 'O Osseo !
O my son, my best beloved !
Broken are the spells that bound you,
All the charms of the magicians,
All the magic powers of evil ;
Come to me ; ascend, Osseo !

"'Taste the food that stands before
   you :
It is blessed and enchanted,
It has magic virtues in it,
It will change you to a spirit.
All your bowls and all your kettles
Shall be wood and clay no longer ;
But the bowls be changed to wampum,
And the kettles shall be silver ;
They shall shine like shells of scarlet,
Like the fire shall gleam and glimmer.

"'And the women shall no longer
Bear the dreary doom of labor,

But be changed to birds, and glisten
With the beauty of the starlight,
Painted with the dusky splendors
Of the skies and clouds of evening !'

"What Osseo heard as whispers,
What as words he comprehended,
Was but music to the others,
Music as of birds afar off,
Of the whippoorwill afar off,
Of the lonely Wawonaissa
Singing in the darksome forest.

"Then the lodge began to tremble,
Straight began to shake and tremble,
And they felt it rising, rising,
Slowly through the air ascending,
From the darkness of the tree-tops
Forth into the dewy starlight,
Till it passed the topmost branches ;
And behold ! the wooden dishes
All were changed to shells of scarlet !
And behold ! the earthen kettles
All were changed to bowls of silver !
And the roof-poles of the wigwam
Were as glittering rods of silver,
And the roof of bark upon them
As the shining shards of beetles.

"Then Osseo gazed around him,
And he saw the nine fair sisters,
All the sisters and their husbands,
Changed to birds of various plumage.
Some were jays and some were mag-
   pies,
Others thrushes, others blackbirds ;
And they hopped, and sang, and twit-
   tered,
Perked and fluttered all their feathers,
Strutted in their shining plumage,
And their tails like fans unfolded.

"Only Oweenee, the youngest,
Was not changed, but sat in silence,
Wasted, wrinkled, old, and ugly.
Looking sadly at the others ;
Till Osseo, gazing upward,
Gave another cry of anguish,
Such a cry as he had uttered
By the oak-tree in the forest.

"Then returned her youth and beauty
And her soiled and tattered garments
Were transformed to robes of ermine,
And her staff became a feather,
Yes, a shining silver feather !

"And again the wigwam trembled,
Swayed and rushed through airy currents,
Through transparent cloud and vapor,
And amid celestial splendors
On the Evening Star alighted,
As a snow-flake falls on snow-flake,

As a leaf drops on a river,
As the thistle-down on water.
    "Forth with cheerful words of welcome
Came the father of Osseo,
He with radiant locks of silver,
He with eyes serene and tender.
And he said : 'My son, Osseo,
Hang the cage of birds you bring there,
Hang the cage with rods of silver,
And the birds with glistening feathers,
At the doorway of my wigwam.'
    "At the door he hung the bird-cage,
And they entered in and gladly
Listened to Osseo's father,
Ruler of the Star of Evening,
As he said : 'O my Osseo !
I have had compassion on you,
Given you back your youth and beauty,
Into birds of various plumage
Changed your sisters and their husbands;
Changed them thus because they mocked you
In the figure of the old man,
In that aspect sad and wrinkled,
Could not see your heart of passion,
Could not see your youth immortal ;
Only Oweenee, the faithful,
Saw your naked heart and loved you.
    "'In the lodge that glimmers yonder,
In the little star that twinkles
Through the vapors, on the left hand,
Lives the envious Evil Spirit,
The Wabeno, the magician,
Who transformed you to an old man.
Take heed lest his beams fall on you,
For the rays he darts around him
Are the power of his enchantment,
Are the arrows that he uses.'
    "Many years, in peace and quiet,
On the peaceful Star of Evening
Dwelt Osseo with his father ;
Many years, in song and flutter,
At the doorway of the wigwam,
Hung the cage with rods of silver,
And fair Oweenee, the faithful,
Bore a son unto Osseo,
With the beauty of his mother,
With the courage of his father.
    "And the boy grew up and prospered,
And Osseo, to delight him,
Made him little bows and arrows,
Opened the great cage of silver,
And let loose his aunts and uncles.
All those birds with glossy feathers,
For his little son to shoot at.

    "Round and round they wheeled and darted,
Filled the Evening Star with music,
With their songs of joy and freedom ;
Filled the Evening Star with splendor,
With the fluttering of their plumage ;
Till the boy, the little hunter,
Bent his bow and shot an arrow,
Shot a swift and fatal arrow,
And a bird, with shining feathers,
At his feet fell wounded sorely.
    "But, O wondrous transformation !
'T was no bird he saw before him,
'T was a beautiful young woman,
With the arrow in her bosom !
    "When her blood fell on the planet,
On the sacred Star of Evening,
Broken was the spell of magic,
Powerless was the strange enchantment,
And the youth, the fearless bowman
Suddenly felt himself descending,
Held by unseen hands, but sinking
Downward through the empty spaces,
Downward through the clouds and vapors,
Till he rested on an island,
On an island, green and grassy,
Yonder in the Big-Sea-Water.
    "After him he saw descending
All the birds with shining feathers,
Fluttering, falling, wafted downward,
Like the painted leaves of Autumn ;
And the lodge with poles of silver,
With its roof like wings of beetles,
Like the shining shards of beetles,
By the winds of heaven uplifted,
Slowly sank upon the island,
Bringing back the good Osseo,
Bringing Oweenee, the faithful.
    "Then the birds, again transfigured,
Reassumed the shape of mortals,
Took their shape, but not their stature ;
They remained as Little People,
Like the pygmies, the Puk-Wudjies,
And on pleasant nights of Summer,
When the Evening Star was shining,
Hand in hand they danced together
On the island's craggy headlands,
On the sand-beach low and level.
    "Still their glittering lodge is seen there,
On the tranquil Summer evenings,
And upon the shore the fisher
Sometimes hears their happy voices,
Sees them dancing in the starlight !"
    When the story was completed,
When the wondrous tale was ended,

Looking round upon his listeners,
Solemnly Iagoo added :
"There are great men, I have known
    such,
Whom their people understand not,
Whom they even make a jest of,
Scoff and jeer at in derision.
From the story of Osseo
Let us learn the fate of jesters !"
   All the wedding guests delighted
Listened to the marvellous story,
Listened laughing and applauding,
And they whispered to each other :
"Does he mean himself, I wonder ?
And are we the aunts and uncles ?"
   Then again sang Chibiabos,
Sang a song of love and longing,
In those accents sweet and tender,
In those tones of pensive sadness,
Sang a maiden's lamentation
For her lover, her Algonquin.
   "When I think of my beloved,
Ah me ! think of my beloved,
When my heart is thinking of him,
O my sweetheart, my Algonquin !
   "Ah me ! when I parted from him,
Round my neck he hung the wampum,
As a pledge, the snow-white wampum,
O my sweetheart, my Algonquin !
   "I will go with you, he whispered,
Ah me ! to your native country ;
Let me go with you, he whispered,
O my sweetheart, my Algonquin !
   "Far away, away, I answered,
Very far away, I answered,
Ah me ! is my native country,
O my sweetheart, my Algonquin !
   "When I looked back to behold him,
Where we parted, to behold him,
After me he still was gazing,
O my sweetheart, my Algonquin !
   "By the tree he still was standing,
By the fallen tree was standing,
That had dropped into the water,
O my sweetheart, my Algonquin !
   "When I think of my beloved,
Ah me ! think of my beloved,
When my heart is thinking of him,
O my sweetheart, my Algonquin !"
   Such was Hiawatha's Wedding,
Such the dance of Pau-Puk-Keewis,
Such the story of Iagoo,
Such the songs of Chibiabos ;
Thus the wedding banquet ended,
And the wedding guests departed,
Leaving Hiawatha happy
With the night and Minnehaha.

XIII.

BLESSING THE CORNFIELDS.

SING, O Song of Hiawatha,
Of the happy days that followed,
In the land of the Ojibways,
In the pleasant land and peaceful !
Sing the mysteries of Mondamin,
Sing the Blessing of the Cornfields !
   Buried was the bloody hatchet,
Buried was the dreadful war-club,
Buried were all warlike weapons,
And the war-cry was forgotten.
There was peace among the nations ;
Unmolested roved the hunters,
Built the birch canoe for sailing,
Caught the fish in lake and river,
Shot the deer and trapped the beaver ;
Unmolested worked the women,
Made their sugar from the maple,
Gathered wild rice in the meadows,
Dressed the skins of deer and beaver.
   All around the happy village
Stood the maize-fields, green and shin-
   ing,
Waved the green plumes of Mondamin,
Waved his soft and sunny tresses,
Filling all the land with plenty.
'T was the women who in Spring-
   time
Planted the broad fields and fruitful,
Buried in the earth Mondamin ;
'T was the women who in Autumn
Stripped the yellow husks of harvest,
Stripped the garments from Mondamin,
Even as Hiawatha taught them.
   Once, when all the maize was planted,
Hiawatha, wise and thoughtful,
Spake and said to Minnehaha,
To his wife, the Laughing Water :
"You shall bless to-night the cornfields,
Draw a magic circle round them,
To protect them from destruction,
Blast of mildew, blight of insect,
Wagemin, the thief of cornfields,
Paimosaid, who steals the maize-ear !
   "In the night, when all is silence,
In the night, when all is darkness,
When the Spirit of Sleep, Nepahwin,
Shuts the doors of all the wigwams,
So that not an ear can hear you,
So that not an eye can see you,
Rise up from your bed in silence,
Lay aside your garments wholly,
Walk around the fields you planted,
Round the borders of the cornfields,

Covered by your tresses only,
Robed with darkness as a garment.
　"Thus the fields shall be more fruitful,
And the passing of your footsteps
Draw a magic circle round them,
So that neither blight nor mildew,
Neither burrowing worm nor insect,
Shall pass o'er the magic circle ;
Not the dragon-fly, Kwo-ne-she,
Nor the spider, Subbekashe,
Nor the grasshopper, Pah-puk-keena,
Nor the mighty caterpillar,
Way-muk-kwana, with the bear-skin,
King of all the caterpillars ! "
　On the tree-tops near the cornfields
Sat the hungry crows and ravens,
Kahgahgee, the King of Ravens,
With his band of black marauders.
And they laughed at Hiawatha,
Till the tree-tops shook with laughter,
With their melancholy laughter,
At the words of Hiawatha.
" Hear him ! " said they ; " hear the Wise
　　Man,
Hear the plots of Hiawatha ! "
　When the noiseless night descended
Broad and dark o'er field and forest,
When the mournful Wawonaissa,
Sorrowing sang among the hemlocks,
And the Spirit of Sleep, Nepahwin,
Shut the doors of all the wigwams,
From her bed rose Laughing Water,
Laid aside her garments wholly,
And with darkness clothed and guarded,
Unashamed and unaffrighted,
Walked securely round the cornfields,
Drew the sacred, magic circle
Of her footprints round the cornfields.
　No one but the Midnight only
Saw her beauty in the darkness, .
No one but the Wawonaissa
Heard the panting of her bosom ;
Guskewau, the darkness, wrapped her
Closely in his sacred mantle,
So that none might see her beauty,
So that none might boast, " I saw her ! "
　On the morrow, as the day dawned,
Kahgahgee, the King of Ravens,
Gathered all his black marauders,
Crows and blackbirds, jays and ravens,
Clamorous on the dusky tree-tops,
And descended, fast and fearless,
On the fields of Hiawatha,
On the grave of the Mondamin.
　" We will drag Mondamin," said they,
" From the grave where he is buried,
Spite of all the magic circles

Laughing Water draws around it,
Spite of all the sacred footprints
Minnehaha stamps upon it ! "
　But the wary Hiawatha,
Ever thoughtful, careful, watchful,
Had o'erheard the scornful laughter
When they mocked him from the tree-
　　tops.
" Kaw ! " he said, " my friends the ra-
　　vens !
Kahgahgee, my King of Ravens !
I will teach you all a lesson
That shall not be soon forgotten ! "
　He had risen before the daybreak,
He had spread o'er all the cornfields
Snares to catch the black marauders,
And was lying now in ambush
In the neighboring grove of pine-trees,
Waiting for the crows and blackbirds,
Waiting for the jays and ravens.
　Soon they came with caw and clamor,
Rush of wings and cry of voices,
To their work of devastation,
Settling down upon the cornfields,
Delving deep with beak and talon,
For the body of Mondamin.
And with all their craft and cunning,
All their skill in wiles of warfare,
They perceived no danger near them,
Till their claws became entangled,
Till they found themselves imprisoned
In the snares of Hiawatha.
　From his place of ambush came he,
Striding terrible among them,
And so awful was his aspect
That the bravest quailed with terror.
Without mercy he destroyed them
Right and left, by tens and twenties,
And their wretched, lifeless bodies
Hung aloft on poles for scarecrows
Round the consecrated cornfields,
As a signal of his vengeance,
As a warning to marauders.
　Only Kahgahgee, the leader,
Kahgahgee, the King of Ravens,
He alone was spared among them
As a hostage for his people.
With his prisoner - string he bound
　　him,
Led him captive to his wigwam,
Tied him fast with cords of elm-bark
To the ridge-pole of his wigwam.
　" Kahgahgee, my raven ! " said he,
" You the leader of the robbers,
You the plotter of this mischief,
The contriver of this outrage,
I will keep you, I will hold you,

As a hostage for your people,
As a pledge of good behavior ! "
    And he left him, grim and sulky,
Sitting in the morning sunshine
On the summit of the wigwam,
Croaking fiercely his displeasure,
Flapping his great sable pinions,
Vainly struggling for his freedom,
Vainly calling on his people !
    Summer passed, and Shawondasee
Breathed his sighs o'er all the landscape,
From the South-land sent his ardors,
Wafted kisses warm and tender ;
And the maize-field grew and ripened,
Till it stood in all the splendor
Of its garments green and yellow,
Of its tassels and its plumage,
And the maize-ears full and shining
Gleamed from bursting sheaths of ver-
        dure.
    Then Nokomis, the old woman,
Spake, and said to Minnehaha :
"'T is the Moon when leaves are falling ;
All the wild-rice has been gathered,
And the maize is ripe and ready ;
Let us gather in the harvest,
Let us wrestle with Mondamin,
Strip him of his plumes and tassels,
Of his garments green and yellow ! "
    And the merry Laughing Water
Went rejoicing from the wigwam,
With Nokomis, old and wrinkled,
And they called the women round them,
Called the young men and the maidens,
To the harvest of the cornfields,
To the husking of the maize-ear.
    On the border of the forest,
Underneath the fragrant pine-trees,
Sat the old men and the warriors
Smoking in the pleasant shadow.
In uninterrupted silence
Looked they at the gamesome labor
Of the young men and the women ;
Listened to their noisy talking,
To their laughter and their singing,
Heard them chattering like the magpies,
Heard them laughing like the blue-jays,
Heard them singing like the robins.
    And whene'er some lucky maiden
Found a red ear in the husking,
Found a maize-ear red as blood is,
"Nushka ! " cried they all together,
"Nushka ! you shall have a sweetheart,
You shall have a handsome husband ! "
"Ugh ! " the old men all responded
From their seats beneath the pine-trees.
    And whene'er a youth or maiden

Found a crooked ear in husking,
Found a maize-ear in the husking
Blighted, mildewed, or misshapen,
Then they laughed and sang together,
Crept and limped about the cornfields,
Mimicked in their gait and gestures
Some old man, bent almost double,
Singing singly or together :
"Wagemin, the thief of cornfields !
Paimosaid, who steals the maize-ear ! "
    Till the cornfields rang with laughter,
Till from Hiawatha's wigwam
Kahgahgee, the King of Ravens,
Screamed and quivered in his anger,
And from all the neighboring tree-tops
Cawed and croaked the black marauders.
"Ugh ! " the old men all responded,
From their seats beneath the pine-trees !

XIV.

PICTURE-WRITING.

In those days said Hiawatha,
"Lo ! how all things fade and perish !
From the memory of the old men
Pass away the great traditions,
The achievements of the warriors,
The adventures of the hunters,
All the wisdom of the Medas,
All the craft of the Wabenos,
All the marvellous dreams and visions
Of the Jossakeeds, the Prophets !
    "Great men die and are forgotten,
Wise men speak ; their words of wis-
        dom
Perish in the ears that hear them,
Do not reach the generations
That, as yet unborn, are waiting
In the great, mysterious darkness
Of the speechless days that shall be !
    "On the grave-posts of our fathers
Are no signs, no figures painted ;
Who are in those graves we know not.
Only know they are our fathers.
Of what kith they are and kindred,
From what old, ancestral Totem,
Be it Eagle, Bear, or Beaver,
They descended, this we know not.
Only know they are our fathers.
    "Face to face we speak together,
But we cannot speak when absent,
Cannot send our voices from us
To the friends that dwell afar off ;
Cannot send a secret message,
But the bearer learns our secret,

May pervert it, may betray it,
May reveal it unto others."
　　Thus said Hiawatha, walking
In the solitary forest,
Pondering, musing in the forest,
On the welfare of his people.
　　From his pouch he took his colors,
Took his paints of different colors,
On the smooth bark of a birch-tree
Painted many shapes and figures,
Wonderful and mystic figures,
And each figure had a meaning,
Each some word or thought suggested.
　　Gitche Manito the Mighty,
He, the Master of Life, was painted
As an egg, with points projecting
To the four winds of the heavens.
Everywhere is the Great Spirit,
Was the meaning of this symbol.
　　Mitche Manito the Mighty,
He the dreadful Spirit of Evil,
As a serpent was depicted,
As Kenabeek, the great serpent.
Very crafty, very cunning,
Is the creeping Spirit of Evil,
Was the meaning of this symbol.
　　Life and Death he drew as circles,
Life was white, but Death was darkened ;
Sun and moon and stars he painted,
Man and beast, and fish and reptile,
Forests, mountains, lakes, and rivers.
　　For the earth he drew a straight line,
For the sky a bow above it ;
White the space between for daytime,
Filled with little stars for night-time ;
On the left a point for sunrise,
On the right a point for sunset,
On the top a point for noontide,
And for rain and cloudy weather
Waving lines descending from it.
　　Footprints pointing towards a wigwam
Were a sign of invitation,
Were a sign of guests assembling ;
Bloody hands with palms uplifted
Were a symbol of destruction,
Were a hostile sign and symbol.
　　All these things did Hiawatha
Show unto his wondering people,
And interpreted their meaning,
And he said : " Behold, your grave-posts
Have no mark, no sign, nor symbol.
Go and paint them all with figures ;
Each one with its household symbol,
With its own ancestral Totem ;
So that those who follow after
May distinguish them and know them."
　　And they painted on the grave-posts

On the graves yet unforgotten,
Each his own ancestral Totem,
Each the symbol of his household ;
Figures of the Bear and Reindeer,
Of the Turtle, Crane, and Beaver,
Each inverted as a token
That the owner was departed,
That the chief who bore the symbol
Lay beneath in dust and ashes.
　　And the Jossakeeds, the Prophets,
The Wabenos, the Magicians,
And the Medicine-men, the Medas,
Painted upon bark and deer-skin
Figures for the songs they chanted,
For each song a separate symbol,
Figures mystical and awful,
Figures strange and brightly colored :
And each figure had its meaning,
Each some magic song suggested.
　　The Great Spirit, the Creator,
Flashing light through all the heaven :
The Great Serpent, the Kenabeek,
With his bloody crest erected,
Creeping, looking into heaven ;
In the sky the sun, that listens,
And the moon eclipsed and dying ;
Owl and eagle, crane and hen-hawk,
And the cormorant, bird of magic ;
Headless men, that walk the heavens,
Bodies lying pierced with arrows,
Bloody hands of death uplifted,
Flags on graves, and great war-captains
Grasping both the earth and heaven !
　　Such as these the shapes they painted
On the birch-bark and the deer-skin ;
Songs of war and songs of hunting,
Songs of medicine and of magic,
All were written in these figures,
For each figure had its meaning,
Each its separate song recorded.
　　Nor forgotten was the Love-Song,
The most subtle of all medicines,
The most potent spell of magic,
Dangerous more than war or hunting !
Thus the Love-Song was recorded,
Symbol and interpretation.
　　First a human figure standing,
Painted in the brightest scarlet ;
'T is the lover, the musician,
And the meaning is, " My painting
Makes me powerful over others."
　　Then the figure seated, singing,
Playing on a drum of magic,
And the interpretation, " Listen !
'T is my voice you hear, my singing !"
　　Then the same red figure seated
In the shelter of a wigwam,

And the meaning of the symbol,
I will come and sit beside you
In the mystery of my passion!"
Then two figures, man and woman,
Standing hand in hand together
With their hands so clasped together
That they seem in one united,
And the words thus represented
Are, "I see your heart within you,
And your cheeks are red with blushes!"
Next the maiden on an island,
In the centre of an island;
And the song this shape suggested
Was, "Though you were at a distance,
Were upon some far-off island,
Such the spell I cast upon you,
Such the magic power of passion,
I could straightway draw you to me!"
Then the figure of the maiden
Sleeping, and the lover near her,
Whispering to her in her slumbers,
Saying, "Though you were far from me
In the land of Sleep and Silence,
Still the voice of love would reach you!"
And the last of all the figures
Was a heart within a circle,
Drawn within a magic circle;
And the image had this meaning:
"Naked lies your heart before me,
To your naked heart I whisper!"
Thus it was that Hiawatha,
In his wisdom, taught the people
All the mysteries of painting,
All the art of Picture-Writing,
On the smooth bark of the birch-tree,
On the white skin of the reindeer,
On the grave-posts of the village.

XV.

HIAWATHA'S LAMENTATION.

In those days the Evil Spirits,
All the Manitos of mischief,
Fearing Hiawatha's wisdom,
And his love for Chibiabos,
Jealous of their faithful friendship,
And their noble words and actions,
Made at length a league against them,
To molest them and destroy them.
Hiawatha, wise and wary,
Often said to Chibiabos,
"O my brother! do not leave me,
Lest the Evil Spirits harm you!"
Chibiabos, young and heedless,
Laughing shook his coal-black tresses,

Answered ever sweet and childlike,
"Do not fear for me, O brother!
Harm and evil come not near me!"
Once when Peboan, the Winter,
Roofed with ice the Big-Sea-Water,
When the snow-flakes, whirling downward,
Hissed among the withered oak-leaves,
Changed the pine-trees into wigwams,
Covered all the earth with silence, —
Armed with arrows, shod with snow-shoes,
Heeding not his brother's warning,
Fearing not the Evil Spirits,
Forth to hunt the deer with antlers
All alone went Chibiabos.
Right across the Big-Sea-Water
Sprang with speed the deer before him.
With the wind and snow he followed,
O'er the treacherous ice he followed,
Wild with all the fierce commotion
And the rapture of the hunting.
But beneath, the Evil Spirits
Lay in ambush, waiting for him,
Broke the treacherous ice beneath him,
Dragged him downward to the bottom,
Buried in the sand his body.
Unktahee, the god of water,
He the god of the Dacotahs,
Drowned him in the deep abysses
Of the lake of Gitche Gumee.
From the headlands Hiawatha
Sent forth such a wail of anguish,
Such a fearful lamentation,
That the bison paused to listen,
And the wolves howled from the prairies,
And the thunder in the distance
Starting answered "Baim-wawa!"
Then his face with black he painted,
With his robe his head he covered,
In his wigwam sat lamenting,
Seven long weeks he sat lamenting,
Uttering still this moan of sorrow:—
"He is dead, the sweet musician!
He the sweetest of all singers!
He has gone from us forever,
He has moved a little nearer
To the Master of all music,
To the Master of all singing!
O my brother, Chibiabos!"
And the melancholy fir-trees
Waved their dark green fans above him,
Waved their purple cones above him,
Sighing with him to console him,
Mingling with his lamentation
Their complaining, their lamenting.

Came the Spring, and all the forest
Looked in vain for Chibiabos ;
Sighed the rivulet, Sebowisha,
Sighed the rushes in the meadow.
From the tree-tops sang the blue-
bird,
Sang the bluebird, the Owaissa,
"Chibiabos ! Chibiabos !
He is dead, the sweet musician !"
From the wigwam sang the robin,
Sang the robin, the Opechee,
"Chibiabos ! Chibiabos !
He is dead, the sweetest singer ! "
And at night through all the forest
Went the whippoorwill complaining,
Wailing went the Wawonaissa,
"Chibiabos ! Chibiabos !
He is dead, the sweet musician !
He the sweetest of all singers ! "
Then the medicine-men, the Medas,
The magicians, the Wabenos,
And the Jossakeeds, the prophets,
Came to visit Hiawatha ;
Built a Sacred Lodge beside him,
To appease him, to console him,
Walked in silent, grave procession,
Bearing each a pouch of healing,
Skin of beaver, lynx, or otter,
Filled with magic roots and simples,
Filled with very potent medicines.
When he heard their steps approach-
ing,
Hiawatha ceased lamenting,
Called no more on Chibiabos ;
Naught he questioned, naught he an-
swered,
But his mournful head uncovered,
From his face the mourning colors
Washed he slowly and in silence,
Slowly and in silence followed
Onward to the Sacred Wigwam.
There a magic drink they gave him,
Made of Nahma-wusk, the spearmint,
And Wabeno-wusk, the yarrow,
Roots of power, and herbs of healing ;
Beat their drums, and shook their rat-
tles ;
Chanted singly and in chorus,
Mystic songs like these, they chanted.
"I myself, myself ! behold me !
'T is the great Gray Eagle talking ;
Come, ye white crows, come and hear
him !
The loud-speaking thunder helps me ;
All the unseen spirits help me ;
I can hear their voices calling,
All around the sky I hear them !

I can blow you strong, my brother,
I can heal you, Hiawatha !"
"Hi-au-ha !" replied the chorus,
Way-ha-way !" the mystic chorus.
"Friends of mine are all the serpents !
Hear me shake my skin of hen-hawk !
Mahng, the white loon, I can kill him ;
I can shoot your heart and kill it !
I can blow you strong, my brother,
I can heal you, Hiawatha !"
"Hi-au-ha !" replied the chorus.
"Way-ha-way !" the mystic chorus.
"I myself, myself ! the prophet !
When I speak the wigwam trembles,
Shakes the Sacred Lodge with terror,
Hands unseen begin to shake it !
When I walk, the sky I tread on
Bends and makes a noise beneath me !
I can blow you strong, my brother !
Rise and speak, O Hiawatha !"
"Hi-au-ha !" replied the chorus,
"Way-ha-way !" the mystic chorus.
Then they shook their medicine-
pouches
O'er the head of Hiawatha,
Danced their medicine-dance around
him ;
And upstarting wild and haggard,
Like a man from dreams awakened,
He was healed of all his madness.
As the clouds are swept from heaven,
Straightway from his brain departed
All his moody melancholy ;
As the ice is swept from rivers,
Straightway from his heart departed
All his sorrow and affliction.
Then they summoned Chibiabos
From his grave beneath the waters,
From the sands of Gitche Gumee
Summoned Hiawatha's brother.
And so mighty was the magic
Of that cry and invocation,
That he heard it as he lay there
Underneath the Big-Sea-Water ;
From the sand he rose and listened,
Heard the music and the singing,
Came, obedient to the summons,
To the doorway of the wigwam,
But to enter they forbade him.
Through a chink a coal they gave him,
Through the door a burning fire-brand :
Ruler in the Land of Spirits,
Ruler o'er the dead, they made him,
Telling him a fire to kindle
For all those that died thereafter,
Camp-fires for their night encampments
On their solitary journey

To the kingdom of Ponemah,
To the land of the Hereafter.
　From the village of his childhood,
From the homes of those who knew him,
Passing silent through the forest,
Like a smoke-wreath wafted sideways,
Slowly vanished Chibiabos !
Where he passed, the branches moved
　　not,
Where he trod, the grasses bent not,
And the fallen leaves of last year
Made no sound beneath his footsteps.
　Four whole days he journeyed onward
Down the pathway of the dead men ;
On the dead-man's strawberry feasted,
Crossed the melancholy river,
On the swinging log he crossed it,
Came unto the Lake of Silver,
In the Stone Canoe was carried
To the Islands of the Blessed,
To the land of ghosts and shadows.
　On that journey, moving slowly,
Many weary spirits saw he,
Panting under heavy burdens,
Laden with war-clubs, bows and arrows,
Robes of fur, and pots and kettles,
And with food that friends had given
For that solitary journey.
　" Ay ! why do the living," said they,
" Lay such heavy burdens on us !
Better were it to go naked,
Better were it to go fasting,
Than to bear such heavy burdens
On our long and weary journey ! "
　Forth then issued Hiawatha,
Wandered eastward, wandered westward,
Teaching men the use of simples
And the antidotes for poisons,
And the cure of all diseases.
Thus was first made known to mortals
All the mystery of Medamin,
All the sacred art of healing.

XVI.

PAU-PUK-KEEWIS.

You shall hear how Pau-Puk-Keewis
He, the handsome Yenadizze,
Whom the people called the Storm Fool,
Vexed the village with disturbance ;
You shall hear of all his mischief,
And his flight from Hiawatha,
And his wondrous transmigrations,
And the end of his adventures.
　On the shores of Gitche Gumee,

On the dunes of Nagow Wudjoo,
By the shining Big-Sea-Water
Stood the lodge of Pau-Puk-Keewis.
It was he who in his frenzy
Whirled these drifting sands together,
On the dunes of Nagow Wudjoo,
When, among the guests assembled,
He so merrily and madly
Danced at Hiawatha's wedding,
Danced the Beggar's Dance to please
　　them.
　Now, in search of new adventures,
From his lodge went Pau-Puk-Keewis,
Came with speed into the village,
Found the young men all assembled
In the lodge of old Iagoo,
Listening to his monstrous stories,
To his wonderful adventures.
　He was telling them the story
Of Ojeeg, the Summer-Maker,
How he made a hole in heaven,
How he climbed up into heaven,
And let out the summer-weather,
The perpetual, pleasant Summer ;
How the Otter first essayed it ;
How the Beaver, Lynx, and Badger
Tried in turn the great achievement,
From the summit of the mountain
Smote their fists against the heavens,
Smote against the sky their foreheads,
Cracked the sky, but could not break it
How the Wolverine, uprising,
Made him ready for the encounter,
Bent his knees down, like a squirrel,
Drew his arms back, like a cricket.
　" Once he leaped," said old Iagoo,
" Once he leaped, and lo ! above him
Bent the sky, as ice in rivers
When the waters rise beneath it ;
Twice he leaped, and lo ! above him
Cracked the sky, as ice in rivers
When the freshet is at highest !
Thrice he leaped, and lo ! above him
Broke the shattered sky asunder,
And he disappeared within it,
And Ojeeg, the Fisher Weasel,
With a bound went in behind him ! "
　" Hark you ! " shouted Pau-Puk-Kee
　　wis
As he entered at the doorway ;
" I am tired of all this talking,
Tired of old Iagoo's stories,
Tired of Hiawatha's wisdom.
Here is something to amuse you,
Better than this endless talking."
　Then from out his pouch of wolf-skin
Forth he drew, with solemn manner,

All the game of Bowl and Counters,
Pugasaing, with thirteen pieces.
White on one side were they painted,
And vermilion on the other ;
Two Kenabeeks or great serpents,
Two Ininewug or wedge-men,
One great war-club, Pugamaugun,
And one slender fish, the Keego,
Four round pieces, Ozawabeeks,
And three Sheshebwug or ducklings.
All were made of bone and painted,
All except the Ozawabeeks ;
These were brass, on one side burnished,
And were black upon the other.

In a wooden bowl he placed them,
Shook and jostled them together,
Threw them on the ground before him.
Thus exclaiming and explaining :
" Red side up are all the pieces,
And one great Kenabeek standing
On the bright side of a brass piece,
On a burnished Ozawabeek ;
Thirteen tens and eight are counted."

Then again he shook the pieces,
Shook and jostled them together,
Threw them on the ground before him,
Still exclaiming and explaining :
" White are both the great Kenabeeks,
White the Ininewug, the wedge-men,
Red are all the other pieces ;
Five tens and an eight are counted."

Thus he taught the game of hazard,
Thus displayed it and explained it,
Running through its various chances,
Various changes, various meanings :
Twenty curious eyes stared at him.
Full of eagerness stared at him.

" Many games," said old Iagoo,
" Many games of skill and hazard
Have I seen in different nations,
Have I played in different countries.
He who plays with old Iagoo
Must have very nimble fingers ;
Though you think yourself so skilful
I can beat you, Pau-Puk-Keewis,
I can even give you lessons
In your game of Bowl and Counters ! "

So they sat and played together,
All the old men and the young men,
Played for dresses, weapons, wampum,
Played till midnight, played till morning,
Played until the Yenadizze,
Till the cunning Pau-Puk-Keewis,
Of their treasures had despoiled them,
Of the best of all their dresses,
Shirts of deer-skin, robes of ermine,

Belts of wampum, crests of feathers,
Warlike weapons, pipes and pouches.
Twenty eyes glared wildly at him,
Like the eyes of wolves glared at him.

Said the lucky Pau-Puk-Keewis :
" In my wigwam I am lonely,
In my wanderings and adventures
I have need of a companion,
Fain would have a Meshinauwa,
An attendant and pipe-bearer.
I will venture all these winnings,
All these garments heaped about me,
All this wampum, all these feathers,
On a single throw will venture
All against the young man yonder ! "
'T was a youth of sixteen summers,
'T was a nephew of Iagoo ;
Face-in-a-Mist, the people called him.

As the fire burns in a pipe-head
Dusky red beneath the ashes,
So beneath his shaggy eyebrows
Glowed the eyes of old Iagoo.
" Ugh ! " he answered very fiercely ;
" Ugh ! " they answered all and each one.

Seized the wooden bowl the old man,
Closely in his bony fingers
Clutched the fatal bowl, Onagon,
Shook it fiercely and with fury,
Made the pieces ring together
As he threw them down before him.

Red were both the great Kenabeeks,
Red the Ininewug, the wedge-men,
Red the Sheshebwug, the ducklings,
Black the four brass Ozawabeeks,
White alone the fish, the Keego ;
Only five the pieces counted !

Then the smiling Pau-Puk-Keewis
Shook the bowl and threw the pieces ;
Lightly in the air he tossed them,
And they fell about him scattered ;
Dark and bright the Ozawabeeks,
Red and white the other pieces,
And upright among the others
One Ininewug was standing,
Even as crafty Pau-Puk-Keewis
Stood alone among the players,
Saying, " Five tens ! mine the game is !"

Twenty eyes glared at him fiercely,
Like the eyes of wolves glared at him,
As he turned and left the wigwam,
Followed by his Meshinauwa,
By the nephew of Iagoo,
By the tall and graceful stripling,
Bearing in his arms the winnings,
Shirts of deer-skin, robes of ermine,
Belts of wampum, pipes and weapons.

12

"Carry them," said Pau-Puk-Keewis,
Pointing with his fan of feathers,
"To my wigwam far to eastward,
On the dunes of Nagow Wudjoo !"
  Hot and red with smoke and gambling
Were the eyes of Pau-Puk-Keewis
As he came forth to the freshness
Of the pleasant Summer morning.
All the birds were singing gayly,
All the streamlets flowing swiftly,
And the heart of Pau-Puk-Keewis
Sang with pleasure as the birds sing,
Beat with triumph like the streamlets,
As he wandered through the village,
In the early gray of morning,
With his fan of turkey-feathers,
With his plumes and tufts of swan's
    down,
Till he reached the farthest wigwam,
Reached the lodge of Hiawatha.
  Silent was it and deserted ;
No one met him at the doorway,
No one came to bid him welcome ;
But the birds were singing round it,
In and out and round the doorway,
Hopping, singing, fluttering, feeding,
And aloft upon the ridge-pole
Kahgahgee, the King of Ravens,
Sat with fiery eyes, and, screaming,
Flapped his wings at Pau-Puk-Keewis.
  "All are gone ! the lodge is empty !"
Thus it was spake Pau-Puk-Keewis,
In his heart resolving mischief ; —
"Gone is wary Hiawatha,
Gone the silly Laughing Water,
Gone Nokomis, the old woman,
And the lodge is left unguarded !"
  By the neck he seized the raven,
Whirled it round him like a rattle,
Like a medicine-pouch he shook it,
Strangled Kahgahgee, the raven,
From the ridge-pole of the wigwam
Left its lifeless body hanging,
As an insult to its master,
As a taunt to Hiawatha.
  With a stealthy step he entered,
Round the lodge in wild disorder
Threw the household things about him,
Piled together in confusion
Bowls of wood and earthen kettles,
Robes of buffalo and beaver,
Skins of otter, lynx, and ermine,
As an insult to Nokomis,
As a taunt to Minnehaha.
  Then departed Pau-Puk-Keewis,
Whistling, singing through the forest,
Whistling gayly to the squirrels,

Who from hollow boughs above him
Dropped their acorn-shells upon him,
Singing gayly to the wood birds,
Who from out the leafy darkness
Answered with a song as merry.
  Then he climbed the rocky headlands,
Looking o'er the Gitche Gumee,
Perched himself upon their summit,
Waiting full of mirth and mischief
The return of Hiawatha.
  Stretched upon his back he lay there ;
Far below him plashed the waters,
Plashed and washed the dreamy waters ;
Far above him swam the heavens,
Swam the dizzy, dreamy heavens ;
Round him hovered, fluttered, rustled,
Hiawatha's mountain chickens,
Flock-wise swept and wheeled about him,
Almost brushed him with their pinions.
  And he killed them as he lay there,
Slaughtered them by tens and twenties,
Threw their bodies down the headland,
Threw them on the beach below him,
Till at length Kayoshk, the sea-gull,
Perched upon a crag above them,
Shouted : "It is Pau-Puk-Keewis !
He is slaying us by hundreds !
Send a message to our brother,
Tidings send to Hiawatha !"

XVII.

THE HUNTING OF PAU-PUK-KEEWIS.

FULL of wrath was Hiawatha
When he came into the village,
Found the people in confusion,
Heard of all the misdemeanors,
All the malice and the mischief,
Of the cunning Pau-Puk-Keewis.
  Hard his breath came through his
    nostrils,
Through his teeth he buzzed and muttered
Words of anger and resentment,
Hot and humming, like a hornet.
"I will slay this Pau-Puk-Keewis,
Slay this mischief-maker !" said he.
"Not so long and wide the world is,
Not so rude and rough the way is,
That my wrath shall not attain him,
That my vengeance shall not reach him !"
  Then in swift pursuit departed
Hiawatha and the hunters
On the trail of Pau-Puk-Keewis,
Through the forest, where he passed it,
To the headlands where he rested ;

But they found not Pau-Puk-Keewis,
Only in the trampled grasses,
In the whortleberry-bushes,
Found the couch where he had rested,
Found the impress of his body.

From the lowlands far beneath them,
From the Muskoday, the meadow,
Pau-Puk-Keewis, turning backward,
Made a gesture of defiance,
Made a gesture of derision ;
And aloud cried Hiawatha,
From the summit of the mountain :
" Not so long and wide the world is,
Not so rude and rough the way is,
But my wrath shall overtake you,
And my vengeance shall attain you ! "

Over rock and over river,
Thorough bush, and brake, and forest,
Ran the cunning Pau-Puk-Keewis ;
Like an antelope he bounded,
Till he came unto a streamlet
In the middle of the forest,
To a streamlet still and tranquil,
That had overflowed its margin,
To a dam made by the beavers,
To a pond of quiet water,
Where knee-deep the trees were standing,
Where the water-lilies floated,
Where the rushes waved and whispered.

On the dam stood Pau-Puk-Keewis,
On the dam of trunks and branches,
Through whose chinks the water spouted,
O'er whose summit flowed the streamlet.
From the bottom rose the beaver,
Looked with two great eyes of wonder,
Eyes that seemed to ask a question,
At the stranger, Pau-Puk-Keewis.

On the dam stood Pau-Puk-Keewis,
O'er his ankles flowed the streamlet,
Flowed the bright and silvery water,
And he spake unto the beaver,
With a smile he spake in this wise :
" O my friend Ahmeek, the beaver,
Cool and pleasant is the water ;
Let me dive into the water,
Let me rest there in your lodges ;
Change me, too, into a beaver ! "

Cautiously replied the beaver,
With reserve he thus made answer :
" Let me first consult the others,
Let me ask the other beavers."
Down he sank into the water,
Heavily sank he, as a stone sinks,
Down among the leaves and branches,
Brown and matted at the bottom.

On the dam stood Pau-Puk-Keewis,
O'er his ankles flowed the streamlet.

Spouted through the chinks below him
Dashed upon the stones beneath him,
Spread serene and calm before him,
And the sunshine and the shadows
Fell in flecks and gleams upon him,
Fell in little shining patches,
Through the waving, rustling branches.

From the bottom rose the beavers,
Silently above the surface
Rose one head and then another,
Till the pond seemed full of beavers,
Full of black and shining faces.

To the beavers Pau-Puk-Keewis
Spake entreating, said in this wise :
" Very pleasant is your dwelling,
O my friends ! and safe from danger ;
Can you not with all your cunning,
All your wisdom and contrivance,
Change me, too, into a beaver ? "

" Yes ! " replied Ahmeek, the beaver,
He the King of all the beavers,
" Let yourself slide down among us,
Down into the tranquil water."

Down into the pond among them
Silently sank Pau-Puk-Keewis ;
Black became his shirt of deer-skin,
Black his moccasins and leggings,
In a broad black tail behind him
Spread his fox-tails and his fringes ;
He was changed into a beaver.

" Make me large," said Pau-Puk-
                          Keewis,
" Make me large and make me larger,
Larger than the other beavers."
" Yes," the beaver chief responded,
" When our lodge below you enter,
In our wigwam we will make you
Ten times larger than the others."

Thus into the clear, brown water
Silently sank Pau-Puk-Keewis ;
Found the bottom covered over
With the trunks of trees and branches,
Hoards of food against the winter,
Piles and heaps against the famine ;
Found the lodge with arching door-
                          way,
Leading into spacious chambers.

Here they made him large and larger,
Made him largest of the beavers,
Ten times larger than the others.
" You shall be our ruler," said they ;
" Chief and King of all the beavers."

But not long had Pau-Puk-Keewis
Sat in state among the beavers,
When there came a voice of warning
From the watchman at his station
In the water-flags and lilies,

Saying, " Here is Hiawatha !
Hiawatha with his hunters ! "
Then they heard a cry above them,
Heard a shouting and a tramping,
Heard a crashing and a rushing,
And the water round and o'er them
Sank and sucked away in eddies,
And they knew their dam was broken.
On the lodge's roof the hunters
Leaped, and broke it all asunder ;
Streamed the sunshine through the
crevice,
Sprang the beavers through the doorway,
Hid themselves in deeper water,
In the channel of the streamlet ;
But the mighty Pau-Puk-Keewis
Could not pass beneath the doorway ;
He was puffed with pride and feeding,
He was swollen like a bladder.
Through the roof looked Hiawatha,
Cried aloud, " O Pau-Puk-Keewis !
Vain are all your craft and cunning,
Vain your manifold disguises !
Well I know you, Pau-Puk-Keewis ! "
With their clubs they beat and bruised
him,
Beat to death poor Pau-Puk-Keewis,
Pounded him as maize is pounded,
Till his skull was crushed to pieces.
Six tall hunters, lithe and limber,
Bore him home on poles and branches,
Bore the body of the beaver ;
But the ghost, the Jeebi in him,
Thought and felt as Pau-Puk-Keewis,
Still lived on as Pau-Puk-Keewis.
And it fluttered, strove, and struggled,
Waving hither, waving thither,
As the curtains of a wigwam
Struggle with their thongs of deer-skin,
When the wintry wind is blowing ;
Till it drew itself together,
Till it rose up from the body,
Till it took the form and features
Of the cunning Pau-Puk-Keewis
Vanishing into the forest.
But the wary Hiawatha
Saw the figure ere it vanished,
Saw the form of Pau-Puk-Keewis
Glide into the soft blue shadow
Of the pine-trees of the forest ;
Toward the squares of white beyond it,
Toward an opening in the forest,
Like a wind it rushed and panted,
Bending all the boughs before it,
And behind it, as the rain comes,
Came the steps of Hiawatha.
To a lake with many islands

Came the breathless Pau-Puk-Keewis,
Where among the water-lilies
Pishnekuh, the brant, were sailing ;
Through the tufts of rushes floating,
Steering through the reedy islands.
Now their broad black beaks they lifted,
Now they plunged beneath the water,
Now they darkened in the shadow,
Now they brightened in the sunshine.
"Pishnekuh !" cried Pau-Puk-Keewis,
" Pishnekuh ! my brothers ! " said he,
" Change me to a brant with plumage,
With a shining neck and feathers,
Make me large, and make me larger,
Ten times larger than the others."
Straightway to a brant they changed
him,
With two huge and dusky pinions,
With a bosom smooth and rounded,
With a bill like two great paddles,
Made him larger than the others,
Ten times larger than the largest,
Just as, shouting from the forest,
On the shore stood Hiawatha.
Up they rose with cry and clamor,
With a whir and beat of pinions,
Rose up from the reedy islands,
From the water-flags and lilies.
And they said to Pau-Puk-Keewis :
" In your flying, look not downward,
Take good heed, and look not downward,
Lest some strange mischance should hap-
pen,
Lest some great mishap befall you ! "
Fast and far they fled to northward,
Fast and far through mist and sunshine,
Fed among the moors and fen-lands,
Slept among the reeds and rushes.
On the morrow as they journeyed,
Buoyed and lifted by the South-wind,
Wafted onward by the South-wind,
Blowing fresh and strong behind them,
Rose a sound of human voices,
Rose a clamor from beneath them,
From the lodges of a village,
From the people miles beneath them.
For the people of the village
Saw the flock of brant with wonder,
Saw the wings of Pau-Puk-Keewis
Flapping far up in the ether,
Broader than two doorway curtains.
Pau-Puk-Keewis heard the shouting,
Knew the voice of Hiawatha,
Knew the outcry of Iagoo,
And, forgetful of the warning,
Drew his neck in, and looked downward,
And the wind that blew behind him

Caught his mighty fan of feathers,
Sent him wheeling, whirling downward !
  All in vain did Pau-Puk-Keewis
Struggle to regain his balance !
Whirling round and round and down-
        ward,
He beheld in turn the village
And in turn the flock above him,
Saw the village coming nearer,
And the flock receding farther,
Heard the voices growing louder,
Heard the shouting and the laughter ;
Saw no more the flock above him,
Only saw the earth beneath him ;
Dead out of the empty heaven,
Dead among the shouting people,
With a heavy sound and sullen,
Fell the brant with broken pinions.
  But his soul, his ghost, his shadow,
Still survived as Pau-Puk-Keewis,
Took again the form and features
Of the handsome Yenadizze,
And again went rushing onward,
Followed fast by Hiawatha,
Crying : " Not so wide the world is,
Not so long and rough the way is,
But my wrath shall overtake you,
But my vengeance shall attain you ! "
  And so near he came, so near him,
That his hand was stretched to seize him,
His right hand to seize and hold him,
When the cunning Pau-Puk-Keewis
Whirled and spun about in circles,
Fanned the air into a whirlwind,
Danced the dust and leaves about him,
And amid the whirling eddies
Sprang into a hollow oak-tree,
Changed himself into a serpent,
Gliding out through root and rubbish.
  With his right hand Hiawatha
Smote amain the hollow oak-tree,
Rent it into shreds and splinters,
Left it lying there in fragments.
But in vain ; for Pau-Puk-Keewis,
Once again in human figure,
Full in sight ran on before him,
Sped away in gust and whirlwind,
On the shores of Gitche Gumee,
Westward by the Big-Sea-Water,
Came unto the rocky headlands,
To the Pictured Rocks of sandstone,
Looking over lake and landscape.
  And the Old Man of the Mountain,
He the Manito of Mountains,
Opened wide his rocky doorways,
Opened wide his deep abysses,
Giving Pau-Puk-Keewis shelter

In his caverns dark and dreary,
Bidding Pau-Puk-Keewis welcome
To his gloomy lodge of sandstone.
  There without stood Hiawatha,
Found the doorways closed against him,
With his mittens, Minjekahwun,
Smote great caverns in the sandstone,
Cried aloud in tones of thunder,
" Open ! I am Hiawatha ! "
But the Old Man of the Mountain
Opened not, and made no answer
From the silent crags of sandstone,
From the gloomy rock abysses.
  Then he raised his hands to heaven,
Called imploring on the tempest,
Called Waywassimo, the lightning,
And the thunder, Annemeekee ;
And they came with night and darkness,
Sweeping down the Big-Sea-Water
From the distant Thunder Mountains ;
And the trembling Pau-Puk-Keewis
Heard the footsteps of the thunder,
Saw the red eyes of the lightning,
Was afraid, and crouched and trembled.
  Then Waywassimo, the lightning,
Smote the doorways of the caverns,
With his war-club smote the doorways,
Smote the jutting crags of sandstone,
And the thunder, Annemeekee,
Shouted down into the caverns,
Saying, " Where is Pau-Puk-Keewis ! "
And the crags fell, and beneath them
Dead among the rocky ruins
Lay the cunning Pau-Puk-Keewis,
Lay the handsome Yenadizze,
Slain in his own human figure.
  Ended were his wild adventures,
Ended were his tricks and gambols,
Ended all his craft and cunning,
Ended all his mischief-making,
All his gambling and his dancing,
All his wooing of the maidens.
  Then the noble Hiawatha
Took his soul, his ghost, his shadow,
Spake and said : " O Pau-Puk-Keewis,
Never more in human figure
Shall you search for new adventures ;
Never more with jest and laughter
Dance the dust and leaves in whirlwinds ;
But above there in the heavens
You shall soar and sail in circles ;
I will change you to an eagle,
To Keneu, the great war-eagle,
Chief of all the fowls with feathers,
Chief of Hiawatha's chickens."
  And the name of Pau-Puk-Keewis
Lingers still among the people,

Lingers still among the singers,
And among the story-tellers ;
And in Winter, when the snow-flakes
Whirl in eddies round the lodges,
When the wind in gusty tumult
O'er the smoke-flue pipes and whistles,
"There," they cry, " comes Pau-Puk-
 Keewis ;
He is dancing through the village,
He is gathering in his harvest ! "

XVIII.

THE DEATH OF KWASIND.

FAR and wide among the nations
Spread the name and fame of Kwasind ;
No man dared to strive with Kwasind,
No man could compete with Kwasind.
But the mischievous Puk-Wudjies,
They the envious Little People,
They the fairies and the pygmies,
Plotted and conspired against him.
 " If this hateful Kwasind," said they,
"If this great, outrageous fellow
Goes on thus a little longer,
Tearing everything he touches,
Rending everything to pieces,
Filling all the world with wonder,
What becomes of the Puk-Wudjies ?
Who will care for the Puk-Wudjies ?
He will tread us down like mushrooms,
Drive us all into the water,
Give our bodies to be eaten
By the wicked Nee-ba-naw-baigs,
By the Spirits of the water ! "
 So the angry Little People
All conspired against the Strong Man,
All conspired to murder Kwasind,
Yes, to rid the world of Kwasind,
The audacious, overbearing,
Heartless, haughty, dangerous Kwasind !
 Now this wondrous strength of Kwa-
 sind
In his crown alone was seated ;
In his crown too was his weakness ;
There alone could he be wounded,
Nowhere else could weapon pierce him,
Nowhere else could weapon harm him.
 Even there the only weapon
That could wound him, that could slay
 him,
Was the seed-cone of the pine-tree,
Was the blue cone of the fir-tree.
This was Kwasind's fatal secret,
Known to no man among mortals ;

But the cunning Little People,
The Puk-Wudjies, knew the secret,
Knew the only way to kill him.
 So they gathered cones together,
Gathered seed-cones of the pine-tree,
Gathered blue cones of the fir-tree,
In the woods by Taquamenaw,
Brought them to the river's margin,
Heaped them in great piles together,
Where the red rocks from the margin
Jutting overhang the river.
There they lay in wait for Kwasind,
The malicious Little People.
 'T was an afternoon in Summer ;
Very hot and still the air was,
Very smooth the gliding river,
Motionless the sleeping shadows :
Insects glistened in the sunshine,
Insects skated on the water,
Filled the drowsy air with buzzing,
With a far resounding war-cry.
 Down the river came the Strong Man,
In his birch canoe came Kwasind,
Floating slowly down the current
Of the sluggish Taquamenaw,
Very languid with the weather,
Very sleepy with the silence.
 From the overhanging branches,
From the tassels of the birch-trees,
Soft the Spirit of Sleep descended ;
By his airy hosts surrounded,
His invisible attendants,
Came the Spirit of Sleep, Nepahwin ;
Like the burnished Dush-kwo-ne-she,
Like a dragon-fly, he hovered
O'er the drowsy head of Kwasind.
 To his ear there came a murmur
As of waves upon a sea-shore,
As of far-off tumbling waters,
As of winds among the pine-trees;
And he felt upon his forehead
Blows of little airy war-clubs,
Wielded by the slumbrous legions
Of the Spirit of Sleep, Nepahwin,
As of some one breathing on him.
 At the first blow of their war-clubs,
Fell a drowsiness on Kwasind ;
At the second blow they smote him,
Motionless his paddle rested ;
At the third, before his vision
Reeled the landscape into darkness,
Very sound asleep was Kwasind.
 So he floated down the river,
Like a blind man seated upright,
Floated down the Taquamenaw,
Underneath the trembling birch-trees,
Underneath the wooded headlands.

Underneath the war encampment
Of the pygmies, the Puk-Wudjies.
    There they stood, all armed and wait-
        ing,
Hurled the pine-cones down upon him,
Struck him on his brawny shoulders,
On his crown defenceless struck him.
"Death to Kwasind!" was the sudden
War-cry of the Little People.
    And he sideways swayed and tumbled,
Sideways fell into the river,
Plunged beneath the sluggish water
Headlong, as an otter plunges;
And the birch-canoe, abandoned,
Drifted empty down the river,
Bottom upward swerved and drifted:
Nothing more was seen of Kwasind.
    But the memory of the Strong Man
Lingered long among the people,
And whenever through the forest
Raged and roared the wintry tempest,
And the branches, tossed and troubled,
Creaked and groaned and split asunder,
"Kwasind!" cried they; "that is
    Kwasind!
He is gathering in his fire-wood!"

XIX.

THE GHOSTS.

NEVER stoops the soaring vulture
On his quarry in the desert,
On the sick or wounded bison,
But another vulture, watching
From his high aerial look-out,
Sees the downward plunge, and follows;
And a third pursues the second,
Coming from the invisible ether,
First a speck, and then a vulture,
Till the air is dark with pinions.
    So disasters come not singly;
But as if they watched and waited,
Scanning one another's motions,
When the first descends, the others
Follow, follow, gathering flock-wise
Round their victim, sick and wounded,
First a shadow, then a sorrow,
Till the air is dark with anguish.
    Now, o'er all the dreary Northland,
Mighty Peboan, the Winter,
Breathing on the lakes and rivers,
Into stone had changed their waters.
From his hair he shook the snow-flakes,
Till the plains were strewn with white-
    ness,

One uninterrupted level,
As if, stooping, the Creator
With his hand had smoothed them over.
    Through the forest, wide and wailing,
Roamed the hunter on his snow-shoes;
In the village worked the women,
Pounded maize, or dressed the deer-skin
And the young men played together
On the ice the noisy ball-play,
On the plain the dance of snow-shoes.
    One dark evening, after sundown,
In her wigwam Laughing Water
Sat with old Nokomis, waiting
For the steps of Hiawatha
Homeward from the hunt returning.
    On their faces gleamed the fire-light,
Painting them with streaks of crimson,
In the eyes of old Nokomis
Glimmered like the watery moonlight,
In the eyes of Laughing Water
Glistened like the sun in water;
And behind them crouched their shadows
In the corners of the wigwam,
And the smoke in wreaths above them
Climbed and crowded through the smoke-
    flue.
    Then the curtain of the doorway
From without was slowly lifted;
Brighter glowed the fire a moment,
And a moment swerved the smoke-
    wreath,
As two women entered softly,
Passed the doorway uninvited,
Without word of salutation,
Without sign of recognition,
Sat down in the farthest corner,
Crouching low among the shadows.
    From their aspect and their garments,
Strangers seemed they in the village;
Very pale and haggard were they,
As they sat there sad and silent,
Trembling, cowering with the shadows.
    Was it the wind above the smoke-flue,
Muttering down into the wigwam?
Was it the owl, the Koko-koho,
Hooting from the dismal forest?
Sure a voice said in the silence:
"These are corpses clad in garments,
These are ghosts that come to haunt you,
From the kingdom of Ponemah,
From the land of the Hereafter!"
    Homeward now came Hiawatha
From his hunting in the forest,
With the snow upon his tresses,
And the red deer on his shoulders.
At the feet of Laughing Water
Down he threw his lifeless burden;

Nobler, handsomer she thought him,
Than when first he came to woo her,
First threw down the deer before her,
As a token of his wishes,
As a promise of the future.

   Then he turned and saw the strangers,
Cowering, crouching with the shadows,
Said within himself, " Who are they ?
What strange guests has Minnehaha ?"
But he questioned not the strangers,
Only spake to bid them welcome
To his lodge, his food, his fireside.

   When the evening meal was ready,
And the deer had been divided,
Both the pallid guests, the strangers,
Springing from among the shadows,
Seized upon the choicest portions,
Seized the white fat of the roebuck,
Set apart for Laughing Water,
For the wife of Hiawatha ;
Without asking, without thanking,
Eagerly devoured the morsels,
Flitted back among the shadows
In the corner of the wigwam.

   Not a word spake Hiawatha,
Not a motion made Nokomis,
Not a gesture Laughing Water ;
Not a change came o'er their features ;
Only Minnehaha softly
Whispered, saying, "They are famished ;
Let them do what best delights them ;
Let them eat, for they are famished."

   Many a daylight dawned and darkened,
Many a night shook off the daylight
As the pine shakes off the snow-flakes
From the midnight of its branches ;
Day by day the guests unmoving
Sat there silent in the wigwam ;
But by night, in storm or starlight,
Forth they went into the forest,
Bringing fire-wood to the wigwam,
Bringing pine-cones for the burning,
Always sad and always silent.

   And whenever Hiawatha
Came from fishing or from hunting,
When the evening meal was ready,
And the food had been divided,
Gliding from their darksome corner,
Came the pallid guests, the strangers,
Seized upon the choicest portions
Set aside for Laughing Water,
And without rebuke or question
Flitted back among the shadows.

   Never once had Hiawatha
By a word or look reproved them ;
Never once had old Nokomis
Made a gesture of impatience ;

Never once had Laughing Water
Shown resentment at the outrage.
All had they endured in silence,
That the rights of guest and stranger,
That the virtue of free-giving,
By a look might not be lessened,
By a word might not be broken.

   Once at midnight Hiawatha,
Ever wakeful, ever watchful,
In the wigwam, dimly lighted
By the brands that still were burning,
By the glimmering, flickering fire-light,
Heard a sighing, oft repeated,
Heard a sobbing, as of sorrow.

   From his couch rose Hiawatha,
From his shaggy hides of bison,
Pushed aside the deer-skin curtain,
Saw the pallid guests, the shadows,
Sitting upright on their couches,
Weeping in the silent midnight.

   And he said : " O guests ! why is it
That your hearts are so afflicted,
That you sob so in the midnight ?
Has perchance the old Nokomis,
Has my wife, my Minnehaha,
Wronged or grieved you by unkindness,
Failed in hospitable duties ?"

   Then the shadows ceased from weeping,
Ceased from sobbing and lamenting,
And they said, with gentle voices •
" We are ghosts of the departed,
Souls of those who once were with
     you.
From the realms of Chibiabos
Hither have we come to try you,
Hither have we come to warn you.

   "Cries of grief and lamentation
Reach us in the Blessed Islands ;
Cries of anguish from the living,
Calling back their friends departed,
Sadden us with useless sorrow.
Therefore have we come to try you ;
No one knows us, no one heeds us.
We are but a burden to you,
And we see that the departed
Have no place among the living.

   "Think of this, O Hiawatha !
Speak of it to all the people,
That henceforward and forever
They no more with lamentations
Sadden the souls of the departed
In the Islands of the Blessed.

   "Do not lay such heavy burdens
In the graves of those you bury,
Not such weight of furs and wampum,
Not such weight of pots and kettles,
For the spirits faint beneath them.

Only give them food to carry,
Only give them fire to light them.
"Four days is the spirit's journey
To the land of ghosts and shadows,
Four its lonely night encampments ;
Four times must their fires be lighted.
Therefore, when the dead are buried,
Let a fire, as night approaches,
Four times on the grave be kindled,
That the soul upon its journey
May not lack the cheerful fire-light,
May not grope about in darkness.

"Farewell, noble Hiawatha !
We have put you to the trial,
To the proof have put your patience,
By the insult of our presence,
By the outrage of our actions.
We have found you great and noble.
Fail not in the greater trial,
Faint not in the harder struggle."

When they ceased, a sudden darkness
Fell and filled the silent wigwam.
Hiawatha heard a rustle
As of garments trailing by him,
Heard the curtain of the doorway
Lifted by a hand he saw not,
Felt the cold breath of the night air,
For a moment saw the starlight ;
But he saw the ghosts no longer,
Saw no more the wandering spirits
From the kingdom of Ponemah,
From the land of the Hereafter.

XX.

THE FAMINE.

O THE long and dreary Winter !
O the cold and cruel Winter !
Ever thicker, thicker, thicker
Froze the ice on lake and river,
Ever deeper, deeper, deeper
Fell the snow o'er all the landscape,
Fell the covering snow, and drifted
Through the forest, round the village.

Hardly from his buried wigwam
Could the hunter force a passage ;
With his mittens and his snow-shoes
Vainly walked he through the forest,
Sought for bird or beast and found none,
Saw no track of deer or rabbit,
In the snow beheld no footprints,
In the ghastly, gleaming forest
Fell, and could not rise from weakness,
Perished there from cold and hunger.

O the famine and the fever !
O the wasting of the famine !
O the blasting of the fever !
O the wailing of the children !
O the anguish of the women !
All the earth was sick and famished ;
Hungry was the air around them,
Hungry was the sky above them,
And the hungry stars in heaven
Like the eyes of wolves glared at them !
Into Hiawatha's wigwam
Came two other guests, as silent
As the ghosts were, and as gloomy,
Waited not to be invited,
Did not parley at the doorway,
Sat there without word of welcome
In the seat of Laughing Water ;
Looked with haggard eyes and hollow
At the face of Laughing Water.

And the foremost said : "Behold me!
I am Famine, Bukadawin !"
And the other said : "Behold me !
I am Fever, Ahkosewin !"
And the lovely Minnehaha
Shuddered as they looked upon her,
Shuddered at the words they uttered,
Lay down on her bed in silence,
Hid her face, but made no answer ;
Lay there trembling, freezing, burning
At the looks they cast upon her,
At the fearful words they uttered.

Forth into the empty forest
Rushed the maddened Hiawatha ;
In his heart was deadly sorrow,
In his face a stony firmness ;
On his brow the sweat of anguish
Started, but it froze and fell not.

Wrapped in furs and armed for hunt
ing,
With his mighty bow of ash-tree,
With his quiver full of arrows,
With his mittens, Minjekahwun,
Into the vast and vacant forest
On his snow-shoes strode he forward.

"Gitche Manito, the Mighty !"
Cried he with his face uplifted
In that bitter hour of anguish,
"Give your children food, O father !
Give us food, or we must perish !
Give me food for Minnehaha,
For my dying Minnehaha !"

Through the far-resounding forest,
Through the forest vast and vacant
Rang that cry of desolation,
But there came no other answer
Than the echo of his crying,
Than the echo of the woodlands,
"Minnehaha ! Minnehaha !"

All day long roved Hiawatha

In that melancholy forest,
Through the shadow of whose thickets,
In the pleasant days of Summer,
Of that ne'er forgotten Summer,
He had brought his young wife homeward
From the land of the Dacotahs ;
When the birds sang in the thickets,
And the streamlets laughed and glistened,
And the air was full of fragrance,
And the lovely Laughing Water
Said with voice that did not tremble,
" I will follow you, my husband ! "
   In the wigwam with Nokomis,
With those gloomy guests, that watched her,
With the Famine and the Fever,
She was lying, the Beloved,
She the dying Minnehaha.
   "Hark ! " she said ; "I hear a rushing,
Hear a roaring and a rushing,
Hear the Falls of Minnehaha
Calling to me from a distance ! "
" No, my child ! " said old Nokomis,
" 'T is the night-wind in the pine-trees ! "
   "Look ! " she said ; "I see my father
Standing lonely at his doorway,
Beckoning to me from his wigwam
In the land of the Dacotahs ! "
" No, my child ! " said old Nokomis,
" 'T is the smoke, that waves and beckons ! "
   "Ah ! " said she, "the eyes of Pauguk
Glare upon me in the darkness,
I can feel his icy fingers
Clasping mine amid the darkness !
Hiawatha ! Hiawatha ! "
   And the desolate Hiawatha,
Far away amid the forest,
Miles away among the mountains,
Heard that sudden cry of anguish,
Heard the voice of Minnehaha
Calling to him in the darkness,
" Hiawatha ! Hiawatha ! "
   Over snow-fields waste and pathless,
Under snow-encumbered branches,
Homeward hurried Hiawatha,
Empty-handed, heavy-hearted,
Heard Nokomis moaning, wailing :
" Wahonowin ! Wahonowin !
Would that I had perished for you,
Would that I were dead as you are !
Wahonowin ! Wahonowin ! "
   And he rushed into the wigwam,
Saw the old Nokomis slowly
Rocking to and fro and moaning,
Saw his lovely Minnehaha
Lying dead and cold before him,

And his bursting heart within him
Uttered such a cry of anguish,
That the forest moaned and shuddered,
That the very stars in heaven
Shook and trembled with his anguish.
   Then he sat down, still and speechless,
On the bed of Minnehaha,
At the feet of Laughing Water,
At those willing feet, that never
More would lightly run to meet him,
Never more would lightly follow.
   With both hands his face he covered,
Seven long days and nights he sat there,
As if in a swoon he sat there,
Speechless, motionless, unconscious
Of the daylight or the darkness.
   Then they buried Minnehaha ;
In the snow a grave they made her,
In the forest deep and darksome,
Underneath the moaning hemlocks ;
Clothed her in her richest garments,
Wrapped her in her robes of ermine ;
Covered her with snow, like ermine,
Thus they buried Minnehaha.
   And at night a fire was lighted,
On her grave four times was kindled,
For her soul upon its journey
To the Islands of the Blessed.
From his doorway Hiawatha
Saw it burning in the forest,
Lighting up the gloomy hemlocks ;
From his sleepless bed uprising,
From the bed of Minnehaha,
Stood and watched it at the doorway,
That it might not be extinguished,
Might not leave her in the darkness.
   " Farewell ! " said he, " Minnehaha !
Farewell, O my Laughing Water !
All my heart is buried with you,
All my thoughts go onward with you !
Come not back again to labor,
Come not back again to suffer,
Where the Famine and the Fever
Wear the heart and waste the body.
Soon my task will be completed,
Soon your footsteps I shall follow
To the Islands of the Blessed,
To the Kingdom of Ponemah,
To the Land of the Hereafter ! "

XXI.

THE WHITE MAN'S FOOT.

IN his lodge beside a river,
Close beside a frozen river,
Sat an old man, sad and lonely.

White his hair was as a snow-drift ;
Dull and low his fire was burning,
And the old man shook and trembled,
Folded in his Waubewyon,
In his tattered white-skin-wrapper,
Hearing nothing but the tempest
As it roared along the forest,
Seeing nothing but the snow-storm,
As it whirled and hissed and drifted.

All the coals were white with ashes,
And the fire was slowly dying,
As a young man, walking lightly,
At the open doorway entered.
Red with blood of youth his cheeks were,
Soft his eyes, as stars in Spring-time,
Bound his forehead was with grasses,
Bound and plumed with scented grasses ;
On his lips a smile of beauty,
Filling all the lodge with sunshine,
In his hand a bunch of blossoms
Filling all the lodge with sweetness.

"Ah, my son ! " exclaimed the old man,
"Happy are my eyes to see you.
Sit here on the mat beside me,
Sit here by the dying embers,
Let us pass the night together.
Tell me of your strange adventures,
Of the lands where you have travelled ;
I will tell you of my prowess,
Of my many deeds of wonder."

From his pouch he drew his peace-pipe,
Very old and strangely fashioned ;
Made of red stone was the pipe-head,
And the stem a reed **with feathers**,
Filled the pipe with bark of willow,
Placed a burning coal upon it,
Gave it to his guest, the stranger,
And began to speak in this wise :

"When I blow my breath about me,
When I breathe upon the landscape,
Motionless are all the rivers,
Hard as stone becomes the water ! "

And the young man answered, smiling :
"When I blow my breath about me,
When I breathe upon the landscape,
Flowers spring up o'er all the meadows,
Singing, onward rush the rivers ! "

"When I shake my hoary tresses,"
Said the old man darkly frowning,
"All the land with snow is covered ;
All the leaves from all the branches
Fall and fade and die and wither,
For I breathe, and lo ! they are not.
From the waters and the marshes
Rise the wild goose and the heron,
Fly away to distant regions,
For I speak, and lo ! they are not.

And where'er my footsteps wander,
All the wild beasts of the forest
Hide themselves in holes and caverns,
And the earth becomes as flintstone ! "

"When I shake my flowing ringlets,"
Said the young man, softly laughing,
"Showers of rain fall warm and welcome
Plants lift up their heads rejoicing,
Back unto their lakes and marshes
Come the wild goose and the heron,
Homeward shoots the arrowy swallow,
Sing the bluebird and the robin,
And where'er my footsteps wander,
All the meadows wave with blossoms,
All the woodlands ring with music,
All the trees are dark with foliage ! "

While they spake, the night departed
From the distant realms of Wabun,
From his shining lodge of silver,
Like a warrior robed and painted,
Came the sun, and said, "Behold me !
Gheezis, the great sun, behold me ! "

Then the old man's tongue was speech-
less
And the air grew warm and pleasant,
And upon the wigwam sweetly
Sang the bluebird and the robin,
And the stream began to murmur,
And a scent of growing grasses
Through the lodge was gently wafted.

And Segwun, the youthful stranger,
More distinctly in the daylight
Saw the icy face before him ;
It was Peboan, the Winter !
From his eyes the tears were flowing,
As from melting lakes the streamlets,
And his body shrunk and dwindled
As the shouting sun ascended,
Till into the air it faded,
Till into the ground it vanished,
And the young man saw before him,
On the hearth-stone of the wigwam,
Where the fire had smoked and smoul-
dered,
Saw the earliest flower of Spring-time,
Saw the Beauty of the Spring-time,
Saw the Miskodeed in blossom.

Thus it was that in the North-land
After that unheard-of coldness,
That intolerable Winter,
Came the Spring with all its splendor,
All its birds and all its blossoms,
All its flowers and leaves and grasses.

Sailing on the wind to northward,
Flying in great flocks, like arrows,
Like huge arrows shot through heaven,
Passed the swan, the Mahnahbezee,

Speaking almost as a man speaks ;
And in long lines waving, bending
Like a bow-string snapped asunder,
Came the white goose, Waw-be-wawa ;
And in pairs, or singly flying,
Mahng the loon, with clangorous pinions,
The blue heron, the Shuh-shuh-gah,
And the grouse, the Mushkodasa.

In the thickets and the meadows
Piped the bluebird, the Owaissa,
On the summit of the lodges
Sang the robin, the Opechee,
In the covert of the pine-trees
Cooed the pigeon, the Omemee,
And the sorrowing Hiawatha,
Speechless in his infinite sorrow,
Heard their voices calling to him,
Went forth from his gloomy doorway,
Stood and gazed into the heaven,
Gazed upon the earth and waters.

From his wanderings far to eastward,
From the regions of the morning,
From the shining land of Wabun,
Homeward now returned Iagoo,
The great traveller, the great boaster,
Full of new and strange adventures,
Marvels many and many wonders.

And the people of the village
Listened to him as he told them
Of his marvellous adventures,
Laughing answered him in this wise :
" Ugh ! it is indeed Iagoo !
No one else beholds such wonders !"

He had seen, he said, a water
Bigger than the Big-Sea-Water,
Broader than the Gitche Gumee,
Bitter so that none could drink it !
At each other looked the warriors,
Looked the women at each other,
Smiled, and said, " It cannot be so !
Kaw !" they said, "it cannot be so !"

O'er it, said he, o'er this water
Came a great canoe with pinions,
A canoe with wings came flying,
Bigger than a grove of pine-trees,
Taller than the tallest tree-tops !
And the old men and the women
Looked and tittered at each other ;
" Kaw !" they said, " we don't believe
   it !"

From its mouth, he said, to greet him,
Came Waywassimo, the lightning,
Came the thunder, Annemeekee !
And the warriors and the women
Laughed aloud at poor Iagoo ;
" Kaw !" they said, " what tales you
   tell us !"

In it, said he, came a people,
In the great canoe with pinions
Came, he said, a hundred warriors ;
Painted white were all their faces
And with hair their chins were covered :
And the warriors and the women
Laughed and shouted in derision,
Like the ravens on the tree-tops,
Like the crows upon the hemlocks.
" Kaw !" they said, " what lies you tell
   us !
Do not think that we believe them !"

Only Hiawatha laughed not,
But he gravely spake and answered
To their jeering and their jesting :
" True is all Iagoo tells us ;
I have seen it in a vision,
Seen the great canoe with pinions,
Seen the people with white faces,
Seen the coming of this bearded
People of the wooden vessel
From the regions of the morning,
From the shining land of Wabun.

" Gitche Manito, the Mighty,
The Great Spirit, the Creator,
Sends them hither on his errand,
Sends them to us with his message.
Wheresoe'er they move, before them
Swarms the stinging fly, the Ahmo,
Swarms the bee, the honey-maker ;
Wheresoe'er they tread, beneath them
Springs a flower unknown among us,
Springs the White-man's Foot in blossom.

" Let us welcome, then, the strangers,
Hail them as our friends and brothers,
And the heart's right hand of friendship
Give them when they come to see us.
Gitche Manito, the Mighty,
Said this to me in my vision.

" I beheld, too, in that vision
All the secrets of the future,
Of the distant days that shall be.
I beheld the westward marches
Of the unknown, crowded nations.
All the land was full of people,
Restless, struggling, toiling, striving,
Speaking many tongues, yet feeling
But one heart-beat in their bosoms.
In the woodlands rang their axes,
Smoked their towns in all the valleys,
Over all the lakes and rivers
Rushed their great canoes of thunder.

" Then a darker, drearier vision
Passed before me, vague and cloud-like
I beheld our nation scattered,
All forgetful of my counsels,
Weakened, warring with each other :

Saw the remnants of our people
Sweeping westward, wild and woful,
Like the cloud-rack of a tempest,
Like the withered leaves of Autumn !"

XXII.

HIAWATHA'S DEPARTURE.

By the shore of Gitche Gumee,
By the shining Big-Sea-Water,
At the doorway of his wigwam,
In the pleasant Summer morning,
Hiawatha stood and waited.
All the air was full of freshness,
All the earth was bright and joyous,
And before him, through the sunshine,
Westward toward the neighboring forest
Passed in golden swarms the Ahmo,
Passed the bees, the honey-makers,
Burning, singing in the sunshine.
Bright above him shone the heavens,
Level spread the lake before him ;
From its bosom leaped the sturgeon,
Sparkling, flashing in the sunshine ;
On its margin the great forest
Stood reflected in the water,
Every tree-top had its shadow,
Motionless beneath the water.
From the brow of Hiawatha
Gone was every trace of sorrow,
As the fog from off the water,
As the mist from off the meadow.
With a smile of joy and triumph,
With a look of exultation,
As of one who in a vision
Sees what is to be, but is not,
Stood and waited Hiawatha.
Toward the sun his hands were lifted,
Both the palms spread out against it,
And between the parted fingers
Fell the sunshine on his features,
Flecked with light his naked shoulders,
As it falls and flecks an oak-tree
Through the rifted leaves and branches.
O'er the water floating, flying,
Something in the hazy distance,
Something in the mists of morning,
Loomed and lifted from the water,
Now seemed floating, now seemed flying,
Coming nearer, nearer, nearer.
Was it Shingebis the diver ?
Or the pelican, the Shada ?
Or the heron, the Shuh-shuh-gah ?
Or the white goose, Waw-be-wawa,

With the water dripping, flashing,
From its glossy neck and feathers ?
It was neither goose nor diver,
Neither pelican nor heron,
O'er the water floating, flying,
Through the shining mist of morning,
But a birch canoe with paddles,
Rising, sinking on the water,
Dripping, flashing in the sunshine ;
And within it came a people
From the distant land of Wabun,
From the farthest realms of morning
Came the Black-Robe chief, the Prophet,
He the Priest of Prayer, the Pale-face,
With his guides and his companions.
And the noble Hiawatha,
With his hands aloft extended,
Held aloft in sign of welcome,
Waited, full of exultation,
Till the birch canoe with paddles
Grated on the shining pebbles,
Stranded on the sandy margin,
Till the Black-Robe chief, the Pale-face,
With the cross upon his bosom,
Landed on the sandy margin.
Then the joyous Hiawatha
Cried aloud and spake in this wise :
"Beautiful is the sun, O strangers,
When you come so far to see us !
All our town in peace awaits you,
All our doors stand open for you ;
You shall enter all our wigwams,
For the heart's right hand we give you.
"Never bloomed the earth so gayly,
Never shone the sun so brightly,
As to-day they shine and blossom
When you come so far to see us !
Never was our lake so tranquil,
Nor so free from rocks and sand-bars ;
For your birch canoe in passing
Has removed both rock and sand-bar.
"Never before had our tobacco
Such a sweet and pleasant flavor,
Never the broad leaves of our cornfields
Were so beautiful to look on,
As they seem to us this morning,
When you come so far to see us !"
And the Black-Robe chief made an
swer,
Stammered in his speech a little,
Speaking words yet unfamiliar :
"Peace be with you, Hiawatha,
Peace be with you and your people,
Peace of prayer, and peace of pardon,
Peace of Christ, and joy of Mary !"
Then the generous Hiawatha
Led the strangers to his wigwam,

Seated them on skins of bison,
Seated them on skins of ermine,
And the careful, old Nokomis
Brought them food in bowls of bass-
wood,
Water brought in birchen dippers,
And the calumet, the peace-pipe,
Filled and lighted for their smoking

All the old men of the village,
All the warriors of the nation,
All the Jossakeeds, the prophets,
The magicians, the Wabenos,
And the medicine-men, the Medas,
Came to bid the strangers welcome ;
" It is well," they said, " O brothers,
That you come so far to see us !"

In a circle round the doorway,
With their pipes they sat in silence,
Waiting to behold the strangers,
Waiting to receive their message ;
Till the Black-Robe chief, the Pale-face,
From the wigwam came to greet them,
Stammering in his speech a little,
Speaking words yet unfamiliar ;
" It is well," they said, " O brother,
That you come so far to see us !"

Then the Black-Robe chief, the
prophet,
Told his message to the people,
Told the purport of his mission,
Told them of the Virgin Mary,
And her blessed Son, the Saviour,
How in distant lands and ages
He had lived on earth as we do ;
How he fasted, prayed, and labored ;
How the Jews, the tribe accursed,
Mocked him, scourged him, crucified
him ;
How he rose from where they laid him,
Walked again with his disciples,
And ascended into heaven.

And the chiefs made answer, saying :
" We have listened to your message,
We have heard your words of wisdom,
We will think on what you tell us.
It is well for us, O brothers,
That you come so far to see us !"

Then they rose up and departed
Each one homeward to his wigwam,
To the young men and the women
Told the story of the strangers
Whom the Master of Life had sent them
From the shining land of Wabun.

Heavy with the heat and silence
Grew the afternoon of Summer ;
With a drowsy sound the forest
Whispered round the sultry wigwam,

With a sound of sleep the water
Rippled on the beach below it ;
From the cornfields shrill and ceaseless
Sang the grasshopper, Pah-puk-keena ;
And the guests of Hiawatha,
Weary with the heat of Summer,
Slumbered in the sultry wigwam.

Slowly o'er the simmering landscape
Fell the evening's dusk and coolness,
And the long and level sunbeams
Shot their spears into the forest,
Breaking through its shields of shadow,
Rushed into each secret ambush,
Searched each thicket, dingle, hollow ;
Still the guests of Hiawatha
Slumbered in the silent wigwam.

From his place rose Hiawatha,
Bade farewell to old Nokomis,
Spake in whispers, spake in this wise,
Did not wake the guests, that slumbered :
" I am going, O Nokomis,
On a long and distant journey,
To the portals of the Sunset,
To the regions of the home-wind,
Of the Northwest wind, Keewaydin.
But these guests I leave behind me,
In your watch and ward I leave them ;
See that never harm comes near them,
See that never fear molests them,
Never danger nor suspicion,
Never want of food or shelter,
In the lodge of Hiawatha !"

Forth into the village went he,
Bade farewell to all the warriors,
Bade farewell to all the young men,
Spake persuading, spake in this wise :
" I am going, O my people,
On a long and distant journey ;
Many moons and many winters
Will have come, and will have vanished,
Ere I come again to see you.
But my guests I leave behind me ;
Listen to their words of wisdom,
Listen to the truth they tell you,
For the Master of Life has sent them
From the land of light and morning !"

On the shore stood Hiawatha,
Turned and waved his hand at parting ;
On the clear and luminous water
Launched his birch canoe for sailing,
From the pebbles of the margin
Shoved it forth into the water ;
Whispered to it, " Westward ! west
ward !"
And with speed it darted forward.

And the evening sun descending
Set the clouds on fire with redness,

Burned the broad sky, like a prairie,
Left upon the level water
One long track and trail of splendor,
Down whose stream, as down a river,
Westward, westward Hiawatha
Sailed into the fiery sunset,
Sailed into the purple vapors,
Sailed into the dusk of evening.
And the people from the margin
Watched him floating, rising, sinking,
Till the birch canoe seemed lifted
High into that sea of splendor,
Till it sank into the vapors
Like the new moon slowly, slowly
Sinking in the purple distance.
And they said, " Farewell forever ! "
Said, " Farewell, O Hiawatha ! "
And the forests, dark and lonely,

Moved through all their depths of dark-
  ness,
Sighed, " Farewell, O Hiawatha ! "
And the waves upon the margin
Rising, rippling on the pebbles,
Sobbed, " Farewell, O Hiawatha ! "
And the heron, the Shuh-shuh-gah,
From her haunts among the fen-lands
Screamed, " Farewell, O Hiawatha ! '
  Thus departed Hiawatha,
Hiawatha the Beloved,
In the glory of the sunset,
In the purple mists of evening,
To the regions of the home-wind,
Of the Northwest wind Keewaydin,
To the Islands of the Blessed,
To the kingdom of Ponemah,
To the land of the Hereafter !

THE COURTSHIP OF MILES STANDISH.

I.

MILES STANDISH.

In the Old Colony days, in Plymouth the land of the Pilgrims,
To and fro in a room of his simple and primitive dwelling,
Clad in doublet and hose, and boots of Cordovan leather,
Strode, with a martial air, Miles Standish the Puritan Captain.
Buried in thought he seemed, with his hands behind him, and pausing
Ever and anon to behold his glittering weapons of warfare,
Hanging in shining array along the walls of the chamber, —
Cutlass and corselet of steel, and his trusty sword of Damascus,
Curved at the point and inscribed with its mystical Arabic sentence,
While underneath, in a corner, were fowling-piece, musket, and matchlock.
Short of stature he was, but strongly built and athletic,
Broad in the shoulders, deep-chested, with muscles and sinews of iron ;
Brown as a nut was his face, but his russet beard was already
Flaked with patches of snow, as hedges sometimes in November.
Near him was seated John Alden, his friend, and household companion,
Writing with diligent speed at a table of pine by the window ;
Fair-haired, azure-eyed, with delicate Saxon complexion,
Having the dew of his youth, and the beauty thereof, as the captives
Whom Saint Gregory saw, and exclaimed, " Not Angles, but Angels."
Youngest of all was he of the men who came in the May Flower.

  Suddenly breaking the silence, the diligent scribe interrupting,
Spake, in the pride of his heart, Miles Standish the Captain of Plymouth.
" Look at these arms," he said, " the warlike weapons that hang here
Burnished and bright and clean, as if for parade or inspection !
This is the sword of Damascus I fought with in Flanders ; this breastplate,
Well I remember the day ! once saved my life in a skirmish ;

Here in front you can see the very dint of the bullet
Fired point-blank at my heart by a Spanish arcabucero.
Had it not been of sheer steel, the forgotten bones of Miles Standish
Would at this moment be mould, in their grave in the Flemish morasses.'
Thereupon answered John Alden, but looked not up from his writing :
"Truly the breath of the Lord hath slackened the speed of the bullet ;
He in his mercy preserved you, to be our shield and our weapon"! "
Still the Captain continued, unheeding the words of the stripling :
"See, how bright they are burnished, as if in an arsenal hanging ;
That is because I have done it myself, and not left it to others.
Serve yourself, would you be well served, is an excellent adage ;
So I take care of my arms, as you of your pens and your inkhorn.
Then, too, there are my soldiers, my great, invincible army,
Twelve men, all equipped, having each his rest and his matchlock,
Eighteen shillings a month, together with diet and pillage,
And, like Cæsar, I know the name of each of my soldiers ! "
This he said with a smile, that danced in his eyes, as the sunbeams
Dance on the waves of the sea, and vanish again in a moment.
Alden laughed as he wrote, and still the Captain continued :
"Look ! you can see from this window my brazen howitzer planted
High on the roof of the church, a preacher who speaks to the purpose,
Steady, straightforward, and strong, with irresistible logic,
Orthodox, flashing conviction right into the hearts of the heathen.
Now we are ready, I think, for any assault of the Indians ;
Let them come, if they like, and the sooner they try it the better, —
Let them come if they like, be it sagamore, sachem, or pow-wow,
Aspinet, Samoset, Corbitant, Squanto, or Tokamahamon ! "

Long at the window he stood, and wistfully gazed on the landscape,
Washed with a cold gray mist, the vapory breath of the east-wind,
Forest and meadow and hill, and the steel-blue rim of the ocean,
Lying silent and sad, in the afternoon shadows and sunshine.
Over his countenance flitted a shadow like those on the landscape,
Gloom intermingled with light ; and his voice was subdued with emotion,
Tenderness, pity, regret, as after a pause he proceeded :
"Yonder there, on the hill by the sea, lies buried Rose Standish ;
Beautiful rose of love, that bloomed for me by the wayside !
She was the first to die of all who came in the May Flower !
Green above her is growing the field of wheat we have sown there,
Better to hide from the Indian scouts the graves of our people,
Lest they should count them and see how many already have perished ! "
Sadly his face he averted, and strode up and down, and was thoughtful.

Fixed to the opposite wall was a shelf of books, and among them
Prominent three, distinguished alike for bulk and for binding ;
Bariffe's Artillery Guide, and the Commentaries of Cæsar
Out of the Latin translated by Arthur Goldinge of London,
And, as if guarded by these, between them was standing the Bible.
Musing a moment before them, Miles Standish paused, as if doubtful
Which of the three he should choose for his consolation and comfort,
Whether the wars of the Hebrews, the famous campaigns of the Romans,
Or the Artillery practice, designed for belligerent Christians.
Finally down from its shelf he dragged the ponderous Roman,
Seated himself at the window, and opened the book, and in silence
Turned o'er the well-worn leaves, where thumb-marks thick on the margin,
Like the trample of feet, proclaimed the battle was hottest,
Nothing was heard in the room but the hurrying pen of the stripling,

Busily writing epistles important, to go by the May Flower,
Ready to sail on the morrow, or next day at latest, God willing!
Homeward bound with the tidings of all that terrible winter,
Letters written by Alden, and full of the name of Priscilla,
Full of the name and the fame of the Puritan maiden Priscilla!

II.

LOVE AND FRIENDSHIP.

NOTHING was heard in the room but the hurrying pen of the stripling,
Or an occasional sigh from the laboring heart of the Captain,
Reading the marvellous words and achievements of Julius Cæsar.
After a while he exclaimed, as he smote with his hand, palm downwards,
Heavily on the page : " A wonderful man was this Cæsar !
You are a writer, and I am a fighter, but here is a fellow
Who could both write and fight, and in both was equally skilful ! "
Straightway answered and spake John Alden, the comely, the youthful :
" Yes, he was equally skilled, as you say, with his pen and his weapons.
Somewhere have I read, but where I forget, he could dictate
Seven letters at once, at the same time writing his memoirs."
" Truly," continued the Captain, not heeding or hearing the other,
" Truly a wonderful man was Caius Julius Cæsar !
Better be first, he said, in a little Iberian village,
Than be second in Rome, and I think he was right when he said it.
Twice was he married before he was twenty, and many times after ;
Battles five hundred he fought, and a thousand cities he conquered ;
He, too, fought in Flanders, as he himself has recorded ;
Finally he was stabbed by his friend, the orator Brutus !
Now, do you know what he did on a certain occasion in Flanders,
When the rear-guard of his army retreated, the front giving way too,
And the immortal Twelfth Legion was crowded so closely together
There was no room for their swords ?   Why, he seized a shield from a soldier,
Put himself straight at the head of his troops, and commanded the captains,
Calling on each by his name, to order forward the ensigns ;
Then to widen the ranks, and give more room for their weapons ;
So he won the day, the battle of something-or-other.
That 's what I always say ; if you wish a thing to be well done,
You must do it yourself, you must not leave it to others ! "

All was silent again ; the Captain continued his reading.
Nothing was heard in the room but the hurrying pen of the stripling
Writing epistles important to go next day by the May Flower,
Filled with the name and the fame of the Puritan maiden Priscilla ;
Every sentence began or closed with the name of Priscilla,
Till the treacherous pen, to which he confided the secret,
Strove to betray it by singing and shouting the name of Priscilla !
Finally closing his book, with a bang of the ponderous cover,
Sudden and loud as the sound of a soldier grounding his musket,
Thus to the young man spake Miles Standish the Captain of Plymouth :
" When you have finished your work, I have something important to tell you.
Be not however in haste ; I can wait ; I shall not be impatient ! "
Straightway Alden replied, as he folded the last of his letters,
Pushing his papers aside, and giving respectful attention :
" Speak ; for whenever you speak, I am always ready to listen,
13

Always ready to hear whatever pertains to Miles Standish."
Thereupon answered the Captain, embarrassed, and culling his phrases :
"'T is not good for a man to be alone, say the Scriptures.
This I have said before, and again and again I repeat it ;
Every hour in the day, I think it, and feel it, and say it.
Since Rose Standish died, my life has been weary and dreary ;
Sick at heart have I been, beyond the healing of friendship.
Oft in my lonely hours have I thought of the maiden Priscilla.
She is alone in the world ; her father and mother and brother
Died in the winter together ; I saw her going and coming,
Now to the grave of the dead, and now to the bed of the dying,
Patient, courageous, and strong, and said to myself, that if ever
There were angels on earth, as there are angels in heaven,
Two have I seen and known ; and the angel whose name is Priscilla
Holds in my desolate life the place which the other abandoned.
Long have I cherished the thought, but never have dared to reveal it,
Being a coward in this, though valiant enough for the most part.
Go to the damsel Priscilla, the loveliest maiden of Plymouth,
Say that a blunt old Captain, a man not of words but of actions,
Offers his hand and his heart, the hand and heart of a soldier.
Not in these words, you know, but this in short is my meaning ;
I am a maker of war, and not a maker of phrases.
You, who are bred as a scholar, can say it in elegant language,
Such as you read in your books of the pleadings and wooings of lovers,
Such as you think best adapted to win the heart of a maiden."

When he had spoken, John Alden, the fair-haired, taciturn stripling,
All aghast at his words, surprised, embarrassed, bewildered,
Trying to mask his dismay by treating the subject with lightness,
Trying to smile, and yet feeling his heart stand still in his bosom,
Just as a timepiece stops in a house that is stricken by lightning,
Thus made answer and spake, or rather stammered than answered :
"Such a message as that, I am sure I should mangle and mar it ;
If you would have it well done, — I am only repeating your maxim, —
You must do it yourself, you must not leave it to others ! "
But with the air of a man whom nothing can turn from his purpose,
Gravely shaking his head, made answer the Captain of Plymouth :
" Truly the maxim is good, and I do not mean to gainsay it ;
But we must use it discreetly, and not waste powder for nothing.
Now, as I said before, I was never a maker of phrases.
I can march up to a fortress and summon the place to surrender,
But march up to a woman with such a proposal, I dare not.
I 'm not afraid of bullets, nor shot from the mouth of a cannon,
But of a thundering " No ! " point-blank from the mouth of a woman,
That I confess I 'm afraid of, nor am I ashamed to confess it !
So you must grant my request, for you are an elegant scholar,
Having the graces of speech, and skill in the turning of phrases."
Taking the hand of his friend, who still was reluctant and doubtful,
Holding it long in his own, and pressing it kindly, he added :
"Though I have spoken thus lightly, yet deep is the feeling that prompts me ,
Surely you cannot refuse what I ask in the name of our friendship ! '
Then made answer John Alden : " The name of friendship is sacred ;
What you demand in that name, I have not the power to deny you ! "
So the strong will prevailed, subduing and moulding the gentler,
Friendship prevailed over love, and Alden went on his errand.

III.

THE LOVER'S ERRAND.

So the strong will prevailed, and Alden went on his errand,
Out of the street of the village, and into the paths of the forest,
Into the tranquil woods, where bluebirds and robins were building
Towns in the populous trees, with hanging gardens of verdure,
Peaceful, aerial cities of joy and affection and freedom.
All around him was calm, but within him commotion and conflict,
Love contending with friendship, and self with each generous impulse.
To and fro in his breast his thoughts were heaving and dashing,
As in a foundering ship, with every roll of the vessel,
Washes the bitter sea, the merciless surge of the ocean !
" Must I relinquish it all," he cried with a wild lamentation, —
" Must I relinquish it all, the joy, the hope, the illusion ?
Was it for this I have loved, and waited, and worshipped in silence ?
Was it for this I have followed the flying feet and the shadow
Over the wintry sea, to the desolate shores of New England ?
Truly the heart is deceitful, and out of its depths of corruption
Rise, like an exhalation, the misty phantoms of passion ;
Angels of light they seem, but are only delusions of Satan.
All is clear to me now ; I feel it, I see it distinctly !
This is the hand of the Lord ; it is laid upon me in anger,
For I have followed too much the heart's desires and devices,
Worshipping Astaroth blindly, and impious idols of Baal.
This is the cross I must bear ; the sin and the swift retribution."

So through the Plymouth woods John Alden went on his errand ;
Crossing the brook at the ford, where it brawled over pebble and shallow
Gathering still, as he went, the May-flowers blooming around him,
Fragrant, filling the air with a strange and wonderful sweetness,
Children lost in the woods, and covered with leaves in their slumber.
" Puritan flowers," he said, " and the type of Puritan maidens,
Modest and simple and sweet, the very type of Priscilla !
So I will take them to her ; to Priscilla the May-flower of Plymouth,
Modest and simple and sweet, as a parting gift will I take them ;
Breathing their silent farewells, as they fade and wither and perish,
Soon to be thrown away as is the heart of the giver."
So through the Plymouth woods John Alden went on his errand ;
Came to an open space, and saw the disk of the ocean,
Sailless, sombre and cold with the comfortless breath of the east-wind ;
Saw the new-built house, and people at work in a meadow ;
Heard, as he drew near the door, the musical voice of Priscilla
Singing the hundredth Psalm, the grand old Puritan anthem,
Music that Luther sang to the sacred words of the Psalmist,
Full of the breath of the Lord, consoling and comforting many.
Then, as he opened the door, he beheld the form of the maiden
Seated beside her wheel, and the carded wool like a snow-drift
Piled at her knee, her white hands feeding the ravenous spindle,
While with her foot on the treadle she guided the wheel in its motion.
Open wide on her lap lay the well-worn psalm-book of Ainsworth,
Printed in Amsterdam, the words and the music together,
Rough-hewn, angular notes, like stones in the wall of a churchyard,
Darkened and overhung by the running vine of the verses.
Such was the book from whose pages she sang the old Puritan anthem,
She, the Puritan girl, in the solitude of the forest,

Making the humble house and the modest apparel of home-spun
Beautiful with her beauty, and rich with the wealth of her being !
Over him rushed, like a wind that is keen and cold and relentless,
Thoughts of what might have been, and the weight and woe of his errand ;
All the dreams that had faded, and all the hopes that had vanished,
All his life henceforth a dreary and tenantless mansion,
Haunted by vain regrets, and pallid, sorrowful faces.
Still he said to himself, and almost fiercely he said it,
" Let not him that putteth his hand to the plough look backwards ;
Though the ploughshare cut through the flowers of life to its fountains,
Though it pass o'er the graves of the dead and the hearths of the living,
It is the will of the Lord ; and his mercy endureth forever ! "

So he entered the house : and the hum of the wheel and the singing
Suddenly ceased ; for Priscilla, aroused by his step on the threshold,
Rose as he entered, and gave him her hand, in signal of welcome,
Saying, " I knew it was you, when I heard your step in the passage ;
For I was thinking of you, as I sat there singing and spinning."
Awkward and dumb with delight, that a thought of him had been mingled
Thus in the sacred psalm, that came from the heart of the maiden,
Silent before her he stood, and gave her the flowers for an answer,
Finding no words for his thought.   He remembered that day in the winter,
After the first great snow, when he broke a path from the village,
Reeling and plunging along through the drifts that encumbered the doorway,
Stamping the snow from his feet as he entered the house, and Priscilla.
Laughed at his snowy locks, and gave him a seat by the fireside,
Grateful and pleased to know he had thought of her in the snow-storm.
Had he but spoken then ! perhaps not in vain had he spoken ;
Now it was all too late ; the golden moment had vanished !
So he stood there abashed, and gave her the flowers for an answer.

Then they sat down and talked of the birds and the beautiful Spring-time,
Talked of their friends at home, and the May Flower that sailed on the morrow.
" I have been thinking all day," said gently the Puritan maiden,
" Dreaming all night, and thinking all day, of the hedge-rows of England, —
They are in blossom now, and the country is all like a garden ;
Thinking of lanes and fields, and the song of the lark and the linnet,
Seeing the village street, and familiar faces of neighbors
Going about as of old, and stopping to gossip together,
And, at the end of the street, the village church, with the ivy
Climbing the old gray tower, and the quiet graves in the churchyard.
Kind are the people I live with, and dear to me my religion ;
Still my heart is so sad, that I wish myself back in Old England.
You will say it is wrong, but I cannot help it : I almost
Wish myself back in Old England, I feel so lonely and wretched."

Thereupon answered the youth : " Indeed I do not condemn you ;
Stouter hearts than a woman's have quailed in this terrible winter.
Yours is tender and trusting, and needs a stronger to lean on ;
So I have come to you now, with an offer and proffer of marriage
Made by a good man and true, Miles Standish the Captain of Plymouth ! "

Thus he delivered his message, the dexterous writer of letters, —
Did not embellish the theme, nor array it in beautiful phrases,
But came straight to the point, and blurted it out like a school-boy ;
Even the Captain himself could hardly have said it more bluntly.

Mute with amazement and sorrow, Priscilla the Puritan maiden
Looked into Alden's face, her eyes dilated with wonder,
Feeling his words like a blow, that stunned her and rendered her speechless;
Till at length she exclaimed, interrupting the ominous silence:
"If the great captain of Plymouth is so very eager to wed me,
Why does he not come himself, and take the trouble to woo me?
If I am not worth the wooing, I surely am not worth the winning!"
Then John Alden began explaining and smoothing the matter,
Making it worse as he went, by saying the Captain was busy,—
Had no time for such things;— such things! the words grating harshly
Fell on the ear of Priscilla; and swift as a flash she made answer ·
"Has no time for such things, as you call it, before he is married,
Would he be likely to find it, or make it, after the wedding?
That is the way with you men; you don't understand us, you cannot.
When you have made up your minds, after thinking of this one and that one,
Choosing, selecting, rejecting, comparing one with another,
Then you make known your desire, with abrupt and sudden avowal,
And are offended and hurt, and indignant perhaps, that a woman
Does not respond at once to a love that she never suspected,
Does not attain at a bound the height to which you have been climbing.
This is not right nor just: for surely a woman's affection
Is not a thing to be asked for, and had for only the asking.
When one is truly in love, one not only says it, but shows it.
Had he but waited awhile, had he only showed that he loved me,
Even this Captain of yours — who knows? — at last might have won me,
Old and rough as he is; but now it never can happen."

Still John Alden went on, unheeding the words of Priscilla,
Urging the suit of his friend, explaining, persuading, expanding;
Spoke of his courage and skill, and of all his battles in Flanders,
How with the people of God he had chosen to suffer affliction,
How, in return for his zeal, they had made him Captain of Plymouth;
He was a gentleman born, could trace his pedigree plainly
Back to Hugh Standish of Duxbury Hall, in Lancashire, England,
Who was the son of Ralph, and the grandson of Thurston de Standish;
Heir unto vast estates, of which he was basely defrauded,
Still bore the family arms, and had for his crest a cock argent
Combed and wattled gules, and all the rest of the blazon.
He was a man of honor, of noble and generous nature;
Though he was rough, he was kindly; she knew how during the winter
He had attended the sick, with a hand as gentle as woman's;
Somewhat hasty and hot, he could not deny it, and headstrong,
Stern as a soldier might be, but hearty, and placable always,
Not to be laughed at and scorned, because he was little of stature;
For he was great of heart, magnanimous, courtly, courageous;
Any woman in Plymouth, nay, any woman in England,
Might be happy and proud to be called the wife of Miles Standish!

But as he warmed and glowed, in his simple and eloquent language,
Quite forgetful of self, and full of the praise of his rival,
Archly the maiden smiled and, with eyes overrunning with laughter,
Said, in a tremulous voice, "Why don't you speak for yourself, John?"

IV.

JOHN ALDEN.

INTO the open air John Alden, perplexed and bewildered,
Rushed like a man insane, and wandered alone by the sea-side ;
Paced up and down the sands, and bared his head to the east-wind,
Cooling his heated brow, and the fire and fever within him.
Slowly as out of the heavens, with apocalyptical splendors,
Sank the City of God, in the vision of John the Apostle,
So, with its cloudy walls of chrysolite, jasper, and sapphire,
Sank the broad red sun, and over its turrets uplifted
Glimmered the golden reed of the angel who measured the city.

"Welcome, O wind of the East !" he exclaimed in his wild exultation,
"Welcome, O wind of the East, from the caves of the misty Atlantic !
Blowing o'er fields of dulse, and measureless meadows of sea-grass,
Blowing o'er rocky wastes, and the grottos and gardens of ocean !
Lay thy cold, moist hand on my burning forehead, and wrap me
Close in thy garments of mist, to allay the fever within me !"

Like an awakened conscience, the sea was moaning and tossing,
Beating remorseful and loud the mutable sands of the sea-shore.
Fierce in his soul was the struggle and tumult of passions contending ;
Love triumphant and crowned, and friendship wounded and bleeding,
Passionate cries of desire, and importunate pleadings of duty !
"Is it my fault," he said, "that the maiden has chosen between us ?
Is it my fault that he failed, — my fault that I am the victor ?"
Then within him there thundered a voice, like the voice of the Prophet :
"It hath displeased the Lord !" — and he thought of David's transgression,
Bathsheba's beautiful face, and his friend in the front of the battle ;
Shame and confusion of guilt, and abasement and self-condemnation,
Overwhelmed him at once ; and he cried in the deepest contrition :
"It hath displeased the Lord !   It is the temptation of Satan !"

Then, uplifting his head, he looked at the sea, and beheld there
Dimly the shadowy form of the May Flower riding at anchor,
Rocked on the rising tide, and ready to sail on the morrow ;
Heard the voices of men through the mist, the rattle of cordage
Thrown on the deck, the shouts of the mate, and the sailors' "Ay, ay, Sir !"
Clear and distinct, but not loud, in the dripping air of the twilight.
Still for a moment he stood, and listened, and stared at the vessel,
Then went hurriedly on, as one who, seeing a phantom,
Stops, then quickens his pace, and follows the beckoning shadow.
"Yes, it is plain to me now," he murmured ; "the hand of the Lord is
Leading me out of the land of darkness, the bondage of error,
Through the sea, that shall lift the walls of its waters around me,
Hiding me, cutting me off, from the cruel thoughts that pursue me.
Back will I go o'er the ocean, this dreary land will abandon,
Her whom I may not love, and him whom my heart has offended.
Better to be in my grave in the green old churchyard in England,
Close by my mother's side, and among the dust of my kindred ;
Better be dead and forgotten, than living in shame and dishonor !
Sacred and safe and unseen, in the dark of the narrow chamber
With me my secret shall lie, like a buried jewel that glimmers
Bright on the hand that is dust, in the chambers of silence and darkness, —
Yes, as the marriage ring of the great espousal hereafter !"

Thus as he spake, he turned, in the strength of his strong resolution,
Leaving behind him the shore, and hurried along in the twilight,
Through the congenial gloom of the forest silent and sombre,
Till he beheld the lights in the seven houses of Plymouth,
Shining like seven stars in the dusk and mist of the evening.
Soon he entered his door, and found the redoubtable Captain
Sitting alone, and absorbed in the martial pages of Cæsar,
Fighting some great campaign in Hainault or Brabant or Flanders.
"Long have you been on your errand," he said with a cheery demeanor,
Even as one who is waiting an answer, and fears not the issue.
"Not far off is the house, although the woods are between us ;
But you have lingered so long, that while you were going and coming
I have fought ten battles and sacked and demolished a city.
Come, sit down, and in order relate to me all that has happened."

Then John Alden spake, and related the wondrous adventure,
From beginning to end, minutely, just as it happened ;
How he had seen Priscilla, and how he had sped in his courtship,
Only smoothing a little, and softening down her refusal.
But when he came at length to the words Priscilla had spoken,
Words so tender and cruel : "Why don't you speak for yourself, John ?"
Up leaped the Captain of Plymouth, and stamped on the floor, till his armor
Clanged on the wall, where it hung, with a sound of sinister omen.
All his pent-up wrath burst forth in a sudden explosion,
E'en as a hand-grenade, that scatters destruction around it.
Wildly he shouted, and loud : "John Alden ! you have betrayed me !
Me, Miles Standish, your friend ! have supplanted, defrauded, betrayed me !
One of my ancestors ran his sword through the heart of Wat Tyler ;
Who shall prevent me from running my own through the heart of a traitor ?
Yours is the greater treason, for yours is a treason to friendship !
You, who lived under my roof, whom I cherished and loved as a brother ;
You, who have fed at my board, and drunk at my cup, to whose keeping
I have intrusted my honor, my thoughts the most sacred and secret, —
You too, Brutus ! ah woe to the name of friendship hereafter !
Brutus was Cæsar's friend, and you were mine, but henceforward
Let there be nothing between us save war, and implacable hatred !"

So spake the Captain of Plymouth, and strode about in the chamber,
Chafing and choking with rage ; like cords were the veins on his temples.
But in the midst of his anger a man appeared at the doorway,
Bringing in uttermost haste a message of urgent importance,
Rumors of danger and war and hostile incursions of Indians !
Straightway the Captain paused, and, without further question or parley,
Took from the nail on the wall his sword with its scabbard of iron,
Buckled the belt round his waist, and, frowning fiercely, departed.
Alden was left alone.   He heard the clank of the scabbard
Growing fainter and fainter, and dying away in the distance.
Then he arose from his seat, and looked forth into the darkness,
Felt the cool air blow on his cheek, that was hot with the insult,
Lifted his eyes to the heavens, and, folding his hands as in childhood,
Prayed in the silence of night to the Father who seeth in secret.

Meanwhile the choleric Captain strode wrathful away to the council,
Found it already assembled, impatiently waiting his coming ;
Men in the middle of life, austere and grave in deportment,
Only one of them old, the hill that was nearest to heaven,
Covered with snow, but erect, the excellent Elder of Plymouth.

God had sifted three kingdoms to find the wheat for this planting,
Then had sifted the wheat, as the living seed of a nation ;
So say the chronicles old, and such is the faith of the people !
Near them was standing an Indian, in attitude stern and defiant,
Naked down to the waist, and grim and ferocious in aspect ;
While on the table before them was lying unopened a Bible,
Ponderous, bound in leather, brass-studded, printed in Holland,
And beside it outstretched the skin of a rattlesnake glittered,
Filled, like a quiver, with arrows ; a signal and challenge of warfare,
Brought by the Indian, and speaking with arrowy tongues of defiance.
This Miles Standish beheld, as he entered, and heard them debating
What were an answer befitting the hostile message and menace,
Talking of this and of that, contriving, suggesting, objecting ;
One voice only for peace, and that the voice of the Elder,
Judging it wise and well that some at least were converted,
Rather than any were slain, for this was but Christian behavior !
Then out spake Miles Standish, the stalwart Captain of Plymouth,
Muttering deep in his throat, for his voice was husky with anger,
"What ! do you mean to make war with milk and the water of roses ?
Is it to shoot red squirrels you have your howitzer planted
There on the roof of the church, or is it to shoot red devils ?
Truly the only tongue that is understood by a savage
Must be the tongue of fire that speaks from the mouth of the cannon !"
Thereupon answered and said the excellent Elder of Plymouth,
Somewhat amazed and alarmed at this irreverent language :
"Not so thought Saint Paul, nor yet the other Apostles ;
Not from the cannon's mouth were the tongues of fire they spake with !"
But unheeded fell this mild rebuke on the Captain,
Who had advanced to the table, and thus continued discoursing :
"Leave this matter to me, for to me by right it pertaineth.
War is a terrible trade ; but in the cause that is righteous,
Sweet is the smell of powder ; and thus I answer the challenge !"

Then from the rattlesnake's skin, with a sudden, contemptuous gesture,
Jerking the Indian arrows, he filled it with powder and bullets
Full to the very jaws, and handed it back to the savage,
Saying, in thundering tones : "Here, take it ! this is your answer !"
Silently out of the room then glided the glistening savage,
Bearing the serpent's skin, and seeming himself like a serpent,
Winding his sinuous way in the dark to the depths of the forest.

V.

THE SAILING OF THE MAY FLOWER.

JUST in the gray of the dawn, as the mists uprose from the meadows,
There was a stir and a sound in the slumbering village of Plymouth ;
Clanging and clicking of arms, and the order imperative, "Forward !"
Given in tone suppressed, a tramp of feet, and then silence.
Figures ten, in the mist, marched slowly out of the village.
Standish the stalwart it was, with eight of his valorous army,
Led by their Indian guide, by Hobomok, friend of the white men,
Northward marching to quell the sudden revolt of the savage.
Giants they seemed in the mist, or the mighty men of King David ;
Giants in heart they were, who believed in God and the Bible, —
Ay, who believed in the smiting of Midianites and Philistines.

Over them gleamed far off the crimson banners of morning ;
Under them loud on the sands, the serried billows, advancing
Fired along the line, and in regular order retreated.

Many a mile had they marched, when at length the village of Plymouth
Woke from its sleep, and arose, intent on its manifold labors.
Sweet was the air and soft ; and slowly the smoke from the chimneys
Rose over roofs of thatch, and pointed steadily eastward ;
Men came forth from the doors, and paused and talked of the weather,
Said that the wind had changed, and was blowing fair for the May Flower ;
Talked of their Captain's departure, and all the dangers that menaced,
He being gone, the town, and what should be done in his absence.
Merrily sang the birds, and the tender voices of women
Consecrated with hymns the common cares of the household.
Out of the sea rose the sun, and the billows rejoiced at his coming ;
Beautiful were his feet on the purple tops of the mountains ;
Beautiful on the sails of the May Flower riding at anchor,
Battered and blackened and worn by all the storms of the winter,
Loosely against her masts was hanging and flapping her canvas,
Rent by so many gales, and patched by the hands of the sailors.
Suddenly from her side, as the sun rose over the ocean,
Darted a puff of smoke, and floated seaward ; anon rang
Loud over field and forest the cannon's roar, and the echoes
Heard and repeated the sound, the signal-gun of departure !
Ah ! but with louder echoes replied the hearts of the people !
Meekly, in voices subdued, the chapter was read from the Bible,
Meekly the prayer was begun, but ended in fervent entreaty !
Then from their houses in haste came forth the Pilgrims of Plymouth,
Men and women and children, all hurrying down to the sea-shore,
Eager, with tearful eyes, to say farewell to the May Flower,
Homeward bound o'er the sea, and leaving them here in the desert.

Foremost among them was Alden.   All night he had lain without slumber,
Turning and tossing about in the heat and unrest of his fever.
He had beheld Miles Standish, who came back late from the council,
Stalking into the room, and heard him mutter and murmur,
Sometimes it seemed a prayer, and sometimes it sounded like swearing.
Once he had come to the bed, and stood there a moment in silence ;
Then he had turned away, and said : "I will not awake him ;
Let him sleep on, it is best ; for what is the use of more talking !"
Then he extinguished the light, and threw himself down on his pallet,
Dressed as he was, and ready to start at the break of the morning, —
Covered himself with the cloak he had worn in his campaigns in Flanders,
Slept as a soldier sleeps in his bivouac, ready for action.
But with the dawn he arose ; in the twilight Alden beheld him
Put on his corselet of steel, and all the rest of his armor,
Buckle about his waist his trusty blade of Damascus,
Take from the corner his musket, and so stride out of the chamber.
Often the heart of the youth had burned and yearned to embrace him,
Often his lips had essayed to speak, imploring for pardon ;
All the old friendship came back, with its tender and grateful emotions ;
But his pride overmastered the nobler nature within him, —
Pride, and the sense of his wrong, and the burning fire of the insult.
So he beheld his friend departing in anger, but spake not,
Saw him go forth to danger, perhaps to death, and he spake not !
Then he arose from his bed, and heard what the people were saying,
Joined in the talk at the door, with Stephen and Richard and Gilbert.

Joined in the morning prayer, and in the reading of Scripture,
And, with the others, in haste went hurrying down to the sea-shore,
Down to the Plymouth Rock, that had been to their feet as a doorstep
Into a world unknown, — the corner-stone of a nation !

There with his boat was the Master, already a little impatient
Lest he should lose the tide, or the wind might shift to the eastward,
Square-built, hearty, and strong, with an odor of ocean about him,
Speaking with this one and that, and cramming letters and parcels
Into his pockets capacious, and messages mingled together
Into his narrow brain, till at last he was wholly bewildered.
Nearer the boat stood Alden, with one foot placed on the gunwale,
One still firm on the rock, and talking at times with the sailors,
Seated erect on the thwarts, all ready and eager for starting.
He too was eager to go, and thus put an end to his anguish,
Thinking to fly from despair, that swifter than keel is or canvas,
Thinking to drown in the sea the ghost that would rise and pursue him.
But as he gazed on the crowd, he beheld the form of Priscilla
Standing dejected among them, unconscious of all that was passing.
Fixed were her eyes upon his, as if she divined his intention,
Fixed with a look so sad, so reproachful, imploring, and patient,
That with a sudden revulsion his heart recoiled from its purpose,
As from the verge of a crag, where one step more is destruction.
Strange is the heart of man, with its quick, mysterious instincts !
Strange is the life of man, and fatal or fated are moments,
Whereupon turn, as on hinges, the gates of the wall adamantine !
" Here I remain !" he exclaimed, as he looked at the heavens above him,
Thanking the Lord whose breath had scattered the mist and the madness
Wherein, blind and lost, to death he was staggering headlong.
" Yonder snow-white cloud, that floats in the ether above me,
Seems like a hand that is pointing and beckoning over the ocean.
There is another hand, that is not so spectral and ghost-like,
Holding me, drawing me back, and clasping mine for protection.
Float, O hand of cloud, and vanish away in the ether !
Roll thyself up like a fist, to threaten and daunt me ; I heed not
Either your warning or menace, or any omen of evil !
There is no land so sacred, no air so pure and so wholesome,
As is the air she breathes, and the soil that is pressed by her footsteps.
Here for her sake will I stay, and like an invisible presence
Hover around her forever, protecting, supporting her weakness ;
Yes ! as my foot was the first that stepped on this rock at the landing,
So, with the blessing of God, shall it be the last at the leaving ! "

Meanwhile the Master alert, but with dignified air and important,
Scanning with watchful eye the tide and the wind and the weather,
Walked about on the sands, and the people crowded around him
Saying a few last words, and enforcing his careful remembrance.
Then, taking each by the hand, as if he were grasping a tiller,
Into the boat he sprang, and in haste shoved off to his vessel,
Glad in his heart to get rid of all this worry and flurry,
Glad to be gone from a land of sand and sickness and sorrow,
Short allowance of victual, and plenty of nothing but Gospel !
Lost in the sound of the oars was the last farewell of the Pilgrims.
O strong hearts and true ! not one went back in the May Flower !
No, not one looked back, who had set his hand to this ploughing !

Soon were heard on board the shouts and songs of the sailors
Heaving the windlass round, and hoisting the ponderous anchor.

Then the yards were braced, and all sails set to the west-wind,
Blowing steady and strong ; and the May Flower sailed from the harbor,
Rounded the point of the Gurnet, and leaving far to the southward
Island and cape of sand, and the Field of the First Encounter,
Took the wind on her quarter, and stood for the open Atlantic,
Borne on the send of the sea, and the swelling hearts of the Pilgrims.

Long in silence they watched the receding sail of the vessel,
Much endeared to them all, as something living and human ;
Then, as if filled with the spirit, and wrapt in a vision prophetic,
Baring his hoary head, the excellent Elder of Plymouth
Said, " Let us pray ! " and they prayed, and thanked the Lord and took courage.
Mournfully sobbed the waves at the base of the rock, and above them
Bowed and whispered the wheat on the hill of death, and their kindred
Seemed to awake in their graves, and to join in the prayer that they uttered.
Sun-illumined and white, on the eastern verge of the ocean
Gleamed the departing sail, like a marble slab in a graveyard ;
Buried beneath it lay forever all hope of escaping.
Lo ! as they turned to depart, they saw the form of an Indian,
Watching them from the hill ; but while they spake with each other,
Pointing with outstretched hands, and saying, " Look ! " he had vanished.
So they returned to their homes ; but Alden lingered a little,
Musing alone on the shore, and watching the wash of the billows
Round the base of the rock, and the sparkle and flash of the sunshine,
Like the spirit of God, moving visibly over the waters.

VI.

PRISCILLA.

Thus for a while he stood, and mused by the shore of the ocean,
Thinking of many things, and most of all of Priscilla ;
And as if thought had the power to draw to itself, like the loadstone,
Whatsoever it touches, by subtile laws of its nature,
Lo ! as he turned to depart, Priscilla was standing beside him.

" Are you so much offended, you will not speak to me ? " said she.
" Am I so much to blame, that yesterday, when you were pleading
Warmly the cause of another, my heart, impulsive and wayward,
Pleaded your own, and spake out, forgetful perhaps of decorum ?
Certainly you can forgive me for speaking so frankly, for saying
What I ought not to have said, yet now I can never unsay it ;
For there are moments in life, when the heart is so full of emotion,
That if by chance it be shaken, or into its depths like a pebble
Drops some careless word, it overflows, and its secret,
Spilt on the ground like water, can never be gathered together.
Yesterday I was shocked, when I heard you speak of Miles Standish,
Praising his virtues, transforming his very defects into virtues,
Praising his courage and strength, and even his fighting in Flanders,
As if by fighting alone you could win the heart of a woman,
Quite overlooking yourself and the rest, in exalting your hero.
Therefore I spake as I did, by an irresistible impulse.
You will forgive me, I hope, for the sake of the friendship between us,
Which is too true and too sacred to be so easily broken ! "
Thereupon answered John Alden, the scholar, the friend of Miles Standish :

"I was not angry with you, with myself alone I was angry,
Seeing how badly I managed the matter I had in my keeping."
"No!" interrupted the maiden, with answer prompt and decisive;
"No; you were angry with me, for speaking so frankly and freely.
It was wrong, I acknowledge; for it is the fate of a woman
Long to be patient and silent, to wait like a ghost that is speechless,
Till some questioning voice dissolves the spell of its silence.
Hence is the inner life of so many suffering women
Sunless and silent and deep, like subterranean rivers
Running through caverns of darkness, unheard, unseen, and unfruitful,
Chafing their channels of stone, with endless and profitless murmurs."
Thereupon answered John Alden, the young man, the lover of women:
"Heaven forbid it, Priscilla; and truly they seem to me always
More like the beautiful rivers that watered the garden of Eden,
More like the river Euphrates, through deserts of Havilah flowing,
Filling the land with delight, and memories sweet of the garden!"
"Ah, by these words, I can see," again interrupted the maiden,
"How very little you prize me, or care for what I am saying.
When from the depths of my heart, in pain and with secret misgiving,
Frankly I speak to you, asking for sympathy only and kindness,
Straightway you take up my words, that are plain and direct and in earnest.
Turn them away from their meaning, and answer with flattering phrases.
This is not right, is not just, is not true to the best that is in you;
For I know and esteem you, and feel that your nature is noble,
Lifting mine up to a higher, a more ethereal level.
Therefore I value your friendship, and feel it perhaps the more keenly
If you say aught that implies I am only as one among many,
If you make use of those common and complimentary phrases
Most men think so fine, in dealing and speaking with women,
But which women reject as insipid, if not as insulting."

Mute and amazed was Alden; and listened and looked at Priscilla,
Thinking he never had seen her more fair, more divine in her beauty.
He who but yesterday pleaded so glibly the cause of another,
Stood there embarrassed and silent, and seeking in vain for an answer.
So the maiden went on, and little divined or imagined
What was at work in his heart, that made him so awkward and speechless.
"Let us, then, be what we are, and speak what we think, and in all things
Keep **ourselves** loyal to truth, and the sacred professions of friendship.
It is no secret I tell you, nor am I ashamed to declare it:
I have liked to be with you, to see you, to speak with you always.
So I was hurt at your words, and a little affronted to hear you
Urge me to marry your friend, though he were the Captain Miles Standish.
For I must tell you the truth: much more to me is your friendship
Than all the love he could give, were he twice the hero you think him."
Then she extended her hand, and Alden, who eagerly grasped it,
Felt all the wounds in his heart, that were aching and bleeding so sorely,
Healed by the touch of that hand, and he said, with a voice full of feeling:
"Yes, we must ever be friends; and of all who offer you friendship
Let me be ever the first, the truest, the nearest and dearest!"

Casting a farewell look at the glimmering sail of the May Flower,
Distant, but still in sight, and sinking below the horizon,
Homeward together they walked, with a strange, indefinite feeling,
That all the rest had departed and left them alone in the desert.
But, as they went through the fields in the blessing and smile of the sunshine
Lighter grew their hearts, and Priscilla said very archly:

"Now that our terrible Captain has gone in pursuit of the Indians,
Where he is happier far than he would be commanding a household,
You may speak boldly, and tell me of all that happened between you,
When you returned last night, and said how ungrateful you found me."
Thereupon answered John Alden, and told her the whole of the story, —
Told her his own despair, and the direful wrath of Miles Standish.
Whereat the maiden smiled, and said between laughing and earnest,
"He is a little chimney, and heated hot in a moment!"
But as he gently rebuked her, and told her how he had suffered, —
How he had even determined to sail that day in the May Flower,
And had remained for her sake, on hearing the dangers that threatened, —
All her manner was changed, and she said with a faltering accent,
"Truly I thank you for this : how good you have been to me always!"

Thus, as a pilgrim devout, who toward Jerusalem journeys,
Taking three steps in advance, and one reluctantly backward,
Urged by importunate zeal, and withheld by pangs of contrition ;
Slowly but steadily onward, receding yet ever advancing,
Journeyed this Puritan youth to the Holy Land of his longings,
Urged by the fervor of love, and withheld by remorseful misgivings.

VII.

THE MARCH OF MILES STANDISH.

MEANWHILE the stalwart Miles Standish was marching steadily northward,
Winding through forest and swamp, and along the trend of the sea-shore,
All day long, with hardly a halt, the fire of his anger
Burning and crackling within, and the sulphurous odor of powder
Seeming more sweet to his nostrils than all the scents of the forest.
Silent and moody he went, and much he revolved his discomfort ;
He who was used to success, and to easy victories always,
Thus to be flouted, rejected, and laughed to scorn by a maiden,
Thus to be mocked and betrayed by the friend whom most he had trusted !
Ah! 't was too much to be borne, and he fretted and chafed in his armor !

"I alone am to blame," he muttered, "for mine was the folly.
What has a rough old soldier, grown grim and gray in the harness,
Used to the camp and its ways, to do with the wooing of maidens?
'T was but a dream, — let it pass, — let it vanish like so many others!
What I thought was a flower, is only a weed, and is worthless ;
Out of my heart will I pluck it, and throw it away, and henceforward
Be but a fighter of battles, a lover and wooer of dangers!"
Thus he revolved in his mind his sorry defeat and discomfort,
While he was marching by day or lying at night in the forest,
Looking up at the trees, and the constellations beyond them.

After a three days' march he came to an Indian encampment
Pitched on the edge of a meadow, between the sea and the forest ;
Women at work by the tents, and the warriors, horrid with war-paint,
Seated about a fire, and smoking and talking together ;
Who, when they saw from afar the sudden approach of the white men,
Saw the flash of the sun on breastplate and sabre and musket,
Straightway leaped to their feet, and two, from among them advancing,
Came to parley with Standish, and offer him furs as a present ;
Friendship was in their looks, but in their hearts there was hatred.

Braves of the tribe were these, and brothers gigantic in stature,
Huge as Goliath of Gath, or the terrible Og, king of Bashan ;
One was Pecksuot named, and the other was called Wattawamat.
Round their necks were suspended their knives in scabbards of wampum,
Two-edged, trenchant knives, with points as sharp as a needle.
Other arms had they none, for they were cunning and crafty.
"Welcome, English !" they said, — these words they had learned from the traders
Touching at times on the coast, to barter and chaffer for peltries.
Then in their native tongue they began to parley with Standish,
Through his guide and interpreter, Hobomok, friend of the white man,
Begging for blankets and knives, but mostly for muskets and powder,
Kept by the white man, they said, concealed, with the plague, in his cellars,
Ready to be let loose, and destroy his brother the red man !
But when Standish refused, and said he would give them the Bible,
Suddenly changing their tone, they began to boast and to bluster.
Then Wattawamat advanced with a stride in front of the other,
And, with a lofty demeanor, thus vauntingly spake to the Captain :
" Now Wattawamat can see, by the fiery eyes of the Captain,
Angry is he in his heart ; but the heart of the brave Wattawamat
Is not afraid at the sight.   He was not born of a woman,
But on a mountain, at night, from an oak-tree riven by lightning,
Forth he sprang at a bound, with all his weapons about him,
Shouting, ' Who is there here to fight with the brave Wattawamat ?' "
Then he unsheathed his knife, and, whetting the blade on his left hand,
Held it aloft and displayed a woman's face on the handle,
Saying, with bitter expression and look of sinister meaning :
" I have another at home, with the face of a man on the handle ;
By and by they shall marry ; and there will be plenty of children ! "

Then stood Pecksuot forth, self-vaunting, insulting Miles Standish :
While with his fingers he patted the knife that hung at his bosom,
Drawing it half from its sheath, and plunging it back, as he muttered,
" By and by it shall see ; it shall eat ; ah, ha ! but shall speak not !
This is the mighty Captain the white men have sent to destroy us !
He is a little man ; let him go and work with the women ! "

Meanwhile Standish had noted the faces and figures of Indians
Peeping and creeping about from bush to tree in the forest,
Feigning to look for game, with arrows set on their bow-strings,
Drawing about him still closer and closer the net of their ambush.
But undaunted he stood, and dissembled and treated them smoothly ;
So the old chronicles say, that were writ in the days of the fathers.
But when he heard their defiance, the boast, the taunt, and the insult,
All the hot blood of his race, of Sir Hugh and of Thurston de Standish,
Boiled and beat in his heart, and swelled in the veins of his temples.
Headlong he leaped on the boaster, and, snatching his knife from its scabbard,
Plunged it into his heart, and, reeling backward, the savage
Fell with his face to the sky, and a fiendlike fierceness upon it.
Straight there arose from the forest the awful sound of the war-whoop,
And, like a flurry of snow on the whistling wind of December,
Swift and sudden and keen came a flight of feathery arrows.
Then came a cloud of smoke, and out of the cloud came the lightning,
Out of the lightning thunder ; and death unseen ran before it.
Frightened the savages fled for shelter in swamp and in thicket,
Hotly pursued and beset ; but their sachem, the brave Wattawamat,
Fled not ; he was dead.   Unswerving and swift had a bullet

Passed through his brain, and he fell with both hands clutching the greensward.
Seeming in death to hold back from his foe the land of his fathers.

There on the flowers of the meadow the warriors lay, and above them,
Silent, with folded arms, stood Hobomok, friend of the white man.
Smiling at length he exclaimed to the stalwart Captain of Plymouth :
"Pecksuot bragged very loud, of his courage, his strength, and his stature, —
Mocked the great Captain, and called him a little man ; but I see now
Big enough have you been to lay him speechless before you ! "

Thus the first battle was fought and won by the stalwart Miles Standish.
When the tidings thereof were brought to the village of Plymouth,
And as a trophy of war the head of the brave Wattawamat
Scowled from the roof of the fort, which at once was a church and a fortress,
All who beheld it rejoiced, and praised the Lord, and took courage.
Only Priscilla averted her face from this spectre of terror,
Thanking God in her heart that she had not married Miles Standish ;
Shrinking, fearing almost, lest, coming home from his battles,
He should lay claim to her hand, as the prize and reward of his valor.

VIII.

THE SPINNING-WHEEL.

MONTH after month passed away, and in Autumn the ships of the merchants
Came with kindred and friends, with cattle and corn for the Pilgrims.
All in the village was peace ; the men were intent on their labors,
Busy with hewing and building, with garden-plot and with merestead,
Busy with breaking the glebe, and mowing the grass in the meadows,
Searching the sea for its fish, and hunting the deer in the forest.
All in the village was peace ; but at times the rumor of warfare
Filled the air with alarm, and the apprehension of danger.
Bravely the stalwart Standish was scouring the land with his forces,
Waxing valiant in fight and defeating the alien armies,
Till his name had become a sound of fear to the nations.
Anger was still in his heart, but at times the remorse and contrition
Which in all noble natures succeed the passionate outbreak,
Came like a rising tide, that encounters the rush of a river,
Staying its current awhile, but making it bitter and brackish.

Meanwhile Alden at home had built him a new habitation,
Solid, substantial, of timber rough-hewn from the firs of the forest.
Wooden-barred was the door, and the roof was covered with rushes ;
Latticed the windows were, and the window-panes were of paper,
Oiled to admit the light, while wind and rain were excluded.
There too he dug a well, and around it planted an orchard :
Still may be seen to this day some trace of the well and the orchard.
Close to the house was the stall, where, safe and secure from annoyance,
Raghorn, the snow-white bull, that had fallen to Alden's allotment
In the division of cattle, might ruminate in the night-time
Over the pastures he cropped, made fragrant by sweet pennyroyal.

Oft when his labor was finished, with eager feet would the dreamer
Follow the pathway that ran through the woods to the house of Priscilla,
Led by illusions romantic and subtile deceptions of fancy,
Pleasure disguised as duty, and love in the semblance of friendship.

Ever of her he thought, when he fashioned the walls of his dwelling ;
Ever of her he thought, when he delved in the soil of his garden ;
Ever of her he thought, when he read in his Bible on Sunday
Praise of the virtuous woman, as she is described in the Proverbs, —
How the heart of her husband doth safely trust in her always,
How all the days of her life she will do him good, and not evil,
How she seeketh the wool and the flax and worketh with gladness,
How she layeth her hand to the spindle and holdeth the distaff,
How she is not afraid of the snow for herself or her household,
Knowing her household are clothed with the scarlet cloth of her weaving !

So as she sat at her wheel one afternoon in the Autumn,
Alden, who opposite sat, and was watching her dexterous fingers,
As if the thread she was spinning were that of his life and his fortune,
After a pause in their talk, thus spake to the sound of the spindle.
"Truly, Priscilla," he said, "when I see you spinning and spinning,
Never idle a moment, but thrifty and thoughtful of others,
Suddenly you are transformed, are visibly changed in a moment ;
You are no longer Priscilla, but Bertha the Beautiful Spinner."
Here the light foot on the treadle grew swifter and swifter ; the spindle
Uttered an angry snarl, and the thread snapped short in her fingers ;
While the impetuous speaker, not heeding the mischief, continued :
"You are the beautiful Bertha, the spinner, the queen of Helvetia ;
She whose story I read at a stall in the streets of Southampton,
Who, as she rode on her palfrey, o'er valley and meadow and mountain,
Ever was spinning her thread from a distaff fixed to her saddle.
She was so thrifty and good, that her name passed into a proverb.
So shall it be with your own, when the spinning-wheel shall no longer
Hum in the house of the farmer, and fill its chambers with music.
Then shall the mothers, reproving, relate how it was in their childhood,
Praising the good old times, and the days of Priscilla the spinner !"
Straight uprose from her wheel the beautiful Puritan maiden,
Pleased with the praise of her thrift from him whose praise was the sweetest,
Drew from the reel on the table a snowy skein of her spinning,
Thus making answer, meanwhile, to the flattering phrases of Alden :
"Come, you must not be idle ; if I am a pattern for housewives,
Show yourself equally worthy of being the model of husbands.
Hold this skein on your hands, while I wind it, ready for knitting ;
Then who knows but hereafter, when fashions have changed and the manners,
Fathers may talk to their sons of the good old times of John Alden !"
Thus, with a jest and a laugh, the skein on his hands she adjusted,
He sitting awkwardly there, with his arms extended before him,
She standing graceful, erect, and winding the thread from his fingers,
Sometimes chiding a little his clumsy manner of holding,
Sometimes touching his hands, as she disentangled expertly
Twist or knot in the yarn, unawares — for how could she help it ? —
Sending electrical thrills through every nerve in his body.

Lo ! in the midst of this scene, a breathless messenger entered,
Bringing in hurry and heat the terrible news from the village.
Yes ; Miles Standish was dead ! — an Indian had brought them the tidings, —
Slain by a poisoned arrow, shot down in the front of the battle,
Into an ambush beguiled, cut off with the whole of his forces ;
All the town would be burned, and all the people be murdered !
Such were the tidings of evil that burst on the hearts of the hearers.
Silent and statue-like stood Priscilla, her face looking backward
Still at the face of the speaker, her arms uplifted in horror ;

But John Alden, upstarting, as if the barb of the arrow
Piercing the heart of his friend had struck his own, and had sundered
Once and forever the bonds that held him bound as a captive,
Wild with excess of sensation, the awful delight of his freedom,
Mingled with pain and regret, unconscious of what he was doing,
Clasped, almost with a groan, the motionless form of Priscilla,
Pressing her close to his heart, as forever his own, and exclaiming :
"Those whom the Lord hath united, let no man put them asunder ! "

    Even as rivulets twain, from distant and separate sources,
Seeing each other afar, as they leap from the rocks, and pursuing
Each one its devious path, but drawing nearer and nearer,
Rush together at last, at their trysting-place in the forest ;
So these lives that had run thus far in separate channels,
Coming in sight of each other, then swerving and flowing asunder,
Parted by barriers strong, but drawing nearer and nearer,
Rushed together at last, and one was lost in the other.

IX.

THE WEDDING-DAY.

FORTH from the curtain of clouds, from the tent of purple and scarlet,
Issued the sun, the great High-Priest, in his garments resplendent,
Holiness unto the Lord, in letters of light, on his forehead,
Round the hem of his robe the golden bells and pomegranates.
Blessing the world he came, and the bars of vapor beneath him
Gleamed like a grate of brass, and the sea at his feet was a laver !

    This was the wedding morn of Priscilla the Puritan maiden.
Friends were assembled together ; the Elder and Magistrate also
Graced the scene with their presence, and stood like the Law and the Gospel,
One with the sanction of earth and one with the blessing of heaven.
Simple and brief was the wedding, as that of Ruth and of Boaz.
Softly the youth and the maiden repeated the words of betrothal,
Taking each other for husband and wife in the Magistrate's presence,
After the Puritan way, and the laudable custom of Holland.
Fervently then, and devoutly, the excellent Elder of Plymouth
Prayed for the hearth and the home, that were founded that day in affection,
Speaking of life and of death, and imploring Divine benedictions.

    Lo ! when the service was ended, a form appeared on the threshold,
Clad in armor of steel, a sombre and sorrowful figure !
Why does the bridegroom start and stare at the strange apparition ?
Why does the bride turn pale, and hide her face on his shoulder ?
Is it a phantom of air, — a bodiless, spectral illusion ?
Is it a ghost from the grave, that has come to forbid the betrothal?
Long had it stood there unseen, a guest uninvited, unwelcomed ;
Over its clouded eyes there had passed at times an expression
Softening the gloom and revealing the warm heart hidden beneath them,
As when across the sky the driving rack of the rain-cloud
Grows for a moment thin, and betrays the sun by its brightness.
Once it had lifted its hand, and moved its lips, but was silent,
As if an iron will had mastered the fleeting intention.
But when were ended the troth and the prayer and the last benediction,
Into the room it strode, and the people beheld with amazement
Bodily there in his armor Miles Standish, the Captain of Plymouth !

Grasping the bridegroom's hand, he said with emotion, "Forgive me !
I have been angry and hurt, — too long have I cherished the feeling ;
I have been cruel and hard, but now, thank God ! it is ended.
Mine is the same hot blood that leaped in the veins of Hugh Standish,
Sensitive, swift to resent, but as swift in atoning for error.
Never so much as now was Miles Standish the friend of John Alden."
Thereupon answered the bridegroom : " Let all be forgotten between us, —
All save the dear, old friendship, and that shall grow older and dearer ! "
Then the Captain advanced, and, bowing, saluted Priscilla,
Gravely, and after the manner of old-fashioned gentry in England,
Something of camp and of court, of town and of country, commingled,
Wishing her joy of her wedding, and loudly lauding her husband.
Then he said with a smile : " I should have remembered the adage, —
If you would be well served, you must serve yourself ; and moreover,
No man can gather cherries in Kent at the season of Christmas ! "

Great was the people's amazement, and greater yet their rejoicing,
Thus to behold once more the sunburnt face of their Captain,
Whom they had mourned as dead ; and they gathered and crowded about him,
Eager to see him and hear him, forgetful of bride and of bridegroom,
Questioning, answering, laughing, and each interrupting the other,
Till the good Captain declared, being quite overpowered and bewildered,
He had rather by far break into an Indian encampment,
Than come again to a wedding to which he had not been invited.

Meanwhile the bridegroom went forth and stood with the bride at the doorway,
Breathing the perfumed air of that warm and beautiful morning.
Touched with autumnal tints, but lonely and sad in the sunshine,
Lay extended before them the land of toil and privation ;
There were the graves of the dead, and the barren waste of the sea-shore,
There the familiar fields, the groves of pine, and the meadows ;
But to their eyes transfigured, it seemed as the Garden of Eden,
Filled with the presence of God, whose voice was the sound of the ocean.

Soon was their vision disturbed by the noise and stir of departure,
Friends coming forth from the house, and impatient of longer delaying,
Each with his plan for the day, and the work that was left uncompleted.
Then from a stall near at hand, amid exclamations of wonder,
Alden the thoughtful, the careful, so happy, so proud of Priscilla,
Brought out his snow-white bull, obeying the hand of its master,
Led by a cord that was tied to an iron ring in its nostrils,
Covered with crimson cloth, and a cushion placed for a saddle.
She should not walk, he said, through the dust and heat of the noonday ;
Nay, she should ride like a queen, not plod along like a peasant.
Somewhat alarmed at first, but reassured by the others,
Placing her hand on the cushion, her foot in the hand of her husband,
Gayly, with joyous laugh, Priscilla mounted her palfrey.
" Nothing is wanting now," he said with a smile, " but the distaff ;
Then you would be in truth my queen, my beautiful Bertha ! "

Onward the bridal procession now moved to their new habitation,
Happy husband and wife, and friends conversing together.
Pleasantly murmured the brook, as they crossed the ford in the forest,
Pleased with the image that passed, like a dream of love through its bosom,
Tremulous, floating in air, o'er the depths of the azure abysses.
Down through the golden leaves the sun was pouring his splendors,
Gleaming on purple grapes, that, from branches above them suspended,

PLYMOUTH, MASS. Page 210.

Mingled their odorous breath with the balm of the pine and the fir-tree,
Wild and sweet as the clusters that grew in the valley of Eshcol.
Like a picture it seemed of the primitive, pastoral ages,
Fresh with the youth of the world, and recalling Rebecca and Isaac,
Old and yet ever new, and simple and beautiful always,
Love immortal and young in the endless succession of lovers.
So through the Plymouth woods passed onward the bridal procession.

BIRDS OF PASSAGE.

. . come i gru van cantando lor lai,
Facendo in aer di sè lunga riga.
DANTE.

PROMETHEUS,

OR THE POET'S FORETHOUGHT.

OF Prometheus, how undaunted
  On Olympus' shining bastions
His audacious foot he planted,
Myths are told and songs are chanted,
  Full of promptings and suggestions.

Beautiful is the tradition
  Of that flight through heavenly portals,
The old classic superstition
Of the theft and the transmission
  Of the fire of the Immortals!

First the deed of noble daring,
  Born of heavenward aspiration,
Then the fire with mortals sharing,
Then the vulture, — the despairing
  Cry of pain on crags Caucasian.

All is but a symbol painted
  Of the Poet, Prophet, Seer;
Only those are crowned and sainted
Who with grief have been acquainted,
  Making nations nobler, freer.

In their feverish exultations,
  In their triumph and their yearning,
In their passionate pulsations,
In their words among the nations,
  The Promethean fire is burning.

Shall it, then, be unavailing,
  All this toil for human culture?
Through the cloud-rack, dark and trailing
Must they see above them sailing
  O'er life's barren crags the vulture?

Such a fate as this was Dante's,
  By defeat and exile maddened;
Thus were Milton and Cervantes,
Nature's priests and Corybantes,
  By affliction touched and saddened.

But the glories so transcendent
  That around their memories cluster,
And, on all their steps attendant,
Make their darkened lives resplendent
  With such gleams of inward lustre!

All the melodies mysterious,
  Through the dreary darkness chanted;
Thoughts in attitudes imperious,
Voices soft, and deep, and serious,
  Words that whispered, songs that
    haunted!

All the soul in rapt suspension,
  All the quivering, palpitating
Chords of life in utmost tension,
With the fervor of invention,
  With the rapture of creating!

Ah, Prometheus! heaven-scaling!
  In such hours of exultation
Even the faintest heart, unquailing,
Might behold the vulture sailing
  Round the cloudy crags Caucasian!

Though to all there is not given
  Strength for such sublime endeavor,
Thus to scale the walls of heaven,
And to leaven with fiery leaven
  All the hearts of men forever;

Yet all bards, whose hearts unblighted
  Honor and believe the presage,

Hold aloft their torches lighted,
Gleaming through the realms benighted,
    As they onward bear the message !

THE LADDER OF ST. AUGUS-TINE.

SAINT AUGUSTINE ! well hast thou said,
    That of our vices we can frame
A ladder, if we will but tread
    Beneath our feet each deed of shame !

All common things, each day's events,
    That with the hour begin and end,
Our pleasures and our discontents,
    Are rounds by which we may ascend.

The low desire, the base design,
    That makes another's virtues less ;
The revel of the ruddy wine,
    And all occasions of excess ;

The longing for ignoble things ;
    The strife for triumph more than truth ;
The hardening of the heart, that brings
    Irreverence for the dreams of youth ;

All thoughts of ill ; all evil deeds,
    That have their root in thoughts of ill ;
Whatever hinders or impedes
    The action of the nobler will ; —

All these must first be trampled down
    Beneath our feet, if we would gain
In the bright fields of fair renown
    The right of eminent domain.

We have not wings, we cannot soar ;
    But we have feet to scale and climb
By slow degrees, by more and more,
    The cloudy summits of our time.

The mighty pyramids of stone
    That wedge-like cleave the desert airs,
When nearer seen, and better known,
    Are but gigantic flights of stairs.

The distant mountains, that uprear
    Their solid bastions to the skies,
Are crossed by pathways, that appear
    As we to higher levels rise.

The heights by great men reached and kept
    Were not attained by sudden flight,
But they, while their companions slept,
    Were toiling upward in the night.

Standing on what too long we bore
    With shoulders bent and downcast eyes,
We may discern — unseen before —
    A path to higher destinies.

Nor deem the irrevocable Past,
    As wholly wasted, wholly vain,
If, rising on its wrecks, at last
    To something nobler we attain.

THE PHANTOM SHIP.

IN Mather's Magnalia Christi,
    Of the old colonial time,
May be found in prose the legend
    That is here set down in rhyme.

A ship sailed from New Haven,
    And the keen and frosty airs,
That filled her sails at parting,
    Were heavy with good men's prayers.

"O Lord ! if it be thy pleasure " —
    Thus prayed the old divine —
"To bury our friends in the ocean,
    Take them, for they are thine ! "

But Master Lamberton muttered,
    And under his breath said he,
"This ship is so crank and walty
    I fear our grave she will be ! "

And the ships that came from England,
    When the winter months were gone,
Brought no tidings of this vessel
    Nor of Master Lamberton.

This put the people to praying
    That the Lord would let them hear
What in his greater wisdom
    He had done with friends so dear.

And at last their prayers were an-
        swered : —
    It was in the month of June,
An hour before the sunset
    Of a windy afternoon,

When, steadily steering landward,
    A ship was seen below,
And they knew it was Lamberton, Mas-
        ter,
    Who sailed so long ago.

On she came, with a cloud of canvas,
  Right against the wind that blew,
Until the eye could distinguish
  The faces of the crew.

Then fell her straining topmasts,
  Hanging tangled in the shrouds,
And her sails were loosened and lifted,
  And blown away like clouds.

And the masts, with all their rigging,
  Fell slowly, one by one,
And the hulk dilated and vanished,
  As a sea-mist in the sun !

And the people who saw this marvel
  Each said unto his friend,
That this was the mould of their vessel,
  And thus her tragic end.

And the pastor of the village
  Gave thanks to God in prayer,
That, to quiet their troubled spirits,
  He had sent this Ship of Air.

THE WARDEN OF THE CINQUE PORTS.

A MIST was driving down the British
      Channel,
  The day was just begun,
And through the window-panes, on floor
      and panel,
  Streamed the red autumn sun.

It glanced on flowing flag and rippling
      pennon,
  And the white sails of ships ;
And, from the frowning rampart, the
      black cannon
  Hailed it with feverish lips.

Sandwich and Romney, Hastings, Hithe,
      and Dover
  Were all alert that day,
To see the French war-steamers speeding
      over,
  When the fog cleared away.

Sullen and silent, and like couchant
      lions,
  Their cannon, through the night,

Holding their breath, had watched, in
      grim defiance,
  The sea-coast opposite.

And now they roared at drum-beat from
      their stations
  On every citadel ;
Each answering each, with morning salu-
      tations,
  That all was well.

And down the coast, all taking up the
      burden,
  Replied the distant forts,
As if to summon from his sleep the
      Warden
  And Lord of the Cinque Ports.

Him shall no sunshine from the fields of
      azure,
  No drum-beat from the wall,
No morning gun from the black fort's
      embrasure,
  Awaken with its call !

No more, surveying with an eye impar-
      tial
  The long line of the coast,
Shall the gaunt figure of the old Field
      Marshal
  Be seen upon his post !

For in the night, unseen, a single war-
      rior,
  In sombre harness mailed,
Dreaded of man, and surnamed the De-
      stroyer,
  The rampart wall had scaled.

He passed into the chamber of the
      sleeper,
  The dark and silent room,
And as he entered, darker grew, and
      deeper,
  The silence and the gloom.

He did not pause to parley or dissemble
  But smote the Warden hoar ;
Ah ! what a blow ! that made all Eng-
      land tremble
  And groan from shore to shore.

Meanwhile, without, the surly cannon
      waited,
  The sun rose bright o'erhead ;
Nothing in Nature's aspect intimated
  That a great man was dead.

HAUNTED HOUSES.

ALL houses wherein men have lived and
      died
   Are haunted houses. Through the
      open doors
The harmless phantoms on their errands
      glide,
   With feet that make no sound upon
      the floors.

We meet them at the doorway, on the
      stair,
   Along the passages they come and go,
Impalpable impressions on the air,
   A sense of something moving to and
      fro.

There are more guests at table, than the
      hosts
   Invited ; the illuminated hall
Is thronged with quiet, inoffensive
      ghosts,
   As silent as the pictures on the wall.

The stranger at my fireside cannot see
   The forms I see, nor hear the sounds
      I hear ;
He but perceives what is ; while unto
      me
   All that has been is visible and clear.

We have no title-deeds to house or
      lands ;
   Owners and occupants of earlier dates
From graves forgotten stretch their
      dusty hands,
   And hold in mortmain still their old
      estates.

The spirit-world around this world of
      sense
   Floats like an atmosphere, and every-
      where
Wafts through these earthly mists and
      vapors dense
   A vital breath of more ethereal air.

Our little lives are kept in equipoise
   By opposite attractions and desires ;
The struggle of the instinct that enjoys,
   And the more noble instinct that as-
      pires.

These perturbations, this perpetual jar
   Of earthly wants and aspirations high,

Come from the influence of an unseen
      star,
   An undiscovered planet in our sky.

And as the moon from some dark gate
      of cloud
   Throws o'er the sea a floating bridge
      of light,
Across whose trembling planks our fan-
      cies crowd
   Into the realm of mystery and night,—

So from the world of spirits there de-
      scends
   A bridge of light, connecting it with
      this,
O'er whose unsteady floor, that sways
      and bends,
   Wander our thoughts above the dark
      abyss.

IN THE CHURCHYARD AT CAM-
BRIDGE.

IN the village churchyard she lies,
Dust is in her beautiful eyes,
   No more she breathes, nor feels, nor
      stirs ;
At her feet and at her head
Lies a slave to attend the dead,
   But their dust is white as hers.

Was she a lady of high degree,
So much in love with the vanity
   And foolish pomp of this world of
      ours ?
Or was it Christian charity,
And lowliness and humility,
   The richest and rarest of all dowers ?

Who shall tell us ? No one speaks ;
No color shoots into those cheeks,
   Either of anger or of pride,
At the rude question we have asked ;
Nor will the mystery be unmasked
   By those who are sleeping at her side.

Hereafter ? — And do you think to look
On the terrible pages of that Book
   To find her failings, faults, and errors ?
Ah, you will then have other cares,
In your own shortcomings and despairs,
   In your own secret sins and terrors !

THE EMPEROR'S BIRD'S—NEST.

ONCE the Emperor Charles of Spain,
  With his swarthy, grave commanders,
I forget in what campaign,
Long besieged, in mud and rain,
  Some old frontier town of Flanders.

Up and down the dreary camp,
  In great boots of Spanish leather,
Striding with a measured tramp,
These Hidalgos, dull and damp,
  Cursed the Frenchmen, cursed the
    weather.

Thus as to and fro they went,
  Over upland and through hollow,
Giving their impatience vent,
Perched upon the Emperor's tent,
  In her nest, they spied a swallow.

Yes, it was a swallow's nest,
  Built of clay and hair of horses,
Mane, or tail, or dragoon's crest,
Found on hedge-rows east and west,
  After skirmish of the forces.

Then an old Hidalgo said,
  As he twirled his gray mustachio,
"Sure this swallow overhead
Thinks the Emperor's tent a shed,
  And the Emperor but a Macho !"

Hearing his imperial name
  Coupled with those words of malice,
Half in anger, half in shame,
Forth the great campaigner came
  Slowly from his canvas palace.

"Let no hand the bird molest,"
  Said he solemnly, "nor hurt her !"
Adding then, by way of jest,
"Golondrina is my guest,
  'T is the wife of some deserter !"

Swift as bowstring speeds a shaft,
  Through the camp was spread the ru-
    mor,
And the soldiers, as they quaffed
Flemish beer at dinner, laughed
  At the Emperor's pleasant humor.

So unharmed and unafraid
  Sat the swallow still and brooded,
Till the constant cannonade
Through the walls a breach had made
  And the siege was thus concluded.

Then the army, elsewhere bent,
  Struck its tents as if disbanding,
Only not the Emperor's tent,
For he ordered, ere he went,
  Very curtly, "Leave it standing !"

So it stood there all alone,
  Loosely flapping, torn and tattered,
Till the brood was fledged and flown,
Singing o'er those walls of stone
  Which the cannon-shot had shattered.

THE TWO ANGELS.

Two angels, one of Life and one of
    Death,
  Passed o'er our village as the morning
    broke ;
The dawn was on their faces, and beneath,
  The sombre houses hearsed with plumes
    of smoke.

Their attitude and aspect were the same,
  Alike their features and their robes of
    white ;
But one was crowned with amaranth, as
    with flame,
  And one with asphodels, like flakes of
    light.

I saw them pause on their celestial way ;
  Then said I, with deep fear and doubt
    oppressed,
"Beat not so loud, my heart, lest thou
    betray
  The place where thy beloved are at
    rest !"

And he who wore the crown of asphodels,
  Descending, at my door began to
    knock,
And my soul sank within me, as in wells
  The waters sink before an earthquake's
    shock.

I recognized the nameless agony,
  The terror and the tremor and the
    pain,
That oft before had filled or haunted me,
  And now returned with threefold
    strength again.

The door I opened to my heavenly guest,
  And listened, for I thought I heard
    God's voice ;

And, knowing whatsoe'er he sent was
    best,
  Dared neither to lament nor to rejoice.

Then with a smile, that filled the house
    with light,
  " My errand is not Death, but Life,"
    he said ;
And ere I answered, passing out of sight,
  On his celestial embassy he sped.

'T was at thy door, O friend ! and not at
    mine,
  The angel with the amaranthine wreath,
Pausing, descended, and with voice di-
    vine,
  Whispered a word that had a sound
    like Death.

Then fell upon the house a sudden gloom,
  A shadow on those features fair and
    thin;
And softly, from that hushed and dark-
    ened room,
  Two angels issued, where but one went
    in.

All is of God ! If he but wave his hand,
  The mists collect, the rain falls thick
    and loud,
Till, with a smile of light on sea and land,
  Lo ! he looks back from the departing
    cloud.

Angels of Life and Death alike are his ;
  Without his leave they pass no thresh-
    old o'er ;
Who, then, would wish or dare, believing
    this,
  Against his messengers to shut the
    door ?

DAYLIGHT AND MOONLIGHT.

In broad daylight, and at noon,
Yesterday I saw the moon
Sailing high, but faint and white,
As a school-boy's paper kite.

In broad daylight, yesterday,
I read a Poet's mystic lay ;
And it seemed to me at most
As a phantom, or a ghost.

But at length the feverish day
Like a passion died away,

And the night, serene and still,
Fell on village, vale, and hill.

Then the moon, in all her pride,
Like a spirit glorified,
Filled and overflowed the night
With revelations of her light.

And the Poet's song again
Passed like music through my brain;
Night interpreted to me
All its grace and mystery.

THE JEWISH CEMETERY AT NEWPORT.

How strange it seems ! These Hebrews
    in their graves,
  Close by the street of this fair seaport
    town,
Silent beside the never-silent waves,
  At rest in all this moving up and
    down !

The trees are white with dust, that o'er
    their sleep
  Wave their broad curtains in the
    south-wind's breath,
While underneath these leafy tents they
    keep
  The long, mysterious Exodus of
    Death.

And these sepulchral stones, so old and
    brown,
  That pave with level flags their burial-
    place,
Seem like the tablets of the Law, thrown
    down
  And broken by Moses at the moun-
    tain's base.

The very names recorded here are
    strange,
  Of foreign accent, and of different
    climes ;
Alvares and Rivera interchange
  With Abraham and Jacob of old
    times.

" Blessed be God ! for he created
    Death ! "
  The mourners said, "and Death is
    rest and peace" ;
Then added, in the certainty of faith,
  "And giveth Life that nevermore
    shall cease."

Closed are the portals of their Synagogue,
　No Psalms of David now the silence
　break,
No Rabbi reads the ancient Decalogue
　In the grand dialect the Prophets
　spake.

Gone are the living, but the dead
remain,
　And not neglected ; for a hand un-
　seen,
Scattering its bounty, like a summer
rain,
　Still keeps their graves and their
　remembrance green.

How came they here? What burst of
　Christian hate,
　What persecution, merciless and
　blind,
Drove o'er the sea — that desert deso-
late—
　These Ishmaels and Hagars of man-
　kind?

They lived in narrow streets and lanes
obscure,
　Ghetto and Judenstrass, in mirk and
　mire ;
Taught in the school of patience to
endure
　The life of anguish and the death of
　fire.

All their lives long, with the unleavened
bread
　And bitter herbs of exile and its fears,
The wasting famine of the heart they
fed,
　And slaked its thirst with marah of
　their tears.

Anathema maranatha ! was the cry
　That rang from town to town, from
　street to street ;
At every gate the accursed Mordecai
　Was mocked and jeered, and spurned
　by Christian feet.

Pride and humiliation hand in hand
　Walked with them through the world
　where'er they went ;
Trampled and beaten were they as the
sand,
　And yet unshaken as the continent.

For in the background figures vague and
vast
　Of patriarchs and of prophets rose
　sublime,
And all the great traditions of the Past
　They saw reflected in the coming
　time.

And thus forever with reverted look
　The mystic volume of the world they
　read,
Spelling it backward, like a Hebrew
book,
　Till life became a Legend of the Dead.

But ah! what once has been shall be no
more !
　The groaning earth in travail and in
　pain
Brings forth its races, but does not
restore,
　And the dead nations never rise again.

OLIVER BASSELIN.

In the Valley of the Vire
　Still is seen an ancient mill,
With its gables quaint and queer,
　And beneath the window-sill,
　　On the stone,
　　These words alone :
" Oliver Basselin lived here."

Far above it, on the steep,
　Ruined stands the old Château ;
Nothing but the donjon-keep
　Left for shelter or for show.
　　Its vacant eyes
　　Stare at the skies,
Stare at the valley green and deep.

Once a convent, old and brown,
　Looked, but ah ! it looks no more,
From the neighboring hillside down
　On the rushing and the roar
　　Of the stream
　　Whose sunny gleam
Cheers the little Norman town.

In that darksome mill of stone,
　To the water's dash and din,
Careless, humble, and unknown,
　Sang the poet Basselin
　　Songs that fill
　　That ancient mill
With a splendor of its own.

Never feeling of unrest
  Broke the pleasant dream he dreamed ;
Only made to be his nest,
  All the lovely valley seemed ;
      No desire
      Of soaring higher
Stirred or fluttered in his breast.

True, his songs were not divine ;
  Were not songs of that high art,
Which, as winds do in the pine,
  Find an answer in each heart ;
      But the mirth
      Of this green earth
Laughed and revelled in his line.

From the alehouse and the inn,
  Opening on the narrow street,
Came the loud, convivial din,
  Singing and applause of feet,
      The laughing lays
      That in those days
Sang the poet Basselin.

In the castle, cased in steel,
  Knights, who fought at Agincourt,
Watched and waited, spur on heel ;
  But the poet sang for sport
      Songs that rang
      Another clang,
Songs that lowlier hearts could feel.

In the convent, clad in gray,
  Sat the monks in lonely cells,
Paced the cloisters, knelt to pray,
  And the poet heard their bells ;
      But his rhymes
      Found other chimes,
Nearer to the earth than they.

Gone are all the barons bold,
  Gone are all the knights and squires,
Gone the abbot stern and cold,
  And the brotherhood of friars ;
      Not a name
      Remains to fame,
From those mouldering days of old !

But the poet's memory here
  Of the landscape makes a part ;
Like the river, swift and clear,
  Flows his song through many a heart ;
      Haunting still
      That ancient mill,
In the Valley of the Vire.

VICTOR GALBRAITH.

UNDER the walls of Monterey
At daybreak the bugles began to play,
      Victor Galbraith !
In the mist of the morning damp and
      gray,
These were the words they seemed to say :
      " Come forth to thy death,
      Victor Galbraith ! "

Forth he came, with a martial tread ;
Firm was his step, erect his head ;
      Victor Galbraith,
He who so well the bugle played,
Could not mistake the words it said :
      " Come forth to thy death,
      Victor Galbraith ! "

He looked at the earth, he looked at the
      sky,
He looked at the files of musketry,
      Victor Galbraith !
And he said, with a steady voice and eye,
" Take good aim ; I am ready to die ! "
      Thus challenges death
      Victor Galbraith.

Twelve fiery tongues flashed straight and
      red,
Six leaden balls on their errand sped ;
      Victor Galbraith !
Falls to the ground, but he is not dead ;
His name was not stamped on those balls
      of lead,
      And they only scath
      Victor Galbraith.

Three balls are in his breast and brain,
But he rises out of the dust again,
      Victor Galbraith !
The water he drinks has a bloody stain ;
" O kill me, and put me out of my pain ! "
      In his agony prayeth
      Victor Galbraith.

Forth dart once more those tongues of
      flame,
And the bugler has died a death of shame,
      Victor Galbraith !
His soul has gone back to whence it came,
And no one answers to the name,
      When the Sergeant saith,
      " Victor Galbraith ! "

Under the walls of Monterey
By night a bugle is heard to play,
      Victor Galbraith !

Through the mist of the valley damp and
    gray
The sentinels hear the sound, and say,
      " That is the wraith
      Of Victor Galbraith ! "

MY LOST YOUTH.

OFTEN I think of the beautiful town
  That is seated by the sea ;
Often in thought go up and down
The pleasant streets of that dear old town,
  And my youth comes back to me.
    And a verse of a Lapland song
    Is haunting my memory still :
" A boy's will is the wind's will,
And the thoughts of youth are long, long
    thoughts."

I can see the shadowy lines of its trees,
  And catch, in sudden gleams,
The sheen of the far-surrounding seas,
And islands that were the Hesperides
  Of all my boyish dreams.
    And the burden of that old song,
    It murmurs and whispers still :
" A boy's will is the wind's will,
And the thoughts of youth are long, long
    thoughts."

I remember the black wharves and the
    slips,
  And the sea-tides tossing free ;
And Spanish sailors with bearded lips,
And the beauty and mystery of the ships,
  And the magic of the sea.
    And the voice of that wayward song
    Is singing and saying still :
" A boy's will is the wind's will,
And the thoughts of youth are long, long
    thoughts."

I remember the bulwarks by the shore,
  And the fort upon the hill ;
The sunrise gun, with its hollow roar
The drum-beat repeated o'er and o'er,
  And the bugle wild and shrill.
    And the music of that old song
    Throbs in my memory still :
" A boy's will is the wind's will,
And the thoughts of youth are long, long
    thoughts."

I remember the sea-fight far away,
  How it thundered o'er the tide !

And the dead captains, as they lay
In their graves, o'erlooking the tranquil
    bay,
  Where they in battle died.
    And the sound of that mournful song
    Goes through me with a thrill :
" A boy's will is the wind's will,
And the thoughts of youth are long, long
    thoughts."

I can see the breezy dome of groves,
  The shadows of Deering's Woods ;
And the friendships old and the early loves
Come back with a sabbath sound, as of
    doves
  In quiet neighborhoods.
    And the verse of that sweet old song,
    It flutters and murmurs still :
" A boy's will is the wind's will,
And the thoughts of youth are long, long
    thoughts."

I remember the gleams and glooms that
    dart
  Across the school-boy's brain ;
The song and the silence in the heart,
That in part are prophecies, and in part
  Are longings wild and vain.
    And the voice of that fitful song
    Sings on, and is never still :
" A boy's will is the wind's will,
And the thoughts of youth are long, long
    thoughts."

There are things of which I may not
    speak ;
  There are dreams that cannot die ;
There are thoughts that make the strong
    heart weak,
And bring a pallor into the cheek,
  And a mist before the eye.
    And the words of that fatal song
    Come over me like a chill :
" A boy's will is the wind's will,
And the thoughts of youth are long, long
    thoughts."

Strange to me now are the forms I meet
  When I visit the dear old town ;
But the native air is pure and sweet,
And the trees that o'ershadow each well-
    known street,
  As they balance up and down,
    Are singing the beautiful song,
    Are sighing and whispering still :
" A boy's will is the wind's will,
And the thoughts of youth are long, long
    thoughts."

And Deering's Woods are fresh and fair,
  And with joy that is almost pain
My heart goes back to wander there,
And among the dreams of the days that
    were,
    I find my lost youth again.
    And the strange and beautiful song,
    The groves are repeating it still :
" A boy's will is the wind's will,
And the thoughts of youth are long, long
    thoughts."

THE ROPEWALK.

In that building, long and low,
With its windows all a-row,
  Like the port-holes of a hulk,
Human spiders spin and spin,
Backward down their threads so thin
  Dropping, each a hempen bulk.

At the end, an open door ;
Squares of sunshine on the floor
  Light the long and dusky lane ;
And the whirring of a wheel,
Dull and drowsy, makes me feel
  All its spokes are in my brain.

As the spinners to the end
Downward go and reascend,
  Gleam the long threads in the sun ;
While within this brain of mine
Cobwebs brighter and more fine
  By the busy wheel are spun.

Two fair maidens in a swing,
Like white doves upon the wing,
  First before my vision pass ;
Laughing, as their gentle hands
Closely clasp the twisted strands,
  At their shadow on the grass.

Then a booth of mountebanks,
With its smell of tan and planks,
  And a girl poised high in air
On a cord, in spangled dress,
With a faded loveliness,
  And a weary look of care.

Then a homestead among farms,
And a woman with bare arms
  Drawing water from a well ;
As the bucket mounts apace,
With it mounts her own fair face,
  As at some magician's spell.

Then an old man in a tower,
Ringing loud the noontide hour,
  While the rope coils round and round
Like a serpent at his feet,
And again, in swift retreat,
  Nearly lifts him from the ground.

Then within a prison-yard,
Faces fixed, and stern, and hard,
  Laughter and indecent mirth ;
Ah ! it is the gallows-tree !
Breath of Christian charity,
  Blow, and sweep it from the earth !

Then a school-boy, with his kite
Gleaming in a sky of light,
  And an eager, upward look ;
Steeds pursued through lane and field ;
Fowlers with their snares concealed ;
  And an angler by a brook.

Ships rejoicing in the breeze,
Wrecks that float o'er unknown seas,
  Anchors dragged through faithless
    sand ;
Sea-fog drifting overhead,
And, with lessening line and lead,
  Sailors feeling for the land.

All these scenes do I behold,
These, and many left untold,
  In that building long and low ;
While the wheel goes round and round,
With a drowsy, dreamy sound,
  And the spinners backward go.

THE GOLDEN MILE-STONE.

Leafless are the trees ; their purple
    branches
Spread themselves abroad, like reefs of
    coral,
    Rising silent
In the Red Sea of the winter sunset.

From the hundred chimneys of the vil-
    lage,
Like the Afreet in the Arabian story,
    Smoky columns
Tower aloft into the air of amber.

At the window winks the flickering fire-
    light ;
Here and there the lamps of evening
    glimmer,
    Social watch-fires
Answering one another through the
    darkness.

On the hearth the lighted logs are glow-
ing,
And like Ariel in the cloven pine-tree
For its freedom
Groans and sighs the air imprisoned in
them.

By the fireside there are old men seated,
Seeing ruined cities in the ashes,
Asking sadly
Of the Past what it can ne'er restore them.

By the fireside there are youthful dreamers,
Building castles fair, with stately stair-
ways,
Asking blindly
Of the Future what it cannot give them.

By the fireside tragedies are acted
In whose scenes appear two actors only,
Wife and husband,
And above them God the sole spectator.

By the fireside there are peace and com-
fort,
Wives and children, with fair, thought-
ful faces,
Waiting, watching
For a well-known footstep in the passage.

Each man's chimney is his Golden Mile-
stone ;
Is the central point, from which he measures
Every distance
Through the gateways of the world
around him.

In his farthest wanderings still he sees it ;
Hears the talking flame, the answering
night-wind,
As he heard them
When he sat with those who were, but
are not.

Happy he whom neither wealth nor fash-
ion,
Nor the march of the encroaching city,
Drives an exile
From the hearth of his ancestral home-
stead.

We may build more splendid habitations,
Fill our rooms with paintings and with
sculptures,
But we cannot
Buy with gold the old associations !

CATAWBA WINE.

THIS song of mine
Is a Song of the Vine,
To be sung by the glowing embers
Of wayside inns,
When the rain begins
To darken the drear Novembers.

It is not a song
Of the Scuppernong,
From warm Carolinian valleys,
Nor the Isabel
And the Muscadel
That bask in our garden alleys.

Nor the red Mustang,
Whose clusters hang
O'er the waves of the Colorado,
And the fiery flood
Of whose purple blood
Has a dash of Spanish bravado.

For richest and best
Is the wine of the West,
That grows by the Beautiful River ;
Whose sweet perfume
Fills all the room
With a benison on the giver.

And as hollow trees
Are the haunts of bees,
Forever going and coming ;
So this crystal hive
Is all alive
With a swarming and buzzing and hum-
ming.

Very good in its way
Is the Verzenay,
Or the Sillery soft and creamy ;
But Catawba wine
Has a taste more divine,
More dulcet, delicious, and dreamy

There grows no vine
By the haunted Rhine,
By Danube or Guadalquivir,
Nor on island or cape,
That bears such a grape
As grows by the Beautiful River.

Drugged is their juice
For foreign use,
When shipped o'er the reeling Atlantic
To rack our brains
With the fever pains,
That have driven the Old World frantic.

To the sewers and sinks
With all such drinks,
And after them tumble the mixer ;
For a poison malign
Is such Borgia wine,
Or at best but a Devil's Elixir.

While pure as a spring
Is the wine I sing,
And to praise it, one needs but name it ;
For Catawba wine
Has need of no sign,
No tavern-bush to proclaim it.

And this Song of the Vine,
This greeting of mine,
The winds and the birds shall deliver
To the Queen of the West,
In her garlands dressed,
On the banks of the Beautiful River.

SANTA FILOMENA.

WHENE'ER a noble deed is wrought,
Whene'er is spoken a noble thought,
      Our hearts, in glad surprise,
      To higher levels rise.

The tidal wave of deeper souls
Into our inmost being rolls,
      And lifts us unawares
      Out of all meaner cares.

Honor to those whose words or deeds
Thus help us in our daily needs,
      And by their overflow
      Raise us from what is low !

Thus thought I, as by night I read
Of the great army of the dead,
      The trenches cold and damp,
      The starved and frozen camp, —

The wounded from the battle-plain,
In dreary hospitals of pain,
      The cheerless corridors,
      The cold and stony floors.

Lo ! in that house of misery
A lady with a lamp I see
      Pass through the glimmering gloom,
      And flit from room to room.

And slow, as in a dream of bliss,
The speechless sufferer turns to kiss
      Her shadow, as it falls
      Upon the darkening walls.

As if a door in heaven should be
Opened and then closed suddenly,
      The vision came and went,
      The light shone and was spent.

On England's annals, through the long
Hereafter of her speech and song,
      That light its rays shall cast
      From portals of the past.

A Lady with a Lamp shall stand
In the great history of the land,
      A noble type of good,
      Heroic womanhood.

Nor even shall be wanting here
The palm, the lily, and the spear,
      The symbols that of yore
      Saint Filomena bore.

THE DISCOVERER OF THE NORTH CAPE.

A LEAF FROM KING ALFRED'S OROSIUS.

OTHERE, the old sea-captain,
   Who dwelt in Helgoland,
To King Alfred, the Lover of Truth,
Brought a snow-white walrus-tooth,
   Which he held in his brown right
      hand.

His figure was tall and stately,
   Like a boy's his eye appeared ;
His hair was yellow as hay,
But threads of a silvery gray
   Gleamed in his tawny beard.

Hearty and hale was Othere,
   His cheek had the color of oak ;
With a kind of laugh in his speech,
Like the sea-tide on a beach,
   As unto the King he spoke.

And Alfred, King of the Saxons,
   Had a book upon his knees,
And wrote down the wondrous tale
Of him who was first to sail
   Into the Arctic seas.

"So far I live to the northward,
   No man lives north of me ;
To the east are wild mountain-chains,
And beyond them meres and plains ;
   To the westward all is sea.

So far I live to the northward,
From the harbor of Skeringes-hale,
If you only sailed by day,
With a fair wind all the way,
  More than a month would you sail.

" I own six hundred reindeer,
  With sheep and swine beside ;
I have tribute from the Finns,
Whalebone and reindeer-skins,
  And ropes of walrus-hide.

" I ploughed the land with horses,
  But my heart was ill at ease,
For the old seafaring men
Came to me now and then,
  With their sagas of the seas ; —

" Of Iceland and of Greenland,
  And the stormy Hebrides,
And the undiscovered deep ; —
O I could not eat nor sleep
  For thinking of those seas.

" To the northward stretched the desert,
  How far I fain would know ;
So at last I sallied forth,
And three days sailed due north,
  As far as the whale-ships go.

" To the west of me was the ocean,
  To the right the desolate shore,
But I did not slacken sail
For the walrus or the whale,
  Till after three days more.

" The days grew longer and longer,
  Till they became as one,
And northward through the haze
I saw the sullen blaze
  Of the red midnight sun.

" And then uprose before me,
  Upon the water's edge,
The huge and haggard shape
Of that unknown North Cape,
  Whose form is like a wedge.

" The sea was rough and stormy,
  The tempest howled and wailed,
And the sea-fog, like a ghost,
Haunted that dreary coast,
  But onward still I sailed.

" Four days I steered to eastward,
  Four days without a night :

Round in a fiery ring
Went the great sun, O King,
  With red and lurid light."

Here Alfred, King of the Saxons,
  Ceased writing for a while ;
And raised his eyes from his book,
With a strange and puzzled look,
  And an incredulous smile.

But Othere, the old sea-captain,
  He neither paused nor stirred,
Till the King listened and then
Once more took up his pen,
  And wrote down every word.

" And now the land," said Othere,
  " Bent southward suddenly,
And I followed the curving shore
And ever southward bore
  Into a nameless sea.

" And there we hunted the walrus,
  The narwhale, and the seal ;
Ha ! 't was a noble game !
And like the lightning's flame
  Flew our harpoons of steel.

" There were six of us all together,
  Norsemen of Helgoland ;
In two days and no more
We killed of them threescore,
  And dragged them to the strand !'

Here Alfred the Truth-Teller
  Suddenly closed his book,
And lifted his blue eyes,
With doubt and strange surmise
  Depicted in their look.

And Othere the old sea-captain
  Stared at him wild and weird,
Then smiled, till his shining teeth
Gleamed white from underneath
  His tawny, quivering beard.

And to the King of the Saxons,
  In witness of the truth,
Raising his noble head,
He stretched his brown hand, and said,
  " Behold this walrus-tooth ! "

DAYBREAK.

A WIND came up out of the sea,
And said, " O mists, make room for me.'

It hailed the ships, and cried, "Sail on,
  Ye mariners, the night is gone."

And hurried landward far away,
  Crying, "Awake! it is the day."

It said unto the forest, "Shout!
  Hang all your leafy banners out!'

It touched the wood-bird's folded wing,
  And said, "O bird, awake and sing."

And o'er the farms, "O chanticleer,
  Your clarion blow; the day is near."

It whispered to the fields of corn,
  "Bow down, and hail the coming morn."

It shouted through the belfry-tower,
  "Awake, O bell! proclaim the hour."

It crossed the churchyard with a sigh,
  And said, "Not yet! in quiet lie."

THE FIFTIETH BIRTHDAY OF AGASSIZ.

MAY 28, 1857.

IT was fifty years ago
  In the pleasant month of May,
In the beautiful Pays de Vaud,
  A child in its cradle lay.

And Nature, the old nurse, took
  The child upon her knee,
Saying: "Here is a story-book
  Thy Father has written for thee."

"Come, wander with me," she said,
  "Into regions yet untrod;
And read what is still unread
  In the manuscripts of God."

And he wandered away and away
  With Nature, the dear old nurse,
Who sang to him night and day
  The rhymes of the universe.

And whenever the way seemed long,
  Or his heart began to fail,
She would sing a more wonderful song,
  Or tell a more marvellous tale.

So she keeps him still a child,
  And will not let him go,

Though at times his heart beats wild
  For the beautiful Pays de Vaud;

Though at times he hears in his dreams
  The Ranz des Vaches of old,
And the rush of mountain streams
  From glaciers clear and cold;

And the mother at home says, "Hark!
  For his voice I listen and yearn;
It is growing late and dark,
  And my boy does not return!"

CHILDREN.

COME to me, O ye children!
  For I hear you at your play,
And the questions that perplexed me
  Have vanished quite away.

Ye open the eastern windows,
  That look towards the sun,
Where thoughts are singing swallows
  And the brooks of morning run.

In your hearts are the birds and the
    sunshine,
  In your thoughts the brooklet's flow
But in mine is the wind of Autumn
  And the first fall of the snow.

Ah! what would the world be to us
  If the children were no more?
We should dread the desert behind us
  Worse than the dark before.

What the leaves are to the forest,
  With light and air for food,
Ere their sweet and tender juices
  Have been hardened into wood, —

That to the world are children;
  Through them it feels the glow
Of a brighter and sunnier climate
  Than reaches the trunks below.

Come to me, O ye children!
  And whisper in my ear
What the birds and the winds are sing-
    ing
  In your sunny atmosphere.

For what are all our contrivings,
  And the wisdom of our books,
When compared with your caresses,
  And the gladness of your looks?

Ye are better than all the ballads
  That ever were sung or said ;
For ye are living poems,
  And all the rest are dead.

SANDALPHON.

HAVE you read in the Talmud of old,
In the Legends the Rabbins have told
  Of the limitless realms of the air,
Have you read it, — the marvellous story
Of Sandalphon, the Angel of Glory,
  Sandalphon, the Angel of Prayer ?

How, erect, at the outermost gates
Of the City Celestial he waits,
  With his feet on the ladder of light,
That, crowded with angels unnumbered,
By Jacob was seen, as he slumbered
  Alone in the desert at night ?

The Angels of Wind and of Fire
Chant only one hymn, and expire
  With the song's irresistible stress ;
Expire in their rapture and wonder,
As harp-strings are broken asunder
  By music they throb to express.

But serene in the rapturous throng,
Unmoved by the rush of the song,
  With eyes unimpassioned and slow,
Among the dead angels, the deathless
Sandalphon stands listening breathless
  To sounds that ascend from below ;—

From the spirits on earth that adore,
From the souls that entreat and implore

In the fervor and passion of prayer ;
From the hearts that are broken with
    losses,
And weary with dragging the crosses
  Too heavy for mortals to bear.

And he gathers the prayers as he stands,
And they change into flowers in his
    hands,
  Into garlands of purple and red ;
And beneath the great arch of the por-
    tal,
Through the streets of the City Immor-
    tal
  Is wafted the fragrance they shed.

It is but a legend, I know, —
A fable, a phantom, a show,
  Of the ancient Rabbinical lore ;
Yet the old mediæval tradition,
The beautiful, strange superstition,
  But haunts me and holds me the
    more.

When I look from my window at night,
And the welkin above is all white,
  All throbbing and panting with
    stars,
Among them majestic is standing
Sandalphon the angel, expanding
  His pinions in nebulous bars.

And the legend, I feel, is a part
Of the hunger and thirst of the heart,
  The frenzy and fire of the brain,
That grasps at the fruitage forbidden,
The golden pomegranates of Eden,
  To quiet its fever and pain.

FLIGHT THE SECOND.

THE CHILDREN'S HOUR.

BETWEEN the dark and the daylight,
  When the night is beginning to lower,
Comes a pause in the day's occupations,
  That is known as the Children's
    Hour.

I hear in the chamber above me
  The patter of little feet,
The sound of a door that is opened,
  And voices soft and sweet.

From my study I see in the lamplight,
  Descending the broad hall stair,
Grave Alice, and laughing Allegra,
  And Edith with golden hair.

A whisper, and then a silence :
  Yet I know by their merry eyes
They are plotting and planning together
  To take me by surprise.

A sudden rush from the stairway,
  A sudden raid from the hall !

By three doors left unguarded
  They enter my castle wall !

They climb up into my turret
  O'er the arms and back of my chair ;
If I try to escape, they surround me ;
  They seem to be everywhere.

They almost devour me with kisses,
  Their arms about me entwine,
Till I think of the Bishop of Bingen
  In his Mouse-Tower on the Rhine !

Do you think, O blue-eyed banditti,
  Because you have scaled the wall,
Such an old mustache as I am
  Is not a match for you all !

I have you fast in my fortress,
  And will not let you depart,
But put you down into the dungeon
  In the round-tower of my heart.

And there will I keep you forever,
  Yes, forever and a day,
Till the walls shall crumble to ruin,
  And moulder in dust away !

ENCELADUS.

UNDER Mount Etna he lies,
  It is slumber, it is not death ;
For he struggles at times to arise,
And above him the lurid skies
  Are hot with his fiery breath.

The crags are piled on his breast,
  The earth is heaped on his head ;
But the groans of his wild unrest,
Though smothered and half suppressed,
  Are heard, and he is not dead.

And the nations far away
  Are watching with eager eyes ;
They talk together and say,
"To-morrow, perhaps to-day,
  Enceladus will arise ! "

And the old gods, the austere
  Oppressors in their strength,
Stand aghast and white with fear
At the ominous sounds they hear,
  And tremble, and mutter, "At length ! "

Ah me ! for the land that is sown
  With the harvest of despair !
Where the burning cinders, blown

From the lips of the overthrown
  Enceladus, fill the air.

Where ashes are heaped in drifts
  Over vineyard and field and town,
Whenever he starts and lifts
His head through the blackened rifts
  Of the crags that keep him down.

See, see ! the red light shines !
  'T is the glare of his awful eyes !
And the storm-wind shouts through the
      pines
Of Alps and of Apennines,
  " Enceladus, arise ! "

THE CUMBERLAND.

AT anchor in Hampton Roads we lay,
  On board of the Cumberland, sloop-of-
      war ;
And at times from the fortress across the
      bay
    The alarum of drums swept past,
    Or a bugle blast
  From the camp on the shore.

Then far away to the south uprose
  A little feather of snow-white smoke,
And we knew that the iron ship of our
      foes
    Was steadily steering its course
    To try the force
  Of our ribs of oak.

Down upon us heavily runs,
  Silent and sullen, the floating fort ;
Then comes a puff of smoke from her
      guns,
    And leaps the terrible death,
    With fiery breath,
  From each open port.

We are not idle, but send her straight
  Defiance back in a full broadside !
As hail rebounds from a roof of slate,
    Rebounds our heavier hail
    From each iron scale
  Of the monster's hide.

"Strike your flag ! " the rebel cries,
  In his arrogant old plantation strain.
"Never ! " our gallant Morris replies ;
    "It is better to sink than to yield ! '
    And the whole air pealed
  With the cheers of our men.

Then, like a kraken huge and black,
  She crushed our ribs in her iron grasp !
Down went the Cumberland all a wrack,
  With a sudden shudder of death,
    And the cannon's breath
  For her dying gasp.

Next morn, as the sun rose over the bay,
  Still floated our flag at the mainmast
    head.
Lord, how beautiful was Thy day !
  Every waft of the air
  Was a whisper of prayer,
  Or a dirge for the dead.

Ho ! brave hearts that went down in the
    seas !
  Ye are at peace in the troubled stream ;
Ho ! brave land ! with hearts like these,
  Thy flag, that is rent in twain,
    Shall be one again,
  And without a seam !

SNOW—FLAKES.

OUT of the bosom of the Air,
  Out of the cloud-folds of her garments
    shaken,
Over the woodlands brown and bare,
  Over the harvest-fields forsaken,
    Silent, and soft, and slow
    Descends the snow.

Even as our cloudy fancies take
  Suddenly shape in some divine expres-
    sion,
Even as the troubled heart doth make
  In the white countenance confession,
    The troubled sky reveals
    The grief it feels.

This is the poem of the air,
  Slowly in silent syllables recorded ;
This is the secret of despair,
  Long in its cloudy bosom hoarded,
    Now whispered and revealed
    To wood and field.

A DAY OF SUNSHINE.

O GIFT of God ! O perfect day :
Whereon shall no man work, but play ;
Whereon it is enough for me,
Not to be doing, but to be !

Through every fibre of my brain,
Through every nerve, through every vein,
I feel the electric thrill, the touch
Of life, that seems almost too much.

I hear the wind among the trees
Playing celestial symphonies ;
I see the branches downward bent,
Like keys of some great instrument.

And over me unrolls on high
The splendid scenery of the sky,
Where through a sapphire sea the sun
Sails like a golden galleon,

Towards yonder cloud-land in the West,
Towards yonder Islands of the Blest,
Whose steep sierra far uplifts
Its craggy summits white with drifts.

Blow, winds ! and waft through all the
    rooms
The snow-flakes of the cherry-blooms !
Blow, winds ! and bend within my reach
The fiery blossoms of the peach !

O Life and Love ! O happy throng
Of thoughts, whose only speech is song !
O heart of man ! canst thou not be
Blithe as the air is, and as free ?

SOMETHING LEFT UNDONE.

LABOR with what zeal we will,
  Something still remains undone,
Something uncompleted still
  Waits the rising of the sun.

By the bedside, on the stair,
  At the threshold, near the gates,
With its menace or its prayer,
  Like a mendicant it waits ;

Waits, and will not go away ;
  Waits, and will not be gainsaid ;
By the cares of yesterday
  Each to-day is heavier made ;

Till at length the burden seems
  Greater than our strength can bear,
Heavy as the weight of dreams,
  Pressing on us everywhere.

And we stand from day to day,
  Like the dwarfs of times gone by,
Who, as Northern legends say,
  On their shoulders held the sky.

WEARINESS.

O LITTLE feet ! that such long years
Must wander on through hopes and fears,
　Must ache and bleed beneath your
　　load ;
I, nearer to the wayside inn
Where toil shall cease and rest begin,
　Am weary, thinking of your road !

O little hands ! that, weak or strong,
Have still to serve or rule so long,
　Have still so long to give or ask ;
I, who so much with book and pen
Have toiled among my fellow-men,
　Am weary, thinking of your task.

O little hearts ! that throb and beat
With such impatient, feverish heat,
　Such limitless and strong desires ;
Mine that so long has glowed and
　　burned,
With passions into ashes turned
　Now covers and conceals its fires.

O little souls ! as pure and white
And crystalline as rays of light
　Direct from heaven, their source di-
　　vine ;
Refracted through the mist of years,
How red my setting sun appears,
　How lurid looks this soul of mine !

FLIGHT THE THIRD.

FATA MORGANA.

O SWEET illusions of Song,
　That tempt me everywhere,
In the lonely fields, and the throng
　Of the crowded thoroughfare !

I approach, and ye vanish away,
　I grasp you, and ye are gone ;
But ever by night and by day,
　The melody soundeth on.

As the weary traveller sees
　In desert or prairie vast,
Blue lakes, overhung with trees,
　That a pleasant shadow cast ;

Fair towns with turrets high,
　And shining roofs of gold,
That vanish as he draws nigh,
　Like mists together rolled, —

So I wander and wander along,
　And forever before me gleams
The shining city of song,
　In the beautiful land of dreams.

But when I would enter the gate
　Of that golden atmosphere,
It is gone, and I wander and wait
　For the vision to reappear.

THE HAUNTED CHAMBER.

EACH heart has its haunted chamber,
　Where the silent moonlight falls !

On the floor are mysterious footsteps,
　There are whispers along the walls !

And mine at times is haunted
　By phantoms of the Past,
As motionless as shadows
　By the silent moonlight cast.

A form sits by the window,
　That is not seen by day,
For as soon as the dawn approaches
　It vanishes away.

It sits there in the moonlight,
　Itself as pale and still,
And points with its airy finger
　Across the window-sill.

Without, before the window,
　There stands a gloomy pine,
Whose boughs wave upward and down-
　　ward
　As wave these thoughts of mine.

And underneath its branches
　Is the grave of a little child,
Who died upon life's threshold,
　And never wept nor smiled.

What are ye, O pallid phantoms !
　That haunt my troubled brain ?
That vanish when day approaches,
　And at night return again ?

What are ye, O pallid phantoms !
  But the statues without breath,
That stand on the bridge overarching
  The silent river of death ?

THE MEETING.

AFTER so long an absence
  At last we meet again :
Does the meeting give us pleasure,
  Or does it give us pain ?

The tree of life has been shaken,
  And but few of us linger now,
Like the Prophet's two or three berries
  In the top of the uppermost bough.

We cordially greet each other
  In the old, familiar tone ;
And we think, though we do not say it,
  How old and gray he is grown !

We speak of a Merry Christmas
  And many a Happy New Year ;
But each in his heart is thinking
  Of those that are not here.

We speak of friends and their fortunes,
  And of what they did and said,
Till the dead alone seem living,
  And the living alone seem dead.

And at last we hardly distinguish
  Between the ghosts and the guests ;
And a mist and shadow of sadness
  Steals over our merriest jests.

VOX POPULI.

WHEN Mazárvan the Magician,
  Journeyed westward through Cathay,
Nothing heard he but the praises
  Of Badoura on his way.

But the lessening rumor ended
  When he came to Khaledan,
There the folk were talking only
  Of Prince Camaralzaman.

So it happens with the poets :
  Every province hath its own ;
Camaralzaman is famous
  Where Badoura is unknown.

THE CASTLE-BUILDER.

A GENTLE boy, with soft and silken
    locks,
  A dreamy boy, with brown and tender
    eyes,
A castle-builder, with his wooden
    blocks,
  And towers that touch imaginary
    skies.

A fearless rider on his father's knee,
  An eager listener unto stories told
At the Round Table of the nursery,
  Of heroes and adventures manifold.

There will be other towers for thee to
    build ;
  There will be other steeds for thee to
    ride ;
There will be other legends, and all
    filled
  With greater marvels and more
    glorified.

Build on, and make thy castles high
    and fair,
  Rising and reaching upward to the
    skies ;
Listen to voices in the upper air,
  Nor lose thy simple faith in mysteries.

CHANGED.

FROM the outskirts of the town,
  Where of old the mile-stone stood,
Now a stranger, looking down
  I behold the shadowy crown
Of the dark and haunted wood.

Is it changed, or am I changed ?
  Ah ! the oaks are fresh and green,
But the friends with whom I ranged
Through their thickets are estranged
  By the years that intervene.

Bright as ever flows the sea,
  Bright as ever shines the sun,
But alas ! they seem to me
Not the sun that used to be,
  Not the tides that used to run.

THE CHALLENGE.

I HAVE a vague remembrance
  Of a story, that is told
In some ancient Spanish legend
  Or chronicle of old.

It was when brave King Sanchez
   Was before Zamora slain,
And his great besieging army
   Lay encamped upon the plain.

Don Diego de Ordoñez
   Sallied forth in front of all,
And shouted loud his challenge
   To the warders on the wall.

All the people of Zamora,
   Both the born and the unborn,
As traitors did he challenge
   With taunting words of scorn.

The living, in their houses,
   And in their graves, the dead !
And the waters of their rivers,
   And their wine, and oil, and bread !

There is a greater army,
   That besets us round with strife,
A starving, numberless army,
   At all the gates of life.

The poverty-stricken millions
   Who challenge our wine and bread,
And impeach us all as traitors,
   Both the living and the dead.

And whenever I sit at the banquet,
   Where the feast and song are high,
Amid the mirth and the music
   I can hear that fearful cry.

And hollow and haggard faces
   Look into the lighted hall,
And wasted hands are extended
   To catch the crumbs that fall.

For within there is light and plenty,
   And odors fill the air ;
But without there is cold and darkness,
   And hunger and despair.

And there in the camp of famine,
   In wind and cold and rain,
Christ, the great Lord of the army,
   Lies dead upon the plain !

THE BROOK AND THE WAVE.

The brooklet came from the mountain,
   As sang the bard of old,
Running with feet of silver
   Over the sands of gold !

Far away in the briny ocean
   There rolled a turbulent wave,
Now singing along the sea-beach,
   Now howling along the cave.

And the brooklet has found the billow,
   Though they flowed so far apart,
And has filled with its freshness an
     sweetness
   That turbulent, bitter heart !

FROM THE SPANISH CANCIONE ROS.

1.

Eyes so tristful, eyes so tristful,
Heart so full of care and cumber,
I was lapped in rest and slumber,
Ye have made me wakeful, wistful !

In this life of labor endless
Who shall comfort my distresses ?
Querulous my soul and friendless
In its sorrow shuns caresses.
Ye have made me, ye have made me
Querulous of you, that care not,
Eyes so tristful, yet I dare not
Say to what ye have betrayed me.

2.

   Some day, some day,
   O troubled breast,
   Shalt thou find rest.

   If Love in thee
   To grief give birth,
   Six feet of earth
   Can more than he ;
   There calm and free
   And unoppressed
   Shalt thou find rest.

   The unattained
   In life at last,
   When life is passed,
   Shall all be gained ;
   And no more pained,
   No more distressed,
   Shalt thou find rest.

3.

Come, O Death, so silent flying
That unheard thy coming be,

Lest the sweet delight of dying
Bring life back again to me.

For thy sure approach perceiving,
In my constancy and pain
I new life should win again,
Thinking that I am not living.
So to me, unconscious lying,
All unknown thy coming be,
Lest the sweet delight of dying
Bring life back again to me.

Unto him who finds thee hateful,
Death, thou art inhuman pain ;
But to me, who dying gain,
Life is but a task ungrateful.
Come, then, with my wish complying,
All unheard thy coming be,
Lest the sweet delight of dying
Bring life back again to me.

4.

Glove of black in white hand bare,
And about her forehead pale
Wound a thin, transparent veil,
That doth not conceal her hair ;
Sovereign attitude and air,
Cheek and neck alike displayed,
With coquettish charms arrayed,
Laughing eyes and fugitive ; —
This is killing men that live,
'T is not mourning for the dead.

AFTERMATH.

WHEN the Summer fields are mown,
When the birds are fledged and flown,
    And the dry leaves strew the path ;
With the falling of the snow,
With the cawing of the crow,
Once again the fields we mow
    And gather in the aftermath.

Not the sweet, new grass with flowers
Is this harvesting of ours ;
    Not the upland clover bloom ;
But the rowen mixed with weeds,
Tangled tufts from marsh and meads,
Where the poppy drops its seeds
    In the silence and the gloom.

EPIMETHEUS,

OR THE POET'S AFTERTHOUGHT.

HAVE I dreamed ? or was it real,
    What I saw as in a vision,

When to marches hymeneal
In the land of the Ideal
    Moved my thought o'er Fields Elysian ?

What ! are these the guests whose glances
    Seemed like sunshine gleaming round
        me ?
These the wild, bewildering fancies,
That with dithyrambic dances
    As with magic circles bound me ?

Ah ! how cold are their caresses !
    Pallid cheeks, and haggard bosoms !
Spectral gleam their snow-white dresses,
And from loose, dishevelled tresses
    Fall the hyacinthine blossoms !

O my songs ! whose winsome measures
    Filled my heart with secret rapture !
Children of my golden leisures !
Must even your delights and pleasures
    Fade and perish with the capture ?

Fair they seemed, those songs sonorous,
    When they came to me unbidden ;
Voices single, and in chorus,
Like the wild birds singing o'er us
    In the dark of branches hidden.

Disenchantment !   Disillusion !
    Must each noble aspiration
Come at last to this conclusion,
Jarring discord, wild confusion,
    Lassitude, renunciation ?

Not with steeper fall nor faster,
    From the sun's serene dominions,
Not through brighter realms nor vaster,
In swift ruin and disaster,
    Icarus fell with shattered pinions !

Sweet Pandora ! dear Pandora !
    Why did mighty Jove create thee
Coy as Thetis, fair as Flora,
Beautiful as young Aurora,
    If to win thee is to hate thee ?

No, not hate thee ! for this feeling
    Of unrest and long resistance
Is but passionate appealing,
A prophetic whisper stealing
    O'er the chords of our existence.

Him whom thou dost once enamor,
    Thou, beloved, never leavest ;
In life's discord, strife, and clamor,
Still he feels thy spell of glamour ;
    Him of Hope thou ne'er bereavest.

Weary hearts by thee are lifted,
  Struggling souls by thee are strength-
    ened,
Clouds of fear asunder rifted,
Truth from falsehood cleansed and sifted,
  Lives, like days in summer, length-
    ened !

Therefore art thou ever dearer,
  O my Sibyl, my deceiver !

For thou makest each mystery clearer,
And the unattained seems nearer,
  When thou fillest my heart with
    fever !

Muse of all the Gifts and Graces !
  Though the fields around us wither,
There are ampler realms and spaces,
Where no foot has left its traces :
  Let us turn and wander thither !

TALES OF A WAYSIDE INN.

PRELUDE.

THE WAYSIDE INN.

ONE Autumn night, in Sudbury town,
Across the meadows bare and brown,
The windows of the wayside inn
Gleamed red with fire-light through the
  leaves
Of woodbine, hanging from the eaves
Their crimson curtains rent and thin.

As ancient is this hostelry
As any in the land may be,
Built in the old Colonial day,
When men lived in a grander way,
With ampler hospitality ;
A kind of old Hobgoblin Hall,
Now somewhat fallen to decay,
With weather-stains upon the wall,
And stairways worn, and crazy doors,
And creaking and uneven floors,
And chimneys huge, and tiled and tall.

A region of repose it seems,
A place of slumber and of dreams,
Re.note among the wooded hills !
For there no noisy railway speeds,
Its torch-race scattering smoke and
  gleeds ;
But noon and night, the panting teams
Stop under the great oaks, that throw
Tangles of light and shade below,
On roofs and doors and window-sills.
Across the road the barns display
Their lines of stalls, their mows of hay,
Through the wide doors the breezes blow,
The wattled cocks strut to and fro,
And, half effaced by rain and shine,
The Red Horse prances on the sign.

Round this old-fashioned, quaint abode
Deep silence reigned, save when a gust
Went rushing down the county road,
And skeletons of leaves, and dust,
A moment quickened by its breath,
Shuddered and danced their dance of
  death,
And through the ancient oaks o'erhead
Mysterious voices moaned and fled.

But from the parlor of the inn
A pleasant murmur smote the ear,
Like water rushing through a weir :
Oft interrupted by the din
Of laughter and of loud applause,
And, in each intervening pause,
The music of a violin.
The fire-light, shedding over all
The splendor of its ruddy glow,
Filled the whole parlor large and low ;
It gleamed on wainscot and on wall,
It touched with more than wonted grace
Fair Princess Mary's pictured face ;
It bronzed the rafters overhead,
On the old spinet's ivory keys
It played inaudible melodies,
It crowned the sombre clock with flame
The hands, the hours, the maker's name,
And painted with a livelier red
The Landlord's coat-of-arms again ;
And, flashing on the window-pane,
Emblazoned with its light and shade
The jovial rhymes, that still remain,
Writ near a century ago,
By the great Major Molineaux,
Whom Hawthorne has immortal made.

Before the blazing fire of wood
Erect the rapt musician stood ;

And ever and anon he bent
His head upon his instrument,
And seemed to listen, till he caught
Confessions of its secret thought, —
The joy, the triumph, the lament,
The exultation and the pain ;
Then, by the magic of his art,
He soothed the throbbings of its heart,
And lulled it into peace again.

Around the fireside at their ease
There sat a group of friends, entranced
With the delicious melodies ;
Who from the far-off noisy town
Had to the wayside inn come down,
To rest beneath its old oak-trees.
The fire-light on their faces glanced,
Their shadows on the wainscot danced,
And, though of different lands and
    speech,
Each had his tale to tell, and each
Was anxious to be pleased and please.
And while the sweet musician plays,
Let me in outline sketch them all,
Perchance uncouthly as the blaze
With its uncertain touch portrays
Their shadowy semblance on the wall.

But first the Landlord will I trace ;
Grave in his aspect and attire ;
A man of ancient pedigree,
A Justice of the Peace was he,
Known in all Sudbury as "The Squire."
Proud was he of his name and race,
Of old Sir William and Sir Hugh,
And in the parlor, full in view,
His coat-of-arms, well framed and glazed,
Upon the wall in colors blazed ;
He beareth gules upon his shield,
A chevron argent in the field,
With three wolf's heads, and for the crest
A Wyvern part-per-pale addressed
Upon a helmet barred ; below
The scroll reads, "By the name of
    Howe."
And over this, no longer bright,
Though glimmering with a latent light,
Was hung the sword his grandsire bore
In the rebellious days of yore,
Down there at Concord in the fight.

A youth was there, of quiet ways,
A Student of old books and days,
To whom all tongues and lands were
    known
And yet a lover of his own ;
With many a social virtue graced,

And yet a friend of solitude ;
A man of such a genial mood
The heart of all things he embraced,
And yet of such fastidious taste,
He never found the best too good.
Books were his passion and delight,
And in his upper room at home
Stood many a rare and sumptuous tome,
In vellum bound, with gold bedight,
Great volumes garmented in white,
Recalling Florence, Pisa, Rome.
He loved the twilight that surrounds
The border-land of old romance ;
Where glitter hauberk, helm, and lance,
And banner waves, and trumpet sounds,
And ladies ride with hawk on wrist,
And mighty warriors sweep along,
Magnified by the purple mist,
The dusk of centuries and of song.
The chronicles of Charlemagne,
Of Merlin and the Mort d'Arthure,
Mingled together in his brain
With tales of Flores and Blanchefleur,
Sir Ferumbras, Sir Eglamour,
Sir Launcelot, Sir Morgadour,
Sir Guy, Sir Bevis, Sir Gawain.

A young Sicilian, too, was there ;
In sight of Etna born and bred,
Some breath of its volcanic air
Was glowing in his heart and brain,
And, being rebellious to his liege,
After Palermo's fatal siege,
Across the western seas he fled,
In good King Bomba's happy reign.
His face was like a summer night,
All flooded with a dusky light ;
His hands were small ; his teeth shone
    white
As sea-shells, when he smiled or spoke ;
His sinews supple and strong as oak ;
Clean shaven was he as a priest,
Who at the mass on Sunday sings,
Save that upon his upper lip
His beard, a good palm's length
    least,
Level and pointed at the tip,
Shot sideways, like a swallow's wings.
The poets read he o'er and o'er,
And most of all the Immortal Four
Of Italy ; and next to those,
The story-telling bard of prose,
Who wrote the joyous Tuscan tales
Of the Decameron, that make
Fiesole's green hills and vales
Remembered for Boccaccio's sake.
Much too of music was his thought :

The melodies and measures fraught
With sunshine and the open air,
Of vineyards and the singing sea
Of his beloved Sicily ;
And much it pleased him to peruse
The songs of the Sicilian muse, —
Bucolic songs by Meli sung
In the familiar peasant tongue,
That made men say, " Behold ! once
    more
The pitying gods to earth restore
Theocritus of Syracuse ! "

A Spanish Jew from Alicant
With aspect grand and grave was there ;
Vender of silks and fabrics rare,
And attar of rose from the Levant.
Like an old Patriarch he appeared,
Abraham or Isaac, or at least
Some later Prophet or High-Priest ;
With lustrous eyes, and olive skin,
And, wildly tossed from cheeks and
    chin,
The tumbling cataract of his beard.
His garments breathed a spicy scent
Of cinnamon and sandal blent,
Like the soft aromatic gales
That meet the mariner, who sails
Through the Moluccas, and the seas
That wash the shores of Celebes.
All stories that recorded are
By Pierre Alphonse he knew by heart,
And it was rumored he could say
The Parables of Sandabar,
And all the Fables of Pilpay,
Or if not all, the greater part !
Well versed was he in Hebrew books,
Talmud and Targum, and the lore
Of Kabala ; and evermore
There was a mystery in his looks ;
His eyes seemed gazing far away,
As if in vision or in trance
He heard the solemn sackbut play,
And saw the Jewish maidens dance.

A Theologian, from the school
Of Cambridge on the Charles, was there ;
Skilful alike with tongue and pen,
He preached to all men everywhere
The Gospel of the Golden Rule,
The New Commandment given to men,
Thinking the deed, and not the creed,
Would help us in our utmost need.
With reverent feet the earth he trod,
Nor banished nature from his plan,
But studied still with deep research
To build the Universal Church,
Lofty as in the love of God,
And ample as the wants of man.

A Poet, too, was there, whose verse
Was tender, musical, and terse ;
The inspiration, the delight,
The gleam, the glory, the swift flight,
Of thoughts so sudden, that they seem
The revelations of a dream,
All these were his ; but with them came
No envy of another's fame ;
He did not find his sleep less sweet
For music in some neighboring street,
Nor rustling hear in every breeze
The laurels of Miltiades.
Honor and blessings on his head
While living, good report when dead,
Who, not too eager for renown,
Accepts, but does not clutch, the crown!

Last the Musician, as he stood
Illumined by that fire of wood ;
Fair-haired, blue-eyed, his aspect blithe,
His figure tall and straight and lithe,
And every feature of his face
Revealing his Norwegian race ;
A radiance, streaming from within,
Around his eyes and forehead beamed,
The Angel with the violin,
Painted by Raphael, he seemed.
He lived in that ideal world
Whose language is not speech, but song ;
Around him evermore the throng
Of elves and sprites their dances whirled ;
The Strömkarl sang, the cataract hurled
Its headlong waters from the height ;
And mingled in the wild delight
The scream of sea-birds in their flight,
The rumor of the forest trees,
The plunge of the implacable seas,
The tumult of the wind at night,
Voices of eld, like trumpets blowing,
Old ballads, and wild melodies
Through mist and darkness pouring
    forth,
Like Elivagar's river flowing
Out of the glaciers of the North.

The instrument on which he played
Was in Cremona's workshops made,
By a great master of the past,
Ere yet was lost the art divine ;
Fashioned of maple and of pine,
That in Tyrolian forests vast
Had rocked and wrestled with the blast :
Exquisite was it in design,
Perfect in each minutest part.

A marvel of the lutist's art;
And in its hollow chamber, thus,
The maker from whose hands it came
Had written his unrivalled name, —
"Antonius Stradivarius."

And when he played, the atmosphere
Was filled with magic, and the ear
Caught echoes of that Harp of Gold,
Whose music had so weird a sound,
The hunted stag forgot to bound,
The leaping rivulet backward rolled,
The birds came down from bush and
   tree,
The dead came from beneath the sea,
The maiden to the harper's knee!

The music ceased; the applause was
   loud,
The pleased musician smiled and bowed;
The wood-fire clapped its hands of flame,
The shadows on the wainscot stirred,
And from the harpsichord there came
A ghostly murmur of acclaim,
A sound like that sent down at night
By birds of passage in their flight,
From the remotest distance heard.

Then silence followed; then began
A clamor for the Landlord's tale, —
The story promised them of old,
They said, but always left untold;
And he, although a bashful man,
And all his courage seemed to fail,
Finding excuse of no avail,
Yielded; and thus the story ran.

THE LANDLORD'S TALE.

PAUL REVERE'S RIDE.

Listen, my children, and you shall
   hear
Of the midnight ride of Paul Revere,
On the eighteenth of April, in Seventy-
   five;
Hardly a man is now alive
Who remembers that famous day and
   year.

He said to his friend, "If the British
   march
By land or sea from the town to-night,
Hang a lantern aloft in the belfry arch
Of the North Church tower as a signal
   light, —

One, if by land, and two, if by sea;
And I on the opposite shore will be,
Ready to ride and spread the alarm
Through every Middlesex village and
   farm,
For the country folk to be up and to
   arm."

Then he said, "Good night!" and with
   muffled oar
Silently rowed to the Charlestown shore,
Just as the moon rose over the bay,
Where swinging wide at her moorings
   lay
The Somerset, British man-of-war;
A phantom ship, with each mast and
   spar
Across the moon like a prison bar,
And a huge black hulk, that was
   magnified
By its own reflection in the tide.

Meanwhile, his friend, through alley
   and street,
Wanders and watches with eager ears,
Till in the silence around him he hears
The muster of men at the barrack door,
The sound of arms, and the tramp of
   feet,
And the measured tread of the grena-
   diers,
Marching down to their boats on the
   shore.

Then he climbed the tower of the Old
   North Church,
By the wooden stairs, with stealthy
   tread,
To the belfry-chamber overhead,
And startled the pigeons from their
   perch
On the sombre rafters, that round him
   made
Masses and moving shapes of shade, —
By the trembling ladder, steep and tall
To the highest window in the wall,
Where he paused to listen and look
   down
A moment on the roofs of the town,
And the moonlight flowing over all.

Beneath, in the churchyard, lay the
   dead,
In their night-encampment on the hill,
Wrapped in silence so deep and still
That he could hear, like a sentinel's
   tread,

The watchful night-wind, as it went
Creeping along from tent to tent,
And seeming to whisper, "All is well!"
A moment only he feels the spell
Of the place and the hour, and the
    secret dread
Of the lonely belfry and the dead ;
For suddenly all his thoughts are bent
On a shadowy something far away,
Where the river widens to meet the
    bay, —
A line of black that bends and floats
On the rising tide, like a bridge of
    boats.

Meanwhile, impatient to mount and
    ride,
Booted and spurred, with a heavy stride
On the opposite shore walked Paul
    Revere.
Now he patted his horse's side,
Now gazed at the landscape far and
    near,
Then, impetuous, stamped the earth,
And turned and tightened his saddle-
    girth ;
But mostly he watched with eager
    search
The belfry-tower of the Old North
    Church,
As it rose above the graves on the hill,
Lonely and spectral and sombre and
    still.
And lo! as he looks, on the belfry's
    height
A glimmer, and then a gleam of light!
He springs to the saddle, the bridle he
    turns,
But lingers and gazes, till full on his
    sight
A second lamp in the belfry burns !

A hurry of hoofs in a village street,
A shape in the moonlight, a bulk in the
    dark,
And beneath, from the pebbles, in pass-
    ing, a spark
Struck out by a steed flying fearless
    and fleet :
That was all ! And yet, through the
    gloom and the light,
The fate of a nation was riding that
    night ;
And the spark struck out by that steed,
    in his flight,
Kindled the land into flame with its
    heat.

He has left the village and mounted
    the steep,
And beneath him, tranquil and broad
    and deep,
Is the Mystic, meeting the ocean tides ;
And under the alders, that skirt its
    edge,
Now soft on the sand, now loud on
    the ledge,
Is heard the tramp of his steed as he
    rides.

It was twelve by the village clock
When he crossed the bridge into Med-
    ford town.
He heard the crowing of the cock,
And the barking of the farmer's dog,
And felt the damp of the river fog,
That rises after the sun goes down.

It was one by the village clock,
When he galloped into Lexington.
He saw the gilded weathercock
Swim in the moonlight as he passed,
And the meeting-house windows, blank
    and bare,
Gaze at him with a spectral glare,
As if they already stood aghast
At the bloody work they would look
    upon.

It was two by the village clock,
When he came to the bridge in Concord
    town.
He heard the bleating of the flock,
And the twitter of birds among the trees,
And felt the breath of the morning
    breeze
Blowing over the meadows brown.
And one was safe and asleep in his bed
Who at the bridge would be first to
    fall,
Who that day would be lying dead,
Pierced by a British musket-ball.

You know the rest. In the books you
    have read,
How the British Regulars fired and
    fled, —
How the farmers gave them ball for
    ball,
From behind each fence and farm-yard
    wall,
Chasing the red-coats down the lane,
Then crossing the fields to emerge again
Under the trees at the turn of the road,
And only pausing to fire and load.

So through the night rode Paul Revere ;
And so through the night went his cry
    of alarm
To every Middlesex village and farm, —
A cry of defiance and not of fear,
A voice in the darkness, a knock at the
    door,
And a word that shall echo forevermore !
For, borne on the night-wind of the
    Past,
Through all our history, to the last,
In the hour of darkness and peril and
    need,
The people will waken and listen to
    hear
The hurrying hoof-beats of that steed,
And the midnight message of Paul
    Revere.

INTERLUDE.

THE Landlord ended thus his tale,
Then rising took down from its nail
The sword that hung there, dim with
    dust,
And cleaving to its sheath with rust,
And said, " This sword was in the
    fight."
The Poet seized it, and exclaimed,
" It is the sword of a good knight,
Though homespun was his coat-of-mail ;
What matter if it be not named
Joyeuse, Colada, Durindale,
Excalibar, or Aroundight,
Or other name the books record ?
Your ancestor, who bore this sword
As Colonel of the Volunteers,
Mounted upon his old gray mare,
Seen here and there and everywhere,
To me a grander shape appears
Than old Sir William, or what not,
Clinking about in foreign lands
With iron gauntlets on his hands,
And on his head an iron pot ! "

All laughed ; the Landlord's face grew
    red
As his escutcheon on the wall ;
He could not comprehend at all
The drift of what the Poet said ;
For those who had been longest dead
Were always greatest in his eyes ;
And he was speechless with surprise
To see Sir William's plumed head
Brought to a level with the rest,
And made the subject of a jest.

And this perceiving, to appease
The Landlord's wrath, the others' fears,
The Student said, with careless ease,
" The ladies and the cavaliers,
The arms, the loves, the courtesies,
The deeds of high emprise, I sing !
Thus Ariosto says, in words
That have the stately stride and ring
Of armed knights and clashing swords.
Now listen to the tale I bring ;
Listen ! though not to me belong
The flowing draperies of his song,
The words that rouse, the voice that
    charms.
The Landlord's tale was one of arms,
Only a tale of love is mine,
Blending the human and divine,
A tale of the Decameron, told
In Palmieri's garden old,
By Fiametta, laurel-crowned,
While her companions lay around,
And heard the intermingled sound
Of airs that on their errands sped,
And wild birds gossiping overhead,
And lisp of leaves, and fountain's fall,
And her own voice more sweet than
    all,
Telling the tale, which, wanting these,
Perchance may lose its power to please."

THE STUDENT'S TALE.

THE FALCON OF SER FEDERIGO.

ONE summer morning, when the sun
    was hot,
Weary with labor in his garden-plot,
On a rude bench beneath his cottage
    eaves,
Ser Federigo sat among the leaves
Of a huge vine, that, with its arms out-
    spread,
Hung its delicious clusters overhead.
Below him, through the lovely valley
    flowed
The river Arno, like a winding road,
And from its banks were lifted high in
    air
The spires and roofs of Florence called
    the Fair ;
To him a marble tomb, that rose above
His wasted fortunes and his buried love.
For there, in banquet and in tourna-
    ment,
His wealth had lavished been, his sub-
    stance spent,

To woo and lose, since ill his wooing
   sped,
Monna Giovanna, who his rival wed,
Yet ever in his fancy reigned supreme,
The ideal woman of a young man's
   dream.

Then he withdrew, in poverty and pain,
To this small farm, the last of his do-
   main,
His only comfort and his only care
To prune his vines, and plant the fig
   and pear ;
His only forester and only guest
His falcon, faithful to him, when the
   rest,
Whose willing hands had found so light
   of yore
The brazen knocker of his palace door,
Had now no strength to lift the wooden
   latch,
That entrance gave beneath a roof of
   thatch.
Companion of his solitary ways,
Purveyor of his feasts on holidays,
On him this melancholy man bestowed
The love with which his nature over-
   flowed.

And so the empty-handed years went
   round,
Vacant, though voiceful with prophetic
   sound,
And so, that summer morn, he sat and
   mused
With folded, patient hands, as he was
   used,
And dreamily before his half-closed sight
Floated the vision of his lost delight.
Beside him, motionless, the drowsy
   bird
Dreamed of the chase, and in his slum-
   ber heard
The sudden, scythe-like sweep of wings,
   that dare
The headlong plunge thro' eddying gulfs
   of air,
Then, starting broad awake upon his
   perch,
Tinkled his bells, like mass-bells in a
   church,
And, looking at his master, seemed to
   say,
" Ser Federigo, shall we hunt to-day ? "

Ser Federigo thought not of the chase ;
The tender vision of her lovely face,

I will not say he seems to see, he sees
In the leaf-shadows of the trellises,
Herself, yet not herself ; a lovely child
With flowing tresses, and eyes wide and
   wild,
Coming undaunted up the garden walk,
And looking not at him, but at the
   hawk.
" Beautiful falcon ! " said he, " would
   that I
Might hold thee on my wrist, or see
   thee fly ! "
The voice was hers, and made strange
   echoes start
Through all the haunted chambers of
   his heart,
As an æolian harp through gusty doors
Of some old ruin its wild music pours.

" Who is thy mother, my fair boy ? " he
   said,
His hand laid softly on that shining
   head.
" Monna Giovanna. Will you let me
   stay
A little while, and with your falcon
   play ?
We live there, just beyond your garden
   wall,
In the great house behind the poplars
   tall."

So he spake on ; and Federigo heard
As from afar each softly uttered word,
And drifted onward through the golden
   gleams
And shadows of the misty sea of dreams,
As mariners becalmed through vapors
   drift,
And feel the sea beneath them sink and
   lift,
And hear far off the mournful breakers
   roar,
And voices calling faintly from the
   shore !
Then, waking from his pleasant reveries
He took the little boy upon his knees,
And told him stories of his gallant bird,
Till in their friendship he became a
   third.

Monna Giovanna, widowed in her prime,
Had come with friends to pass the sum-
   mer time
In her grand villa, half-way up the hill,
O'erlooking Florence, but retired and
   still ;

With iron gates, that opened through
    long lines
Of sacred ilex and centennial pines,
And terraced gardens, and broad steps
    of stone,
And sylvan deities, with moss o'ergrown,
And fountains palpitating in the heat,
And all Val d'Arno stretched beneath
    its feet.

Here in seclusion, as a widow may,
The lovely lady whiled the hours away,
Pacing in sable robes the statued hall,
Herself the stateliest statue among all,
And seeing more and more, with secret
    joy,
Her husband risen and living in her boy,
Till the lost sense of life returned again,
Not as delight, but as relief from pain.
Meanwhile the boy, rejoicing in his
    strength,
Stormed down the terraces from length
    to length ;
The screaming peacock chased in hot
    pursuit,
And climbed the garden trellises for fruit.
But his chief pastime was to watch the
    flight
Of a gerfalcon, soaring into sight,
Beyond the trees that fringed the garden
    wall,
Then downward stooping at some distant
    call ;
And as he gazed full often wondered he
Who might the master of the falcon be,
Until that happy morning, when he found
Master and falcon in the cottage ground.

And now a shadow and a terror fell
On the great house, as if a passing-bell
Tolled from the tower, and filled each
    spacious room
With secret awe, and preternatural
    gloom ;
The petted boy grew ill, and day by day
Pined with mysterious malady away.
The mother's heart would not be com-
    forted ;
Her darling seemed to her already dead,
And often, sitting by the sufferer's side,
"What can I do to comfort thee ? " she
    cried.
At first the silent lips made no reply,
But, moved at length by her importu-
    nate cry,
" Give me," he answered, with implor-
    ing tone,
" Ser Federigo's falcon for my own ! "

No answer could the astonished mother
    make ;
How could she ask, e'en for her darling's
    sake,
Such favor at a luckless lover's hand,
Well knowing that to ask was to com-
    mand ?
Well knowing, what all falconers con-
    fessed,
In all the land that falcon was the best,
The master's pride and passion and
    delight,
And the sole pursuivant of this poor
    knight.
But yet, for her child's sake, she could
    no less
Than give assent, to soothe his restless-
    ness,
So promised, and then promising to keep
Her promise sacred, saw him fall asleep.

The morrow was a bright September morn ;
The earth was beautiful as if new-born ;
There was that nameless splendor every-
    where,
That wild exhilaration in the air,
Which makes the passers in the city
    street
Congratulate each other as they meet.
Two lovely ladies, clothed in cloak and
    hood,
Passed through the garden gate into the
    wood,
Under the lustrous leaves, and through
    the sheen
Of dewy sunshine showering down be-
    tween.

The one, close-hooded, had the attractive
    grace
Which sorrow sometimes lends a woman's
    face ;
Her dark eyes moistened with the mists
    that roll
From the gulf-stream of passion in the
    soul ;
The other with her hood thrown back,
    her hair
Making a golden glory in the air,
Her cheeks suffused with an auroral
    blush,
Her young heart singing louder than the
    thrush.
So walked, that morn, through mingled
    light and shade,
Each by the other's presence lovelier
    made,

Monna Giovanna and her bosom friend,
Intent upon their errand and its end.

They found Ser Federigo at his toil,
Like banished Adam, delving in the soil ;
And when he looked and these fair wo-
    men spied,
The garden suddenly was glorified ;
His long-lost Eden was restored again,
And the strange river winding through
    the plain
No longer was the Arno to his eyes,
But the Euphrates watering Paradise !

Monna Giovanna raised her stately head,
And with fair words of salutation said :
"Ser Federigo, we come here as friends,
Hoping in this to make some poor amends
For past unkindness.   I who ne'er before
Would even cross the threshold of your
    door,
I who in happier days such pride main-
    tained,
Refused your banquets, and your gifts
    disdained,
This morning come, a self-invited guest,
To put your generous nature to the test,
And breakfast with you under your own
    vine."
To which he answered : "Poor desert of
    mine,
Not your unkindness call it, for if aught
Is good in me of feeling or of thought,
From you it comes, and this last grace
    outweighs
All sorrows, all regrets of other days."

And after further compliment and talk,
Among the **asters in the** garden walk
He left his guests ; and to his cottage
    turned,
And as he entered for a moment yearned
For the lost splendors of the days of old,
The ruby glass, the silver and the gold,
And felt how piercing is the sting of pride,
By want embittered and intensified.
He looked about him for some means or
    way
To keep this unexpected holiday ;
Searched every cupboard, and then
    searched again,
Summoned the maid, who came, but
    came in vain ;
"The Signor did not hunt to-day," she
    said,
"There's nothing in the house but wine
    and bread."

Then suddenly the drowsy falcon shook
His little bells, with that sagacious look,
Which said, as plain as language to the
    ear,
"If anything is wanting, I am here !"
Yes, everything is wanting, gallant bird !
The master seized thee without further
    word.
Like thine own lure, he whirled thee
    round ; ah me !
The pomp and flutter of brave falconry,
The bells, the jesses, the bright scarlet
    hood,
The flight and the pursuit o'er field and
    wood,
All these forevermore are ended now ;
No longer victor, but the victim thou !

Then on the board a snow-white cloth
    he spread,
Laid on its wooden dish the loaf of bread,
Brought purple grapes with autumn sun-
    shine hot,
The fragrant peach, the juicy bergamot ;
Then in the midst a flask of wine he
    placed,
And with autumnal flowers the banquet
    graced.
Ser Federigo, would not these suffice
Without thy falcon stuffed with cloves
    and spice ?

When all was ready, and the courtly
    dame
With her companion to the cottage came,
Upon Ser Federigo's brain there fell
The wild enchantment of a magic spell !
The room they entered, mean and low
    and small,
Was changed into a sumptuous banquet-
    hall,
With fanfares by aerial trumpets blown ;
The rustic chair she sat on was a throne ;
He ate celestial food, and a divine
Flavor was given to his country wine,
And the poor falcon, fragrant with his
    spice,
A peacock was, or bird of paradise !

When the repast was ended, they arose
And passed again into the garden-close.
Then said the lady, "Far too well I
    know,
Remembering still the days of long ago,
Though you betray it not, with what
    surprise
You see me here in this familiar wise.

You have no children, and you cannot
  guess
What anguish, what unspeakable dis-
  tress
A mother feels, whose child is lying ill,
Nor how her heart anticipates his will.
And yet for this, you see me lay aside
All womanly reserve and check of pride,
And ask the thing most precious in your
  sight,
Your falcon, your sole comfort and de-
  light,
Which if you find it in your heart to give,
My poor, unhappy boy perchance may
  live."

Ser Federigo listens, and replies,
With tears of love and pity in his eyes:
"Alas, dear lady! there can be no task
So sweet to me, as giving when you ask.
One little hour ago, if I had known
This wish of yours, it would have been
  my own.
But thinking in what manner I could
  best
Do honor to the presence of my guest,
I deemed that nothing worthier could be
Than what most dear and precious was
  to me,
And so my gallant falcon breathed his
  last
To furnish forth this morning our repast."

In mute contrition, mingled with dismay,
The gentle lady turned her eyes away,
Grieving that he such sacrifice should
  make,
And kill his falcon for a woman's sake,
Yet feeling in her heart a woman's pride,
That nothing she could ask for was
  denied;
Then took her leave, and passed out at
  the gate
With footstep slow and soul disconsolate.

Three days went by, and lo! a passing-
  bell
Tolled from the little chapel in the dell;
Ten strokes Ser Federigo heard, and said,
Breathing a prayer, "Alas! her child is
  dead!"
Three months went by; and lo! a mer-
  rier chime
Rang from the chapel bells at Christmas
  time;
The cottage was deserted, and no more
Ser Federigo sat beside its door,

But now, with servitors to do his will,
In the grand villa, half-way up the hill,
Sat at the Christmas feast, and at his side
Monna Giovanna, his beloved bride,
Never so beautiful, so kind, so fair,
Enthroned once more in the old rustic
  chair,
High-perched upon the back of which
  there stood
The image of a falcon carved in wood,
And underneath the inscription, with
  date,
"All things come round to him who will
  but wait."

INTERLUDE.

Soon as the story reached its end,
One, over eager to commend,
Crowned it with injudicious praise;
And then the voice of blame found vent,
And fanned the embers of dissent
Into a somewhat lively blaze.

The Theologian shook his head;
"These old Italian tales," he said,
"From the much-praised Decameron
  down
Through all the rabble of the rest,
Are either trifling, dull, or lewd;
The gossip of a neighborhood
In some remote provincial town,
A scandalous chronicle at best!
They seem to me a stagnant fen,
Grown rank with rushes and with reeds,
Where a white lily, now and then,
Blooms in the midst of noxious weeds
And deadly nightshade on its banks."

To this the Student straight replied,
"For the white lily, many thanks!
One should not say, with too much pride,
Fountain, I will not drink of thee!
Nor were it grateful to forget,
That from these reservoirs and tanks
Even imperial Shakespeare drew
His Moor of Venice, and the Jew,
And Romeo and Juliet,
And many a famous comedy."

Then a long pause; till some one said,
"An Angel is flying overhead!"
At these words spake the Spanish Jew,
And murmured with an inward breath:
"God grant, if what you say be true,
It may not be the Angel of Death!"

And then another pause ; and then,
Stroking his beard, he said again :
" This brings back to my memory
A story in the Talmud told,
That book of gems, that book of gold,
Of wonders many and manifold,
A tale that often comes to me,
And fills my heart, and haunts my brain,
And never wearies nor grows old."

THE SPANISH JEW'S TALE.

THE LEGEND OF RABBI BEN LEVI.

RABBI BEN LEVI, on the Sabbath, read
A volume of the Law, in which it said,
" No man shall look upon my face and
live."
And as he read, he prayed that God
would give
His faithful servant grace with mortal
eye
To look upon His face and yet not die.

Then fell a sudden shadow on the page,
And, lifting up his eyes, grown dim with
age,
He saw the Angel of Death before him
stand,
Holding a naked sword in his right hand.
Rabbi Ben Levi was a righteous man,
Yet through his veins a chill of terror
ran.
With trembling voice he said, " What
wilt thou here ? "
The angel answered, " Lo ! the time
draws near
When thou must die ; yet first, by God's
decree,
Whate'er thou askest shall be granted
thee."
Replied the Rabbi, " Let these living
eyes
First look upon my place in Paradise."

Then said the Angel, " Come with me
and look."
Rabbi Ben Levi closed the sacred book,
And rising, and uplifting his gray head,
" Give me thy sword," he to the Angel
said,
" Lest thou shouldst fall upon me by the
way."
The angel smiled and hastened to obey,
Then led him forth to the Celestial Town,
And set him on the wall, whence, gazing
down,

Rabbi Ben Levi, with his living eyes,
Might look upon his place in Paradise.

Then straight into the city of the Lord
The Rabbi leaped with the Death-Angel's
sword,
And through the streets there swept a
sudden breath
Of something there unknown, which men
call death.
Meanwhile the Angel stayed without,
and cried,
" Come back ! " To which the Rabbi's
voice replied,
" No ! in the name of God, whom I
adore,
I swear that hence I will depart no
more ! "

Then all the Angels cried, " O Holy One,
See what the son of Levi here hath done !
The kingdom of Heaven he takes by
violence,
And in Thy name refuses to go hence ! "
The Lord replied, " My Angels, be not
wroth ;
Did e'er the son of Levi break his oath ?
Let him remain ; for he with mortal eye
Shall look upon my face and yet not die."

Beyond the outer wall the Angel of Death
Heard the great voice, and said, with
panting breath,
" Give back the sword, and let me go
my way."
Whereat the Rabbi paused, and answered,
" Nay !
Anguish enough already hath it caused
Among the sons of men." And while
he paused
He heard the awful mandate of the
Lord
Resounding through the air, " Give back
the sword ! "

The Rabbi bowed his head in silent
prayer ;
Then said he to the dreadful Angel,
" Swear,
No human eye shall look on it again ;
But when thou takest away the souls of
men,
Thyself unseen, and with an unseen
sword,
Thou wilt perform the bidding of the
Lord."

The Angel took the sword again, and
  swore,
And walks on earth unseen forevermore.

INTERLUDE.

He ended: and a kind of spell
Upon the silent listeners fell.
His solemn manner and his words
Had touched the deep, mysterious
  chords,
That vibrate in each human breast
Alike, but not alike confessed.
The spiritual world seemed near;
And close above them, full of fear,
Its awful adumbration passed,
A luminous shadow, vague and vast.
They almost feared to look, lest there,
Embodied from the impalpable air,
They might behold the Angel stand,
Holding the sword in his right hand.

At last, but in a voice subdued,
Not to disturb their dreamy mood,
Said the Sicilian : " While you spoke,
Telling your legend marvellous,
Suddenly in my memory woke
The thought of one, now gone from
  us, —
An old Abate, meek and mild,
My friend and teacher, when a child,
Who sometimes in those days of old
The legend of an Angel told,
Which ran, as I remember, thus."

THE SICILIAN'S TALE.

KING ROBERT OF SICILY.

Robert of Sicily, brother of Pope Ur-
  bane
And Valmond, Emperor of Allemaine,
Apparelled in magnificent attire,
With retinue of many a knight and
  squire,
On St. John's eve, at vespers, proudly
  sat
And heard the priests chant the Mag-
  nificat.
And as he listened, o'er and o'er again
Repeated, like a burden or refrain,
He caught the words, " *Deposuit poten-
tes
De sede, et exaltavit humiles*";
And slowly lifting up his kingly head
He to a learned clerk beside him said,

" What mean these words?"   The clerk
  made answer meet,
" He has put down the mighty from
  their seat,
And has exalted them of low degree."
Thereat King Robert muttered scorn-
  fully,
" 'T is well that such seditious words are
  sung
Only by priests and in the Latin tongue;
For unto priests and people be it known,
There is no power can push me from
  my throne!"
And leaning back, he yawned and fell
  asleep,
Lulled by the chant monotonous and
  deep.

When he awoke, it was already night;
The church was empty, and there was
  no light,
Save where the lamps, that glimmered
  few and faint,
Lighted a little space before some saint.
He started from his seat and gazed
  around,
But saw no living thing and heard no
  sound.
He groped towards the door, but it was
  locked;
He cried aloud, and listened, and then
  knocked,
And uttered awful threatenings and
  complaints,
And imprecations upon men and saints.
The sounds re-echoed from the roof and
  walls
As if dead priests were laughing in their
  stalls.

At length the sexton, hearing from
  without
The tumult of the knocking and the
  shout,
And thinking thieves were in the house
  of prayer,
Came with his lantern, asking, " Who
  is there?"
Half choked with rage, King Robert
  fiercely said,
" Open: 't is I, the King! Art thou
  afraid?"
The frightened sexton, muttering, with
  a curse,
" This is some drunken vagabond, or
  worse!"
Turned the great key and flung the portal wide;

A man rushed by him at a single stride,
Haggard, half naked, without hat or
    cloak,
Who neither turned, nor looked at him,
    nor spoke,
But leaped into the blackness of the
    night,
And vanished like a spectre from his
    sight.

Robert of Sicily, brother of Pope Urbane
And Valmond, Emperor of Allemaine,
Despoiled of his magnificent attire,
Bareheaded, breathless, and besprent
    with mire,
With sense of wrong and outrage desper-
    ate,
Strode on and thundered at the palace
    gate ;
Rushed through the courtyard, thrust-
    ing in his rage
To right and left each seneschal and
    page,
And hurried up the broad and sounding
    stair,
His white face ghastly in the torches'
    glare.
From hall to hall he passed with breath-
    less speed ;
Voices and cries he heard, but did not
    heed,
Until at last he reached the banquet-
    room,
Blazing with light, and breathing with
    perfume.

There on the dais sat another king,
Wearing his robes, his crown, his signet-
    ring,
King Robert's self in features, form, and
    height,
But all transfigured with angelic light !
It was an Angel ; and his presence there
With a divine effulgence filled the air,
An exaltation, piercing the disguise,
Though none the hidden Angel recognize.

A moment speechless, motionless,
    amazed,
The throneless monarch on the Angel
    gazed,
Who met his look of anger and surprise
With the divine compassion of his eyes ;
Then said, " Who art thou ? and why
    com'st thou here ? "
To which King Robert answered, with a
    sneer,

"I am the King, and come to claim my own
From an impostor, who usurps my
    throne ! "
And suddenly, at these audacious words,
Up sprang the angry guests, and drew
    their swords ;
The Angel answered, with unruffled brow,
" Nay, not the King, but the King's Jes-
    ter, thou
Henceforth shall wear the bells and
    scalloped cape,
And for thy counsellor shalt lead an ape ;
Thou shalt obey my servants when they
    call,
And wait upon my henchmen in the hall ! "

Deaf to King Robert's threats and cries
    and prayers,
They thrust him from the hall and down
    the stairs ;
A group of tittering pages ran before,
And as they opened wide the folding-
    door,
His heart failed, for he heard, with
    strange alarms,
The boisterous laughter of the men-at-
    arms,
And all the vaulted chamber roar and ring
With the mock plaudits of " Long live
    the King ! "

Next morning, waking with the day's
    first beam,
He said within himself, " It was a
    dream ! "
But the straw rustled as he turned his
    head,
There were the cap and bells beside his bed,
Around him rose the bare, discolored walls,
Close by, the steeds were champing in
    their stalls,
And in the corner, a revolting shape,
Shivering and chattering sat the wretch-
    ed ape.
It was no dream ; the world he loved so
    much
Had turned to dust and ashes at his
    touch !

Days came and went ; and now returned
    again
To Sicily the old Saturnian reign ;
Under the Angel's governance benign
The happy island danced with corn and
    wine,
And deep within the mountain's burn-
    ing breast
Enceladus, the giant, was at rest.

Meanwhile King Robert yielded to his
fate,
Sullen and silent and disconsolate.
Dressed in the motley garb that Jesters
wear,
With look bewildered and a vacant stare,
Close shaven above the ears, as monks
are shorn,
By courtiers mocked, by pages laughed
to scorn,
His only friend the ape, his only food
What others left, — he still was unsub-
dued.
And when the Angel met him on his way,
And half in earnest, half in jest, would
say,
Sternly, though tenderly, that he might
feel
The velvet scabbard held a sword of steel,
"Art thou the King?" the passion of
his woe
Burst from him in resistless overflow,
And, lifting high his forehead, he would
fling
The haughty answer back, " I am, I am
the King!"

Almost three years were ended; when
there came
Ambassadors of great repute and name
From Valmond, Emperor of Allemaine,
Unto King Robert, saying that Pope
Urbane
By letter summoned them forthwith to
come
On Holy Thursday to his city of Rome.
The Angel with great joy received his
guests,
And gave them presents of embroidered
vests,
And velvet mantles with rich ermine
lined,
And rings and jewels of the rarest kind.
Then he departed with them o'er the sea
Into the lovely land of Italy,
Whose loveliness was more resplendent
made
By the mere passing of that cavalcade,
With plumes, and cloaks, and housings,
and the stir
Of jewelled bridle and of golden spur.

And lo! among the menials, in mock
state,
Upon a piebald steed, with shambling
gait,
His cloak of fox-tails flapping in the wind,

The solemn ape demurely perched behind,
King Robert rode, making huge merriment
In all the country towns through which
they went.

The Pope received them with great pomp
and blare
Of bannered trumpets, on Saint Peter's
square,
Giving his benediction and embrace,
Fervent, and full of apostolic grace.
While with congratulations and with
prayers
He entertained the Angel unawares,
Robert, the Jester, bursting through the
crowd,
Into their presence rushed, and cried
aloud,
" I am the King! Look, and behold in
me
Robert, your brother, King of Sicily!
This man, who wears my semblance to
your eyes,
Is an impostor in a king's disguise.
Do you not know me? does no voice
within
Answer my cry, and say we are akin?"
The Pope in silence, but with troubled
mien,
Gazed at the Angel's countenance serene;
The Emperor, laughing, said, " It is
strange sport
To keep a madman for thy Fool at court!"
And the poor, baffled Jester in disgrace
Was hustled back among the populace.

In solemn state the Holy Week went by,
And Easter Sunday gleamed upon the
sky;
The presence of the Angel, with its light,
Before the sun rose, made the city bright,
And with new fervor filled the hearts
of men,
Who felt that Christ indeed had risen
again.
Even the Jester, on his bed of straw,
With haggard eyes the unwonted splen-
dor saw,
He felt within a power unfelt before,
And, kneeling humbly on his chamber
floor,
He heard the rushing garments of the
Lord
Sweep through the silent air, ascending
heavenward.

And now the visit ending, and once more
Valmond returning to the Danube's shore,
Homeward the Angel journeyed, and again
The land was made resplendent with his train,
Flashing along the towns of Italy
Unto Salerno, and from thence by sea.
And when once more within Palermo's wall,
And, seated on the throne in his great hall,
He heard the Angelus from convent towers,
As if the better world conversed with ours,
He beckoned to King Robert to draw nigher,
And with a gesture bade the rest retire ;
And when they were alone, the Angel said,
"Art thou the King ?"   Then, bowing down his head,
King Robert crossed both hands upon his breast,
And meekly answered him : "Thou knowest best !
My sins as scarlet are ; let me go hence,
And in some cloister's school of penitence,
Across those stones, that pave the way to heaven,
Walk barefoot, till my guilty soul be shriven ! "

The Angel smiled, and from his radiant face
A holy light illumined all the place,
And through the open window, loud and clear,
They heard the monks chant in the chapel near,
Above the stir and tumult of the street :
"He has put down the mighty from their seat,
And has exalted them of low degree ! "
And through the chant a second melody
Rose like the throbbing of a single string :
" I am an Angel, and thou art the King ! "

King Robert, who was standing near the throne,
Lifted his eyes, and lo ! he was alone !
But all apparelled as in days of old,
With ermined mantle and with cloth of gold ;

And when his courtiers came, they found him there
Kneeling upon the floor, absorbed in silent prayer.

INTERLUDE.

AND then the blue-eyed Norseman told
A Saga of the days of old.
"There is," said he, "a wondrous book
Of Legends in the old Norse tongue,
Of the dead kings of Norroway, —
Legends that once were told or sung
In many a smoky fireside nook
Of Iceland, in the ancient day,
By wandering Saga-man or Scald ;
Heimskringla is the volume called ;
And he who looks may find therein
The story that I now begin."

And in each pause the story made
Upon his violin he played,
As an appropriate interlude,
Fragments of old Norwegian tunes
That bound in one the separate runes,
And held the mind in perfect mood,
Entwining and encircling all
The strange and antiquated rhymes
With melodies of olden times ;
As over some half-ruined wall,
Disjointed and about to fall,
Fresh woodbines climb and interlace,
And keep the loosened stones in place.

THE MUSICIAN'S TALE.

THE SAGA OF KING OLAF.

I.

THE CHALLENGE OF THOR.

I AM the God Thor,
I am the War God,
I am the Thunderer !
Here in my Northland,
My fastness and fortress,
Reign I forever !

Here amid icebergs
Rule I the nations ;
This is my hammer,
Miölner the mighty ;
Giants and sorcerers
Cannot withstand it !

"And his ships went sailing, sailing."   Page 247.

These are the gauntlets
Wherewith I wield it,
And hurl it afar off;
This is my girdle;
Whenever I brace it,
Strength is redoubled!

The light thou beholdest
Stream through the heavens,
In flashes of crimson,
Is but my red beard
Blown by the night-wind,
Affrighting the nations!

Jove is my brother;
Mine eyes are the lightning;
The wheels of my chariot
Roll in the thunder,
The blows of my hammer
Ring in the earthquake!

Force rules the world still,
Has ruled it, shall rule it;
Meekness is weakness,
Strength is triumphant,
Over the whole earth
Still is it Thor's-Day!

Thou art a God too,
O Galilean!
And thus single-handed
Unto the combat,
Gauntlet or Gospel,
Here I defy thee!

II.

KING OLAF'S RETURN.

And King Olaf heard the cry,
Saw the red light in the sky,
    Laid his hand upon his sword,
As he leaned upon the railing,
And his ships went sailing, sailing
    Northward into Drontheim fiord.

There he stood as one who dreamed;
And the red light glanced and gleamed
    On the armor that he wore;
And he shouted, as the rifted
Streamers o'er him shook and shifted,
    "I accept thy challenge, Thor!"

To avenge his father slain,
And reconquer realm and reign,
    Came the youthful Olaf home,
Through the midnight sailing, sailing,

Listening to the wild wind's wailing,
    And the dashing of the foam.

To his thoughts the sacred name
Of his mother Astrid came,
    And the tale she oft had told
Of her flight by secret passes
Through the mountains and morasses,
    To the home of Hakon old.

Then strange memories crowded back
Of Queen Gunhild's wrath and wrack,
    And a hurried flight by sea;
Of grim Vikings, and the rapture
Of the sea-fight, and the capture,
    And the life of slavery.

How a stranger watched his face
In the Esthonian market-place,
    Scanned his features one by one,
Saying, "We should know each other;
I am Sigurd, Astrid's brother,
    Thou art Olaf, Astrid's son!"

Then as Queen Allogia's page,
Old in honors, young in age,
    Chief of all her men-at-arms;
Till vague whispers, and mysterious,
Reached King Valdemar, the imperious,
    Filling him with strange alarms.

Then his cruisings o'er the seas,
Westward to the Hebrides,
    And to Scilly's rocky shore;
And the hermit's cavern dismal,
Christ's great name and rites baptismal
    In the ocean's rush and roar.

All these thoughts of love and strife
Glimmered through his lurid life,
    As the stars' intenser light
Through the red flames o'er him trailing,
As his ships went sailing, sailing,
    Northward in the summer night.

Trained for either camp or court,
Skilful in each manly sport,
    Young and beautiful and tall;
Art of warfare, craft of chases,
Swimming, skating, snow-shoe races
    Excellent alike in all.

When at sea, with all his rowers,
He along the bending oars
    Outside of his ship could run.
He the Smalsor Horn ascended,
And his shining shield suspended
    On its summit, like a sun.

On the ship-rails he could stand,
Wield his sword with either hand,
    And at once two javelins throw ;
At all feasts where ale was strongest
Sat the merry monarch longest,
    First to come and last to go.

Norway never yet had seen
One so beautiful of mien,
    One so royal in attire,
When in arms completely furnished,
Harness gold-inlaid and burnished,
    Mantle like a flame of fire.

Thus came Olaf to his own,
When upon the night-wind blown
    Passed that cry along the shore ;
And he answered, while the rifted
Streamers o'er him shook and shifted,
    " I accept thy challenge, Thor ! "

III.

THORA OF RIMOL.

" THORA of Rimol ! hide me ! hide me !
Danger and shame and death betide me !
For Olaf the King is hunting me down
Through field and forest, through thorp
    and town ! "
        Thus cried Jarl Hakon
        To Thora, the fairest of women.

" Hakon Jarl ! for the love I bear thee
Neither shall shame nor death come
    near thee !
But the hiding-place wherein thou must
    lie
Is the cave underneath the swine in the
    sty."
        Thus to Jarl Hakon
        Said Thora, the fairest of women.

So Hakon Jarl and his base thrall Karker
Crouched in the cave, than a dungeon
    darker,
As Olaf came riding, with men in mail,
Through the forest roads into Orkadale,
        Demanding Jarl Hakon
        Of Thora, the fairest of women.

" Rich and honored shall be whoever
The head of Hakon Jarl shall dissever ! "
Hakon heard him, and Karker the slave,
Through the breathing-holes of the dark-
    some cave.
        Alone in her chamber
        Wept Thora, the fairest of women.

Said Karker, the crafty, " I will not slay
    thee !
For all the king's gold I will never betray
    thee ! "
" Then why dost thou turn so pale, O
    churl,
And then again black as the earth ? " said
    the Earl.
        More pale and more faithful
        Was Thora, the fairest of women.

From a dream in the night the thrall
    started, saying,
" Round my neck a gold ring King Olaf
    was laying ! "
And Hakon answered, " Beware of the
    king !
He will lay round thy neck a blood-red
    ring."
        At the ring on her finger
        Gazed Thora, the fairest of women.

At daybreak slept Hakon, with sorrows
    encumbered,
But screamed and drew up his feet as he
    slumbered ;
The thrall in the darkness plunged with
    his knife,
And the Earl awakened no more in this
    life.
        But wakeful and weeping
        Sat Thora, the fairest of women.

At Nidarholm the priests are all singing,
Two ghastly heads on the gibbet are
    swinging ;
One is Jarl Hakon's and one is his
    thrall's,
And the people are shouting from win-
    dows and walls ;
        While alone in her chamber
        Swoons Thora, the fairest of women.

IV.

QUEEN SIGRID THE HAUGHTY.

QUEEN Sigrid the Haughty sat proud
    and aloft
In her chamber, that looked over meadow
    and croft.
        Heart's dearest,
        Why dost thou sorrow so ?

The floor with tassels of fir was besprent,
Filling the room with their fragrant
    scent.

She heard the birds sing, she saw the sun
shine,
The air of summer was sweeter than wine.

Like a sword without scabbard the bright
river lay
Between her own kingdom and Norroway.

But Olaf the King had sued for her hand,
The sword would be sheathed, the river
be spanned.

Her maidens were seated around her
knee,
Working bright figures in tapestry.

And one was singing the ancient rune
Of Brynhilda's love and the wrath of
Gudrun.

And through it, and round it, and over
it all
Sounded incessant the waterfall.

The Queen in her hand held a ring of
gold,
From the door of Ladé's Temple old.

King Olaf had sent her this wedding gift,
But her thoughts as arrows were keen
and swift.

She had given the ring to her goldsmiths
twain,
Who smiled, as they handed it back
again.

And Sigrid the Queen, in her haughty way,
Said, "Why do you smile, my goldsmiths, say?"

And they answered: "O Queen! if the
truth must be told,
The ring is of copper, and not of gold!"

The lightning flashed o'er her forehead
and cheek,
She only murmured, she did not speak:

"If in his gifts he can faithless be,
There will be no gold in his love to me."

A footstep was heard on the outer stair,
And in strode King Olaf with royal air.

He kissed the Queen's hand, and he
whispered of love,
And swore to be true as the stars are
above.

But she smiled with contempt as she
answered : "O King,
Will you swear it, as Odin once swore,
on the ring?"

And the King : "O speak not of Odin
to me,
The wife of King Olaf a Christian must
be."

Looking straight at the King, with her
level brows,
She said, "I keep true to my faith and
my vows."

Then the face of King Olaf was darkened
with gloom,
He rose in his anger and strode through
the room.

"Why, then, should I care to have
thee?" he said, —
"A faded old woman, a heathenish
jade!"

His zeal was stronger than fear or love,
And he struck the Queen in the face with
his glove.

Then forth from the chamber in anger he
fled,
And the wooden stairway shook with his
tread.

Queen Sigrid the Haughty said under
her breath,
"This insult, King Olaf, shall be thy
death!"
　　　Heart's dearest,
　　　Why dost thou sorrow so?

v.

THE SKERRY OF SHRIEKS.

Now from all King Olaf's farms
　　　His men-at-arms
Gathered on the Eve of Easter;
To his house at Angvalds-ness
　　　Fast they press,
Drinking with the royal feaster.

Loudly through the wide-flung door
　　　Came the roar
Of the sea upon the Skerry;
And its thunder loud and near
　　　Reached the ear,
Mingling with their voices merry.

"Hark!" said Olaf to his Scald,
        Halfred the Bald,
"Listen to that song, and learn it!
Half my kingdom would I give,
        As I live,
If by such songs you would earn it!

"For of all the runes and rhymes
        Of all times,
Best I like the ocean's dirges,
When the old harper heaves and rocks,
        His hoary locks
Flowing and flashing in the surges!"

Halfred answered: "I am called
        The Unappalled!
Nothing hinders me or daunts me.
Hearken to me, then, O King,
        While I sing
The great Ocean Song that haunts me."

"I will hear your song sublime
        Some other time,"
Says the drowsy monarch, yawning,
And retires; each laughing guest
        Applauds the jest;
Then they sleep till day is dawning.

Pacing up and down the yard,
        King Olaf's guard
Saw the sea-mist slowly creeping
O'er the sands, and up the hill,
        Gathering still
Round the house where they were
        sleeping.

It was not the fog he saw,
        Nor misty flaw,
That above the landscape brooded;
It was Eyvind Kallda's crew
        Of warlocks blue
With their caps of darkness hooded!

Round and round the house they go,
        Weaving slow
Magic circles to encumber
And imprison in their ring
        Olaf the King,
As he helpless lies in slumber.

Then athwart the vapors dun
        The Easter sun
Streamed with one broad track of splen-
        dor!
In their real forms appeared
        The warlocks weird,
        Awful as the Witch of Endor.

Blinded by the light that glared,
        They groped and stared
Round about with steps unsteady;
From his window Olaf gazed,
        And, amazed,
"Who are these strange people?" said
        he.

"Eyvind Kallda and his men!"
        Answered then
From the yard a sturdy farmer;
While the men-at-arms apace
        Filled the place,
Busily buckling on their armor.

From the gates they sallied forth,
        South and north,
Scoured the island coast around them,
Seizing all the warlock band,
        Foot and hand
On the Skerry's rocks they bound them.

And at eve the king again
        Called his train,
And, with all the candles burning,
Silent sat and heard once more
        The sullen roar
Of the ocean tides returning.

Shrieks and cries of wild despair
        Filled the air,
Growing fainter as they listened;
Then the bursting surge alone
        Sounded on; —
Thus the sorcerers were christened!

"Sing, O Scald, your song sublime,
        Your ocean-rhyme,"
Cried King Olaf: "it will cheer me!"
Said the Scald, with pallid cheeks,
        "The Skerry of Shrieks
Sings too loud for you to hear me!"

VI.

THE WRAITH OF ODIN.

THE guests were loud, the ale was
        strong,
King Olaf feasted late and long;
The hoary Scalds together sang;
O'erhead the smoky rafters rang.
        Dead rides Sir Morten of Fogelsang.

The door swung wide, with creak and
        din;
A blast of cold night-air came in,

And on the threshold shivering stood
A one-eyed guest, with cloak and hood.
    Dead rides Sir Morten of Fogelsang.

The King exclaimed, "O graybeard
    pale !
Come warm thee with this cup of ale."
The foaming draught the old man
    quaffed,
The noisy guests looked on and laughed.
    Dead rides Sir Morten of Fogelsang.

Then spake the King : " Be not afraid ;
Sit here by me." The guest obeyed,
And, seated at the table, told
Tales of the sea, and Sagas old.
    Dead rides Sir Morten of Fogelsang.

And ever, when the tale was o'er,
The King demanded yet one more ;
Till Sigurd the Bishop smiling said,
"'T is late, O King, and time for bed."
    Dead rides Sir Morten of Fogelsang.

The King retired ; the stranger guest
Followed and entered with the rest ;
The lights were out, the pages gone,
But still the garrulous guest spake on.
    Dead rides Sir Morten of Fogelsang.

As one who from a volume reads,
He spake of heroes and their deeds,
Of lands and cities he had seen,
And stormy gulfs that tossed between.
    Dead rides Sir Morten of Fogelsang.

Then from his lips in music rolled
The Havamal of Odin old,
With sounds mysterious as the roar
Of billows on a distant shore.
    Dead rides Sir Morten of Fogelsang.

" Do we not learn from runes and
    rhymes
Made by the gods in elder times,
And do not still the great Scalds teach
That silence better is than speech ?"
    Dead rides Sir Morten of Fogelsang.

Smiling at this, the King replied,
" Thy lore is by thy tongue belied ;
For never was I so enthralled
Either by Saga-man or Scald."
    Dead rides Sir Morten of Fogelsang.

The Bishop said, " Late hours we keep !
Night wanes, O King ! 't is time for
    sleep ! "

Then slept the King, and when he woke
The guest was gone, the morning broke.
    Dead rides Sir Morten of Fogelsang.

They found the doors securely barred,
They found the watch-dog in the yard,
There was no footprint in the grass,
And none had seen the stranger pass.
    Dead rides Sir Morten of Fogelsang

King Olaf crossed himself and said :
" I know that Odin the Great is dead ;
Sure is the triumph of our Faith,
The one-eyed stranger was his wraith."
    Dead rides Sir Morten of Fogelsang

VII.

IRON-BEARD.

OLAF the King, one summer morn,
Blew a blast on his bugle-horn,
Sending his signal through the land of
    Drontheim.

And to the Hus-Ting held at Mere
Gathered the farmers far and near,
With their war weapons ready to confront
    him.

Ploughing under the morning star,
Old Iron-Beard in Yriar
Heard the summons, chuckling with a
    low laugh.

He wiped the sweat-drops from his
    brow,
Unharnessed his horses from the
    plough,
And clattering came on horseback to
    King Olaf.

He was the churliest of the churls ;
Little he cared for king or earls ;
Bitter as home-brewed ale were his foam-
    ing passions.

Hodden-gray was the garb he wore,
And by the Hammer of Thor he
    swore ;
He hated the narrow town, and all its
    fashions.

But he loved the freedom of his
    farm,
His ale at night, by the fireside
    warm,
Gudrun his daughter, with her flaxen
    tresses.

He loved his horses and his herds,
The smell of the earth, and the song
    of birds,
His well-filled barns, his brook with its
    water-cresses.

Huge and cumbersome was his frame ;
His beard, from which he took his
    name,
Frosty and fierce, like that of Hymer the
    Giant.

So at the Hus-Ting he appeared,
The farmer of Yriar, Iron-Beard,
On horseback, in an attitude defiant.

And to King Olaf he cried aloud,
Out of the middle of the crowd,
That tossed about him like a stormy
    ocean :

" Such sacrifices shalt thou bring ;
To Odin and to Thor, O King,
As other kings have done in their devo-
    tion ! "

King Olaf answered : " I command
This land to be a Christian land ;
Here is my Bishop who the folk bap-
    tizes !

" But if you ask me to restore
Your sacrifices, stained with gore,
Then will I offer human sacrifices !

" Not slaves and peasants shall they
    be,
But men of note and high degree,
Such men as Orm of Lyra and Kar of
    Gryting ! "

Then to their Temple strode he in,
And loud behind him heard the din
Of his men-at-arms and the peasants
    fiercely fighting.

There in the Temple, carved in wood,
The image of great Odin stood,
And other gods, with Thor supreme
    among them.

King Olaf smote them with the
    blade
Of his huge war-axe, gold inlaid,
And downward shattered to the pavement
    flung them.

At the same moment rose without,
From the contending crowd, a shout,
A mingled sound of triumph and of wail-
    ing.

And there upon the trampled plain
The farmer Iron-Beard lay slain,
Midway between the assailed and the
    assailing.

King Olaf from the doorway spoke
" Choose ye between two things, my
    folk,
To be baptized or given up to slaughter ! "

And seeing their leader stark and
    dead,
The people with a murmur said,
" O King, baptize us with thy holy
    water " ;

So all the Drontheim land became
A Christian land in name and fame,
In the old gods no more believing and
    trusting.

And as a blood-atonement, soon
King Olaf wed the fair Gudrun ;
And thus in peace ended the Drontheim
    Hus-Ting !

VIII.

GUDRUN.

On King Olaf's bridal night
Shines the moon with tender light,
And across the chamber streams
    Its tide of dreams.

At the fatal midnight hour,
When all evil things have power,
In the glimmer of the moon
    Stands Gudrun.

Close against her heaving breast,
Something in her hand is pressed ·
Like an icicle, its sheen
    Is cold and keen.

On the cairn are fixed her eyes
Where her murdered father lies,
And a voice remote and drear
    She seems to hear.

What a bridal night is this !
Cold will be the dagger's kiss ;

Laden with the chill of death
    Is its breath.

Like the drifting snow she sweeps
To the couch where Olaf sleeps;
Suddenly he wakes and stirs,
    His eyes meet hers.

"What is that," King Olaf said,
"Gleams so bright above thy head?
Wherefore standest thou so white
    In pale moonlight?"

"'T is the bodkin that I wear
When at night I bind my hair;
It woke me falling on the floor;
    'T is nothing more."

"Forests have ears, and fields have eyes;
Often treachery lurking lies
Underneath the fairest hair!
    Gudrun beware!"

Ere the earliest peep of morn
Blew King Olaf's bugle-horn;
And forever sundered ride
    Bridegroom and bride!

IX.

THANGBRAND THE PRIEST.

SHORT of stature, large of limb,
  Burly face and russet beard,
All the women stared at him,
  When in Iceland he appeared.
    "Look!" they said,
    With nodding head,
"There goes Thangbrand, Olaf's Priest."

All the prayers he knew by rote,
  He could preach like Chrysostome,
From the Fathers he could quote,
  He had even been at Rome.
    A learned clerk,
    A man of mark,
Was this Thangbrand, Olaf's Priest.

He was quarrelsome and loud,
  And impatient of control,
Boisterous in the market crowd,
  Boisterous at the wassail-bowl,
    Everywhere
    Would drink and swear,
Swaggering Thangbrand. Olaf's Priest.

In his house this malcontent
  Could the King no longer bear,
So to Iceland he was sent
  To convert the heathen there,
    And away
    One summer day
Sailed this Thangbrand, Olaf's Priest.

There in Iceland, o'er their books
  Pored the people day and night,
But he did not like their looks,
  Nor the songs they used to write.
    "All this rhyme
    Is waste of time!"
Grumbled Thangbrand, Olaf's Priest.

To the alehouse, where he sat,
  Came the Scalds and Saga-men;
Is it to be wondered at,
  That they quarrelled now and then,
    When o'er his beer
    Began to leer
Drunken Thangbrand, Olaf's Priest?

All the folk in Altafiord
  Boasted of their island grand;
Saying in a single word,
  "Iceland is the finest land
    That the sun
    Doth shine upon!"
Loud laughed Thangbrand, Olaf's Priest

And he answered: "What's the use
Of this bragging up and down,
When three women and one goose
  Make a market in your town!"
    Every Scald
    Satires scrawled
On poor Thangbrand, Olaf's Priest.

Something worse they did than that;
  And what vexed him most of all
Was a figure in shovel hat,
  Drawn in charcoal on the wall;
    With words that go
    Sprawling below,
"This is Thangbrand, Olaf's Priest."

Hardly knowing what he did,
  Then he smote them might and main
Thorvald Veile and Veterlid
  Lay there in the alehouse slain.
    "To-day we are gold,
    To-morrow mould!"
Muttered Thangbrand, Olaf's Priest.

Much in fear of axe and rope,
  Back to Norway sailed he then.

" O, King Olaf ! little hope
  Is there of these Iceland men ! "
    Meekly said,
      With bending head,
Pious Thangbrand, Olaf's Priest.

x.

RAUD THE STRONG.

" ALL the old gods are dead,
All the wild warlocks fled ;
But the White Christ lives and reigns,
And throughout my wide domains
His Gospel shall be spread ! "
    On the Evangelists
      Thus swore King Olaf.

But still in dreams of the night
Beheld he the crimson light,
And heard the voice that defied
Him who was crucified,
And challenged him to the fight.
    To Sigurd the Bishop
      King Olaf confessed it.

And Sigurd the Bishop said,
" The old gods are not dead,
For the great Thor still reigns,
And among the Jarls and Thanes
The old witchcraft still is spread."
    Thus to King Olaf
      Said Sigurd the Bishop.

" Far north in the Salten Fiord,
By rapine, fire, and sword,
Lives the Viking, Raud the Strong ;
All the Godoe Isles belong
To him and his heathen horde."
    Thus went on speaking
      Sigurd the Bishop.

" A warlock, a wizard is he,
And lord of the wind and the sea ;
And whichever way he sails,
He has ever favoring gales,
By his craft in sorcery."
    Here the sign of the cross
      Made devoutly King Olaf.

" With rites that we both abhor,
He worships Odin and Thor ;
So it cannot yet be said,
That all the old gods are dead,
And the warlocks are no more,"
    Flushing with anger
      Said Sigurd the Bishop.

Then King Olaf cried aloud :
" I will talk with this mighty Raud,
And along the Salten Fiord
Preach the Gospel with my sword,
Or be brought back in my shroud ! "
    So northward from Drontheim
      Sailed King Olaf !

XI.

BISHOP SIGURD AT SALTEN FIORD.

LOUD the angry wind was wailing
As King Olaf's ships came sailing
Northward out of Drontheim haven
    To the mouth of Salten Fiord.

Though the flying sea-spray drenches
Fore and aft the rowers' benches,
Not a single heart is craven
    Of the champions there on board.

All without the Fiord was quiet,
But within it storm and riot,
Such as on his Viking cruises
    Raud the Strong was wont to ride.

And the sea through all its tide-ways
Swept the reeling vessels sideways,
As the leaves are swept through sluices,
    When the flood-gates open wide.

" 'T is the warlock ! 't is the demon
Raud ! " cried Sigurd to the seamen :
" But the Lord is not affrighted
    By the witchcraft of his foes."

To the ship's bow he ascended,
By his choristers attended,
Round him were the tapers lighted,
    And the sacred incense rose.

On the bow stood Bishop Sigurd,
In his robes, as one transfigured,
And the Crucifix he planted
    High amid the rain and mist.

Then with holy water sprinkled
All the ship ; the mass-bells tinkled ;
Loud the monks around him chanted,
    Loud he read the Evangelist.

As into the Fiord they darted,
On each side the water parted ;
Down a path like silver molten
    Steadily rowed King Olaf's ships ;

Steadily burned all night the tapers,
And the White Christ through the vapors
Gleamed across the Fiord of Salten,
    As through John's Apocalypse, —

Till at last they reached Raud's dwelling
On the little isle of Gelling ;
Not a guard was at the doorway,
    Not a glimmer of light was seen.

But at anchor, carved and gilded,
Lay the dragon-ship he builded ;
T was the grandest ship in Norway,
    With its crest and scales of green.

Up the stairway, softly creeping,
To the loft where Raud was sleeping,
With their fists they burst asunder
    Bolt and bar that held the door.

Drunken with sleep and ale they found
        him,
Dragged him from his bed and bound him,
While he stared with stupid wonder,
    At the look and garb they wore.

Then King Olaf said : "O Sea-King !
Little time have we for speaking,
Choose between the good and evil ;
    Be baptized, or thou shalt die !

But in scorn the heathen scoffer
Answered : "I disdain thine offer ;
Neither fear I God nor Devil ;
    Thee and thy Gospel I defy ! "

Then between his jaws distended,
When his frantic struggles ended,
Through King Olaf's horn an adder,
    Touched by fire, they forced to
        glide.

Sharp his tooth was as an arrow,
As he gnawed through bone and marrow ;
But without a groan or shudder,
    Raud the Strong blaspheming died.

Then baptized they all that region,
Swarthy Lap and fair Norwegian,
Far as swims the salmon, leaping,
    Up the streams of Salten Fiord.

In their temples Thor and Odin
Lay in dust and ashes trodden,
As King Olaf, onward sweeping,
    Preached the Gospel with his sword.

Then he took the carved and gilded
Dragon-ship that Raud had builded,
And the tiller single-handed,
    Grasping, steered into the main.

Southward sailed the sea-gulls o'er him,
Southward sailed the ship that bore him,
Till at Drontheim haven landed
    Olaf and his crew again.

XII.

KING OLAF'S CHRISTMAS.

AT Drontheim, Olaf the King
Heard the bells of Yule-tide ring,
    As he sat in his banquet-hall,
Drinking the nut-brown ale,
With his bearded Berserks hale
    And tall.

Three days his Yule-tide feasts
He held with Bishops and Priests,
    And his horn filled up to the brim ;
But the ale was never too strong,
Nor the Saga-man's tale too long,
    For him.

O'er his drinking-horn, the sign
He made of the cross divine,
    As he drank, and muttered his
        prayers ;
But the Berserks evermore
Made the sign of the Hammer of Thor
    Over theirs.

The gleams of the fire-light dance
Upon helmet and hauberk and lance,
    And laugh in the eyes of the King .
And he cries to Halfred the Scald,
Gray-bearded, wrinkled, and bald,
    "Sing ! "

"Sing me a song divine,
With a sword in every line,
    And this shall be thy reward."
And he loosened the belt at his waist,
And in front of the singer placed
    His sword.

"Quern-biter of Hakon the Good,
Wherewith at a stroke he hewed
    The millstone through and through,
And Foot-breadth of Thoralf the Strong,
Were neither so broad nor so long,
    Nor so true."

Then the Scald took his harp and sang,
And loud through the music rang
    The sound of that shining word ;
And the harp-strings a clangor made,
As if they were struck with the blade
    Of a sword.

And the Berserks round about
Broke forth into a shout
    That made the rafters ring :
They smote with their fists on the board,
And shouted, " Long live the Sword,
    And the King ! "

But the King said, " O my son,
I miss the bright word in one
    Of thy measures and thy rhymes."
And Halfred the Scald replied,
" In another 't was multiplied
    Three times."

Then King Olaf raised the hilt
Of iron, cross-shaped and gilt,
    And said, " Do not refuse ;
Count well the gain and the loss,
Thor's hammer or Christ's cross :
    Choose ! "

And Halfred the Scald said, " This
In the name of the Lord I kiss,
    Who on it was crucified ! "
And a shout went round the board,
" In the name of Christ the Lord,
    Who died ! "

Then over the waste of snows
The noonday sun uprose,
    Through the driving mists revealed,
Like the lifting of the Host,
By incense-clouds almost
    Concealed.

On the shining wall a vast
And shadowy cross was cast
    From the hilt of the lifted sword,
And in foaming cups of ale
The Berserks drank " Was-hael !
    To the Lord ! "

XIII.

THE BUILDING OF THE LONG SERPENT.

THORBERG SKAFTING, master-builder,
    In his ship-yard by the sea,
Whistling, said, " It would bewilder
Any man but Thorberg Skafting,
    Any man but me ! "

Near him lay the Dragon stranded,
    Built of old by Raud the Strong,
And King Olaf had commanded
He should build another Dragon,
    Twice as large and long.

Therefore whistled Thorberg Skafting,
    As he sat with half-closed eyes,
And his head turned sideways, drafting
That new vessel for King Olaf
    Twice the Dragon's size.

Round him busily hewed and hammered
    Mallet huge and heavy axe ;
Workmen laughed and sang and clam-
    ored ;
Whirred the wheels, that into rigging
    Spun the shining flax !

All this tumult heard the master, —
    It was music to his ear ;
Fancy whispered all the faster,
" Men shall hear of Thorberg Skafting
    For a hundred year ! "

Workmen sweating at the forges
    Fashioned iron bolt and bar,
Like a warlock's midnight orgies
Smoked and bubbled the black caldron
    With the boiling tar.

Did the warlocks mingle in it,
    Thorberg Skafting, any curse ?
Could you not be gone a minute
But some mischief must be doing,
    Turning bad to worse ?

'T was an ill wind that came wafting,
    From his homestead words of woe
To his farm went Thorberg Skafting,
Oft repeating to his workmen,
    Build ye thus and so.

After long delays returning
    Came the master back by night ·
To his ship-yard longing, yearning,
Hurried he, and did not leave it
    Till the morning's light.

" Come and see my ship, my darling
    On the morrow said the King ;
" Finished now from keel to carling ;
Never yet was seen in Norway
    Such a wondrous thing ! "

In the ship-yard, idly talking,
    At the ship the workmen stared :

Some one, all their labor balking,
Down her sides had cut deep gashes,
  Not a plank was spared !

" Death be to the evil-doer ! "
  With an oath King Olaf spoke ;
" But rewards to his pursuer ! "
And with wrath his face grew redder
  Than his scarlet cloak.

Straight the master-builder, smiling,
  Answered thus the angry King :
" Cease blaspheming and reviling,
Olaf, it was Thorberg Skafting
  Who has done this thing ! "

Then he chipped and smoothed the plank-
  ing,
  Till the King, delighted, swore,
With much lauding and much thanking,
" Handsomer is now my Dragon
  Than she was before ! "

Seventy ells and four extended
  On the grass the vessel's keel ;
High above it, gilt and splendid,
Rose the figure-head ferocious
  With its crest of steel.

Then they launched her from the tressels,
  In the ship-yard by the sea ;
She was the grandest of all vessels,
Never ship was built in Norway
  Half so fine as she !

The Long Serpent was she christened,
  'Mid the roar of cheer on cheer !
They who to the Saga listened
Heard the name of Thorberg Skafting
  For a hundred year !

XIV.

THE CREW OF THE LONG SERPENT.

SAFE at anchor in Drontheim bay
King Olaf's fleet assembled lay,
  And, striped with white and blue,
Downward fluttered sail and banner,
As alights the screaming lanner ;
Lustily cheered, in their wild manner,
  The Long Serpent's crew

Her torecastle man was Ulf the Red
Like a wolf's was his shaggy head,

  His teeth as large and white ;
His beard, of gray and russet blended,
Round as a swallow's nest descended :
As standard-bearer he defended
  Olaf's flag in the fight.

Near him Kolbiorn had his place,
Like the King in garb and face,
  So gallant and so hale ;
Every cabin-boy and varlet
Wondered at his cloak of scarlet ;
Like a river, frozen and star-lit,
  Gleamed his coat of mail.

By the bulkhead, tall and dark,
Stood Thrand Rame of Thelemark,
  A figure gaunt and grand ;
On his hairy arm imprinted
Was an anchor, azure-tinted ;
Like Thor's hammer, huge and dinted
  Was his brawny hand.

Einar Tamberskelver, bare
To the winds his golden hair,
  By the mainmast stood ;
Graceful was his form, and slender,
And his eyes were deep and tender
As a woman's, in the splendor
  Of her maidenhood.

In the fore-hold Biorn and Bork
Watched the sailors at their work :
  Heavens ! how they swore !
Thirty men they each commanded,
Iron-sinewed, horny-handed,
Shoulders broad, and chests expanded,
  Tugging at the oar.

These, and many more like these,
With King Olaf sailed the seas,
  Till the waters vast
Filled them with a vague devotion,
With the freedom and the motion,
With the roll and roar of ocean
  And the sounding blast.

When they landed from the fleet,
How they roared through Drontheim's
  street,
  Boisterous as the gale !
How they laughed and stamped and
  pounded,
Till the tavern roof resounded,
And the host looked on astounded
  As they drank the ale !

Never saw the wild North Sea
Such a gallant company
   Sail its billows blue !
Never, while they cruised and quarrelled,
Old King Gorm, or Blue-Tooth Harald,
Owned a ship so well apparelled,
   Boasted such a crew !

XV.

A LITTLE BIRD IN THE AIR.

A LITTLE bird in the air
Is singing of Thyri the fair,
   The sister of Svend the Dane ;
And the song of the garrulous bird
In the streets of the town is heard,
   And repeated again and again.
      Hoist up your sails of silk,
      And flee away from each other.

To King Burislaf, it is said,
Was the beautiful Thyri wed,
   And a sorrowful bride went she ;
And after a week and a day,
She has fled away and away,
   From his town by the stormy sea.
      Hoist up your sails of silk,
      And flee away from each other.

They say, that through heat and through
   cold,
Through weald, they say, and through
   wold,
   By day and by night, they say,
She has fled ; and the gossips report
She has come to King Olaf's court,
   And the town is all in dismay.
      Hoist up your sails of silk,
      And flee away from each other.

It is whispered King Olaf has seen,
Has talked with the beautiful Queen ;
   And they wonder how it will end ;
For surely, if here she remain,
It is war with King Svend the Dane,
   And King Burislaf the Vend !
      Hoist up your sails of silk,
      And flee away from each other.

O, greatest wonder of all !
It is published in hamlet and hall,
   It roars like a flame that is fanned !
The King — yes, Olaf the King —
Has wedded her with his ring,
   And Thyri is Queen in the land !
      Hoist up your sails of silk,
      And flee away from each other.

XVI.

QUEEN THYRI AND THE ANGELICA STALKS.

NORTHWARD over Drontheim,
Flew the clamorous sea-gulls,
Sang the lark and linnet
   From the meadows green ;

Weeping in her chamber,
Lonely and unhappy,
Sat the Drottning Thyri,
   Sat King Olaf's Queen.

In at all the windows
Streamed the pleasant sunshine,
On the roof above her
   Softly cooed the dove ;

But the sound she heard not,
Nor the sunshine heeded,
For the thoughts of Thyri
   Were not thoughts of love.

Then King Olaf entered,
Beautiful as morning,
Like the sun at Easter
   Shone his happy face ;

In his hand he carried
Angelicas uprooted,
With delicious fragrance
   Filling all the place.

Like a rainy midnight
Sat the Drottning Thyri,
Even the smile of Olaf
   Could not cheer her gloom ;

Nor the stalks he gave her
With a gracious gesture,
And with words as pleasant
   As their own perfume.

In her hands he placed them,
And her jewelled fingers
Through the green leaves glistened
   Like the dews of morn ;

But she cast them from her,
Haughty and indignant,
On the floor she threw them
   With a look of scorn.

" Richer presents," said she,
" Gave King Harald Gormson

To the Queen, my mother,
  Than such worthless weeds ;

"When he ravaged Norway,
Laying waste the kingdom,
Seizing scatt and treasure
  For her royal needs.

"But thou darest not venture
Through the Sound to Vendland,
My domains to rescue
  From King Burislaf ;

"Lest King Svend of Denmark,
Forked Beard, my brother,
Scatter all thy vessels
  As the wind the chaff."

Then up sprang King Olaf,
Like a reindeer bounding,
With an oath he answered
  Thus the luckless Queen :

"Never yet did Olaf
Fear King Svend of Denmark ;
This right hand shall hale him
  By his forked chin !"

Then he left the chamber,
Thundering through the doorway,
Loud his steps resounded
  Down the outer stair.

Smarting with the insult,
Through the streets of Drontheim
Strode he red and wrathful,
  With his stately air.

All his ships he gathered,
Summoned all his forces,
Making his war levy
  In the region round ;

Down the coast of Norway,
Like a flock of sea-gulls,
Sailed the fleet of Olaf
  Through the Danish Sound.

With his own hand fearless,
Steered he the Long Serpent,
Strained the creaking cordage,
  Bent each boom and gaff ;

Till in Vendland landing,
The domains of Thyri
He redeemed and rescued
  From King Burislaf.

Then said Olaf, laughing,
"Not ten yoke of oxen
Have the power to draw us
  Like a woman's hair !

"Now will I confess it,
Better things are jewels
Than angelica stalks are
  For a Queen to wear."

XVII.

KING SVEND OF THE FORKED BEARD.

LOUDLY the sailors cheered
Svend of the Forked Beard,
As with his fleet he steered
  Southward to Vendland ;
Where with their courses hauled
All were together called,
Under the Isle of Svald
  Near to the mainland.

After Queen Gunhild's death,
So the old Saga saith,
Plighted King Svend his faith
  To Sigrid the Haughty ;
And to avenge his bride,
Soothing her wounded pride,
Over the waters wide
  King Olaf sought he.

Still on her scornful face,
Blushing with deep disgrace,
Bore she the crimson trace
  Of Olaf's gauntlet ;
Like a malignant star,
Blazing in heaven afar,
Red shone the angry scar
  Under her frontlet.

Oft to King Svend she spake,
"For thine own honor's sake
Shalt thou swift vengeance take
  On the vile coward !"
Until the King at last,
Gusty and overcast,
Like a tempestuous blast
  Threatened and lowered.

Soon as the Spring appeared,
Svend of the Forked Beard
High his red standard reared,
  Eager for battle ;
While every warlike Dane,
Seizing his arms again,

Left all unsown the grain,
  Unhoused the cattle.

Likewise the Swedish King
Summoned in haste a Thing,
Weapons and men to bring
  In aid of Denmark ;
Eric the Norseman, too,
As the war-tidings flew,
Sailed with a chosen crew
  From Lapland and Finmark.

So upon Easter day
Sailed the three kings away,
Out of the sheltered bay,
  In the bright season ;
With them Earl Sigvald came,
Eager for spoil and fame ;
Pity that such a name
  Stooped to such treason !

Safe under Svald at last,
Now were their anchors cast,
Safe from the sea and blast,
  Plotted the three kings ;
While, with a base intent,
Southward Earl Sigvald went,
On a foul errand bent,
  Unto the Sea-kings.

Thence to hold on his course,
Unto King Olaf's force,
Lying within the hoarse
  Mouths of Stet-haven ;
Him to ensnare and bring,
Unto the Danish king,
Who his dead corse would fling
  Forth to the raven !

XVIII.

KING OLAF AND EARL SIGVALD.

On the gray sea-sands
King Olaf stands,
Northward and seaward
He points with his hands.

With eddy and whirl
The sea-tides curl,
Washing the sandals
Of Sigvald the Earl.

The mariners shout,
The ships swing about,
The yards are all hoisted,
The sails flutter out.

The war-horns are played,
The anchors are weighed,
Like moths in the distance
The sails flit and fade.

The sea is like lead,
The harbor lies dead,
As a corse on the sea-shore,
Whose spirit has fled !

On that fatal day,
The histories say,
Seventy vessels
Sailed out of the bay.

But soon scattered wide
O'er the billows they ride,
While Sigvald and Olaf
Sail side by side.

Cried the Earl : " Follow me !
I your pilot will be,
For I know all the channels
Where flows the deep sea ! "

So into the strait
Where his foes lie in wait,
Gallant King Olaf
Sails to his fate !

Then the sea-fog veils
The ships and their sails ;
Queen Sigrid the Haughty,
Thy vengeance prevails !

XIX.

KING OLAF'S WAR-HORNS.

" Strike the sails ! " King Olaf said ;
" Never shall men of mine take flight ;
Never away from battle I fled,
Never away from my foes !
    Let God dispose
Of my life in the fight ! "

" Sound the horns ! " said Olaf the King ;
And suddenly through the drifting brume
The blare of the horns began to ring,
Like the terrible trumpet shock
    Of Regnarock,
On the Day of Doom !

Louder and louder the war-horns sang
Over the level floor of the flood ;

All the sails came down with a clang,
And there in the mist overhead
    The sun hung red
As a drop of blood.

Drifting down on the Danish fleet
Three together the ships were lashed,
So that neither should turn and retreat ;
In the midst, but in front of the rest
    The burnished crest
Of the Serpent flashed.

King Olaf stood on the quarter-deck,
With bow of ash and arrows of oak,
His gilded shield was without a fleck,
His helmet inlaid with gold,
    And in many a fold
Hung his crimson cloak.

On the forecastle Ulf the Red
Watched the lashing of the ships ;
"If the Serpent lie so far ahead,
We shall have hard work of it here,
    Said he with a sneer
On his bearded lips.

King Olaf laid an arrow on string,
"Have I a coward on board ? " said he.
"Shoot it another way, O King ! "
Sullenly answered Ulf,
    The old sea-wolf ;
"You have need of me ! "

In front came Svend, the King of the
    Danes,
Sweeping down with his fifty rowers ;
To the right, the Swedish king with his
    thanes ;
And on board of the Iron Beard
    Earl Eric steered
To the left with his oars.

"These soft Danes and Swedes," said the
    King,
"At home with their wives had better
    stay,
Than come within reach of my Serpent's
    sting :
But where Eric the Norseman leads
    Heroic deeds
Will be done to-day ! "

Then as together the vessels crashed,
Eric severed the cables of hide,
With which King Olaf's ships were
    lashed,

And left them to drive and drift
    With the currents swift
Of the outward tide.

Louder the war-horns growl and snarl,
Sharper the dragons bite and sting !
Eric the son of Hakon Jarl
A death-drink salt as the sea
    Pledges to thee,
Olaf the King !

XX.

EINAR TAMBERSKELVER.

IT was Einar Tamberskelver
    Stood beside the mast ;
From his yew-bow, tipped with silver,
    Flew the arrows fast ;
Aimed at Eric unavailing,
    As he sat concealed,
Half behind the quarter-railing,
    Half behind his shield.

First an arrow struck the tiller,
    Just above his head ;
"Sing, O Eyvind Skaldaspiller,"
    Then Earl Eric said.
"Sing the song of Hakon dying,
    Sing his funeral wail ! "
And another arrow flying
    Grazed his coat of mail.

Turning to a Lapland yeoman,
    As the arrow passed,
Said Earl Eric, "Shoot that bowman
    Standing by the mast."
Sooner than the word was spoken
    Flew the yeoman's shaft ;
Einar's bow in twain was broken,
    Einar only laughed.

"What was that ? " said Olaf, standing
    On the quarter-deck.
"Something heard I like the stranding
    Of a shattered wreck."
Einar then, the arrow taking
    From the loosened string,
Answered, "That was Norway breaking
    From thy hand, O King ! "

"Thou art but a poor diviner,"
    Straightway Olaf said ;
"Take my bow, and swifter, Einar,
    Let thy shafts be sped."

Of his bows the fairest choosing,
   Reached he from above ;
Einar saw the blood-drops oozing
   Through his iron glove.

But the bow was thin and narrow ;
   At the first assay,
O'er its head he drew the arrow,
   Flung the bow away ;
Said, with hot and angry temper
   Flushing in his cheek,
 ·Olaf ! for so great a Kämper
   Are thy bows too weak ! "

Then, with smile of joy defiant
   On his beardless lip,
Scaled he, light and self-reliant,
   Eric's dragon-ship.
Loose his golden locks were flowing,
   Bright his armor gleamed ;
Like Saint Michael overthrowing
   Lucifer he seemed.

XXI.

KING OLAF'S DEATH-DRINK.

ALL day has the battle raged,
All day have the ships engaged,
But not yet is assuaged
   The vengeance of Eric the Earl.

The decks with blood are red,
The arrows of death are sped,
The ships are filled with the dead,
   And the spears the champions hurl.

They drift as wrecks on the tide,
The grappling-irons are plied,
The boarders climb up the side,
   The shouts are feeble and few.

Ah ! never shall Norway again
See her sailors come back o'er the main ;
They all lie wounded or slain,
   Or asleep in the billows blue !

On the deck stands Olaf the King,
Around him whistle and sing
The spears that the foemen fling,
   And the stones they hurl with their
      hands.

In the midst of the stones and the spears,
Kolbiorn, the marshal, appears,
His shield in the air he uprears,
   By the side of King Olaf he stands.

Over the slippery wreck
Of the Long Serpent's deck
Sweeps Eric with hardly a check,
   His lips with anger are pale ;

He hews with his axe at the mast,
Till it falls, with the sails overcast,
Like a snow-covered pine in the vast
   Dim forests of Orkadale.

Seeking King Olaf then,
He rushes aft with his men,
As a hunter into the den
   Of the bear, when he stands at bay.

" Remember Jarl Hakon ! " he cries ;
When lo ! on his wondering eyes,
Two kingly figures arise,
   Two Olafs in warlike array !

Then Kolbiorn speaks in the ear
Of King Olaf a word of cheer,
In a whisper that none may hear,
   With a smile on his tremulous lip ;

Two shields raised high in the air,
Two flashes of golden hair,
Two scarlet meteors' glare,
   And both have leaped from the ship.

Earl Eric's men in the boats
Seize Kolbiorn's shield as it floats,
And cry, from their hairy throats,
   " See ! it is Olaf the King ! "

While far on the opposite side
Floats another shield on the tide,
Like a jewel set in the wide
   Sea-current's eddying ring.

There is told a wonderful tale,
How the King stripped off his mail,
Like leaves of the brown sea-kale,
   As he swam beneath the main ;

But the young grew old and gray,
And never, by night or by day,
In his kingdom of Norroway
   Was King Olaf seen again !

XXII.

THE NUN OF NIDAROS.

IN the convent of Drontheim,
Alone in her chamber
Knelt Astrid the Abbess,
At midnight, adoring,

Beseeching, entreating
The Virgin and Mother.

She heard in the silence
The voice of one speaking,
Without in the darkness,
In gusts of the night-wind
Now louder, now nearer,
Now lost in the distance.

The voice of a stranger
It seemed as she listened,
Of some one who answered,
Beseeching, imploring,
A cry from afar off
She could not distinguish.

The voice of Saint John,
The beloved disciple,
Who wandered and waited
The Master's appearance.
Alone in the darkness,
Unsheltered and friendless.

"It is accepted
The angry defiance,
The challenge of battle !
It is accepted,
But not with the weapons
Of war that thou wieldest !

"Cross against corselet,
Love against hatred,
Peace-cry for war-cry !
Patience is powerful ;
He that o'ercometh
Hath power o'er the nations \

"As torrents in summer,
Half dried in their channels,
Suddenly rise, though the
Sky is still cloudless,
For rain has been falling
Far off at their fountains ;

So hearts that are fainting
Grow full to o'erflowing,
And they that behold it
Marvel, and know not
That God at their fountains
Far off has been raining !

"Stronger than steel
Is the sword of the Spirit ;
Swifter than arrows
The light of the truth is,
Greater than anger
Is love, and subdueth !

"Thou art a phantom,
A shape of the sea-mist,
A shape of the brumal
Rain, and the darkness
Fearful and formless ;
Day dawns and thou art not !

"The dawn is not distant,
Nor is the night starless ;
Love is eternal !
God is still God, and
His faith shall not fail us ;
Christ is eternal !"

INTERLUDE.

A STRAIN of music closed the tale,
A low, monotonous, funeral wail,
That with its cadence, wild and sweet,
Made the long Saga more complete.

"Thank God," the Theologian said,
"The reign of violence is dead,
Or dying surely from the world ;
While Love triumphant reigns instead,
And in a brighter sky o'erhead
His blessed banners are unfurled.
And most of all thank God for this :
The war and waste of clashing creeds
Now end in words, and not in deeds,
And no one suffers loss, or bleeds,
For thoughts that men call heresies.

"I stand without here in the porch,
I hear the bell's melodious din,
I hear the organ peal within,
I hear the prayer, with words that
        scorch
Like sparks from an inverted torch,
I hear the sermon upon sin,
With threatenings of the last account.
And all, translated in the air,
Reach me but as our dear Lord's Prayer,
And as the Sermon on the Mount.

"Must it be Calvin, and not Christ ?
Must it be Athanasian creeds,
Or holy water, books, and beads ?
Must struggling souls remain content
With councils and decrees of Trent ?
And can it be enough for these
The Christian Church the year embalms
With evergreens and boughs of palms,
And fills the air with litanies ?

"I know that yonder Pharisee
Thanks God that he is not like me ;

In my humiliation dressed,
I only stand and beat my breast,
And pray for human charity.

" Not to one church alone, but seven,
The voice prophetic spake from heaven ;
And unto each the promise came,
Diversified, but still the same ;
For him that overcometh are
The new name written on the stone,
The raiment white, the crown, the throne,
And I will give him the Morning Star !

" Ah ! to how many Faith has been
No evidence of things unseen,
But a dim shadow, that recasts
The creed of the Phantasiasts,
For whom no Man of Sorrows died,
For whom the Tragedy Divine
Was but a symbol and a sign,
And Christ a phantom crucified !

" For others a diviner creed
Is living in the life they lead.
The passing of their beautiful feet
Blesses the pavement of the street,
And all their looks and words repeat
Old Fuller's saying, wise and sweet,
Not as a vulture, but a dove,
The Holy Ghost came from above.

" And this brings back to me a tale
So sad the hearer well may quail,
And question if such things can be ;
Yet in the chronicles of Spain
Down the dark pages runs this stain,
And naught can wash them white again,
So fearful is the tragedy."

THE THEOLOGIAN'S TALE.

TORQUEMADA.

IN the heroic days when Ferdinand
And Isabella ruled the Spanish land,
And Torquemada, with his subtle brain,
Ruled them, as Grand Inquisitor of
    Spain,
In a great castle near Valladolid,
Moated and high and by fair woodlands
    hid,
There dwelt, as from the chronicles we
    learn,
An old Hidalgo proud and taciturn,
Whose name has perished, with his tow-
    ers of stone,
And all his actions save this one alone ;

This one, so terrible, perhaps 't were best
If it, too, were forgotten with the rest ;
Unless, perchance, our eyes can see
    therein
The martyrdom triumphant o'er the sin ;
A double picture, with its gloom and
    glow,
The splendor overhead, the death below.

This sombre man counted each day as lost
On which his feet no sacred threshold
    crossed ;
And when he chanced the passing Host
    to meet,
He knelt and prayed devoutly in the
    street ;
Oft he confessed ; and with each muti-
    nous thought,
As with wild beasts at Ephesus, he fought.
In deep contrition scourged himself in
    Lent,
Walked in processions, with his head
    down bent,
At plays of Corpus Christi oft was seen,
And on Palm Sunday bore his bough of
    green.
His sole diversion was to hunt the boar
Through tangled thickets of the forest
    hoar,
Or with his jingling mules to hurry
    down
To some grand bull-fight in the neigh-
    boring town,
Or in the crowd with lighted taper stand,
When Jews were burned, or banished
    from the land.
Then stirred within him a tumultuous
    joy ;
The demon whose delight is to destroy
Shook him, and shouted with a trum-
    pet tone,
Kill ! kill ! and let the Lord find out
    his own !"

And now, in that old castle in the wood,
His daughters, in the dawn of woman-
    hood,
Returning from their convent school,
    had made
Resplendent with their bloom the forest
    shade,
Reminding him of their dead mother's
    face,
When first she came into that gloomy
    place, —
A memory in his heart as dim and sweet
As moonlight in a solitary street,

Where the same rays, that lift the sea,
 are thrown
Lovely but powerless upon walls of stone.
These two fair daughters of a mother
 dead
Were all the dream had left him as it
 fled.
A joy at first, and then a growing care,
As if a voice within him cried, "Be-
 ware!"
A vague presentiment of impending
 doom,
Like ghostly footsteps in a vacant room,
Haunted him day and night; a formless
 fear
That death to some one of his house was
 near,
With dark surmises of a hidden crime,
Made life itself a death before its time.
Jealous, suspicious, with no sense of
 shame,
A spy upon his daughters he became;
With velvet slippers, noiseless on the
 floors,
He glided softly through half-open doors;
Now in the room, and now upon the
 stair,
He stood beside them ere they were
 aware;
He listened in the passage when they
 talked,
He watched them from the casement
 when they walked,
He saw the gypsy haunt the river's side,
He saw the monk among the cork-trees
 glide;
And, tortured by the mystery and the
 doubt
Of some dark secret, past his finding out,
Baffled he paused; then reassured again
Pursued the flying phantom of his brain.
He watched them even when they knelt
 in church;
And then, descending lower in his search,
Questioned the servants, and with eager
 eyes
Listened incredulous to their replies;
The gypsy? none had seen her in the
 wood!
The monk? a mendicant in search of
 food!

At length the awful revelation came,
Crushing at once his pride of birth and
 name;
The hopes his yearning bosom forward
 cast,

And the ancestral glories of the past,
All fell together, crumbling in disgrace,
A turret rent from battlement to base.
His daughters talking in the dead of
 night
In their own chamber, and without a
 light,
Listening, as he was wont, he overheard,
And learned the dreadful secret, word by
 word;
And hurrying from his castle, with a
 cry
He raised his hands to the unpitying
 sky,
Repeating one dread word, till bush and
 tree
Caught it, and shuddering answered,
 "Heresy!"

Wrapped in his cloak, his hat drawn
 o'er his face,
Now hurrying forward, now with lin-
 gering pace,
He walked all night the alleys of his
 park,
With one unseen companion in the dark,
The Demon who within him lay in wait,
And by his presence turned his love to
 hate,
Forever muttering in an undertone,
"Kill! kill! and let the Lord find out
 his own!"

Upon the morrow, after early Mass,
While yet the dew was glistening on the
 grass,
And all the woods were musical with
 birds,
The old Hidalgo, uttering fearful words,
Walked homeward with the Priest, and
 in his room
Summoned his trembling daughters to
 their doom.
When questioned, with brief answers
 they replied,
Nor when accused evaded or denied;
Expostulations, passionate appeals,
All that the human heart most fears or
 feels,
In vain the Priest with earnest voice es-
 sayed;
In vain the father threatened, wept, and
 prayed;
Until at last he said, with haughty
 mien,
"The Holy Office, then, must inter-
 vene!"

And now the Grand Inquisitor of Spain,
With all the fifty horsemen of his train,
His awful name resounding, like the
    blast
Of funeral trumpets, as he onward
    passed,
Came to Valladolid, and there began
To harry the rich Jews with fire and
    ban.
To him the Hidalgo went, and at the
    gate
Demanded audience on affairs of state,
And in a secret chamber stood before
A venerable graybeard of fourscore,
Dressed in the hood and habit of a friar;
Out of his eyes flashed a consuming fire,
And in his hand the mystic horn he
    held,
Which poison and all noxious charms
    dispelled.
He heard in silence the Hidalgo's tale,
Then answered in a voice that made him
    quail:
" Son of the Church! when Abraham
    of old
To sacrifice his only son was told,
He did not pause to parley nor protest,
But hastened to obey the Lord's behest.
In him it was accounted righteousness;
The Holy Church expects of thee no
    less!"

A sacred frenzy seized the father's brain,
And Mercy from that hour implored in
    vain.
Ah! who will e'er believe the words I
    say?
His daughters he accused, and the same
    day
They both were cast into the dungeon's
    gloom,
That dismal antechamber of the tomb,
Arraigned, condemned, and sentenced
    to the flame,
The secret torture and the public shame.

Then to the Grand Inquisitor once more
The Hidalgo went, more eager than be-
    fore,
And said: " When Abraham offered up
    his son,
He clave the wood wherewith it might
    be done.
By his example taught, let me too bring
Wood from the forest for my offering!"
And the deep voice, without a pause,
    replied:

"Son of the Church! by faith now jus-
    tified,
Complete thy sacrifice, even as thou
    wilt;
The Church absolves thy conscience from
    all guilt!"

Then this most wretched father went
    his way
Into the woods, that round his castle
    lay,
Where once his daughters in their child-
    hood played
With their young mother in the sun
    and shade.
Now all the leaves had fallen; the
    branches bare
Made a perpetual moaning in the air,
And screaming from their eyries over-
    head
The ravens sailed athwart the sky of
    lead.
With his own hands he lopped the
    boughs and bound
Fagots, that crackled with foreboding
    sound,
And on his mules, caparisoned and
    gay
With bells and tassels, sent them on
    their way.

Then with his mind on one dark purpose
    bent,
Again to the Inquisitor he went,
And said: " Behold, the fagots I have
    brought,
And now, lest my atonement be as
    naught,
Grant me one more request, one last de-
    sire, —
With my own hand to light the funeral
    fire!"
And Torquemada answered from his
    seat,
"Son of the Church! Thine offering is
    complete;
Her servants through all ages shall not
    cease
To magnify thy deed. Depart in
    peace!"

Upon the market-place, builded of stone
The scaffold rose, whereon Death claimed
    his own.
At the four corners, in stern attitude,
Four statues of the Hebrew Prophets
    stood,

Gazing with calm indifference in their
   eyes
Upon this place of human sacrifice,
Round which was gathering fast the ea-
   ger crowd,
With clamor of voices dissonant and
   loud,
And every roof and window was alive
With restless gazers, swarming like a
   hive.

The church-bells tolled, the chant of
   monks drew near,
Loud trumpets stammered forth their
   notes of fear,
A line of torches smoked along the
   street,
There was a stir, a rush, a tramp of feet,
And, with its banners floating in the air,
Slowly the long procession crossed the
   square,
And, to the statues of the Prophets
   bound,
The victims stood, with fagots piled
   around.
Then all the air a blast of trumpets
   shook,
And louder sang the monks with bell
   and book,
And the Hidalgo, lofty, stern, and
   proud,
Lifted his torch, and, bursting through
   the crowd,
Lighted in haste the fagots, and then
   fled,
Lest those imploring eyes should strike
   him dead !

O pitiless skies ! why did your clouds
   retain
For peasants' fields their floods of hoard-
   ed rain ?
O pitiless earth ! why open no abyss
To bury in its chasm a crime like this ?

That night, a mingled column of fire
   and smoke
From the dark thickets of the forest
   broke,
And, glaring o'er the landscape leagues
   away,
Made all the fields and hamlets bright
   as day.
Wrapped in a sheet of flame the castle
   blazed,
And as the villagers in terror gazed,
They saw the figure of that cruel knight

Lean from a window in the turret's
   height,
His ghastly face illumined with the
   glare,
His hands upraised above his head in
   prayer,
Till the floor sank beneath him, and he
   fell
Down the black hollow of that burning
   well.

Three centuries and more above his
   bones
Have piled the oblivious years like fu-
   neral stones ;
His name has perished with him, and
   no trace
Remains on earth of his afflicted race ;
But Torquemada's name, with clouds
   o'ercast,
Looms in the distant landscape of the
   Past,
Like a burnt tower upon a blackened
   heath,
Lit by the fires of burning woods be-
   neath !

INTERLUDE.

THUS closed the tale of guilt and
   gloom,
That cast upon each listener's face
Its shadow, and for some brief space
Unbroken silence filled the room.
The Jew was thoughtful and distressed ;
Upon his memory thronged and pressed
The persecution of his race,
Their wrongs and sufferings and dis-
   grace ;
His head was sunk upon his breast,
And from his eyes alternate came
Flashes of wrath and tears of shame.

The student first the silence broke,
As one who long has lain in wait,
With purpose to retaliate,
And thus he dealt the avenging stroke.
" In such a company as this,
A tale so tragic seems amiss,
That by its terrible control
O'ermasters and drags down the soul
Into a fathomless abyss.
The Italian Tales that you disdain,
Some merry Night of Straparole,
Or Machiavelli's Belphagor,
Would cheer us and delight us more,

Give greater pleasure and less pain
Than your grim tragedies of Spain ! ''

And here the Poet raised his hand,
With such entreaty and command,
It stopped discussion at its birth,
And said : '' The story I shall tell
Has meaning in it, if not mirth ;
Listen, and hear what once befell
The merry birds of Killingworth ! ''

THE POET'S TALE.

THE BIRDS OF KILLINGWORTH.

It was the season, when through all the
        land
    The merle and mavis build, and build-
        ing sing
Those lovely lyrics, written by His hand,
    Whom Saxon Cædmon calls the Blithe-
        heart King ;
When on the boughs the purple buds ex-
        pand,
    The banners of the vanguard of the
        Spring,
And rivulets, rejoicing, rush and leap,
And wave their fluttering signals from
    the steep.

The robin and the bluebird, piping loud,
    Filled all the blossoming orchards
        with their glee ;
The sparrows chirped as if they still were
        proud
    Their race in Holy Writ should men-
        tioned be ;
And hungry crows assembled in a crowd,
    Clamored their piteous prayer inces-
        santly,
Knowing who hears the ravens cry, and
        said :
'' Give us, O Lord, this day our daily
    bread ! ''

Across the Sound the birds of passage
    sailed,
    Speaking some unknown language
        strange and sweet
Of tropic isle remote, and passing hailed
    The village with the cheers of all their
        fleet ;
Or quarrelling together, laughed and
    railed
    Like foreign sailors, landed in the
        street

Of seaport town, and with outlandish
        noise
Of oaths and gibberish frightening girls
    and boys.

Thus came the jocund Spring in Killing-
        worth,
    In fabulous days, some hundred years
        ago ;
And thrifty farmers, as they tilled the
        earth,
    Heard with alarm the cawing of the
        crow,
That mingled with the universal mirth,
    Cassandra-like, prognosticating woe ;
They shook their heads, and doomed
        with dreadful words
To swift destruction the whole race of
    birds.

And a town-meeting was convened
        straightway
    To set a price upon the guilty heads
Of these marauders, who, in lieu of pay,
    Levied black-mail upon the garden
        beds
And cornfields, and beheld without dis-
        may
    The awful scarecrow, with his flutter-
        ing shreds ;
The skeleton that waited at their feast,
Whereby their sinful pleasure was in-
    creased.

Then from his house, a temple painted
        white,
    With fluted columns, and a roof of red,
The Squire came forth, august and splen-
        did sight !
    Slowly descending, with majestic tread,
Three flights of steps, nor looking left
        nor right,
    Down the long street he walked, as
        one who said,
'' A town that boasts inhabitants like me
Can have no lack of good society ! ''

The Parson, too, appeared, a man aus-
        tere,
    The instinct of whose nature was to
        kill ;
The wrath of God he preached from year
        to year,
    And read, with fervor, Edwards on the
        Will ;
His favorite pastime was to slay the deer
    In Summer on some Adirondac hill ;

E'en now, while walking down the rural
  lane,
He lopped the wayside lilies with his
  cane.

From the Academy, whose belfry crowned
  The hill of Science with its vane of
    brass,
Came the Preceptor, gazing idly round,
  Now at the clouds, and now at the
    green grass,
And all absorbed in reveries profound
  Of fair Almira in the upper class,
Who was, as in a sonnet he had said,
As pure as water, and as good as bread.

And next the Deacon issued from his
  door,
  In his voluminous neck-cloth, white
    as snow ;
A suit of sable bombazine he wore ;
  His form was ponderous, and his step
    was slow ;
There never was so wise a man before ;
  He seemed the incarnate "Well, I
    told you so ! "
And to perpetuate his great renown
There was a street named after him in
  town.

These came together in the new town-
  hall,
  With sundry farmers from the region
    round.
The Squire presided, dignified and tall,
  His air impressive and his reasoning
    sound ;
Ill fared it with the birds, both great
  and small ;
  Hardly a friend in all that crowd they
    found,
But enemies enough, who every one
Charged them with all the crimes be-
  neath the sun.

When they had ended, from his place
  apart,
  Rose the Preceptor, to redress the
    wrong,
And, trembling like a steed before the
  start,
  Looked round bewildered on the ex-
    pectant throng ;
Then thought of fair Almira, and took
  heart
  To speak out what was in him, clear
    and strong,

Alike regardless of their smile or frown,
And quite determined not to be laughed
  down.

"Plato, anticipating the Reviewers,
  From his Republic banished without
    pity
The Poets ; in this little town of yours,
  You put to death, by means of a Com-
    mittee,
The ballad-singers and the Troubadours,
  The street-musicians of the heavenly
    city,
The birds, who make sweet music for us
  all
In our dark hours, as David did for Saul.

"The thrush that carols at the dawn of
  day
  From the green steeples of the piny
    wood ;
The oriole in the elm ; the noisy jay,
  Jargoning like a foreigner at his food ;
The bluebird balanced on some topmost
  spray,
  Flooding with melody the neighbor-
    hood ;
Linnet and meadow-lark, and all the
  throng
That dwell in nests, and have the gift of
  song.

"You slay them all ! and wherefore ?
  for the gain
  Of a scant handful more or less of
    wheat,
Or rye, or barley, or some other grain,
  Scratched up at random by industri-
    ous feet,
Searching for worm or weevil after rain !
  Or a few cherries, that are not so sweet
As are the songs these uninvited guests
Sing at their feast with comfortable
  breasts.

"Do you ne'er think what wondrous
  beings these ?
  Do you ne'er think who made them
    and who taught
The dialect they speak, where melodies
  Alone are the interpreters of thought ?
Whose household words are songs in
  many keys,
  Sweeter than instrument of man e'er
    caught !
Whose habitations in the tree-tops even
Are half-way houses on the road to heaven !

'Think, every morning when the sun
    peeps through
The dim, leaf-latticed windows of the
    grove,
How jubilant the happy birds renew
    Their old, melodious madrigals of love!
And when you think of this, remember
    too
'T is always morning somewhere, and
    above
The awakening continents, from shore
    to shore,
Somewhere the birds are singing ever-
    more.

"Think of your woods and orchards
    without birds!
    Of empty nests that cling to boughs
        and beams
As in an idiot's brain remembered words
    Hang empty 'mid the cobwebs of his
        dreams!
Will bleat of flocks or bellowing of herds
    Make up for the lost music, when your
        teams
Drag home the stingy harvest, and no
    more
The feathered gleaners follow to your
    door?

"What! would you rather see the inces-
    sant stir
Of insects in the windrows of the hay,
And hear the locust and the grasshopper
    Their melancholy hurdy-gurdies play?
Is this more pleasant to you than the
    whir
Of meadow-lark, and her sweet rounde-
    lay,
Or twitter of little field-fares, as you
    take
Your nooning in the shade of bush and
    brake?

"You call them thieves and pillagers;
    but know,
    They are the winged wardens of your
        farms,
Who from the cornfields drive the insid-
    ious foe,
    And from your harvests keep a hun-
        dred harms;
Even the blackest of them all, the crow,
    Renders good service as your man-at-
        arms,
Crushing the beetle in his coat of mail,
And crying havoc on the slug and snail.

"How can I teach your children gentle-
    ness,
    And mercy to the weak, and reverence
For Life, which, in its weakness or
    excess,
    Is still a gleam of God's omnipotence,
Or Death, which, seeming darkness, is
    no less
    The selfsame light, although averted
        hence,
When by your laws, your actions, and
    your speech,
You contradict the very things I teach?"

With this he closed; and through the
    audience went
    A murmur, like the rustle of dead
        leaves;
The farmers laughed and nodded, and
    some bent
    Their yellow heads together like their
        sheaves;
Men have no faith in fine-spun senti-
    ment
    Who put their trust in bullocks and
        in beeves.
The birds were doomed; and, as the rec-
    ord shows,
A bounty offered for the heads of crows.

There was another audience out of reach,
    Who had no voice nor vote in making
        laws,
But in the papers read his little speech,
    And crowned his modest temples with
        applause;
They made him conscious, each one more
    than each,
    He still was victor, vanquished in
        their cause.
Sweetest of all the applause he won from
    thee,
O fair Almira at the Academy!

And so the dreadful massacre began;
    O'er fields and orchards, and o'er
        woodland crests,
The ceaseless fusillade of terror ran.
    Dead fell the birds, with blood-stains
        on their breasts,
Or wounded crept away from sight of
    man,
    While the young died of famine in
        their nests;
A slaughter to be told in groans, not
    words,
The very St. Bartholomew of Birds!

The Summer came, and all the birds
  were dead ;
  The days were like hot coals ; the
    very ground
Was burned to ashes ; in the orchards
  fed
Myriads of caterpillars, and around
The cultivated fields and garden beds
  Hosts of devouring insects crawled,
    and found
No foe to check their march, till they
  had made
The land a desert without leaf or shade.

Devoured by worms, like Herod, was the
  town,
  Because, like Herod, it had ruthlessly
Slaughtered the Innocents.   From the
  trees spun down
  The canker-worms upon the passers-
    by,
Upon each woman's bonnet, shawl, and
  gown,
  Who shook them off with just a little
    cry ;
They were the terror of each favorite
  walk,
The endless theme of all the village talk.

The farmers grew impatient, but a few
  Confessed their error, and would not
    complain,
For after all, the best thing one can do
  When it is raining, is to let it rain.
Then they repealed the law, although
  they knew
  It would not call the dead to life again ;
As school-boys, finding their mistake too
  late,
Draw a wet sponge across the accusing
  slate.

That year in Killingworth the Autumn
  came
  Without the light of his majestic
    look,
The wonder of the falling tongues of
  flame,
  The illumined pages of his Doom's-
    Day book.
A few lost leaves blushed crimson with
  their shame,
  And drowned themselves despairing
    in the brook,
While the wild wind went moaning
  everywhere,
Lamenting the dead children of the air !

But the next Spring a stranger sight was
  seen,
  A sight that never yet by bard was
    sung,
As great a wonder as it would have been
  If some dumb animal had found a
    tongue !
A wagon, overarched with evergreen,
  Upon whose boughs were wicker cages
    hung,
All full of singing birds, came down the
  street,
Filling the air with music wild and
  sweet.

From all the country round these birds
  were brought,
  By order of the town, with anxious
    quest,
And, loosened from their wicker prisons,
  sought
  In woods and fields the places they
    loved best,
Singing loud canticles, which many
  thought
  Were satires to the authorities ad-
    dressed,
While others, listening in green lanes,
  averred
Such lovely music never had been heard !

But blither still and louder carolled they
  Upon the morrow, for they seemed to
    know
It was the fair Almira's wedding-day,
  And everywhere, around, above, be-
    low,
When the Preceptor bore his bride away,
  Their songs burst forth in joyous over-
    flow,
And a new heaven bent over a new earth
Amid the sunny farms of Killingworth.

FINALE.

The hour was late ; the fire burned
  low,
The Landlord's eyes were closed in sleep,
And near the story's end a deep
Sonorous sound at times was heard,
As when the distant bagpipes blow.
At this all laughed ; the Landlord
  stirred,
As one awaking from a swound,
And, gazing anxiously around,
Protested that he had not slept,

But only shut his eyes, and kept
His ears attentive to each word.

Then all arose, and said "Good Night."
Alone remained the drowsy Squire
To rake the embers of the fire,
And quench the waning parlor light :

While from the windows, here and there,
The scattered lamps a moment gleamed,
And the illumined hostel seemed
The constellation of the Bear,
Downward, athwart the misty air,
Sinking and setting toward the sun.
Far off the village clock struck one.

PART SECOND.

PRELUDE.

A COLD, uninterrupted rain,
That washed each southern window-
pane,
And made a river of the road ;
A sea of mist that overflowed
The house, the barns, the gilded vane,
And drowned the upland and the plain,
Through which the oak-trees, broad and
high,
Like phantom ships went drifting by ;
And, hidden behind a watery screen,
The sun unseen, or only seen
As a faint pallor in the sky ; —
Thus cold and colorless and gray,
The morn of that autumnal day,
As if reluctant to begin,
Dawned on the silent Sudbury Inn,
And all the guests that in it lay.

Full late they slept. They did not
hear
The challenge of Sir Chanticleer,
Who on the empty threshing-floor,
Disdainful of the rain outside,
Was strutting with a martial stride,
As if upon his thigh he wore
The famous broadsword of the Squire,
And said, " Behold me, and admire ! "

Only the Poet seemed to hear,
In drowse or dream, more near and near
Across the border-land of sleep
The blowing of a blithesome horn,
That laughed the dismal day to scorn ;
A splash of hoofs and rush of wheels
Through sand and mire like stranding
keels,
As from the road with sudden sweep
The Mail drove up the little steep,
And stopped beside the tavern door ;
A moment stopped, and then again

With crack of whip and bark of dog
Plunged forward through the sea of fog,
And all was silent as before, —
All silent save the dripping rain.

Then one by one the guests came down,
And greeted with a smile the Squire,
Who sat before the parlor fire,
Reading the paper fresh from town.
First the Sicilian, like a bird,
Before his form appeared, was heard
Whistling and singing down the stair ;
Then came the Student, with a look
As placid as a meadow-brook ;
The Theologian, still perplexed
With thoughts of this world and the
next ;
The Poet then, as one who seems
Walking in visions and in dreams ;
Then the Musician, like a fair
Hyperion from whose golden hair
The radiance of the morning streams ;
And last the aromatic Jew
Of Alicant, who, as he threw
The door wide open, on the air
Breathed round about him a perfume
Of damask roses in full bloom,
Making a garden of the room.

The breakfast ended, each pursued
The promptings of his various mood
Beside the fire in silence smoked
The taciturn, impassive Jew,
Lost in a pleasant revery ;
While, by his gravity provoked,
His portrait the Sicilian drew,
And wrote beneath it " Edrehi,
At the Red Horse in Sudbury."

By far the busiest of them all,
The Theologian in the hall
Was feeding robins in a cage, —
Two corpulent and lazy birds,

Vagrants and pilferers at best,
If one might trust the hostler's words,
Chief instrument of their arrest ;
Two poets of the Golden Age,
Heirs of a boundless heritage
Of fields and orchards, east and west,
And sunshine of long summer days,
Though outlawed now and dispos-
    sessed ! —
Such was the Theologian's phrase.

Meanwhile the Student held discourse
With the Musician, on the source
Of all the legendary lore
Among the nations, scattered wide
Like silt and seaweed by the force
And fluctuation of the tide ;
The tale repeated o'er and o'er,
With change of place and change of
    name,
Disguised, transformed, and yet the same
We 've heard a hundred times before.

The Poet at the window mused,
And saw, as in a dream confused,
The countenance of the Sun, discrowned,
And haggard with a pale despair,
And saw the cloud-rack trail and drift
Before it, and the trees uplift
Their leafless branches, and the air
Filled with the arrows of the rain,
And heard amid the mist below,
Like voices of distress and pain,
That haunt the thoughts of men insane,
The fateful cawings of the crow.

Then down the road, with mud besprent,
And drenched with rain from head to
    hoof,
The rain-drops dripping from his mane
And tail as from a pent-house roof,
A jaded horse, his head down bent,
Passed slowly, limping as he went.

The young Sicilian — who had grown
Impatient longer to abide
A prisoner, greatly mortified
To see completely overthrown
His plans for angling in the brook,
And, leaning o'er the bridge of stone,
To watch the speckled trout glide by,
And float through the inverted sky,
Still round and round the baited hook —
Now paced the room with rapid stride,
And, pausing at the Poet's side,
Looked forth, and saw the wretched
    steed,

And said : " Alas for human greed,
That with cold hand and stony eye
Thus turns an old friend out to die,
Or beg his food from gate to gate !
This brings a tale into my mind,
Which, if you are not disinclined
To listen, I will now relate."

All gave assent ; all wished to hear,
Not without many a jest and jeer,
The story of a spavined steed ;
And even the Student with the rest
Put in his pleasant little jest
Out of Malherbe, that Pegasus
Is but a horse that with all speed
Bears poets to the hospital ;
While the Sicilian, self-possessed,
After a moment's interval
Began his simple story thus.

THE SICILIAN'S TALE.

THE BELL OF ATRI.

AT Atri in Abruzzo, a small town
Of ancient Roman date, but scant
    renown,
One of those little places that have run
Half up the hill, beneath a blazing sun,
And then sat down to rest, as if to say,
" I climb no farther upward, come what
    may," —
The Re Giovanni, now unknown to fame,
So many monarchs since have borne the
    name,
Had a great bell hung in the market-
    place
Beneath a roof, projecting some small
    space,
By way of shelter from the sun and rain.
Then rode he through the streets with
    all his train,
And, with the blast of trumpets loud
    and long,
Made proclamation, that whenever
    wrong
Was done to any man, he should but ring
The great bell in the square, and he, the
    King,
Would cause the Syndic to decide thereon.
Such was the proclamation of King John.

How swift the happy days in Atri sped,
What wrongs were righted, need not
    here be said.
Suffice it that, as all things must decay,

The hempen rope at length was worn
    away,
Unravelled at the end, and, strand by
    strand,
Loosened and wasted in the ringer's hand,
Till one, who noted this in passing by,
Mended the rope with braids of briony,
So that the leaves and tendrils of the
    vine
Hung like a votive garland at a shrine.

By chance it happened that in Atri dwelt
A knight, with spur on heel and sword
    in belt,
Who loved to hunt the wild-boar in the
    woods,
Who loved his falcons with their crim-
    son hoods,
Who loved his hounds and horses, and
    all sports
And prodigalities of camps and courts ; —
Loved, or had loved them ; for at last,
    grown old,
His only passion was the love of gold.

He sold his horses, sold his hawks and
    hounds,
Rented his vineyards and his garden-
    grounds,
Kept but one steed, his favorite steed of
    all,
To starve and shiver in a naked stall,
And day by day sat brooding in his chair,
Devising plans how best to hoard and
    spare.

At length he said : " What is the use
    or need
To keep at my own cost this lazy steed,
Eating his head off in my stables here,
When rents are low and provender is
    dear ?
Let him go feed upon the public ways ;
I want him only for the holidays."
So the old steed was turned into the
    heat
Of the long, lonely, silent, shadeless
    street ;
And wandered in suburban lanes forlorn,
Barked at by dogs, and torn by brier
    and thorn.

One afternoon, as in that sultry clime
It is the custom in the summer time,
With bolted doors and window-shutters
    closed,
The inhabitants of Atri slept or dozed ;

When suddenly upon their senses fell
The loud alarum of the accusing bell !
The Syndic started from his deep repose,
Turned on his couch, and listened, and
    then rose
And donned his robes, and with reluc-
    tant pace
Went panting forth into the market-
    place,
Where the great bell upon its cross-beam
    swung
Reiterating with persistent tongue,
In half-articulate jargon, the old song :
" Some one hath done a wrong, hath
    done a wrong ! "

But ere he reached the belfry's light ar-
    cade
He saw, or thought he saw, beneath its
    shade,
No shape of human form of woman born,
But a poor steed dejected and forlorn,
Who with uplifted head and eager eye
Was tugging at the vines of briony.
" Domeneddio ! " cried the Syndic
    straight,
" This is the Knight of Atri's steed of
    state !
He calls for justice, being sore distressed,
And pleads his cause as loudly as the
    best."

Meanwhile from street and lane a noisy
    crowd
Had rolled together like a summer cloud,
And told the story of the wretched beast
In five-and-twenty different ways at
    least,
With much gesticulation and appeal
To heathen gods, in their excessive zeal.
The Knight was called and questioned ;
    in reply
Did not confess the fact, did not deny ;
Treated the matter as a pleasant jest,
And set at naught the Syndic and the
    rest,
Maintaining, in an angry undertone,
That he should do what pleased him
    with his own.

And thereupon the Syndic gravely read
The proclamation of the King ; then
    said :
" Pride goeth forth on horseback grand
    and gay,
But cometh back on foot, and begs its way ;
Fame is the fragrance of heroic deeds,

Of flowers of chivalry and not of weeds !
These are familiar proverbs ; but I fear
They never yet have reached your
    knightly ear.
What fair renown, what honor, what re-
    pute
Can come to you from starving this poor
    brute ?
He who serves well and speaks not,
    merits more
Than they who clamor loudest at the
    door.
Therefore the law decrees that as this
    steed
Served you in youth, henceforth you
    shall take heed
To comfort his old age, and to provide
Shelter in stall, and food and field be-
    side."

The Knight withdrew abashed ; the
    people all
Led home the steed in triumph to his
    stall.
The King heard and approved, and
    laughed in glee,
And cried aloud : "Right well it pleas-
    eth me !
Church-bells at best but ring us to the
    door ;
But go not in to mass ; my bell doth
    more :
It cometh into court and pleads the cause
Of creatures dumb and unknown to the
    laws ;
And this shall make, in every Christian
    clime,
The Bell of Atri famous for all time."

INTERLUDE.

"YES, well your story pleads the cause
Of those dumb mouths that have no
    speech,
Only a cry from each to each
In its own kind, with its own laws ;
Something that is beyond the reach
Of human power to learn or teach, —
An inarticulate moan of pain,
Like the immeasurable main
Breaking upon an unknown beach."

Thus spake the Poet with a sigh ;
Then added, with impassioned cry,
As one who feels the words he speaks,
The color flushing in his cheeks,

The fervor burning in his eye :
"Among the noblest in the land,
Though he may count himself the least,
That man I honor and revere
Who without favor, without fear,
In the great city dares to stand
The friend of every friendless beast,
And tames with his unflinching hand
The brutes that wear our form and face,
The were-wolves of the human race !"
Then paused, and waited with a frown,
Like some old champion of romance,
Who, having thrown his gauntlet down,
Expectant leans upon his lance ;
But neither Knight nor Squire is found
To raise the gauntlet from the ground,
And try with him the battle's chance.

"Wake from your dreams, O Edrehi !
Or dreaming speak to us, and make
A feint of being half awake,
And tell us what your dreams may be.
Out of the hazy atmosphere
Of cloud-land deign to reappear
Among us in this Wayside Inn ;
Tell us what visions and what scenes
Illuminate the dark ravines
In which you grope your way.   Begin !"

Thus the Sicilian spake.   The Jew
Made no reply, but only smiled,
As men unto a wayward child,
Not knowing what to answer, do.
As from a cavern's mouth, o'ergrown
With moss and intertangled vines,
A streamlet leaps into the light
And murmurs over root and stone
In a melodious undertone ;
Or as amid the noonday night
Of sombre and wind-haunted pines,
There runs a sound as of the sea ;
So from his bearded lips there came
A melody without a name,
A song, a tale, a history,
Or whatsoever it may be,
Writ and recorded in these lines.

THE SPANISH JEW'S TALE.

KAMBALU.

INTO the city of Kambalu,
By the road that leadeth to Ispahan,
At the head of his dusty caravan,
Laden with treasure from realms afar,
Baldacca and Kelat and Kandahar,
Rode the great captain Alau.

The Khan from his palace-window gazed,
And saw in the thronging street beneath,
In the light of the setting sun, that
    blazed
Through the clouds of dust by the cara-
    van raised,
The flash of harness and jewelled sheath,
And the shining scymitars of the guard,
And the weary camels that bared their
    teeth,
As they passed and passed through the
    gates unbarred
Into the shade of the palace-yard.

Thus into the city of Kambalu
Rode the great captain Alau ;
And he stood before the Khan, and said :
"The enemies of my lord are dead ;
All the Kalifs of all the West
Bow and obey thy least behest ;
The plains are dark with the mulberry-
    trees,
The weavers are busy in Samarcand,
The miners are sifting the golden sand,
The divers plunging for pearls in the
    seas,
And peace and plenty are in the land.

"Baldacca's Kalif, and he alone,
Rose in revolt against thy throne :
His treasures are at thy palace-door,
With the swords and the shawls and the
    jewels he wore ;
His body is dust o'er the desert blown.

"A mile outside of Baldacca's gate
I left my forces to lie in wait,
Concealed by forests and hillocks of sand,
And forward dashed with a handful of
    men,
To lure the old tiger from his den
Into the ambush I had planned.
Ere we reached the town the alarm was
    spread,
For we heard the sound of gongs from
    within ;
And with clash of cymbals and warlike
    din
The gates swung wide ; and we turned
    and fled ;
And the garrison sallied forth and pur-
    sued,
With the gray old Kalif at their head,
And above them the banner of Moham-
    med :
So we snared them all, and the town was
    subdued.

"As in at the gate we rode, behold,
A tower that is called the Tower of Gold !
For there the Kalif had hidden his
    wealth,
Heaped and hoarded and piled on high,
Like sacks of wheat in a granary ;
And thither the miser crept by stealth
To feel of the gold that gave him health,
And to gaze and gloat with his hungry
    eye
On jewels that gleamed like a glow-
    worm's spark,
Or the eyes of a panther in the dark.

"I said to the Kalif : 'Thou art old,
Thou hast no need of so much gold.
Thou shouldst not have heaped and hid-
    den it here,
Till the breath of battle was hot and
    near,
But have sown through the land these
    useless hoards
To spring into shining blades of swords,
And keep thine honor sweet and clear.
These grains of gold are not grains of
    wheat ;
These bars of silver thou canst not eat ;
These jewels and pearls and precious
    stones
Cannot cure the aches in thy bones,
Nor keep the feet of Death one hour
From climbing the stairways of thy
    tower !'

"Then into his dungeon I locked the
    drone,
And left him to feed there all alone
In the honey-cells of his golden hive :
Never a prayer, nor a cry, nor a groan
Was heard from those massive walls of
    stone,
Nor again was the Kalif seen alive !

"When at last we unlocked the door,
We found him dead upon the floor ;
The rings had dropped from his withered
    hands,
His teeth were like bones in the desert
    sands :
Still clutching his treasure he had died ;
And as he lay there, he appeared
A statue of gold with a silver beard,
His arms outstretched as if crucified."

This is the story, strange and true,
That the great captain Alau
Told to his brother the Tartar Khan,

When he rode that day into Kambalu
By the road that leadeth to Ispahan.

INTERLUDE.

I THOUGHT before your tale began,"
The Student murmured, "we should
    have
Some legend written by Judah Rav
In his Gemara of Babylon ;
Or something from the Gulistan, —
The tale of the Cazy of Hamadan,
Or of that King of Khorasan
Who saw in dreams the eyes of one
That had a hundred years been dead
Still moving restless in his head,
Undimmed, and gleaming with the lust
Of power, though all the rest was dust.

" But lo ! your glittering caravan
On the road that leadeth to Ispahan
Hath led us farther to the East
Into the regions of Cathay.
Spite of your Kalif and his gold,
Pleasant has been the tale you told,
And full of color ; that at least
No one will question or gainsay.
And yet on such a dismal day
We need a merrier tale to clear
The dark and heavy atmosphere.
So listen, Lordlings, while I tell,
Without a preface, what befell
A simple cobbler, in the year —
No matter ; it was long ago ;
And that is all we need to know."

THE STUDENT'S TALE.

THE COBBLER OF HAGENAU.

I TRUST that somewhere and somehow
You all have heard of Hagenau,
A quiet, quaint, and ancient town
Among the green Alsatian hills,
A place of valleys, streams, and mills,
Where Barbarossa's castle, brown
With rust of centuries, still looks down
On the broad, drowsy land below, —
On shadowy forests filled with game,
And the blue river winding slow
Through meadows, where the hedges
    grow
That give this little town its name.

It happened in the good old times,
While yet the Master-singers filled

The noisy workshop and the guild
With various melodies and rhymes,
That here in Hagenau there dwelt
A cobbler, — one who loved debate,
And, arguing from a postulate,
Would say what others only felt ;
A man of forecast and of thrift,
And of a shrewd and careful mind
In this world's business, but inclined
Somewhat to let the next world drift.

Hans Sachs with vast delight he read,
And Regenbogen's rhymes of love,
For their poetic fame had spread
Even to the town of Hagenau ;
And some Quick Melody of the Plough,
Or Double Harmony of the Dove,
Was always running in his head.
He kept, moreover, at his side,
Among his leathers and his tools,
Reynard the Fox, the Ship of Fools,
Or Eulenspiegel, open wide ;
With these he was much edified :
He thought them wiser than the Schools.

His good wife, full of godly fear,
Liked not these worldly themes to hear ;
The Psalter was her book of songs ;
The only music to her ear
Was that which to the Church belongs,
When the loud choir on Sunday chanted,
And the two angels carved in wood,
That by the windy organ stood,
Blew on their trumpets loud and clear,
And all the echoes, far and near,
Gibbered as if the church were haunted.
Outside his door, one afternoon,
This humble votary of the muse
Sat in the narrow strip of shade
By a projecting cornice made,
Mending the Burgomaster's shoes,
And singing a familiar tune : —

" Our ingress into the world
    Was naked and bare ;
Our progress through the world
    Is trouble and care ;
Our egress from the world
    Will be nobody knows where ;
But if we do well here
    We shall do well there ;
And I could tell you no more,
    Should I preach a whole year ! "

Thus sang the cobbler at his work ;
And with his gestures marked the
    time

Closing together with a jerk
Of his waxed thread the stitch and
    rhyme.
Meanwhile his quiet little dame
Was leaning o'er the window-sill,
Eager, excited, but mouse-still,
Gazing impatiently to see
What the great throng of folk might be
That onward in procession came,
Along the unfrequented street,
With horns that blew, and drums that
    beat,
And banners flying, and the flame
Of tapers, and, at times, the sweet
Voices of nuns ; and as they sang
Suddenly all the church-bells rang.

In a gay coach, above the crowd,
There sat a monk in ample hood,
Who with his right hand held aloft
A red and ponderous cross of wood,
To which at times he meekly bowed.
In front three horsemen rode, and oft,
With voice and air importunate,
A boisterous herald cried aloud :
"The grace of God is at your gate !"
So onward to the church they passed.

The cobbler slowly turned his last,
And, wagging his sagacious head,
Unto his kneeling housewife said :
"'T is the monk Tetzel. I have heard
The cawings of that reverend bird.
Don't let him cheat you of your gold ;
Indulgence is not bought and sold."

The church of Hagenau, that night,
Was full of people, full of light ;
An odor of incense filled the air,
The priest intoned, the organ groaned
Its inarticulate despair ;
The candles on the altar blazed,
And full in front of it upraised
The red cross stood against the glare.
Below, upon the altar-rail
Indulgences were set to sale,
Like ballads at a country fair.
A heavy strong-box, iron-bound
And carved with many a quaint device,
Received, with a melodious sound,
The coin that purchased Paradise.

Then from the pulpit overhead,
Tetzel the monk, with fiery glow,
Thundered upon the crowd below.
"Good people all, draw near !" he
    said ;

"Purchase these letters, signed and
    sealed,
By which all sins, though unrevealed
And unrepented, are forgiven !
Count but the gain, count not the loss
Your gold and silver are but dross,
And yet they pave the way to heaven.
I hear your mothers and your sires
Cry from their purgatorial fires,
And will ye not their ransom pay ?
O senseless people ! when the gate
Of heaven is open, will ye wait ?
Will ye not enter in to-day ?
To-morrow it will be too late ;
I shall be gone upon my way.
Make haste ! bring money while ye may !'

The women shuddered, and turned
    pale ;
Allured by hope or driven by fear,
With many a sob and many a tear,
All crowded to the altar-rail.
Pieces of silver and of gold
Into the tinkling strong-box fell
Like pebbles dropped into a well ;
And soon the ballads were all sold.
The cobbler's wife among the rest
Slipped into the capacious chest
A golden florin ; then withdrew,
Hiding the paper in her breast ;
And homeward through the darkness
    went
Comforted, quieted, content ;
She did not walk, she rather flew,
A dove that settles to her nest,
When some appalling bird of prey
That scared her has been driven away.

The days went by, the monk was gone,
The summer passed, the winter came ;
Though seasons changed, yet still the
    same
The daily round of life went on ;
The daily round of household care,
The narrow life of toil and prayer.
But in her heart the cobbler's dame
Had now a treasure beyond price,
A secret joy without a name,
The certainty of Paradise.
Alas, alas ! Dust unto dust !
Before the winter wore away,
Her body in the churchyard lay,
Her patient soul was with the Just !
After her death, among the things
That even the poor preserve with
    care, —
Some little trinkets and cheap rings,

A locket with her mother's hair,
Her wedding gown, the faded flowers
She wore upon her wedding day, —
Among these memories of past hours,
That so much of the heart reveal,
Carefully kept and put away,
The Letter of Indulgence lay
Folded, with signature and seal.

Meanwhile the Priest, aggrieved and
    pained,
Waited and wondered that no word
Of mass or requiem he heard,
As by the Holy Church ordained :
Then to the Magistrate complained,
That as this woman had been dead
A week or more, and no mass said,
It was rank heresy, or at least
Contempt of Church ; thus said the
    Priest ;
And straight the cobbler was arraigned.

He came, confiding in his cause,
But rather doubtful of the laws.
The Justice from his elbow-chair
Gave him a look that seemed to say :
"Thou standest before a Magistrate,
Therefore do not prevaricate !"
Then asked him in a business way,
Kindly but cold : "Is thy wife dead?"
The cobbler meekly bowed his head ;
"She is," came struggling from his
    throat
Scarce audibly. The Justice wrote
The words down in a book, and then
Continued, as he raised his pen :
"She is; and hath a mass been said
For the salvation of her soul ?
Come, speak the truth ! confess the
    whole !"
The cobbler without pause replied :
"Of mass or prayer there was no need ;
For at the moment when she died
Her soul was with the glorified !"
And from his pocket with all speed
He drew the priestly title-deed,
And prayed the Justice he would read.

The Justice read, amused, amazed ;
And as he read his mirth increased ;
At times his shaggy brows he raised,
Now wondering at the cobbler gazed,
Now archly at the angry Priest.
"From all excesses, sins, and crimes
Thou hast committed in past times
Thee I absolve ! And furthermore,
Purified from all earthly taints,

To the communion of the Saints
And to the sacraments restore !
All stains of weakness, and all trace
Of shame and censure I efface ;
Remit the pains thou shouldst endure,
And make thee innocent and pure,
So that in dying, unto thee
The gates of heaven shall open be !
Though long thou livest, yet this grace
Until the moment of thy death
Unchangeable continueth !"

Then said he to the Priest : "I find
This document is duly signed
Brother John Tetzel, his own hand.
At all tribunals in the land
In evidence it may be used ;
Therefore acquitted is the accused."
Then to the cobbler turned : "My
    friend,
Pray tell me, didst thou ever read
Reynard the Fox ?" — "O yes, in-
    deed !" —
"I thought so. Don't forget the end."

INTERLUDE.

"WHAT was the end ? I am ashamed
Not to remember Reynard's fate ;
I have not read the book of late ;
Was he not hanged ?" the Poet said.
The Student gravely shook his head,
And answered : "You exaggerate.
There was a tournament proclaimed,
And Reynard fought with Isegrim
The Wolf, and having vanquished him,
Rose to high honor in the State,
And Keeper of the Seals was named !"

At this the gay Sicilian laughed :
"Fight fire with fire, and craft with
    craft ;
Successful cunning seems to be
The moral of your tale," said he.
"Mine had a better, and the Jew's
Had none at all, that I could see ;
His aim was only to amuse."

Meanwhile from out its ebon case
His violin the Minstrel drew,
And having tuned its strings anew,
Now held it close in his embrace,
And poising in his outstretched hand
The bow, like a magician's wand,
He paused, and said, with beaming face:
"Last night my story was too long ;

To-day I give you but a song,
An old tradition of the North;
But first, to put you in the mood,
I will a little while prelude,
And from this instrument draw forth
Something by way of overture."

He played ; at first the tones were pure
And tender as a summer night,
The full moon climbing to her height,
The sob and ripple of the seas,
The flapping of an idle sail ;
And then by sudden and sharp degrees
The multiplied, wild harmonies
Freshened and burst into a gale ;
A tempest howling through the dark,
A crash as of some shipwrecked bark,
A loud and melancholy wail.

Such was the prelude to the tale
Told by the Minstrel ; and at times
He paused amid its varying rhymes,
And at each pause again broke in
The music of his violin,
With tones of sweetness or of fear,
Movements of trouble or of calm,
Creating their own atmosphere ;
As sitting in a church we hear
Between the verses of the psalm
The organ playing soft and clear,
Or thundering on the startled ear.

THE MUSICIAN'S TALE.

THE BALLAD OF CARMILHAN.

I.

At Stralsund, by the Baltic Sea,
    Within the sandy bar,
At sunset of a summer's day,
Ready for sea, at anchor lay
    The good ship Valdemar.

The sunbeams danced upon the waves,
    And played along her side ;
And through the cabin windows
        streamed
In ripples of golden light, that seemed
    The ripple of the tide.

There sat the captain with his friends,
    Old skippers brown and hale,
Who smoked and grumbled o'er their
        grog,
And talked of iceberg and of fog,
    Of calm and storm and gale.

And one was spinning a sailor's yarn
    About Klaboterman,
The Kobold of the sea ; a spright
Invisible to mortal sight,
    Who o'er the rigging ran.

Sometimes he hammered in the hold,
    Sometimes upon the mast,
Sometimes abeam, sometimes abaft,
Or at the bows he sang and laughed,
    And made all tight and fast.

He helped the sailors at their work,
    And toiled with jovial din ;
He helped them hoist and reef the
        sails,
He helped them stow the casks and
        bales,
    And heave the anchor in.

But woe unto the lazy louts,
    The idlers of the crew ;
Them to torment was his delight,
And worry them by day and night,
    And pinch them black and blue.

And woe to him whose mortal eyes
    Klaboterman behold.
It is a certain sign of death ! —
The cabin-boy here held his breath,
    He felt his blood run cold.

II.

The jolly skipper paused awhile,
    And then again began ;
" There is a Spectre Ship," quoth he,
" A ship of the Dead that sails the
        sea,
    And is called the Carmilhan.

" A ghostly ship, with a ghostly crew,
    In tempests she appears ;
And before the gale, or against the
        gale,
She sails without a rag of sail,
    Without a helmsman steers.

" She haunts the Atlantic north and
        south,
    But mostly the mid-sea,
Where three great rocks rise bleak and
        bare
Like furnace-chimneys in the air,
    And are called the Chimneys Three.

" And ill betide the luckless ship
    That meets the Carmilhan :

Over her decks the seas will leap,
She must go down into the deep,
  And perish mouse and man."

The captain of the Valdemar
  Laughed loud with merry heart.
"I should like to see this ship," said
    he ;
"I should like to find these Chimneys
    Three,
  That are marked down in the chart.

"I have sailed right over the spot," he
    said,
  "With a good stiff breeze behind,
When the sea was blue, and the sky was
    clear, —
You can follow my course by these pin-
    holes here, —
  And never a rock could find."

And then he swore a dreadful oath,
  He swore by the Kingdoms Three,
That, should he meet the Carmilhan,
He would run her down, although he ran
  Right into Eternity !

All this, while passing to and fro,
  The cabin-boy had heard ;
He lingered at the door to hear,
And drank in all with greedy ear,
  And pondered every word.

He was a simple country lad,
  But of a roving mind.
"O, it must be like heaven," thought
    he,
"Those far-off foreign lands to see,
  And fortune seek and find ! "

But in the fo'castle, when he heard
  The mariners blaspheme,
He thought of home, he thought of God,
And his mother under the churchyard
    sod,
  And wished it were a dream.

One friend on board that ship had he ;
  'T was the Klaboterman,
Who saw the Bible in his chest,
And made a sign upon his breast,
  All evil things to ban.

III.

THE cabin windows have grown blank
  As eyeballs of the dead ;

No more the glancing sunbeams burn
On the gilt letters of the stern,
  But on the figure-head ;

On Valdemar Victorious,
  Who looketh with disdain
To see his image in the tide
Dismembered float from side to side,
  And reunite again.

"It is the wind," those skippers said,
  "That swings the vessel so ;
It is the wind ; it freshens fast,
'T is time to say farewell at last,
  'T is time for us to go."

They shook the captain by the hand,
  "Good luck ! good luck ! " they cried ;
Each face was like the setting sun,
As, broad and red, they one by one
  Went o'er the vessel's side.

The sun went down, the full moon rose,
  Serene o'er field and flood ;
And all the winding creeks and bays
And broad sea-meadows seemed ablaze,
  The sky was red as blood.

The southwest wind blew fresh and fair,
  As fair as wind could be ;
Bound for Odessa, o'er the bar,
With all sail set, the Valdemar
  Went proudly out to sea.

The lovely moon climbs up the sky
  As one who walks in dreams ;
A tower of marble in her light,
A wall of black, a wall of white,
  The stately vessel seems.

Low down upon the sandy coast
  The lights begin to burn ;
And now, uplifted high in air,
They kindle with a fiercer glare,
  And now drop far astern.

The dawn appears, the land is gone,
  The sea is all around ;
Then on each hand low hills of sand
Emerge and form another land ;
  She steereth through the Sound.

Through Kattegat and Skager-rack
  She flitteth like a ghost ;
By day and night, by night and day,
She bounds, she flies upon her way
  Along the English coast.

Cape Finisterre is drawing near,
  Cape Finisterre is past ;
Into the open ocean stream
She floats, the vision of a dream
  Too beautiful to last.

Suns rise and set, and rise, and yet
  There is no land in sight ;
The liquid planets overhead
Burn brighter now the moon is dead,
  And longer stays the night.

IV.

AND now along the horizon's edge
  Mountains of cloud uprose,
Black as with forests underneath,
Above their sharp and jagged teeth
  Were white as drifted snows.

Unseen behind them sank the sun,
  But flushed each snowy peak
A little while with rosy light
That faded slowly from the sight
  As blushes from the cheek.

Black grew the sky, — all black, all
    black ;
  The clouds were everywhere ;
There was a feeling of suspense
In nature, a mysterious sense
  Of terror in the air.

And all on board the Valdemar
  Was still as still could be ;
Save when the dismal ship-bell tolled,
As ever and anon she rolled,
  And lurched into the sea.

The captain up and down the deck
  Went striding to and fro ;
Now watched the compass at the wheel,
Now lifted up his hand to feel
  Which way the wind might blow.

And now he looked up at the sails,
  And now upon the deep ;
In every fibre of his frame
He felt the storm before it came,
  He had no thought of sleep.

Eight bells ! and suddenly abaft,
  With a great rush of rain,
Making the ocean white with spume,
In darkness like the day of doom,
  On came the hurricane.

The lightning flashed from cloud to
    cloud,
  And rent the sky in two ;
A jagged flame, a single jet
Of white fire, like a bayonet,
  That pierced the eyeballs through.

Then all around was dark again,
  And blacker than before ;
But in that single flash of light
He had beheld a fearful sight,
  And thought of the oath he swore.

For right ahead lay the Ship of the Dead,
  The ghostly Carmilhan !
Her masts were stripped, her yards were
    bare,
And on her bowsprit, poised in air,
  Sat the Klaboterman.

Her crew of ghosts was all on deck
  Or clambering up the shrouds ;
The boatswain's whistle, the captain's
    hail,
Were like the piping of the gale,
  And thunder in the clouds.

And close behind the Carmilhan
  There rose up from the sea,
As from a foundered ship of stone,
Three bare and splintered masts alone :
  They were the Chimneys Three.

And onward dashed the Valdemar
  And leaped into the dark ;
A denser mist, a colder blast,
A little shudder, and she had passed
  Right through the Phantom Bark.

She cleft in twain the shadowy hulk,
  But cleft it unaware ;
As when, careering to her nest,
The sea-gull severs with her breast
  The unresisting air.

Again the lightning flashed ; again
  They saw the Carmilhan,
Whole as before in hull and spar ;
But now on board of the Valdemar
  Stood the Klaboterman.

And they all knew their doom was sealed ;
  They knew that death was near ;
Some prayed who never prayed before,
And some they wept, and some they
    swore,
  And some were mute with fear.

"Stood Mistress Stavers in her furbelows." Page 283.

Then suddenly there came a shock,
 And louder than wind or sea
A cry burst from the crew on deck,
As she dashed and crashed, a hopeless
      wreck,
 Upon the Chimneys Three.

The storm and night were passed, the
      light
 To streak the east began ;
The cabin-boy, picked up at sea,
Survived the wreck, and only he,
 To tell of the Carmilhan.

INTERLUDE.

WHEN the long murmur of applause
That greeted the Musician's lay
Had slowly buzzed itself away,
And the long talk of Spectre Ships
That followed died upon their lips
And came unto a natural pause,
" These tales you tell are one and all
Of the Old World," the Poet said,
" Flowers gathered from a crumbling
      wall,
Dead leaves that rustle as they fall ;
Let me present you in their stead
Something of our New England earth,
A tale which, though of no great worth,
Has still this merit, that it yields
A certain freshness of the fields,
A sweetness as of home-made bread."

The Student answered : " Be discreet ;
For if the flour be fresh and sound,
And if the bread be light and sweet,
Who careth in what mill 't was ground,
Or of what oven felt the heat,
Unless, as old Cervantes said,
You are looking after better bread
Than any that is made of wheat ?
You know that people nowadays
To what is old give little praise ;
All must be new in prose and verse :
They want hot bread, or something
      worse,
Fresh every morning, and half baked ;
The wholesome bread of yesterday,
Too stale for them, is thrown away,
Nor is their thirst with water slaked.

As oft we see the sky in May
Threaten to rain, and yet not rain,
The Poet's face, before so gay,

Was clouded with a look of pain,
But suddenly brightened up again ;
And without further let or stay
He told his tale of yesterday.

THE POET'S TALE.

LADY WENTWORTH.

ONE hundred years ago, and something
      more,
In Queen Street, Portsmouth, at her tav-
      ern door,
Neat as a pin, and blooming as a rose,
Stood Mistress Stavers in her furbelows,
Just as her cuckoo-clock was striking
      nine.
Above her head, resplendent on the sign,
The portrait of the Earl of Halifax,
In scarlet coat and periwig of flax,
Surveyed at leisure all her varied charms,
Her cap, her bodice, her white folded
      arms,
And half resolved, though he was past
      his prime,
And rather damaged by the lapse of time,
To fall down at her feet, and to declare
The passion that had driven him to
      despair.
For from his lofty station he had seen
Stavers, her husband, dressed in bottle-
      green,
Drive his new Flying Stage-coach, four
      in hand,
Down the long lane, and out into the
      land,
And knew that he was far upon the way
To Ipswich and to Boston on the Bay !

Just then the meditations of the Earl
Were interrupted by a little girl,
Barefooted, ragged, with neglected hair,
Eyes full of laughter, neck and shoulders
      bare,
A thin slip of a girl, like a new moon,
Sure to be rounded into beauty soon,
A creature men would worship and adore,
Though now in mean habiliments she
      bore
A pail of water, dripping, through the
      street,
And bathing, as she went, her naked
      feet.

It was a pretty picture, full of grace, —
The slender form, the delicate, thin face ;

The swaying motion, as she hurried by ;
The shining feet, the laughter in her eye,
That o'er her face in ripples gleamed and
　　glanced,
As in her pail the shifting sunbeam
　　danced :
And with uncommon feelings of delight
The Earl of Halifax beheld the sight.
Not so Dame Stavers, for he heard her
　　say
These words, or thought he did, as plain
　　as day :
"O Martha Hilton !　Fie ! how dare you
　　go
About the town half dressed, and looking
　　so ! "
At which the gypsy laughed, and straight
　　replied :
" No matter how I look ;　I yet shall ride
In my own chariot, ma'am."　And on
　　the child
The Earl of Halifax benignly smiled,
As with her heavy burden she passed on,
Looked back, then turned the corner,
　　and was gone.

What next, upon that memorable day,
Arrested his attention was a gay
And brilliant equipage, that flashed and
　　spun,
The silver harness glittering in the sun,
Outriders with red jackets, lithe and
　　lank,
Pounding the saddles as they rose and
　　sank,
While all alone within the chariot sat
A portly person with three-cornered hat,
A crimson velvet coat, head high in air,
Gold-headed cane, and nicely powdered
　　hair,
And diamond buckles sparkling at his
　　knees,
Dignified, stately, florid, much at ease.
Onward the pageant swept, and as it
　　passed,
Fair Mistress Stavers courtesied low and
　　fast ;
For this was Governor Wentworth, driv-
　　ing down
To Little Harbor, just beyond the town,
Where his Great House stood looking
　　out to sea,
A goodly place, where it was good to be.

It was a pleasant mansion, an abode
Near and yet hidden from the great high-
　　road,

Sequestered among trees, a noble pile,
Baronial and colonial in its style ;
Gables and dormer-windows everywhere,
And stacks of chimneys rising high in
　　air, —
Pandæan pipes, on which all winds that
　　blew
Made mournful music the whole winter
　　through.
Within, unwonted splendors met the
　　eye,
Panels, and floors of oak, and tapes-
　　try ;
Carved chimney-pieces, where on brazen
　　dogs
Revelled and roared the Christmas fires
　　of logs ;
Doors opening into darkness unawares,
Mysterious passages, and flights of
　　stairs ;
And on the walls, in heavy gilded
　　frames,
The ancestral Wentworths with Old-
　　Scripture names.

Such was the mansion where the great
　　man dwelt,
A　widower and childless ;　and he
　　felt
The loneliness, the uncongenial gloom,
That like a presence haunted every
　　room ;
For though not given to weakness, he
　　could feel
The pain of wounds, that ache because
　　they heal.

The years came and the years went, —
　　seven in all,
And passed in cloud and sunshine o'er
　　the Hall ;
The dawns their splendor through its
　　chambers shed,
The sunsets flushed its western windows
　　red ;
The snow was on its roofs, the wind, the
　　rain ;
Its woodlands were in leaf and bare
　　again ;
Moons waxed and waned, the lilacs
　　bloomed and died,
In the broad river ebbed and flowed the
　　tide,
Ships went to sea, and ships came home
　　from sea,
And the slow years sailed by and ceased
　　to be.

And all these years had Martha Hilton
    served
In the Great House, not wholly unob-
    served :
By day, by night, the silver crescent
    grew,
Though hidden by clouds, her light
    still shining through ;
A maid of all work, whether coarse or
    fine,
A servant who made service seem divine !
Through her each room was fair to look
    upon ;
The mirrors glistened, and the brasses
    shone,
The very knocker on the outer door,
If she but passed, was brighter than be-
    fore.

And now the ceaseless turning of the
    mill
Of Time, that never for an hour stands
    still,
Ground out the Governor's sixtieth
    birthday,
And powdered his brown hair with sil-
    ver-gray.
The robin, the forerunner of the spring,,
The bluebird with his jocund carolling,
The restless swallows building in the
    eaves,
The golden buttercups, the grass, the
    leaves,
The lilacs tossing in the winds of May,
All welcomed this majestic holiday !
He gave a splendid banquet, served on
    plate,
Such as became the Governor of the
    State,
Who represented England and the King,
And was magnificent in everything.
He had invited all his friends and
    peers, —
The Pepperels, the Langdons, and the
    Lears,
The Sparhawks, the Penhallows, and the
    rest ;
For why repeat the name of every
    guest ?
But I must mention one, in bands and
    gown,
The rector there, the Reverend Arthur
    Brown
Of the Established Church ; with smil-
    ing face
He sat beside the Governor and said
    grace ;

And then the feast went on, as others do,
But ended as none other I e'er knew.

When they had drunk the King, with
    many a cheer,
The Governor whispered in a servant's
    ear,
Who disappeared, and presently there
    stood
Within the room, in perfect womanhood,
A maiden, modest and yet self-possessed,
Youthful and beautiful, and simply
    dressed.
Can this be Martha Hilton ? It must
    be !
Yes, Martha Hilton, and no other she !
Dowered with the beauty of her twenty
    years,
How ladylike, how queenlike she ap-
    pears ;
The pale, thin crescent of the days gone
    by
Is Dian now in all her majesty !
Yet scarce a guest perceived that she
    was there,
Until the Governor, rising from his
    chair,
Played slightly with his ruffles, then
    looked down,
And said unto the Reverend Arthur
    Brown :
" This is my birthday : it shall likewise
    be
My wedding-day ; and you shall marry
    me ! "

The listening guests were greatly mysti-
    fied,
None more so than the rector, who re-
    plied :
" Marry you ? Yes, that were a pleas-
    ant task,
Your Excellency ; but to whom ? I
    ask."
The Governor answered : " To this lady
    here " ;
And beckoned Martha Hilton to draw
    near.
She came and stood, all blushes, at his
    side.
The rector paused. The impatient Gov-
    ernor cried :
" This is the lady ; do you hesitate ?
Then I command you as Chief Magis-
    trate."
The rector read the service loud and
    clear :

" Dearly beloved, we are gathered here,"
And so on to the end.   At his command
On the fourth finger of her fair left hand
The Governor placed the ring ; and that
    was all :
Martha was Lady Wentworth of the
    Hall !

INTERLUDE.

WELL pleased the audience heard the
    tale.
The Theologian said : " Indeed,
To praise you there is little need ;
One almost hears the farmer's flail
Thresh out your wheat, nor does there fail
A certain freshness, as you said,
And sweetness as of home-made bread.
But not less sweet and not less fresh
Are many legends that I know,
Writ by the monks of long-ago,
Who loved to mortify the flesh,
So that the soul might purer grow,
And rise to a diviner state ;
And one of these — perhaps of all
Most beautiful — I now recall,
And with permission will narrate ;
Hoping thereby to make amends
For that grim tragedy of mine,
As strong and black as Spanish wine,
I told last night, and wish almost
It had remained untold, my friends ;
For Torquemada's awful ghost
Came to me in the dreams I dreamed,
And in the darkness glared and gleamed
Like a great lighthouse on the coast."

The Student laughing said : " Far more
Like to some dismal fire of bale
Flaring portentous on a hill ;
Or torches lighted on a shore
By wreckers in a midnight gale.
No matter ; be it as you will,
Only go forward with your tale."

THE THEOLOGIAN'S TALE.

THE LEGEND BEAUTIFUL.

" HADST thou stayed, I must have
    fled ! "
That is what the Vision said.

In his chamber all alone,
Kneeling on the floor of stone,

Prayed the Monk in deep contrition
For his sins of indecision,
Prayed for greater self-denial
In temptation and in trial ;
It was noonday by the dial,
And the Monk was all alone.

Suddenly, as if it lightened,
An unwonted splendor brightened
All within him and without him
In that narrow cell of stone ;
And he saw the Blessed Vision
Of our Lord, with light Elysian
Like a vesture wrapped about him,
Like a garment round him thrown.

Not as crucified and slain,
Not in agonies of pain,
Not with bleeding hands and feet,
Did the Monk his Master see ;
But as in the village street,
In the house or harvest-field,
Halt and lame and blind he healed,
When he walked in Galilee.

In an attitude imploring,
Hands upon his bosom crossed,
Wondering, worshipping, adoring,
Knelt the Monk in rapture lost.
Lord, he thought, in heaven that reign
    est,
Who am I, that thus thou deignest
To reveal thyself to me ?
Who am I, that from the centre
Of thy glory thou shouldst enter
This poor cell, my guest to be ?

Then amid his exaltation,
Loud the convent bell appalling,
From its belfry calling, calling,
Rang through court and corridor
With persistent iteration
He had never heard before.
It was now the appointed hour
When alike in shine or shower,
Winter's cold or summer's heat,
To the convent portals came
All the blind and halt and lame,
All the beggars of the street,
For their daily dole of food
Dealt them by the brotherhood ;
And their almoner was he
Who upon his bended knee,
Rapt in silent ecstasy
Of divinest self-surrender,
Saw the Vision and the Splendor.

Deep distress and hesitation
Mingled with his adoration ;
Should he go, or should he stay ?
Should he leave the poor to wait
Hungry at the convent gate,
Till the Vision passed away ?
Should he slight his radiant guest,
Slight this visitant celestial,
For a crowd of ragged, bestial
Beggars at the convent gate ?
Would the Vision there remain ?
Would the Vision come again ?
Then a voice within his breast
Whispered, audible and clear
As if to the outward ear :
" Do thy duty ; that is best ;
Leave unto thy Lord the rest ! "

Straightway to his feet he started,
And with longing look intent
On the Blessed Vision bent,
Slowly from his cell departed,
Slowly on his errand went.

At the gate the poor were waiting,
Looking through the iron grating,
With that terror in the eye
That is only seen in those
Who amid their wants and woes
Hear the sound of doors that close,
And of feet that pass them by ;
Grown familiar with disfavor,
Grown familiar with the savor
Of the bread by which men die !
But to-day, they knew not why,
Like the gate of Paradise
Seemed the convent gate to rise,
Like a sacrament divine
Seemed to them the bread and wine.
In his heart the Monk was praying,
Thinking of the homeless poor,
What they suffer and endure ;
What we see not, what we see ;
And the inward voice was saying :
" Whatsoever thing thou doest
To the least of mine and lowest,
That thou doest unto me ! "

Unto me ! but had the Vision
Come to him in beggar's clothing,
Come a mendicant imploring,
Would he then have knelt adoring,
Or have listened with derision,
And have turned away with loathing ?

Thus his conscience put the question,
Full of troublesome suggestion,

As at length, with hurried pace,
Towards his cell he turned his face,
And beheld the convent bright
With a supernatural light,
Like a luminous cloud expanding
Over floor and wall and ceiling.

But he paused with awe-struck feeling
At the threshold of his door,
For the Vision still was standing
As he left it there before,
When the convent bell appalling,
From its belfry calling, calling,
Summoned him to feed the poor.
Through the long hour intervening
It had waited his return,
And he felt his bosom burn,
Comprehending all the meaning,
When the Blessed Vision said,
" Hadst thou stayed, I must have
fled ! "

INTERLUDE.

ALL praised the Legend more or less ;
Some liked the moral, some the verse ;
Some thought it better, and some worse
Than other legends of the past ;
Until, with ill-concealed distress
At all their cavilling, at last
The Theologian gravely said :
" The Spanish proverb, then, is right ;
Consult your friends on what you do,
And one will say that it is white,
And others say that it is red."
And " Amen ! " quoth the Spanish Jew.

" Six stories told ! We must have
seven,
A cluster like the Pleiades,
And lo ! it happens, as with these,
That one is missing from our heaven.
Where is the Landlord ? Bring him
here ;
Let the Lost Pleiad reappear."

Thus the Sicilian cried, and went
Forthwith to seek his missing star,
But did not find him in the bar,
A place that landlords most frequent,
Nor yet beside the kitchen fire,
Nor up the stairs, nor in the hall ;
It was in vain to ask or call,
There were no tidings of the Squire.

So he came back with downcast head,
Exclaiming : " Well, our bashful host

Hath surely given up the ghost.
Another proverb says the dead
Can tell no tales ; and that is true.
It follows, then, that one of you
Must tell a story in his stead.
You must," he to the Student said,
" Who know so many of the best,
And tell them better than the rest."

Straight, by these flattering words be-
　　guiled,
The Student, happy as a child
When he is called a little man,
Assumed the double task imposed,
And without more ado unclosed
His smiling lips, and thus began.

THE STUDENT'S SECOND TALE.

THE BARON OF ST. CASTINE.

BARON CASTINE of St. Castine
Has left his château in the Pyrenees,
And sailed across the western seas.
When he went away from his fair demesne
The birds were building, the woods were
　　green ;
And now the winds of winter blow
Round the turrets of the old château,
The birds are silent and unseen,
The leaves lie dead in the ravine,
And the Pyrenees are white with snow.

His father, lonely, old, and gray,
Sits by the fireside day by day,
Thinking ever one thought of care ;
Through the southern windows, narrow
　　and tall,
The sun shines into the ancient hall,
And makes a glory round his hair.
The house-dog, stretched beneath his
　　chair,
Groans in his sleep as if in pain,
Then wakes, and yawns, and sleeps
　　again,
So silent is it everywhere, —
So silent you can hear the mouse
Run and rummage along the beams
Behind the wainscot of the wall ;
And the old man rouses from his dreams,
And wanders restless through the house,
As if he heard strange voices call.

His footsteps echo along the floor
Of a distant passage, and pause awhile ;
He is standing by an open door
Looking long, with a sad, sweet smile,

Into the room of his absent son.
There is the bed on which he lay,
There are the pictures bright and gay,
Horses and hounds and sun-lit seas ;
There are his powder-flask and gun,
And his hunting-knives in shape of a fan ;
The chair by the window where he sat,
With the clouded tiger-skin for a mat,
Looking out on the Pyrenees,
Looking out on Mount Marboré
And the Seven Valleys of Lavedan.
Ah me ! he turns away and sighs ;
There is a mist before his eyes.

At night, whatever the weather be,
Wind or rain or starry heaven,
Just as the clock is striking seven,
Those who look from the windows see
The village Curate, with lantern and
　　maid,
Come through the gateway from the park
And cross the courtyard damp and
　　dark, —
A ring of light in a ring of shade.

And now at the old man's side he stands,
His voice is cheery, his heart expands,
He gossips pleasantly, by the blaze
Of the fire of fagots, about old days,
And Cardinal Mazarin and the Fronde,
And the Cardinal's nieces fair and fond,
And what they did, and what they said,
When they heard his Eminence was dead.

And after a pause the old man says,
His mind still coming back again
To the one sad thought that haunts his
　　brain,
" Are there any tidings from over sea ?
Ah, why has that wild boy gone from
　　me ? "
And the Curate answers, looking down,
Harmless and docile as a lamb,
" Young blood ! young blood ! It must
　　so be ! "
And draws from the pocket of his gown
A handkerchief like an oriflamb,
And wipes his spectacles, and they play
Their little game of lansquenet
In silence for an hour or so,
Till the clock at nine strikes loud and
　　clear
From the village lying asleep below,
And across the courtyard, into the dark
Of the winding pathway in the park,
Curate and lantern disappear,
And darkness reigns in the old château.

The ship has come back from over
    sea,
She has been signalled from below,
And into the harbor of Bordeaux
She sails with her gallant company.
But among them is nowhere seen
The brave young Baron of St. Castine;
He hath tarried behind, I ween,
In the beautiful land of Acadie !

And the father paces to and fro
Through the chambers of the old château,
Waiting, waiting to hear the hum
Of wheels on the road that runs below,
Of servants hurrying here and there,
The voice in the courtyard, the step on
    the stair,
Waiting for some one who doth not
    come !
But letters there are, which the old man
    reads
To the Curate, when he comes at night,
Word by word, as an acolyte
Repeats his prayers and tells his beads ;
Letters full of the rolling sea,
Full of a young man's joy to be
Abroad in the world, alone and free ;
Full of adventures and wonderful scenes
Of hunting the deer through forests
    vast
In the royal grant of Pierre du Gast ;
Of nights in the tents of the Tarratines ;
Of Madocawando the Indian chief,
And his daughters, glorious as queens,
And beautiful beyond belief ;
And so soft the tones of their native
    tongue,
The words are not spoken, they are sung !

And the Curate listens, and smiling says:
"Ah yes, dear friend ! in our young days
We should have liked to hunt the deer
All day amid those forest scenes,
And to sleep in the tents of the Tarra-
    tines ;
But now it is better sitting here
Within four walls, and without the fear
Of losing our hearts to Indian queens ;
For man is fire and woman is tow,
And the Somebody comes and begins to
    blow."
Then a gleam of distrust and vague sur-
    mise
Shines in the father's gentle eyes,
As fire-light on a window-pane
Glimmers and vanishes again ;
But naught he answers ; he only sighs,

And for a moment bows his head ;
Then, as their custom is, they play
Their little game of lansquenet,
And another day is with the dead.

Another day, and many a day
And many a week and month depart,
When a fatal letter wings its way
Across the sea, like a bird of prey,
And strikes and tears the old man's
    heart.
Lo ! the young Baron of St. Castine,
Swift as the wind is, and as wild,
Has married a dusky Tarratine,
Has married Madocawando's child !

The letter drops from the father's hand ;
Though the sinews of his heart are
    wrung,
He utters no cry, he breathes no prayer.
No malediction falls from his tongue :
But his stately figure, erect and grand,
Bends and sinks like a column of sand
In the whirlwind of his great despair.
Dying, yes, dying ! His latest breath
Of parley at the door of death
Is a blessing on his wayward son.
Lower and lower on his breast
Sinks his gray head ; he is at rest ;
No longer he waits for any one.

For many a year the old château
Lies tenantless and desolate ;
Rank grasses in the courtyard grow,
About its gables caws the crow ;
Only the porter at the gate
Is left to guard it, and to wait
The coming of the rightful heir ;
No other life or sound is there ;
No more the Curate comes at night,
No more is seen the unsteady light,
Threading the alleys of the park ;
The windows of the hall are dark,
The chambers dreary, cold, and bare !

At length, at last, when the winter is
    past,
And birds are building, and woods are
    green,
With flying skirts is the Curate seen
Speeding along the woodland way,
Humming gayly, " No day is so long
But it comes at last to vesper-song."
He stops at the porter's lodge to say
That at last the Baron of St. Castine
Is coming home with his Indian queen,
Is coming without a week's delay ;

And all the house must be swept and
    clean,
And all things set in good array !
And the solemn porter shakes his head ;
And the answer he makes is : "Lacka-
    day !
We will see, as the blind man said ! "

Alert since first the day began,
The cock upon the village church
Looks northward from his airy perch,
As if beyond the ken of man
To see the ships come sailing on,
And pass the Isle of Oléron,
And pass the Tower of Cordouan.

In the church below is cold in clay
The heart that would have leaped for
    joy —
O tender heart of truth and trust ! —
To see the coming of that day ;
In the church below the lips are dust ;
Dust are the hands, and dust the feet,
That would have been so swift to meet
The coming of that wayward boy.

At night the front of the old château
Is a blaze of light above and below ;
There 's a sound of wheels and hoofs in
    the street,
A cracking of whips, and scamper of
    feet,
Bells are ringing, and horns are blown,
And the Baron hath come again to his
    own.
The Curate is waiting in the hall,
Most eager and alive of all
To welcome the Baron and Baroness ;
But his mind is full of vague distress,
For he hath read in Jesuit books
Of those children of the wilderness,
And now, good, simple man ! he looks
To see a painted savage stride
Into the room, with shoulders bare,
And eagle feathers in her hair,
And around her a robe of panther's hide.

Instead, he beholds with secret shame
A form of beauty undefined,
A loveliness without a name,
Not of degree, but more of kind ;
Nor bold nor shy, nor short nor tall,
But a new mingling of them all.
Yes, beautiful beyond belief,
Transfigured and transfused, he sees
The lady of the Pyrenees,
The daughter of the Indian chief.

Beneath the shadow of her hair
The gold-bronze color of the skin
Seems lighted by a fire within,
As when a burst of sunlight shines
Beneath a sombre grove of pines, —
A dusky splendor in the air.
The two small hands, that now are
    pressed
In his, seem made to be caressed,
They lie so warm and soft and still,
Like birds half hidden in a nest,
Trustful, and innocent of ill.
And ah ! he cannot believe his ears
When her melodious voice he hears
Speaking his native Gascon tongue ;
The words she utters seem to be
Part of some poem of Goudouli,
They are not spoken, they are sung !
And the Baron smiles, and says, "You
    see,
I told you but the simple truth ;
Ah, you may trust the eyes of youth !"

Down in the village day by day
The people gossip in their way,
And stare to see the Baroness pass
On Sunday morning to early Mass ;
And when she kneeleth down to pray,
They wonder, and whisper together, and
    say,
"Surely this is no heathen lass !"
And in course of time they learn to
    bless
The Baron and the Baroness.

And in course of time the Curate learns
A secret so dreadful, that by turns
He is ice and fire, he freezes and burns.
The Baron at confession hath said,
That though this woman be his wife,
He hath wed her as the Indians wed,
He hath bought her for a gun and a
    knife !
And the Curate replies : "O profligate,
O Prodigal Son ! return once more
To the open arms and the open door
Of the Church, or ever it be too late.
Thank God, thy father did not live
To see what he could not forgive ;
On thee, so reckless and perverse,
He left his blessing, not his curse.
But the nearer the dawn the darker the
    night,
And by going wrong all things come
    right ;
Things have been mended that were
    worse,

And the worse, the nearer they are to
    mend.
For the sake of the living and the dead,
Thou shalt be wed as Christians wed,
And all things come to a happy end."

O sun, that followest the night,
In yon blue sky, serene and pure,
And pourest thine impartial light
Alike on mountain and on moor,
Pause for a moment in thy course,
And bless the bridegroom and the bride !
O Gave, that from thy hidden source
In yon mysterious mountain-side
Pursuest thy wandering way alone,
And leaping down its steps of stone,
Along the meadow-lands demure
Stealest away to the Adour,
Pause for a moment in thy course
To bless the bridegroom and the bride ?

The choir is singing the matin song,
The doors of the church are opened
    wide,
The people crowd, and press, and throng
To see the bridegroom and the bride.
They enter and pass along the nave ;
They stand upon the father's grave ;
The bells are ringing soft and slow ;
The living above and the dead below
Give their blessing on one and twain ;
The warm wind blows from the hills of
    Spain,
The birds are building, the leaves are
    green,
And Baron Castine of St. Castine
Hath come at last to his own again.

FINALE.

'*Nunc plaudite !*" the Student cried,
When he had finished; "now applaud,

As Roman actors used to say
At the conclusion of a play";
And rose, and spread his hands abroad,
And smiling bowed from side to side,
As one who bears the palm away.
And generous was the applause and loud,
But less for him than for the sun,
That even as the tale was done
Burst from its canopy of cloud,
And lit the landscape with the blaze
Of afternoon on autumn days,
And filled the room with light, and
    made
The fire of logs a painted shade.

A sudden wind from out the west
Blew all its trumpets loud and shrill ;
The windows rattled with the blast,
The oak-trees shouted as it passed,
And straight, as if by fear possessed,
The cloud encampment on the hill
Broke up, and fluttering flag and tent
Vanished into the firmament,
And down the valley fled amain
The rear of the retreating rain.

Only far up in the blue sky
A mass of clouds, like drifted snow
Suffused with a faint Alpine glow,
Was heaped together, vast and high,
On which a shattered rainbow hung,
Not rising like the ruined arch
Of some aerial aqueduct,
But like a roseate garland plucked
From an Olympian god, and flung
Aside in his triumphal march.

Like prisoners from their dungeon gloom,
Like birds escaping from a snare,
Like school-boys at the hour of play,
All left at once the pent-up room,
And rushed into the open air ;
And no more tales were told that day.

PART THIRD.

PRELUDE.

THE evening came ; the golden vane
A moment in the sunset glanced,
Then darkened, and then gleamed again,
As from the east the moon advanced
And touched it with a softer light ;
While underneath, with flowing mane,
Upon the sign the Red Horse pranced,
And galloped forth into the night.

But brighter than the afternoon
That followed the dark day of rain,
And brighter than the golden vane
That glistened in the rising moon,
Within the ruddy fire-light gleamed ;
And every separate window-pane,
Backed by the outer darkness, showed
A mirror, where the flamelets gleamed
And flickered to and fro, and seemed
A bonfire lighted in the road.

Amid the hospitable glow,
Like an old actor on the stage,
With the uncertain voice of age,
The singing chimney chanted low
The homely songs of long ago.

The voice that Ossian heard of yore,
When midnight winds were in his hall ;
A ghostly and appealing call,
A sound of days that are no more !
And dark as Ossian sat the Jew,
And listened to the sound, and knew
The passing of the airy hosts,
The gray and misty cloud of ghosts
In their interminable flight ;
And listening muttered in his beard,
With accent indistinct and weird,
"Who are ye, children of the Night ?"

Beholding his mysterious face,
"Tell me," the gay Sicilian said,
"Why was it that in breaking bread
At supper, you bent down your head
And, musing, paused a little space,
As one who says a silent grace ?"

The Jew replied, with solemn air,
"I said the Manichæan's prayer.
It was his faith, — perhaps is mine, —
That life in all its forms is one,
And that its secret conduits run

Unseen, but in unbroken line,
From the great fountain-head divine
Through man and beast, through grain
        and grass.
Howe'er we struggle, strive, and cry,
From death there can be no escape,
And no escape from life, alas !
Because we cannot die, but pass
From one into another shape :
It is but into life we die.

"Therefore the Manichæan said
This simple prayer on breaking bread,
Lest he with hasty hand or knife
Might wound the incarcerated life,
The soul in things that we call dead :
'I did not reap thee, did not bind thee,
I did not thrash thee, did not grind
        thee,
Nor did I in the oven bake thee !
It was not I, it was another
Did these things unto thee, O brother ;
I only have thee, hold thee, break
        thee !' "

"That birds have souls I can concede,"
The poet cried, with glowing cheeks ;
"The flocks that from their beds of reed
Uprising north or southward fly,
And flying write upon the sky
The biforked letter of the Greeks,
As hath been said by Rucellai ;
All birds that sing or chirp or cry,
Even those migratory bands,
The minor poets of the air,
The plover, peep, and sanderling,
That hardly can be said to sing,
But pipe along the barren sands, —
All these have souls akin to ours ;
So hath the lovely race of flowers :
Thus much I grant, but nothing more.
The rusty hinges of a door
Are not alive because they creak ;
This chimney, with its dreary roar,
These rattling windows, do not speak !"
"To me they speak," the Jew replied ;
"And in the sounds that sink and soar,
I hear the voices of a tide
That breaks upon an unknown shore !"

Here the Sicilian interfered :
"That was your dream, then, as you
        dozed

A moment since, with eyes half-closed,
And murmured something in your
    beard."
The Hebrew smiled, and answered,
    "Nay ;
Not that, but something very near ;
Like, and yet not the same, may seem
The vision of my waking dream ;
Before it wholly dies away,
Listen to me, and you shall hear."

THE SPANISH JEW'S TALE.

AZRAEL.

KING SOLOMON, before his palace gate
At evening, on the pavement tessellate
Was walking with a stranger from the
    East,
Arrayed in rich attire as for a feast,
The mighty Runjeet-Sing, a learned man,
And Rajah of the realms of Hindostan.
And as they walked the guest became
    aware
Of a white figure in the twilight air,
Gazing intent, as one who with surprise
His form and features seemed to recog-
    nize ;
And in a whisper to the king he said :
"What is yon shape, that, pallid as the
    dead,
Is watching me, as if he sought to trace
In the dim light the features of my face ?"

The king looked, and replied : "I know
    him well ;
It is the Angel men call Azrael,
'T is the Death Angel ; what hast thou
    to fear ?"
And the guest answered : "Lest he
    should come near,
And speak to me, and take away my
    breath !
Save me from Azrael, save me from
    death !
O king, that hast dominion o'er the wind,
Bid it arise and bear me hence to Ind."

The king gazed upward at the cloudless
    sky,
Whispered a word, and raised his hand
    on high,
And lo ! the signet-ring of chrysoprase
On his uplifted finger seemed to blaze
With hidden fire, and rushing from the
    west

There came a mighty wind, and seized
    the guest
And lifted him from earth, and on they
    passed,
His shining garments streaming in the
    blast,
A silken banner o'er the walls upreared,
A purple cloud, that gleamed and disap-
    peared.
Then said the Angel, smiling : "If this
    man
Be Rajah Runjeet-Sing of Hindostan,
Thou hast done well in listening to his
    prayer ;
I was upon my way to seek him there."

INTERLUDE.

"O EDREHI, forbear to-night
Your ghostly legends of affright,
And let the Talmud rest in peace ;
Spare us your dismal tales of death
That almost take away one's breath ;
So doing, may your tribe increase."

Thus the Sicilian said ; then went
And on the spinet's rattling keys
Played Marianina, like a breeze
From Naples and the Southern seas,
That brings us the delicious scent
Of citron and of orange trees,
And memories of soft days of ease
At Capri and Amalfi spent.

"Not so," the eager Poet said ;
"At least, not so before I tell
The story of my Azrael,
An angel mortal as ourselves,
Which in an ancient tome I found
Upon a convent's dusty shelves,
Chained with an iron chain, and bound
In parchment, and with clasps of brass,
Lest from its prison, some dark day,
It might be stolen or steal away,
While the good friars were singing mass.

"It is a tale of Charlemagne,
When like a thunder-cloud, that lowers
And sweeps from mountain-crest to
    coast,
With lightning flaming through its
    showers,
He swept across the Lombard plain,
Beleaguering with his warlike train
Pavia, the country's pride and boast,
The City of the Hundred Towers."

Thus heralded the tale began,
And thus in sober measure ran.

THE POET'S TALE

CHARLEMAGNE.

OLGER the Dane and Desiderio,
King of the Lombards, on a lofty tower
Stood gazing northward o'er the rolling
    plains,
League after league of harvests, to the
    foot
Of the snow-crested Alps, and saw ap-
    proach
A mighty army, thronging all the
    roads
That led into the city. And the
    King
Said unto Olger, who had passed his
    youth
As hostage at the court of France, and
    knew
The Emperor's form and face : " Is
    Charlemagne
Among that host ? " And Olger an-
    swered : " No."

And still the innumerable multitude
Flowed onward and increased, until the
    King
Cried in amazement : " Surely Charle-
    magne
Is coming in the midst of all these
    knights ! "
And Olger answered slowly : " No ; not
    yet ;
He will not come so soon." Then much
    disturbed
King Desiderio asked : " What shall we
    do,
If he approach with a still greater
    army ? "
And Olger answered : " When he shall
    appear,
You will behold what manner of man
    he is ;
But what will then befall us I know
    not."

Then came the guard that never knew
    repose,
The Paladins of France ; and at the
    sight
The Lombard King o'ercome with terror
    cried :

" This must be Charlemagne ! " and as
    before
Did Olger answer : " No ; not yet, not
    yet."

And then appeared in panoply complete
The Bishops and the Abbots and the
    Priests
Of the imperial chapel, and the Counts
And Desiderio could no more endure
The light of day, nor yet encounter
    death,
But sobbed aloud and said : " Let us
    go down
And hide us in the bosom of the earth,
Far from the sight and anger of a foe
So terrible as this ! " And Olger said :
" When you behold the harvests in the
    fields
Shaking with fear, the Po and the
    Ticino
Lashing the city walls with iron waves,
Then may you know that Charlemagne
    is come."
And even as he spake, in the northwest,
Lo ! there uprose a black and threaten-
    ing cloud,
Out of whose bosom flashed the light of
    arms
Upon the people pent up in the city ;
A light more terrible than any dark-
    ness ;
And Charlemagne appeared ; — a Man
    of Iron !

His helmet was of iron, and his gloves
Of iron, and his breastplate and his
    greaves
And tassets were of iron, and his shield.
In his left hand he held an iron spear,
In his right hand his sword invincible.
The horse he rode on had the strength
    of iron,
And color of iron. All who went before
    him,
Beside him and behind him, his whole
    host,
Were armed with iron, and their hearts
    within them
Were stronger than the armor that they
    wore.
The fields and all the roads were filled
    with iron,
And points of iron glistened in the
    sun
And shed a terror through the city
    streets.

This at a single glance Olger the Dane
Saw from the tower, and turning to the
    King
Exclaimed in haste : " Behold ! this is
    the man
You looked for with such eagerness ! "
    and then
Fell as one dead at Desiderio's feet.

INTERLUDE.

WELL pleased all listened to the tale,
That drew, the Student said, its pith
And marrow from the ancient myth
Of some one with an iron flail ;
Or that portentous Man of Brass
Hephæstus made in days of yore,
Who stalked about the Cretan shore,
And saw the ships appear and pass,
And threw stones at the Argonauts,
Being filled with indiscriminate ire
That tangled and perplexed his thoughts ;
But, like a hospitable host,
When strangers landed on the coast,
Heated himself red-hot with fire,
And hugged them in his arms, and
    pressed
Their bodies to his burning breast.

The Poet answered : " No, not thus
The legend rose ; it sprang at first
Out of the hunger and the thirst
In all men for the marvellous.
And thus it filled and satisfied
The imagination of mankind,
And this ideal to the mind
Was truer than historic fact.
Fancy enlarged and multiplied
The terrors of the awful name
Of Charlemagne, till he became
Armipotent in every act,
And, clothed in mystery, appeared
Not what men saw, but what they
    feared.

The Theologian said : " Perchance
Your chronicler in writing this
Had in his mind the Anabasis,
Where Xenophon describes the advance
Of Artaxerxes to the fight ;
At first the low gray cloud of dust,
And then a blackness o'er the fields
As of a passing thunder-gust,
Then flash of brazen armor bright,
And ranks of men, and spears up-thrust,

Bowmen and troops with wicker shields,
And cavalry equipped in white,
And chariots ranged in front of these
With scythes upon their axle-trees."

To this the Student answered : " Well,
I also have a tale to tell
Of Charlemagne ; a tale that throws
A softer light, more tinged with rose,
Than your grim apparition cast
Upon the darkness of the past.
Listen, and hear in English rhyme
What the good Monk of Lauresheim
Gives as the gossip of his time,
In mediæval Latin prose."

THE STUDENT'S TALE.

EMMA AND EGINHARD.

WHEN Alcuin taught the sons of Char-
    lemagne,
In the free schools of Aix, how kings
    should reign,
And with them taught the children of
    the poor
How subjects should be patient and en-
    dure,
He touched the lips of some, as best be-
    fit,
With honey from the hives of Holy
    Writ ;
Others intoxicated with the wine
Of ancient history, sweet but less divine ;
Some with the wholesome fruits of gram-
    mar fed ;
Others with mysteries of the stars o'er-
    head,
That hang suspended in the vaulted
    sky
Like lamps in some fair palace vast and
    high.

In sooth, it was a pleasant sight to see
That Saxon monk, with hood and ro-
    sary,
With inkhorn at his belt, and pen and
    book,
And mingled love and reverence in his
    look,
Or hear the cloister and the court repeat
The measured footfalls of his sandaled
    feet,
Or watch him with the pupils of his
    school,
Gentle of speech, but absolute of rule.

* See page 340.

Among them, always earliest in his place,
Was Eginhard, a youth of Frankish race,
Whose face was bright with flashes that
    forerun
The splendors of a yet unrisen sun.
To him all things were possible, and
    seemed
Not what he had accomplished, but had
    dreamed,
And what were tasks to others were his
    play,
The pastime of an idle holiday.

Smaragdo, Abbot of St. Michael's, said,
With many a shrug and shaking of the
    head,
Surely some demon must possess the lad,
Who showed more wit than ever school-
    boy had,
And learned his Trivium thus without
    the rod ;
But Alcuin said it was the grace of God.

Thus he grew up, in Logic point-device,
Perfect in Grammar, and in Rhetoric nice ;
Science of Numbers, Geometric art,
And lore of Stars, and Music knew by
    heart ;
A Minnesinger, long before the times
Of those who sang their love in Suabian
    rhymes.

The Emperor, when he heard this good
    report
Of Eginhard much buzzed about the
    court,
Said to himself, "This stripling seems
    to be
Purposely sent into the world for me ;
He shall become my scribe, and shall be
    schooled
In all the arts whereby the world is
    ruled."
Thus did the gentle Eginhard attain
To honor in the court of Charlemagne ;
Became the sovereign's favorite, his right
    hand,
So that his fame was great in all the land,
And all men loved him for his modest
    grace
And comeliness of figure and of face.
An inmate of the palace, yet recluse,
A man of books, yet sacred from abuse
Among the armed knights with spur on
    heel,
The tramp of horses and the clang of
    steel ;

And as the Emperor promised he was
    schooled
In all the arts by which the world is
    ruled.
But the one art supreme, whose law is
    fate,
The Emperor never dreamed of till too
    late.

Home from her convent to the palace
    came
The lovely Princess Emma, whose sweet
    name,
Whispered by seneschal or sung by bard,
Had often touched the soul of Eginhard.
He saw her from his window, as in state
She came, by knights attended through
    the gate ;
He saw her at the banquet of that day,
Fresh as the morn, and beautiful as May ;
He saw her in the garden, as she strayed
Among the flowers of summer with her
    maid,
And said to him, "O Eginhard, disclose
The meaning and the mystery of the
    rose" ;
And trembling he made answer : "In
    good sooth,
Its mystery is love, its meaning youth !"

How can I tell the signals and the signs
By which one heart another heart di-
    vines ?
How can I tell the many thousand ways
By which it keeps the secret it betrays ?

O mystery of love ! O strange romance !
Among the Peers and Paladins of France,
Shining in steel, and prancing on gay
    steeds,
Noble by birth, yet nobler by great deeds,
The Princess Emma had no words nor
    looks
But for this clerk, this man of thought
    and books.

The summer passed, the autumn came;
    the stalks
Of lilies blackened in the garden walks ;
The leaves fell, russet-golden and blood-
    red,
Love-letters thought the poet fancy-led,
Or Jove descending in a shower of gold
Into the lap of Danae of old ;
For poets cherish many a strange conceit,
And love transmutes all nature by its
    heat.

No more the garden lessons, nor the dark
And hurried meetings in the twilight
    park ;
But now the studious lamp, and the de-
    lights
Of firesides in the silent winter nights,
And watching from his window hour by
    hour
The light that burned in Princess Emma's
    tower.

At length one night, while musing by
    the fire,
O'ercome at last by his insane desire, —
For what will reckless love not do and
    dare ? —
He crossed the court, and climbed the
    winding stair,
With some feigned message in the Em-
    peror's name ;
But when he to the lady's presence came
He knelt down at her feet, until she
    laid
Her hand upon him, like a naked blade,
And whispered in his ear : " Arise, Sir
    Knight,
To my heart's level, O my heart's de-
    light."

And there he lingered till the crowing
    cock,
The Alectryon of the farmyard and the
    flock,
Sang his aubade with lusty voice and
    clear,
To tell the sleeping world that dawn was
    near.
And then they parted ; but at parting, lo !
They saw the palace courtyard white
    with snow,
And, placid as a nun, the moon on high
Gazing from cloudy cloisters of the sky.
" Alas ! " he said, " how hide the fatal
    line
Of footprints leading from thy door to
    mine,
And none returning ! " Ah, he little
    knew
What woman's wit, when put to proof,
    can do !

That night the Emperor, sleepless with
    the cares
And troubles that attend on state affairs,
Had risen before the dawn, and musing
    gazed
Into the silent night, as one amazed

To see the calm that reigned o'er all
    supreme,
When his own reign was but a troubled
    dream.
The moon lit up the gables capped with
    snow,
And the white roofs, and half the court
    below,
And he beheld a form, that seemed to
    cower
Beneath a burden, come from Emma's
    tower, —
A woman, who upon her shoulders bore
Clerk Eginhard to his own private door,
And then returned in haste, but still
    essayed
To tread the footprints she herself had
    made ;
And as she passed across the lighted
    space,
The Emperor saw his daughter Emma's
    face !

He started not ; he did not speak or
    moan,
But seemed as one who hath been turned
    to stone ;
And stood there like a statue, nor awoke
Out of his trance of pain, till morning
    broke,
Till the stars faded, and the moon went
    down,
And o'er the towers and steeples of the
    town
Came the gray daylight ; then the sun,
    who took
The empire of the world with sovereign
    look,
Suffusing with a soft and golden glow
All the dead landscape in its shroud of
    snow,
Touching with flame the tapering chapel
    spires,
Windows and roofs, and smoke of house-
    hold fires,
And kindling park and palace as he
    came ;
The stork's nest on the chimney seemed
    in flame.
And thus he stood till Eginhard ap-
    peared,
Demure and modest with his comely
    beard
And flowing flaxen tresses, come to
    ask,
As was his wont, the day's appointed
    task.

The Emperor looked upon him with a
     smile,
And gently said : "My son, wait yet
     awhile ;
This hour my council meets upon some
     great
And very urgent business of the state.
Come back within the hour. On thy
     return
The work appointed for thee shalt thou
     learn."

Having dismissed this gallant Trouba-
     dour,
He summoned straight his council, and
     secure
And steadfast in his purpose, from the
     throne
All the adventure of the night made
     known ;
Then asked for sentence ; and with eager
     breath
Some answered banishment, and others
     death.

Then spake the king : "Your sentence
     is not mine ;
Life is the gift of God, and is divine ;
Nor from these palace walls shall one
     depart
Who carries such a secret in his heart ;
My better judgment points another way.
Good Alcuin, I remember how one day
When my Pepino asked you, 'What
     are men ?'
You wrote upon his tablets with your
     pen,
'Guests of the grave and travellers that
     pass !'
This being true of all men, we, alas !
Being all fashioned of the selfsame dust,
Let us be merciful as well as just ;
This passing traveller, who hath stolen
     away
The brightest jewel of my crown to-day,
Shall of himself the precious gem restore ;
By giving it, I make it mine once more.
Over those fatal footprints I will throw
My ermine mantle like another snow."

Then Eginhard was summoned to the
     hall,
And entered, and in presence of them
     all,
The Emperor said : "My son, for thou
     to me
Hast been a son, and evermore shalt be,

Long hast thou served thy sovereign,
     and thy zeal
Pleads to me with importunate appeal,
While I have been forgetful to requite
Thy service and affection as was right.
But now the hour is come, when I, thy
     Lord,
Will crown thy love with such supreme
     reward,
A gift so precious kings have striven in
     vain
To win it from the hands of Charle-
     magne."

Then sprang the portals of the chamber
     wide,
And Princess Emma entered, in the
     pride
Of birth and beauty, that in part o'er-
     came
The conscious terror and the blush of
     shame.
And the good Emperor rose up from his
     throne,
And taking her white hand within his
     own
Placed it in Eginhard's, and said : "My
     son,
This is the gift thy constant zeal hath
     won ;
Thus I repay the royal debt I owe,
And cover up the footprints in the snow."

INTERLUDE.

Thus ran the Student's pleasant rhyme
Of Eginhard and love and youth ;
Some doubted its historic truth,
But while they doubted, ne'ertheless
Saw in it gleams of truthfulness,
And thanked the Monk of Lauresheim.

This they discussed in various mood ;
Then in the silence that ensued
Was heard a sharp and sudden sound
As of a bowstring snapped in air ;
And the Musician with a bound
Sprang up in terror from his chair,
And for a moment listening stood,
Then strode across the room, and found
His dear, his darling violin
Still lying safe asleep within
Its little cradle, like a child
That gives a sudden cry of pain,
And wakes to fall asleep again ;
And as he looked at it and smiled,

By the uncertain light beguiled,
Despair ! two strings were broken in
    twain.

While all lamented and made moan,
With many a sympathetic word
As if the loss had been their own,
Deeming the tones they might have
    heard
Sweeter than they had heard before,
They saw the Landlord at the door,
The missing man, the portly Squire !
He had not entered, but he stood
With both arms full of seasoned wood,
To feed the much-devouring fire,
That like a lion in a cage
Lashed its long tail and roared with rage.

The missing man ! Ah, yes, they said,
Missing, but whither had he fled ?
Where had he hidden himself away ?
No farther than the barn or shed ;
He had not hidden himself, nor fled ;
How should he pass the rainy day
But in his barn with hens and hay,
Or mending harness, cart, or sled ?
Now, having come, he needs must stay
And tell his tale as well as they.

The Landlord answered only : "These
Are logs from the dead apple-trees
Of the old orchard planted here
By the first Howe of Sudbury.
Nor oak nor maple has so clear
A flame, or burns so quietly,
Or leaves an ash so clean and white " ;
Thinking by this to put aside

The impending tale that terrified ;
When suddenly, to his delight,
The Theologian interposed,
Saying that when the door was closed,
And they had stopped that draft of cold,
Unpleasant night air, he proposed
To tell a tale world-wide apart
From that the Student had just told ;
World-wide apart, and yet akin,
As showing that the human heart
Beats on forever as of old,
As well beneath the snow-white fold
Of Quaker kerchief, as within
Sendal or silk or cloth of gold,
And without preface would begin.

And then the clamorous clock struck
    eight,
Deliberate, with sonorous chime
Slow measuring out the march of time,
Like some grave Consul of old Rome
In Jupiter's temple driving home
The nails that marked the year and date.
Thus interrupted in his rhyme,
The Theologian needs must wait ;
But quoted Horace, where he sings
The dire Necessity of things,
That drives into the roofs sublime
Of new-built houses of the great
The adamantine nails of Fate.

When ceased the little carillon
To herald from its wooden tower
The important transit of the hour,
The Theologian hastened on,
Content to be allowed at last
To sing his Idyl of the Past.

THE THEOLOGIAN'S TALE.

ELIZABETH.

I.

" AH, how short are the days ! How soon the night overtakes us !
In the old country the twilight is longer ; but here in the forest
Suddenly comes the dark, with hardly a pause in its coming,
Hardly a moment between the two lights, the day and the lamplight ;
Yet how grand is the winter ! How spotless the snow is, and perfect ! "

Thus spake Elizabeth Haddon at nightfall to Hannah the housemaid,
As in the farm-house kitchen, that served for kitchen and parlor,
By the window she sat with her work, and looked on a landscape
White as the great white sheet that Peter saw in his vision,
By the four corners let down and descending out of the heavens.
Covered with snow were the forests of pine, and the fields and the meadows.

Nothing was dark but the sky, and the distant Delaware flowing
Down from its native hills, a peaceful and bountiful river.

Then with a smile on her lips made answer Hannah the housemaid :
"Beautiful winter ! yea, the winter is beautiful, surely,
If one could only walk like a fly with one's feet on the ceiling.
But the great Delaware River is not like the Thames, as we saw it
Out of our upper windows in Rotherhithe Street in the Borough,
Crowded with masts and sails of vessels coming and going ;
Here there is nothing but pines, with patches of snow on their branches.
There is snow in the air, and see ! it is falling already ;
All the roads will be blocked, and I pity Joseph to-morrow,
Breaking his way through the drifts, with his sled and oxen ; and then, too,
How in all the world shall we get to Meeting on First-Day ?"

But Elizabeth checked her, and answered, mildly reproving :
"Surely the Lord will provide ; for unto the snow he sayeth,
Be thou on the earth, the good Lord sayeth ; he is it
Giveth snow like wool, like ashes scatters the hoar-frost."
So she folded her work and laid it away in her basket.

Meanwhile Hannah the housemaid had closed and fastened the shutters,
Spread the cloth, and lighted the lamp on the table, and placed there
Plates and cups from the dresser, the brown rye loaf, and the butter
Fresh from the dairy, and then, protecting her hand with a holder,
Took from the crane in the chimney the steaming and simmering kettle,
Poised it aloft in the air, and filled up the earthen teapot,
Made in Delft, and adorned with quaint and wonderful figures.

Then Elizabeth said, "Lo ! Joseph is long on his errand.
I have sent him away with a hamper of food and of clothing
For the poor in the village. A good lad and cheerful is Joseph ;
In the right place is his heart, and his hand is ready and willing."

Thus in praise of her servant she spake, and Hannah the housemaid
Laughed with her eyes, as she listened, but governed her tongue, and was silent,
While her mistress went on : "The house is far from the village ;
We should be lonely here, were it not for Friends that in passing
Sometimes tarry o'ernight, and make us glad by their coming."

Thereupon answered Hannah the housemaid, the thrifty, the frugal :
"Yea, they come and they tarry, as if thy house were a tavern ;
Open to all are its doors, and they come and go like the pigeons
In and out of the holes of the pigeon-house over the hayloft,
Cooing and smoothing their feathers and basking themselves in the sunshine."

But in meekness of spirit, and calmly, Elizabeth answered :
"All I have is the Lord's, not mine to give or withhold it ;
I but distribute his gifts to the poor, and to those of his people
Who in journeyings often surrender their lives to his service.
His, not mine, are the gifts, and only so far can I make them
Mine, as in giving I add my heart to whatever is given.
Therefore my excellent father first built this house in the clearing ;
Though he came not himself, I came ; for the Lord was my guidance,
Leading me here for this service. We must not grudge, then, to others
Ever the cup of cold water, or crumbs that fall from our table."

Thus rebuked, for a season was silent the penitent housemaid ;
And Elizabeth said in tones even sweeter and softer :
" Dost thou remember, Hannah, the great May-Meeting in London,
When I was still a child, how we sat in the silent assembly,
Waiting upon the Lord in patient and passive submission ?
No one spake, till at length a young man, a stranger, John Estaugh,
Moved by the Spirit, rose, as if he were John the Apostle,
Speaking such words of power that they bowed our hearts, as a strong wind
Bends the grass of the fields, or grain that is ripe for the sickle.
Thoughts of him to-day have been oft borne inward upon me,
Wherefore I do not know ; but strong is the feeling within me
That once more I shall see a face I have never forgotten."

II.

E'en as she spake they heard the musical jangle of sleigh-bells,
First far off, with a dreamy sound and faint in the distance,
Then growing nearer and louder, and turning into the farmyard,
Till it stopped at the door, with sudden creaking of runners.
Then there were voices heard as of two men talking together,
And to herself, as she listened, upbraiding said Hannah the housemaid,
" It is Joseph come back, and I wonder what stranger is with him."

Down from its nail she took and lighted the great tin lantern
Pierced with holes, and round, and roofed like the top of a lighthouse,
And went forth to receive the coming guest at the doorway,
Casting into the dark a network of glimmer and shadow
Over the falling snow, the yellow sleigh, and the horses,
And the forms of men, snow-covered, looming gigantic.
Then giving Joseph the lantern, she entered the house with the stranger.
Youthful he was and tall, and his cheeks aglow with the night air ;
And as he entered, Elizabeth rose, and, going to meet him,
As if an unseen power had announced and preceded his presence,
And he had come as one whose coming had long been expected,
Quietly gave him her hand, and said, " Thou art welcome, John Estaugh.
And the stranger replied, with staid and quiet behavior,
" Dost thou remember me still, Elizabeth ?   After so many
Years have passed, it seemeth a wonderful thing that I find thee.
Surely the hand of the Lord conducted me here to thy threshold.
For as I journeyed along, and pondered alone and in silence
On his ways, that are past finding out, I saw in the snow-mist,
Seemingly weary with travel, a wayfarer, who by the wayside
Paused and waited.   Forthwith I remembered Queen Candace's eunuch
How on the way that goes down from Jerusalem unto Gaza,
Reading Esaias the Prophet, he journeyed, and spake unto Philip,
Praying him to come up and sit in his chariot with him.
So I greeted the man, and he mounted the sledge beside me,
And as we talked on the way he told me of thee and thy homestead,
How, being led by the light of the Spirit, that never deceiveth,
Full of zeal for the work of the Lord, thou hadst come to this country.
And I remembered thy name, and thy father and mother in England,
And on my journey have stopped to see thee, Elizabeth Haddon,
Wishing to strengthen thy hand in the labors of love thou art doing."

And Elizabeth answered with confident voice, and serenely
Looking into his face with her innocent eyes as she answered,

"Surely the hand of the Lord is in it; his Spirit hath led thee
Out of the darkness and storm to the light and peace of my fireside."

Then, with stamping of feet, the door was opened, and Joseph
Entered, bearing the lantern, and, carefully blowing the light out,
Hung it up on its nail, and all sat down to their supper;
For underneath that roof was no distinction of persons,
But one family only, one heart, one hearth, and one household.

When the supper was ended they drew their chairs to the fireplace,
Spacious, open-hearted, profuse of flame and of firewood,
Lord of forests unfelled, and not a gleaner of fagots,
Spreading its arms to embrace with inexhaustible bounty
All who fled from the cold, exultant, laughing at winter!
Only Hannah the housemaid was busy in clearing the table,
Coming and going, and bustling about in closet and chamber.

Then Elizabeth told her story again to John Estaugh,
Going far back to the past, to the early days of her childhood;
How she had waited and watched, in all her doubts and besetments
Comforted with the extendings and holy, sweet inflowings
Of the spirit of love, till the voice imperative sounded,
And she obeyed the voice, and cast in her lot with her people
Here in the desert land, and God would provide for the issue.

Meanwhile Joseph sat with folded hands, and demurely
Listened, or seemed to listen, and in the silence that followed
Nothing was heard for a while but the step of Hannah the housemaid
Walking the floor overhead, and setting the chambers in order.
And Elizabeth said, with a smile of compassion, "The maiden
Hath a light heart in her breast, but her feet are heavy and awkward."
Inwardly Joseph laughed, but governed his tongue, and was silent.

Then came the hour of sleep, death's counterfeit, nightly rehearsal
Of the great Silent Assembly, the Meeting of shadows, where no man
Speaketh, but all are still, and the peace and rest are unbroken!
Silently over that house the blessing of slumber descended.
But when the morning dawned, and the sun uprose in his splendor,
Breaking his way through clouds that encumbered his path in the heavens,
Joseph was seen with his sled and oxen breaking a pathway
Through the drifts of snow; the horses already were harnessed,
And John Estaugh was standing and taking leave at the threshold,
Saying that he should return at the Meeting in May; while above them
Hannah the housemaid, the homely, was looking out of the attic,
Laughing aloud at Joseph, then suddenly closing the casement,
As the bird in a cuckoo-clock peeps out of its window,
Then disappears again, and closes the shutter behind it.

III.

Now was the winter gone, and the snow; and Robin the Redbreast,
Boasted on bush and tree it was he, it was he and no other
That had covered with leaves the Babes in the Wood, and blithely
All the birds sang with him, and little cared for his boasting,
Or for his Babes in the Wood, or the Cruel Uncle, and only
Sang for the mates they had chosen, and cared for the nests they were building.

With them, but more sedately and meekly, Elizabeth Haddon
Sang in her inmost heart, but her lips were silent and songless.
Thus came the lovely spring with a rush of blossoms and music,
Flooding the earth with flowers, and the air with melodies vernal.

Then it came to pass, one pleasant morning, that slowly
Up the road there came a cavalcade, as of pilgrims,
Men and women, wending their way to the Quarterly Meeting
In the neighboring town ; and with them came riding John Estaugh.
At Elizabeth's door they stopped to rest, and alighting
Tasted the currant wine, and the bread of rye, and the honey
Brought from the hives, that stood by the sunny wall of the garden ;
Then remounted their horses, refreshed, and continued their journey,
And Elizabeth with them, and Joseph, and Hannah the housemaid.
But, as they started, Elizabeth lingered a little, and leaning
Over her horse's neck, in a whisper said to John Estaugh :
"Tarry awhile behind, for I have something to tell thee,
Not to be spoken lightly, nor in the presence of others ;
Them it concerneth not, only thee and me it concerneth."
And they rode slowly along through the woods, conversing together.
It was a pleasure to breathe the fragrant air of the forest ;
It was a pleasure to live on that bright and happy May morning !

Then Elizabeth said, though still with a certain reluctance,
As if impelled to reveal a secret she fain would have guarded :
"I will no longer conceal what is laid upon me to tell thee ;
I have received from the Lord a charge to love thee, John Estaugh."

And John Estaugh made answer, surprised by the words she had spoken,
"Pleasant to me are thy converse, thy ways, thy meekness of spirit ;
Pleasant thy frankness of speech, and thy soul's immaculate whiteness,
Love without dissimulation, a holy and inward adorning.
But I have yet no light to lead me, no voice to direct me.
When the Lord's work is done, and the toil and the labor completed
He hath appointed to me, I will gather into the stillness
Of my own heart awhile, and listen and wait for his guidance."

Then Elizabeth said, not troubled nor wounded in spirit,
"So is it best, John Estaugh. We will not speak of it further.
It hath been laid upon me to tell thee this, for to-morrow
Thou art going away, across the sea, and I know not
When I shall see thee more ; but if the Lord hath decreed it,
Thou wilt return again to seek me here and to find me."
And they rode onward in silence, and entered the town with the others.

IV.

Ships that pass in the night, and speak each other in passing,
Only a signal shown and a distant voice in the darkness ;
So on the ocean of life we pass and speak one another,
Only a look and a voice, then darkness again and a silence.

Now went on as of old the quiet life of the homestead.
Patient and unrepining Elizabeth labored, in all things
Mindful not of herself, but bearing the burdens of others,
Always thoughtful and kind and untroubled ; and Hannah the housemaid
Diligent early and late, and rosy with washing and scouring,

Still as of old disparaged the eminent merits of Joseph,
And was at times reproved for her light and frothy behavior,
For her shy looks, and her careless words, and her evil surmisings,
Being pressed down somewhat, like a cart with sheaves overladen,
As she would sometimes say to Joseph, quoting the Scriptures.

Meanwhile John Estaugh departed across the sea, and departing
Carried hid in his heart a secret sacred and precious,
Filling its chambers with fragrance, and seeming to him in its sweetness
Mary's ointment of spikenard, that filled all the house with its odor.
O lost days of delight, that are wasted in doubting and waiting !
O lost hours and days in which we might have been happy !
But the light shone at last, and guided his wavering footsteps,
And at last came the voice, imperative, questionless, certain.

Then John Estaugh came back o'er the sea for the gift that was offered,
Better than houses and lands, the gift of a woman's affection.
And on the First-Day that followed, he rose in the Silent Assembly,
Holding in his strong hand a hand that trembled a little,
Promising to be kind and true and faithful in all things.
Such were the marriage-rites of John and Elizabeth Estaugh.

And not otherwise Joseph, the honest, the diligent servant,
Sped in his bashful wooing with homely Hannah the housemaid ;
For when he asked her the question, she answered, " Nay " ; and then added
" But thee may make believe, and see what will come of it, Joseph."

INTERLUDE.

" A PLEASANT and a winsome tale,"
The Student said, " though somewhat
        pale
And quiet in its coloring,
As if it caught its tone and air
From the gray suits that Quakers wear ;
Yet worthy of some German bard,
Hebel, or Voss, or Eberhard,
Who love of humble themes to sing,
In humble verse ; but no more true
Than was the tale I told to you."

The Theologian made reply,
And with some warmth, " That I deny ;
'T is no invention of my own,
But something well and widely known
To readers of a riper age,
Writ by the skilful hand that wrote
The Indian tale of Hobomok,
And Philothea's classic page.
I found it like a waif afloat,
Or dulse uprooted from its rock,
On the swift tides that ebb and flow
In daily papers, and at flood
Bear freighted vessels to and fro,
But later, when the ebb is low,
Leave a long waste of sand and mud."

" It matters little," quoth the Jew ;
" The cloak of truth is lined with lies,
Sayeth some proverb old and wise ;
And Love is master of all arts,
And puts it into human hearts
The strangest things to say and do."

And here the controversy closed
Abruptly, ere 't was well begun ;
For the Sicilian interposed
With, " Lordlings, listen, every one
That listen may, unto a tale
That 's merrier than the nightingale ;
A tale that cannot boast, forsooth,
A single rag or shred of truth ;
That does not leave the mind in doubt
As to the with it or without ;
A naked falsehood and absurd
As mortal ever told or heard.
Therefore I tell it ; or, maybe,
Simply because it pleases me."

THE SICILIAN'S TALE.

THE MONK OF CASAL-MAGGIORE.

ONCE on a time, some centuries ago,
    In the hot sunshine two Franciscan
        friars

Wended their weary way with footsteps
   slow
Back to their convent, whose white
   walls and spires
Gleamed on the hillside like a patch of
   snow ;
Covered with dust they were, and torn
   by briers,
And bore like sumpter-mules upon their
   backs
The badge of poverty, their beggar's
   sacks.

The first was Brother Anthony, a spare
   And silent man, with pallid cheeks and
   thin,
Much given to vigils, penance, fasting,
   prayer,
   Solemn and gray, and worn with dis-
   cipline,
As if his body but white ashes were,
   Heaped on the living coals that glowed
   within ;
A simple monk, like many of his day,
Whose instinct was to listen and obey.

A different man was Brother Timothy,
   Of larger mould and of a coarser paste ;
A rubicund and stalwart monk was he,
   Broad in the shoulders, broader in the
   waist,
Who often filled the dull refectory
   With noise by which the convent was
   disgraced,
But to the mass-book gave but little
   heed,
By reason he had never learned to read.

Now, as they passed the outskirts of a
   wood,
   They saw, with mingled pleasure and
   surprise,
Fast tethered to a tree an ass, that stood
   Lazily winking his large, limpid eyes.
The farmer Gilbert   that neighborhood
   His owner was, who, looking for sup-
   plies
Of fagots, deeper in the wood had strayed,
Leaving his beast to ponder in the shade.

As soon as Brother Timothy espied
   The patient animal, he said : " Good-
   lack !
Thus for our needs doth Providence provide ;
   We 'll lay our wallets on the creature's
   back."

20

This being done, he leisurely untied
   From head and neck the halter of the
   jack,
And put it round his own, and to the
   tree
Stood tethered fast as if the ass were he.

And, bursting forth into a merry laugh,
   He cried to Brother Anthony: "Away !
And drive the ass before you with your
   staff ;
   And when you reach the convent you
   may say
You left me at a farm, half tired and
   half
   Ill with a fever, for a night and day,
And that the farmer lent this ass to bear
Our wallets, that are heavy with good
   fare."

Now Brother Anthony, who knew the
   pranks
   Of Brother Timothy, would not persuade
Or reason with him on his quirks and
   cranks,
   But, being obedient, silently obeyed ;
And, smiting with his staff the ass's
   flanks,
   Drove him before him over hill and
   glade,
Safe with his provend to the convent
   gate,
Leaving poor Brother Timothy to his
   fate.

Then Gilbert, laden with fagots for his
   fire,
   Forth issued from the wood, and stood
   aghast
To see the ponderous body of the friar
   Standing where he had left his donkey
   last.
Trembling he stood, and dared not ven-
   ture nigher,
   But stared, and gaped, and crossed
   himself full fast ;
For, being credulous and of little wit,
He thought it was some demon from the
   pit.

While speechless and bewildered thus he
   gazed,
   And dropped his load of fagots on the
   ground,
Quoth Brother Timothy : " Be not
   amazed

That where you left a donkey should
    be found
A poor Franciscan friar, half-starved, and
    crazed,
    Standing demure and with a halter
        bound ;
But set me free, and hear the piteous
    story
Of Brother Timothy of Casal-Maggiore.

" I am a sinful man, although you see
    I wear the consecrated cowl and cape ;
You never owned an ass, but you owned
    me,
    Changed and transformed from my
        own natural shape
All for the deadly sin of gluttony,
    From which I could not otherwise
        escape,
Than by this penance, dieting on grass,
And being worked and beaten as an ass.

" Think of the ignominy I endured ;
    Think of the miserable life I led,
The toil and blows to which I was inured,
    My wretched lodging in a windy shed,
My scanty fare so grudgingly procured,
    The damp and musty straw that formed
        my bed !
But, having done this penance for my
    sins,
My life as man and monk again begins."

The simple Gilbert, hearing words like
    these,
    Was conscience-stricken, and fell down
        apace
Before the friar upon his bended knees,
    And with a suppliant voice implored
        his grace ;
And the good monk, now very much at
    ease,
    Granted him pardon with a smiling
        face,
Nor could refuse to be that night his
    guest,
It being late, and he in need of rest.

Upon a hillside, where the olive thrives,
    With figures painted on its white-
        washed walls,
The cottage stood ; and near the hum-
    ming hives
    Made murmurs as of far-off water-
        falls ;
A place where those who love secluded
    lives

Might live content, and, free from
    noise and brawls,
Like Claudian's Old Man of Verona here
Measure by fruits the slow-revolving
    year.

And, coming to this cottage of content,
    They found his children, and the
        buxom wench
His wife, Dame Cicely, and his father,
    bent
    With years and labor, seated on a
        bench,
Repeating over some obscure event
    In the old wars of Milanese and
        French ;
All welcomed the Franciscan, with a sense
Of sacred awe and humble reverence.

When Gilbert told them what had come
    to pass,
    How beyond question, cavil, or sur-
        mise,
Good Brother Timothy had been their ass,
    You should have seen the wonder in
        their eyes ;
You should have heard them cry,
    " Alas ! alas ! "
Have heard their lamentations and
    their sighs !
For all believed the story, and began
To see a saint in this afflicted man.

Forthwith there was prepared a grand
    repast,
    To satisfy the craving of the friar
After so rigid and prolonged a fast ;
    The bustling housewife stirred the
        kitchen fire ;
Then her two barnyard fowls, her best
    and last,
    Were put to death, at her express de-
        sire,
And served up with a salad in a bowl,
And flasks of country wine to crown the
    whole.

It would not be believed should I repeat
    How hungry Brother Timothy ap-
        peared ;
It was a pleasure but to see him eat,
    His white teeth flashing through his
        russet beard,
His face aglow and flushed with wine
    and meat,
    His roguish eyes that rolled and
        laughed and leered !

Lord ! how he drank the blood-red country wine
As if the village vintage were divine !

And all the while he talked without sur-
cease,
And told his merry tales with jovial
glee
That never flagged, but rather did in-
crease,
And laughed aloud as if insane were he,
And wagged his red beard, matted like a
fleece,
And cast such glances at Dame Cicely
That Gilbert now grew angry with his
guest,
And thus in words his rising wrath ex-
pressed.

" Good father," said he, "easily we see
How needful in some persons, and how
right,
Mortification of the flesh may be.
The indulgence you have given it to-
night,
After long penance, clearly proves to me
Your strength against temptation is
but slight,
And shows the dreadful peril you are in
Of a relapse into your deadly sin.

"To-morrow morning, with the rising
sun,
Go back unto your convent, nor refrain
From fasting and from scourging, for you
run
Great danger to become an ass again,
Since monkish flesh and asinine are one ;
Therefore be wise, nor longer here re-
main,
Unless you wish the scourge should be
applied
By other hands, that will not spare your
hide.'"

When this the monk had heard, his
color fled
And then returned, like lightning in
the air,
Till he was all one blush from foot to
head,
And even the bald spot in his russet
hair
Turned from its usual pallor to bright
red !
The old man was asleep upon his chair.
Then all retired, and sank into the deep
And helpless imbecility of sleep.

They slept until the dawn of day drew
near,
Till the cock should have crowed, but
did not crow,
For they had slain the shining chanti-
cleer
And eaten him for supper, as you know.
The monk was up betimes and of good
cheer,
And, having breakfasted, made haste
to go,
As if he heard the distant matin bell,
And had but little time to say farewell.

Fresh was the morning as the breath of
kine ;
Odors of herbs commingled with the
sweet
Balsamic exhalations of the pine ;
A haze was in the air presaging heat ;
Uprose the sun above the Apennine,
And all the misty valleys at its feet
Were full of the delirious song of birds,
Voices of men, and bells, and low of
herds.

All this to Brother Timothy was naught ;
He did not care for scenery, nor here
His busy fancy found the thing it
sought ;
But when he saw the convent walls
appear,
And smoke from kitchen chimneys up-
ward caught
And whirled aloft into the atmos-
phere,
He quickened his slow footsteps, like a
beast
That scents the stable a league off at
least.

And as he entered through the convent
gate
He saw there in the court the ass,
who stood
Twirling his ears about, and seemed to
wait,
Just as he found him waiting in the
wood ;
And told the Prior that, to alleviate
The daily labors of the brotherhood,
The owner, being a man of means and
thrift,
Bestowed him on the convent as a gift.

And thereupon the Prior for many days
Revolved this serious matter in his
mind,

And turned it over many different
    ways,
  Hoping that some safe issue he might
    find ;
But stood in fear of what the world
    would say,
  If he accepted presents of this kind,
Employing beasts of burden for the
    packs,
  That lazy monks should carry on their
    backs.

Then, to avoid all scandal of the sort,
  And stop the mouth of cavil, he
    decreed
That he would cut the tedious matter
    short,
  And sell the ass with all convenient
    speed,
Thus saving the expense of his sup-
    port,
  And hoarding something for a time of
    need.
So he despatched him to the neighbor-
    ing Fair,
And freed himself from cumber and from
    care.

It happened now by chance, as some
    might say,
  Others perhaps would call it destiny,
Gilbert was at the Fair ; and heard a
    bray,
  And nearer came, and saw that it was
    he,
And whispered in his ear, "Ah, lacka-
    day !
  Good father, the rebellious flesh, I
    see,
Has changed you back into an ass
    again,
And all my admonitions were in vain."

The ass, who felt this breathing in his
    ear,
  Did not turn round to look, but
    shook his head,
As if he were not pleased these words to
    hear,
  And contradicted all that had been
    said.
And this made Gilbert cry in voice more
    clear,
  "I know you well ; your hair is
    russet-red ;
Do not deny it ; for you are the same
Franciscan friar, and Timothy by name."

The ass, though now the secret had
    come out,
  Was obstinate, and shook his head
    again ;
Until a crowd was gathered round about
  To hear this dialogue between the
    twain ;
And raised their voices in a noisy shout
  When Gilbert tried to make the
    matter plain,
And flouted him and mocked him all
    day long
With laughter and with jibes and scraps
    of song.

"If this be Brother Timothy," they
    cried,
  "Buy him, and feed him on the
    tenderest grass ;
Thou canst not do too much for one so
    tried
  As to be twice transformed into an
    ass."
So simple Gilbert bought him, and un-
    tied
  His halter, and o'er mountain and
    morass
He led him homeward, talking as he
    went
Of good behavior and a mind content.

The children saw them coming, and
    advanced,
  Shouting with joy, and hung about
    his neck, —
Not Gilbert's, but the ass's, — round
    him danced,
  And wove green garlands where-
    withal to deck
His sacred person ; for again it chanced
  Their childish feelings, without rein
    or check,
Could not discriminate in any way
A donkey from a friar of Orders Gray.

"O Brother Timothy," the children
    said,
  "You have come back to us just as
    before ;
We were afraid, and thought that you
    were dead,
  And we should never see you any
    more."
And then they kissed the white star on
    his head,
  That like a birth-mark or a badge he
    wore,

And patted him upon the neck and face,
And said a thousand things with child-
    ish grace.

Thenceforward and forever he was known
As Brother Timothy, and led alway
A life of luxury, till he had grown
    Ungrateful, being stuffed with corn
      and hay,
And very vicious.   Then in angry tone,
    Rousing himself, poor Gilbert said one
      day,
" When simple kindness is misunder-
    stood
A little flagellation may do good."

His many vices need not here be told ;
    Among them was a habit that he
      had
Of flinging up his heels at young and
    old,
    Breaking his halter, running off like
      mad
O'er pasture-lands and meadow, wood
    and wold,
    And other misdemeanors quite as
      bad ;
But worst of all was breaking from his
    shed
At night, and ravaging the cabbage-bed.

So Brother Timothy went back once
    more
To his old life of labor and distress ;
Was beaten worse than he had been be-
    fore.
    And now, instead of comfort and ca-
      ress,
Came labors manifold and trials sore ;
    And as his toils increased his food
      grew less,
Until at last the great consoler, Death,
Ended his many sufferings with his
    breath.

Great was the lamentation when he died ;
    And mainly that he died impenitent ;
Dame Cicely bewailed, the children cried,
    The old man still remembered the
      event
In the French war, and Gilbert magni-
    fied
    His many virtues, as he came and
      went,
And said : " Heaven pardon Brother
    Timothy,
And keep us from the sin of gluttony."

INTERLUDE.

" SIGNOR LUIGI," said the Jew,
When the Sicilian's tale was told,
" The were-wolf is a legend old,
But the were-ass is something new,
And yet for one I think it true.
The days of wonder have not ceased ;
If there are beasts in forms of men,
As sure it happens now and then,
Why may not man become a beast,
In way of punishment at least ?

" But this I will not now discuss ,
I leave the theme, that we may thus
Remain within the realm of song.
The story that I told before,
Though not acceptable to all,
At least you did not find too long.
I beg you, let me try again,
With something in a different vein,
Before you bid the curtain fall.
Meanwhile keep watch upon the door,
Nor let the Landlord leave his chair,
Lest he should vanish into air,
And thus elude our search once more."

Thus saying, from his lips he blew
A little cloud of perfumed breath,
And then, as if it were a clew
To lead his footsteps safely through,
Began his tale as followeth.

THE SPANISH JEW'S SECOND TALE.

SCANDERBEG.

THE battle is fought and won
By King Ladislaus the Hun,
In fire of hell and death's frost
On the day of Pentecost.
And in rout before his path
From the field of battle red
Flee all that are not dead
Of the army of Amurath.

In the darkness of the night
Iskander, the pride and boast
Of that mighty Othman host,
With his routed Turks, takes flight
From the battle fought and lost
On the day of Pentecost ;
Leaving behind him dead
The army of Amurath,
The vanguard as it led,

The rearguard as it fled,
Mown down in the bloody swath
Of the battle's aftermath.

But he cared not for Hospodars,
Nor for Baron or Voivode,
As on through the night he rode
And gazed at the fateful stars,
That were shining overhead ;
But smote his steed with his staff,
And smiled to himself, and said :
" This is the time to laugh."

In the middle of the night,
In a halt of the hurrying flight,
There came a Scribe of the King
Wearing his signet ring,
And said in a voice severe :
" This is the first dark blot
On thy name, George Castriot !
Alas ! why art thou here,
And the army of Amurath slain,
And left on the battle plain ? "

And Iskander answered and said :
" They lie on the bloody sod
By the hoofs of horses trod ;
But this was the decree
Of the watchers overhead ;
For the war belongeth to God,
And in battle who are we,
Who are we, that shall withstand
The wind of his lifted hand ? "

Then he bade them bind with chains
This man of books and brains ;
And the Scribe said : " What misdeed
Have I done, that, without need,
Thou doest to me this thing ? "
And Iskander answering
Said unto him : " Not one
Misdeed to me hast thou done ;
But for fear that thou shouldst run
And hide thyself from me,
Have I done this unto thee.

" Now write me a writing, O Scribe,
And a blessing be on thy tribe !
A writing sealed with thy ring,
To King Amurath's Pasha
In the city of Croia,
The city moated and walled,
That he surrender the same
In the name of my master, the King ;
For what is writ in his name
Can never be recalled."

And the Scribe bowed low in dread,
And unto Iskander said :
" Allah is great and just,
But we are as ashes and dust ;
How shall I do this thing,
When I know that my guilty head
Will be forfeit to the King ? "

Then swift as a shooting star
The curved and shining blade
Of Iskander's scimetar
From its sheath, with jewels bright,
Shot, as he thundered : " Write ! "
And the trembling Scribe obeyed,
And wrote in the fitful glare
Of the bivouac fire apart,
With the chill of the midnight air
On his forehead white and bare,
And the chill of death in his heart.

Then again Iskander cried :
" Now follow whither I ride,
For here thou must not stay.
Thou shalt be as my dearest friend,
And honors without end
Shall surround thee on every side,
And attend thee night and day."
But the sullen Scribe replied :
" Our pathways here divide ;
Mine leadeth not thy way."

And even as he spoke
Fell a sudden scimetar-stroke,
When no one else was near ;
And the Scribe sank to the ground,
As a stone, pushed from the brink
Of a black pool, might sink
With a sob and disappear ;
And no one saw the deed ;
And in the stillness around
No sound was heard but the sound
Of the hoofs of Iskander's steed,
As forward he sprang with a bound.

Then onward he rode and afar,
With scarce three hundred men,
Through river and forest and fen,
O'er the mountains of Argentar ;
And his heart was merry within,
When he crossed the river Drin,
And saw in the gleam of the morn
The White Castle Ak-Hissar,
The city Croia called,
The city moated and walled,
The city where he was born, —
And above it the morning star.

Then his trumpeters in the van
On their silver bugles blew,
And in crowds about him ran
Albanian and Turkoman,
That the sound together drew.
And he feasted with his friends,
And when they were warm with wine,
He said : " O friends of mine,
Behold what fortune sends,
And what the fates design !
King Amurath commands
That my father's wide domain,
This city and all its lands,
Shall be given to me again."

Then to the Castle White
He rode in regal state,
And entered in at the gate
In all his arms bedight,
And gave to the Pasha
Who ruled in Croia
The writing of the King,
Sealed with his signet ring.
And the Pasha bowed his head,
And after a silence said :
" Allah is just and great !
I yield to the will divine,
The city and lands are thine ;
Who shall contend with fate ?"

Anon from the castle walls
The crescent banner falls,
And the crowd beholds instead,
Like a portent in the sky,
Iskander's banner fly,
The Black Eagle with double head ;
And a shout ascends on high,
For men's souls are tired of the Turks,
And their wicked ways and works,
That have made of Ak-Hissar
A city of the plague ;
And the loud, exultant cry
That echoes wide and far
Is : " Long live Scanderbeg !"

It was thus Iskander came
Once more unto his own ;
And the tidings, like the flame
Of a conflagration blown
By the winds of summer, ran,
Till the land was in a blaze,
And the cities far and near,
Sayeth Ben Joshua Ben Meir,
In his Book of the Words of the
      Days,
" Were taken as a man
Would take the tip of his ear."

INTERLUDE.

" Now that is after my own heart,"
The Poet cried ; " one understands
Your swarthy hero Scanderbeg,
Gauntlet on hand and boot on leg,
And skilled in every warlike art,
Riding through his Albanian lands,
And following the auspicious star
That shone for him o'er Ak-Hissar."

The Theologian added here
His word of praise not less sincere,
Although he ended with a jibe ;
" The hero of romance and song
Was born," he said, " to right the
            wrong ;
And I approve ; but all the same
That bit of treason with the Scribe
Adds nothing to your hero's fame."

The Student praised the good old times,
And liked the canter of the rhymes,
That had a hoofbeat in their sound ;
But longed some further word to hear
Of the old chronicler Ben Meir,
And where his volume might be found.
The tall Musician walked the room
With folded arms and gleaming eyes,
As if he saw the Vikings rise,
Gigantic shadows in the gloom ;
And much he talked of their emprise,
And meteors seen in Northern skies,
And Heimdal's horn, and day of doom
But the Sicilian laughed again ;
" This is the time to laugh," he said,
For the whole story he well knew
Was an invention of the Jew,
Spun from the cobwebs in his brain,
And of the same bright scarlet thread
As was the Tale of Kambalu.

Only the Landlord spake no word ;
'T was doubtful whether he had heard
The tale at all, so full of care
Was he of his impending fate,
That, like the sword of Damocles,
Above his head hung blank and bare,
Suspended by a single hair,
So that he could not sit at ease,
But sighed and looked disconsolate,
And shifted restless in his chair,
Revolving how he might evade
The blow of the descending blade.

The Student came to his relief
By saving in his easy way

To the Musician : "Calm your grief,
My fair Apollo of the North,
Balder the Beautiful and so forth ;
Although your magic lyre or lute
With broken strings is lying mute,
Still you can tell some doleful tale
Of shipwreck in a midnight gale,
Or something of the kind to suit
The mood that we are in to-night
For what is marvellous and strange ;
So give your nimble fancy range,
And we will follow in its flight."

But the Musician shook his head ;
"No tale I tell to-night," he said,
"While my poor instrument lies there,
Even as a child with vacant stare
Lies in its little coffin dead."

Yet, being urged, he said at last :
"There comes to me out of the Past
A voice, whose tones are sweet and wild,
Singing a song almost divine,
And with a tear in every line ;
An ancient ballad, that my nurse
Sang to me when I was a child,
In accents tender as the verse ;
And sometimes wept, and sometimes
    smiled
While singing it, to see arise
The look of wonder in my eyes,
And feel my heart with terror beat.
This simple ballad I retain
Clearly imprinted on my brain,
And as a tale will now repeat."

THE MUSICIAN'S TALE.

THE MOTHER'S GHOST.

SVEND DYRING he rideth adown the
    glade ;
   I myself was young !
There he hath wooed him so winsome a
    maid ;
   Fair words gladden so many a heart.

Together were they for seven years,
And together children six were theirs.

Then came Death abroad through the
    land,
And blighted the beautiful lily-wand.

Svend Dyring he rideth adown the glade,
And again hath he wooed him another
    maid.

He hath wooed him a maid and brought
    home a bride,
But she was bitter and full of pride.

When she came driving into the yard,
There stood the six children weeping so
    hard.

There stood the small children with sor-
    rowful heart ;
From before her feet she thrust them
    apart.

She gave to them neither ale nor bread ;
"Ye shall suffer hunger and hate," she
    said.

She took from them their quilts of blue,
And said : Ye shall lie on the straw we
    strew."

She took from them the great waxlight ;
"Now ye shall lie in the dark at night."

In the evening late they cried with cold ;
The mother heard it under the mould.

The woman heard it the earth below :
"To my little children I must go."

She standeth before the Lord of all :
"And may I go to my children small ?"

She prayed him so long, and would not
    cease,
Until he bade her depart in peace.

"At cock-crow thou shalt return again ;
Longer thou shalt not there remain !"

She girded up her sorrowful bones,
And rifted the walls and the marble
    stones.

As through the village she flitted by,
The watch-dogs howled aloud to the sky.

When she came to the castle gate,
There stood her eldest daughter in wait.

"Why standest thou here, dear daughter
    mine ?
How fares it with brothers and sisters
    thine ?"

"Never art thou mother of mine,
For my mother was both fair and fine.

" My mother was white, with cheeks of
red,
But thou art pale, and like to the dead."

" How should I be fair and fine ?
I have been dead ; pale cheeks are mine.

" How should I be white and red,
So long, so long have I been dead ? "

When she came in at the chamber door,
There stood the small children weeping
sore.

One she braided, another she brushed,
The third she lifted, the fourth she
hushed.

The fifth she took on her lap and pressed,
As if she would suckle it at her breast.

Then to her eldest daughter said she,
" Do thou bid Svend Dyring come hither
to me."

Into the chamber when he came
She spake to him in anger and shame.

" I left behind me both ale and bread ;
My children hunger and are not fed.

" I left behind me quilts of blue ;
My children lie on the straw ye strew.

" I left behind me the great waxlight ;
My children lie in the dark at night.

" If I come again unto your hall,
As cruel a fate shall you befall !

" Now crows the cock with feathers red ;
Back to the earth must all the dead.

" Now crows the cock with feathers
swart ;
The gates of heaven fly wide apart.

" Now crows the cock with feathers
white ;
I can abide no longer to-night."

Whenever they heard the watch-dogs
wail,
They gave the children bread and ale.

Whenever they heard the watch-dogs
bay,
They feared lest the dead were on their
way.

Whenever they heard the watch-dogs
bark ;
I myself was young !
They feared the dead out there in the
dark.
Fair words gladden so many a heart.

INTERLUDE.

TOUCHED by the pathos of these rhymes,
The Theologian said : " All praise
Be to the ballads of old times
And to the bards of simple ways,
Who walked with Nature hand in hand,
Whose country was their Holy Land,
Whose singing robes were homespun
brown
From looms of their own native town,
Which they were not ashamed to wear,
And not of silk or sendal gay,
Nor decked with fanciful array
Of cockle-shells from Outre-Mer."

To whom the Student answered : " Yes ;
All praise and honor !   I confess
That bread and ale, home-baked, home-
brewed,
Are wholesome and nutritious food,
But not enough for all our needs ;
Poets — the best of them — are birds
Of passage ; where their instinct leads
They range abroad for thoughts and
words,
And from all climes bring home the seeds
That germinate in flowers or weeds.
They are not fowls in barnyards born
To cackle o'er a grain of corn ;
And, if you shut the horizon down
To the small limits of their town,
What do you but degrade your bard
Till he at last becomes as one
Who thinks the all-encircling sun
Rises and sets in his back yard ? "

The Theologian said again :
" It may be so ; yet I maintain
That what is native still is best,
And little care I for the rest.
'T is a long story ; time would fail
To tell it, and the hour is late ;
We will not waste it in debate,
But listen to our Landlord's tale."

And thus the sword of Damocles
Descending not by slow degrees,
But suddenly, on the Landlord fell,
Who blushing, and with much demur
And many vain apologies,
Plucking up heart, began to tell
The Rhyme of one Sir Christopher.

THE LANDLORD'S TALE.

THE RHYME OF SIR CHRISTOPHER.

It was Sir Christopher Gardiner,
Knight of the Holy Sepulchre,
From Merry England over the sea,
Who stepped upon this continent
As if his august presence lent
A glory to the colony.

You should have seen him in the street
Of the little Boston of Winthrop's time,
His rapier dangling at his feet,
Doublet and hose and boots complete,
Prince Rupert hat with ostrich plume,
Gloves that exhaled a faint perfume,
Luxuriant curls and air sublime,
And superior manners now obsolete !

He had a way of saying things
That made one think of courts and
          kings,
And lords and ladies of high degree ;
So that not having been at court
Seemed something very little short
Of treason or lese-majesty,
Such an accomplished knight was he.

His dwelling was just beyond the town,
At what he called his country-seat ;
For, careless of Fortune's smile or
          frown,
And weary grown of the world and its
          ways,
He wished to pass the rest of his days
In a private life and a calm retreat.

But a double life was the life he led,
And, while professing to be in search
Of a godly course, and willing, he said,
Nay, anxious to join the Puritan
          church,
He made of all this but small account,
And passed his idle hours instead
With roystering Morton of Merry
          Mount,
That pettifogger from Furnival's Inn,

Lord of misrule and riot and sin,
Who looked on the wine when it wa-
          red.

This country-seat was little more
Than a cabin of logs ; but in front of the
          door
A modest flower-bed thickly sown
With sweet alyssum and columbine
Made those who saw it at once divine
The touch of some other hand than his
          own.
And first it was whispered, and then it
          was known,
That he in secret was harboring there
A little lady with golden hair,
Whom he called his cousin, but whom
          he had wed
In the Italian manner, as men said,
And great was the scandal everywhere.

But worse than this was the vague
          surmise,
Though none could vouch for it or
          aver,
That the Knight of the Holy Sepulchre
Was only a Papist in disguise ;
And the more to imbitter their bitter
          lives,
And the more to trouble the public
          mind,
Came letters from England, from two
          other wives,
Whom he had carelessly left behind ;
Both of them letters of such a kind
As made the governor hold his breath ;
The one imploring him straight to send
The husband home, that he might
          amend ;
The other asking his instant death,
As the only way to make an end.

The wary governor deemed it right,
When all this wickedness was revealed,
To send his warrant signed and sealed,
And take the body of the knight.
Armed with this mighty instrument,
The marshal, mounting his gallant
          steed,
Rode forth from town at the top of his
          speed,
And followed by all his bailiffs bold,
As if on high achievement bent,
To storm some castle or stronghold,
Challenge the warders on the wall,
And seize in his ancestral hall
A robber-baron grim and old.

"A little lady with golden hair."   Page 314.

But when through all the dust and
  heat
He came to Sir Christopher's country-
  seat,
No knight he found, nor warder there,
But the little lady with golden hair,
Who was gathering in the bright sun-
  shine
The sweet alyssum and columbine ;
While gallant Sir Christopher, all so
  gay,
Being forewarned, through the postern
  gate
Of his castle wall had tripped away,
And was keeping a little holiday
In the forests, that bounded his estate.

Then as a trusty squire and true
The marshal searched the castle through,
Not crediting what the lady said ;
Searched from cellar to garret in vain,
And, finding no knight, came out again
And arrested the golden damsel instead,
And bore her in triumph into the town,
While from her eyes the tears rolled down
On the sweet alyssum and columbine,
That she held in her fingers white and
  fine.

The governor's heart was moved to see
So fair a creature caught within
The snares of Satan and of sin,
And he read her a little homily
On the folly and wickedness of the lives
Of women, half cousins and half wives ;
But, seeing that naught his words
  availed,
He sent her away in a ship that sailed
For Merry England over the sea,
To the other two wives in the old coun-
  tree,
To search her further, since he had failed
To come at the heart of the mystery.

Meanwhile Sir Christopher wandered
  away
Through pathless woods for a month and
  a day,
Shooting pigeons, and sleeping at night
With the noble savage, who took delight
In his feathered hat and his velvet vest,
His gun and his rapier and the rest.
But as soon as the noble savage heard
That a bounty was offered for this gay
  bird,
He wanted to slay him out of hand,

And bring in his beautiful scalp for a
  show,
Like the glossy head of a kite or crow,
Until he was made to understand
They wanted the bird alive, not dead ;
Then he followed him whithersoever he
  fled,
Through forest and field, and hunted
  him down,
And brought him prisoner into the town.

Alas ! it was a rueful sight,
To see this melancholy knight
In such a dismal and hapless case ;
His hat deformed by stain and dent,
His plumage broken, his doublet rent,
His beard and flowing locks forlorn,
Matted, dishevelled, and unshorn,
His boots with dust and mire besprent ;
But dignified in his disgrace,
And wearing an unblushing face.
And thus before the magistrate
He stood to hear the doom of fate.
In vain he strove with wonted ease
To modify and extenuate
His evil deeds in church and state,
For gone was now his power to please ;
And his pompous words had no more
  weight
Than feathers flying in the breeze.

With suavity equal to his own
The governor lent a patient ear
To the speech evasive and highflown,
In which he endeavored to make clear
That colonial laws were too severe
When applied to a gallant cavalier,
A gentleman born, and so well known,
And accustomed to move in a higher
  sphere.

All this the Puritan governor heard,
And deigned in answer never a word ;
But in summary manner shipped away,
In a vessel that sailed from Salem bay,
This splendid and famous cavalier,
With his Rupert hat and his popery,
To Merry England over the sea,
As being unmeet to inhabit here.

Thus endeth the Rhyme of Sir Christopher,
Knight of the Holy Sepulchre,
The first who furnished this barren
  land
With apples of Sodom and ropes of
  sand.

FINALE.

THESE are the tales those merry guests
Told to each other, well or ill ;
Like summer birds that lift their crests
Above the borders of their nests
And twitter, and again are still.

These are the tales, or new or old,
In idle moments idly told ;
Flowers of the field with petals thin,
Lilies that neither toil nor spin,
And tufts of wayside weeds and gorse
Hung in the parlor of the inn
Beneath the sign of the Red Horse.

And still, reluctant to retire,
The friends sat talking by the fire
And watched the smouldering embers
        burn
To ashes, and flash up again
Into a momentary glow,
Lingering like them when forced to go,
And going when they would remain ;
For on the morrow they must turn
Their faces homeward, and the pain
Of parting touched with its unrest
A tender nerve in every breast.

But sleep at last the victory won ;
They must be stirring with the sun,
And drowsily good night they said,
And went still gossiping to bed,
And left the parlor wrapped in gloom.
The only live thing in the room
Was the old clock, that in its pace
Kept time with the revolving spheres
And constellations in their flight,
And struck with its uplifted mace

The dark, unconscious hours of night,
To senseless and unlistening ears.

Uprose the sun ; and every guest,
Uprisen, was soon equipped and dressed
For journeying home and city-ward ;
The old stage-coach was at the door,
With horses harnessed, long before
The sunshine reached the withered sward
Beneath the oaks, whose branches hoar
Murmured : "Farewell forevermore."

"Farewell!" the portly Landlord cried ;
"Farewell!" the parting guests replied,
But little thought that nevermore
Their feet would pass that threshold
        o'er ;
That nevermore together there
Would they assemble, free from care,
To hear the oaks' mysterious roar,
And breathe the wholesome country air.

Where are they now ?   What lands and
        skies
Paint pictures in their friendly eyes ?
What hope deludes, what promise
        cheers,
What pleasant voices fill their ears ?
Two are beyond the salt sea waves,
And three already in their graves.
Perchance the living still may look
Into the pages of this book,
And see the days of long ago
Floating and fleeting to and fro,
As in the well-remembered brook
They saw the inverted landscape gleam,
And their own faces like a dream
Look up upon them from below.

FLOWER-DE-LUCE.

FLOWER-DE-LUCE.

BEAUTIFUL lily, dwelling by still riv-
ers,
   Or solitary mere,
Or where the sluggish meadow-brook
delivers
   Its waters to the weir !

Thou laughest at the mill, the whir and
worry
   Of spindle and of loom,
And the great wheel that toils amid the
hurry
   And rushing of the flume.

Born in the purple, born to joy and
pleasance,
   Thou dost not toil nor spin,
But makest glad and radiant with thy
presence
   The meadow and the lin.

The wind blows, and uplifts thy droop-
ing banner,
   And round thee throng and run
The rushes, the green yeomen of thy
manor,
   The outlaws of the sun.

The burnished dragon-fly is thine at-
tendant,
   And tilts against the field,
And down the listed sunbeam rides re-
splendent
   With steel-blue mail and shield.

Thou art the Iris, fair among the fair-
est,
   Who, armed with golden rod
And winged with the celestial azure,
bearest
   The message of some God.

Thou art the Muse, who far from crowded
cities
   Hauntest the sylvan streams,
Playing on pipes of reed the artless dit-
ties
   That come to us as dreams.

O flower-de-luce, bloom on, and let the
river
   Linger to kiss thy feet !
O flower of song, bloom on, and make
forever
   The world more fair and sweet.

PALINGENESIS.

I LAY upon the headland-height, and
listened
To the incessant sobbing of the sea
   In caverns under me,
And watched the waves, that tossed and
fled and glistened,
Until the rolling meadows of amethyst
   Melted away in mist.

Then suddenly, as one from sleep, I
started ;
For round about me all the sunny
capes
   Seemed peopled with the shapes
Of those whom I had known in days de-
parted,
Apparelled in the loveliness which
gleams
   On faces seen in dreams.

A moment only, and the light and glory
Faded away, and the disconsolate shore
   Stood lonely as before ;
And the wild-roses of the promontory
Around me shuddered in the wind, and
shed
   Their petals of pale red.

There was an old belief that in the em-
bers
Of all things their primordial form exists,
   And cunning alchemists
Could re-create the rose with all its
members
From its own ashes, but without the
bloom,
   Without the lost perfume.

Ah me ! what wonder-working, occult
science

Can from the ashes in our hearts once
        more
    The rose of youth restore ?
What craft of alchemy can bid defiance
To time and change, and for a single
        hour
    Renew this phantom-flower ?

"O, give me back," I cried, "the van-
        ished splendors,
The breath of morn, and the exultant
        strife,
    When the swift stream of life
Bounds o'er its rocky channel, and sur-
        renders
The pond, with all its lilies, for the leap
    Into the unknown deep !"

And the sea answered, with a lamenta-
        tion,
Like some old prophet wailing, and it
        said,
    "Alas ! thy youth is dead !
It breathes no more, its heart has no
        pulsation ;
In the dark places with the dead of old
    It lies forever cold !"

Then said I , " From its consecrated
        cerements
I will not drag this sacred dust again,
    Only to give me pain ;
But, still remembering all the lost en-
        dearments,
Go on my way, like one who looks be-
        fore,
    And turns to weep no more."

Into what land of harvests, what planta-
        tions
Bright with autumnal foliage and the
        glow
    Of sunsets burning low ;
Beneath what midnight skies, whose con-
        stellations
Light up the spacious avenues between
    This world and the unseen !

Amid what friendly greetings and ca-
        resses,
What households, though not alien, yet
        not mine,
    What bowers of rest divine ;
To what temptations in lone wildernesses,
What famine of the heart, what pain and
        loss,
    The bearing of what cross !

I do not know ; nor will I vainly ques-
        tion
Those pages of the mystic book which
        hold
    The story still untold,
But without rash conjecture or suggestion
Turn its last leaves in reverence and
        good heed,
    Until "The End" I read.

THE BRIDGE OF CLOUD.

BURN, O evening hearth, and waken
    Pleasant visions, as of old !
Though the house by winds be shaken,
    Safe I keep this room of gold !

Ah, no longer wizard Fancy
    Builds her castles in the air,
Luring me by necromancy
    Up the never-ending stair !

But, instead, she builds me bridges
    Over many a dark ravine,
Where beneath the gusty ridges
    Cataracts dash and roar unseen.

And I cross them, little heeding
    Blast of wind or torrent's roar,
As I follow the receding
    Footsteps that have gone before.

Naught avails the imploring gesture,
    Naught avails the cry of pain !
When I touch the flying vesture,
    'T is the gray robe of the rain.

Baffled I return, and, leaning
    O'er the parapets of cloud,
Watch the mist that intervening
    Wraps the valley in its shroud.

And the sounds of life ascending
    Faintly, vaguely, meet the ear,
Murmur of bells and voices blending
    With the rush of waters near.

Well I know what there lies hidden,
    Every tower and town and farm,
And again the land forbidden
    Reassumes its vanished charm.

Well I know the secret places,
    And the nests in hedge and tree ;
At what doors are friendly faces,
    In what hearts are thoughts of me.

Through the mist and darkness sinking,
  Blown by wind and beaten by shower,
Down I fling the thought I 'm thinking,
  Down I toss this Alpine flower.

HAWTHORNE.

MAY 23, 1864.

How beautiful it was, that one bright
    day
  In the long week of rain !
Though all its splendor could not chase
    away
  The omnipresent pain.

The lovely town was white with apple-
    blooms,
  And the great elms o'erhead
Dark shadows wove on their aerial looms
  Shot through with golden thread.

Across the meadows, by the gray old
    manse,
  The historic river flowed :
I was as one who wanders in a trance,
  Unconscious of his road.

The faces of familiar friends seemed
    strange ;
  Their voices I could hear,
And yet the words they uttered seemed
    to change
  Their meaning to my ear.

For the one face I looked for was not
    there,
  The one low voice was mute ;
Only an unseen presence filled the air,
  And baffled my pursuit.

Now I look back, and meadow, manse,
    and stream
  Dimly my thought defines ;
I only see — a dream within a dream —
  The hill-top hearsed with pines.

I only hear above his place of rest
  Their tender undertone,
The infinite longings of a troubled breast,
  The voice so like his own.

There in seclusion and remote from men
  The wizard hand lies cold,

Which at its topmost speed let fall the
    pen,
  And left the tale half told.

Ah ! who shall lift that wand of magic
    power,
  And the lost clew regain ?
The unfinished window in Aladdin's
    tower
  Unfinished must remain !

CHRISTMAS BELLS.

I HEARD the bells on Christmas Day
Their old, familiar carols play,
        And wild and sweet
        The words repeat
Of peace on earth, good-will to men !

And thought how, as the day had come,
The belfries of all Christendom
        Had rolled along
        The unbroken song
Of peace on earth, good-will to men !

Till, ringing, singing on its way,
The world revolved from night to day,
        A voice, a chime,
        A chant sublime
Of peace on earth, good-will to men !

Then from each black, accursed mouth
The cannon thundered in the South,
        And with the sound
        The carols drowned
Of peace on earth, good-will to men !

It was as if an earthquake rent
The hearth-stones of a continent,
        And made forlorn
        The households born
Of peace on earth, good-will to men !

And in despair I bowed my head ;
"There is no peace on earth," I said :
        "For hate is strong,
        And mocks the song
Of peace on earth, good-will to men ! "

Then pealed the bells more loud and deep :
"God is not dead ; nor doth he sleep !
        The Wrong shall fail,
        The Right prevail,
With peace on earth, good-will to men ! "

THE WIND OVER THE CHIMNEY.

SEE, the fire is sinking low,
Dusky red the embers glow,
  While above them still I cower,
While a moment more I linger,
Though the clock, with lifted finger,
  Points beyond the midnight hour.

Sings the blackened log a tune
Learned in some forgotten June
  From a school-boy at his play,
When they both were young together,
Heart of youth and summer weather
  Making all their holiday.

And the night-wind rising, hark !
How above there in the dark,
  In the midnight and the snow,
Ever wilder, fiercer, grander,
Like the trumpets of Iskander,
  All the noisy chimneys blow !

Every quivering tongue of flame
Seems to murmur some great name,
  Seems to say to me, " Aspire ! "
But the night-wind answers, " Hollow
Are the visions that you follow,
  Into darkness sinks your fire ! "

Then the flicker of the blaze
Gleams on volumes of old days,
  Written by masters of the art,
Loud through whose majestic pages
Rolls the melody of ages,
  Throb the harp-strings of the heart.

And again the tongues of flame
Start exulting and exclaim :
  " These are prophets, bards, and seers ;
In the horoscope of nations,
Like ascendant constellations,
  They control the coming years."

But the night-wind cries : " Despair !
Those who walk with feet of air
  Leave no long-enduring marks ;
At God's forges incandescent
Mighty hammers beat incessant,
  These are but the flying sparks.

" Dust are all the hands that wrought ;
Books are sepulchres of thought ;
  The dead laurels of the dead
Rustle for a moment only,
Like the withered leaves in lonely
  Churchyards at some passing tread."

Suddenly the flame sinks down ;
Sink the rumors of renown ;
  And alone the night-wind drear
Clamors louder, wilder, vaguer, —
" 'T is the brand of Meleager
  Dying on the hearth-stone here ! "

And I answer, — " Though it be,
Why should that discomfort me ?
  No endeavor is in vain ;
Its reward is in the doing,
And the rapture of pursuing
  Is the prize the vanquished gain."

THE BELLS OF LYNN

HEARD AT NAHANT.

O CURFEW of the setting sun !   O Bells
  of Lynn !
O requiem of the dying day !   O Bells
  of Lynn !

From the dark belfries of yon cloud-
  cathedral wafted,
Your sounds aerial seem to float, O Bells
  of Lynn !

Borne on the evening wind across the
  crimson twilight,
O er land and sea they rise and fall, O
  Bells of Lynn !

The fisherman in his boat, far out beyond
  the headland,
Listens, and leisurely rows ashore, O Bells
  of Lynn !

Over the shining sands the wandering
  cattle homeward
Follow each other at your call, O Bells
  of Lynn !

The distant lighthouse hears, and with
  his flaming signal
Answers you, passing the watchword on,
  O Bells of Lynn !

And down the darkening coast run the
  tumultuous surges,
And clap their hands, and shout to you,
  . O Bells of Lynn !

Till from the shuddering sea, with your
  wild incantations,
Ye summon up the spectral moon, O
  Bells of Lynn !

And startled at the sight, like the weird
    woman of Endor,
Ye cry aloud, and then are still, O Bells
    of Lynn !

KILLED AT THE FORD.

HE is dead, the beautiful youth,
The heart of honor, the tongue of truth,
He, the life and light of us all,
Whose voice was blithe as a bugle-call,
Whom all eyes followed with one consent,
The cheer of whose laugh, and whose
    pleasant word,
Hushed all murmurs of discontent.

Only last night, as we rode along,
Down the dark of the mountain gap,
To visit the picket-guard at the ford,
Little dreaming of any mishap,
He was humming the words of some old
    song :
"Two red roses he had on his cap,
And another he bore at the point of his
    sword."

Sudden and swift a whistling ball
Came out of a wood, and the voice was
    still ;
Something I heard in the darkness fall,
And for a moment my blood grew chill ;
I spake in a whisper, as he who speaks
In a room where some one is lying dead ;
But he made no answer to what I said.

We lifted him up to his saddle again,
And through the mire and the mist and
    the rain
Carried him back to the silent camp,
And laid him as if asleep on his bed ;
And I saw by the light of the surgeon's
    lamp
Two white roses upon his cheeks,
And one, just over his heart, blood-red !

And I saw in a vision how far and fleet
That fatal bullet went speeding forth,
Till it reached a town in the distant
    North,
Till it reached a house in a sunny street,
Till it reached a heart that ceased to beat
Without a murmur, without a cry ;
And a bell was tolled, in that far-off town,
For one who had passed from cross to
    crown,
And the neighbors wondered that she
    should die.

GIOTTO'S TOWER.

How many lives, made beautiful and
    sweet
By self-devotion and by self-restraint,
Whose pleasure is to run without
    complaint
On unknown errands of the Paraclete,
Wanting the reverence of unshodden
    feet,
Fail of the nimbus which the artists
    paint
Around the shining forehead of the
    saint,
And are in their completeness incom-
    plete !
In the old Tuscan town stands Giotto's
    tower,
The lily of Florence blossoming in
    stone, —
A vision, a delight, and a desire, —
The builder's perfect and centennial
    flower,
That in the night of ages bloomed
    alone,
But wanting still the glory of the spire.

TO-MORROW.

'T IS late at night, and in the realm of
    sleep
My little lambs are folded like the
    flocks ;
From room to room I hear the wakeful
    clocks
Challenge the passing hour, like guards
    that keep
Their solitary watch on tower and
    steep ;
Far off I hear the crowing of the
    cocks,
And through the opening door that
    time unlocks
Feel the fresh breathing of To-morrow
    creep.
To-morrow ! the mysterious, unknown
    guest,
Who cries to me : "Remember Bar-
    mecide,
And tremble to be happy with the
    rest."
And I make answer : "I am satisfied ;
I dare not ask ; I know not what is
    best ;
God hath already said what shall be-
    tide."

DIVINA COMMEDIA.

I.

OFT have I seen at some cathedral door
    A laborer, pausing in the dust and
        heat,
    Lay down his burden, and with rever-
        ent feet
    Enter, and cross himself, and on the
        floor
Kneel to repeat his paternoster o'er ;
    Far off the noises of the world retreat ;
    The loud vociferations of the street
Become an undistinguishable roar.
So, as I enter here from day to day,
    And leave my burden at this minster
        gate,
    Kneeling in prayer, and not ashamed
        to pray,
The tumult of the time disconsolate
    To inarticulate murmurs dies away,
    While the eternal ages watch and wait.

II.

How strange the sculptures that adorn
    these towers !
    This crowd of statues, in whose folded
        sleeves
Birds build their nests ; while canopied
    with leaves
Parvis and portal bloom like trellised
    bowers,
And the vast minster seems a cross of
    flowers !
    But fiends and dragons on the gar-
        goyled eaves
    Watch the dead Christ between the
        living thieves,
And, underneath, the traitor Judas
    lowers !
Ah ! from what agonies of heart and
    brain,
    What exultations trampling on de-
        spair,
    What tenderness, what tears, what
        hate of wrong,
What passionate outcry of a soul in pain,
    Uprose this poem of the earth and air,
    This mediæval miracle of song !

III.

I ENTER, and I see thee in the gloom
    Of the long aisles, O poet saturnine !
    And strive to make my steps keep
        pace with thine.

The air is filled with some unknown
    perfume ;
The congregation of the dead make room
    For thee to pass ; the votive tapers
        shine ;
    Like rooks that haunt Ravenna's
        groves of pine
    The hovering echoes fly from tomb to
        tomb.
From the confessionals I hear arise
    Rehearsals of forgotten tragedies,
    And lamentations from the crypts be-
        low ;
And then a voice celestial, that begins
    With the pathetic words, " Although
        your sins
    As scarlet be," and ends with " as the
        snow."

IV.

WITH snow-white veil and garments as
    of flame,
    She stands before thee, who so long
        ago
    Filled thy young heart with passion
        and the woe
    From which thy song and all its splen-
        dors came ;
And while with stern rebuke she speaks
    thy name,
    The ice about thy heart melts as the
        snow
    On mountain heights, and in swift
        overflow
    Comes gushing from thy lips in sobs
        of shame.
Thou makest full confession ; and a
    gleam,
    As of the dawn on some dark forest
        cast,
    Seems on thy lifted forehead to in-
        crease ;
Lethe and Eunoe — the remembered
    dream
    And the forgotten sorrow — bring at
        last
    That perfect pardon which is perfect
        peace.

V.

I LIFT mine eyes, and all the windows
    blaze
    With forms of saints and holy men
        who died,
    Here martyred and hereafter glorified ;

And the great Rose upon its leaves
displays
Christ's Triumph, and the angelic roun-
delays,
With splendor upon splendor multi-
plied ;
And Beatrice again at Dante's side
No more rebukes, but smiles her
words of praise.
And then the organ sounds, and unseen
choirs
Sing the old Latin hymns of peace
and love,
And benedictions of the Holy Ghost ;
And the melodious bells among the spires
O'er all the house-tops and through
heaven above
Proclaim the elevation of the Host !

VI.

O STAR of morning and of liberty !
O bringer of the light, whose splendor
shines
Above the darkness of the Apennines,
Forerunner of the day that is to be !
The voices of the city and the sea,
The voices of the mountains and the
pines,
Repeat thy song, till the familiar lines
Are footpaths for the thought of Italy !
Thy fame is blown abroad from all the
heights,
Through all the nations, and a sound
is heard,
As of a mighty wind, and men devout,
Strangers of Rome, and the new prose-
lytes,
In their own language hear thy won-
drous word,
And many are amazed and many
doubt.

NOËL.

ENVOYÉ À M. AGASSIZ, LA VEILLE DE
NOËL 1864, AVEC UN PANIER DE
VINS DIVERS.

L'Académie en respect,
Nonobstant l'incorrection
A la faveur du sujet,
Ture-lure,
N'y fera point de rature,
Noël ! ture-lure-lure.
GUI BARÔZAI

QUAND les astres de Noël
Brillaient, palpitaient au ciel,

Six gaillards, et chacun ivre,
Chantaient gaîment dans le givre,
" Bons amis
Allons donc chez Agassiz ! "

Ces illustres Pèlerins
D'Outre-Mer adroits et fins,
Se donnant des airs de prêtre,
A l'envi se vantaient d'être
" Bons amis
De Jean Rudolphe Agassiz ! "

Œil-de-Perdrix, grand farceur,
Sans reproche et sans pudeur,
Dans son patois de Bourgogne,
Bredouillait comme un ivrogne,
" Bons amis,
J'ai dansé chez Agassiz ! "

Verzenay le Champenois,
Bon Français, point New-Yorquois,
Mais des environs d'Avize,
Fredonne à mainte reprise,
" Bons amis,
J'ai chanté chez Agassiz ! "

A côté marchait un vieux
Hidalgo, mais non mousseux ;
Dans le temps de Charlemagne
Fut son père Grand d'Espagne !
" Bons amis
J'ai dîné chez Agassiz ! "

Derrière eux un Bordelais,
Gascon, s'il en fut jamais,
Parfumé de poésie
Riait, chantait, plein de vie,
" Bons amis,
J'ai soupé chez Agassiz ! "

Avec ce beau cadet roux,
Bras dessus et bras dessous,
Mine altière et couleur terne,
Vint le Sire de Sauterne ;
" Bons amis,
J'ai couché chez Agassiz ! "

Mais le dernier de ces preux,
Était un pauvre Chartreux,
Qui disait, d'un ton robuste,
" Bénédictions sur le Juste !
Bons amis
Bénissons Père Agassiz ! "

Ils arrivent trois à trois,
Montent l'escalier de bois
Clopin-clopant ! quel gendarme
Peut permettre ce vacarme,
    Bons amis,
A la porte d'Agassiz !

"Ouvrez donc, mon bon Seigneur,
Ouvrez vite et n'ayez peur ;
Ouvrez, ouvrez, car nous sommes

Gens de bien et gentilshommes,
    Bons amis
De la famille Agassiz !"

Chut, ganaches ! taisez-vous !
C'en est trop de vos glouglous ;
Epargnez aux Philosophes
Vos abominables strophes !
    Bons amis,
Respectez mon Agassiz !

JUDAS MACCABÆUS.

ACT I.

The Citadel of Antiochus at Jerusalem.

SCENE I. — ANTIOCHUS ; JASON.

Antiochus. O Antioch, my Antioch, my city !
Queen of the East ! my solace, my delight !
The dowry of my sister Cleopatra
When she was wed to Ptolemy, and now
Won back and made more wonderful by me !
I love thee, and I long to be once more
Among the players and the dancing women
Within thy gates, and bathe in the Orontes,
Thy river and mine. O Jason, my High-Priest,
For I have made thee so, and thou art mine,
Hast thou seen Antioch the Beautiful ?
Jason. Never, my Lord.
Ant. Then hast thou never seen
The wonder of the world. This city of David
Compared with Antioch is but a village,
And its inhabitants compared with Greeks
Are mannerless boors.
Jason. They are barbarians,
And mannerless.
Ant. They must be civilized.
They must be made to have more gods than one ;
And goddesses besides.

Jason. They shall have more.
Ant. They must have hippodromes, and games, and baths,
Stage-plays and festivals, and most of all
The Dionysia.
Jason. They shall have them all.
Ant. By Heracles ! but I should like to see
These Hebrews crowned with ivy, and arrayed
In skins of fawns, with drums and flutes and thyrsi,
Revel and riot through the solemn streets
Of their old town. Ha, ha ! It makes me merry
Only to think of it ! — Thou dost not laugh.
Jason. Yea, I laugh inwardly.
Ant. The new Greek leaven
Works slowly in this Israelitish dough !
Have I not sacked the Temple, and on the altar
Set up the statue of Olympian Zeus
To Hellenize it ?
Jason. Thou hast done all this.
Ant. As thou wast Joshua once and now art Jason,
And from a Hebrew hast become a Greek,
So shall this Hebrew nation be translated,
Their very natures and their names be changed,
And all be Hellenized.
Jason. It shall be done.
Ant. Their manners and their laws and way of living
Shall all be Greek. They shall unlearn their language,

And learn the lovely speech of Antioch.
Where hast thou been to-day ? Thou
    comest late.
   Jason. Playing at discus with the
    other priests
In the Gymnasium.
   Ant.   Thou hast done well.
There's nothing better for you lazy
    priests
Than discus-playing with the common
    people.
Now tell me, Jason, what these Hebrews
    call me
When they converse together at their
    games.
   Jason. Antiochus Epiphanes, my
    Lord ;
Antiochus the Illustrious.
   Ant.   O, not that ;
That is the public cry ; I mean the
    name
They give me when they talk among
    themselves,
And think that no one listens ; what is
    that ?
   Jason. Antiochus Epimanes, my Lord !
   Ant. Antiochus the Mad ! Ay, that
    is it.
And who hath said it ? Who hath set
    in motion
That sorry jest ?
   Jason.   The Seven Sons insane
Of a weird woman, like themselves in-
    sane.
   Ant. I like their courage, but it shall
    not save them.
They shall be made to eat the flesh of
    swine,
Or they shall die. Where are they ?
   Jason.   In the dungeons
Beneath this tower.
   Ant. There let them stay and starve,
Till I am ready to make Greeks of them,
After my fashion.
   Jason. They shall stay and starve. —
My Lord, the Ambassadors of Samaria
Await thy pleasure.
   Ant.   Why not my displeasure ?
Ambassadors are tedious. They are
    men
Who work for their own ends, and not
    for mine ;
There is no furtherance in them. Let
    them go
To Apollonius, my governor
There in Samaria, and not trouble me.
What do they want ?

   Jason.   Only the royal sanction
To give a name unto a nameless temple
Upon Mount Gerizim.
   Ant.   Then bid them enter.
This pleases me, and furthers my designs.
The occasion is auspicious. Bid them
    enter.

SCENE II. — ANTIOCHUS; JASON ; *the* SA
    MARITAN AMBASSADORS.

   Ant. Approach. Come forward ; stand
    not at the door
Wagging your long beards, but demean
    yourselves
As doth become Ambassadors. What
    seek ye ?
   An Ambassador. An audience from
    the King.
   Ant.   Speak, and be brief.
Waste not the time in useless rhetoric.
Words are not things.
   Ambassador (*reading*). " To   King
    Antiochus,
The God, Epiphanes ; a Memorial
From the Sidonians, who live at Sichem."
   Ant. Sidonians ?
   Ambassador.   Ay, my Lord.
   Ant.   Go on, go on !
And do not tire thyself and me with
    bowing !
   Ambassador (*reading*). " We are a col-
    ony of Medes and Persians."
   Ant. No, ye are Jews from one of the
    Ten Tribes ;
Whether Sidonians or Samaritans
Or Jews of Jewry, matters not to me ;
Ye are all Israelites, ye are all Jews.
When the Jews prosper, ye claim kindred
    with them ;
When the Jews suffer, ye are Medes and
    Persians :
I know that in the days of Alexander
Ye claimed exemption from the annual
    tribute
In the Sabbatic Year, because, ye said,
Your fields had not been planted in that
    year.
   Ambassador (*reading*). " Our fathers,
    upon certain frequent plagues,
And following an ancient superstition,
Were long accustomed to observe that
    day
Which by the Israelites is called the
    Sabbath,
And in a temple on Mount Gerizim

Without a name, they offered sacrifice.
Now we, who are Sidonians, beseech
thee,
Who art our benefactor and our savior,
Not to confound us with these wicked
Jews,
But to give royal order and injunction
To Apollonius in Samaria.
Thy governor, and likewise to Nicanor,
Thy procurator, no more to molest us ;
And let our nameless temple now be
named
The Temple of Jupiter Hellenius."
　　Ant. This shall be done. Full well
it pleaseth me
Ye are not Jews, or are no longer Jews,
But Greeks ; if not by birth, yet Greeks
by custom.
Your nameless temple shall receive the
name
Of Jupiter Hellenius. Ye may go !

SCENE III. — ANTIOCHUS ; JASON.

　　Ant. My task is easier than I dreamed.
These people
Meet me half-way. Jason, didst thou
take note
How these Samaritans of Sichem said
They were not Jews ? that they were
Medes and Persians,
They were Sidonians, anything but Jews ?
'T is of good augury. The rest will fol-
low
Till the whole land is Hellenized.
　　Jason.　　　　　　　　My Lord,
These are Samaritans. The tribe of
Judah
Is of a different temper, and the task
Will be more difficult.
　　Ant.　　　Dost thou gainsay me ?
　　Jason. I know the stubborn nature
of the Jew.
Yesterday, Eleazer, an old man,
Being fourscore years and ten, chose
rather death
By torture than to eat the flesh of swine.
　　Ant. The life is in the blood, and the
whole nation
Shall bleed to death, or it shall change
its faith !
　　Jason. Hundreds have fled already to
the mountains
Of Ephraim, where Judas Maccabæus
Hath raised the standard of revolt against
thee.

　　Ant. I will burn down their city, and
will make it
Waste as a wilderness. Its thoroughfares
Shall be but furrows in a field of ashes.
It shall be sown with salt as Sodom is !
This hundred and fifty-third Olympiad
Shall have a broad and blood-red seal
upon it,
Stamped with the awful letters of my
name,
Antiochus the God, Epiphanes ! —
Where are those Seven Sons ?
　　Jason.　　　　　　My Lord, they wait
Thy royal pleasure.
　　Ant.　　　They shall wait no longer !

ACT II.

The Dungeons in the Citadel.

SCENE I. — THE MOTHER *of the* SEVEN SONS
alone, listening.

　　The Mother. Be strong, my heart !
Break not till they are dead,
All, all my Seven Sons ; then burst
asunder,
And let this tortured and tormented soul
Leap and rush out like water through the
shards
Of earthen vessels broken at a well.
O my dear children, mine in life and
death,
I know not how ye came into my womb ;
I neither gave you breath, nor gave you
life,
And neither was it I that formed the
members
Of every one of you. But the Creator,
Who made the world, and made the
heavens above us,
Who formed the generation of man-
kind,
And found out the beginning of all
things,
He gave you breath and life, and will
again
Of his own mercy, as ye now regard
Not your own selves, but his eternal
law.
I do not murmur, nay, I thank thee,
God,
That I and mine have not been deemed
unworthy
To suffer for thy sake, and for thy law,
And for the many sins of Israel.

Hark ! I can hear within the sound of
scourges !
I feel them more than ye do, O my
sons !
But cannot come to you. I, who was
wont
To wake at night at the least cry ye
made,
To whom ye ran at every slightest
hurt, —
I cannot take you now into my lap
And soothe your pain, but God will take
you all
Into his pitying arms, and comfort you,
And give you rest.
   A Voice (*within*). What wouldst thou
ask of us ?
Ready are we to die, but we will never
Transgress the law and customs of our
fathers.
   The Mother. It is the voice of my
first-born ! O brave
And noble boy ! Thou hast the
privilege
Of dying first, as thou wast born the
first.
The same Voice (*within*). God looketh
on us, and hath comfort in us ;
As Moses in his song of old declared,
He in his servants shall be comforted.
   The Mother. I knew thou wouldst not
fail ! — He speaks no more,
He is beyond all pain !
   Ant. (*within*).   If thou eat not
Thou shalt be tortured throughout all
the members
Of thy whole body. Wilt thou eat
then ?
   Second Voice (*within*). No.
   The Mother. It is Adaiah's voice. I
tremble for him.
I know his nature, devious as the
wind,
And swift to change, gentle and
yielding always.
Be steadfast, O my son !
   The same Voice (*within*). Thou, like
a fury,
Takest us from this present life, but
God,
Who rules the world, shall raise us up
again
Into life everlasting.
   The Mother.   God, I thank thee
That thou hast breathed into that timid
heart
Courage to die for thee.   O my Adaiah,

Witness of God ! if thou for whom I
feared
Canst thus encounter death, I need not
fear ;
The others will not shrink.
   Third Voice (*within*). Behold these
hands
Held out to thee, O King Antiochus,
Not to implore thy mercy, but to show
That I despise them.   He who gave
them to me
Will give them back again.
   The Mother.   O Avilan,
It is thy voice.   For the last time I
hear it ;
For the last time on earth, but not the
last.
To death it bids defiance and to torture.
It sounds to me as from another world,
And makes the petty miseries of this
Seem unto me as naught, and less than
naught.
Farewell, my Avilan ; nay, I should say
Welcome, my Avilan ; for I am dead
Before thee.   I am waiting for the
others.
Why do they linger ?
   Fourth Voice (*within*). It is good, O
King,
Being put to death by men, to look for
hope
From God, to be raised up again by him.
But thou — no resurrection shalt thou
have
To life hereafter.
   The Mother.   Four ! already four !
Three are still living ; nay, they all are
living,
Half here, half there.   Make haste,
Antiochus,
To reunite us ; for the sword that
cleaves
These miserable bodies makes a door
Through which our souls, impatient of
release,
Rush to each other's arms.
   Fifth Voice (*within*). Thou hast the
power ;
Thou doest what thou wilt.   Abide
awhile,
And thou shalt see the power of God,
and how
He will torment thee and thy seed.
   The Mother.   O hasten ;
Why dost thou pause ?   Thou who hast
slain already
So many Hebrew women, and hast hung

328   MACCABÆUS.

Their murdered infants round their
    necks, slay me,
For I too am a woman, and these boys
Are mine.   Make haste to slay us all,
And hang my lifeless babes about my
    neck.
    Sixth Voice (within).   Think not,
        Antiochus, that takest in hand
To strive against the God of Israel,
Thou shalt escape unpunished, for his
    wrath
Shall overtake thee and thy bloody house.
    The Mother.   One more, my Sirion, and
        then all is ended.
Having put all to bed, then in my turn
I will lie down and sleep as sound as they.
My Sirion, my youngest, best beloved !
And those bright golden locks, that I so
    oft
Have curled about these fingers, even now
Are foul with blood and dust, like a
    lamb's fleece,
Slain in the shambles. — Not a sound I
    hear.
This silence is more terrible to me
Than any sound, than any cry of pain,
That might escape the lips of one who
    dies.
Doth his heart fail him ?   Doth he fall
    away
In the last hour from God ?   O Sirion,
    Sirion,
Art thou afraid ?   I do not hear thy
    voice.
Die as thy brothers died.   Thou must
    not live !

SCENE II. — THE MOTHER ; ANTIOCHUS;
    SIRION.

The Mother.   Are they all dead ?
Ant.   Of all thy Seven Sons
One only lives.   Behold them where they
    lie ;
How dost thou like this picture ?
The Mother.   God in heaven !
Can a man do such deeds, and yet not die
By the recoil of his own wickedness ?
Ye murdered, bleeding, mutilated bodies
That were my children once, and still
    are mine,
I cannot watch o'er you as Rispah watched
In sackcloth o'er the seven sons of Saul,
Till water drop upon you out of heaven
And wash this blood away !   I cannot
    mourn

As she, the daughter of Aiah, mourned
    the dead,
From the beginning of the barley-harvest
Until the autumn rains, and suffered not
The birds of air to rest on them by day,
Nor the wild beasts by night.   For ye
    have died
A better death, a death so full of life
That I ought rather to rejoice than
    mourn. —
Wherefore art thou not dead, O Sirion ?
Wherefore art thou the only living thing
Among thy brothers dead ?   Art thou
    afraid ?
    Ant.   O woman, I have spared him for
        thy sake,
For he is fair to look upon and comely ;
And I have sworn to him by all the
    gods
That I would crown his life with joy and
    honor,
Heap treasures on him, luxuries, de-
    lights,
Make him my friend and keeper of my
    secrets,
If he would turn from your Mosaic Law
And be as we are ; but he will not listen.
    The Mother.   My noble Sirion !
    Ant.   Therefore I beseech thee,
Who art his mother, thou wouldst speak
    with him,
And wouldst persuade him.   I am sick
    of blood.
    The Mother.   Yea, I will speak with
        him and will persuade him.
O Sirion, my son ! have pity on me,
On me that bare thee, and that gave thee
    suck,
And fed and nourished thee, and brought
    thee up
With the dear trouble of a mother's care
Unto this age.   Look on the heavens
    above thee,
And on the earth and all that is therein ;
Consider that God made them out of
    things
That were not ; and that likewise in this
    manner
Mankind was made.   Then fear not this
    tormentor ;
But, being worthy of thy brethren, take
Thy death as they did, that I may re-
    ceive thee
Again in mercy with them.
    Ant.   I am mocked,
Yea, I am laughed to scorn.
    Sirion.   Whom wait ye for ?

Never will I obey the King's command-
    ment,
But the commandment of the ancient
    Law,
That was by Moses given unto our fa-
    thers.
And thou, O godless man, that of all
    others
Art the most wicked, be not lifted
    up,
Nor puffed up with uncertain hopes, up-
    lifting
Thy hand against the servants of the
    Lord,
For thou hast not escaped the righteous
    judgment
Of the Almighty God, who seeth all
    things!
    Ant. He is no God of mine; I fear
    him not.
    Sirion. My brothers, who have suf-
    fered a brief pain,
Are dead; but thou, Antiochus, shalt
    suffer
The punishment of pride. I offer up
My body and my life, beseeching God
That he would speedily be merciful
Unto our nation, and that thou by
    plagues
Mysterious and by torments mayest con-
    fess
That he alone is God.
    Ant.   Ye both shall perish
By torments worse than any that your
    God,
Here or hereafter, hath in store for me.
    The Mother. My Sirion, I am proud
    of thee!
    Ant.   Be silent!
Go to thy bed of torture in yon cham-
    ber,
Where lie so many sleepers, heartless
    mother!
Thy footsteps will not wake them, nor
    thy voice,
Nor wilt thou hear, amid thy troubled
    dreams,
Thy children crying for thee in the night!
    The Mother. O Death, that stretchest
    thy white hands to me,
I fear them not, but press them to my
    lips,
That are as white as thine; for I am
    Death,
Nay, am the Mother of Death, seeing
    these sons
All lying lifeless. — Kiss me, Sirion.

ACT III.

The Battle-field of Beth-horon.

SCENE I. — JUDAS MACCABÆUS *in armor
    before his tent.*

    Judas. The trumpets sound; the
        echoes of the mountains
Answer them, as the Sabbath morning
    breaks
Over Beth-horon and its battle-field,
Where the great captain of the hosts of
    God,
A slave brought up in the brick-fields of
    Egypt,
O'ercame the Amorites. There was no
    day
Like that, before or after it, nor shall be.
The sun stood still; the hammers of the
    hail
Beat on their harness; and the captains
    set
Their weary feet upon the necks of kings,
As I will upon thine, Antiochus,
Thou man of blood! — Behold the rising
    sun
Strikes on the golden letters of my banner,
Be Elohim Yehovah! Who is like
To thee, O Lord, among the gods?
            — Alas!
I am not Joshua, I cannot say,
"Sun, stand thou still on Gibeon, and
    thou Moon,
In Ajalon!" Nor am I one who wastes
The fateful time in useless lamentation;
But one who bears his life upon his hand
To lose it or to save it, as may best
Serve the designs of Him who giveth
    life.

SCENE II. — JUDAS MACCABÆUS; JEWISH
    FUGITIVES.

    Judas. Who and what are ye, that
        with furtive steps
Steal in among our tents?
    Fugitives.   O Maccabæus,
Outcasts are we, and fugitives as thou art,
Jews of Jerusalem, that have escaped
From the polluted city, and from death.
    Judas. None can escape from death.
        Say that ye come
To die for Israel, and ye are welcome.
What tidings bring ye?
    Fugitives.   Tidings of despair.

The Temple is laid waste ; the precious vessels,
Censers of gold, vials and veils and crowns,
And golden ornaments, and hidden treasures,
Have all been taken from it, and the Gentiles
With revelling and with riot fill its courts,
And dally with harlots in the holy places.
　Judas. All this I knew before.
　Fugitives.　　　Upon the altar
Are things profane, things by the law forbidden ;
Nor can we keep our Sabbaths or our Feasts,
But on the festivals of Dionysus
Must walk in their processions, bearing ivy
To crown a drunken god.
　Judas.　　　This too I know.
But tell me of the Jews. How fare the Jews ?
　Fugitives. The coming of this mischief hath been sore
And grievous to the people. All the land
Is full of lamentation and of mourning.
The Princes and the Elders weep and wail ;
The young men and the maidens are made feeble ;
The beauty of the women hath been changed.
　Judas. And are there none to die for Israel ?
'T is not enough to mourn. Breastplate and harness
Are better things than sackcloth. Let the women
Lament for Israel ; the men should die.
　Fugitives. Both men and women die ; old men and young :
Old Eleazer died : and Máhala
With all her Seven Sons.
　Judas.　　　Antiochus,
At every step thou takest there is left
A bloody footprint in the street, by which
The avenging wrath of God will track thee out !
It is enough. Go to the sutler's tents :
Those of you who are men, put on such armor
As ye may find ; those of you who are women,

Buckle that armor on ; and for a watchword
Whisper, or cry aloud, "The Help of God."

SCENE III. — JUDAS MACCABÆUS ; NICANOR.

　Nicanor. Hail, Judas Maccabæus !
　Judas.　　　Hail ! — Who art thou
That comest here in this mysterious guise
Into our camp unheralded ?
　Nic.　　　A herald
Sent from Nicanor.
　Judas.　　　Heralds come not thus.
Armed with thy shirt of mail from head to heel,
Thou glidest like a serpent silently
Into my presence. Wherefore dost thou turn
Thy face from me ? A herald speaks his errand
With forehead unabashed. Thou art a spy
Sent by Nicanor.
　Nic.　　　No disguise avails !
Behold my face ; I am Nicanor's self.
　Judas. Thou art indeed Nicanor. I salute thee.
What brings thee hither to this hostile camp
Thus unattended ?
　Nic.　　　Confidence in thee.
Thou hast the nobler virtues of thy race,
Without the failings that attend those virtues.
Thou canst be strong, and yet not tyrannous,
Canst righteous be and not intolerant.
Let there be peace between us.
　Judas.　　　What is peace ?
Is it to bow in silence to our victors ?
Is it to see our cities sacked and pillaged,
Our people slain, or sold as slaves, or fleeing
At night-time by the blaze of burning towns ;
Jerusalem laid waste ; the Holy Temple
Polluted with strange gods ? Are these things peace ?
　Nic. These are the dire necessities that wait
On war, whose loud and bloody enginery
I seek to stay. Let there be peace between
Antiochus and thee.

Judas.   Antiochus ?
What is Antiochus, that he should prate
Of peace to me, who am a fugitive ?
To-day he shall be lifted up ; to-morrow
Shall not be found, because he is re-
    turned
Unto his dust ; his thought has come to
    nothing.
There is no peace between us, nor can
    be,
Until this banner floats upon the walls
Of our Jerusalem.
    Nic.   Between that city
And thee there lies a waving wall of
    tents,
Held by a host of forty thousand foot,
And horsemen seven thousand.   What
    hast thou
To bring against all these ?
    Judas.   The power of God,
Whose breath shall scatter your white
    tents abroad,
As flakes of snow.
    Nic.   Your Mighty One in heaven
Will not do battle on the Seventh Day ;
It is his day of rest.
    Judas.   Silence, blasphemer.
Go to thy tents.
    Nic.   Shall it be war or peace ?
    Judas.   War, war, and only war.   Go
    to thy tents
That shall be scattered, as by you were
    scattered
The torn and trampled pages of the Law,
Blown through the windy streets.
    Nic.   Farewell, brave foe !
    Judas. Ho, there, my captains ! Have
    safe-conduct given
Unto Nicanor's herald through the camp,
And come yourselves to me. — Farewell,
    Nicanor !   .

SCENE IV. — JUDAS MACCABÆUS ; CAP-
    TAINS AND SOLDIERS.

    Judas. The hour is come.   Gather
    the host together
For battle. Lo, with trumpets and with
    songs
The army of Nicanor comes against us.
Go forth to meet them, praying in your
    hearts,
And fighting with your hands.
    Captains.   Look forth and see !
The morning sun is shining on their
    shields

Of gold and brass ; the mountains glis-
    ten with them,
And shine like lamps.   And we who are
    so few
And poorly armed, and ready to faint
    with fasting,
How shall we fight against this multi-
    tude ?
    Judas. The victory of a battle stand-
    eth not
In multitudes, but in the strength that
    cometh
From heaven above.   The Lord forbid
    that I
Should do this thing, and flee away from
    them.
Nay, if our hour be come, then let us
    die ;
Let us not stain our honor.
    Captains.   'T is the Sabbath.
Wilt thou fight on the Sabbath, Macca-
    bæus ?
    Judas. Ay ; when I fight the battles
    of the Lord,
I fight them on his day, as on all others.
Have ye forgotten certain fugitives
That fled once to these hills, and hid
    themselves
In caves ?   How their pursuers camped
    against them
Upon the Seventh Day, and challenged
    them ?
And how they answered not, nor cast a
    stone,
Nor stopped the places where they lay
    concealed,
But meekly perished with their wives
    and children,
Even to the number of a thousand souls ?
We who are fighting for our laws and
    lives
Will not so perish.
    Captains.   Lead us to the battle !
    Judas. And let our watchword be,
    "The Help of God ! "
Last night I dreamed a dream ; and in
    my vision
Beheld Onias, our High-Priest of old,
Who holding up his hands prayed for
    the Jews.
This done, in the like manner there ap-
    peared
An old man, and exceeding glorious,
With hoary hair, and of a wonderful
And excellent majesty.   And Onias said :
"This is a lover of the Jews, who pray-
    eth

Much for the people and the Holy
  City, —
God's prophet Jeremias." And the
  prophet
Held forth his right hand and gave
  unto me
A sword of gold ; and giving it he said :
"Take thou this holy sword, a gift from
  God,
And with it thou shalt wound thine
  adversaries."
  Captains. The Lord is with us !
  Judas.   Hark ! I hear the trumpets
Sound from Beth-horon ; from the bat-
  tle-field
Of Joshua, where he smote the Amorites,
Smote the Five Kings of Eglon and of
  Jarmuth,
Of Hebron, Lachish, and Jerusalem,
As we to-day will smite Nicanor's hosts
And leave a memory of great deeds be-
  hind us.
  Captains and Soldiers. The Help of
  God !
  Judas.   *Be Elohim Yehovah !*
Lord, thou didst send thine Angel in the
  time
Of Esekias, King of Israel,
And in the armies of Sennacherib
Didst slay a hundred fourscore and five
  thousand.
Wherefore, O Lord of heaven, now also
  send
Before us a good angel for a fear,
And through the might of thy right arm
  let those
Be stricken with terror that have come
  this day
Against thy holy people to blaspheme !

ACT IV.

*The outer Courts of the Temple at Jeru-
  salem.*

SCENE I. — JUDAS MACCABÆUS ; CAP-
        TAINS ; JEWS.

  Judas. Behold, our enemies are dis-
  comfited.
Jerusalem is fallen ; and our banners
Float from her battlements, and o'er her
  gates
Nicanor's severed head, a sign of terror,
Blackens in wind and sun.
  Captains.   O Maccabæus,

The citadel of Antiochus, wherein
The Mother with her Seven Sons was
  murdered,
Is still defiant.
  Judas.   Wait.
  Captains.   Its hateful aspect
Insults us with the bitter memories
Of other days.
  Judas.   Wait ; it shall disappear
And vanish as a cloud. First let us
  cleanse
The Sanctuary. See, it is become
Waste like a wilderness. Its golden
  gates
Wrenched from their hinges and con-
  sumed by fire ;
Shrubs growing in its courts as in a for-
  est ;
Upon its altars hideous and strange
  idols ;
And strewn about its pavement at my
  feet
Its Sacred Books, half burned and paint-
  ed o'er
With images of heathen gods.
  Jews.   Woe ! woe !
Our beauty and our glory are laid waste !
The Gentiles have profaned our holy
  places !

  (*Lamentation and alarm of trumpets.*)

  Judas. This sound of trumpets, and
  this lamentation,
The heart-cry of a people toward the
  heavens,
Stir me to wrath and vengeance. Go,
  my captains ;
I hold you back no longer. Batter
  down
The citadel of Antiochus, while here
We sweep away his altars and his gods.

SCENE II. — JUDAS MACCABÆUS ; JASON ;
            JEWS.

  Jews. Lurking among the ruins of the
  Temple,
Deep in its inner courts, we found this
  man,
Clad as High-Priest.
  Judas.   I ask not who thou art.
I know thy face, writ over with deceit
As are these tattered volumes of the Law
With heathen images. A priest of God
Wast thou in other days, but thou art
  now

A priest of Satan. Traitor, thou art Jason.

Jason. I am thy prisoner, Judas Maccabæus,
And it would ill become me to conceal
My name or office.

Judas. Over yonder gate
There hangs the head of one who was a
Greek.
What should prevent me now, thou man
of sin,
From hanging at its side the head of
one
Who born a Jew hath made himself a
Greek?

Jason. Justice prevents thee.

Judas. Justice? Thou art stained
With every crime 'gainst which the Decalogue
Thunders with all its thunder.

Jason. If not Justice,
Then Mercy, her handmaiden.

Judas. When hast thou
At any time, to any man or woman,
Or even to any little child, shown mercy?

Jason. I have but done what King
Antiochus
Commanded me.

Judas. True, thou hast been
the weapon
With which he struck; but hast been
such a weapon,
So flexible, so fitted to his hand,
It tempted him to strike. So thou hast
urged him
To double wickedness, thine own and
his.
Where is this King? Is he in Antioch
Among his women still, and from his
windows
Throwing down gold by handfuls, for
the rabble
To scramble for?

Jason. Nay, he is gone from there,
Gone with an army into the far East.

Judas. And wherefore gone?

Jason. I know not. For the space
Of forty days almost were horsemen
seen
Running in air, in cloth of gold, and
armed
With lances, like a band of soldiery;
It was a sign of triumph.

Judas. Or of death.
Wherefore art thou not with him?

Jason. I was left
For service in the Temple.

Judas. To pollute
And to corrupt the Jews; for there are
men
Whose presence is corruption; to be
with them
Degrades us and deforms the things we
do.

Jason. I never made a boast, as some
men do,
Of my superior virtue, nor denied
The weakness of my nature, that hath
made me
Subservient to the will of other men.

Judas. Upon this day, the five and-
twentieth day
Of the month Caslan, was the Temple
here
Profaned by strangers, — by Antiochus
And thee, his instrument. Upon this
day
Shall it be cleansed. Thou, who didst
lend thyself
Unto this profanation, canst not be
A witness of these solemn services.
There can be nothing clean where thou
art present.
The people put to death Callisthenes,
Who burned the Temple gates; and if
they find thee
Will surely slay thee. I will spare thy
life
To punish thee the longer. Thou shalt
wander
Among strange nations. Thou, that
hast cast out
So many from their native land, shalt
perish
In a strange land. Thou, that hast left
so many
Unburied, shalt have none to mourn for
thee,
Nor any solemn funerals at all,
Nor sepulchre with thy fathers. — Get
thee hence!

*(Music. Procession of Priests and people,
with citherns, harps, and cymbals. Judas Maccabæus puts himself at their
head, and they go into the inner courts.)*

SCENE III. — JASON, *alone.*

Jason. Through the Gate Beautiful I
see them come
With branches and green boughs and
leaves of palm,
And pass into the inner courts. Alas!

I should be with them, should be one of them,
But in an evil hour, an hour of weakness,
That cometh unto all, I fell away
From the old faith, and did not clutch the new,
Only an outward semblance of belief ;
For the new faith I cannot make mine own,
Not being born to it.   It hath no root
Within me.   I am neither Jew nor Greek,
But stand between them both, a renegade
To each in turn ; having no longer faith
In gods or men.   Then what mysterious charm,
What fascination is it chains my feet,
And keeps me gazing like a curious child
Into the holy places, where the priests
Have raised their altar ? — Striking stones together,
They take fire out of them, and light the lamps
In the great candlestick.   They spread the veils,
And set the loaves of showbread on the table.
The incense burns ; the well-remembered odor
Comes wafted unto me, and takes me back
To other days.   I see myself among them
As I was then ; and the old superstition
Creeps over me again ! — A childish fancy ! —
And hark ! they sing with citherns and with cymbals,
And all the people fall upon their faces,
Praying and worshipping ! — I will away
Into the East, to meet Antiochus
Upon his homeward journey, crowned with triumph.
Alas ! to-day I would give everything
To see a friend's face, or to hear a voice
That had the slightest tone of comfort in it !

ACT V.

The Mountains of Ecbatana.

SCENE I. — ANTIOCHUS ; PHILIP ; ATTENDANTS.

Ant. Here let us rest awhile.   Where are we, Philip ?
What place is this ?

Philip.   Ecbatana, my Lord ;
And yonder mountain range is the Orontes.
Ant. The Orontes is my river at Antioch.
Why did I leave it ?   Why have I been tempted
By coverings of gold and shields and breastplates
To plunder Elymais, and be driven
From out its gates, as by a fiery blast
Out of a furnace ?
Philip.   These are fortune's changes.
Ant. What a defeat it was !   The Persian horsemen
Came like a mighty wind, the wind Khamáseen,
And melted us away, and scattered us
As if we were dead leaves, or desert sand.
Philip. Be comforted, my Lord ; for thou hast lost
But what thou hadst not.
Ant.   I, who made the Jews
Skip like the grasshoppers, am made myself
To skip among these stones.
Philip.   Be not discouraged.
Thy realm of Syria remains to thee ;
That is not lost nor marred.
Ant.   O, where are now
The splendors of my court, my baths and banquets ?
Where are my players and my dancing women ?
Where are my sweet musicians with their pipes,
That made me merry in the olden time ?
I am a laughing-stock to man and brute.
The very camels, with their ugly faces,
Mock me and laugh at me.
Philip.   Alas ! my Lord,
It is not so.   If thou wouldst sleep awhile,
All would be well.
Ant.   Sleep from mine eyes is gone,
And my heart faileth me for very care.
Dost thou remember, Philip, the old fable
Told us when we were boys, in which the bear
Going for honey overturns the hive,
And is stung blind by bees ?   I am that beast,
Stung by the Persian swarms of Elymais.
Philip. When thou art come again to Antioch

These thoughts will be as covered and
forgotten
As are the tracks of Pharaoh's chariot-
wheels
In the Egyptian sands.
 Ant.   Ah! when I come
Again to Antioch! When will that be?
Alas! alas!

SCENE II. — ANTIOCHUS; PHILIP; A MES-
SENGER.

 Messenger. May the King live forever!
 Ant. Who art thou, and whence com-
est thou?
 Messenger. My Lord,
I am a messenger from Antioch,
Sent here by Lysias.
 Ant. A strange foreboding
Of something evil overshadows me.
I am no reader of the Jewish Scriptures;
I know not Hebrew; but my High-
Priest Jason,
As I remember, told me of a Prophet
Who saw a little cloud rise from the
sea
Like a man's hand, and soon the heaven
was black
With clouds and rain. Here, Philip,
read; I cannot;
I see that cloud. It makes the letters
dim
Before mine eyes.
 Philip (*reading*). "To King Antio-
chus,
The God, Epiphanes."
 Ant. O mockery!
Even Lysias laughs at me! — Go on, go
on!
 Philip (*reading*). "We pray thee
hasten thy return. The realm
Is falling from thee. Since thou hast
gone from us
The victories of Judas Maccabæus
Form all our annals. First he overthrew
Thy forces at Beth-horon, and passed on,
And took Jerusalem, the Holy City.
And then Emmaus fell; and then Beth-
sura;
Ephron and all the towns of Galaad,
And Maccabæus marched to Carnion."
 Ant. Enough, enough! Go call my
chariot-men;
We will drive forward, forward, without
ceasing,
Until we come to Antioch. My captains,

My Lysias, Gorgias, Seron, and Nica-
nor,
Are babes in battle, and this dreadful
Jew
Will rob me of my kingdom and my
crown.
My elephants shall trample him to dust;
I will wipe out his nation, and will
make
Jerusalem a common burying-place,
And every home within its walls a
tomb!

(*Throws up his hands, and sinks into the
arms of attendants, who lay him upon
a bank.*)

 Philip. Antiochus! Antiochus! Alas,
The King is ill! What is it, O my Lord?
 Ant. Nothing. A sudden and sharp
spasm of pain,
As if the lightning struck me, or the
knife
Of an assassin smote me to the heart.
'T is passed, even as it came. Let us
set forward.
 Philip. See that the chariots be in
readiness;
We will depart forthwith.
 Ant. A moment more.
I cannot stand. I am become at once
Weak as an infant. Ye will have to
lead me.
Jove, or Jehovah, or whatever name
Thou wouldst be named, — it is alike to
me, —
If I knew how to pray, I would entreat
To live a little longer.
 Philip. O my Lord,
Thou shalt not die; we will not let thee
die!
 Ant. How canst thou help it, Philip?
O the pain!
Stab after stab. Thou hast no shield
against
This unseen weapon. God of Israel,
Since all the other gods abandon me,
Help me. I will release the Holy City
Garnish with goodly gifts the Holy
Temple.
Thy people, whom I judged to be un-
worthy
To be so much as buried, shall be equal
Unto the citizens of Antioch.
I will become a Jew, and will declare
Through all the world that is inhabited
The power of God!
 Philip. He faints. It is like death.

Bring here the royal litter. We will
  bear him
Into the camp, while yet he lives.
  Ant.   O Philip,
Into what tribulation am I come !
Alas ! I now remember all the evil
That I have done the Jews ; and for this
  cause
These troubles are upon me, and behold
I perish through great grief in a strange
  land.
  Philip. Antiochus ! my King !
  Ant.   Nay, King no longer.
Take thou my royal robes, my signet-
  ring,
My crown and sceptre, and deliver them

Unto my son, Antiochus Eupator ;
And unto the good Jews, my citizens,
In all my towns, say that their dying
  monarch
Wisheth them joy, prosperity, and
  health.
I who, puffed up with pride and arro-
  gance,
Thought all the kingdoms of the earth
  mine own,
If I would but outstretch my hand and
  take them,
Meet face to face a greater potentate,
King Death — Epiphanes — the Illus-
  trious !

                                        [*Dies.*

A HANDFUL OF TRANSLATIONS.

THE FUGITIVE.

*Tartar Song from the Prose Version of
Chodzko.*

I.

"HE is gone to the desert land !
I can see the shining mane
Of his horse on the distant plain,
As he rides with his Kossak band !

" Come back, rebellious one !
Let thy proud heart relent ;
Come back to my tall, white tent,
Come back, my only son !·

" Thy hand in freedom shall
Cast thy hawks, when morning breaks,
On the swans of the Seven Lakes,
On the lakes of Karajal.

" I will give thee leave to stray
And pasture thy hunting steeds
In the long grass and the reeds
Of the meadows of Karaday.

" I will give thee my coat of mail,
Of softest leather made,
With choicest steel inlaid ;
Will not all this prevail ? "

II.

" This hand no longer shall
Cast my hawks, when morning breaks,

On the swans of the Seven Lakes,
On the lakes of Karajal.

" I will no longer stray
And pasture my hunting steeds
In the long grass and the reeds
Of the meadows of Karaday.

" Though thou give me thy coat of mail,
Of softest leather made,
With choicest steel inlaid,
All this cannot prevail.

" What right hast thou, O Khan,
To me, who am mine own,
Who am slave to God alone,
And not to any man ?

" God will appoint the day
When I again shall be
By the blue, shallow sea,
Where the steel-bright sturgeons play.

" God, who doth care for me,
In the barren wilderness,
On unknown hills, no less
Will my companion be.

" When I wander lonely and lost
In the wind ; when I watch at night
Like a hungry wolf, and am white
And covered with hoar-frost ;

" Yea, wheresoever I be,
In the yellow desert sands,

In mountains or unknown lands,
Allah will care for me!"

III.

Then Sobra, the old, old man, —
Three hundred and sixty years
Had he lived in this land of tears,
Bowed down and said, "O Khan!

"If you bid me, I will speak.
There's no sap in dry grass,
No marrow in dry bones! Alas,
The mind of old men is weak!

"I am old, I am very old:
I have seen the primeval man,
I have seen the great Gengis Khan,
Arrayed in his robes of gold.

"What I say to you is the truth;
And I say to you, O Khan,
Pursue not the star-white man,
Pursue not the beautiful youth.

"Him the Almighty made,
And brought him forth of the light,
At the verge and end of the night,
When men on the mountain prayed.

"He was born at the break of day,
When abroad the angels walk;
He hath listened to their talk,
And he knoweth what they say.

"Gifted with Allah's grace,
Like the moon of Ramazan
When it shines in the skies, O Khan,
Is the light of his beautiful face.

"When first on earth he trod,
The first words that he said
Were these, as he stood and prayed,
There is no God but God!

"And he shall be king of men,
For Allah hath heard his prayer,
And the Archangel in the air,
Gabriel, hath said, Amen!"

THE SIEGE OF KAZAN.

Tartar Song, from the Prose Version of Chodzko.

BLACK are the moors before Kazan,
And their stagnant waters smell of
blood:

22

I said in my heart, with horse and man,
I will swim across this shallow flood.

Under the feet of Argamack,
Like new moons were the shoes he
bare,
Silken trappings hung on his back,
In a talisman on his neck, a prayer.

My warriors, thought I, are followin
me;
But when I looked behind, alas!
Not one of all the band could I see,
All had sunk in the black morass!

Where are our shallow fords? and where
The power of Kazan with its fourfold
gates?
From the prison windows our maidens
fair
Talk of us still through the iron grates.

We cannot hear them; for horse and man
Lie buried deep in the dark abyss!
Ah! the black day hath come down on
Kazan!
Ah! was ever a grief like this?

THE BOY AND THE BROOK.

Armenian Popular Song, from the Prose Version of Alishan.

DOWN from yon distant mountain
height
The brooklet flows through the village
street;
A boy comes forth to wash his hands,
Washing, yes washing, there he stands,
In the water cool and sweet.

Brook, from what mountain dost thou
come,
O my brooklet cool and sweet!
I come from yon mountain high and
cold,
Where lieth the new snow on the old,
And melts in the summer heat.

Brook, to what river dost thou go?
O my brooklet cool and sweet!
I go to the river there below
Where in bunches the violets grow,
And sun and shadow meet.

Brook, to what garden dost thou go?
O my brooklet cool and sweet!

I go to the garden in the vale
Where all night long the nightingale
Her love-song doth repeat.

Brook, to what fountain dost thou go ?
O my brooklet cool and sweet !
I go to the fountain at whose brink
The maid that loves thee comes to
    drink,
And whenever she looks therein,
I rise to meet her, and kiss her chin,
And my joy is then complete.

TO THE STORK.

*Armenian Popular Song, from the Prose
Version of Alishan.*

WELCOME, O Stork ! that dost wing
Thy flight from the far-away !
Thou hast brought us the signs of
    Spring,
Thou hast made our sad hearts gay.

Descend, O Stork ! descend
Upon our roof to rest ;
In our ash-tree, O my friend,
My darling, make thy nest.

To thee, O Stork, I complain,
O Stork, to thee I impart
The thousand sorrows, the pain
And aching of my heart.

When thou away didst go,
Away from this tree of ours,
The withering winds did blow,
And dried up all the flowers.

Dark grew the brilliant sky,
Cloudy and dark and drear ;
They were breaking the snow on high,
And winter was drawing near.

From Varaca's rocky wall,
From the rock of Varaca unrolled,
The snow came and covered all,
And the green meadow was cold.

O Stork, our garden with snow
Was hidden away and lost,
And the rose-trees that in it grow
Were withered by snow and frost.

CONSOLATION.

*To M. Duperrier, Gentleman of Aix
in Provence, on the Death of his
Daughter.*

FROM MALHERBE.

WILL then, Duperrier, thy sorrow be
    eternal ?
    And shall the sad discourse
Whispered within thy heart, by tender
    ness paternal,
    Only augment its force ?

Thy daughter's mournful fate, into the
    tomb descending
    By death's frequented ways,
Has it become to thee a labyrinth never
    ending,
    Where thy lost reason strays ?

I know the charms that made her youth
    a benediction :
    Nor should I be content,
As a censorious friend, to solace thine
    affliction
    By her disparagement.

But she was of the world, which fairest
    things exposes
    To fates the most forlorn ;
A rose, she too hath lived as long as live
    the roses,
    The space of one brief morn.

*   *   *   *   *

Death has his rigorous laws, unparal-
    leled, unfeeling ;
    All prayers to him are vain ;
Cruel, he stops his ears, and, deaf to our
    appealing,
    He leaves us to complain.

The poor man in his hut, with only thatch
    for cover,
    Unto these laws must bend ;
The sentinel that guards the barriers
    the Louvre
    Cannot our kings defend.

To murmur against death, in petulant
    defiance,
    Is never for the best ;
To will what God doth will, that is the
    only science
    That gives us any rest.

TO CARDINAL RICHELIEU.

FROM MALHERBE.

THOU mighty Prince of Church and
 State,
Richelieu ! until the hour of death,
Whatever road man chooses, Fate
Still holds him subject to her breath.
Spun of all silks, our days and nights
Have sorrows woven with delights ;
And of this intermingled shade
Our various destiny appears,
Even as one sees the course of years
Of summers and of winters made.

Sometimes the soft, deceitful hours
Let us enjoy the halcyon wave ;
Sometimes impending peril lowers
Beyond the seaman's skill to save.
The Wisdom, infinitely wise,
That gives to human destinies
Their foreordained necessity,
Has made no law more fixed below,
Than the alternate ebb and flow
Of Fortune and Adversity.

THE ANGEL AND THE CHILD.

FROM JEAN REBOUL, THE BAKER OF NISMES.

AN angel with a radiant face,
 Above a cradle bent to look,
Seemed his own image there to trace,
 As in the waters of a brook.

" Dear child ! who me resemblest so,"
 It whispered, " come, O come with
  me !
Happy together let us go,
 The earth unworthy is of thee !

" Here none to perfect bliss attain ;
 The soul in pleasure suffering lies ;
Joy hath an undertone of pain,
 And even the happiest hours their
  sighs.

" Fear doth at every portal knock ;
 Never a day serene and pure
From the o'ershadowing tempest's shock
 Hath made the morrow's dawn secure.

" What, then, shall sorrows and shall
 fears
 Come to disturb so pure a brow ?)

And with the bitterness of tears
 These eyes of azure troubled grow ?

" Ah no ! into the fields of space,
 Away shalt thou escape with me ;
And Providence will grant thee grace
 Of all the days that were to be.

" Let no one in thy dwelling cower,
 In sombre vestments draped and
  veiled ;
But let them welcome thy last hour,
 As thy first moments once they hailed.

" Without a cloud be there each
 brow ;
 There let the grave no shadow cast ;
When one is pure as thou art now,
 The fairest day is still the last."

And waving wide his wings of white,
 The angel, at these words, had
  sped
Towards the eternal realms of light ! —
 Poor mother ! see, thy son is dead !

TO ITALY.

FROM FILICAJA.

ITALY ! Italy ! thou who 'rt doomed to
 wear
The fatal gift of beauty, and possess
The dower funest of infinite wretched-
 ness
Written upon thy forehead by despair ;
Ah ! would that thou wert stronger, or
 less fair.
That they might fear thee more, or love
 thee less,
Who in the splendor of thy loveli-
 ness
Seem wasting, yet to mortal combat
 dare !
Then from the Alps I should not see de-
 scending
Such torrents of armed men, nor Gallic
 horde
Drinking the wave of Po, distained
 with gore,
Nor should I see thee girded with a
 sword
Not thine, and with the stranger's arm
 contending,
Victor or vanquished, slave forevermore.

WANDERER'S NIGHT-SONGS.

FROM GOETHE.

I.

THOU that from the heavens art,
Every pain and sorrow stillest,
And the doubly wretched heart
Doubly with refreshment fillest,
I am weary with contending !
Why this rapture and unrest ?
Peace descending
Come, ah, come into my breast !

II.

O'er all the hill-tops
Is quiet now,
In all the tree-tops
Hearest thou
Hardly a breath ;
The birds are asleep in the trees :
Wait ; soon like these
Thou too shalt rest.

REMORSE.

FROM AUGUST VON PLATEN.

How I started up in the night, in the
    night,
Drawn on without rest or reprieval !
The streets, with their watchmen, were
    lost to my sight,
    As I wandered so light
    In the night, in the night,
Through the gate with the arch mediæ-
    val.

The mill-brook rushed from the rocky
    height,
    I leaned o'er the bridge in my yearn-
    ing ;

Deep under me watched I the waves in
    their flight,
    As they glided so light
    In the night, in the night,
Yet backward not one was returning.

O'erhead were revolving, so countless
    and bright,
    The stars in melodious existence ;
And with them the moon, more serenely
    bedight ;—
    They sparkled so light
    In the night, in the night,
Through the magical, measureless dis-
    tance.

And upward I gazed in the night, in the
    night,
    And again on the waves in their fleet-
    ing ;
Ah woe ! thou hast wasted thy days in
    delight,
    Now silence thou light,
    In the night, in the night,
The remorse in thy heart that is beating.

SANTA TERESA'S BOOK-MARK.

FROM THE SPANISH OF SANTA TERESA.

LET nothing disturb thee,
Nothing affright thee ;
All things are passing ;
God never changeth ;
Patient endurance
Attaineth to all things;
Who God possesseth
In nothing is wanting ;
Alone God sufficeth.

Add to Interlude, p. 295, after the line, " Not what men saw, but what they feared."

Besides, unless my memory fail,
Your some one with an iron flail
Is not an ancient myth at all,
But comes much later on the scene
As Talus in the Faerie Queene,

The iron groom of Artegall,
Who threshed out falsehood and deceit,
And truth upheld, and righted wrong,
As was, as is the swallow, fleet,
And as the lion is, was strong."

THE MASQUE OF PANDORA.

I.

THE WORKSHOP OF HEPHÆSTUS.

HEPHÆSTUS, *standing before the statue of* PANDORA.

NOT fashioned out of gold, like Hera's
throne,
Nor forged of iron like the thunderbolts
Of Zeus omnipotent, or other works
Wrought by my hands at Lemnos or
Olympus,
But moulded in soft clay, that unresist-
ing
Yields itself to the touch, this lovely
form
Before me stands, perfect in every part.
Not Aphrodite's self appeared more fair,
When first upwafted by caressing winds
She came to high Olympus, and the gods
Paid homage to her beauty. Thus her
hair
Was cinctured; thus her floating dra-
pery
Was like a cloud about her, and her face
Was radiant with the sunshine and the
sea.

THE VOICE OF ZEUS.

Is thy work done, Hephæstus?

HEPHÆSTUS.
It is finished!

THE VOICE.

Not finished till I breathe the breath of
life
Into her nostrils, and she moves and
speaks.

HEPHÆSTUS.

Will she become immortal like ourselves?

THE VOICE.

The form that thou hast fashioned out
of clay
Is of the earth and mortal; but the spirit,

The life, the exhalation of my breath,
Is of diviner essence and immortal.
The gods shall shower on her their ben-
efactions,
She shall possess all gifts : the gift of
song,
The gift of eloquence, the gift of beauty,
The fascination and the nameless charm
That shall lead all men captive.

HEPHÆSTUS.

Wherefore? wherefore?

A wind shakes the house.

I hear the rushing of a mighty wind
Through all the halls and chambers of
my house!
Her parted lips inhale it, and her bosom
Heaves with the inspiration.   As a reed
Beside a river in the rippling current
Bends to and fro, she bows or lifts her
head.
She gazes round about as if amazed;
She is alive; she breathes, but yet she
speaks not!

PANDORA *descends from the pedestal.*

CHORUS OF THE GRACES.

AGLAIA.

In the workshop of Hephæstus
What is this I see?
Have the Gods to four increased us
Who were only three?
Beautiful in form and feature,
Lovely as the day,
Can there be so fair a creature
Formed of common clay?

THALIA.

O sweet, pale face! O lovely eyes of
azure,
Clear as the waters of a brook that run
Limpid and laughing in the summer
sun!

O golden hair that like a miser's treas-
    ure
In its abundance overflows the measure !
    O graceful form, that cloudlike floatest
        on
With the soft, undulating gait of one
Who moveth as if motion were a pleas-
    ure !
By what name shall I call thee ? Nymph
    or Muse,
Callirrhoë or Urania ? Some sweet
    name
Whose every syllable is a caress
Would best befit thee ; but I cannot
    choose,
Nor do I care to choose ; for still the
    same,
Nameless or named, will be thy love-
    liness.

EUPHROSYNE.

Dowered with all celestial gifts,
    Skilled in every art
That ennobles and uplifts
    And delights the heart,
Fair on earth shall be thy fame
    As thy face is fair,
And Pandora be the name
    Thou henceforth shalt bear.

II.

OLYMPUS.

HERMES, *putting on his sandals.*

MUCH must he toil who serves the Im-
    mortal Gods,
And I, who am their herald, most of all.
No rest have I, nor respite.   I no sooner
Unclasp the winged sandals from my
    feet,
Than I again must clasp them, and de-
    part
Upon some foolish errand.   But to-day
The errand is not foolish.   Never yet
With greater joy did I obey the summons
That sends me earthward.   I will fly so
    swiftly
That my caduceus in the whistling air
Shall make a sound like the Pandæan
    pipes,
Cheating the shepherds ; for to-day I go,
Commissioned by high-thundering Zeus,
    to lead
A maiden to Prometheus, in his tower,

And by my cunning arguments persuade
    him
To marry her.   What mischief lies con-
    cealed
In this design I know not ; but I know
Who thinks of marrying hath already
    taken
One step upon the road to penitence.
Such embassies delight me.   Forth I
    launch
On the sustaining air, nor fear to fall
Like Icarus, nor swerve aside like him
Who drove amiss Hyperion's fiery steeds.
I sink, I fly ! The yielding element
Folds itself round about me like an arm,
And holds me as a mother holds her
    child.

III.

TOWER OF PROMETHEUS ON MOUNT CAUCASUS.

PROMETHEUS.

I HEAR the trumpet of Alectryon
Proclaim the dawn.   The stars begin to
    fade,
And all the heavens are full of prophecies
And evil auguries.   Blood-red last night
I saw great Kronos rise ; the crescent
    moon
Sank through the mist, as if it were the
    scythe
His parricidal hand had flung far down
The western steeps.   O ye Immortal
    Gods,
What evil are ye plotting and contriving ?

HERMES *and* PANDORA *at the threshold.*

PANDORA.

I cannot cross the threshold.   An unseen
And icy hand repels me.   These blank
    walls
Oppress me with their weight !

PROMETHEUS.

                    Powerful ye are,
But not omnipotent.   Ye cannot fight
Against Necessity.   The Fates control
    you,
As they do us, and so far we are equals !

PANDORA.

Motionless, passionless, companionless,

He sits there muttering in his beard.
His voice
Is like a river flowing underground !

HERMES.

Prometheus, hail !

PROMETHEUS.
                Who calls me ?

HERMES.
                It is I.

Dost thou not know me ?

PROMETHEUS.
                By thy winged cap
And winged heels I know thee. Thou
    art Hermes,
Captain of thieves! Hast thou again
    been stealing
The heifers of Admetus in the sweet
Meadows of asphodel ? or Hera's girdle ?
Or the earth-shaking trident of Poseidon ?

HERMES.

And thou, Prometheus ; say, hast thou
    again
Been stealing fire from Helios' chariot-
    wheels
To light thy furnaces ?

PROMETHEUS.
                Why comest thou hither
So early in the dawn ?

HERMES.
                The Immortal Gods
Know naught of late or early. Zeus
    himself
The omnipotent hath sent me.

PROMETHEUS.
                For what purpose ?

HERMES.

To bring this maiden to thee.

PROMETHEUS.
                I mistrust
The Gods and all their gifts. If they
    have sent her
It is for no good purpose.

HERMES.
                What disaster
Could she bring on thy house, who is a
    woman ?

PROMETHEUS.

The Gods are not my friends, nor am I
    theirs.
Whatever comes from them, though in
    a shape
As beautiful as this, is evil only.
Who art thou ?

PANDORA.
                One who, though to thee unknown,
Yet knoweth thee.

PROMETHEUS.

How shouldst thou know me, woman ?

PANDORA.

Who knoweth not Prometheus the hu-
    mane ?

PROMETHEUS.

Prometheus the unfortunate ; to whom
Both Gods and men have shown them-
    selves ungrateful.
When every spark was quenched on every
    hearth
Throughout the earth, I brought to man
    the fire
And all its ministrations.   My reward
Hath been the rock and vulture.

HERMES.
                But the Gods
At last relent and pardon.

PROMETHEUS.
                They relent not;
They pardon not ; they are implacable,
Revengeful, unforgiving !

HERMES.
                As a pledge
Of reconciliation they have sent to thee
This divine being, to be thy companion,
And bring into thy melancholy house
The sunshine and the fragrance of her
    youth.

PROMETHEUS.

I need them not. I have within myself
All that my heart desires ; the ideal
    beauty
Which the creative faculty of mind
Fashions and follows in a thousand
    shapes
More lovely than the real.   My own
    thoughts

Are my companions; my designs and
labors
And aspirations are my only friends.

HERMES.

Decide not rashly.   The decision made
Can never be recalled.   The Gods im-
plore not,
Plead not, solicit not; they only offer
Choice and occasion, which once being
passed
Return no more.   Dost thou accept the
gift?

PROMETHEUS.

No gift of theirs, in whatsoever shape
It comes to me, with whatsoever charm
To fascinate my sense, will I receive.
Leave me.

PANDORA.

Let us go hence.   I will not stay.

HERMES.

We leave thee to thy vacant dreams, and
all
The silence and the solitude of thought,
The endless bitterness of unbelief,
The loneliness of existence without love.

CHORUS OF THE FATES.

CLOTHO.

How the Titan, the defiant,
The self-centred, self-reliant,
Wrapped in visions and illusions,
Robs himself of life's best gifts!
Till by all the storm-winds shaken,
By the blast of fate o'ertaken,
Hopeless, helpless, and forsaken,
In the mists of his confusions
To the reefs of doom he drifts!

LACHESIS.

Sorely tried and sorely tempted,
From no agonies exempted,
In the penance of his trial,
And the discipline of pain;
Often by illusions cheated,
Often baffled and defeated
In the tasks to be completed,
He, by toil and self-denial,
To the highest shall attain.

ATROPOS.

Tempt no more the noble schemer;
Bear unto some idle dreamer

This new toy and fascination,
This new dalliance and delight!
To the garden where reposes
Epimetheus crowned with roses,
To the door that never closes
Upon pleasure and temptation,
Bring this vision of the night!

IV.

THE AIR.

HERMES, *returning to Olympus.*

As lonely as the tower that he inhabits,
As firm and cold as are the crags about
him,
Prometheus stands.   The thunderbolts
of Zeus
Alone can move him; but the tender
heart
Of Epimetheus, burning at white heat,
Hammers and flames like all his broth-
er's forges!
Now as an arrow from Hyperion's bow,
My errand done, I fly, I float, I soar
Into the air, returning to Olympus.
O joy of motion!   O delight to cleave
The infinite realms of space, the liquid
ether,
Through the warm sunshine and the
cooling cloud,
Myself as light as sunbeam or as cloud!
With one touch of my swift and winged
feet,
I spurn the solid earth, and leave it
rocking
As rocks the bough from which a bird
takes wing.

V.

THE HOUSE OF EPIMETHEUS.

EPIMETHEUS.

BEAUTIFUL apparition! go not hence!
Surely thou art a Goddess, for thy voice
Is a celestial melody, and thy form
Self-poised as if it floated on the air!

PANDORA.

No Goddess am I, nor of heavenly birth,
But a mere woman fashioned out of clay
And mortal as the rest.

EPIMETHEUS.

              Thy face is fair;
There is a wonder in thine azure eyes
That fascinates me. Thy whole pres-
    ence seems
A soft desire, a breathing thought of love.
Say, would thy star like Merope's grow
    dim
If thou shouldst wed beneath thee?

PANDORA.

              Ask me not;
I cannot answer thee. I only know
The Gods have sent me hither.

EPIMETHEUS.

              I believe,
And thus believing am most fortunate.
It was not Hermes led thee here, but
    Eros,
And swifter than his arrows were thine
    eyes
In wounding me. There was no mo-
    ment's space
Between my seeing thee and loving thee.
O, what a telltale face thou hast! Again
I see the wonder in thy tender eyes.

PANDORA.

They do but answer to the love in thine,
Yet secretly I wonder thou shouldst
    love me.
Thou knowest me not.

EPIMETHEUS.

        Perhaps I know thee better
Than had I known thee longer. Yet it
    seems
That I have always known thee, and
    but now
Have found thee. Ah, I have been
    waiting long.

PANDORA.

How beautiful is this house! The at-
    mosphere
Breathes rest and comfort, and the many
    chambers
Seem full of welcomes.

EPIMETHEUS.

        They not only seem,
But truly are. This dwelling and its
    master
Belong to thee.

PANDORA.

        Here let me stay forever!
There is a spell upon me.

EPIMETHEUS.

             Thou thyself
Art the enchantress, and I feel thy
    power
Envelop me, and wrap my soul and sense
In an Elysian dream.

PANDORA.

            O, let me stay.
How beautiful are all things round about
    me,
Multiplied by the mirrors on the walls!
What treasures hast thou here! Yon
    oaken chest,
Carven with figures and embossed with
    gold,
Is wonderful to look upon! What choice
And precious things dost thou keep hid-
    den in it?

EPIMETHEUS.

I know not. 'T is a mystery.

PANDORA.

           Hast thou never
Lifted the lid?

EPIMETHEUS.

        The oracle forbids.
Safely concealed there from all mortal
    eyes
Forever sleeps the secret of the Gods.
Seek not to know what they have hidden
    from thee,
Till they themselves reveal it.

PANDORA.

            As thou wilt.

EPIMETHEUS.

Let us go forth from this mysterious
    place.
The garden walks are pleasant at this
    hour;
The nightingales among the sheltering
    boughs
Of populous and many-nested trees
Shall teach me how to woo thee, and
    shall tell me
By what resistless charms or incantations
They won their mates.

PANDORA.

Thou dost not need a teacher.

They go out.

CHORUS OF THE EUMENIDES.

What the Immortals
Confide to thy keeping,
Tell unto no man ;
Waking or sleeping,
Closed be thy portals
To friend as to foeman.

Silence conceals it ;
The word that is spoken
Betrays and reveals it ;
By breath or by token
The charm may be broken.

With shafts of their splendors
The Gods unforgiving
Pursue the offenders,
The dead and the living !
Fortune forsakes them,
Nor earth shall abide them,
Nor Tartarus hide them ;
Swift wrath overtakes them !

With useless endeavor,
Forever, forever,
Is Sisyphus rolling
His stone up the mountain !
Immersed in the fountain,
Tantalus tastes not
The water that wastes not !
Through ages increasing
The pangs that afflict him,
With motion unceasing
The wheel of Ixion
Shall torture its victim !

VI.

IN THE GARDEN.

EPIMETHEUS.

YON snow-white cloud that sails sublime
in ether
Is but the sovereign Zeus, who like a
swan
Flies to fair-ankled Leda !

PANDORA.

Or perchance
Ixion's cloud, the shadowy shape of Hera,
That bore the Centaurs.

EPIMETHEUS.

The divine and human

CHORUS OF BIRDS.

Gently swaying to and fro,
Rocked by all the winds that blow,
Bright with sunshine from above
Dark with shadow from below,
Beak to beak and breast to breast
In the cradle of their nest,
Lie the fledglings of our love.

ECHO.

Love ! love !

EPIMETHEUS.

Hark ! listen !   Hear how sweetly overhead
The feathered flute-players pipe their
songs of love,
And echo answers, love and only love.

CHORUS OF BIRDS.

Every flutter of the wing,
Every note of song we sing,
Every murmur, every tone,
Is of love and love alone.

ECHO.

Love alone !

EPIMETHEUS.

Who would not love, if loving she might
be
Changed like Callisto to a star in heaven ?

PANDORA.

Ah, who would love, if loving she might
be
Like Semele consumed and burnt to
ashes ?

EPIMETHEUS.

Whence knowest thou these stories ?

PANDORA.

Hermes taught me ;
He told me all the history of the Gods.

CHORUS OF REEDS.

Evermore a sound shall be
In the reeds of Arcady,
Evermore a low lament
Of unrest and discontent,

As the story is retold
Of the nymph so coy and cold,
Who with frightened feet outran
The pursuing steps of Pan.

EPIMETHEUS.

The pipe of Pan out of these reeds is
    made,
And when he plays upon it to the shep-
    herds
They pity him, so mournful is the sound.
Be thou not coy and cold as Syrinx was.

PANDORA.

Nor thou as Pan be rude and mannerless.

PROMETHEUS, *without.*

Ho! Epimetheus!

EPIMETHEUS.

'T is my brother's voice;
A sound unwelcome and inopportune
As was the braying of Silenus' ass,
Once heard in Cybele's garden.

PANDORA.

                    Let me go.
I would not be found here. I would
    not see him.

She escapes among the trees.

CHORUS OF DRYADES.

Haste and hide thee,
Ere too late,
In these thickets intricate;
Lest Prometheus
See and chide thee,
Lest some hurt
Or harm betide thee,
Haste and hide thee!

PROMETHEUS, *entering.*

Who was it fled from here? I saw a
    shape
Flitting among the trees.

EPIMETHEUS.

              It was Pandora.

PROMETHEUS.

O Epimetheus! Is it then in vain

That I have warned thee? Let me now
    implore.
Thou harborest in thy house a dangerous
    guest.

EPIMETHEUS.

Whom the Gods love they honor with
    such guests.

PROMETHEUS.

Whom the Gods would destroy they first
    make mad.

EPIMETHEUS.

Shall I refuse the gifts they send to me?

PROMETHEUS.

Reject all gifts that come from higher
    powers.

EPIMETHEUS.

Such gifts as this are not to be rejected.

PROMETHEUS.

Make not thyself the slave of any woman.

EPIMETHEUS.

Make not thyself the judge of any man.

PROMETHEUS.

I judge thee not; for thou art more than
    man;
Thou art descended from Titanic race,
And hast a Titan's strength, and faculties
That make thee godlike; and thou sittest
    here
Like Heracles spinning Omphale's flax,
And beaten with her sandals.

EPIMETHEUS.

                    O my brother!
Thou drivest me to madness with thy
    taunts.

PROMETHEUS.

And me thou drivest to madness with thy
    follies.
Come with me to my tower on Caucasus:
See there my forges in the roaring cav-
    erns,
Beneficent to man, and taste the joy
That springs from labor. Read with me
    the stars,
And learn the virtues that lie hidden in
    plants,
And all things that are useful.

EPIMETHEUS.
O my brother!
I am not as thou art. Thou dost inherit
Our father's strength, and I our mother's
weakness:
The softness of the Oceanides,
The yielding nature that cannot resist.

PROMETHEUS.
Because thou wilt not.

EPIMETHEUS.
Nay; because I cannot.

PROMETHEUS.
Assert thyself; rise up to thy full height;
Shake from thy soul these dreams effemi-
nate,
These passions born of indolence and
ease.
Resolve, and thou art free. But breathe
the air
Of mountains, and their unapproachable
summits
Will lift thee to the level of themselves.

EPIMETHEUS.
The roar of forests and of waterfalls,
The rushing of a mighty wind, with loud
And undistinguishable voices calling,
Are in my ear!

PROMETHEUS.
O, listen and obey.

EPIMETHEUS.
Thou leadest me as a child. I follow
thee.
They go out.

CHORUS OF OREADES.

Centuries old are the mountains;
Their foreheads wrinkled and rifted
Helios crowns by day,
Pallid Selene by night;
From their bosoms uptossed
The snows are driven and drifted,
Like Tithonus' beard
Streaming dishevelled and white.

Thunder and tempest of wind
Their trumpets blow in the vastness;
Phantoms of mist and rain,
Cloud and the shadow of cloud,

Pass and repass by the gates
Of their inaccessible fastness;
Ever unmoved they stand,
Solemn, eternal, and proud.

VOICES OF THE WATERS.

Flooded by rain and snow
In their inexhaustible sources,
Swollen by affluent streams
Hurrying onward and hurled
Headlong over the crags,
The impetuous water-courses,
Rush and roar and plunge
Down to the nethermost world.

Say, have the solid rocks
Into streams of silver been melted,
Flowing over the plains,
Spreading to lakes in the fields?
Or have the mountains, the giants,
The ice-helmed, the forest-belted,
Scattered their arms abroad;
Flung in the meadows their shields?

VOICES OF THE WINDS.

High on their turreted cliffs
That bolts of thunder have shattered,
Storm-winds muster and blow
Trumpets of terrible breath;
Then from the gateways rush,
And before them routed and scattered
Sullen the cloud-rack flies,
Pale with the pallor of death.

Onward the hurricane rides,
And flee for shelter the shepherds;
White are the frightened leaves,
Harvests with terror are white;
Panic seizes the herds,
And even the lions and leopards,
Prowling no longer for prey,
Crouch in their caverns with fright.

VOICES OF THE FOREST.

Guarding the mountains around
Majestic the forests are standing,
Bright are their crested helms,
Dark is their armor of leaves;
Filled with the breath of freedom
Each bosom subsiding, expanding,
Now like the ocean sinks,
Now like the ocean upheaves.

Planted firm on the rock,
With foreheads stern and defiant,
Loud they shout to the winds,
Loud to the tempest they call;
Naught but Olympian thunders,
That blasted Titan and Giant,
Them can uproot and o'erthrow,
Shaking the earth with their fall.

CHORUS OF OREADES.

These are the Voices Three
Of winds and forests and fountains,
Voices of earth and of air,
Murmur and rushing of streams,
Making together one sound,
The mysterious voice of the mountains,
Waking the sluggard that sleeps,
Waking the dreamer of dreams.

These are the Voices Three,
That speak of endless endeavor,
Speak of endurance and strength,
Triumph and fulness of fame,
Sounding about the world,
An inspiration forever,
Stirring the hearts of men,
Shaping their end and their aim.

VII.

THE HOUSE OF EPIMETHEUS.

PANDORA.

LEFT to myself I wander as I will,
And as my fancy leads me, through this
　　house,
Nor could I ask a dwelling more com-
　　plete
Were I indeed the Goddess that he
　deems me.
No mansion of Olympus, framed to be
The habitation of the Immortal Gods,
Can be more beautiful. And this is mine
And more than this, the love wherewith
　　he crowns me.
As if impelled by powers invisible
And irresistible, my steps return
Unto this spacious hall. All corridors
And passages lead hither, and all doors
But open into it. Yon mysterious chest
Attracts and fascinates me. Would I
　　knew
What there lies hidden! But the oracle

Forbids. Ah me! The secret then is
　　safe.
So would it be if it were in my keeping.
A crowd of shadowy faces from the mir-
　　rors
That line these walls are watching me.
　　I dare not
Lift up the lid. A hundred times the
　　act
Would be repeated, and the secret seen
By twice a hundred incorporeal eyes.

She walks to the other side of the hall.

My feet are weary, wandering to and
　　fro,
My eyes with seeing and my heart with
　　waiting.
I will lie here and rest till he returns,
Who is my dawn, my day, my Helios.

*Throws herself upon a couch, and falls
　　asleep.*

ZEPHYRUS.

Come from thy caverns dark and deep,
O son of Erebus and Night;
All sense of hearing and of sight
Enfold in the serene delight
And quietude of sleep!

Set all thy silent sentinels
To bar and guard the Ivory Gate,
And keep the evil dreams of fate
And falsehood and infernal hate
Imprisoned in their cells.

But open wide the Gate of Horn,
Whence, beautiful as planets, rise
The dreams of truth, with starry eyes,
And all the wondrous prophecies
And visions of the morn.

CHORUS OF DREAMS FROM THE IVORY
GATE.

Ye sentinels of sleep,
　It is in vain ye keep
Your drowsy watch before the Ivory
　　Gate;
　Though closed the portal seems,
　The airy feet of dreams
Ye cannot thus in walls incarcerate.

We phantoms are and dreams
Born by Tartarean streams,
As ministers of the infernal powers;

O son of Erebus
And Night, behold ! we thus
Elude your watchful warders on the
    towers !

From gloomy Tartarus
The Fates have summoned us
To whisper in her ear, who lies asleep,
    A tale to fan the fire
    Of her insane desire
To know a secret that the Gods would
    keep.

This passion, in their ire,
The Gods themselves inspire,
To vex mankind with evils manifold,
    So that disease and pain
    O'er the whole earth may reign,
And nevermore return the Age of Gold.

PANDORA, *waking.*

A voice said in my sleep: " Do not de-
    lay :
Do not delay ; the golden moments fly !
The oracle hath forbidden ; yet not thee
Doth it forbid, but Epimetheus only ! "
I am alone.   These faces in the mirrors
Are but the shadows and phantoms of
    myself ;
They cannot help nor hinder.   No one
    sees me,
Save the all-seeing Gods, who, knowing
    good
And knowing evil, have created me
Such as I am, and filled me with desire
Of knowing good and evil like them-
    selves.

She approaches the chest.

I hesitate no longer.   Weal or woe,
Or life or death, the moment shall de-
    cide.

*She lifts the lid.   A dense mist rises from
the chest, and fills the room.   PANDORA
falls senseless on the floor.   Storm without.*

CHORUS OF DREAMS FROM THE GATE
OF HORN.

Yes, the moment shall decide !
It already hath decided ;
And the secret once confided
To the keeping of the Titan
Now is flying far and wide,
Whispered, told on every side,
To disquiet and to frighten.

Fever of the heart and brain,
Sorrow, pestilence, and pain,
Moans of anguish, maniac laughter,
All the evils that hereafter
Shall afflict and vex mankind,
All into the air have risen
From the chambers of their prison :
Only Hope remains behind.

VIII.

IN THE GARDEN.

EPIMETHEUS.

THE storm is past, but it hath left be-
    hind it
Ruin and desolation.   All the walks
Are strewn with shattered boughs; the
    birds are silent ;
The flowers, downtrodden by the wind,
    lie dead ;
The swollen rivulet sobs with secret pain,
The melancholy reeds whisper together
As if some dreadful deed had been com-
    mitted
They dare not name, and all the air is
    heavy
With an unspoken sorrow !   Premoni-
    tions,
Foreshadowings of some terrible disaster
Oppress my heart.   Ye Gods, avert the
    omen !

PANDORA, *coming from the house.*

O Epimetheus, I no longer dare
To lift mine eyes to thine, nor hear thy
    voice,
Being no longer worthy of thy love.

EPIMETHEUS.

What hast thou done?

PANDORA.

Forgive me not, but kill me.

EPIMETHEUS.

What hast thou done?

PANDORA.

I pray for death, not pardon.

EPIMETHEUS.

What hast thou done?

PANDORA.

I dare not speak of it.

EPIMETHEUS.

Thy pallor and thy silence terrify me !

PANDORA.

I have brought wrath and ruin on thy
house !
My heart hath braved the oracle that
guarded
The fatal secret from us, and my hand
Lifted the lid of the mysterious chest !

EPIMETHEUS.

Then all is lost ! I am indeed undone.

PANDORA.

I pray for punishment, and not for pardon.

EPIMETHEUS.

Mine is the fault, not thine. On me
shall fall
The vengeance of the Gods, for I betrayed
Their secret when, in evil hour, I said
It was a secret; when, in evil hour,
I left thee here alone to this temptation.
Why did I leave thee?

PANDORA.

Why didst thou return?
Eternal absence would have been to me
The greatest punishment. To be left
alone
And face to face with my own crime, had
been
Just retribution. Upon me, ye Gods,
Let all your vengeance fall !

EPIMETHEUS.

On thee and me.
I do not love thee less for what is done,
And cannot be undone. Thy very weak-
ness
Hath brought thee nearer to me, and
henceforth
My love will have a sense of pity in it,
Making it less a worship than before.

PANDORA.

Pity me not; pity is degradation.
Love me and kill me.

EPIMETHEUS.

Beautiful Pandora !
Thou art a Goddess still !

PANDORA.

I am a woman;
And the insurgent demon in my nature,

That made me brave the oracle, revolts
At pity and compassion.   Let me die;
What else remains for me?

EPIMETHEUS.

Youth, hope, and love :
To build a new life on a ruined life,
To make the future fairer than the past,
And make the past appear a troubled
dream.
Even now in passing through the garden
walks
Upon the ground I saw a fallen nest
Ruined and full of rain ; and over me
Beheld the uncomplaining birds already
Busy in building a new habitation.

PANDORA.

Auspicious omen!

EPIMETHEUS.

May the Eumenides
Put out their torches and behold us not,
And fling away their whips of scorpions
And touch us not.

PANDORA.

Me let them punish.
Only through punishment of our evil
deeds,
Only through suffering, are we reconciled
To the immortal Gods and to ourselves.

CHORUS OF THE EUMENIDES.

Never shall souls like these
Escape the Eumenides,
The daughters dark of Acheron and
Night !
Unquenched our torches glare,
Our scourges in the air
Send forth prophetic sounds before they
smite.

Never by lapse of time
The soul defaced by crime
Into its former self returns again ;
For every guilty deed
Holds in itself the seed
Of retribution and undying pain.

Never shall be the loss
Restored, till Helios
Hath purified them with his heavenly
fires ;
Then what was lost is won,
And the new life begun,
Kindled with nobler passions and desires.

THE HANGING OF THE CRANE.

I.

THE lights are out, and gone are all the
    guests
That thronging came with merriment
    and jests
    To celebrate the Hanging of the Crane
In the new house, — into the night are
    gone ;
But still the fire upon the hearth burns on,
    And I alone remain.

O fortunate, O happy day,
When a new household finds its place
Among the myriad homes of earth,
Like a new star just sprung to birth,
And rolled on its harmonious way
Into the boundless realms of space !

So said the guests in speech and song,
As in the chimney, burning bright,
We hung the iron crane to-night,
And merry was the feast and long.

II.

AND now I sit and muse on what may be,
And in my vision see, or seem to see,
    Through floating vapors interfused
      with light,
Shapes indeterminate, that gleam and
    fade,
As shadows passing into deeper shade
    Sink and elude the sight.

For two alone, there in the hall,
Is spread the table round and small ;
Upon the polished silver shine
The evening lamps, but, more divine,
The light of love shines over all ;
Of love, that says not mine and thine,
But ours, for ours is thine and mine.

They want no guests, to come between
Their tender glances like a screen,
And tell them tales of land and sea,
And whatsoever may betide
The great, forgotten world outside ;
They want no guests ; they needs must
    be
Each other's own best company.

III.

THE picture fades ; as at a village fair
A showman's views, dissolving into air,
    Again appear transfigured on the
      screen,
So in my fancy this ; and now once more,
In part transfigured, through the open
    door
    Appears the selfsame scene.

Seated, I see the two again,
But not alone ; they entertain
A little angel unaware,
With face as round as is the moon ;
A royal guest with flaxen hair,
Who, throned upon his lofty chair,
Drums on the table with his spoon,
Then drops it careless on the floor,
To grasp at things unseen before.

Are these celestial manners ? these
The ways that win, the arts that please?
Ah yes ; consider well the guest,
And whatsoe'er he does seems best ;
He ruleth by the right divine
Of helplessness, so lately born
In purple chambers of the morn,
As sovereign over thee and thine.
He speaketh not ; and yet there lies
A conversation in his eyes ;
The golden silence of the Greek,
The gravest wisdom of the wise,
Not spoken in language, but in looks
More legible than printed books,
As if he could but would not speak.
And now, O monarch absolute,
Thy power is put to proof ; for, lo !
Resistless, fathomless, and slow,
The nurse comes rustling like the sea,
And pushes back thy chair and thee,
And so good night to King Canute.

IV.

As one who walking in a forest sees
A lovely landscape through the parted
    trees,

"I see the table wider grown."   Page 353.

Then sees it not, for boughs that in-
        tervene ;
Or as we see the moon sometimes revealed
Through drifting clouds, and then again
        concealed,
    So I behold the scene.

There are two guests at table now ;
The king, deposed and older grown,
No longer occupies the throne, —
The crown is on his sister's brow ;
A Princess from the Fairy Isles,
The very pattern girl of girls,
All covered and embowered in curls,
Rose-tinted from the Isle of Flowers,
And sailing with soft, silken sails
From far-off Dreamland into ours.
Above their bowls with rims of blue
Four azure eyes of deeper hue
Are looking, dreamy with delight ;
Limpid as planets that emerge
Above the ocean's rounded verge,
Soft-shining through the summer
        night.
Steadfast they gaze, yet nothing see
Beyond the horizon of their bowls ;
Nor care they for the world that rolls
With all its freight of troubled souls
Into the days that are to be.

V.

AGAIN the tossing boughs shut out the
        scene,
Again the drifting vapors intervene,
    And the moon's pallid disk is hidden
        quite ;
And now I see the table wider grown,
As round a pebble into water thrown
    Dilates a ring of light.

I see the table wider grown,
I see it garlanded with guests,
As if fair Ariadne's Crown
Out of the sky had fallen down ;
Maidens within whose tender breasts
A thousand restless hopes and fears,
Forth reaching to the coming years,
Flutter awhile, then quiet lie,
Like timid birds that fain would fly,
But do not dare to leave their nests ;—
And youths, who in their strength elate
Challenge the van and front of fate,
Eager as champions to be
In the divine knight-errantry
Of youth, that travels sea and land
28

Seeking adventures, or pursues,
Through cities, and through solitudes
Frequented by the lyric Muse,
The phantom with the beckoning hand,
That still allures and still eludes.
O sweet illusions of the brain !
O sudden thrills of fire and frost !
The world is bright while ye remain,
And dark and dead when ye are lost !

VI.

THE meadow-brook, that seemeth to
        stand still,
Quickens its current as it nears the mill ;
    And so the stream of Time that lin-
        gereth
In level places, and so dull appears,
Runs with a swifter current as it nears
        The gloomy mills of Death.

And now, like the magician's scroll,
That in the owner's keeping shrinks
With every wish he speaks or thinks,
Till the last wish consumes the whole,
The table dwindles, and again
I see the two alone remain.
The crown of stars is broken in parts ;
Its jewels, brighter than the day,
Have one by one been stolen away
To shine in other homes and hearts.
One is a wanderer now afar
In Ceylon or in Zanzibar,
Or sunny regions of Cathay ;
And one is in the boisterous camp
Mid clink of arms and horses' tramp,
And battle's terrible array.
I see the patient mother read,
With aching heart, of wrecks that float
Disabled on those seas remote,
Or of some great heroic deed
On battle-fields, where thousands bleed
To lift one hero into fame.
Anxious she bends her graceful head
Above these chronicles of pain,
And trembles with a secret dread
Lest there among the drowned or slain
She find the one beloved name.

VII.

AFTER a day of cloud and wind and rain
Sometimes the setting sun breaks out
        again,

And, touching all the darksome woods
with light,
Smiles on the fields, until they laugh
and sing,
Then like a ruby from the horizon's ring
Drops down into the night.

What see I now ? The night is fair,
The storm of grief, the clouds of care,
The wind, the rain, have passed away ;
The lamps are lit, the fires burn bright,
The house is full of life and light :
It is the Golden Wedding day.
The guests come thronging in once more,
Quick footsteps sound along the floor,
The trooping children crowd the stair,
And in and out and everywhere
Flashes along the corridor
The sunshine of their golden hair.

On the round table in the hall
Another Ariadne's Crown
Out of the sky hath fallen down;
More than one Monarch of the Moon
Is drumming with his silver spoon ;
The light of love shines over all.

O fortunate, O happy day !
The people sing, the people say.
The ancient bridegroom and the bride,
Smiling contented and serene
Upon the blithe, bewildering scene,
Behold, well pleased, on every side
Their forms and features multiplied,
As the reflection of a light
Between two burnished mirrors gleams,
Or lamps upon a bridge at night
Stretch on and on before the sight,
Till the long vista endless seems.

MORITURI SALUTAMUS.

POEM FOR THE FIFTIETH ANNIVERSARY OF THE CLASS OF 1825 IN BOWDOIN COLLEGE.

Tempora labuntur, tacitisque senescimus annis,
Et fugiunt freno non remorante dies.
OVID, *Fastorum*, Lib. vi.

"O CÆSAR, we who are about to die
Salute you ! " was the gladiators' cry
In the arena, standing face to face
With death and with the Roman popu-
lace.

O ye familiar scenes, — ye groves of
pine,
That once were mine and are no longer
mine, —
Thou river, widening through the mead-
ows green
To the vast sea, so near and yet un-
seen, —
Ye halls, in whose seclusion and repose
Phantoms of fame, like exhalations, rose
And vanished, — we who are about to
die
Salute you ; earth and air and sea and
sky,
And the Imperial Sun that scatters
down
His sovereign splendors upon grove and
town.

Ye do not answer us ! ye do not hear !
We are forgotten ; and in your austere
And calm indifference, ye little care
Whether we come or go, or whence or
where.
What passing generations fill these
halls,
What passing voices echo from these
walls,
Ye heed not ; we are only as the blast,
A moment heard, and then forever past.

Not so the teachers who in earlier days
Led our bewildered feet through learn-
ing's maze ;
They answer us — alas ! what have I
said ?
What greetings come there from the
voiceless dead ?
What salutation, welcome, or reply ?
What pressure from the hands that life-
less lie ?
They are no longer here ; they all are
gone

Into the land of shadows, — all save
   one.
Honor and reverence, and the good re-
   pute
That follows faithful service as its fruit,
Be unto him, whom living we salute.

The great Italian poet, when he made
His dreadful journey to the realms of
   shade,
Met there the old instructor of his
   youth,
And cried in tones of pity and of ruth :
" O, never from the memory of my
   heart
Your dear, paternal image shall depart,
Who while on earth, ere yet by death
   surprised,
Taught me how mortals are immortal-
   ized ;
How grateful am I for that patient care
All my life long my language shall de-
   clare."

To-day we make the poet's words our
   own,
And utter them in plaintive undertone ;
Nor to the living only be they said,
But to the other living called the dead,
Whose dear, paternal images appear
Not wrapped in gloom, but robed in sun-
   shine here ;
Whose simple lives, complete and with-
   out flaw,
Were part and parcel of great Nature's
   law ;
Who said not to their Lord, as if afraid,
" Here is thy talent in a napkin laid,"
But labored in their sphere, as men who
   live
In the delight that work alone can give.
Peace be to them ; eternal peace and rest,
And the fulfilment of the great behest :
" Ye have been faithful over a few
   things,
Over ten cities shall ye reign as kings."

And ye who fill the places we once filled,
And follow in the furrows that we tilled,
Young men, whose generous hearts are
   beating high,
We who are old, and are about to die,
Salute you ; hail you ; take your hands
   in ours,
And crown you with our welcome as
   with flowers !

How beautiful is youth ! how bright it
   gleams
With its illusions, aspirations, dreams !
Book of Beginnings, Story without End,
Each maid a heroine, and each man a
   friend !
Aladdin's Lamp, and Fortunatus' Purse,
That holds the treasures of the universe !
All possibilities are in its hands,
No danger daunts it, and no foe with-
   stands ;
In its sublime audacity of faith,
" Be thou removed ! " it to the moun-
   tain saith,
And with ambitious feet, secure and
   proud,
Ascends the ladder leaning on the
   cloud !

As ancient Priam at the Scæan gate
Sat on the walls of Troy in regal state
With the old men, too old and weak to
   fight,
Chirping like grasshoppers in their de-
   light
To see the embattled hosts, with spear
   and shield,
Of Trojans and Achaians in the field ;
So from the snowy summits of our years
We see you in the plain, as each appears,
And question of you ; asking, "Who is
   he
That towers above the others ?   Which
   may be
Atreides, Menelaus, Odysseus,
Ajax the great, or bold Idomeneus ?"

Let him not boast who puts his armor
   on
As he who puts it off, the battle done.
Study yourselves ; and most of all note
   well
Wherein kind Nature meant you to
   excel.
Not every blossom ripens into fruit ;
Minerva, the inventress of the flute,
Flung it aside, when she her face sur-
   veyed
Distorted in a fountain as she played ;
The unlucky Marsyas found it, and his
   fate
Was one to make the bravest hesitate.

Write on your doors the saying wise and
   old,
" Be bold ! be bold ! " and everywhere
   — " Be bold ;

Be not too bold!" Yet better the excess
Than the defect ; better the more than less ;
Better like Hector in the field to die,
Than like a perfumed Paris turn and fly.

And now, my classmates ; ye remaining few
That number not the half of those we knew,
Ye, against whose familiar names not yet
The fatal asterisk of death is set,
Ye I salute ! The horologe of Time
Strikes the half-century with a solemn chime,
And summons us together once again,
The joy of meeting not unmixed with pain.

Where are the others ? Voices from the deep
Caverns of darkness answer me : "They sleep !"
I name no names ; instinctively I feel
Each at some well-remembered grave will kneel,
And from the inscription wipe the weeds and moss,
For every heart best knoweth its own loss.
I see their scattered gravestones gleaming white
Through the pale dusk of the impending night ;
O'er all alike the impartial sunset throws
Its golden lilies mingled with the rose ;
We give to each a tender thought, and pass
Out of the graveyards with their tangled grass,
Unto these scenes frequented by our feet
When we were young, and life was fresh and sweet.

What shall I say to you ? What can I say
Better than silence is ? When I survey
This throng of faces turned to meet my own,
Friendly and fair, and yet to me unknown,
Transformed the very landscape seems to be ;
It is the same, yet not the same to me.

So many memories crowd upon my brain,
So many ghosts are in the wooded plain,
I fain would steal away, with noiseless tread,
As from a house where some one lieth dead.
I cannot go ; — I pause ; — I hesitate ;
My feet reluctant linger at the gate ;
As one who struggles in a troubled dream
To speak and cannot, to myself I seem.

Vanish the dream ! Vanish the idle fears !
Vanish the rolling mists of fifty years !
Whatever time or space may intervene,
I will not be a stranger in this scene.
Here every doubt, all indecision, ends ;
Hail, my companions, comrades, classmates, friends !

Ah me ! the fifty years since last we met
Seem to me fifty folios bound and set
By Time, the great transcriber, on his shelves,
Wherein are written the histories of ourselves.
What tragedies, what comedies, are there ;
What joy and grief, what rapture and despair !
What chronicles of triumph and defeat,
Of struggle, and temptation, and retreat !
What records of regrets, and doubts, and fears !
What pages blotted, blistered by our tears !
What lovely landscapes on the margin shine,
What sweet, angelic faces, what divine
And holy images of love and trust,
Undimmed by age, unsoiled by damp or dust !

Whose hand shall dare to open and explore
These volumes, closed and clasped forevermore ?
Not mine. With reverential feet I pass ;
I hear a voice that cries, " Alas ! alas !
Whatever hath been written shall remain,
Nor be erased nor written o'er again ;
The unwritten only still belongs to thee :
Take heed, and ponder well what that shall be."

As children frightened by a thunder-
cloud
Are reassured if some one reads aloud
A tale of wonder, with enchantment
fraught,
Or wild adventure, that diverts their
thought,
Let me endeavor with a tale to chase
The gathering shadows of the time and
place,
And banish what we all too deeply feel
Wholly to say, or wholly to conceal.

In mediæval Rome, I know not where,
There stood an image with its arm in
air,
And on its lifted finger, shining clear,
A golden ring with the device, "Strike
here!"
Greatly the people wondered, though
none guessed
The meaning that these words but half
expressed,
Until a learned clerk, who at noonday
With downcast eyes was passing on his
way,
Paused, and observed the spot, and
marked it well,
Whereon the shadow of the finger fell;
And, coming back at midnight, delved,
and found
A secret stairway leading under ground.
Down this he passed into a spacious
hall,
Lit by a flaming jewel on the wall;
And opposite in threatening attitude
With bow and shaft a brazen statue
stood.
Upon its forehead, like a coronet,
Were these mysterious words of menace
set:
"That which I am, I am; my fatal aim
None can escape, not even yon lumi-
nous flame!"

Midway the hall was a fair table placed,
With cloth of gold, and golden cups en-
chased
With rubies, and the plates and knives
were gold,
And gold the bread and viands mani-
fold.
Around it, silent, motionless, and sad,
Were seated gallant knights in armor
clad,
And ladies beautiful with plume and
zone,

But they were stone, their hearts within
were stone;
And the vast hall was filled in every part
With silent crowds, stony in face and
heart.

Long at the scene, bewildered and
amazed
The trembling clerk in speechless won-
der gazed;
Then from the table, by his greed made
bold,
He seized a goblet and a knife of gold,
And suddenly from their seats the guests
upsprang,
The vaulted ceiling with loud clamors
rang,
The archer sped his arrow, at their call,
Shattering the lambent jewel on the
wall,
And all was dark around and overhead;—
Stark on the floor the luckless clerk lay
dead!

The writer of this legend then records
Its ghostly application in these words:
The image is the Adversary old,
Whose beckoning finger points to realms
of gold;
Our lusts and passions are the down-
ward stair
That leads the soul from a diviner air;
The archer, Death; the flaming jewel,
Life;
Terrestrial goods, the goblet and the
knife;
The knights and ladies, all whose flesh
and bone
By avarice have been hardened into
stone;
The clerk, the scholar whom the love
of pelf
Tempts from his books and from his
nobler self.

The scholar and the world! The end-
less strife,
The discord in the harmonies of life!
The love of learning, the sequestered
nooks,
And all the sweet serenity of books;
The market-place, the eager love of gain,
Whose aim is vanity, and whose end is
pain!

But why, you ask me, should this tale be
told

To men grown old, or who are growing
    old ?
It is too late ! Ah, nothing is too late
Till the tired heart shall cease to palpi-
    tate.
Cato learned Greek at eighty ; Sophocles
Wrote his grand Œdipus, and Simonides
Bore off the prize of verse from his com-
    peers,
When each had numbered more than
    fourscore years,
And Theophrastus, at fourscore and ten,
Had but begun his Characters of Men
Chaucer, at Woodstock with the night-
    ingales,
At sixty wrote the Canterbury Tales ;
Goethe at Weimar, toiling to the last,
Completed Faust when eighty years were
    past.
These are indeed exceptions ; but they
    show
How far the gulf-stream of our youth
    may flow
Into the arctic regions of our lives,
Where little else than life itself survives.

As the barometer foretells the storm
While still the skies are clear, the
    weather warm,
So something in us, as old age draws
    near,
Betrays the pressure of the atmosphere.
The nimble mercury, ere we are aware,
Descends the elastic ladder of the air ;
The telltale blood in artery and vein

Sinks from its higher levels in the brain ;
Whatever poet, orator, or sage
May say of it, old age is still old age.
It is the waning, not the crescent moon ;
The dusk of evening, not the blaze of
    noon :
It is not strength, but weakness ; not de-
    sire,
But its surcease ; not the fierce heat of
    fire,
The burning and consuming element,
But that of ashes and of embers spent,
In which some living sparks we still
    discern,
Enough to warm, but not enough to burn.

What then ? Shall we sit idly down
    and say
The night hath come ; it is no longer day ?
The night hath not yet come ; we are
    not quite
Cut off from labor by the failing light ;
Something remains for us to do or dare ;
Even the oldest tree some fruit may bear ;
Not Œdipus Coloneus, or Greek Ode,
Or tales of pilgrims that one morning rode
Out of the gateway of the Tabard Inn,
But other something, would we but be-
    gin ;
For age is opportunity no less
Than youth itself, though in another
    dress,
And as the evening twilight fades away
The sky is filled with stars, invisible by
    day.

BIRDS OF PASSAGE.

FLIGHT THE FOURTH.

CHARLES SUMNER.

GARLANDS upon his grave,
    And flowers upon his hearse,
And to the tender heart and brave
    The tribute of this verse.

His was the troubled life,
    The conflict and the pain,
The grief, the bitterness of strife,
    The honor without stain.

Like Winkelried, he took
    Into his manly breast
The sheaf of hostile spears, and broke
    A path for the oppressed.

Then from the fatal field
    Upon a nation's heart
Borne like a warrior on his shield ! —
    So should the brave depart.

Death takes us by surprise,
    And stays our hurrying feet ;

The great design unfinished lies,
  Our lives are incomplete.

But in the dark unknown
  Perfect their circles seem,
Even as a bridge's arch of stone
  Is rounded in the stream.

Alike are life and death,
  When life in death survives,
And the uninterrupted breath
  Inspires a thousand lives.

Were a star quenched on high,
  For ages would its light,
Still travelling downward from the sky,
  Shine on our mortal sight.

So when a great man dies,
  For years beyond our ken,
The light he leaves behind him lies
  Upon the paths of men.

TRAVELS BY THE FIRESIDE.

The ceaseless rain is falling fast,
  And yonder gilded vane,
Immovable for three days past,
  Points to the misty main.

It drives me in upon myself
  And to the fireside gleams,
To pleasant books that crowd my shelf,
  And still more pleasant dreams.

I read whatever bards have sung
  Of lands beyond the sea,
And the bright days when I was young
  Come thronging back to me.

In fancy I can hear again
  The Alpine torrent's roar,
The mule-bells on the hills of Spain,
  The sea at Elsinore.

I see the convent's gleaming wall
  Rise from its groves of pine,
And towers of old cathedrals tall,
  And castles by the Rhine.

I journey on by park and spire,
  Beneath centennial trees,
Through fields with poppies all on fire,
  And gleams of distant seas.

I fear no more the dust and heat,
  No more I feel fatigue,
While journeying with another's feet
  O'er many a lengthening league.

Let others traverse sea and land,
  And toil through various climes,
I turn the world round with my hand
  Reading these poets' rhymes.

From them I learn whatever lies
  Beneath each changing zone,
And see, when looking with their eyes,
  Better than with mine own.

CADENABBIA.

LAKE OF COMO.

No sound of wheels or hoof-beat breaks
  The silence of the summer day,
As by the loveliest of all lakes
  I while the idle hours away.

I pace the leafy colonnade
  Where level branches of the plane
Above me weave a roof of shade
  Impervious to the sun and rain.

At times a sudden rush of air
  Flutters the lazy leaves o'erhead,
And gleams of sunshine toss and flare
  Like torches down the path I tread.

By Somariva's garden gate
  I make the marble stairs my seat,
And hear the water, as I wait,
  Lapping the steps beneath my feet.

The undulation sinks and swells
  Along the stony parapets,
And far away the floating bells
  Tinkle upon the fisher's nets.

Silent and slow, by tower and town
  The freighted barges come and go,
Their pendent shadows gliding down
  By town and tower submerged below.

The hills sweep upward from the shore,
  With villas scattered one by one
Upon their wooded spurs, and lower
  Bellaggio blazing in the sun.

And dimly seen, a tangled mass
  Of walls and woods, of light and shade,

Stands beckoning up the Stelvio Pass
  Varenna with its white cascade.

I ask myself, Is this a dream?
  Will it all vanish into air?
Is there a land of such supreme
  And perfect beauty anywhere?

Sweet vision! Do not fade away:
  Linger until my heart shall take
Into itself the summer day,
  And all the beauty of the lake.

Linger until upon my brain
  Is stamped an image of the scene,
Then fade into the air again,
  And be as if thou hadst not been.

MONTE CASSINO.

TERRA DI LAVORO.

BEAUTIFUL valley! through whose ver-
    dant meads
Unheard the Garigliano glides along;—
The Liris, nurse of rushes and of reeds,
  The river taciturn of classic song.

The Land of Labor and the Land of Rest,
  Where mediæval towns are white on all
The hillsides, and where every moun-
    tain's crest
  Is an Etrurian or a Roman wall.

There is Alagna, where Pope Boniface
  Was dragged with contumely from his
    throne;
Sciàrra Colonna, was that day's disgrace
  The Pontiff's only, or in part thine
    own?

There is Ceprano, where a renegade
  Was each Apulian, as great Dante
    saith,
When Manfred by his men-at-arms be-
    trayed
  Spurred on to Benevento and to death.

There is Aquinum, the old Volscian town,
  Where Juvenal was born, whose lurid
    light
Still hovers o'er his birthplace like the
    crown
  Of splendor seen o'er cities in the night.

Doubled the splendor is, that in its
    streets
  The Angelic Doctor as a school-boy
    played,
And dreamed perhaps the dreams, that
    he repeats
  In ponderous folios for scholastics made.

And there, uplifted, like a passing cloud
  That pauses on a mountain summit
    high,
Monte Cassino's convent rears its proud
  And venerable walls against the sky.

Well I remember how on foot I climbed
  The stony pathway leading to its gate;
Above, the convent bells for vespers
    chimed,
  Below, the darkening town grew des-
    olate.

Well I remember the low arch and dark,
  The court-yard with its well, the ter-
    race wide,
From which, **far down, the valley** like a
    park
  Veiled in the evening mists, was dim
    descried.

The day was dying, and with feeble
    hands
  Caressed the mountain-tops; the vales
    between
Darkened; the river in the meadow-
    lands
  Sheathed itself as a sword, and was
    not seen.

The silence of the place was like a sleep,
  So full of rest it seemed; each passing
    tread
Was a reverberation from the deep
  Recesses of the ages that are dead.

For, more than thirteen centuries ago,
  Benedict fleeing from the gates of
    Rome,
A youth disgusted with its vice and woe,
  Sought in these mountain solitudes a
    home.

He founded here his Convent and his
    Rule
  Of prayer and work, and counted
    work as prayer;
The pen became a clarion, and his school
  Flamed like a beacon in the midnight
    air.

What though Boccaccio, in his reckless
way,
  Mocking the lazy brotherhood, de-
  plores
The illuminated manuscripts, that lay
  Torn and neglected on the dusty floors?

Boccaccio was a novelist, a child
  Of fancy and of fiction at the best !
This the urbane librarian said, and smiled
  Incredulous, as at some idle jest.

Upon such themes as these, with one
  young friar
I sat conversing late into the night,
Till in its cavernous chimney the wood-
  fire
    Had burnt its heart out like an ancho-
    rite.

And then translated, in my convent cell,
  Myself yet not myself, in dreams I lay,
And, as a monk who hears the matin bell,
  Started from sleep ; already it was day.

From the high window I beheld the scene
  On which Saint Benedict so oft had
  gazed, —
The mountains and the valley in the
  sheen
    Of the bright sun, — and stood as one
    amazed.

Gray mists were rolling, rising, vanish-
  ing ;
  The woodlands glistened with their
  jewelled crowns ;
Far off the mellow bells began to ring
For matins in the half-awakened towns.

The conflict of the Present and the Past,
  The ideal and the actual in our life,
As on a field of battle held me fast,
  Where this world and the next world
  were at strife.

For, as the valley from its sleep awoke,
  I saw the iron horses of the steam
Toss to the morning air their plumes of
  smoke,
  And woke, as one awaketh from a
  dream.

AMALFI.

SWEET the memory is to me
Of a land beyond the sea,
Where the waves and mountains meet,

Where, amid her mulberry-trees
Sits Amalfi in the heat,
Bathing ever her white feet
In the tideless summer seas.

In the middle of the town,
From its fountains in the hills,
Tumbling through the narrow gorge,
The Canneto rushes down,
Turns the great wheels of the mills,
Lifts the hammers of the forge.

'T is a stairway, not a street,
That ascends the deep ravine,
Where the torrent leaps between
Rocky walls that almost meet.
Toiling up from stair to stair
Peasant girls their burdens bear ;
Sunburnt daughters of the soil,
Stately figures tall and straight,
What inexorable fate
Dooms them to this life of toil ?

Lord of vineyards and of lands,
Far above the convent stands.
On its terraced walk aloof
Leans a monk with folded hands,
Placid, satisfied, serene,
Looking down upon the scene
Over wall and red-tiled roof ;
Wondering unto what good end
All this toil and traffic tend,
And why all men cannot be
Free from care and free from pain,
And the sordid love of gain,
And as indolent as he.

Where are now the freighted barks
From the marts of east and west ?
Where the knights in iron sarks
Journeying to the Holy Land,
Glove of steel upon the hand,
Cross of crimson on the breast ?
Where the pomp of camp and court ?
Where the pilgrims with their prayers ?
Where the merchants with their wares,
And their gallant brigantines
Sailing safely into port
Chased by corsair Algerines ?

Vanished like a fleet of cloud,
Like a passing trumpet-blast,
Are those splendors of the past,
And the commerce and the crowd !
Fathoms deep beneath the seas
Lie the ancient wharves and quays,
Swallowed by the engulfing waves :

Silent streets and vacant halls,
Ruined roofs and towers and walls;
Hidden from all mortal eyes
Deep the sunken city lies:
Even cities have their graves!

This is an enchanted land!
Round the headlands far away
Sweeps the blue Salernian bay
With its sickle of white sand:
Further still and furthermost
On the dim discovered coast
Pæstum with its ruins lies,
And its roses all in bloom
Seem to tinge the fatal skies
Of that lonely land of doom.

On his terrace, high in air,
Nothing doth the good monk care
For such worldly themes as these.
From the garden just below
Little puffs of perfume blow,
And a sound is in his ears
Of the murmur of the bees
In the shining chestnut-trees;
Nothing else he heeds or hears.
All the landscape seems to swoon
In the happy afternoon;
Slowly o'er his senses creep
The encroaching waves of sleep,
And he sinks as sank the town,
Unresisting, fathoms down,
Into caverns cool and deep!

Walled about with drifts of snow,
Hearing the fierce north-wind blow,
Seeing all the landscape white,
And the river cased in ice,
Comes this memory of delight,
Comes this vision unto me
Of a long-lost Paradise
In the land beyond the sea.

THE SERMON OF ST. FRANCIS.

Up soared the lark into the air,
A shaft of song, a winged prayer,
As if a soul, released from pain,
Were flying back to heaven again.

St. Francis heard; it was to him
An emblem of the Seraphim;
The upward motion of the fire,
The light, the heat, the heart's desire.

Around Assisi's convent gate
The birds, God's poor who cannot wait,
From moor and mere and darksome wood
Came flocking for their dole of food.

"O brother birds," St. Francis said,
"Ye come to me and ask for bread,
But not with bread alone to-day
Shall ye be fed and sent away.

"Ye shall be fed, ye happy birds,
With manna of celestial words;
Not mine, though mine they seem to be,
Not mine, though they be spoken through
    me.

"O, doubly are ye bound to praise
The great Creator in your lays;
He giveth you your plumes of down,
Your crimson hoods, your cloaks of brown.

"He giveth you your wings to fly
And breathe a purer air on high,
And careth for you everywhere,
Who for yourselves so little care!"

With flutter of swift wings and songs
Together rose the feathered throngs,
And singing scattered far apart;
Deep peace was in St. Francis' heart.

He knew not if the brotherhood
His homily had understood;
He only knew that to one ear
The meaning of his words was clear.

BELISARIUS.

I am poor and old and blind;
The sun burns me, and the wind
    Blows through the city gate
And covers me with dust
From the wheels of the august
    Justinian the Great.

It was for him I chased
The Persians o'er wild and waste,
    As General of the East;
Night after night I lay
In their camps of yesterday;
    Their forage was my feast.

For him, with sails of red,
And torches at mast-head,
    Piloting the great fleet,

I swept the Afric coasts
And scattered the Vandal hosts,
    Like dust in a windy street.

For him I won again
The Ausonian realm and reign,
    Rome and Parthenope ;
And all the land was mine
From the summits of Apennine
    To the shores of either sea.

For him, in my feeble age,
I dared the battle's rage,
    To save Byzantium's state,
When the tents of Zabergan,
Like snow-drifts overran
    The road to the Golden Gate.

And for this, for this, behold !
Infirm and blind and old,
    With gray, uncovered head,
Beneath the very arch
Of my triumphal march,
    I stand and beg my bread !

Methinks I still can hear,
Sounding distinct and near,
    The Vandal monarch's cry,
As, captive and disgraced,
With majestic step he paced, —
    " All, all is Vanity ! "

Ah ! vainest of all things
Is the gratitude of kings ;
    The plaudits of the crowd
Are but the clatter of feet
At midnight in the street,
    Hollow and restless and loud.

But the bitterest disgrace
Is to see forever the face
    Of the Monk of Ephesus !
The unconquerable will
This, too, can bear ; — I still
    Am Belisarius !

SONGO RIVER.

NOWHERE such a devious stream,
Save in fancy or in dream,

Winding slow through bush and brake
Links together lake and lake.

Walled with woods or sandy shelf,
Ever doubling on itself
Flows the stream, so still and slow
That it hardly seems to flow.

Never errant knight of old,
Lost in woodland or on wold,
Such a winding path pursued
Through the sylvan solitude.

Never school-boy in his quest
After hazel-nut or nest,
Through the forest in and out
Wandered loitering thus about.

In the mirror of its tide
Tangled thickets on each side
Hang inverted, and between
Floating cloud or sky serene.

Swift or swallow on the wing
Seems the only living thing,
Or the loon, that laughs and flies
Down to those reflected skies.

Silent stream ! thy Indian name
Unfamiliar is to fame ;
For thou hidest here alone,
Well content to be unknown.

But thy tranquil waters teach
Wisdom deep as human speech,
Moving without haste or noise
In unbroken equipoise.

Though thou turnest no busy mill,
And art ever calm and still,
Even thy silence seems to say
To the traveller on his way : —

" Traveller, hurrying from the heat
Of the city, stay thy feet !
Rest awhile, nor longer waste
Life with inconsiderate haste !

" Be not like a stream that brawls
Loud with shallow waterfalls,
But in quiet self-control
Link together soul and soul."

A BOOK OF SONNETS.

THREE FRIENDS OF MINE.

I.

WHEN I remember them, those friends
  of mine,
  Who are no longer here, the noble
    three,
  Who half my life were more than
    friends to me,
  And whose discourse was like a gener-
    ous wine,
I most of all remember the divine
  Something, that shone in them, and
    made us see
  The archetypal man, and what might
    be
  The amplitude of Nature's first design.
In vain I stretch my hands to clasp
    their hands ;
  I cannot find them.   Nothing now is
    left
  But a majestic memory.   They mean-
    while
Wander together in Elysian lands,
  Perchance remembering me, who am
    bereft
  Of their dear presence, and, remem-
    bering, smile.

II.

IN Attica thy birthplace should have
    been,
  Or the Ionian Isles, or where the seas
  Encircle in their arms the Cyclades,
  So wholly Greek wast thou in thy se-
    rene
And childlike joy of life, O Philhellene !
  Around thee would have swarmed the
    Attic bees ;
  Homer had been thy friend, or Soc-
    rates,
  And Plato welcomed thee to his de-
    mesne.
For thee old legends breathed historic
    breath ;
  Thou sawest Poseidon in the purple
    sea,

And in the sunset Jason's fleece of
    gold !
O, what hadst thou to do with cruel
    Death,
  Who wast so full of life, or Death
    with thee,
  That thou shouldst die before thou
    hadst grown old !

III.

I STAND again on the familiar shore,
  And hear the waves of the distracted
    sea
  Piteously calling and lamenting thee,
  And waiting restless at thy cottage
    door.
The rocks, the sea-weed on the ocean
    floor,
  The willows in the meadow, and the
    free
  Wild winds of the Atlantic welcome
    me ;
  Then why shouldst thou be dead, and
    come no more ?
Ah, why shouldst thou be dead, when
    common men
  Are busy with their trivial affairs,
  Having and holding ?   Why, when
    thou hadst read
Nature's mysterious manuscript, and
    then
  Wast ready to reveal the truth it bears,
  Why art thou silent ?   Why shouldst
    thou be dead ?

IV.

RIVER, that stealest with such silent
    pace
  Around the City of the Dead, where
    lies
  A friend who bore thy name, and
    whom these eyes
  Shall see no more in his accustomed
    place,
Linger and fold him in thy soft embrace

And say good night, for now the western skies
Are red with sunset, and gray mists arise
Like damps that gather on a dead man's face.
Good night! good night! as we so oft have said
Beneath this roof at midnight, in the days
That are no more, and shall no more return.
Thou hast but taken thy lamp and gone to bed ;
I stay a little longer, as one stays
To cover up the embers that still burn.

V.

THE doors are all wide open; at the gate
The blossomed lilacs counterfeit a blaze,
And seem to warm the air; a dreamy haze
Hangs o'er the Brighton meadows like a fate,
And on their margin, with sea-tides elate,
The flooded Charles, as in the happier days,
Writes the last letter of his name, and stays
His restless steps, as if compelled to wait.
I also wait; but they will come no more,
Those friends of mine, whose presence satisfied
The thirst and hunger of my heart. Ah me!
They have forgotten the pathway to my door!
Something is gone from nature since they died,
And summer is not summer, nor can be.

CHAUCER.

AN old man in a lodge within a park ;
The chamber walls depicted all around
With portraitures of huntsman, hawk, and hound.

And the hurt deer. He listeneth to the lark,
Whose song comes with the sunshine through the dark
Of painted glass in leaden lattice bound ;
He listeneth and he laugheth at the sound,
Then writeth in a book like any clerk.
He is the poet of the dawn, who wrote
The Canterbury Tales, and his old age
Made beautiful with song ; and as I read
I hear the crowing cock, I hear the note
Of lark and linnet, and from every page
Rise odors of ploughed field or flowery mead.

SHAKESPEARE.

A VISION as of crowded city streets,
With human life in endless overflow;
Thunder of thoroughfares ; trumpets that blow
To battle; clamor, in obscure retreats,
Of sailors landed from their anchored fleets;
Tolling of bells in turrets, and below
Voices of children, and bright flowers that throw
O'er garden-walls their intermingled sweets !
This vision comes to me when I unfold
The volume of the Poet paramount,
Whom all the Muses loved, not one alone ;—
Into his hands they put the lyre of gold,
And, crowned with sacred laurel at their fount,
Placed him as Musagetes on their throne.

MILTON.

I PACE the sounding sea-beach and behold
How the voluminous billows roll and run,
Upheaving and subsiding, while the sun
Shines through their sheeted emerald far unrolled,
And the ninth wave, slow gathering fold by fold

All its loose-flowing garments into one,
Plunges upon the shore, and floods the dun
Pale reach of sands, and changes them to gold.
So in majestic cadence rise and fall
The mighty undulations of thy song,
O sightless bard, England's Mæonides!
And ever and anon, high over all
Uplifted, a ninth wave superb and strong,
Floods all the soul with its melodious seas.

His patron saint descended in the sheen
Of his celestial armor, on serene
And quiet nights, when all the heavens were fair.
Not this I see, nor yet the ancient fable
Of Phaeton's wild course, that scorched the skies
Where'er the hoofs of his hot coursers trod;
But the white drift of worlds o'er chasms of sable,
The star-dust, that is whirled aloft and flies
From the invisible chariot-wheels of God.

KEATS.

THE young Endymion sleeps Endymion's sleep;
The shepherd-boy whose tale was left half told!
The solemn grove uplifts its shield of gold
To the red rising moon, and loud and deep
The nightingale is singing from the steep;
It is midsummer, but the air is cold;
Can it be death? Alas, beside the fold
A shepherd's pipe lies shattered near his sheep.
Lo! in the moonlight gleams a marble white,
On which I read: "Here lieth one whose name
Was writ in water." And was this the meed
Of his sweet singing? Rather let me write:
"The smoking flax before it burst to flame
Was quenched by death, and broken the bruised reed."

THE GALAXY.

TORRENT of light and river of the air,
Along whose bed the glimmering stars are seen
Like gold and silver sands in some ravine
Where mountain streams have left their channels bare!
The Spaniard sees in thee the pathway, where

THE SOUND OF THE SEA.

THE sea awoke at midnight from its sleep,
And round the pebbly beaches far and wide
I heard the first wave of the rising tide
Rush onward with uninterrupted sweep;
A voice out of the silence of the deep,
A sound mysteriously multiplied
As of a cataract from the mountain's side,
Or roar of winds upon a wooded steep.
So comes to us at times, from the unknown
And inaccessible solitudes of being,
The rushing of the sea-tides of the soul;
And inspirations, that we deem our own,
Are some divine foreshadowing and foreseeing
Of things beyond our reason or control.

A SUMMER DAY BY THE SEA.

THE sun is set; and in his latest beams
Yon little cloud of ashen gray and gold,
Slowly upon the amber air unrolled,
The falling mantle of the Prophet seems.
From the dim headlands many a light-house gleams,
The street-lamps of the ocean; and behold,
O'erhead the banners of the night unfold;
The day hath passed into the land of dreams.
O summer day beside the joyous sea!
O summer day so wonderful and white,

So full of gladness and so full of pain!
Forever and forever shalt thou be
  To some the gravestone of a dead de-
    light,
  To some the landmark of a new do-
    main.

THE TIDES.

I saw the long line of the vacant shore,
  The sea-weed and the shells upon the
    sand,
  And the brown rocks left bare on every
    hand,
  As if the ebbing tide would flow no
    more.
Then heard I, more distinctly than before,
  The ocean breathe and its great breast
    expand,
  And hurrying came on the defenceless
    land
  The insurgent waters with tumultuous
    roar.
All thought and feeling and desire, I
    said,
  Love, laughter, and the exultant joy of
    song
  Have ebbed from me forever! Sud-
    denly o'er me
They swept again from their deep ocean
    bed,
  And in a tumult of delight, and strong
  As youth, and beautiful as youth, up-
    bore me.

A SHADOW.

I said unto myself, if I were dead,
  What would befall these children?
    What would be
  Their fate, who now are looking up to
    me
  For help and furtherance? Their lives,
    I said,
Would be a volume wherein I have read
  But the first chapters, and no longer
    see
  To read the rest of their dear history,
  So full of beauty and so full of dread.
Be comforted; the world is very old,
  And generations pass, as they have
    passed,
  A troop of shadows moving with the
    sun;

Thousands of times has the old tale been
    told;
  The world belongs to those who come
    the last,
  They will find hope and strength as
    we have done.

A NAMELESS GRAVE.

"A soldier of the Union mustered out,'
  Is the inscription on an unknown grave
  At Newport News, beside the salt-sea
    wave,
  Nameless and dateless; sentinel or
    scout
Shot down in skirmish, or disastrous rout
  Of battle, when the loud artillery drave
  Its iron wedges through the ranks of
    brave
  And doomed battalions, storming the
    redoubt.
Thou unknown hero sleeping by the sea
  In thy forgotten grave! with secret
    shame
I feel my pulses beat, my forehead burn,
When I remember thou hast given for me
  All that thou hadst, thy life, thy very
    name,
  And I can give thee nothing in return.

SLEEP.

Lull me to sleep, ye winds, whose fitful
    sound
  Seems from some faint Æolian harp-
    string caught;
  Seal up the hundred wakeful eyes of
    thought
  As Hermes with his lyre in sleep pro-
    found
The hundred wakeful eyes of Argus
    bound;
  For I am weary, and am overwrought
  With too much toil, with too much
    care distraught,
  And with the iron crown of anguish
    crowned.
Lay thy soft hand upon my brow and
    cheek,
  O peaceful Sleep! until from pain re-
    leased
I breathe again uninterrupted breath!
Ah, with what subtile meaning did the
    Greek
  Call thee the lesser mystery at the feast
  Whereof the greater mystery is death!

THE OLD BRIDGE AT FLORENCE.

Taddeo Gaddi built me.   I am old,
    Five centuries old.   I plant my foot
        of stone
    Upon the Arno, as St. Michael's own
    Was planted on the dragon.   Fold by
        fold
Beneath me as it struggles, I behold
    Its glistening scales.   Twice hath it
        overthrown
    My kindred and companions.   Me
        alone
    It moveth not, but is by me controlled.
I can remember when the Medici
    Were driven from Florence; longer
        still ago
    The final wars of Ghibelline and Guelf.
Florence adorns me with her jewelry;
    And when I think that Michael Angelo
    Hath leaned on me, I glory in myself.

IL PONTE VECCHIO DI FIRENZE.

Gaddi mi fece; il Ponte Vecchio sono;
    Cinquecent' anni già sull' Arno pi-
        anto
    Il piede, come il suo Michele Santo
    Piantò sal draco.   Mentre ch' io ra-
        giono
Lo vedo torcere con flebil suono
    Le rilucenti scaglie.   Ha questi af-
        franto
    Due volte i miei maggior.   Me solo
        intanto
    Neppure muove, ed io non l' abban-
        dono.
Io mi rammento quando fur cacciati
    I Medici; pur quando Ghibellino
    E Guelfo fecer pace mi rammento.
Fiorenza i suoi giojelli m' ha prestati;
    E quando penso ch' Agnolo il divino
    Su me posava, insuperbir mi sento.

KÉRAMOS.

Turn, turn, my wheel!   Turn round
        and round
Without a pause, without a sound:
    So spins the flying world away!
This clay, well mixed with marl and sand,
Follows the motion of my hand;
For some must follow, and some com-
        mand,
    Though all are made of clay!

Thus sang the Potter at his task
Beneath the blossoming hawthorn-tree,
While o'er his features, like a mask,
The quilted sunshine and leaf-shade
Moved, as the boughs above him swayed,
And clothed him, till he seemed to be
A figure woven in tapestry,
So sumptuously was he arrayed
In that magnificent attire
Of sable tissue flaked with fire.
Like a magician he appeared,
A conjurer without book or beard;
And while he plied his magic art —
For it was magical to me —
I stood in silence and apart,
And wondered more and more to see
That shapeless, lifeless mass of clay

Rise up to meet the master's hand,
And now contract and now expand,
And even his slightest touch obey;
While ever in a thoughtful mood
He sang his ditty, and at times
Whistled a tune between the rhymes,
As a melodious interlude.

Turn, turn, my wheel!   All things mus:
        change
To something new, to something strange;
    Nothing that is can pause or stay;
The moon will wax, the moon will wane,
The mist and cloud will turn to rain,
The rain to mist and cloud again,
    To-morrow be to-day.

Thus still the Potter sang, and still,
By some unconscious act of will,
The melody and even the words
Were intermingled with my thought,
As bits of colored thread are caught
And woven into nests of birds.
And thus to regions far remote,
Beyond the ocean's vast expanse,
This wizard in the motley coat
Transported me on wings of song,

And by the northern shores of France
Bore me with restless speed along.
What land is this that seems to be
A mingling of the land and sea?
This land of sluices, dikes, and dunes?
This water-net, that tessellates
The landscape? this unending maze
Of gardens, through whose latticed gates
The imprisoned pinks and tulips gaze;
Where in long summer afternoons
The sunshine, softened by the haze,
Comes streaming down as through a
      screen;
Where over fields and pastures green
The painted ships float high in air,
And over all and everywhere
The sails of windmills sink and soar
Like wings of sea-gulls on the shore?

What land is this? Yon pretty town
Is Delft, with all its wares displayed;
The pride, the market-place, the crown
And centre of the Potter's trade.
See! every house and room is bright
With glimmers of reflected light
From plates that on the dresser shine;
Flagons to foam with Flemish beer,
Or sparkle with the Rhenish wine,
And pilgrim flasks with fleurs-de-lis,
And ships upon a rolling sea,
And tankards pewter topped, and queer
With comic mask and musketeer!
Each hospitable chimney smiles
A welcome from its painted tiles;
The parlor walls, the chamber floors,
The stairways and the corridors,
The borders of the garden walks,
Are beautiful with fadeless flowers,
That never droop in winds or showers,
And never wither on their stalks.

Turn, turn, my wheel! All life is brief;
What now is bud will soon be leaf,
   What now is leaf will soon decay;
The wind blows east, the wind blows west;
The blue eggs in the robin's nest
Will soon have wings and beak and breast,
   And flutter and fly away.

Now southward through the air I glide,
The song my only pursuivant,
And see across the landscape wide
The blue Charente, upon whose tide
The belfries and the spires of Saintes
Ripple and rock from side to side,
As, when an earthquake rends its walls,
A crumbling city reels and falls.

Who is it in the suburbs here,
This Potter, working with such cheer,
In this mean house, this mean attire,
His manly features bronzed with fire,
Whose figulines and rustic wares
Scarce find him bread from day to day?
This madman, as the people say,
Who breaks his tables and his chairs
To feed his furnace fires, nor cares
Who goes unfed if they are fed,
Nor who may live if they are dead?
This alchemist with hollow cheeks
And sunken, searching eyes, who seeks,
By mingled earths and ores combined
With potency of fire, to find
Some new enamel, hard and bright,
His dream, his passion, his delight?

O Palissy! within thy breast
Burned the hot fever of unrest;
Thine was the prophet's vision, thine
The exultation, the divine
Insanity of noble minds,
That never falters nor abates,
But labors and endures and waits,
Till all that it foresees it finds,
Or what it cannot find creates!

Turn, turn, my wheel! This earthen jar
A touch can make, a touch can mar;
   And shall it to the Potter say,
What makest thou? Thou hast no hand?
As men who think to understand
A world by their Creater planned,
   Who wiser is than they.

Still guided by the dreamy song,
As in a trance I float along
Above the Pyrenean chain,
Above the fields and farms of Spain,
Above the bright Majorcan isle,
That lends its softened name to art,—
A spot, a dot upon the chart,
Whose little towns, red-roofed with tile,
Are ruby-lustred with the light
Of blazing furnaces by night,
And crowned by day with wreaths of
      smoke.
Then eastward, wafted in my flight
On my enchanter's magic cloak,
I sail across the Tyrrhene Sea
Into the land of Italy,
And o'er the windy Apennines,
Mantled and musical with pines.

The palaces, the princely halls,
The doors of houses and the walls

Of churches and of belfry towers,
Cloister and castle, street and mart,
Are garlanded and gay with flowers
That blossom in the fields of art.
Here Gubbio's workshops gleam and glow
With brilliant, iridescent dyes,
The dazzling whiteness of the snow,
The cobalt blue of summer skies;
And vase and scutcheon, cup and plate,
In perfect finish emulate
Faenza, Florence, Pesaro.

Forth from Urbino's gate there came
A youth with the angelic name
Of Raphael, in form and face
Himself angelic, and divine
In arts of color and design.
From him Francesco Xanto caught
Something of his transcendent grace,
And into fictile fabrics wrought
Suggestions of the master's thought.
Nor less Maestro Giorgio shines
With madre-perl and golden lines
Of arabesques, and interweaves
His birds and fruits and flowers and leaves
About some landscape, shaded brown,
With olive tints on rock and town.
Behold this cup within whose bowl,
Upon a ground of deepest blue
With yellow-lustred stars o'erlaid,
Colors of every tint and hue
Mingle in one harmonious whole!
With large blue eyes and steadfast gaze,
Her yellow hair in net and braid,
Necklace and ear-rings all ablaze
With golden lustre o'er the glaze,
A woman's portrait; on the scroll,
Cana, the Beautiful! A name
Forgotten save for such brief fame
As this memorial can bestow, —
A gift some lover long ago
Gave with his heart to this fair dame.

A nobler title to renown
Is thine, O pleasant Tuscan town,
Seated beside the Arno's stream;
For Lucca della Robbia there
Created forms so wondrous fair,
They made thy sovereignty supreme.
These choristers with lips of stone,
Whose music is not heard, but seen,
Still chant, as from their organ-screen,
Their Maker's praise; nor these alone,
But the more fragile forms of clay,
Hardly less beautiful than they,
These saints and angels that adorn
The walls of hospitals, and tell

The story of good deeds so well
That poverty seems less forlorn,
And life more like a holiday.

Here in this old neglected church,
That long eludes the traveller's search,
Lies the dead bishop on his tomb;
Earth upon earth he slumbering lies,
Life-like and death-like in the gloom;
Garlands of fruit and flowers in bloom
And foliage deck his resting place;
A shadow in the sightless eyes,
A pallor on the patient face,
Made perfect by the furnace heat;
All earthly passions and desires
Burnt out by purgatorial fires;
Seeming to say, "Our years are fleet,
And to the weary death is sweet."

But the most wonderful of all
The ornaments on tomb or wall
That grace the fair Ausonian shores
Are those the faithful earth restores,
Near some Apulian town concealed,
In vineyard or in harvest field, —
Vases and urns and bas-reliefs,
Memorials of forgotten griefs,
Or records of heroic deeds
Of demigods and mighty chiefs:
Figures that almost move and speak,
And, buried amid mould and weeds,
Still in their attitudes attest
The presence of the graceful Greek, —
Achilles in his armor dressed,
Alcides with the Cretan bull,
And Aphrodite with her boy,
Or lovely Helena of Troy,
Still living and still beautiful.

Turn, turn, my wheel! 'T is nature's plan
The child should grow into the man,
The man grow wrinkled, old, and gray;
In youth the heart exults and sings,
The pulses leap, the feet have wings;
In age the cricket chirps, and brings
The harvest home of day.

And now the winds that southward blow,
And cool the hot Sicilian isle,
Bear me away. I see below
The long line of the Libyan Nile,
Flooding and feeding the parched land
With annual ebb and overflow,
A fallen palm whose branches lie
Beneath the Abyssinian sky,
Whose roots are in Egyptian sands.
On either bank huge water-wheels,

Belted with jars and dripping weeds,
Send forth their melancholy moans,
As if, in their gray mantles hid,
Dead anchorites of the Thebaid
Knelt on the shore and told their beads,
Beating their breasts with loud appeals
And penitential tears and groans.

This city, walled and thickly set
With glittering mosque and minaret,
Is Cairo, in whose gay bazaars
The dreaming traveller first inhales
The perfume of Arabian gales,
And sees the fabulous earthen jars,
Huge as were those wherein the maid
Morgiana found the Forty Thieves
Concealed in midnight ambuscade ;
And seeing, more than half believes
The fascinating tales that run
Through all the Thousand Nights and
      One,
Told by the fair Scheherezade.

More strange and wonderful than these
Are the Egyptian deities,
Ammon, and Emeth, and the grand
Osiris, holding in his hand
The lotus ; Isis, crowned and veiled ;
The sacred Ibis, and the Sphinx ;
Bracelets with blue enamelled links ;
The Scarabee in emerald mailed,
Or spreading wide his funeral wings ;
Lamps that perchance their night-watch
      kept
O'er Cleopatra while she slept, —
All plundered from the tombs of kings.

Turn, turn, my wheel! The human race,
Of every tongue, of every place,
  Caucasian, Coptic, or Malay,
All that inhabit this great earth,
Whatever be their rank or worth,
  Are kindred and allied by birth,
    And made of the same clay.

O'er desert sands, o'er gulf and bay,
O'er Ganges and o'er Himalay,
Bird-like I fly, and flying sing,
To flowery kingdoms of Cathay,
And bird-like poise on balanced wing
Above the town of King-te-tching,
A burning town, or seeming so, —
Three thousand furnaces that glow
Incessantly, and fill the air
With smoke uprising, gyre on gyre
And painted by the lurid glare,
Of jets and flashes of red fire.

As leaves that in the autumn fall,
Spotted and veined with various hues,
Are swept along the avenues,
And lie in heaps by hedge and wall,
So from this grove of chimneys whirled
To all the markets of the world,
These porcelain leaves are wafted on, —
Light yellow leaves with spots and stains
Of violet and of crimson dye,
Or tender azure of a sky
Just washed by gentle April rains,
And beautiful with celadon.

Nor less the coarser household wares, —
The willow pattern, that we knew
In childhood, with its bridge of blue
Leading to unknown thoroughfares ;
The solitary man who stares
At the white river flowing through
Its arches, the fantastic trees
And wild perspective of the view ;
And intermingled among these
The tiles that in our nurseries
Filled us with wonder and delight,
Or haunted us in dreams at night.

And yonder by Nankin, behold !
The Tower of Porcelain, strange and old,
Uplifting to the astonished skies
Its ninefold painted balconies,
With balustrades of twining leaves,
And roofs of tile, beneath whose eaves
Hang porcelain bells that all the time
Ring with a soft, melodious chime ;
While the whole fabric is ablaze
With varied tints, all fused in one
Great mass of color, like a maze
Of flowers illumined by the sun.

Turn, turn, my wheel ! What is begun
At daybreak must at dark be done,
  To-morrow will be another day ;
To-morrow the hot furnace flame
Will search the heart and try the frame,
And stamp with honor or with shame
    These vessels made of clay.

Cradled and rocked in Eastern seas,
The islands of the Japanese
Beneath me lie ; o'er lake and plain
The stork, the heron, and the crane
Through the clear realms of azure drift,
And on the hillside I can see
The villages of Imari,
Whose thronged and flaming workshops
      lift
Their twisted columns of smoke on high

Cloud cloisters that in ruins lie,
With sunshine streaming through each
    rift,
And broken arches of blue sky.

All the bright flowers that fill the land,
Ripple of waves on rock or sand,
The snow on Fusiyama's cone,
The midnight heaven so thickly sown
With constellations of bright stars,
The leaves that rustle, the reeds that make
A whisper by each stream and lake,
The saffron dawn, the sunset red,
Are painted on these lovely jars ;
Again the skylark sings, again
The stork, the heron, and the crane
Float through the azure overhead,
The counterfeit and counterpart
Of Nature reproduced in Art.

Art is the child of Nature ; yes,
Her darling child, in whom we trace
The features of the mother's face,
Her aspect and her attitude,
All her majestic loveliness
Chastened and softened and subdued
Into a more attractive grace,
And with a human sense imbued.
He is the greatest artist, then,
Whether of pencil or of pen,

Who follows Nature.   Never man,
As artist or as artisan,
Pursuing his own fantasies,
Can touch the human heart, or please,
Or satisfy our nobler needs,
As he who sets his willing feet
In Nature's footprints, light and fleet,
And follows fearless where she leads.

Thus mused I on that morn in May,
Wrapped in my visions like the Seer,
Whose eyes behold not what is near,
But only what is far away,
When, suddenly sounding peal on peal,
The church-bell from the neighboring
    town
Proclaimed the welcome hour of noon.
The Potter heard, and stopped his wheel,
His apron on the grass threw down,
Whistled his quiet little tune,
Not overloud nor overlong,
And ended thus his simple song:

Stop, stop, my wheel ! Too soon, too soon
The noon will be the afternoon,
    Too soon to-day be yesterday ;
Behind us in our path we cast
The broken potsherds of the past,
And all are ground to dust at last,
    And trodden into clay !

BIRDS OF PASSAGE.

FLIGHT THE FIFTH.

THE HERONS OF ELMWOOD.

WARM and still is the summer night,
    As here by the river's brink I wander ;
White overhead are the stars, and white
    The glimmering lamps on the hillside
        yonder.

Silent are all the sounds of day ;
    Nothing I hear but the chirp of crickets,
And the cry of the herons winging their
        way
    O'er the poet's house in the Elmwood
        thickets.

Call to him, herons, as slowly you pass
    To your roosts in the haunts of the
        exiled thrushes,

Sing him the song of the green morass,
    And the tides that water the reeds and
        rushes.

Sing him the mystical Song of the Hern,
    And the secret that baffles our utmost
        seeking ;
For only a sound of lament we discern,
    And cannot interpret the words you
        are speaking.

Sing of the air, and the wild delight
    Of wings that uplift and winds that
        uphold you,
The joy of freedom, the rapture of flight
    Through the drift of the floating mists
        that infold you :

Of the landscape lying so far below,
    With its towns and rivers and desert places;
And the splendor of light above, and the glow
    Of the limitless, blue, ethereal spaces.

Ask him if songs of the Troubadours,
    Or of Minnesingers in old black-letter,
Sound in his ears more sweet than yours,
    And if yours are not sweeter and wilder and better.

Sing to him, say to him, here at his gate,
    Where the boughs of the stately elms are meeting,
Some one hath lingered to meditate,
    And send him unseen this friendly greeting;

That many another hath done the same,
    Though not by a sound was the silence broken;
The surest pledge of a deathless name
    Is the silent homage of thoughts unspoken.

A DUTCH PICTURE.

Simon Danz has come home again,
    From cruising about with his buccaneers;
He has singed the beard of the King of Spain,
And carried away the Dean of Jaen
    And sold him in Algiers.

In his house by the Maese, with its roof of tiles,
    And weathercocks flying aloft in air,
There are silver tankards of antique styles,
Plunder of convent and castle, and piles
    Of carpets rich and rare.

In his tulip-garden there by the town,
    Overlooking the sluggish stream,
With his Moorish cap and dressing-gown,
The old sea-captain, hale and brown,
    Walks in a waking dream.

A smile in his gray mustachio lurks
    Whenever he thinks of the King of Spain,
And the listed tulips look like Turks,
And the silent gardener as he works
    Is changed to the Dean of Jaen.

The windmills on the outermost
    Verge of the landscape in the haze,
To him are towers on the Spanish coast,
With whiskered sentinels at their post,
    Though this is the river Maese.

But when the winter rains begin,
    He sits and smokes by the blazing brands,
And old seafaring men come in,
Goat-bearded, gray, and with double chin,
    And rings upon their hands.

They sit there in the shadow and shine
    Of the flickering fire of the winter night;
Figures in color and design
Like those by Rembrandt of the Rhine,
    Half darkness and half light.

And they talk of ventures lost or won,
    And their talk is ever and ever the same,
While they drink the red wine of Tarragon,
From the cellars of some Spanish Don,
    Or convent set on flame.

Restless at times with heavy strides
    He paces his parlor to and fro;
He is like a ship that at anchor rides,
And swings with the rising and falling tides,
    And tugs at her anchor-tow.

Voices mysterious far and near,
    Sound of the wind and sound of the sea,
Are calling and whispering in his ear,
"Simon Danz! Why stayest thou here?
    Come forth and follow me!"

So he thinks he shall take to the sea again
    For one more cruise with his buccaneers,
To singe the beard of the King of Spain,
And capture another Dean of Jaen
    And sell him in Algiers.

CASTLES IN SPAIN.

How much of my young heart, O Spain,
    Went out to thee in days of yore!
What dreams romantic filled my brain,
And summoned back to life again
The Paladins of Charlemagne
    The Cid Campeador!

And shapes more shadowy than these,
   In the dim twilight half revealed ;
Phœnician galleys on the seas,
The Roman camps like hives of bees,
The Goth uplifting from his knees
   Pelayo on his shield.

It was these memories perchance,
   From annals of remotest eld,
That lent the colors of romance
To every trivial circumstance,
And changed the form and countenance
   Of all that I beheld.

Old towns, whose history lies hid
   In monkish chronicle or rhyme, -
Burgos, the birthplace of the Cid,
Zamora and Valladolid,
Toledo, built and walled amid
   The wars of Wamba's time ;

The long, straight line of the high-
      way,
   The distant town that seems so near,
The peasants in the fields, that stay
Their toil to cross themselves and pray,
When from the belfry at midday
   The Angelus they hear ;

White crosses in the mountain pass,
   Mules gay with tassels, the loud din
Of muleteers, the tethered ass
That crops the dusty wayside grass,
And cavaliers with spurs of brass
   Alighting at the inn ;

White hamlets hidden in fields of wheat,
   White cities slumbering by the sea,
White sunshine flooding square and
      street,
Dark mountain-ranges, at whose feet
The river-beds are dry with heat, —
   All was a dream to me.

Yet something sombre and severe
   O'er the enchanted landscape reigned ;
A terror in the atmosphere
As if King Philip listened near,
Or Torquemada, the austere,
   His ghostly sway maintained.

The softer Andalusian skies
   Dispelled the sadness and the gloom ;
There Cadiz by the seaside lies,
And Seville's orange-orchards rise,
Making the land a paradise
   Of beauty and of bloom.

There Cordova is hidden among
   The palm, the olive, and the vine ;
Gem of the South, by poets sung,
And in whose Mosque Almanzor hung
As lamps the bells that once had rung
   At Compostella's shrine.

But over all the rest supreme,
   The star of stars, the cynosure,
The artist's and the poet's theme,
The young man's vision, the old man's
      dream,
Granada by its winding stream,
   The city of the Moor !

And there the Alhambra still recalls
   Aladdin's palace of delight :
Allah il Allah ! through its halls
Whispers the fountain as it falls,
The Darro darts beneath its walls,
   The hills with snow are white. .

Ah yes, the hills are white with snow,
   And cold with blasts that bite and
      freeze ;
But in the happy vale below
The orange and pomegranate grow,
And wafts of air toss to and fro
   The blossoming almond-trees.

The Vega cleft by the Xenil,
   The fascination and allure
Of the sweet landscape chains the will ;
The traveller lingers on the hill,
His parted lips are breathing still
   The last sigh of the Moor.

How like a ruin overgrown
   With flowers that hide the rents of time,
Stands now the Past that I have known,
Castles in Spain, not built of stone
But of white summer clouds, and blown
   Into this little mist of rhyme !

VITTORIA COLONNA.

VITTORIA COLONNA, on the death of her husband, the Marchese di Pescara, retired to her
castle at Ischia (Inarimé), and there wrote the
Ode upon his death, which gained her the title
of Divine.

ONCE more, once more, Inarimé,
   I see thy purple hills ! — once more
I hear the billows of the bay
   Wash the white pebbles on thy shore.

High o'er the sea-surge and the sands,
   Like a great galleon wrecked and
     cast
Ashore by storms, thy castle stands,
   A mouldering landmark of the Past.

Upon its terrace-walk I see
   A phantom gliding to and fro ;
It is Colonna, — it is she
   Who lived and loved so long ago.

Pescara's beautiful young wife,
   The type of perfect womanhood,
Whose life was love, the life of life,
   That time and change and death with-
     stood.

For death, that breaks the marriage
     band
   In others, only closer pressed
The wedding-ring upon her hand
   And closer locked and barred her
     breast.

She knew the life-long martyrdom,
   The weariness, the endless pain
Of waiting for some one to come
   Who nevermore would come again.

The shadows of the chestnut-trees,
   The odor of the orange blooms,
The song of birds, and, more than
    these,
   The silence of deserted rooms ;

The respiration of the sea,
   The soft caresses of the air,
All things in nature seemed to be
   But ministers of her despair ;

Till the o'erburdened heart, so long
   Imprisoned in itself, found vent
And voice in one impassioned song
   Of inconsolable lament.

Then as the sun, though hidden from
    sight,
   Transmutes to gold the leaden mist,
Her life was interfused with light,
   From realms that, though unseen,
    exist.

Inarimé ! Inarimé !
   Thy castle on the crags above
In dust shall crumble and decay,
   But not the memory of her love.

THE REVENGE OF RAIN-IN-THE-FACE.

In that desolate land and lone,
Where the Big Horn and Yellowstone
   Roar down their mountain path,
By their fires the Sioux Chiefs
Muttered their woes and griefs
   And the menace of their wrath.

" Revenge ! " cried Rain-in-the-Face,
" Revenge upon all the race
   Of the White Chief with yellow hair ! '
And the mountains dark and high
From their crags re-echoed the cry
   Of his anger and despair.

In the meadow, spreading wide
By woodland and riverside
   The Indian village stood ;
All was silent as a dream,
Save the rushing of the stream
   And the blue-jay in the wood.

In his war paint and his beads,
Like a bison among the reeds,
   In ambush the Sitting Bull
Lay with three thousand braves
Crouched in the clefts and caves,
   Savage, unmerciful !

Into the fatal snare
The White Chief with yellow hair
   And his three hundred men
Dashed headlong, sword in hand ;
But of that gallant band
   Not one returned again.

The sudden darkness of death
Overwhelmed them like the breath
   And smoke of a furnace fire:
By the river's bank, and between
The rocks of the ravine,
   They lay in their bloody attire.

But the foemen fled in the night,
And Rain-in-the-Face, in his flight
   Uplifted high in air
As a ghastly trophy, bore
The brave heart, that beat no more,
   Of the White Chief with yellow hair

Whose was the right and the wrong ?
Sing it, O funeral song,
   With a voice that is full of tears,
And say that our broken faith
Wrought all this ruin and scathe,
   In the Year of a Hundred Years.

TO THE RIVER YVETTE.

O LOVELY river of Yvette !
    O darling river ! like a bride,
Some dimpled, bashful, fair Lisette,
    Thou goest to wed the Orge's tide.

Maincourt, and lordly Dampierre,
    See and salute thee on thy way,
And, with a blessing and a prayer,
    Ring the sweet bells of St. Forget.

The valley of Chevreuse in vain
    Would hold thee in its fond embrace ;
Thou glidest from its arms again
    And hurriest on with swifter pace.

Thou wilt not stay ; with restless feet
    Pursuing still thine onward flight, —
Thou goest as one in haste to meet
    Her sole desire, her heart's delight.

O lovely river of Yvette !
    O darling stream ! on balanced wings
The wood-birds sang the chansonnette
    That here a wandering poet sings.

THE EMPEROR'S GLOVE.

COMBIEN faudrait-il de peaux d'Espagne pour
faire un gant de cette grandeur? A play upon
the words *gant*, a glove, and *Gand*, the French
for Ghent.

ON St. Bavon's tower, commanding
    Half of Flanders, his domain,
Charles the Emperor once was standing,
While beneath him on the landing
    Stood Duke Alva and his train.

Like a print in books of fables,
    Or a model made for show,
With its pointed roofs and gables,
Dormer windows, scrolls and labels,
    Lay the city far below.

Through its squares and streets and alleys
    Poured the populace of Ghent;
As a routed army rallies,
Or as rivers run through valleys,
    Hurrying to their homes they went.

" Nest of Lutheran misbelievers ! "
    Cried Duke Alva as he gazed ;
" Haunt of traitors and deceivers,
Stronghold of insurgent weavers,
    Let it to the ground be razed ! "

On the Emperor's cap the feather
    Nods, as laughing he replies:
" How many skins of Spanish leather,
Think you, would, if stitched together
    Make a glove of such a size ? "

A BALLAD OF THE FRENCH FLEET.

OCTOBER, 1746.

MR. THOMAS PRINCE *loquitur*.

A FLEET with flags arrayed
    Sailed from the port of Brest,
And the Admiral's ship displayed
    The signal : " Steer southwest."
For this Admiral D'Anville
    Had sworn by cross and crown
To ravage with fire and steel
    Our helpless Boston Town.

There were rumors in the street,
    In the houses there was fear
Of the coming of the fleet,
    And the danger hovering near.
And while from mouth to mouth
    Spread the tidings of dismay,
I stood in the Old South,
    Saying humbly : " Let us pray !

" O Lord ! we would not advise ;
    But if in thy Providence
A tempest should arise
    To drive the French Fleet hence,
And scatter it far and wide,
    Or sink it in the sea,
We should be satisfied,
    And thine the glory be."

This was the prayer I made,
    For my soul was all on flame,
And even as I prayed
    The answering tempest came ;
It came with a mighty power,
    Shaking the windows and walls,
And tolling the bell in the tower,
    As it tolls at funerals.

The lightning suddenly
    Unsheathed its flaming sword,
And I cried : " Stand still, and see
    The salvation of the Lord ! "
The heavens were black with cloud,
    The sea was white with hail,
And ever more fierce and loud
    Blew the October gale.

The fleet it overtook,
  And the broad sails in the van
Like the tents of Cushan shook,
  Or the curtains of Midian.
Down on the reeling decks
  Crashed the o'erwhelming seas ;
Ah, never were there wrecks
  So pitiful as these !

Like a potter's vessel broke
  The great ships of the line ;
They were carried away as a smoke,
  Or sank like lead in the brine.
O Lord ! before thy path
  They vanished and ceased to be,
When thou didst walk in wrath
  With thine horses through the sea !

THE LEAP OF ROUSHAN BEG.

MOUNTED on Kyrat strong and fleet,
His chestnut steed with four white feet,
  Roushan Beg, called Kurroglou,
Son of the road and bandit chief,
Seeking refuge and relief,
  Up the mountain pathway flew.

Such was Kyrat's wondrous speed,
Never yet could any steed
  Reach the dust-cloud in his course.
More than maiden, more than wife,
More than gold and next to life
  Roushan the Robber loved his horse.

In the land that lies beyond
Erzeroum and Trebizond,
  Garden-girt his fortress stood ;
Plundered khan, or caravan
Journeying north from Koordistan,
  Gave him wealth and wine and food.

Seven hundred and fourscore
Men at arms his livery wore,
  Did his bidding night and day.
Now, through regions all unknown,
He was wandering, lost, alone,
  Seeking without guide his way.

Suddenly the pathway ends,
Sheer the precipice descends,
  Loud the torrent roars unseen ;
Thirty feet from side to side
Yawns the chasm ; on air must ride
  He who crosses this ravine.

Following close in his pursuit,
At the precipice's foot,

Reyhan the Arab of Orfah
Halted with his hundred men,
Shouting upward from the glen,
  " La Illâh illa Allâh ! "

Gently Roushan Beg caressed
Kyrat's forehead, neck, and breast ;
  Kissed him upon both his eyes ;
Sang to him in his wild way,
As upon the topmost spray
  Sings a bird before it flies.

"O my Kyrat, O my steed,
Round and slender as a reed,
  Carry me this peril through !
Satin housings shall be thine,
Shoes of gold, O Kyrat mine,
  O thou soul of Kurroglou !

"Soft thy skin as silken skein,
Soft as woman's hair thy mane,
  Tender are thine eyes and true ;
All thy hoofs like ivory shine,
Polished bright ; O, life of mine,
  Leap, and rescue Kurroglou ! "

Kyrat, then, the strong and fleet,
Drew together his four white feet,
  Paused a moment on the verge,
Measured with his eye the space,
And into the air's embrace
  Leaped as leaps the ocean surge.

As the ocean surge o'er sand
Bears a swimmer safe to land,
  Kyrat safe his rider bore ;
Rattling down the deep abyss
Fragments of the precipice
  Rolled like pebbles on a shore.

Roushan's tasselled cap of red
Trembled not upon his head,
  Careless sat he and upright ;
Neither hand nor bridle shook,
Nor his head he turned to look,
  As he galloped out of sight.

Flash of harness in the air,
Seen a moment like the glare
  Of a sword drawn from its sheath ;
Thus the phantom horseman passed,
And the shadow that he cast
  Leaped the cataract underneath.

Reyhan the Arab held his breath
While this vision of life and death
  Passed above him. "Allahu ! "

Cried he. "In all Koordistan
Lives there not so brave a man
As this Robber Kurroglou ! "

HAROUN AL RASCHID.

ONE day, Haroun Al Raschid read
A book wherein the poet said : —

" Where are the kings, and where the rest
Of those who once the world possessed ?

"They 're gone with all their pomp and
    show,
They 're gone the way that thou shalt go.

" O thou who choosest for thy share
The world, and what the world calls fair,

" Take all that it can give or lend,
But know that death is at the end ! "

Haroun Al Raschid bowed his head :
Tears fell upon the page he read.

KING TRISANKU.

VISWAMITRA the Magician,
    By his spells and incantations,
Up to Indra's realms elysian
    Raised Trisanku, king of nations.

Indra and the gods offended
    Hurled him downward, and descending
In the air he hung suspended,
    With these equal powers contending.

Thus by aspirations lifted,
    By misgivings downward driven,
Human hearts are tossed and drifted
    Midway between earth and heaven.

A WRAITH IN THE MIST.

"SIR, I should build me a fortification, if I
came to live here." — BOSWELL'S *Johnson.*

ON the green little isle of Inchkenneth,
    Who is it that walks by the shore,
So gay with his Highland blue bonnet,
    So brave with his targe and claymore ?

His form is the form of a giant,
    But his face wears an aspect of pain ;
Can this be the Laird of Inchkenneth ?
Can this be Sir Allan McLean ?

Ah, no ! It is only the Rambler,
    The Idler, who lives in Bolt Court,
And who says, were he Laird of Inchken·
    neth,
    He would wall himself round with a
        fort.

THE THREE KINGS.

THREE Kings came riding from far away,
    Melchior and Gaspar and Baltasar ;
Three Wise Men out of the East were they,
And they travelled by night and they slept
        by day,
    For their guide was a beautiful, won·
        derful star.

The star was so beautiful, large, and clear,
    That all the other stars of the sky
Became a white mist in the atmosphere,
And by this they knew that the coming
        was near
    Of the Prince foretold in the prophecy.

Three caskets they bore on their saddle-
        bows,
    Three caskets of gold with golden keys ;
Their robes were of crimson silk with rows
Of bells and pomegranates and furbelows,
    Their turbans like blossoming almond-
        trees.

And so the Three Kings rode into the
        West,
    Through the dusk of night, over hill
        and dell,
And sometimes they nodded with beard
        on breast,
And sometimes talked, as they paused to
        rest,
    With the people they met at some way-
        side well.

"Of the child that is born," said Baltasar,
    "Good people, I pray you, tell us the
        news ;
For we in the East have seen his star,
And have ridden fast, and have ridden far,
    To find and worship the King of the
        Jews."

And the people answered, "You ask in
        vain ;
    We know of no king but Herod the
        Great ! "

They thought the Wise Men were men
    insane,
As they spurred their horses across the
    plain,
    Like riders in haste, and who cannot
    wait.

And when they came to Jerusalem,
    Herod the Great, who had heard this
    thing,
Sent for the Wise Men and questioned
    them ;
And said, "Go down unto Bethlehem,
    And bring me tidings of this new king."

So they rode away ; and the star stood
    still,
    The only one in the gray of morn ;
Yes, it stopped, it stood still of its own
    free will,
Right over Bethlehem on the hill,
    The city of David where Christ was
    born.

And the Three Kings rode through the
    gate and the guard,
    Through the silent street, till their
    horses turned
And neighed as they entered the great
    inn-yard ;
But the windows were closed, and the
    doors were barred,
    And only a light in the stable burned.

And cradled there in the scented hay,
    In the air made sweet by the breath of
    kine,
The little child in the manger lay,
The child, that would be king one day
    Of a kingdom not human but divine.

His mother Mary of Nazareth
    Sat watching beside his place of rest,
Watching the even flow of his breath,
For the joy of life and the terror of
    death
    Were mingled together in her breast.

They laid their offerings at his feet :
    The gold was their tribute to a King,
The frankincense, with its odor sweet,
Was for the Priest, the Paraclete,
    The myrrh for the body's burying.

And the mother wondered and bowed
    her head,
    And sat as still as a statue of stone ;

Her heart was troubled yet comforted,
Remembering what the Angel had said
    Of an endless reign and of David'
    throne.

Then the Kings rode out of the city gate,
    With a clatter of hoofs in proud array ;
But they went not back to Herod the
    Great,
For they knew his malice and feared his
    hate,
    And returned to their homes by an-
    other way.

SONG.

STAY, stay at home, my heart, and rest ;
Home-keeping hearts are happiest,
For those that wander they know not
    where
Are full of trouble and full of care ;
    To stay at home is best.

Weary and homesick and distressed,
They wander east, they wander west,
And are baffled and beaten and blown
    about
By the winds of the wilderness of doubt ;
    To stay at home is best.

Then stay at home, my heart, and rest ;
The bird is safest in its nest ;
O'er all that flutter their wings and fly
A hawk is hovering in the sky ;
    To stay at home is best.

THE WHITE CZAR.

THE White Czar is Peter the Great. Baty-
ushka, *Father dear,* and Gosudar, *Sovereign,*
are titles the Russian people are fond of giving
to the Czar in their popular songs.

DOST thou see on the rampart's height
That wreath of mist, in the light
Of the midnight moon ?   O, hist !
It is not a wreath of mist ;
It is the Czar, the White Czar,
    Batyushka ! Gosudar !

He has heard, among the dead,
The artillery roll o'erhead ;
The drums and the tramp of feet
Of his soldiery in the street ;
He is awake ! the White Czar,
    Batyushka ! Gosudar !

He has heard in the grave the cries
Of his people : "Awake ! arise !"
He has rent the gold brocade
Whereof his shroud was made ;
He is risen ! the White Czar,
    Batyushka ! Gosudar !

From the Volga and the Don
He has led his armies on,
Over river and morass,
Over desert and mountain pass ;
The Czar, the Orthodox Czar,
    Batyushka ! Gosudar !

He looks from the mountain-chain
Toward the seas, that cleave in twain
The continents ; his hand
Points southward o'er the land
Of Roumili ! O Czar,
    Batyushka ! Gosudar !

And the words break from his lips :
"I am the builder of ships,
And my ships shall sail these seas
To the Pillars of Hercules !
I say it ; the White Czar,
    Batyushka ! Gosudar !

"The Bosphorus shall be free ;
It shall make room for me ;
And the gates of its water-streets
Be unbarred before my fleets.
I say it ; the White Czar,
    Batyushka ! Gosudar !

"And the Christian shall no more
Be crushed, as heretofore,
Beneath thine iron rule,
O Sultan of Istamboul !
I swear it ; I the Czar,
    Batyushka ! Gosudar !

DELIA.

SWEET as the tender fragrance that survives,
When martyred flowers breathe out their little lives,
Sweet as a song that once consoled our pain,
But never will be sung to us again,
Is thy remembrance. Now the hour of rest
Hath come to thee. Sleep, darling ; it is best.

A BOOK OF SONNETS.

PART SECOND.

NATURE.

As a fond mother, when the day is o'er,
Leads by the hand her little child to bed,
Half willing, half reluctant to be led,
And leave his broken playthings on the floor,
Still gazing at them through the open door,
Nor wholly reassured and comforted
By promises of others in their stead,
Which, though more splendid, may not please him more ;
So Nature deals with us, and takes away
Our playthings one by one, and by the hand
Leads us to rest so gently, that we go
Scarce knowing if we wish to go or stay,
Being too full of sleep to understand
How far the unknown transcends the what we know.

IN THE CHURCHYARD AT TARRYTOWN.

HERE lies the gentle humorist, who died
In the bright Indian Summer of his fame !
A simple stone, with but a date and name,
Marks his secluded resting-place beside
The river that he loved and glorified.
Here in the autumn of his days he came,
But the dry leaves of life were all aflame
With tints that brightened and were multiplied.
How sweet a life was his ; how sweet a death !
Living, to wing with mirth the weary hours,
Or with romantic tales the heart to cheer ;

Dying, to leave a memory like the breath
  Of summers full of sunshine and of
    showers,
A grief and gladness in the atmosphere.

ELIOT'S OAK.

THOU ancient oak ! whose myriad leaves
    are loud
  With sounds of unintelligible speech,
  Sounds as of surges on a shingly beach,
  Or multitudinous murmurs of a crowd ;
With some mysterious gift of tongues
    endowed,
  Thou speakest a different dialect to
    each ;
  To me a language that no man can teach,
  Of a lost race, long vanished like a
    cloud.
For underneath thy shade, in days remote,
  Seated like Abraham at eventide
  Beneath the oaks of Mamre, the un-
    known
Apostle of the Indians, Eliot, wrote
  His Bible in a language that hath died
  And is forgotten, save by thee alone.

THE DESCENT OF THE MUSES.

NINE sisters, beautiful in form and
    face,
  Came from their convent on the shining
    heights
  Of Pierus, the mountain of delights,
To dwell among the people at its base.
Then seemed the world to change. All
    time and space,
  Splendor of cloudless days and starry
    nights,
  And men and manners, and all sounds
    and sights,
  Had a new meaning, a diviner grace.
Proud were these sisters, but were not too
    proud
  To teach in schools of little country
    towns
  Science and song, and all the arts that
    please ;
So that while housewives span, and
    farmers ploughed,
  Their comely daughters, clad in home-
    spun gowns,
  Learned the sweet songs of the Pier-
    ides.

VENICE.

WHITE swan of cities, slumbering in thy
    nest
  So wonderfully built among the reeds
  Of the lagoon, that fences thee and
    feeds,
  As sayeth thy old historian and thy
    guest !
White water-lily, cradled and caressed
  By ocean streams, and from the silt
    and weeds
  Lifting thy golden filaments and seeds,
  Thy sun-illumined spires, thy crown
    and crest !
White phantom city, whose untrodden
    streets
  Are rivers, and whose pavements are
    the shifting
  Shadows of palaces and strips of sky ;
I wait to see thee vanish like the fleets
  Seen in mirage, or towers of cloud up-
    lifting
  In air their unsubstantial masonry.

THE POETS.

O YE dead Poets, who are living still
  Immortal in your verse, though life be
    fled,
  And ye, O living Poets, who are dead
  Though ye are living, if neglect can kill,
Tell me if in the darkest hours of ill,
  With drops of anguish falling fast and
    red
  From the sharp crown of thorns upon
    your head,
  Ye were not glad your errand to fulfil ?
Yes ; for the gift and ministry of Song
  Have something in them so divinely
    sweet,
  It can assuage the bitterness of wrong ;
Not in the clamor of the crowded street,
  Not in the shouts and plaudits of the
    throng,
  But in ourselves, are triumph and
    defeat.

PARKER CLEAVELAND.

WRITTEN ON REVISITING BRUNSWICK IN
    THE SUMMER OF 1875.

AMONG the many lives that I have known,
  None I remember more serene and
    sweet,

More rounded in itself and more com-
plete,
Than his, who lies beneath this funeral
stone.
These pines, that murmur in low mono-
tone,
These walks frequented by scholastic
feet,
Were all his world ; but in this calm
retreat
For him the Teacher's chair became
a throne.
With fond affection memory loves to dwell
On the old days, when his example
made
A pastime of the toil of tongue and pen ;
And now, amid the groves he loved so well
That naught could lure him from their
grateful shade,
He sleeps, but wakes elsewhere, for
God hath said, Amen !

THE HARVEST MOON.

It is the Harvest Moon ! On gilded vanes
And roofs of villages, on woodland
crests
And their aerial neighborhoods of nests
Deserted, on the curtained window-
panes
Of rooms where children sleep, on country
lanes
And harvest-fields, its mystic splendor
rests !
Gone are the birds that were our sum-
mer guests,
With the last sheaves return the labor-
ing wains !
All things are symbols : the external
shows
Of Nature have their image in the mind,
As flowers and fruits and falling of the
leaves ;
The song-birds leave us at the summer's
close,
Only the empty nests are left behind,
And pipings of the quail among the
sheaves.

TO THE RIVER RHONE.

Thou Royal River, born of sun and shower
In chambers purple with the Alpine
glow,

Wrapped in the spotless ermine of the
snow
And rocked by tempests ! — at the
appointed hour
Forth, like a steel-clad horseman from a
tower,
With clang and clink of harness dost
thou go
To meet thy vassal torrents, that below
Rush to receive thee and obey thy
power.
And now thou movest in triumphal
march,
A king among the rivers ! On thy
way
A hundred towns await and welcome
thee ;
Bridges uplift for thee the stately
arch,
Vineyards encircle thee with garlands
gay,
And fleets attend thy progress to the
sea !

THE THREE SILENCES OF MOLI-
NOS.

TO JOHN GREENLEAF WHITTIER.

Three Silences there are : the first of
speech,
The second of desire, the third of
thought ;
This is the lore a Spanish monk, dis-
traught
With dreams and visions, was the first
to teach.
These Silences, commingling each with
each,
Made up the perfect Silence, that he
sought
And prayed for, and wherein at times
he caught
Mysterious sounds from realms beyond
our reach.
O thou, whose daily life anticipates
The life to come, and in whose thought
and word
The spiritual world preponderates,
Hermit of Amesbury ! thou too hast
heard
Voices and melodies from beyond the
gates,
And speakest only when thy soul is
stirred !

THE TWO RIVERS.

I.

Slowly the hour-hand of the clock moves
round ;
So slowly that no human eye hath
power
To see it move ! Slowly in shine or
shower
The painted ship above it, homeward
bound,
Sails, but seems motionless, as if aground ;
Yet both arrive at last ; and in his tower
The slumberous watchman wakes and
strikes the hour,
A mellow, measured, melancholy
sound.
Midnight ! the outpost of advancing day !
The frontier town and citadel of night !
The watershed of Time, from which
the streams
Of Yesterday and To-morrow take their
way,
One to the land of promise and of light,
One to the land of darkness and of
dreams !

II.

O River of Yesterday, with current swift
Through chasms descending, and soon
lost to sight,
I do not care to follow in their flight
The faded leaves, that on thy bosom
drift !
O River of To-morrow, I uplift
Mine eyes, and thee I follow, as the
night
Wanes into morning, and the dawn-
ing light
Broadens, and all the shadows fade
and shift !
I follow, follow, where thy waters run
Through unfrequented, unfamiliar
fields,
Fragrant with flowers and musical
with song ;
Still follow, follow ; sure to meet the sun,
And confident, that what the future
yields
Will be the right, unless myself be
wrong.

III.

Yet not in vain, O River of Yesterday,
Through chasms of darkness to the
deep descending,

I heard thee sobbing in the rain, and
blending
Thy voice with other voices far away.
I called to thee, and yet thou wouldst
not stay,
But turbulent, and with thyself con-
tending,
And torrent-like thy force on pebbles
spending,
Thou wouldst not listen to a poet's lay.
Thoughts, like a loud and sudden rush
of wings,
Regrets and recollections of things past,
With hints and prophecies of things
to be,
And inspirations, which, could they be
things,
And stay with us, and we could hold
them fast,
Were our good angels, — these I owe
to thee.

IV.

And thou, O River of To-morrow, flowing
Between thy narrow adamantine walls,
But beautiful, and white with water-
falls,
And wreaths of mist, like hands the
pathway showing ;
I hear the trumpets of the morning blow-
ing,
I hear thy mighty voice, that calls and
calls,
And see, as Ossian saw in Morven's
halls,
Mysterious phantoms, coming, beck-
oning, going !
It is the mystery of the unknown
That fascinates us ; we are children
still,
Wayward and wistful ; with one hand
we cling
To the familiar things we call our own,
And with the other, resolute of will,
Grope in the dark for what the day
will bring.

BOSTON.

St. Botolph's Town ! Hither across
the plains
And fens of Lincolnshire, in garb austere,
There came a Saxon monk, and founded
here

A Priory, pillaged by marauding Danes,
So that thereof no vestige now remains ;
Only a name, that, spoken loud and
clear,
And echoed in another hemisphere,
Survives the sculptured walls and
painted panes.
St. Botolph's Town ! Far over leagues
of land
And leagues of sea looks forth its no-
ble tower,
And far around the chiming bells are
heard ;
So may that sacred name forever stand
A landmark, and a symbol of the power,
That lies concentred in a single word.

ST. JOHN'S, CAMBRIDGE.

I STAND beneath the tree, whose branches
shade
Thy western window, Chapel of St.
John !
And hear its leaves repeat their benison
On him, whose hand thy stones me-
morial laid ;
Then I remember one of whom was said
In the world's darkest hour, "Behold
thy son !"
And see him living still, and wander-
ing on
And waiting for the advent long de-
layed.
Not only tongues of the apostles teach
Lessons of love and light, but these
expanding
And sheltering boughs with all their
leaves implore,
And say in language clear as human
speech,
"The peace of God, that passeth un-
derstanding,
Be and abide with you forevermore !"

MOODS.

O THAT a Song would sing itself to me
Out of the heart of Nature, or the heart
Of man, the child of Nature, not of Art,
Fresh as the morning, salt as the salt
sea,
With just enough of bitterness to be
A medicine to this sluggish mood, and
start

The life-blood in my veins, and so
impart
Healing and help in this dull lethargy !
Alas ! not always doth the breath of song
Breathe on us. It is like the wind
that bloweth
At its own will, not ours, nor tarries
long ;
We hear the sound thereof, but no man
knoweth
From whence it comes, so sudden and
swift and strong,
Nor whither in its wayward course it
goeth.

WOODSTOCK PARK.

HERE in a little rustic hermitage
Alfred the Saxon King, Alfred the
Great,
Postponed the cares of king-craft to
translate
The Consolations of the Roman sage.
Here Geoffrey Chaucer in his ripe old age
Wrote the unrivalled Tales, which soon
or late
The venturous hand that strives to
imitate
Vanquished must fall on the unfin-
ished page.
Two kings were they, who ruled by right
divine,
And both supreme ; one in the realm
of Truth,
One in the realm of Fiction and of
Song.
What prince hereditary of their line,
Uprising in the strength and flush of
youth,
Their glory shall inherit and prolong ?

THE FOUR PRINCESSES AT WILNA.

A PHOTOGRAPH.

SWEET faces, that from pictured casements lean
As from a castle window, looking down
On some gay pageant passing through
a town,
Yourselves the fairest figures in the
scene ;
With what a gentle grace, with what
serene

Unconsciousness ye wear the triple
  crown
Of youth and beauty and the fair re-
  nown
Of a great name, that ne'er hath tar-
  nished been !
From your soft eyes, so innocent and
  sweet,
  Four spirits, sweet and innocent as
    they,
Gaze on the world below, the sky above;
Hark ! there is some one singing in the
  street ;
  "Faith, Hope, and Love ! these three,"
    he seems to say ;
" These three ; and greatest of the three
  is Love."

HOLIDAYS.

THE holiest of all holidays are those
  Kept by ourselves in silence and apart ;
  The secret anniversaries of the heart,
  When the full river of feeling over-
    flows ; —
The happy days unclouded to their close ;
  The sudden joys that out of darkness
    start
  As flames from ashes ; swift desires
    that dart
  Like swallows singing down each wind
    that blows !
White as the gleam of a receding sail,
  White as a cloud that floats and fades
    in air,
  White as the whitest lily on a stream,
These tender memories are ; — a Fairy
    Tale
  Of some enchanted land we know not
    where,
  But lovely as a landscape in a dream.

WAPENTAKE.

TO ALFRED TENNYSON.

POET ! I come to touch thy lance with
  mine ;
  Not as a knight, who on the listed field

Of tourney touched his adversary's
  shield
  In token of defiance, but in sign
Of homage to the mastery, which is
  thine,
  In English song ; nor will 1 keep
    concealed,
  And voiceless as a rivulet frost-con-
    gealed,
  My admiration for thy verse divine.
Not of the howling dervishes of song,
  Who craze the brain with their de-
    lirious dance,
  Art thou, O sweet historian of the
    heart !
Therefore to thee the laurel-leaves be-
  long,
  To thee our love and our allegiance,
  For thy allegiance to the poet's art.

THE BROKEN OAR.

ONCE upon Iceland's solitary strand
  A poet wandered with his book and
    pen,
  Seeking some final word, some sweet
    Amen,
  Wherewith to close the volume in his
    hand.
The billows rolled and plunged upon the
  sand,
  The circling sea-gulls swept beyond
    his ken,
  And from the parting cloud-rack now
    and then
  Flashed the red sunset over sea and
    land.
Then by the billows at his feet was
  tossed
  A broken oar ; and carved thereon he
    read,
  " Oft was I weary, when I toiled at
    thee " ;
And like a man, who findeth what was
  lost,
  He wrote the words, then lifted up his
    head,
  And flung his useless pen into the
    sea.

TRANSLATIONS.

VIRGIL'S FIRST ECLOGUE.

MELIBŒUS.

TITYRUS, thou in the shade of a spreading beech-tree reclining,
Meditatest, with slender pipe, the Muse
of the woodlands.
We our country's bounds and pleasant
pastures relinquish,
We our country fly ; thou, Tityrus,
stretched in the shadow,
Teachest the woods to resound with the
name of the fair Amaryllis.

TITYRUS.

O Melibœus, a god for us this leisure
created,
For he will be unto me a god forever ;
his altar
Oftentimes shall imbue a tender lamb from
our sheepfolds.
He, my heifers to wander at large, and
myself, as thou seest,
On my rustic reed to play what I will,
hath permitted.

MELIBŒUS.

Truly I envy not, I marvel rather ; on
all sides
In all the fields is such trouble.   Behold,
my goats I am driving,
Heartsick, further away ; this one scarce,
Tityrus, lead I ;
For having here yeaned twins just now
among the dense hazels,
Hope of the flock, ah me ! on the naked
flint she hath left them.
Often this evil to me, if my mind had
not been insensate,
Oak-trees stricken by heaven predicted,
as now I remember ;
Often the sinister crow from the hollow
ilex predicted.
Nevertheless, who this god may be, O
Tityrus, tell me.

TITYRUS.

O Melibœus, the city that they call
Rome, I imagined,
Foolish I ! to be like this of ours, where
often we shepherds

Wonted are to drive down of our ewes the
delicate offspring.
Thus whelps like unto dogs had I known,
and kids to their mothers,
Thus to compare great things with small
had I been accustomed.
But this among other cities its head as
far hath exalted
As the cypresses do among the lissome
viburnums.

MELIBŒUS.

And what so great occasion of seeing
Rome hath possessed thee ?

TITYRUS.

Liberty, which, though late, looked upon
me in my inertness,
After the time when my beard fell whiter
from me in shaving, —
Yet she looked upon me, and came to me
after a long while,
Since Amaryllis possesses and Galatea
hath left me.
For I will even confess that while Galatea
possessed me
Neither care of my flock nor hope of liberty was there.
Though from my wattled folds there
went forth many a victim,
And the unctuous cheese was pressed for
the city ungrateful,
Never did my right hand return home
heavy with money.

MELIBŒUS.

I have wondered why sad thou invok-
edst the gods, Amaryllis,
And for whom thou didst suffer the apples
to hang on the branches !
Tityrus hence was absent !   Thee, Tityrus, even the pine-trees,
Thee, the very fountains, the very copses
were calling.

TITYRUS.

What could I do ?   No power had I to
escape from my bondage,
Nor had I power elsewhere to recognize
gods so propitious.

Here I beheld that youth, to whom each
year, Meliboeus,
During twice six days ascends the smoke
of our altars.
Here first gave he response to me solicit-
ing favor :
" Feed as before your heifers, ye boys,
and yoke up your bullocks."

MELIBOEUS.

Fortunate old man !   So then thy fields
will be left thee,
And large enough for thee, though naked
stone and the marish
All thy pasture-lands with the dreggy
rush may encompass.
No unaccustomed food thy gravid ewes
shall endanger,
Nor of the neighboring flock the dire
contagion infect them.
Fortunate old man ! Here among familiar
rivers,
And these sacred founts, shalt thou take
the shadowy coolness.
On this side, a hedge along the neighboring cross-road,
Where Hyblæan bees ever feed on the
flower of the willow,
Often with gentle susurrus to fall asleep
shall persuade thee.
Yonder, beneath the high rock, the
pruner shall sing to the breezes,
Nor meanwhile shall thy heart's delight,
the hoarse wood-pigeons,
Nor the turtle-dove cease to mourn from
aerial elm-trees.

TITYRUS.

Therefore the agile stags shall sooner feed
in the ether,
And the billows leave the fishes bare on
the sea-shore,
Sooner, the border-lands of both over-
passed, shall the exiled
Parthian drink of the Soane, or the German drink of the Tigris,
Than the face of him shall glide away
from my bosom !

MELIBOEUS.

But we hence shall go, a part to the
thirsty Africs,
Part to Scythia come, and the rapid
Cretan Oaxes,
And to the Britons from all the universe
utterly sundered.

Ah, shall I ever, a long time hence, the
bounds of my country
And the roof of my lowly cottage cov-
ered with greensward
Seeing, with wonder behold, — my king-
doms, a handful of wheat-ears !
Shall an impious soldier possess these
lands newly cultured,
And these fields of corn a barbarian ?
Lo, whither discord
Us wretched people hath brought ! for
whom our fields we have planted !
Graft, Meliboeus, thy pear-trees now, put
in order thy vineyards.
Go, my goats, go hence, my flocks so
happy aforetime.
Never again henceforth outstretched in
my verdurous cavern
Shall I behold you afar from the bushy
precipice hanging.
Songs no more shall I sing; not with me,
ye goats, as your shepherd,
Shall ye browse on the bitter willow or
blooming laburnum.

TITYRUS.

Nevertheless, this night together with
me canst thou rest thee
Here on the verdant leaves ; for us there
are mellowing apples,
Chestnuts soft to the touch, and clouted
cream in abundance ;
And the high roofs now of the villages
smoke in the distance,
And from the lofty mountains are falling
larger the shadows.

OVID IN EXILE,

AT TOMIS, IN BESSARABIA, NEAR THE MOUTHS OF THE DANUBE.

TRISTIA, Book III., Elegy X.

SHOULD any one there in Rome remember Ovid the exile,
And, without me, my name still in the
city survive ;

Tell him that under stars which never set
in the ocean
I am existing still, here in a barbarous
land.

Fierce Sarmatians encompass me round,
and the Bessi and Getæ ;
Names how unworthy to be sung by a
genius like mine !

Yet when the air is warm, intervening
    Ister defends us :
He, as he flows, repels inroads of war
    with his waves.

But when the dismal winter reveals its
    hideous aspect,
  When all the earth becomes white with
    a marble-like frost ;

And when Boreas is loosed, and the snow
    hurled under Arcturus,
Then these nations, in sooth, shudder
    and shiver with cold.

Deep lies the snow, and neither the sun
    nor the rain can dissolve it ;
Boreas hardens it still, makes it for-
    ever remain.

Hence, ere the first has melted away,
    another succeeds it,
And two years it is wont, in many
    places, to lie.

And so great is the power of the North-
    wind awakened, it levels
Lofty towers with the ground, roofs
    uplifted bears off.

Wrapped in skins, and with trousers sewed,
    they contend with the weather,
And their faces alone of the whole
    body are seen.

Often their tresses, when shaken, with
    pendent icicles tinkle,
And their whitened beards shine with
    the gathering frost.

Wines consolidate stand, preserving the
    form of the vessels ;
No more draughts of wine, — pieces
    presented they drink.

Why should I tell you how all the rivers
    are frozen and solid,
And from out of the lake frangible
    water is dug ?

Ister, — no narrower stream than the
    river that bears the papyrus, —
Which through its many mouths min-
    gles its waves with the deep ;

Ister, with hardening winds, congeals its
    cerulean waters,
Under a roof of ice, winding its way to
    the sea.

There where ships have sailed, men go on
    foot ; and the billows,
Solid made by the frost, hoof-beats of
    horses indent.

Over unwonted bridges, with water glid-
    ing beneath them,
The Sarmatian steers drag their bar-
    barian carts.

Scarcely shall I be believed ; yet when
    naught is gained by a falsehood,
Absolute credence then should to a
    witness be given.

I have beheld the vast Black Sea of ice
    all compacted,
And a slippery crust pressing its mo-
    tionless tides.

'T is not enough to have seen, I have
    trodden this indurate ocean ;
Dry shod passed my foot over its up-
    permost wave.

If thou hadst had of old such a sea as this
    is, Leander !
Then thy death had not been charged
    as a crime to the Strait.

Nor can the curvéd dolphins uplift them-
    selves from the water ;
All their struggles to rise merciless
    winter prevents ;

And though Boreas sound with roar of
    wings in commotion,
In the blockaded gulf never a wave
    will there be ;

And the ships will stand hemmed in by
    the frost, as in marble,
Nor will the oar have power through
    the stiff waters to cleave.

Fast-bound in the ice have I seen the
    fishes adhering,
Yet notwithstanding this some of them
    still were alive.

Hence, if the savage strength of omnipo-
    tent Boreas freezes
Whether the salt-sea wave, whether
    the refluent stream, —

Straightway, — the Ister made level by
    arid blasts of the North-wind, —
Comes the barbaric foe borne on his
    swift-footed steed ;

Foe, that powerful made by his steed and
   his far-flying arrows,
   All the neighboring land void of in-
      habitants makes.

Some take flight, and none being left to
      defend their possessions,
   Unprotected, their goods pillage and
      plunder become ;

Cattle and creaking carts, the little wealth
      of the country,
   And what riches beside indigent peas-
      ants possess.

Some as captives are driven along, their
      hands bound behind them,
   Looking backward in vain toward their
      Lares and lands.

Others, transfixed with barbéd arrows, in
      agony perish,
   For the swift arrow-heads all have in
      poison been dipped.

What they cannot carry or lead away
      they demolish,
   And the hostile flames burn up the
      innocent cots.

Even when there is peace, the fear of war
      is impending,
   None, with the ploughshare pressed,
      furrows the soil any more.

Either this region sees, or fears a foe that
      it sees not,
   And the sluggish land slumbers in utter
      neglect.

No sweet grape lies hidden here in the
      shade of its vine-leaves,
   No fermenting must fills and o'erflows
      the deep vats.

Apples the region denies ; nor would
      Acontius have found here
   Aught upon which to write words for
      his mistress to read.

Naked and barren plains without leaves
      or trees we behold here, —
   Places, alas ! unto which no happy
      man would repair.

Since then this mighty orb lies open so
      wide upon all sides,
   Has this region been found only my
      prison to be ?

TRISTIA, Book III., Elegy XII.

Now the zephyrs diminish the cold, and
      the year being ended,
   Winter Mæotian seems longer than ever
      before ;

And the Ram that bore unsafely the
      burden of Helle,
   Now makes the hours of the day equal
      with those of the night.

Now the boys and the laughing girls the
      violet gather,
   Which the fields bring forth, nobody
      sowing the seed.

Now the meadows are blooming with
      flowers of various colors,
   And with untaught throats carol the
      garrulous birds.

Now the swallow, to shun the crime of
      her merciless mother,
   Under the rafters builds cradles and
      dear little homes ;

And the blade that lay hid, covered up in
      the furrows of Ceres,
   Now from the tepid ground raises its
      delicate head.

Where there is ever a vine, the bud
      shoots forth from the tendrils,
   But from the Getic shore distant afar
      is the vine !

Where there is ever a tree, on the tree
      the branches are swelling,
   But from the Getic land distant afar
      is the tree !

Now it is holiday there in Rome, and to
      games in due order
   Give place the windy wars of the vocif-
      erous bar.

Now they are riding the horses ; with
      light arms now they are playing,
   Now with the ball, and now round
      rolls the swift-flying hoop :

Now, when the young athlete with flow-
      ing oil is anointed,
   He in the Virgin's Fount bathes, over-
      wearied, his limbs.

Thrives the stage ; and applause, with
　　voices at variance, thunders,
　And the Theatres three for the three
　　Forums resound.

Four times happy is he, and times with-
　　out number is happy,
　Who the city of Rome, uninterdicted,
　　enjoys.

But all I see is the snow in the vernal
　　sunshine dissolving,
　And the waters no more delved from
　　the indurate lake.

Nor is the sea now frozen, nor as before
　　o'er the Ister
　Comes the Sarmatian boor driving his
　　stridulous cart.

Hitherward, nevertheless, some keels
　　already are steering,
　And on this Pontic shore alien vessels
　　will be.

Eagerly shall I run to the sailor, and,
　　having saluted,
　Who he may be, I shall ask ; where-
　　fore and whence he hath come.

Strange indeed will it be, if he come not
　　from regions adjacent,
　And incautious unless ploughing the
　　neighboring sea.

Rarely a mariner over the deep from Italy
　　passes,
　Rarely he comes to these shores, wholly
　　of harbors devoid.

Whether he knoweth Greek, or whether
　　in Latin he speaketh,
　Surely on this account he the more
　　welcome will be.

Also perchance from the mouth of the
　　Strait and the waters Propontic,
　Unto the steady South-wind, some one
　　is spreading his sails.

Whosoever he is, the news he can faith-
　　fully tell me,
　Which may become a part and an ap-
　　proach to the truth.

He, I pray, may be able to tell me the
　　triumphs of Cæsar,
　Which he has heard of, and vows paid
　　to the Latian Jove ;

And that thy sorrowful head, Germania,
　　thou, the rebellious,
　Under the feet, at last, of the Great
　　Captain hast laid.

Whoso shall tell me these things, that
　　not to have seen will afflict me,
　Forthwith unto my house welcomed as
　　guest shall he be.

Woe is me ! Is the house of Ovid in
　　Scythian lands now ?
　And doth punishment now give me its
　　place for a home ?

Grant, ye gods, that Cæsar make this not
　　my house and my homestead,
　But decree it to be only the inn of my
　　pain.

ON THE TERRACE OF THE AIGA-
LADES.

FROM THE FRENCH OF MÉRY.

FROM this high portal, where upsprings
The rose to touch our hands in play,
We at a glance behold three things, —
The Sea, the Town, and the Highway.

And the Sea says : My shipwrecks fear ;
I drown my best friends in the deep ;
And those who braved my tempests, here
Among my sea-weeds lie asleep !

The Town says : I am filled and fraught
With tumult and with smoke and care ;
My days with toil are overwrought,
And in my nights I gasp for air.

The Highway says : My wheel-tracks
　　guide
To the pale climates of the North ;
Where my last milestone stands abide
The people to their death gone forth.

Here, in the shade, this life of ours,
Full of delicious air, glides by
Amid a multitude of flowers
As countless as the stars on high ;

These red-tiled roofs, this fruitful soil,
Bathed with an azure all divine,
Where springs the tree that gives us oil,
The grape that giveth us the wine ;

Beneath these mountains stripped of trees,
Whose tops with flowers are covered o'er,
Where springtime of the Hesperides
Begins, but endeth nevermore ;

Under these leafy vaults and walls,
That unto gentle sleep persuade ;
This rainbow of the waterfalls,
Of mingled mist and sunshine made ;

Upon these shores, where all invites,
We live our languid life apart ;
This air is that of life's delights,
The festival of sense and heart ;

This limpid space of time prolong,
Forget to-morrow in to-day,
And leave unto the passing throng
The Sea, the Town, and the Highway.

TO MY BROOKLET.

FROM THE FRENCH OF DUCIS.

THOU brooklet, all unknown to song,
Hid in the covert of the wood !
Ah, yes, like thee I fear the throng,
Like thee I love the solitude.

O brooklet, let my sorrows past
Lie all forgotten in their graves,
Till in my thoughts remain at last
Only thy peace, thy flowers, thy waves.

The lily by thy margin waits ; —
The nightingale, the marguerite ;
In shadow here he meditates
His nest, his love, his music sweet.

Near thee the self-collected soul
Knows naught of error or of crime ;
Thy waters, murmuring as they roll,
Transform his musings into rhyme.

Ah, when, on bright autumnal eves,
Pursuing still thy course, shall I
Lisp the soft shudder of the leaves,
And hear the lapwing's plaintive cry ?

BARRÉGES.

FROM THE FRENCH OF LEFRANC DE POMPIGNAN.

I LEAVE you, ye cold mountain chains,
Dwelling of warriors stark and frore !
You, may these eyes behold no more,
Save on the horizon of our plains.

Vanish, ye frightful, gloomy views !
Ye rocks that mount up to the clouds !
Of skies, enwrapped in misty shrouds,
Impracticable avenues !

Ye torrents, that with might and main
Break pathways through the rocky walls,
With your terrific waterfalls
Fatigue no more my weary brain !

Arise, ye landscapes full of charms,
Arise, ye pictures of delight !
Ye brooks, that water in your flight
The flowers and harvests of our farms !

You I perceive, ye meadows green,
Where the Garonne the lowland fills,
Not far from that long chain of hills,
With intermingled vales between.

Yon wreath of smoke, that mounts so
    high,
Methinks from my own hearth must come ;
With speed, to that beloved home,
Fly, ye too lazy coursers, fly !

And bear me thither, where the soul
In quiet may itself possess,
Where all things soothe the mind's dis-
    tress,
Where all things teach me and console.

FORSAKEN.

FROM THE GERMAN.

SOMETHING the heart must have to
    cherish,
    Must love and joy and sorrow learn,
Something with passion clasp, or perish,
    And in itself to ashes burn.

So to this child my heart is clinging,
    And its frank eyes, with look intense,
Me from a world of sin are bringing
    Back to a world of innocence.

Disdain must thou endure forever ;
    Strong may thy heart in danger be !
Thou shalt not fail ! but ah, be never
    False as thy father was to me.

Never will I forsake thee, faithless,
    And thou thy mother ne'er forsake,
Until her lips are white and breathless,
    Until in death her eyes shall break.

ALLAH.

FROM THE GERMAN OF MAHLMANN.

ALLAH gives light in darkness,
  Allah gives rest in pain,
Cheeks that are white with weeping
  Allah paints red again.

The flowers and the blossoms wither,
  Years vanish with flying fleet ;
But my heart will live on forever,
  That here in sadness beat.

Gladly to Allah's dwelling
  Yonder would I take flight ;
There will the darkness vanish,
  There will my eyes have sight.

SEVEN SONNETS

AND A CANZONE, FROM THE ITALIAN OF MICHAEL ANGELO.

[THE following translations are from the poems of Michael Angelo as revised by his nephew Michael Angelo the Younger, and were made before the publication of the original text by Guasti.]

I.

THE ARTIST.

NOTHING the greatest artist can conceive
  That every marble block doth not
      confine
  Within itself ; and only its design
  The hand that follows intellect can
      achieve.
The ill I flee, the good that I believe,
  In thee, fair lady, lofty and divine,
  Thus hidden lie ; and so that death be
      mine
  Art, of desired success, doth me be-
      reave.
Love is not guilty, then, nor thy fair face,
  Nor fortune, cruelty, nor great disdain,
  Of my disgrace, nor chance, nor destiny,
If in thy heart both death and love find
      place
  At the same time, and if my humble
      brain,
  Burning, can nothing draw but death
      from thee.

II.

FIRE.

NOT without fire can any workman mould
  The iron to his preconceived design,
  Nor can the artist without fire refine
  And purify from all its dross the gold ;
Nor can revive the phœnix, we are told,

Except by fire.   Hence if such death
      be mine
I hope to rise again with the divine,
  Whom death augments, and time can-
      not make old.
O sweet, sweet death !   O fortunate fire
      that burns
  Within me still to renovate my days,
  Though I am almost numbered with
      the dead !
If by its nature unto heaven returns
  This element, me, kindled in its blaze,
  Will it bear upward when my life is fled.

III.

YOUTH AND AGE.

O GIVE me back the days when loose and
      free
  To my blind passion were the curb and
      rein,
  O give me back the angelic face again,
  With which all virtue buried seems
      to be !
O give my panting footsteps back to me,
  That are in age so slow and fraught
      with pain,
  And fire and moisture in the heart and
      brain,
  If thou wouldst have me burn and
      weep for thee !
If it be true thou livest alone, Amor,
  On the sweet-bitter tears of human
      hearts,

In an old man thou canst not wake
    desire ;
Souls that have almost reached the other
    shore
Of a diviner love should feel the darts,
And be as tinder to a holier fire.

IV.

OLD AGE.

THE course of my long life hath reached
    at last,
    In fragile bark o'er a tempestuous sea,
    The common harbor, where must ren-
        dered be
Account of all the actions of the past.
The impassioned phantasy, that, vague
        and vast,
    Made art an idol and a king to me,
    Was an illusion, and but vanity
Were the desires that lured me and
        harassed.
The dreams of love, that were so sweet
        of yore,
    What are they now, when two deaths
        may be mine, —
    One sure, and one forecasting its
        alarms ?
Painting and sculpture satisfy no more
    The soul now turning to the Love
        Divine,
    That oped, to embrace us, on the cross
        its arms.

V.

TO VITTORIA COLONNA.

LADY, how can it chance — yet this we
        see
    In long experience — that will longer
        last
    A living image carved from quarries
        vast
Than its own maker, who dies presently ?
Cause yieldeth to effect if this so be,
    And even Nature is by Art surpassed ;
    This know I, who to Art have given
        the past,
    But see that Time is breaking faith
        with me.
Perhaps on both of us long life can I
    Either in color or in stone bestow,
    By now portraying each in look and
        mien ;

So that a thousand years after we die,
    How fair thou wast, and I how full of
        woe,
    And wherefore I so loved thee, may be
        seen.

VI.

TO VITTORIA COLONNA.

WHEN the prime mover of my many sighs
    Heaven took through death from out
        her earthly place,
    Nature, that never made so fair a face,
    Remained ashamed, and tears were in
        all eyes.
O fate, unheeding my impassioned cries !
    O hopes fallacious !   O thou spirit of
        grace,
    Where art thou now ?   Earth holds
        in its embrace
    Thy lovely limbs, thy holy thoughts
        the skies.
Vainly did cruel death attempt to stay
    The rumor of thy virtuous renown,
    That Lethe's waters could not wash
        away !
A thousand leaves, since he hath stricken
        thee down,
    Speak of thee, nor to thee could
        Heaven convey,
    Except through death, a refuge and a
        crown.

VII.

DANTE.

WHAT should be said of him cannot be
        said ;
    By too great splendor is his name at-
        tended ;
    To blame is easier those who him of-
        fended,
    Than reach the faintest glory round
        him shed.
This man descended to the doomed and
        dead
    For our instruction ; then to God as-
        cended ;
    Heaven opened wide to him its portals
        splendid,
    Who from his country's, closed against
        him, fled.
Ungrateful land !   To its own prejudice

Nurse of his fortunes ; and this show-
eth well,
That the most perfect most of grief
shall see.
Among a thousand proofs let one suffice,
That as his exile hath no parallel,
Ne'er walked the earth a greater man
than he.

VIII.

CANZONE.

Ah me ! ah me ! when thinking of the
years,
The vanished years, alas, I do not find

Among them all one day that was my
own !
Fallacious hopes, desires of the unknown,
Lamenting, loving, burning, and in
tears
(For human passions all have stirred
my mind),
Have held me, now I feel and know,
confined
Both from the true and good still far
away.
I perish day by day ;
The sunshine fails, the shadows grow
more dreary,
And I am near to fall, infirm and
weary.

ULTIMA THULE.

DEDICATION.

TO G. W. G.

WITH favoring winds, o'er sunlit seas,
We sailed for the Hesperides,
The land where golden apples grow ;
But that, ah ! that was long ago.

How far, since then, the ocean streams
Have swept us from that land of dreams,
That land of fiction and of truth,
The lost Atlantis of our youth !

Whither, ah, whither ?   Are not these
The tempest-haunted Hebrides,
Where sea-gulls scream, and breakers
roar,
And wreck and sea-weed line the shore ?

Ultima Thule !   Utmost Isle !
Here in thy harbors for a while
We lower our sails ; a while we rest
From the unending, endless quest.

BAYARD TAYLOR.

DEAD he lay among his books !
The peace of God was in his looks.

As the statues in the gloom
Watch o'er Maximilian's tomb,[1]

So those volumes from their shelves
Watched him, silent as themselves.

Ah ! his hand will nevermore
Turn their storied pages o'er ;

Nevermore his lips repeat
Songs of theirs, however sweet.

Let the lifeless body rest !
He is gone, who was its guest ;

Gone, as travellers haste to leave
An inn, nor tarry until eve.

Traveller ! in what realms afar,
In what planet, in what star,

In what vast, aerial space,
Shines the light upon thy face ?

In what gardens of delight
Rest thy weary feet to-night ?

Poet ! thou, whose latest verse
Was a garland on thy hearse ;

Thou hast sung, with organ tone,
In Deukalion's life, thine own ;

On the ruins of the Past
Blooms the perfect flower at last.

[1] In the Hofkirche at Innsbruck.

Friend! but yesterday the bells
Rang for thee their loud farewells;

And to-day they toll for thee,
Lying dead beyond the sea;

Lying dead among thy books,
The peace of God in all thy looks!

THE CHAMBER OVER THE GATE.

Is it so far from thee
Thou canst no longer see,
In the Chamber over the Gate,
That old man desolate,
Weeping and wailing sore
For his son, who is no more?
　　O Absalom, my son!

Is it so long ago
That cry of human woe
From the walled city came,
Calling on his dear name,
That it has died away
In the distance of to-day?
　　O Absalom, my son!

There is no far or near,
There is neither there nor here,
There is neither soon nor late,
In that Chamber over the Gate,
Nor any long ago
To that cry of human woe,
　　O Absalom, my son!

From the ages that are past
The voice sounds like a blast,
Over seas that wreck and drown,
Over tumult of traffic and town;
And from ages yet to be
Come the echoes back to me,
　　O Absalom, my son!

Somewhere at every hour
The watchman on the tower
Looks forth, and sees the fleet
Approach of the hurrying feet
Of messengers, that bear
The tidings of despair.
　　O Absalom, my son!

He goes forth from the door
Who shall return no more.
With him our joy departs;
The light goes out in our hearts;

In the Chamber over the Gate
We sit disconsolate.
　　O Absalom, my son!

That 't is a common grief
Bringeth but slight relief;
Ours is the bitterest loss,
Ours is the heaviest cross;
And forever the cry will be
"Would God I had died for thee,
　　O Absalom, my son!"

FROM MY ARM-CHAIR.

TO THE CHILDREN OF CAMBRIDGE,

Who presented to me, on my Seventy-second
Birth-day, February 27, 1879, this Chair, made
from the Wood of the Village Blacksmith's
Chestnut Tree.

Am I a king, that I should call my own
　　This splendid ebon throne?
Or by what reason, or what right divine,
　　Can I proclaim it mine?

Only, perhaps, by right divine of song
　　It may to me belong;
Only because the spreading chestnut
　　tree
　　Of old was sung by me.

Well I remember it in all its prime,
　　When in the summer-time
The affluent foliage of its branches made
　　A cavern of cool shade.

There, by the blacksmith's forge, beside
　　the street,
　　Its blossoms white and sweet
Enticed the bees, until it seemed alive,
　　And murmured like a hive.

And when the winds of autumn, with a
　　shout,
　　Tossed its great arms about,
The shining chestnuts, bursting from the
　　sheath,
　　Dropped to the ground beneath.

And now some fragments of its branches
　　bare,
　　Shaped as a stately chair,
Have by my hearthstone found a home
　　at last,
　　And whisper of the past

The Danish king could not in all his pride
  Repel the ocean tide,
But, seated in this chair, I can in rhyme
  Roll back the tide of Time.

I see again, as one in vision sees,
  The blossoms and the bees,
And hear the children's voices shout and
    call,
  And the brown chestnuts fall.

I see the smithy with its fires aglow,
  I hear the bellows blow,
And the shrill hammers on the anvil
    beat
  The iron white with heat!

And thus, dear children, have ye made
    for me
  This day a jubilee,
And to my more than three-score years
    and ten
  Brought back my youth again.

The heart hath its own memory, like the
    mind,
  And in it are enshrined
The precious keepsakes, into which is
    wrought
  The giver's loving thought.

Only your love and your remembrance
    could
  Give life to this dead wood,
And make these branches, leafless now so
    long,
  Blossom again in song.

JUGURTHA.

How cold are thy baths, Apollo!
  Cried the African monarch, the splen-
    did,
As down to his death in the hollow
  Dark dungeons of Rome he descended,
  Uncrowned, unthroned, unattended;
How cold are thy baths, Apollo!

How cold are thy baths, Apollo!
  Cried the Poet, unknown, unbefriended,
As the vision, that lured him to follow,
  With the mist and the darkness
    blended,
  And the dream of his life was ended;
How cold are thy baths, Apollo!

THE IRON PEN,

Made from a fetter of Bonnivard, the Prisoner
of Chillon; the handle of wood from the Frigate Constitution, and bound with a circlet of
gold, inset with three precious stones from
Siberia, Ceylon, and Maine.

I THOUGHT this Pen would arise
From the casket where it lies—
  Of itself would arise and write
My thanks and my surprise.

When you gave it me under the pines,
I dreamed these gems from the mines
  Of Siberia, Ceylon, and Maine
Would glimmer as thoughts in the lines;

That this iron link from the chain
Of Bonnivard might retain
  Some verse of the Poet who sang
Of the prisoner and his pain;

That this wood from the frigate's mast
Might write me a rhyme at last,
  As it used to write on the sky
The song of the sea and the blast.

But motionless as I wait,
Like a Bishop lying in state
  Lies the Pen, with its mitre of gold,
And its jewels inviolate.

Then must I speak, and say
That the light of that summer day
  In the garden under the pines
Shall not fade and pass away.

I shall see you standing there,
Caressed by the fragrant air,
  With the shadow on your face,
And the sunshine on your hair.

I shall hear the sweet low tone
Of a voice before unknown,
  Saying, "This is from me to you—
From me, and to you alone."

And in words not idle and vain
I shall answer and thank you again
  For the gift, and the grace of the
    gift,
O beautiful Helen of Maine!

And forever this gift will be
As a blessing from you to me,
  As a drop of the dew of your youth
On the leaves of an aged tree.

ROBERT BURNS.

I SEE amid the fields of Ayr
A ploughman, who, in foul and fair,
    Sings at his task
So clear, we know not if it is
The laverock's song we hear, or his,
    Nor care to ask.

For him the ploughing of those fields
A more ethereal harvest yields
    Than sheaves of grain ;
Songs flush with purple bloom the rye,
The plover's call, the curlew's cry,
    Sing in his brain.

Touched by his hand, the wayside weed
Becomes a flower ; the lowliest reed
    Beside the stream
Is clothed with beauty ; gorse and grass
And heather, where his footsteps pass,
    The brighter seem.

He sings of love, whose flame illumes
The darkness of lone cottage rooms ;
    He feels the force,
The treacherous undertow and stress
Of wayward passions, and no less
    The keen remorse.

At moments, wrestling with his fate,
His voice is harsh, but not with hate ;
    The brushwood, hung
Above the tavern door, lets fall
Its bitter leaf, its drop of gall
    Upon his tongue.

But still the music of his song
Rises o'er all elate and strong ;
    Its master-chords
Are Manhood, Freedom, Brotherhood,
Its discords but an interlude
    Between the words.

And then to die so young and leave
Unfinished what he might achieve !
    Yet better sure
Is this, than wandering up and down
An old man in a country town,
    Infirm and poor.

For now he haunts his native land
As an immortal youth ; his hand
    Guides every plough ;
He sits beside each ingle-nook,
His voice is in each rushing brook,
    Each rustling bough.

His presence haunts this room to-night,
A form of mingled mist and light
    From that far coast.
Welcome beneath this roof of mine !
Welcome ! this vacant chair is thine,
    Dear guest and ghost !

HELEN OF TYRE.

WHAT phantom is this that appears
Through the purple mist of the years,
    Itself but a mist like these ?
A woman of cloud and of fire ;
It is she ; it is Helen of Tyre,
    The town in the midst of the seas

O Tyre ! in thy crowded streets
The phantom appears and retreats,
    And the Israelites that sell
Thy lilies and lions of brass,
Look up as they see her pass,
    And murmur " Jezebel ! "

Then another phantom is seen
At her side, in a gray gabardine,
    With beard that floats to his waist ;
It is Simon Magus, the Seer ;
He speaks, and she pauses to hear
    The words he utters in haste.

He says : " From this evil fame,
From this life of sorrow and shame,
    I will lift thee and make thee mine,
Thou hast been Queen Candace,
And Helen of Troy, and shalt be
    The Intelligence Divine ! "

Oh, sweet as the breath of morn,
To the fallen and forlorn
    Are whispered words of praise ;
For the famished heart believes
The falsehood that tempts and deceives,
    And the promise that betrays.

So she follows from land to land
The wizard's beckoning hand,
    As a leaf is blown by the gust,
Till she vanishes into night.
O reader, stoop down and write
    With thy finger in the dust.

O town in the midst of the seas,
With thy rafts of cedar trees,
    Thy merchandise and thy ships,
Thou, too, art become as naught,
A phantom, a shadow, a thought,
    A name upon men's lips.

ELEGIAC.

DARK is the morning with mist ; in the
　　narrow mouth of the harbor
　Motionless lies the sea, under its cur-
　　tain of cloud ;
Dreamily glimmer the sails of ships on
　　the distant horizon,
　Like to the towers of a town, built on
　　the verge of the sea.

Slowly and stately and still, they sail
　　forth into the ocean ;
　With them sail my thoughts over the
　　limitless deep,
Farther and farther away, borne on by
　　unsatisfied longings,
　Unto Hesperian isles, unto Ausonian
　　shores.

Now they have vanished away, have dis-
　　peared in the ocean ;
　Sunk are the towers of the town into
　　the depths of the sea !
All have vanished but those that, moored
　　in the neighboring roadstead,
　Sailless at anchor ride, looming so
　　large in the mist.

Vanished, too, are the thoughts, the dim,
　　unsatisfied longings ;
　Sunk are the turrets of cloud into the
　　ocean of dreams ;
While in a haven of rest my heart is rid-
　　ing at anchor,
　Held by the chains of love, held by the
　　anchors of trust !

OLD ST. DAVID'S AT RADNOR.

WHAT an image of peace and rest
　Is this little church among its graves !
All is so quiet ; the troubled breast,
The wounded spirit, the heart oppressed,
　Here may find the repose it craves.

See, how the ivy climbs and expands
　Over this humble hermitage,
And seems to caress with its little hands
The rough, gray stones, as a child that
　　stands
　Caressing the wrinkled cheeks of age !

You cross the threshold ; and dim and
　　small
　Is the space that serves for the Shep-
　　herd's Fold ;
The narrow aisle, the bare, white wall,
The pews, and the pulpit quaint and
　　tall,
　Whisper and say : " Alas ! we are old."

Herbert's chapel at Bemerton
　Hardly more spacious is than this ;
But Poet and Pastor, blent in one,
Clothed with a splendor, as of the sun,
　That lowly and holy edifice.

It is not the wall of stone without
　That makes the building small or
　　great
But the soul's light shining round about,
And the faith that overcometh doubt,
　And the love that stronger is than
　　hate.

Were I a pilgrim in search of peace,
　Were I a pastor of Holy Church,
More than a Bishop's diocese
Should I prize this place of rest, and re-
　　lease
　From farther longing and farther
　　search.

Here would I stay, and let the world
　With its distant thunder roar and
　　roll ;
Storms do not rend the sail that is
　　furled ;
Nor like a dead leaf, tossed and whirled
　In an eddy of wind, is the anchored
　　soul.

FOLK SONGS.

THE SIFTING OF PETER.

In St. Luke's Gospel we are told
How Peter in the days of old
  Was sifted;
And now, though ages intervene,
Sin is the same, while time and scene
  Are shifted.

Satan desires us, great and small,
As wheat to sift us, and we all
  Are tempted;
Not one, however rich or great,
Is by his station or estate
  Exempted.

No house so safely guarded is
But he, by some device of his,
  Can enter;
No heart hath armor so complete
But he can pierce with arrows fleet
  Its centre.

For all at last the cock will crow,
Who hear the warning voice, but go
  Unheeding,
Till thrice and more they have denied
The Man of Sorrows, crucified
  And bleeding.

One look of that pale suffering face
Will make us feel the deep disgrace
  Of weakness;
We shall be sifted till the strength
Of self-conceit be changed at length
  To meekness.

Wounds of the soul, though healed will
  ache;
The reddening scars remain, and make
  Confession;
Lost innocence returns no more;
We are not what we were before
  Transgression.

But noble souls, through dust and heat,
Rise from disaster and defeat
  The stronger,
And conscious still of the divine
Within them, lie on earth supine
  No longer.

MAIDEN AND WEATHERCOCK.

MAIDEN.

O Weathercock on the village spire,
With your golden feathers all on fire,
Tell me, what can you see from your
  perch
Above there over the tower of the church?

WEATHERCOCK.

I can see the roofs and the streets below,
And the people moving to and fro,
And beyond, without either roof or street,
The great salt sea, and the fisherman's
  fleet.

I can see a ship come sailing in
Beyond the headlands and harbor of
  Lynn,
And a young man standing on the deck,
With a silken kerchief round his neck.

Now he is pressing it to his lips,
And now he is kissing his finger-tips,
And now he is lifting and waving his
  hand,
And blowing the kisses toward the land.

MAIDEN.

Ah, that is the ship from over the sea,
That is bringing my lover back to me,
Bringing my lover so fond and true,
Who does not change with the wind like
  you.

WEATHERCOCK.

If I change with all the winds that blow,
It is only because they made me so,
And people would think it wondrous
  strange,
If I, a Weathercock, should not change.

O pretty Maiden, so fine and fair,
With your dreamy eyes and your golden
  hair,
When you and your lover meet to-day
You will thank me for looking some other
  way.

THE WINDMILL.

BEHOLD! a giant am I!
   Aloft here in my tower,
   With my granite jaws I devour
The maize, and the wheat, and the rye,
   And grind them into flour.

I look down over the farms;
   In the fields of grain I see
   The harvest that is to be,
And I fling to the air my arms,
   For I know it is all for me.

I hear the sound of flails
   Far off, from the threshing-floors
   In barns, with their open doors,
And the wind, the wind in my sails,
   Louder and louder roars.

I stand here in my place,
   With my foot on the rock below,
   And whichever way it may blow
I meet it face to face,
   As a brave man meets his foe.

And while we wrestle and strive
   My master, the miller, stands
   And feeds me with his hands;
For he knows who makes him thrive,
   Who makes him lord of lands.

On Sundays I take my rest;
   Church-going bells begin
   Their low, melodious din;
I cross my arms on my breast,
   And all is peace within.

THE TIDE RISES, THE TIDE FALLS.

THE tide rises, the tide falls,
The twilight darkens, the curlew calls;
Along the sea-sands damp and brown
The traveller hastens toward the town,
   And the tide rises, the tide falls.

Darkness settles on roofs and walls,
But the sea in the darkness calls and
   calls;
The little waves, with their soft, white
   hands,
Efface the footprints in the sands,
   And the tide rises, the tide falls.

The morning breaks; the steeds in their
   stalls
Stamp and neigh, as the hostler calls;
The day returns, but nevermore
Returns the traveller to the shore,
   And the tide rises, the tide falls.

SONNETS.

MY CATHEDRAL.

LIKE two cathedral towers these stately
   pines
   Uplift their fretted summits tipped
    with cones;
The arch beneath them is not built
   with stones,
   Not Art but Nature traced these lovely
   lines,
And carved this graceful arabesque of
   vines;
   No organ but the wind here sighs and
   moans.

No sepulchre conceals a martyr's bones.
No marble bishop on his tomb re-
   clines.
Enter! the pavement, carpeted with
   leaves,
   Gives back a softened echo to thy
   tread!
   Listen! the choir is singing; all the
   birds,
In leafy galleries beneath the eaves,
   Are singing! listen, ere the sound be
   fled,
   And learn there may be worship with-
   out words.

THE BURIAL OF THE POET.

RICHARD HENRY DANA.

In the old churchyard of his native town,
  And in the ancestral tomb beside the
    wall,
  We laid him in the sleep that comes
    to all,
And left him to his rest and his renown.
The snow was falling, as if Heaven drop-
    ped down
  White flowers of Paradise to strew his
    pall ; —
  The dead around him seemed to wake,
    and call
  His name, as worthy of so white a
    crown.
And now the moon is shining on the
    scene,
  And the broad sheet of snow is written
    o'er
  With shadows cruciform of leafless
    trees,
As once the winding-sheet of Saladin
  With chapters of the Koran ; but, ah !
    more
  Mysterious and triumphant signs are
    these.

NIGHT.

Into the darkness and the hush of
    night
Slowly the landscape sinks, and fades
    away,
And with it fade the phantoms of the
    day,
The ghosts of men and things, that
    haunt the light.
The crowd, the clamor, the pursuit, the
    flight,
The unprofitable splendor and display,
The agitations, and the cares that
    prey
Upon our hearts, all vanish out of
    sight.
The better life begins ; the world no
    more
Molests us ; all its records we erase
From the dull common-place book of
    our lives,
That like a palimpsest is written o'er
With trivial incidents of time and
    place,
And lo ! the ideal, hidden beneath, re-
    vives.

L'ENVOI.

THE POET AND HIS SONGS.

As the birds come in the Spring,
  We know not from where ;
As the stars come at evening
  From depths of the air ;

As the rain comes from the cloud,
  And the brook from the ground ;
As suddenly, low or loud,
  Out of silence a sound ;

As the grape comes to the vine,
  The fruit to the tree ;
As the wind comes to the pine,
  And the tide to the sea ;

As come the white sails of ships
  O'er the ocean's verge ;

As comes the smile to the lips,
  The foam to the surge ;

So come to the Poet his songs,
  All hitherward blown
From the misty realm, that belongs
  To the vast Unknown.

His, and not his. are the lays
  He sings ; and their fame
Is his, and not his ; and the praise
  And the pride of a name.

For voices pursue him by day,
  And haunt him by night,
And he listens, and needs must obey,
  When the Angel says : " Write ! "

IN THE HARBOR.

ULTIMA THULE. — PART II.

BECALMED.

BECALMED upon the sea of Thought,
Still unattained the land it sought,
My mind, with loosely-hanging sails,
Lies waiting the auspicious gales.

On either side, behind, before,
The ocean stretches like a floor, —
A level floor of amethyst,
Crowned by a golden dome of mist.

Blow, breath of inspiration, blow !
Shake and uplift this golden glow !
And fill the canvas of the mind
With wafts of thy celestial wind.

Blow, breath of song ! until I feel
The straining sail, the lifting keel,
The life of the awakening sea,
Its motion and its mystery !

HERMES TRISMEGISTUS.

As Seleucus narrates, Hermes describes the
principles that rank as wholes in two myriads
of books; or, as we are informed by Manetho,
he perfectly unfolded these principles in three
myriads six thousand five hundred and twenty-
five volumes. . . .
. . . Our ancestors dedicated the inventions
of their wisdom to this deity, inscribing all
their own writings with the name of Hermes. —
IAMBLICUS.

STILL through Egypt's desert places
    Flows the lordly Nile,
From its banks the great stone faces
    Gaze with patient smile.
Still the pyramids imperious
    Pierce the cloudless skies,
And the Sphinx stares with mysterious,
    Solemn, stony eyes.

But where are the old Egyptian
    Demi-gods and kings ?
Nothing left but an inscription
    Graven on stones and rings.

Where are Helios and Hephæstus,
    Gods of eldest eld ?
Where is Hermes Trismegistus,
    Who their secrets held ?

Where are now the many hundred
    Thousand books he wrote ?
By the Thaumaturgists plundered,
    Lost in lands remote ;
In oblivion sunk forever,
    As when o'er the land
Blows a storm-wind, in the river
    Sinks the scattered sand.

Something unsubstantial, ghostly,
    Seems this Theurgist,
In deep meditation mostly
    Wrapped, as in a mist.
Vague, phantasmal, and unreal
    To our thought he seems,
Walking in a world ideal,
    In a land of dreams.

Was he one, or many, merging
    Name and fame in one,
Like a stream, to which, converging
    Many streamlets run ?
Till, with gathered power proceeding
    Ampler sweep it takes,
Downward the sweet waters leading
    From unnumbered lakes.

By the Nile I see him wandering,
    Pausing now and then,
On the mystic union pondering
    Between gods and men ;
Half believing, wholly feeling,
    With supreme delight,
How the gods, themselves concealing,
    Lift men to their height.

Or in Thebes, the hundred-gated,
    In the thoroughfare
Breathing, as if consecrated,
    A diviner air ;
And amid discordant noises,
    In the jostling throng,

Hearing far, celestial voices
  Of Olympian song.

Who shall call his dreams fallacious ?
  Who has searched or sought
All the unexplored and spacious
  Universe of thought ?
Who, in his own skill confiding,
  Shall with rule and line
Mark the border-land dividing
  Human and divine ?

Trismegistus ! three times greatest !
  How thy name sublime
Has descended to this latest
  Progeny of time !
Happy they whose written pages
  Perish with their lives,
If amid the crumbling ages
  Still their name survives !

Thine, O priest of Egypt, lately
  Found I in the vast,
Weed-encumbered, sombre, stately,
  Grave-yard of the Past ;
And a presence moved before me
  On that gloomy shore,
As a waft of wind, that o'er me
  Breathed, and was no more.

THE POET'S CALENDAR.

JANUARY.

I.

Janus am I ; oldest of potentates ;
  Forward I look, and backward, and
    below
I count, as god of avenues and gates,
  The years that through my portals
    come and go.

II.

I block the roads, and drift the fields
  with snow ;
  I chase the wild-fowl from the frozen
    fen ;
My frosts congeal the rivers in their
  flow,
  My fires light up the hearths and
    hearts of men.

FEBRUARY.

I am lustration , and the sea is mine.
  I wash the sands and headlands with
    my tide ;

My brow is crowned with branches of
  the pine ;
  Before my chariot-wheels the fishes
    glide.
By me all things unclean are purified,
  By me the souls of men washed white
    again ;
E'en the unlovely tombs of those who
  died
  Without a dirge, I cleanse from every
    stain.

MARCH.

I Martius am ! Once first, and now the
  third !
  To lead the Year was my appointed
    place ;
A mortal dispossessed me by a word,
  And set there Janus with the double
    face.
Hence I make war on all the human
  race ;
  I shake the cities with my hurricanes ;
I flood the rivers and their banks efface,
  And drown the farms and hamlets
    with my rains.

APRIL.

I open wide the portals of the Spring
  To welcome the procession of the
    flowers,
With their gay banners, and the birds
  that sing
  Their song of songs from their aerial
    towers.
I soften with my sunshine and my show-
  ers
  The heart of earth ; with thoughts of
    love I glide
Into the hearts of men ; and with the
  Hours
  Upon the Bull with wreathèd horns I
    ride.

MAY.

Hark ! The sea-faring wild-fowl loud
  proclaim
  My coming, and the swarming of the
    bees.
These are my heralds, and behold ! my
  name
  Is written in blossoms on the haw-
    thorn-trees.
I tell the mariner when to sail the
  seas ;
  I waft o'er all the land from far away

The breath and bloom of the Hesper-
    ides,
    My birthplace. I am Maia. I am
    May.

JUNE.

Mine is the Month of Roses; yes, and
    mine
    The Month of Marriages! All pleas-
    ant sights
And scents, the fragrance of the blos-
    soming vine,
    The foliage of the valleys and the
    heights.
Mine are the longest days, the loveliest
    nights;
    The mower's scythe makes music to
    my ear;
I am the mother of all dear delights;
    I am the fairest daughter of the year.

JULY.

My emblem is the Lion, and I breathe
    The breath of Libyan deserts o'er the
    land;
My sickle as a sabre I unsheathe,
    And bent before me the pale harvests
    stand.
The lakes and rivers shrink at my com-
    mand,
    And there is thirst and fever in the
    air;
The sky is changed to brass, the earth
    to sand;
    I am the Emperor whose name I bear.

AUGUST.

The Emperor Octavian, called the Au-
    gust,
    I being his favorite, bestowed his
    name
Upon me, and I hold it still in trust,
    In memory of him and of his fame.
I am the Virgin, and my vestal flame
    Burns less intensely than the Lion's
    rage;
Sheaves are my only garlands, and I
    claim
    The golden Harvests as my heritage.

SEPTEMBER.

I bear the Scales, where hang in equi-
    poise
    The night and day; and when unto
    my lips

I put my trumpet, with its stress and
    noise
    Fly the white clouds like tattered sails
    of ships;
The tree-tops lash the air with sounding
    whips;
    Southward the clamorous sea-fowl
    wing their flight;
The hedges are all red with haws and
    hips,
    The Hunter's Moon reigns empress of
    the night.

OCTOBER.

My ornaments are fruits; my garments
    leaves,
    Woven like cloth of gold, and crim-
    son dyed;
I do not boast the harvesting of sheaves,
    O'er orchards and o'er vineyards I
    preside.
Though on the frigid Scorpion I ride,
    The dreamy air is full, and over-
    flows
With tender memories of the summer-
    tide,
    And mingled voices of the doves and
    crows.

NOVEMBER.

The Centaur, Sagittarius, am I,
    Born of Ixion's and the cloud's em-
    brace;
With sounding hoofs across the earth I
    fly,
    A steed Thessalian with a human face.
Sharp winds the arrows are with which
    I chase
    The leaves, half dead already with
    affright;
I shroud myself in gloom; and to the
    race
    Of mortals bring nor comfort nor
    delight.

DECEMBER.

Riding upon the Goat, with snow-white
    hair,
    I come, the last of all. This crown of
    mine
Is of the holly; in my hand I bear
    The thyrsus, tipped with fragrant
    cones of pine.
I celebrate the birth of the Divine,
    And the return of the Saturnian
    reign: —

My songs are carols sung at every
    shrine,
  Proclaiming " Peace on earth, good
    will to men.''

MAD RIVER,

IN THE WHITE MOUNTAINS.

TRAVELLER.

WHY dost thou wildly rush and roar,
    Mad River, O Mad River?
Wilt thou not pause and cease to pour
Thy hurrying, headlong waters o'er
    This rocky shelf forever?

What secret trouble stirs thy breast?
    Why all this fret and flurry?
Dost thou not know that what is best
In this too restless world is rest
    From over-work and worry?

THE RIVER.

What wouldst thou in these mountains
    seek,
    O stranger from the city?
Is it perhaps some foolish freak
Of thine, to put the words I speak
    Into a plaintive ditty?

TRAVELLER.

Yes ; I would learn of thee thy song,
    With all its flowing numbers,
And in a voice as fresh and strong
As thine is, sing it all day long,
    And hear it in my slumbers.

THE RIVER.

A brooklet nameless and unknown
    Was I at first, resembling
A little child, that all alone
Comes venturing down the stairs of
    stone,
    Irresolute and trembling.

Later, by wayward fancies led,
    For the wide world I panted ;
Out of the forest dark and dread
Across the open fields I fled,
    Like one pursued and haunted

I tossed my arms, I sang aloud,
    My voice exultant blending

With thunder from the passing cloud,
The wind, the forest bent and bowed,
    The rush of rain descending.

I heard the distant ocean call,
    Imploring and entreating;
Drawn onward, o'er this rocky wall
I plunged, and the loud waterfall
    Made answer to the greeting.

And now, beset with many ills,
    A toilsome life I follow;
Compelled to carry from the hills
These logs to the impatient mills
    Below there in the hollow.

Yet something ever cheers and charms
    The rudeness of my labors;
Daily I water with these arms
The cattle of a hundred farms,
    And have the birds for neighbors

Men call me Mad, and well they may,
    When, full of rage and trouble,
I burst my banks of sand and clay,
And sweep their wooden bridge away,
    Like withered reeds or stubble.

Now go and write thy little rhyme,
    As of thine own creating.
Thou seest the day is past its prime ;
I can no longer waste my time ;
    The mills are tired of waiting

AUF WIEDERSEHEN.

IN MEMORY OF J. T. F.

UNTIL we meet again! That is the
    meaning
Of the familiar words, that men repeat
    At parting in the street.
Ah yes, till then ! but when death in-
    tervening
Rends us asunder, with what ceaseless
    pain
    We wait for the Again!

The friends who leave us do not feel the
    sorrow
Of parting, as we feel it, who must stay
    Lamenting day by day,
And knowing, when we wake upon the
    morrow,
We shall not find in its accustomed
    place
    The one beloved face.

It were a double grief, if the departed,
Being released from earth, should still
  retain
    A sense of earthly pain;
It were a double grief, if the true-
  hearted,
Who loved us here, should on the farther shore
    Remember us no more.

Believing, in the midst of our afflictions,
That death is a beginning, not an end,
    We cry to them, and send
Farewells, that better might be called
  predictions,
Being fore-shadowings of the future,
  thrown
    Into the vast Unknown.

Faith overleaps the confines of our reason,
And if by faith, as in old times was said,
    Women received their dead
Raised up to life, then only for a season
Our partings are, nor shall we wait in
  vain
    Until we meet again!

THE CHILDREN'S CRUSADE.

[A FRAGMENT.]

I.

WHAT is this I read in history,
Full of marvel, full of mystery,
Difficult to understand?
Is it fiction, is it truth?
Children in the flower of youth,
Heart in heart, and hand in hand,
Ignorant of what helps or harms,
Without armor, without arms,
Journeying to the Holy Land!

Who shall answer or divine?
Never since the world was made
Such a wonderful crusade
Started forth for Palestine.
Never while the world shall last
Will it reproduce the past;
Never will it see again
Such an army, such a band,
Over mountain, over main,
Journeying to the Holy Land.

Like a shower of blossoms blown
From the parent trees were they;

Like a flock of birds that fly
Through the unfrequented sky,
Holding nothing as their own,
Passed they into lands unknown,
Passed to suffer and to die.

O the simple, child-like trust!
O the faith that could believe
What the harnessed, iron-mailed
Knights of Christendom had failed,
By their prowess, to achieve,
They, the children, could and must!

Little thought the Hermit, preaching
Holy Wars to knight and baron,
That the words dropped in his teach-
  ing,
His entreaty, his beseeching,
Would by children's hands be gleaned,
And the staff on which he leaned
Blossom like the rod of Aaron.

As a summer wind upheaves
The innumerable leaves
In the bosom of a wood, —
Not as separate leaves, but massed
All together by the blast, —
So for evil or for good
His resistless breath upheaved
All at once the many-leaved,
Many-thoughted multitude.

In the tumult of the air
Rock the boughs with all the nests
Cradled on their tossing crests;
By the fervor of his prayer
Troubled hearts were everywhere
Rocked and tossed in human breasts.

For a century, at least,
His prophetic voice had ceased;
But the air was heated still
By his lurid words and will,
As from fires in far-off woods,
In the autumn of the year,
An unwonted fever broods
In the sultry atmosphere.

II.

In Cologne the bells were ringing,
In Cologne the nuns were singing
Hymns and canticles divine;
Loud the monks sang in their stalls,
And the thronging streets were loud
With the voices of the crowd; —
Underneath the city walls
Silent flowed the river Rhine.

From the gates, that summer day,
Clad in robes of hodden gray,
With the red cross on the breast,
Azure-eyed and golden-haired,
Forth the young crusaders fared :
While above the band devoted
Consecrated banners floated,
Fluttered many a flag and streamer,
And the cross o'er all the rest !
Singing lowly, meekly, slowly,
" Give us, give us back the holy
Sepulchre of the Redeemer ! "
On the vast procession pressed,
Youths and maidens. . . .

III.

Ah ! what master hand shall paint
How they journeyed on their way,
How the days grew long and dreary,
How their little feet grew weary,
How their little hearts grew faint !

Ever swifter day by day
Flowed the homeward river ; ever
More and more its whitening current
Broke and scattered into spray,
Till the calmly-flowing river
Changed into a mountain torrent,
Rushing from its glacier green
Down through chasm and black ravine.
Like a phœnix in its nest,
Burned the red sun in the West,
Sinking in an ashen cloud ;
In the East, above the crest
Of the sea-like mountain chain,
Like a phœnix from its shroud,
Came the red sun back again.

Now around them, white with snow,
Closed the mountain peaks. Below,
Headlong from the precipice
Down into the dark abyss,
Plunged the cataract, white with foam ;
And it said, or seemed to say :
" Oh return, while yet you may,
Foolish children, to your home,
There the Holy City is ! "

But the dauntless leader said :
" Faint not, though your bleeding feet
O'er these slippery paths of sleet
Move but painfully and slowly ;
Other feet than yours have bled ;
Other tears than yours been shed.
Courage ! lose not heart or hope ;
On the mountains' southern slope
Lies Jerusalem the Holy ! "

As a white rose in its pride,
By the wind in summer-tide
Tossed and loosened from the branch,
Showers its petals o'er the ground,
From the distant mountain's side,
Scattering all its snows around,
With mysterious, muffled sound,
Loosened, fell the avalanche.
Voices, echoes far and near,
Roar of winds and waters blending,
Mists uprising, clouds impending,
Filled them with a sense of fear,
Formless, nameless, never ending.

. . . .

THE CITY AND THE SEA.

THE panting City cried to the Sea,
" I am faint with heat, — O breathe on
me ! "

And the Sea said, " Lo, I breathe ! but
my breath
To some will be life, to others death ! '

As to Prometheus, bringing ease
In pain, come the Oceanides,

So to the City, hot with the flame
Of the pitiless sun, the east wind came.

It came from the heaving breast of the
deep,
Silent as dreams are, and sudden a
sleep.

Life-giving, death-giving, which will it
be ;
O breath of the merciful, merciless Sea ?

SUNDOWN.

THE summer sun is sinking low ;
Only the tree-tops redden and glow :
Only the weathercock on the spire
Of the neighboring church is a flame o
fire ;
All is in shadow below.

O beautiful, awful summer day,
What hast thou given, what taken away ?
Life and death, and love and hate,
Homes made happy or desolate,
Hearts made sad or gay !

On the road of life one mile-stone more ;
In the book of life one leaf turned o'er

Like a red seal is the setting sun
On the good and the evil men have
    done, —
    Naught can to-day restore !
July 24, 1879.

PRESIDENT GARFIELD.

" E VENNI DAL MARTIRIO A QUESTA
            PACE."

THESE words the poet heard in Para-
    dise,
    Uttered by one who, bravely dying
        here,
    In the true faith was living in that
        sphere
Where the celestial cross of sacrifice
Spread its protecting arms athwart the
    skies ;
    And set thereon, like jewels crystal
        clear,
    The souls magnanimous, that knew
        not fear,
    Flashed their effulgence on his daz-
        zled eyes.
Ah me ! how dark the discipline of pain,
    Were not the suffering followed by
        the sense
Of infinite rest and infinite release !
This is our consolation ; and again
    A great soul cries to us in our sus-
        pense,
    " I came from martyrdom unto this
        peace ! "

DECORATION DAY.

SLEEP, comrades, sleep and rest
    On this Field of the Grounded Arms,
Where foes no more molest,
    Nor sentry's shot alarms !

Ye have slept on the ground before,
    And started to your feet
At the cannon's sudden roar,
    Or the drum's redoubling beat.

But in this camp of Death
    No sound your slumber breaks ;
Here is no fevered breath,
    No wound that bleeds and aches.

All is repose and peace,
    Untrampled lies the sod ;
The shouts of battle cease,
    It is the Truce of God !

Rest, comrades, rest and sleep !
    The thoughts of men shall be
As sentinels to keep
    Your rest from danger free.

Your silent tents of green
    We deck with fragrant flowers ;
Yours has the suffering been,
    The memory shall be ours.
February 3, 1882.

CHIMES.

SWEET chimes ! that in the loneliness
        of night
    Salute the passing hour, and in the
        dark
    And silent chambers of the house-
        hold mark
    The movements of the myriad orbs
        of light !
Through my closed eyelids, by the inner
        sight,
    I see the constellations in the arc
    Of their great circles moving on, and
        hark !
    I almost hear them singing in their
        flight.
Better than sleep it is to lie awake
    O'er-canopied by the vast starry dome
Of the immeasurable sky ; to feel
The slumbering world sink under us,
        and make
    Hardly an eddy, — a mere rush of
        foam
    On the great sea beneath a sinking
        keel.
August 28, 1879.

FOUR BY THE CLOCK.

FOUR by the clock ! and yet not day ;
But the great world rolls and wheels
        away,
With its cities on land, and its ships at
        sea,
Into the dawn that is to be !

Only the lamp in the anchored bark
Sends its glimmer across the dark,
And the heavy breathing of the sea
Is the only sound that comes to me.

NAHANT, *September* 8, 1880,
    Four o'clock in the morning.

THE FOUR LAKES OF MADISON.

FOUR limpid lakes, — four Naiades
Or sylvan deities are these,
  In flowing robes of azure dressed;
Four lovely handmaids, that uphold
Their shining mirrors, rimmed with
  gold,
  To the fair city in the West.

By day the coursers of the sun
Drink of these waters as they run
  Their swift diurnal round on high;
By night the constellations glow
Far down the hollow deeps below,
  And glimmer in another sky.

Fair lakes, serene and full of light,
Fair town, arrayed in robes of white,
  How visionary ye appear!
All like a floating landscape seems
In cloud-land or the land of dreams,
  Bathed in a golden atmosphere!

MOONLIGHT.

As a pale phantom with a lamp
  Ascends some ruin's haunted stair,
So glides the moon along the damp
  Mysterious chambers of the air.

Now hidden in cloud, and now revealed,
  As if this phantom, full of pain,
Were by the crumbling walls concealed,
  And at the windows seen again.

Until at last, serene and proud
  In all the splendor of her light,
She walks the terraces of cloud,
  Supreme as Empress of the Night.

I look, but recognize no more
  Objects familiar to my view;
The very pathway to my door
  Is an enchanted avenue.

All things are changed. One mass of
  shade,
  The elm-trees drop their curtains
  down ;
By palace, park, and colonnade
  I walk as in a foreign town.

The very ground beneath my feet
  Is clothed with a diviner air ;
White marble paves the silent street
  And glimmers in the empty square

Illusion! Underneath there lies
  The common life of every day ;
Only the spirit glorifies
  With its own tints the sober gray.

In vain we look, in vain uplift
  Our eyes to heaven, if we are blind
We see but what we have the gift
  Of seeing ; what we bring we find.

December 20, 1878.

TO THE AVON.

FLOW on, sweet river ! like his verse
Who lies beneath this sculptured hearse
Nor wait beside the churchyard wall
For him who cannot hear thy call.

Thy playmate once ; I see him now
A boy with sunshine on his brow,
And hear in Stratford's quiet street
The patter of his little feet.

I see him by thy shallow edge
Wading knee-deep amid the sedge ;
And lost in thought, as if thy stream
Were the swift river of a dream.

He wonders whitherward it flows;
And fain would follow where it goes,
To the wide world, that shall erelong
Be filled with his melodious song.

Flow on, fair stream ! That dream is
  o'er ;
He stands upon another shore ;
A vaster river near him flows,
And still he follows where it goes.

ELEGIAC VERSE.

I.

PERADVENTURE of old, some bard in
  Ionian Islands,
  Walking alone by the sea, hearing the
  wash of the waves,
Learned the secret from them of the
  beautiful verse elegiac,
  Breathing into his song motion and
  sound of the sea.

For as the wave of the sea, upheaving in
  long undulations,
  Plunges loud on the sands, pauses, and
  turns, and retreats,

So the Hexameter, rising and singing,
  with cadence sonorous,
Falls; and in refluent rhythm back
  the Pentameter flows.[1]

II.

Not in his youth alone, but in age, may
  the heart of the poet
Bloom into song, as the gorse blossoms
  in autumn and spring.

III.

Not in tenderness wanting, yet rough are
  the rhymes of our poet;
Though it be Jacob's voice, Esau's,
  alas! are the hands.

IV.

Let us be grateful to writers for what is
  left in the inkstand;
When to leave off is an art only attained by the few.

V.

How can the Three be One? you ask
  me; I answer by asking,
Hail and snow and rain, are they not
  three, and yet one?

VI.

By the mirage uplifted the land floats
  vague in the ether,
  Ships and the shadows of ships hang
    in the motionless air;
So by the art of the poet our common
  life is uplifted,
  So, transfigured, the world floats in a
    luminous haze.

VII.

Like a French poem is Life; being only
  perfect in structure
When with the masculine rhymes mingled the feminine are.

VIII.

Down from the mountain descends the
  brooklet, rejoicing in freedom;
Little it dreams of the mill hid in the
  valley below;

[1] Compare Schiller.

Im Hexameter steigt des Springquells flüssige Säule;
Im Pentameter drauf fällt sie melodisch herab.

See also Coleridge's translation.

Glad with the joy of existence, the child
  goes singing and laughing,
Little dreaming what toils lie in the
  future concealed.

IX.

As the ink from our pen, so flow our
  thoughts and our feelings
When we begin to write, however
  sluggish before.

X.

Like the Kingdom of Heaven, the Fountain of Youth is within us;
If we seek it elsewhere, old shall we
  grow in the search.

XI.

If you would hit the mark, you must
  aim a little above it;
Every arrow that flies feels the attraction of earth.

XII.

Wisely the Hebrews admit no Present
  tense in their language;
While we are speaking the word, it is
  is already the Past.

XIII.

In the twilight of age all things seem
  strange and phantasmal,
As between daylight and dark ghost-
  like the landscape appears.

XIV.

Great is the art of beginning, but greater
  the art is of ending;
Many a poem is marred by a superfluous verse.

1881.

A FRAGMENT.

AWAKE! arise! the hour is late!
  Angels are knocking at thy door!
They are in haste and cannot wait,
  And once departed come no more.

Awake! arise! the athlete's arm
  Loses its strength by too much rest;
The fallow land, the untilled farm
  Produces only weeds at best.

THE BELLS OF SAN BLAS.[1]

WHAT say the Bells of San Blas
To the ships that southward pass
From the harbor of Mazatlan?
To them it is nothing more
Than the sound of surf on the shore, —
Nothing more to master or man.

But to me, a dreamer of dreams,
To whom what is and what seems
Are often one and the same, —
The Bells of San Blas to me
Have a strange, wild melody,
And are something more than a
name.

For bells are the voice of the church;
They have tones that touch and search
The hearts of young and old;
One sound to all, yet each
Lends a meaning to their speech,
And the meaning is manifold.

They are a voice of the Past,
Of an age that is fading fast,
Of a power austere and grand,
When the flag of Spain unfurled
Its folds o'er this western world,
And the Priest was lord of the land.

The chapel that once looked down
On the little seaport town
Has crumbled into the dust;
And on oaken beams below
The bells swing to and fro,
And are green with mould and rust.

"Is, then, the old faith dead,"
They say, " and in its stead
Is some new faith proclaimed,

That we are forced to remain
Naked to sun and rain,
Unsheltered and ashamed?

"Once, in our tower aloof,
We rang over wall and roof
Our warnings and our complaints;
And round about us there
The white doves filled the air,
Like the white souls of the saints.

"The saints! Ah, have they grown
Forgetful of their own?
Are they asleep, or dead,
That open to the sky
Their ruined Missions lie,
No longer tenanted?

"Oh, bring us back once more
The vanished days of yore,
When the world with faith was
filled;
Bring back the fervid zeal,
The hearts of fire and steel,
The hands that believe and build.

"Then from our tower again
We will send over land and main
Our voices of command,
Like exiled kings who return
To their thrones, and the people learn
That the Priest is lord of th'
land!"

O Bells of San Blas, in vain
Ye call back the Past again;
The Past is deaf to your prayer!
Out of the shadows of night
The world rolls into light;
It is daybreak everywhere.

[1] The last poem written by Mr. Longfellow

March 15, 1882

TRANSLATIONS.

PRELUDE.

As treasures that men seek,
  Deep-buried in sea-sands,
Vanish if they but speak,
  And elude their eager hands,

So ye escape and slip,
  O songs, and fade away,
When the word is on my lip
  To interpret what ye say.

Were it not better, then,
  To let the treasures rest
Hid from the eyes of men,
  Locked in their iron chest ?

I have but marked the place,
  But half the secret told,
That, following this slight trace,
  Others may find the gold.

FROM THE FRENCH.

WILL ever the dear days come back
    again,
  Those days of June, when lilacs were
    in bloom,
  And bluebirds sang their sonnets in
    the gloom
  Of leaves that roofed them in from
    sun or rain ?
I know not ; but a presence will re-
    main
  Forever and forever in this room,
  Formless, diffused in air, like a per-
    fume, —
  A phantom of the heart, and not the
    brain.
Delicious days ! when every spoken
    word
  Was like a foot-fall nearer and more
    near,
  And a mysterious knocking at the
    gate
Of the heart's secret places, and we
    heard

In the sweet tumult of delight and
    fear
A voice that whispered, "Open, I
    cannot wait ! "

THE WINE OF JURANÇON.

FROM THE FRENCH OF CHARLES CORAN.

LITTLE sweet wine of Jurançon,
  You are dear to my memory still !
With mine host and his merry song,
  Under the rose-tree I drank my fill.

Twenty years after, passing that way,
  Under the trellis I found again
Mine host, still sitting there *au frais*,
  And singing still the same refrain.

The Jurançon, so fresh and bold,
  Treats me as one it used to know ;
Souvenirs of the days of old
  Already from the bottle flow.

With glass in hand our glances met ;
  We pledge, we drink. How sour it is
Never Argenteuil piquette
  Was to my palate sour as this !

And yet the vintage was good, in sooth ;
  The self-same juice, the self-same
    cask !
It was you, O gayety of my youth,
  That failed in the autumnal flask !

AT LA CHAUDEAU.

FROM THE FRENCH OF XAVIER MAR-
MIER.

AT La Chaudeau, — ' t is long since
    then :
I was young, — my years twice ten ;
All things smiled on the happy boy,
Dreams of love and songs of joy,
Azure of heaven and wave below,
    At La Chaudeau.

To La Chaudeau I come back old :
My head is gray, my blood is cold ;
Seeking along the meadow ooze,
Seeking beside the river Seymouse,
The days of my spring-time of long
ago
    At La Chaudeau.

At La Chaudeau nor heart nor brain
Ever grows old with grief and pain ;
A sweet remembrance keeps off age ;
A tender friendship doth still assuage
The burden of sorrow that one may
know
    At La Chaudeau.

At La Chaudeau, had fate decreed
To limit the wandering life I lead,
Peradventure I still, forsooth,
Should have preserved my fresh green
youth,
Under the shadows the hill-tops throw
    At La Chaudeau.

At La Chaudeau, live on, my friends,
Happy to be where God intends ;
And sometimes, by the evening fire,
Think of him whose sole desire
    again to sit in the old château
    At La Chaudeau.

A QUIET LIFE.

FROM THE FRENCH.

LET him who will, by force or fraud in-
    nate,
  Of courtly grandeurs gain the slippery
    height ;
I, leaving not the home of my delight,
  Far from the world and noise will
    meditate.
Then, without pomps or perils of the
    great,
  I shall behold the day succeed the
    night ;
Behold the alternate seasons take their
    flight,
  And in serene repose old age await.
And so, whenever Death shall come to
    close
  The happy moments that my days
    compose,
  I, full of years, shall die, obscure,
    alone !
How wretched is the man, with honors
    crowned,
  Who, having not the one thing need-
    ful found,
  Dies, known to all, but to himself un
    known.

September 11, 1879

PERSONAL POEMS.

LOSS AND GAIN.

WHEN I compare
What I have lost with what I have
    gained,
What I have missed with what attained,
  Little room do I find for pride.

I am aware
How many days have been idly spent ;
How like an arrow the good intent
  Has fallen short or been turned aside.

But who shall dare
To measure loss and gain in this wise ?
Defeat may be victory in disguise ;
  The lowest ebb is the turn of the tide.

AUTUMN WITHIN.

IT is autumn ; not without,
  But within me is the cold.
Youth and spring are all about ;
  It is I that have grown old.

Birds are darting through the air,
  Singing, building without rest ;
Life is stirring everywhere,
  Save within my lonely breast.

There is silence : the dead leaves
  Fall and rustle and are still ;
Beats no flail upon the sheaves,
  Comes no murmur from the mill.

April 9, 1874.

VICTOR AND VANQUISHED.

As one who long hath fled with panting
    breath
    Before his foe, bleeding and near to
      fall,
    I turn and set my back against the
      wall,
    And look thee in the face, triumphant
      Death,
I call for aid, and no one answereth;
    I am alone with thee, who conquerest
      all;
    Yet me thy threatening form doth not
      appall,
    For thou art but a phantom and a
      wraith.
Wounded and weak, sword broken at
    the hilt,
    With armor shattered, and without a
      shield,
    I stand unmoved; do with me what
      thou wilt;
I can resist no more, but will not yield.
    This is no tournament where cowards
      tilt ;
    The vanquished here is victor of the
      field.
April 4, 1876.

MEMORIES.

OFT I remember those whom I have
    known
    In other days, to whom my heart was
      led
    As by a magnet, and who are not dead,
    But absent, and their memories over-
      grown
With other thoughts and troubles of
    my own,
    As graves with grasses are, and at
      their head

The stone with moss and lichens so
    o'erspread,
Nothing is legible but the name alone.
And is it so with them ? After long
    years,
    Do they remember me in the same
      way,
    And is the memory pleasant as to me ?
I fear to ask; yet wherefore are my
    fears ?
    Pleasures, like flowers, may wither
      and decay,
    And yet the root perennial may be.
September 23, 1881.

MY BOOKS.

SADLY as some old mediæval knight
    Gazed at the arms he could no longer
      wield,
    The sword two-handed and the shin-
      ing shield
    Suspended in the hall, and full in
      sight,
While secret longings for the lost de-
    light
    Of tourney or adventure in the field
    Came over him, and tears but half
      concealed
    Trembled and fell upon his beard of
      white,
So I behold these books upon their shelf,
    My ornaments and arms of other
      days;
    Not wholly useless, though no longer
      used,
For they remind me of my other self,
    Younger and stronger, and the pleas-
      ant ways
    In which I walked, now clouded and
      confused.
December 27, 1881.

L'ENVOI.

POSSIBILITIES.

WHERE are the Poets, unto whom be-
    long
    The Olympian heights; whose sing-
      ing shafts were sent

Straight to the mark, and not from
    bows half bent,
    But with the utmost tension of the
      thong ?
Where are the stately argosies of
    song.

Whose rushing keels made music as
  they went
Sailing in search of some new continent,
With all sail set, and steady winds and
  strong ?
Perhaps there lives some dreamy boy,
  untaught
In schools, some graduate of the field
  or street,

Who shall become a master of the
  art,
An admiral sailing the high seas of
  thought,
Fearless and first and steering with
  his fleet
For lands not yet laid down in any
  chart.

January 17, 1882.

MICHAEL ANGELO.

Michel, più che mortal, Angel divino.
ARIOSTO.

Similamente operando all' artista
Ch' a l'abito dell' arte e man che trema.
DANTE, *Par.* xiii., *st.* 77.

DEDICATION.

NOTHING that is shall perish utterly,
  But perish only to revive again
  In other forms, as clouds restore in
    rain
  The exhalations of the land and sea.
Men build their houses from the ma-
    sonry
  Of ruined tombs ; the passion and the
    pain
  Of hearts, that long have ceased to
    beat, remain
  To throb in hearts that are, or are to
    be.
So from old chronicles, where sleep in
    dust
  Names that once filled the world with
    trumpet tones,
  I build this verse ; and flowers of song
    have thrust
Their roots among the loose disjointed
    stones,
  Which to this end I fashion as I must.
  Quickened are they that touch the
    Prophet's bones.

PART FIRST.

I.

PROLOGUE AT ISCHIA.

The Castle Terrace. VITTORIA CO-
LONNA, *and* JULIA GONZAGA

VITTORIA.

Will you then leave me, Julia, and so
    soon,
To pace alone this terrace like a ghost ?

JULIA.

To-morrow, dearest.

VITTORIA.

                    Do not say to-morrow.
A whole month of to-morrows were too
    soon.
You must not go.   You are a part of
    me.

JULIA.

I must return to Fondi.

VITTORIA.

                    The old castle
Needs not your presence.   No one waits
    for you.
Stay one day longer with me.   They
    who go
Feel not the pain of parting ; it is they
Who stay behind that suffer.   I was
    thinking
But yesterday how like and how unlike
Have been, and are, our destinies.   Your
    husband,
The good Vespasian, an old man, who
    seemed
A father to you rather than a husband,
Died in your arms ; but mine, in all the
    flower
And promise of his youth, was taken
    from me
As by a rushing wind.   The breath of
    battle
Breathed on him, and I saw his face no
    more,
Save as in dreams it haunts me.   As our
    love

Was for these men, so is our sorrow for them.
Yours a child's sorrow, smiling through its tears;
But mine the grief of an impassioned woman,
Who drank her life up in one draught of love.

JULIA.

Behold this locket. This is the white hair
Of my Vespasian. This is the flower-of-love,
This amaranth, and beneath it the device
Non moritura. Thus my heart remains
True to his memory; and the ancient castle,
Where we have lived together, where he died,
Is dear to me as Ischia is to you.

VITTORIA.

I did not mean to chide you.

JULIA.

Let your heart
Find, if it can, some poor apology
For one who is too young, and feels too keenly
The joy of life, to give up all her days
To sorrow for the dead. While I am true
To the remembrance of the man I loved
And mourn for still, I do not make a show
Of all the grief I feel, nor live secluded
And, like Veronica da Gámbara,
Drape my whole house in mourning, and drive forth
In coach of sable drawn by sable horses,
As if I were a corpse. Ah, one to-day
Is worth for me a thousand yesterdays.

VITTORIA.

Dear Julia! Friendship has its jealousies
As well as love. Who waits for you at Fondi?

JULIA.

A friend of mine and yours; a friend and friar.
You have at Naples your Fra Bernadino;
And I at Fondi have my Fra Bastiano,

The famous artist, who has come from Rome
To paint my portrait. That is not a sin.

VITTORIA.

Only a vanity.

JULIA.

He painted yours.

VITTORIA.

Do not call up to me those days departed
When I was young, and all was bright about me,
And the vicissitudes of life were things
But to be read of in old histories,
Though as pertaining unto me or mine
Impossible. Ah, then I dreamed your dreams,
And now, grown older, I look back and see
They were illusions.

JULIA.

Yet without illusions
What would our lives become, what we ourselves?
Dreams or illusions, call them what you will,
They lift us from the commonplace of life
To better things.

VITTORIA.

Are there no brighter dreams,
No higher aspirations, than the wish
To please and to be pleased?

JULIA.

For you there are:
I am no saint; I feel the world we live in
Comes before that which is to be here after,
And must be dealt with first.

VITTORIA.

But in what way?

JULIA.

Let the soft wind that wafts to us the odor
Of orange blossoms, let the laughing sea
And the bright sunshine bathing all the world,
Answer the question.

VITTORIA.

                    And for whom is meant
This portrait that you speak of ?

JULIA.

                    For my friend
The Cardinal Ippolito.

VITTORIA.

                    For him ?

JULIA

Yes, for Ippolito the Magnificent.
'T is always flattering to a woman's
     pride
To be admired by one whom all admire.

VITTORIA.

Ah, Julia, she that makes herself a
     dove
Is eaten by the hawk. Be on your
     guard.
He is a Cardinal ; and his adoration
Should be elsewhere directed.

JULIA.

                    You forget
The horror of that night, when Barba-
     rossa,
The Moorish corsair, landed on our
     coast
To seize me for the Sultan Soliman ;
How in the dead of night, when all were
     sleeping,
He scaled the castle wall ; how I es-
     caped,
And in my night-dress, mounting a swift
     steed,
Fled to the mountains, and took refuge
     there
Among the brigands. Then of all my
     friends
The Cardinal Ippolito was first
To come with his retainers to my res-
     cue.
Could I refuse the only boon he asked
At such a time, my portrait ?

VITTORIA.

                    I have heard
Strange stories of the splendors of his
     palace,
And how, apparelled like a Spanish
     Prince,
He rides through Rome with a long
     retinue
Of Ethiopians and Numidians

And Turks and Tartars, in fantastic
     dresses,
Making a gallant show.   Is this the
     way
A Cardinal should live ?

JULIA.

                    He is so young ;
Hardly of age, or little more than that ;
Beautiful, generous, fond of arts and
     letters,
A poet, a musician, and a scholar ;
Master of many languages, and a player
On many instruments.   In Rome, his
     palace
Is the asylum of all men distinguished
In art or science, and all Florentines
Escaping from the tyranny of his cousin,
Duke Alessandro.

VITTORIA.

                    I have seen his portrait,
Painted by Titian.   You have painted it
In brighter colors.

JULIA.

                    And my Cardinal,
At Itri, in the courtyard of his palace,
Keeps a tame lion !

VITTORIA.

                    And so counterfeits
St. Mark, the Evangelist !

JULIA.

                    Ah, your tame lion
Is Michael Angelo.

VITTORIA.

                    You speak a name
That always thrills me with a noble
     sound,
As of a trumpet ! Michael Angelo !
A lion all men fear and none can tame ;
A man that all men honor, and the
     model
That all should follow ; one who works
     and prays,
For work is prayer, and consecrates his
     life
To the sublime ideal of his art,
Till art and life are one ; a man who
     holds
Such place in all men's thoughts, that
     when they speak
Of great things done, or to be done, his
     name
Is ever on their lips.

JULIA.

                        You too can paint
The portrait of your hero, and in colors
Brighter than Titian's; I might warn
    you also
Against the dangers that beset your
    path;
But I forbear.

VITTORIA.

                    If I were made of marble,
Of Fior di Persico or Pavonazzo,
He might admire me : being but flesh
    and blood,
I am no more to him than other women;
That is, am nothing.

JULIA.

                    Does he ride through Rome
Upon his little mule, as he was wont,
With his slouched hat, and boots of Cor-
    dovan,
As when I saw him last ?

VITTORIA.

                        Pray do not jest.
I cannot couple with his noble name
A trivial word ! Look, how the setting
    sun
Lights up Castel-a-mare ana Sorrento,
And changes Capri to a purple cloud !
And there Vesuvius with its plume of
    smoke,
And the great city stretched upon the
    shore
As in a dream !

JULIA.

Parthenope the Siren !

VITTORIA.

And yon long line of lights, those sun-
    lit windows
Blaze like the torches carried in pro-
    cession
To do her honor ! It is beautiful !

JULIA.

I have no heart to feel the beauty of it !
My feet are weary, pacing up and down
These level flags, and wearier still my
    thoughts
Treading the broken pavement of the
    Past.
It is too sad. I will go in and rest,
And make me ready for to-morrow's
    journey.

VITTORIA.

I will go with you; for I would not lose
One hour of your dear presence. 'T is
    enough
Only to be in the same room with you.
I need not speak to you, nor hear you
    speak;
If I but see you, I am satisfied.
                        [*They go in*

II.

MONOLOGUE.

MICHAEL ANGELO'S *Studio. He is at
work on the cartoon of the Last Judg
ment.*

MICHAEL ANGELO.

Why did the Pope and his ten Cardinals
Come here to lay this heavy task upon
    me ?
Were not the paintings on the Sistine
    ceiling
Enough for them ? They saw the He
    brew leader
Waiting, and clutching his tempestuous
    beard,
But heeded not. The bones of Julius
Shook in their sepulchre. I heard the
    sound ;
They only heard the sound of their own
    voices.

Are there no other artists here in Rome
To do this work, that they must needs
    seek me ?
Fra Bastian, my Fra Bastian, might
    have done it ;
But he is lost to art. The Papal Seals,
Like leaden weights upon a dead man's
    eyes,
Press down his lids ; and so the burden
    falls
On Michael Angelo, Chief Architect
And Painter of the Apostolic Palace.
That is the title they cajole me with,
To make me do their work and leave my
    own ;
But having once begun, I turn not back
Blow, ye bright angels, on your golden
    trumpets
To the four corners of the earth, and
    wake
The dead to judgment ! Ye recording
    angels,
Open your books and read ! Ye dead
    awake !

Rise from your graves, drowsy and
    drugged with death,
As men who suddenly aroused from
    sleep
Look round amazed, and know not
    where they are!

In happy hours, when the imagination
Wakes like a wind at midnight, and the
    soul
Trembles in all its leaves, it is a joy
To be uplifted on its wings, and listen
To the prophetic voices in the air
That call us onward. Then the work
    we do
Is a delight, and the obedient hand
Never grows weary. But how different
    is it
In the disconsolate, discouraged hours,
When all the wisdom of the world ap-
    pears
As trivial as the gossip of a nurse
In a sick-room, and all our work seems
    useless.

What is it guides my hand, what
    thoughts possess me,
That I have drawn her face among the
    angels,
Where she will be hereafter? O sweet
    dreams,
That through the vacant chambers of
    my heart
Walk in the silence, as familiar phan-
    toms
Frequent an ancient house, what will ye
    with me?
'T is said that Emperors write their
    names in green
When under age, but when of age in
    purple.
So Love, the greatest Emperor of them
    all,
Writes his in green at first, but after-
    wards
In the imperial purple of our blood.
First love or last love, — which of these
    two passions
Is more omnipotent? Which is more
    fair,
The star of morning or the evening star?
The sunrise or the sunset of the heart?
The hour when we look forth to the un-
    known,
And the advancing day consumes the
    shadows,
Or that when all the landscape of our
    lives

Lies stretched behind us, and familiar
    places
Gleam in the distance, and sweet mem-
    ories
Rise like a tender haze, and magnify
The objects we behold, that soon must
    vanish?

What matters it to me, whose counte-
    nance
Is like the Laocoön's, full of pain; whose
    forehead
Is a ploughed harvest-field, where three-
    score years
Have sown in sorrow and have reaped in
    anguish;
To me, the artisan, to whom all women
Have been as if they were not, or at most
A sudden rush of pigeons in the air,
A flutter of wings, a sound, and then a
    silence?
I am too old for love; I am too old
To flatter and delude myself with visions
Of never-ending friendship with fair
    women,
Imaginations, fantasies, illusions,
In which the things that cannot be take
    shape,
And seem to be, and for the moment
    are.   [Convent bells ring.

Distant and near and low and loud the
    bells,
Dominican, Benedictine, and Franciscan,
Jangle and wrangle in their airy towers,
Discordant as the brotherhoods them-
    selves
In their dim cloisters. The descending
    sun
Seems to caress the city that he loves,
And crowns it with the aureole of a
    saint.
I will go forth and breathe the air a
    while.

III.

SAN SILVESTRO.

*A Chapel in the Church of San Silvestro
on Monte Cavallo.*

VITTORIA COLONNA, CLAUDIO TO-
    LOMMEI, *and others.*

VITTORIA.

Here let us rest a while, until the crowd
Has left the church. I have already
    sent
For Michael Angelo to join us here.

MESSER CLAUDIO.

After Fra Bernardino's wise discourse
On the Pauline Epistles, certainly
Some words of Michael Angelo on Art
Were not amiss, to bring us back to
    earth.

MICHAEL ANGELO, *at the door.*

How like a Saint or Goddess she ap-
    pears ;
Diana or Madonna, which I know not !
In attitude and aspect formed to be
At once the artist's worship and despair !

VITTORIA.

Welcome, Maestro. We were waiting for
    you.

MICHAEL ANGELO.

I met your messenger upon the way,
And hastened hither.

VITTORIA.

           It is kind of you
To come to us, who linger here like gos-
    sips
Wasting the afternoon in idle talk.
These are all friends of mine and friends
    of yours.

MICHAEL ANGELO.

If friends of yours, then are they friends
    of mine.
Pardon me, gentlemen. But when I
    entered
I saw but the Marchesa.

VITTORIA.

           Take this seat
Between me and Ser Claudio Tolommei,
Who still maintains that our Italian
    tongue
Should be called Tuscan. But for that
    offence
We will not quarrel with him.

MICHAEL ANGELO.

           Eccellenza —

VITTORIA.

Ser Claudio has banished Eccellenza
And all such titles from the Tuscan
    tongue.

MESSER CLAUDIO.

'T is the abuse of them and not the use
I deprecate.

MICHAEL ANGELO.

           The use or the abuse
It matters not. Let them all go to-
    gether,
As empty phrases and frivolities,
And common as gold-lace upon the col-
    lar
Of an obsequious lackey.

VITTORIA.

           That may be
But something of politeness would go
    with them.;
We should lose something of the stately
    manners
Of the old school.

MESSER CLAUDIO.

           Undoubtedly.

VITTORIA.

           But that
Is not what occupies my thoughts at
    present,
Nor why I sent for you, Messer Michele.
It was to counsel me. His Holiness
Has granted me permission, long desired,
To build a convent in this neighbor-
    hood,
Where the old tower is standing, from
    whose top
Nero looked down upon the burning city.

MICHAEL ANGELO.

It is an inspiration !

VITTORIA.

           I am doubtful
How I shall build; how large to make
    the convent,
And which way fronting.

MICHAEL ANGELO.

           Ah, to build, to build
That is the noblest art of all the arts.
Painting and sculpture are but images,
Are merely shadows cast by outward
    things
On stone or canvas, having in them-
    selves
No separate existence. Architecture,
Existing in itself, and not in seeming
A something it is not, surpasses them
As substance shadow. Long, long years
    ago,
Standing one morning near the Baths of
    Titus,
I saw the statue of Laocoön

Rise from its grave of centuries, like a
    ghost
Writhing in pain ; and as it tore away
The knotted serpents from its limbs, I
    heard,
Or seemed to hear, the cry of agony
From its white, parted lips.   And still I
    marvel
At the three Rhodian artists, by whose
    hands
This miracle was wrought.   Yet he be-
    holds
Far nobler works who looks upon the
    ruins
Of temples in the Forum here in Rome.
If God should give me power in my old
    age
To build for Him a temple half as grand
As those were in their glory, I should
    count
My age more excellent than youth itself,
And all that I have hitherto accom-
    plished
As only vanity.

VITTORIA.
                    I understand you.
Art is the gift of God, and must be
    used
Unto His glory.   That in art is highest
Which aims at this.   When St. Hilarion
    blessed
The horses of Italicus, they won
The race at Gaza, for his benediction
O'erpowered all magic ; and the people
    shouted
That Christ had conquered Marnas.   So
    that art
Which bears the consecration and the
    seal
Of holiness upon it will prevail
Over all others.   Those few words of
    yours
Inspire me with new confidence to build.
What think you ?   The old walls might
    serve, perhaps,
Some purpose still.   The tower can hold
    the bells.

MICHAEL ANGELO.
If strong enough.

VITTORIA.
If not, it can be strengthened.

MICHAEL ANGELO.
I see no bar nor drawback to this build-
    ing,

And on our homeward way, if it shall
    please you,
We may together view the site.

VITTORIA.
                    I thank you.
I did not venture to request so much.

MICHAEL ANGELO.
Let us now go to the old walls you
    spake of,
Vossignoria —

VITTORIA.
                    What, again, Maestro ?

MICHAEL ANGELO.
Pardon me, Messer Claudio, if once
    more
I use the ancient courtesies of speech.
I am too old to change.

IV.

CARDINAL IPPOLITO.

A richly furnished apartment in the Pal
ace of CARDINAL IPPOLITO.   *Night.*

JACOPO NARDI, *an old man, alone.*

NARDI.
I am bewildered.   These Numidian
    slaves,
In strange attire ; these endless ante-
    chambers ;
This lighted hall, with all its golden
    splendors,
Pictures, and statues !   Can this be the
    dwelling
Of a disciple of that lowly Man
Who had not where to lay his head ?
    These statues
Are not of Saints ; nor is this a Ma-
    donna,
This lovely face, that with such tender
    eyes
Looks down upon me from the painted
    canvas.
My heart begins to fail me.   What can
    he
Who lives in boundless luxury at Rome
Care for the imperilled liberties of Flor-
    ence,
Her people, her Republic ?   Ah, the
    rich
Feel not the pangs of banishment.   All
    doors

Are open to them, and all hands extended,
The poor alone are outcasts ; they who
risked
All they possessed for liberty, and lost ;
And wander through the world without
a friend,
Sick, comfortless, distressed, unknown,
uncared for.

Enter CARDINAL IPPOLITO, *in Spanish
cloak and slouched hat.*

IPPOLITO.

I pray you pardon me that I have kept
you
Waiting so long alone.

NARDI.
          I wait to see
The Cardinal.

IPPOLITO.
      I am the Cardinal ,
And you ?

NARDI.
Jacopo Nardi.

IPPOLITO.
        You are welcome.
I was expecting you. Philippo Strozzi
Had told me of your coming.

NARDI.
        'T was his son
That brought me to your door.

IPPOLITO.
        Pray you, be seated.
You seem astonished at the garb I wear,
But at my time of life, and with my
habits,
The petticoats of a Cardinal would be —
Troublesome ; I could neither ride nor
walk,
Nor do a thousand things, if I were
dressed
Like an old dowager. It were putting
wine
Young as the young Astyanax into gob-
lets
As old as Priam.

NARDI.
        Oh, your Eminence
Knows best what you should wear.

IPPOLITO.
        Dear Messer Nardi,

You are no stranger to me. I have read
Your excellent translation of the books
Of Titus Livius, the historian
Of Rome, and model of all historians
That shall come after him. It does you
honor ;
But greater honor still the love you bear
To Florence, our dear country, and
whose annals
I hope your hand will write, in happier
days
Than we now see.

NARDI.
        Your Eminence will pardon
The lateness of the hour.

IPPOLITO.
        The hours I count not
As a sun-dial ; but am like a clock,
That tells the time as well by night as
day.
So. no excuse. I know what brings you
here.
You come to speak of Florence.

NARDI.
        And her woes.

IPPOLITO.
The Duke, my cousin, the black Ales-
sandro,
Whose mother was a Moorish slave,
that fed
The sheep upon Lorenzo's farm, still
lives
And reigns.

NARDI.
        Alas, that such a scourge
Should fall on such a city !

IPPOLITO.
        When he dies,
The Wild Boar in the gardens of Lo-
renzo,
The beast obscene, should be the monu
ment
Of this bad man.

NARDI
        He walks the streets at night
With revellers, insulting honest men.
No house is sacred from his lusts. The
convents
Are turned by him to brothels, and the
honor
Of women and all ancient pious customs

Are quite forgotten now. The offices
Of the Priori and Gonfalonieri
Have been abolished. All the magis-
trates
Are now his creatures. Liberty is dead.
The very memory of all honest living
Is wiped away, and even our Tuscan
tongue
Corrupted to a Lombard dialect.

IPPOLITO.

And worst of all his impious hand has
broken
The Martinella, — our great battle bell,
That, sounding through three centuries,
has led
The Florentines to victory, — lest its
voice
Should waken in their souls some mem-
ory
Of far-off times of glory.

NARDI.

What a change
Ten little years have made ! We all re-
member
Those better days, when Niccolà Cap-
poni,
The Gonfaloniere, from the windows
Of the Old Palace, with the blast of
trumpets,
Proclaimed to the inhabitants that
Christ
Was chosen King of Florence ; and al-
ready
Christ is dethroned, and slain, and in
his stead
Reigns Lucifer ! Alas, alas, for Flor-
ence !

IPPOLITO.

Lilies with lilies, said Savonarola ;
Florence and France ! But I say Flor-
ence only,
Or only with the Emperor's hand to help
us
In sweeping out the rubbish.

NARDI.

Little hope
Of help is there from him. He has be-
trothed
His daughter Margaret to this shameless
Duke.
What hope have we from such an Em-
peror ?

IPPOLITO.

Baccio Valori and Philippo Strozzi,
Once the Duke's friends and intimates
are with us,
And Cardinals Salvati and Ridolfi.
We shall soon see, then, as Valori says,
Whether the Duke can best spare hon-
est men,
Or honest men the Duke.

NARDI.

We have determined
To send ambassadors to Spain, and lay
Our griefs before the Emperor, though
I fear
More than I hope.

IPPOLITO.

The Emperor is busy
With this new war against the Alge-
rines,
And has no time to listen to complaints
From our ambassadors ; nor will I trust
them,
But go myself. All is in readiness
For my departure, and to-morrow morn-
ing
I shall go down to Itri, where I meet
Dante da Castiglione and some others,
Republicans and fugitives from Flor-
ence,
And then take ship at Gaëta, and go
To join the Emperor in his new crusade
Against the Turk. I shall have time
enough
And opportunity to plead our cause.

NARDI, rising.

It is an inspiration, and I hail it
As of good omen. May the power that
sends it
Bless our beloved country, and restore
Its banished citizens. The soul of Flor-
ence
Is now outside its gates. What lies
within
Is but a corpse, corrupted and corrupt-
ing.
Heaven help us all. I will not tarry
longer,
For you have need of rest. Good-night

IPPOLITO.

Good-night

Enter FRA SEBASTIANO; *Turkish attendants.*

IPPOLITO.

Fra Bastiano, how your portly presence
Contrasts with that of the spare Florentine
Who has just left me !

FRA SEBASTIANO.

          As we passed each other,
I saw that he was weeping.

IPPOLITO.

               Poor old man !

FRA SEBASTIANO.

Who is he ?

IPPOLITO.

Jacopo Nardi. A brave soul;
One of the Fuoruseiti, and the best
And noblest of them all ; but he has
     made me
Sad with his sadness. As I look on you
My heart grows lighter. I behold a
     man
Who lives in an ideal world, apart
From all the rude collisions of our life,
In a calm atmosphere.

FRA SEBASTIANO.

          Your Eminence
Is surely jesting. If you knew the life
Of artists as I know it, you might think
Far otherwise.

IPPOLITO.

          But wherefore should I jest ?
The world of art is an ideal world, —
The world I love, and that I fain would
     live in ;
So speak to me of artists and of art,
Of all the painters, sculptors, and musicians
That now illustrate Rome.

FRA SEBASTIANO.

          Of the musicians,
I know but Goudimel, the brave maestro
And chapel-master of his Holiness,
Who trains the Papal choir.

IPPOLITO.

          In church this morning,
I listened to a mass of Goudimel,
Divinely chanted. In the Incarnatus,
In lieu of Latin words, the tenor sang

With infinite tenderness, in plain Italian,
A Neapolitan love-song.

FRA SEBASTIANO.

          You amaze me
Was it a wanton song ?

IPPOLITO.

          Not a divine one .
I am not over-scrupulous, as you know,
In word or deed, yet such a song as that
Sung by the tenor of the Papal choir,
And in a Papal mass, seemed out of
     place ;
There 's something wrong in it.

FRA SEBASTIANO.

          There 's something wrong
In everything. We cannot make the
     world
Go right. 'T is not my business to reform
The Papal choir.

IPPOLITO.

Nor mine, thank Heaven.
Then tell me of the artists.

FRA SEBASTIANO.

          Naming one
I name them all ; for there is only one :
His name is Messer Michael Angelo.
All art and artists of the present day
Centre in him.

IPPOLITO.

You count yourself as nothing

FRA SEBASTIANO.

Or less than nothing, since I am at best
Only a portrait-painter ; one who draws
With greater or less skill, as best he may,
The features of a face.

IPPOLITO.

          And you have had
The honor, nay, the glory, of portraying
Julia Gonzaga ! Do you count as nothing
A privilege like that? See there the
     portrait
Rebuking you with its divine expression.
Are you not penitent ? He whose skilful
     hand
Painted that lovely picture has not right
To vilipend the art of portrait-painting.
But what of Michael Angelo ?

FRA SEBASTIANO.

          But lately

Strolling together down the crowded
    Corso,
We stopped, well pleased, to see your
    Eminence
Pass on an Arab steed, a noble crea-
    ture,
Which Michael Angelo, who is a lover
Of all things beautiful, especially
When they are Arab horses, much ad-
    mired,
And could not praise enough.

IPPOLITO, *to an attendant.*

                    Hassan, to-morrow,
When I am gone, but not till I am
    gone, —
Be careful about that, — take Barba-
    rossa
To Messer Michael Angelo, the sculp-
    tor,
Who lives there at Macello dei Corvi,
Near to the Capitol; and take besides
Some ten mule-loads of provender, and
    say
Your master sends them to him as a
    present.

FRA SEBASTIANO.

A princely gift. Though Michael An-
    gelo
Refuses presents from his Holiness,
Yours he will not refuse.

IPPOLITO.

                    You think him like
Thymœtes, who received the wooden
    horse
Into the walls of Troy. That book of
    Virgil
Have I translated in Italian verse,
And shall, some day, when we have lei-
    sure for it,
Be pleased to read you. When I speak
    of Troy
I am reminded of another town
And of a lovelier Helen, our dear Count-
    ess
Julia Gonzaga. You remember, surely,
The adventure with the corsair Barba-
    rossa,
And all that followed?

FRA SEBASTIANO.

                    A most strange adventure;
A tale as marvellous and full of wonder
As any in Boccaccio or Sacchetti;
Almost incredible!

IPPOLITO.

                    Were I a painter
I should not want a better theme than
    that :
The lovely lady fleeing through the
    night
In wild disorder; and the brigands'
    camp
With the red fire-light on their swarthy
    faces.
Could you not paint it for me?

FRA SEBASTIANO.

                    No, not I.
It is not in my line.

IPPOLITO.

                    Then you shall paint
The portrait of the corsair, when we
    bring him
A prisoner chained to Naples: for I feel
Something like admiration for a man
Who dared this strange adventure.

FRA SEBASTIANO.

                    I will do it
But catch the corsair first.

IPPOLITO.

                    You may begin
To-morrow with the sword. Hassan,
    come hither ;
Bring me the Turkish scimitar that
    hangs
Beneath the picture yonder. Now un-
    sheathe it.
'T is a Damascus blade ; you see the in-
    scription
In Arabic : *La Allah illa Allah,* —
There is no God but God.

FRA SEBASTIANO.

                    How beautiful
In fashion and in finish! It is perfect.
The Arsenal of Venice cannot boast
A finer sword.

IPPOLITO.

                    You like it ? It is yours.

FRA SEBASTIANO.

You do not mean it.

IPPOLITO.

                    I am not a Spaniard,
To say that it is yours and not to mean
    it.

I have at Itri a whole armory
Full of such weapons. When you paint
    the portrait
Of Barbarossa, it will be of use.
You have not been rewarded as you
    should be
For painting the Gonzaga. Throw this
    bauble
Into the scale, and make the balance
    equal.
Till then suspend it in your studio;
You artists like such trifles.

FRA SEBASTIANO.

                    I will keep it
In memory of the donor. Many thanks.

IPPOLITO.

Fra Bastian, I am growing tired of
    Rome,
The old dead city, with the old dead
    people;
Priests everywhere, like shadows on a
    wall,
And morning, noon, and night the
    ceaseless sound
Of convent bells. I must be gone from
    here;
Though Ovid somewhere says that
    Rome is worthy
To be the dwelling-place of all the Gods,
I must be gone from here. To-morrow
    morning
I start for Itri, and go thence by sea
To join the Emperor, who is making
    war
Upon the Algerines; perhaps to sink
Some Turkish galleys, and bring back
    in chains
The famous corsair. Thus would I
    avenge
The beautiful Gonzaga.

FRA SEBASTIANO.

                    An achievement
Worthy of Charlemagne, or of Orlando.
Berni and Ariosto both shall add
A canto to their poems, and describe
    you
As Furioso and Innamorato.
Now I must say good-night.

IPPOLITO.

                    You must not go;
First you shall sup with me. My senes-
    chal,
Giovan Andrea dal Borgo a San Sepol-
    cro.

I like to give the whole sonorous name,
It sounds so like a verse of the Æneid, ·
Has brought me eels fresh from the
    Lake of Fondi,
And Lucrine oysters cradled in their
    shells:
These, with red Fondi wine, the Cæcu-
    ban
That Horace speaks of, under a hundred
    keys
Kept safe, until the heir of Posthumus
Shall stain the pavement with it, make a
    feast
Fit for Lucullus, or Fra Bastian even;
So we will go to supper, and be merry.

FRA SEBASTIANO.

Beware! Remember that Bolsena's
    eels
And Vernage wine once killed a Pope of
    Rome!

IPPOLITO.

'T was a French Pope; and then so long
    ago;
Who knows? — perhaps the story is not
    true.

V.

BORGO DELLE VERGINE AT NAPLES.

Room in the Palace of JULIA GONZAGA.
Night.

JULIA GONZAGA, GIOVANNI VALDESSO.

JULIA.

Do not go yet.

VALDESSO.

            The night is far advanced;
I fear to stay too late, and weary you
With these discussions.

JULIA.

                I have much to say.
I speak to you, Valdesso, with that
    frankness
Which is the greatest privilege of
    friendship, —
Speak as I hardly would to my confes-
    sor,
Such is my confidence in you.

VALDESSO.

                    Dear Countess

"I will keep it
In memory of the donor. Many thanks."   Page 426.

If loyalty to friendship be a claim
Upon your confidence, then I may claim
  it.

JULIA.

Then sit again, and listen unto things
That nearer are to me than life itself.

VALDESSO.

In all things I am happy to obey you,
And happiest then when you command
  me most.

JULIA.

Laying aside all useless rhetoric,
That is superfluous between us two,
I come at once unto the point, and say,
You know my outward life, my rank
  and fortune ;
Countess of Fondi, Duchess of Trajetto,
A widow rich and flattered, for whose
  hand
In marriage princes ask, and ask it only
To be rejected. All the world can offer
Lies at my feet. If I remind you of it,
It is not in the way of idle boasting,
But only to the better understanding
Of what comes after.

VALDESSO.

              God hath given you also
Beauty and intellect; and the signal
  grace
To lead a spotless life amid temptations,
That others yield to.

JULIA.

              But the inward life, —
That you know not ; 't is known but to
  myself,
And is to me a mystery and a pain.
A soul disquieted, and ill at ease,
A mind perplexed with doubts and ap-
  prehensions,
A heart dissatisfied with all around me,
And with myself, so that sometimes I
  weep,
Discouraged and disgusted with the
  world.

VALDESSO.

Whene'er we cross a river at a ford,
If we would pass in safety, we must
  keep
Our eyes fixed steadfast on the shore
  beyond,
For if we cast them on the flowing
  stream,

The head swims with it ; so if we would
  cross
The running flood of things here in the
  world,
Our souls must not look down, but fix
  their sight
On the firm land beyond.

JULIA.

              I comprehend you.
You think I am too worldly ; that my
  head
Swims with the giddying whirl of life
  about me.
Is that your meaning ?

VALDESSO.

              Yes ; your meditations
Are more of this world and its vanities
Than of the world to come.

JULIA.

              Between the two
I am confused.

VALDESSO.

              Yet have I seen you listen
Enraptured when Fra Bernardino
  preached
Of faith and hope and charity.

JULIA.

              I listen,
But only as to music without meaning.
It moves me for the moment, and I think
How beautiful it is to be a saint,
As dear Vittoria is ; but I am weak
And wayward, and I soon fall back
  again
To my old ways, so very easily.
There are too many week-days for one
  Sunday.

VALDESSO.

Then take the Sunday with you through
  the week,
And sweeten with it all the other days.

JULIA.

In part I do so ; for to put a stop
To idle tongues, what men might say of
  me
If I lived all alone here in my palace,
And not from a vocation that I feel
For the monastic life, I now am living
With Sister Caterina at the convent
Of Santa Chiara, and I come here only

On certain days, for my affairs, or visits
Of ceremony, or to be with friends.
For I confess, to live among my friends
Is Paradise to me ; my Purgatory
Is living among people I dislike.
And so I pass my life in these two worlds,
This palace and the convent.

VALDESSO.

It was then
The fear of man, and not the love of
God,
That led you to this step. Why will you
not
Give all your heart to God ?

JULIA.

If God commands it,
Wherefore hath He not made me capable
Of doing for Him what I wish to do
As easily as I could offer Him
This jewel from my hand, this gown I
wear,
Or aught else that is mine ?

VALDESSO.

The hindrance lies
In that original sin, by which all fell.

JULIA.

Ah me, I cannot bring my troubled mind
To wish well to that Adam, our first
parent,
Who by his sin lost Paradise for us,
And brought such ills upon us.

VALDESSO.

We ourselves,
When we commit a sin, lose Paradise,
As much as he did. Let us think of this,
And how we may regain it.

JULIA.

Teach me, then,
To harmonize the discord of my life,
And stop the painful jangle of these
wires.

VALDESSO.

That is a task impossible, until
You tune your heart-strings to a higher
key
Than earthly melodies.

JULIA.

How shall I do it ?
Point out to me the way of this perfection,

And I will follow you ; for you have
made
My soul enamored with it, and I can-
not
Rest satisfied until I find it out.
But lead me privately, so that the world
Hear not my steps ; I would not give
occasion
For talk among the people.

VALDESSO.

Now at last
I understand you fully. Then, what
need
Is there for us to beat about the bush ?
I know what you desire of me.

JULIA.

What rudeness !
If you already know it, why not tell me ?

VALDESSO.

Because I rather wait for you to ask it
With your own lips.

JULIA.

Do me the kindness, then,
To speak without reserve ; and with all
frankness,
If you divine the truth, will I confess it.

VALDESSO.

I am content.

JULIA.

Then speak.

VALDESSO.

You would be free
From the vexatious thoughts that come
and go
Through your imagination, and would
have me
Point out some royal road and lady-like
Which you may walk in, and not wound
your feet ;
You would attain to the divine perfec-
tion,
And yet not turn your back upon the
world ;
You would possess humility within,
But not reveal it in your outward ac-
tions ;
You would have patience, but without
the rude
Occasions that require its exercise ;
You would despise the world, but in such
fashion

The world snould not despise you in re-
    turn ;
Would clothe the soul with all the Chris-
    tian graces,
Yet not despoil the body of its gauds ;
Would feed the soul with spiritual food,
Yet not deprive the body of its feasts ;
Would seem angelic in the sight of
    God,
Yet not too saint-like in the eyes of
    men ;
In short, would lead a holy Christian
    life
In such a way that even your nearest
    friend
Would not detect therein one circum-
    stance
To show a change from what it was be-
    fore.
Have I divined your secret ?

JULIA.

                You have drawn
The portrait of my inner self as truly
As the most skilful painter ever painted
A human face.

VALDESSO.

        This warrants me in saying
You think you can win heaven by com-
    promise,
And not by verdict.

JULIA

        You have often told me
That a bad compromise was better even
Than a good verdict.

VALDESSO.

                Yes, in suits at law ;
Not in religion.   With the human soul
There is no compromise.   By faith alone
Can man be justified.

JULIA.

        Hush, dear Valdesso ;
That is a heresy.   Do not, I pray you,
Proclaim it from the house-top, but pre-
    serve it
As something precious, hidden in your
    heart,
As I, who half believe and tremble at it.

VALDESSO.

I must proclaim the truth.

JULIA.

                Enthusiast !

Why must you ?   You imperil both
    yourself
And friends by your imprudence.   Pray,
    be patient.
You have occasion now to show that vir-
    tue
Which you lay stress upon.   Let us re-
    turn
To our lost pathway.   Show me by what
    steps
I shall walk in it.

            [Convent bells are heard.

VALDESSO.

            Hark ! the convent bells
Are ringing ; it is midnight ; I must
    leave you.
And yet I linger.   Pardon me, dear
    Countess,
Since you to-night have made me your
    confessor,
If I so far may venture, I will warn you
Upon one point.

JULIA.

        What is it ?   Speak, I pray you,
For I have no concealments in my con-
    duct ;
All is as open as the light of day.
What is it you would warn me of ?

VALDESSO.

                Your friendship
With Cardinal Ippolito.

JULIA.

                What is there
To cause suspicion or alarm in that,
More than in friendships that I enter-
    tain
With you and others ?   I ne'er sat with
    him
Alone at night, as I am sitting now
With you, Valdesso.

VALDESSO.

        Pardon me ; the portrait
That Fra Bastiano painted was for him.
Is that quite prudent ?

JULIA.

            That is the same question
Vittoria put to me, when I last saw her.
I make you the same answer.   That was
    not
A pledge of love, but of pure gratitude
Recall the adventure of that dreadful
    night

When Barbarossa with two thousand
   Moors
Landed upon the coast, and in the dark-
   ness
Attacked my castle.   Then, without de-
   lay,
The Cardinal came hurrying down from
   Rome
To rescue and protect me. Was it wrong
That in an hour like that I did not weigh
Too nicely this or that, but granted him
A boon that pleased him, and that flat-
   tered me ?

        VALDESSO.

Only beware lest, in disguise of friend-
   ship
Another corsair, worse than Barbarossa,
Steal in and seize the castle, not by storm
But strategy. And now I take my leave.

        JULIA.

Farewell ; but ere you go look forth and
   see
How night hath hushed the clamor and
   the stir
Of the tumultuous streets.   The cloud-
   less moon
Roofs the whole city as with tiles of sil-
   ver ;
The dim, mysterious sea in silence sleeps;
And straight into the air Vesuvius lifts
His plume of smoke.   How beautiful it
   is !   [*Voices in the street.*

      GIOVAN ANDREA.

Poisoned at Itri.

      ANOTHER VOICE.

Poisoned ?   Who is poisoned ?

      GIOVAN ANDREA.

The Cardinal Ippolito, my master.
Call it malaria. It was very sudden.
            [*Julia swoons.*

         VI.

   VITTORIA COLONNA.

   A room in the Torre Argentina.

VITTORIA COLONNA *and* JULIA GON-
   ZAGA.
        VITTORIA.

Come to my arms and to my heart once
   more ;
My soul goes out to meet you and embrace you,

For we are of the sisterhood of sorrow.
I know what you have suffered.

        JULIA.

             Name it not
Let me forget it.

        VITTORIA.

          I will say no more
Let me look at you.   What a joy it is
To see your face, to hear your voice
   again !
You bring with you a breath as of the
   morn,
A memory of the far-off happy days
When we were young.   When did you
   come from Fondi ?

        JULIA.

I have not been at Fondi since —

        VITTORIA.

            Ah me !
You need not speak the word ; I under
   stand you.

        JULIA.

I came from Naples by the lovely valley
The Terra di Lavoro.

        VITTORIA.

         And you find me
But just returned from a long journey
   northward.
I have been staying with that noble
   woman
Renée of France, the Duchess of Ferrara.

        JULIA.

Oh, tell me of the Duchess. I have heard
Flaminio speak her praises with such
   warmth
That I am eager to hear more of her
And of her brilliant court.

        VITTORIA.

         You shall hear all
But first sit down and listen patiently
While I confess myself.

        JULIA.

         What deadly sin
Have you committed ?

        VITTORIA.

         Not a sin ; a folly.
I chid you once at Ischia, when you told
   me

That brave Fra Bastian was to paint
    your portrait.

JULIA

Well I remember it.

VITTORIA.

                    Then chide me now,
For I confess to something still more
    strange.
Old as I am, I have at last consented
To the entreaties and the supplications
Of Michael Angelo —

JULIA

                    To marry him?

VITTORIA.

I pray you, do not jest with me! You
    know,
Or you should know, that never such a
    thought
Entered my breast. I am already mar-
    ried.
The Marquis of Pescara is my husband,
And death has not divorced us.

JULIA.

                    Pardon me.
Have I offended you?

VITTORIA.

            No, but have hurt me.
Unto my buried lord I give myself,
Unto my friend the shadow of myself,
My portrait. It is not from vanity,
But for the love I bear him.

JULIA.

                    I rejoice
To hear these words. Oh, this will be a
    portrait
Worthy of both of you!   [A knock.

VITTORIA.

            Hark! he is coming.

JULIA.

And shall I go or stay?

VITTORIA.

            By all means, stay.
The drawing will be better for your pres-
    ence;
You will enliven me.

JULIA.

            I shall not speak;
The presence of great men doth take
    from me

All power of speech. I only gaze at
    them
In silent wonder, as if they were gods
Or the inhabitants of some other planet

Enter MICHAEL ANGELO.

VITTORIA.

Come in.

MICHAEL ANGELO.

            I fear my visit is ill-timed;
I interrupt you.

VITTORIA.

                No; this is a friend
Of yours as well as mine, — the Lady
    Julia,
The Duchess of Trajetto.

MICHAEL ANGELO *to* JULIA.

                    I salute you.
'T is long since I have seen your face, my
    lady;
Pardon me if I say that having seen it,
One never can forget it.

JULIA.

                You are kind
To keep me in your memory.

MICHAEL ANGELO.

                    It is
The privilege of age to speak with frank-
    ness
You will not be offended when I say
That never was your beauty more divine

JULIA.

When Michael Angelo condescends to
    flatter
Or praise me, I am proud, and not of-
    fended.

VITTORIA.

Now this is gallantry enough for one;
Show me a little.

MICHAEL ANGELO.

                Ah, my gracious lady,
You know I have not words to speak
    your praise.
I think of you in silence. You conceal
Your manifold perfections from all
    eyes,
And make yourself more saint-like day
    by day.
And day by day men worship you the
    more.

But now your hour of martyrdom has
    come.
You know why I am here.

VITTORIA.

                    Ah yes, I know it,
And meet my fate with fortitude.   You
    find me
Surrounded by the labors of your hands :
The Woman of Samaria at the Well,
The Mater Dolorosa, and the Christ
Upon the Cross, beneath which you have
    written
Those memorable words of Alighieri,
"Men have forgotten how much blood
    it costs."

MICHAEL ANGELO.

And now I come to add one labor more,
If you will call that labor which is pleas-
    ure,
And only pleasure.

VITTORIA.

                How shall I be seated ?

MICHAEL ANGELO, *opening his portfolio.*

Just as you are.   The light falls well
    upon you.

VITTORIA.

I am ashamed to steal the time from you
That should be given to the Sistine
    Chapel.
How does that work go on ?

MICHAEL ANGELO, *drawing.*

                    But tardily.
Old men work slowly.   Brain and hand
    alike
Are dull and torpid.   To die young is
    best,
And not to be remembered as old men
Tottering about in their decrepitude.

VITTORIA.

My dear Maestro ! have you, then, for-
    gotten
The story of Sophocles in his old age ?

MICHAEL ANGELO.

What story is it ?

VITTORIA.

            When his sons accused him,
Before the Areopagus, of dotage,
For all defence, he read there to his
    Judges

The Tragedy of Œdipus Coloneus,—
The work of his old age.

MICHAEL ANGELO.

                    'T is an illusion
A fabulous story, that will lead old men
Into a thousand follies and conceits.

VITTORIA.

So you may show to cavilers your paint-
    ing
Of the Last Judgment in the Sistine
    Chapel.

MICHAEL ANGELO.

Now you and Lady Julia shall resume
The conversation that I interrupted.

VITTORIA.

It was of no great import ; nothing more
Nor less than my late visit to Ferrara,
And what I saw there in the ducal pal-
    ace.
Will it not interrupt you ?

MICHAEL ANGELO.

                    Not the least.

VITTORIA.

Well, first, then, of Duke Ercole : a man
Cold in his manners, and reserved and
    silent,
And yet magnificent in all his ways ;
Not hospitable unto new ideas,
But from state policy, and certain rea-
    sons
Concerning the investiture of the duchy,
A partisan of Rome, and consequently
Intolerant of all the new opinions.

JULIA.

I should not like the Duke.   These silent
    men,
Who only look and listen, are like wells
That have no water in them, deep and
    empty.
How could the daughter of a king of
    France
Wed such a duke ?

MICHAEL ANGELO.

            The men that women marry,
And why they marry them, will always
    be
A marvel and a mystery to the world.

VITTORIA.

And then the Duchess, — how shall I de-
    scribe her,

Or tell the merits of that happy nature,
Which pleases most when least it thinks
    of pleasing?
Not beautiful, perhaps, in form and fea-
    ture,
Yet with an inward beauty, that shines
    through
Each look and attitude and word and
    gesture;
A kindly grace of manner and behav-
    ior,
A something in her presence and her
    ways
That makes her beautiful beyond the
    reach
Of mere external beauty; and in heart
So noble and devoted to the truth,
And so in sympathy with all who strive
After the higher life.

JULIA.

            She draws me to her
As much as her Duke Ercole repels me.

VITTORIA.

Then the devout and honorable women
That grace her court, and make it good
    to be there;
Francesca Bucyronia, the true-hearted,
Lavinia della Rovere and the Orsini,
The Magdalena and the Cherubina,
And Anne de Parthenai, who sings so
    sweetly;
All lovely women, full of noble thoughts
And aspirations after noble things.

JULIA.

Boccaccio would have envied you such
    dames.

VITTORIA

No; his Fiammettas and his Philomenas
Are fitter company for Ser Giovanni;
I fear he hardly would have comprehen-
    ded
The women that I speak of.

MICHAEL ANGELO.

                Yet he wrote
The story of Griselda. That is some-
    thing
To set down in his favor.

VITTORIA.

            With these ladies
Was a young girl, Olympia Morata,
Daughter of Fulvio, the learned scholar,
Famous in all the universities ·

A marvellous child, who at the spinning
    wheel,
And in the daily round of household
    cares,
Hath learned both Greek and Latin
    and is now
A favorite of the Duchess and compan-
    ion
Of Princess Anne. This beautiful young
    Sappho
Sometimes recited to us Grecian odes
That she had written, with a voice whose
    sadness
Thrilled and o'ermastered me, and made
    me look
Into the future time, and ask myself
What destiny will be hers.

JULIA.

            A sad one, surely.
Frost kills the flowers that blossom out
    of season;
And these precocious intellects portend
A life of sorrow or an early death.

VITTORIA.

About the court were many learned
    men;
Chilian Sinapius from beyond the Alps,
And Celio Curione, and Manzolli,
The Duke's physician; and a pale young
    man,
Charles d'Espeville of Geneva, whom the
    Duchess
Doth much delight to talk with and to
    read,
For he hath written a book of Institutes
The Duchess greatly praises, though
    some call it
The Koran of the heretics.

JULIA.

            And what poets
Were there to sing you madrigals, and
    praise
Olympia's eyes and Cherubina's tresses?

VITTORIA.

No; for great Ariosto is no more.
The voice that filled those halls with mel-
    ody
Has long been hushed in death.

JULIA.

            You should have made
A pilgrimage unto the poet's tomb,
And laid a wreath upon it, for the words
He spake of you.

VITTORIA.

And of yourself no less,
And of our master, Michael Angelo.

MICHAEL ANGELO.

Of me ?

VITTORIA.

Have you forgotten that he calls you
Michael, less man than angel, and divine?
You are ungrateful.

MICHAEL ANGELO.

A mere play on words.
That adjective he wanted for a rhyme,
To match with Gian Bellino and Urbino.

VITTORIA.

Bernardo Tasso is no longer there,
Nor the gay troubadour of Gascony,
Clement Marot, surnamed by flatterers
The Prince of Poets and the Poet of
Princes,
Who, being looked upon with much dis-
favor
By the Duke Ercole, has fled to Venice.

MICHAEL ANGELO.

There let him stay with Pietro Aretino,
The Scourge of Princes, also called Di-
vine.
The title is so common in our mouths,
That even the Pifferari of Abruzzi,
Who play their bag-pipes in the streets
of Rome
At the Epiphany, will bear it soon,
And will deserve it better than some po-
ets.

VITTORIA.

What bee hath stung you ?

MICHAEL ANGELO.

One that makes no honey ;
One that comes buzzing in through ev-
ery window,
And stabs men with his sting.   A bitter
thought
Passed through my mind, but it is gone
again ;
I spake too hastily.

JULIA.

I pray you, show me
What you have done.

MICHAEL ANGELO.

Not yet ; it is not finished.

PART SECOND.

I.

MONOLOGUE.

A room in MICHAEL ANGELO'S *house.*

MICHAEL ANGELO.

FLED to Viterbo, the old Papal city
Where once an Emperor, humbled in
his pride,
Held the Pope's stirrup, as his Holiness
Alighted from his mule !   A fugitive
From Cardinal Caraffa's hate, who hurls
His thunders at the house of the Co-
lonna,
With endless bitterness ! — Among the
nuns
In Santa Catarina's convent hidden,
Herself in soul a nun ! And now she
chides me
For my too frequent letters, that disturb
Her meditations, and that hinder me
And keep me from my work ; now gra-
ciously
She thanks me for the crucifix I sent her,
And says that she will keep it: with
one hand
Inflicts a wound, and with the othe\
heals it.   [*Reading.*

" Profoundly I believed that God would
grant you
A supernatural faith to paint this
Christ ;
I wished for that which I now see ful-
filled
So marvellously, exceeding all my
wishes.
Nor more could be desired, or even so
much.
And greatly I rejoice that you have
made
The angel on the right so beautiful ;
For the Archangel Michael will place
you,
You, Michael Angelo, on that new day
Upon the Lord's right hand ! And
waiting that,
How can I better serve you than to pray
To this sweet Christ for you, and to
beseech you
To hold me altogether yours in all
things."

Well, I will write less often, or no more
But wait her coming. No one born in
Rome

Can live elsewhere; but he must pine
    for Rome,
And must return to it. I, who am born
And bred a Tuscan and a Florentine,
Feel the attraction, and I linger here
As if I were a pebble in the pavement
Trodden by priestly feet. This I en-
    dure,
Because I breathe in Rome an atmos-
    phere
Heavy with odors of the laurel leaves
That crowned great heroes of the sword
    and pen,
In ages past. I feel myself exalted
To walk the streets in which a Virgil
    walked,
Or Trajan rode in triumph; but far
    more,
And most of all, because the great Co-
    lonna
Breathes the same air I breathe, and is
    to me
An inspiration. Now that she is gone,
Rome is no longer Rome till she return.
This feeling overmasters me. I know
    not
If it be love, this strong desire to be
Forever in her presence; but I know
That I, who was the friend of solitude,
And ever was best pleased when most
    alone,
Now weary grow of my own company.
For the first time old age seems lonely
    to me.
        [*Opening the Divina Commedia.*
I turn for consolation to the leaves
Of the great master of our Tuscan
    tongue,
Whose words, like colored garnet-shirls
    in lava,
Betray the heat in which they were en-
    gendered.
A mendicant, he ate the bitter bread
Of others, but repaid their meagre gifts
With immortality. In courts of princes
He was a by-word, and in streets of
    towns
Was mocked by children, like the He-
    brew prophet,
Himself a prophet. I too know the cry,
Go up, thou bald head! from a genera-
    tion
That, wanting reverence, wanteth the
    best food
The soul can feed on. There's not
    room enough
For age and youth upon this little
    planet.

Age must give way. There was not
    room enough
Even for this great poet. In his song
I hear reverberate the gates of Florence,
Closing upon him, never more to open;
But mingled with the sound are melo-
    dies
Celestial from the gates of paradise.
He came, and he is gone. The people
    knew not
What manner of man was passing by
    their doors,
Until he passed no more; but in his
    vision
He saw the torments and beatitudes
Of souls condemned or pardoned, and
    hath left
Behind him this sublime Apocalypse.

I strive in vain to draw here on the
    margin
The face of Beatrice. It is not hers,
But the Colonna's. Each hath his ideal,
The image of some woman excellent,
That is his guide. No Grecian art, nor
    Roman,
Hath yet revealed such loveliness as hers

II.

VITERBO.

VITTORIA COLONNA *at the convent win-
    dow.*

VITTORIA.

Parting with friends is temporary death,
As all death is. We see no more their
    faces,
Nor hear their voices, save in memory;
But messages of love give us assurance
That we are not forgotten. Who shall
    say
That from the world of spirits comes no
    greeting,
No message of remembrance? It may
    be
The thoughts that visit us, we know not
    whence,
Sudden as inspiration, are the whispers
Of disembodied spirits, speaking to us
As friends, who wait outside a prison
    wall,
Through the barred windows speak to
    those within.   [*A pause.*

As quiet as the lake that lies beneath
    me,

As quiet as the tranquil sky above me,
As quiet as a heart that beats no more,
This convent seems.   Above, below, all
    peace !
Silence and solitude, the soul's best
    friends,
Are with me here, and the tumultuous
    world
Makes no more noise than the remotest
    planet.
O gentle spirit, unto the third circle
Of heaven among the blessed souls as-
    cended,
Who, living in the faith and dying for
    it,
Have gone to their reward, I do not
    sigh
For thee as being dead, but for my-
    self
That I am still alive.   Turn those dear
    eyes,
Once so benignant to me, upon mine,
That open to their tears such uncon-
    trolled
And such continual issue.   Still awhile
Have patience ; I will come to thee at
    last.
A few more goings in and out these
    doors,
A few more chimings of these convent
    bells,
A few more prayers, a few more sighs
    and tears,
And the long agony of this life will
    end,
And I shall be with thee.   If I am want-
    ing
To thy well-being, as thou art to mine,
Have patience ; I will come to thee at
    last.
Ye minds that loiter in these cloister
    gardens,
Or wander far above the city walls,
Bear unto him this message, that I ever
Or speak or think of him, or weep for
    him.

By unseen hands uplifted in the light
Of sunset, yonder solitary cloud
Floats, with its white apparel blown
    abroad,
And wafted up to heaven.   It fades
    away,
And melts into the air.   Ah, would
    that I
Could thus be wafted unto thee, Fran-
    cesco,
A cloud of white, an incorporeal spirit !

III.

MICHAEL ANGELO AND BEN- VENUTO CELLINI.

MICHAEL ANGELO, BENVENUTO CEL-
LINI *in gay attire.*

BENVENUTO.

A good day and good year to the divine
Maestro Michael Angelo, the sculptor !

MICHAEL ANGELO.

Welcome, my Benvenuto.

BENVENUTO.

                    That is what
My father said, the first time he beheld
This handsome face.   But say farewell,
    not welcome.
I come to take my leave   I start for
    Florence
As fast as horse can carry me.   I long
To set once more upon its level flags
These feet, made sore by your vile Ro-
    man pavements.
Come with me ; you are wanted there
    in Florence.
The Sacristy is not finished.

MICHAEL ANGELO.

                    Speak not of it !
How damp and cold it was !   How my
    bones ached
And my head reeled, when I was work-
    ing there !
I am too old   I will stay here in Rome,
Where all is old and crumbling, like
    myself,
To hopeless ruin.   All roads lead to
    Rome.

BENVENUTO.

And all lead out of it.

MICHAEL ANGELO.

                    There is a charm
A certain something in the atmosphere,
That all men feel, and no man can de-
    scribe.

BENVENUTO.

Malaria ?

MICHAEL ANGELO.

        Yes, malaria of the mind,
Out of this tomb of the majestic Past ?

The fever to accomplish some great
        work
That will not let us sleep. I must go
        on
Until I die.

BENVENUTO.

Do you ne'er think of Florence ?

MICHAEL ANGELO.
                        Yes; whenever
I think of anything beside my work,
I think of Florence. I remember, too,
The bitter days I passed among the
        quarries
Of Seravezza and Pietrasanta;
Road-building in the marshes; stupid
        people,
And cold and rain incessant, and mad
        gusts
Of mountain wind, like howling der-
        vishes,
That spun and whirled the eddying
        snow about them
As if it were a garment ; aye, vexations
And troubles of all kinds, that ended
        only
In loss of time and money.

BENVENUTO.
                        True; Maestro;
But that was not in Florence. You
        should leave
Such work to others. Sweeter memo-
        ries
Cluster about you, in the pleasant city
Upon the Arno.

MICHAEL ANGELO.
                In my waking dreams
I see the marvellous dome of Brunel-
        leschi,
Ghiberti's gates of bronze, and Giotto's
        tower ;
And Ghirlandajo's lovely Benci glides
With folded hands amid my troubled
        thoughts,
A splendid vision ! Time rides with the
        old
At a great pace. As travellers on swift
        steeds
See the near landscape fly and flow be-
        hind them,
While the remoter fields and dim hori-
        zons
Go with them, and seem wheeling round
        to meet them,
So in old age things near us slip away,

And distant things go with us. Pleas-
        antly
Come back to me the days when, as a
        youth,
I walked with Ghirlandajo in the gar-
        dens
Of Medici, and saw the antique statues,
The forms august of gods and godlike
        men,
And the great world of art revealed
        itself
To my young eyes. Then all that man
        hath done
Seemed possible to me. Alas! how
        little
Of all I dreamed of has my hand
        achieved !

BENVENUTO.
Nay, let the Night and Morning, let
        Lorenzo
And Julian in the Sacristy at Flor-
        ence,
Prophets and Sibyls in the Sistine
        Chapel,
And the Last Judgment answer. Is it
        finished ?

MICHAEL ANGELO.
The work is nearly done. But this
        Last Judgment
Has been the cause of more vexation to
        me
Than it will be of honor. Ser Biagio,
Master of ceremonies at the Papal
        court,
A man punctilious and over nice,
Calls it improper; says that those nude
        forms,
Showing their nakedness in such shame-
        less fashion,
Are better suited to a common bagnio,
Or wayside wine-shop, than a Papal
        Chapel.
To punish him I painted him as Minos
And leave him there as master of cere-
        monies
In the Infernal Regions. What would
        you
Have done to such a man ?

BENVENUTO.
                I would have killed him.
When any one insults me, if I can
I kill him, kill him.

MICHAEL ANGELO.
                Oh, you gentlemen

Who dress in silks and velvets, and
    wear swords,
Are ready with your weapons, and have
    all
A taste for homicide.

BENVENUTO.

                    I learned that lesson
Under Pope Clement at the siege of
    Rome,
Some twenty years ago.   As I was
    standing
Upon the ramparts of the Campo Santo
With Alessandro Bene, I beheld
A sea of fog, that covered all the
    plain,
And hid from us the foe; when sud-
    denly,
A misty figure, like an apparition,
Rose up above the fog, as if on horse-
    back.
At this I aimed my arquebus, and fired.
The figure vanished; and there rose a
    cry
Out of the darkness, long and fierce and
    loud,
With imprecations in all languages.
It was the Constable of France, the
    Bourbon,
That I had slain.

MICHAEL ANGELO.

Rome should be grateful to you.

BENVENUTO.

But has not been; you shall hear pres-
    ently.
During the siege I served as bombardier,
There in St. Angelo.   His Holiness,
One day, was walking with his Cardi-
    nals
On the round bastion, while I stood
    above
Among my falconets.   All thought and
    feeling,
All skill in art and all desire of fame,
Were swallowed up in the delightful
    music
Of that artillery.   I saw far off,
Within the enemy's trenches on the
    Prati,
A Spanish cavalier in scarlet cloak;
And firing at him with due aim and
    range,
I cut the gay Hidalgo in two pieces.
The eyes are dry that wept for him in
    Spain.
His Holiness, delighted beyond measure

With such display of gunnery, and
    amazed
To see the man in scarlet cut in two,
Gave me his benediction, and absolved
    me
From all the homicides I had commit-
    ted
In service of the Apostolic Church,
Or should commit thereafter.   From
    that day
I have not held in very high esteem
The life of man.

MICHAEL ANGELO.

        And who absolved Pope Clement?
Now let us speak of Art.

BENVENUTO.

                    Of what you will

MICHAEL ANGELO.

Say, have you seen our friend Fra
    Bastian lately,
Since by a turn of fortune he became
Friar of the Signet?

BENVENUTO.

                    Faith, a pretty artist
To pass his days in stamping leaden
    seals
On Papal bulls!

MICHAEL ANGELO.

            He has grown fat and lazy,
As if the lead clung to him like a sinker.
He paints no more, since he was sent to
    Fondi
By Cardinal Ippolito to paint
The fair Gonzaga.   Ah, you should have
    seen him
As I did, riding through the city gate,
In his brown hood, attended by four
    horsemen,
Completely armed, to frighten the ban-
    ditti.
I think he would have frightened them
    alone,
For he was rounder than the O of Giotto

BENVENUTO.

He must have looked more like a sack
    of meal
Than a great painter.

MICHAEL ANGELO.

            Well, he is not great
But still I like him greatly.   Benvenuto
Have faith in nothing but in industry.

Be at it late and early ; persevere,
And work right on through censure and
    applause,
Or else abandon Art.

BENVENUTO.

No man works harder
Than I do. 1 am not a moment idle.

MICHAEL ANGELO.

And what have you to show me ?

BENVENUTO.

This gold ring,
Made for his Holiness, — my latest
    work,
And I am proud of it. A single dia-
    mond,
Presented by the Emperor to the Pope.
Targhetta of Venice set and tinted it ;
I have reset it, and retinted it
Divinely, as you see. The jewellers
Say I've surpassed Targhetta.

MICHAEL ANGELO.

Let me see it.
A pretty jewel.

BENVENUTO.

That is not the expression.
Pretty is not a very pretty word
To be applied to such a precious stone,
Given by an Emperor to a Pope, and
    set
By Benvenuto !

MICHAEL ANGELO.

Messer Benvenuto,
I lose all patience with you ; for the
    gifts
That God hath given you are of such a
    kind,
They should be put to far more noble
    uses
Than setting diamonds for the Pope of
Rome.
You can do greater things.

BENVENUTO.

The God who made me
Knows why he made me what I am, —
    a goldsmith,
A mere artificer.

MICHAEL ANGELO.

Oh no ; an artist,
Richly endowed by nature, but who
    wraps

His talent in a napkin, and consumes
His life in vanities.

BENVENUTO.

Michael Angelo
May say what Benvenuto would not
    bear
From any other man. He speaks the
    truth.
I know my life is wasted and consumed
In vanities ; but I have better hours
And higher aspirations than you think.
Once, when a prisoner at St. Angelo,
Fasting and praying in the midnight
    darkness,
In a celestial vision I beheld
A crucifix in the sun, of the same sub
    stance
As is the sun itself. And since that
    hour
There is a splendor round about my
    head,
That may be seen at sunrise and at sun·
    set
Above my shadow on the grass. And
    now
I know that I am in the grace of God,
And none henceforth can harm me.

MICHAEL ANGELO.

None but one, —
None but yourself, who are your great-
    est foe.
He that respects himself is safe from
    others ;
He wears a coat of mail that none can
    pierce.

BENVENUTO.

I always wear one.

MICHAEL ANGELO.

O incorrigible !
At least, forget not the celestial vision.
Man must have something higher than
    himself
To think of.

BENVENUTO.

That I know full well. Now listen.
I have been sent for into France, where
    grow
The Lilies that illumine heaven and
    earth,
And carry in mine equipage the model
Of a most marvellous golden salt-cellar
For the king's table ; and here in my
    brain

A statue of Mars Armipotent for the
    fountain
Of Fontainebleau, colossal, wonderful.
I go a goldsmith, to return a sculptor.
And so farewell, great Master. Think
    of me
As one who, in the midst of all his fol-
    lies,
Had also his ambition, and aspired
To better things.

MICHAEL ANGELO.

            Do not forget the vision.
[*Sitting down again to the Divina
    Commedia.*

Now in what circle of his poem sacred
Would the great Florentine have placed
    this man ?
Whether in Phlegethon, the river of
    blood,
Or in the fiery belt of Purgatory,
I know not, but most surely not with
    those
Who walk in leaden cloaks. Though
    he is one
Whose passions, like a potent alkahest,
Dissolve his better nature, he is not
That despicable thing, a hypocrite ;
He doth not cloak his vices, nor deny
    them.
Come back, my thoughts, from him to
    Paradise.

IV.

FRA SEBASTIANO DEL PIOMBO.

MICHAEL ANGELO ; FRA SEBASTIANO
    DEL PIOMBO.

MICHAEL ANGELO, *not turning round.*
Who is it ?

FRA SEBASTIANO.

            Wait, for I am out of breath
In climbing your steep stairs.

MICHAEL ANGELO.

            Ah, my Bastiano,
If you went up and down as many stairs
As I do still, and climbed as many lad-
    ders,
It would be better for you. Pray sit
    down.
Your idle and luxurious way of living
Will one day take your breath away
    entirely.
And you will never find it.

FRA SEBASTIANO.

            Well, what then ?
That would be better, in my apprehen
    sion,
Than falling from a scaffold.

MICHAEL ANGELO.

            That was nothing
It did not kill me ; only lamed me
    slightly ;
I am quite well again.

FRA SEBASTIANO.

            But why, dear Master,
Why do you live so high up in your
    house,
When you could live below and have a
    garden,
As I do ?

MICHAEL ANGELO.

        From this window I can look
On many gardens ; o'er the city roofs
See the Campagna and the Alban hills :
And all are mine.

FRA SEBASTIANO.

            Can you sit down in them,
On summer afternoons, and play the
    lute,
Or sing, or sleep the time away ?

MICHAEL ANGELO.

            I never
Sleep in the day-time ; scarcely sleep at
    night.
I have not time. Did you meet Ben-
    venuto
As you came up the stair ?

FRA SEBASTIANO.

            He ran against me
On the first landing, going at full speed ;
Dressed like the Spanish captain in a
    play,
With his long rapier and his short red
    cloak.
Why hurry through the world at such a
    pace ?
Life will not be too long.

MICHAEL ANGELO.

            It is his nature, —
A restless spirit, that consumes itself
With useless agitations. He o'erleaps
The goal he aims at. Patience is a
    plant

That grows not in all gardens. You are made
Of quite another clay.

FRA SEBASTIANO.

And thank God for it.
And now, being somewhat rested, I will tell you
Why I have climbed these formidable stairs.
I have a friend, Francesco Berni, here,
A very charming poet and companion,
Who greatly honors you and all your doings,
And you must sup with us.

MICHAEL ANGELO.

Not I, indeed.
I know too well what artists' suppers are.
You must excuse me.

FRA SEBASTIANO.

I will not excuse you.
You need repose from your incessant work;
Some recreation, some bright hours of pleasure.

MICHAEL ANGELO.

To me, what you and other men call pleasure
Is only pain. Work is my recreation,
The play of faculty; a delight like that
Which a bird feels in flying, or a fish
In darting through the water, — nothing more.
I cannot go. The Sibylline leaves of life
Grow precious now, when only few remain.
I cannot go.

FRA SEBASTIANO.

Berni, perhaps, will read
A canto of the Orlando Inamorato.

MICHAEL ANGELO.

That is another reason for not going.
If aught is tedious and intolerable,
It is a poet reading his own verses.

FRA SEBASTIANO.

Berni thinks somewhat better of your verses
Than you of his. He says that you speak things,
And other poets words. So, pray you, come.

MICHAEL ANGELO.

If it were now the Improvisatore,
Luigia Pulci, whom I used to hear
With Benvenuto, in the streets of Florence,
I might be tempted. I was younger then,
And singing in the open air was pleasant.

FRA SEBASTIANO.

There is a Frenchman here, named Rabelais,
Once a Franciscan friar, and now a doctor,
And secretary to the embassy:
A learned man, who speaks all languages,
And wittiest of men; who wrote a book
Of the Adventures of Gargantua,
So full of strange conceits one roars with laughter
At every page; a jovial boon-companion
And lover of much wine. He too is coming.

MICHAEL ANGELO.

Then you will not want me, who am not witty,
And have no sense of mirth, and love not wine.
I should be like a dead man at your banquet.
Why should I seek this Frenchman, Rabelais?
And wherefore go to hear Francesco Berni,
When I have Dante Alighieri here,
The greatest of all poets?

FRA SEBASTIANO.

And the dullest;
And only to be read in episodes.
His day is past. Petrarca is our poet.

MICHAEL ANGELO.

Petrarca is for women and for lovers.
And for those soft Abati, who delight
To wander down long garden walks in summer,
Tinkling their little sonnets all day long,
As lap dogs do their bells.

FRA SEBASTIANO.

I love Petrarca
How sweetly of his absent love he sings

When journeying in the forest of Ar-
    dennes!
"I seem to hear her, hearing the boughs
    and breezes
And leaves and birds lamenting, and the
    waters
Murmuring flee along the verdant herb-
    age."

MICHAEL ANGELO.

Enough. It is all seeming, and no be-
    ing.
If you would know how a man speaks
    in earnest,
Read here this passage, where St. Peter
    thunders
In Paradise against degenerate Popes
And the corruptions of the church, till
    all
The heaven about him blushes like a
    sunset.
I beg you to take note of what he
    says
About the Papal seals, for that concerns
Your office and yourself.

FRA SEBASTIANO, *reading.*

                    Is this the passage?
"Nor I be made the figure of a seal
To privileges venal and mendacious,
Whereat I often redden and flash with
    fire!" —
That is not poetry.

MICHAEL ANGELO.

                    What is it, then?

FRA SEBASTIANO.

Vituperation; gall that might have
    spirted
From Aretino's pen.

MICHAEL ANGELO.

                    Name not that man!
A profligate, whom your Francesco
    Berni
Describes as having one foot in the
    brothel
And the other in the hospital; who
    lives
By flattering or maligning, as best serves
His purpose at the time. He writes to
    me
With easy arrogance of my Last Judg-
    ment,
In such familiar tone that one would
    say
The great event already had occurred,

And he was present, and from observa
    tion
Informed me how the picture should be
    painted.

FRA SEBASTIANO.

What unassuming, unobtrusive men
These critics are! Now, to have Are
    tino
Aiming his shafts at you brings back to
    mind
The Gascon archers in the square of
    Milan,
Shooting their arrows at Duke Sforza's
    statue,
By Leonardo, and the foolish rabble
Of envious Florentines, that at your
    David
Threw stones at night. But Aretino
    praised you.

MICHAEL ANGELO.

His praises were ironical. He knows
How to use words as weapons, and to
    wound
While seeming to defend. But look,
    Bastiano,
See how the setting sun lights up that
    picture!

FRA SEBASTIANO.

My portrait of Vittoria Colonna.

MICHAEL ANGELO.

It makes her look as she will look here-
    after,
When she becomes a saint!

FRA SEBASTIANO.

                    A noble woman!

MICHAEL ANGELO.

Ah, these old hands can fashion fairer
    shapes
In marble, and can paint diviner pic-
    tures,
Since I have known her.

FRA SEBASTIANO.

                    And you like this picture,
And yet it is in oils, which you detest.

MICHAEL ANGELO.

When that barbarian Jan Van Eyck
    discovered
The use of oil in painting, he degraded
His art into a handicraft, and made it
Sign-painting, merely, for a country inn

Or wayside wine-shop. 'T is an art for
    women,
Or for such leisurely and idle people
As you, Fra Bastiano. Nature paints
    not
In oils, but frescoes the great dome of
    heaven
With sunsets, and the lovely forms of
    clouds
And flying vapors.

FRA SEBASTIANO.

        And how soon they fade !
Behold yon line of roofs and belfries
    painted
Upon the golden background of the
    sky,
Like a Byzantine picture, or a portrait
Of Cimabue. See how hard the out-
    line,
Sharp-cut and clear, not rounded into
    shadow.
Yet that is nature.

MICHAEL ANGELO.

          She is always right.
The picture that approaches sculpture
    nearest
Is the best picture.

FRA SEBASTIANO.

        Leonardo thinks
The open air too bright. We ought to
    paint
As if the sun were shining through a
    mist.
'T is easier done in oil than in distem-
    per.

MICHAEL ANGELO.

Do not revive again the old dispute ;
I have an excellent memory for forget-
    ting,
But I still feel the hurt. Wounds are
    not healed
By the unbending of the bow that made
    them.

FRA SEBASTIANO.

So say Petrarca and the ancient prov-
    erb.

MICHAEL ANGELO.

But that is past. Now I am angry with
    you,
Not that you paint in oils, but that,
    grown fat
And indolent, you do not paint at all.

FRA SEBASTIANO.

Why should I paint ? Why should I
    toil and sweat,
Who now am rich enough to live at
    ease,
And take my pleasure ?

MICHAEL ANGELO.

         When Pope Leo died,
He who had been so lavish of the
    wealth
His predecessors left him, who received
A basket of gold-pieces every morning,
Which every night was empty, left be-
    hind
Hardly enough to pay his funeral.

FRA SEBASTIANO.

I care for banquets, not for funerals,
As did his Holiness. I have forbidden
All tapers at my burial, and procession
Of priests and friars and monks ; and
    have provided
The cost thereof be given to the poor !

MICHAEL ANGELO.

You have done wisely, but of that I
    speak not.
Ghiberti left behind him wealth and chil-
    dren ;
But who to-day would know that he had
    lived,
If he had never made those gates of
    bronze
In the old Baptistery, — those gates of
    bronze,
Worthy to be the gates of Paradise.
His wealth is scattered to the winds ; his
    children
Are long since dead ; but those celestial
    gates
Survive, and keep his name and memory
    green.

FRA SEBASTIANO.

But why should I fatigue myself ? I
    think
That all things it is possible to paint
Have been already painted ; and if not,
Why, there are painters in the world at
    present
Who can accomplish more in two short
    months
Than I could in two years ; so it is well
That some one is contented to do noth-
    ing,
And leave the field to others.

MICHAEL ANGELO.

　　　　　　　　O blasphemer !
Not without reason do the people call
　　you
Sebastian del Piombo, for the lead
Of all the Papal bulls is heavy upon you,
And wraps you like a shroud.

FRA SEBASTIANO.

　　　　　　　　Misericordia !
Sharp is the vinegar of sweet wine, and
　　sharp
The words you speak, because the heart
　　within you
Is sweet unto the core.

MICHAEL ANGELO.

　　　　　　　　How changed you are
From the Sebastiano I once knew,
When poor, laborious, emulous to excel,
You strove in rivalry with Badassare
And Raphael Sanzio.

FRA SEBASTIANO.

　　　　　　　　Raphael is dead ;
He is but dust and ashes in his grave,
While I am living and enjoying life,
And so am victor. One live Pope is
　　worth
A dozen dead ones.

MICHAEL ANGELO.

　　　　　　　　Raphael is not dead ;
He doth but sleep ; for how can he be
　　dead
Who lives immortal in the hearts of
　　men ?
He only drank the precious wine of
　　youth,
The outbreak of the grapes, before the
　　vintage
Was trodden to bitterness by the feet of
　　men.
The gods have given him sleep. We
　　never were
Nor could be foes, although our follow-
　　ers,
Who are distorted shadows of ourselves,
Have striven to make us so ; but each
　　one worked
Unconsciously upon the other's thoughts,
Both giving and receiving. He per-
　　chance
Caught strength from me, and I some
　　greater sweetness
And tenderness from his more gentle na-
　　ture.

I have but words of praise and admira-
　　tion
For his great genius ; and the world is
　　fairer
That he lived in it.

FRA SEBASTIANO.

　　　　　　　　We at least are friends ;
So come with me.

MICHAEL ANGELO.

　　　　　　　　No, no ; I am best pleased
When I 'm not asked to banquets. I
　　have reached
A time of life when daily walks are
　　shortened,
And even the houses of our dearest
　　friends,
That used to be so near, seem far away.

FRA SEBASTIANO.

Then we must sup without you. We
　　shall laugh
At those who toil for fame, and make
　　their lives
A tedious martyrdom, that they may
　　live
A little longer in the mouths of men !
And so, good-night.

MICHAEL ANGELO.

　　　　　　　　Good-night, my Fra Bastiano
　　　　　　　　[Returning to his work
How will men speak of me when I am
　　gone,
When all this colorless, sad life is ended,
And I am dust ? They will remember
　　only
The wrinkled forehead, the marred
　　countenance,
The rudeness of my speech, and my
　　rough manners,
And never dream that underneath them
　　all
There was a woman's heart of tender-
　　ness.
They will not know the secret of my
　　life,
Locked up in silence, or but vaguely
　　hinted
In uncouth rhymes, that may perchance
　　survive
Some little space in memories of men !
Each one performs his life-work, and
　　then leaves it ;
Those that come after him will estimate
His influence on the age in which he
　　lived.

V.

MICHAEL ANGELO AND TITIAN.

Palazzo Belvedere. TITIAN'S *studio. A painting of Danaë with a curtain before it.* TITIAN, MICHAEL ANGELO, *and* GIORGIO VASARI.

MICHAEL ANGELO.

So you have left at last your still· lagoons,
Your City of Silence floating in the sea,
And come to us in Rome.

TITIAN.

                I come to learn,
But I have come too late. I should
        have seen
Rome in my youth, when all my mind
        was open
To new impressions. Our Vasari here
Leads me about, a blind man, groping
        darkly
Among the marvels of the past. I touch
        them,
But do not see them.

MICHAEL ANGELO.

                There are things in Rome
That one might walk bare-footed here
        from Venice
But to see once, and then to die content.

TITIAN.

I must confess that these majestic ruins
Oppress me with their gloom. I feel
        as one
Who in the twilight stumbles among
        tombs,
And cannot read the inscriptions carved
        upon them.

MICHAEL ANGELO.

I felt so once; but I have. grown familiar
With desolation, and it has become
No more a pain to me, but a delight.

TITIAN.

I could not live here. I must have the
        sea,
And the sea-mist, with sunshine interwoven
Like cloth of gold ; must have beneath
        my windows

The laughter of the waves, and at my
        door
Their pattering footsteps, or I am not
        happy.

MICHAEL ANGELO.

Then tell me of your city in the sea,
Paved with red basalt of the Paduan
        hills.
Tell me of art in Venice. Three great
        names,
Giorgione, Titian, and the Tintoretto,
Illustrate your Venetian school, and
        send
A challenge to the world. The first is
        dead,
But Tintoretto lives.

TITIAN.

                And paints with fire,
Sudden and splendid, as the lightning
        paints
The cloudy vault of heaven.

GIORGIO.

                Does he still keep
Above his door the arrogant inscription
That once was painted there, — " The
        color of Titian,
With the design of Michael Angelo " ?

TITIAN.

Indeed, I know not. 'T was a foolish
        boast,
And does no harm to any but himself.
Perhaps he has grown wiser.

MICHAEL ANGELO.

                When you two
Are gone, who is there that remains behind
To seize the pencil falling from your
        fingers?

GIORGIO.

Oh there are many hands upraised already
To clutch at such a prize, which hardly
        wait
For death to loose your grasp, — a hundred of them :
Schiavone, Bonifazio, Campagnola,
Moretto. and Moroni ; who can count
        them,
Or measure their ambition ?

TITIAN.

                When we are gone

The generation that comes after us
Will have far other thoughts than ours.
    Our ruins
Will serve to build their palaces or
    tombs.
They will possess the world that we
    think ours,
And fashion it far otherwise.

MICHAEL ANGELO.

            I hear
Your son Orazio and your nephew Marco
Mentioned with honor.

TITIAN.

         Ay, brave lads, brave lads.
But time will show. There is a youth
    in Venice,
One Paul Cagliari, called the Veronese,
Still a mere stripling, but of such rare
    promise
That we must guard our laurels, or may
    lose them.

MICHAEL ANGELO.

These are good tidings ; for I sometimes
    fear
That, when we die, with us all art will
    die.
T is but a fancy. Nature will provide
Others to take our places. I rejoice
To see the young spring forward in the
    race,
Eager as we were, and as full of hope
And the sublime audacity of youth.

TITIAN.

Men die and are forgotten. The great
    world
Goes on the same. Among the myriads
Of men that live, or have lived, or shall
    live,
What is a single life, or thine or mine,
That we should think all nature would
    stand still
If we were gone ? We must make room
    for others.

MICHAEL ANGELO.

And now, Maestro, pray unveil your
    picture
Of Danaë, of which I hear such praise.

TITIAN, *drawing back the curtain.*

What think you ?

MICHAEL ANGELO.

        That Acrisius did well

To lock such beauty in a brazen tower
And hide it from all eyes.

TITIAN.

            The model truly
Was beautiful.

MICHAEL ANGELO.

      And more, that you were present,
And saw the showery Jove from high
    Olympus
Descend in all his splendor.

TITIAN.

           From your lips
Such words are full of sweetness.

MICHAEL ANGELO.

          You have caught
These golden hues from your Venetian
    sunsets.

TITIAN.

Possibly.

MICHAEL ANGELO.

    Or from sunshine through a shower
On the lagoons, or the broad Adriatic.
Nature reveals herself in all our arts.
The pavements and the palaces of cities
Hint at the nature of the neighboring
    hills.
Red lavas from the Euganean quarries
Of Padua pave your streets ; your pal
    aces
Are the white stones of Istria, and
    gleam
Reflected in your waters and your pic-
    tures.
And thus the works of every artist show
Something of his surroundings and his
    habits.
The uttermost that can be reached by
    color
Is here accomplished. Warmth and
    light and softness
Mingle together. Never yet was flesh
Painted by hand of artist, dead or living,
With such divine perfection.

TITIAN.

          I am grateful
For so much praise from you, who are
    a master ;
While mostly those who praise and those
    who blame
Know nothing of the matter, so that
    mainly
Their censure sounds like praise, their
    praise like censure.

MICHAEL ANGELO.

Wonderful! wonderful! The charm of
color
Fascinates me the more that in myself
The gift is wanting. I am not a painter.

GIORGIO.

Messer Michele, all the arts are yours,
Not one alone; and therefore I may
venture
To put a question to you.

MICHAEL ANGELO.

    Well, speak on.

GIORGIO.

Two nephews of the Cardinal Farnese
Have made me umpire in dispute be-
tween them
Which is the greater of the sister arts,
Painting or sculpture. Solve for me
the doubt.

MICHAEL ANGELO.

Sculpture and painting have a common
goal,
And whosoever would attain to it,
Whichever path he take, will find that
goal
Equally hard to reach.

GIORGIO.

    No doubt, no doubt;
But you evade the question.

MICHAEL ANGELO.

    When I stand
In presence of this picture, I concede
That painting has attained its uttermost;
But in the presence of my sculptured
figures
I feel that my conception soars beyond
All limit I have reached.

GIORGIO.

    You still evade me.

MICHAEL ANGELO.

Giorgio Vasari, I have often said
That I account that painting as the
best
Which most resembles sculpture. Here
before us
We have the proof. Behold those
rounded limbs!
How from the canvas they detach themselves,

Till they deceive the eye, and one would
say,
It is a statue with a screen behind it!

TITIAN.

Signori, pardon me; but all such ques
tions
Seem to me idle.

MICHAEL ANGELO.

    Idle as the wind.
And now, Maestro, I will say once more
How admirable I esteem your work,
And leave you, without further inter-
ruption.

TITIAN.

Your friendly visit hath much honored
me.

GIORGIO.

Farewell.

MICHAEL ANGELO *to* GIORGIO, *going out*.

    If the Venetian painters knew
But half as much of drawing as of
color,
They would indeed work miracles in
art,
And the world see what it hath never
seen.

VI.

PALAZZO CESARINI.

VITTORIA COLONNA, *seated in an arm-
chair;* JULIA GONZAGA, *standing near
her.*

JULIA.

It grieves me that I find you still so
weak
And suffering.

VITTORIA.

    No, not suffering; only dying.
Death is the chillness that precedes the
dawn;
We shudder for a moment, then awake
In the broad sunshine of the other life.
I am a shadow, merely, and these hands,
These cheeks, these eyes, these tresses
that my husband
Once thought so beautiful, and I was
proud of
Because he thought them so, are faded
quite, —
All beauty gone from them.

JULIA.

               Ah, no, not that.
Paler you are, but not less beautiful.

VITTORIA.

Hand me the mirror. I would fain be-
    hold
What change comes o'er our features
    when we die.
Thank you. And now sit down beside
    me here.
How glad I am that you have come to-
    day,
Above all other days, and at the hour
When most I need you!

JULIA.

            Do you ever need me?

VITTORIA.

Always, and most of all to-day and
    now.
Do you remember, Julia, when we
    walked,
One afternoon, upon the castle terrace
At Ischia, on the day before you left
    me?

JULIA.

Well I remember; but it seems to me
Something unreal, that has never
    been, —
Something that I have read of in a
    book,
Or heard of some one else.

VITTORIA.

          Ten years and more
Have passed since then; and many
    things have happened
In those ten years, and many friends
    have died;
Marco Flaminio, whom we all admired
And loved as our Catullus; dear Val-
    desso,
The noble champion of free thought and
    speech;
And Cardinal Ippolito, your friend.

JULIA.

Oh, do not speak of him! His sudden
    death
O'ercomes me now, as it o'ercame me
    then.
Let me forget it; for my memory
Serves me too often as an unkind
    friend,

And I remember things I would forget,
While I forget the things I would re
    member.

VITTORIA.

Forgive me; I will speak of him no
    more,
The good Fra Bernardino has departed,
Has fled from Italy, and crossed the
    Alps,
Fearing Caraffa's wrath, because he
    taught
That He who made us all without our
    help
Could also save us without aid of ours.
Renee of France, the Duchess of Fer
    rara,
That Lily of the Loire, is bowed by
    winds
That blow from Rome; Olympia Mo-
    rata
Banished from court because of this
    new doctrine.
Therefore be cautious. Keep your se-
    cret thought
Locked in your breast.

JULIA.

          I will be very prudent.
But speak no more, I pray; it wearies
    you.

VITTORIA.

Yes, I am very weary. Read to me.

JULIA.

Most willingly. What shall I read?

VITTORIA.

             Petrarca's
Triumph of Death. The book lies on
    the table;
Beside the casket there. Read where
    you find
The leaf turned down. 'T was there I
    left off reading.

JULIA, reads.

"Not as a flame that by some force is
    spent,
    But one that of itself consumeth
      quite,
    Departed hence in peace the soul
      content,
In fashion of a soft and lucent light
    Whose nutriment by slow gradation
      goes,
    Keeping until the end its lustre
      bright.

Not pale, but whiter than the sheet of
snows
 That without wind on some fair
  hill-top lies.
 Her weary body seemed to find repose.
Like a sweet slumber in her lovely
  eyes,
 When now the spirit was no longer
  there,
 Was what is dying called by the
  unwise.
E'en Death itself in her fair face
  seemed fair." —

Is it of Laura that he here is speak-
 ing ? —
She doth not answer, yet is not asleep;
Her eyes are full of light and fixed on
 something
Above her in the air. I can see naught
Except the painted angels on the ceil-
 ing.
Vittoria! speak! What is it? An-
 swer me ! —
She only smiles, and stretches out her
 hands.
   [The mirror falls and breaks.

VITTORIA

Not disobedient to the heavenly vision !
Pescara ! my Pescara !   [Dies

JULIA.

    Holy Virgin !
Her body sinks together, — she is
 dead !
 [Kneels, and hides her face in Vittoria's lap.

Enter MICHAEL ANGELO.

JULIA.

Hush ! make no noise.

MICHAEL ANGELO.

    How is she ?

JULIA.

    Never better.

MICHAEL ANGELO.

Then she is dead !

JULIA

   Alas ! yes, she is dead !
Even death itself in her fair face seems
 fair.

MICHAEL ANGELO.

How wonderful ! The light upon her
 face
Shines from the windows of another
 world.
Saints only have such faces. Holy
 Angels !
Bear her like sainted Catherine to her
 rest ! [Kisses Vittoria's hand.

PART THIRD.

I.

MONOLOGUE.

Macello de' Corvi. A room in MICHAEL
ANGELO'S *house.* MICHAEL ANGELO,
standing before a model of St. Peter's.

MICHAEL ANGELO.

Better than thou I cannot, Brunelleschi,
And less than thou I will not ! If the
 thought
Could, like a windlass, lift the ponder-
 ous stones.
And swing them to their places; if a
 breath
Could blow this rounded dome into the
 air,
As if it were a bubble, and these stat-
 ues
Spring at a signal to their sacred sta-
 tions,
As sentinels mount guard upon a wall.
Then were my task completed. Now,
 alas !
Naught am I but a Saint Sebaldus, hold-
 ing
Upon his hand the model of a church,
As German artists paint him ; and what
 years,
What weary years, must drag them-
 selves along,
Ere this be turned to stone ! What
 hindrances
Must block the way ; what idle interfer-
 ences
Of Cardinals and Canons of St. Peter's,
Who nothing know of art beyond the
 color
Of cloaks and stockings, nor of any
 building
Save that of their own fortunes ! And
 what then ?

I must then the short-coming of my
     means
Piece out by stepping forward, as the
     Spartan
Was told to add a step to his short sword.
                              [A pause.
And is Fra Bastian dead? Is all that
     light
Gone out, that sunshine darkened; all
     that music
And merriment, that used to make our
     lives
Less melancholy, swallowed up in si-
     lence
Like madrigals sung in the street at
     night
By passing revellers? It is strange in-
     deed
That he should die before me. 'T is
     against
The laws of nature that the young
     should die,
And the old live; unless it be that some
Have long been dead who think them-
     selves alive,
Because not buried. Well, what mat-
     ters it,
Since now that greater light, that was
     my sun,
Is set, and all is darkness, all is dark-
     ness!
Death's lightnings strike to right and
     left of me,
And, like a ruined wall, the world around
     me
Crumbles away, and I am left alone.
I have no friends, and want none. My
     own thoughts
Are now my sole companions,—thoughts
     of her,
That like a benediction from the skies
Come to me in my solitude and soothe
     me.
When men are old, the incessant thought
     of Death
Follows them like their shadow; sits
     with them
At every meal; sleeps with them when
     they sleep;
And when they wake already is awake,
And standing by their bedside. Then,
     what folly
It is in us to make an enemy
Of this importunate follower, not a
     friend!
To me a friend, and not an enemy,
Has he become since all my friends are
     dead.

II.

VIGNA DI PAPA GIULIO.

POPE JULIUS III. *seated by the Fountain
     of Acqua Vergine, surrounded by Car-
     dinals.*

JULIUS.

Tell me, why is it ye are discontent,
You, Cardinals Salviati and Marcello,
With Michael Angelo? What has he
     done,
Or left undone, that ye are set against
     him?
When one Pope dies, another is soon
     made;
And I can make a dozen Cardinals,
But cannot make one Michael Angelo.

CARDINAL SALVIATI.

Your Holiness, we are not set against
     him;
We but deplore his incapacity.
He is too old.

JULIUS.

                    You, Cardinal Salviati,
Are an old man. Are you incapable?
'T is the old ox that draws the straight-
     est furrow.

CARDINAL MARCELLO.

Your Holiness remembers he was
     charged
With the repairs upon St. Mary's bridge;
Made cofferdams, and heaped up load
     on load
Of timber and travertine; and yet for
     years
The bridge remained unfinished, till we
     gave it
To Baccio Bigio.

JULIUS.

                    Always Baccio Bigio!
Is there no other architect on earth?
Was it not he that sometime had in
     charge
The harbor of Ancona.

CARDINAL MARCELLO.

                              Ay, the same

JULIUS.

Then let me tell you that your Baccio
     Bigio
Did greater damage in a single day

To that fair harbor than the sea had
   done
Or would do in ten years. And him you
   think
To put in place of Michael Angelo,
In building the Basilica of St. Peter!
The ass that thinks himself a stag dis-
   covers
His error when he comes to leap the
   ditch.

CARDINAL MARCELLO.

He does not build; he but demolishes
The labors of Bramante and San Gallo.

JULIUS.

Only to build more grandly.

CARDINAL MARCELLO.

                   But time passes:
Year after year goes by, and yet the
   work
Is not completed. Michael Angelo
Is a great sculptor, but no architect.
His plans are faulty.

JULIUS.

              I have seen his model,
And have approved it. But here comes
   the artist.
Beware of him. He may make Persians
   of you,
To carry burdens on your backs forever.

The same: MICHAEL ANGELO.

JULIUS.

Come forward, dear Maestro! In these
   gardens
All ceremonies of our court are banished.
Sit down beside me here.

MICHAEL ANGELO, *sitting down.*

                   How graciously
Your Holiness commiserates old age
And its infirmities!

JULIUS.

              Say its privileges.
Art I respect. The building of this
   palace
And laying out these pleasant garden
   walks
Are my delight, and if I have not asked
Your aid in this, it is that I forbear
To lay new burdens on you at an age
When you need rest. Here I escape
   from Rome

To be at peace. The tumult of the city
Scarce reaches here.

MICHAEL ANGELO.

                   How beautiful it is
And quiet almost as a hermitage!

JULIUS.

We live as hermits here; and from
   these heights
O'erlook all Rome and see the yellow
   Tiber
Cleaving in twain the city, like a sword,
As far below there as St. Mary's bridge.
What think you of that bridge?

MICHAEL ANGELO.

                   I would advise
Your Holiness not to cross it, or not of-
   ten;
It is not safe.

JULIUS.

              It was repaired of late.

MICHAEL ANGELO.

Some morning you will look for it in
   vain;
It will be gone. The current of the
   river
Is undermining it.

JULIUS.

              But you repaired it.

MICHAEL ANGELO.

I strengthened all its piers, and paved
   its road
With travertine. He who came after
   me
Removed the stone, and sold it, and filled
   in
The space with gravel.

JULIUS.

                   Cardinal Salviati
And Cardinal Marcello, do you listen?
This is your famous Nanni Baccio Bigio.

MICHAEL ANGELO, *aside.*

There is some mystery here. These
   Cardinals
Stand lowering at me with unfriendly
   eyes.

JULIUS.

Now let us come to what concerns us
   more

Than bridge or gardens. Some complaints are made
Concerning the Three Chapels in St. Peter's;
Certain supposed defects or imperfections,
You doubtless can explain.

MICHAEL ANGELO.

This is no longer
The golden age of art. Men have become
Iconoclasts and critics. They delight not
In what an artist does, but set themselves
To censure what they do not comprehend.
You will not see them bearing a Madonna
Of Cimabue to the church in triumph,
But tearing down the statue of a Pope
To cast it into cannon. Who are they
That bring complaints against me?

JULIUS.

Deputies
Of the commissioners; and they complain
Of insufficient light in the Three Chapels.

MICHAEL ANGELO.

Your Holiness, the insufficient light
Is somewhere else, and not in the Three Chapels.
Who are the deputies that make complaint?

JULIUS.

The Cardinals Salviati and Marcello,
Here present.

MICHAEL ANGELO, rising.

With permission, Monsignori,
What is it ye complain of?

CARDINAL MARCELLO.

We regret
You have departed from Bramante's plan,
And from San Gallo's.

MICHAEL ANGELO.

Since the ancient time
No greater architect has lived on earth
Than Lazzari Bramante. His design,
Without confusion, simple, clear, well-lighted,

Merits all praise, and to depart from it
Would be departing from the truth
San Gallo,
Building about with columns, took all light
Out of this plan; left in the choir dark corners
For infinite ribaldries, and lurking places
For rogues and robbers; so that when the church
Was shut at night, not five and twenty men
Could find them out. It was San Gallo, then,
That left the church in darkness, and not I.

CARDINAL MARCELLO.

Excuse me; but in each of the Three Chapels
Is but a single window.

MICHAEL ANGELO.

Monsignore,
Perhaps you do not know that in the vaulting
Above there are to go three other windows.

CARDINAL SALVIATI.

How should we know? You never told us of it.

MICHAEL ANGELO.

I neither am obliged, nor will I be,
To tell your Eminence or any other
What I intend or ought to do. Your office
Is to provide the means, and see that thieves
Do not lay hands upon them. The designs
Must all be left to me.

CARDINAL MARCELLO.

Sir architect,
You do forget yourself, to speak thus rudely
In presence of his Holiness, and to us
Who are his cardinals.

MICHAEL ANGELO, putting on his hat.

I do not forget
I am descended from the Counts Canossa,
Linked with the Imperial line, and with Matilda,

Who gave the Church Saint Peter's Pat-
rimony.
I, too, am proud to give unto the Church
The labor of these hands, and what of
life
Remains to me.   My father Buonarotti
Was Podestà of Chiusi and Caprese.
I am not used to have men speak to
me
As if I were a mason, hired to build
A garden wall, and paid on Saturdays
So much an hour.

CARDINAL SALVIATI, *aside*.

                No wonder that Pope Clement
Never sat down in presence of this man,
Lest he should do the same ; and always
bade him
Put on his hat, lest he unasked should
do it !

MICHAEL ANGELO.

If any one could die of grief and shame,
I should.   This labor was imposed upon
me ;
I did not seek it ; and if I assumed it,
'T was not for love of fame or love of
gain,
But for the love of God.   Perhaps old
age
Deceived me, or self-interest, or ambi-
tion ;
I may be doing harm instead of good.
Therefore, I pray your Holiness, release
me ;
Take off from me the burden of this
work ;
Let me go back to Florence.

JULIUS.

                        Never, never,
While I am living.

MICHAEL ANGELO.

                Doth your Holiness
Remember what the Holy Scriptures
say
Of the inevitable time, when those
Who look out of the windows shall be
darkened,
And the almond-tree shall flourish ?

JULIUS.

                        That is in
Ecclesiastes.

MICHAEL ANGELO.

                And the grasshopper

Shall be a burden, and desire shall fail,
Because man goeth unto his long home.
Vanity of vanities, saith the Preacher ;
all
Is vanity.

JULIUS.

                Ah, were to do a thing
As easy as to dream of doing it,
We should not want for artists.   But
the men
Who carry out in act their great designs
Are few in number ; ay, they may be
counted
Upon the fingers of this hand.   Your
place
Is at St. Peter's.

MICHAEL ANGELO.

                I have had my dream,
And cannot carry out my great concep-
tion,
And put it into act.

JULIUS.

                Then who can do it ?
You would but leave it to some Baccio
Bigio
To mangle and deface.

MICHAEL ANGELO.

                        Rather than that,
I will still bear the burden on my shoul-
ders
A little longer.   If your Holiness
Will keep the world in order, and will
leave
The building of the church to me, the
work
Will go on better for it.   Holy Father,
If all the labors that I have endured,
And shall endure, advantage not my
soul,
I am but losing time.

JULIUS, *laying his hands on* MICHAEL
ANGELO'S *shoulders*.

                        You will be gainer
Both for your soul and body.

MICHAEL ANGELO.

                        Not events
Exasperate me, but the funest conclu-
sions
I draw from these events ; the sure decline
Of art, and all the meaning of that
word :

All that embellishes and sweetens life,
And lifts it from the level of low cares
Into the purer atmosphere of beauty ;
The faith in the Ideal ; the inspiration
That made the canons of the church of
    Seville
Say, " Let us build, so that all men here-
    after
Will say that we were madmen." Holy
    Father,
I beg permission to retire from here.

JULIUS.

Go ; and my benediction be upon you.
            [*Michael Angelo goes out.*
My Cardinals, this Michael Angelo
Must not be dealt with as a common
    mason.
He comes of noble blood, and for his
    crest
Bear two bull's horns ; and he has given
    us proof
That he can toss with them. From this
    day forth
Unto the end of time, let no man utter
The name of Baccio Bigio in my pres-
    ence.
All great achievements are the natural
    fruits
Of a great character. As trees bear not
Their fruits of the same size and qual-
    ity,
But each one in its kind with equal
    ease,
So are great deeds as natural to great
    men
As mean things are to small ones. By
    his work
We know the master. Let us not per-
    plex him.

III.

BINDO ALTOVITI.

A street in Rome. BINDO ALTOVITI,
    standing at the door of his house. MI-
    CHAEL ANGELO, *passing.*

BINDO.

Good-morning, Messer Michael Angelo !

MICHAEL ANGELO.

Good-morning, Messer Bindo Altoviti !

BINDO.

What brings you forth so early ?

MICHAEL ANGELO.

                    The same reason
That keeps you standing sentinel at your
    door, —
The air of this delicious summer morn-
    ing.
What news have you from Florence ?

BINDO.

                    Nothing new ;
The same old tale of violence and
    wrong.
Since the disastrous day at Monte
    Murlo,
When in procession, through San Gallo's
    gate,
Bareheaded, clothed in rags, on sorry
    steeds,
Philippo Strozzi and the good Valori
Were led as prisoners down the streets
    of Florence,
Amid the shouts of an ungrateful peo-
    ple,
Hope is no more, and liberty no more.
Duke Cosimo, the tyrant, reigns su-
    preme.

MICHAEL ANGELO.

Florence is dead : her houses are but
    tombs ;
Silence and solitude are in her streets.

BINDO.

Ah yes ; and often I repeat the words
You wrote upon your statue of the
    Night,
There in the Sacristy of San Lorenzo :
" Grateful to me is sleep ; to be of
    stone
More grateful, while the wrong and
    shame endure ;
To see not, feel not, is a benediction ;
Therefore awake me not ; oh, speak in
    whispers."

MICHAEL ANGELO.

Ah, Messer Bindo, the calamities,
The fallen fortunes, and the desolation
Of Florence are to me a tragedy
Deeper than words, and darker than
    despair.
I, who have worshipped freedom from
    my cradle,
Have loved her with the passion of a
    lover,
And clothed her with all lovely attrib
    utes

That the imagination can conceive,
Or the heart conjure up, now see her
     dead,
And trodden in the dust beneath the
     feet
Of an adventurer! It is a grief
Too great for me to bear in my old
     age.

BINDO.

I say no news from Florence: I am
     wrong,
For Benvenuto writes that he is coming
To be my guest in Rome.

MICHAEL ANGELO.

              Those are good tidings.
He hath been many years away from
     us.

BINDO.

Pray you, come in.

MICHAEL ANGELO.

              I have not time to stay,
And yet I will. I see from here your
     house
Is filled with works of art. That bust
     in bronze
Is of yourself. Tell me, who is the
     master
That works in such an admirable way,
And with such power and feeling?

BINDO.
                   Benvenuto.

MICHAEL ANGELO.

Ah? Benvenuto? 'T is a master-
     piece!
It pleases me as much, and even more,
Than the antiques about it; and yet
     they
Are of the best one sees. But you have
     placed it
By far too high. The light comes from
     below,
And injures the expression. Were
     these windows
Above and not beneath it, then indeed
It would maintain its own among these
     works
Of the old masters, noble as they are.
I will go in and study it more closely.
I always prophesied that Benvenuto,
With all his follies and fantastic ways,
Would show his genius in some work of
     art

That would amaze the world, and be a
     challenge
Unto all other artists of his time.
                    [*They go in.*

IV.

IN THE COLISEUM.

MICHAEL ANGELO *and* TOMASO DE
          CAVALIERI.

CAVALIERI.

What have you here alone, Messer Mi-
     chele?

MICHAEL ANGELO.

I come to learn.

CAVALIERI.

              You are already master,
And teach all other men.

MICHAEL ANGELO.

              Nay, I know nothing;
Not even my own ignorance, as some
Philosopher hath said. I am a school-
     boy
Who hath not learned his lesson, and
     who stands
Ashamed and silent in the awful pres-
     ence
Of the great master of antiquity
Who built these walls cyclopean.

CAVALIERI.
              Gaudentius
His name was, I remember. His re-
     ward
Was to be thrown alive to the wild
     beasts
Here where we now are standing.

MICHAEL ANGELO.
                   Idle tales.

CAVALIERI.

But you are greater than Gaudentius
     was,
And your work nobler.

MICHAEL ANGELO.
              Silence, I beseech you.

CAVALIERI.

Tradition says that fifteen thousand
     men

Were toiling for ten years incessantly
Upon this amphitheatre.

MICHAEL ANGELO.

Behold
How wonderful it is! The queen of
        flowers,
The marble rose of Rome! Its petals
        torn
By wind and rain of thrice five hundred
        years;
Its mossy sheath half rent away, and
        sold
To ornament our palaces and churches,
Or to be trodden under feet of man
Upon the Tiber's bank; yet what re-
        mains
Still opening its fair bosom to the sun,
And to the constellations that at night
Hang poised above it like a swarm of
        bees.

CAVALIERI.

The rose of Rome, but not of Para-
        dise;
Not the white rose our Tuscan poet saw,
With saints for petals.   When this rose
        was perfect
Its hundred thousand petals were not
        saints,
But senators in their Thessalian caps,
And all the roaring populace of Rome;
And even an Empress and the Vestal
        Virgins,
Who came to see the gladiators die,
Could not give sweetness to a rose like
        this.

MICHAEL ANGELO.

I spake not of its uses, but its beauty.

CAVALIERI.

The sand beneath our feet is saturate
With blood of martyrs; and these rifted
        stones
Are awful witnesses against a people
Whose pleasure was the pain of dying
        men.

MICHAEL ANGELO.

Tomaso Cavalieri, on my word,
You should have been a preacher, not a
        painter!
Think you that I approve such cruel-
        ties,
Because I marvel at the architects
Who built these walls, and curved these
        noble arches?

Oh, I am put to shame, when I consider
How mean our work is, when compared
        with theirs!
Look at these walls about us and above
        us!
They have been shaken by earthquakes,
        have been made
A fortress, and been battered by long
        sieges;
The iron clamps, that held the stones
        together,
Have been wrenched from them; but
        they stand erect
And firm, as if they had been hewn and
        hollowed
Out of the solid rock, and were a part
Of the foundations of the world itself.

CAVALIERI.

Your work, I say again, is nobler work,
In so far as its end and aim are nobler;
And this is but a ruin, like the rest.
Its vaulted passages are made the cav-
        erns
Of robbers, and are haunted by the
        ghosts
Of murdered men.

MICHAEL ANGELO.

        A thousand wild flowers bloom
From every chink, and the birds build
        their nests
Among the ruined arches, and suggest
New thoughts of beauty to the architect.
Now let us climb the broken stairs that
        lead
Into the corridors above, and study
The marvel and the mystery of that art
In which I am a pupil, not a master.
All things must have an end; the world
        itself
Must have an end, as in a dream I saw
        it.
There came a great hand out of heaven,
        and touched
The earth, and stopped it in its course
        The seas
Leaped, a vast cataract, into the abyss;
The forests and the fields slid off, and
        floated
Like wooded islands in the air.   The
        dead
Were hurled forth from their sepulchres;
        the living
Were mingled with them, and them
        selves were dead, —
All being dead; and the fair, shining
        cities

Dropped out like jewels from a broken
    crown.
Naught but the core of the great globe
    remained,
A skeleton of stone. And over it
The wrack of matter drifted like a
    cloud,
And then recoiled upon itself, and fell
Back on the empty world, that with the
    weight
Reeled, staggered, righted, and then
    headlong plunged
Into the darkness, as a ship, when
    struck
By a great sea, throws off the waves at
    first
On either side, then settles and goes
    down
Into the dark abyss, with her dead crew.

CAVALIERI.

But the earth does not move.

MICHAEL ANGELO.

        Who knows ? who knows?
There are great truths that pitch their
    shining tents
Outside our walls, and though but
    dimly seen
In the gray dawn, they will be mani-
    fest
When the light widens into perfect day.
A certain man, Copernicus by name,
Sometime professor here in Rome, has
    whispered
It is the earth, and not the sun, that
    moves.
What I beheld was only in a dream,
Yet dreams sometimes anticipate events,
Being unsubstantial images of things
As yet unseen.

V.

BENVENUTO AGAIN.

Macello de' Corri. MICHAEL ANGELO,
BENVENUTO CELLINI.

MICHAEL ANGELO.

So, Benvenuto, you return once more
To the Eternal City   'T is the centre
To which all gravitates   One finds no
    rest
Elsewhere than here.   There may be
    other cities

That please us for a while, but Rome
    alone
Completely satisfies. It becomes to all
A second native land by predilection,
And not by accident of birth alone.

BENVENUTO.

I am but just arrived, and am now lodg
    ing
With Bindo Altoviti. I have been
To kiss the feet of our most Holy Father,
And now am come in haste to kiss the
    hands
Of my miraculous Master.

MICHAEL ANGELO.

                And to find him
Grown very old.

BENVENUTO.

            You know that precious stones
Never grow old.

MICHAEL ANGELO.

         Half sunk beneath the horizon,
And yet not gone. Twelve years are
    a long while.
Tell me of France.

BENVENUTO.

             It were too long a tale
To tell you all. Suffice in brief to say
The King received me well, and loved
    me well ;
Gave me the annual pension that before
    me
Our Leonardo had, nor more nor less,
And for my residence the Tour de
    Nesle,
Upon the river-side.

MICHAEL ANGELO.

               A princely lodging

BENVENUTO.

What in return I did now matters
    not,
For there are other things, of greater
    moment,
I wish to speak of. First of all, the
    letter
You wrote me, not long since, about
    my bust
Of Bindo Altoviti, here in Rome. You
    said,
"My Benvenuto, I for many years
Have known you as the greatest of all
    goldsmiths,

And now I know you as no less a sculp-
    tor."
Ah, generous Master! How shall I e'er
    thank you
For such kind language ?

MICHAEL ANGELO.

                    By believing it.
I saw the bust at Messer Bindo's house,
And thought it worthy of the ancient
    masters,
And said so. That is all.

BENVENUTO.

                    It is too much ;
And I should stand abashed here in your
    presence,
Had I done nothing worthier of your
    praise
Than Bindo's bust.

MICHAEL ANGELO.

What have you done that 's better ?

BENVENUTO.

When I left Rome for Paris, you re-
    member
I promised you that if I went a gold-
    smith
I would return a sculptor. I have kept
The promise I then made.

MICHAEL ANGELO.

                    Dear Benvenuto,
I recognized the latent genius in you,
But feared your vices.

BENVENUTO.

                    I have turned them all
To virtues. My impatient, wayward
    nature,
That made me quick in quarrel, now
    has served me
Where meekness could not, and where
    patience could not,
As you shall hear now. I have cast in
    bronze
A statue of Perseus, holding thus aloft
In his left hand the head of the Medusa,
And in his right the sword that severed it;
His right foot planted on the lifeless
    corse ;
His face superb and pitiful, with eyes
Down-looking on the victim of his ven-
    geance.

MICHAEL ANGELO.

I see it as it should be.

BENVENUTO.

                    As it will be
When it is placed upon the Ducal
    Square,
Half-way between your David and the
    Judith
Of Donatello.

MICHAEL ANGELO.

            Rival of them both !

BENVENUTO.

But ah, what infinite trouble have I had
With Bandinello, and that stupid beast,
The major-domo of Duke Cosimo,
Francesco Ricci, and their wretched
    agent
Gorini, who came crawling round about
    me
Like a black spider, with his whining
    voice
That sounded like the buzz of a mos-
    quito !
Oh, I have wept in utter desperation,
And wished a thousand times I had not
    left
My Tour de Nesle, nor e'er returned to
    Florence,
Or thought of Perseus. What malignant
    falsehoods
They told the Grand Duke, to impede
    my work,
And make me desperate !

MICHAEL ANGELO.

                    The nimble lie
Is like the second-hand upon a clock ;
We see it fly; while the hour-hand of
    truth
Seems to stand still, and yet it moves
    unseen,
And wins at last, for the clock will not
    strike
Till it has reached the goal.

BENVENUTO.

                    My obstinacy
Stood me in stead, and helped me to
    o'ercome
The hindrances that envy and ill-will
Put in my way.

MICHAEL ANGELO.

            When anything is done,
People see not the patient doing of it,
Nor think how great would be the loss
    to man

If it had not been done. As in a build-
ing
Stone rests on stone, and wanting the
foundation
All would be wanting, so in human life
Each action rests on the foregone event,
That made it possible, but is forgotten
And buried in the earth.

BENVENUTO.

Even Bandinello,
Who never yet spake well of anything,
Speaks well of this; and yet he told the
Duke
That, though I cast small figures well
enough,
I never could cast this.

MICHAEL ANGELO.

But you have done it,
And proved Ser Bandinello a false
prophet.
That is the wisest way.

BENVENUTO.

And ah, that casting!
What a wild scene it was, as late at
night,
A night of wind and rain, we heaped
the furnace
With pine of Serristori, till the flames
Caught in the rafters over us, and threat-
ened
To send the burning roof upon our
heads;
And from the garden side the wind and
rain
Poured in upon us, and half quenched
our fires.
I was beside myself with desperation.
A shudder came upon me, then a fever;
I thought that I was dying, and was
forced
To leave the work-shop, and to throw
myself
Upon my bed, as one who has no hope.
And as I lay there, a deformed old man
Appeared before me, and with dismal
voice,
Like one who doth exhort a criminal
Led forth to death, exclaimed, " Poor
Benvenuto,
Thy work is spoiled! There is no rem-
edy!"
Then, with a cry so loud it might have
reached
The heaven of fire, I bounded to my
feet.

And rushed back to my workmen. They
all stood
Bewildered and desponding; and I
looked
Into the furnace, and beheld the mass
Half molten only, and in my despair
I fed the fire with oak, whose terrible
heat
Soon made the sluggish metal shine and
sparkle.
Then followed a bright flash, and an
explosion,
As if a thunderbolt had fallen among us.
The covering of the furnace had been
rent
Asunder, and the bronze was flowing
over;
So that I straightway opened all the
sluices
To fill the mould. The metal ran like
lava,
Sluggish and heavy; and I sent my
workmen
To ransack the whole house, and bring
together
My pewter plates and pans, two hundred
of them,
And cast them one by one into the fur-
nace
To liquefy the mass, and in a moment
The mould was filled! I fell upon my
knees
And thanked the Lord; and then we
ate and drank
And went to bed, all hearty and con-
tented.
It was two hours before the break of day.
My fever was quite gone.

MICHAEL ANGELO.

A strange adventure,
That could have happened to no man
alive
But you, my Benvenuto.

BENVENUTO.

As my workmen said
To major-domo Ricci afterward,
When he inquired of them: " 'T was
not a man,
But an express great devil."

MICHAEL ANGELO.

And the statue?

BENVENUTO.

Perfect in every part, save the right
foot

Of Perseus, as I had foretold the Duke.
There was just bronze enough to fill the
    mould ;
Not a drop over, not a drop too little.
I looked upon it as a miracle
Wrought by the hand of God.

MICHAEL ANGELO.

                    And now I see
How you have turned your vices into
    virtues.

BENVENUTO.

But wherefore do I prate of this ? I
    came
To speak of other things. Duke Co-
    simo
Through me invites you to return to
    Florence,
And offers you great honors, even to
    make you
One of the Forty-Eight, his Senators.

MICHAEL ANGELO.

His Senators ! That is enough. Since
    Florence
Was changed by Clement Seventh from
    a Republic
Into a Dukedom, I no longer wish
To be a Florentine.   That dream is
    ended.
The Grand Duke Cosimo now reigns
    supreme ;
All liberty is dead. Ah, woe is me !
I hoped to see my country rise to
    heights
Of happiness and freedom yet unreached
By other nations, but the climbing wave
Pauses, lets go its hold, and slides again
Back to the common level, with a hoarse
Death rattle in its throat.   I am too old
To hope for better days. I will stay here
And die in Rome. The very weeds,
    that grow
Among the broken fragments of her
    ruins,
Are sweeter to me than the garden
    flowers
Of other cities ; and the desolate ring
Of the Campagna round about her walls
Fairer than all the villas that encircle
The towns of Tuscany.

BENVENUTO.

                    But your old friends !

MICHAEL ANGELO.

All dead by violence. Baccio Valori

Has been beheaded ; Guicciardini poi
    soned ;
Philippo Strozzi strangled in his prison.
Is Florence then a place for honest men
To flourish in ?   What is there to pre-
    vent
My sharing the same fate ?

BENVENUTO.

                    Why, this : if all
Your friends are dead, so are your ene
    mies.

MICHAEL ANGELO.

Is Aretino dead ?

BENVENUTO.

                    He lives in Venice,
And not in Florence.

MICHAEL ANGELO.

                    'T is the same to me.
This wretched mountebank, whom flat-
    terers
Call the Divine, as if to make the word
Unpleasant in the mouths of those who
    speak it
And in the ears of those who hear it,
    sends me
A letter written for the public eye,
And with such subtle and infernal mal-
    ice,
I wonder at his wickedness.   'T is he
Is the express great devil, and not you.
Some years ago he told me how to paint
The scenes of the Last Judgment.

BENVENUTO.

                    I remember

MICHAEL ANGELO.

Well, now he writes to me that, as a
    Christian,
He is ashamed of the unbounded free-
    dom
With which I represent it.

BENVENUTO.

                    Hypocrite !

MICHAEL ANGELO.

He says I show mankind that I am
    wanting
In piety and religion, in proportion
As I profess perfection in my art.
Profess perfection ?   Why, 't is only
    men
Like Bugiardini who are satisfied

With what they do. I never am con-
  tent,
But always see the labors of my hand
Fall short of my conception.

BENVENUTO.

                  I perceive
The malice of this creature. He would
  taint you
With heresy, and in a time like this!
'T is infamous!

MICHAEL ANGELO.

               I represent the angels
Without their heavenly glory, and the
  saints
Without a trace of earthly modesty.

BENVENUTO.

Incredible audacity!

MICHAEL ANGELO.

                  The heathen
Veiled their Diana with some drapery,
And when they represented Venus
  naked
They made her by her modest attitude,
Appear half clothed. But I, who am a
  Christian,
Do so subordinate belief to art
That I have made the very violation
Of modesty in martyrs and in virgins
A spectacle at which all men would
  gaze
With half-averted eyes even in a brothel.

BENVENUTO.

He is at at home there, and he ought to
  know
What men avert their eyes from in such
  places;
From the Last Judgment chiefly, I imagine.

MICHAEL ANGELO.

But divine Providence will never leave
The boldness of my marvellous work un-
  punished;
And the more marvellous it is, the more
'T is sure to prove the ruin of my
  fame!
And finally, if in this composition
I had pursued the instructions that he
  gave me
Concerning heaven and hell and para-
  dise,
In that same letter, known to all the
  world.

Nature would not be forced, as she is
  now,
To feel ashamed that she invested me
With such great talent; that I stand
  myself
A very idol in the world of art.
He taunts me also with the Mauso-
  leum
Of Julius, still unfinished, for the rea-
  son
That men persuaded the inane old man
It was of evil augury to build
His tomb while he was living; and he
  speaks
Of heaps of gold this Pope bequeathed
  to me,
And calls it robbery; — that is what he
  says.
What prompted such a letter?

BENVENUTO.

                  Vanity.
He is a clever writer, and he likes
To draw his pen, and flourish it in the
  face
Of every honest man, as swordsmen do
Their rapiers on occasion, but to show
How skilfully they do it. Had you fol-
  lowed
The advice he gave, or even thanked
  him for it,
You would have seen another style of
  fence.
'T is but his wounded vanity, and the
  wish
To see his name in print. So give it
  not
A moment's thought; it soon will be
  forgotten.

MICHAEL ANGELO.

I will not think of it, but let it pass
For a rude speech thrown at me in the
  street,
As boys threw stones at Dante.

BENVENUTO.

              And what answer
Shall I take back to Grand Duke Cosimo?
He does not ask your labor or your service;
Only your presence in the city of Florence,
With such advice upon his work in
  hand
As he may ask, and you may choose to
  give.

MICHAEL ANGELO.

You have my answer.   Nothing he can
    offer
Shall tempt me to leave Rome. My work
    is here,
And only here, the building of St. Pe-
    ter's.
What other things I hitherto have done
Have fallen from me, are no longer mine ;
I have passed on beyond them, and
    have left them
As milestones on the way. What lies
    before me,
That is still mine, and while it is unfin-
    ished
No one shall draw me from it, or per-
    suade me,
By promises of ease, or wealth, or honor,
Till I behold the finished dome uprise
Complete, as now I see it in my thought.

BENVENUTO.

And will you paint no more ?

MICHAEL ANGELO.

                    No more.

BENVENUTO.

                    'T is well.
Sculpture is more divine, and more like
    Nature,
That fashions all her works in high re-
    lief,
And that is sculpture. This vast ball,
    the Earth,
Was moulded out of clay, and baked in
    fire ;
Men, women, and all animals that
    breathe
Are statues, and not paintings. Even
    the plants,
The flowers, the fruits, the grasses, were
    first sculptured,
And colored later. Painting is a lie,
A shadow merely.

MICHAEL ANGELO.

                    Truly, as you say,
Sculpture is more than painting. It is
    greater
To raise the dead to life than to create
Phantoms that seem to live. The most
    majestic
Of the three sister arts is that which
    builds ;
The eldest of them all, to whom the
    others

Are but the hand-maids and the servi-
    tors,
Being but imitation, not creation.
Henceforth I dedicate myself to her.

BENVENUTO.

And no more from the marble hew those
    forms
That fill us all with wonder ?

MICHAEL ANGELO.

                    Many statues
Will there be room for in my work.
    Their station
Already is assigned them in my mind.
But things move slowly. There are
    hindrances,
Want of material, want of means, delays
And interruptions, endless interference
Of Cardinal Commissioners, and dis-
    putes
And jealousies of artists, that annoy me.
But I will persevere until the work
Is wholly finished, or till I sink down
Surprised by death, that unexpected
    guest,
Who waits for no man's leisure, but steps
    in,
Unasked and unannounced, to put a stop
To all our occupations and designs.
And then perhaps I may go back to
    Florence ;
This is my answer to Duke Cosimo.

VI.

URBINO'S FORTUNE.

MICHAEL ANGELO'S *Studio*. MICHAEL
    ANGELO *and* URBINO.

MICHAEL ANGELO, *pausing in his work*.

Urbino, thou and I are both old men.
My strength begins to fail me.

URBINO.

                    Eccellenza,
That is impossible. Do I not see you
Attack the marble blocks with the same
    fury
As twenty years ago ?

MICHAEL ANGELO.

                    'T is an old habit.
I must have learned it early from my
    nurse
At Setignano, the stone-mason's wife :

For the first sounds I heard were of the chisel
Chipping away the stone.

URBINO.

At every stroke
You strike fire with your chisel.

MICHAEL ANGELO.

Ay, because
The marble is too hard.

URBINO.

It is a block
That Topolino sent you from Carrara.
He is a judge of marble.

MICHAEL ANGELO.

I remember.
With it he sent me something of his making, —
A Mercury, with long body and short legs,
As if by any possibility
A messenger of the gods could have short legs.
It was no more like Mercury than you are,
But rather like those little plaster figures
That peddlers hawk about the villages
As images of saints. But luckily
For Topolino, there are many people
Who see no difference between what is best
And what is only good, or not even good ;
So that poor artists stand in their esteem
On the same level with the best, or higher.

URBINO.

How Eccellenza laughed !

MICHAEL ANGELO.

Poor Topolino !
All men are not born artists, nor will labor
E'er make them artists.

URBINO.

No, no more
Than Emperors, or Popes, or Cardinals.
One must be chosen for it. I have been
Your color-grinder six and twenty years,
And am not yet an artist.

MICHAEL ANGELO.

Some have eyes
That see not; but in every block of marble

I see a statue, — see it as distinctly
As if it stood before me shaped and perfect
In attitude and action. I have only
To hew away the stone walls that imprison
The lovely apparition, and reveal it
To other eyes as mine already see it.
But I grow old and weak. What wilt thou do
When I am dead, Urbino ?

URBINO.

Eccellenza,
I must then serve another master.

MICHAEL ANGELO.

Never !
Bitter is servitude at best. Already
So many years hast thou been serving me ;
But rather as a friend than as a servant.
We have grown old together. Dost thou think
So meanly of this Michael Angelo
As to imagine he would let thee serve.
When he is free from service ? Take this purse,
Two thousand crowns in gold.

URBINO.

Two thousand crowns !

MICHAEL ANGELO.

Ay, it will make thee rich. Thou shalt not die
A beggar in a hospital.

URBINO.

Oh, Master !

MICHAEL ANGELO.

I cannot have them with me on the journey
That I am undertaking. The last garment
That men will make for me will have no pockets.

URBINO, kissing the hand of MICHAEL ANGELO.

My generous master !

MICHAEL ANGELO.

Hush !

URBINO.

My Providence !

464 MICHAEL ANGELO.

MICHAEL ANGELO.

Not a word more.   Go now to bed, old
man.
Thou hast served Michael Angelo.   Remember,
Henceforward thou shalt serve no other
master.

VII.

THE OAKS OF MONTE LUCA.

MICHAEL ANGELO, *alone in the woods.*

MICHAEL ANGELO.

How still it is among these ancient
oaks!
Surges and undulations of the air
Uplift the leafy boughs, and let them
fall
With scarce a sound.   Such sylvan
quietudes
Become old age.   These huge centen-
nial oaks,
That may have heard in infancy the
trumpets
Of Barbarossa's cavalry, deride
Man's brief existence, that with all his
strength
He cannot stretch beyond the hundredth
year.
This little acorn, turbaned like the
Turk,
Which with my foot I spurn, may be an
oak
Hereafter, feeding with its bitter mast
The fierce wild boar, and tossing in its
arms
The cradled nests of birds, when all the
men
That now inhabit this vast universe,
They and their children, and their chil-
dren's children,
Shall be but dust and mould, and noth-
ing more.
Through openings in the trees I see be-
low me
The valley of Clitumnus, with its farms
And snow-white oxen grazing in the
shade
Of the tall poplars on the river's brink.
O Nature, gentle mother, tender nurse!
I, who have never loved thee as I ought,
But wasted all my years immured in
cities,
And breathed the stifling atmosphere of
streets.

Now come to thee for refuge.   Here is
peace.
Yonder I see the little hermitages
Dotting the mountain side with points
of light,
And here St. Julian's convent, like a
nest
Of curlews, clinging to some windy cliff.
Beyond the broad, illimitable plain
Down sinks the sun, red as Apollo's
quoit,
That, by the envious Zephyr blown
aside,
Struck Hyacinthus dead, and stained
the earth
With his young blood, that blossomed
into flowers.
And now, instead of these fair deities,
Dread demons haunt the earth; hermits
inhabit
The leafy homes of sylvan Hama-
dryads;
And jovial friars, rotund and rubicund,
Replace the old Silenus with his ass.

Here underneath these venerable oaks,
Wrinkled and brown and gnarled like
them with age,
A brother of the monastery sits,
Lost in his meditations.   What may be
The questions that perplex, the hopes
that cheer him?
Good-evening, holy father.

MONK.
God be with you.

MICHAEL ANGELO.

Pardon a stranger if he interrupt
Your meditations.

MONK.
It was but a dream,—
The old, old dream, that never will come
true;
The dream that all my life I have been
dreaming,
And yet is still a dream.

MICHAEL ANGELO.

All men have dreams:
I have had mine; but none of them
came true;
They were but vanity.   Sometimes I
think
The happiness of man lies in pursuing,
Not in possessing; for the things pos-
sessed

Lose half their value.   Tell me of your
 dream.

MONK.

The yearning of my heart, my sole de-
 sire,
That like the sheaf of Joseph stands
 upright,
While all the others bend and bow to it;
The passion that torments me, and that
 breathes
New meaning into the dead forms of
 prayer,
Is that with mortal eyes I may behold
The Eternal City.

MICHAEL ANGELO.

Rome?

MONK.

There is but one;
The rest are merely names.   I think
 of it
As the Celestial City, paved with gold,
And sentinelled with angels.

MICHAEL ANGELO.

Would it were.
I have just fled from it.   It is be-
 leaguered
By Spanish troops, led by the Duke of
 Alva.

MONK.

But still for me 't is the Celestial City,
And I would see it once before I die.

MICHAEL ANGELO.

Each one must bear his cross.

MONK.

Were it a cross
That had been laid upon me, I could
 bear it,
Or fall with it.   It is a crucifix;
I am nailed hand and foot, and I am
 dying!

MICHAEL ANGELO.

What would you see in Rome?

MONK.

His Holiness.

MICHAEL ANGELO.

Him that was once the Cardinal Caraffa?
You would but see a man of fourscore
 years,

With sunken eyes, burning like carbun-
 cles,
Who sits at table with his friends for
 hours,
Cursing the Spaniards as a race of
 Jews
And miscreant Moors.   And with what
 soldiery
Think you he now defends the Eternal
 City?

MONK.

With legions of bright angels.

MICHAEL ANGELO.

So he calls them;
And yet in fact these bright angelic
 legions
Are only German Lutherans.

MONK, *crossing himself.*

Heaven protect us!

MICHAEL ANGELO.

What further would you see?

MONK.

The Cardinals,
Going in their gilt coaches to High
 Mass.

MICHAEL ANGELO.

Men do not go to Paradise in coaches.

MONK.

The catacombs, the convents, and the
 churches;
The ceremonies of the Holy Week
In all their pomp, or, at the Epiphany,
The Feast of the Santissima Bambino
At Ara Cœli.   But I shall not see
 them.

MICHAEL ANGELO.

These pompous ceremonies of the
 Church
Are but an empty show to him who
 knows
The actors in them.   Stay here in your
 convent,
For he who goes to Rome may see too
 much.
What would you further?

MONK.

I would see the painting
Of the Last Judgment in the Sistine
 Chapel.

MICHAEL ANGELO.

The smoke of incense and of altar candles
Has blackened it already.

MONK.
                              Woe is me!
Then I would hear Allegri's Miserere,
Sung by the Papal choir.

MICHAEL ANGELO.
                         A dismal dirge!
I am an old, old man, and I have lived
In Rome for thirty years and more, and
know
The jarring of the wheels of that great
world,
Its jealousies, its discords, and its strife.
Therefore I say to you, remain content
Here in your convent, here among your
woods,
Where only there is peace. Go not to
Rome.
There was of old a monk of Wittenberg
Who went to Rome; you may have
heard of him;
His name was Luther; and you know
what followed.
                    [The convent bell rings.

MONK, rising.

It is the convent bell; it rings for vespers.
Let us go in; we both will pray for
peace.

VIII.

THE DEAD CHRIST.

MICHAEL ANGELO'S studio. MICHAEL
ANGELO, with a light, working upon
the Dead Christ. Midnight.

MICHAEL ANGELO.

O Death, why is it I cannot portray
Thy form and features? Do I stand
too near thee?
Or dost thou hold my hand, and draw
me back,
As being thy disciple, not thy master?
Let him who knows not what old age is
like
Have patience till it comes, and he will
know.
I once had skill to fashion Life and
Death

And Sleep, which is the counterfeit of
Death;
And I remember what Giovanni Strozzi
Wrote underneath my statue of the
Night
In San Lorenzo, ah, so long ago!

Grateful to me is sleep! More grateful
now
Than it was then; for all my friends
are dead;
And she is dead, the noblest of them
all.
I saw her face, when the great sculptor
Death,
Whom men should call Divine, had at a
blow
Stricken her into marble; and I kissed
Her cold white hand. What was it
held me back
From kissing her fair forehead, and
those lips,
Those dead, dumb lips? Grateful to
me is sleep!

Enter GIORGIO VASARI.

GIORGIO.

Good-evening, or good-morning, for I
know not
Which of the two it is.

MICHAEL ANGELO.
                    How came you in?

GIORGIO.

Why, by the door, as all men do.

MICHAEL ANGELO.
                              Ascanio
Must have forgotten to bolt it.

GIORGIO.
                    Probably.
Am I a spirit, or so like a spirit,
That I could slip through bolted door
or window?
As I was passing down the street, I saw
A glimmer of light, and heard the well-
known chink
Of chisel upon marble. So I entered,
To see what keeps you from your bed
so late.

MICHAEL ANGELO, *coming forward with
the lamp.*

You have been revelling with your boon
companions,

Giorgio Vasari, and you come to me
At an untimely hour.

GIORGIO.

The Pope hath sent me.
His Holiness desires to see again
The drawing you once showed him of
the dome
Of the Basilica.

MICHAEL ANGELO.

We will look for it.

GIORGIO.

What is the marble group that glimmers there
Behind you ?

MICHAEL ANGELO.

Nothing, and yet everything, —
As one may take it. It is my own
tomb,
That I am building.

GIORGIO.

Do not hide it from me.
By our long friendship and the love I
bear you,
Refuse me not !

MICHAEL ANGELO, *letting fall the lamp.*

Life hath become to me
An empty theatre, — its lights extin-
guished,
The music silent, and the actors gone ;
And I alone sit musing on the scenes
That once have been. I am so old that
Death
Oft plucks me by the cloak, to come
with him ;
And some day, like this lamp, shall I
fall down,
And my last spark of life will be extin-
guished.
Ah me ! ah me ! what darkness of de-
spair !
So near to death, and yet so far from
God !

CHRISTUS: A MYSTERY.

INTROITUS.

The ANGEL *bearing the* PROPHET HA-
BAKKUK *through the air.*

PROPHET.

WHY dost thou bear me aloft,
O Angel of God, on thy pinions
O'er realms and dominions ?
Softly I float as a cloud
In air, for thy right hand upholds me,
Thy garment enfolds me !

ANGEL.

Lo ! as I passed on my way
In the harvest-field I beheld thee,
When no man compelled thee,
Bearing with thine own hands
This food to the famishing reapers,
A flock without keepers !

The fragrant sheaves of the wheat
Made the air above them sweet ;
Sweeter and more divine
Was the scent of the scattered grain,

That the reaper's hand let fall
To be gathered again
By the hand of the gleaner !
Sweetest, divinest of all,
Was the humble deed of thine,
And the meekness of thy demeanor !

PROPHET.

Angel of Light,
I cannot gainsay thee,
I can but obey thee !

ANGEL.

Beautiful was it in the Lord's sight,
To behold his Prophet
Feeding those that toil,
The tillers of the soil.
But why should the reapers eat of it
And not the Prophet of Zion
In the den of the lion ?
The Prophet should feed the Prophet !
Therefore I thee have uplifted,
And bear thee aloft by the hair
Of thy head, like a cloud that is drifted
Through the vast unknown of the air !

Five days ·hath the Prophet been ly-
ing
In Babylon, in the den
Of the lions, death-defying,
Defying hunger and thirst;
But the worst
Is the mockery of men!
Alas! how full of fear
Is the fate of Prophet and Seer!
Forevermore, forevermore,
It shall be as it hath been heretofore;
The age in which they live
Will not forgive
The splendor of the everlasting light,
That makes their foreheads bright,
Nor the sublime
Fore-running of their time!

PROPHET.

Oh tell me, for thou knowest,
Wherefore and by what grace,
Have I, who am least and lowest,
Been chosen to this place,
To this exalted part?

ANGEL.

Because thou art
The Struggler; and from thy youth
Thy humble and patient life
Hath been a strife
And battle for the Truth;
Nor hast thou paused nor halted,
Nor ever in thy pride
Turned from the poor aside,
But with deed and word and pen
Hast served thy fellow-men;
Therefore art thou exalted!

PROPHET.

By thine arrow's light
Thou goest onward through the night,
And by the clear
Sheen of thy glittering spear!
When will our journey end?

ANGEL.

Lo, it is ended!
Yon silver gleam
Is the Euphrates' stream.
Let us descend
Into the city splendid,
Into the City of Gold!

PROPHET.

Behold!
As if the stars had fallen from their
places
Into the firmament below,

The streets, the gardens, and the vacant
spaces
With light are all aglow;
And hark!
As we draw near,
What sound is it I hear
Ascending through the dark?

ANGEL.

The tumultuous noise of the nations,
Their rejoicings and lamentations,
The pleadings of their prayer,
The groans of their despair,
The cry of their imprecations,
Their wrath, their love, their hate!

PROPHET.

Surely the world doth wait
The coming of its Redeemer!

ANGEL.

Awake from thy sleep, O dreamer!
The hour is near, though late;
Awake! write the vision sublime,
The vision, that is for a time,
Though it tarry, wait; it is nigh;
In the end it will speak and not lie.

PART ONE.

THE DIVINE TRAGEDY.

THE FIRST PASSOVER.

I.

VOX CLAMANTIS.

JOHN THE BAPTIST.

REPENT! repent! repent!
For the kingdom of God is at hand
And all the land
Full of the knowledge of the Lord shall
be
As the waters cover the sea,
And encircle the continent!

Repent! repent! repent!
For lo, the hour appointed,
The hour so long foretold
By the Prophets of old,
Of the coming of the Anointed,
The Messiah, the Paraclete,
The Desire of the Nations, is nigh!
He shall not strive nor cry,
Nor his voice be heard in the street;
Nor the bruised reed shall He break,

Nor quench the smoking flax;
And many of them that sleep
In the dust of earth shall awake,
On that great and terrible day,
And the wicked shall wail and weep,
And be blown like a smoke away,
And be melted away like wax.
Repent! repent! repent!

O Priest, and Pharisee,
Who hath warned you to flee
From the wrath that is to be?
From the coming anguish and ire?
The axe is laid at the root
Of the trees, and every tree
That bringeth not forth good fruit
Is hewn down and cast into the fire!

Ye Scribes, why come ye hither?
In the hour that is uncertain,
In the day of anguish and trouble,
He that stretcheth the heavens as a curtain
And spreadeth them out as a tent,
Shall blow upon you, and ye shall wither,
And the whirlwind shall take you away as stubble!
Repent! repent! repent!

PRIEST.

Who art thou, O man of prayer!
In raiment of camel's hair,
Begirt with leathern thong,
That here in the wilderness,
With a cry as of one in distress,
Preachest unto this throng?
Art thou the Christ?

JOHN.

Priest of Jerusalem,
In meekness and humbleness,
I deny not, I confess
I am not the Christ!

PRIEST.

What shall we say unto them
That sent us here?   Reveal
Thy name, and naught conceal!
Art thou Elias?

JOHN.

No!

PRIEST.

Art thou that Prophet, then,
Of lamentation and woe,
Who, as a symbol and sign

Of impending wrath divine
Upon unbelieving men,
Shattered the vessel of clay
In the Valley of Slaughter?

JOHN.

Nay.
I am not he thou namest!

PRIEST.

Who art thou, and what is the word
That here thou proclaimest?

JOHN.

I am the voice of one
Crying in the wilderness alone:
Prepare ye the way of the Lord;
Make his paths straight
In the land that is desolate!

PRIEST.

If thou be not the Christ,
Nor yet Elias, nor he
That, in sign of the things to be,
Shattered the vessel of clay
In the Valley of Slaughter,
Then declare unto us, and say
By what authority now
Baptizest thou?

JOHN.

I indeed baptize you with water
Unto repentance; but He,
That cometh after me,
Is mightier than I and higher;
The latchet of whose shoes
I am not worthy to unloose;
He shall baptize you with fire,
And with the Holy Ghost!
Whose fan is in his hand;
He will purge to the uttermost
His floor, and garner his wheat,
But will burn the chaff in the brand
And fire of unquenchable heat!
Repent! repent! repent!

II.

MOUNT QUARANTANIA.

I.

LUCIFER.

Not in the lightning's flash, nor in the thunder,
Not in the tempest, nor the cloudy storm,
Will I array my form;

But part invisible these boughs asunder,
And move and murmur, as the wind up-
heaves
And whispers in the leaves.

Not as a terror and a desolation,
Not in my natural shape, inspiring fear
And dread, will I appear;
But in soft tones of sweetness and per-
suasion,
A sound as of the fall of mountain
streams,
Or voices heard in dreams.

He sitteth there in silence, worn and
wasted
With famine, and uplifts his hollow eyes
To the unpitying skies;
For forty days and nights he hath not
tasted
Of food or drink, his parted lips are
pale,
Surely his strength must fail.

Wherefore dost thou in penitential fast-
ing
Waste and consume the beauty of thy
youth?
Ah, if thou be in truth
The Son of the Unnamed, the Everlast-
ing,
Command these stones beneath thy feet
to be
Changed into bread for thee!

CHRISTUS.

'T is written! Man shall not live by
bread alone,
But by each word that from God's
mouth proceedeth!

II.

LUCIFER.

Too weak, alas! too weak is the temp-
tation
For one whose soul to nobler things
aspires
Than sensual desires!
Ah, could I, by some sudden aberra-
tion,
Lead and delude to suicidal death
This Christ of Nazareth!

Unto the holy Temple on Moriah,
With its resplendent domes, and mani-
fold
Bright pinnacles of gold,
Where they await thy coming, O Mes-
siah!
Lo, I have brought thee! Let thy
glory here
Be manifest and clear.

Reveal thyself by royal act and gesture
Descending with the bright triumphant
host
Of all the highermost
Archangels, and about thee as a vesture
The shining clouds, and all thy splen-
dors show
Unto the world below!

Cast thyself down, it is the hour ap-
pointed;
And God hath given his angels charge
and care
To keep thee and upbear
Upon their hands his only Son, the
Anointed,
Lest he should dash his foot against a
stone
And die, and be unknown.

CHRISTUS.

'T is written: Thou shalt not tempt the
Lord thy God!

III.

LUCIFER.

I cannot thus delude him to perdition!
But one temptation still remains un-
tried,
The trial of his pride,
The thirst of power, the fever of ambition!
Surely by these a humble peasant's son
At last may be undone!

Above the yawning chasms and deep
abysses,
Across the headlong torrents, I have
brought
Thy footsteps, swift as thought;
And from the highest of these preci-
pices,
The Kingdoms of the world thine eyes
behold,
Like a great map unrolled.

From far-off Lebanon, with cedars
crested,
To where the waters of the Asphalt
Lake

On its white pebbles break,
And the vast desert, silent, sand-invested,
These kingdoms all are mine, and thine shall be,
If thou wilt worship me!

CHRISTUS.

Get thee behind me, Satan! thou shalt worship
The Lord thy God; Him only shalt thou serve!

ANGELS MINISTRANT.

The sun goes down; the evening shadows lengthen,
The fever and the struggle of the day
Abate and pass away;
Thine Angels Ministrant, we come to strengthen
And comfort thee, and crown thee with the palm,
The silence and the calm.

III.

THE MARRIAGE IN CANA.

THE MUSICIANS.

Rise up, my love, my fair one,
Rise up, and come away,
For lo! the winter is past,
The rain is over and gone,
The flowers appear on the earth,
The time of the singing of birds is come,
And the voice of the turtle is heard in our land.

THE BRIDEGROOM.

Sweetly the minstrels sing the Song of Songs!
My heart runs forward with it, and I say:
Oh set me as a seal upon thine heart,
And set me as a seal upon thine arm;
For love is strong as life, and strong as death,
And cruel as the grave is jealousy!

THE MUSICIANS.

I sleep, but my heart awaketh;
'T is the voice of my beloved
Who knocketh, saying: Open to me,
My sister, my love, my dove,
For my head is filled with dew,
My locks with the drops of the night!

THE BRIDE.

Ah yes, I sleep, and yet my heart awaketh.
It is the voice of my beloved who knocks.

THE BRIDEGROOM.

O beautiful as Rebecca at the fountain,
O beautiful as Ruth among the sheaves!
O fairest among women! O undefiled!
Thou art all fair, my love, there's no spot in thee!

THE MUSICIANS.

My beloved is white and ruddy,
The chiefest among ten thousand
His locks are black as a raven,
His eyes are the eyes of doves,
Of doves by the rivers of water,
His lips are like unto lilies,
Dropping sweet-smelling myrrh.

ARCHITRICLINUS.

Who is that youth with the dark azure eyes,
And hair, in color like unto the wine,
Parted upon his forehead, and behind
Falling in flowing locks?

PARANYMPHUS.

        The Nazarene
Who preacheth to the poor in field and village
The coming of God's Kingdom.

ARCHITRICLINUS.

        How serene
His aspect is! manly yet womanly.

PARANYMPHUS.

Most beautiful among the sons of men!
Oft known to weep, but never known to laugh.

ARCHITRICLINUS.

And tell me, she with eyes of olive tint,
And skin as fair as wheat, and pale brown hair,
The woman at his side?

PARANYMPHUS.

        His mother, Mary.

ARCHITRICLINUS.

And the tall figure standing close behind them,
Clad all in white, with face and beard like ashes,

As if he were Elias, the White Witness,
Come from his cave on Carmel to fore-
    tell
The end of all things ?

PARANYMPHUS.

                    That is Manahem
The Essenian, he who dwells among
    the palms
Near the Dead Sea.

ARCHITRICLINUS.

            He who foretold to Herod
He should one day be King ?

PARANYMPHUS.

                    The same.

ARCHITRICLINUS.

                    Then why
Doth he come here to sadden with his
    presence
Our marriage feast, belonging to a sect
Haters of women, and that taste not
    wine ?

THE MUSICIANS.

My undefiled is but one,
The only one of her mother,
The choice of her that bare her ;
The daughters saw her and blessed
    her ;
The queens and the concubines praised
    her ;
Saying, Lo ! who is this
That looketh forth as the morning ?

MANAHEM, aside.

The Ruler of the Feast is gazing at me,
As if he asked, why is that old man here
Among the revellers ? And thou, the
    Anointed !
Why art thou here ? I see as in a vision
A figure clothed in purple, crowned
    with thorns ;
I see a cross uplifted in the darkness,
And hear a cry of agony, that shall echo
Forever and forever through the world !

ARCHITRICLINUS.

Give us more wine. These goblets are
    all empty.

MARY to CHRISTUS.

They have no wine !

CHRISTUS.

            O woman, what have I

To do with thee ?   Mine hour is not yet
    come.

MARY to the servants.

Whatever he shall say to you, that do.

CHRISTUS.

Fill up these pots with water.

THE MUSICIANS.

Come, my beloved,
Let us go forth into the field,
Let us lodge in the villages ;
Let us get up early to the vineyards,
Let us see if the vine flourish,
Whether the tender grape appear,
And the pomegranates bud forth.

CHRISTUS.

                    Draw out now
And bear unto the Ruler of the Feast.

MANAHEM, aside.

O thou, brought up among the Essenians,
Nurtured in abstinence, taste not the
    wine !
It is the poison of dragons from the
    vineyards
Of Sodom, and the taste of death is in
    it !

ARCHITRICLINUS to the BRIDEGROOM.

All men set forth good wine at the be-
    ginning,
And when men have well drunk, that
    which is worse ;
But thou hast kept the good wine until
    now.

MANAHEM, aside.

The things that have been and shall be
    no more,
The things that are, and that hereafter
    shall be,
The things that might have been, and
    yet were not,
The fading twilight of great joys de-
    parted,
The daybreak of great truths as yet un-
    risen,
The intuition and the expectation
Of something, which, when come, is not
    the same,
But only like its forecast in men's
    dreams,
The longing, the delay, and the delight,
Sweeter for the delay ; youth, hope,
    love, death,

And disappointment which is also death,
All these make up the sum of human
life;
A dream within a dream, a wind at
night
Howling across the desert in despair,
Seeking for something lost it cannot
find.
Fate or foreseeing, or whatever name
Men call it, matters not; what is to be
Hath been fore-written in the thought
divine
From the beginning. None can hide
from it,
But it will find him out; nor run from it,
But it o'ertaketh him! The Lord hath
said it.

THE BRIDEGROOM *to the* BRIDE, *on the
balcony.*

When Abraham went with Sarah into
Egypt,
The land was all illumined with her
beauty;
But thou dost make the very night itself
Brighter than day! Behold, in glad
procession,
Crowding the threshold of the sky above
us,
The stars come forth to meet thee with
their lamps;
And the soft winds, the ambassadors of
flowers,
From neighboring gardens and from
fields unseen,
Come laden with odors unto thee, my
Queen!

THE MUSICIANS.

Awake, O north-wind,
And come, thou wind of the South.
Blow, blow upon my garden,
That the spices thereof may flow out.

IV.

IN THE CORNFIELDS.

PHILIP.

Onward through leagues of sun-illum-
ined corn,
As if through parted seas, the pathway
runs,
And crowned with sunshine as the Prince
of Peace
Walks the beloved Master, leading us,
As Moses led our fathers in old times
Out of the land of bondage! We have
found
Him of whom Moses and the Prophets
wrote,
Jesus of Nazareth, the Son of Joseph.

NATHANAEL.

Can any good come out of Nazareth?
Can this be the Messiah?

PHILIP.

Come and see

NATHANAEL.

The summer sun grows hot: I am an-
hungered.
How cheerily the Sabbath-breaking quail
Pipes in the corn, and bids us to his
Feast
Of Wheat Sheaves! How the bearded,
ripening ears
Toss in the roofless temple of the air;
As if the unseen hand of some High-
Priest
Waved them before Mount Tabor as an
altar!
It were no harm, if we should pluck and
eat.

PHILIP.

How wonderful it is to walk abroad
With the Good Master! Since the
miracle
He wrought at Cana, at the marriage
feast,
His fame hath gone abroad through all
the land,
And when we come to Nazareth, thou
shalt see
How his own people will receive their
Prophet,
And hail him as Messiah! See, he
turns
And looks at thee.

CHRISTUS.

Behold an Israelite
In whom there is no guile.

NATHANAEL.

Whence knowest thou me?

CHRISTUS.

Before that Philip called thee, when
thou wast
Under the fig-tree, I beheld thee.

NATHANAEL.

Rabbi !
Thou art the Son of God, thou art the King
Of Israel !

CHRISTUS.

Because I said I saw thee
Under the fig-tree, before Philip called thee,
Believest thou ?   Thou shalt see greater things.
Hereafter thou shalt see the heavens unclosed,
The angels of God ascending and descending
Upon the Son of Man !

PHARISEES, *passing.*

Hail, Rabbi !

CHRISTUS.

Hail !

PHARISEES.

Behold how thy disciples do a thing
Which is not lawful on the Sabbath-day,
And thou forbiddest them not !

CHRISTUS.

Have ye not read
What David did when he anhungered was,
And all they that were with him ?   How he entered
Into the house of God, and ate the shew-bread,
Which was not lawful, saving for the priests ?
Have ye not read, how on the Sabbath-days
The priests profane the Sabbath in the Temple,
And yet are blameless ?   But I say to you,
One in this place is greater than the Temple !
And had ye known the meaning of the words,
I will have mercy and not sacrifice,
The guiltless ye would not condemn.
The Sabbath
Was made for man, and not man for for the Sabbath.

Passes on with the disciples.

PHARISEES.

This is, alas ! some poor demoniac
Wandering about the fields, and uttering
His unintelligible blasphemies
Among the common people, who receive
As prophecies the words they comprehend not !
Deluded folk !   The incomprehensible
Alone excites their wonder.   There is none
So visionary, or so void of sense,
But he will find a crowd to follow him !

V.

NAZARETH.

CHRISTUS, *reading in the Synagogue.*

The Spirit of the Lord God is upon me.
He hath anointed me to preach good tidings
Unto the poor; to heal the broken-hearted ;
To comfort those that mourn, and to throw open
The prison doors of captives, and proclaim
The Year Acceptable of the Lord, our God !

He closes the book and sits down.

A PHARISEE.

Who is this youth ?   He hath taken the Teacher's seat !
Will he instruct the Elders ?

A PRIEST.

Fifty years
Have I been Priest here in the Synagogue,
And never have I seen so young a man
Sit in the Teacher's seat !

CHRISTUS.

Behold, to-day
This scripture is fulfilled.   One is appointed
And hath been sent to them that mourn in Zion,
To give them beauty for ashes, and the oil
Of joy for mourning !   They shall build again
The old waste-places ; and again raise up

NAZARETH. Page 474.

The former desolations, and repair
The cities that are wasted! As a bride-
groom
Decketh himself with ornaments; as a
bride
Adorneth herself with jewels, so the
Lord
Hath clothed me with the robe of right-
eousness!

A PRIEST.

He speaks the Prophet's words; but
with an air
As if himself had been foreshadowed in
them!

CHRISTUS.

For Zion's sake I will not hold my
peace,
And for Jerusalem's sake I will not
rest
Until its righteousness be as a bright-
ness,
And its salvation as a lamp that burn-
eth!
Thou shalt be called no longer the For-
saken,
Nor any more thy land the Desolate.
The Lord hath sworn, by his right hand
hath sworn,
And by his arm of strength: I will no
more
Give to thine enemies thy corn as meat;
The sons of strangers shall not drink
thy wine.
Go through, go through the gates!
Prepare a way
Unto the people! Gather out the
stones!
Lift up a standard for the people!

A PRIEST.
Ah!
These are seditious words!

CHRISTUS.
And they shall call them
The holy people; the redeemed of God!
And thou, Jerusalem, shalt be called
Sought out,
A city not forsaken!

A PHARISEE.
Is not this
The carpenter Joseph's son? Is not
his mother
Called Mary? and his brethren and his
sisters

Are they not with us? Doth he make
himself
To be a Prophet?

CHRISTUS.
No man is a Prophet
In his own country, and among his kin.
In his own house no Prophet is accepted.
I say to you, in the land of Israel
Were many widows in Elijah's day,
When for three years and more the
heavens were shut,
And a great famine was throughout the
land;
But unto no one was Elijah sent
Save to Sarepta, to a city of Sidon,
And to a woman there that was a widow.
And many lepers were there in the land
Of Israel, in the time of Eliseus
The Prophet, and yet none of them was
cleansed,
Save Naaman the Syrian!

A PRIEST.
Say no more!
Thou comest here into our Synagogue
And speakest to the Elders and the
Priests,
As if the very mantle of Elijah
Had fallen upon thee! Are thou not
ashamed?

A PHARISEE.

We want no Prophets here! Let him
be driven
From Synagogue and city! Let him go
And prophesy to the Samaritans!

AN ELDER.

The world is changed. We Elders are
as nothing!
We are but yesterdays, that have no
part
Or portion in to-day! Dry leaves that
rustle,
That make a little sound, and then are
dust!

A PHARISEE.

A carpenter's apprentice! a mechanic,
Whom we have seen at work here in
the town
Day after day; a stripling without
learning,
Shall he pretend to unfold the Word of
God
To men grown old in study of the Law?
CHRISTUS *is thrust out.*

VI.

THE SEA OF GALILEE.

PETER *and* ANDREW *mending their nets.*

PETER.

Never was such a marvellous draught of
fishes
Heard of in Galilee ! The market-
places
Both of Bethsaida and Capernaum
Are full of them ! Yet we had toiled
all night
And taken nothing, when the Master
said :
Launch out into the deep, and cast your
nets ;
And doing this, we caught such multi-
tudes,
Our nets like spiders' webs were snapped
asunder,
And with the draught we filled two
ships so full
That they began to sink. Then I knelt
down
Amazed, and said : O Lord, depart from
me,
I am a sinful man. And he made
answer :
Simon, fear not ; henceforth thou shalt
catch men !
What was the meaning of those words ?

ANDREW.

　　　　　　　I know not.
But here is Philip, come from Nazareth.
He hath been with the Master. Tell us,
Philip,
What tidings dost thou bring ?

PHILIP.

　　　　　　Most wonderful !
As we drew near to Nain, out of the
gate
Upon a bier was carried the dead body
Of a young man, his mother's only son,
And she a widow, who with lamentation
Bewailed her loss, and the much people
with her ;
And when the Master saw her he was
filled
With pity ; and he said to her : Weep
not !
And came and touched the bier, and
they that bare it
Stood still ; and then he said : Young
man, arise !

And he that had been dead sat up, and
soon
Began to speak ; and he delivered him
Unto his mother. And there came a
fear
On all the people, and they glorified
The Lord, and said, rejoicing : A
great Prophet
Is risen up among us ! and the Lord
Hath visited his people !

PETER.

　　　　　　　A great Prophet ?
Ay, greater than a Prophet : greater
even
Than John the Baptist !

PHILIP.

　　　　　　Yet the Nazarenes
Rejected him.

PETER.

　　　　　　The Nazarenes are dogs !
As natural brute beasts, they growl at
things
They do not understand ; and they shall
perish,
Utterly perish in their own corruption.
The Nazarenes are dogs !

PHILIP.

　　　　　　They drave him forth
Out of their Synagogue, out of their
city,
And would have cast him down a preci-
pice,
But, passing through the midst of them,
he vanished
Out of their hands.

PETER.

　　　　　　Wells are they without water,
Clouds carried with a tempest, unto
whom
The mist of darkness is reserved forever.

PHILIP.

Behold, he cometh. There is one man
with him
I am amazed to see !

ANDREW.

　　　　　　What man is that ?

PHILIP.

Judas Iscariot ; he that cometh last,
Girt with a leathern apron. No one
knoweth

His history; but the rumor of him is
He had an unclean spirit in his youth.
It hath not left him yet.

CHRISTUS, *passing.*

Come unto me,
All ye that labor and are heavy laden,
And I will give you rest! Come unto
me,
And take my yoke upon you and learn
of me,
For I am meek, and I am lowly in
heart,
And ye shall all find rest unto your
souls!

PHILIP.

Oh, there is something in that voice
that reaches
The innermost recesses of my spirit!
I feel that it might say unto the blind:
Receive your sight! and straightway
they would see!
I feel that it might say unto the dead,
Arise! and they would hear it and
obey!
Behold, he beckons to us!

CHRISTUS *to* PETER *and* ANDREW.

Follow me!

PETER.

Master, I will leave all and follow thee.

VII.

THE DEMONIAC OF GADARA.

A GADARENE.

He hath escaped, hath plucked his
chains asunder,
And broken his fetters; always night
and day
Is in the mountains here, and in the
tombs,
Crying aloud, and cutting himself with
stones,
Exceeding fierce, so that no man can
tame him!

THE DEMONIAC *from above, unseen.*

O Aschmedai! O Aschmedai, have
pity!

A GADARENE.

Listen! It is his voice! Go warn the
people
Just landing from the lake!

THE DEMONIAC.

O Aschmedai!
Thou angel of the bottomless pit, have
pity!
It was enough to hurl King Solomon,
On whom be peace! two hundred leagues
away
Into the country, and to make him scul-
lion
In the kitchen of the King of Maschke-
men!
Why dost thou hurl me here among
these rocks,
And cut me with these stones?

A GADARENE.

He raves and mutters
He knows not what.

THE DEMONIAC, *appearing from a tomb
among the rocks.*

The wild cock Tarnegal
Singeth to me, and bids me to the ban-
quet,
Where all the Jews shall come; for they
have slain
Behemoth the great ox, who daily
cropped
A thousand hills for food, and at a
draught
Drank up the river Jordan, and have
slain
The huge Leviathan, and stretched his
skin
Upon the high walls of Jerusalem,
And made them shine from one end of
the world
Unto the other; and the fowl Barjuchne,
Whose outspread wings eclipse the sun,
and make
Midnight at noon o'er all the continents!
And we shall drink the wine of Paradise
From Adam's cellars.

A GADARENE.

O thou unclean spirit!

THE DEMONIAC, *hurling down a stone.*

This is the wonderful Barjuchne's egg,
That fell out of her nest, and broke to
pieces
And swept away three hundred cedar-
trees,
And threescore villages! — Rabbi Elie-
zer,
How thou didst sin there in that seaport
town

When thou hadst carried safe thy chest
  of silver
Over the seven rivers for her sake !
I too have sinned beyond the reach of
  pardon.
Ye hills and mountains, pray for mercy
  on me !
Ye stars and planets, pray for mercy on
  me !
Ye sun and moon, oh pray for mercy on
  me !
CHRISTUS *and his disciples pass.*

A GADARENE.

There is a man here of Decapolis,
Who hath an unclean spirit; so that
  none
Can pass this way. He lives among
  the tombs
Up there upon the cliffs, and hurls down
  stones
On those who pass beneath.

CHRISTUS.

                        Come out of him,
Thou unclean spirit !

THE DEMONIAC.

                        What have I to do
With thee, thou Son of God ? Do not
  torment us.

CHRISTUS.

What is thy name ?

THE DEMONIAC.

            Legion ; for we are many.
Cain, the first murderer ; and the King
  Belshazzar,
And Evil Merodach of Babylon,
And Admatha, the death-cloud, prince
  of Persia ;
And Aschmedai, the angel of the pit,
And many other devils. We are Legion.
Send us not forth beyond Decapolis ;
Command us not to go into the deep !
There is a herd of swine here in the
  pastures,
Let us go into them.

CHRISTUS.

                        Come out of him,
Thou unclean spirit !

A GADARENE.

                        See, how stupefied,
How motionless he stands ! He cries no
  more ;

He seems bewildered and in silence
  stares
As one who, walking in his sleep, awakes
And knows not where he is, and looks
  about him,
And at his nakedness, and is ashamed.

THE DEMONIAC.

Why am I here alone among the tombs ?
What have they done to me, that I am
  naked ?
Ah, woe is me !

CHRISTUS.

                Go home unto thy friends
And tell them how great things the Lord
  hath done
For thee, and how He had compassion
  on thee !

A SWINEHERD, *running.*

The herds ! the herd ! O most unlucky
  day !
They were all feeding quiet in the sun,
When suddenly they started, and grew
  savage
As the wild boars of Tabor, and to-
  gether
Rushed down a precipice into the sea !
They are all drowned !

PETER.

                Thus righteously are punished
The apostate Jews, that eat the flesh of
  swine,
And broth of such abominable things !

GREEKS OF GADARA.

We sacrifice a sow unto Demeter
At the beginning of harvest, and another
To Dionysus at the vintage-time.
Therefore we prize our herds of swine,
  and count them
Not as unclean, but as things conse-
  crate
To the immortal gods. O great magi-
  cian,
Depart out of our coasts ; let us alone,
We are afraid of thee.

PETER.

                        Let us depart ;
For they that sanctify and purify
Themselves in gardens, eating flesh of
  swine,
And the abomination, and the mouse,
Shall be consumed together, saith the
  Lord !

VIII.

TALITHA CUMI.

JAIRUS *at the feet of* CHRISTUS.

O Master! I entreat thee! I implore
    thee!
My daughter lieth at the point of death;
I pray thee come and lay thy hands
    upon her,
And she shall live!

CHRISTUS.

Who was it touched my garments?

SIMON PETER.

Thou seest the multitude that throng
    and press thee,
And sayest thou: Who touched me?
'T was not I.

CHRISTUS.

Some one hath touched my garments; I
    perceive
That virtue is gone out of me.

A WOMAN.

             O Master!
Forgive me! For I said within my-
    self,
If I so much as touch his garment's
    hem,
I shall be whole.

CHRISTUS.

    Be of good comfort, daughter!
Thy faith hath made thee whole. De-
    part in peace.

A MESSENGER *from the house.*

Why troublest thou the Master? Hear-
    est thou not
The flute-players, and the voices of the
    women
Singing their lamentation? She is
    dead!

THE MINSTRELS AND MOURNERS.

We have girded ourselves with sack-
    cloth!
We have covered our heads with ashes!
For our young men die, and our maid-
    ens
Swoon in the streets of the city;
And into their mother's bosom
They pour out their souls like water!

CHRISTUS, *going in.*

Give place. Why make ye this ado,
    and weep?
She is not dead, but sleepeth.

THE MOTHER, *from within.*

           Cruel Death!
To take away from me this tender blos-
    som!
To take away my dove, my lamb, my
    darling!

THE MINSTRELS AND MOURNERS.

He hath led me and brought into dark-
    ness,
Like the dead of old in dark places!
He hath bent his bow, and hath set me
Apart as a mark for his arrow!
He hath covered himself with a cloud,
That our prayer should not pass through
    and reach him!

THE CROWD.

He stands beside her bed! He takes
    her hand!
Listen, he speaks to her!

CHRISTUS, *within.*

           Maiden, arise!

THE CROWD.

See, she obeys his voice! She stirs!
    She lives!
Her mother holds her folded in her
    arms!
O miracle of miracles! O marvel!

IX.

THE TOWER OF MAGDALA.

MARY MAGDALENE.

Companionless, unsatisfied, forlorn,
I sit here in this lonely tower, and look
Upon the lake below me, and the hills
That swoon with heat, and see as in a
    vision
All my past life unroll itself before me.
The princes and the merchants come to
    me,
Merchants of Tyre and Princes of Da-
    mascus,
And pass, and disappear, and are no
    more;
But leave behind their merchandise and
    jewels,

Their perfumes, and their gold, and
    their disgust.
I loathe them, and the very memory of
    them
Is unto me as thought of food to one
Cloyed with the luscious figs of Dalma-
    nutha !
What if hereafter, in the long hereafter
Of endless joy or pain, or joy in pain,
It were my punishment to be with them
Grown hideous and decrepit in their
    sins,
And hear them say : Thou that hast
    brought us here,
Be unto us as thou hast been of old !
I look upon this raiment that I wear,
These silks, and these embroideries, and
    they seem
Only as cerements wrapped about my
    limbs !
I look upon these rings thick set with
    pearls,
And emerald and amethyst and jasper,
And they are burning coals upon my
    flesh !
This serpent on my wrist becomes
    alive !
Away, thou viper ! and away, ye gar-
    lands,
Whose odors bring the swift remem-
    brance back
Of the unhallowed revels in these cham-
    bers !
But yesterday, — and yet it seems to
    me
Something remote, like a pathetic song
Sung long ago by minstrels in the
    street, —
But yesterday, as from this tower I
    gazed,
Over the olive and the walnut trees
Upon the lake and the white ships, and
    wondered
Whither and whence they steered, and
    who was in them,
A fisher's boat drew near the landing-
    place
Under the oleanders, and the people
Came up from it, and passed beneath
    the tower,
Close under me. In front of them, as
    leader,
Walked one of royal aspect, clothed in
    white,
Who lifted up his eyes, and looked at
    me,
And all at once the air seemed filled
    and living

With a mysterious power, that streamed
    from him,
And overflowed me with an atmosphere
Of light and love. As one entranced I
    stood,
And when I woke again, lo ! he was
    gone ;
So that I said : Perhaps it is a dream.
But from that very hour the seven de-
    mons
That had their habitation in this body
Which men call beautiful, departed
    from me !

This morning, when the first gleam of
    the dawn
Made Lebanon a glory in the air,
And all below was darkness, I beheld
An angel, or a spirit glorified,
With wind-tossed garments walking on
    the lake.
The face I could not see, but I distin-
    guished
The attitude and gesture, and I knew
'T was he that healed me. And the
    gusty wind
Brought to mine ears a voice, which
    seemed to say :
Be of good cheer ! 'T is I ! Be not
    afraid !
And from the darkness, scarcely heard,
    the answer :
If it be thou, bid me come unto thee
Upon the water ! And the voice said :
    Come !
And then I heard a cry of fear : Lord,
    save me !
As of a drowning man. And then the
    voice :
Why didst thou doubt, O thou of little
    faith !
At this all vanished, and the wind was
    hushed,
And the great sun came up above the
    hills,
And the swift-flying vapors hid them-
    selves
In caverns among the rocks ! Oh, I
    must find him
And follow him, and be with him for-
    ever !

Thou box of alabaster, in whose walls
The souls of flowers lie pent, the pre-
    cious balm
And spikenard of Arabian farms, the
    spirits
Of aromatic herbs, ethereal natures

Nursed by the sun and dew, not all un-
worthy
To bathe his consecrated feet, whose
step
Makes every threshold holy that he
crosses;
Let us go forth upon our pilgrimage,
Thou and I only! Let us search for
him
Until we find him, and pour out our
souls
Before his feet, till all that's left of us
Shall be the broken caskets that once
held us!

X.

THE HOUSE OF SIMON THE PHARISEE.

A GUEST *at table.*

Are ye deceived? Have any of the
Rulers
Believed on him? or do they know
indeed
This man to be the very Christ? How-
beit
We know whence this man is, but when
the Christ
Shall come, none knoweth whence he is.

CHRISTUS.

Whereunto shall I liken, then, the men
Of this generation? and what are they
like?
They are like children sitting in the
markets,
And calling unto one another, saying:
We have piped unto you, and ye have
not danced;
We have mourned unto you, and ye
have not wept!
This say I unto you, for John the Bap-
tist
Came neither eating bread nor drinking
wine;
Ye say he hath a devil. The Son of
Man
Eating and drinking cometh, and ye
say:
Behold a gluttonous man, and a wine-
bibber;
Behold a friend of publicans and sin-
ners!

A GUEST *aside to* SIMON.

Who is that woman yonder, gliding in
So silently behind him?

SIMON.

It is Mary,
Who dwelleth in the Tower of Magdala.

THE GUEST.

See, how she kneels there weeping, and
her tears
Fall on his feet; and her long, golden
hair
Waves to and fro and wipes them dry
again.
And now she kisses them, and from a
box
Of alabaster is anointing them
With precious ointment, filling all the
house
With its sweet odor!

SIMON, *aside.*

Oh, this man, forsooth,
Were he indeed a Prophet, would have
known
Who and what manner of woman this
may be
That toucheth him! would know she is
a sinner!

CHRISTUS.

Simon, somewhat have I to say to thee.

SIMON.

Master, say on.

CHRISTUS.

A certain creditor
Had once two debtors; and the one of
them
Owed him five hundred pence; the
other, fifty.
They having naught to pay withal, he
frankly
Forgave them both. Now tell me
which of them
Will love him most?

SIMON.

He, I suppose to whom
He most forgave.

CHRISTUS.

Yea, thou hast rightly judged.
Seest thou this woman? When thine
house I entered,
Thou gavest me no water for my feet,
But she hath washed them with her
tears, and wiped them
With her own hair. Thou gavest me
no kiss;

This woman hath not ceased, since I
came in,
To kiss my feet. My head with oil
didst thou
Anoint not; but this woman hath
anointed
My feet with ointment. Hence I say to
thee,
Her sins, which have been many, are
forgiven,
For she loved much.

THE GUESTS.

Oh, who, then, is this man
That pardoneth also sins without atonement ?

CHRISTUS.

Woman, thy faith hath saved thee ! Go
in peace !

THE SECOND PASSOVER.

I.

BEFORE THE GATES OF MACHÆRUS.

MANAHEM.

WELCOME, O wilderness, and welcome,
night
And solitude, and ye swift-flying stars
That drift with golden sands the barren
heavens,
Welcome once more ! The Angels of
the Wind
Hasten across the desert to receive me ;
And sweeter than men's voices are to me
The voices of these solitudes ; the sound
Of unseen rivulets, and the far-off cry
Of bitterns in the reeds of water-pools.
And lo ! above me, like the Prophet's
arrow
Shot from the eastern window, high in
air
The clamorous cranes go singing through
the night.
O ye mysterious pilgrims of the air,
Would I had wings that I might follow
you !

I look forth from these mountains, and
behold
The omnipotent and omnipresent night,
Mysterious as the future and the fate
That hangs o'er all men's lives ! I see
beneath me

The desert stretching to the Dead Sea
shore,
And westward, faint and far away, the
glimmer
Of torches on Mount Olivet, announ-
cing
The rising of the Moon of Passover.
Like a great cross it seems, on which
suspended,
With head bowed down in agony, I see
A human figure ! Hide, O merciful
heaven,
The awful apparition from my sight !

And thou, Machærus, lifting high and
black
Thy dreadful walls against the rising
moon,
Haunted by demons and by apparitions,
Lilith, and Jezerhara, and Bedargon,
How grim thou showest in the uncertain
light,
A palace and a prison, where King
Herod
Feasts with Herodias, while the Baptist
John
Fasts, and consumes his unavailing life !
And in thy court-yard grows the un-
tithed rue,
Huge as the olives of Gethsemane,
And ancient as the terebinth of He-
bron,
Coeval with the world. Would that its
leaves
Medicinal could purge thee of the
demons
That now possess thee, and the cunning
fox
That burrows in thy walls, contriving
mischief !

Music is heard from within.

Angels of God ! Sandalphon, thou that
weavest
The prayers of men into immortal garlands,
And thou, Metatron, who dost gather
up
Their songs, and bear them to the gates
of heaven,
Now gather up together in your hands
The prayers that fill this prison, and the
songs
That echo from the ceiling of this palace,
And lay them side by side before God's
feet !

He enters the castle.

II.

HEROD'S BANQUET-HALL.

MANAHEM.

Thou hast sent for me, O King, and I
am here.

HEROD.

Who art thou?

MANAHEM.

Manahem, the Essenian.

HEROD.

I recognize thy features, but what mean
These torn and faded garments? On
thy road
Have demons crowded thee, and rubbed
against thee,
And given thee weary knees? A cup
of wine!

MANAHEM.

The Essenians drink no wine.

HEROD.

What wilt thou, then?

MANAHEM.

Nothing.

HEROD.

Not even a cup of water?

MANAHEM.

Nothing.
Why hast thou sent for me?

HEROD.

Dost thou remember
One day when I, a schoolboy in the
streets
Of the great city, met thee on my way
To school, and thou didst say to me:
Hereafter
Thou shalt be king?

MANAHEM.

Yea, I remember it.

HEROD.

Thinking thou didst not know me, I
replied:
I am of humble birth; whereat thou,
smiling,
Didst smite me with thy hand, and
saidst again:

Thou shalt be king; and let the friendly
blows
That Manahem hath given thee on this
day
Remind thee of the fickleness of fortune.

MANAHEM.

What more?

HEROD.

No more.

MANAHEM.

Yea, for I said to thee:
It shall be well with thee if thou love
justice
And clemency towards thy fellow-men.
Hast thou done this, O King?

HEROD.

Go, ask my people.

MANAHEM.

And then, foreseeing all thy life, I
added:
But these thou wilt forget; and at the
end
Of life the Lord will punish thee.

HEROD.

The end!
When will that come? For this I sent
to thee.
How long shall I still reign? Thou
dost not answer!
Speak! shall I reign ten years?

MANAHEM.

Thou shalt reign twenty,
Nay, thirty years. I cannot name the
end.

HEROD.

Thirty? I thank thee, good Essenian!
This is my birthday, and a happier
one
Was never mine. We hold a banquet
here.
See, yonder are Herodias and her daughter.

MANAHEM, *aside*.

'T is said that devils sometimes take the
shape
Of ministering angels, clothed with air,
That they may be inhabitants of earth,
And lead man to destruction. Such are
these.

HEROD.

Knowest thou John the Baptist?

MANAHEM.

Yea, I know him;
Who knows him not?

HEROD.

Know, then, this John the Baptist
Said that it was not lawful I should
marry
My brother Philip's wife, and John the
Baptist
Is here in prison. In my father's time
Matthias Margaloth was put to death
For tearing the golden eagle from its
station
Above the Temple Gate, — a slighter
crime
Than John is guilty of. These things
are warnings
To intermeddlers not to play with eagles,
Living or dead. I think the Essenians
Are wiser, or more wary, are they not?

MANAHEM.

The Essenians do not marry.

HEROD.

Thou hast given
My words a meaning foreign to my
thought.

MANAHEM.

Let me go hence, O King!

HEROD.

Stay yet awhile,
And see the daughter of Herodias dance.
Cleopatra of Jerusalem, my mother,
In her best days, was not more beautiful.
Music. THE DAUGHTER OF HERODIAS
dances.

HEROD.

Oh. what was Miriam dancing with her
timbrel,
Compared to this one?

MANAHEM, *aside.*

O thou Angel of Death,
Dancing at funerals among the women,
When men bear out the dead! The
air is hot
And stifles me! Oh for a breath of
air!
Bid me depart, O King!

HEROD.

Not yet. Come hither,
Salome, thou enchantress! Ask of me
Whate'er thou wilt; and even unto
the half
Of all my kingdom, I will give it thee,
As the Lord liveth!

DAUGHTER OF HERODIAS, *kneeling.*

Give me here the head
Of John the Baptist on this silver
charger!

HEROD.

Not that, dear child! I dare not; for
the people
Regard John as a prophet.

DAUGHTER OF HERODIAS.

Thou hast sworn it.

HEROD.

For mine oath's sake, then. Send unto
the prison;
Let him die quickly. Oh, accursed
oath!

MANAHEM.

Bid me depart, O King!

HEROD.

Good Manahem,
Give me thy hand. I love the Essenians.
He's gone and hears me not! The
guests are dumb,
Awaiting the pale face, the silent wit-
ness.
The lamps flare; and the curtains of the
doorways
Wave to and fro as if a ghost were
passing!
Strengthen my heart, red wine of
Ascalon!

III.

UNDER THE WALLS OF MACHÆRUS.

MANAHEM, *rushing out.*

Away from this Palace of sin!
The demons, the terrible powers
Of the air, that haunt its towers
And hide in its water-spouts,
Deafen me with the din
Of their laughter and their shouts
For the crimes that are done within!

Sink back into the earth,
Or vanish into the air,
Thou castle of despair !
Let it all be but a dream
Of the things of monstrous birth,
Of the things that only seem !
White Angel of the Moon,
Onafiel ! be my guide
Out of this hateful place
Of sin and death, nor hide
In yon black cloud too soon
Thy pale and tranquil face !
       A trumpet is blown from the walls.
Hark ! hark ! It is the breath
Of the trump of doom and death,
From the battlements overhead
Like a burden of sorrow cast
On the midnight and the blast,
A wailing for the dead,
That the gusts drop and uplift !
O Herod, thy vengeance is swift !
O Herodias, thou hast been
The demon, the evil thing,
That in place of Esther the Queen,
In place of the lawful bride,
Hast lain at night by the side
Of Ahasuerus the king !
       The trumpet again.
The Prophet of God is dead !
At a drunken monarch's call,
At a dancing-woman's beck,
They have severed that stubborn neck
And into the banquet-hall
Are bearing the ghastly head !
       A body is thrown from the tower.
A torch of red
Lights the window with its glow ;
And a white mass as of snow
Is hurled into the abyss
Of the black precipice,
That yawns for it below !
O hand of the Most High,
O hand of Adonai !
Bury it, hide it away
From the birds and beasts of prey,
And the eyes of the homicide,
More pitiless than they,
As thou didst bury of yore
The body of him that died
On the mountain of Peor !
Even now I behold a sign,
A threatening of wrath divine,
A watery, wandering star,
Through whose streaming hair, and the
       white
Unfolding garments of light,
That trail behind it afar,
The constellations shine !

And the whiteness and brightness ap-
       pear
Like the Angel bearing the Seer
By the hair of his head, in the might
And rush of his vehement flight.
And I listen until I hear
From fathomless depths of the sky
The voice of his prophecy
Sounding louder and more near !

Malediction ! malediction !
May the lightnings of heaven fall
On palace and prison wall,
And their desolation be
As the day of fear and affliction,
As the day of anguish and ire,
With the burning and fuel of fire,
In the Valley of the Sea !

IV.

NICODEMUS AT NIGHT.

NICODEMUS.

The streets are silent. The dark houses
       seem
Like sepulchres, in which the sleepers
       lie
Wrapped in their shrouds, and for the
       moment dead.
The lamps are all extinguished ; only
       one
Burns steadily, and from the door its
       light
Lies like a shining gate across the street.
He waits for me. Ah, should this be
       at last
The long-expected Christ ! I see him
       there
Sitting alone, deep-buried in his thought,
As if the weight of all the world were
       resting
Upon him, and thus bowed him down.
       O Rabbi,
We know thou art a Teacher come from
       God,
For no man can perform the miracles
Thou dost perform, except the Lord be
       with him.
Thou art a Prophet, sent here to pro-
       claim
The Kingdom of the Lord. Behold in
       me
A Ruler of the Jews, who long have
       waited
The coming of that kingdom. Tell me
       of it.

CHRISTUS.

Verily, verily I say unto thee,
Except a man be born again, he cannot
Behold the Kingdom of God !

NICODEMUS.

                    Be born again ?
How can a man be born when he is
    old ?
Say, can he enter for a second time
Into his mother's womb, and so be born ?

CHRISTUS.

Verily I say unto thee, except
A man be born of water and the spirit,
He cannot enter into the Kingdom of
    God.
For that which of the flesh is born, is
    flesh ;
And that which of the spirit is born, is
    spirit.

NICODEMUS.

We Israelites from the Primeval Man
Adam Ahelion derive our bodies ;
Our souls are breathings of the Holy
    Ghost.
No more than this we know, or need to
    know.

CHRISTUS.

Then marvel not, that I said unto thee
Ye must be born again.

NICODEMUS.

                    The mystery
Of birth and death we cannot compre-
    hend.

CHRISTUS.

The wind bloweth where it listeth, and
    we hear
The sound thereof, but know not whence
    it cometh,
Nor whither it goeth.   So is every one
Born of the spirit !

NICODEMUS, *aside.*

                    How can these things be ?
He seems to speak of some vague realm
    of shadows,
Some unsubstantial kingdom of the air !
It is not this the Jews are waiting for,
Nor can this be the Christ, the Son of
    David,
Who shall deliver us !

CHRISTUS.

                    Art thou a master
Of Israel, and knowest not these things ?
We speak that we do know, and tes-
    tify
That we have seen, and ye will not
    receive
Our witness.   If I tell you earthly
    things,
And ye believe not, how shall ye be-
    lieve,
If I should tell you of things heavenly ?
And no man hath ascended up to
    heaven,
But he alone that first came down from
    heaven,
Even the Son of Man which is in
    heaven !

NICODEMUS, *aside.*

This is a dreamer of dreams ; a vision-
    ary,
Whose brain is overtasked, until he
    deems
The unseen world to be a thing sub-
    stantial,
And this we live in, an unreal vision !
And yet his presence fascinates and fills
    me
With wonder, and I feel myself ex-
    alted
Into a higher region, and become
Myself in part a dreamer of his dreams,
A seer of his visions !

CHRISTUS.

                    And as Moses
Uplifted the serpent in the wilderness,
So must the Son of Man be lifted up ;
That whosoever shall believe in Him
Shall perish not, but have eternal life.
He that believes in Him is not con-
    demned ;
He that believes not, is condemned
    already.

NICODEMUS, *aside.*

He speaketh like a Prophet of the Lord !

CHRISTUS.

This is the condemnation ; that the
    light
Is come into the world, and men loved
    darkness
Rather than light, because their deeds
    are evil !

NICODEMUS, *aside.*

Of me he speaketh! He reproveth me,
Because I come by night to question
him!

CHRISTUS.

For every one that doeth evil deeds
Hateth the light, nor cometh to the
light
Lest he should be reproved.

NICODEMUS, *aside.*

Alas, how truly
He readeth what is passing in my heart!

CHRISTUS.

But he that doeth truth comes to the
light,
So that his deeds may be made manifest,
That they are wrought in God.

NICODEMUS

Alas! alas!

V.

BLIND BARTIMEUS.

BARTIMEUS.

Be not impatient, Chilion; it is pleasant
To sit here in the shadow of the walls
Under the palms, and hear the hum of
bees,
And rumor of voices passing to and fro,
And drowsy bells of caravans on their
way
To Sidon or Damascus. This is still
The City of Palms, and yet the walls
thou seest
Are not the old walls, not the walls
where Rahab
Hid the two spies, and let them down
by cords
Out of the window, when the gates were
shut,
And it was dark. Those walls were
overthrown
When Joshua's army shouted, and the
priests
Blew with their seven trumpets.

CHILION.

When was that?

BARTIMEUS.

O my sweet rose of Jericho, I know not.
Hundreds of years ago. And over there

Beyond the river, the great prophet
Elijah
Was taken by a whirlwind up to heaven
In chariot of fire, with fiery horses.
That is the plain of Moab; and beyond it
Rise the blue summits of Mount Abarim,
Nebo and Pisgah and Peor, where Moses
Died, whom the Lord knew face to face,
and whom.
He buried in a valley, and no man
Knows of his sepulchre unto this day.

CHILION.

Would thou couldst see these places, as
I see them.

BARTIMEUS.

I have not seen a glimmer of the light
Since thou wast born. I never saw thy
face,
And yet I seem to see it; and one day
Perhaps shall see it; for there is a
Prophet
In Galilee, the Messiah, the Son of
David,
Who heals the blind, if I could only
find him.
I hear the sound of many feet approach-
ing,
And voices, like the murmur of a
crowd!
What seest thou?

CHILION.

A young man clad in white
Is coming through the gateway, and a
crowd
Of people follow.

BARTIMEUS.

Can it be the Prophet!
O neighbors, tell me who it is that
passes?

ONE OF THE CROWD.

Jesus of Nazareth.

BARTIMEUS, *crying.*

O Son of David!
Have mercy on me!

MANY OF THE CROWD.

Peace, Blind Bartimeus!
Do not disturb the Master.

BARTIMEUS, *crying more vehemently.*

Son of David,
Have mercy on me!

ONE OF THE CROWD.

See, the Master stops.
Be of good comfort; rise, He calleth
    thee !

BARTIMEUS, *casting away his cloak.*

Chilion ! good neighbors ! lead me on.

CHRISTUS.

What wilt thou
That I should do to thee ?

BARTIMEUS.

Good Lord ! my sight —
That I receive my sight !

CHRISTUS.

Receive thy sight !
Thy faith hath made thee whole !

THE CROWD.

He sees again !
CHRISTUS *passes on. The crowd gathers
    round* BARTIMEUS.

BARTIMEUS.

I see again ; but sight bewilders me !
Like a remembered dream, familiar
    things
Come back to me. I see the tender sky
Above me, see the trees, the city walls,
And the old gateway, through whose
    echoing arch
I groped so many years ; and you, my
    neighbors ;
But know you by your friendly voices
    only.
How beautiful the world is ! and how
    wide !
Oh, I am miles away, if I but look !
Where art thou, Chilion ?

CHILION.

Father, I am here.

BARTIMEUS.

Oh let me gaze upon thy face, dear
    child !
For I have only seen thee with my
    hands !
How beautiful thou art ! I should have
    known thee ;
Thou hast her eyes whom we shall see
    hereafter !
O God of Abraham ! Elion ! Adonai !
Who art thyself a Father, pardon me

If for a moment I have thee postponed
To the affections and the thoughts of
    earth,
Thee, and the adoration that I owe
    thee,
When by thy power alone these dark-
    ened eyes
Have been unsealed again to see thy
    light !

VI.

JACOB'S WELL.

A SAMARITAN WOMAN.

The sun is hot ; and the dry east-wind
    blowing
Fills all the air with dust. The birds
    are silent ;
Even the little fieldfares in the corn
No longer twitter ; only the grasshop-
    pers
Sing their incessant song of sun and
    summer.
I wonder who those strangers were I
    met
Going into the city ? Galileans
They seemed to me in speaking, when
    they asked
The short way to the market-place.
    Perhaps
They are fishermen from the lake ; or
    travellers,
Looking to find the inn. And here is
    some one
Sitting beside the well ; another stran-
    ger ;
A Galilean also by his looks.
What can so many Jews be doing here
Together in Samaria ? Are they going
Up to Jerusalem to the Passover ?
Our Passover is better here at Sychem,
For here is Ebal ; here is Gerizim,
The mountain where our father Abra-
    ham
Went up to offer Isaac ; here the tomb
Of Joseph, — for they brought his bones
    from Egypt
And buried them in this land, and it is
    holy.

CHRISTUS.

Give me to drink.

SAMARITAN WOMAN.

How can it be that thou,
Being a Jew, askest to drink of me

Which am a woman of Samaria ?
You Jews despise us ; have no dealings
  with us ;
Make us a byword ; call us in derision
The silly folk of Sychar.   Sir, how is
  it
Thou askest drink of me ?

CHRISTUS.

                  If thou hadst known
The gift of God, and who it is that
  sayeth
Give me to drink, thou wouldst have
  asked of Him ;
He would have given thee the living
  water.

SAMARITAN WOMAN.

Sir, thou hast naught to draw with, and
  the well
Is deep ! Whence hast thou living
  water ?
Say, art thou greater than our father
  Jacob,
Which gave this well to us, and drank
  thereof
Himself, and all his children and his
  cattle ?

CHRISTUS.

Ah, whosoever drinketh of this water
Shall thirst again ; but whosoever
  drinketh
The water I shall give him shall not
  thirst
Forevermore, for it shall be within him
A well of living water, springing up
Into life everlasting.

SAMARITAN WOMAN.

                  Every day
I must go to and fro, in heat and cold,
And I am weary.   Give me of this
  water,
That I may thirst not, nor come here to
  draw.

CHRISTUS.

Go call thy husband, woman, and come
  hither.

SAMARITAN WOMAN.

I have no husband, Sir.

CHRISTUS.

                  Thou hast well said
I have no husband.   Thou hast had five
  husbands ;

And he whom now thou hast is not thy
  husband.

SAMARITAN WOMAN.

Surely thou art a Prophet, for thou
  readest
The hidden things of life !   Our fathers
  worshipped
Upon this mountain Gerizim ; and ye
  say
The only place in which men ought to
  worship
Is at Jerusalem.

CHRISTUS.

                  Believe me, woman,
The hour is coming, when ye neither
  shall
Upon this mount, nor at Jerusalem,
Worship the Father ; for the hour is
  coming,
And is now come, when the true wor-
  shippers
Shall worship the Father in spirit and
  in truth !
The Father seeketh such to worship
  Him.
God is a spirit ; and they that worship
  Him
Must worship Him in spirit and in truth.

SAMARITAN WOMAN.

Master, I know that the Messiah cometh,
Which is called Christ ; and he will tell
  us all things.

CHRISTUS.

I that speak unto thee am He !

THE DISCIPLES, *returning.*

                  Behold,
The Master sitting by the well, and
  talking
With a Samaritan woman !   With a
  woman
Of Sychar, the silly people, always
  boasting
Of their Mount Ebal, and Mount Geri-
  zim,
Their Everlasting Mountain, which they
  think
Higher and holier than our Mount
  Moriah !
Why, once upon the Feast of the New
  Moon,
When our great Sanhedrim of Jerusalem
Had all its watch-fires kindled on the
  hills

To warn the distant villages, these
    people
Lighted up others to mislead the Jews,
And make a mockery of their festival!
See, she has left the Master; and is
    running
Back to the city!

SAMARITAN WOMAN.

                Oh, come see a man
Who hath told me all things that I ever
    did!
Say, is not this the Christ?

THE DISCIPLES.

                Lo, Master, here
Is food, that we have brought thee from
    the city.
We pray thee eat it.

CHRISTUS.

                I have food to eat
Ye know not of.

THE DISCIPLES, *to each other.*

        Hath any man been here,
And brought Him aught to eat, while
    we were gone?

CHRISTUS.

The food I speak of is to do the will
Of Him that sent me, and to finish his
    work.
Do ye not say, Lo! there are yet four
    months
And cometh harvest? I say unto you,
Lift up your eyes, and look upon the
    fields,
For they are white already unto har-
    vest!

VII.

THE COASTS OF CÆSAREA PHILIPPI.

CHRISTUS, *going up the mountain.*

Who do the people say I am?

JOHN.

                Some say
That thou art John the Baptist; some,
    Elias;
And others Jeremiah.

JAMES.

                Or that one
Of the old Prophets is risen again.

CHRISTUS.

But who say ye I am?

PETER.

                Thou art the Christ!
Thou art the Son of God!

CHRISTUS.

                Blessed art thou,
Simon Barjona! Flesh and blood hath
    not
Revealed it unto thee, but even my
    Father,
Which is in Heaven. And I say unto
    thee
That thou art Peter; and upon this
    rock
I build my Church, and all the gates of
    Hell
Shall not prevail against it. But take
    heed
Ye tell no man that I am the Christ.
For I must go up to Jerusalem,
And suffer many things, and be re-
    jected
Of the Chief Priests, and of the Scribes
    and Elders,
And must be crucified, and the third
    day
Shall rise again!

PETER.

        Be it far from thee, Lord!
This shall not be!

CHRISTUS.

        Get thee behind me, Satan!
Thou savorest not the things that be of
    God,
But those that be of men! If any will
Come after me, let him deny himself,
And daily take his cross, and follow me.
For whosoever will save his life shall
    lose it,
And whosoever will lose his life shall
    find it.
For wherein shall a man be profited
If he shall gain the whole world, and
    shall lose
Himself or be a castaway?

JAMES, *after a long pause.*

                Why doth
The Master lead us up into this moun-
    tain?

PETER.

He goeth up to pray.

JOHN.

See where He standeth
Above us on the summit of the hill!
His face shines as the sun! and all his
    raiment
Exceeding white as snow, so as no
    fuller
On earth can white them! He is not
    alone;
There are two with him there; two
    men of eld,
Their white beards blowing on the
    mountain air,
Are talking with him.

JAMES.

I am sore afraid!

PETER.

Who and whence are they?

JOHN.

Moses and Elias!

PETER.

O Master! it is good for us to be here!
If thou wilt, let us make three taberna-
    cles;
For thee one, and for Moses and Elias!

JOHN.

Behold a bright cloud sailing in the
    sun!
It overshadows us. A golden mist
Now hides them from us, and envelops
    us
And all the mountains in a luminous
    shadow!
I see no more. The nearest rocks are
    hidden.

VOICE *from the cloud.*

Lo! this is my beloved Son! Hear
    Him!

PETER.

It is the voice of God. He speaketh to
    us,
As from the burning bush He spake to
    Moses!

JOHN.

The cloud-wreaths roll away. The veil
    is lifted;
We see again. Behold! He is alone.
It was a vision that our eyes beheld,
And it hath vanished into the unseen.

CHRISTUS, *coming down from the moun-
    tain.*

I charge ye, tell the vision unto no one,
Till the Son of Man is risen from the
    dead!

PETER, *aside.*

Again He speaks of it! What can it
    mean,
This rising from the dead?

JAMES.

Why say the Scribes
Elias must first come?

CHRISTUS.

He cometh first,
Restoring all things. But I say to you,
That this Elias is already come.
They knew him not, but have done unto
    him
Whate'er they listed, as is written of
    him.

PETER, *aside.*

It is of John the Baptist He is speak-
    ing.

JAMES.

As we descend, see, at the mountain's
    foot,
A crowd of people; coming, going,
    thronging
Round the disciples, that we left behind
    us,
Seeming impatient, that we stay so long.

PETER.

It is some blind man, or some paralytic
That waits the Master's coming to be
    healed.

JAMES.

I see a boy, who struggles and demeans
    him
As if an unclean spirit tormented him!

A CERTAIN MAN, *running forward.*

Lord! I beseech thee, look upon my
    son.
He is mine only child; a lunatic,
And sorely vexed; for oftentimes he
    falleth
Into the fire and oft into the water.
Wherever the dumb spirit taketh him
He teareth him. He gnasheth with his
    teeth,

And pines away. I spake to thy dis-
    ciples
That they should cast him out, and they
    could not.

CHRISTUS.

O faithless generation and perverse !
How long shall I be with you, and suffer
    you ?
Bring thy son hither.

BYSTANDERS.

        How the unclean spirit
Seizes the boy, and tortures him with
    pain !
He falleth to the ground and wallows,
    foaming !
He cannot live.

CHRISTUS.

        How long is it ago
Since this came unto him ?

THE FATHER.

        Even of a child.
Oh, have compassion on us, Lord, and
    help us,
If thou canst help us.

CHRISTUS.

        If thou canst believe.
For unto him that verily believeth,
All things are possible.

THE FATHER.

        Lord, I believe !
Help thou mine unbelief !

CHRISTUS.

        Dumb and deaf spirit,
Come out of him, I charge thee, and no
    more
Enter thou into him !

*The boy utters a loud cry of pain, and
    then lies still.*

BYSTANDERS.

        How motionless
He lieth there. No life is left in him.
His eyes are like a blind man's, that see
    not.
The boy is dead !

OTHERS.

        Behold ! the Master stoops,
And takes him by the hand, and lifts
    him up.
He is not dead.

DISCIPLES.

        But one word from those lips,
But one touch of that hand, and he is
    healed !
Ah, why could we not do it ?

THE FATHER.

        My poor child !
Now thou art mine again. The un-
    clean spirit
Shall never more torment thee ! Look
    at me !
Speak unto me ! Say that thou know-
    est me !

DISCIPLES *to* CHRISTUS *departing.*

Good Master, tell us, for what reason
    was it
We could not cast him out ?

CHRISTUS.

        Because of your unbelief !

VIII.

THE YOUNG RULER.

CHRISTUS.

Two men went up into the temple to
    pray.
The one was a self-righteous Pharisee,
The other a Publican. And the Phar-
    isee
Stood and prayed thus within himself :
    O God,
I thank thee I am not as other men,
Extortioners, unjust, adulterers,
Or even as this Publican. I fast
Twice in the week, and also I give
    tithes
Of all that I possess ! The Publican,
Standing afar off, would not lift so
    much
Even as his eyes to heaven, but smote
    his breast,
Saying : God be merciful to me a sinner !
I tell you that this man went to his
    house
More justified than the other. Every
    one
That doth exalt himself shall be abased,
And he that humbleth himself shall be
    exalted !

CHILDREN, *among themselves.*

Let us go nearer ! He is telling stories !
Let us go listen to them.

AN OLD JEW.

Children, children!
What are ye doing here? Why do ye
   crowd us?
It was such little vagabonds as you
That followed Elisha, mocking him and
   crying:
Go up, thou bald-head! But the bears
   — the bears
Came out of the wood, and tare them!

A MOTHER.

Speak not thus!
We brought them here, that He might
   lay his hands
On them, and bless them.

CHRISTUS.

Suffer little children
To come unto me, and forbid them
   not;
Of such is the kingdom of heaven; and
   their angels
Look always on my Father's face.

Takes them in his arms and blesses them.

A YOUNG RULER, *running.*

Good Master!
What good thing shall I do, that I may
   have
Eternal life?

CHRISTUS.

Why callest thou me good?
There is none good but one, and that is
   God.
If thou wilt enter into life eternal,
Keep the commandments.

YOUNG RULER.

Which of them?

CHRISTUS.

Thou shalt not
Commit adultery; thou shalt not kill;
Thou shalt not steal; thou shalt not
   bear false witness;
Honor thy father and thy mother; and
   love
Thy neighbor as thyself.

YOUNG RULER.

From my youth up
All these things have I kept. What
   lack I yet?

JOHN.

With what divine compassion in his
   eyes
The Master looks upon this eager
   youth,
As if he loved him!

CHRISTUS.

Wouldst thou perfect be,
Sell all thou hast, and give it to the
   poor,
And come, take up thy cross, and follow
   me,
And thou shalt have thy treasure in the
   heavens.

JOHN.

Behold, how sorrowful he turns away!

CHRISTUS.

Children! how hard it is for them that
   trust
In riches to enter into the kingdom of
   God!
'T is easier for a camel to go through
A needle's eye, than for the rich to enter
The kingdom of God!

JOHN.

Ah, who then can be saved?

CHRISTUS.

With men this is indeed impossible,
But unto God all things are possible!

PETER.

Behold, we have left all, and followed
   thee.
What shall we have therefor?

CHRISTUS.

Eternal life.

IX.

AT BETHANY.

MARTHA *busy about household affairs.*
MARY *sitting at the feet of* CHRISTUS.

MARTHA.

She sitteth idly at the Master's feet,
And troubles not herself with household cares.
'T is the old story. When a guest
   arrives

She gives up all to be with him; while I
Must be the drudge, make ready the
          guest-chamber,
Prepare the food, set everything in
          order,
And see that naught is wanting in the
          house.
She shows her love by words, and I by
          works.

MARY.

O Master! when thou comest, it is
          always
A Sabbath in the house. I cannot
          work;
I must sit at thy feet; must see thee,
          hear thee!
I have a feeble, wayward, doubting
          heart,
Incapable of endurance or great
          thoughts,
Striving for something that it cannot
          reach,
Baffled and disappointed, wounded,
          hungry;
And only when I hear thee am I happy,
And only when I see thee am at peace!
Stronger than I, and wiser, and far
          better
In every manner, is my sister Martha.
Thou seest how well she orders every-
          thing
To make thee welcome; how she comes
          and goes,
Careful and cumbered ever with much
          serving,
While I but welcome thee with foolish
          words!
Whene'er thou speakest to me, I am
          happy;
When thou art silent, I am satisfied.
Thy presence is enough. I ask no
          more.
Only to be with thee, only to see thee,
Sufficeth me. My heart is then at rest.
I wonder I am worthy of so much.

MARTHA.

Lord, dost thou care not that my sister
          Mary
Hath left me thus to wait on thee
          alone?
I pray thee, bid her help me.

CHRISTUS.

                    Martha, Martha,
Careful and troubled about many things

Art thou, and yet one thing alone is
          needful!
Thy sister Mary hath chosen that good
          part,
Which never shall be taken away from
          her!

X.

BORN BLIND.

A JEW.

Who is this beggar blinking in the sun ?
Is it not he who used to sit and beg
By the Gate Beautiful ?

ANOTHER.

                    It is the same.

A THIRD.

It is not he, but like him, for that
          beggar
Was blind from birth. It cannot be the
          same.

THE BEGGAR.

Yea, I am he.

A JEW.

          How have thine eyes been opened ?

THE BEGGAR.

A man that is called Jesus made a clay
And put it on mine eyes, and said to
          me :
Go to Siloam's Pool and wash thyself.
I went and washed, and I received my
          sight.

A JEW.

Where is he ?

THE BEGGAR.

          I know not.

PHARISEES.

                    What is this crowd
Gathered about a beggar? What has
          happened ?

A JEW.

Here is a man who hath been blind from
          birth,
And now he sees. He says a man
          called Jesus
Hath healed him.

PHARISEES.

As God liveth, the Nazarene!
How was this done?

THE BEGGAR.

Rabboni, he put clay
Upon mine eyes; I washed, and now I
see.

PHARISEES.

When did he this?

THE BEGGAR.

Rabboni, yesterday.

PHARISEES.

The Sabbath day. This man is not of
God,
Because he keepeth not the Sabbath
day!

A JEW.

How can a man that is a sinner do
Such miracles?

PHARISEES.

What dost thou say of him
That hath restored thy sight?

THE BEGGAR.

He is a Prophet.

A JEW.

This is a wonderful story, but not true,
A beggar's fiction. He was not born
blind,
And never has been blind!

OTHERS.

Here are his parents.
Ask them.

PHARISEES.

Is this your son?

THE PARENTS.

Rabboni, yea;
We know this is our son.

PHARISEES.

Was he born blind?

THE PARENTS.

He was born blind.

PHARISEES.

Then how doth he now see?

THE PARENTS, *aside.*

What answer shall we make? If we
confess
It was the Christ, we shall be driven
forth
Out of the Synagogue!
We know, Rabboni,
This is our son, and that he was born
blind;
But by what means he seeth, we know
not,
Or who his eyes hath opened, we know
not.
He is of age; ask him; we cannot say;
He shall speak for himself.

PHARISEES.

Give God the praise!
We know the man that healed thee is a
sinner!

THE BEGGAR.

Whether He be a sinner, I know not;
One thing I know; that whereas I was
blind,
I now do see.

PHARISEES.

How opened he thine eyes?
What did he do?

THE BEGGAR.

I have already told you.
Ye did not hear: why would ye hear
again?
Will ye be his disciples?

PHARISEES.

God of Moses!
Are we demoniacs, are we halt or blind,
Or palsy-stricken, or lepers, or the like,
That we should join the Synagogue of
Satan,
And follow jugglers? Thou art his
disciple,
But we are disciples of Moses; and we
know
That God spake unto Moses; but this
fellow,
We know not whence he is!

THE BEGGAR.

Why, herein is
A marvellous thing! Ye know not
whence he is,
Yet he hath opened mine eyes! We
know that God

Heareth not sinners; but if any man
Doeth God's will, and is his worship-
  per,
Him doth he hear. Oh, since the world
  began
It was not heard that any man hath
  opened
The eyes of one that was born blind.
  If He
Were not of God, surely he could do
  nothing !

PHARISEES.

Thou, who wast altogether born in sins
And in iniquities, dost thou teach us ?
Away with thee out of the holy places,
Thou reprobate, thou beggar, thou blas-
  phemer !

THE BEGGAR *is cast out.*

XI.

SIMON MAGUS AND HELEN OF TYRE.

*On the house-top at Endor. Night. A
lighted lantern on a table.*

SIMON.

Swift are the blessed Immortals to the
  mortal
That perseveres ! So doth it stand re-
  corded
In the divine Chaldæan Oracles
Of Zoroaster, once Ezekiel's slave,
Who in his native East betook himself
To lonely meditation, and the writing
On the dried skins of oxen the Twelve
  Books
Of the Avesta and the Oracles !
Therefore I persevere; and I have
  brought thee
From the great city of Tyre, where men
  deride
The things they comprehend not, to
  this plain
Of Esdraelon, in the Hebrew tongue
Called Armageddon, and this town of
  Endor,
Where men believe; where all the air is
  full
Of marvellous traditions, and the En-
  chantress
That summoned up the ghost of Samuel
Is still remembered. Thou hast seen
  the land ;
Is it not fair to look on ?

HELEN.

                        It is fair,
Yet not so fair as Tyre.

SIMON.

                        Is not Mount Tabor
As beautiful as Carmel by the Sea ?

HELEN.

It is too silent and too solitary ;
I miss the tumult of the street; the
  sounds
Of traffic, and the going to and fro
Of people in gay attire, with cloaks of
  purple,
And gold and silver jewelry !

SIMON.

                        Inventions
Of Ahriman, the spirit of the dark,
The Evil Spirit !

HELEN.

                I regret the gossip
Of friends and neighbors at the open
  door
On summer nights.

SIMON.

                An idle waste of time.

HELEN.

The singing and the dancing, the delight
Of music and of motion. Woe is me,
To give up all these pleasures, and to
  lead
The life we lead !

SIMON.

                Thou canst not raise thyself
Up to the level of my higher thought,
And though possessing thee, I still re
  main
Apart from thee, and with thee, am
  alone
In my high dreams.

HELEN.

                Happier was I in Tyre.
Oh, I remember how the gallant ships
Came sailing in, with ivory, gold, and
  silver,
And apes and peacocks ; and the singing
  sailors,
And the gay captains with their silken
  dresses,
Smelling of aloes, myrrh, and cinnamon !

SIMON.

But the dishonor, Helen! Let the ships
Of Tarshish howl for that!

HELEN.

And what dishonor?
Remember Rahab, and how she became
The ancestress of the great Psalmist
David;
And wherefore should not I, Helen of
Tyre,
Attain like honor?

SIMON.

Thou art Helen of Tyre,
And hast been Helen of Troy, and hast
been Rahab,
The Queen of Sheba, and Semiramis,
And Sara of seven husbands, and Jezebel,
And other women of the like allure-
ments;
And now thou art Minerva, the first
Æon,
The Mother of Angels!

HELEN.

And the concubine
Of Simon the Magician! Is it honor
For one who has been all these noble
dames,
To tramp about the dirty villages
And cities of Samaria with a juggler?
A charmer of serpents?

SIMON.

He who knows himself
Knows all things in himself. I have
charmed thee,
Thou beautiful asp: yet am I no ma-
gician.
I am the Power of God, and the Beauty
of God!
I am the Paraclete, the Comforter!

HELEN.

Illusions! Thou deceiver, self-deceived!
Thou dost usurp the titles of another;
Thou art not what thou sayest.

SIMON.

Am I not?
Then feel my power.

HELEN.

Would I had ne'er left Tyre!
*He looks at her, and she sinks into a deep
sleep.*

SIMON.

Go, see it in thy dreams, fair unbeliever!
And leave me unto mine, if they be
dreams,
That take such shapes before me, that I
see them;
These effable and ineffable impressions
Of the mysterious world, that come to
me
From the elements of Fire and Earth
and Water,
And the all-nourishing Ether! It is
written,
Look not on Nature, for her name is
fatal!
Yet there are Principles, that make ap-
parent
The images of unapparent things,
And the impression of vague charac-
ters
And visions most divine appear in ether.
So speak the Oracles; then wherefore
fatal?
I take this orange-bough, with its five
leaves,
Each equidistant on the upright stem;
And I project them on a plane below,
In the circumference of a circle drawn
About a centre where the stem is planted,
And each still equidistant from the other,
As if a thread of gossamer were drawn
Down from each leaf, and fastened with
a pin.
Now if from these five points a line be
traced
To each alternate point, we shall obtain
The Pentagram, or Solomon's Pentan-
gle,
A charm against all witchcraft, and a
sign,
Which on the banner of Antiochus
Drove back the fierce barbarians of the
North,
Demons esteemed, and gave the Syrian
King
The sacred name of Soter, or of Savior.
Thus Nature works mysteriously with
man;
And from the Eternal One, as from a
centre,
All things proceed, in fire, air, earth,
and water,
And all are subject to one law, which,
broken
Even in a single point, is broken in
all;
Demons rush in, and chaos comes again.

By this will I compel the stubborn spirits,
That guard the treasures, hid in caverns
    deep
On Gerizim, by Uzzi the High-Priest,
The ark and holy vessels, to reveal
Their secret unto me, and to restore
These precious things to the Samaritans.
A mist is rising from the plain below
    me,
And as I look, the vapors shape them-
    selves
Into strange figures, as if unawares
My lips had breathed the Tetragramma-
    ton,
And from their graves, o'er all the
    battlefields
Of Armageddon, the long-buried cap-
    tains
Had started, with their thousands, and
    ten thousands,
And rushed together to renew their
    wars,
Powerless, and weaponless, and without
    a sound !
Wake, Helen, from thy sleep ! The
    air grows cold ;
Let us go down.

HELEN, *awaking*.

                    Oh, would I were at home !

SIMON.

Thou sayest that I usurp another's
    titles.
In youth I saw the Wise Men of the
    East,
Magalath and Pangalath and Saracen,
Who followed the bright star, but home
    returned
For fear of Herod by another way.
O shining worlds above me ! in what
    deep
Recesses of your realms of mystery
Lies hidden now that star ? and where
    are they
That brought the gifts of frankincense
    and myrrh ?

HELEN.

The Nazarene still liveth.

SIMON.

                    We have heard
His name in many towns, but have not
    seen Him.
He flits before us ; tarries not ; is gone
When we approach, like something un-
    substantial,

Made of the air, and fading into air.
He is at Nazareth, He is at Nain,
Or at the Lovely Village on the Lake,
Or sailing on its waters.

HELEN.

                    So say those
Who do not wish to find Him.

SIMON.

                    Can this be
The King of Israel, whom the Wise
    Men worshipped ?
Or does He fear to meet me ?   It would
    seem so.
We should soon learn which of us twain
    usurps
The titles of the other, as thou sayest.

    They go down.

THE THIRD PASSOVER.

I.

THE ENTRY INTO JERUSALEM.

THE SYRO-PHŒNICIAN WOMAN *and
her* DAUGHTER *on the house-top at
Jerusalem.*

THE DAUGHTER, *singing*.

BLIND Bartimeus at the gates
Of Jericho in darkness waits ;
He hears the crowd ; — he hears a
    breath
Say, It is Christ of Nazareth !
And calls, in tones of agony,
Ἰησοῦ ἐλέησόν με !

The thronging multitudes increase :
Blind Bartimeus, hold thy peace !
But still, above the noisy crowd,
The beggar's cry is shrill and loud ;
Until they say, he calleth thee !
Θάρσει · ἔγειραι, φωνεῖ σε !

Then saith the Christ, as silent stands
The crowd, What wilt thou at my
    hands ?
And he replies, Oh, give me light !
Rabbi, restore the blind man's sight !
And Jesus answers, Ὕπαγε ·
Ἡ πίστις σου σέσωκέ σε !

Ye that have eyes, yet cannot see,
In darkness and in misery,
Recall those mighty voices three,

Ἰησοῦ, ἐλέησόν με!
Θάρσει · ἔγειραι, ὕπαγε!
Ἡ πίστις σου σέσωκέ σε!

THE MOTHER.

Thy faith hath saved thee! Ah, how
    true that is!
For I had faith; and when the Master
    came
Into the coasts of Tyre and Sidon, fleeing
From those who sought to slay him, I
    went forth
And cried unto Him, saying: Have
    mercy on me,
O Lord, thou Son of David! for my
    daughter
Is grievously tormented with a devil.
But he passed on, and answered not a
    word.
And his disciples said, beseeching Him:
Send her away! She crieth after us!
And then the Master answered them
    and said:
I am not sent but unto the lost sheep
Of the House of Israel! Then I wor-
    shipped Him,
Saying: Lord help me! And He an-
    swered me,
It is not meet to take the children's
    bread
And cast it unto dogs! Truth, Lord, I
    said;
And yet the dogs may eat the crumbs
    which fall
From off their master's table; and He
    turned,
And answered me; and said to me: O
    woman,
Great is thy faith; then be it unto thee
Even as thou wilt. And from that very
    hour
Thou wast made whole, my darling!
    my delight!

THE DAUGHTER.

There came upon my dark and troubled
    mind
A calm, as when the tumult of the city
Suddenly ceases, and I lie and hear
The silver trumpets of the Temple
    blowing
Their welcome to the Sabbath. Still I
    wonder,
That one who was so far away from me
And could not see me, by his thought
    alone
Had power to heal me. Oh that I
    could see Him!

THE MOTHER.

Perhaps thou wilt; for I have brought
    thee here
To keep the holy Passover, and lay
Thine offering of thanksgiving on the
    altar.
Thou mayst both see and hear Him.
    Hark!

VOICES *afar off.*

Hosanna!

THE DAUGHTER.

A crowd comes pouring through the
    city gate!
O mother, look!

VOICES *in the street.*

Hosanna to the Son
Of David!

THE DAUGHTER.

A great multitude of people
Fills all the street; and riding on an
    ass
Comes one of noble aspect, like a king!
The people spread their garments in the
    way,
And scatter branches of the palm-trees!

VOICES.

Blessed
Is He that cometh in the name of the
    Lord!
Hosanna in the highest!

OTHER VOICES.

Who is this?

VOICES.

Jesus of Nazareth!

THE DAUGHTER.

Mother, it is he!

VOICES.

He hath called Lazarus of Bethany
Out of his grave, and raised him from
    the dead!
Hosanna in the highest!

PHARISEES.

Ye perceive
That nothing we prevail. Behold, the
    world
Is all gone after him!

THE DAUGHTER.

What majesty,
What power is in that care-worn countenance!
What sweetness, what compassion! I no longer
Wonder that he hath healed me!

VOICES.

Peace in heaven,
And glory in the highest!

PHARISEES.

Rabbi! Rabbi!
Rebuke thy followers!

CHRISTUS.

Should they hold their peace
The very stones beneath us would cry out!

THE DAUGHTER.

All hath passed by me like a dream of wonder!
But I have seen Him, and have heard his voice,
And I am satisfied! I ask no more!

II.

SOLOMON'S PORCH.

GAMALIEL THE SCRIBE.

When Rabban Simeon — upon whom be peace! —
Taught in these Schools, he boasted that his pen
Had written no word that he could call his own,
But wholly and always had been consecrated
To the transcribing of the Law and Prophets.
He used to say, and never tired of saying,
The world itself was built upon the Law.
And ancient Hillel said, that whosoever
Gains a good name gains something for himself,
But he who gains a knowledge of the Law
Gains everlasting life. And they spake truly.

Great is the Written Law; but greater still
The Unwritten, the Traditions of the Elders,
The lovely words of Levites, spoken first
To Moses on the Mount, and handed down
From mouth to mouth, in one unbroken sound
And sequence of divine authority,
The voice of God resounding through the ages.

The Written Law is water; the Unwritten
Is precious wine; the Written Law is salt,
The Unwritten costly spice; the Written Law
Is but the body; the Unwritten, the soul
That quickens it and makes it breathe and live.
I can remember, many years ago,
A little bright-eyed school-boy, a mere stripling,
Son of a Galilean carpenter,
From Nazareth, I think, who came one day
And sat here in the Temple with the Scribes,
Hearing us speak, and asking many questions,
And we were all astonished at his quickness.
And when his mother came, and said: Behold
Thy father and I have sought thee, sorrowing;
He looked as one astonished, and made answer,
How is it that ye sought me? Wist ye not
That I must be about my Father's business?
Often since then I see him here among us,
Or dream I see him, with his upraised face
Intent and eager, and I often wonder
Unto what manner of manhood he hath grown!
Perhaps a poor mechanic like his father,
Lost in his little Galilean village
And toiling at his craft, to die unknown
And be no more remembered among men.

CHRISTUS, *in the outer court.*

The Scribes and Pharisees sit in Moses'
seat;
All, therefore, whatsoever they command
you,
Observe and do; but follow not their
works;
They say and do not. They bind heavy
burdens
And very grievous to be borne, and lay
them
Upon men's shoulders, but they move
them not
With so much as a finger!

GAMALIEL, *looking forth.*

Who is this
Exhorting in the outer courts so loudly?

CHRISTUS.

Their works they do for to be seen of
men.
They make broad their phylacteries,
and enlarge
The borders of their garments, and they
love
The uppermost rooms at feasts, and the
chief seats
In Synagogues, and greetings in the
markets,
And to be called of all men Rabbi,
Rabbi!

GAMALIEL.

It is that loud and turbulent Galilean,
That came here at the Feast of Dedica-
tion,
And stirred the people up to break the
Law!

CHRISTUS.

Woe unto you, ye Scribes and Pharisees,
Ye hypocrites! for ye shut up the kingdom
Of heaven, and neither go ye in yourselves
Nor suffer them that are entering to go
in!

GAMALIEL.

How eagerly the people throng and
listen,
As if his ribald words were words of
wisdom!

CHRISTUS.

Woe unto you, ye Scribes and Pharisees,

Ye hypocrites! for ye devour the houses
Of widows, and for pretence ye make
long prayers;
Therefore shall ye receive the more
damnation.

GAMALIEL.

This brawler is no Jew, — he is a vile
Samaritan, and hath an unclean spirit!

CHRISTUS.

Woe unto you, ye Scribes and Phari-
sees,
Ye hypocrites! ye compass sea and land
To make one proselyte, and when he is
made
Ye make him twofold more the child of
hell
Than you yourselves are!

GAMALIEL.

O my father's father!
Hillel of blessed memory, hear and
judge!

CHRISTUS.

Woe unto you, ye Scribes and Pharisees,
Ye hypocrites! for ye pay tithe of mint,
Of anise, and of cumin, and omit
The weightier matters of the law of
God,
Judgment and faith and mercy; and all
these
Ye ought to have done, nor leave undone
the others!

GAMALIEL.

O Rabban Simeon! how must thy bones
Stir in their grave to hear such blasphemies!

CHRISTUS.

Woe unto you, ye Scribes, and Pharisees,
Ye hypocrites! for ye make clean and
sweet
The outside of the cup and of the
platter,
But they within are full of all excess!

GAMALIEL.

Patience of God! canst thou endure so
long?
Or art thou deaf, or gone upon a journey?

CHRISTUS.

Woe unto you, ye Scribes and Pharisees,
Ye hypocrites! for ye are very like

To whited sepulchres, which indeed appear
Beautiful outwardly, but are within
Filled full of dead men's bones and all
    uncleanness!

GAMALIEL.

Am I awake? Is this Jerusalem?
And are these Jews that throng and
    stare and listen?

CHRISTUS.

Woe unto you, ye Scribes and Pharisees,
Ye hypocrites! because ye build the
    tombs
Of prophets, and adorn the sepulchres
Of righteous men, and say: If we had
    lived
When lived our fathers, we would not
    have been
Partakers with them in the blood of
    Prophets.
So ye be witnesses unto yourselves,
That ye are children of them that
    killed the Prophets!
Fill ye up then the measure of your
    fathers.
I send unto you Prophets and Wise
    Men,
And Scribes, and some ye crucify, and
    some
Scourge in your Synagogues, and persecute
From city to city; that on you may
    come
The righteous blood that hath been shed
    on earth,
From the blood of righteous Abel to
    the blood
Of Zacharias, son of Barachias,
Ye slew between the Temple and the
    altar!

GAMALIEL.

Oh, had I here my subtle dialectician,
My little Saul of Tarsus, the tentmaker,
Whose wit is sharper than his needle's
    point,
He would delight to foil this noisy
    wrangler!

CHRISTUS.

Jerusalem! Jerusalem! O thou
That killest the Prophets, and that
    stonest them
Which are sent unto thee, how often
    would I

Have gathered together thy children, as
    a hen
Gathereth her chickens underneath her
    wing,
And ye would not! Behold, your house
    is left
Unto you desolate!

THE PEOPLE.

           This is a Prophet!
This is the Christ that was to come!

GAMALIEL.

             Ye fools!
Think ye, shall Christ come out of
    Galilee?

III.

LORD, IS IT I?

CHRISTUS.

One of you shall betray me.

THE DISCIPLES.

             Is it I?
Lord, is it I?

CHRISTUS.

      One of the Twelve it is
That dippeth with me in this dish his
    hand;
He shall betray me. Lo, the Son of
    Man
Goeth indeed as it is written of Him;
But woe shall be unto that man by
    whom
He is betrayed! Good were it for that
    man
If he had ne'er been born!

JUDAS ISCARIOT.

           Lord, is it I?

CHRISTUS.

Ay, thou hast said. And that thou
    doest, do quickly.

JUDAS ISCARIOT, *going out.*

Ah, woe is me!

CHRISTUS.

        All ye shall be offended
Because of me this night; for it is
    written:
Awake, O sword, against my shepherd!
    Smite

The shepherd, saith the Lord of hosts,
and scattered
Shall be the sheep! — But after I am
risen
I go before you into Galilee.

PETER.

O Master! though all men shall be offended
Because of thee, yet will not I be!

CHRISTUS.

Simon,
Behold how Satan hath desired to have
you,
That he may sift you as one sifteth
wheat!
Whither I go thou canst not follow
me —
Not now; but thou shalt follow me
hereafter.

PETER.

Wherefore can I not follow thee? I
am ready
To go with thee to prison and to death.

CHRISTUS.

Verily I say unto thee, this night,
Ere the cock crow, thou shalt deny me
thrice!

PETER.

Though I should die, yet will I not
deny thee.

CHRISTUS.

When first I sent you forth without a
purse,
Or scrip, or shoes, did ye lack anything?

THE DISCIPLES.

Not anything.

CHRISTUS.

But he that hath a purse,
Now let him take it, and likewise his
scrip;
And he that hath no sword, let him go
sell
His clothes and buy one. That which
hath been written
Must be accomplished now: He hath
poured out
His soul even unto death; he hath been
numbered
With the transgressors, and himself hath
borne

The sin of many, and made intercession
For the transgressors. And here have
an end
The things concerning me.

PETER.

Behold, O Lord,
Behold here are two swords!

CHRISTUS.

It is enough.

IV.

THE GARDEN OF GETHSEMANE.

CHRISTUS.

My spirit is exceeding sorrowful
Even unto death! Tarry ye here and
watch.

He goes apart.

PETER.

Under this ancient olive-tree, that
spreads
Its broad centennial branches like a
tent,
Let us lie down and rest.

JOHN.

What are those torches,
That glimmer on Brook Kedron there
below us?

JAMES.

It is some marriage feast; the joyful
maidens
Go out to meet the bridegroom.

PETER.

I am weary.
The struggles of this day have overcome
me.

They sleep.

CHRISTUS, *falling on his face.*

Father! all things are possible to thee, —
Oh let this cup pass from me! Never-
theless
Not as I will, but as thou wilt, be done!

Returning to the Disciples.

What! could ye not watch with me for
one hour?
Oh watch and pray, that ye may enter
not
Into temptation. For the spirit indeed
Is willing, but the flesh is weak!

JOHN.

Alas!
It is for sorrow that our eyes are
heavy. —
I see again the glimmer of those torches
Among the olives; they are coming
hither.

JAMES.

Outside the garden wall the path
divides;
Surely they come not hither.
They sleep again.

CHRISTUS, *as before.*

O my Father!
If this cup may not pass away from
me,
Except I drink of it, thy will be done.
Returning to the Disciples.
Sleep on; and take your rest!

JOHN.

Beloved Master,
Alas! we know not what to answer
thee!
It is for sorrow that our eyes are
heavy. —
Behold, the torches now encompass us.

JAMES.

They do but go about the garden wall,
Seeking for some one, or for something
lost.
They sleep again.

CHRISTUS, *as before.*

If this cup may not pass away from me,
Except I drink of it, thy will be done.
Returning to the Disciples.
It is enough! Behold, the Son of Man
Hath been betrayed into the hands of
sinners!
The hour is come. Rise up, let us be
going;
For he that shall betray me is at hand.

JOHN.

Ah me! See, from his forehead, in the
torchlight,
Great drops of blood are falling to the
ground!

PETER.

What lights are these? What torches
glare and glisten

Upon the swords and armor of these
men?
And there among them Judas Iscariot!
*He smites the servant of the High-Priest
with his sword.*

CHRISTUS.

Put up thy sword into its sheath; for
they
That take the sword shall perish with
the sword.
The cup my Father hath given me to
drink,
Shall I not drink it? Think'st thou
that I cannot
Pray to my Father, and that He shall
give me
More than twelve legions of angels
presently?

JUDAS *to* CHRISTUS, *kissing him.*

Hail, Master! hail!

CHRISTUS.

Friend, wherefore art thou come?
Whom seek ye?

CAPTAIN OF THE TEMPLE.

Jesus of Nazareth.

CHRISTUS.

I am he.
Are ye come hither as against a thief,
With swords and staves to take me?
When I daily
Was with you in the Temple, ye
stretched forth
No hands to take me! But this is your
hour,
And this the power of darkness. If ye
seek
Me only, let these others go their way.
The Disciples depart. CHRISTUS *is
bound and led away. A certain young
man follows Him, having a linen cloth
cast about his body. They lay hold of
him, and the young man flees from them
naked.*

V.

THE PALACE OF CAIAPHAS.

PHARISEES.

What do we? Clearly something must
we do,
For this man worketh many miracles.

CAIAPHAS.

I am informed that he is a mechanic ;
A carpenter's son ; a Galilean peasant,
Keeping disreputable company.

PHARISEES.

The people say that here in Bethany
He hath raised up a certain Lazarus,
Who had been dead three days.

CAIAPHAS.

Impossible !
There is no resurrection of the dead ;
This Lazarus should be taken, and put
to death
As an impostor. If this Galilean
Would be content to stay in Galilee,
And preach in country towns, I should
not heed him.
But when he comes up to Jerusalem
Riding in triumph, as I am informed,
And drives the money-changers from
the Temple,
That is another matter.

PHARISEES.

If we thus
Let him alone, all will believe on him,
And then the Romans come and take
away
Our place and nation.

CAIAPHAS.

Ye know nothing at all.
Simon Ben Camith, my great predeces-
sor,
On whom be peace ! would have dealt
presently
With such a demagogue. I shall no
less.
The man must die. Do ye consider not
It is expedient that one man should die,
Not the whole nation perish ? What is
death ?
It differeth from sleep but in duration.
We sleep and wake again ; an hour or
two
Later or earlier, and it matters not,
And if we never wake it matters not ;
When we are in our graves we are at
peace,
Nothing can wake us or disturb us more.
There is no resurrection.

PHARISEES, aside.

O most faithful
Disciple of Hircanus Maccabæus,

Will nothing but complete annihilation
Comfort and satisfy thee ?

CAIAPHAS.

While ye are talking
And plotting, and contriving how to
take him,
Fearing the people, and so doing naught,
I, who fear not the people, have been
acting ;
Have taken this Prophet, this young
Nazarene,
Who by Beelzebub the Prince of devils
Casteth out devils, and doth raise the
dead,
That might as well be dead, and left in
peace.
Annas my father-in-law hath sent him
hither.
I hear the guard. Behold your Gali-
lean !

CHRISTUS *is brought in bound.*

SERVANT, *in the vestibule.*

Why art thou up so late, my pretty
damsel ?

DAMSEL.

Why art thou up so early, pretty man ?
It is not cock-crow yet, and art thou
stirring ?

SERVANT.

What brings thee here ?

DAMSEL.

What brings the rest of you ?

SERVANT.

Come here and warm thy hands.

DAMSEL *to* PETER.

Art thou not also
One of this man's disciples ?

PETER.

I am not.

DAMSEL.

Now surely thou art also one of them ;
Thou art a Galilean, and thy speech
Bewrayeth thee.

PETER.

Woman, I know him not !

CAIAPHAS *to* CHRISTUS, *in the Hall.*

Who art thou ? Tell us plainly of thyself

And of thy doctrines, and of thy disciples.

CHRISTUS.

Lo, I have spoken openly to the world,
I have taught ever in the Synagogue,
And in the Temple, where the Jews resort ;
In secret have said nothing.   Wherefore then
Askest thou me of this ?   Ask them that heard me
What I have said to them.   Behold, they know
What I have said !

OFFICER, *striking him.*

What, fellow ! answerest thou
The High-Priest so ?

CHRISTUS.

If I have spoken evil,
Bear witness of the evil ; but if well,
Why smitest thou me ?

CAIAPHAS.

Where are the witnesses ?
Let them say what they know.

THE TWO FALSE WITNESSES.

We heard him say :
I will destroy this Temple made with hands,
And will within three days build up another
Made without hands.

SCRIBES *and* PHARISEES.

He is o'erwhelmed with shame
And cannot answer !

CAIAPHAS.

Dost thou answer nothing ?
What is this thing they witness here against thee ?

SCRIBES *and* PHARISEES.

He holds his peace.

CAIAPHAS.

Tell us, art thou the Christ ?
I do adjure thee by the living God,
Tell us, art thou indeed the Christ ?

CHRISTUS.

I am.
Hereafter shall ye see the Son of Man

Sit on the right hand of the power of God,
And come in clouds of heaven !

CAIAPHAS, *rending his clothes.*

It is enough.
He hath spoken blasphemy !   What further need
Have we of witnesses ?   Now ye have heard
His blasphemy.   What think ye ?   Is he guilty ?

SCRIBES *and* PHARISEES.

Guilty of death !

KINSMAN OF MALCHUS *to* PETER *in the vestibule.*

Surely I know thy face,
Did I not see thee in the garden with him ?

PETER.

How couldst thou see me ?   I swear unto thee
I do not know this man of whom ye speak !

The cock crows.

Hark ! the cock crows !   That sorrowful, pale face
Seeks for me in the crowd, and looks at me,
As if He would remind me of those words :
Ere the cock crow thou shalt deny me thrice !
Goes out weeping. CHRISTUS *is blindfolded and buffeted.*

AN OFFICER, *striking him with his palm.*

Prophesy unto us, thou Christ, thou Prophet !
Who is it smote thee ?

CAIAPHAS.

Lead him unto Pilate !

VI.

PONTIUS PILATE.

PILATE.

Wholly incomprehensible to me,
Vainglorious, obstinate, and given up
To unintelligible old traditions,
And proud, and self-conceited are these Jews !

Not long ago, I marched the legions
Down from Cæsarea to their winter-
  quarters
Here in Jerusalem, with the effigies
Of Cæsar on their ensigns, and a tumult
Arose among these Jews, because their
  Law
Forbids the making of all images !
They threw themselves upon the ground
  with wild
Expostulations, bared their necks, and
  cried
That they would sooner die than have
  their Law
Infringed in any manner; as if Numa
Were not as great as Moses, and the
  Laws
Of the Twelve Tables as their Penta-
  teuch !

And then, again, when I desired to span
Their valley with an aqueduct, and
  bring
A rushing river in to wash the city
And its inhabitants, — they all rebelled
As if they had been herds of unwashed
  swine !
Thousands and thousands of them got
  together
And raised so great a clamor round my
  doors,
That, fearing violent outbreak, I de-
  sisted,
And left them to their wallowing in
  the mire.

And now here comes the reverend San-
  hedrim
Of lawyers, priests, and Scribes and
  Pharisees,
Like old and toothless mastiffs, that can
  bark
But cannot bite, howling their accusa-
  tions
Against a mild enthusiast, who hath
  preached
I know not what new doctrine, being
  King
Of some vague kingdom in the other
  world,
That hath no more to do with Rome
  and Cæsar
Than I have with the patriarch Abra-
  ham !
Finding this man to be a Galilean
I sent him straight to Herod, and I
  hope
That is the last of it; but if it be not,

I still have power to pardon and release
  him,
As is the custom at the Passover,
And so accommodate the matter
  smoothly,
Seeming to yield to them, yet saving
  him,
A prudent and sagacious policy
For Roman Governors in the Provinces.

Incomprehensible, fanatic people !
Ye have a God, who seemeth like your-
  selves
Incomprehensible, dwelling apart,
Majestic, cloud-encompassed, clothed in
  darkness !
One whom ye fear, but love not; yet ye
  have
No Goddesses to soften your stern lives,
And make you tender unto human weak-
  ness,
While we of Rome have everywhere
  around us
Our amiable divinities, that haunt
The woodlands, and the waters, and fre-
  quent
Our households, with their sweet and
  gracious presence !
I will go in, and, while these Jews are
  wrangling,
Read my Ovidius on the Art of Love.

VII.

BARABBAS IN PRISON.

BARABBAS, *to his fellow-prisoners.*

Barabbas is my name,
Barabbas, the Son of Shame,
  Is the meaning, I suppose;
I 'm no better than the best,
And whether worse than the rest
  Of my fellow-men, who knows ?

I was once, to say it in brief,
A highwayman, a robber-chief,
  In the open light of day.
So much I am free to confess ;
But all men, more or less,
  Are robbers in their way.

From my cavern in the crags,
From my lair of leaves and flags,
  I could see, like ants, below,
The camels with their load
Of merchandise, on the road
  That leadeth to Jericho.

And I struck them unaware,
As an eagle from the air
    Drops down upon bird or beast;
And I had my heart's desire
Of the merchants of Sidon and Tyre,
    And Damascus and the East.

But it is not for that I fear;
It is not for that I am here
    In these iron fetters bound ;
Sedition ! that is the word
That Pontius Pilate heard,
    And he liketh not the sound.

What think ye, would he care
For a Jew slain here or there,
    Or a plundered caravan ?
But Cæsar ! — ah, that is a crime,
To the uttermost end of time
    Shall not be forgiven to man.

Therefore was Herod wroth
With Matthias Margaloth,
    And burned him for a show !
Therefore his wrath did smite
Judas the Gaulonite,
    And his followers, as ye know.

For that cause and no more,
Am I here, as I said before;
    For one unlucky night,
Jucundus, the captain of horse,
Was upon us with all his force,
    And I was caught in the fight.

I might have fled with the rest,
But my dagger was in the breast
    Of a Roman equerry ,
As we rolled there in the street,
They bound me, hands and feet;
    And this is the end of me.

Who cares for death ? Not I !
A thousand times I would die,
    Rather than suffer wrong !
Already those women of mine
Are mixing the myrrh and the wine ;
    I shall not be with you long.

VIII.

ECCE HOMO.

PILATE, *on the tessellated pavement in
    front of his palace.*

Ye have brought unto me this man, as
    one

Who doth pervert the people ; and be-
    hold !
I have examined him, and found no
    fault
Touching the things whereof ye do
    accuse him.
No, nor yet Herod ; for I sent you to
    him,
And nothing worthy of death he findeth
    in him.
Ye have a custom at the Passover,
That one condemned to death shall be
    released.
Whom will ye, then, that I release to
    you ?
Jesus Barabbas, called the Son of
    Shame,
Or Jesus, Son of Joseph, called the
    Christ ?

THE PEOPLE, *shouting.*

Not this man, but Barabbas !

PILATE.

                What then will ye
That I should do with him that is
    called Christ ?

THE PEOPLE.

Crucify him !

PILATE.

            Why, what evil hath he done ?
Lo, I have found no cause of death in
    him ;
I will chastise him, and then let him go.

THE PEOPLE, *more vehemently.*

Crucify him ! crucify him !

A MESSENGER, *to* PILATE.

                Thy wife sends
This message to thee, — Have thou
    naught to do
With that just man ; for I this day in
    dreams
Have suffered many things because of
    him.

PILATE, *aside.*

The Gods speak to us in our dreams !
    I tremble
At what I have to do ! O Claudia,
How shall I save him ? Yet one effort
    more,
Or he must perish !

    Washes his hands before them.

I am innocent
Of the blood of this just person; see ye
to it!

THE PEOPLE.

Let his blood be on us and on our
children!

VOICES, *within the palace.*

Put on thy royal robes; put on thy
crown,
And take thy sceptre! Hail, thou
King of the Jews!

PILATE.

I bring him forth to you, that ye may
know
I find no fault in him. Behold the
man!

CHRISTUS *is led in with the purple robe
and crown of thorns.*

CHIEF PRIESTS *and* OFFICERS.

Crucify him! crucify him!

PILATE.

								Take ye him;
I find no fault in him.

CHIEF PRIESTS.

								We have a Law,
And by our Law he ought to die; be-
cause
He made himself to be the Son of God.

PILATE, *aside.*

Ah! there are Sons of God, and demi-
gods
More than ye know, ye ignorant High-
Priests!

To CHRISTUS.

Whence art thou?

CHIEF PRIESTS.

								Crucify him! crucify him!

PILATE, *to* CHRISTUS.

Dost thou not answer me? Dost thou
not know
That I have power enough to crucify
thee?
That I have also power to set thee free?

CHRISTUS.

Thou couldst have no power at all
against me

Except that it were given thee from
above;
Therefore hath he that sent me unto
thee
The greater sin.

CHIEF PRIESTS.

								If thou let this man go,
Thou art not Cæsar's friend. For who-
soever
Maketh himself a King, speaks against
Cæsar.

PILATE.

Ye Jews, behold your King!

CHIEF PRIESTS.

								Away with him!
Crucify him!

PILATE.

								Shall I crucify your King?

CHIEF PRIESTS.

We have no King but Cæsar!

PILATE.

								Take him, then.
Take him, ye cruel and bloodthirsty
priests,
More merciless than the plebeian mob,
Who pity and spare the fainting gladi-
ator
Blood-stained in Roman amphithea-
tres,—
Take him, and crucify him if ye will;
But if the immortal Gods do ever min-
gle
With the affairs of mortals, which I
doubt not,
And hold the attribute of justice dear,
They will commission the Eumenides
To scatter you to the four winds of
heaven,
Exacting tear for tear, and blood for
blood.
Here, take ye this inscription, Priests,
and nail it
Upon the cross, above your victim's
head:
Jesus of Nazareth, King of the Jews.

CHIEF PRIESTS.

Nay, we entreat! write not, the King of
the Jews!
But that he said: I am the King of the
Jews!

PILATE.

Enough. What I have written, I have written.

IX.

ACELDAMA.

JUDAS ISCARIOT.

Lost ! Lost ! Forever lost ! I have be-
trayed
The innocent blood ! O God ! if thou
art love,
Why didst thou leave me naked to the
tempter ?
Why didst thou not commission thy
swift lightning
To strike me dead ? or why did I not
perish
With those by Herod slain, the innocent
children,
Who went with playthings in their little
hands
Into the darkness of the other world,
As if to bed ? Or wherefore was I born,
If thou in thy foreknowledge didst per-
ceive
All that I am, and all that I must be ?
I know I am not generous, am not
gentle,
Like other men ; but I have tried to be,
And I have failed. I thought by fol-
lowing Him
I should grow like him ; but the unclean
spirit
That from my childhood up hath tor-
tured me
Hath been too cunning and too strong
for me.
Am I to blame for this ? Am I to blame
Because I cannot love, and ne'er have
known
The love of woman or the love of chil-
dren ?
It is a curse and a fatality,
A mark that hath been set upon my
forehead,
That none shall slay me, for it were a
mercy
That I were dead, or never had been
born.

Too late ! too late ! I shall not see Him
more
Among the living. That sweet, patient
face

Will never more rebuke me, nor those
lips
Repeat the words : One of you shall
betray me !
It stung me into madness. How I
loved,
Yet hated Him : But in the other
world !
I will be there before Him, and will
wait
Until he comes, and fall down on my
knees
And kiss his feet, jmploring pardon,
pardon !

I heard Him say : All sins shall be for-
given,
Except the sin against the Holy Ghost.
That shall not be forgiven in this world,
Nor in the world to come. Is that my
sin ?
Have I offended so there is no hope
Here nor hereafter ? That I soon shall
know.
O God, have mercy ! Christ have
mercy on me !

Throws himself headlong from the cliff.

X.

THE THREE CROSSES.

MANAHEM, THE ESSENIAN.

Three crosses in this noonday night up-
lifted,
Three human figures that in mortal
pain
Gleam white against the supernatural
darkness ;
Two thieves, that writhe in torture, and
between them
The Suffering Messiah, the Son of
Joseph,
Ay, the Messiah Triumphant, Son of
David !
A crown of thorns on that dishonored
head !
Those hands that healed the sick now
pierced with nails,
Those feet that wandered homeless
through the world
Now crossed and bleeding, and at rest
forever !
And the three faithful Maries, over-
whelmed
By this great sorrow, kneeling, praying
weeping !

O Joseph Caiaphas, thou great High-
Priest,
How wilt thou answer for this deed of
blood ?

SCRIBES *and* ELDERS.

Thou that destroyest the Temple, and
dost build it
In three days, save thyself ; and if thou
be
The Son of God, come down now from
the cross.

CHIEF PRIESTS.

Others he saved, himself he cannot save !
Let Christ the King of Israel descend
That we may see and believe !

SCRIBES *and* ELDERS.

In God he trusted ;
Let Him deliver him, if He will have
him,
And we will then believe.

CHRISTUS.

Father ! forgive them ;
They know not what they do.

THE IMPENITENT THIEF.

If thou be Christ,
Oh save thyself and us !

THE PENITENT THIEF.

Remember me,
Lord, when thou comest into thine own
kingdom.

CHRISTUS.

This day shalt thou be with me in
Paradise.

MANAHEM.

Golgotha ! Golgotha ! Oh the pain
and darkness !
Oh the uplifted cross, that shall forever
Shine through the darkness, and shall
conquer pain
By the triumphant memory of this
hour !

SIMON MAGUS.

O Nazarene ! I find thee here at last !
Thou art no more a phantom unto
me !
This is the end of one who called himself
The Son of God ! Such is the fate of
those

Who preach new doctrines. 'T is not
what he did,
But what he said, hath brought him
unto this.
I will speak evil of no dignitaries.
This is my hour of triumph, Nazarene !

THE YOUNG RULER.

This is the end of him who said to me :
Sell that thou hast, and give unto the
poor !
This is the treasure in heaven he promised me !

CHRISTUS.

Eloi, Eloi, lama sabachthani !

A SOLDIER, *preparing the hyssop.*

He calleth for Elias !

ANOTHER.

Nay, let be !
See if Elias will now come to save him !

CHRISTUS.

I thirst.

A SOLDIER.

Give him the wormwood !

CHRISTUS, *with a loud cry, bowing his head.*

It is finished !

XI.

THE TWO MARIES.

MARY MAGDALENE.

We have risen early, yet the sun
O'ertakes us ere we reach the sepulchre,
To wrap the body of our blessed Lord
With our sweet spices.

MARY, MOTHER OF JAMES.

Lo, this is the garden,
And yonder is the sepulchre. But who
Shall roll away the stone for us to
enter ?

MARY MAGDALENE.

It hath been rolled away ! The sepulchre
Is open ! Ah, who hath been here before us,
When we rose early, wishing to be
first ?

MARY, MOTHER OF JAMES.

I am affrighted!

MARY MAGDALENE.

Hush! I will stoop down
And look within. There is a young
   man sitting
On the right side, clothed in a long
   white garment!
It is an angel!

THE ANGEL.

Fear not; ye are seeking
Jesus of Nazareth, which was crucified.
Why do ye seek the living among the
   dead?
He is no longer here; He is arisen!
Come see the place where the Lord lay!
   Remember
How He spake unto you in Galilee,
Saying: The Son of Man must be de-
   livered
Into the hands of sinful men; by them
Be crucified, and the third day rise
   again!
But go your way, and say to his disci-
   ples,
He goeth before you into Galilee;
There shall ye see Him as He said to
   you.

MARY, MOTHER OF JAMES.

I will go swiftly for them.

MARY MAGDALENE, alone, weeping.

They have taken
My Lord away from me, and now I
   know not
Where they have laid Him! Who is
   there to tell me?
This is the gardener. Surely he must
   know.

CHRISTUS.

Woman, why weepest thou? Whom
   seekest thou?

MARY MAGDALENE.

They have taken my Lord away; I
   cannot find Him.
O sir, if thou have borne Him hence, I
   pray thee
Tell me where thou hast laid Him.

CHRISTUS.

Mary!

MARY MAGDALENE.

Rabboni!

XII.

THE SEA OF GALILEE.

NATHANIEL, in the ship.

All is now ended.

JOHN.

Nay, He is arisen,
I ran unto the tomb, and stooping down
Looked in, and saw the linen grave-
   clothes lying,
Yet dared not enter.

PETER.

I went in, and saw
The napkin that had been about his
   head,
Not lying with the other linen clothes,
But wrapped together in a separate
   place.

THOMAS.

And I have seen Him. I have seen the
   print
Of nails upon his hands, and thrust my
   hands
Into his side. I know He is arisen;
But where are now the kingdom and the
   glory
He promised unto us? We have all
   dreamed
That we were princes, and we wake to
   find
We are but fishermen.

PETER.

Who should have been
Fishers of men!

JOHN.

We have come back again
To the old life, the peaceful life, among
The white towns of the Galilean lake.

PETER.

They seem to me like silent sepulchres
In the gray light of morning! The old
   life,
Yea, the old life! for we have toiled all
   night
And have caught nothing.

JOHN.

Do ye see a man
Standing upon the beach and beckon-
ing?
'T is like an apparition. He hath kin-
dled
A fire of coals, and seems to wait for
us.
He calleth.

CHRISTUS, *from the shore.*

Children, have ye any meat?

PETER.

Alas! We have caught nothing.

CHRISTUS.

Cast the net
On the right side of the ship, and ye
shall find.

PETER.

How that reminds me of the days gone
by,
And one who said : Launch out into the
deep,
And cast your nets!

NATHANAEL.

We have but let them down
And they are filled, so that we cannot
draw them!

JOHN.

It is the Lord!

PETER, *girding his fisher's coat about him.*

He said : When I am risen
I will go before you into Galilee!
He casts himself into the lake.

JOHN.

There is no fear in love; for perfect
love
Casteth out fear. Now then, if ye are
men,
Put forth your strength; we are not far
from shore;
The net is heavy, but breaks not. All
is safe.

PETER, *on the shore.*

Dear Lord ! I heard thy voice and could
not wait.
Let me behold thy face, and kiss thy
feet !

Thou art not dead, thou livest! Again
I see thee.
Pardon, dear Lord! I am a sinful
man;
I have denied thee thrice. Have mercy
on me !

THE OTHERS, *coming to land.*

Dear Lord! stay with us! cheer us!
comfort us!
Lo! we again have found thee! Leave
us not!

CHRISTUS.

Bring hither of the fish that ye have
caught,
And come and eat!

JOHN.

Behold! He breaketh bread
As He was wont. From his own blessed
hands
Again we take it.

CHRISTUS.

Simon, son of Jonas,
Lovest thou me, more than these others?

PETER.

Yea,
More, Lord, than all men, even more
than these.
Thou knowest that I love thee.

CHRISTUS.

Feed my lambs.

THOMAS, *aside.*

How more than we do? He remaineth
ever
Self-confident and boastful as before.
Nothing will cure him.

CHRISTUS.

Simon, son of Jonas,
Lovest thou me?

PETER.

Yea, dearest Lord, I love thee.
Thou knowest that I love thee.

CHRISTUS.

Feed my sheep

THOMAS, *aside.*

Again, the selfsame question, and the
answer

Repeated with more vehemence. Can the Master
Doubt if we love Him?

CHRISTUS.

Simon, son of Jonas,
Lovest thou me?

PETER, *grieved.*

Dear Lord, thou knowest all things.
Thou knowest that I love thee.

CHRISTUS.

Feed my sheep.
When thou wast young thou girdedst thyself, and walkedst
Whither thou wouldst; but when thou shalt be old,
Thou shalt stretch forth thy hands, and other men
Shall gird and carry thee whither thou wouldst not.
Follow thou me!

JOHN, *aside.*

It is a prophecy
Of what death he shall die.

PETER, *pointing to* JOHN.

Tell me, O Lord,
And what shall this man do?

CHRISTUS.

And if I will
He tarry till I come, what is it to thee?
Follow thou me!

PETER.

Yea, I will follow thee, dear Lord and Master!
Will follow thee through fasting and temptation,
Through all thine agony and bloody sweat,
Thy cross and passion, even unto death!

EPILOGUE.

SYMBOLUM APOSTOLORUM.

PETER.

I BELIEVE in God the Father Almighty;

JOHN.

Maker of Heaven and Earth;

JAMES.

And in Jesus Christ his only Son, our Lord;

ANDREW.

Who was conceived by the Holy Ghost, born of the Virgin Mary;

PHILIP.

Suffered under Pontius Pilate, was crucified, dead, and buried;

THOMAS.

And the third day He rose again from the dead;

BARTHOLOMEW.

He ascended into Heaven, and sitteth on the right hand of God, the Father Almighty;

MATTHEW.

From thence He shall come to judge the quick and the dead.

JAMES, THE SON OF ALPHEUS.

I believe in the Holy Ghost; the holy Catholic Church;

SIMON ZELOTES.

The communion of Saints; the forgiveness of sins;

JUDE.

The resurrection of the body;

MATTHIAS.

And the Life Everlasting.

FIRST INTERLUDE.

THE ABBOT JOACHIM.

A ROOM IN THE CONVENT OF FLORA IN CALABRIA. NIGHT.

JOACHIM.

THE wind is rising; it seizes and shakes
The doors and window-blinds and makes
Mysterious moanings in the halls;
The convent-chimneys seem almost
The trumpets of some heavenly host,
Setting its watch upon our walls!
Where it listeth, there it bloweth;
We hear the sound, but no man knoweth
Whence it cometh or whither it goeth.

And thus it is with the Holy Ghost.
O breath of God! O my delight
In many a vigil of the night,
Like the great voice in Patmos heard
By John, the Evangelist of the Word,
I hear thee behind me saying: Write
In a book the things that thou hast
    seen,
The things that are, and that have been,
And the things that shall hereafter be!

This convent, on the rocky crest
Of the Calabrian hills, to me
A Patmos is wherein I rest;
While round about me like a sea
The white mists roll, and overflow
The world that lies unseen below
In darkness and in mystery.
Here in the Spirit, in the vast
Embrace of God's encircling arm,
Am I uplifted from all harm;
The world seems something far away,
Something belonging to the Past,
A hostelry, a peasant's farm,
That lodged me for a night or day,
In which I care not to remain,
Nor, having left, to see again.

Thus, in the hollow of God's hand
I dwelt on sacred Tabor's height,
When as a simple acolyte
I journeyed to the Holy Land,
A pilgrim for my master's sake,
And saw the Galilean Lake,
And walked through many a village
    street
That once had echoed to his feet.
There first I heard the great com-
    mand,
The voice behind me saying: Write!
And suddenly my soul became
Illumined by a flash of flame,
That left imprinted on my thought
The image I in vain had sought,
And which forever shall remain;
As sometimes from these windows high,
Gazing at midnight on the sky
Black with a storm of wind and rain,
I have beheld a sudden glare
Of lightning lay the landscape bare,
With tower and town and hill and plain
Distinct and burnt into my brain,
Never to be effaced again!

And I have written. These volumes
    three,
The Apocalypse, the Harmony
Of the Sacred Scriptures, new and old,

And the Psalter with Ten Strings, en-
    fold
Within their pages, all and each,
The Eternal Gospel that I teach.
Well I remember the Kingdom of
    Heaven
Hath been likened to a little leaven
Hidden in two measures of meal,
Until it leavened the whole mass;
So likewise will it come to pass
With the doctrines that I here conceal.

Open and manifest to me
The truth appears, and must be told;
All sacred mysteries are threefold;
Three Persons in the Trinity,
Three ages of Humanity,
And holy Scriptures likewise three,
Of Fear, of Wisdom, and of Love;
For Wisdom that begins in Fear
Endeth in Love; the atmosphere
In which the soul delights to be
And finds that perfect liberty
Which cometh only from above.

In the first Age, the early prime
And dawn of all historic time,
The Father reigned; and face to face
He spake with the primeval race.
Bright Angels, on his errands sent,
Sat with the patriarch in his tent;
His prophets thundered in the street;
His lightnings flashed, his hailstorms
    beat;
In earthquake and in flood and flame,
In tempest and in cloud He came!
The fear of God is in his Book;
The pages of the Pentateuch
Are full of the terror of his name.

Then reigned the Son; his Covenant
Was peace on earth, good-will to man;
With Him the reign of Law began.
He was the Wisdom and the Word,
And sent his Angels Ministrant,
Unterrified and undeterred,
To rescue souls forlorn and lost,
The troubled, tempted, tempest-tost
To heal, to comfort, and to teach.
The fiery tongues of Pentecost
His symbols were, that they should
    preach
In every form of human speech
From continent to continent.
He is the Light Divine, whose rays
Across the thousand years unspent
Shine through the darkness of our days,
And touch with their celestial fires

Our churches and our convent spires.
His Book is the New Testament.

These Ages now are of the Past;
And the Third Age begins at last.
The coming of the Holy Ghost,
The reign of Grace, the reign of Love
Brightens the mountain-tops above,
And the dark outline of the coast.
Already the whole land is white
With convent walls, as if by night
A snow had fallen on hill and height !
Already from the streets and marts
Of town and traffic, and low cares,
Men climb the consecrated stairs
With weary feet, and bleeding hearts ;
And leave the world and its delights,
Its passions, struggles, and despairs,
For contemplation and for prayers
In cloister-cells of cœnobites.

Eternal benedictions rest
Upon thy name, Saint Benedict !
Founder of convents in the West,
Who built on Mount Cassino's crest
In the Land of Labor, thine eagle's
   nest !
May I be found not derelict
In aught of faith or godly fear,
If I have written, in many a page,
The Gospel of the coming age,
The Eternal Gospel men shall hear.
Oh may I live resembling thee,
And die at last as thou hast died ;
So that hereafter men may see,
Within the choir, a form of air,
Standing with arms outstretched in
   prayer,
As one that hath been crucified !
My work is finished ; I am strong
In faith and hope and charity ;
For I have written the things I see,
The things that have been and shall
   be,
Conscious of right, nor fearing wrong ;
Because I am in love with Love,
And the sole thing I hate is Hate ;
For Hate is death ; and Love is life,
A peace, a splendor from above ;
And Hate, a never-ending strife,
A smoke, a blackness from the abyss
Where unclean serpents coil and hiss !
Love is the Holy Ghost within ;
Hate the unpardonable sin !
Who preaches otherwise than this
Betrays his Master with a kiss !

PART TWO.

THE GOLDEN LEGEND.

PROLOGUE.

THE SPIRE OF STRASBURG CATHEDRAL.

Night and storm. LUCIFER, *with the Powers of the Air, trying to tear down the Cross.*

LUCIFER.

HASTEN ! hasten !
O ye spirits !
From its station drag the ponderous
Cross of iron, that to mock us
Is uplifted high in air !

VOICES.

Oh, we cannot !
For around it
All the Saints and Guardian Angels
Throng in legions to protect it ;
They defeat us everywhere !

THE BELLS.

Laudo Deum verum !
Plebem voco !
Congrego clerum !

LUCIFER.

Lower ! lower !
Hover downward !
Seize the loud, vociferous bells, and
Clashing, clanging to the pavement,
Hurl them from their windy tower.

VOICES.

All thy thunders
Here are harmless !
For these bells have been anointed,
And baptized with holy water !
They defy our utmost power.

THE BELLS.

Defunctos ploro !
Pestem fugo !
Festa decoro !

LUCIFER.

Shake the casements !
Break the painted
Panes, that flame with gold and crimson;

Scatter them like leaves of Autumn,
Swept away before the blast !

VOICES.

Oh, we cannot !
The Archangel
Michael flames from every window,
With the sword of fire that drove us
Headlong, out of heaven, aghast !

THE BELLS.

Funera plango !
Fulgura frango !
Sabbata pango !

LUCIFER.

Aim your lightnings
At the oaken,
Massive, iron-studded portals !
Sack the house of God, and scatter
Wide the ashes of the dead !

VOICES.

Oh, we cannot !
The Apostles
And the Martyrs, wrapped in mantles,
Stand as warders at the entrance,
Stand as sentinels o'erhead !

THE BELLS.

Excito lentos !
Dissipo ventos !
Paco cruentos !

LUCIFER.

Baffled ! baffled !
Inefficient,
Craven spirits ! leave this labor
Unto Time, the great Destroyer !
Come away, ere night is gone !

VOICES

Onward ! onward !
With the night-wind,
Over field and farm and forest,
Lonely homestead, darksome hamlet,
Blighting all we breathe upon !

*They sweep away.   Organ and Gregorian
Chant.*

CHOIR.

Nocte surgentes
Vigilemus omnes !

I.

THE CASTLE OF VAUTSBERG ON THE
RHINE.

A chamber in a tower. PRINCE HENRY
sitting alone, ill and restless.   Midnight.

PRINCE HENRY.

I cannot sleep ! my fervid brain
Calls up the vanished Past again,
And throws its misty splendors deep
Into the pallid realms of sleep !
A breath from that far-distant shore
Comes freshening ever more and more,
And wafts o'er intervening seas
Sweet odors from the Hesperides !
A wind, that through the corridor
Just stirs the curtain, and no more,
And, touching the æolian strings,
Faints with the burden that it brings !
Come back ! ye friendships long de-
                parted !
That like o'erflowing streamlets started,
And now are dwindled, one by one,
To stony channels in the sun !
Come back ! ye friends, whose lives are
                ended,
Come back, with all that light attended,
Which seemed to darken and decay
When ye arose and went away !

They come, the shapes of joy and woe,
The airy crowds of long ago,
The dreams and fancies known of yore,
That have been, and shall be no more.
They change the cloisters of the night
Into a garden of delight ;
They make the dark and dreary hours
Open and blossom into flowers !
I would not sleep ! I love to be
Again in their fair company ;
But ere my lips can bid them stay,
They pass and vanish quite away !
Alas ! our memories may retrace
Each circumstance of time and place,
Season and scene come back again,
And outward things unchanged remain ;
The rest we cannot reinstate ;
Ourselves we cannot re-create ;
Nor set our souls to the same key
Of the remembered harmony !

Rest ! rest ! Oh, give me rest and
                peace !
The thought of life that ne'er shall
                cease

Has something in it like despair,
A weight I am too weak to bear !
Sweeter to this afflicted breast
The thought of never-ending rest !
Sweeter the undisturbed and deep
Tranquillity of endless sleep !

A flash of lightning, out of which LUCI-
FER appears, in the garb of a travelling
Physician.

LUCIFER.

All hail, Prince Henry !

PRINCE HENRY, *starting.*

            Who is it speaks ?
Who and what are you ?

LUCIFER.

            One who seeks
A moment's audience with the Prince.

PRINCE HENRY.

When came you in ?

LUCIFER.

          A moment since.
I found your study door unlocked,
And thought you answered when I
    knocked.

PRINCE HENRY.

I did not hear you.

LUCIFER.

        You heard the thunder ;
It was loud enough to waken the dead.
And it is not a matter of special wonder
That, when God is walking overhead,
You should not hear my feeble tread.

PRINCE HENRY.

What may your wish or purpose be ?

LUCIFER.

Nothing or everything, as it pleases
Your Highness. You behold in me
Only a travelling Physician ;
One of the few who have a mission
To cure incurable diseases,
Or those that are called so.

PRINCE HENRY.

          Can you bring
The dead to life ?

LUCIFER.

      Yes ; very nearly.
And, what is a wiser and better thing,

Can keep the living from ever needing
Such an unnatural, strange proceeding,
By showing conclusively and clearly
That death is a stupid blunder merely,
And not a necessity of our lives.
My being here is accidental ;
The storm, that against your casement
    drives,
In the little village below waylaid me.
And there I heard, with a secret delight,
Of your maladies physical and mental,
Which neither astonished nor dismayed
    me.
And I hastened hither, though late in
    the night,
To proffer my aid !

PRINCE HENRY, *ironically.*

         For this you came !
Ah, how can I ever hope to requite
This honor from one so erudite ?

LUCIFER.

The honor is mine, or will be when
I have cured your disease.

PRINCE HENRY.

          But not till then.

LUCIFER.

What is your illness ?

PRINCE HENRY.

         It has no name.
A smouldering, dull, perpetual flame,
As in a kiln, burns in my veins,
Sending up vapors to the head ;
My heart has become a dull lagoon,
Which a kind of leprosy drinks and
    drains ;
I am accounted as one who is dead,
And, indeed, I think that I shall be
    soon.

LUCIFER.

And has Gordonius the Divine,
In his famous Lily of Medicine, —
I see the book lies open before you, —
No remedy potent enough to restore
    you ?

PRINCE HENRY.

None whatever !

LUCIFER.

        The dead are dead,
And their oracles dumb, when ques-
    tionèd

Of the new diseases that human life
Evolves in its progress, rank and rife.
Consult the dead upon things that were,
But the living only on things that are.
Have you done this, by the appliance
And aid of doctors ?

PRINCE HENRY.

Ay, whole schools
Of doctors, with their learned rules ;
But the case is quite beyond their
science.
Even the doctors of Salern
Send me back word they can discern
No cure for a malady like this,
Save one which in its nature is
Impossible and cannot be !

LUCIFER.

That sounds oracular !

PRINCE HENRY.

Unendurable !

LUCIFER.

What is their remedy ?

PRINCE HENRY.

You shall see ;
Writ in this scroll is the mystery.

LUCIFER, *reading.*

" Not to be cured, yet not incurable !
The only remedy that remains
Is the blood that flows from a maiden's
veins,
Who of her own free will shall die,
And give her life as the price of yours ! "

That is the strangest of all cures,
And one, I think, you will never try ;
The prescription you may well put by,
As something impossible to find
Before the world itself shall end !
And yet who knows ? One cannot say
That into some maiden's brain that kind
Of madness will not find its way.
Meanwhile permit me to recommend,
As the matter admits of no delay,
My wonderful Catholicon,
Of very subtile and magical powers !

PRINCE HENRY.

Purge with your nostrums and drugs
infernal
The spouts and gargoyles of these
towers,
Not me ! My faith is utterly gone

In every power but the Power Supernal !
Pray tell me, of what school are you ?

LUCIFER.

Both of the Old and of the New !
The school of Hermes Trismegistus,
Who uttered his oracles sublime
Before the Olympiads, in the dew
Of the early dusk and dawn of time,
The reign of dateless old Hephæstus !
As northward, from its Nubian springs,
The Nile, forever new and old,
Among the living and the dead,
Its mighty mystic stream has rolled ;
So, starting from its fountain-head
Under the lotus-leaves of Isis,
From the dead demigods of eld,
Through long unbroken lines of kings
Its course the sacred art has held,
Unchecked, unchanged by man's devices.
This art the Arabian Geber taught,
And in alembics, finely wrought,
Distilling herbs and flowers, discovered
The secret that so long had hovered
Upon the misty verge of Truth,
The Elixir of Perpetual Youth,
Called Alcohol, in the Arab speech !
Like him, this wondrous lore I teach !

PRINCE HENRY.

What ! an adept ?

LUCIFER.

Nor less, nor more !

PRINCE HENRY.

I am a reader of your books,
A lover of that mystic lore !
With such a piercing glance it looks
Into great Nature's open eye,
And sees within it trembling lie
The portrait of the Deity !
And yet, alas ! with all my pains,
The secret and the mystery
Have baffled and eluded me,
Unseen the grand result remains !

LUCIFER, *showing a flask.*

Behold it here ! this little flask
Contains the wonderful quintessence,
The perfect flower and efflorescence,
Of all the knowledge man can ask !
Hold it up thus against the light !

PRINCE HENRY.

How limpid, pure, and crystalline,
How quick, and tremulous, and bright

The little wavelets dance and shine,
As were it the Water of Life in sooth!

LUCIFER.

It is! It assuages every pain,
Cures all disease, and gives again
To age the swift delights of youth.
Inhale its fragrance.

PRINCE HENRY.

It is sweet.
A thousand different odors meet
And mingle in its rare perfume,
Such as the winds of summer waft
At open windows through a room!

LUCIFER.

Will you not taste it?

PRINCE HENRY.

Will one draught
Suffice?

LUCIFER.

If not, you can drink more.

PRINCE HENRY.

Into this crystal goblet pour
So much as safely I may drink.

LUCIFER, *pouring.*

Let not the quantity alarm you;
You may drink all; it will not harm
you.

PRINCE HENRY.

I am as one who on the brink
Of a dark river stands and sees
The waters flow, the landscape dim
Around him waver, wheel, and swim,
And, ere he plunges, stops to think
Into what whirlpools he may sink;
One moment pauses, and no more,
Then madly plunges from the shore!
Headlong into the mysteries
Of life and death I boldly leap,
Nor fear the fateful current's sweep,
Nor what in ambush lurks below!
For death is better than disease!

An ANGEL with an æolian harp hovers in the air.

ANGEL.

Woe! woe! eternal woe!
Not only the whispered prayer
Of love,
But the imprecations of hate,
Reverberate

For ever and ever through the air
Above!
This fearful curse
Shakes the great universe!

LUCIFER, *disappearing.*

Drink! drink!
And thy soul shall sink
Down into the dark abyss,
Into the infinite abyss,
From which no plummet nor rope
Ever drew up the silver sand of hope!

PRINCE HENRY, *drinking.*

It is like a draught of fire!
Through every vein
I feel again
The fever of youth, the soft desire;
A rapture that is almost pain
Throbs in my heart and fills my brain!
O joy! O joy! I feel
The band of steel
That so long and heavily has pressed
Upon my breast
Uplifted, and the malediction
Of my affliction
Is taken from me, and my weary breast
At length finds rest.

THE ANGEL.

It is but the rest of the fire, from which
the air has been taken!
It is but the rest of the sand, when the
hour-glass is not shaken!
It is but the rest of the tide between the
ebb and the flow!
It is but the rest of the wind between
the flaws that blow!
With fiendish laughter,
Hereafter,
This false physician
Will mock thee in thy perdition.

PRINCE HENRY.

Speak! speak!
Who says that I am ill?
I am not ill! I am not weak!
The trance, the swoon, the dream, is
o'er!
I feel the chill of death no more!
At length,
I stand renewed in all my strength!
Beneath me I can feel
The great earth stagger and reel,
As if the feet of a descending God
Upon its surface trod,
And like a pebble it rolled beneath his
heel!

This, O brave physician! this
Is thy great Palingenesis!
Drinks again.

THE ANGEL.

Touch the goblet no more!
It will make thy heart sore
To its very core!
Its perfume is the breath
Of the Angel of Death,
And the light that within it lies
Is the flash of his evil eyes.
Beware! Oh, beware!
For sickness, sorrow, and care
All are there!

PRINCE HENRY, *sinking back.*

O thou voice within my breast!
Why entreat me, why upbraid me,
When the steadfast tongues of truth
And the flattering hopes of youth
Have all deceived me and betrayed me?
Give me, give me rest, oh rest!
Golden visions wave and hover,
Golden vapors, waters streaming,
Landscapes moving, changing, gleaming,
I am like a happy lover,
Who illumines life with dreaming!
Brave physician! Rare physician!
Well hast thou fulfilled thy mission!
His head falls on his book.

THE ANGEL, *receding.*

Alas! alas!
Like a vapor the golden vision
Shall fade and pass,
And thou wilt find in thy heart again
Only the blight of pain,
And bitter, bitter, bitter contrition!

COURT-YARD OF THE CASTLE.

HUBERT *standing by the gateway.*

HUBERT.

How sad the grand old castle looks!
O'erhead, the unmolested rooks
Upon the turret's windy top
Sit, talking of the farmer's crop;
Here in the court-yard springs the grass,
So few are now the feet that pass;
The stately peacocks, bolder grown,
Come hopping down the steps of stone,
As if the castle were their own;
And I, the poor old seneschal,
Haunt, like a ghost, the banquet-hall.

Alas! the merry guests no more
Crowd through the hospitable door;
No eyes with youth and passion shine,
No cheeks glow redder than the wine;
No song, no laugh, no jovial din
Of drinking wassail to the pin;
But all is silent, sad, and drear,
And now the only sounds I hear
Are the hoarse rooks upon the walls,
And horses stamping in their stalls!

A horn sounds.

What ho! that merry, sudden blast
Reminds me of the days long past!
And, as of old resounding, grate
The heavy hinges of the gate,
And, clattering loud, with iron clank,
Down goes the sounding bridge of plank,
As if it were in haste to greet
The pressure of a traveller's feet!

Enter WALTER the Minnesinger.

WALTER.

How now, my friend! This looks
quite lonely!
No banner flying from the walls,
No pages and no seneschals,
No warders, and one porter only!
Is it you, Hubert?

HUBERT.

Ah! Master Walter!

WALTER.

Alas! how forms and faces alter!
I did not know you. You look older!
Your hair has grown much grayer and
thinner,
And you stoop a little in the shoulder!

HUBERT.

Alack! I am a poor old sinner,
And, like these towers, begin to moulder;
And you have been absent many a
year!

WALTER.

How is the Prince?

HUBERT.

He is not here;
He has been ill: and now has fled.

WALTER.

Speak it out frankly; say he's dead!
Is it not so?

HUBERT.

No; if you please,
A strange, mysterious disease
Fell on him with a sudden blight.
Whole hours together he would stand
Upon the terrace in a dream,
Resting his head upon his hand,
Best pleased when he was most alone,
Like Saint John Nepomuck in stone,
Looking down into a stream.
In the Round Tower, night after night,
He sat and bleared his eyes with books;
Until one morning we found him there
Stretched on the floor, as if in a swoon
He had fallen from his chair.
We hardly recognized his sweet looks!

WALTER.

Poor Prince!

HUBERT.

I think he might have mended;
And he did mend; but very soon
The priests came flocking in, like rooks,
With all their crosiers and their crooks,
And so at last the matter ended.

WALTER.

How did it end ?

HUBERT.

Why, in Saint Rochus
They made him stand and wait his
     doom ;
And, as if he were condemned to the
     tomb,
Began to mutter their hocus-pocus.
First, the Mass for the Dead they
     chanted,
Then three times laid upon his head
A shovelful of churchyard clay,
Saying to him, as he stood undaunted,
" This is a sign that thou art dead,
So in thy heart be penitent ! "
And forth from the chapel door he
     went
Into disgrace and banishment,
Clothed in a cloak of hodden gray,
And bearing a wallet, and a bell,
Whose sound should be a perpetual
     knell
To keep all travellers away.

WALTER.

Oh, horrible fate !   Outcast, rejected,
As one with pestilence infected !

HUBERT.

Then was the family tomb unsealed,
And broken helmet, sword, and shield
Buried together, in common wreck,
As is the custom when the last
Of any princely house has passed,
And thrice, as with a trumpet-blast,
A herald shouted down the stair
The words of warning and despair, —
" O Hoheneck !   O Hoheneck ! "

WALTER.

Still in my soul that cry goes on, —
Forever gone ! forever gone !
Ah, what a cruel sense of loss,
Like a black shadow, would fall across
The hearts of all, if he should die !
His gracious presence upon earth
Was as a fire upon a hearth;
As pleasant songs, at morning sung,
The words that dropped from his sweet
     tongue
Strengthened our hearts; or heard at
     night
Made all our slumbers soft and light.
Where is he ?

HUBERT.

In the Odenwald.
Some of his tenants, unappalled
By fear of death, or priestly word, —
A holy family, that make
Each meal a Supper of the Lord, —
Have him beneath their watch and
     ward,
For love of him, and Jesus' sake !
Pray you come in.   For why should I
With out-door hospitality
My prince's friend thus entertain ?

WALTER.

I would a moment here remain.
But you, good Hubert, go before,
Fill me a goblet of May-drink,
As aromatic as the May
From which it steals the breath away,
And which he loved so well of yore;
It is of him that I would think.
You shall attend me, when I call,
In the ancestral banquet-hall.
Unseen companions, guests of air,
You cannot wait on, will be there ;
They taste not food, they drink not
     wine,
But their soft eyes look into mine,
And their lips speak to me, and all

The vast and shadowy banquet-hall
Is full of looks and words divine!

Leaning over the parapet.

The day is done; and slowly from the
scene
The stooping sun up-gathers his spent
shafts,
And puts them back into his golden
quiver!
Below me in the valley, deep and green
As goblets are, from which in thirsty
draughts
We drink its wine, the swift and man-
tling river
Flows on triumphant through these
lovely regions,
Etched with the shadows of its sombre
margent,
And soft, reflected clouds of gold and
argent!
Yes, there it flows, forever, broad and
still
As when the vanguard of the Roman
legions
First saw it from the top of yonder
hill!
How beautiful it is! Fresh fields of
wheat,
Vineyard and town, and tower with
fluttering flag,
The consecrated chapel on the crag,
And the white hamlet gathered round
its base,
Like Mary sitting at her Saviour's feet,
And looking up at his beloved face!
O friend! O best of friends! Thy ab-
sence more
Than the impending night darkens the
landscape o'er!

II

A FARM IN THE ODENWALD.

A garden; morning; PRINCE HENRY
seated, with a book. ELSIE *at a distance gathering flowers.*

PRINCE HENRY, *reading.*

One morning, all alone,
Out of his convent of gray stone,
Into the forest older, darker, grayer,
His lips moving, as if in prayer,
His head sunken upon his breast
As in a dream of rest,
Walked the Monk Felix. All about

The broad, sweet sunshine lay without,
Filling the summer air;
And within the woodlands as he trod,
The dusk was like the truce of God
With worldly woe and care;
Under him lay the golden moss;
And above him the boughs of hoary
trees
Waved, and made the sign of the cross,
And whispered their Benedicites;
And from the ground
Rose an odor sweet and fragrant
Of the wild-flowers and the vagrant
Vines that wandered,
Seeking the sunshine, round and round.

These he heeded not, but pondered
On the volume in his hand,
Wherein amazed he read:
"A thousand years in thy sight
Are but as yesterday when it is past,
And as a watch in the night!"
And with his eyes downcast
In humility he said:
"I believe, O Lord,
What is written in thy Word,
But alas! I do not understand!"

And lo! he heard
The sudden singing of a bird,
A snow-white bird, that from a cloud
Dropped down,
And among the branches brown
Sat singing,
So sweet, and clear, and loud,
It seemed a thousand harp-strings ring-
ing.
And the Monk Felix closed his book,
And long, long,
With rapturous look,
He listened to the song,
And hardly breathed or stirred,
Until he saw, as in a vision,
The land Elysian,
And in the heavenly city heard
Angelic feet
Fall on the golden flagging of the street
And he would fain
Have caught the wondrous bird,
But strove in vain;
For it flew away, away,
Far over hill and dell,
And instead of its sweet singing
He heard the convent bell
Suddenly in the silence ringing
For the service of noonday.
And he retraced
His pathway sadly and in haste.

In the convent there was a change !
He looked for each well-known face,
But the faces were new and strange ;
New figures sat in the oaken stalls,
New voices chanted in the choir ;
Yet the place was the same place,
The same dusky walls
Of cold, gray stone,
The same cloisters and belfry and spire.

A stranger and alone
Among that brotherhood
The Monk Felix stood.
" Forty years." said a Friar,
" Have I been Prior
Of this convent in the wood,
But for that space
Never have I beheld thy face ! "

The heart of the Monk Felix fell :
And he answered, with submissive tone,
" This morning after the hour of Prime,
I left my cell,
And wandered forth alone,
Listening all the time
To the melodious singing
Of a beautiful white bird,
Until I heard
The bells of the convent ringing
Noon from their noisy towers.
It was as if I dreamed ;
For what to me had seemed
Moments only, had been hours ! "

" Years ! " said a voice close by.
It was an aged monk who spoke,
From a bench of oak
Fastened against the wall ; —
He was the oldest monk of all.
For a whole century
Had he been there,
Serving God in prayer,
The meekest and humblest of his crea-
tures.
He remembered well the features
Of Felix, and he said,
Speaking distinct and slow :
" One hundred years ago,
When I was a novice in this place,
There was here a monk, full of God's
grace,
Who bore the name
Of Felix, and this man must be the
same."

And straightway
They brought forth to the light of day
A volume old and brown,

A huge tome, bound
In brass and wild-boar's hide,
Wherein were written down
The names of all who had died
In the convent, since it was edified.
And there they found,
Just as the old monk said,
That on a certain day and date,
One hundred years before,
Had gone forth from the convent gate
The Monk Felix, and never more
Had entered that sacred door.
He had been counted among the dead !
And they knew, at last,
That, such had been the power
Of that celestial and immortal song,
A hundred years had passed,
And had not seemed so long
As a single hour !

ELSIE *comes in with flowers.*

ELSIE.

Here are flowers for you,
But they are not all for you.
Some of them are for the Virgin
And for Saint Cecilia.

PRINCE HENRY.

As thou standest there,
Thou seemest to me like the angel
That brought the immortal roses
To Saint Cecilia's bridal chamber.

ELSIE.

But these will fade.

PRINCE HENRY.

Themselves will fade,
But not their memory,
And memory has the power
To re-create them from the dust.
They remind me, too,
Of martyred Dorothea,
Who from Celestial gardens sent
Flowers as her witnesses
To him who scoffed and doubted.

ELSIE.

Do you know the story
Of Christ and the Sultan's daughter ?
That is the prettiest legend of them all

PRINCE HENRY.

Then tell it to me.
But first come hither.
Lay the flowers down beside me,
And put both thy hands in mine.
Now tell me the story.

ELSIE.

Early in the morning
The Sultan's daughter
Walked in her father's garden,
Gathering the bright flowers,
All full of dew.

PRINCE HENRY.

Just as thou hast been doing
This morning, dearest Elsie.

ELSIE.

And as she gathered them
She wondered more and more
Who was the Master of the Flowers,
And made them grow
Out of the cold, dark earth.
" In my heart," she said,
" I love him ; and for him
Would leave my father's palace,
To labor in his garden."

PRINCE HENRY.

Dear, innocent child !
How sweetly thou recallest
The long-forgotten legend,
That in my early childhood
My mother told me !
Upon my brain
It reappears once more,
As a birth-mark on the forehead
When a hand suddenly
Is raised upon it, and removed !

ELSIE.

And at midnight,
As she lay upon her bed,
She heard a voice
Call to her from the garden,
And, looking forth from her window,
She saw a beautiful youth
Standing among the flowers.
It was the Lord Jesus ;
And she went down to Him,
And opened the door for Him ;
And He said to her, " O maiden !
Thou hast thought of me with love,
And for thy sake
Out of my Father's kingdom
Have I come hither :
I am the Master of the Flowers.
My garden is in Paradise,
And if thou wilt go with me,
Thy bridal garland
Shall be of bright red flowers."
And then He took from his finger
A golden ring,

And asked the Sultan's daughter
If she would be his bride.
And when she answered Him with love,
His wounds began to bleed,
And she said to Him,
" O Love ! how red thy heart is,
And thy hands are full of roses."
" For thy sake," answered He,
" For thy sake is my heart so red,
For thee I bring these roses ;
I gathered them at the cross
Whereon I died for thee !
Come, for my Father calls.
Thou art my elected bride ! "
And the Sultan's daughter
Followed Him to his Father's garden.

PRINCE HENRY.

Wouldst thou have done so, Elsie ?

ELSIE.

Yes, very gladly.

PRINCE HENRY.

Then the Celestial Bridegroom
Will come for thee also.
Upon thy forehead He will place,
Not his crown of thorns,
But a crown of roses.
In thy bridal chamber,
Like Saint Cecilia,
Thou shalt hear sweet music,
And breathe the fragrance
Of flowers immortal !
Go now and place these flowers
Before her picture.

A ROOM IN THE FARM-HOUSE.

Twilight. URSULA *spinning.* GOTTLIEB *asleep in his chair.*

URSULA.

Darker and darker ! Hardly a glimmer
Of light comes in at the window-pane ;
Or is it my eyes are growing dimmer ?
I cannot disentangle this skein,
Nor wind it rightly upon the reel.
Elsie !

GOTTLIEB, *starting.*

The stopping of thy wheel
Has awakened me out of a pleasant
dream.
I thought I was sitting beside a stream,
And heard the grinding of a mill,
When suddenly the wheels stood still,
And a voice cried "Elsie," in my ear !
It startled me, it seemed so near.

URSULA.

I was calling her : I want a light.
I cannot see to spin my flax.
Bring the lamp, Elsie. Dost thou
   hear ?

ELSIE, *within.*

In a moment !

GOTTLIEB.

Where are Bertha and Max ?

URSULA.

They are sitting with Elsie at the door.
She is telling them stories of the wood,
And the Wolf, and little Red Riding-
   hood.

GOTTLIEB.

And where is the Prince ?

URSULA.

In his room overhead ;
I heard him walking across the floor,
As he always does, with a heavy tread.

ELSIE *comes in with a lamp.* MAX *and*
   BERTHA *follow her ; and they all sing
   the Evening Song on the lighting of the
   lamps.*

EVENING SONG.

O gladsome light
Of the Father Immortal,
And of the celestial
Sacred and blessed
Jesus, our Saviour !

Now to the sunset
Again hast thou brought us ;
And seeing the evening
Twilight, we bless thee !
Praise thee, adore thee !

Father omnipotent !
Son, the Life-giver !
Spirit, the Comforter !
Worthy at all times
Of worship and wonder !

PRINCE HENRY, *at the door.*

Amen !

URSULA.

Who was it said Amen ?

ELSIE.

It was the Prince : he stood at the door,
And listened a moment, as we chanted
The evening song.   He is gone again.
I have often seen him there before.

URSULA.

Poor Prince !

GOTTLIEB.

I thought the house was haunted !
Poor Prince, alas ! and yet as mild
And patient as the gentlest child !

MAX.

I love him because he is so good,
And makes me such fine bows and ar-
   rows,
To shoot at the robins and the spar
   rows,
And the red squirrels in the wood !

BERTHA.

I love him, too !

GOTTLIEB.

Ah, yes ! we all
Love him from the bottom of our
   hearts ;
He gave us the farm, the house, and
   the grange,
He gave us the horses and the carts,
And the great oxen in the stall,
The vineyard, and the forest range !
We have nothing to give him but our
   love !

BERTHA.

Did he give us the beautiful stork above
On the chimney-top, with its large,
   round nest ?

GOTTLIEB.

No, not the stork ; by God in heaven,
As a blessing, the dear white stork was
   given,
But the Prince has given us all the
   rest.
God bless him, and make him well
   again.

ELSIE.

Would I could do something for his
   sake,
Something to cure his sorrow and pain !

GOTTLIEB.

That no one can ; neither thou nor I,
Nor any one else.

ELSIE.

And must he die ?

URSULA.

Yes ; if the dear God does not take
Pity upon him in his distress,
And work a miracle !

GOTTLIEB.

Or unless
Some maiden, of her own accord,
Offers her life for that of her lord,
And is willing to die in his stead.

ELSIE.

I will !

URSULA.

Prithee, thou foolish child, be still !
Thou shouldst not say what thou dost
not mean !

ELSIE.

I mean it truly !

MAX.

O father ! this morning,
Down by the mill, in the ravine,
Hans killed a wolf, the very same
That in the night to the sheepfold came,
And ate up my lamb, that was left out-
side.

GOTTLIEB.

I am glad he is dead.   It will be a warning
To the wolves in the forest, far and wide.

MAX.

And I am going to have his hide !

BERTHA.

I wonder if this is the wolf that ate
Little Red Ridinghood !

URSULA.

Oh, no !
That wolf was killed a long while ago.
Come, children, it is growing late.

MAX.

Ah, how I wish I were a man,
As stout as Hans is, and as strong !

I would do nothing else, the whole day
long,
But just kill wolves.

GOTTLIEB.

Then go to bed,
And grow as fast as a little boy can.
Bertha is half asleep already.
See how she nods her heavy head,
And her sleepy feet are so unsteady
She will hardly be able to creep upstairs.

URSULA.

Good night, my children.   Here 's the
light.
And do not forget to say your prayers
Before you sleep.

GOTTLIEB.

Good night !

MAX *and* BERTHA.

Good night !
They go out with ELSIE.

URSULA, *spinning.*

She is a strange and wayward child,
That Elsie of ours.   She looks so old,
And thoughts and fancies weird and
wild
Seem of late to have taken hold
Of her heart, that was once so docile
and mild !

GOTTLIEB.

She is like all girls.

URSULA.

Ah no, forsooth !
Unlike all I have ever seen.
For she has visions and strange dreams,
And in all her words and ways, she
seems
Much older than she is in truth.
Who would think her but fifteen ?
And there has been of late such a
change !
My heart is heavy with fear and doubt
That she may not live till the year is
out.
She is so strange, — so strange, — so
strange !

GOTTLIEB.

I am not troubled with any such fear ;
She will live and thrive for many a
year.

ELSIE'S CHAMBER.

Night. ELSIE *praying.*

ELSIE.

My Redeemer and my Lord,
I beseech thee, I entreat thee,
Guide me in each act and word,
That hereafter I may meet thee,
Watching, waiting, hoping, yearning,
With my lamp well trimmed and burn-
    ing!

Interceding
With these bleeding
Wounds upon thy hands and side,
For all who have lived and errèd
Thou hast suffered, thou hast died,
Scourged, and mocked, and crucified,
And in the grave hast thou been buried!

If my feeble prayer can reach thee,
O my Saviour, I beseech thee,
Even as thou hast died for me,
More sincerely
Let me follow where thou leadest,
Let me, bleeding as thou bleedest,
Die, if dying I may give
Life to one who asks to live,
And more nearly,
Dying thus, resemble thee!

THE CHAMBER OF GOTTLIEB AND
URSULA.

Midnight. ELSIE *standing by their bedside, weeping.*

GOTTLIEB.

The wind is roaring; the rushing rain
Is loud upon roof and window-pane,
As if the Wild Huntsman of Rodenstein,
Boding evil to me and mine,
Were abroad to-night with his ghostly
    train!
In the brief lulls of the tempest wild,
The dogs howl in the yard; and hark!
Some one is sobbing in the dark,
Here in the chamber!

ELSIE.

It is I.

URSULA.

Elsie! what ails thee, my poor child?

ELSIE.

I am disturbed and much distressed,
In thinking our dear Prince must die;
I cannot close mine eyes, nor rest.

GOTTLIEB.

What wouldst thou? In the Power
    Divine
His healing lies, not in our own;
It is in the hand of God alone.

ELSIE.

Nay, He has put it into mine,
And into my heart!

GOTTLIEB.

    Thy words are wild!

URSULA.

What dost thou mean? my child! my
    child!

ELSIE.

That for our dear Prince Henry's sake
I will myself the offering make,
And give my life to purchase his.

URSULA.

Am I still dreaming, or awake?
Thou speakest carelessly of death,
And yet thou knowest not what it is.

ELSIE.

'T is the cessation of our breath.
Silent and motionless we lie;
And no one knoweth more than this.
I saw our little Gertrude die;
She left off breathing, and no more
I smoothed the pillow beneath her head.
She was more beautiful than before.
Like violets faded were her eyes;
By this we knew that she was dead.
Through the open window looked the
    skies
Into the chamber where she lay,
And the wind was like the sound of
    wings,
As if angels came to bear her away.
Ah! when I saw and felt these things,
I found it difficult to stay;
I longed to die, as she had died,
And go forth with her, side by side.
The Saints are dead, the Martyrs dead,
And Mary, and our Lord; and I
Would follow in humility
The way by them illuminèd!

URSULA.

My child! my child! thou must not die!

ELSIE.

Why should I live ?   Do I not know
The life of woman is full of woe ?
Toiling on and on and on,
With breaking heart, and tearful eyes,
And silent lips, and in the soul
The secret longings that arise,
Which this world never satisfies !
Some more, some less, but of the whole
Not one quite happy, no, not one !

URSULA.

It is the malediction of Eve!

ELSIE.

In place of it, let me receive
The benediction of Mary, then.

GOTTLIEB.

Ah, woe is me!   Ah, woe is me!
Most wretched am I among men !

URSULA.

Alas! that I should live to see
Thy death, beloved, and to stand
Above thy grave!   Ah, woe the day?

ELSIE.

Thou wilt not see it.   I shall lie
Beneath the flowers of another land,
For at Salerno, far away
Over the mountains, over the sea,
It is appointed me to die !
And it will seem no more to thee
Than if at the village on market-day
I should a little longer stay
Than I am wont.

URSULA.

            Even as thou sayest !
And how my heart beats, when thou
    stayest !
I cannot rest until my sight
Is satisfied with seeing thee.
What, then, if thou wert dead ?

GOTTLIEB.

            Ah me !
Of our old eyes thou art the light !
The joy of our old hearts art thou !
And wilt thou die ?

URSULA.

            Not now ! not now !

ELSIE.

Christ died for me, and shall not I
Be willing for my Prince to die ?
You both are silent ; you cannot speak
This said I at our Saviour's feast
After confession, to the priest,
And even he made no reply.
Does he not warn us all to seek
The happier, better land on high,
Where flowers immortal never wither ;
And could he forbid me to go thither ?

GOTTLIEB.

In God's own time, my heart's delight !
When He shall call thee, not before !

ELSIE.

I heard Him call.   When Christ as-
    cended
Triumphantly, from star to star,
He left the gates of heaven ajar.
I had a vision in the night,
And saw Him standing at the door
Of his Father's mansion, vast and splen-
    did,
And beckoning to me from afar.
I cannot stay!

GOTTLIEB.

            She speaks almost
As if it were the Holy Ghost
Spake through her lips, and in her
    stead :
What if this were of God ?

URSULA.

            Ah, then
Gainsay it dare we not.

GOTTLIEB.

            Amen !
Elsie ! the words that thou hast said
Are strange and new for us to hear,
And fill our hearts with doubt and fear.
Whether it be a dark temptation
Of the Evil One, or God's inspiration,
We in our blindness cannot say.
We must think upon it, and pray ;
For evil and good it both resembles.
If it be of God, his will be done !
May He guard us from the Evil One !
How hot thy hand is! how it trembles !
Go to thy bed, and try to sleep.

URSULA.

Kiss me.   Good night; and do not
weep !

ELSIE *goes out.*

Ah, what an awful thing is this!
I almost shuddered at her kiss,
As if a ghost had touched my cheek,
I am so childish and so weak!
As soon as I see the earliest gray
Of morning glimmer in the east,
I will go over to the priest,
And hear what the good man has to
say!

A VILLAGE CHURCH.

A woman kneeling at the confessional.

THE PARISH PRIEST, *from within.*

Go, sin no more! Thy penance o'er,
A new and better life begin!
God maketh thee forever free
From the dominion of thy sin!
Go, sin no more! He will restore
The peace that filled thy heart before,
And pardon thine iniquity!

*The woman goes out. The Priest comes
forth, and walks slowly up and down the
church.*

O blessed Lord! how much I need
Thy light to guide me on my way!
So many hands, that, without heed,
Still touch thy wounds and make them
bleed!
So many feet, that, day by day,
Still wander from thy fold astray!
Unless thou fill me with thy light,
I cannot lead thy flock aright;
Nor without thy support can bear
The burden of so great a care,
But am myself a castaway!

A pause.

The day is drawing to its close;
And what good deeds, since first it rose,
Have I presented, Lord, to thee,
As offsprings of my ministry?
What wrong repressed, what right main-
tained,
What struggle passed, what victory
gained,
What good attempted and attained?
Feeble, at best, is my endeavor!
I see, but cannot reach, the height
That lies forever in the light,
And yet forever and forever,
When seeming just within my grasp,
I feel my feeble hands unclasp,

And sink discouraged into night!
For thine own purpose, thou hast sent
The strife and the discouragement!

A pause.

Why stayest thou, Prince of Hoheneck?
Why keep me pacing to and fro
Amid these aisles of sacred gloom,
Counting my footsteps as I go,
And marking with each step a tomb?
Why should the world for thee make
room,
And wait thy leisure and thy beck?
Thou comest in the hope to hear
Some word of comfort and of cheer.
What can I say? I cannot give
The counsel to do this and live;
But rather, firmly to deny
The tempter, though his power be
strong,
And, inaccessible to wrong,
Still like a martyr live and die!

A pause.

The evening air grows dusk and brown;
I must go forth into the town,
To visit beds of pain and death,
Of restless limbs, and quivering breath,
And sorrowing hearts, and patient eyes
That see, through tears, the sun go
down,
But never more shall see it rise.
The poor in body and estate,
The sick and the disconsolate,
Must not on man's convenience wait.

Goes out.

Enter LUCIFER, *as a Priest.*

LUCIFER, *with a genuflexion, mocking.*

This is the Black Pater-noster.
God was my foster,
He fostered me
Under the book of the Palm-tree!
St. Michael was my dame.
He was born at Bethlehem,
He was made of flesh and blood.
God send me my right food,
My right food, and shelter too,
That I may to yon kirk go,
To read upon yon sweet book
Which the mighty God of heaven shook
Open, open, hell's gates!
Shut, shut, heaven's gates!
All the devils in the air
The stronger be, that hear the Black
Prayer!

Looking round the church.

What a darksome and dismal place!
I wonder that any man has the face
To call such a hole the House of the
Lord,
And the gate of Heaven, — yet such is
the word.
Ceiling, and walls, and windows old,
Covered with cobwebs, blackened with
mould;
Dust on the pulpit, dust on the stairs,
Dust on the benches, and stalls, and
chairs!
The pulpit, from which such ponderous
sermons
Have fallen down on the brains of the
Germans,
With about as much real edification
As if a great Bible, bound in lead,
Had fallen, and struck them on the
head;
And I ought to remember that sensation!
Here stands the holy-water stoup!
Holy-water it may be to many,
But to me, the veriest Liquor Gehennæ!
It smells like a filthy fast-day soup!
Near it stands the box for the poor,
With its iron padlock, safe and sure.
I and the priest of the parish know
Whither all these charities go;
Therefore, to keep up the institution,
I will add my little contribution!

He puts in money.

Underneath this mouldering tomb,
With statue of stone, and scutcheon of
brass,
Slumbers a great lord of the village.
All his life was riot and pillage,
But at length, to escape the threatened
doom
Of the everlasting penal fire,
He died in the dress of a mendicant
friar,
And bartered his wealth for a daily
mass.
But all that afterwards came to pass,
And whether he finds it dull or pleasant,
Is kept a secret for the present,
At his own particular desire.

And here, in a corner of the wall,
Shadowy, silent, apart from all,
With its awful portal open wide,
And its latticed windows on either side,
And its step well worn by the bended
knees
Of one or two pious centuries,
Stands the village confessional!

Within it, as an honored guest,
I will sit down awhile and rest!

Seats himself in the confessional.

Here sits the priest; and faint and low,
Like the sighing of an evening breeze,
Comes through these painted lattices
The ceaseless sound of human woe;
Here, while her bosom aches and throbs
With deep and agonizing sobs,
That half are passion, half contrition,
The luckless daughter of perdition
Slowly confesses her secret shame!
The time, the place, the lover's name!
Here the grim murderer, with a groan,
From his bruised conscience rolls the
stone,
Thinking that thus he can atone
For ravages of sword and flame!

Indeed, I marvel, and marvel greatly,
How a priest can sit here so sedately,
Reading, the whole year out and in,
Naught but the catalogue of sin,
And still keep any faith whatever
In human virtue! Never! never!

I cannot repeat a thousandth part
Of the horrors and crimes and sins and
woes
That arise, when with palpitating throes
The graveyard in the human heart
Gives up its dead, at the voice of the
priest,
As if he were an archangel, at least.
It makes a peculiar atmosphere,
This odor of earthly passions and crimes,
Such as I like to breathe, at times,
And such as often brings me here
In the hottest and most pestilential sea-
son.
To-day, I come for another reason;
To foster and ripen an evil thought
In a heart that is almost to madness
wrought,
And to make a murderer out of a prince,
A sleight of hand I learned long since!
He comes. In the twilight he will not
see
The difference between his priest and
me!
In the same net was the mother caught!

PRINCE HENRY, *entering and kneeling at
the confessional.*

Remorseful, penitent, and lowly,
I come to crave, O Father noly,
Thy benediction on my head.

LUCIFER.

The benediction shall be said
After confession, not before!
'T is a God-speed to the parting guest,
Who stands already at the door,
Sandalled with holiness, and dressed
In garments pure from earthly stain.
Meanwhile, hast thou searched well thy
    breast?
Does the same madness fill thy brain?
Or have thy passion and unrest
Vanished forever from thy mind?

PRINCE HENRY.

By the same madness still made blind,
By the same passion still possessed,
I come again to the house of prayer,
A man afflicted and distressed!
As in a cloudy atmosphere,
Through unseen sluices of the air,
A sudden and impetuous wind
Strikes the great forest white with fear,
And every branch, and bough, and
    spray,
Points all its quivering leaves one way,
And meadows of grass, and fields of
    grain,
And the clouds above, and the slanting
    rain,
And smoke from chimneys of the town,
Yield themselves to it, and bow down,
So does this dreadful purpose press
Onward, with irresistible stress,
And all my thoughts and faculties,
Struck level by the strength of this,
From their true inclination turn
And all stream forward to Salern!

LUCIFER.

Alas! we are but eddies of dust,
Uplifted by the blast, and whirled
Along the highway of the world
A moment only, then to fall
Back to a common level all,
At the subsiding of the gust!

PRINCE HENRY.

O holy Father! pardon in me
The oscillation of a mind
Unsteadfast, and that cannot find
Its centre of rest and harmony!
For evermore before mine eyes
This ghastly phantom flits and flies,
And as a madman through a crowd,
With frantic gestures and wild cries,
It hurries onward, and aloud
Repeats its awful prophecies!

Weakness is wretchedness! To be
    strong
Is to be happy! I am weak,
And cannot find the good I seek,
Because I feel and fear the wrong!

LUCIFER.

Be not alarmed! The church is kind,
And in her mercy and her meekness
She meets half-way her children's
    weakness,
Writes their transgressions in the dust!
Though in the Decalogue we find
The mandate written, "Thou shalt not
    kill!"
Yet there are cases when we must.
In war, for instance, or from scathe
To guard and keep the one true faith
We must look at the Decalogue in the
    light
Of an ancient statute, that was meant
For a mild and general application,
To be understood with the reservation
That in certain instances the Right
Must yield to the Expedient!
Thou art a Prince. If thou shouldst
    die
What hearts and hopes would prostrate
    lie!
What noble deeds, what fair renown,
Into the grave with thee go down!
What acts of valor and courtesy
Remain undone, and die with thee!
Thou art the last of all thy race!
With thee a noble name expires,
And vanishes from the earth's face
The glorious memory of thy sires!
She is a peasant. In her veins
Flows common and plebeian blood;
It is such as daily and hourly stains
The dust and the turf of battle plains,
By vassals shed, in a crimson flood,
Without reserve and without reward,
At the slightest summons of their lord!
But thine is precious; the fore-ap-
    pointed
Blood of kings, of God's anointed!
Moreover, what has the world in store
For one like her, but tears and toil?
Daughter of sorrow, serf of the soil,
A peasant's child and a peasant's wife,
And her soul within her sick and sore
With the roughness and barrenness of
    life!
I marvel not at the heart's recoil
From a fate like this, in one so tender,
Nor at its eagerness to surrender
All the wretchedness, want, and woe

That await it in this world below,
For the unutterable splendor
Of the world of rest beyond the skies.
So the Church sanctions the sacrifice :
Therefore inhale this healing balm,
And breathe this fresh life into thine ;
Accept the comfort and the calm
She offers, as a gift divine ;
Let her fall down and anoint thy feet
With the ointment costly and most sweet
Of her young blood, and thou shalt live.

PRINCE HENRY.

And will the righteous Heaven forgive ?
No action, whether foul or fair,
Is ever done, but it leaves somewhere
A record, written by fingers ghostly,
As a blessing or a curse, and mostly
In the greater weakness or greater
strength
Of the acts which follow it, till at length
The wrongs of ages are redressed,
And the justice of God made manifest !

LUCIFER.

In ancient records it is stated
That, whenever an evil deed is done,
Another devil is created
To scourge and torment the offending
one !
But evil is only good perverted,
And Lucifer, the bearer of Light,
But an angel fallen and deserted,
Thrust from his Father's house with a
curse
Into the black and endless night.

PRINCE HENRY.

If justice rules the universe,
From the good actions of good men
Angels of light should be begotten,
And thus the balance restored again.

LUCIFER.

Yes ; if the world were not so rotten,
And so given over to the Devil !

PRINCE HENRY.

But this deed, is it good or evil ?
Have I thine absolution free
To do it, and without restriction ?

LUCIFER.

Ay ; and from whatsoever sin
Lieth around it and within,
From all crimes in which it may involve
thee,
I now release thee and absolve thee !

PRINCE HENRY.

Give me thy holy benediction.

LUCIFER, *stretching forth his hand and
muttering.*

Maledictione perpetua
Maledicat vos
Pater eternus !

THE ANGEL, *with the æolian harp.*

Take heed ! take heed !
Noble art thou in thy birth,
By the good and the great of earth
Hast thou been taught !
Be noble in every thought
And in every deed !
Let not the illusion of thy senses
Betray thee to deadly offences.
Be strong ! be good ! be pure !
The right only shall endure,
All things else are but false pretences.
I entreat thee, I implore,
Listen no more
To the suggestions of an evil spirit,
That even now is there,
Making the foul seem fair,
And selfishness itself a virtue and a
merit !

A ROOM IN THE FARM-HOUSE.

GOTTLIEB.

It is decided ! For many days,
And nights as many, we have had
A nameless terror in our breast,
Making us timid, and afraid
Of God, and his mysterious ways !
We have been sorrowful and sad ;
Much have we suffered, much have
prayed
That He would lead us as is best,
And show us what his will required.
It is decided ; and we give
Our child, O Prince, that you may live !

URSULA.

It is of God. He has inspired
This purpose in her : and through pain,
Out of a world of sin and woe,
He takes her to Himself again.
The mother's heart resists no longer ;
With the Angel of the Lord in vain
It wrestled, for he was the stronger.

GOTTLIEB.

As Abraham offered long ago

His son unto the Lord, and even
The Everlasting Father in heaven
Gave his, as a lamb unto the slaughter,
So do I offer up my daughter!

URSULA *hides her face.*

ELSIE.

My life is little,
Only a cup of water,
But pure and limpid.
Take it, O my Prince!
Let it refresh you,
Let it restore you.
It is given willingly,
It is given freely;
May God bless the gift!

PRINCE HENRY.

And the giver!

GOTTLIEB.

Amen!

PRINCE HENRY.

I accept it!

GOTTLIEB.

Where are the children?

URSULA.

They are already asleep.

GOTTLIEB.

What if they were dead?

IN THE GARDEN.

ELSIE.

I have one thing to ask of you.

PRINCE HENRY.

What is it?
It is already granted.

ELSIE.

Promise me,
When we are gone from here, and on
    our way
Are journeying to Salerno, you will not,
By word or deed, endeavor to dissuade
    me
And turn me from my purpose; but
    remember
That as a pilgrim to the Holy City
Walks unmolested, and with thoughts
    of pardon

Occupied wholly, so would I approach
The gates of Heaven, in this great
    jubilee,
With my petition, putting off from me
All thoughts of earth, as shoes from off
    my feet.
Promise me this.

PRINCE HENRY.

Thy words fall from thy lips
Like roses from the lips of Angelo: and
    angels
Might stoop to pick them up!

ELSIE.

Will you not promise?

PRINCE HENRY.

If ever we depart upon this journey,
So long to one or both of us, I promise.

ELSIE.

Shall we not go, then? Have you lifted
    me
Into the air, only to hurl me back
Wounded upon the ground? and offered
    me
The waters of eternal life, to bid me
Drink the polluted puddles of the world?

PRINCE HENRY.

O Elsie! what a lesson thou dost teach
    me!
The life which is, and that which is to
    come,
Suspended hang in such nice equipoise
A breath disturbs the balance; and that
    scale
In which we throw our hearts pre-
    ponderates,
And the other, like an empty one, flies
    up,
And is accounted vanity and air!
To me the thought of death is terri-
    ble,
Having such hold on life. To thee it is
    not
So much even as the lifting of a latch;
Only a step into the open air
Out of a tent already luminous
With light that shines through its trans-
    parent walls!
O pure in heart! from thy sweet dust
    shall grow
Lilies, upon whose petals will be writ-
    ten
"Ave Maria" in characters of gold!

III.

A STREET IN STRASBURG.

Night. PRINCE HENRY *wandering alone, wrapped in a cloak.*

PRINCE HENRY.

Still is the night. The sound of feet
Has died away from the empty street,
And like an artisan, bending down
His head on his anvil, the dark town
Sleeps, with a slumber deep and sweet.
Sleepless and restless, I alone,
In the dusk and damp of these walls of
stone,
Wander and weep in my remorse!

CRIER OF THE DEAD, *ringing a bell.*

Wake! wake!
All ye that sleep!
Pray for the Dead!
Pray for the Dead!

PRINCE HENRY.

Hark! with what accents loud and
hoarse
This warder on the walls of death
Sends forth the challenge of his breath!
I see the dead that sleep in the grave!
They rise up and their garments wave,
Dimly and spectral, as they rise,
With the light of another world in
their eyes!

CRIER OF THE DEAD.

Wake! wake!
All ye that sleep!
Pray for the Dead!
Pray for the Dead!

PRINCE HENRY.

Why for the dead, who are at rest?
Pray for the living, in whose breast
The struggle between right and wrong
Is raging terrible and strong,
As when good angels war with devils!
This is the Master of the Revels,
Who, at Life's flowing feast, proposes
The health of absent friends, and
pledges,
Not in bright goblets crowned with
roses,
And tinkling as we touch their edges,
But with his dismal, tinkling bell,
That mocks and mimics their funeral
knell.

CRIER OF THE DEAD.

Wake! wake!
All ye that sleep!
Pray for the Dead!
Pray for the Dead!

PRINCE HENRY.

Wake not, beloved! be thy sleep
Silent as night is, and as deep!
There walks a sentinel at thy gate
Whose heart is heavy and desolate,
And the heavings of whose bosom num
ber
The respirations of thy slumber,
As if some strange, mysterious fate
Had linked two hearts in one, and mine
Went madly wheeling about thine,
Only with wider and wilder sweep!

CRIER OF THE DEAD, *at a distance.*

Wake! wake!
All ye that sleep!
Pray for the Dead!
Pray for the Dead!

PRINCE HENRY.

Lo! with what depth of blackness
thrown
Against the clouds, far up the skies
The walls of the cathedral rise,
Like a mysterious grove of stone,
With fitful lights and shadows blend-
ing,
As from behind, the moon ascending,
Lights its dim aisles and paths un-
known!
The wind is rising; but the boughs
Rise not and fall not with the wind,
That through their foliage sobs and
soughs;
Only the cloudy rack behind,
Drifting onward, wild and ragged,
Gives to each spire and buttress jagged
A seeming motion undefined.
Below on the square, an armèd knight,
Still as a statue and as white,
Sits on his steed, and the moonbeams
quiver
Upon the points of his armor bright
As on the ripples of a river.
He lifts the visor from his cheek,
And beckons, and makes as he would
speak.

WALTER *the Minnesinger.*

Friend! can you tell me where alight
Thuringia's horsemen for the night?

For I have lingered in the rear,
And wander vainly up and down.

PRINCE HENRY.

I am a stranger in the town,
As thou art; but the voice I hear
Is not a stranger to mine ear.
Thou art Walter of the Vogelweid!

WALTER.

Thou hast guessed rightly; and thy name
Is Henry of Hoheneck!

PRINCE HENRY.

Ay, the same.

WALTER, *embracing him.*

Come closer, closer to my side!
What brings thee hither?   What potent charm
Has drawn thee from thy German farm
Into the old Alsatian city?

PRINCE HENRY.

A tale of wonder and of pity!
A wretched man, almost by stealth
Dragging my body to Salern,
In the vain hope and search for health,
And destined never to return.
Already thou hast heard the rest.
But what brings thee, thus armed and dight
In the equipments of a knight?

WALTER.

Dost thou not see upon my breast
The cross of the Crusaders shine?
My pathway leads to Palestine.

PRINCE HENRY.

Ah, would that way were also mine!
O noble poet! thou whose heart
Is like a nest of singing-birds
Rocked on the topmost bough of life,
Wilt thou, too, from our sky depart,
And in the clangor of the strife
Mingle the music of thy words?

WALTER.

My hopes are high, my heart is proud,
And like a trumpet long and loud,
Thither my thoughts all clang and ring!
My life is in my hand, and lo!
I grasp and bend it as a bow,
And shoot forth from its trembling string   •
An arrow, that shall be, perchance,

Like the arrow of the Israelite king
Shot from the window towards the east,
That of the Lord's deliverance!

PRINCE HENRY.

My life, alas! is what thou seest!
O enviable fate! to be
Strong, beautiful, and armed like thee
With lyre and sword, with song and steel;
A hand to smite, a heart to feel!
Thy heart, thy hand, thy lyre, thy sword,
Thou givest all unto thy Lord;
While I, so mean and abject grown,
Am thinking of myself alone.

WALTER.

Be patient: Time will reinstate
Thy health and fortunes.

PRINCE HENRY.

'T is too late!
I cannot strive against my fate!

WALTER.

Come with me; 'for my steed is weary;
Our journey has been long and dreary,
And, dreaming of his stall, he dints
With his impatient hoofs the flints.

PRINCE HENRY, *aside.*

I am ashamed, in my disgrace,
To look into that noble face!
To-morrow, Walter, let it be.

WALTER.

To-morrow, at the dawn of day,
I shall again be on my way.
Come with me to the hostelry,
For I have many things to say.
Our journey into Italy
Perchance together we may make;
Wilt thou not do it for my sake?

PRINCE HENRY.

A sick man's pace would but impede
Thine eager and impatient speed.
Besides, my pathway leads me round
To Hirschau, in the forest's bound,
Where I assemble man and steed,
And all things for my journey's need.

They go out.

LUCIFER, *flying over the city.*

Sleep, sleep, O city! till the light
Wake you to sin and crime again,
Whilst on your dreams, like dismal rain,

I scatter downward through the night
My maledictions dark and deep.
I have more martyrs in your walls
Than God has; and they cannot sleep;
They are my bond-men and my thralls;
Their wretched lives are full of pain,
Wild agonies of nerve and brain;
And every heart-beat, every breath,
Is a convulsion worse than death!
Sleep, sleep, O city! though within
The circuit of your walls there be
No habitation free from sin,
And all its nameless misery;
The aching heart, the aching head,
Grief for the living and the dead,
And foul corruption of the time,
Disease, distress, and want, and woe,
And crimes, and passions that may
    grow
Until they ripen into crime!

SQUARE IN FRONT OF THE CATHEDRAL.

Easter Sunday. FRIAR CUTHBERT
*preaching to the crowd from a pulpit in
the open air.* PRINCE HENRY *and
Elsie crossing the square.*

PRINCE HENRY.

This is the day, when from the dead
Our Lord arose; and everywhere,
Out of their darkness and despair,
Triumphant over fears and foes,
The hearts of his disciples rose,
When to the women, standing near,
The Angel in shining vesture said,
"The Lord is risen; he is not here!"
And, mindful that the day is come,
On all the hearths in Christendom
The fires are quenched, to be again
Rekindled from the sun, that high
Is dancing in the cloudless sky.
The churches are all decked with flow-
    ers,
The salutations among men
Are but the Angel's words divine,
"Christ is arisen!" and the bells
Catch the glad murmur, as it swells,
And chant together in their towers.
All hearts are glad; and free from care
The faces of the people shine.
See what a crowd is in the square,
Gayly and gallantly arrayed!

ELSIE.

Let us go back; I am afraid!

PRINCE HENRY.

Nay, let us mount the church-steps
    here,
Under the doorway's sacred shadow;
We can see all things, and be freer
From the crowd that madly heaves and
    presses!

ELSIE.

What a gay pageant! what bright
    dresses!
It looks like a flower - besprinkled
    meadow.
What is that yonder on the square?

PRINCE HENRY.

A pulpit in the open air,
And a Friar, who is preaching to the
    crowd
In a voice so deep and clear and loud,
That, if we listen, and give heed,
His lowest words will reach the ear.

FRIAR CUTHBERT, *gesticulating and
cracking a postilion's whip.*

What ho! good people! do you not hear?
Dashing along at the top of his speed,
Booted and spurred, on his jaded steed,
A courier comes with words of cheer.
Courier! what is the news, I pray?
"Christ is arisen!" Whence come you?
    "From court."
Then I do not believe it; you say it in
    sport.

Cracks his whip again.

Ah, here comes another, riding this
    way;
We soon shall know what he has to
    say.
Courier! what are the tidings to-day?
"Christ is arisen!" Whence come you?
    "From town."
Then I do not believe it; away with
    you, clown.

Cracks his whip more violently.

And here comes a third, who is spur-
    ring amain;
What news do you bring, with your
    loose-hanging rein,
Your spurs wet with blood, and your
    bridle with foam?
"Christ is arisen!" Whence come you?
    "From Rome."
Ah, now I believe. He is risen, indeed.

Ride on with the news, at the top of
your speed!

Great applause among the crowd.

To come back to my text! When the
news was first spread
That Christ was arisen indeed from the
dead,
Very great was the joy of the angels in
heaven;
And as great the dispute as to who
should carry
The tidings thereof to the Virgin Mary,
Pierced to the heart with sorrows seven.
Old Father Adam was first to propose,
As being the author of all our woes;
But he was refused, for fear, said they,
He would stop to eat apples on the way!
Abel came next, but petitioned in vain,
Because he might meet with his brother
Cain!
Noah, too, was refused, lest his weakness
for wine
Should delay him at every tavern-sign;
And John the Baptist could not get a
vote,
On account of his old-fashioned camel's-
hair coat;
And the Penitent Thief, who died on the
cross,
Was reminded that all his bones were
broken!
Till at last, when each in turn had
spoken,
The company being still at loss,
The Angel, who rolled away the stone,
Was sent to the sepulchre, all alone.
And filled with glory that gloomy
prison,
And said to the Virgin, "The Lord is
arisen!"

The Cathedral bells ring.

But hark! the bells are beginning to
chime;
And I feel that I am growing hoarse.
I will put an end to my discourse,
And leave the rest for some other time.
For the bells themselves are the best of
preachers;
Their brazen lips are learned teachers,
From their pulpits of stone, in the upper
air,
Sounding aloft, without crack or flaw,
Shriller than trumpets under the Law,
Now a sermon, and now a prayer.
The clangorous hammer is the tongue,
This way, that way, beaten and swung,

That from mouth of brass, as from Mouth
of Gold,
May be taught the Testaments, New
and Old.
And above it the great cross-beam of
wood
Representeth the Holy Rood,
Upon which, like the bell, our hopes are
hung.
And the wheel wherewith it is swayed
and rung
Is the mind of man, that round and
round
Sways, and maketh the tongue to
sound!
And the rope, with its twisted cordage
three,
Denoteth the Scriptural Trinity
Of Morals, and Symbols, and History;
And the upward and downward motion
show
That we touch upon matters high and
low;
And the constant change and transmu-
tation
Of action and of contemplation,
Downward, the Scripture brought from
on high,
Upward, exalted again to the sky;
Downward, the literal interpretation,
Upward, the Vision and Mystery!

And now, my hearers, to make an end,
I have only one word more to say;
In the church, in honor of Easter day
Will be presented a Miracle Play;
And I hope you will have the grace to
attend.
Christ bring us at last to his felicity!
Pax vobiscum! et Benedicite!

IN THE CATHEDRAL.

CHANT.

Kyrie Eleison!
Christe Eleison!

ELSIE.

I am at home here in my Father's
house!
These paintings of the Saints upon the
walls
Have all familiar and benignant faces.

PRINCE HENRY.

The portraits of the family of God!

Thine own hereafter shall be placed
    among them.

ELSIE.

How very grand it is and wonderful!
Never have I beheld a church so
    splendid!
Such columns, and such arches, and such
    windows,
So many tombs and statues in the
    chapels,
And under them so many confessionals.
They must be for the rich. I should
    not like
To tell my sins in such a church as this.
Who built it?

PRINCE HENRY.

        A great master of his craft,
Erwin von Steinbach; but not he alone,
For many generations labored with him.
Children that came to see these Saints
    in stone,
As day by day out of the blocks they
    rose,
Grew old and died, and still the work
    went on,
And on, and on, and is not yet com-
    pleted.
The generation that succeeds our own
Perhaps may finish it. The architect
Built his great heart into these sculp-
    tured stones,
And with him toiled his children, and
    their lives
Were builded, with his own, into the
    walls,
As offerings unto God. You see that
    statue
Fixing its joyous, but deep-wrinkled eyes
Upon the Pillars of the Angels yonder.
That is the image of the master, carved
By the fair hand of his own child,
    Sabina.

ELSIE.

How beautiful is the column that he
    looks at!

PRINCE HENRY.

That, too, she sculptured. At the base
    of it
Stand the Evangelists; above their
    heads
Four Angels blowing upon marble
    trumpets,
And over them the blessed Christ, sur-
    rounded

By his attendant ministers, upholding
The instruments of his passion.

ELSIE.

                O my Lord!
Would I could leave behind me upon
    earth
Some monument to thy glory, such as
    this!

PRINCE HENRY.

A greater monument than this thou
    leavest
In thine own life, all purity and love!
See, too, the Rose, above the western
    portal
Resplendent with a thousand gorgeous
    colors,
The perfect flower of Gothic loveliness!

ELSIE.

And, in the gallery, the long line of
    statues,
Christ with his twelve Apostles watch-
    ing us!

*A BISHOP in armor, booted and spurred,
    passes with his train.*

PRINCE HENRY.

But come away; we have not time to
    look,
The crowd already fills the church, and
    yonder
Upon a stage, a herald with a trumpet,
Clad like the Angel Gabriel, proclaims
The Mystery that will now be repre-
    sented.

THE NATIVITY.

A MIRACLE-PLAY.

INTROITUS.

PRÆCO.

Come, good people, all and each,
Come and listen to our speech!
In your presence here I stand,
With a trumpet in my hand,
To announce the Easter Play,
Which we represent to-day!
First of all we shall rehearse,
In our action and our verse,
The Nativity of our Lord,
As written in the old record
Of the Protevangelion,
So that he who reads may run!
    Blows his trumpet.

I. HEAVEN.

MERCY, *at the feet of God.*

Have pity, Lord ! be not afraid
To save mankind, whom thou hast made,
Nor let the souls that were betrayed
  Perish eternally !

JUSTICE.

It cannot be, it must not be !
When in the garden placed by thee,
The fruit of the forbidden tree
  He ate, and he must die !

MERCY.

Have pity, Lord ! let penitence
Atone for disobedience,
Nor let the fruit of man's offence
  Be endless misery !

JUSTICE.

What penitence proportionate
Can e'er be felt for sin so great ?
Of the forbidden fruit he ate,
  And damnèd must he be !

GOD.

He shall be saved, if that within
The bounds of earth one free from sin
Be found, who for his kith and kin
  Will suffer martyrdom.

THE FOUR VIRTUES.

Lord ! we have searched the world
    around,
From centre to the utmost bound,
But no such mortal can be found ;
  Despairing, back we come.

WISDOM.

No mortal, but a God-made man,
Can ever carry out this plan,
Achieving what none other can,
  Salvation unto all !

GOD.

Go, then, O my beloved Son !
It can by thee alone be done ;
By thee the victory shall be won
  O'er Satan and the Fall !

Here the ANGEL GABRIEL *shall leave
  Paradise and fly towards the earth ;
  the jaws of Hell open below, and the
  Devils walk about, making a great noise.*

II. MARY AT THE WELL.

MARY.

Along the garden walk, and thence
Through the wicket in the garden fence,
  I steal with quiet pace,
My pitcher at the well to fill,
That lies so deep and cool and still
  In this sequestered place.

These sycamores keep guard around ;
I see no face, I hear no sound,
  Save bubblings of the spring,
And my companions, who, within,
The threads of gold and scarlet spin,
  And at their labor sing.

THE ANGEL GABRIEL.

Hail, Virgin Mary, full of grace !

Here MARY *looketh around her, trembling, and then saith :*

MARY.

Who is it speaketh in this place,
  With such a gentle voice ?

GABRIEL.

The Lord of heaven is with thee now !
Blessed among all women thou,
  Who art his holy choice !

MARY, *setting down the pitcher.*

What can this mean ? No one is near,
And yet, such sacred words I hear,
  I almost fear to stay.

Here the ANGEL, *appearing to her, shall
  say :*

GABRIEL.

Fear not, O Mary ! but believe !
For thou, a Virgin, shalt conceive
  A child this very day.

Fear not, O Mary ! from the sky
The Majesty of the Most High
  Shall overshadow thee !

MARY.

Behold the handmaid of the Lord !
According to thy holy word,
  So be it unto me !

*Here the Devils shall again make a great
  noise, under the stage.*

III. THE ANGELS OF THE SEVEN PLANETS, BEARING THE STAR OF BETHLEHEM.

THE ANGELS.

The Angels of the Planets Seven,
Across the shining fields of heaven
  The natal star we bring!
Dropping our sevenfold virtues down
As priceless jewels in the crown
  Of Christ, our new-born King.

RAPHAEL.

I am the Angel of the Sun,
Whose flaming wheels began to run
  When God Almighty's breath
Said to the darkness and the Night,
Let there be light! and there was light!
  I bring the gift of Faith.

ONAFIEL.

I am the Angel of the Moon,
Darkened to be rekindled soon
  Beneath the azure cope!
Nearest to earth, it is my ray
That best illumes the midnight way;
  I bring the gift of Hope!

ANAEL.

The Angel of the Star of Love,
The Evening Star, that shines above
  The place where lovers be,
Above all happy hearths and homes,
On roofs of thatch, or golden domes,
  I give him Charity!

ZOBIACHEL.

The Planet Jupiter is mine!
The mightiest star of all that shine,
  Except the sun alone!
He is the High Priest of the Dove,
And sends, from his great throne above,
  Justice, that shall atone!

MICHAEL.

The Planet Mercury, whose place
Is nearest to the sun in space,
  Is my allotted sphere!
And with celestial ardor swift
I bear upon my hands the gift
  Of heavenly Prudence here!

URIEL.

I am the Minister of Mars,
The strongest star among the stars!
  My songs of power prelude
The march and battle of man's life,
And for the suffering and the strife,
  I give him Fortitude!

ORIFEL.

The Angel of the uttermost
Of all the shining, heavenly host,
  From the far-off expanse
Of the Saturnian, endless space
I bring the last, the crowning grace,
  The gift of Temperance!

*A sudden light shines from the windows of
the stable in the village below.*

IV. THE WISE MEN OF THE EAST.

The stable of the Inn. The VIRGIN *and*
CHILD. *Three Gypsy Kings,* GASPAR,
MELCHIOR, *and* BELSHAZZAR, *shall
come in.*

GASPAR.

Hail to thee, Jesus of Nazareth!
Though in a manger thou draw breath,
Thou art greater than Life and Death,
  Greater than Joy or Woe!
This cross upon the line of life
Portendeth struggle, toil, and strife,
And through a region with peril rife
  In darkness shalt thou go!

MELCHIOR.

Hail to thee, King of Jerusalem!
Though humbly born in Bethlehem,
A sceptre and a diadem
  Await thy brow and hand!
The sceptre is a simple reed,
The crown will make thy temples bleed,
And in thine hour of greatest need,
  Abashed thy subjects stand!

BELSHAZZAR.

Hail to thee, Christ of Christendom!
O'er all the earth thy kingdom come!
From distant Trebizond to Rome
  Thy name shall men adore!
Peace and good-will among all men,
The Virgin has returned again,
Returned the old Saturnian reign
  And Golden Age once more.

THE CHILD CHRIST.

Jesus, the Son of God, am I,
Born here to suffer and to die
According to the prophecy,
  That other men may live!

THE VIRGIN.

And now these clothes, that wrapped
    Him, take
And keep them precious, for his sake;
Our benediction thus we make,
    Naught else have we to give.

*She gives them swaddling-clothes and they
    depart.*

V. THE FLIGHT INTO EGYPT.

Here JOSEPH *shall come in, leading an
ass, on which are seated* MARY *and the*
CHILD.

MARY.

Here will we rest us, under these
O'erhanging branches of the trees,
Where robins chant their Litanies
    And canticles of joy.

JOSEPH.

My saddle-girths have given way
With trudging through the heat to-day;
To you I think it is but play
    To ride and hold the boy.

MARY.

Hark! how the robins shout and sing,
As if to hail their infant King!
I will alight at yonder spring
    To wash his little coat.

JOSEPH.

And I will hobble well the ass,
Lest, being loose upon the grass,
He should escape; for, by the mass,
    He's nimble as a goat.

Here MARY *shall alight and go to the
    spring.*

MARY.

O Joseph! I am much afraid,
For men are sleeping in the shade;
I fear that we shall be waylaid,
    And robbed and beaten sore!

*Here a band of robbers shall be seen sleep-
ing, two of whom shall rise and come
forward.*

DUMACHUS.

Cock's soul! deliver up your gold!

JOSEPH.

I pray you, sirs, let go your hold!

You see that I am weak and old,
    Of wealth I have no store.

DUMACHUS.

Give up your money!

TITUS.

              Prithee cease.
Let these people go in peace.

DUMACHUS.

First let them pay for their release,
    And then go on their way.

TITUS.

These forty groats I give in fee,
If thou wilt only silent be.

MARY.

May God be merciful to thee
    Upon the Judgment Day!

JESUS.

When thirty years shall have gone
    by,
I at Jerusalem shall die,
By Jewish hands exalted high
    On the accursed tree,
Then on my right and my left side,
These thieves shall both be crucified,
And Titus thenceforth shall abide
    In paradise with me.

*Here a great rumor of trumpets and
horses, like the noise of a king with his
army, and the robbers shall take flight.*

VI. THE SLAUGHTER OF THE INNO-
CENTS.

KING HEROD.

Potz-tausend! Himmel-sacrament!
Filled am I with great wonderment
    At this unwelcome news!
Am I not Herod? Who shall dare
My crown to take, my sceptre bear,
    As king among the Jews?

*Here he shall stride up and down and
flourish his sword.*

What ho! I fain would drink a can
Of the strong wine of Canaan!
    The wine of Helbon bring
I purchased at the Fair of Tyre,
As red as blood, as hot as fire,
    And fit for any king!

He quaffs great goblets of wine.

Now at the window will I stand,
While in the street the armèd band
The little children slay;
The babe just born in Bethlehem
Will surely slaughtered be with them,
Nor live another day!

*Here a voice of lamentation shall be heard
in the street.*

RACHEL.

O wicked king! O cruel speed!
To do this most unrighteous deed!
My children all are slain!

HEROD.

Ho, seneschal! another cup!
With wine of Sorek fill it up!
I would a bumper drain!

RAHAB.

May maledictions fall and blast
Thyself and lineage to the last
Of all thy kith and kin!

HEROD.

Another goblet! quick! and stir
Pomegranate juice and drops of myrrh
And calamus therein!

SOLDIERS, *in the street.*

Give up thy child into our hands!
It is King Herod who commands
That he should thus be slain!

THE NURSE MEDUSA.

O monstrous men! What have ye
done!
It is King Herod's only son
That ye have cleft in twain!

HEROD.

Ah, luckless day! What words of
fear
Are these that smite upon my ear
With such a doleful sound!
What torments rack my heart and
head!
Would I were dead! would I were
dead,
And buried in the ground!

*He falls down and writhes as though eaten
by worms. Hell opens, and* SATAN *and*
ASTAROTH *come forth and drag him
down.*

VII. JESUS AT PLAY WITH HIS
SCHOOLMATES.

JESUS.

The shower is over.   Let us play,
And make some sparrows out of clay,
Down by the river's side.

JUDAS.

See, how the stream has overflowed
Its banks, and o'er the meadow road
Is spreading far and wide!

*They draw water out of the river by chan-
nels and form little pools.* JESUS *makes
twelve sparrows of clay, and the other
boys do the same.*

JESUS.

Look! look how prettily I make
These little sparrows by the lake
Bend down their necks and drink!
Now will I make them sing and soar
So far, they shall return no more
Unto this river's brink.

JUDAS.

That canst thou not! They are but
clay,
They cannot sing, nor fly away
Above the meadow lands!

JESUS.

Fly, fly! ye sparrows! you are free!
And while you live, remember me,
Who made you with my hands.

Here JESUS *shall clap his hands, and the
sparrows shall fly away, chirruping.*

JUDAS.

Thou art a sorcerer, I know;
Oft has my mother told me so,
I will not play with thee!

He strikes JESUS *in the right side.*

JESUS.

Ah, Judas! thou hast smote my side,
And when I shall be crucified,
There shall I piercèd be!

Here JOSEPH *shall come in and say:*

JOSEPH.

Ye wicked boys! why do ye play,
And break the holy Sabbath day?
What, think ye, will your mothers say
To see you in such plight!
In such a sweat and such a heat,

With all that mud upon your feet !
There's not a beggar in the street
    Makes such a sorry sight !

VIII. THE VILLAGE SCHOOL.

The RABBI BEN ISRAEL, *sitting on a
high stool, with a long beard, and a rod
in his hand.*

RABBI.

I am the Rabbi Ben Israel,
Throughout this village known full well,
And, as my scholars all will tell,
    Learned in things divine ;
The Cabala and Talmud hoar
Than all the prophets prize I more,
For water is all Bible lore,
    But Mishna is strong wine.

My fame extends from West to East,
And always, at the Purim feast,
I am as drunk as any beast
    That wallows in his sty ;
The wine it so elateth me,
That I no difference can see
Between " Accursed Haman be ! "
    And " Blessed be Mordecai ! "

Come hither, Judas Iscariot ;
Say, if thy lesson thou hast got
From the Rabbinical Book or not.
    Why howl the dogs at night ?

JUDAS.

In the Rabbinical Book, it saith
The dogs howl, when with icy breath
Great Sammael, the Angel of Death,
    Takes through the town his flight !

RABBI.

Well, boy ! now say, if thou art wise,
When the Angel of Death, who is full
    of eyes,
Comes where a sick man dying lies,
    What doth he to the wight ?

JUDAS.

He stands beside him, dark and tall,
Holding a sword, from which doth fall
Into his mouth a drop of gall,
    And so he turneth white.

RABBI.

And now, my Judas, say to me
What the great Voices Four may be,
That quite across the world do flee,
    And are not heard by men ?

JUDAS.

The Voice of the Sun in heaven's dome,
The Voice of the Murmuring of Rome,
The Voice of a Soul that goeth home,
    And the Angel of the Rain !

RABBI.

Right are thine answers every one !
Now, little Jesus, the carpenter's son,
Let us see how thy task is done ;
    Canst thou thy letters say ?

JESUS.

Aleph.

RABBI.

        What next ?   Do not stop yet !
Go on with all the alphabet.
Come, Aleph, Beth ; dost thou forget ?
    Cock's soul ! thou 'dst rather play !

JESUS.

What Aleph means I fain would know
Before I any farther go !

RABBI.

Oh, by Saint Peter ! wouldst thou so ?
    Come hither, boy, to me.
As surely as the letter Jod
Once cried aloud, and spake to God,
So surely shalt thou feel this rod,
    And punished shalt thou be !

Here RABBI BEN ISRAEL *shall lift up
his rod to strike Jesus, and his right
arm shall be paralyzed.*

IX. CROWNED WITH FLOWERS.

JESUS *sitting among his playmates,
crowned with flowers as their King.*

BOYS.

We spread our garments on the ground !
With fragrant flowers thy head is
    crowned
While like a guard we stand around,
    And hail thee as our King !
Thou art the new King of the Jews !
Nor let the passers-by refuse
To bring that homage which men use
    To majesty to bring.

*Here a traveller shall go by, and the boys
shall lay hold of his garments and say :*

BOYS.

Come hither ! and all reverence pay
Unto our monarch, crowned to-day !

Then go rejoicing on your way,
In all prosperity!

TRAVELLER.

Hail to the King of Bethlehem,
Who weareth in his diadem
The yellow crocus for the gem
Of his authority!

He passes by; and others come in, bearing on a litter a sick child.

BOYS.

Set down the litter and draw near!
The King of Bethlehem is here!
What ails the child, who seems to fear
That we shall do him harm?

THE BEARERS.

He climbed up to the robin's nest,
And out there darted, from his rest,
A serpent with a crimson crest,
And stung him in the arm.

JESUS.

Bring him to me, and let me feel
The wounded place; my touch can heal
The sting of serpents, and can steal
The poison from the bite!

He touches the wound, and the boy begins to cry.

Cease to lament! I can foresee
That thou hereafter known shalt be,
Among the men who follow me,
As Simon the Canaanite!

EPILOGUE.

In the after part of the day
Will be represented another play,
Of the Passion of our Blessed Lord,
Beginning directly after Nones!
At the close of which we shall accord,
By way of benison and reward,
The sight of a holy Martyr's bones!

IV.

THE ROAD TO HIRSCHAU.

PRINCE HENRY *and* ELSIE, *with their attendants on horseback.*

ELSIE.

Onward and onward the highway runs
to the distant city, impatiently
bearing

Tidings of human joy and disaster, of
love and of hate, of doing and
daring!

PRINCE HENRY.

This life of ours is a wild æolian harp
of many a joyous strain,
But under them all there runs a loud
perpetual wail, as of souls in
pain.

ELSIE.

Faith alone can interpret life, and the
heart that aches and bleeds with
the stigma
Of pain, alone bears the likeness of
Christ, and can comprehend its
dark enigma.

PRINCE HENRY.

Man is selfish, and seeketh pleasure with
little care of what may betide,
Else why am I travelling here beside
thee, a demon that rides by an
angel's side?

ELSIE.

All the hedges are white with dust, and
the great dog under the creaking
wain
Hangs his head in the lazy heat, while
onward the horses toil and strain.

PRINCE HENRY.

Now they stop at the wayside inn, and
the wagoner laughs with the
landlord's daughter,
While out of the dripping trough the
horses distend their leathern
sides with water.

ELSIE.

All through life there are wayside inns,
where man may refresh his soul
with love;
Even the lowest may quench his thirst
at rivulets fed by springs from
above.

PRINCE HENRY.

Yonder, where rises the cross of stone,
our journey along the highway
ends,
And over the fields, by a bridle path,
down into the broad green valley
descends.

ELSIE.

I am not sorry to leave behind the
　　beaten road with its dust and
　　heat ;
The air will be sweeter far, and the turf
　　will be softer under our horses'
　　feet.

They turn down a green lane.

ELSIE.

Sweet is the air with the budding haws,
　　and the valley stretching for
　　miles below
Is white with blossoming cherry-trees,
　　as if just covered with lightest
　　snow.

PRINCE HENRY.

Over our heads a white cascade is
　　gleaming against the distant
　　hill ;
We cannot hear it, nor see it move, but
　　it hangs like a banner when
　　winds are still.

ELSIE.

Damp and cool is this deep ravine, and
　　cool the sound of the brook by
　　our side !
What is this castle that rises above us,
　　and lords it over a land so wide ?

PRINCE HENRY.

It is the home of the Counts of Calva ;
　　well have I known these scenes
　　of old,
Well I remember each tower and tur-
　　ret, remember the brooklet, the
　　wood, and the wold.

ELSIE.

Hark ! from the little village below us
　　the bells of the church are ring-
　　ing for rain !
Priests and peasants in long procession
　　come forth and kneel on the arid
　　plain.

PRINCE HENRY.

They have not long to wait, for I see
　　in the south uprising a little
　　cloud,
That before the sun shall be set will
　　cover the sky above us as with a
　　shroud.

They pass on.

THE CONVENT OF HIRSCHAU IN THE
BLACK FOREST.

The Convent cellar. FRIAR CLAUS *comes
in with a light and a basket of empty
flagons.*

FRIAR CLAUS.

I always enter this sacred place
With a thoughtful, solemn, and reverent
　　pace,
Pausing long enough on each stair
To breathe an ejaculatory prayer,
And a benediction on the vines
That produce these various sorts of
　　wines !
For my part, I am well content
That we have got through with the
　　tedious Lent !
Fasting is all very well for those
Who have to contend with invisible
　　foes ;
But I am quite sure it does not agree
With a quiet, peaceable man like me,
Who am not of that nervous and meagre
　　kind,
That are always distressed in body and
　　mind !
And at times it really does me good
To come down among this brotherhood,
Dwelling forever underground,
Silent, contemplative, round and sound ;
Each one old, and brown with mould,
But filled to the lips with the ardor of
　　youth,
With the latent power and love of truth,
And with virtues fervent and manifold.

I have heard it said, that at Easter-tide,
When buds are swelling on every side,
And the sap begins to move in the vine,
Then in all cellars, far and wide,
The oldest as well as the newest wine
Begins to stir itself, and ferment,
With a kind of revolt and discontent
At being so long in darkness pent,
And fain would burst from its sombre
　　tun
To bask on the hillside in the sun ;
As in the bosom of us poor friars,
The tumult of half-subdued desires
For the world that we have left behind
Disturbs at times all peace of mind !
And now that we have lived through
　　Lent,
My duty it is, as often before,
To open awhile the prison-door,
And give these restless spirits vent.

Now here is a cask that stands alone,
And has stood a hundred years or more,
Its beard of cobwebs, long and hoar,
Trailing and sweeping along the floor,
Like Barbarossa, who sits in his cave,
Taciturn, sombre, sedate, and grave,
Till his beard has grown through the
    table of stone !
It is of the quick and not of the dead !
In its veins the blood is hot and red,
And a heart still beats in those ribs of
    oak
That time may have tamed, but has not
    broke !
It comes from Bacharach on the Rhine,
Is one of the three best kinds of wine,
And costs some hundred florins the
    ohm ;
But that I do not consider dear,
When I remember that every year
Four butts are sent to the Pope of
    Rome.
And whenever a goblet thereof I drain,
The old rhyme keeps running in my
    brain ;

At Bacharach on the Rhine,
At Hochheim on the Main,
And at Würzburg on the Stein,
Grow the three best kinds of wine !

They are all good wines, and better far
Than those of the Neckar, or those of
    the Ahr.
In particular, Würzburg well may boast
Of its blessed wine of the Holy Ghost,
Which of all wines I like the most.
This I shall draw for the Abbot's drink-
    ing,
Who seems to be much of my way of
    thinking.

Fills a flagon.

Ah ! how the streamlet laughs and
    sings !
What a delicious fragrance springs
From the deep flagon, while it fills,
As of hyacinths and daffodils !
Between this cask and the Abbot's lips
Many have been the sips and slips ;
Many have been the draughts of wine,
On their way to his, that have stopped
    at mine ;
And many a time my soul has hankered
For a deep draught out of his silver
    tankard,
When it should have been busy with
    other affairs,

Less with its longings and more with
    its prayers.
But now there is no such awkward con-
    dition,
No danger of death and eternal perdi-
    tion ;
So here 's to the Abbot and Brothers
    all,
Who dwell in this convent of Peter and
    Paul !

He drinks.

O cordial delicious ! O soother of pain !
It flashes like sunshine into my brain !
A benison rest on the Bishop who sends
Such a fudder of wine as this to his
    friends !
And now a flagon for such as may ask
A draught from the noble Bacharach
    cask,
And I will be gone, though I know full
    well
The cellar 's a cheerfuller place than
    the cell.
Behold where he stands, all sound and
    good,
Brown and old in his oaken hood ;
Silent he seems externally
As any Carthusian monk may be ;
But within, what a spirit of deep un-
    rest !
What a seething and simmering in his
    breast !
As if the heaving of his great heart
Would burst his belt of oak apart !
Let me unloose this button of wood,
And quiet a little his turbulent mood.

Sets it running.

See ! how its currents gleam and shine,
As if they had caught the purple hues
Of autumn sunsets on the Rhine,
Descending and mingling with the
    dews ;
Or as if the grapes were stained with
    the blood
Of the innocent boy, who, some years
    back,
Was taken and crucified by the Jews,
In that ancient town of Bacharach !
Perdition upon those infidel Jews,
In that ancient town of Bacharach !
The beautiful town, that gives us wine
With the fragrant odor of Muscadine !
I should deem it wrong to let this pass
Without first touching my lips to the
    glass,
For here in the midst of the current I
    stand

Like the stone Pfalz in the midst of the
river,
Taking toll upon either hand,
And much more grateful to the giver.

He drinks.

Here, now, is a very inferior kind,
Such as in any town you may find,
Such as one might imagine would suit
The rascal who drank wine out of a
boot.
And, after all, it was not a crime,
For he won thereby Dorf Hüffelsheim.
A jolly old toper! who at a pull
Could drink a postilion's jack-boot full,
And ask with a laugh, when that was
done,
If the fellow had left the other one!
This wine is as good as we can afford
To the friars who sit at the lower board,
And cannot distinguish bad from good,
And are far better off than if they could,
Being rather the rude disciples of beer,
Than of anything more refined and
dear!

Fills the flagon and departs.

THE SCRIPTORIUM.

FRIAR PACIFICUS *transcribing and illu-
minating.*

FRIAR PACIFICUS.

It is growing dark! Yet one line more,
And then my work for to-day is o'er.
I come again to the name of the Lord!
Ere I that awful name record,
That is spoken so lightly among men,
Let me pause awhile and wash my pen;
Pure from blemish and blot must it be
When it writes that word of mystery!

Thus have I labored on and on,
Nearly through the Gospel of John.
Can it be that from the lips
Of this same gentle Evangelist,
That Christ himself perhaps has kissed,
Came the dread Apocalypse!
It has a very awful look,
As it stands there at the end of the
book,
Like the sun in an eclipse.
Ah me! when I think of that vision di-
vine,
Think of writing it, line by line,
I stand in awe of the terrible curse,

Like the trump of doom, in the closing
verse!
God forgive me! if ever I
Take aught from the book of that
Prophecy,
Lest my part too should be taken away
From the Book of Life on the Judg-
ment Day.
This is well written, though I say it!
I should not be afraid to display it
In open day, on the selfsame shelf
With the writings of St. Thecla herself,
Or of Theodosius, who of old
Wrote the Gospels in letters of gold!
That goodly folio standing yonder,
Without a single blot or blunder,
Would not bear away the palm from
mine,
If we should compare them line for line.

There, now, is an initial letter!
Saint Ulric himself never made a better!
Finished down to the leaf and the snail,
Down to the eyes on the peacock's tail!
And now, as I turn the volume over,
And see what lies between cover and
cover,
What treasures of art these pages hold,
All ablaze with crimson and gold,
God forgive me! I seem to feel
A certain satisfaction steal
Into my heart, and into my brain,
As if my talent had not lain
Wrapped in a napkin, and all in vain.
Yes, I might almost say to the Lord,
Here is a copy of thy Word,
Written out with much toil and pain;
Take it, O Lord, and let it be
As something I have done for thee!

He looks from the window.

How sweet the air is! How fair the
scene!
I wish I had as lovely a green
To paint my landscapes and my leaves!
How the swallows twitter under the
eaves!
There, now, there is one in her nest;
I can just catch a glimpse of her head
and breast,
And will sketch her thus, in her quiet
nook,
For the margin of my Gospel book.

He makes a sketch.

I can see no more. Through the valley
yonder
A shower is passing; I hear the thunder

Mutter its curses in the air,
The devil's own and only prayer!
The dusty road is brown with rain,
And, speeding on with might and main,
Hitherward rides a gallant train.
They do not parley, they cannot wait,
But hurry in at the convent gate.
What a fair lady! and beside her
What a handsome, graceful, noble rider!
Now she gives him her hand to alight;
They will beg a shelter for the night.
I will go down to the corridor,
And try to see that face once more;
It will do for the face of some beautiful
Saint,
Or for one of the Maries I shall paint.

Goes out.

THE CLOISTERS.

The ABBOT ERNESTUS *pacing to and fro.*

ABBOT.

Slowly, slowly up the wall
Steals the sunshine, steals the shade;
Evening damps begin to fall,
Evening shadows are displayed.
Round me, o'er me, everywhere,
All the sky is grand with clouds,
And athwart the evening air
Wheel the swallows home in crowds.
Shafts of sunshine from the west
Paint the dusky windows red;
Darker shadows, deeper rest,
Underneath and overhead.
Darker, darker, and more wan,
In my breast the shadows fall;
Upward steals the life of man,
As the sunshine from the wall.
From the wall into the sky,
From the roof along the spire;
Ah, the souls of those that die
Are but sunbeams lifted higher.

Enter PRINCE HENRY.

PRINCE HENRY.

Christ is arisen!

ABBOT.

Amen! He is arisen!
His peace be with you!

PRINCE HENRY.

Here it reigns forever!
The peace of God, that passeth understanding,

Reigns in these cloisters and these corridors.
Are you Ernestus, Abbot of the convent?

ABBOT.

I am.

PRINCE HENRY.

And I Prince Henry of Hoheneck,
Who crave your hospitality to-night.

ABBOT.

You are thrice welcome to our humble
walls.
You do us honor; and we shall requite
it,
I fear, but poorly, entertaining you
With Paschal eggs, and our poor con-
vent wine,
The remnants of our Easter holidays.

PRINCE HENRY.

How fares it with the holy monks of
Hirschau?
Are all things well with them?

ABBOT.

All things are well.

PRINCE HENRY.

A noble convent! I have known it
long
By the report of travellers. I now see
Their commendations lag behind the
truth.
You lie here in the valley of the Nagold
As in a nest: and the still river, gliding
Along its bed, is like an admonition
How all things pass. Your lands are
rich and ample,
And your revenues large. God's bene-
diction
Rests on your convent.

ABBOT.

By our charities
We strive to merit it. Our Lord and
Master,
When He departed, left us in his will,
As our best legacy on earth, the poor!
These we have always with us; had we
not,
Our hearts would grow as hard as are
these stones.

PRINCE HENRY.

If I remember right, the Counts of
Calva
Founded your convent.

ABBOT.

Even as you say.

PRINCE HENRY.

And, if I err not, it is very old.

ABBOT.

Within these cloisters lie already buried
Twelve holy Abbots. Underneath the
flags
On which we stand, the Abbot William
lies,
Of blessed memory.

PRINCE HENRY.

And whose tomb is that,
Which bears the brass escutcheon?

ABBOT.

A benefactor's.
Conrad, a Count of Calva, he who stood
Godfather to our bells.

PRINCE HENRY.

Your monks are learned
And holy men, I trust.

ABBOT.

There are among them
Learned and holy men. Yet in this age
We need another Hildebrand, to shake
And purify us like a mighty wind.
The world is wicked, and sometimes I
wonder
God does not lose his patience with it
wholly,
And shatter it like glass! Even here,
at times,
Within these walls, where all should be
at peace,
I have my trials. Time has laid his
hand
Upon my heart, gently, not smiting it,
But as a harper lays his open palm
Upon his harp to deaden its vibrations.
Ashes are on my head, and on my lips
Sackcloth, and in my breast a heaviness
And weariness of life, that makes me
ready
To say to the dead Abbots under us,
"Make room for me!" Only I see the
dusk
Of evening twilight coming, and have
not
Completed half my task; and so at
times

The thought of my shortcomings in this
life
Falls like a shadow on the life to come.

PRINCE HENRY.

We must all die, and not the old alone;
The young have no exemption from
that doom.

ABBOT.

Ah, yes! the young may die, but the old
must!
That is the difference.

PRINCE HENRY.

I have heard much laud
Of your transcribers. Your Scriptorium
Is famous among all; your manuscripts
Praised for their beauty and their excellence.

ABBOT.

That is indeed our boast. If you desire
it,
You shall behold these treasures. And
meanwhile
Shall the Refectorarius bestow
Your horses and attendants for the
night.
They go in. The Vesper-bell rings.

THE CHAPEL.

*Vespers: after which the monks retire, a
chorister leading an old monk who is
blind.*

PRINCE HENRY.

They are all gone, save one who lin-
gers,
Absorbed in deep and silent prayer.
As if his heart could find no rest,
At times he beats his heaving breast
With clenchèd and convulsive fingers,
Then lifts them trembling in the air.
A chorister, with golden hair,
Guides hitherward his heavy pace.
Can it be so? Or does my sight
Deceive me in the uncertain light?
Ah no! I recognize that face,
Though Time has touched it in his
flight,
And changed the auburn hair to white.
It is Count Hugo of the Rhine,

The deadliest foe of all our race,
And hateful unto me and mine!

THE BLIND MONK.

Who is it that doth stand so near
His whispered words I almost hear?

PRINCE HENRY.

I am Prince Henry of Hoheneck,
And you, Count Hugo of the Rhine!
I know you, and I see the scar,
The brand upon your forehead, shine
And redden like a baleful star!

THE BLIND MONK.

Count Hugo once, but now the wreck
Of what I was. O Hoheneck!
The passionate will, the pride, the wrath
That bore me headlong on my path,
Stumbled and staggered into fear,
And failed me in my mad career,
As a tired steed some evil-doer,
Alone upon a desolate moor,
Bewildered, lost, deserted, blind,
And hearing loud and close behind
The o'ertaking steps of his pursuer.
Then suddenly from the dark there came
A voice that called me by my name,
And said to me, "Kneel down and pray!"
And so my terror passed away,
Passed utterly away forever.
Contrition, penitence, remorse,
Came on me, with o'erwhelming force;
A hope, a longing, an endeavor,
By days of penance and nights of prayer,
To frustrate and defeat despair!
Calm, deep, and still is now my heart,
With tranquil waters overflowed;
A lake whose unseen fountains start,
Where once the hot volcano glowed.
And you, O Prince of Hoheneck!
Have known me in that earlier time,
A man of violence and crime,
Whose passions brooked no curb nor check.
Behold me now, in gentler mood,
One of this holy brotherhood.
Give me your hand; here let me kneel;
Make your reproaches sharp as steel;
Spurn me, and smite me on each cheek;
No violence can harm the meek,
There is no wound Christ cannot heal!
Yes; lift your princely hand, and take
Revenge, if 't is revenge you seek;
Then pardon me, for Jesus' sake!

PRINCE HENRY.

Arise, Count Hugo! let there be
No further strife nor enmity
Between us twain; we both have erred!
Too rash in act, too wroth in word,
From the beginning have we stood
In fierce, defiant attitude,
Each thoughtless of the other's right,
And each reliant on his might.
But now our souls are more subdued;
The hand of God, and not in vain,
Has touched us with the fire of pain.
Let us kneel down and side by side
Pray till our souls are purified,
And pardon will not be denied!

They kneel.

THE REFECTORY.

Gaudiolum of Monks at midnight. LU-
CIFER *disguised as a Friar.*

FRIAR PAUL *sings.*

Ave! color vini clari,
Dulcis potus, non amari,
Tua nos inebriari
Digneris potentia!

FRIAR CUTHBERT.

Not so much noise, my worthy frères,
You'll disturb the Abbot at his prayers.

FRIAR PAUL *sings.*

O! quam placens in colore!
O! quam fragrans in odore!
O! quam sapidum in ore!
Dulce linguæ vinculum!

FRIAR CUTHBERT.

I should think your tongue had broken
its chain!

FRIAR PAUL *sings.*

Felix venter quem intrabis!
Felix guttur quod rigabis!
Felix os quod tu lavabis!
Et beata labia!

FRIAR CUTHBERT.

Peace! I say, peace!
Will you never cease!
You will rouse up the Abbot, I tell you,
again!

FRIAR JOHN.

No danger! to-night he will let us
alone,

As I happen to know he has guests of
his own.

FRIAR CUTHBERT.

Who are they ?

FRIAR JOHN.

A German Prince and his train,
Who arrived here just before the rain.
There is with him a damsel fair to
see,
As slender and graceful as a reed !
When she alighted from her steed,
It seemed like a blossom blown from a
tree.

FRIAR CUTHBERT.

None of your pale-faced girls for me !
None of your damsels of high degree !

FRIAR JOHN.

Come, old fellow, drink down to your
peg !
But do not drink any further, I beg !

FRIAR PAUL *sings.*

In the days of gold,
The days of old,
Crosier of wood
And bishop of gold !

FRIAR CUTHBERT.

What an infernal racket and riot !
Can you not drink your wine in quiet ?
Why fill the convent with such scan-
dals,
As if we were so many drunken Van-
dals ?

FRIAR PAUL *continues.*

Now we have changed
That law so good
To crosier of gold
And bishop of wood !

FRIAR CUTHBERT.

Well, then, since you are in the mood
To give your noisy humors vent,
Sing and howl to your heart's content !

CHORUS OF MONKS.

Funde vinum, funde !
Tanquam sint fluminis undæ,
Nec quæras unde,
Sed fundas semper abunde !

FRIAR JOHN.

What is the name of yonder friar,
With an eye that glows like a coal of
fire,
And such a black mass of tangled hair ?

FRIAR PAUL.

He who is sitting there,
With a rollicking,
Devil may care,
Free and easy look and air,
As if he were used to such feasting and
frolicking ?

FRIAR JOHN.

The same.

FRIAR PAUL.

He 's a stranger. You had better ask
his name,
And where he is going and whence he
came.

FRIAR JOHN.

Hallo ! Sir Friar !

FRIAR PAUL.

You must raise your voice a little
higher,
He does not seem to hear what you
say.
Now, try again ! He is looking this
way.

FRIAR JOHN.

Hallo ! Sir Friar,
We wish to inquire
Whence you came, and where you are
going,
And anything else that is worth the
knowing.
So be so good as to open your head.

LUCIFER.

I am a Frenchman born and bred,
Going on a pilgrimage to Rome.
My home
Is the convent of St. Gildas de Rhuys,
Of which, very like, you never have
heard.

MONKS.

Never a word.

LUCIFER.

You must know, then, it is in the dio-
cese
Called the Diocese of Vannes,
In the province of Brittany.
From the gray rocks of Morbihan

It overlooks the angry sea;
The very sea-shore where,
In his great despair,
Abbot Abelard walked to and fro,
Filling the night with woe,
And wailing aloud to the merciless seas
The name of his sweet Heloise,
Whilst overhead
The convent windows gleamed as red
As the fiery eyes of the monks within,
Who with jovial din
Gave themselves up to all kinds of
sin!
Ha! that is a convent! that is an
abbey!
Over the doors,
None of your death-heads carved in
wood,
None of your Saints looking pious and
good,
None of your Patriarchs old and
shabby!
But the heads and tusks of boars,
And the cells
Hung all round with the fells
Of the fallow-deer.
And then what cheer!
What jolly, fat friars,
Sitting round the great, roaring fires,
Roaring louder than they,
With their strong wines,
And their concubines,
And never a bell,
With its swagger and swell,
Calling you up with a start of affright
In the dead of night,
To send you grumbling down dark
stairs,
To mumble your prayers;
But the cheery crow
Of cocks in the yard below,
After daybreak, an hour or so,
And the barking of deep-mouthed
hounds,
These are the sounds
That, instead of bells, salute the ear.
And then all day
Up and away
Through the forest, hunting the deer!
Ah, my friends, I'm afraid that here
You are a little too pious, a little too
tame,
And the more is the shame.
'T is the greatest folly
Not to be jolly;
That's what I think!
Come, drink, drink,
Drink, and die game!

MONKS.

And your Abbot What's-his-name?

LUCIFER.

Abelard!

MONKS.

Did he drink hard?

LUCIFER.

Oh, no! Not he!
He was a dry old fellow,
Without juice enough to get thoroughly
mellow.
There he stood,
Lowering at us in sullen mood,
As if he had come into Brittany
Just to reform our brotherhood!

A roar of laughter

But you see
It never would do!
For some of us knew a thing or two,
In the Abbey of St. Gildas de Rhuys!
For instance, the great ado
With old Fulbert's niece,
The young and lovely Heloise.

FRIAR JOHN.

Stop there, if you please,
Till we drink to the fair Heloise.

ALL, *drinking and shouting.*

Heloise! Heloise!

The Chapel-bell tolls.

LUCIFER, *starting.*

What is that bell for! Are you such
asses
As to keep up the fashion of midnight
masses?

FRIAR CUTHBERT.

It is only a poor unfortunate brother,
Who is gifted with most miraculous
powers
Of getting up at all sorts of hours,
And, by way of penance and Christian
meekness,
Of creeping silently out of his cell
To take a pull at that hideous bell;
So that all monks who are lying awake
May murmur some kind of prayer for
his sake,
And adapted to his peculiar weakness!

FRIAR JOHN.

From frailty and fall —

ALL.

Good Lord, deliver us all!

FRIAR CUTHBERT.

And before the bell for matins sounds,
He takes his lantern, and goes the
    rounds,
Flashing it into our sleepy eyes,
Merely to say it is time to arise.
But enough of that. Go on, if you
    please,
With your story about St. Gildas de
    Rhuys.

LUCIFER.

Well, it finally came to pass
That, half in fun and half in malice,
One Sunday at Mass
We put some poison into the chalice.
But, either by accident or design,
Peter Abelard kept away
From the chapel that day,
And a poor young friar, who in his
    stead
Drank the sacramental wine,
Fell on the steps of the altar, dead!
But look! do you see at the window
    there
That face, with a look of grief and
    despair,
That ghastly face, as of one in pain?

MONKS.

Who? where?

LUCIFER.

As I spoke, it vanished away again.

FRIAR CUTHBERT.

It is that nefarious
Siebald the Refectorarius.
That fellow is always playing the scout,
Creeping and peeping and prowling
    about;
And then he regales
The Abbot with scandalous tales.

LUCIFER.

A spy in the convent? One of the
    brothers
Telling scandalous tales of the others?
Out upon him, the lazy loon!
I would put a stop to that pretty soon,
In a way he should rue it.

MONKS.

How shall we do it?

LUCIFER.

Do you, brother Paul,
Creep under the window, close to the
    wall,
And open it suddenly when I call.
Then seize the villain by the hair,
And hold him there,
And punish him soundly, once for all.

FRIAR CUTHBERT.

As Saint Dunstan of old,
We are told,
Once caught the Devil by the nose!

LUCIFER.

Ha! ha! that story is very clever,
But has no foundation whatsoever.
Quick! for I see his face again
Glaring in at the window-pane;
Now! now! and do not spare your
    blows.

FRIAR PAUL opens the window suddenly,
    and seizes SIEBALD.

They beat him.

FRIAR SIEBALD.

Help! help! are you going to slay me?

FRIAR PAUL.

That will teach you again to betray
    me!

FRIAR SIEBALD.

Mercy! mercy!

FRIAR PAUL, shouting and beating.

Rumpas bellorum lorum
Vim confer amorum
Morum verorum rorum
Tu plena polorum!

LUCIFER.

Who stands in the doorway yonder,
Stretching out his trembling hand,
Just as Abelard used to stand,
The flash of his keen, black eyes
Forerunning the thunder?

THE MONKS, in confusion.

The Abbot! the Abbot!

FRIAR CUTHBERT.

                And what is the wonder!
He seems to have taken you by sur
    prise.

FRIAR FRANCIS.

Hide the great flagon
From the eyes of the dragon!

FRIAR CUTHBERT.

Pull the brown hood over your face!
This will bring us into disgrace!

ABBOT.

What means this revel and carouse?
Is this a tavern and drinking-house?
Are you Christian monks, or heathen
    devils,
To pollute this convent with your
    revels?
Were Peter Damian still upon earth,
To be shocked by such ungodly mirth,
He would write your names, with pen of
.   gall,
In his Book of Gomorrah, one and all!
Away, you drunkards! to your cells,
And pray till you hear the matin-bells;
You, Brother Francis, and you, Brother
    Paul!
And as a penance mark each prayer
With the scourge upon your shoulders
    bare;
Nothing atones for such a sin
But the blood that follows the dis-
    cipline.
And you, Brother Cuthbert, come with
    me
Alone into the sacristy;
You, who should be a guide to your
    brothers,
And are ten times worse than all the
    others,
For you I've a draught that has long
    been brewing,
You shall do a penance worth the
    doing!
Away to your prayers, then, one and all!
I wonder the very convent wall
Does not crumble and crush you in its
    fall!

THE NEIGHBORING NUNNERY.

The ABBESS IRMINGARD *sitting with*
    ELSIE *in the moonlight.*

IRMINGARD.

The night is silent, the wind is still,
The moon is looking from yonder hill
Down upon convent, and grove, and
    garden;

The clouds have passed away from her
    face,
Leaving behind them no sorrowful
    trace,
Only the tender and quiet grace
Of one whose heart has been healed
    with pardon!

And such am I. My soul within
Was dark with passion and soiled with
    sin.
But now its wounds are healed again;
Gone are the anguish, the terror, and
    pain;
For across that desolate land of woe,
O'er whose burning sands I was forced
    to go,
A wind from heaven began to blow;
And all my being trembled and shook,
As the leaves of the tree, or the grass
    of the field,
And I was healed, as the sick are
    healed,
When fanned by the leaves of the Holy
    Book!

As thou sittest in the moonlight there,
Its glory flooding thy golden hair,
And the only darkness that which lies
In the haunted chambers of thine eyes,
I feel my soul drawn unto thee,
Strangely, and strongly, and more and
    more,
As to one I have known and loved
    before;
For every soul is akin to me
That dwells in the land of mystery!
I am the Lady Irmingard,
Born of a noble race and name!
Many a wandering Suabian bard,
Whose life was dreary, and bleak, and
    hard,
Has found through me the way to fame.

Brief and bright were those days, and
    the night
Which followed was full of a lurid light.
Love, that of every woman's heart
Will have the whole, and not a part,
That is to her, in Nature's plan,
More than ambition is to man,
Her light, her life, her very breath,
With no alternative but death,
Found me a maiden soft and young,
Just from the convent's cloistered
    school,
And seated on my lowly stool,
Attentive while the minstrels sung.

Gallant, graceful, gentle, tall,
Fairest, noblest, best of all,
Was Walter of the Vogelweid;
And, whatsoever may betide,
Still I think of him with pride!
His song was of the summer-time,
The very birds sang in his rhyme;
The sunshine, the delicious air,
The fragrance of the flowers, were
 there;
And I grew restless as I heard,
Restless and buoyant as a bird,
Down soft, aerial currents sailing,
O'er blossomed orchards and fields in
 bloom,
And through the momentary gloom,
Of shadows o'er the landscape trailing,
Yielding and borne I knew not where,
But feeling resistance unavailing.

And thus, unnoticed and apart,
And more by accident than choice,
I listened to that single voice
Until the chambers of my heart
Were filled with it by night and day.
One night, — it was a night in May, —
Within the garden, unawares,
Under the blossoms in the gloom,
I heard it utter my own name
With protestations and wild prayers;
And it rang through me, and became
Like the archangel's trump of doom,
Which the soul hears, and must obey;
And mine arose as from a tomb.
My former life now seemed to me
Such as hereafter death may be,
When in the great Eternity
We shall awake and find it day.

It was a dream, and would not stay;
A dream, that in a single night
Faded and vanished out of sight.
My father's anger followed fast
This passion, as a freshening blast
Seeks out and fans the fire, whose rage
It may increase, but not assuage.
And he exclaimed: "No wandering
 bard
Shall win thy hand, O Irmingard!
For which Prince Henry of Hoheneck
By messenger and letter sues."

Gently, but firmly, I replied:
"Henry of Hoheneck I discard!
Never the hand of Irmingard
Shall lie in his as the hand of a bride!"
This said I, Walter, for thy sake;
This said I, for I could not choose.

After a pause, my father spake
In that cold and deliberate tone
Which turns the hearer into stone,
And seems itself the act to be
That follows with such dread certainty
"This or the cloister and the veil!"
No other words than these he said,
But they were like a funeral wail;
My life was ended, my heart was dead.

That night from the castle-gate went
 down
With silent, slow, and stealthy pace,
Two shadows, mounted on shadowy
 steeds,
Taking the narrow path that leads
Into the forest dense and brown.
In the leafy darkness of the place,
One could not distinguish form nor face,
Only a bulk without a shape,
A darker shadow in the shade;
One scarce could say it moved or stayed.
Thus it was we made our escape!
A foaming brook, with many a bound,
Followed us like a playful hound;
Then leaped before us, and in the hollow
Paused, and waited for us to follow,
And seemed impatient, and afraid
That our tardy flight should be be-
 trayed
By the sound our horses' hoof-beats
 made.
And when we reached the plain below,
We paused a moment and drew rein
To look back at the castle again;
And we saw the windows all aglow
With lights, that were passing to and
 fro;
Our hearts with terror ceased to beat;
The brook crept silent to our feet;
We knew what most we feared to
 know.
Then suddenly horns began to blow;
And we heard a shout, and a heavy
 tramp,
And our horses snorted in the damp
Night-air of the meadows green and
 wide,
And in a moment, side by side,
So close, they must have seemed but
 one,
The shadows across the moonlight run,
And another came, and swept behind,
Like the shadow of clouds before the
 wind!

How I remember that breathless flight
Across the moors, in the summer night!

How under our feet the long, white
   road
Backward like a river flowed,
Sweeping with it fences and hedges,
Whilst farther away and overhead,
Paler than I, with fear and dread,
The moon fled with us as we fled
Along the forest's jagged edges!

All this I can remember well;
But of what afterwards befell
I nothing further can recall
Than a blind, desperate, headlong fall;
The rest is a blank and darkness all.
When I awoke out of this swoon,
The sun was shining, not the moon,
Making a cross upon the wall
With the bars of my windows narrow
   and tall;
And I prayed to it, as I had been wont
   to pray,
From early childhood, day by day,
Each morning, as in bed I lay!
I was lying again in my own room!
And I thanked God, in my fever and
   pain,
That those shadows on the midnight
   plain
Were gone, and could not come again!
I struggled no longer with my doom!

This happened many years ago.
I left my father's home to come
Like Catherine to her martyrdom,
For blindly I esteemed it so.
And when I heard the convent door
Behind me close, to ope no more,
I felt it smite me like a blow.
Through all my limbs a shudder ran,
And on my bruisèd spirit fell
The dampness of my narrow cell
As night-air on a wounded man,
Giving intolerable pain.

But now a better life began.
I felt the agony decrease
By slow degrees, then wholly cease,
Ending in perfect rest and peace!
It was not apathy, nor dulness,
That weighed and pressed upon my
   brain,
But the same passion I had given
To earth before, now turned to heaven
With all its overflowing fulness.

Alas! the world is full of peril!
The path that runs through the fairest
   meads,

On the sunniest side of the valley, leads
Into a region bleak and sterile!
Alike in the high-born and the lowly,
The will is feeble, and passion strong.
We cannot sever right from wrong;
Some falsehood mingles with all truth;
Nor is it strange the heart of youth
Should waver and comprehend but
   slowly
The things that are holy and unholy!
But in this sacred, calm retreat,
We are all well and safely shielded
From winds that blow, and waves that
   beat,
From the cold, and rain, and blighting
   heat,
To which the strongest hearts have
   yielded.
Here we stand as the Virgins Seven,
For our celestial bridegroom yearning;
Our hearts are lamps forever burning,
With a steady and unwavering flame,
Pointing upward, forever the same,
Steadily upward toward the heaven!

The moon is hidden behind a cloud;
A sudden darkness fills the room,
And thy deep eyes, amid the gloom,
Shine like jewels in a shroud.
On the leaves is a sound of falling rain;
A bird, awakened in its nest,
Gives a faint twitter of unrest,
Then smooths its plumes and sleeps
   again.
No other sounds than these I hear;
The hour of midnight must be near.
Thou art o'erspent with the day's
   fatigue
Of riding many a dusty league;
Sink, then, gently to thy slumber;
Me so many cares encumber,
So many ghosts, and forms of fright,
Have started from their graves to-night,
They have driven sleep from mine eyes
   away:
I will go down to the chapel and pray

V.

A COVERED BRIDGE AT LUCERNE.

PRINCE HENRY.

God's blessing on the architects who
   build
The bridges o'er swift rivers and abysses
Before impassable to human feet,
No less than on the builders of cathe-
   drals,

Whose massive walls are bridges thrown
    across
The dark and terrible abyss of Death.
Well has the name of Pontifex been
    given
Unto the Church's head, as the chief
    builder
And architect of the invisible bridge
That leads from earth to heaven.

ELSIE.

            How dark it grows !
What are these paintings on the walls
    around us ?

PRINCE HENRY.

The Dance Macaber !

ELSIE.

            What ?

PRINCE HENRY.

            The Dance of Death !
All that go to and fro must look upon
    it,
Mindful of what they shall be, while
    beneath,
Among the wooden piles, the turbulent
    river
Rushes, impetuous as the river of life,
With dimpling eddies, ever green and
    bright,
Save where the shadow of this bridge
    falls on it.

ELSIE.

Oh yes ! I see it now !

PRINCE HENRY.

            The grim musician
Leads all men through the mazes of
    that dance,
To different sounds in different meas-
    ures moving ;
Sometimes he plays a lute, sometimes a
    drum,
To tempt or terrify.

ELSIE.

            What is this picture ?

PRINCE HENRY.

It is a young man singing to a nun,
Who kneels at her devotions, but in
    kneeling
Turns round to look at him ; and
    Death, meanwhile,
Is putting out the candles on the altar !

ELSIE.

Ah, what a pity 't is that she should
    listen
Unto such songs, when in her orisons
She might have heard in heaven the
    angels singing !

PRINCE HENRY.

Here he has stolen a jester's cap and
    bells
And dances with the Queen.

ELSIE.

            A foolish jest !

PRINCE HENRY.

And here the heart of the new-wedded
    wife,
Coming from church with her beloved
    lord,
He startles with the rattle of his drum.

ELSIE.

Ah, that is sad ! And yet perhaps 't is
    best
That she should die, with all the sun-
    shine on her,
And all the benedictions of the morn-
    ing,
Before this affluence of golden light
Shall fade into a cold and clouded gray.
Then into darkness !

PRINCE HENRY.

            Under it is written
" Nothing but death shall separate thee
    and me ! "

ELSIE.

And what is this, that follows close
    upon it ?

PRINCE HENRY.

Death playing on a dulcimer. Behind
    him,
A poor old woman, with a rosary,
Follows the sound, and seems to wish
    her feet
Were swifter to o'ertake him. Under-
    neath,
The inscription reads, " Better is Death
    than Life."

ELSIE.

Better is Death than Life ! Ah yes !
    to thousands
Death plays upon a dulcimer, and sings

That song of consolation, till the air
Rings with it, and they cannot choose
    but follow
Whither he leads.   And not the old
    alone,
But the young also hear it, and are
    still.

PRINCE HENRY.

Yes, in their sadder moments.   'T is
    the sound
Of their own hearts they hear, half full
    of tears,
Which are like crystal cups, half filled
    with water,
Responding to the pressure of a finger
With music sweet and low and melan-
    choly.
Let us go forward, and no longer stay
In this great picture-gallery of Death !
I hate it ! ay, the very thought of it !

ELSIE.

Why is it hateful to you ?

PRINCE HENRY.

                          For the reason
That life, and all that speaks of life, is
    lovely,
And death, and all that speaks of death,
    is hateful.

ELSIE.

The grave itself is but a covered bridge,
Leading from light to light, through a
    brief darkness !

PRINCE HENRY, *emerging from the bridge.*

I breathe again more freely !   Ah, how
    pleasant
To come once more into the light of day,
Out of that shadow of death !   To hear
    again
The hoof-beats of our horses on firm
    ground,
And not upon those hollow planks,
    resounding
With a sepulchral echo, like the clods
On coffins in a churchyard !   Yonder lies
The Lake of the Four Forest-Towns,
    apparelled
In light, and lingering, like a village
    maiden,
Hid in the bosom of her native moun-
    tains,
Then pouring all her life into another's,
Changing her name and being !   Over-
    head,

Shaking his cloudy tresses loose in air,
Rises Pilatus, with his windy pines.

They pass on.

THE DEVIL'S BRIDGE.

PRINCE HENRY *and* ELSIE *crossing with
    attendants.*

GUIDE.

This bridge is called the Devil's Bridge.
With a single arch, from ridge to ridge,
It leaps across the terrible chasm
Yawning beneath us, black and deep,
As if, in some convulsive spasm,
The summits of the hills had cracked,
And made a road for the cataract
That raves and rages down the steep !

LUCIFER, *under the bridge.*

Ha ! ha !

GUIDE.

Never any bridge but this
Could stand across the wild abyss ;
All the rest, of wood or stone,
By the Devil's hand were overthrown.
He toppled crags from the precipice,
And whatsoe'er was built by day
In the night was swept away ;
None could stand but this alone.

LUCIFER, *under the bridge.*

Ha ! ha !

GUIDE.

I showed you in the valley a bowlder
Marked   with   the   imprint   of   his
    shoulder ;
As he was bearing it up this way,
A peasant, passing, cried, " Herr Jé ! "
And the Devil dropped it in his fright,
And vanished suddenly out of sight !

LUCIFER, *under the bridge.*

Ha ! ha !

GUIDE.

Abbot Giraldus of Einsiedel,
For pilgrims on their way to Rome,
Built this at last, with a single arch,
Under which, on its endless march,
Runs the river, white with foam,
Like a thread through the eye of a
    needle.
And the Devil promised to let it stand,

Under compact and condition
That the first living thing which crossed
Should be surrendered into his hand,
And be beyond redemption lost.

LUCIFER, *under the bridge.*

Ha! ha! perdition!

GUIDE.

At length, the bridge being all com-
    pleted,
The Abbot, standing at its head,
Threw across it a loaf of bread,
Which a hungry dog sprang after,
And the rocks reëchoed with the peals
    of laughter,
To see the Devil thus defeated!

They pass on.

LUCIFER, *under the bridge.*

Ha! ha! defeated!
For journeys and for crimes like this
I let the bridge stand o'er the abyss!

THE ST. GOTHARD PASS.

PRINCE HENRY.

This is the highest point. Two ways
    the rivers
Leap down to different seas, and as
    they roll
Grow deep and still, and their majestic
    presence
Becomes a benefaction to the towns
They visit, wandering silently among
    them,
Like patriarchs old among their shining
    tents.

ELSIE.

How bleak and bare it is! Nothing but
    mosses
Grow on these rocks.

PRINCE HENRY.

            Yet are they not forgotten;
Beneficent Nature sends the mists to
feed them.

ELSIE.

See yonder little cloud, that, borne
    aloft
So tenderly by the wind, floats fast
    away
Over the snowy peaks! It seems to me
The body of St. Catherine, borne by
    angels!

PRINCE HENRY.

Thou art St. Catherine, and invisible
    angels
Bear thee across these chasms and
    precipices,
Lest thou shouldst dash thy feet against
    a stone!

ELSIE.

Would I were borne unto my grave, as
    she was,
Upon angelic shoulders! Even now
I seem uplifted by them, light as air!
What sound is that?

PRINCE HENRY.

            The tumbling avalanches,

ELSIE.

How awful, yet how beautiful!

PRINCE HENRY.

                    These are
The voices of the mountains! Thus
    they ope
Their snowy lips, and speak unto each
    other,
In the primeval language, lost to man.

ELSIE.

What land is this that spreads itself
    beneath us?

PRINCE HENRY.

Italy! Italy!

ELSIE.

            Land of the Madonna!
How beautiful it is! It seems a garden
Of Paradise!

PRINCE HENRY.

            Nay, of Gethsemane
To thee and me, of passion and of
    prayer!
Yet once of Paradise. Long years ago
I wandered as a youth among its
    bowers,
And never from my heart has faded
    quite
Its memory, that, like a summer sunset,
Encircles with a ring of purple light
All the horizon of my youth.

GUIDE.

                O friends!
The days are short, the way before us
    long:

We must not linger, if we think to reach
The inn at Belinzona before vespers!
They pass on.

AT THE FOOT OF THE ALPS.

A halt under the trees at noon.

PRINCE HENRY.

Here let us pause a moment in the trembling
Shadow and sunshine of the roadside trees,
And, our tired horses in a group assembling,
Inhale long draughts of this delicious breeze.
Our fleeter steeds have distanced our attendants;
They lag behind us with a slower pace;
We will await them under the green pendants
Of the great willows in this shady place.
Ho, Barbarossa! how thy mottled haunches
Sweat with this canter over hill and glade!
Stand still, and let these overhanging branches
Fan thy hot sides and comfort thee with shade!

ELSIE.

What a delightful landscape spreads before us,
Marked with a whitewashed cottage here and there!
And, in luxuriant garlands drooping o'er us,
Blossoms of grape-vines scent the sunny air.

PRINCE HENRY.

Hark! what sweet sounds are those, whose accents holy
Fill the warm noon with music sad and sweet!

ELSIE.

It is a band of pilgrims, moving slowly
On their long journey, with uncovered feet.

PILGRIMS, *chanting the Hymn of St. Hildebert.*

Me receptet Sion illa,
Sion David, urbs tranquilla,

Cujus faber auctor lucis,
Cujus portæ lignum crucis,
Cujus claves lingua Petri,
Cujus cives semper læti,
Cujus muri lapis vivus,
Cujus custos Rex festivus!

LUCIFER, *as a Friar in the procession.*

Here am I, too, in the pious band,
In the garb of a barefooted Carmelite dressed!
The soles of my feet are as hard and tanned
As the conscience of old Pope Hildebrand,
The Holy Satan, who made the wives
Of the bishops lead such shameful lives.
All day long I beat my breast,
And chant with a most particular zest
The Latin hymns, which I understand
Quite as well, I think, as the rest.
And at night such lodging in barns and sheds,
Such a hurly-burly in country inns,
Such a clatter of tongues in empty heads,
Such a helter-skelter of prayers and sins!
Of all the contrivances of the time
For sowing broadcast the seeds of crime,
There is none so pleasing to me and mine
As a pilgrimage to some far-off shrine!

PRINCE HENRY.

If from the outward man we judge the inner,
And cleanliness is godliness, I fear
A hopeless reprobate, a hardened sinner,
Must be that Carmelite now passing near.

LUCIFER.

There is my German Prince again,
Thus far on his journey to Salern,
And the lovesick girl, whose heated brain
Is sowing the cloud to reap the rain;
But it 's a long road that has no turn!
Let them quietly hold their way,
I have also a part in the play.
But first I must act to my heart's content
This mummery and this merriment,
And drive this motley flock of sheep
Into the fold, where drink and sleep

The jolly old friars of Benevent.
Of a truth, it often provokes me to laugh
To see these beggars hobble along,
Lamed and maimed, and fed upon chaff,
Chanting their wonderful piff and paff,
And, to make up for not understanding
  the song,
Singing it fiercely, and wild, and strong!
Were it not for my magic garters and
  staff,
And the goblets of goodly wine I quaff,
And the mischief I make in the idle
  throng,
I should not continue the business long.

PILGRIMS, *chanting.*

In hâc urbe, lux solennis,
Ver æternum, pax perennis;
In hâc odor implens cælos,
In hâc semper festum melos!

PRINCE HENRY.

Do you observe that monk among the
  train,
Who pours from his great throat the
  roaring bass,
As a cathedral spout pours out the rain,
And this way turns his rubicund, round
  face ?

ELSIE.

It is the same who, on the Strasburg
  square,
Preached to the people in the open air.

PRINCE HENRY.

And he has crossed o'er mountain, field,
  and fell,
On that good steed, that seems to bear
  him well,
The hackney of the Friars of Orders
  Gray,
His own stout legs! He, too, was in
  the play,
Both as King Herod and Ben Israel.
Good morrow, Friar !

FRIAR CUTHBERT.

          Good morrow, noble Sir !

PRINCE HENRY.

I speak in German, for, unless I err,
You are a German.

FRIAR CUTHBERT.

            I cannot gainsay you.
But by what instinct, or what secret
  sign,

Meeting me here, do you straightway
  divine
That northward of the Alps my country
  lies ?

PRINCE HENRY.

Your accent, like St. Peter's, would betray you,
Did not your yellow beard and your
  blue eyes.
Moreover, we have seen your face be-
  fore,
And heard you preach at the Cathedral
  door
On Easter Sunday, in the Strasburg
  square.
We were among the crowd that gath-
  ered there,
And saw you play the Rabbi with great
  skill,
As if, by leaning o'er so many years
To walk with little children, your own
  will
Had caught a childish attitude from
  theirs,
A kind of stooping in its form and
  gait,
And could no longer stand erect and
  straight.
Whence come you now ?

FRIAR CUTHBERT.

          From the old monastery
Of Hirschau, in the forest; being sent
Upon a pilgrimage to Benevent,
To see the image of the Virgin Mary,
That moves its holy eyes, and some-
  times speaks,
And lets the piteous tears run down its
  cheeks,
To touch the hearts of the impenitent.

PRINCE HENRY.

Oh, had I faith, as in the days gone by,
That knew no doubt, and feared no
  mystery !

LUCIFER, *at a distance.*

Ho, Cuthbert ! Friar Cuthbert !

FRIAR CUTHBERT.

          Farewell, Prince;
I cannot stay to argue and convince.

PRINCE HENRY.

This is indeed the blessed Mary's land,
Virgin and mother of our dear Redeemer !

All hearts are touched and softened at
    her name,
Alike the bandit, with the bloody hand,
The priest, the prince, the scholar, and
    the peasant,
The man of deeds, the visionary
    dreamer,
Pay homage to her as one ever present !
And even as children, who have much
    offended
A too indulgent father, in great shame,
Penitent, and yet not daring unat-
    tended
To go into his presence, at the gate
Speak with their sister, and confiding
    wait
Till she goes in before and intercedes ;
So men, repenting of their evil deeds,
And yet not venturing rashly to draw
    near
With their requests an angry father's
    ear,
Offer to her their prayers and their con-
    fession,
And she for them in heaven makes in-
    tercession.
And if our faith had given us nothing
    more
Than this example of all womanhood,
So mild, so merciful, so strong, so good,
So patient, peaceful, loyal, loving, pure,
This were enough to prove it higher and
    truer
Than all the creeds the world had known
    before.

PILGRIMS, *chanting afar off.*

Urbs cœlestis, urbs beata,
Supra petram collocata,
Urbs in portu satis tuto
De longinquo te saluto,
Te saluto, te suspiro,
Te affecto, te requiro!

THE INN AT GENOA.

A terrace overlooking the sea. Night.

PRINCE HENRY.

It is the sea, it is the sea,
In all its vague immensity,
Fading and darkening in the distance !
Silent, majestical, and slow,
The white ships haunt it to and fro,
With all their ghostly sails unfurled,
As phantoms from another world
Haunt the dim confines of existence !

But ah ! how few can comprehend
Their signals, or to what good end
From land to land they come and go !
Upon a sea more vast and dark
The spirits of the dead embark,
All voyaging to unknown coasts.
We wave our farewells from the shore,
And they depart, and come no more,
Or come as phantoms and as ghosts.

Above the darksome sea of death
Looms the great life that is to be,
A land of cloud and mystery,
A dim mirage, with shapes of men
Long dead and passed beyond our
    ken.
Awe-struck we gaze, and hold our
    breath
Till the fair pageant vanisheth,
Leaving us in perplexity,
And doubtful whether it has been
A vision of the world unseen,
Or a bright image of our own
Against the sky in vapors thrown.

LUCIFER, *singing from the sea.*

Thou didst not make it, thou canst not
    mend it,
But thou hast the power to end it !
The sea is silent, the sea is discreet,
Deep it lies at thy very feet ;
There is no confessor like unto Death !
Thou canst not see him, but he is near ;
Thou needst not whisper above thy
    breath,
And he will hear ;
He will answer the questions,
The vague surmises and suggestions,
That fill thy soul with doubt and fear !

PRINCE HENRY.

The fisherman, who lies afloat,
With shadowy sail, in yonder boat,
Is singing softly to the Night !
But do I comprehend aright
The meaning of the words he sung
So sweetly in his native tongue ?
Ah yes ! the sea is still and deep.
All things within its bosom sleep !
A single step, and all is o'er ;
A plunge, a bubble, and no more ;
And thou, dear Elsie, wilt be free
From martyrdom and agony.

ELSIE, *coming from her chamber upon the
terrace.*

The night is calm and cloudless,
And still as still can be,

And the stars come forth to listen
To the music of the sea.
They gather, and gather, and gather,
Until they crowd the sky,
And listen, in breathless silence,
To the solemn litany.
It begins in rocky caverns,
As a voice that chants alone
To the pedals of the organ
In monotonous undertone ;
And anon from shelving beaches,
And shallow sands beyond,
In snow-white robes uprising
The ghostly choirs respond.
And sadly and unceasing
The mournful voice sings on,
And the snow-white choirs still answer
Christe eleison !

PRINCE HENRY.

Angel of God ! thy finer sense perceives
Celestial and perpetual harmonies !
Thy purer soul, that trembles and be-
    lieves,
Hears the archangel's trumpet in the
    breeze,
And where the forest rolls, or ocean
    heaves,
Cecilia's organ sounding in the seas,
And tongues of prophets speaking in
    the leaves.
But I hear discord only and despair,
And whispers as of demons in the air !

AT SEA.

IL PADRONE.

The wind upon our quarter lies,
And on before the freshening gale,
That fills the snow-white lateen sail,
Swiftly our light felucca flies.
Around, the billows burst and foam ;
They lift her o'er the sunken rock,
They beat her sides with many a shock,
And then upon their flowing dome
They poise her, like a weathercock !
Between us and the western skies
The hills of Corsica arise ;
Eastward in yonder long blue line,
The summits of the Apennine,
And southward, and still far away,
Salerno, on its sunny bay.
You cannot see it, where it lies.

PRINCE HENRY.

Ah, would that never more mine eyes
Might see its towers by night or day !

ELSIE.

Behind us, dark and awfully,
There comes a cloud out of the sea,
That bears the form of a hunted deer,
With hide of brown, and hoofs of
    black
And antlers laid upon its back,
And fleeing fast and wild with fear,
As if the hounds were on its track !

PRINCE HENRY.

Lo ! while we gaze, it breaks and falls
In shapeless masses, like the walls
Of a burnt city. Broad and red
The fires of the descending sun
Glare through the windows, and o'er-
    head,
Athwart the vapors, dense and dun,
Long shafts of silvery light arise,
Like rafters that support the skies !

ELSIE.

See ! from its summit the lurid levin
Flashes downward without warning,
As Lucifer, son of the morning,
Fell from the battlements of heaven !

IL PADRONE.

I must entreat you, friends, below !
The angry storm begins to blow,
For the weather changes with the
    moon.
All this morning, until noon,
We had baffling winds, and sudden
    flaws
Struck the sea with their cat's-paws.
Only a little hour ago
I was whistling to Saint Antonio
For a capful of wind to fill our sail,
And instead of a breeze he has sent a
    gale.
Last night I saw St. Elmo's stars,
With their glimmering lanterns, all at
    play
On the tops of the masts and the tips of
    the spars,
And I knew we should have foul
    weather to-day.
Cheerily, my hearties ! yo heave ho !
Brail up the mainsail, and let her go
As the winds will and Saint Antonio !

Do you see that Livornese felucca,
That vessel to the windward yonder,
Running with her gunwale under ?
I was looking when the wind o'ertook
    her.

She had all sail set, and the only won-
der
Is that at once the strength of the blast
Did not carry away her mast.
She is a galley of the Gran Duca,
That, through the fear of the Algerines,
Convoys those lazy brigantines,
Laden with wine and oil from Lucca.
Now all is ready, high and low;
Blow, blow, good Saint Antonio!

Ha! that is the first dash of the rain,
With a sprinkle of spray above the
rails,
Just enough to moisten our sails,
And make them ready for the strain.
See how she leaps, as the blasts o'er-
take her,
And speeds away with a bone in her
mouth!
Now keep her head toward the south,
And there is no danger of bank or
breaker.
With the breeze behind us, on we go;
Not too much, good Saint Antonio!

VI.

THE SCHOOL OF SALERNO.

*A travelling Scholastic affixing his
Theses to the gate of the College.*

SCHOLASTIC.

There, that is my gauntlet, my banner,
my shield,
Hung up as a challenge to all the field!
One hundred and twenty-five proposi-
tions,
Which I will maintain with the sword
of the tongue
Against all disputants, old and young.
Let us see if doctors or dialecticians
Will dare to dispute my definitions,
Or attack any one of my learned theses.
Here stand I; the end shall be as God
pleases.
I think I have proved, by profound re-
searches,
The error of all those doctrines so
vicious
Of the old Areopagite Dionysius,
That are making such terrible work in
the churches,
By Michael the Stammerer sent from
the East,

And done into Latin by that Scottish
beast,
Johannes Duns Scotus, who dares to
maintain,
In the face of the truth, the error infer-
nal,
That the universe is and must be eter-
nal;
At first laying down, as a fact funda-
mental,
That nothing with God can be acciden-
tal;
Then asserting that God before the crea-
tion
Could not have existed, because it is
plain
That, had He existed, He would have
created;
Which is begging the question that
should be debated,
And moveth me less to anger than
laughter.
All nature, he holds, is a respiration
Of the Spirit of God, who, in breathing,
hereafter
Will inhale it into his bosom again,
So that nothing but God alone will re-
main.
And therein he contradicteth himself;
For he opens the whole discussion by
stating,
That God can only exist in creating.
That question I think I have laid on
the shelf!

*He goes out. Two Doctors come in disput-
ing, and followed by pupils.*

DOCTOR SERAFINO.

I, with the Doctor Seraphic, maintain,
That a word which is only conceived in
the brain
Is a type of eternal Generation;
The spoken word is the Incarnation.

DOCTOR CHERUBINO.

What do I care for the Doctor Seraphic,
With all his wordy chaffer and traffic?

DOCTOR SERAFINO.

You make but a paltry show of resistance;
Universals have no real existence!

DOCTOR CHERUBINO.

Your words are but idle and empty
chatter;
Ideas are eternally joined to matter!

DOCTOR SERAFINO.

May the Lord have mercy on your position,
You wretched, wrangling culler of herbs !

DOCTOR CHERUBINO.

May he send your soul to eternal perdition,
For your Treatise on the Irregular Verbs !

They rush out fighting. Two Scholars come in.

FIRST SCHOLAR.

Monte Cassino, then, is your College.
What think you of ours here at Salern ?

SECOND SCHOLAR.

To tell the truth, I arrived so lately,
I hardly yet have had time to discern.
So much, at least, I am bound to acknowledge:
The air seems healthy, the buildings stately,
And on the whole I like it greatly.

FIRST SCHOLAR.

Yes, the air is sweet; the Calabrian hills
Send us down puffs of mountain air ;
And in summer-time the sea-breeze fills
With its coolness cloister, and court, and square.
Then at every season of the year
There are crowds of guests and travellers here ;
Pilgrims, and mendicant friars, and traders
From the Levant, with figs and wine,
And bands of wounded and sick Crusaders,
Coming back from Palestine.

SECOND SCHOLAR.

And what are the studies you pursue ?
What is the course you here go through ?

FIRST SCHOLAR.

The first three years of the college course
Are given to Logic alone, as the source
Of all that is noble, and wise, and true.

SECOND SCHOLAR.

That seems rather strange, I must confess,

In a Medical School; yet, nevertheless,
You doubtless have reasons for that.

FIRST SCHOLAR.

Oh yes
For none but a clever dialectician
Can hope to become a great physician;
That has been settled long ago.
Logic makes an important part
Of the mystery of the healing art ;
For without it how could you hope to show
That nobody knows so much as you know ?
After this there are five years more
Devoted wholly to medicine,
With lectures on chirurgical lore,
And dissections of the bodies of swine,
As likest the human form divine.

SECOND SCHOLAR.

What are the books now most in vogue ?

FIRST SCHOLAR.

Quite an extensive catalogue ;
Mostly, however, books of our own ;
As Gariopontus' Passionarius,
And the writings of Matthew Platearius ;
And a volume universally known
As the Regimen of the School of Salern,
For Robert of Normandy written in terse
And very elegant Latin verse.
Each of these writings has its turn.
And when at length we have finished these
Then comes the struggle for degrees,
With all the oldest and ablest critics ;
The public thesis and disputation,
Question, and answer, and explanation
Of a passage out of Hippocrates,
Or Aristotle's Analytics.
There the triumphant Magister stands !
A book is solemnly placed in his hands,
On which he swears to follow the rule
And ancient forms of the good old School ;
To report if any confectionarius
Mingles his drugs with matters various,
And to visit his patients twice a day,
And once in the night, if they live in town,
And if they are poor, to take no pay.
Having faithfully promised these,
His head is crowned with a laurel crown ;

" Let us see what the learned wag maintains." Page 567.

A kiss on his cheek, a ring on his hand,
The Magister Artium et Physices
Goes forth from the school like a lord
    of the land.
And now, as we have the whole morn-
    ing before us,
Let us go in, if you make no objection,
And listen awhile to a learned prelec-
    tion
On Marcus Aurelius Cassiodorus.

They go in. Enter LUCIFER *as a Doctor.*

LUCIFER.

This is the great School of Salern!
A land of wrangling and of quarrels,
Of brains that seethe, and hearts that
    burn,
Where every emulous scholar hears,
In every breath that comes to his ears,
The rustling of another's laurels!
The air of the place is called salubrious;
The neighborhood of Vesuvius lends it
An odor volcanic, that rather mends it,
And the buildings have an aspect lugu-
    brious,
That inspires a feeling of awe and terror
Into the heart of the beholder,
And befits such an ancient homestead
    of error,
Where the old falsehoods moulder and
    smoulder,
And yearly by many hundred hands
Are carried away in the zeal of youth,
And sown like tares in the field of
    truth,
To blossom and ripen in other lands.

What have we here, affixed to the gate?
The challenge of some scholastic wight,
Who wishes to hold a public debate
On sundry questions wrong or right!
Ah, now this is my great delight!
For I have often observed of late
That such discussions end in a fight.
Let us see what the learned wag main-
    tains
With such a prodigal waste of brains.

Reads.

" Whether angels in moving from place
    to place
Pass through the intermediate space.
Whether God himself is the author of
    evil,
Or whether that is the work of the
    Devil.
When, where, and wherefore Lucifer
    fell,

And whether he now is chained in
    hell."
I think I can answer that question well:
So long as the boastful human mind
Consents in such mills as this to grind,
I sit very firmly upon my throne!
Of a truth it almost makes me laugh,
To see men leaving the golden grain
To gather in piles the pitiful chaff
That old Peter Lombard thrashed with
    his brain,
To have it caught up and tossed again
On the horns of the Dumb Ox of
    Cologne!

But my guests approach! there is in the
    air
A fragrance, like that of the Beautiful
    Garden
Of Paradise, in the days that were!
An odor of innocence and of prayer,
And of love, and faith that never fails,
Such as the fresh young heart exhales
Before it begins to wither and harden!
I cannot breathe such an atmosphere!
My soul is filled with a nameless fear,
That, after all my trouble and pain,
After all my restless endeavor,
The youngest, fairest soul of the twain,
The most ethereal, most divine,
Will escape from my hands for ever and
    ever.
But the other is already mine!
Let him live to corrupt his race,
Breathing among them, with every
    breath,
Weakness, selfishness, and the base
And pusillanimous fear of death.
I know his nature, and I know
That of all who in my ministry
Wander the great earth to and fro,
And on my errands come and go,
The safest and subtlest are such as he.

Enter PRINCE HENRY *and* ELSIE, *with
    attendants.*

PRINCE HENRY.

Can you direct us to Friar Angelo?

LUCIFER.

He stands before you.

PRINCE HENRY.

            Then you know our purpose.
I am Prince Henry of Hoheneck, and
    this
The maiden that I spake of in my
    letters.

LUCIFER.

It is a very grave and solemn business !
We must not be precipitate.   Does she
Without compulsion, of her own free
     will,
Consent to this ?

PRINCE HENRY.

                 Against all opposition,
Against all prayers, entreaties, protesta-
     tions,
She will not be persuaded.

LUCIFER.

               That is strange !
Have you thought well of it ?

ELSIE.

              I come not here
To argue, but to die.   Your business is
     not
To question, but to kill me.   I am
     ready.
I am impatient to be gone from here
Ere any thoughts of earth disturb again
The spirit of tranquillity within me.

PRINCE HENRY.

Would I had not come here !   Would I
     were dead,
And thou wert in thy cottage in the
     forest,
And hadst not known me !   Why have
     I done this ?
Let me go back and die.

ELSIE.

              It cannot be ;
Not if these cold, flat stones on which
     we tread
Were coulters heated white, and yonder
     gateway
Flamed like a furnace with a sevenfold
     heat.
I must fulfil my purpose.

PRINCE HENRY.

               I forbid it !
Not one step further.   For I only meant
To put thus far thy courage to the
     proof.
It is enough.   I, too, have strength to
     die,
For thou hast taught me !

ELSIE.

O my Prince ! remember

Your promises.   Let me fulfil my er-
     rand.
You do not look on life and death as I
     do.
There are two angels, that attend unseen
Each one of us, and in great books
     record
Our good and evil deeds.   He who
     writes down
The good ones, after every action closes
His volume, and ascends with it to God.
The other keeps his dreadful day-book
     open
Till sunset, that we may repent ; which
     doing,
The record of the action fades away,
And leaves a line of white across the
     page.
Now if my act be good, as I believe,
It cannot be recalled.   It is already
Sealed up in heaven, as a good deed
     accomplished.
The rest is yours.   Why wait you ?   I
     am ready.

                 To her attendants.

Weep not, my friends ! rather rejoice
     with me.
I shall not feel the pain, but shall be
     gone,
And you will have another friend in
     heaven.
Then start not at the creaking of the
     door
Through which I pass.   I see what lies
     beyond it.

                 To PRINCE HENRY.

And you, O Prince ! bear back my
     benison
Unto my father's house, and all within
     it.
This morning in the church I prayed for
     them,
After confession, after absolution,
When my whole soul was white, I
     prayed for them.
God will take care of them, they need
     me not.
And in your life let my remembrance
     linger,
As something not to trouble and disturb
     it,
But to complete it, adding life to life.
And if at times beside the evening fire,
You see my face among the other faces,
Let it not be regarded as a ghost
That haunts your house, but as a guest
     that loves you.

Nay, even as one of your own family,
Without whose presence there were
    something wanting.
I have no more to say.   Let us go in.

PRINCE HENRY.

Friar Angelo! I charge you on your
    life,
Believe not what she says, for she is
    mad,
And comes here not to die, but to be
    healed.

ELSIE.

Alas! Prince Henry!

LUCIFER.

Come with me; this way.

ELSIE *goes in with* LUCIFER, *who thrusts*
PRINCE HENRY *back and closes the
door.*

PRINCE HENRY.

Gone! and the light of all my life gone
    with her!
A sudden darkness falls upon the world!
Oh, what a vile and abject thing am I
That purchase length of days at such a
    cost!
Not by her death alone, but by the death
Of all that's good and true and noble in
    me!
All   manhood,   excellence,   and   self-
    respect,
All love, and faith, and hope, and heart
    are dead!
All my divine nobility of nature
By this one act is forfeited forever.
I am a Prince in nothing but in name!

To the attendants.

Why did you let this horrible deed be
    done ?
Why did you not lay hold on her, and
    keep her
From self-destruction?   Angelo! mur-
    derer!

Struggles at the door, but cannot open it.

ELSIE, *within.*

Farewell, dear Prince! farewell!

PRINCE HENRY.

Unbar the door!

LUCIFER.

It is too late!

PRINCE HENRY.

It shall not be too late
They burst the door open and rush in.

THE FARM-HOUSE IN THE ODENWALD.

URSULA *spinning.   A summer afternoon.
A table spread.*

URSULA.

I have marked it well, — it must be
    true, —
Death never takes one alone, but two!
Whenever he enters in at a door,
Under roof of gold or roof of thatch,
He always leaves it upon the latch,
And comes again ere the year is o'er.
Never one of a household only!
Perhaps it is a mercy of God,
Lest the dead there under the sod,
In the land of strangers, should be
    lonely!
Ah me! I think I am lonelier here!
It is hard to go, — but harder to stay!
Were it not for the children, I should
    pray
That Death would take me within the
    year!
And Gottlieb! — he is at work all day,
In the sunny field, or the forest murk,
But I know that his thoughts are far
    away,
I know that his heart is not in his
    work!
And when he comes home to me at
    night
He is not cheery, but sits and sighs,
And I see the great tears in his eyes,
And try to be cheerful for his sake.
Only the children's hearts are light.
Mine is weary, and ready to break.
God help us! I hope we have done
    right;
We thought we were acting for the
    best!

Looking through the open door.

Who is it coming under the trees ?
A man, in the Prince's livery dressed!
He looks about him with doubtful face,
As if uncertain of the place.
He stops at the beehives; — now he
    sees
The garden gate; — he is going past!
Can he be afraid of the bees ?

No ; he is coming in at last !
He fills my heart with strange alarm !

Enter a Forester.

FORESTER.

Is this the tenant Gottlieb's farm ?

URSULA.

This is his farm, and I his wife.
Pray sit.   What may your business be ?

FORESTER.

News from the Prince !

URSULA.

                    Of death or life ?

FORESTER.

You put your questions eagerly !

URSULA.

Answer me, then !   How is the Prince ?

FORESTER.

I left him only two hours since
Homeward returning down the river,
As strong and well as if God, the Giver,
Had given him back his youth again.

URSULA, *despairing.*

Then Elsie, my poor child, is dead !

FORESTER.

That, my good woman, I have not said.
Don't cross the bridge till you come
    to it,
Is a proverb old, and of excellent wit.

URSULA.

Keep me no longer in this pain !

FORESTER.

It is true your daughter is no more ; —
That is, the peasant she was before.

URSULA.

Alas ! I am simple and lowly bred,
I am poor, distracted, and forlorn.
And it is not well that you of the court
Should mock me thus, and make a sport
Of a joyless mother whose child is dead,
For you, too, were of mother born !

FORESTER.

Your daughter lives, and the Prince is
    well !
You will learn erelong how it all befell.
Her heart for a moment never failed ;

But when they reached Salerno's gate,
The Prince's nobler self prevailed,
And saved her for a noble fate.
And he was healed, in his despair,
By the touch of St. Matthew's sacred
    bones ;
Though I think the long ride in the
    open air,
That pilgrimage over stocks and stones,
In the miracle must come in for a
    share.

URSULA.

Virgin ! who lovest the poor and lowly,
If the loud cry of a mother's heart
Can ever ascend to where thou art,
Into thy blessed hands and holy
Receive my prayer of praise and thanks-
    giving !
Let the hands that bore our Saviour
    bear it
Into the awful presence of God ;
For thy feet with holiness are shod,
And if thou bearest it He will hear it.
Our child who was dead again is living !

FORESTER.

I did not tell you she was dead ;
If you thought so 't was no fault of
    mine ;
At this very moment while I speak,
They are sailing homeward down the
    Rhine,
In a splendid barge, with golden prow,
And decked with banners white and
    red
As the colors on your daughter's cheek.
They call her the Lady Alicia now ;
For the Prince in Salerno made a vow
That Elsie only would he wed.

URSULA.

Jesu Maria ! what a change !
All seems to me so weird and strange !

FORESTER.

I saw her standing on the deck,
Beneath an awning cool and shady ;
Her cap of velvet could not hold
The tresses of her hair of gold,
That flowed and floated like the stream,
And fell in masses down her neck.
As fair and lovely did she seem
As in a story or a dream
Some beautiful and foreign lady.
And the Prince looked so grand and
    proud,
And waved his hand thus to the crowd

That gazed and shouted from the shore,
All down the river, long and loud.

URSULA.

We shall behold our child once more ;
She is not dead ! She is not dead !
God, listening, must have overheard
The prayers, that, without sound or
    word,
Our hearts in secrecy have said !
Oh, bring me to her ; for mine eyes
Are hungry to behold her face ;
My very soul within me cries ;
My very hands seem to caress her,
To see her, gaze at her, and bless her ;
Dear Elsie, child of God and grace !

Goes out toward the garden.

FORESTER.

There goes the good woman out of her
    head ;
And Gottlieb's supper is waiting here ;
A very capacious flagon of beer,
And a very portentous loaf of bread.
One would say his grief did not much
    oppress him.
Here 's to the health of the Prince, God
    bless him !

He drinks.

Ha ! it buzzes and stings like a hornet !
And what a scene there, through the
    door !
The forest behind and the garden be-
    fore,
And midway an old man of threescore,
With a wife and children that caress
    him.
Let me try still further to cheer and
    adorn it
With a merry, echoing blast of my
    cornet !

Goes out blowing his horn.

THE CASTLE OF VAUTSBERG ON THE RHINE.

PRINCE HENRY *and* ELSIE *standing on
    the terrace at evening.*

The sound of bells heard from a distance.

PRINCE HENRY.

We are alone. The wedding guests
Ride down the hill, with plumes and
    cloaks,
And the descending dark invests

The Niederwald, and all the nests
Among its hoar and haunted oaks.

ELSIE.

What bells are those, that ring so slow,
So mellow, musical, and low ?

PRINCE HENRY.

They are the bells of Geisenheim,
That with their melancholy chime
Ring out the curfew of the sun.

ELSIE.

Listen, beloved.

PRINCE HENRY.

            They are done !
Dear Elsie ! many years ago
Those same soft bells at eventide
Rang in the ears of Charlemagne,
As, seated by Fastrada's side
At Ingelheim, in all his pride
He heard their sound with secret pain.

ELSIE.

Their voices only speak to me
Of peace and deep tranquillity,
And endless confidence in thee !

PRINCE HENRY.

Thou knowest the story of her ring,
How, when the court went back to Aix,
Fastrada died ; and how the king
Sat watching by her night and day,
Till into one of the blue lakes,
Which water that delicious land,
They cast the ring, drawn from her
    hand :
And the great monarch sat serene
And sad beside the fated shore,
Nor left the land forevermore.

ELSIE.

That was true love.

PRINCE HENRY.

            For him the queen
Ne'er did what thou hast done for me.

ELSIE.

Wilt thou as fond and faithful be ?
Wilt thou so love me after death ?

PRINCE HENRY.

In life's delight, in death's dismay,
In storm and sunshine, night and day,
In health, in sickness, in decay,
Here and hereafter, I am thine !

Thou hast Fastrada's ring. Beneath
The calm, blue waters of thine eyes,
Deep in thy steadfast soul it lies,
And, undisturbed by this world's breath,
With magic light its jewels shine!
This golden ring, which thou hast
          worn
Upon thy finger since the morn,
Is but a symbol and a semblance,
An outward fashion, a remembrance,
Of what thou wearest within unseen,
O my Fastrada, O my queen!
Behold! the hill-tops all aglow
With purple and with amethyst;
While the whole valley deep below
Is filled, and seems to overflow,
With a fast-rising tide of mist.
The evening air grows damp and chill;
Let us go in.

ELSIE.

          Ah, not so soon.
See yonder fire! It is the moon
Slow rising o'er the eastern hill.
It glimmers on the forest tips,
And through the dewy foliage drips
In little rivulets of light,
And makes the heart in love with
          night.

PRINCE HENRY.

Oft on this terrace, when the day
Was closing, have I stood and gazed,
And seen the landscape fade away,
And the white vapors rise and drown
Hamlet and vineyard, tower and town,
While far above the hill-tops blazed.
But then another hand than thine
Was gently held and clasped in mine;
Another head upon my breast
Was laid, as thine is now, at rest.
Why dost thou lift those tender eyes
With so much sorrow and surprise?
A minstrel's, not a maiden's hand,
Was that which in my own was
          pressed,
A manly form usurped thy place,
A beautiful, but bearded face,
That now is in the Holy Land,
Yet in my memory from afar
Is shining on us like a star.
But linger not. For while I speak,
A sheeted spectre white and tall,
The cold mist climbs the castle wall,
And lays his hand upon thy cheek!

          They go in.

EPILOGUE.

THE   TWO   RECORDING   ANGELS   AS CENDING.

THE ANGEL OF GOOD DEEDS, *with closed book.*

GOD sent his messenger the rain,
And said unto the mountain brook,
" Rise up, and from thy caverns look
And leap, with naked, snow-white feet,
From the cool hills into the heat
Of the broad, arid plain."

God sent his messenger of faith,
And whispered in the maiden's heart,
" Rise up and look from where thou art,
And scatter with unselfish hands
Thy freshness on the barren sands
And solitudes of Death."

O beauty of holiness,
Of self-forgetfulness, of lowliness!
O power of meekness,
Whose very gentleness and weakness
Are like the yielding, but irresistible air!
Upon the pages
Of the sealed volume that I bear,
The deed divine
Is written in characters of gold,
That never shall grow old,
But through all ages
Burn and shine,
With soft effulgence!
O God! it is thy indulgence
That fills the world with the bliss
Of a good deed like this!

THE ANGEL OF EVIL DEEDS, *with open book.*

Not yet, not yet
Is the red sun wholly set,
But evermore recedes,
While open still I bear
The Book of Evil Deeds,
To let the breathings of the upper air
Visit its pages and erase
The records from its face!
Fainter and fainter as I gaze
In the broad blaze
The glimmering landscape shines,
And below me the black river
Is hidden by wreaths of vapor!
Fainter and fainter the black lines
Begin to quiver
Along the whitening surface of the
          paper;

Shade after shade
The terrible words grow faint and fade,
And in their place
Runs a white space!

Down goes the sun!
But the soul of one,
Who by repentance
Hath escaped the dreadful sentence,
Shines bright below me as I look.
It is the end!
With closèd Book
To God do I ascend.
Lo! over the mountain steeps
A dark, gigantic shadow sweeps
Beneath my feet;
A blackness inwardly brightening
With sullen heat,
As a storm-cloud lurid with lightning.
And a cry of lamentation,
Repeated and again repeated,
Deep and loud
As the reverberation
Of cloud answering unto cloud,
Swells and rolls away in the distance,
As if the sheeted
Lightning retreated,
Baffled and thwarted by the wind's re-
sistance.

It is Lucifer,
The son of mystery;
And since God suffers him to be,
He, too, is God's minister,
And labors for some good
By us not understood!

SECOND INTERLUDE.

MARTIN LUTHER.

A CHAMBER IN THE WARTBURG. MORN-
ING. MARTIN LUTHER WRITING.

MARTIN LUTHER.

Our God, a Tower of Strength is He,
A goodly wall and weapon;
From all our need He helps us free,
That now to us doth happen.
  The old evil foe
  Doth in earnest grow,
  In grim armor dight,
  Much guile and great might;
On earth there is none like him.

OH yes; a tower of strength indeed,
A present help in all our need,
A sword and buckler is our God.
Innocent men have walked unshod
O'er burning ploughshares, and have
    trod
Unharmed on serpents in their path,
And laughed to scorn the Devil's wrath!

Safe in this Wartburg tower I stand
Where God hath led me by the hand,
And look down, with a heart at ease,
Over the pleasant neighborhoods,
Over the vast Thuringian Woods,
With flash of river, and gloom of trees,
With castles crowning the dizzy heights,
And farms and pastoral delights,
And the morning pouring everywhere
Its golden glory on the air.
Safe, yes, safe am I here at last,
Safe from the overwhelming blast
Of the mouths of Hell, that followed me
    fast,
And the howling demons of despair
That hunted me like a beast to his lair.

  Of our own might we nothing can;
  We soon are unprotected;
  There fighteth for us the right Man,
  Whom God himself elected.
    Who is He; ye exclaim?
    Christus is his name,
    Lord of Sabaoth,
    Very God in troth;
  The field He holds forever.

Nothing can vex the Devil more
Than the name of Him whom we adore
Therefore doth it delight me best
To stand in the choir among the rest,
With the great organ trumpeting
Through its metallic tubes, and sing:
Et verbum caro factum est!
These words the Devil cannot endure,
For he knoweth their meaning well!
Him they trouble and repel,
Us they comfort and allure,
And happy it were, if our delight
Were as great as his affright!

Yea, music is the Prophet's art;
Among the gifts that God hath sent,
One of the most magnificent!
It calms the agitated heart;
Temptations, evil thoughts, and all
The passions that disturb the soul,
Are quelled by its divine control,
As the evil spirit fled from Saul,
And his distemper was allayed,
When David took his harp and played

This world may full of Devils be,
All ready to devour us;
Yet not so sore afraid are we,
They shall not overpower us.
   This World's Prince, howe'er
   Fierce he may appear,
   He can harm us not,
   He is doomed, God wot!
   One little word can slay him!

Incredible it seems to some
And to myself a mystery,
That such weak flesh and blood as
   we,
Armed with no other shield or sword,
Or other weapon than the Word,
Should combat and should overcome
A spirit powerful as he!
He summons forth the Pope of Rome
With all his diabolic crew,
His shorn and shaven retinue
Of priests and children of the dark ;
Kill ! kill ! they cry, the Heresiarch,
Who rouseth up all Christendom
Against us; and at one fell blow
Seeks the whole Church to overthrow!
Not yet ; my hour is not yet come.

Yesterday in an idle mood,
Hunting with others in the wood,
I did not pass the hours in vain,
For in the very heart of all
The joyous tumult raised around,
Shouting of men, and baying of hound,
And the bugle's blithe and cheery
   call,
And echoes answering back again,
From crags of the distant mountain
   chain, —
In the very heart of this, I found
A mystery of grief and pain.
It was an image of the power
Of Satan, hunting the world about,
With his nets and traps and well-
   trained dogs,
His bishops and priests and theologues,
And all the rest of the rabble rout,
Seeking whom he may devour!
Enough I have had of hunting hares,
Enough of these hours of idle mirth,
Enough of nets and traps and gins !
The only hunting of any worth
Is where I can pierce with javelins
The cunning foxes and wolves and
   bears,
The whole iniquitous troop of beasts,
The Roman Pope and the Roman
   priests
That sorely infest and afflict the earth !

Ye nuns, ye singing birds of the air !
The fowler hath caught you in his snare
And keeps you safe in his gilded cage,
Singing the song that never tires,
To lure down others from their nests ;
How ye flutter and beat your breasts,
Warm and soft with young desires,
Against the cruel, pitiless wires,
Reclaiming your lost heritage !
Behold ! a hand unbars the door,
Ye shall be captives held no more.

   The Word they shall perforce let stand,
   And little thanks they merit!
   For He is with us in the land,
   With gifts of his own Spirit!
      Though they take our life,
      Goods, honors, child and wife,
      Let these pass away,
      Little gain have they;
   The Kingdom still remaineth !

Yea, it remaineth forevermore,
However Satan may rage and roar,
Though often he whispers in my ears :
What if thy doctrines false should be ?
And wrings from me a bitter sweat.
Then I put him to flight with jeers,
Saying : Saint Satan ! pray for me ;
If thou thinkest I am not saved yet !

And my mortal foes that lie in wait
In every avenue and gate!
As to that odious monk John Tetzel,
Hawking about his hollow wares
Like a huckster at village fairs,
And those mischievous fellows, Wetzel,
Campanus, Carlstadt, Martin Cellarius,
And all the busy, multifarious
Heretics, and disciples of Arius,
Half-learned, dunce-bold, dry and hard,
They are not worthy of my regard,
Poor and humble as I am.

But ah ! Erasmus of Rotterdam,
He is the vilest miscreant
That ever walked this world below !
A Momus, making his mock and mow,
At Papist and at Protestant,
Sneering at St. John and St. Paul,
At God and Man, at one and all;
And yet as hollow and false and drear,
As a cracked pitcher to the ear,
And ever growing worse and worse !
Whenever I pray, I pray for a curse
On Erasmus, the Insincere !

Philip Melancthon ! thou alone
Faithful among the faithless known,

Thee I hail, and only thee!
Behold the record of us three!
   Res et verba Philippus,
   Res sine verbis Lutherus ;
   Erasmus verba sine re!

My Philip, prayest thou for me?
Lifted above all earthly care,
From these high regions of the air,
Among the birds that day and night
Upon the branches of tall trees
Sing their lauds and litanies,
Praising God with all their might,
My Philip, unto thee I write.

My Philip! thou who knowest best
All that is passing in this breast;
The spiritual agonies,
The inward deaths, the inward hell,
And the divine new births as well,
That surely follow after these,
As after winter follows spring;
My Philip, in the night-time sing
This song of the Lord I send to thee;
And I will sing it for thy sake,
Until our answering voices make
A glorious antiphony,
And choral chant of victory!

PART THREE.

THE NEW ENGLAND TRAGE-
DIES.

JOHN ENDICOTT.

DRAMATIS PERSONÆ.

John Endicott . .	*Governor.*
John Endicott . .	*His son.*
Richard Bellingham .	*Deputy Governor.*
John Norton . . .	*Minister of the Gospel.*
Edward Butter . .	*Treasurer.*
Walter Merry . . .	*Tithing-man.*
Nicholas Upsall . .	*An old citizen.*
Samuel Cole . . .	*Landlord of the Three Mariners.*
Simon Kempthorn } **Ralph Goldsmith** } .	*Sea-Captains.*
Wenlock Christison) **Edith,** *his daughter* } **Edward Wharton**)	*Quakers.*

Assistants, Halberdiers, Marshal, etc.

The Scene is in Boston in the year 1665.

PROLOGUE.

To-night we strive to read, as we may
   best,
This city, like an ancient palimpsest;

And bring to light, upon the blotted
   page,
The mournful record of an earlier age,
That, pale and half effaced, lies hidden
   away
Beneath the fresher writing of to-day.

Rise, then, O buried city that hast been;
Rise up, rebuilded in the painted scene,
And let our curious eyes behold once
   more
The pointed gable and the pent-house
   door,
The Meeting-house with leaden-latticed
   panes,
The narrow thoroughfares, the crooked
   lanes!

Rise, too, ye shapes and shadows of the
   Past,
Rise from your long-forgotten graves at
   last;
Let us behold your faces, let us hear
The words ye uttered in those days of
   fear!
Revisit your familiar haunts again, —
The scenes of triumph, and the scenes
   of pain,
And leave the footprints of your bleeding
   feet
Once more upon the pavement of the
   street!

Nor let the Historian blame the Poet
   here,
If he perchance misdate the day or
   year,
And group events together, by his art,
That in the Chronicles lie far apart;
For as the double stars, though sun-
   dered far,
Seem to the naked eye a single star,
So facts of history, at a distance seen,
Into one common point of light con-
   vene.

"Why touch upon such themes?" per-
   haps some friend
May ask, incredulous; "and to what
   good end?
Why drag again into the light of day
The errors of an age long passed away?"
I answer: "For the lessons that they
   teach:
The tolerance of opinion and of speech.
Hope, Faith, and Charity remain, —
   these three;
And greatest of them all is Charity."

Let us remember, if these words be true,
That unto all men Charity is due;
Give what we ask; and pity, while we blame,
Lest we become copartners in the shame,
Lest we condemn, and yet ourselves partake,
And persecute the dead for conscience' sake.

Therefore it is the author seeks and strives
To represent the dead as in their lives,
And lets at times his characters unfold
Their thoughts in their own language, strong and bold;
He only asks of you to do the like;
To hear him first, and, if you will, then strike.

ACT I.

SCENE I. — *Sunday afternoon. The interior of the Meeting-house. On the pulpit, an hour-glass; below, a box for contributions.* JOHN NORTON *in the pulpit.* GOVERNOR ENDICOTT *in a canopied seat, attended by four halberdiers. The congregation singing.*

The Lord descended from above,
    And bowed the heavens high;
And underneath his feet He cast
    The darkness of the sky.

On Cherubim and Seraphim
    Right royally He rode,
And on the wings of mighty winds
    Came flying all abroad.

NORTON (*rising and turning the hour-glass on the pulpit*).

I heard a great voice from the temple saying
Unto the Seven Angels, Go your ways;
Pour out the vials of the wrath of God
Upon the earth. And the First Angel went
And poured his vial on the earth; and straight
There fell a noisome and a grievous sore
On them which had the birth-mark of the Beast,
And them which worshipped and adored his image.

On us hath fallen this grievous pestilence.
There is a sense of terror in the air;
And apparitions of things horrible
Are seen by many; from the sky above us
The stars fall; and beneath us the earth quakes!
The sound of drums at midnight from afar,
The sound of horsemen riding to and fro,
As if the gates of the invisible world
Were opened, and the dead came forth to warn us, —
All these are omens of some dire disaster
Impending over us, and soon to fall.
Moreover, in the language of the Prophet,
Death is again come up into our windows,
To cut off little children from without,
And young men from the streets. And in the midst
Of all these supernatural threats and warnings
Doth Heresy uplift its horrid head;
A vision of Sin more awful and appalling
Than any phantasm, ghost, or apparition,
As arguing and portending some enlargement
Of the mysterious Power of Darkness!

EDITH, *barefooted, and clad in sackcloth, with her hair hanging loose upon her shoulders, walks slowly up the aisle, followed by* WHARTON *and other Quakers. The congregation starts up in confusion.*

EDITH (*to* NORTON, *raising her hand*).

                            Peace!

NORTON.

Anathema maranatha! The Lord cometh!

EDITH.

Yea, verily He cometh, and shall judge
The shepherds of Israel who do feed themselves,
And leave their flocks to eat what they have trodden
Beneath their feet.

NORTON.

            Be silent, babbling woman!

St. Paul commands all women to keep
   silence
Within the churches.

EDITH.

        Yet the women prayed
And prophesied at Corinth in his day;
And, among those on whom the fiery
   tongues
Of Pentecost descended, some were
   women!

NORTON.

The Elders of the Churches, by our
   law,
Alone have power to open the doors of
   speech
And silence in the Assembly. I command you!

EDITH.

The law of God is greater than your
   laws!
Ye build your church with blood, your
   town with crime;
The heads thereof give judgment for
   reward;
The priests thereof teach only for their
   hire;
Your laws condemn the innocent to
   death;
And against this I bear my testimony!

NORTON.

What testimony?

EDITH.

        That of the Holy Spirit,
Which, as your Calvin says, surpasseth
   reason.

NORTON.

The laborer is worthy of his hire.

EDITH.

Yet our great Master did not teach for
   hire,
And the Apostles without purse or scrip
Went forth to do his work. Behold
   this box
Beneath thy pulpit. Is it for the poor?
Thou canst not answer. It is for the
   Priest;
And against this I bear my testimony.

NORTON.

Away with all these Heretics and
   Quakers!

Quakers, forsooth! Because a quaking
   fell
On Daniel, at beholding of the Vision,
Must ye needs shake and quake? Be-
   cause Isaiah
Went stripped and barefoot, must ye
   wail and howl?
Must ye go stripped and naked? must ye
   make
A wailing like the dragons, and a mourn-
   ing
As of the owls? Ye verify the adage
That Satan is God's ape! Away with
   them!

*Tumult. The Quakers are driven out
with violence,* EDITH *following slowly.
The congregation retires in confusion.*

Thus freely do the Reprobates commit
Such measure of iniquity as fits them
For the intended measure of God's
   wrath,
And even in violating God's commands
Are they fulfilling the divine decree!
The will of man is but an instrument
Disposed and predetermined to its ac-
   tion
According unto the decree of God,
Being as much subordinate thereto
As is the axe unto the hewer's hand!

He descends from the pulpit, and joins
GOVERNOR ENDICOTT, *who comes forward to meet him.*

The omens and the wonders of the
   time,
Famine, and fire, and shipwreck, and
   disease,
The blast of corn, the death of our
   young men,
Our sufferings in all precious, pleasant
   things,
Are manifestations of the wrath divine,
Signs of God's controversy with New
   England.
These emissaries of the Evil One,
These servants and ambassadors of
   Satan,
Are but commissioned executioners
Of God's vindictive and deserved dis-
   pleasure.
We must receive them as the Roman
   Bishop
Once received Attila, saying, I rejoice
You have come safe, whom I esteem to
   be
The scourge of God, sent to chastise his
   people.

This very heresy, perchance, may serve
The purposes of God to some good end.
With you I leave it; but do not neg-
    lect
The holy tactics of the civil sword.

ENDICOTT.

And what more can be done?

NORTON.

                    The hand that cut
The Red Cross from the colors of the
    king
Can cut the red heart from this heresy.
Fear not. All blasphemies immediate
And heresies turbulent must be sup-
    pressed
By civil power.

ENDICOTT.

                But in what way suppressed?

NORTON.

The Book of Deuteronomy declares
That if thy son, thy daughter, or thy
    wife,
Ay, or the friend which is as thine own
    soul,
Entice thee secretly, and say to thee,
Let us serve other gods, then shall thine
    eye
Not pity him, but thou shalt surely kill
    him,
And thine own hand shall be the first
    upon him
To slay him.

ENDICOTT.

                Four already have been slain;
And others banished upon pain of
    death.
But they come back again to meet their
    doom,
Bringing the linen for their winding-
    sheets.
We must not go too far. In truth, I
    shrink
From shedding of more blood. The
    people murmur
At our severity.

NORTON.

                Then let them murmur!
Truth is relentless; justice never wa-
    vers;
The greatest firmness is the greatest
    mercy;
The noble order of the Magistracy

Cometh immediately from God, and yet
This noble order of the Magistracy
Is by these Heretics despised and out-
    raged.

ENDICOTT.

To-night they sleep in prison. If they
    die,
They cannot say that we have caused
    their death.
We do but guard the passage, with the
    sword
Pointed towards them; if they dash
    upon it,
Their blood will be on their own heads,
    not ours.

NORTON.

Enough. I ask no more. My prede-
    cessor
Coped only with the milder heresies
Of Antinomians and of Anabaptists.
He was not born to wrestle with these
    fiends.
Chrysostom in his pulpit; Augustine
In disputation; Timothy in his house!
The lantern of St. Botolph's ceased to
    burn
When from the portals of that church
    he came
To be a burning and a shining light
Here in the wilderness. And, as he lay
On his death-bed, he saw me in a vision
Ride on a snow-white horse into this
    town.
His vision was prophetic; thus I came,
A terror to the impenitent, and Death
On the pale horse of the Apocalypse
To all the accursed race of Heretics!
                                    [Exeunt.

SCENE II. — A street. On one side,
    NICHOLAS UPSALL'S house; on the
    other, WALTER MERRY'S, with a flock
    of pigeons on the roof. UPSALL seated
    in the porch of his house.

UPSALL.

O day of rest! How beautiful, how
    fair,
How welcome to the weary and the
    old!
Day of the Lord! and truce to earthly
    cares!
Day of the Lord, as all our days should
    be!
Ah, why will man by his austerities

Shut out the blessed sunshine and the
light,
And make of thee a dungeon of despair!

WALTER MERRY (*entering and looking
round him*).

All silent as a graveyard! No one stir-
ring;
No footfall in the street, no sound of
voices!
By righteous punishment and persever-
ance,
And perseverance in that punishment,
At last I have brought this contuma-
cious town
To strict observance of the Sabbath
day.
Those wanton gospellers, the pigeons
yonder,
Are now the only Sabbath-breakers
left.
I cannot put them down. As if to
taunt me,
They gather every Sabbath afternoon
In noisy congregation on my roof,
Billing and cooing. Whir! take that,
ye Quakers.

Throws a stone at the pigeons. Sees
UPSALL.

Ah! Master Nicholas!

UPSALL.

Good afternoon,
Dear neighbor Walter.

MERRY.

Master Nicholas,
You have to-day withdrawn yourself
from meeting.

UPSALL.

Yea, I have chosen rather to worship
God
Sitting in silence here at my own door.

MERRY.

Worship the Devil! You this day
have broken
Three of our strictest laws. First, by
abstaining
From public worship. Secondly, by
walking
Profanely on the Sabbath.

UPSALL.

Not one step.

I have been sitting still here, seeing the
pigeons
Feed in the street and fly about the
roofs.

MERRY.

You have been in the street with other
intent
Than going to and from the Meeting-
house.
And, thirdly, you are harboring Quakers
here.
I am amazed!

UPSALL.

Men sometimes, it is said,
Entertain angels unawares.

MERRY.

Nice angels!
Angels in broad-brimmed hats and
russet cloaks,
The color of the Devil's nutting-bag.
They came
Into the Meeting-house this afternoon
More in the shape of devils than of
angels.
The women screamed and fainted; and
the boys
Made such an uproar in the gallery
I could not keep them quiet.

UPSALL.

Neighbor Walter,
Your persecution is of no avail.

MERRY.

'T is prosecution, as the Governor says,
Not persecution.

UPSALL.

Well, your prosecution
Your hangings do no good.

MERRY.

The reason is,
We do not hang enough. But, mark
my words,
We 'll scour them; yea, I warrant ye,
we 'll scour them!
And now go in and entertain your
angels,
And don't be seen here in the street
again
Till after sundown! There they are
again!

Exit UPSALL. MERRY *throws another
stone at the pigeons, and then goes into
his house.*

SCENE III. — *A room in* UPSALL'S *house. Night.* EDITH, WHARTON, *and other Quakers seated at a table.* UPSALL *seated near them. Several books on the table.*

WHARTON.

William and Marmaduke, our martyred brothers,
Sleep in untimely graves, if aught untimely
Can find place in the providence of God,
Where nothing comes too early or too late.
I saw their noble death. They to the scaffold
Walked hand in hand. Two hundred armèd men
And many horsemen guarded them, for fear
Of rescue by the crowd, whose hearts were stirred.

EDITH.

O holy martyrs !

WHARTON.

When they tried to speak,
Their voices by the roll of drums were drowned.
When they were dead they still looked fresh and fair,
The terror of death was not upon their faces.
Our sister Mary, likewise, the meek woman,
Has passed through martyrdom to her reward ;
Exclaiming, as they led her to her death,
" These many days I 've been in Paradise."
And, when she died, Priest Wilson threw the hangman
His handkerchief, to cover the pale face
He dared not look upon.

EDITH.

As persecuted,
Yet not forsaken; as unknown, yet known ;
As dying, and behold we are alive ;
As sorrowful, and yet rejoicing always ;
As having nothing, yet possessing all !

WHARTON.

And Leddra, too, is dead. But from his prison,

The day before his death, he sent these words
Unto the little flock of Christ : " Whatever
May come upon the followers of the Light, —
Distress, affliction, famine, nakedness,
Or perils in the city or the sea,
Or persecution, or even death itself, —
I am persuaded that God's armor of Light,
As it is loved and lived in, will preserve you.
Yea, death itself ; through which you will find entrance
Into the pleasant pastures of the fold,
Where you shall feed forever as the herds
That roam at large in the low valleys of Achor.
And as the flowing of the ocean fills
Each creek and branch thereof, and then retires,
Leaving behind a sweet and wholesome savor ;
So doth the virtue and the life of God
Flow evermore into the hearts of those
Whom He hath made partakers of His nature ;
And, when it but withdraws itself a little,
Leaves a sweet savor after it, that many
Can say they are made clean by every word
That He hath spoken to them in their silence."

EDITH (*rising and breaking into a kind of chant*).

Truly we do but grope here in the dark,
Near the partition-wall of Life and Death,
At every moment dreading or desiring
To lay our hands upon the unseen door !
Let us, then, labor for an inward stillness, —
An inward stillness and an inward healing ;
That perfect silence where the lips and heart
Are still, and we no longer entertain
Our own imperfect thoughts and vain opinions,
But God alone speaks in us, and we wait
In singleness of heart, that we may know
His will, and in the silence of our spirits,
That we may do His will, and do that only !

A long pause, interrupted by the sound of a drum approaching; then shouts in the street, and a loud knocking at the door.

MARSHAL.

Within there! Open the door!

MERRY.

Will no one answer?

MARSHAL.

In the King's name! Within there!

MERRY.

Open the door!

UPSALL (*from the window*).

It is not barred. Come in. Nothing prevents you.
The poor man's door is ever on the latch.
He needs no bolt nor bar to shut out thieves;
He fears no enemies, and has no friends
Importunate enough to need a key.

Enter JOHN ENDICOTT, *the* MARSHAL, MERRY, *and a crowd. Seeing the Quakers silent and unmoved, they pause, awe-struck.* ENDICOTT *opposite* EDITH.

MARSHAL.

In the King's name do I arrest you all!
Away with them to prison. Master Upsall,
You are again discovered harboring here
These ranters and disturbers of the peace.
You know the law.

UPSALL.

I know it, and am ready
To suffer yet again its penalties.

EDITH (*to* ENDICOTT).

Why dost thou persecute me, Saul of Tarsus?

ACT II.

SCENE I. — JOHN ENDICOTT'S *room. Early morning.*

JOHN ENDICOTT.

"Why dost thou persecute me, Saul of Tarsus?"
All night these words were ringing in mine ears!

A sorrowful sweet face; a look that pierced me
With meek reproach; a voice of resignation
That had a life of suffering in its tone;
And that was all! And yet I could not sleep,
Or, when I slept, I dreamed that awful dream!
I stood beneath the elm-tree on the Common,
On which the Quakers have been hanged, and heard
A voice, not hers, that cried amid the darkness,
"This is Aceldama, the field of blood!
I will have mercy, and not sacrifice!'"

Opens the window and looks out.

The sun is up already; and my heart
Sickens and sinks within me when I think
How many tragedies will be enacted
Before his setting. As the earth rolls round,
It seems to me a huge Ixion's wheel,
Upon whose whirling spokes we are bound fast,
And must go with it! Ah, how bright the sun
Strikes on the sea and on the masts of vessels,
That are uplifted, in the morning air,
Like crosses of some peaceable crusade!
It makes me long to sail for lands unknown,
No matter whither! Under me, in shadow,
Gloomy and narrow, lies the little town,
Still sleeping, but to wake and toil awhile,
Then sleep again. How dismal looks the prison,
How grim and sombre in the sunless street, —
The prison where she sleeps, or wakes and waits
For what I dare not think of, — death, perhaps!
A word that has been said may be unsaid:
It is but air. But when a deed is done
It cannot be undone, nor can our thoughts
Reach out to all the mischiefs that may follow.
'T is time for morning prayers. I will go down.

My father, though severe, is kind and
        just;
And when his heart is tender with de-
        votion, —
When from his lips have fallen the
        words, "Forgive us
As we forgive," — then will I intercede
For these poor people, and perhaps may
        save them.   [*Exit.*

SCENE II. — *Dock Square. On one side,
the tavern of the Three Mariners. In
the background, a quaint building with
gables; and, beyond it, wharves and
shipping.* CAPTAIN KEMPTHORN *and
others seated at a table before the door.*
SAMUEL COLE *standing near them.*

KEMPTHORN.

Come, drink about! Remember Parson
        Melham,
And bless the man who first invented
        flip!

They drink.

COLE.

Pray, Master Kempthorn, where were
        you last night?

KEMPTHORN.

On board the Swallow, Simon Kemp-
        thorn, master,
Up for Barbadoes, and the Windward
        Islands.

COLE.

The town was in a tumult.

KEMPTHORN.

                      And for what?

COLE.

Your Quakers were arrested.

KEMPTHORN.

                      How my Quakers?

COLE.

These you brought in your vessel from
        Barbadoes.
They made an uproar in the Meeting-
        house
Yesterday, and they're now in prison
        for it.
I owe you little thanks for bringing them
To the Three Mariners.

KEMPTHORN.

        They have not harmed you.
I tell you, Goodman Cole, that Quaker
        girl
Is precious as a sea-bream's eye. I tell
        you
It was a lucky day when first she set
Her little foot upon the Swallow's deck,
Bringing good luck, fair winds, and
        pleasant weather.

COLE.

I am a law-abiding citizen;
I have a seat in the new Meeting-house,
A cow-right on the Common; and,
        besides,
Am corporal in the Great Artillery.
I rid me of the vagabonds at once.

KEMPTHORN.

Why should you not have Quakers at
        your tavern
If you have fiddlers?

COLE.

                Never! never! never!
If you want fiddling you must go else-
        where,
To the Green Dragon and the Admiral
        Vernon,
And other such disreputable places.
But the Three Mariners is an orderly
        house,
Most orderly, quiet, and respectable.
Lord Leigh said he could be as quiet
        here
As at the Governor's. And have I not
King Charles's Twelve Good Rules, all
        framed and glazed,
Hanging in my best parlor?

KEMPTHORN.

                        Here 's a health
To good King Charles. Will you not
        drink the King?
Then drink confusion to old Parson
        Palmer.

COLE.

And who is Parson Palmer? I don't
        know him.

KEMPTHORN.

He had his cellar underneath his pulpit,
And so preached o'er his liquor, just as
        you do.

        A drum within.

COLE.

Here comes the Marshal.

MERRY (*within*).

Make room for the Marshal.

KEMPTHORN.

How pompous and imposing he appears!
His great buff doublet bellying like a
    mainsail,
And all his streamers fluttering in the
    wind.
What holds he in his hand?

COLE.

A proclamation.

Enter the MARSHAL, *with a proclamation;
and* MERRY, *with a halberd. They are
preceded by a drummer, and followed
by the hangman, with an armful of
books, and a crowd of people, among
whom are* UPSALL *and* JOHN ENDI-
COTT. *A pile is made of the books.*

MERRY.

Silence, the drum! Good citizens, attend
To the new laws enacted by the Court.

MARSHAL (*reads*).

" Whereas a cursed sect of Heretics
Has lately risen, commonly called
    Quakers,
Who take upon themselves to be com-
    missioned
Immediately of God, and furthermore
Infallibly assisted by the Spirit
To write and utter blasphemous opinions,
Despising Government and the order of
    God
In Church and Commonwealth, and
    speaking evil
Of Dignities, reproaching and reviling
The Magistrates and Ministers, and
    seeking
To turn the people from their faith, and
    thus
Gain proselytes to their pernicious
    ways; —
This Court, considering the premises,
And to prevent like mischief as is
    wrought
By their means in our land, doth hereby
    order,
That whatsoever master or commander
Of any ship, bark, pink, or catch shall
    bring

To any roadstead, harbor, creek, or
    cove
Within this Jurisdiction any Quakers,
Or other blasphemous Heretics, shall
    pay
Unto the Treasurer of the Common-
    wealth
One hundred pounds, and for default
    thereof
Be put in prison, and continue there
Till the said sum be satisfied and paid.'

COLE.

Now, Simon Kempthorn, what say you
to that?

KEMPTHORN.

I pray you, Cole, lend me a hundred
    pounds!

MARSHAL (*reads*).

" If any one within this Jurisdiction
Shall henceforth entertain, or shall con-
    ceal
Quakers or other blasphemous Heretics,
Knowing them so to be, every such
    person
Shall forfeit to the country forty shil-
    lings
For each hour's entertainment or con-
    cealment,
And shall be sent to prison, as afore-
    said,
Until the forfeiture be wholly paid."
    Murmurs in the crowd.

KEMPTHORN.

Now, Goodman Cole, I think your turn
has come!

COLE.

Knowing them so to be!

KEMPTHORN.

                    At forty shillings
The hour, your fine will be some forty
    pounds!

COLE.

Knowing them so to be! That is the
law.

MARSHAL (*reads*).

" And it is further ordered and enacted,
If any Quaker or Quakers shall pre-
    sume
To come henceforth into this Jurisdic-
    tion,

Every male Quaker for the first offence
Shall have one ear cut off; and shall be
  kept
At labor in the Workhouse, till such
  time
As he be sent away at his own charge.
And for the repetition of the offence
Shall have his other ear cut off, and
  then
Be branded in the palm of his right
  hand.
And every woman Quaker shall be
  whipt
Severely in three towns; and every
  Quaker,
Or he or she, that shall for a third
  time
Herein again offend, shall have their
  tongues
Bored through with a hot iron, and
  shall be
Sentenced to Banishment on pain of
  Death."

Loud murmurs. The voice of CHRIST-
  ISON *in the crowd.*

O patience of the Lord! How long,
  how long,
Ere thou avenge the blood of Thine
  Elect?

MERRY.

Silence, there, silence! Do not break
  the peace!

MARSHAL (*reads*).

" Every inhabitant of this Jurisdiction
Who shall defend the horrible opinions
Of Quakers, by denying due respect
To equals and superiors, and withdraw-
  ing
From Church Assemblies, and thereby
  approving
The abusive and destructive practices
Of this accursed sect, in opposition
To all the orthodox received opinions
Of godly men, shall be forthwith com-
  mitted
Unto close prison for one month; and
  then
Refusing to retract and to reform
The opinions as aforesaid, he shall be
Sentenced to Banishment on pain of
  Death.
By the Court. Edward Rawson, Sec-
  retary."

Now, hangman, do your duty. Burn
  those books.

*Loud murmurs in the crowd. The pile of
  books is lighted.*

UPSALL.

I testify against these cruel laws!
Forerunners are they of some judgment
  on us;
And, in the love and tenderness I
  bear
Unto this town and people, I beseech
  you,
O Magistrates, take heed, lest ye be
  found
As fighters against God!

JOHN ENDICOTT (*taking* UPSALL'S *hand*).

                              Upsall, I thank you
For speaking words such as some
  younger man,
I, or another, should have said before
  you.
Such laws as these are cruel and op-
  pressive;
A blot on this fair town, and a disgrace
To any Christian people.

MERRY (*aside, listening behind them*).

                              Here's sedition!
I never thought that any good would
  come
Of this young popinjay, with his long
  hair
And his great boots, fit only for the
  Russians
Or barbarous Indians, as his father says!

THE VOICE.

Woe to the bloody town! And right-
  fully
Men call it the Lost Town! The blood
  of Abel
Cries from the ground, and at the final
  judgment
The Lord will say, " Cain, Cain! where
  is thy brother?"

MERRY.

Silence there in the crowd!

UPSALL (*aside*).

                              'T is Christison!

THE VOICE.

O foolish people, ye that think to burn
And to consume the truth of God, I tell
  you
That every flame is a loud tongue of fire

To publish it abroad to all the world
Louder than tongues of men!

KEMPTHORN (*springing to his feet*).

        Well said, my hearty!
There's a brave fellow! There's a man
   of pluck!
A man who's not afraid to say his
   say,
Though a whole town's against him.
   Rain, rain, rain,
Bones of St. Botolph, and put out this
   fire!

The drum beats. Exeunt all but MERRY,
   KEMPTHORN, *and* COLE.

MERRY.

And now that matter's ended, Goodman Cole,
Fetch me a mug of ale, your strongest
   ale.

KEMPTHORN (*sitting down*).

And me another mug of flip; and
   put
Two gills of brandy in it.
               [*Exit* COLE.

MERRY.

          No; no more.
Not a drop more, I say. You've had
   enough.

KEMPTHORN.

And who are you, sir?

MERRY.

         I'm a Tithing-man,
And Merry is my name.

KEMPTHORN.

         A merry name!
I like it; and I'll drink your merry
   health
Till all is blue.

MERRY.

       And then you will be clapped
Into the stocks, with the red letter D
Hung round about your neck for drunk-
   enness.
You're a free-drinker, — yes, and a free-
   thinker!

KEMPTHORN.

And you are Andrew Merry, or Merry
   Andrew.

MERRY.

My name is Walter Merry, and not Andrew.

KEMPTHORN.

Andrew or Walter, you're a merry fellow;
I'll swear to that.

MERRY.

       No swearing, let me tell you.
The other day one Shorthose had his
   tongue
Put into a cleft stick for profane swearing.

        COLE *brings the ale.*

KEMPTHORN.

Well, where's my flip? As sure as my
   name's Kempthorn —

MERRY.

Is your name Kempthorn?

KEMPTHORN.

        That's the name I go by.

MERRY.

What, Captain Simon Kempthorn of the
   Swallow?

KEMPTHORN.

No other.

MERRY (*touching him on the shoulder.*)

       Then you're wanted. I arrest you
In the King's name.

KEMPTHORN.

       And where's your warrant?

MERRY (*unfolding a paper, and reading*).

               Here.
Listen to me. "Hereby you are re-
   quired,
In the King's name, to apprehend the
   body
Of Simon Kempthorn, mariner, and
   him
Safely to bring before me, there to
   answer
All such objections as are laid to him,
Touching the Quakers." Signed, John
   Endicott.

KEMPTHORN.

Has it the Governor's seal?

MERRY.

Ay, here it is.

KEMPTHORN.

Death's head and cross-bones. That's
a pirate's flag!

MERRY.

Beware how you revile the Magistrates;
You may be whipped for that.

KEMPTHORN.

Then mum's the word.

Exeunt MERRY *and* KEMPTHORN.

COLE.

There's mischief brewing! Sure, there's
mischief brewing.
I feel like Master Josselyn when he
found
The hornet's nest, and thought it some
strange fruit,
Until the seeds came out, and then he
dropped it.   [*Exit.*

SCENE III. — *A room in the Governor's
house. Enter* GOVERNOR ENDICOTT
and MERRY.

ENDICOTT.

My son, you say?

MERRY.

Your Worship's eldest son.

ENDICOTT.

Speaking against the laws?

MERRY.

Ay, worshipful sir.

ENDICOTT.

And in the public market-place?

MERRY.

I saw him
With my own eyes, heard him with my
own ears.

ENDICOTT.

Impossible!

MERRY.

He stood there in the crowd
With Nicholas Upsall, when the laws
were read

To-day against the Quakers, and I heard
him
Denounce and vilipend them as unjust,
And cruel, wicked, and abominable.

ENDICOTT.

Ungrateful son!   O God! thou layest
upon me
A burden heavier than I can bear!
Surely the power of Satan must be
great
Upon the earth, if even the elect
Are thus deceived and fall away from
grace!

MERRY.

Worshipful sir! I meant no harm —

ENDICOTT.

'T is well.
You've done your duty, though you've
done it roughly,
And every word you've uttered since
you came
Has stabbed me to the heart!

MERRY.

I do beseech
Your Worship's pardon!

ENDICOTT.

He whom I have nurtured
And brought up in the reverence of the
Lord!
The child of all my hopes and my af-
fections!
He upon whom I leaned as a sure staff
For my old age! It is God's chastise-
ment
For leaning upon any arm but His!

MERRY.

Your Worship! —

ENDICOTT.

And this comes from holding parley
With the delusions and deceits of Satan.
At once, forever, must they be crushed
out,
Or all the land will reek with heresy!
Pray, have you any children?

MERRY.

No, not any.

ENDICOTT.

Thank God for that. He has delivered
you

"Worshipful sir! I meant no harm."   Page 586.

From a great care. Enough; my private griefs
Too long have kept me from the public service.

Exit MERRY. ENDICOTT *seats himself at the table and arranges his papers.*

The hour has come; and I am eager now
To sit in judgment on these Heretics.

A knock.

Come in. Who is it? (*Not looking up.*)

JOHN ENDICOTT.

It is I.

ENDICOTT (*restraining himself*).

Sit down!

JOHN ENDICOTT (*sitting down*).

I come to intercede for these poor people
Who are in prison, and await their trial.

ENDICOTT.

It is of them I wished to speak with you.
I have been angry with you, but 't is passed.
For when I hear your footsteps come or go,
See in your features your dead mother's face,
And in your voice detect some tone of hers,
All anger vanishes, and I remember
The days that are no more, and come no more,
When as a child you sat upon my knee,
And prattled of your playthings, and the games
You played among the pear trees in the orchard!

JOHN ENDICOTT.

Oh, let the memory of my noble mother
Plead with you to be mild and merciful!
For mercy more becomes a Magistrate
Than the vindictive wrath which men call justice!

ENDICOTT.

The sin of heresy is a deadly sin.
'T is like the falling of the snow, whose crystals
The traveller plays with, thoughtless of his danger,

Until he sees the air so full of light
That it is dark; and blindly staggering onward,
Lost and bewildered, he sits down to rest;
There falls a pleasant drowsiness upon him,
And what he thinks is sleep, alas! is death.

JOHN ENDICOTT.

And yet who is there that has never doubted?
And doubting and believing, has not said,
"Lord, I believe; help thou my unbelief"?

ENDICOTT.

In the same way we trifle with our doubts,
Whose shining shapes are like the stars descending;
Until at last, bewildered and dismayed,
Blinded by that which seemed to give us light,
We sink to sleep, and find that it is death,

Rising.

Death to the soul through all eternity!
Alas that I should see you growing up
To man's estate, and in the admonition
And nurture of the law, to find you now
Pleading for Heretics!

JOHN ENDICOTT (*rising*).

In the sight of God,
Perhaps all men are Heretics. Who dares
To say that he alone has found the truth?
We cannot always feel and think and act
As those who go before us. Had you done so,
You would not now be here.

ENDICOTT.

Have you forgotten
The doom of Heretics, and the fate of those
Who aid and comfort them? Have you forgotten
That in the market-place this very day
You trampled on the laws? What right have you,

An inexperienced and untravelled youth,
To sit in judgment here upon the acts
Of older men and wiser than yourself,
Thus stirring up sedition in the streets,
And making me a byword and a jest?

JOHN ENDICOTT.

Words of an inexperienced youth like
   me
Were powerless if the acts of older men
Were not before them. 'T is these laws
   themselves
Stir up sedition, not my judgment of
   them.

ENDICOTT.

Take heed, lest I be called, as Brutus
   was,
To be the judge of my own son. Be-
   gone!
When you are tired of feeding upon
   husks,
Return again to duty and submission,
But not till then.

JOHN ENDICOTT.

      I hear and I obey!
                    [Exit.

ENDICOTT.

Oh happy, happy they who have no
   children!
He's gone! I hear the hall door shut
   behind him.
It sends a dismal echo through my
   heart,
As if forever it had closed between us,
And I should look upon his face no
   more!
Oh, this will drag me down into my
   grave, —
To that eternal resting-place wherein
Man lieth down, and riseth not again!
Till the heavens be no more, he shall
   not wake,
Nor be roused from his sleep; for Thou
   dost change
His countenance and sendest him away!
                    [Exit.

ACT III.

SCENE I. — The Court of Assistants.
   ENDICOTT, BELLINGHAM, ATHER-
   TON, and other magistrates. KEMP-
   THORN, MERRY, and constables. Af-
   terwards WHARTON, EDITH, and
   CHRISTISON.

ENDICOTT.

Call Captain Simon Kempthorn.

MERRY.

            Simon Kempthorn,
Come to the bar!
   KEMPTHORN comes forward.

ENDICOTT.

            You are accused of bringing
Into this Jurisdiction, from Barbadoes,
Some persons of that sort and sect of
   people
Known by the name of Quakers, and
   maintaining
Most dangerous and heretical opinions,
Purposely coming here to propagate
Their heresies and errors; bringing
   with them
And spreading sundry books here,
   which contain
Their doctrines most corrupt and blas-
   phemous,
And contrary to the truth professed
   among us.
What say you to this charge?

KEMPTHORN.

            I do acknowledge,
Among the passengers on board the
   Swallow
Were certain persons saying Thee and
   Thou.
They seemed a harmless people, most-
   ways silent,
Particularly when they said their
   prayers.

ENDICOTT.

Harmless and silent as the pestilence!
You'd better have brought the fever or
   the plague
Among us in your ship! Therefore,
   this Court,
For preservation of the Peace and
   Truth,
Hereby commands you speedily to
   transport,
Or cause to be transported speedily,
The aforesaid persons hence unto Bar-
   badoes,
From whence they came; you paying
   all the charges
Of their imprisonment.

KEMPTHORN.

            Worshipful sir

No ship e'er prospered that has carried
    Quakers
Against their will! I knew a vessel
    once —

ENDICOTT.

And for the more effectual perform-
    ance
Hereof you are to give security
In bonds amounting to one hundred
    pounds.
On your refusal, you will be committed
To prison till you do it.

KEMPTHORN.   .

                    But you see
I cannot do it. The law, sir, of Barba-
    does
Forbids the landing Quakers on the
    island.

ENDICOTT.

Then you will be committed. Who
    comes next ?

MERRY.

There is another charge against the
    Captain.

ENDICOTT.

What is it ?

MERRY.

Profane swearing, please your Worship.
He cursed and swore from Dock Square
    to the Court-house.

ENDICOTT.

Then let him stand in the pillory for
    one hour.
    [*Exit* KEMPTHORN *with constable.*
Who 's next ?

MERRY.

    The Quakers.

ENDICOTT.

        Call them.

MERRY.

                Edward Wharton,
Come to the bar !

WHARTON.

        Yea, even to the bench.

ENDICOTT.

Take off your hat.

WHARTON.

            My hat offendeth not.
If it offendeth any, let him take it ;
For I shall not resist.

ENDICOTT.

            Take off his hat.
Let him be fined ten shillings for con-
    tempt.
    MERRY *takes off* WHARTON's *hat.*

WHARTON.

What evil have I done ?

ENDICOTT.

            Your hair 's too long ;
And in not putting off your hat to us
You 've disobeyed and broken that
    commandment
Which sayeth " Honor thy father and
    thy mother."

WHARTON.

John Endicott, thou art become too
    proud ;
And lovest him who putteth off the hat,
And honoreth thee by bowing of the
    body,
And sayeth " Worshipful sir ! " 'T is
    time for thee
To give such follies over, for thou may-
    est
Be drawing very near unto thy grave.

ENDICOTT.

Now, sirrah, leave your canting. Take
    the oath.

WHARTON.

Nay, sirrah me no sirrahs !

ENDICOTT.

                Will you swear ?

WHARTON.

Nay, I will not.

ENDICOTT.

            You made a great disturbance
And uproar yesterday in the Meeting-
    house,
Having your hat on.

WHARTON.

            I made no disturbance ;
For peacefully I stood, like other peo-
    ple.

I spake no words; moved against none
    my hand;
But by the hair they haled me out, and
    dashed
Their books into my face.

ENDICOTT.

                You, Edward Wharton,
On pain of death, depart this Jurisdic-
    tion
Within ten days. Such is your sen-
    tence. Go.

WHARTON.

John Endicott, it had been well for thee
If this day's doings thou hadst left
    undone.
But, banish me as far as thou hast
    power,
Beyond the guard and presence of my
    God
Thou canst not banish me.

ENDICOTT.

                Depart the Court;
We have no time to listen to your bab-
    ble.
Who 's next?   [*Exit* WHARTON.

MERRY.

    This woman, for the same offence.
    EDITH *comes forward.*

ENDICOTT.

What is your name?

EDITH.

        'T is to the world unknown,
But written in the Book of Life.

ENDICOTT.

                Take heed
It be not written in the Book of Death!
What is it?

EDITH.

    Edith Christison.

ENDICOTT (*with eagerness*).

                The daughter
Of Wenlock Christison?

EDITH.

            I am his daughter.

ENDICOTT.

Your father hath given us trouble many
    times.
A bold man and a violent, who sets

At naught the authority of our Church
    and State,
And is in banishment on pain of death.
Where are you living?

EDITH.

        In the Lord.

ENDICOTT.

                Make answer
Without evasion.   Where?

EDITH.

                My outward being
Is in Barbadoes.

ENDICOTT.

        Then why come you here?

EDITH.

I come upon an errand of the Lord.

ENDICOTT.

'T is not the business of the Lord you 're
    doing;
It is the Devil's. Will you take the
    oath?
Give her the Book.
        MERRY *offers the Book.*

EDITH.

            You offer me this Book
To swear on; and it saith, "Swear not
    at all,
Neither by heaven, because it is God's
    Throne,
Nor by the earth, because it is his foot-
    stool!"
I dare not swear.

ENDICOTT.

    You dare not?   Yet you Quakers
Deny this book of Holy Writ, the
    Bible,
To be the Word of God.

EDITH (*reverentially*).

                Christ is the Word,
The everlasting oath of God.   I dare
    not.

ENDICOTT.

You own yourself a Quaker, — do you
    not?

EDITH.

I own that in derision and reproach
I am so called.

ENDICOTT.

Then you deny the Scripture
To be the rule of life.

EDITH.

Yea, I believe
The Inner Light, and not the Written
Word,
To be the rule of life.

ENDICOTT.

And you deny
That the Lord's Day is holy.

EDITH.

Every day
Is the Lord's Day. It runs through all
our lives,
As through the pages of the Holy Bible,
" Thus saith the Lord."

ENDICOTT.

You are accused of making
An horrible disturbance, and affright-
ing
The people in the Meeting-house on
Sunday.
What answer make you?

EDITH.

I do not deny
That I was present in your Steeple-
house
On the First Day; but I made no disturbance.

ENDICOTT.

Why came you there?

EDITH.

Because the Lord commanded.
His word was in my heart, a burning
fire
Shut up within me and consuming me,
And I was very weary with forbearing;
I could not stay.

ENDICOTT.

'T was not the Lord that sent you;
As an incarnate devil did you come!

EDITH.

On the First Day, when, seated in my
chamber,
I heard the bells toll, calling you together,

The sound struck at my life, as once at
his,
The holy man, our Founder, when he
heard
The far-off bells toll in the Vale of Bea-
vor.
It sounded like a market bell to call
The folk together, that the Priest might
set
His wares to sale. And the Lord said
within me,
" Thou must go cry aloud against that
Idol,
And all the worshippers thereof." I
went
Barefooted, clad in sackcloth, and I
stood
And listened at the threshold; and I
heard
The praying and the singing and the
preaching,
Which were but outward forms, and
without power.
Then rose a cry within me, and my
heart
Was filled with admonitions and re-
proofs.
Remembering how the Prophets and
Apostles
Denounced the covetous hirelings and
diviners,
I entered in, and spake the words the
Lord
Commanded me to speak. I could no
less.

ENDICOTT.

Are you a Prophetess?

EDITH.

Is it not written,
" Upon my handmaidens will I pour out
My spirit, and they shall prophesy "?

ENDICOTT.

Enough;
For out of your own mouth are you
condemned!
Need we hear further?

THE JUDGES.

We are satisfied.

ENDICOTT.

It is sufficient. Edith Christison,
The sentence of the Court is, that you
be

Scourged in three towns, with forty
   stripes save one,
Then banished upon pain of death!

EDITH.

          Your sentence
Is truly no more terrible to me
Than had you blown a feather into the
   the air,
And, as it fell upon me, you had said,
"Take heed it hurt thee not!" God's
   will be done!

WENLOCK CHRISTISON (*unseen in the
   crowd*).

Woe to the city of blood! The stone
   shall cry
Out of the wall; the beam from out the
   timber
Shall answer it! Woe unto him that
   buildeth
A town with blood, and stablisheth a
   city
By his iniquity!

ENDICOTT.

          Who is it makes
Such outcry here?

CHRISTISON (*coming forward*).

          I, Wenlock Christison!

ENDICOTT.

Banished on pain of death, why come
   you here?

CHRISTISON.

I come to warn you that you shed no
   more
The blood of innocent men! It cries
   aloud
For vengeance to the Lord!

ENDICOTT.

          Your life is forfeit
Unto the law; and you shall surely die,
And shall not live.

CHRISTISON.

          Like unto Eleazer,
Maintaining the excellence of ancient
   years
And the honor of his gray head, I stand
   before you;
Like him disdaining all hypocrisy,
Lest, through desire to live a little
   longer,
I get a stain to my old age and name!

ENDICOTT.

Being in banishment, on pain of death,
You come now in among us in rebellion.

CHRISTISON.

I come not in among you in rebellion,
But in obedience to the Lord of Heaven.
Not in contempt to any Magistrate,
But only in the love I bear your souls,
As ye shall know hereafter, when all
   men
Give an account of deeds done in the
   body!
God's righteous judgments ye cannot
   escape.

ONE OF THE JUDGES.

Those who have gone before you said
   the same,
And yet no judgment of the Lord hath
   fallen
Upon us.

CHRISTISON.

          He but waiteth till the measure
Of your iniquities shall be filled up,
And ye have run your race. Then will
   his wrath
Descend upon you to the uttermost!
For thy part, Humphrey Atherton, it
   hangs
Over thy head already. It shall come
Suddenly, as a thief doth in the night,
And in the hour when least thou thinkest
   of it!

ENDICOTT.

We have a law, and by that law you
   die.

CHRISTISON.

I, a free man of England and freeborn,
Appeal unto the laws of mine own
   nation!

ENDICOTT.

There's no appeal to England from this
   Court!
What! do you think our statutes are
   but paper?
Are but dead leaves that rustle in the
   wind?
Or litter to be trampled under foot?
What say ye, Judges of the Court, —
   what say ye?
Shall this man suffer death? Speak
   your opinions.

ONE OF THE JUDGES.

I am a mortal man, and die I must,
And that erelong; and I must then
  appear
Before the awful judgment-seat of
  Christ,
To give account of deeds done in the
  body.
My greatest glory on that day will be,
That I have given my vote against this
  man.

CHRISTISON.

If, Thomas Danforth, thou hast nothing
  more
To glory in upon that dreadful day
Than blood of innocent people, then thy
  glory
Will be turned into shame ! The Lord
  hath said it !

ANOTHER JUDGE.

I cannot give consent, while other men
Who have been banished upon pain of
  death
Are now in their own houses here
  among us.

ENDICOTT.

Ye that will not consent, make record
  of it.
I thank my God that I am not afraid
To give my judgment. Wenlock Chris-
  tison,
You must be taken back from hence to
  prison,
Thence to the place of public execution,
There to be hanged till you be dead —
  dead, — dead.

CHRISTISON.

If ye have power to take my life from
  me, —
Which I do question, — God hath power
  to raise
The principle of life in other men,
And send them here among you. There
  shall be
No peace unto the wicked, saith my
  God.
Listen, ye Magistrates, for the Lord
  hath said it !
The day ye put his servitors to death,
That day the Day of your own Visita-
  tion,
The Day of Wrath shall pass above
  your heads,

And ye shall be accursed forevermore !
  To EDITH, *embracing her.*

Cheer up, dear heart ! they have not
  power to harm us.
[*Exeunt* CHRISTISON *and* EDITH
  guarded. The Scene closes.

SCENE II. — *A street. Enter* JOHN
ENDICOTT *and* UPSALL.

JOHN ENDICOTT.

Scourged in three towns ! and yet the
  busy people
Go up and down the streets on their
  affairs
Of business or of pleasure, as if nothing
Had happened to disturb them or their
  thoughts !
When bloody tragedies like this are
  acted,
The pulses of a nation should stand
  still ;
The town should be in mourning, and
  the people
Speak only in low whispers to each
  other.

UPSALL.

I know this people ; and that underneath
A cold outside there burns a secret fire
That will find vent and will not be put
  out,
Till every remnant of these barbarous
  laws
Shall be to ashes burned, and blown
  away.

JOHN ENDICOTT.

Scourged in three towns ! It is incredible
Such things can be ! I feel the blood
  within me
Fast mounting in rebellion, since in vain
Have I implored compassion of my father !

UPSALL.

You know your father only as a father ;
I know him better as a Magistrate.
He is a man both loving and severe ;
A tender heart ; a will inflexible.
None ever loved him more than I have
  loved him.
He is an upright man and a just man
In all things save the treatment of the
  Quakers.

JOHN ENDICOTT.

Yet I have found him cruel and unjust
Even as a father. He has driven me
  forth
Into the street ; has shut his door upon
  me,
With words of bitterness.   I am as
  homeless
As these poor Quakers are.

UPSALL.

                    Then come with me.
You shall be welcome for your father's
  sake,
And the old friendship that has been be-
  tween us.
He will relent erelong. A father's
  anger
Is like a sword without a handle, pier-
  cing
Both ways alike, and wounding him that
  wields it
No less than him that it is pointed at.
                              [*Exeunt.*

SCENE III. — *The prison. Night.* EDITH
  reading the Bible by a lamp.

EDITH.

" Blessed are ye when men shall persecute you,
And shall revile you, and shall say
  against you
All manner of evil falsely for my sake !
Rejoice, and be exceeding glad, for
  great
Is your reward in heaven. For so the
  prophets,
Which were before you, have been persecuted."

Enter JOHN ENDICOTT.

JOHN ENDICOTT.

Edith !

EDITH.

Who is it that speaketh ?

JOHN ENDICOTT.

                    Saul of Tarsus :
As thou didst call me once.

EDITH (*coming forward*).

                    Yea, I remember.
Thou art the Governor's son.

JOHN ENDICOTT.

                    I am ashamed
Thou shouldst remember me.

EDITH.

                    Why comest thou
Into this dark guest-chamber in the
  night ?
What seekest thou ?

JOHN ENDICOTT.

          Forgiveness !

EDITH.

                    I forgive
All who have injured me. What hast
  thou done ?

JOHN ENDICOTT.

I have betrayed thee, thinking that in
  this
I did God service. Now, in deep contrition,
I come to rescue thee.

EDITH.

          From what ?

JOHN ENDICOTT.

                    From prison.

EDITH.

I am safe here within these gloomy
  walls.

JOHN ENDICOTT.

From scourging in the streets, and in
  three towns !

EDITH.

Remembering who was scourged for
  me, I shrink not
Nor shudder at the forty stripes save
  one.

JOHN ENDICOTT.

Perhaps from death itself !

EDITH.

                    I fear not death,
Knowing who died for me.

JOHN ENDICOTT (*aside*).

                    Surely some divine
Ambassador is speaking through those
    lips
And looking through those eyes ! I
  cannot answer !

EDITH.

If all these prison doors stood opened
wide
I would not cross the threshold, — not
one step.
There are invisible bars I cannot break;
There are invisible doors that shut me in,
And keep me ever steadfast to my pur-
pose.

JOHN ENDICOTT.

Thou hast the patience and the faith of
Saints!

EDITH.

Thy Priest hath been with me this day
to save me,
Not only from the death that comes to
all,
But from the second death!

JOHN ENDICOTT.

The Pharisee!
My heart revolts against him and his
creed!
Alas! the coat that was without a seam
Is rent asunder by contending sects;
Each bears away a portion of the gar-
ment,
Blindly believing that he has the whole!

EDITH.

When Death, the Healer, shall have
touched our eyes
With moist clay of the grave, then shall
we see
The truth as we have never yet beheld
it.
But he that overcometh shall not be
Hurt of the second death. Has he forgotten
The many mansions in our father's
house?

JOHN ENDICOTT.

There is no pity in his iron heart!
The hands that now bear stamped upon
their palms
The burning sign of Heresy, hereafter
Shall be uplifted against such accusers,
And then the imprinted letter and its
meaning
Will not be Heresy, but Holiness!

EDITH.

Remember, thou condemnest thine own
father!

JOHN ENDICOTT.

I have no father! He has cast me off.
I am as homeless as the wind that
moans
And wanders through the streets. Oh,
come with me!
Do not delay. Thy God shall be my
God,
And where thou goest I will go.

EDITH.

I cannot.
Yet will I not deny it, nor conceal it;
From the first moment I beheld thy face
I felt a tenderness in my soul towards
thee.
My mind has since been inward to the
Lord,
Waiting his word. It has not yet been
spoken.

JOHN ENDICOTT.

I cannot wait. Trust me. Oh, come
with me!

EDITH.

In the next room, my father, an old
man,
Sitteth imprisoned and condemned to
death,
Willing to prove his faith by martyrdom;
And thinkest thou his daughter would
do less?

JOHN ENDICOTT.

Oh, life is sweet, and death is terrible!

EDITH.

I have too long walked hand in hand
with death
To shudder at that pale familiar face.
But leave me now. I wish to be alone.

JOHN ENDICOTT.

Not yet. Oh, let me stay.

EDITH.

Urge me no more.

JOHN ENDICOTT.

Alas! good-night. I will not say good-
by!

EDITH.

Put this temptation underneath thy feet.
To him that overcometh shall be given

The white stone with the new name
   written on it,
That no man knows save him that doth
   receive it,
And I will give thee a new name, and
   call thee
Paul of Damascus, and not Saul of
   Tarsus.

[*Exit* ENDICOTT. EDITH *sits down again
   to read the Bible.*

ACT IV.

SCENE I. — *King Street, in front of the
town-house.* KEMPTHORN *in the pillory.*
MERRY *and a crowd of lookers-on.*

KEMPTHORN (*sings*).

The world is full of care,
   Much like unto a bubble;
Women and care, and care and women,
   And women and care and trouble.

Good Master Merry, may I say confound?

MERRY.

Ay, that you may.

KEMPTHORN.

Well, then, with your permission,
Confound the Pillory!

MERRY.

                   That's the very thing
The joiner said who made the Shrews-
   bury stocks.
He said, Confound the stocks, because
   they put him
Into his own. He was the first man in
   them.

KEMPTHORN.

For swearing, was it?

MERRY.

               No, it was for charging;
He charged the town too much; and so
   the town,
To make things square, set him in his
   own stocks,
And fined him five pounds sterling, —
   just enough
To settle his own bill.

KEMPTHORN.

               And served him right;

But, Master Merry, is it not eight
   bells?

MERRY.

Not quite.

KEMPTHORN.

   For, do you see? I'm getting tired
Of being perched aloft here in this cro'
   nest
Like the first mate of a whaler, or a
   Middy
Mast-headed, looking out for land!
   Sail ho!
Here comes a heavy-laden merchant-
   man
With the lee clews eased off, and run-
   ning free
Before the wind. A solid man of
   Boston.
A comfortable man, with dividends,
And the first salmon, and the first green
   peas.

A gentleman passes.

He does not even turn his head to look.
He's gone without a word. Here
   comes another,
A different kind of craft on a taut bow-
   line, —
Deacon Giles Firmin the apothecary,
A pious and a ponderous citizen,
Looking as rubicund and round and
   splendid
As the great bottle in his own shop
   window!

DEACON FIRMIN *passes.*

And here's my host of the Three Mari-
   ners,
My creditor and trusty taverner,
My corporal in the Great Artillery!
He's not a man to pass me without
   speaking.

COLE *looks away and passes.*

Don't yaw so; keep your luff, old hypo-
   crite!
Respectable, ah yes, respectable,
You, with your seat in the new Meet-
   ing-house,
Your cow-right on the Common! But
   who's this?
I did not know the Mary Ann was in!
And yet this is my old friend, Captain
   Goldsmith,
As sure as I stand in the bilboes here.
Why, Ralph, my boy!

Enter RALPH GOLDSMITH.

GOLDSMITH.

Why, Simon, is it you?
Set in the bilboes?

KEMPTHORN.

Chock-a-block, you see,
And without chafing-gear.

GOLDSMITH.

And what's it for?

KEMPTHORN.

Ask that starbowline with the boat-
hook there,
That handsome man.

MERRY (*bowing*).

For swearing.

KEMPTHORN.

In this town
They put sea-captains in the stocks for
swearing,
And Quakers for not swearing. So
look out.

GOLDSMITH.

I pray you set him free; he meant no
harm;
'T is an old habit he picked up afloat.

MERRY.

Well, as your time is out, you may
come down.
The law allows you now to go at large
Like Elder Oliver's horse upon the
Common.

KEMPTHORN.

Now, hearties, bear a hand! Let go
and haul.

KEMPTHORN *is set free, and comes forward, shaking* GOLDSMITH's *hand.*

KEMPTHORN.

Give me your hand, Ralph. Ah, how
good it feels!
The hand of an old friend.

GOLDSMITH.

God bless you, Simon!

KEMPTHORN.

Now let us make a straight wake for
the tavern

Of the Three Mariners, Samuel Cole
commander;
Where we can take our ease, and see
the shipping,
And talk about old times.

GOLDSMITH.

First I must pay
My duty to the Governor, and take him
His letters and despatches.   Come with
me.

KEMPTHORN.

I'd rather not.   I saw him yesterday.

GOLDSMITH.

Then wait for me at the Three Nuns
and Comb.

KEMPTHORN.

I thank you.   That's too near to the
town pump.
I will go with you to the Governor's,
And wait outside there, sailing off and
on;
If I am wanted, you can hoist a signal.

MERRY.

Shall I go with you and point out the
way?

GOLDSMITH.

Oh no, I thank you.   I am not a stranger
Here in your crooked little town.

MERRY.

How now, sir?
Do you abuse our town?   [*Exit.*

GOLDSMITH.

Oh, no offence.

KEMPTHORN.

Ralph, I am under bonds for a hundred
pound.

GOLDSMITH.

Hard lines.   What for?

KEMPTHORN.

To take some Quakers back
I brought here from Barbadoes in the
Swallow.
And how to do it I don't clearly see,
For one of them is banished, and
another
Is sentenced to be hanged!   What shall
I do?

GOLDSMITH.

Just slip your hawser on some cloudy
  night ;
Sheer off, and pay it with the topsail,
  Simon !   [*Exeunt.*

SCENE II. — *Street in front of the prison.
  In the background a gateway and several flights of steps leading up terraces
  to the Governor's house. A pump on
  one side of the street.* JOHN ENDI-
  COTT, MERRY, UPSALL, *and others.
  A drum beats.*

JOHN ENDICOTT.

Oh shame, shame, shame !

MERRY.

                Yes, it would be a shame
But for the damnable sin of Heresy !

JOHN ENDICOTT.

A woman scourged and dragged about
  our streets !

MERRY.

Well, Roxbury and Dorchester must
  take
Their share of shame. She will be
  whipped in each !
Three towns, and Forty Stripes save
  one ; that makes
Thirteen in each.

JOHN ENDICOTT.

              And are we Jews or Christians ?
See where she comes, amid a gaping
  crowd !
And she a child. Oh, pitiful ! pitiful !
There 's blood upon her clothes, her
  hands, her feet !

Enter MARSHAL *and a drummer.* EDITH,
  *stripped to the waist, followed by the
  hangman with a scourge, and a noisy
  crowd.*

EDITH.

Here let me rest one moment. I am
  tired.
Will some one give me water ?

MERRY.

                        At his peril.
UPSALL.

Alas ! that I should live to see this
  day !

A WOMAN.

Did I forsake my father and my mother
And come here to New England to see
  this ?

EDITH.

I am athirst. Will no one give me
  water ?

JOHN ENDICOTT (*making his way through
  the crowd with water*).

In the Lord's name !

EDITH (*drinking*).

          In his name I receive it !
Sweet as the water of Samaria's well
This water tastes. I thank thee. Is it
  thou ?
I was afraid thou hadst deserted me.

JOHN ENDICOTT.

Never will I desert thee, nor deny thee.
Be comforted.

MERRY.

          O Master Endicott,
Be careful what you say.

JOHN ENDICOTT.

                Peace, idle babbler !

MERRY.

You 'll rue these words !

JOHN ENDICOTT.

            Art thou not better now ?

EDITH.

They 've struck me as with roses.

JOHN ENDICOTT.

              Ah, these wounds !
These bloody garments !

EDITH.

              It is granted me
To seal my testimony with my blood.

JOHN ENDICOTT.

O blood-red seal of man's vindictive
  wrath !
O roses in the garden of the Lord !
I, of the household of Iscariot,
I have betrayed in thee my Lord and
  Master.

WENLOCK CHRISTISON *appears above, at the window of the prison, stretching out his hands through the bars.*

CHRISTISON.

Be of good courage, O my child! my child!
Blessed art thou when men shall perse-cute thee!
Fear not their faces, saith the Lord, fear not,
For I am with thee to deliver thee.

A CITIZEN.

Who is it crying from the prison yonder?

MERRY.

It is old Wenlock Christison.

CHRISTISON.

Remember
Him who was scourged, and mocked, and crucified!
I see his messengers attending thee.
Be steadfast, oh, be steadfast to the end!

EDITH (*with exultation*).

I cannot reach thee with these arms, O father!
But closely in my soul do I embrace thee
And hold thee. In thy dungeon and thy death
I will be with thee, and will comfort thee!

MARSHAL.

Come, put an end to this. Let the drum beat.

The drum beats. Exeunt all but JOHN ENDICOTT, UPSALL, *and* MERRY.

CHRISTISON.

Dear child, farewell! Never shall I be-hold
Thy face again with these bleared eyes of flesh;
And never wast thou fairer, lovelier, dearer
Than now, when scourged and bleeding, and insulted
For the truth's sake. O pitiless, pitiless town!
The wrath of God hangs over thee; and the day
Is near at hand when thou shalt be abandoned

To desolation and the breeding of net-tles.
The bittern and the cormorant shall lodge
Upon thine upper lintels, and their voice
Sing in thy windows. Yea, thus saith the Lord!

JOHN ENDICOTT.

Awake! awake! ye sleepers, ere too late,
And wipe these bloody statutes from your books!   [*Exit.*

MERRY.

Take heed; the walls have ears!

UPSALL.

At last, the heart
Of every honest man must speak or break!
Enter GOVERNOR ENDICOTT *with his halberdiers.*

ENDICOTT.

What is this stir and tumult in the street?

MERRY.

Worshipful sir, the whipping of a girl,
And her old father howling from the prison.

ENDICOTT (*to his halberdiers*).

Go on.

CHRISTISON.

Antiochus! Antiochus!
O thou that slayest the Maccabees! The Lord
Shall smite thee with incurable disease,
And no man shall endure to carry thee!

MERRY.

Peace, old blasphemer!

CHRISTISON.

I both feel and see
The presence and the waft of death go forth
Against thee, and already thou dost look
Like one that's dead!

MERRY (*pointing*).

And there is your own son,
Worshipful sir, abetting the sedition.

ENDICOTT.

Arrest him. Do not spare him.

MERRY (*aside*).

        His own child !
There is some special providence takes
   care
That none shall be too happy in this
   world !
His own first-born.

ENDICOTT.

        O Absalom, my son !

[*Exeunt ; the Governor with his halberdiers
ascending the steps of his house.*

SCENE III. — *The Governor's private
room. Papers upon the table.* ENDI-
COTT *and* BELLINGHAM.

ENDICOTT.

There is a ship from England has come
   in,
Bringing despatches and much news
   from home.
His majesty was at the Abbey crowned ;
And when the coronation was complete
There passed a mighty tempest o'er the
   city,
Portentous with great thunderings and
   lightnings.

BELLINGHAM.

After his father's, if I well remember,
There was an earthquake, that foreboded
   evil.

ENDICOTT.

Ten of the Regicides have been put to
   death !
The bodies of Cromwell, Ireton, and
   Bradshaw
Have been dragged from their graves,
   and publicly
Hanged in their shrouds at Tyburn.

BELLINGHAM.

        Horrible !

ENDICOTT.

Thus the old tyranny revives again !
Its arm is long enough to reach us here,
As you will see. For, more insulting
   still
Than flaunting in our faces dead men's
   shrouds,
Here is the King's Mandamus, taking
   from us,
From this day forth, all power to punish
   Quakers.

BELLINGHAM.

That takes from us all power ; we are
   but puppets,
And can no longer execute our laws.

ENDICOTT.

His Majesty begins with pleasant words,
"Trusty and well-beloved, we greet you
   well ;"
Then with a ruthless hand he strips from
   me
All that which makes me what I am ;
   as if
From some old general in the field,
   grown gray
In service, scarred with many wounds,
Just at the hour of victory, he should
   strip
His badge of office and his well-gained
   honors,
And thrust him back into the ranks
   again.

Opens the Mandamus and hands it to
BELLINGHAM ; *and, while he is reading,*
ENDICOTT *walks up and down the room.*

Here, read it for yourself ; you see his
   words
Are pleasant words — considerate — not
   reproachful —
Nothing could be more gentle — or
   more royal ;
But then the meaning underneath the
   words,
Mark that. He says all people known
   as Quakers
Among us, now condemned to suffer
   death
Or any corporal punishment whatever,
Who are imprisoned, or may be obnox-
   ious
To the like condemnation, shall be sent
Forthwith to England, to be dealt with
   there
In such wise as shall be agreeable
Unto the English law and their demer
   its.
Is it not so ?

BELLINGHAM (*returning the paper*).

        Ay, so the paper says.

ENDICOTT.

It means we shall no longer rule the
   Province ;
It means farewell to law and liberty,
Authority, respect for Magistrates,

The peace and welfare of the Common-
wealth.
If all the knaves upon this continent
Can make appeal to England, and so
thwart
The ends of truth and justice by delay,
Our power is gone forever. We are
nothing
But ciphers, valueless save when we
follow
Some unit ; and our unit is the King !
'T is he that gives us value.

BELLINGHAM.

I confess
Such seems to be the meaning of this
paper,
But being the King's Mandamus,
signed and sealed,
We must obey, or we are in rebellion.

ENDICOTT.

I tell you, Richard Bellingham, — I tell
you,
That this is the beginning of a struggle
Of which no mortal can foresee the end.
I shall not live to fight the battle for
you,
I am a man disgraced in every way;
This order takes from me my self-
respect
And the respect of others. 'T is my
doom,
Yes, my death-warrant, but must be
obeyed !
Take it, and see that it is executed
So far as this, that all be set at large ;
But see that none of them be sent to
England
To bear false witness, and to spread
reports
That might be prejudicial to ourselves.
                                    [*Exit* BELLINGHAM.

There's a dull pain keeps knocking at
my heart,
Dolefully saying, "Set thy house in
order,
For thou shalt surely die, and shalt not
live ! "
For me the shadow on the dial-plate
Goeth not back, but on into the dark !
                                    [*Exit.*

SCENE .IV. — *The street. A crowd,
reading a placard on the door of the
Meeting - house.* NICHOLAS UPSALL
among them. Enter John Norton.

NORTON.

What is this gathering here ?

UPSALL.

One William Brand,
An old man like ourselves, and weak in
body,
Has been so cruelly tortured in his
prison,
The people are excited, and they
threaten
To tear the prison down.

NORTON.

What has been done ?

UPSALL.

He has been put in irons, with his neck
And heels tied close together, and so
left
From five in the morning until nine at
night.

NORTON.

What more was done ?

UPSALL.

He has been kept five days
In prison without food, and cruelly
beaten,
So that his limbs were cold, his senses
stopped.

NORTON.

What more ?

UPSALL.

And is this not enough ?

NORTON.

Now hear me.
This William Brand of yours has tried
to beat
Our Gospel Ordinances black and blue ;
And, if he has been beaten in like man-
ner,
It is but justice, and I will appear
In his behalf that did so. I suppose
That he refused to work.

UPSALL.

He was too weak.
How could an old man work, when he
was starving ?

NORTON.

And what is this placard ?

UPSALL.

The Magistrates,
To appease the people and prevent a
tumult,
Have put up these placards throughout
the town,
Declaring that the jailer shall be dealt
with
Impartially and sternly by the Court.

NORTON (*tearing down the placard*).

Down with this weak and cowardly con-
cession,
This flag of truce with Satan and with
Sin !
I fling it in his face ! I trample it
Under my feet ! It is his cunning craft,
The masterpiece of his diplomacy,
To cry and plead for boundless tolera-
tion.
But toleration is the first-born child
Of all abominations and deceits.
There is no room in Christ's triumphant
army
For tolerationists. And if an Angel
Preach any other gospel unto you
Than that ye have received, God's male-
diction
Descend upon him ! Let him be ac-
cursed !   [*Exit.*

UPSALL.

Now, go thy ways, John Norton, go thy
ways,
Thou Orthodox Evangelist, as men call
thee !
But even now there cometh out of Eng-
land,
Like an o'ertaking and accusing con-
science,
An outraged man, to call thee to ac-
count
For the unrighteous murder of his son !
[*Exit.*

SCENE V. — *The Wilderness.* Enter
EDITH.

EDITH.

How beautiful are these autumnal
woods !
The wilderness doth blossom like the
rose,
And change into a garden of the Lord !
How silent everywhere ! Alone and lost
Here in the forest, there comes over
me

An inward awfulness. I recall the
words
Of the Apostle Paul : " In journeyings
often,
Often in perils in the wilderness,
In weariness, in painfulness, in watch-
ings,
In hunger and thirst, in cold and naked-
ness ; "
And I forget my weariness and pain,
My watchings, and my hunger and my
thirst.
The Lord hath said that He will seek his
flock
In cloudy and dark days, and they shall
dwell
Securely in the wilderness, and sleep
Safe in the woods ! Whichever way I
turn,
I come back with my face towards the
town.
Dimly I see it, and the sea beyond it.
O cruel town ! I know what waits me
there,
And yet I must go back ; for ever louder
I hear the inward calling of the Spirit,
And must obey the voice. O woods that
wear
Your golden crown of martyrdom, blood-
stained,
From you I learn a lesson of submission,
And am obedient even unto death,
If God so wills it.   [*Exit.*

JOHN ENDICOTT (*within*).

Edith ! Edith ! Edith !

He enters.

It is in vain ! I call, she answers not ;
I follow, but I find no trace of her !
Blood ! blood ! The leaves above me
and around me
Are red with blood ! The pathways of
the forest,
The clouds that canopy the setting sun,
And even the little river in the mead-
ows
Are stained with it ! Where'er I look,
I see it !
Away, thou horrible vision ! Leave me !
leave me !
Alas ! yon winding stream, that gropes
its way
Through mist and shadow, doubling on
itself,
At length will find, by the unerring law
Of nature, what it seeks. O soul of
man,

Groping through mist and shadow, and
recoiling
Back on thyself, are, too, thy devious
ways
Subject to law ? and when thou seemest
to wander
The farthest from thy goal, art thou
still drawing
Nearer and nearer to it, till at length
Thou findest, like the river, what thou
seekest ?   [*Exit.*

ACT V.

SCENE I. — *Daybreak. Street in front
of* UPSALL'S *house. A light in the window. Enter* JOHN ENDICOTT.

JOHN ENDICOTT.

O silent, sombre, and deserted streets,
To me ye 're peopled with a sad proces-
sion,
And echo only to the voice of sor-
row !
O houses full of peacefulness and sleep,
Far better were it to awake no more
Than wake to look upon such scenes
again !
There is a light in Master Upsall's
window.
The good man is already risen, for sleep
Deserts the couches of the old.

Knocks at UPSALL'S *door.*

UPSALL (*at the window*).
                    Who 's there ?

JOHN ENDICOTT.

Am I so changed you do not know my
voice ?

UPSALL.

I know you. Have you heard what
things have happened ?

JOHN ENDICOTT.

I have heard nothing.

UPSALL.

          Stay ; I will come down.

JOHN ENDICOTT.

I am afraid some dreadful news awaits
me !
I do not dare to ask, yet am impatient
To know the worst. Oh, I am very
weary

With waiting and with watching and
pursuing !

Enter UPSALL.

UPSALL.

Thank God, you have come back ! I 've
much to tell you.
Where have you been ?

JOHN ENDICOTT.

          You know that I was seized,
Fined, and released again. You know
that Edith,
After her scourging in three towns, was
banished
Into the wilderness, into the land
That is not sown ; and there I followed
her,
But found her not. Where is she ?

UPSALL.

          She is here.

JOHN ENDICOTT.

Oh, do not speak that word, for it
means death !

UPSALL.

No, it means life. She sleeps in yonder
chamber.
Listen to me. When news of Leddra's
death
Reached England, Edward Burroughs,
having boldly
Got access to the presence of the King,
Told him there was a vein of innocent
blood
Opened in his dominions here, which
threatened
To overrun them all. The King re-
plied,
"But I will stop that vein !" and he
forthwith
Sent his Mandamus to our Magistrates,
That they proceed no further in this
business.
So all are pardoned, and all set at large.

JOHN ENDICOTT.

Thank God ! This is a victory for
truth !
Our thoughts are free. They cannot be
shut up
In prison wall, nor put to death on
scaffolds !

UPSALL.

Come in; the morning air blows sharp
    and cold
Through the damp streets.

JOHN ENDICOTT.

                    It is the dawn of day
That chases the old darkness from our
    sky,
And fills the land with liberty and light.
                                [Exeunt.

SCENE II. — *The parlor of the Three
Mariners. Enter* KEMPTHORN.

KEMPTHORN.

A dull life this, — a dull life anyway !
Ready for sea ; the cargo all aboard,
Cleared for Barbadoes, and a fair wind
    blowing
From nor'-nor'-west ; and I, an idle
    lubber,
Laid neck and heels by that confounded
    bond !
I said to Ralph, says I, " What 's to be
    done ? "
Says he : " Just slip your hawser in the
    night ;
Sheer off, and pay it with the topsail,
    Simon."
But that won't do ; because, you see, the
    owners
Somehow or other are mixed up with it.
Here are King Charles's Twelve Good
    Rules, that Cole
Thinks as important as the Rule of
    Three.

Reads.

" Make no comparisons ; make no long
    meals."
Those are good rules and golden for a
    landlord
To hang in his best parlor, framed and
    glazed !
" Maintain no ill opinions ; urge no
    healths."
I drink to the King's, whatever he may
    say,
And, as to ill opinions, that depends.
Now of Ralph Goldsmith I 've a good
    opinion,
And of the bilboes I 've an ill opinion ;
And both of these opinions I 'll maintain
As long as there 's a shot left in the
    locker.

Enter EDWARD BUTTER, *with an ear-
    trumpet.*

BUTTER.

Good morning, Captain Kempthorn.

KEMPTHORN.

                            Sir, to you.
You 've the advantage of me. I don't
    know you.
What may I call your name ?

BUTTER.

                    That 's not your name ?

KEMPTHORN.

Yes, that 's my name.   What 's yours ?

BUTTER.

                    My name is Butter.
I am the treasurer of the Commonwealth.

KEMPTHORN.

Will you be seated ?

BUTTER.

        What say ?   Who 's conceited ?

KEMPTHORN.

Will you sit down ?

BUTTER.

                Oh, thank you.

KEMPTHORN.

                        Spread yourself
Upon this chair, sweet Butter.

        BUTTER (*sitting down*).

                        A fine morning.

KEMPTHORN.

Nothing 's the matter with it that I
    know of.
I have seen better, and I have seen
    worse.
The wind 's nor'west.   That 's fair for
    them that sail.

BUTTER.

You need not speak so loud ; I under-
    stand you.
You sail to-day.

KEMPTHORN.

            No, I don't sail to-day.
So, be it fair or foul, it matters not.
Say, will you smoke ?   There 's choice
    tobacco here.

BUTTER.

No, thank you. It 's against the law to smoke.

KEMPTHORN.

Then, will you drink? There 's good ale at this inn.

BUTTER.

No, thank you. It 's against the law to drink.

KEMPTHORN.

Well, almost everything 's against the law
In this good town. Give a wide berth to one thing,
You 're sure to fetch up soon on something else.

BUTTER.

And so you sail to-day for dear Old England.
I am not one of those who think a sup
Of this New England air is better worth
Than a whole draught of our Old England's ale.

KEMPTHORN.

Nor I. Give me the ale and keep the air.
But, as I said, I do not sail to-day.

BUTTER.

Ah yes; you sail to-day.

KEMPTHORN.

I 'm under bonds
To take some Quakers back to the Barbadoes;
And one of them is banished, and another
Is sentenced to be hanged.

BUTTER.

No, all are pardoned,
All are set free by order of the Court;
But some of them would fain return to England.
You must not take them. Upon that condition
Your bond is cancelled.

KEMPTHORN.

Ah, the wind has shifted!
I pray you, do you speak officially?

BUTTER.

I always speak officially. To prove it,
Here is the bond.

Rising and giving a paper.

KEMPTHORN.

And here 's my hand upon it.
And look you, when I say I 'll do a thing
The thing is done. Am I now free to go?

BUTTER.

What say?

KEMPTHORN.

I say, confound the tedious man
With his strange speaking-trumpet!
Can I go?

BUTTER.

You 're free to go, by order of the Court.
Your servant, sir.

[*Exit.*

KEMPTHORN (*shouting from the window*).

Swallow, ahoy! Hallo!
If ever a man was happy to leave Boston,
That man is Simon Kempthorn of the Swallow!

Reënter BUTTER.

BUTTER.

Pray, did you call?

KEMPTHORN.

Call? Yes, I hailed the Swallow.

BUTTER.

That 's not my name. My name is Edward Butter.
You need not speak so loud.

KEMPTHORN (*shaking hands*).

Good-by! Good-by!

BUTTER.

Your servant, sir.

KEMPTHORN.

And yours a thousand times!
[*Exeunt.*

Scene III. — Governor Endicott's *private room. An open window.* Endicott *seated in an arm-chair.* Bellingham *standing near.*

ENDICOTT.

O lost, O loved! wilt thou return no
    more?
O loved and lost, and loved the more
    when lost!
How many men are dragged into their
    graves
By their rebellious children! I now
    feel
The agony of a father's breaking heart
In David's cry, "O Absalom, my son!"

BELLINGHAM.

Can you not turn your thoughts a little
    while
To public matters? There are papers
    here
That need attention.

ENDICOTT.

                Trouble me no more!
My business now is with another world.
Ah, Richard Bellingham! I greatly
    fear
That in my righteous zeal I have been
    led
To doing many things which, left un-
    done,
My mind would now be easier. Did I
    dream it,
Or has some person told me, that John
    Norton
Is dead?

BELLINGHAM.

You have not dreamed it. He is dead,
And gone to his reward. It was no
    dream.

ENDICOTT.

Then it was very sudden; for I saw him
Standing where you now stand, not long
    ago.

BELLINGHAM.

By his own fireside, in the afternoon,
A faintness and a giddiness came o'er
    him;
And, leaning on the chimney-piece, he
    cried,
"The hand of God is on me!" and fell
    dead.

ENDICOTT.

And did not some one say, or have I
    dreamed it,
That Humphrey Atherton is dead?

BELLINGHAM.

                        Alas!
He too is gone, and by a death as sud-
    den.
Returning home one evening, at the
    place
Where usually the Quakers have been
    scourged,
His horse took fright, and threw him to
    the ground,
So that his brains were dashed about
    the street.

ENDICOTT.

I am not superstitious, Bellingham,
And yet I tremble lest it may have
    been
A judgment on him.

BELLINGHAM.

                So the people think.
They say his horse saw standing in the
    way
The ghost of William Leddra, and was
    frightened.
And furthermore, brave Richard Daven-
    port,
The captain of the Castle, in the storm
Has been struck dead by lightning.

ENDICOTT.

                    Speak no more.
For as I listen to your voice it seems
As if the Seven Thunders uttered their
    voices,
And the dead bodies lay about the
    streets
Of the disconsolate city! Bellingham,
I did not put those wretched men to
    death.
I did but guard the passage with the
    sword
Pointed towards them, and they rushed
    upon it!
Yet now I would that I had taken no
    part
In all that bloody work.

BELLINGHAM.

                The guilt of it
Be on their heads, not ours.

ENDICOTT.

Are all set free ?

BELLINGHAM.

All are at large.

ENDICOTT.

And none have been sent back
To England to malign us with the
King ?

BELLINGHAM.

The ship that brought them sails this
very hour,
But carries no one back.

A distant cannon.

ENDICOTT.

What is that gun ?

BELLINGHAM.

Her parting signal. Through the window there,
Look, you can see her sails, above the
roofs,
Dropping below the Castle, outward
bound.

ENDICOTT.

O white, white, white ! Would that my
soul had wings
As spotless as those shining sails to fly
with !
Now lay this cushion straight. I thank
you. Hark !
I thought I heard the hall door open
and shut !
I thought I heard the footsteps of my
boy !

BELLINGHAM.

It was the wind. There 's no one in the
passage.

ENDICOTT.

O Absalom, my son ! I feel the world
Sinking beneath me, sinking, sinking,
sinking !
Death knocks ! I go to meet him !
Welcome, Death !

*Rises, and sinks back dead ; his head
falling aside upon his shoulder.*

BELLINGHAM.

O ghastly sight ! Like one who has
been hanged !

Endicott ! Endicott ! He makes no
answer !
Raises ENDICOTT's *head.*

He breathes no more ! How bright this
signet-ring
Glitters upon his hand, where he has
worn it
Through such long years of trouble, as
if Death
Had given him this memento of affection,
And whispered in his ear, " Remember
me ! "
How placid and how quiet is his face,
Now that the struggle and the strife are
ended !
Only the acrid spirit of the times
Corroded this true steel. Oh, rest in
peace,
Courageous heart ! Forever rest in
peace !

GILES COREY OF THE SALEM FARMS.

DRAMATIS PERSONÆ.

GILES COREY	. . .	*Farmer.*
JOHN HATHORNE	. .	*Magistrate.*
COTTON MATHER	. .	*Minister of the Gospel.*
JONATHAN WALCOT	.	*A youth.*
RICHARD GARDNER	.	*Sea-Captain.*
JOHN GLOYD	. . . .	*Corey's hired man.*
MARTHA	. . . . .	*Wife of Giles Corey.*
TITUBA	. . . . .	*An Indian woman.*
MARY WALCOT	. . .	*One of the Afflicted.*

The Scene is in Salem in the year 1692.

PROLOGUE.

DELUSIONS of the days that once have
been,
Witchcraft and wonders of the world
unseen,
Phantoms of air, and necromantic arts
That crushed the weak and awed the
stoutest hearts, —
These are our theme to-night ; and
vaguely here,
Through the dim mists that crowd the
atmosphere,
We draw the outlines of weird figures
cast
In shadow on the background of the
Past.

Who would believe that in the quiet
town

Of Salem, and amid the. woods that crown
The neighboring hillsides, and the sunny farms
That fold it safe in their paternal arms, —
Who would believe that in those peaceful streets,
Where the great elms shut out the summer heats,
Where quiet reigns, and breathes through brain and breast
The benediction of unbroken rest, —
Who would believe such deeds could find a place
As these whose tragic history we retrace?

'T was but a village then: the goodman ploughed
His ample acres under sun or cloud;
The goodwife at her doorstep sat and spun,
And gossiped with her neighbors in the sun;
The only men of dignity and state
Were then the Minister and the Magistrate,
Who ruled their little realm with iron rod,
Less in the love than in the fear of God;
And who believed devoutly in the Powers
Of Darkness, working in this world of ours,
In spells of Witchcraft, incantations dread,
And shrouded apparitions of the dead.

Upon this simple folk "with fire and flame,"
Saith the old chronicle, "the Devil came;
Scattering his firebrands and his poisonous darts,
To set on fire of Hell all tongues and hearts!
And 't is no wonder; for, with all his host,
There most he rages where he hateth most,
And is most hated; so on us he brings
All these stupendous and portentous things!"

Something of this our scene to-night will show;
And ye who listen to the Tale of Woe,

Be not too swift in casting the first stone,
Nor think New England bears the guilt alone.
This sudden burst of wickedness and crime
Was but the common madness of the time,
When in all lands, that lie within the sound
Of Sabbath bells, a Witch was burned or drowned.

ACT I.

SCENE I. — *The woods near Salem Village. Enter* TITUBA, *with a basket of herbs.*

TITUBA.

Here's monk's-hood, that breeds fever in the blood;
And deadly nightshade, that makes men see ghosts;
And henbane, that will shake them with convulsions;
And meadow-saffron and black hellebore,
That rack the nerves, and puff the skin with dropsy;
And bitter-sweet, and briony, and eyebright,
That cause eruptions, nosebleed, rheumatisms;
I know them, and the places where they hide
In field and meadow; and I know their secrets,
And gather them because they give me power
Over all men and women. Armed with these,
I, Tituba, an Indian and a slave,
Am stronger than the captain with his sword,
Am richer than the merchant with his money,
Am wiser than the scholar with his books,
Mightier than Ministers and Magistrates,
With all the fear and reverence that attend them!
For I can fill their bones with aches and pains,
Can make them cough with asthma, shake with palsy,

Can make their daughters see and talk
  with ghosts,
Or fall into delirium and convulsions;
I have the Evil Eye, the Evil Hand;
A touch from me and they are weak
  with pain,
A look from me, and they consume and
  die.
The death of cattle and the blight of
  corn,
The shipwreck, the tornado, and the
  fire, —
These are my doings, and they know
  it not.
Thus I work vengeance on mine ene-
  mies
Who, while they call me slave, are
  slaves to me!

Exit TITUBA. *Enter* MATHER, *booted
  and spurred, with a riding-whip in his
  hand.*

MATHER.

Methinks that I have come by paths
  unknown
Into the land and atmosphere of
  Witches;
For, meditating as I journeyed on,
Lo! I have lost my way! If I remem-
  ber
Rightly, it is Scribonius the learned
That tells the story of a man who, pray-
  ing
For one that was possessed by Evil
  Spirits,
Was struck by Evil Spirits in the face;
I, journeying to circumvent the Witches,
Surely by Witches have been led astray.
I am persuaded there are few affairs
In which the Devil doth not interfere.
We cannot undertake a journey even,
But Satan will be there to meddle with
  it
By hindering or by furthering. He
  hath led me
Into this thicket, struck me in the face
With branches of the trees, and so en-
  tangled
The fetlocks of my horse with vines and
  brambles,
That I must needs dismount, and search
  on foot
For the lost pathway leading to the vil-
  lage.

Reënter TITUBA.

What shape is this? What monstrous
  apparition,

Exceeding fierce, that none may pass
  that way?
Tell me, good woman, if you are a
  woman —

TITUBA.

I am a woman, but I am not good,
I am a Witch!

MATHER.

Then tell me, Witch and woman,
For you must know the pathways
  through this wood,
Where lieth Salem Village?

TITUBA.

                   Reverend sir,
The village is near by. I'm going
  there
With these few herbs. I'll lead you.
  Follow me.

MATHER.

First say, who are you? I am loath to
  follow
A stranger in this wilderness, for fear
Of being misled, and left in some
  morass.
Who are you?

TITUBA.

        I am Tituba the Witch,
Wife of John Indian.

MATHER.

            You are Tituba?
I know you then. You have renounced
  the Devil,
And have become a penitent confessor.
The Lord be praised! Go on, I'll fol-
  low you.
Wait only till I fetch my horse, that
  stands
Tethered among the trees, not far from
  here.

TITUBA.

Let me get up behind you, reverend
  sir.

MATHER.

The Lord forbid! What would the
  people think,
If they should see the Reverend Cotton
  Mather
Ride into Salem with a Witch behind
  him?
The Lord forbid!

TITUBA.

          I do not need a horse!
I can ride through the air upon a stick,
Above the tree-tops and above the
    houses,
And no one see me, no one overtake
    me.   [*Exeunt.*

SCENE II. — *A room at* JUSTICE
HATHORNE'S. *A clock in the corner.*
Enter HATHORNE *and* MATHER.

HATHORNE.

You are welcome, reverend sir, thrice
    welcome here
Beneath my humble roof.

MATHER.

         I thank your Worship.

HATHORNE.

Pray you be seated. You must be fa-
    tigued
With your long ride through unfre-
    quented woods.
        They sit down.

MATHER.

You know the purport of my visit
    here, —
To be advised by you, and counsel with
    you,
And with the Reverend Clergy of the
    village,
Touching these witchcrafts that so much
    afflict you;
And see with mine own eyes the won-
    ders told
Of spectres and the shadows of the dead,
That come back from their graves to
    speak with men.

HATHORNE.

Some men there are, I have known such,
    who think
That the two worlds — the seen and the
    unseen,
The world of matter and the world of
    spirit —
Are like the hemispheres upon our maps,
And touch each other only at a point.
But these two worlds are not divided
    thus,
Save for the purposes of common speech.
They form one globe, in which the
    parted seas
All flow together and are intermingled,

While the great continents remain dis-
    tinct.

MATHER.

I doubt it not. The spiritual world
Lies all about us, and its avenues
Are open to the unseen feet of phan-
    toms
That come and go, and we perceive
    them not,
Save by their influence, or when at
    times
A most mysterious Providence permits
    them
To manifest themselves to mortal eyes.

HATHORNE.

You, who are always welcome here
    among us,
Are doubly welcome now. We need
    your wisdom,
Your learning in these things to be our
    guide.
The Devil hath come down in wrath
    upon us,
And ravages the land with all his hosts.

MATHER.

The Unclean Spirit said, "My name is
    Legion!"
Multitudes in the Valley of Destruction!
But when our fervent, well-directed
    prayers,
Which are the great artillery of Heaven,
Are brought into the field, I see them
    scattered
And driven like autumn leaves before
    the wind.

HATHORNE.

You, as a Minister of God, can meet
    them
With spiritual weapons: but, alas!
I, as a Magistrate, must combat them
With weapons from the armory of the
    flesh.

MATHER.

These wonders of the world invisible, —
These spectral shapes that haunt our
    habitations, —
The multiplied and manifold afflictions
With which the aged and the dying
    saints
Have their death prefaced and their age
    imbittered, —
Are but prophetic trumpets that pro-
    claim

The Second Coming of our Lord on
    earth.
The evening wolves will be much more
    abroad,
When we are near the evening of the
    world.

HATHORNE.

When you shall see, as I have hourly
    seen,
The sorceries and the witchcrafts that
    torment us,
See children tortured by invisible spir-
    its,
And wasted and consumed by powers
    unseen,
You will confess the half has not been
    told you.

MATHER.

It must be so.   The death-pangs of the
    Devil
Will make him more a Devil than be-
    fore ;
And Nebuchadnezzar's furnace will be
    heated
Seven times more hot before its putting
    out.

HATHORNE.

Advise me, reverend sir.   I look to you
For counsel and for guidance in this
    matter.
What further shall we do ?

MATHER.

               Remember this,
That as a sparrow falls not to the
    ground
Without the will of God, so not a Devil
Can come down from the air without
    his leave.
We must inquire.

HATHORNE.

         Dear sir, we have inquired ;
Sifted the matter thoroughly through
    and through,
And then resifted it.

MATHER.

           If God permits
These Evil Spirits from the unseen re-
    gions
To visit us with surprising informa-
    tions,
We must inquire what cause there is for
    this,

But not receive the testimony borne
By spectres as conclusive proof of guilt
In the accused.

HATHORNE.

           Upon such evidence
We do not rest our case.   The ways are
    many
In which the guilty do betray them-
    selves.

MATHER.

Be careful.   Carry the knife with such
    exactness,
That on one side no innocent blood be
    shed
By too excessive zeal, and on the other
No shelter given to any work of darkness.

HATHORNE.

For one, I do not fear excess of zeal.
What do we gain by parleying with the
    Devil ?
You reason, but you hesitate to act !
Ah, reverend sir ! believe me, in such
    cases
The only safety is in acting promptly.
'T is not the part of wisdom to delay
In things where not to do is still to do
A deed more fatal than the deed we
    shrink from.
You are a man of books and meditation,
But I am one who acts.

MATHER.

           God give us wisdom
In the directing of this thorny business,
And guide us, lest New England should
    become
Of an unsavory and sulphurous odor
In the opinion of the world abroad !

The clock strikes.

I never hear the striking of a clock
Without a warning and an admonition
That time is on the wing, and we must
    quicken
Our tardy pace in journeying Heaven-
    ward,
As Israel did in journeying Canaan-
    ward !

They rise.

HATHORNE.

Then let us make all haste ; and I will
    show you
In what disguises and what fearful
    shapes

The Unclean Spirits haunt this neigh-
    borhood,
And you will pardon my excess of zeal.

MATHER.

Ah, poor New England ! He who
    hurricanoed
The house of Job is making now on
    thee
One last assault, more deadly and more
    snarled
With unintelligible circumstances
Than any thou hast hitherto encoun-
    tered !   [*Exeunt.*

SCENE III. — *A room in* WALCOT'S
    house. MARY WALCOT *seated in an
    arm-chair.* TITUBA *with a mirror.*

MARY.

Tell me another story, Tituba.
A drowsiness is stealing over me
Which is not sleep ; for, though I close
    mine eyes,
I am awake, and in another world.
Dim faces of the dead and of the absent
Come floating up before me, — floating,
    fading,
And disappearing.

TITUBA.

                Look into this glass.
What see you ?

MARY.

                Nothing but a golden vapor.
Yes, something more. An island, with
    the sea
Breaking all round it, like a blooming
    hedge.
What land is this ?

TITUBA.

                It is San Salvador,
Where Tituba was born. What see you
    now ?

MARY.

A man all black and fierce.

TITUBA.

                That is my father.
He was an Obi man, and taught me
    magic, —
Taught me the use of herbs and images.
What is he doing ?

MARY.

                Holding in his hand
A waxen figure. He is melting it
Slowly before a fire.

TITUBA.

                And now what see you ?

MARY.

A woman lying on a bed of leaves,
Wasted and worn away. Ah, she is
    dying !

TITUBA.

That is the way the Obi men destroy
The people they dislike ! That is the
    way
Some one is wasting and consuming you.

MARY.

You terrify me, Tituba ! Oh, save me
From those who make me pine and
    waste away !
Who are they ? Tell me.

TITUBA.

                That I do not know,
But you will see them. They will come
    to you.

MARY.

No, do not let them come ! I cannot
    bear it !
I am too weak to bear it ! I am dying.

                Falls into a trance.

TITUBA.

Hark ! there is some one coming !
    Enter HATHORNE, MATHER, *and*
        WALCOT.

WALCOT.

                There she lies,
Wasted and worn by devilish incanta-
    tions !
O my poor sister !

MATHER.

                Is she always thus ?

WALCOT.

Nay, she is sometimes tortured by con-
    vulsions.

MATHER.

Poor child ! How thin she is ! How
    wan and wasted !

HATHORNE.

Observe her. She is troubled in her sleep.

MATHER.

Some fearful vision haunts her.

HATHORNE.

You now see
With your own eyes, and touch with your own hands,
The mysteries of this Witchcraft.

MATHER.

One would need
The hands of Briareus and the eyes of Argus
To see and touch them all.

HATHORNE.

You now have entered
The realm of ghosts and phantoms, — the vast realm
Of the unknown and the invisible,
Through whose wide-open gates there blows a wind
From the dark valley of the shadow of Death,
That freezes us with horror.

MARY (starting).

Take her hence!
Take her away from me. I see her there!
She 's coming to torment me!

WALCOT (taking her hand).

O my sister!
What frightens you ? She neither hears nor sees me.
She 's in a trance.

MARY.

Do you not see her there ?

TITUBA.

My child, who is it ?

MARY.

Ah, I do not know,
I cannot see her face.

TITUBA.

How is she clad ?

MARY.

She wears a crimson bodice. In her hand

She holds an image, and is pinching it
Between her fingers. Ah, she tortures me!
I see her face now. It is Goodwife Bishop!
Why does she torture me? I never harmed her!
And now she strikes me with an iron rod!
Oh, I am beaten!

MATHER.

This is wonderful!
I can see nothing! Is this apparition
Visibly there, and yet we cannot see it?

HATHORNE.

It is. The spectre is invisible
Unto our grosser senses, but she sees it.

MARY.

Look! look! there is another clad in gray!
She holds a spindle in her hand, and threatens
To stab me with it! It is Goodwife Corey!
Keep her away! Now she is coming at me!
Oh, mercy! mercy!

WALCOT (thrusting with his sword).

There is nothing there!

MATHER to HATHORNE.

Do you see anything ?

HATHORNE.

The laws that govern
The spiritual world prevent our seeing
Things palpable and visible to her.
These spectres are to us as if they were not.
Mark her; she wakes.

TITUBA touches her, and she awakes.

MARY.

Who are these gentlemen ?

WALCOT.

They are our friends. Dear Mary, are you better ?

MARY.

Weak, very weak.
Taking a spindle from her lap, and holding it up.
How came this spindle here ?

TITUBA.

You wrenched it from the hand of
Goodwife Corey
When she rushed at you.

HATHORNE.

Mark that, reverend sir!

MATHER.

It is most marvellous, most inexpli-
cable!

TITUBA (*picking up a bit of gray cloth
from the floor*).

And here, too, is a bit of her gray dress,
That the sword cut away.

MATHER.

Beholding this,
It were indeed by far more credulous
To be incredulous than to believe.
None but a Sadducee, who doubts of all
Pertaining to the spiritual world,
Could doubt such manifest and damn-
ing proofs!

HATHORNE.

Are you convinced?

MATHER *to* MARY.

Dear child, be comforted!
Only by prayer and fasting can you
drive
These Unclean Spirits from you. An
old man
Gives you his blessing. God be with
you, Mary!

ACT II.

SCENE I. — GILES COREY'S *farm.
Morning. Enter COREY, with a horseshoe and a hammer.*

COREY.

The Lord hath prospered me. The
rising sun
Shines on my Hundred Acres and my
woods
As if he loved them. On a morn like
this
I can forgive mine enemies, and thank
God
For all his goodness unto me and mine.
My orchard groans with russets and
pearmains;

My ripening corn shines golden in the
sun;
My barns are crammed with hay, my
cattle thrive;
The birds sing blithely on the trees
around me!
And blither than the birds my heart
within me.
But Satan still goes up and down the
earth;
And to protect this house from his as-
saults,
And keep the powers of darkness from
my door,
This horseshoe will I nail upon the
threshold.
Nails down the horseshoe.
There, ye night-hags and witches that
torment
The neighborhood, ye shall not enter
here! —
What is the matter in the field? — John
Gloyd!
The cattle are all running to the
woods! —
John Gloyd! Where is the man?

Enter JOHN GLOYD.

Look there!
What ails the cattle? Are they all be-
witched?
They run like mad.

GLOYD.

They have been overlooked.

COREY.

The Evil Eye is on them sure enough.
Call all the men. Be quick. Go after
them!

Exit GLOYD *and enter* MARTHA.

MARTHA.

What is amiss?

COREY.

The cattle are bewitched.
They are broken loose and making for
the woods.

MARTHA.

Why will you harbor such delusions,
Giles?
Bewitched? Well, then it was John
Gloyd bewitched them;
I saw him even now take down the bars
And turn them loose! They're only
frolicsome.

COREY.

The rascal!

MARTHA.

I was standing in the road,
Talking with Goodwife Proctor, and I
saw him.

COREY.

With Proctor's wife? And what says
Goodwife Proctor?

MARTHA.

Sad things indeed; the saddest you can
hear
Of Bridget Bishop. She's cried out
upon!

COREY.

Poor soul! I've known her forty year
or more.
She was the widow Wasselby, and then
She married Oliver, and Bishop next.
She's had three husbands. I remember
well
My games of shovel-board at Bishop's
tavern
In the old merry days, and she so gay
With her red paragon bodice and her
ribbons!
Ah, Bridget Bishop always was a Witch!

MARTHA.

They'll little help her now, — her caps
and ribbons,
And her red paragon bodice and her
plumes,
With which she flaunted in the Meeting-
house!
When next she goes there, it will be for
trial.

COREY.

When will that be?

MARTHA.

This very day at ten.

COREY,

Then get you ready. We'll go and see
it.
Come; you shall ride behind me on the
pillion.

MARTHA.

Not I. You know I do not like such
things.

I wonder you should. I do not believe
In Witches nor in Witchcraft.

COREY.

Well, I do.
There's a strange fascination in it all,
That draws me on and on, I know not
why.

MARTHA.

What do we know of spirits good or ill,
Or of their power to help us or to harm
us?

COREY.

Surely what's in the Bible must be
true.
Did not an Evil Spirit come on Saul?
Did not the Witch of Endor bring the
ghost
Of Samuel from his grave? The Bible
says so.

MARTHA.

That happened very long ago.

COREY.

With God
There is no long ago.

MARTHA.

There is with us.

COREY.

And Mary Magdalene had seven devils,
And he who dwelt among the tombs a
legion!

MARTHA.

God's power is infinite. I do not doubt
it.
If in His providence He once permitted
Such things to be among the Israelites,
It does not follow He permits them now,
And among us who are not Israelites.
But we will not dispute about it, Giles.
Go to the village if you think it best,
And leave me here; I'll go about my
work.   [Exit into the house.

COREY.

And I will go and saddle the gray mare.
The last word always. That is woman's
nature.
If an old man will marry a young wife,
He must make up his mind to many
things.
It's putting new cloth into an old gar-
ment,

When the strain comes, it is the old
gives way.

Goes to the door.

Oh, Martha! I forgot to tell you some-
thing.
I've had a letter from a friend of mine,
A certain Richard Gardner of Nan-
tucket,
Master and owner of a whaling-vessel;
He writes that he is coming down to
see us.
I hope you 'll like him.

MARTHA.

I will do my best.

COREY.

That 's a good woman. Now I will be
gone.
I 've not seen Gardner for this twenty
year;
But there is something of the sea about
him, —
Something so open, generous, large, and
strong,
It makes me love him better than a brother.   [*Exit.*

MARTHA *comes to the door.*

MARTHA.

Oh these old friends and cronies of my
husband,
These captains from Nantucket and the
Cape,
That come and turn my house into a
tavern
With their carousing! Still, there 's
something frank
In these seafaring men that makes me
like them.
Why, here 's a horseshoe nailed upon
the doorstep!
Giles has done this to keep away the
Witches.
I hope this Richard Gardner will bring
him
A gale of good sound common-sense to
blow
The fog of these delusions from his
brain!

COREY (*within*).

Ho! Martha! Martha!

Enter COREY.

Have you seen my saddle?

MARTHA.

I saw it yesterday.

COREY.

Where did you see it?

MARTHA.

On a gray mare, that somebody was
riding
Along the village road.

COREY.

Who was it? Tell me.

MARTHA.

Some one who should have stayed at
home.

COREY (*restraining himself*).

I see!
Don't vex me, Martha. Tell me where
it is.

MARTHA.

I 've hidden it away.

COREY.

Go fetch it me.

MARTHA.

Go find it.

COREY.

No. I 'll ride down to the village
Bareback; and when the people stare
and say,
"Giles Corey, where 's your saddle?"
I will answer,
"A Witch has stolen it." How shall
you like that?

MARTHA.

I shall not like it.

COREY.

Then go fetch the saddle.
                                   [*Exit* MARTHA.

If an old man will marry a young wife,
Why then — why then — why then —
he must spell Baker!

Enter MARTHA *with the saddle, which
she throws down.*

MARTHA.

There! There 's the saddle.

COREY.

Take it up.

MARTHA.

I won't!

COREY.

Then let it lie there. I'll ride to the village,
And say you are a Witch.

MARTHA.

No, not that, Giles.

She takes up the saddle.

COREY.

Now come with me, and saddle the gray mare
With your own hands; and you shall see me ride
Along the village road as is becoming
Giles Corey of the Salem Farms, your husband!   [*Exeunt.*

SCENE II. — *The Green in front of the Meeting-house in Salem Village. People coming and going. Enter* GILES COREY.

COREY.

A melancholy end! Who would have thought
That Bridget Bishop e'er would come to this?
Accused, convicted, and condemned to death
For Witchcraft! And so good a woman too!

A FARMER.

Good morrow, neighbor Corey.

COREY (*not hearing him*).

Who is safe?
How do I know but under my own roof
I too may harbor Witches, and some Devil
Be plotting and contriving against me?

FARMER.

He does not hear. Good morrow, neighbor Corey!

COREY.

Good morrow.

FARMER.

Have you seen John Proctor lately?

COREY.

No, I have not.

FARMER.

Then do not see him, Corey.

COREY.

Why should I not?

FARMER.

Because he's angry with you.
So keep out of his way. Avoid a quarrel.

COREY.

Why does he seek to fix a quarrel on me?

FARMER.

He says you burned his house.

COREY.

I burn his house?
If he says that, John Proctor is a liar!
The night his house was burned I was in bed,
And I can prove it! Why, we are old friends!
He could not say that of me.

FARMER.

He did say it.
I heard him say it.

COREY.

Then he shall unsay it.

FARMER.

He said you did it out of spite to him
For taking part against you in the quarrel
You had with your John Gloyd about his wages.
He says you murdered Goodell; that you trampled
Upon his body till he breathed no more.
And so beware of him; that's my advice!   [*Exit.*

COREY.

By Heaven! this is too much! I'll seek him out,
And make him eat his words, or strangle him.

I 'll not be slandered at a time like this,
When every word is made an accusa-
tion,
When every whisper kills, and every
man
Walks with a halter round his neck !

Enter GLOYD *in haste.*

What now ?

GLOYD.

I came to look for you.   The cattle —

COREY.

Well,
What of them ?   Have you found
them ?

GLOYD.

They are dead.
I followed them through the woods,
across the meadows ;
Then they all leaped into the Ipswich
River,
And swam across, but could not climb
the bank,
And so were drowned.

COREY.

You are to blame for this ;
For you took down the bars, and let
them loose.

GLOYD.

That I deny.   They broke the fences
down.
You know they were bewitched.

COREY.

Ah, my poor cattle !
The Evil Eye was on them ; that is
true.
Day of disaster !   Most unlucky day !
Why did I leave my ploughing and my
reaping
To plough and reap this Sodom and
Gomorrah ?
Oh, I could drown myself for sheer
vexation !   [*Exit.*

GLOYD.

He 's going for his cattle.   He won't
find them.
By this time they have drifted out to
sea.
They will not break his fences any more,
Though they may break his heart.
And what care I ?   [*Exit.*

SCENE III. — COREY'S *kitchen.   A table
with supper.*   MARTHA *knitting.*

MARTHA.

He 's come at last.   I hear him in the
passage.
Something has gone amiss with him to-
day ;
I know it by his step, and by the sound
The door made as he shut it.   He is
angry.

Enter COREY *with his riding-whip.   As
he speaks he takes off his hat and gloves
and throws them down violently.*

COREY.

I say if Satan ever entered man
He 's in John Proctor !

MARTHA.

Giles, what is the matter ?
You frighten me.

COREY.

I say if any man
Can have a Devil in him, then that man
Is Proctor, — is John Proctor, and no
other !

MARTHA.

Why, what has he been doing ?

COREY.

Everything !
What do you think I heard there in the
village ?

MARTHA.

I 'm sure I cannot guess.   What did you
hear ?

COREY.

He says I burned his house !

MARTHA.

Does he say that ?

COREY.

He says I burned his house.   I was in
bed
And fast asleep that night ; and I can
prove it.

MARTHA.

If he says that, I think the Father of
Lies
Is surely in the man.

COREY.

He does say that,
And that I did it to wreak vengeance on
　him
For taking sides against me in the
　quarrel
I had with that John Gloyd about his
　wages.
And God knows that I never bore him
　malice
For that, as I have told him twenty
　times!

MARTHA.

It is John Gloyd has stirred him up to
　this.
I do not like that Gloyd. I think him
　crafty,
Not to be trusted, sullen and untruth-
　ful.
Come, have your supper. You are tired
　and hungry.

COREY.

I 'm angry, and not hungry.

MARTHA.

　　　　Do eat something.
You 'll be the better for it.

COREY (sitting down).

　　　　　I 'm not hungry.

MARTHA.

Let not the sun go down upon your
　wrath.

COREY.

It has gone down upon it, and will rise
To-morrow, and go down again upon
　it.
They have trumped up against me the
　old story
Of causing Goodell's death by tram-
　pling on him.

MARTHA.

Oh, that is false. I know it to be false.

COREY.

He has been dead these fourteen years
　or more.
Why can't they let him rest? Why
　must they drag him
Out of his grave to give me a bad
　name?

I did not kill him. In his bed he died,
As most men die, because his hour had
　come.
I have wronged no man. Why should
　Proctor say
Such things about me? I will not for-
　give him
Till he confesses he has slandered me.
Then, I 've more trouble. All my cat-
　tle gone.

MARTHA.

They will come back again.

COREY.

　　　　Not in this world.
Did I not tell you they were over-
　looked?
They ran down through the woods, into
　the meadows,
And tried to swim the river, and were
　drowned.
It is a heavy loss.

MARTHA.

　　　　I 'm sorry for it.

COREY.

All my dear oxen dead. I loved them,
　Martha,
Next to yourself. I liked to look at
　them,
And watch the breath come out of their
　wide nostrils,
And see their patient eyes. Somehow I
　thought
It gave me strength only to look at
　them.
And how they strained their necks
　against the yoke
If I but spoke, or touched them with
　the goad!
They were my friends; and when Gloyd
　came and told me
They were all drowned, I could have
　drowned myself
From sheer vexation; and I said as
　much
To Gloyd and others.

MARTHA.

　　　　Do not trust John Gloyd
With anything you would not have re-
　peated.

COREY.

As I came through the woods this after-
　noon,

Impatient at my loss, and much per-
     plexed
With all that I had heard there in the
     village,
The yellow leaves lit up the trees about
     me
Like an enchanted palace, and I wished
I knew enough of magic or of Witch-
     craft
To change them into gold.   Then sud-
     denly
A tree shook down some crimson leaves
     upon me,
Like drops of blood, and in the path be-
     fore me
Stood Tituba the Indian, the old crone.

MARTHA.

Were you not frightened ?

COREY.

                           No, I do not think
I know the meaning of that word.   Why
     frightened ?
I am not one of those who think the
     Lord
Is waiting till He catches them some
     day
In the back yard alone !   What should
     I fear ?
She started from the bushes by the
     path,
And had a basket full of herbs and roots
For some witch-broth or other, — the
     old hag.

MARTHA.

She has been here to-day.

COREY.

                           With hand outstretched
She said : " Giles Corey, will you sign
     the Book ? "
" Avaunt ! " I cried : " Get thee behind
     me, Satan ! "
At which she laughed and left me.   But
     a voice
Was whispering in my ear contin-
     ually :
" Self-murder is no crime.   The life of
     man
Is his, to keep it or to throw away ! "

MARTHA.

'T was a temptation of the Evil One !
Giles, Giles ! why will you harbor these
     dark thoughts ?

COREY (rising).

I am too tired to talk.   I 'll go to bed.

MARTHA.

First tell me something about Bridget
     Bishop.
How did she look ?   You saw her ?   You
     were there ?

COREY.

I 'll tell you that to-morrow, not to
     night.
I 'll go to bed.

MARTHA.

          First let us pray together.

COREY.

I cannot pray to-night.

MARTHA.

                    Say the Lord's Prayer,
And that will comfort you.

COREY.

               I cannot say,
" As we forgive those that have sinned
     against us,"
When I do not forgive them.

MARTHA (kneeling on the hearth).

                         God forgive you !

COREY.

I will not make believe !   I say to-night
There 's something thwarts me when I
     wish to pray,
And thrusts into my mind, instead of
     prayers,
Hate and revenge, and things that are
     not prayers.
Something of my old self, — my old,
     bad life, —
And the old Adam in me rises up,
And will not let me pray.   I am afraid
The Devil hinders me.   You know I
     say
Just what I think, and nothing more
     nor less,
And, when I pray, my heart is in my
     prayer.
I cannot say one thing and mean an-
     other.
If I can't pray, I will not make believe !

[Exit COREY.   MARTHA contin-
                    ues kneeling.

ACT III.

SCENE I. — GILES COREY'S *kitchen. Morning.* COREY *and* MARTHA *sitting at the breakfast-table.*

COREY (*rising*).

Well, now I 've told you all I saw and heard
Of Bridget Bishop ; and I must be gone.

MARTHA.

Don't go into the village, Giles, to-day.
Last night you came back tired and out of humor.

COREY.

Say, angry ; say, right angry.   I was never
In a more devilish temper in my life.
All things went wrong with me.

MARTHA.

    You were much vexed ;
So don't go to the village.

COREY (*going*).

      No, I won't.
I won't go near it.   We are going to mow
The Ipswich meadows for the aftermath,
The crop of sedge and rowens.

MARTHA.

     Stay a moment.
I want to tell you what I dreamed last night.
Do you believe in dreams ?

COREY.

     Why, yes and no.
When they come true, then I believe in them ;
When they come false, I don't believe in them.
But let me hear.   What did you dream about ?

MARTHA.

I dreamed that you and I were both in prison ;
That we had fetters on our hands and feet ;
That we were taken before the Magistrates,
And tried for Witchcraft, and condemned to death !

I wished to pray ; they would not let me pray ;
You tried to comfort me, and they forbade it.
But the most dreadful thing in all my dream
Was that they made you testify against me !
And then there came a kind of mist between us ;
I could not see you ; and I woke in terror.
I never was more thankful in my life
Than when I found you sleeping at my side !

COREY (*with tenderness*).

It was our talk last night that made you dream.
I 'm sorry for it.   I 'll control myself
Another time, and keep my temper down !
I do not like such dreams. — Remember, Martha,
I 'm going to mow the Ipswich River meadows ;
If Gardner comes, you 'll tell him where to find me.   [*Exit.*

MARTHA.

So this delusion grows from bad to worse.
First, a forsaken and forlorn old woman,
Ragged and wretched, and without a friend ;
Then something higher.   Now it 's Bridget Bishop ;
God only knows whose turn it will be next !
The Magistrates are blind, the people mad !
If they would only seize the Afflicted Children,
And put them in the Workhouse, where they should be,
There 'd be an end of all this wickedness.   [*Exit.*

SCENE II. — *A street in Salem Village. Enter* MATHER *and* HATHORNE.

MATHER.

Yet one thing troubles me.

HATHORNE.

     And what is that ?

MATHER.

May not the Devil take the outward
    shape
Of innocent persons ? Are we not in
    danger,
Perhaps, of punishing some who are not
    guilty ?

HATHORNE.

As I have said, we do not trust alone
To spectral evidence.

MATHER.

                    And then again,
If any shall be put to death for Witch-
    craft,
We do but kill the body, not the soul.
The Unclean Spirits that possessed them
    once
Live still, to enter into other bodies.
What have we gained ? Surely, there 's
    nothing gained.

HATHORNE.

Doth not the Scripture say, " Thou
    shalt not suffer
A Witch to live " ?

MATHER.

                    The Scripture sayeth it,
But speaketh to the Jews ; and we are
    Christians.
What say the laws of England ?

HATHORNE.

                    They make Witchcraft
Felony without the benefit of Clergy.
Witches are burned in England. You
    have read —
For you read all things, not a book es-
    capes you —
The famous Demonology of King
    James ?

MATHER.

A curious volume. I remember also
The plot of the Two Hundred, with
    one Fian,
The Registrar of the Devil, at their
    head,
To drown his Majesty on his return
From Denmark ; how they sailed in
    sieves or riddles
Unto North Berwick Kirk in Lothian,
And, landing there, danced hand in
    hand, and sang,

" Goodwife, go ye berore ! goodwife, go
    ye !
If ye 'll not go before, goodwife, let
    me ! "
While   Geilis   Duncan   played   the
    Witches' Reel
Upon a jews-harp.

HATHORNE.

                    Then you know full well
The English law, and that in England
    Witches,
When lawfully convicted and attainted,
Are put to death.

MATHER.

                    When lawfully convicted ;
That is the point.

HATHORNE.

                    You heard the evidence
Produced before us yesterday at the
    trial
Of Bridget Bishop.

MATHER.

                    One of the Afflicted,
I know, bore witness to the apparition
Of ghosts unto the spectre of this
    Bishop,
Saying, " You murdered us ! " of the
    truth whereof
There was in matter of fact too much
    suspicion.

HATHORNE.

And when she cast her eyes on the
    Afflicted,
They were struck down ; and this in
    such a manner
There could be no collusion in the
    business.
And when the accused but laid her
    hand upon them,
As they lay in their swoons, they
    straight revived,
Although they stirred not when the
    others touched them.

MATHER.

What most convinced me of the wo-
    man's guilt
Was finding hidden in her cellar wall
Those poppets made of rags, with head-
    less pins
Stuck into them point outwards, and
    whereof
She could not give a reasonable ac-
    count.

HATHORNE.

When you shall read the testimony given
Before the Court in all the other cases,
I am persuaded you will find the proof
No less conclusive than it was in this.
Come, then, with me, and I will tax your patience
With reading of the documents so far
As may convince you that these sorcerers
Are lawfully convicted and attainted.
Like doubting Thomas, you shall lay your hand
Upon these wounds, and you will doubt no more.   [*Exeunt.*

SCENE III. — *A room in* COREY's *house.* MARTHA *and two Deacons of the church.*

MARTHA.

Be seated. I am glad to see you here.
I know what you are come for. You are come
To question me, and learn from my own lips
If I have any dealings with the Devil;
In short, if I 'm a Witch.

DEACON (*sitting down*).

                    Such is our purpose.
How could you know beforehand why we came?

MARTHA.

'T was only a surmise.

DEACON.

                    We came to ask you,
You being with us in church covenant,
What part you have, if any, in these matters.

MARTHA.

And I make answer, No part whatsoever.
I am a farmer's wife, a working woman;
You see my spinning-wheel, you see my loom,
You know the duties of a farmer's wife,
And are not ignorant that my life among you
Has been without reproach until this day.
Is it not true?

DEACON.

                    So much we 're bound to own;
And say it frankly, and without reserve.

MARTHA.

I 've heard the idle tales that are abroad;
I 've heard it whispered that I am a Witch;
I cannot help it. I do not believe
In any Witchcraft. It is a delusion.

DEACON.

How can you say that it is a delusion,
When all our learned and good men believe it, —
Our Ministers and worshipful Magistrates?

MARTHA.

Their eyes are blinded and see not the truth.
Perhaps one day they will be open to it.

DEACON.

You answer boldly. The Afflicted Children
Say you appeared to them.

MARTHA.

                    And did they say
What clothes I came in?

DEACON.

                    No, they could not tell.
They said that you foresaw our visit here,
And blinded them, so that they could not see
The clothes you wore.

MARTHA.

                    The cunning, crafty girls!
I say to you, in all sincerity,
I never have appeared to any one
In my own person. If the Devil takes
My shape to hurt these children, or afflict them,
I am not guilty of it. And I say
It 's all a mere delusion of the senses.

DEACON.

I greatly fear that you will find too late
It is not so.

MARTHA (*rising*).

                    They do accuse me falsely

It is delusion, or it is deceit.
There is a story in the ancient Scriptures
Which I much wonder comes not to your minds.
Let me repeat it to you.

DEACON.

We will hear it.

MARTHA.

It came to pass that Naboth had a vineyard
Hard by the palace of the King called Ahab.
And Ahab, King of Israel, spake to Naboth,
And said to him, Give unto me thy vineyard,
That I may have it for a garden of herbs,
And I will give a better vineyard for it,
Or, if it seemeth good to thee, its worth
In money. And then Naboth said to Ahab,
The Lord forbid it me that I should give
The inheritance of my fathers unto thee.
And Ahab came into his house displeased
And heavy at the words which Naboth spake,
And laid him down upon his bed, and turned
His face away; and he would eat no bread.
And Jezebel, the wife of Ahab, came
And said to him, Why is thy spirit sad?
And he said unto her, Because I spake
To Naboth, to the Jezreelite, and said,
Give me thy vineyard; and he answered, saying,
I will not give my vineyard unto thee.
And Jezebel, the wife of Ahab, said,
Dost thou not rule the realm of Israel?
Arise, eat bread, and let thy heart be merry;
I will give Naboth's vineyard unto thee.
So she wrote letters in King Ahab's name,
And sealed them with his seal, and sent the letters
Unto the elders that were in his city
Dwelling with Naboth, and unto the nobles;
And in the letters wrote, Proclaim a fast;
And set this Naboth high among the people,

And set two men, the sons of Belial,
Before him, to bear witness and to say,
Thou didst blaspheme against God and the King;
And carry him out and stone him, that he die!
And the elders and the nobles in the city
Did even as Jezebel, the wife of Ahab,
Had sent to them and written in the letters.

And then it came to pass, when Ahab heard
Naboth was dead, that Ahab rose to go
Down unto Naboth's vineyard, and to take
Possession of it. And the word of God
Came to Elijah, saying to him, Arise,
Go down to meet the King of Israel
In Naboth's vineyard, whither he hath gone
To take possession. Thou shalt speak to him,
Saying, Thus saith the Lord! What! hast thou killed
And also taken possession? In the place
Wherein the dogs have licked the blood of Naboth
Shall the dogs lick thy blood, — ay, even thine!

Both of the Deacons start from their seats.

And Ahab then, the King of Israel,
Said, Hast thou found me, O mine enemy?
Elijah the Prophet answered, I have found thee!
So will it be with those who have stirred up
The Sons of Belial here to bear false witness
And swear away the lives of innocent people;
Their enemy will find them out at last,
The Prophet's voice will thunder, I have found thee!   [*Exeunt.*

SCENE IV. — *Meadows on Ipswich River.*
COREY *and his men mowing;* COREY *in advance.*

COREY.

Well done, my men. You see, I lead the field!

I 'm an old man, but I can swing a scythe
Better than most of you, though you be younger.

Hangs his scythe upon a tree.

GLOYD (*aside to the others*).

How strong he is! It 's supernatural.
No man so old as he is has such strength.
The Devil helps him!

COREY (*wiping his forehead*).

Now we 'll rest awhile,
And take our nooning. What 's the matter with you?
You are not angry with me, — are you, Gloyd?
Come, come, we will not quarrel. Let 's be friends.
It 's an old story, that the Raven said,
" Read the Third of Colossians and fifteenth."

GLOYD.

You 're handier at the scythe, but I can beat you
At wrestling.

COREY.

Well, perhaps so. I don't know.
I never wrestled with you. Why, you 're vexed!
Come, come, don't bear a grudge.

GLOYD.

You are afraid.

COREY.

What should I be afraid of? All bear witness
The challenge comes from him. Now, then, my man.

They wrestle, and GLOYD *is thrown.*

ONE OF THE MEN.

That 's a fair fall.

ANOTHER.

'T was nothing but a foil!

OTHERS.

You 've hurt him!

COREY (*helping* GLOYD *rise*).

No; this meadow-land is soft.
You 're not hurt, — are you, Gloyd?

GLOYD (*rising*).

No, not much hurt.

COREY.

Well, then, shake hands; and there 's an end of it.
How do you like that Cornish hug, my lad?
And now we 'll see what 's in our basket here.

GLOYD (*aside*).

The Devil and all his imps are in that man!
The clutch of his ten fingers burns like fire!

COREY (*reverentially taking off his hat*).

God bless the food He hath provided for us,
And make us thankful for it, for Christ's sake!

He lifts up a keg of cider, and drinks from it.

GLOYD.

Do you see that? Don't tell me it 's not Witchcraft.
Two of us could not lift that cask as he does!

COREY *puts down the keg, and opens a basket. A voice is heard calling.*

VOICE.

Ho! Corey, Corey!

COREY.

What is that? I surely
Heard some one calling me by name!

VOICE.

Giles Corey!

Enter a boy, running, and out of breath.

BOY.

Is Master Corey here?

COREY.

Yes, here I am.

BOY.

O Master Corey!

COREY.

Well?

BOY.

Your wife — your wife —

COREY.

What 's happened to my wife ?

BOY.

She 's sent to prison !

COREY.

The dream ! the dream ! O God, be
    merciful !

BOY.

She sent me here to tell you.

COREY (*putting on his jacket*).

Where 's my horse ?
Don't stand there staring, fellows.
    Where 's my horse ?
                [*Exit* COREY.

GLOYD.

Under the trees there. Run, old man,
    run, run !
You 've got some one to wrestle with
    you now
Who 'll trip your heels up, with your
    Cornish hug.
If there 's a Devil, he has got you now.
Ah, there he goes ! His horse is snort-
    ing fire !

ONE OF THE MEN.

John Gloyd, don't talk so ! It 's a
    shame to talk so !
He 's a good master, though you quar-
    rel with him.

GLOYD.

If hard work and low wages make good
    masters,
Then he is one. But I think otherwise.
Come, let us have our dinner and be
    merry,
And talk about the old man and the
    Witches.
I know some stories that will make you
    laugh.

They sit down on the grass, and eat.

Now there are Goody Cloyse and Goody
    Good,
Who have not got a decent tooth be-
    tween them,
And yet these children — the Afflicted
    Children —

Say that they bite them, and show
    marks of teeth
Upon their arms !

ONE OF THE MEN.

That makes the wonder greater.
That 's Witchcraft. Why, if they had
    teeth like yours,
'T would be no wonder if the girls were
    bitten !

GLOYD.

And then those ghosts that come out of
    their graves
And cry, "You murdered us ! you mur-
    dered us ! "

ONE OF THE MEN.

And all those Apparitions that stick
    pins
Into the flesh of the Afflicted Chil-
    dren !

GLOYD.

Oh those Afflicted Children ! They
    know well
Where the pins come from. I can tell
    you that.
And there 's old Corey, he has got a
    horseshoe
Nailed on his doorstep to keep off the
    Witches,
And all the same his wife has gone to
    prison.

ONE OF THE MEN.

Oh, she 's no Witch. I 'll swear that
    Goodwife Corey
Never did harm to any living creature.
She 's a good woman, if there ever was
    one.

GLOYD.

Well, we shall see. As for that Bridget
    Bishop,
She has been tried before ; some years
    ago
A negro testified he saw her shape
Sitting upon the rafters in a barn,
And holding in its hand an egg ; and
    while
He went to fetch his pitchfork, she had
    vanished.
And now be quiet, will you ? I am
    tired,
And want to sleep here on the grass a
    little.

They stretch themselves on the grass

ONE OF THE MEN.

There may be Witches riding through
the air
Over our heads on broomsticks at this
moment,
Bound for some Satan's Sabbath in the
woods
To be baptized.

GLOYD.

I wish they 'd take you with them,
And hold you under water, head and
ears,
Till you were drowned ; and that would
stop your talking,
If nothing else will. Let me sleep, I
say.

ACT IV.

SCENE I. — *The Green in front of the village Meeting-house. An excited crowd
gathering. Enter* JOHN GLOYD.

A FARMER.

Who will be tried to-day ?

A SECOND.

I do not know.
Here is John Gloyd. Ask him; he
knows.

FARMER.

John Gloyd,
Whose turn is it to-day ?

GLOYD.

It 's Goodwife Corey's.

FARMER.

Giles Corey's wife ?

GLOYD.

The same. She is not mine.
It will go hard with her with all her
praying.
The hypocrite ! She 's always on her
knees ;
But she prays to the Devil when she
prays.
Let us go in.

A trumpet blows.

FARMER.

Here come the Magistrates.

SECOND FARMER.

Who 's the tall man in front ?

GLOYD.

Oh, that is Hathorne,
A Justice of the Court, and a Quarter-
master
In the Three County Troop. He 'll sift
the matter.
That 's Corwin with him ; and the man
in black
Is Cotton Mather, Minister of Boston.

Enter HATHORNE *and other Magistrates
on horseback, followed by the Sheriff,
constables, and attendants on foot. The
Magistrates dismount, and enter the
Meeting-house, with the rest.*

FARMER.

The Meeting-house is full. I never saw
So great a crowd before.

GLOYD.

No matter. Come.
We shall find room enough by elbow-
ing
Our way among them. Put your
shoulder to it.

FARMER.

There were not half so many at the trial
Of Goodwife Bishop.

GLOYD.

Keep close after me.
I 'll find a place for you. They 'll want
me there.
I am a friend of Corey's, as you know,
And he can't do without me just at
present. [*Exeunt.*

SCENE II. — *Interior of the Meeting-
house.* MATHER *and the Magistrates
seated in front of the pulpit. Before
them a raised platform.* MARTHA *in
chains.* COREY *near her.* MARY
WALCOT *in a chair. A crowd of spectators, among them* GLOYD. *Confusion
and murmurs during the scene.*

HATHORNE.

Call Martha Corey.

MARTHA.

I am here.

HATHORNE.

　　　　Come forward.
She ascends the platform.

The Jurors of our Sovereign Lord and
　　Lady
The King and Queen, here present, do
　　accuse you
Of having on the tenth of June last past,
And divers other times before and after,
Wickedly used and practised certain
　　arts
Called Witchcrafts, Sorceries, and In-
　　cantations,
Against one Mary Walcot, single woman,
Of Salem Village ; by which wicked arts
The aforesaid Mary Walcot was tor-
　　mented,
Tortured, afflicted, pined, consumed, and
　　wasted,
Against the peace of our Sovereign
　　Lord and Lady
The King and Queen, as well as of the
　　Statute
Made and provided in that case. What
　　say you ?

MARTHA.

Before I answer, give me leave to pray.

HATHORNE.

We have not sent for you, nor are we
　　here,
To hear you pray, but to examine you
In whatsoever is alleged against you.
Why do you hurt this person ?

MARTHA.

　　　　　　I do not.
I am not guilty of the charge against
　　me.

MARY.

Avoid, she-devil ! You may torment me
　　now !
Avoid, avoid, Witch !

MARTHA.

　　　　I am innocent.
I never had to do with any Witchcraft
Since I was born. I am a gospel woman.

MARY.

You are a gospel Witch !

MARTHA (*clasping her hands*).

　　　　　Ah me ! ah me !
Oh, give me leave to pray !

MARY (*stretching out her hands*).

　　　　She hurts me now.
See, she has pinched my hands !

HATHORNE.

　　　　Who made these marks
Upon her hands ?

MARTHA.

　　　　I do not know. I stand
Apart from her. I did not touch her
　　hands.

HATHORNE.

Who hurt her then ?

MARTHA.

I know not.

HATHORNE.

　　　　　　Do you think
She is bewitched ?

MARTHA.

　　　　Indeed I do not think so.
I am no Witch, and have no faith in
　　Witches.

HATHORNE.

Then answer me : When certain per-
　　sons came
To see you yesterday, how did you
　　know
Beforehand why they came ?

MARTHA.

　　　　　　I had had speech ;
The children said I hurt them, and I
　　thought
These people came to question me about
　　it.

HATHORNE.

How did you know the children had
　　been told
To note the clothes you wore ?

MARTHA.

　　　　　My husband told me
What others said about it.

HATHORNE.

　　　　　Goodman Corey,
Say, did you tell her ?

COREY.

　　　　I must speak the truth ;

I did not tell her. It was some one else.

HATHORNE.

Did you not say your husband told you so?
How dare you tell a lie in this assembly?
Who told you of the clothes? Confess the truth.

MARTHA *bites her lips, and is silent.*

You bite your lips, but do not answer me!

MARY.

Ah, she is biting me! Avoid, avoid!

HATHORNE.

You said your husband told you.

MARTHA.

Yes, he told me
The children said I troubled them.

HATHORNE.

Then tell me,
Why do you trouble them?

MARTHA.

I have denied it.

MARY.

She threatened me; stabbed at me with her spindle;
And, when my brother thrust her with his sword,
He tore her gown, and cut a piece away.
Here are they both, the spindle and the cloth.

Shows them.

HATHORNE.

And there are persons here who know the truth
Of what has now been said. What answer make you?

MARTHA.

I make no answer. Give me leave to pray.

HATHORNE.

Whom would you pray to?

MARTHA.

To my God and Father.

HATHORNE.

Who is your God and Father?

MARTHA.

The Almighty!

HATHORNE.

Doth he you pray to say that he is God?
It is the Prince of Darkness, and not God.

MARY.

There is a dark shape whispering in her ear.

HATHORNE.

What does it say to you?

MARTHA.

I see no shape.

HATHORNE.

Did you not hear it whisper?

MARTHA.

I heard nothing.

MARY.

What torture! Ah, what agony I suffer!

Falls into a swoon.

HATHORNE.

You see this woman cannot stand before you.
If you would look for mercy, you **must** look
In God's way, by confession of your guilt.
Why does your spectre haunt and **hurt** this person?

MARTHA.

I do not know. He who appeared **of** old
In Samuel's shape, a saint and glorified,
May come in whatsoever shape he chooses.
I cannot help it. I am sick at heart!

COREY.

O Martha, Martha! let me hold **your** hand.

HATHORNE.

No; stand aside, old man.

MARY (*starting up*).

Look there! Look there!
I see a little bird, a yellow bird,
Perched on her finger; and it pecks at
    me.
Ah, it will tear mine eyes out!

MARTHA.

I see nothing.

HATHORNE.

'T is the Familiar Spirit that attends
    her.

MARY.

Now it has flown away. It sits up
    there
Upon the rafters. It is gone; is van-
    ished.

MARTHA.

Giles, wipe these tears of anger from
    mine eyes.
Wipe the sweat from my forehead. I
    am faint.

She leans against the railing.

MARY.

Oh, she is crushing me with all her
    weight!

HATHORNE.

Did you not carry once the Devil's
    Book
To this young woman?

MARTHA.

Never.

HATHORNE.

Have you signed it,
Or touched it?

MARTHA.

No; I never saw it.

HATHORNE.

Did you not scourge her with an iron
    rod?

MARTHA.

No, I did not. If any Evil Spirit
Has taken my shape to do these evil
    deeds,
I cannot help it. I am innocent.

HATHORNE.

Did you not say the Magistrates were
    blind?
That you would open their eyes?

MARTHA (*with a scornful laugh*).

Yes, I said that;
If you call me a sorceress, you are
    blind!
If you accuse the innocent, you are
    blind!
Can the innocent be guilty?

HATHORNE.

Did you not
On one occasion hide your husband's
    saddle
To hinder him from coming to the ses-
    sions?

MARTHA.

I thought it was a folly in a farmer
To waste his time pursuing such illu-
    sions.

HATHORNE.

What was the bird that this young wo-
    man saw
Just now upon your hand?

MARTHA.

I know no bird.

HATHORNE.

Have you not dealt with a Familiar
    Spirit?

MARTHA.

No, never, never!

HATHORNE.

What then was the Book
You showed to this young woman, and
    besought her
To write in it?

MARTHA.

Where should I have a book?
I showed her none, nor have none.

MARY.

The next Sabbath
Is the Communion Day, but Martha
    Corey
Will not be there!

"Oh! She is crushing me with all her weight."   Page 630.

MARTHA.

Ah, you are all against me.
What can I do or say?

HATHORNE.

You can confess.

MARTHA.

No, I cannot, for I am innocent.

HATHORNE.

We have the proof of many witnesses
That you are guilty.

MARTHA.

Give me leave to speak.
Will you condemn me on such evi-
dence, —
You who have known me for so many
years?
Will you condemn me in this house of
God,
Where I so long have worshipped with
you all?
Where I have eaten the bread and
drunk the wine
So many times at our Lord's Table with
you?
Bear witness, you that hear me; you all
know
That I have led a blameless life among
you,
That never any whisper of suspicion
Was breathed against me till this accu-
sation.
And shall this count for nothing? Will
you take
My life away from me, because this girl,
Who is distraught, and not in her right
mind,
Accuses me of things I blush to name?

HATHORNE.

What! is it not enough? Would you
hear more?
Giles Corey!

COREY.

I am here.

HATHORNE.

Come forward, then.
COREY ascends the platform.
Is it not true, that on a certain night
You were impeded strangely in your
prayers?

That something hindered you? and that
you left
This woman here, your wife, kneeling
alone
Upon the hearth?

COREY.

Yes; I cannot deny it.

HATHORNE.

Did you not say the Devil hindered
you?

COREY.

I think I said some words to that effect.

HATHORNE.

Is it not true, that fourteen head of
cattle,
To you belonging, broke from their enclosure
And leaped into the river, and were
drowned?

COREY.

It is most true.

HATHORNE.

And did you not then say
That they were overlooked?

COREY.

So much I said.
I see; they're drawing round me closer,
closer,
A net I cannot break, cannot escape
from!   (Aside.)

HATHORNE.

Who did these things?

COREY.

I do not know who did them.

HATHORNE.

Then I will tell you. It is some one
near you;
You see her now; this woman, your
own wife.

COREY.

I call the heavens to witness, it is false!
She never harmed me, never hindered
me
In anything but what I should not do.
And I bear witness in the sight of
heaven,

And in God's house here, that I never
    knew her
As otherwise than patient, brave, and
    true,
Faithful, forgiving, full of charity,
A virtuous and industrious and good
    wife!

HATHORNE.

Tut, tut, man; do not rant so in your
    speech;
You are a witness, not an advocate!
Here, Sheriff, take this woman back to
    prison.

MARTHA.

O Giles, this day you 've sworn away my
    life!

MARY.

Go, go and join the Witches at the
    door.
Do you not hear the drum? Do you
    not see them?
Go quick. They 're waiting for you.
    You are late.
    [*Exit* MARTHA ; COREY *following.*

COREY.

The dream! the dream! the dream!

HATHORNE.

             What does he say?
Giles Corey, go not hence. You are
    yourself
Accused of Witchcraft and of Sorcery
By many witnesses. Say, are you
    guilty?

COREY.

I know my death is foreordained by
    you, —
Mine and my wife's. Therefore I will
    not answer.

*During the rest of the scene he remains
silent.*

HATHORNE.

Do you refuse to plead? — 'T were
    better for you
To make confession, or to plead Not
    Guilty. —
Do you not hear me? — Answer, are
    you guilty?
Do you not know a heavier doom awaits
    you,

If you refuse to plead, than if found
    guilty?
Where is John Gloyd?

GLOYD (*coming forward*).

             Here am I.

HATHORNE.

             Tell the Court ;
Have you not seen the supernatural
    power
Of this old man? Have you not seen
    him do
Strange feats of strength?

GLOYD.

            I 've seen him lead the field,
On a hot day, in mowing, and against
Us younger men ; and I have wrestled
    with him.
He threw me like a feather. I have
    seen him
Lift up a barrel with his single hands,
Which two strong men could hardly
    lift together,
And, holding it above his head, drink
    from it.

HATHORNE.

That is enough; we need not question
    further.
What answer do you make to this, Giles
    Corey?

MARY.

See there! See there!

HATHORNE.

            What is it? I see nothing.

MARY.

Look! Look! It is the ghost of Robert
    Goodell,
Whom fifteen years ago this man did
    murder
By stamping on his body! In his shroud
He comes here to bear witness to the
    crime!
The crowd shrinks back from COREY *in
horror.*

HATHORNE.

Ghosts of the dead and voices of the
    living
Bear witness to your guilt, and you
    must die!
It might have been an easier death.
    Your doom

Will be on your own head, and not on
ours.
Twice more will you be questioned of
these things;
Twice more have room to plead or to
confess.
If you are contumacious to the Court,
And if, when questioned, you refuse to
answer,
Then by the Statute you will be condemned
To the *peine forte et dure!* To have
your body
Pressed by great weights until you
shall be dead!
And may the Lord have mercy on your
soul!

ACT V.

SCENE I. — COREY's *farm as in Act II.,
Scene I. Enter* RICHARD GARDNER,
looking round him.

GARDNER.

Here stands the house as I remember
it.
The four tall poplar-trees before the
door;
The house, the barn, the orchard, and
the well,
With its moss-covered bucket and its
trough;
The garden, with its hedge of currant-
bushes;
The woods, the harvest-fields; and, far
beyond,
The pleasant landscape stretching to
the sea.
But everything is silent and deserted!
No bleat of flocks, no bellowing of
herds,
No sound of flails, that should be beat-
ing now;
Nor man nor beast astir. What can
this mean?
Knocks at the door.
What ho! Giles Corey! Hillo-ho! Giles
Corey! —
No answer but the echo from the barn,
And the ill-omened cawing of the crow,
That yonder wings his flight across the
fields,
As if he scented carrion in the air.
Enter TITUBA *with a basket.*
What woman's this, that, like an ap-
parition,

Haunts this deserted homestead in
broad day?
Woman, who are you?

TITUBA.

I'm Tituba.
I am John Indian's wife. I am a
Witch.

GARDNER.

What are you doing here?

TITUBA.

I am gathering herbs, —
Cinquefoil, and saxifrage, and pennyroyal.

GARDNER (*looking at the herbs*).
This is not cinquefoil, it is deadly
nightshade!
This is not saxifrage, but hellebore!
This is not pennyroyal, it is henbane!
Do you come here to poison these good
people?

TITUBA.

I get these for the Doctor in the Vil-
lage.
Beware of Tituba. I pinch the chil-
dren;
Make little poppets and stick pins in
them,
And then the children cry out they are
pricked.
The Black Dog came to me and said,
"Serve me!"
I was afraid. He made me hurt the
children.

GARDNER.

Poor soul! She's crazed, with all these
Devil's doings.

TITUBA.

Will you, sir, sign the book?

GARDNER.

No, I'll not sign it.
Where is Giles Corey? Do you know
Giles Corey?

TITUBA.

He's safe enough. He's down there in
the prison.

GARDNER.

Corey in prison? What is he accused
of?

TITUBA.

Giles Corey and Martha Corey are in
    prison
Down there in Salem Village. Both
    are witches.
She came to me and whispered, " Kill
    the children ! "
Both signed the Book !

GARDNER.

        Begone, you imp of darkness !
You Devil's dam !

TITUBA.

        Beware of Tituba !
            [Exit.

GARDNER.

How often out at sea on stormy nights,
When the waves thundered round me,
    and the wind
Bellowed, and beat the canvas, and my
    ship
Clove through the solid darkness, like a
    wedge,
I 've thought of him upon his pleasant
    farm,
Living in quiet with his thrifty house-
    wife,
And envied him, and wished his fate
    were mine !
And now I find him shipwrecked ut-
    terly,
Drifting upon this sea of sorceries,
And lost, perhaps, beyond all aid of
    man !   [Exit.

SCENE II. — The prison. GILES COREY
    at a table on which are some papers.

COREY.

Now I have done with earth and all its
    cares ;
I give my worldly goods to my dear
    children ;
My body I bequeath to my tormentors,
And my immortal soul to Him who
    made it.
O God ! who in thy wisdom dost afflict
    me
With an affliction greater than most men
Have ever yet endured or shall endure,
Suffer me not in this last bitter hour
For any pains of death to fall from Thee!

MARTHA is heard singing.

Arise, O righteous Lord !
    And disappoint my foes ;

They are but thine avenging sword,
    Whose wounds are swift to close.

COREY.

Hark, hark ! it is her voice ! She is not
    dead !
She lives ! I am not utterly forsaken !

MARTHA, singing.

By thine abounding grace,
    And mercies multiplied,
I shall awake, and see thy face ;
    I shall be satisfied.

COREY hides his face in his hands. En-
    ter the JAILER, followed by RICHARD
    GARDNER.

JAILER.

Here 's a seafaring man, one Richard
    Gardner,
A friend of yours, who asks to speak
    with you.
    COREY rises.   They embrace.

COREY.

I 'm glad to see you, ay, right glad to
    see you.

GARDNER.

And I am most sorely grieved to see
    you thus.

COREY.

Of all the friends I had in happier days,
You are the first, ay, and the only one,
That comes to seek me out in my dis-
    grace !
And you but come in time to say fare-
    well.
They 've dug my grave already in the
    field.
I thank you.   There is something in
    your presence,
I know not what it is, that gives me
    strength.
Perhaps it is the bearing of a man
Familiar with all dangers of the deep,
Familiar with the cries of drowning
    men,
With fire, and wreck, and foundering
    ships at sea !

GARDNER.

Ah, I have never known a wreck like
    yours !
Would I could save you !

COREY.

                    Do not speak of that.
It is too late.   I am resolved to die.

GARDNER.

Why would you die who have so much
    to live for ? —
Your daughters, and —

COREY.

                    You cannot say the word.
My daughters have gone from me.
    They are married ;
They have their homes, their thoughts,
    apart from me ;
I will not say their hearts, — that were
    too cruel.
What would you have me do ?

GARDNER.

                    Confess and live.

COREY.

That 's what they said who came here
    yesterday
To lay a heavy weight upon my con-
    science
By telling me that I was driven forth
As an unworthy member of their church.

GARDNER.

It is an awful death.

COREY.

                    'T is but to drown,
And have the weight of all the seas
    upon you.

GARDNER.

Say something ; say enough to fend off
    death
Till this tornado of fanaticism
Blows itself out.   Let me come in be-
    tween you
And your severer self, with my plain
    sense ;
Do not be obstinate.

COREY.

                    I will not plead.
If I deny, I am condemned already,
In courts where ghosts appear as wit-
    nesses,
And swear men's lives away.   If I con-
    fess,
Then I confess a lie, to buy a life
Which is not life, but only death in life.

I will not bear false witness against any,
Not even against myself, whom I count
    least.

GARDNER (aside).

Ah, what a noble character is this !

COREY.

I pray you, do not urge me to do that
You would not do yourself.   I have
    already
The bitter taste of death upon my lips ;
I feel the pressure of the heavy weight
That will crush out my life within this
    hour ;
But if a word could save me, and that
    word
Were not the Truth ; nay, if it did but
    swerve
A hair's-breadth from the Truth, I
    would not say it !

GARDNER (aside).

How mean I seem beside a man like
    this !

COREY.

As for my wife, my Martha and my
    Martyr, —
Whose virtues, like the stars, unseen by
    day,
Though numberless, do but await the
    dark
To manifest themselves unto all eyes, —
She who first won me from my evil ways,
And taught me how to live by her
    example,
By her example teaches me to die,
And leads me onward to the better
    life !

SHERIFF (without).

Giles Corey !   Come !   The hour has
    struck !

COREY.

                    I come !
Here is my body ; ye may torture it,
But the immortal soul ye cannot crush !
                    [Exeunt.

SCENE III. — A street in the Village.
    Enter GLOYD and others.

GLOYD.

Quick, or we shall be late !

A MAN.

That's not the way.
Come here; come up this lane.

GLOYD.

I wonder now
If the old man will die, and will not
    speak?
He's obstinate enough and tough enough
For anything on earth.

A bell tolls.

Hark! What is that?

A MAN.

The passing bell. He's dead!

GLOYD.

We are too late.
[*Exeunt in haste.*

SCENE IV. — *A field near the graveyard.*
GILES COREY *lying dead, with a great
stone on his breast. The Sheriff at his
head,* RICHARD GARDNER *at his feet.
A crowd behind. The bell tolling.
Enter* HATHORNE *and* MATHER.

HATHORNE.

This is the Potter's Field. Behold the
    fate
Of those who deal in Witchcrafts, and,
    when questioned,
Refuse to plead their guilt or innocence,
And stubbornly drag death upon them-
    selves.

MATHER.

O sight most horrible! In a land like
    this,
Spangled with Churches Evangelical,
Inwrapped in our salvations, must we
    seek
In mouldering statute-books of English
    Courts
Some old forgotten Law, to do such
    deeds?
Those who lie buried in the Potter's
    Field
Will rise again, as surely as ourselves
That sleep in honored graves with epi-
    taphs;
And this poor man, whom we have
    made a victim,
Hereafter will be counted as a martyr!

FINALE.

SAINT JOHN.

SAINT JOHN *wandering over the face of
the Earth.*

SAINT JOHN.

THE Ages come and go,
The Centuries pass as Years;
My hair is white as the snow,
My feet are weary and slow,
The earth is wet with my tears!
The kingdoms crumble, and fall
Apart, like a ruined wall,
Or a bank that is undermined
By a river's ceaseless flow,
And leave no trace behind!
The world itself is old;
The portals of Time unfold
On hinges of iron, that grate
And groan with the rust and the weight,
Like the hinges of a gate
That hath fallen to decay;
But the evil doth not cease;
There is war instead of peace,
Instead of Love there is hate;
And still I must wander and wait,
Still I must watch and pray,
Not forgetting in whose sight,
A thousand years in their flight
Are as a single day.

The life of man is a gleam
Of light, that comes and goes
Like the course of the Holy Stream,
The cityless river, that flows
From fountains no one knows,
Through the Lake of Galilee,
Through forests and level lands,
Over rocks, and shallows, and sands
Of a wilderness wild and vast,
Till it findeth its rest at last
In the desolate Dead Sea!
But alas! alas for me
Not yet this rest shall be!

What, then! doth Charity fail?
Is Faith of no avail?
Is Hope blown out like a light
By a gust of wind in the night?
The clashing of creeds, and the strife
Of the many beliefs, that in vain
Perplex man's heart and brain,
Are naught but the rustle of leaves,
When the breath of God upheaves
The boughs of the Tree of Life,

And they subside again!
And I remember still
The words, and from whom they came,
Not he that repeateth the name,
But he that doeth the will!

And Him evermore I behold
Walking in Galilee,
Through the cornfield's waving gold,
In hamlet, in wood, and in wold,
By the shores of the Beautiful Sea.
He toucheth the sightless eyes;
Before Him the demons flee;
To the dead He sayeth: Arise!
To the living: Follow me!
And that voice still soundeth on
From the centuries that are gone,
To the centuries that shall be!

From all vain pomps and shows,
From the pride that overflows,
And the false conceits of men;
From all the narrow rules
And subtleties of Schools,
And the craft of tongue and pen;
Bewildered in its search,
Bewildered with the cry,
Lo, here! lo, there, the Church!
Poor, sad Humanity
Through all the dust and heat
Turns back with bleeding feet,
By the weary road it came,
Unto the simple thought
By the great Master taught,
And that remaineth still:
Not he that repeateth the name,
But he that doeth the will!

FRAGMENTS AND TRANSLATIONS.

FRAGMENTS.

October 22, 1838.

NEGLECTED record of a mind neglected,
Unto what "lets and stops" art thou
    subjected!
The day with all its toils and occupa-
    tions,
The night with its reflections and sen-
    sations,
The future, and the present, and the
    past, —
All I remember, feel, and hope at last,
All shapes of joy and sorrow, as they
    pass, —
Find but a dusty image in this glass.

August 18, 1847.

O faithful, indefatigable tides,
That evermore upon God's errands go, —
Now seaward bearing tidings of the
    land, —
Now landward bearing tidings of the
    sea, —
And filling every frith and estuary,
Each arm of the great sea, each little
    creek,
Each thread and filament of water-
    courses,

Full with your ministration of delight!
Under the rafters of this wooden bridge
I see you come and go; sometimes in
    haste
To reach your journey's end, which be-
    ing done
With feet unrested ye return again
And recommence the never-ending task;
Patient, whatever burdens ye may bear,
And fretted only by the impeding rocks.

December 18, 1847.

Soft through the silent air descend the
    feathery snow-flakes;
White are the distant hills, white are
    the neighboring fields;
Only the marshes are brown, and the
    river rolling among them
Weareth the leaden hue seen in the
    eyes of the blind.

August 4, 1856.

A lovely morning, without the glare of the
sun, the sea in great commotion, chafing and
foaming.

So from the bosom of darkness our
    days come roaring and gleaming,
Chafe and break into foam, sink into
    darkness again.

But on the shores of Time each leaves
    some trace of its passage,
Though the succeeding wave washes
    it out from the sand.

INSCRIPTION ON THE SHANK-LIN FOUNTAIN.

O TRAVELLER, stay thy weary feet;
Drink of this fountain, pure and sweet;
    It flows for rich and poor the same.
Then go thy way, remembering still
The wayside well beneath the hill,
    The cup of water in His name.

TRANSLATIONS.

FROM THE SPANISH.

ANCIENT SPANISH BALLADS.

In the chapter with this title in *Outre-Mer*, besides illustrations from Byron and Lockhart are the three following examples, contributed by Mr. Longfellow.

I.

RIO VERDE, Rio Verde!
    Many a corpse is bathed in thee,
Both of Moors and eke of Christians,
    Slain with swords most cruelly.

And thy pure and crystal waters
    Dappled are with crimson gore;
For between the Moors and Christians
    Long has been the fight and sore.

Dukes and counts fell bleeding near
    thee,
    Lords of high renown were slain,
Perished many a brave hidalgo
    Of the noblemen of Spain.

II.

"King Alfonso the Eighth, having exhausted his treasury in war, wishes to lay a tax of five farthings upon each of the Castilian hidalgos, in order to defray the expenses of a journey from Burgos to Cuenca. This proposition of the king was met with disdain by the noblemen who had been assembled on the occasion."

DON NUNO, Count of Lara,
    In anger and in pride,

Forgot all reverence for the king,
    And thus in wrath replied:

"Our noble ancestors," quoth he,
    "Ne'er such a tribute paid;
Nor shall the king receive of us
    What they have once gainsaid.

"The base-born soul who deems it just
    May here with thee remain;
But follow me, ye cavaliers,
    Ye noblemen of Spain."

Forth followed they the noble Count,
    They marched to Glera's plain;
Out of three thousand gallant knights
    Did only three remain.

They tied the tribute to their spears,
    They raised it in the air,
And they sent to tell their lord the
    king
That his tax was ready there.

"He may send and take by force," said
    they,
    "This paltry sum of gold;
But the goodly gift of liberty
    Cannot be bought and sold."

III.

"One of the finest of the historic ballads is that which describes Bernardo's march to Roncesvalles. He sallies forth 'with three thousand Leonese and more,' to protect the glory and freedom of his native land. From all sides, the peasantry of the land flock to the hero's standard."

THE peasant leaves his plough afield,
    The reaper leaves his hook,
And from his hand the shepherd-boy
    Lets fall the pastoral crook.

The young set up a shout of joy,
    The old forget their years,
The feeble man grows stout of heart,
    No more the craven fears.

All rush to Bernard's standard,
    And on liberty they call;
They cannot brook to wear the yoke,
    When threatened by the Gaul.

"Free were we born," 't is thus they cry,
    "And willingly pay we
The duty that we owe our king
    By the divine decree.

" But God forbid that we obey
   The laws of foreign knaves,
Tarnish the glory of our sires,
   And make our children slaves.

" Our hearts have not so craven grown,
   So bloodless all our veins,
So vigorless our brawny arms,
   As to submit to chains.

" Has the audacious Frank, forsooth,
   Subdued these seas and lands ?
Shall he a bloodless victory have ?
   No, not while we have hands.

" He shall learn that the gallant Leonese
   Can bravely fight and fall,
But that they know not how to yield ;
   They are Castilians all.

" Was it for this the Roman power
   Of old was made to yield
Unto Numantia's valiant hosts
   On many a bloody field ?

" Shall the bold lions that have bathed
   Their paws in Libyan gore,
Crouch basely to a feebler foe,
   And dare the strife no more ?

" Let the false king sell town and tower,
   But not his vassals free ;
For to subdue the free-born soul
   No royal power hath he ! "

VIDA DE SAN MILLAN.

BY GONZALO DE BERCEO.

AND when the kings were in the field, —
   their squadrons in array, —
With lance in rest they onward pressed
   to mingle in the fray ;
But soon upon the Christians fell a terror of their foes, —
These were a numerous army, — a little
   handful those.

And while the Christian people stood in
   this uncertainty,
Upward to heaven they turned their
   eyes, and fixed their thoughts on
   high ;
And there two figures they beheld, all
   beautiful and bright,
Even than the pure new-fallen snow
   their garments were more white.

They rode upon two horses more white
   than crystal sheen,
And arms they bore such as before no
   mortal man had seen ;
The one, he held a crosier, — a pontiff's
   mitre wore ;
The other held a crucifix, — such man
   ne'er saw before.

Their faces were angelical, celestial
   forms had they, —
And downward through the fields of air
   they urged their rapid way ;
They looked upon the Moorish host
   with fierce and angry look,
And in their hands, with dire portent,
   their naked sabres shook.

The Christian host, beholding this,
   straightway take heart again ;
They fall upon their bended knees, all
   resting on the plain,
And each one with his clenchèd fist to
   smite his breast begins,
And promises to God on high he will
   forsake his sins.

And when the heavenly knights drew
   near unto the battle-ground,
They dashed among the Moors and dealt
   unerring blows around ;
Such deadly havoc there they made the
   foremost ranks along,
A panic terror spread unto the hindmost
   of the throng.

Together with these two good knights,
   the champions of the sky,
The Christians rallied and began to
   smite full sore and high ;
The Moors raised up their voices and by
   the Koran swore
That in their lives such deadly fray they
   ne'er had seen before.

Down went the misbelievers, — fast sped
   the bloody fight, —
Some ghastly and dismembered lay, and
   some half dead with fright :
Full sorely they repented that to the
   field they came,
For they saw that from the battle they
   should retreat with shame.

Another thing befell them, — they
   dreamed not of such woes, —

The very arrows that the Moors shot
from their twanging bows
Turned back against them in their flight
and wounded them full sore,
And every blow they dealt the foe was
paid in drops of gore.

. . . .

Now he that bore the crosier, and the
papal crown had on,
Was the glorified Apostle, the brother
of Saint John;
And he that held the crucifix, and wore
the monkish hood,
Was the holy San Millan of Cogolla's
neighborhood.

SAN MIGUEL, THE CONVENT.

(SAN MIGUEL DE LA TUMBA.)

BY GONZALO DE BERCEO.

SAN MIGUEL DE LA TUMBA is a convent vast and wide;
The sea encircles it around, and groans
on every side:
It is a wild and dangerous place, and
many woes betide
The monks who in that burial-place in
penitence abide.

Within those dark monastic walls, amid
the ocean flood,
Of pious, fasting monks there dwelt a
holy brotherhood;
To the Madonna's glory there an altar
high was placed,
And a rich and costly image the sacred
altar graced.

Exalted high upon a throne, the Virgin
Mother smiled,
And, as the custom is, she held within
her arms the Child;
The kings and wise men of the East
were kneeling by her side;
Attended was she like a queen whom
God had sanctified.

. . . .

Descending low before her face a screen
of feathers hung, —
A *moscader*, or fan for flies, 't is called in
vulgar tongue;

From the feathers of the peacock's wing
't was fashioned bright and fair,
And glistened like the heaven above
when all its stars are there.

It chanced that, for the people's sins, fell
the lightning's blasting stroke:
Forth from all four the sacred walls the
flames consuming broke;
The sacred robes were all consumed,
missal and holy book;
And hardly with their lives the monks
their crumbling walls forsook.

. . . .

But though the desolating flame raged
fearfully and wild,
It did not reach the Virgin Queen, it did
not reach the Child;
It did not reach the feathery screen before her face that shone,
Nor injure in a farthing's worth the
image or the throne.

The image it did not consume, it did not
burn the screen;
Even in the value of a hair they were
not hurt, I ween;
Not even the smoke did reach them, nor
injure more the shrine
Than the bishop hight Don Tello has
been hurt by hand of mine.

. . . .

SONG.

SHE is a maid of artless grace,
Gentle in form, and fair of face.

Tell me, thou ancient mariner,
That sailest on the sea,
If ship, or sail, or evening star
Be half so fair as she!

Tell me, thou gallant cavalier,
Whose shining arms I see,
If steel, or sword, or battle-field
Be half so fair as she!

Tell me, thou swain, that guard'st thy
flock
Beneath the shadowy tree,
If flock, or vale, or mountain-ridge
Be half so fair as she!

FROM THE SWEDISH AND DANISH.

PASSAGES FROM FRITHIOF'S SAGA.

BY ESAIAS TEGNÉR.

I.

FRITHIOF'S HOMESTEAD.

THREE miles extended around the fields
of the homestead, on three sides
Valleys and mountains and hills, but on
the fourth side was the ocean.
Birch woods crowned the summits, but
down the slope of the hillsides
Flourished the golden corn, and man-
high was waving the rye-field.
Lakes, full many in number, their mirror held up for the mountains,
Held for the forests up, in whose depths
the high-horned reindeers
Had their kingly walk, and drank of a
hundred brooklets.
But in the valleys widely around, there
fed on the greensward
Herds with shining hides and udders
that longed for the milk-pail.
'Mid these scattered, now here and now
there, were numberless flocks of
Sheep with fleeces white, as thou seest
the white-looking stray clouds,
Flock - wise spread o'er the heavenly
vault when it bloweth in spring-
time.
Coursers two times twelve, all mettle-
some, fast fettered storm-winds,
Stamping stood in the line of stalls, and
tugged at their fodder.
Knotted with red were their manes, and
their hoofs all white with steel
shoes.
Th' banquet-hall, a house by itself, was
timbered of hard fir.
Not five hundred men (at ten times
twelve to the hundred)
Filled up the roomy hall, when assembled
for drinking, at Yule-tide.
Thorough the hall, as long as it was,
went a table of holm-oak,
Polished and white, as of steel; the columns twain of the High-seat
Stood at the end thereof, two gods
carved out of an elm-tree:
Odin with lordly look, and Frey with
the sun on his frontlet.

Lately between the two, on a bear-skin
(the skin it was coal-black,
Scarlet-red was the throat, but the paws
were shodden with silver),
Thorsten sat with his friends. Hospital-
ity sitting with Gladness.
Oft, when the moon through the cloud-
rack flew, related the old man
Wonders from distant lands he had seen,
and cruises of Vikings
Far away on the Baltic, and Sea of the
West, and the White Sea.
Hushed sat the listening bench, and their
glances hung on the graybeard's
Lips, as a bee on the rose; but the Scald
was thinking of Brage,
Where, with his silver beard, and runes
on his tongue, he is seated
Under the leafy beech, and tells a tradi-
tion by Mimer's
Ever-murmuring wave, himself a living
tradition.
Midway the floor (with thatch was it
strewn) burned ever the fire-flame
Glad on its stone-built hearth; and thor-
ough the wide-mouthed smoke-flue
Looked the stars, those heavenly friends,
down into the great hall.
Round the walls, upon nails of steel,
were hanging in order
Breastplate and helmet together, and
here and there among them
Downward lightened a sword, as in winter evening a star shoots.
More than helmets and swords the shields
in the hall were resplendent,
White as the orb of the sun, or white as
the moon's disk of silver.
Ever and anon went a maid round the
board, and filled up the drink-
horns,
Ever she cast down her eyes and blushed;
in the shield her reflection
Blushed, too, even as she; this gladdened the drinking champions.

II.

A SLEDGE-RIDE ON THE ICE.

KING RING with his queen to the banquet did fare,
On the lake stood the ice so mirror-clear.

"Fare not o'er the ice," the stranger
cries;
"It will burst, and full deep the cold
bath lies."

"The king drowns not easily," Ring
 outspake;
"He who's afraid may go round the
 lake."

Threatening and dark looked the stranger round,
His steel shoes with haste on his feet he
 bound.

The sledge-horse starts forth strong and
 free;
He snorteth flames, so glad is he.

"Strike out," screamed the king, "my
 trotter good,
Let us see if thou art of Sleipner's
 blood."

They go as a storm goes over the
 lake,
No heed to his queen doth the old man
 take.

But the steel-shod champion standeth
 not still,
He passeth them by as swift as he will.

He carves many runes in the frozen
 tide,
Fair Ingeborg o'er her own name doth
 glide.

III.

FRITHIOF'S TEMPTATION.

Spring is coming, birds are twittering,
 forests leaf, and smiles the sun,
And the loosened torrents downward,
 singing, to the ocean run;
Glowing like the cheek of Freya, peeping rosebuds 'gin to ope,
And in human hearts awaken love of
 life, and joy, and hope.

Now will hunt the ancient monarch, and
 the queen shall join the sport:
Swarming in its gorgeous splendor, is
 assembled all the court;
Bows ring loud, and quivers rattle, stal-
 lions paw the ground alway,
And, with hoods upon their eyelids,
 scream the falcons for their prey.

See, the Queen of the chase advances!
 Frithiof, gaze not at the sight!

Like a star upon a spring-cloud sits she
 on her palfrey white.
Half of Freya, half of Rota, yet more
 beauteous than these two,
And from her light hat of purple wave
 aloft the feathers blue.

Gaze not at her eyes' blue heaven, gaze
 not at her golden hair!
Oh beware! her waist is slender, full
 her bosom is, beware!
Look not at the rose and lily on her
 cheek that shifting play,
List not to the voice beloved, whispering like the wind of May.

Now the huntsman's band is ready.
 Hurrah! over hill and dale!
Horns ring, and the hawks right up-
 ward to the hall of Odin sail.
All the dwellers in the forest seek in
 fear their cavern homes,
But, with spear outstretched before her,
 after them the Valkyr comes.

. . . .

Then threw Frithiof down his mantle, and upon the greensward
 spread,
And the ancient king so trustful laid on
 Frithiof's knee his head,
Slept as calmly as the hero sleepeth,
 after war's alarm,
On his shield, or as an infant sleeps
 upon its mother's arm.

As he slumbers, hark! there sings a
 coal-black bird upon the bough;
"Hasten, Frithiof, slay the old man,
 end your quarrel at a blow:
Take his queen, for she is thine, and
 once the bridal kiss she gave,
Now no human eye beholds thee, deep
 and silent is the grave."

Frithiof listens; hark! there sings a
 snow-white bird upon the bough:
"Though no human eye beholds thee,
 Odin's eye beholds thee now.
Coward! wilt thou murder sleep, and a
 defenceless old man slay!
Whatsoe'er thou winn'st, thou canst not
 win a hero's fame this way."

Thus the two wood-birds did warble:
 Frithiof took his war-sword good,

With a shudder hurled it from him, far
  into the gloomy wood.
Coal-black bird flies down to Nastrand,
  but on light, unfolded wings,
Like the tone of harps, the other, sounding towards the sun, upsprings.

Straight the ancient king awakens.
  "Sweet has been my sleep," he
  said;
"Pleasantly sleeps one in the shadow,
  guarded by a brave man's blade.
But where is thy sword, O stranger?
  Lightning's brother, where is
  he?
Who thus parts you, who should never
  from each other parted be?"

"It avails not," Frithiof answered; "in
  the North are other swords:
Sharp, O monarch! is the sword's
  tongue, and it speaks not peaceful
  words;
Murky spirits dwell in steel blades,
  spirits from the Niffelhem;
Slumber is not safe before them, silver
  locks but anger them."

IV.

FRITHIOF'S FAREWELL.

No more shall I see
In its upward motion
The smoke of the Northland.   Man is a
  slave:
The fates decree.
On the waste of the ocean
There is my fatherland, there is my
  grave.

Go not to the strand,
Ring, with thy bride,
After the stars spread their light through
  the sky.
Perhaps in the sand,
Washed up by the tide,
The bones of the outlawed Viking may
  lie.

Then, quoth the king,
"'T is mournful to hear
A man like a whimpering maiden cry.
The death-song they sing
Even now in mine ear.
What avails it?   He who is born must
  die."

CHILDHOOD.

(DA JEG VAR LILLE.)

BY JENS IMMANUEL BAGGESEN.

THERE was a time when I was very
  small,
  When my whole frame was but an ell
    in height;
Sweetly, as I recall it, tears do fall,
  And therefore I recall it with delight.

I sported in my tender mother's arms,
  And rode a-horseback on best father's
    knee;
Alike were sorrows, passions and alarms,
  And gold, and Greek, and love, un-
    known to me.

Then seemed to me this world far less in
  size,
  Likewise it seemed to me less wicked
    far;
Like points in heaven, I saw the stars
  arise,
  And longed for wings that I might
    catch a star.

I saw the moon behind the island fade,
  And thought, "Oh, were I on that
    island there,
I could find out of what the moon is
  made,
  Find out how large it is, how round,
    how fair!"

Wondering, I saw God's sun, through
  western skies,
  Sink in the ocean's golden lap at
    night,
And yet upon the morrow early rise,
  And paint the eastern heaven with
    crimson light;

And thought of God, the gracious
  Heavenly Father,
  Who made me, and that lovely sun on
    high,
And all those pearls of heaven thick-
  strung together,
  Dropped, clustering, from his hand
    o'er all the sky.

With childish reverence, my young lips
  did say
  The prayer my pious mother taught
    to me:

"O gentle God! oh, let me strive alway
  Still to be wise, and good, and follow
    Thee!"

So prayed I for my father and my
    mother,
  And for my sister, and for all the
    town;
The king I knew not, and the beggar-
    brother,
  Who, bent with age, went, sighing,
    up and down.

They perished, the blithe days of boy-
    hood perished,
  And all the gladness, all the peace I
    knew!
Now have I but their memory, fondly
    cherished; —
  God! may I never lose that too!

FROM THE GERMAN.

SILENT LOVE.

Who love would seek,
  Let him love evermore
And seldom speak;
  For in love's domain
  Silence must reign;
Or it brings the heart
  Smart
      And pain.

BLESSED ARE THE DEAD.

(Selig sind, die in dem Herrn sterben.)

BY SIMON DACH.

Oh, how blest are ye whose toils are
    ended!
Who, through death, have unto God
    ascended!
Ye have arisen
From the cares which keep us still in
    prison.

We are still as in a dungeon living,
Still oppressed with sorrow and misgiv-
    ing;
Our undertakings
Are but toils, and troubles, and heart-
    breakings.

Ye meanwhile, are in your chambers
    sleeping,

Quiet, and set free from all our weep-
    ing;
No cross nor trial
Hinders your enjoyments with denial.

Christ has wiped away your tears for
    ever;
Ye have that for which we still endeavor.
To you are chanted
Songs which yet no mortal ear have
    haunted.

Ah! who would not, then, depart with
    gladness,
To inherit heaven for earthly sadness?
Who here would languish
Longer in bewailing and in anguish?

Come, O Christ, and loose the chains
    that bind us!
Lead us forth, and cast this world be-
    hind us!
With Thee, the Anointed,
Finds the soul its joy and rest appointed.

FROM THE ANGLO-SAXON.

BEOWULF'S EXPEDITION TO HEORT.

Thus then, much care-worn,
The son of Healfden
Sorrowed evermore,
Nor might the prudent hero
His woes avert.
The war was too hard,
Too loath and longsome,
That on the people came,
Dire wrath and grim,
Of night-woes the worst.
This from home heard
Higelac's Thane,
Good among the Goths,
Grendel's deeds.
He was of mankind
In might the strongest,
At that day
Of this life,
Noble and stalwart.
He bade him a sea-ship,
A goodly one, prepare.
Quoth he, the war-king,
Over the swan's road,
Seek he would
The mighty monarch,
Since he wanted men.

For him that journey
His prudent fellows
Straight made ready,
Those that loved him.
They excited their souls,
The omen they beheld.
Had the good-man
Of the Gothic people
Champions chosen,
Of those that keenest
He might find,
Some fifteen men.
The sea-wood sought he.
The warrior showed,
Sea-crafty man!
The land-marks,
And first went forth.
The ship was on the waves,
Boat under the cliffs.
The barons ready
To the prow mounted.
The streams they whirled
The sea against the sands.
The chieftains bore
On the naked breast
Bright ornaments,
War-gear, Goth-like.
The men shoved off,
Men on their willing way,
The bounden wood.
Then went over the sea-waves,
Hurried by the wind,
The ship with foamy neck,
Most like a sea-fowl,
Till about one hour
Of the second day
The curved prow
Had passed onward
So that the sailors
The land saw,
The shore-cliffs shining,
Mountains steep,
And broad sea-noses.
Then was the sea-sailing
Of the Earl at an end.
Then up speedily
The Weather people
On the land went,
The sea-bark moored,
Their mail-sarks shook,
Their war-weeds.
God thanked they,
That to them the sea-journey
Easy had been.
Then from the wall beheld
The warden of the Scyldings,
He who the sea-cliffs
Had in his keeping,

Bear o'er the balks
The bright shields,
The war-weapons speedily.
Him the doubt disturbed
In his mind's thought,
What these men might be.
Went then to the shore,
On his steed riding,
The Thane of Hrothgar.
Before the host he shook
His warden's-staff in hand,
In measured words demanded:
"What men are ye
War-gear wearing,
Host in harness,
Who thus the brown keel
Over the water-street
Leading come
Hither over the sea?
I these boundaries
As shore-warden hold,
That in the Land of the Danes
Nothing loathsome
With a ship-crew
Scathe us might. . . .
Ne'er saw I mightier
Earl upon earth
Than is your own,
Hero in harness.
Not seldom this warrior
Is in weapons distinguished;
Never his beauty belies him,
His peerless countenance!
Now would I fain
Your origin know,
Ere ye forth
As false spies
Into the Land of the Danes
Farther fare.
Now, ye dwellers afar-off!
Ye sailors of the sea!
Listen to my
One-fold thought.
Quickest is best
To make known
Whence your coming may be."

THE SOUL'S COMPLAINT AGAINST THE BODY.

MUCH it behoveth
Each one of mortals,
That he his soul's journey
In himself ponder,
How deep it may be.
When Death cometh,
The bonds he breaketh

By which were united
The soul and the body.

Long it is thenceforth
Ere the soul taketh
From God himself
Its woe or its weal;
As in the world erst,
Even in its earth-vessel,
It wrought before.

The soul shall come
Wailing with loud voice,
After a sennight,
The soul, to find
The body
That it erst dwelt in; —
Three hundred winters,
Unless ere that worketh
The Eternal Lord,
The Almighty God,
The end of the world.

Crieth then, so care-worn,
With cold utterance,
And speaketh grimly,
The ghost to the dust:
"Dry dust! thou dreary one!
How little didst thou labor for me!
In the foulness of earth
Thou all wearest away
Like to the loam!
Little didst thou think
How thy soul's journey
Would be thereafter,
When from the body
It should be led forth."

FROM THE FRENCH.

SONG, FROM THE PARADISE OF LOVE.

Hark! hark!
Pretty lark!
Little heedest thou my pain!
But if to these longing arms
Pitying Love would yield the charms
Of the fair
With smiling air,
Blithe would beat my heart again.

Hark! hark!
Pretty lark!
Little heedest thou my pain!
Love may force me still to bear,

While he lists, consuming care;
But in anguish
Though I languish,
Faithful shall my heart remain.

Hark! hark!
Pretty lark!
Little heedest thou my pain!
Then cease, Love, to torment me so;
But rather than all thoughts forego
Of the fair
With flaxen hair,
Give me back her frowns again.

Hark! hark!
Pretty lark!
Little heedest thou my pain!

SONG.

And whither goest thou, gentle sigh,
    Breathed so softly in my ear?
    Say, dost thou bear his fate severe
To Love's poor martyr doomed to die?
Come, tell me quickly, — do not lie;
    What secret message bring'st thou
        here?
And whither goest thou, gentle sigh,
    Breathed so softly in my ear?
May Heaven conduct thee to thy will
    And safely speed thee on thy way;
    This only I would humbly pray, —
Pierce deep, — but oh! forbear to kill.
And whither goest thou, gentle sigh,
    Breathed so softly in my ear?

THE RETURN OF SPRING.

(Renouveau.)

BY CHARLES D'ORLEANS.

Now Time throws off his cloak again
Of ermined frost, and wind, and rain,
And clothes him in the embroidery
Of glittering sun and clear blue sky.
With beast and bird the forest rings,
Each in his jargon cries or sings;
And Time throws off his cloak again.
Of ermined frost, and wind, and rain.

River, and fount, and tinkling brook
Wear in their dainty livery
Drops of silver jewelry;
In new-made suit they merry look;
And Time throws off his cloak again
Of ermined frost, and wind, and rain.

DEATH OF ARCHBISHOP TURPIN.

FROM THE CHANSON DE ROLAND.

THE Archbishop, whom God loved in high degree,
Beheld his wounds all bleeding fresh and free;
And then his cheek more ghastly grew and wan,
And a faint shudder through his members ran.
Upon the battle-field his knee was bent;
Brave Roland saw, and to his succor went,
Straightway his helmet from his brow unlaced,
And tore the shining hauberk from his breast.
Then raising in his arms the man of God,
Gently he laid him on the verdant sod.
"Rest, Sire," he cried, — "for rest thy suffering needs."
The priest replied, "Think but of warlike deeds!
The field is ours; well may we boast this strife!
But death steals on, — there is no hope of life;
In paradise, where Almoners live again,
There are our couches spread, there shall we rest from pain."

Sore Roland grieved; nor marvel I, alas!
That thrice he swooned upon the thick green grass.
When he revived, with a loud voice cried he,
"O Heavenly Father! Holy Saint Marie!
Why lingers death to lay me in my grave!
Beloved France! how have the good and brave
Been torn from thee, and left thee weak and poor!"
Then thoughts of Aude, his lady-love, came o'er
His spirit, and he whispered soft and slow,
"My gentle friend! — what parting full of woe!
Never so true a liegeman shalt thou see; —
Whate'er my fate, Christ's benison on thee!
Christ, who did save from realms of woe beneath,

The Hebrew Prophets from the second death."
Then to the Paladins, whom well he knew,
He went, and one by one unaided drew
To Turpin's side, well skilled in ghostly lore; —
No heart had he to smile, but, weeping sore,
He blessed them in God's name, with faith that He
Would soon vouchsafe to them a glad eternity.

The Archbishop, then, on whom God's benison rest,
Exhausted, bowed his head upon his breast; —
His mouth was full of dust and clotted gore,
And many a wound his swollen visage bore.
Slow beats his heart, his panting bosom heaves,
Death comes apace, — no hope of cure relieves.
Towards heaven he raised his dying hands and prayed
That God, who for our sins was mortal made,
Born of the Virgin, scorned and crucified,
In paradise would place him by His side.

Then Turpin died in service of Charlon,
In battle great and eke great orison; —
'Gainst Pagan host alway strong champion;
God grant to him His holy benison.

FRIAR LUBIN.

(LE FRÈRE LUBIN.)

BY CLEMENT MAROT.

To gallop off to town post-haste,
  So oft, the times I cannot tell;
To do vile deed, nor feel disgraced, —
  Friar Lubin will do it well.
But a sober life to lead,
  To honor virtue, and pursue it,
That 's a pious, Christian deed, —
  Friar Lubin cannot do it.

To mingle, with a knowing smile,
  The goods of others with his own,
And leave you without cross or pile,

Friar Lubin stands alone.
To say 't is yours is all in vain,
  If once he lays his finger to it;
For as to giving back again,
  Friar Lubin cannot do it.

With flattering words and gentle tone,
  To woo and win some guileless maid,
Cunning pander need you none, —
  Friar Lubin knows the trade.
Loud preacheth he sobriety,
  But as for water, doth eschew it;
Your dog may drink it, — but not he;
  Friar Lubin cannot do it.

ENVOY.

When an evil deed 's to do
  Friar Lubin is stout and true;
Glimmers a ray of goodness through it,
  Friar Lubin cannot do it.

RONDEL.

BY JEAN FROISSART.

LOVE, love, what wilt thou with this
    heart of mine?
  Naught see I fixed or sure in thee!
I do not know thee, — nor what deeds
    are thine:
Love, love, what wilt thou with this heart
    of mine?
  Naught see I fixed or sure in thee!

Shall I be mute, or vows with prayers
    combine?
  Ye who are blessed in loving, tell it
    me:
Love, love, what wilt thou with this heart
    of mine?
  Naught see I permanent or sure in
    thee!

MY SECRET.

BY FÉLIX ARVERS.

MY soul its secret has, my life too has
    its mystery,
A love eternal in a moment's space con-
    ceived;
Hopeless the evil is, I have not told its
    history,
And she who was the cause nor knew it
    nor believed.
Alas! I shall have passed close by her
    unperceived,

Forever at her side, and yet forever
    lonely,
I shall unto the end have made life's
    journey, only
Daring to ask for naught, and having
    naught received.
For her, though God has made her gentle
    and endearing,
She will go on her way distraught and
    without hearing
These murmurings of love that round
    her steps ascend,
Piously faithful still unto her austere
    duty,
Will say, when she shall read these lines
    full of her beauty,
"Who can this woman be?" and will
    not comprehend.

FROM THE ITALIAN.

THE NATURE OF LOVE.

BY GUIDO GUINIZELLI.

To noble heart Love doth for shelter
    fly,
As seeks the bird the forest's leafy shade;
Love was not felt till noble heart beat
    high,
Nor before love the noble heart was
    made.
  Soon as the sun's broad flame
Was formed, so soon the clear light
    filled the air;
  Yet was not till he came:
So love springs up in noble breasts, and
    there
  Has its appointed space,
As heat in the bright flames finds its
    allotted place.
Kindles in noble heart the fire of love,
As hidden virtue in the precious stone:
This virtue comes not from the stars
    above,
Till round it the ennobling sun has
    shone;
  But when his powerful blaze
Has drawn forth what was vile, the stars
    impart
  Strange virtue in their rays;
And thus when Nature doth create the
    heart
  Noble and pure and high,
Like virtue from the star, love comes
    from woman's eye.

NOTES.

NOTES.

Page 11. *Coplas de Manrique.*

This poem of Manrique is a great favorite in Spain. No less than four poetic Glosses, or running commentaries, upon it have been published, no one of which, however, possesses great poetic merit. That of the Carthusian monk, Rodrigo de Valdepeñas, is the best. It is known as the *Closa del Cartujo.* There is also a prose Commentary by Luis de Aranda.

The following stanzas of the poem were found in the author's pocket, after his death on the field of battle.

" O World! so few the years we live,
Would that the life which thou dost give
Were life indeed '
Alas! thy sorrows fall so fast,
Our happiest hour is when at last
The soul is freed.

" Our days are covered o'er with grief,
And sorrows neither few nor brief
Veil all in gloom;
Left desolate of real good,
Within this cheerless solitude
No pleasures bloom.

" Thy pilgrimage begins in tears,
And ends in bitter doubts and fears,
Or dark despair;
Midway so many toils appear,
That he who lingers longest here
Knows most of care.

" Thy goods are bought with many a groan,
By the hot sweat of toil alone,
And weary hearts;
Fleet-footed is the approach of woe,
But with a lingering step and slow
Its form departs."

Page 21. *King Christian.*

Nils Juel was a celebrated Danish Admiral, and Peder Wessel, a Vice-Admiral, who for his great prowess received the popular title of Tordenskiold, or Thundershield. In childhood he was a tailor's apprentice, and rose to his high rank before the age of twenty-eight, when he was killed in a duel.

Page 25. *The Skeleton in Armor.*

This Ballad was suggested to me while riding on the sea-shore at Newport. A year or two previous a skeleton had been dug up at Fall River, clad in broken and corroded armor; and the idea occurred to me of connecting it with the Round Tower at Newport, generally known hitherto as the Old Windmill, though now claimed by the Danes as a work of their early ancestors. Professor Rafn, in the *Mémoires de la Société Royale des Antiquaires du Nord,* for 1838-1839, says: —

" There is no mistaking in this instance the style in which the more ancient stone edifices of the North were constructed, — the style which belongs to the Roman or Ante-Gothic architecture, and which, especially after the time of Charlemagne, diffused itself from Italy over the whole of the West and North of Europe, where it continued to predominate until the close of the twelfth century, — that style which some authors have, from one of its most striking characteristics, called the round arch style, the same which in England is denominated Saxon and sometimes Norman architecture.

" On the ancient structure in Newport there are no ornaments remaining, which might possibly have served to guide us in assigning the probable date of its erection. That no vestige whatever is found of the pointed arch, nor any approximation to it, is indicative of an earlier rather than of a later period. From such characteristics as remain, however, we can scarcely form any other inference than one, in which I am persuaded that all who are familiar with Old - Northern architecture will concur, THAT THIS BUILDING WAS ERECTED AT A PERIOD DECIDEDLY NOT LATER THAN THE TWELFTH CENTURY. This remark applies, of course, to the original building only, and not to the alterations that it subsequently received; for there are several such alterations in the upper part of the building which cannot be mistaken, and which were most likely occasioned by its being adapted in modern times to various uses ; for example, as the substructure of a windmill, and latterly as a hay magazine. To the same times may be referred the windows, the fireplace, and the apertures made above the columns. That this building could not have been erected for a windmill, is what an architect will easily discern."

I will not enter into a discussion of the point. It is sufficiently well established for the purpose of a ballad ; though doubtless many a citizen of Newport, who has passed his days within sight of the Round Tower, will be ready to exclaim, with Sancho : " God bless me ! did I not warn you to have a care of what you were doing, for that it was nothing but a windmill ; and nobody could mistake it, but one who had the like in his head."

Page 27. *Skoal !*

In Scandinavia, this is the customary salutation when drinking a health. I have slightly changed the orthography of the word, in order to preserve the correct pronunciation.

Page 28. *The Luck of Edenhall.*

The tradition upon which this ballad is founded, and the " shards of the Luck of Edenhall," still exist in England. The goblet is in the possession of Sir Christopher Musgrave, Bart., of Eden Hall, Cumberland ; and is not so entirely shattered as the ballad leaves it.

Page 29. *The Elected Knight.*

This strange and somewhat mystical ballad is from Nyerup and Rahbek's *Danske Viser* of the Middle Ages. It seems to refer to the first preaching of Christianity in the North, and to the institution of Knight-Errantry. The three maidens I suppose to be Faith, Hope, and Charity. The irregularities of the original have been carefully preserved in the translation.

Page 29. *The Children of the Lord's Supper.*

There is something patriarchal still lingering about rural life in Sweden, which renders it a fit theme for song. Almost primeval simplicity reigns over that Northern land, — almost primeval solitude and stillness. You pass out from the gate of the city, and, as if by magic, the scene changes to a wild, woodland landscape. Around you are forests of fir. Overhead hang the long, fan-like branches, trailing with moss, and heavy with red and blue cones. Under foot is a carpet of yellow leaves ; and the air is warm and balmy. On a wooden bridge you cross a little silver stream ; and anon come forth into a pleasant and sunny land of farms. Wooden fences divide the adjoining fields. Across the road are gates, which are opened by troops of children. The peasants take off their hats as you pass ; you sneeze, and they cry, " God bless you ! " The houses in the villages and smaller towns are all built of hewn timber, and for the most part painted red. The floors of the taverns are strewn with the fragrant tips of fir boughs. In many villages there are no taverns, and the peasants take turns in receiving travellers. The thrifty housewife shows you into the best chamber, the walls of which are hung round with rude pictures from the Bible ; and brings you her heavy silver spoons, — an heirloom, — to dip the curdled milk from the pan. You have oaten cakes baked some months before, or bread with anise-seed and coriander in it, or perhaps a little pine bark.

Meanwhile the sturdy husband has brought his horses from the plough, and harnessed them to your carriage. Solitary travellers come and go in uncouth one-horse chaises. Most of them have pipes in their mouths, and, hanging around their necks in front, a leather wallet, in which they carry tobacco, and the great bank-notes of the country, as large as your two hands. You meet, also, groups of Dalekarlian peasant-women, travelling homeward or townward in pursuit of work. They walk barefoot, carrying in their hands their shoes, which have high heels under the hollow of the foot, and soles of birch bark.

Frequent, too, are the village churches, standing by the roadside, each in its own little Garden of Gethsemane. In the parish register great events are doubtless recorded. Some old king was christened or buried in that church ; and a little sexton, with a rusty key, shows you the baptismal font, or the coffin. In the churchyard are a few flowers, and much green grass ; and daily the shadow of the church spire, with its long, tapering finger, counts the tombs, representing a dial-plate of human life, on which the hours and minutes are the graves of men. The stones are flat, and large, and low, and perhaps sunken, like the roofs of old houses. On some are armorial bearings ; on others only the initials of the poor tenants, with a date, as on the roofs of Dutch cottages. They all sleep with their heads to the westward. Each held a lighted taper in his hand when he died ; and in his coffin were placed his lit tle heart-treasures, and a piece of money for his last journey. Babes that came lifeless into the world were carried in the arms of gray-haired old men to the only cradle they ever slept in; and in the shroud of the dead mother were laid the little garments of the child that lived and died in her bosom. And over this scene the village pastor looks from his window in the stillness of midnight, and says in his heart, "How quietly they rest, all the departed!"

Near the churchyard gate stands a poor-box, fastened to a post by iron bands, and secured by a padlock, with a sloping wooden roof to keep off the rain. If it be Sunday, the peasants sit on the church steps and con their psalm-books. Others are coming down the road with their beloved pastor, who talks to them of holy things from beneath his broad-brimmed hat. He speaks of fields and harvests, and of the parable of the sower, that went forth to sow. He leads them to the Good Shepherd, and to the pleasant pastures of the spirit-land. He is their patriarch, and, like Melchizedek, both priest and king, though he has no other throne than the church pulpit. The women carry psalm-books in their hands, wrapped in silk handkerchiefs, and listen devoutly to the good man's words. But the young men, like Gallio, care for none of these things. They are busy counting the plaits in the kirtles of the peasant-girls, their number being an indication of the wearer's wealth. It may end in a wedding.

I will endeavor to describe a village wedding in Sweden. It shall be in summertime, that there may be flowers, and in a southern province, that the bride may be fair. The early song of the lark and of chanticleer are mingling in the clear morning air, and the sun, the heavenly bridegroom with golden locks, arises in the east, just as our earthly bridegroom with yellow hair arises in the south. In the yard there is a sound of voices and trampling of hoofs, and horses are led forth and saddled. The steed that is to bear the bridegroom has a bunch of flowers upon his forehead, and a garland of corn-flowers around his neck. Friends from the neighboring farms come riding in, their blue cloaks streaming to the wind; and finally the happy bridegroom, with a whip in his hand, and a monstrous nosegay in the breast of his black jacket, comes forth from his chamber; and then to horse and away, towards the village where the bride already sits and waits.

Foremost rides the spokesman, followed by some half-dozen village musicians. Next comes the bridegroom between his two groomsmen, and then forty or fifty friends and wedding guests, half of them perhaps with pistols and guns in their hands. A kind of baggage-wagon brings up the rear, laden with food and drink for these merry pilgrims. At the entrance of every village stands a triumphal arch, adorned with flowers and ribbons and evergreens; and as they pass beneath it the wedding guests fire a salute, and the whole procession stops. And straight from every pocket flies a black-jack, filled with punch or brandy. It is passed from hand to hand among the crowd; provisions are brought from the wagon, and after eating and drinking and hurrahing the procession moves forward again, and at length draws near the house of the bride. Four heralds ride forward to announce that a knight and his attendants are in the neighboring forest, and pray for hospitality. "How many are you?" asks the bride's father. "At least three hundred," is the answer; and to this the host replies, "Yes; were you seven times as many, you should all be welcome: and in token thereof receive this cup." Whereupon each herald receives a can of ale; and soon after the whole jovial company comes storming into the farmer's yard, and, riding round the May-pole, which stands in the centre, alights amid a grand salute and flourish of music.

In the hall sits the bride, with a crown upon her head and a tear in her eye, like the Virgin Mary in old church paintings. She is dressed in a red bodice and kirtle with loose linen sleeves. There is a gilded belt around her waist; and around her neck strings of golden beads, and a golden chain. On the crown rests a wreath of wild roses, and below it another of cypress. Loose over her shoulders falls her flaxen hair: and her blue innocent eyes are fixed upon the ground. O thou good soul! thou hast hard hands, but a soft heart! Thou art poor. The very ornaments thou wearest are not thine. They have been hired for this great day. Yet art thou rich; rich in health, rich in hope, rich in thy first, young, fervent love. The blessing of Heaven be upon thee! So thinks the parish priest, as he joins together the hands of bride and bridegroom, saying in deep, solemn tones, — "I give thee in marriage this damsel, to be thy wedded wife in all honor, and to share the half of thy bed, thy lock and key, and every third penny which you two may possess, or may inherit, and all the rights which Upland's laws provide, and the holy King Erik gave."

The dinner is now served, and the bride sits between the bridegroom and the priest. The spokesman delivers an oration after the ancient custom of his fathers. He interlards it well with quotations from the Bible ; and invites the Saviour to be present at this marriage feast, as he was at the marriage feast in Cana of Galilee. The table is not sparingly set forth. Each makes a long arm and the feast goes cheerly on. Punch and brandy pass round between the courses, and here and there a pipe is smoked while waiting for the next dish. They sit long at table ; but, as all things must have an end, so must a Swedish dinner. Then the dance begins. It is led off by the bride and the priest, who perform a solemn minuet together. Not till after midnight comes the last dance. The girls form a ring around the bride, to keep her from the hands of the married women, who endeavor to break through the magic circle, and seize their new sister. After long struggling they succeed ; and the crown is taken from her head and the jewels from her neck, and her bodice is unlaced and her kirtle taken off ; and like a vestal virgin clad all in white she goes, but it is to her marriage chamber, not to her grave ; and the wedding guests follow her with lighted candles in their hands. And this is a village bridal.

Nor must I forget the suddenly changing seasons of the Northern clime. There is no long and lingering spring, unfolding leaf and blossom one by one ; no long and lingering autumn, pompous with many-colored leaves and the glow of Indian summers. But winter and summer are wonderful, and pass into each other. The quail has hardly ceased piping in the corn, when winter from the folds of trailing clouds sows broadcast over the land snow, icicles, and rattling hail. The days wane apace. Erelong the sun hardly rises above the horizon, or does not rise at all. The moon and the stars shine through the day ; only, at noon, they are pale and wan, and in the southern sky a red, fiery glow, as of sunset, burns along the horizon, and then goes out. And pleasantly under the silver moon, and under the silent, solemn stars, ring the steel-shoes of the skaters on the frozen sea, and voices, and the sound of bells.

And now the Northern Lights begin to burn, faintly at first, like sunbeams playing in the waters of the blue sea. Then a soft crimson glow tinges the heavens. There is a blush on the cheek of night. The colors come and go, and change from crimson to gold, from gold to crimson. The snow is stained with rosy light. Two-

fold from the zenith, east and west, flames a fiery sword ; and a broad band passes athwart the heavens like a summer sunset. Soft purple clouds come sailing over the sky, and through their vapory folds the winking stars shine white as silver. With such pomp as this is Merry Christmas ushered in, though only a single star heralded the first Christmas. And in memory of that day the Swedish peasants dance on straw ; and the peasant-girls throw straws at the timbered roof of the hall, and for every one that sticks in a crack shall a groomsman come to their wedding. Merry Christmas indeed ! For pious souls there shall be church songs and sermons, but for Swedish peasants, brandy and nut-brown ale in wooden bowls ; and the great Yule-cake crowned with a cheese, and garlanded with apples, and upholding a three-armed candlestick over the Christmas feast. They may tell tales, too, of Jöns Lundsbracka, and Lunkenfus, and the great Riddar Finke of Pingsdaga.*

And now the glad, leafy midsummer full of blossoms and the song of nightingales, is come ! Saint John has taken the flowers and festival of heathen Balder ; and in every village there is a May-pole fifty feet high, with wreaths and roses and ribbons streaming in the wind, and a noisy weather-cock on top, to tell the village whence the wind cometh and whither it goeth. The sun does not set till ten o'clock at night ; and the children are at play in the streets an hour later. The windows and doors are all open, and you may sit and read till midnight without a candle. O, how beautiful is the summer night, which is not night, but a sunless yet unclouded day, descending upon earth with dews and shadows and refreshing coolness ! How beautiful the long, mild twilight, which like a silver clasp unites to-day with yesterday ! How beautiful the silent hour, when Morning and Evening thus sit together, hand in hand, beneath the starless sky of midnight ! From the church-tower in the public square the bell tolls the hour, with a soft, musical chime ; and the watchman, whose watch-tower is the belfry, blows a blast in his horn, for each stroke of the hammer, and four times, to the four corners of the heavens, in a sonorous voice he chants, —

> " Ho ! watchman, ho !
> Twelve is the clock !
> God keep our town
> From fire and brand
> And hostile hand !
> Twelve is the clock ! "

From his swallow's nest in the belfry he

* Titles of Swedish popular tales.

can see the sun all night long ; and farther north the priest stands at his door in the warm midnight, and lights his pipe with a common burning-glass.

Page 30. *The Feast of the Leafy Pavilions.*

In Swedish, *Löfhyddohögtiden*, the Leaf-huts'-high-tide.

Page 30. *Hörberg.*

The peasant-painter of Sweden. He is known chiefly by his altar-pieces in the village churches.

Page 30. *Wallin.*

A distinguished pulpit-orator and poet. He is particularly remarkable for the beauty and sublimity of his psalms.

Page 45. *As Lope says.*

" La cólera
de un Español sentado no se templa,
sino le representan en dos horas
hasta el final juicio desde el Génesis."
Lope de Vega.

Page 46. *Abrenuncio Satanas!*

" Digo, Señora, respondió Sancho, lo que tengo dicho, que de los azotes abernuncio. Abrenuncio, habeis de decir, Sancho, y no como decis, dijo el Duque." — *Don Quixote,* Part II. ch. 35.

Page 50. *Fray Carrillo.*

The allusion here is to a Spanish Epigram.

" Siempre Fray Carrillo estás
cansándonos acá fuera ;
quien en tu celda estuviera
para no verte jamas ! "
Böhl de Faber. Floresta, No. 611.

Page 50. *Padre Francisco.*

This is from an Italian popular song.

" ' Padre Francesco,
Padre Francesco ! '
— Cosa volete del Padre Francesco ? —
' V' è una bella ragazzina
Che si vuole confessar ! '
Fatte l' entrare, fatte l' entrare !
Che la voglio confessare."
Kopisch. Volksthümliche Poesien aus allen Mundarten Italiens und seiner Inseln, p. 194.

Page 51. *Ave ! cujus calcem clare.*

From a monkish hymn of the twelfth century, in Sir Alexander Croke's *Essay on the Origin, Progress, and Decline of Rhyming Latin Verse,* p. 109.

Page 54. *The gold of the Busné.*

Busné is the name given by the Gypsies to all who are not of their race.

Page 54. *Count of the Calés.*

The Gypsies call themselves Calés. See Borrow's valuable and extremely interesting work, *The Zincali; or an Account of the Gypsies in Spain.* London, 1841.

Page 56. *Asks if his money-bags would rise.*

" ¿ Y volviéndome á un lado, ví á un Avariento, que estaba preguntando á otro, (que por haber sido embalsamado, y estar léxos sus tripas no hablaba, porque no habian llegado si habian de resucitar aquel dia todos los enterrados) si resucitarian unos bolsones suyos ? " — *El Sueño de las Calaveras.*

Page 56. *And amen ! said my Cid the Campeador.*

A line from the ancient *Poema del Cid.*

" Amen, dixo Mio Cid el Campeador."
Line 3044

Page 56. *The river of his thoughts.*

This expression is from Dante ;

" Si che chiaro
Per essa scenda della mente il fiume."

Byron has likewise used the expression ; though I do not recollect in which of his poems.

Page 57. *Mari Franca.*

A common Spanish proverb, used to turn aside a question one does not wish to answer ;

" Porque casó Mari Franca
quatro leguas de Salamanca."

Page 57. *Ay, soft, emerald eyes.*

The Spaniards, with good reason, consider this color of the eye as beautiful, and celebrate it in song ; as, for example, in the well-known *Villancico :*

" Ay ojuelos verdes,
ay los mis ojuelos,
ay hagan los cielos
que de mí te acuerdes !

Tengo confianza
de mis verdes ojos."
Böhl de Faber. Floresta, No. 255

Dante speaks of Beatrice's eyes as emeralds. *Purgatorio,* xxxi. 116. Lami says, in his *Annotazioni,* " Erano i suoi occhi d' un turchino verdiccio, simile a quel del mare."

Page 58. *The Avenging Child.*

See the ancient Ballads of *El Infante Vengador,* and *Calaynos.*

Page 58. *All are sleeping.*

From the Spanish. *Böhl de Faber. Floresta,* No. 282.

Page 63. *Good night.*

From the Spanish ; as are likewise the
songs immediately following, and that
which commences the first scene of Act III.

Page 70. *The evil eye.*

" In the Gitano language, casting the
evil eye is called *Querelar nasula*, which
simply means making sick, and which, according to the common superstition, is
accomplished by casting an evil look at
people, especially children, who, from the
tenderness of their constitution, are supposed to be more easily blighted than those
of a more mature age. After receiving the
evil glance, they fall sick, and die in a few
hours.

" The Spaniards have very little to say
respecting the evil eye, though the belief
in it is very prevalent, especially in Andalusia, amongst the lower orders. A stag's
horn is considered a good safeguard, and
on that account a small horn, tipped with
silver, is frequently attached to the children's necks by means of a cord braided
from the hair of a black mare's tail.
Should the evil glance be cast, it is imagined that the horn receives it, and instantly snaps asunder. Such horns may
be purchased in some of the silversmiths'
shops at Seville." — BORROW'S *Zincali*,
Vol. I. ch. ix.

Page 70. *On the top of a mountain I
stand.*

This and the following scraps of song
are from Borrow's *Zincali ; or an Account
of the Gypsies in Spain.*
The Gypsy words in the same scene may
be thus interpreted : —
John-Dorados, pieces of gold.
Pigeon, a simpleton.
In your morocco, stripped.
Doves, sheets.
Moon, a shirt.
Chirelin, a thief.
Murcigalleros, those who steal at night-
fall.
Rastilleros, footpads.
Hermit, highway-robber.
Planets, candles.
Commandments, the fingers.
Saint Martin asleep, to rob a person
asleep.
Lanterns, eyes.
Goblin, police officer.
Papagayo, a spy.
Vineyards and Dancing John, to take
flight.

Page 74. *If thou art sleeping, maiden.*

From the Spanish ; as is likewise the
song of the Contrabandista on page 75.

Page 77. *All the Foresters of Flanders.*

The title of Foresters was given to the
early governors of Flanders, appointed by
the kings of France. Lyderick du Bucq,
in the days of Clotaire the Second, was the
first of them ; and Beaudoin Bras-de-Fer,
who stole away the fair Judith, daughter
of Charles the Bald, from the French
court, and married her in Bruges, was the
last. After him the title of Forester was
changed to that of Count. Philippe d'Alsace, Guy de Dampierre, and Louis de
Crécy, coming later in the order of time,
were therefore rather Counts than Foresters. Philippe went twice to the Holy
Land as a Crusader, and died of the plague
at St. Jean-d'Acre, shortly after the capture of the city by the Christians. Guy
de Dampierre died in the prison of Compiègne. Louis de Crécy was son and successor of Robert de Béthune, who strangled
his wife, Yolande de Bourgogne, with the
bridle of his horse, for having poisoned, at
the age of eleven years, Charles, his son
by his first wife, Blanche d'Anjou.

Page 77. *Stately dames, like queens attended.*

When Philippe-le-Bel, king of France,
visited Flanders with his queen, she was
so astonished at the magnificence of the
dames of Bruges, that she exclaimed :
" Je croyais être seule reine ici, mais il
paraît que ceux de Flandre qui se trouvent
dans nos prisons sont tous des princes, car
leurs femmes sont habillées comme des
princesses et des reines."
When the burgomasters of Ghent, Bruges, and Ypres went to Paris to pay
homage to King John, in 1351, they were
received with great pomp and distinction ;
but, being invited to a festival, they observed that their seats at table were not
furnished with cushions ; whereupon, to
make known their displeasure at this want
of regard to their dignity, they folded
their richly embroidered cloaks and seated
themselves upon them. On rising from
table, they left their cloaks behind them,
and, being informed of their apparent forgetfulness, Simon van Eertrycke, burgomaster of Bruges, replied, " We Flemings
are not in the habit of carrying away our
cushions after dinner."

Page 77. *Knights who bore the Fleece
of Gold.*

Philippe de Bourgogne, surnamed Le
Bon, espoused Isabella of Portugal on the
10th of January, 1430 ; and on the same
day instituted the famous order of the
Fleece of Gold.

Page 77. *I beheld the gentle Mary.*

Marie de Valois, Duchess of Burgundy, was left by the death of her father, Charles-le-Téméraire, at the age of twenty, the richest heiress of Europe. She came to Bruges, as Countess of Flanders, in 1477, and in the same year was married by proxy to the Archduke Maximilian. According to the custom of the time, the Duke of Bavaria, Maximilian's substitute, slept with the princess. They were both in complete dress, separated by a naked sword, and attended by four armed guards. Marie was adored by her subjects for her gentleness and her many other virtues.

Maximilian was son of the Emperor Frederick the Third, and is the same person mentioned afterwards in the poem of *Nuremberg* as the Kaiser Maximilian, and the hero of Pfinzing's poem of *Teuerdank.* Having been imprisoned by the revolted burghers of Bruges, they refused to release him, till he consented to kneel in the public square, and to swear on the Holy Evangelists and the body of Saint Donatus, that he would not take vengeance upon them for their rebellion.

Page 77. *The bloody battle of the Spurs of Gold.*

This battle, the most memorable in Flemish history, was fought under the walls of Courtray, on the 11th of July, 1302, between the French and the Flemings, the former commanded by Robert, Comte d'Artois, and the latter by Guillaume de Juliers, and Jean, Comte de Namur. The French army was completely routed, with a loss of twenty thousand infantry and seven thousand cavalry; among whom were sixty-three princes, dukes, and counts, seven hundred lords-banneret, and eleven hundred noblemen. The flower of the French nobility perished on that day; to which history has given the name of the *Journée des Eperons d'Or*, from the great number of golden spurs found on the field of battle. Seven hundred of them were hung up as a trophy in the church of Notre Dame de Courtray; and, as the cavaliers of that day wore but a single spur each, these vouched to God for the violent and bloody death of seven hundred of his creatures.

Page 77. *Saw the fight at Minnewater.*

When the inhabitants of Bruges were digging a canal at Minnewater, to bring the waters of the Lys from Deynze to their city, they were attacked and routed by the citizens of Ghent, whose commerce would have been much injured by the canal. They were led by Jean Lyons, captain of a military company at Ghent, called the *Chaperons Blancs.* He had great sway over the turbulent populace, who, in those prosperous times of the city, gained an easy livelihood by laboring two or three days in the week, and had the remaining four or five to devote to public affairs. The fight at Minnewater was followed by open rebellion against Louis de Maele, the Count of Flanders and Protector of Bruges. His superb château of Wondelghem was pillaged and burnt; and the insurgents forced the gates of Bruges, and entered in triumph, with Lyons mounted at their head. A few days afterwards he died suddenly, perhaps by poison.

Meanwhile the insurgents received a check at the village of Nevèle; and two hundred of them perished in the church, which was burned by the Count's orders. One of the chiefs, Jean de Lannoy, took refuge in the belfry. From the summit of the tower he held forth his purse filled with gold, and begged for deliverance. It was in vain. His enemies cried to him from below to save himself as best he might; and, half suffocated with smoke and flame, he threw himself from the tower and perished at their feet. Peace was soon afterwards established, and the Count retired to faithful Bruges.

Page 77. *The Golden Dragon's nest.*

The Golden Dragon, taken from the church of St. Sophia, at Constantinople, in one of the Crusades, and placed on the belfry of Bruges, was afterwards transported to Ghent by Philip van Artevelde, and still adorns the belfry of that city.

The inscription on the alarm-bell at Ghent is, " *Mynen naem is Roland ; als ik klep is er brand, and als ik luy is er victorie in het land.*" My name is Roland; when I toll there is fire, and when I ring there is victory in the land.

Page 79. *That their great imperial city stretched its hand through every clime.*

An old popular proverb of the town runs thus: —

" *Nürnberg's Hand*
Geht durch alle Land."

Nuremberg's hand
Goes through every land.

Page 79. *Sat the poet Melchior singing Kaiser Maximilian's praise.*

Melchior Pfinzing was one of the most celebrated German poets of the sixteenth century. The hero of his *Teuerdank* was the reigning emperor, Maximilian; and the poem was to the Germans of that day what the *Orlando Furioso* was to the Ital-

ians. Maximilian is mentioned before, in
the *Belfry of Bruges.* See page 77.

Page 79. *In the church of sainted Sebald sleeps enshrined his holy dust.*

The tomb of Saint Sebald, in the church
which bears his name, is one of the richest
works of art in Nuremberg. It is of
bronze, and was cast by Peter Vischer and
his sons, who labored upon it thirteen
years. It is adorned with nearly one
hundred figures, among which those of the
Twelve Apostles are conspicuous for size
and beauty.

Page 80. *In the church of sainted Lawrence stands a pix of sculpture rare.*

This pix, or tabernacle for the vessels of
the sacrament, is by the hand of Adam
Kraft. It is an exquisite piece of sculpture in white stone, and rises to the height
of sixty-four feet. It stands in the choir,
whose richly painted windows cover it
with varied colors.

Page 80. *Wisest of the Twelve Wise
Masters.*

The Twelve Wise Masters was the title
of the original corporation of the Master-
singers. Hans Sachs, the cobbler of Nuremberg, though not one of the original
Twelve, was the most renowned of the
Mastersingers, as well as the most voluminous. He flourished in the sixteenth century ; and left behind him thirty-four folio
volumes of manuscript, containing two
hundred and eight plays, one thousand
and seven hundred comic tales, and between four and five thousand lyric poems.

Page 80. *As in Adam Puschman's
song.*

Adam Puschman, in his poem on the
death of Hans Sachs, describes him as he
appeared in a vision : —

> "An old man,
> Gray and white, and dove-like,
> Who had, in sooth, a great beard,
> And read in a fair, great book,
> Beautiful with golden clasps."

Page 84. *The Occultation of Orion.*

Astronomically speaking, this title is
incorrect ; as I apply to a constellation
what can properly be applied to some of
its stars only. But my observation is
made from the hill of song, and not from
that of science ; and will, I trust, be found
sufficiently accurate for the present purpose.

Page 86. *Who, unharmed, on his tusks
once caught the bolts of the thunder.*

"A delegation of warriors from the Del-

aware tribe having visited the governor of
Virginia, during the Revolution, on matters of business, after these had been discussed and settled in council, the governor
asked them some questions relative to
their country, and among others, what
they knew or had heard of the animal
whose bones were found at the Saltlicks
on the Ohio. Their chief speaker immediately put himself into an attitude of ora-
tory, and with a pomp suited to what he
conceived the elevation of his subject, informed him that it was a tradition handed
down from their fathers, 'that in ancient
times a herd of these tremendous animals
came to the Big-bone licks, and began an
universal destruction of the bear, deer,
elks, buffaloes, and other animals which
had been created for the use of the Indians :
that the Great Man above, looking down
and seeing this, was so enraged that he
seized his lightning, descended on the earth,
seated himself on a neighboring mountain,
on a rock of which his seat and the print
of his feet are still to be seen, and hurled
his bolts among them till the whole were
slaughtered, except the big bull, who, pre-
senting his forehead to the shafts, shook
them off as they fell ; but missing one at
length, it wounded him in the side;
whereon, springing round, he bounded
over the Ohio, over the Wabash, the Illinois, and finally over the great lakes,
where he is living at this day.'" — JEF-
FERSON'S *Notes on Virginia*, Query VI.

Page 88. *Walter von der Vogelweid.*

Walter von der Vogelweid, or Bird-
Meadow, was one of the principal Minnesingers of the thirteenth century. He
triumphed over Heinrich von Ofterdingen
in that poetic contest at Wartburg Castle,
known in literary history as the War of
Wartburg.

Page 91. *Like imperial Charlemagne.*

Charlemagne may be called by pre-emi-
nence the monarch of farmers. According
to the German tradition, in seasons of great
abundance, his spirit crosses the Rhine on
a golden bridge at Bingen, and blesses the
cornfields and the vineyards. During his
lifetime, he did not disdain, says Montes-
quieu, "to sell the eggs from the farm-
yards of his domains, and the superfluous
vegetables of his gardens ; while he distrib-
uted among his people the wealth of the
Lombards and the immense treasures of
the Huns."

Page 124.

> *Behold, at last,
> Each tall and tapering mast
> Is swung into its place.*

I wish to anticipate a criticism on this passage, by stating, that sometimes, though not usually, vessels are launched fully sparred and rigged. I have availed myself of the exception as better suited to my purposes than the general rule; but the reader will see that it is neither a blunder nor a poetic license. On this subject a friend in Portland, Maine, writes me thus:—

"In this State, and also, I am told, in New York, ships are sometimes rigged upon the stocks, in order to save time, or to make a show. There was a fine, large ship launched last summer at Ellsworth, fully sparred and rigged. Some years ago a ship was launched here, with her rigging, spars, sails, and cargo aboard. She sailed the next day and — was never heard of again! I hope this will not be the fate of your poem!"

Page 127. *Sir Humphrey Gilbert.*

"When the wind abated and the vessels were near enough, the Admiral was seen constantly sitting in the stern, with a book in his hand. On the 9th of September he was seen for the last time, and was heard by the people of the Hind to say, 'We are as near heaven by sea as by land.' In the following night, the lights of the ship suddenly disappeared. The people in the other vessel kept a good lookout for him during the remainder of the voyage. On the 22d of September they arrived, through much tempest and peril, at Falmouth. But nothing more was seen or heard of the Admiral." — BELKNAP'S *American Biography*, I. 203.

Page 135. *The Blind Girl of Castèl-Cuillè.*

Jasmin, the author of this beautiful poem, is to the South of France what Burns is to the South of Scotland, — the representative of the heart of the people, — one of those happy bards who are born with their mouths full of birds (*la bouco pleno d'aouzelous*). He has written his own biography in a poetic form, and the simple narrative of his poverty, his struggles, and his triumphs, is very touching. He still lives at Agen, on the Garonne; and long may he live there to delight his native land with native songs!

The following description of his person and way of life is taken from the graphic pages of "Béarn and the Pyrenees," by Louisa Stuart Costello, whose charming pen has done so much to illustrate the French provinces and their literature.

"At the entrance of the promenade, Du Gravier, is a row of small houses, — some cafés, others shops, the indication of which

is a painted cloth placed across the way, with the owner's name in bright gold letters, in the manner of the arcades in the streets, and their announcements. One of the most glaring of these was, we observed, a bright blue flag, bordered with gold; on which, in large gold letters, appeared the name of 'Jasmin, Coiffeur.' We entered, and were welcomed by a smiling, dark-eyed woman, who informed us that her husband was busy at that moment dressing a customer's hair, but he was desirous to receive us, and begged we would walk into his parlor at the back of the shop.

. . . . . .

"She exhibited to us a laurel crown of gold, of delicate workmanship, sent from the city of Clemence Isaure, Toulouse, to the poet; who will probably one day take his place in the *capitoul.* Next came a golden cup, with an inscription in his honor, given by the citizens of Auch; a gold watch, chain, and seals, sent by the king, Louis Philippe; an emerald ring worn and presented by the lamented Duke of Orleans; a pearl pin, by the graceful Duchess, who, on the poet's visit to Paris accompanied by his son, received him in the words he puts into the mouth of Henri Quatre:—

'Brabes Gascous!
A moun amou per bous aou dibes creyre:
Benès! benès! ey plazé de bous beyre:
Aproucha bous!'

A fine service of linen, the offering of the town of Pau, after its citizens had given fêtes in his honor, and loaded him with caresses and praises; and knickknacks and jewels of all descriptions offered to him by lady-ambassadresses, and great lords; English 'misses' and 'miladis'; and French, and foreigners of all nations who did or did not understand Gascon.

"All this, though startling, was not convincing; Jasmin, the barber, might only be a fashion, a *furore*, a caprice, after all; and it was evident that he knew how to get up a scene well. When we had become nearly tired of looking over these tributes to his genius, the door opened, and the poet himself appeared. His manner was free and unembarrassed, well-bred, and lively; he received our compliments naturally, and like one accustomed to homage; said he was ill, and unfortunately too hoarse to read anything to us, or should have been delighted to do so. He spoke with a broad Gascon accent, and very rapidly and eloquently; ran over the story of his successes; told us that his grandfather had been a beggar, and all his family very poor; that he was now as rich as he wished to be; his son placed in a good position at Nantes; then showed us his son's picture, and spoke of his disposition; to which his brisk little wife added, that, though no fool, he had not his father's genius, to which truth Jasmin assented as a matter of course. I told him of having seen mention made of him in an English review; which he said had been sent him by Lord Durham, who had paid him a visit; and I then spoke of 'Me cal mouri' as known to me. This was enough to make him forget his hoarseness and every other evil: it would never do for me to imagine that that little song was his best composition; it was merely his first; he must try to read to me a little of 'L'Abuglo,' — a few verses of 'Françouneto.' 'You will be charmed,' said he; 'but if I were well, and you would give me the pleasure of your company for some time, if you were not merely running through Agen, I would kill you with weeping, — I would make you die with distress for my poor Margarido, — my pretty Françouneto!'

"He caught up two copies of his book, from a pile lying on the table, and making us sit close to him, he pointed out the French translation on one side, which he told us to follow while he read in Gascon. He began in a rich, soft voice, and as he advanced, the surprise of Hamlet on hearing the player-king recite the disasters of Hecuba was but a type of ours, to find ourselves carried away by the spell of his enthusiasm. His eyes swam in tears; he became pale and red; he trembled; he recovered himself; his face was now joyous, now exulting, gay, jocose; in fact, he was twenty actors in one; he rang the changes from Rachel to Bouffé; and he finished by delighting us, besides beguiling us of our tears, and overwhelming us with astonishment.

"He would have been a treasure on the stage; for he is still, though his first youth is past, remarkably good-looking and striking; with black, sparkling eyes, of intense expression; a fine, ruddy complexion; a countenance of wondrous mobility; a good figure; and action full of fire and grace; he has handsome hands, which he uses with infinite effect; and, on the whole, he is the best actor of the kind I ever saw. I could now quite understand what a troubadour or *jongleur* might be, and I look upon Jasmin as a revived specimen of that extinct race. Such as he is might have been Gaucelm Faidit, of Avignon, the friend of Cœur de Lion, who lamented the death of the hero in such moving strains; such might have been Bernard de Ventadour, who sang the praises of Queen Elinore's beauty; such Geoffrey Rudel, of Blaye, on his own Garonne such the wild Vidal: certain it is,

that none of these troubadours of old could more move, by their singing or reciting, than Jasmin, in whom all their long-smothered fire and traditional magic seems re-illumined.

"We found we had stayed hours instead of minutes with the poet; but he would not hear of any apology, — only regretted that his voice was so out of tune, in consequence of a violent cold, under which he was really laboring, and hoped to see us again. He told us our countrywomen of Pau had laden him with kindness and attention, and spoke with such enthusiasm of the beauty of certain 'misses,' that I feared his little wife would feel somewhat piqued; but, on the contrary, she stood by, smiling and happy, and enjoying the stories of his triumphs. I remarked that he had restored the poetry of the troubadours; asked him if he knew their songs; and said he was worthy to stand at their head. 'I am, indeed, a troubadour,' said he, with energy; 'but I am far beyond them all: they were but beginners; they never composed a poem like my Françouneto! there are no poets in France now, — there cannot be; the language does not admit of it; where is the fire, the spirit, the expression, the tenderness, the force of the Gascon? French is but the ladder to reach to the first floor of Gascon, — how can you get up to a height except by a ladder!'

. . . .

"I returned by Agen, after an absence in the Pyrenees of some months, and renewed my acquaintance with Jasmin and his dark-eyed wife. I did not expect that I should be recognized; but the moment I entered the little shop I was hailed as an old friend. 'Ah!' cried Jasmin, 'enfin la voilà encore!' I could not but be flattered by this recollection, but soon found it was less on my own account that I was thus welcomed, than because a circumstance had occurred to the poet which he thought I could perhaps explain. He produced several French newspapers, in which he pointed out to me an article headed 'Jasmin à Londres'; being a translation of certain notices of himself, which had appeared in a leading English literary journal. He had, he said, been informed of the honor done him by numerous friends, and assured me his fame had been much spread by this means; and he was so delighted on the occasion, that he had resolved to learn English, in order that he might judge of the translations from his works, which, he had been told, were well done. I enjoyed his surprise, while I informed him that I knew who was the reviewer and translator; and explained the reason for the verses giving pleasure in an English dress to be the superior simplicity of the English language over Modern French, for which he has a great contempt, as unfitted for lyrical composition. He inquired of me respecting Burns, to whom he had been likened; and begged me to tell him something of Moore. The delight of himself and his wife was amusing, at having discovered a secret which had puzzled them so long.

"He had a thousand things to tell me; in particular, that he had only the day before received a letter from the Duchess of Orleans, informing him that she had ordered a medal of her late husband to be struck, the first of which would be sent to him: she also announced to him the agreeable news of the king having granted him a pension of a thousand francs. He smiled and wept by turns, as he told us all this; and declared, much as he was elated at the possession of a sum which made him a rich man for life, the kindness of the Duchess gratified him even more.

"He then made us sit down while he read us two new poems; both charming, and full of grace and naiveté; and one very affecting, being an address to the king, alluding to the death of his son. As he read, his wife stood by, and fearing we did not quite comprehend his language, she made a remark to that effect : to which he answered impatiently, 'Nonsense, — don't you see they are in tears?' This was unanswerable ; and we were allowed to hear the poem to the end; and I certainly never listened to anything more feelingly and energetically delivered.

"We had much conversation, for he was anxious to detain us, and, in the course of it, he told me he had been by some accused of vanity. 'O,' he rejoined, 'what would you have! I am a child of nature, and cannot conceal my feelings; the only difference between me and a man of refinement is, that he knows how to conceal his vanity and exultation at success, which I let everybody see.' " — Béarn and the Pyrenees, I. 369, et seq.

Page 140. A Christmas Carol.

The following description of Christmas in Burgundy is from M. Fertiault's Coup d'Œil sur les Noels en Bourgogne, prefixed to the Paris edition of Les Noels Bourguignons de Bernard de la Monnoye (Gui Barôzai), 1842.

"Every year at the approach of Advent, people refresh their memories, clear their throats, and begin preluding, in the long evenings by the fireside, those carols whose invariable and eternal theme is the coming of the Messiah. They take from old clos-

ets pamphlets, little collections begrimed with dust and smoke, to which the press, and sometimes the pen, has consigned these songs ; and as soon as the first Sunday of Advent sounds, they gossip, they gad about, they sit together by the fireside, sometimes at one house, sometimes at another, taking turns in paying for the chestnuts and white wine, but singing with one common voice the grotesque praises of the Little Jesus. There are very few villages even, which, during all the evenings of Advent, do not hear some of these curious canticles shouted in their streets, to the nasal drone of bagpipes. In this case the minstrel comes as a reinforcement to the singers at the fireside; he brings and adds his dose of joy (spontaneous or mercenary, it matters little which) to the joy which breathes around the hearth-stone; and when the voices vibrate and resound, one voice more is always welcome. There, it is not the purity of the notes which makes the concert, but the quantity, — non qualitas, sed quantitas ; then (to finish at once with the minstrel), when the Saviour has at length been born in the manger, and the beautiful Christmas Eve is passed, the rustic piper makes his round among the houses, where every one compliments and thanks him, and, moreover, gives him in small coin the price of the shrill notes with which he has enlivened the evening entertainments.

"More or less until Christmas Eve, all goes on in this way among our devout singers, with the difference of some gallons of wine or some hundreds of chestnuts. But this famous eve once come, the scale is pitched upon a higher key; the closing evening must be a memorable one. The toilet is begun at nightfall ; then comes the hour of supper, admonishing divers appetites; and groups, as numerous as possible, are formed to take together this comfortable evening repast. The supper finished, a circle gathers around the hearth, which is arranged and set in order this evening after a particular fashion, and which at a later hour of the night is to become the object of special interest to the children. On the burning brands an enormous log has been placed. This log assuredly does not change its nature, but it changes its name during this evening : it is called the Suche (the Yule-log). 'Look you,' say they to the children, 'if you are good this evening, Noel' (for with children one must always personify) 'will rain down sugar-plums in the night.' And the children sit demurely, keeping as quiet as their turbulent little natures will permit. The groups of older persons, not always as orderly as the children, seize this good opportunity to surrender themselves with merry hearts and boisterous voices to the chanted worship of the miraculous Noel. For this final solemnity, they have kept the most powerful, the most enthusiastic, the most electrifying carols. Noel! Noel! Noel! This magic word resounds on all sides; it seasons every sauce, it is served up with every course. Of the thousands of canticles which are heard on this famous eve, ninety-nine in a hundred begin and end with this word; which is, one may say, their Alpha and Omega, their crown and footstool. This last, evening, the merry-making is prolonged. Instead of retiring at ten or eleven o'clock, as is generally done on all the preceding evenings, they wait for the stroke of midnight: this word sufficiently proclaims to what ceremony they are going to repair. For ten minutes or a quarter of an hour, the bells have been calling the faithful with a triple-bob-major; and each one, furnished with a little taper streaked with various colors (the Christmas Candle), goes through the crowded streets, where the lanterns are dancing like Will-o'-the-Wisps, at the impatient summons of the multitudinous chimes. It is the Midnight Mass. Once inside the church, they hear with more or less piety the Mass, emblematic of the coming of the Messiah. Then in tumult and great haste they return homeward, always in numerous groups; they salute the Yule-log; they pay homage to the hearth; they sit down at table; and, amid songs which reverberate louder than ever, make this meal of after-Christmas, so long looked for, so cherished, so joyous, so noisy, and which it has been thought fit to call, we hardly know why, *Rossignon*. The supper eaten at nightfall is no impediment, as you may imagine, to the appetite's returning; above all, if the going to and from church has made the devout eaters feel some little shafts of the sharp and biting north-wind. *Rossignon* then goes on merrily, — sometimes far into the morning hours; but, nevertheless, gradually throats grow hoarse, stomachs are filled, the Yule-log burns out, and at last the hour arrives when each one, as best he may, regains his domicile and his bed, and puts with himself between the sheets the material for a good sore-throat, or a good indigestion, for the morrow. Previous to this, care has been taken to place in the slippers, or wooden shoes of the children, the sugar-plums, which shall be for them, on their waking, the welcome fruits of the Christmas log."

In the Glossary, the *Suche*, or Yule-log, is thus defined : —

"This is a huge log, which is placed on the fire on Christmas Eve, and which in Burgundy is called, on this account, *lai Suche de Noei*. Then the father of the family, particularly among the middle classes, sings solemnly Christmas carols with his wife and children, the smallest of whom he sends into the corner to pray that the Yule-log may bear him some sugar-plums. Meanwhile, little parcels of them are placed under each end of the log, and the children come and pick them up, believing, in good faith, that the great log has borne them."

Page 141. THE SONG OF HIAWATHA. This Indian Edda — if I may so call it — is founded on a tradition prevalent among the North American Indians, of a personage of miraculous birth, who was sent among them to clear their rivers, forests, and fishing-grounds, and to teach them the arts of peace. He was known among different tribes by the several names of Michabou, Chiabo, Manabozo, Tarenyawagon, and Hiawatha. Mr. Schoolcraft gives an account of him in his *Algic Researches*, Vol. I. p. 134; and in his *History, Condition, and Prospects of the Indian Tribes of the United States*, Part III. p. 314, may be found the Iroquois form of the tradition, derived from the verbal narrations of an Onondaga chief.

Into this old tradition I have woven other curious Indian legends, drawn chiefly from the various and valuable writings of Mr. Schoolcraft, to whom the literary world is greatly indebted for his indefatigable zeal in rescuing from oblivion so much of the legendary lore of the Indians.

The scene of the poem is among the Ojibways on the southern shore of Lake Superior, in the region between the Pictured Rocks and the Grand Sable.

VOCABULARY

Adjidau'mo, *the red squirrel.*
Ahdeek', *the reindeer.*
Ahkose'win, *fever.*
Ahmeek', *the beaver.*
Algon'quin, *Ojibway.*
Annemee'kee, *the thunder.*
Apuk'wa, *a bulrush.*
Baim-wa'wa, *the sound of the thunder.*
Bemah'gut, *the grapevine.*
Be'na, *the pheasant.*
Big-Sea-Water, *Lake Superior.*
Bukada'win, *famine.*
Cheemaun', *a birch canoe.*
Chetowaik', *the plover.*
Chibia'bos, *a musician; friend of Hiawatha; ruler in the Land of Spirits.*
Dahin'da, *the bull-frog.*
Dush-kwo-ne'she, *or* Kwo-ne'she, *the dragon-fly*
Esa, *shame upon you.*
Ewa-yea', *lullaby.*

Ghee'zis, *the sun.*

Gitche Gu'mee, *the Big-Sea-Water, Lake Superior.*

Gitche Man'ito, *the Great Spirit, the Master of Life.*

Gushkewau', *the darkness.*

Hiawa'tha, *the Wise Man, the Teacher; son of Mudjekeewis, the West-Wind, and Wenonah, daughter of Nokomis.*

Ia'goo, *a great boaster and story-teller.*

Inin'ewug, *men, or pawns in the Game of the Bowl.*

Ishkoodah', *fire; a comet.*

Jee'bi, *a ghost, a spirit.*

Joss'akeed, *a prophet.*

Kabibonok'ka, *the North-Wind.*

Kagh, *the hedge-hog.*

Ka'go, *do not.*

Kahgahgee', *the raven.*

Kaw, *no.*

Kaween', *no indeed.*

Kayoshk', *the sea-gull.*

Kee'go, *a fish.*

Keeway'din, *the Northwest-Wind, the Home-wind.*

Kena'beek, *a serpent.*

Keneu', *the great war-eagle.*

Keno'zha, *the pickerel.*

Ko'ko-ko'ho, *the owl.*

Kuntasoo', *the Game of Plum-stones.*

Kwa'sind, *the Strong Man.*

Kwo-ne'she, *or* Dush-kwo-ne'she, *the dragon-fly.*

Mahnahbe'zee, *the swan.*

Mahng, *the loon.*

Mahn-go-tay'see, *loon-hearted, brave.*

Mahnomo'nee, *wild rice.*

Ma'ma, *the woodpecker.*

Maskeno'zha, *the pike.*

Me'da, *a medicine-man.*

Meenah'ga, *the blueberry.*

Megissog'won, *the great Pearl-Feather, a magician, and the Manito of Wealth.*

Meshinau'wa, *a pipe-bearer.*

Minjekah'wun, *Hiawatha's mittens.*

Minneha'ha, *Laughing Water; a water-fall on a stream running into the Mississippi, between Fort Snelling and the Falls of St. Anthony.*

Minneha'ha, *Laughing Water; wife of Hiawatha.*

Minne-wa'wa, *a pleasant sound, as of the wind in the trees.*

Mishe-Mo'kwa, *the Great Bear.*

Mishe-Nah'ma, *the Great Sturgeon.*

Miskodeed', *the Spring-Beauty, the Claytonia Virginica.*

Monda'min, *Indian corn.*

Moon of Bright Nights, *April.*

Moon of Leaves, *May.*

Moon of Strawberries, *June.*

Moon of the Falling Leaves, *September.*

Moon of Snow-Shoes, *November.*

Mudjekee'wis, *the West-Wind; father of Hiawatha.*

Mudway-aush'ka, *sound of waves on a shore.*

Mushkoda'sa, *the grouse.*

Nah'ma, *the sturgeon.*

Nah'ma-wusk, *spearmint.*

Na'gow Wudj'oo, *the Sand Dunes of Lake Superior.*

Nee-ba-naw'baigs, *water spirits.*

Nenemoo'sha, *sweetheart.*

Nepah'win, *sleep.*

Noko'mis, *a grandmother; mother of Wenonah.*

No'sa, *my father.*

Nush'ka, *look! look!*

Odah'min, *the strawberry.*

Okahah'wis, *the fresh-water herring.*

Ome'me, *the pigeon.*

Ona'gon, *a bowl.*

Onaway', *awake.*

Ope'chee, *the robin.*

Osse'o, *Son of the Evening Star.*

Owais'sa, *the bluebird.*

Oweenee', *wife of Osseo.*

Ozawa'beek, *a round piece of brass or copper in the Game of the Bowl.*

Pah-puk-kee'na, *the grasshopper.*

Pau'guk, *death.*

Pau-Puk-Kee'wis, *the handsome Yenadizze, the Storm Fool.*

Pauwa'ting, *Saut Sainte Marie.*

Pe'boan, *Winter.*

Pem'ican, *meat of the deer or buffalo dried and pounded.*

Pezhekee', *the bison.*

Pishnekuh', *the brant.*

Pone'mah, *hereafter.*

Pugasaing', *Game of the Bowl.*

Puggawau'gun, *a war-club.*

Puk-Wudj'ies, *little wild men of the woods; pygmies.*

Sah-sah-je'wun, *rapids.*

Sah'wa, *the perch.*

Segwun', *Spring.*

Sha'da, *the pelican.*

Shahbo'min, *the gooseberry.*

Shah-shah, *long ago.*

Shaugoda'ya, *a coward.*

Shawgashee', *the craw-fish.*

Shawonda'see, *the South-Wind.*

Shaw-shaw, *the swallow.*

Shesh'ebwug, *ducks; pieces in the Game of the Bowl.*

Shin'gebis, *the diver or grebe.*

Showain' neme'shin, *pity me.*

Shuh-shuh'gah, *the blue heron.*

Soan-ge-ta'ha, *strong-hearted.*

Subbeka'she, *the spider.*

Sugge'ma, *the mosquito.*

To'tem, *family coat-of-arms.*

Ugh, *yes.*

Ugudwash', *the sun-fish.*

Unktahee', *the God of Water.*

Wabas'so, *the rabbit; the North.*

Wabe'no, *a magician, a juggler.*

Wabe'no-wusk, *yarrow.*

Wa'bun, *the East-Wind.*

Wa'bun An'nung, *the Star of the East, the Morning Star.*

Wahono'win, *a cry of lamentation.*

Wah-wah-tay'see, *the fire-fly.*

Wam'pum, *beads of shell.*

Waubewy'on, *a white skin wrapper.*

Wa'wa, *the wild-goose.*

Waw'beek, *a rock.*

Waw-be-wa'wa, *the white goose.*

Wawonais'sa, *the whippoorwill.*

Way-muk-kwa'na, *the caterpillar.*

Wen'digoes, *giants.*

Weno'nah, *Hiawatha's mother, daughter of Nokomis.*

Yenadiz'ze, *an idler and gambler; an Indian dandy.*

Page 142. *In the Vale of Tawasentha.*

This valley, now called Norman's Kill, is in Albany County, New York.

Page 142. *On the Mountains of the Prairie.*

Mr. Catlin, in his *Letters and Notes on the Manners, Customs, and Condition of the North American Indians*, Vol. II. p. 160, gives an interesting account of the *Côteau des Prairies*, and the Red Pipe-stone Quarry. He says : —

"Here (according to their traditions) happened the mysterious birth of the red pipe, which has blown its fumes of peace and war to the remotest corners of the continent ; which has visited every war-rior, and passed through its reddened stem the irrevocable oath of war and desolation. And here, also, the peace-breathing calu-met was born, and fringed with the eagle's quills, which has shed its thrilling fumes over the land, and soothed the fury of the relentless savage.

"The Great Spirit at an ancient period here called the Indian nations together, and, standing on the precipice of the red pipe-stone rock, broke from its wall a piece, and made a huge pipe by turning it in his hand, which he smoked over them, and to the North, the South, the East, and the West, and told them that this stone was red, — that it was their flesh, — that they must use it for their pipes of peace, — that it belonged to them all, and that the war-club and scalping-knife must not be raised on its ground. At the last whiff of his pipe his head went into a great cloud, and the whole surface of the rock for sev-eral miles was melted and glazed ; two great ovens were opened beneath, and two women (guardian spirits of the place) en-tered them in a blaze of fire ; and they are heard there yet (Tso-mec-cos-tee and Tso-me-cos-te-won-dee), answering to the invo-cations of the high-priests or medicine-men, who consult them when they are visitors to this sacred place."

Page 144. *Hark you, Bear ! you are a coward.*

This anecdote is from Heckewelder. In his account of the *Indian Nations*, he de-scribes an Indian hunter as addressing a bear in nearly these words. "I was pres-ent," he says, "at the delivery of this cu-rious invective ; when the hunter had de-spatched the bear, I asked him how he thought that poor animal could under-stand what he said to it. 'O,' said he in answer, 'the bear understood me very well ; did you not observe how *ashamed* he looked while I was upbraiding him ?'" — *Transactions of the American Philosoph-ical Society*, Vol. I. p. 240.

Page 147. *Hush ! the Naked Bear will hear thee !*

Heckewelder, in a letter published in the *Transactions of the American Philo-sophical Society*, Vol. IV. p. 260, speaks of this tradition as prevalent among the Mohicans and Delawares.

"Their reports," he says, "run thus: that among all animals that had been for-merly in this country, this was the most ferocious ; that it was much larger than the largest of the common bears, and remark-ably long-bodied ; all over (except a spot of hair on its back of a white color) na-ked. . . . .

"The history of this animal used to be a subject of conversation among the Indians, especially when in the woods a hunting. I have also heard them say to their chil-dren when crying : 'Hush ! the naked bear will hear you, be upon you, and devour you.'"

Page 151. *Where the Falls of Minne-haha*, etc.

"The scenery about Fort Snelling is rich in beauty. The Falls of St. Anthony are familiar to travellers, and to readers of Indian sketches. Between the fort and these falls are the 'Little Falls,' forty feet in height, on a stream that empties into the Mississippi. The Indians called them Mine-hah-hah, or 'laughing waters.'" — MRS. EASTMAN'S *Dacotah, or Legends of the Sioux*, Introd., p. ii.

Page 165. *Sand Hills of the Nagow Wudjoo.*

A description of the *Grand Sable*, or great sand-dunes of Lake Superior, is given in Foster and Whitney's *Report on the Ge-ology of the Lake Superior Land District*, Part II. p. 131.

"The Grand Sable possesses a scenic in-terest little inferior to that of the Pictured Rocks. The explorer passes abruptly from a coast of consolidated sand to one of loose materials ; and although in the one case the cliffs are less precipitous, yet in the other they attain a higher altitude. He sees before him a long reach of coast, re-sembling a vast sand-bank, more than three hundred and fifty feet in height, without a trace of vegetation. Ascending to the top, rounded hillocks of blown sand are ob-served, with occasional clumps of trees, standing out like oases in the desert."

Page 166. *Onaway ! Awake, beloved !*

The original of this song may be found in Littell's *Living Age*, Vol. XXV. p. 45.

Page 167. *On the Red Swan floating,
flying.*

The fanciful tradition of the Red Swan
may be found in Schoolcraft's *Algic Researches,* Vol. II. p. 9. Three brothers
were hunting on a wager to see who would
bring home the first game.

"They were to shoot no other animal,"
so the legend says, " but such as each was
in the habit of killing. They set out different ways : Odjibwa, the youngest, had
not gone far before he saw a bear, an animal he was not to kill, by the agreement.
He followed him close, and drove an arrow
through him, which brought him to the
ground. Although contrary to the bet, he
immediately commenced skinning him,
when suddenly something red tinged all
the air around him. He rubbed his eyes,
thinking he was perhaps deceived; but
without effect, for the red hue continued.
At length he heard a strange noise at a
distance. It first appeared like a human
voice, but after following the sound for
some distance, he reached the shores of a
lake, and soon saw the object he was looking for. At a distance out in the lake sat
a most beautiful Red Swan, whose plumage
glittered in the sun, and who would now
and then make the same noise he had heard.
He was within long bow-shot, and, pulling
the arrow from the bowstring up to his ear,
took deliberate aim and shot. The arrow
took no effect; and he shot and shot again
till his quiver was empty. Still the swan
remained, moving round and round,
stretching its long neck and dipping its
bill into the water, as if heedless of the
arrows shot at it. Odjibwa ran home, and
got all his own and his brother's arrows,
and shot them all away. He then stood
and gazed at the beautiful bird. While
standing, he remembered his brother's saying that in their deceased father's medicine-sack were three magic arrows. Off he
started, his anxiety to kill the swan over-
coming all scruples. At any other time,
he would have deemed it sacrilege to open
his father's medicine-sack ; but now he
hastily seized the three arrows and ran
back, leaving the other contents of the
sack scattered over the lodge. The swan
was still there. He shot the first arrow
with great precision, and came very near
to it. The second came still closer; as he
took the last arrow, he felt his arm firmer,
and, drawing it up with vigor, saw it pass
through the neck of the swan a little above
the breast. Still it did not prevent the
bird from flying off, which it did, however,
at first slowly, flapping its wings and rising gradually into the air, and then flying

off toward the sinking of the sun." — pp.
10 – 12.

Page 170. *When I think of my beloved.*
The original of this song may be found
in *Oneóta,* p. 15.

Page 170. *Sing the mysteries of Mondamin.*

The Indians hold the maize, or Indian
corn, in great veneration. "They esteem
it so important and divine a grain," says
Schoolcraft, "that their story-tellers invented various tales, in which this idea is
symbolized under the form of a special gift
from the Great Spirit. The Odjibwa-Al-
gonquins, who call it Mon-dá-min, that is,
the Spirit's grain or berry, have a pretty
story of this kind, in which the stalk in
full tassel is represented as descending
from the sky, under the guise of a handsome youth, in answer to the prayers of a
young man at his fast of virility, or
coming to manhood.

"It is well known that corn-planting
and corn-gathering, at least among all the
still *uncolonized* tribes, are left entirely to
the females and children, and a few super-
annuated old men. It is not generally
known, perhaps, that this labor is not
compulsory, and that it is assumed by the
females as a just equivalent, in their view,
for the onerous and continuous labor of
the other sex, in providing meats, and
skins for clothing, by the chase, and in
defending their villages against their enemies, and keeping intruders off their terri-
tories. A good Indian housewife deems
this a part of her prerogative, and prides
herself to have a store of corn to exercise
her hospitality, or duly honor her husband's hospitality, in the entertainment of
the lodge guests." — *Oneóta,* p. 82.

Page 171. *Thus the fields shall be more
fruitful.*

"A singular proof of this belief, in both
sexes, of the mysterious influence of the
steps of a woman on the vegetable and in
sect creation, is found in an ancient cus
tom, which was related to me, respecting
corn-planting. It was the practice of the
hunter's wife, when the field of corn had
been planted, to choose the first dark or
overclouded evening to perform a secret
circuit, *sans habillement,* around the field.
For this purpose she slipped out of the
lodge in the evening, unobserved, to some
obscure nook, where she completely dis-
robed. Then, taking her matchecota, or
principal garment, in one hand, she dragged
it around the field. This was thought to
insure a prolific crop, and to prevent the

assaults of insects and worms upon the grain. It was supposed they could not creep over the charmed line." — *Oneóta*, p. 83.

Page 171. *With his prisoner-string he bound him.*

"These cords," says Mr. Tanner, "are made of the bark of the elm-tree, by boiling and then immersing it in cold water. . . . . The leader of a war party commonly carries several fastened about his waist, and if, in the course of the fight, any one of his young men takes a prisoner, it is his duty to bring him immediately to the chief, to be tied, and the latter is responsible for his safe keeping." — *Narrative of Captivity and Adventures*, p. 412.

Page 172.
Wagemin, the thief of cornfields,
Paimosaid, who steals the maize-ear.

"If one of the young female huskers finds a *red* ear of corn, it is typical of a brave admirer, and is regarded as a fitting present to some young warrior. But if the ear be *crooked*, and tapering to a point, no matter what color, the whole circle is set in a roar, and *wa-ge-min* is the word shouted aloud. It is the symbol of a thief in the cornfield. It is considered as the image of an old man stooping as he enters the lot. Had the chisel of Praxiteles been employed to produce this image, it could not more vividly bring to the minds of the merry group the idea of a pilferer of their favorite *mondámin*. . . . .

"The literal meaning of the term is, a mass, or crooked ear of grain; but the ear of corn so called is a conventional type of a little old man pilfering ears of corn in a cornfield. It is in this manner that a single word or term, in these curious languages, becomes the fruitful parent of many ideas. And we can thus perceive why it is that the word *wagemin* is alone competent to excite merriment in the husking circle.

"This term is taken as the basis of the cereal chorus, or corn song, as sung by the Northern Algonquin tribes. It is coupled with the phrase *Paimosaid*, — a permutative form of the Indian substantive, made from the verb *pim-o-sa*, to walk. Its literal meaning is, *he who walks*, or *the walker;* but the ideas conveyed by it are, he who walks by night to pilfer corn. It offers, therefore, a kind of parallelism in expression to the preceding term." — *Oneóta*, p. 254.

Page 177. *Pugasaing, with thirteen pieces.*

This Game of the Bowl is the principal game of hazard among the Northern tribes of Indians. Mr. Schoolcraft gives a particular account of it in *Oneóta*, p. 85. "This game," he says, "is very fascinating to some portions of the Indians. They stake at it their ornaments, weapons, clothing, canoes, horses, everything in fact they possess; and have been known, it is said, to set up their wives and children, and even to forfeit their own liberty. Of such desperate stakes I have seen no examples, nor do I think the game itself in common use. It is rather confined to certain persons, who hold the relative rank of gamblers in Indian society, — men who are not noted as hunters or warriors, or steady providers for their families. Among these are persons who bear the term of *Ienadizze-wug*, that is, wanderers about the country, braggadocios, or fops. It can hardly be classed with the popular games of amusement, by which skill and dexterity are acquired. I have generally found the chiefs and graver men of the tribes, who encouraged the young men to play ball, and are sure to be present at the customary sports, to witness, and sanction, and applaud them, speak lightly and disparagingly of this game of hazard. Yet it cannot be denied that some of the chiefs, distinguished in war and the chase, at the West, can be referred to as lending their example to its fascinating power."

See also his *History, Condition, and Prospects of the Indian Tribes*, Part II. p. 72.

Page 181. *To the Pictured Rocks of sandstone.*

The reader will find a long description of the Pictured Rocks in Foster and Whitney's *Report on the Geology of the Lake Superior Land District*, Part II. p. 124. From this I make the following extract : —

"The Pictured Rocks may be described, in general terms, as a series of sandstone bluffs extending along the shore of Lake Superior for about five miles, and rising, in most places, vertically from the water, without any beach at the base, to a height varying from fifty to nearly two hundred feet. Were they simply a line of cliffs, they might not, so far as relates to height or extent, be worthy of a rank among great natural curiosities, although such an assemblage of rocky strata, washed by the waves of the great lake, would not, under any circumstances, be destitute of grandeur. To the voyager, coasting along their base in his frail canoe, they would, at all times, be an object of dread ; the recoil of the surf, the rock-bound coast, affording, for miles, no place of refuge, — the lowering sky, the rising wind, — all these would excite his apprehension, and induce him to ply a vigorous oar until the dreaded wall was passed. But in the Pictured Rocks there are two features which communicate to the scenery a wonderful and almost unique character. These are, first, the curious manner in which the cliffs have been excavated and worn away by the action of the lake, which, for centuries, has dashed an ocean-like surf against their base; and, second, the equally curious manner in which large portions of the surface have been colored by bands of brilliant hues.

"It is from the latter circumstance that the name, by which these cliffs are known to the American traveller, is derived; while that applied to them by the French voyageurs ('Les Portails') is derived from the former, and by far the most striking peculiarity.

"The term *Pictured Rocks* has been in use for a great length of time; but when it was first applied, we have been unable to discover. It would seem that the first travellers were more impressed with the novel and striking distribution of colors on the surface than with the astonishing variety of form into which the cliffs themselves have been worn. . . . .

"Our voyageurs had many legends to relate of the pranks of the *Menni-bojou* in these caverns, and, in answer to our inquiries, seemed disposed to fabricate stories, without end, of the achievements of this Indian deity."

Page 189. *Toward the sun his hands were lifted.*

In this manner, and with such salutations, was Father Marquette received by the Illinois. See his *Voyages et Découvertes*, Section V.

Page 212.

That of our vices we can frame A ladder.

The words of St. Augustine are, — "De vitiis nostris scalam nobis facimus, si vitia ipsa calcamus."

Sermon III. *De Ascensione.*

Page 212. *The Phantom Ship.*

A detailed account of this "apparition of a Ship in the Air" is given by Cotton Mather in his *Magnalia Christi*, Book I. Ch. VI. It is contained in a letter from the Rev. James Pierpont, Pastor of New Haven. To this account Mather adds these words ; —

"Reader, there being yet living so many credible gentlemen that were eyewitnesses of this wonderful thing, I venture to publish it for a thing as undoubted as 't is wonderful."

Page 215. *And the Emperor but a Macho.*

Macho, in Spanish, signifies a mule. *Golondrina* is the feminine form of *Golondrino*, a swallow, and also a cant name for a deserter.

Page 217. *Oliver Basselin.*

Oliver Basselin, the "*Père joyeux du Vaudeville*," flourished in the fifteenth century, and gave to his convivial songs the name of his native valleys, in which he sang them, Vaux-de-Vire. This name was afterwards corrupted into the modern *Vaudeville*.

Page 218. *Victor Galbraith.*

This poem is founded on fact. Victor Galbraith was a bugler in a company of volunteer cavalry, and was shot in Mexico for some breach of discipline. It is a common superstition among soldiers, that no balls will kill them unless their names are written on them. The old proverb says, "Every bullet has its billet."

Page 219. *I remember the sea-fight far away.*

This was the engagement between the Enterprise and Boxer, off the harbor of Portland, in which both captains were slain. They were buried side by side, in the cemetery on Mountjoy.

Page 222. *Santa Filomena.*

"At Pisa the church of San Francisco contains a chapel dedicated lately to Santa Filomena; over the altar is a picture, by Sabatelli, representing the Saint as a beautiful, nymph-like figure, floating down from heaven, attended by two angels bearing the lily, palm, and javelin, and beneath, in the foreground, the sick and maimed, who are healed by her intercession." — MRS. JAMESON, *Sacred and Legendary Art*, II. 298.

Page 406. *The Children's Crusade.*

"The Children's Crusade" was left unfinished by Mr. Longfellow. It is founded upon an event which occurred in the year 1212. An army of twenty thousand children, mostly boys, under the lead of a boy of ten years, named Nicolas, set out from

Cologne for the Holy Land. When they reached Genoa only seven thousand remained. There, as the sea did not divide to allow them to march dry-shod to the East, they broke up. Some got as far as Rome ; two ship-loads sailed from Pisa, and were not heard of again; the rest straggled back to Germany.

Page 516.   *The Golden Legend.*

The old *Legenda Aurea,* or Golden Legend, was originally written in Latin, in the thirteenth century, by Jacobus de Voragine, a Dominican friar, who afterwards became Archbishop of Genoa, and died in 1292.

He called his book simply *Legends of the Saints.* The epithet of Golden was given it by his admirers; for, as Wynkin de Worde says, " Like as passeth gold in value all other metals, so this Legend exceedeth all other books." But Edward Leigh, in much distress of mind, calls it " a book written by a man of a leaden heart for the basenesse of the errours, that are without wit or reason, and of a brazen forehead, for his impudent boldnesse in reporting things so fabulous and incredible."

This work, the great text-book of the legendary lore of the Middle Ages, was translated into French in the fourteenth century by Jean de Vignay, and in the fifteenth into English by William Caxton. It has lately been made more accessible by a new French translation: *La Legende Dorée, traduite du Latin, par M. G. B.* Paris, 1850. There is a copy of the original, with the *Gesta Longobardorum* appended, in the Harvard College Library, Cambridge, printed at Strasburg, 1496. The title-page is wanting; and the volume begins with the *Tabula Legendorum.*

I have called this poem the *Golden Legend,* because the story upon which it is founded seems to me to surpass all other legends in beauty and significance. It exhibits, amid the corruptions of the Middle Ages, the virtue of disinterestedness and self-sacrifice, and the power of Faith, Hope, and Charity, sufficient for all the exigencies of life and death. The story is told, and perhaps invented, by Hartmann von der Aue, a Minnesinger of the twelfth century. The original may be found in Mailáth's *Altdeutsche Gedichte,* with a modern German version There is another in Marbach's *Volksbücher,* No. 32.

Page 516.

> *For these bells have been anointed,*
> *And baptized with holy water!*

The consecration and baptism of bells is one of the most curious ceremonies of the Church in the Middle Ages. The Council of Cologne ordained as follows: —

"Let the bells be blessed, as the trumpets of the Church militant, by which the people are assembled to hear the word of God ; the clergy to announce his mercy by day, and his truth in their nocturnal vigils: that by their sound the faithful may be invited to prayers, and that the spirit of devotion in them may be increased. The fathers have also maintained that demons, affrighted by the sound of bells calling Christians to prayers, would flee away; and when they fled, the persons of the faithful would be secure: that the destruction of lightnings and whirlwinds would be averted, and the spirits of the storm defeated." — *Edinburgh Encyclopædia,* Art. " Bells."

See also Scheible's *Kloster,* vi. 776.

Page 529.   *It is the malediction of Eve !*

" Nec esses plus quam femina, quæ nunc etiam viros transcendis, et quæ maledictionem Evæ in benedictionem vertisti Mariæ." — *Epistola Abælardi Heloissæ.*

Page 538.   *To come back to my text !*

In giving this sermon of Friar Cuthbert as a specimen of the *Risus Paschales,* or street-preaching of the monks at Easter, I have exaggerated nothing. This very anecdote, offensive as it is, comes from a discourse of Father Barletta, a Dominican friar of the fifteenth century, whose fame as a popular preacher was so great that it gave rise to the proverb, —

> *Nescit predicare*
> *Qui nescit Barlettare.*

"Among the abuses introduced in this century," says Tiraboschi, "was that of exciting from the pulpit the laughter of the hearers; as if that were the same thing as converting them. We have examples of this, not only in Italy, but also in France, where the sermons of Menot and Maillard, and of others, who would make a better appearance on the stage than in the pulpit, are still celebrated for such follies."

If the reader is curious to see how far the freedom of speech was carried in these popular sermons, he is referred to Scheible's *Kloster,* vol. i., where he will find extracts from Abraham a Sancta Clara, Sebastian Frank, and others; and in particular an anonymous discourse called *Der Gräuel der Verwüstung,* The Abomination of Desolation, preached at Ottakring, a village west of Vienna, November 25, 1782, in which the license of language is carried to its utmost limit.

See also *Prédicatoriana, ou Révélations singulières et amusantes sur les Prédicateurs; par G. P. Philomneste.* (Menin.) This work contains extracts from the popular sermons of St. Vincent Ferrier, Barletta, Menot, Maillard, Marini, Raulin, Valladier, De Besse, Camus, Père André, Bening, and the most eloquent of all, Jacques Brydaine.

My authority for the spiritual interpretation of bell-ringing, which follows, is Durandus, *Ration. Divin. Offic.*, Lib. I., cap. 4.

Page 539. *The Nativity: a Miracle-Play.*

A singular chapter in the history of the Middle Ages is that which gives account of the early Christian Drama, the Mysteries, Moralities, and Miracle-Plays, which were at first performed in churches, and afterwards in the streets, on fixed or movable stages. For the most part, the Mysteries were founded on the historic portions of the Old and New Testaments, and the Miracle-Plays on the lives of Saints; a distinction not always observed, however, for in Mr. Wright's *Early Mysteries and other Latin Poems of the Twelfth and Thirteenth Centuries,* the Resurrection of Lazarus is called a Miracle, and not a Mystery. The Moralities were plays in which the Virtues and Vices were personified.

The earliest religious play which has been preserved is the *Christos Paschon* of Gregory Nazianzen, written in Greek, in the fourth century. Next to this come the remarkable Latin plays of Roswitha, the Nun of Gandersheim, in the tenth century, which, though crude and wanting in artistic construction, are marked by a good deal of dramatic power and interest. A handsome edition of these plays, with a French translation, has been lately published, entitled *Théâtre de Rotsvitha, Religieuse allemande du Xe Siècle. Par Charles Magnin.* Paris, 1845.

The most important collections of English Mysteries and Miracle-Plays are those known as the Townley, the Chester, and the Coventry Plays. The first of these collections has been published by the Surtees Society, and the other two by the Shakespeare Society. In his Introduction to the Coventry Mysteries, the editor, Mr. Halliwell, quotes the following passage from Dugdale's *Antiquities of Warwickshire*: —

"Before the suppression of the monasteries, this city was very famous for the pageants, that were played therein, upon Corpus-Christi day; which, occasioning very great confluence of people thither, from far and near, was of no small benefit thereto; which pageants being acted with mighty state and reverence by the friars of this house, had theaters for the severall scenes, very large and high, placed upon wheels, and drawn to all the eminent parts of the city, for the better advantage of spectators: and contain'd the story of the New Testament, composed into old English Rithme, as appeareth by an ancient MS. intituled *Ludus Corporis Christi,* or *Ludus Conventriæ.* I have been told by some old people, who in their younger years were eyewitnesses of these pageants so acted, that the yearly confluence of people to see that shew was extraordinary great, and yielded no small advantage to this city."

The representation of religious plays has not yet been wholly discontinued by the Roman Church. At Ober-Ammergau, in the Tyrol, a grand spectacle of this kind is exhibited once in ten years. A very graphic description of that which took place in the year 1850 is given by Miss Anna Mary Howitt, in her *Art-Student in Munich,* vol. i., chap. 4. She says:—

"We had come expecting to feel our souls revolt at so material a representation of Christ, as any representation of him we naturally imagined must be in a peasant's Miracle-Play. Yet so far, strange to confess, neither horror, disgust, nor contempt was excited in our minds. Such an earnest solemnity and simplicity breathed throughout the whole of the performance, that to me, at least, anything like anger, or a perception of the ludicrous, would have seemed more irreverent on my part than was this simple, childlike rendering of the sublime Christian tragedy. We felt at times as though the figures of Cimabue's, Giotto's, and Perugino's pictures had become animated, and were moving before us; there was the same simple arrangement and brilliant color of drapery, — the same earnest, quiet dignity about the heads, whilst the entire absence of all theatrical effect wonderfully increased the illusion. There were scenes and groups so extraordinarily like the early Italian pictures, that you could have declared they were the works of Giotto and Perugino, and not living men and women, had not the figures moved and spoken, and the breeze stirred their richly colored drapery, and the sun cast long, moving shadows behind them on the stage. These effects of sunshine and shadow, and of drapery fluttered by the wind, were very striking and beautiful; one could imagine how the Greeks must have availed themselves of such striking effects in their theatres open to the sky."

Mr. Bayard Taylor, in his *Eldorado*, gives a description of a Mystery he saw performed at San Lionel, in Mexico. See vol. ii., chap. 11.

"Against the wing-wall of the Hacienda del Mayo, which occupied one end of the plaza, was raised a platform, on which stood a table covered with scarlet cloth. A rude bower of cane-leaves on one end of the platform represented the manger of Bethlehem; while a cord, stretched from its top across the plaza to a hole in the front of the church, bore a large tinsel star, suspended by a hole in its centre. There was quite a crowd in the plaza, and very soon a procession appeared, coming up from the lower part of the village. The three kings took the lead; the Virgin, mounted on an ass that gloried in a gilded saddle and rose-besprinkled mane and tail, followed them, led by the angel; and several women, with curious masks of paper, brought up the rear. Two characters of the harlequin sort — one with a dog's head on his shoulders, and the other a bald-headed friar, with a huge hat hanging on his back — played all sorts of antics for the diversion of the crowd. After making the circuit of the plaza, the Virgin was taken to the platform, and entered the manger. King Herod took his seat at the scarlet table, with an attendant in blue coat and red sash, whom I took to be his Prime Minister. The three kings remained on their horses in front of the church; but between them and the platform, under the string on which the star was to slide, walked two men in long white robes and blue hoods, with parchment folios in their hands. These were the Wise Men of the East, as one might readily know from their solemn air and the mysterious glances which they cast towards all quarters of the heavens.

"In a little while, a company of women on the platform, concealed behind a curtain, sang an angelic chorus to the tune of 'O pescator dell' onda.' At the proper moment, the Magi turned towards the platform, followed by the star, to which a string was conveniently attached, that it might be slid along the line. The three kings followed the star till it reached the manger, when they dismounted, and inquired for the sovereign whom it had led them to visit. They were invited upon the platform, and introduced to Herod, as the only king; this did not seem to satisfy them, and, after some conversation, they retired. By this time the star had receded to the other end of the line, and commenced moving forward again, they following. The angel called them into the manger, where,

upon their knees, they were shown a small wooden box, supposed to contain the sacred infant; they then retired, and the star brought them back no more. After this departure, King Herod declared himself greatly confused by what he had witnessed, and was very much afraid this newly found king would weaken his power. Upon consultation with his Prime Minister, the Massacre of the Innocents was decided upon, as the only means of security.

"The angel, on hearing this, gave warning to the Virgin, who quickly got down from the platform, mounted her bespangled donkey, and hurried off. Herod's Prime Minister directed all the children to be handed up for execution. A boy, in a ragged serape, was caught and thrust forward; the Minister took him by the heels in spite of his kicking, and held his head on the table. The little brother and sister of the boy, thinking he was really to be decapitated, yelled at the top of their voices, in an agony of terror, which threw the crowd into a roar of laughter. King Herod brought down his sword with a whack on the table, and the Prime Minister, dipping his brush into a pot of white paint which stood before him, made a flaring cross on the boy's face. Several other boys were caught and served likewise; and finally the two harlequins, whose kicks and struggles nearly shook down the platform. The procession then went off up the hill, followed by the whole population of the village. All the evening there were fandangoes in the méson, bonfires and rockets on the plaza, ringing of bells, and high mass in the church, with the accompaniment of two guitars, tinkling to lively polkas."

In 1852 there was a representation of this kind by Germans in Boston: and I have now before me the copy of a play-bill, announcing the performance, on June 10, 1852, in Cincinnati, of the *Great Biblico-Historical Drama, the Life of Jesus Christ*, with the characters and the names of the performers.

Page 548. *The Scriptorium.*

A most interesting volume might be written on the Calligraphers and Chrysographers, the transcribers and illuminators of manuscripts in the Middle Ages. These men were for the most part monks, who labored, sometimes for pleasure and sometimes for penance, in multiplying copies of the classics and the Scriptures.

"Of all bodily labors which are proper for us," says Cassiodorus, the old Calabrian monk, "that of copying books has always been more to my taste than any other.

The more so, as in this exercise the mind is instructed by the reading of the Holy Scriptures, and it is a kind of homily to the others, whom these books may reach. It is preaching with the hand, by converting the fingers into tongues; it is publishing to men in silence the words of salvation; in fine, it is fighting against the demon with pen and ink. As many words as a transcriber writes, so many wounds the demon receives. In a word, a recluse, seated in his chair to copy books, travels into different provinces without moving from the spot, and the labor of his hands is felt even where he is not."

Nearly every monastery was provided with its Scriptorium. Nicolas de Clairvaux, St. Bernard's secretary, in one of his letters describes his cell, which he calls Scriptoriolum, where he copied books. And Mabillon, in his *Etudes Monastiques*, says that in his time were still to be seen at Citeaux "many of those little cells, where the transcribers and bookbinders worked."

Silvestre's *Paléographie Universelle* contains a vast number of fac-similes of the most beautiful illuminated manuscripts of all ages and all countries; and Montfaucon, in his *Palæographia Græca*, gives the names of over three hundred calligraphers. He also gives an account of the books they copied, and the colophons with which, as with a satisfactory flourish of the pen, they closed their long-continued labors. Many of these are very curious; expressing joy, humility, remorse; entreating the reader's prayers and pardon for the writer's sins; and sometimes pronouncing a malediction on any one who should steal the book. A few of these I subjoin: —

"As pilgrims rejoice, beholding their native land, so are transcribers made glad, beholding the end of a book."

"Sweet is it to write the end of any book."

"Ye who read, pray for me, who have written this book, the humble and sinful Theodulus."

"As many therefore as shall read this book, pardon me, I beseech you, if aught I have erred in accent acute and grave, in apostrophe, in breathing soft or aspirate; and may God save you all! Amen."

"If anything is well, praise the transcriber; if ill, pardon his unskilfulness."

"Ye who read, pray for me, the most sinful of all men, for the Lord's sake."

"The hand that has written this book shall decay, alas! and become dust, and go down to the grave, the corrupter of all bodies. But all ye who are of the portion of Christ, pray that I may obtain the pardon of my sins. Again and again I beseech you with tears, brothers and fathers, accept my miserable supplication, O holy choir! I am called John, woe is me! I am called Hiereus, or Sacerdos, in name only, not in unction."

"Whoever shall carry away this book, without permission of the Pope, may he incur the malediction of the Holy Trinity, of the Holy Mother of God, of Saint John the Baptist, of the one hundred and eighteen holy Nicene Fathers, and of all the Saints; the fate of Sodom and Gomorrah; and the halter of Judas! Anathema, amen."

"Keep safe, O Trinity, Father, Son, and Holy Ghost, my three fingers, with which I have written this book."

"Mathusalas Machir transcribed this divinest book in toil, infirmity, and dangers many."

"Bacchius Barbardorius and Michael Sophianus wrote this book in sport and laughter, being the guests of their noble and common friend Vincentius Pinellus, and Petrus Nunnius, a most learned man."

This last colophon Montfaucon does not suffer to pass without reproof. "Other calligraphers," he remarks, "demand only the prayers of their readers, and the pardon of their sins; but these glory in their wantonness."

Page 552. *Drink down to your peg!*

One of the canons of Archbishop Anselm, promulgated at the beginning of the twelfth century, ordains "that priests go not to drinking-bouts, nor drink to pegs." In the times of the hard-drinking Danes, King Edgar ordained that "pins or nails should be fastened into the drinking-cups or horns at stated distances, and whosoever should drink beyond those marks at one draught should be obnoxious to a severe punishment."

Sharpe, in his *History of the Kings of England*, says: "Our ancestors were formerly famous for compotation; their liquor was ale, and one method of amusing themselves in this way was with the peg-tankard. I had lately one of them in my hand. It had on the inside a row of eight pins, one above another, from top to bottom. It held two quarts, and was a noble piece of plate, so that there was a gill of ale, half a pint Winchester measure, between each peg. The law was, that every person that drank was to empty the space between pin and pin, so that the pins were so many measures to make the company all drink alike, and to swallow the same quantity of liquor. This was a pretty sure method of making all the company drunk, especially if it be considered that the rule was, that whoever drank short of his pin, or beyond it, was obliged to drink again, and even as deep as to the next pin."

Page 552. *The convent of St. Gildas de Rhuys.*

Abelard, in a letter to his friend Philintus, gives a sad picture of this monastery. "I live," he says, "in a barbarous country, the language of which I do not understand; I have no conversation but with the rudest people. my walks are on the inaccessible shore of a sea, which is perpetually stormy. my monks are only known by their dissoluteness, and living without any rule or order. could you see the abby, Philintus, you would not call it one. the doors and walls are without any ornament, except the heads of wild boars and hinds feet, which are nailed up against them, and the hides of frightful animals. the cells are hung with the skins of deer. the monks have not so much as a bell to wake them, the cocks and dogs supply that defect. in short, they pass their whole days in hunting; would to heaven that were their greatest fault! or that their pleasure terminated there! I endeavor in vain to recall them to their duty; they all combine against me, and I only expose myself to continual vexations and dangers. I imagine I see every moment a naked sword hang over my head. sometimes they surround me, and load me with infinite abuses; sometimes they abandon me, and I am left alone to my own tormenting thoughts. I make it my endeavor to merit by my sufferings, and to appease an angry God. sometimes I grieve for the loss of the house of the Paraclete, and wish to see it again. ah Philintus, does not the love of Heloise still burn in my heart? I have not yet triumphed over that unhappy passion. in the midst of my retirement I sigh, I weep, I pine, I speak the dear name Heloise, and am pleased to hear the sound." — *Letters of the Celebrated Abelard and Heloise. Translated by Mr. John Hughes.* Glasgow, 1751.

Page 562. *Were it not for my magic garters and staff.*

The method of making the Magic Garters and the Magic Staff is thus laid down in *Les Secrets Merveilleux au Petit Albert*, a French translation of *Alberti Parvi Lucii Libellus de Mirabilibus Naturæ Arcanis:*—

"Gather some of the herb called motherwort, when the sun is entering the first degree of the sign of Capricorn; let it dry a little in the shade, and make some garters of the skin of a young hare; that is to say, having cut the skin of the hare into strips two inches wide, double them, sew the before-mentioned herb between, and wear them on your legs. No horse can long keep up with a man on foot, who is furnished with these garters." — Page 128.

"Gather on the morrow of All-Saints, a strong branch of willow, of which you will make a staff, fashioned to your liking. Hollow it out by removing the pith from within, after having furnished the lower end with an iron ferule. Put into the bottom of the staff the two eyes of a young wolf, the tongue and heart of a dog, three green lizards, and the hearts of three swallows. These must all be dried in the sun, between two papers, having been first sprinkled with finely pulverized saltpetre. Besides all these, put into the staff seven leaves of vervain, gathered on the eve of St. John the Baptist, with a stone of divers colors, which you will find in the nest of the lapwing, and stop the end of the staff with a pomel of box, or of any other material you please, and be assured that this staff will guarantee you from the perils and mishaps which too often befall travellers, either from robbers, wild beasts, mad dogs, or venomous animals. It will also procure you the good-will of those with whom you lodge." — Page 130.

Page 564. *Saint Elmo's stars.*

So the Italian sailors call the phosphorescent gleams that sometimes play about the masts and rigging of ships.

Page 565. *The School of Salerno.*

For a history of the celebrated schools of Salerno and Monte-Cassino, the reader is referred to Sir Alexander Croke's Introduction to the *Regimen Sanitatis Salernitanum;* and to Kurt Sprengel's *Geschichte der Arzneikunde,* i. 463, or Jourdan's French translation of it, *Histoire de la Médecine,* ii. 354.

INDEX OF FIRST LINES

INDEX OF TITLES.

[The titles in small capital letters are those of the principal divisions of the work, those in lower-case are single poems, or the subdivisions of long poems.]